MW01015058

THE OXFORD HANDBOOK OF

ROMAN LAW AND SOCIETY

THE OXFORD HANDBOOK OF

ROMAN LAW AND SOCIETY

Edited by

PAUL J. DU PLESSIS

CLIFFORD ANDO

and

KAIUS TUORI

UNIVERSITY PRESS

Great Clarendon Street, Oxford, OX2 6DP,
United Kingdom

Oxford University Press is a department of the University of Oxford. It furthers the University's objective of excellence in research, scholarship, and education by publishing worldwide. Oxford is a registered trade mark of Oxford University Press in the UK and in certain other countries

© Oxford University Press 2016

The moral rights of the authors have been asserted

Impression: 2

All rights reserved. No part of this publication may be reproduced, stored in a retrieval system, or transmitted, in any form or by any means, without the prior permission in writing of Oxford University Press, or as expressly permitted by law, by licence or under terms agreed with the appropriate reprographics rights organization. Enquiries concerning reproduction outside the scope of the above should be sent to the Rights Department, Oxford University Press, at the address above

You must not circulate this work in any other form
and you must impose this same condition on any acquirer

Published in the United States of America by Oxford University Press
198 Madison Avenue, New York, NY 10016, United States of America

British Library Cataloguing in Publication Data

Data available

Library of Congress Control Number: 2016933500

ISBN 978–0–19–872868–9

Printed in Great Britain by
CPI Group (UK) Ltd, Croydon, CR0 4YY

Links to third party websites are provided by Oxford in good faith and for information only. Oxford disclaims any responsibility for the materials contained in any third party website referenced in this work.

Acknowledgements

THE editors of this handbook would like to express their gratitude towards the Socio-Legal Studies Association (UK); the Edinburgh Legal Education Trust; the School of Law, University of Edinburgh; the Faculty of Law and the Faculty of Social Sciences, University of Helsinki; and the Center for the Study of Ancient Religions, University of Chicago, for their financial assistance during the course of this project.

Clifford Ando wishes to acknowledge the Notre Dame Institute for Advanced Study, the American Academy in Rome, and the Forschungskolleg Humanwissenschaften of the University of Frankfurt, all of which provided hospitality during the final year of the editorial process. Kaius Tuori would like to thank the New York University Department of Classics for their hospitality during the editing process. Paul J. du Plessis wishes to thank the University of Cincinnati Department of Classics for their hospitality during the editing process.

The editors would like to express a special word of thanks to Heta Björklund and Aleksandra Guminiak, who acted as project assistants. Furthermore, Paul J. du Plessis wishes to thank Ilya Kotlyar, Justine Bendel, Benedikt Forschner and Alberto Lorusso for their assistance with the organising of the conference and in the preparation of the manuscript.

A number of chapters in this volume have been translated. In each case, the name of the translator is cited underneath that of the original author. The editors wish to thank the translators for their patience and professionalism.

Finally, this project would not have seen the light of day were it not for the expert guidance of Charlotte Loveridge at Oxford University Press.

Contents

List of Abbreviations xiii
List of Contributors xv
A Note on Terms and Translations xvii

PART I INTRODUCTION

1. A Word from the Editors 3
PAUL J. DU PLESSIS, CLIFFORD ANDO AND KAIUS TUORI

2. Framing "Law and Society" in the Roman World 8
JANNE PÖLÖNEN

PART II READING ROMAN LAW

3. More than Codes: Roman Ways of Organising and Giving Access to Legal Information 23
DARIO MANTOVANI

4. Epigraphy 43
TOMMASO BEGGIO

5. Juristic Papyrology and Roman Law 56
JOSÉ LUIS ALONSO

6. Roman Law and Latin Literature 70
MICHÈLE LOWRIE

PART III THE CONSTITUTIONAL STRUCTURE OF THE ROMAN STATE

7. SPQR: Institutions and Popular Participation in the Roman Republic 85
FRANCISCO PINA POLO

8. The Emperor, the Law and Imperial Administration 98
WERNER ECK

9. Provincial Administration 111
JOHN RICHARDSON

10. Local Administration 124
SASKIA T. ROSELAAR

11. *Collegia* and their Impact on the Constitutional Structure of the Roman State 137
JONATHAN S. PERRY

PART IV LEGAL PROFESSIONALS AND LEGAL CULTURE

12. Legal Education and Training of Lawyers 151
JILL HARRIES

13. Lawyers in Administration 164
MICHAEL PEACHIN

14. Legal Writing and Legal Reasoning 176
ULRIKE BABUSIAUX

15. Greek Philosophy and Classical Roman Law: A Brief Overview 188
JACOB GILTAIJ

16. Rhetoric and Roman Law 200
AGNIESZKA KACPRZAK

PART V SETTLING DISPUTES

CIVIL ACTIONS AND CIVIL PROCEDURE

17. Magistrates who Made and Applied the Law 219
FREDERIK J. VERVAET

18. Roman Courts and Private Arbitration 234
LEANNE BABLITZ

19. Republican Civil Procedure: Sanctioning Reluctant Defendants 245
ERNEST METZGER

20. Imperial *Cognitio* Process 257
THOMAS RÜFNER

21. Evidence and Argument: The Truth of Prestige and its Performance 270
ELIZABETH A. MEYER

22. Legal Pluralism in Practice 283
CLIFFORD ANDO

CRIMINAL LAW AND SOCIAL ORDER

23. Police Functions and Public Order 297
CHRISTOPHER J. FUHRMANN

24. Public and Private Criminal Law 310
ANDREW RIGGSBY

25. Crimes against the Individual: Violence and Sexual Crimes 322
ARI Z. BRYEN

26. Crimes against the State 333
CALLIE WILLIAMSON

PART VI PERSONS BEFORE THE LAW

STATUS

27. Social Status, Legal Status and Legal Privilege 349
TRISTAN S. TAYLOR

28. Legally Marginalised Groups—The Empire 362
ROBERT KNAPP

29. Repression, Resistance and Rebellion 374
BENJAMIN KELLY

30. Slavery: Social Position and Legal Capacity 386
RICHARD GAMAUF

31. Manumission 402
HENRIK MOURITSEN

GENDER

32. Women and Patriarchy in Roman Law 419
Eva Cantarella

33. Defining Gender 432
Matthew J. Perry

34. Women as Legal Actors 443
Verena Halbwachs

PART VII LEGAL RELATIONS

PERSONS AND FAMILY

35. Family 461
Suzanne Dixon

36. Husband and Wife 473
Jakub Urbanik

37. Child and Parent in Roman Law 487
Ville Vuolanto

38. Inheritance 498
Éva Jakab

PROPERTY

39. The Economic Structure of Roman Property Law 513
Richard A. Epstein

40. Ownership and Power in Roman Law 524
Luigi Capogrossi Colognesi

41. Possession in Roman Law 537
Christian Baldus

42. Possession and Provincial Practice 553
Andrea Jördens

OBLIGATIONS

43. *Obligatio* in Roman Law and Society 569
David Ibbetson

44. Contracts, Commerce and Roman Society 581
Roberto Fiori

45. The Scope and Function of Civil Wrongs in Roman Society 596
M. Floriana Cursi

ECONOMICS

46. Price Setting and Other Attempts to Control the Economy 609
Egbert Koops

47. Law, Business Ventures and Trade 621
Jean-Jacques Aubert

48. Urban Landlords and Tenants 635
Paul J. du Plessis

49. Tenure of Land and Agricultural Regulation 646
Dennis P. Kehoe

50. Roman Law, Markets and Market Prices 660
Luuk de Ligt

Index 671
Index Locorum 701

List of Abbreviations

Where abbreviated, all references to texts from classical Antiquity follow the guidelines of the *Oxford Classical Dictionary* (third edition, 2003). Where the *OCD* does not supply an abbreviation for an author or work, we have crafted one that is easily disambiguated. We have also followed the list of general abbreviations appearing in this work. Citations of epigraphic sources follow the abbreviations in Bérard et al., *Guide de l'épigraphiste* (fourth edition; 2010). For papyrological material, references follow *Checklist of Abbreviations of Greek, Latin, Demotic, and Coptic Papyri, Ostraca and Tablets* (http://library.duke.edu/rubenstein/scriptorium/papyrus/texts/clist.html) (accessed 25 March 2016).

In a small number of cases we have diverged from the abbreviations in the *OCD*. These are listed below. Furthermore, in two instances (RS and FIRA), while the abbreviations do form part of the *OCD* list, they are so ubiquitous in this volume that they deserve specific mention:

C.	*Codex Iustinianus*
Coll.	*Collatio legum mosaicarum et romanarum*
cos. suff.	consul suffectus
cos./cos. ord.	consul/consul ordinarius
CTh.	*Codex Theodosianus*
D.	*Digesta*
Epit.Ulp.	*Epitome Ulpiani* (cf. *Tituli*)
FIRA	S. Riccobono et al., eds., *Fontes iuris romani antejustiniani* (Florence: 1941–1943)
Fr.Vat.	*Fragmenta Vaticana*
Frg. Dosith.	*Fragmentum Dositheanum*
Inst.	*Institutiones* of Justinian
Inst.Gai.	*Institutiones* of Gaius
lex Irn.	*lex Irnitana*
lex Malac.	*lex Malacitana*
lex Salp.	*lex Salpensana*
lex Urs.	*lex Ursonensis*
ms.	manuscript
n.	note
Nov.	*Novellae Iustiniani*
Nov. Theod.	*Novellae Theodosiani*
nr./no.	number
Reg.Ulp.	*Regulae Ulpiani* (cf. *Tituli*)
Repr.	reprint
RG/RGDA	*Res Gestae Divi Augusti*

RS	M. H. Crawford, ed., *Roman statutes* (Bulletin of the Institute of Classical Studies, Supplement 64. London: 1996).
s.c.	*senatus consultum*
SCU	*senatus consultum ultimum*
Sent.Paul.	*Sententiae Pauli*
T.H.	*Tabulae Herculanenses*
Tab. Her.	*Tabula Heracleensis*
Tit.Ulp.	*Tituli ex corpore Ulpiani*
TPSulp	*Tabulae Pompeianae Sulpiciorum*
trib. pl.	*tribunus plebis*

List of Contributors

José Luis Alonso, San Sebastian, Spain: joseluis.alonso@ehu.es

Clifford Ando, Chicago, Ill., United States of America: cando@uchicago.edu

Jean-Jacques Aubert, Neuchâtel, Switzerland: Jean-Jacques Aubert@unine.ch

Leanne Bablitz, Vancouver, BC, Canada: leanne.bablitz@ubc.ca

Ulrike Babusiaux, Zurich, Switzerland: ulrike.babusiaux@uzh.ch

Christian Baldus, Heidelberg, Germany: baldus@igr.uni-heidelberg.de

Tommaso Beggio, Helsinki, Finland: tommaso.beggio@gmail.com

Ari Z. Bryen, Morgantown, W.Va., United States of America: azbryen@gmail.com

Eva Cantarella, Milan, Italy: eva.cantarella@unimi.it

Luigi Capogrossi Colognesi, Rome, Italy: luigi.capogrossicolognesi@jus.uniroma1.it

M. Floriana Cursi, Teramo, Italy: fcursi@unite.it

Luuk de Ligt, Leiden, the Netherlands: L.de.Ligt@hum.leidenuniv.nl

Suzanne Dixon, Pt Lookout, North Stradbroke Island, QLD, Australia: suzanndixon@gmail.com

Paul J. du Plessis, Edinburgh, United Kingdom: p.duplessis@ed.ac.uk

Werner Eck, Cologne, Germany: Werner.Eck@uni-koeln.de

Richard A. Epstein, Chicago, Ill., United States of America: repstein@uchicago.edu

Roberto Fiori, Rome, Italy: roberto.fiori@uniroma2.it

Christopher J. Fuhrmann, Denton, Tex., United States of America: cfuhrmann@unt.edu

Richard Gamauf, Vienna, Austria: richard.gamauf@univie.ac.at

Jacob Giltaij, Helsinki, Finland: jacob.giltaij@gmail.com

Verena Halbwachs, Vienna, Austria: verena.halbwachs@univie.ac.at

Jill Harries, St. Andrews, United Kingdom: jdh2@st-andrews.ac.uk

David Ibbetson, Cambridge, United Kingdom: dji22@cam.ac.uk

Éva Jakab, Szeged, Hungary: jakabeva@juris.u-szeged.hu

Andrea Jördens, Heidelberg, Germany: andrea.joerdens@urz.uni-heidelberg.de

Agnieszka Kacprzak, Warsaw, Poland: a.e.kacprzak@gmail.com

Dennis P. Kehoe, New Orleans, La., United States of America: kehoe@tulane.edu

Benjamin Kelly, Toronto, ON, Canada: benkelly@yorku.ca

Robert Knapp, Berkeley, Calif., United States of America: rcknapp2@gmail.com

Egbert Koops, Leiden, the Netherlands: e.koops@law.leidenuniv.nl

Michèle Lowrie, Chicago, Ill., United States of America: mlowrie@uchicago.edu

Dario Mantovani, Pavia, Italy: dario.mantovani@unipv.it

Ernest Metzger, Glasgow, United Kingdom: Ernest.Metzger@glasgow.ac.uk

Elizabeth A. Meyer, Charlottesville, Va., United States of America: eam2n@virginia.edu

Henrik Mouritsen, London, United Kingdom: henrik.mouritsen@kcl.ac.uk

Michael Peachin, New York, N.Y., United States of America: mp8@nyu.edu

Jonathan S. Perry, Tampa, Fla., United States of America: perryjonat@gmail.com

Matthew J. Perry, New York, N.Y., United States of America: mperry@jjay.cuny.edu

Francisco Pina Polo, Zaragoza, Spain: franpina@unizar.es

Janne Pölönen, Helsinki, Finland: jpolonen@hotmail.com

John Richardson, Edinburgh, United Kingdom: j.richardson@ed.ac.uk

Andrew Riggsby, Austin, Tex., United States of America: ariggsby@mail.utexas.edu

Saskia T. Roselaar, Delft, the Netherlands: saskiaroselaar@gmail.com

Thomas Rüfner, Trier, Germany: ruefner@uni-trier.de

Tristan S. Taylor, Armidale, NSW, Australia: ttaylo33@une.edu.au

Kaius Tuori, Helsinki, Finland: kaius.tuori@gmail.com

Jakub Urbanik, Warsaw, Poland: Jakub.Urbanik@adm.uw.edu.pl

Frederik J. Vervaet, Melbourne, Vic., Australia: fvervaet@unimelb.edu.au

Ville Vuolanto, Tampere, Finland: ville.vuolanto@uta.fi

Callie Williamson, Spring Hope, N.C., United States of America: chwillia.att@gmail.com

A Note on Terms and Translations

Instead of a conventional glossary of terms, we have opted to explain Latin and Greek technical terms in the text where they appear. It is our belief that this mode of explanation is more useful than a voluminous glossary added at the front or the rear of a volume of this size. For those wishing to delve deeper into Roman legal terms, we recommend Adolf Berger's 1953 *Encyclopedic Dictionary of Roman Law* (Philadelphia), a book that despite its age has stood the test of time. It is also now available via JSTOR.

As is the convention for handbooks of this kind, many chapter authors have chosen to produce their own translations of passages from legal and other works from the Graeco-Roman world. Where published translations have been used, these have been clearly signposted. In addition, citations to the Digest are to that text alone and include neither reference to the work whence the Justinianic editors excerpted the text nor fragment numbers in Lenel. The editors acknowledge the difficulty of this decision. However, that information is most useful in connection with palingenetic research, and our system will allow those conducting such inquiries to pursue their projects without undue inefficiency.

Finally, readers of this work will notice certain Anglo-American legal terminology such as "distraint", "bailment", "lien" and "personal injury" in some of the chapters. This is a testament to the diversity of scholarship and of the legal traditions represented by the chapter authors. These terms have been employed with due sensitivity to the concepts that they seek to describe. It is also an acknowledgement that all engagement with classical Antiquity is mediated and accomplished by acts of conceptual and linguistic translation. The dangers of misapprehension are greatest not when translation is explicit, but when the distance between ourselves and Antiquity is naturalised and effaced.

PART I

INTRODUCTION

CHAPTER 1

A WORD FROM THE EDITORS

PAUL J. DU PLESSIS, CLIFFORD ANDO AND KAIUS TUORI

THE Roman legal tradition that is the focus of this volume developed through centuries of debate, contestation and interaction between magistrates, legislative authorities, legal experts and lay users. Without exaggeration, its breadth and depth are without rival in the ancient world. The different sources of Roman law form a vast body of literature that has come down to us in the form of manuscripts of the works of Roman jurists, texts inscribed in bronze, stone and wax that contain legal texts, the immense corpus of papyri with legally relevant material, as well as references to legal issues in Roman and Greek literature. What sets the Roman legal tradition apart is the combination of the self-understanding of legal experts who argued on a highly conceptual level about the interpretation of law, and their social, political, cultural and religious contexts, which were equally shaped by, and themselves shaped, the law. The timeframe of the present inquiry is the historical era known as the long classical period, from roughly the second century BC to the sixth century AD. The geographical coverage of this volume follows that of the Roman world in the Mediterranean basin and beyond. While the Roman legal tradition has played a defining role in the formation of the Western legal heritage through its reception and reuse, this will be outside our scope.

This tradition was and remains the site of learned study in the history of doctrine. What is more, doctrinal approaches to Roman legal history have, throughout the years, been subject to repeated, learned and valuable restatement in the form of handbooks. Although this work engages that tradition and, indeed, would not exist without it, ours is not a handbook of doctrine. As its title suggests, this Handbook studies law and legal institutions as products of human institution building, deeply imbricated with and shaped by the very social practices they were created to regulate. Many societies have crafted ideological justifications for law's authority, and the effective autonomy of legal interpretative communities, by assigning law a transcendent or superordinate authority: it was delivered on Sinai, for example, or written by a lawgiver who then removed himself from the society for which the law was written, which then lacked authority to change it.

In what follows, we seek briefly to contextualise this project in relation to such theories of law and practices of legal history. This might be accomplished in multiple perspectives.

We concentrate on three: Roman theories of law; historical inquiries into the autonomy of law; and the practice of law and society scholarship in the study of ancient societies.

To begin with, we argue that a rich contextualisation of law in the circumstances of its production and subsequent interpretation accords with deeply held Roman beliefs about the nature of law. In contrast with post-exilic Jewish literatures or Greek accounts of nomothetic law, to which we alluded above, Roman jurists and historians emphatically insisted that any individual law, to say nothing of any given society's law writ large, was the product of historical forces (Ando 2015a, 53–86). This historical awareness is a key feature of what may be described as "Roman legal culture" and ties in with the Roman understanding of historical *exempla* and their purpose more generally. Law was but part of the understanding of heritage and remembrance that defined the Roman self-image and the possibility of change. Not simply positive law, but also law-making and law-applying institutions evolved in direct response to social and demographic change. Claims to this effect are widely visible both in general terms and in specific application. This is so not in least in regard to the role of the praetor in "correcting" statute law, which betimes fell so afoul of social practice or had proved so improperly designed that its rigid application produced injustice, even as it might be corrected with all due respect for the legitimacy of the multiple sources of law in operation at any given time (Inst.Gai.3.25–26, 28, 32; D.1.1.7.1; Ando 2011, 1–18; cf. Schiavone 2012, 133–153). Such argumentation is also visible in reflection on the historical nature of language and custom, such that "the passage of time rendered the words and customs of Antiquity obscure, even while it was in light of words and customs that the meaning of laws was to be understood" (Gell. *NA* 20.1.5–8; see also Inst. Gai.1.122). Finally, such emphasis on the contingency of social norms achieves a particular valence in provincial contexts, where different conditions of knowledge of law obtained. There, jurists supposed that Roman magistrates might have to enforce norms that were merely immanent in practice; to know what these were, it was optimistically supposed that evidence of their content would be available in records of proceedings, where the norms might have been cited and upheld (Ando, ch. 22).

Our approach is also informed by the extraordinary achievements of recent historical research into ideologies of law in general and the autonomy of law in particular. Of particular relevance is Bruce Frier's analysis of the rise of the Roman jurists and their law (Frier 1985; see also Schiavone 2012, 177–225). Frier advances a fourfold argument concerning the rationalising tendencies of Roman jurisprudence in the late Republic; the legal security that a scientific jurisprudence could provide; the social authority provided (and secured) by the professionalisation of legal acumen; this last rested in part on the emergence and insistence on a distinction between public and private law and the focus of jurisprudence on the latter, which was then bracketed from the chaos of political life and public law in the period. It is crucial to observe, however, that neither the autonomy nor the rationality of the jurists' law was ever secured absolutely: the nature of law, its relationship to notions of substantive justice, and the social, political and institutional position of authoritative interpretation were contested once again in the high and late Empire. In that later contest, the stakeholders were emperors, on the one hand, who naturally held a sovereigntist commitment to positive law, and jurists and judges, on the other, whose commitment to traditions of interpretation as embodied in case law may be understood as seeking to wrest and retain authority independent of the sovereign (Ando 2015b). The idea of the autonomy or independence of law existed thus in particular social and political contexts, and the striving to maintain that independence may be seen as a part of the legal culture and the cohesion of the group of legal experts who defined themselves as such.

Such a contextualisation of legal theory and practice serves to align debates over interpretative authority and the proper sources of law of the high and late Roman Empire with the long history of contests over jurisdiction and sources of law in England. There, the emergence of a strong emphasis on positive law, which is to say, law promulgated by the sovereign, has been shown by Marianne Constable to be the product of a long and complex history of negotiation and contestation among varied sites of legal authority (Constable 1994). The attempt to insist upon the immanence of custom in highly localised contexts was thus not simply reflective of some pluralism inherent in pre-modern and pre-statal context; it enacted a resistance to precisely the centralising tendencies of royal authority and early modern étatism. What is more, the history analysed by Constable should be viewed alongside the long history of the ideology of common law charted in the classic work of J. G. A. Pocock (Pocock 1957), where *inter alia* the localness of local custom emerges in part as an expression of Englishness over against the perceived foreignness of many contemporary monarchs.

A final tradition of research concerns the scientific autonomy of the Roman legal tradition itself. It now seems fundamentally clear that the modern science of Roman law—its conception of its own practice—arose in a precise context and developed instrumentally, in order to arrogate the social authority of scientistic knowledge in pursuit of specific ends (Whitman 1990; Tuori 2007). Nineteenth- and early twentieth-century ways of reading Roman law—in particular, the continued privileging of jurisprudence as the pre-eminent source—thus find their origin in interested efforts on the part of German Romanists to craft a picture of ancient practice in justificatory mimesis of themselves. It has been the difficult task of contextual historical scholarship to separate ancient Roman law from the Romanistic tradition that built upon it and legitimised itself through the authority of the classical heritage.

This raises a further point. As should be clear, when we speak of "ways of reading Roman law", we refer also to inclusive and exclusive choices in respect of what counts as evidence of law. A standard narrative holds that it was the emergence of the field of legal papyrology that exploded the conceit that the Digest gave sufficient access to the totality of ancient experience even of private law (Alonso, ch. 5). The narrative is in many respects true. But one should not neglect the long history of discovery, publication and collation of inscribed sources for Roman law, which had its first great product in the collection of inscribed laws and decrees of the senate by Antonio Augustín (Augustín 1583).

In light of such histories of claims for and against the autonomy of law, and contests over the legitimate vehicles for promulgation and knowledge of law, it becomes clear that conventions about method and the very intellectual style of the history of doctrine were in part sustained by a priori decisions about what counted as evidence, inquiry into doctrine being focused on sources labelled doctrinal. By contrast, sociological and anthropological study or, more broadly speaking, law and society approaches to law, recognise no such limits (du Plessis 2013). The boundaries between law and social conduct, between authorised and lay interpreters of norms, between statal and semi-autonomous social fields, are recognised as porous. They are drawn and contested contingently, as relevant to the question one poses and the answers one crafts, and entertained and contested by one's fellow inquirers. In this sense, legal history has increasingly partaken in the extraordinary expansion of the imaginative and epistemic horizons of historical inquiry writ large (Cairns and du Plessis 2007). One may point here to the exciting scholarship being undertaken in the emergent fields of "law and economics" as well as "comparative legal institutions" with reference to the Graeco-Roman world. Largely outside the domain of handbooks, legal history of the Roman world has partaken of this extraordinary and exciting expansion in the horizons of inquiry, and Janne Pölönen's contribution to this volume reflects on the relationship of Roman legal studies to this dynamic.

This volume seeks to embrace the extraordinary richness of Roman legal culture and the different lines of inquiry that shed light on it and its interactions with the political, economic, social, intellectual and religious cultures of the ancient world. The different chapters seek to provide various viewpoints and alternative readings on issues like the ways Roman legal texts were drafted, presented and preserved and how their authors thought about law. They explore how the institutions of Roman state and society were structured and shaped by law and how legislative activities took place. One section debates Roman legal culture, the contested conception of the legal profession and the formation of legal expertise, as an intellectual exercise and in relation to both the administrative structures and other intellectual pursuits. While some chapters discuss how courts and magistrates applied the law and settled disputes, others look at ways in which the legal procedure was avoided and alternative measures were taken. A particular emphasis has been on the way that law defined and structured social status and relations, marginalising and privileging different groups, but also how it enabled movement in status. Investigations into issues of family relations and inheritance, as well as property and contract, demonstrate how law and legal practice formed the structure of social and legal interaction between individuals as well as in the Roman economy.

In the composition of this volume, we as editors have sought to give voice to alternative views and issues. Dogmatic inquiries into the rules of Roman law and historical inquiries into the effect of those rules within the Roman world are seen as complementary. The success of any field lies in its capacity to reform and reconfigure, to present new questions and seek answers to them. We hope that this volume will contribute in its own way to this process.

This Handbook results from collaboration among scholars working in fifteen countries, who participate in a great range of national and disciplinary traditions. It is intended to celebrate that diversity. In consequence, as editors we have adhered to as open-ended a view of the field as possible. We have emphatically not imposed any uniformity of approach in respect of theory. Instead, our object has been to engage each text sympathetically but also critically and, within the material limits imposed by the volume, to make it as strong as possible. We exhort readers to engage the volume as a whole, and also its individual chapters, in the same spirit.

Work on the volume commenced with an effort to enlist contributors that reflected the fullest possible range of scholarly approaches to the historical study of Roman law and society. The editors hosted a conference in Edinburgh in June 2014, at which drafts were presented by as many of the contributors as could attend. In this way, substantive and theoretical differences were aired and discussed before a dedicated and critical audience.

Final drafts, prepared in light of those conversations, were submitted in the following months, and each chapter was then read by at least two editors, one exercising primary responsibility for a section, another secondary.

It should be obvious from even this brief narrative that the Handbook reflects the efforts and dedication of an extraordinary range of scholars. To them, and to all those in the wider world whose interest and care sustains the field, the editors are extremely grateful.

Clifford Ando
Paul J. du Plessis
Kaius Tuori

Bibliography

Ando, C. 2011. *Law, language and empire in the Roman tradition*. Philadelphia.

Ando, C. 2015a. *Roman social imaginaries: language and thought in contexts of empire*. Toronto.

Ando, C. 2015b. "*Exemplum*, analogy and precedent in Roman law." In M. Lowrie and S. Lüdemann, eds., *Between exemplarity and singularity: literature, philosophy, law*. New York. 111–122.

Augustín, A. 1583. *De legibus et senatus consultis liber*. Rome.

Cairns, J. W. and P. J. du Plessis, eds. 2007. *Beyond dogmatics: law and society in the Roman world*. Edinburgh.

Constable, M. 1994. *The law of the other: the mixed jury and changing conceptions of citizenship, law and knowledge*. Chicago.

du Plessis, P. J., ed. 2013. *New frontiers: law and society in the Roman world*. Edinburgh.

Frier, B. W. 1985. *The rise of the Roman jurists: studies in Cicero's* Pro Caecina. Princeton.

Pocock, J. G. A. 1957. *The ancient constitution and the feudal law: a study of English historical thought in the seventeenth century*. Cambridge.

Schiavone, A. 2012. *The invention of law in the west*. Translated by J. Carden and A. Shugaar. Cambridge.

Tuori, K. 2007. *Ancient Roman lawyers and modern legal ideals: studies on the impact of contemporary concerns in the interpretation of ancient Roman legal history*. Frankfurt.

Whitman, J. Q. 1990. *The legacy of Roman law in the German romantic era: historical vision and legal change*. Princeton.

CHAPTER 2

FRAMING "LAW AND SOCIETY" IN THE ROMAN WORLD

JANNE PÖLÖNEN

2.1 Introduction

> Almost everyone concedes that law on the books and the law in action are not invariably the same. Rules and structures alone do not tell us how the machine really works. These provide no way to sort out dead law from the living law. They do not tell us how and why rules are made and what effect they have on people's lives.
>
> (Friedman 1975, 1–2)

Historians of Roman law expect a close relationship between law and society. Law reflects the prevailing social, economic and moral conditions, and regulates the conduct and conflict of the populace. Understanding law aids the historical reconstruction of Roman society, and understanding society is beneficial for the reconstruction of historical Roman law. From the perspective of practice, the relationship between law and society appears more problematic. Abstract legal rules (law) and what courts and people actually do (facts) are frequently observed to differ. This raises the question of the utility of facts in the reconstruction of Roman law, and the utility of legal rules in the reconstruction of facts about Roman law and society. Historians, with and without legal training, tend to value the importance of practice and facts in the study of Roman law differently, and not without controversy.

The purpose of this chapter is to frame the history of Roman law and society as an interdisciplinary field of socio-legal research in a way to reconcile lawyers' and historians' approaches to Roman law. In the introduction, I briefly describe these two approaches, pointing out the underlying assumptions about law and practice that separate lawyers' and historians' histories. In sections 2.2 and 2.3, I explore those approaches and assumptions by relating them to two well-established research traditions in law: formal legal science and empirical socio-legal research, respectively. Although Roman legal history has been dominated by the former tradition, the history of law and society should build on the theoretical and methodological foundations of the latter. The final section, 2.4, outlines the landscape of a socio-legal approach to Roman law.

Contemporary Roman-law scholarship is shaped by needs both internal and external to law as an academic discipline. The study of Roman law played a key role in the formation of Western legal science, which has educated most specialists in the field. The history of Roman law as a field of study has gradually extended beyond civil law to comprise public law, criminal law, the history of sources, the legal culture of the Roman jurists, and—most recently—the critical appraisal of the Roman legal tradition itself. To understand the substance and development of Roman doctrine, lawyers specialising in the study of Roman law (Romanists) have complemented legal dogmatics with philological and historical methods and materials (Orestano 1987; Crifò 1998). Common interests in Roman law have brought Romanists and historians to a close and invaluable dialogue (Cairns and du Plessis 2007).

The field of ancient history has expanded to cover all aspects of Roman life, including the role played by law in Roman society and culture. Law is an area of knowledge about Roman society that has been systematically documented and commented on by Roman legal specialists, whose writings happen to survive in Justinian's sixth-century compilation. In reconstructing Roman society, historians use reflections of social phenomena in legal concepts and definitions, as well as behavioural implications of legal rules, as data. Legal cases arguably describe events in daily life of a wider social range of people than elitist literary sources (Matthews 2006, 483). Roman law and legal writings have become indispensable historical sources (Frier 2000, 447; Treggiari 2002, 33), increasingly studied by classical scholars acquainted with Roman law but without legal training.

Whether it is understanding law in a social context or society in light of law, scholars have to deal with the relationship between law and society. Roman legal history is grounded in the idea that law and society develop hand in hand, from the rudimentary forms of the archaic community to the somewhat modern legal system of the world Empire (Jolowicz and Nicholas 1972; Schiavone 2012). Legal specialists—*iuris periti*—steered Roman law towards an internally coherent set of legal rules and principles that was independent of other (social, ethical, religious) norms in society. It has been argued that the Roman elite jurists isolated law from the realities of daily life (Watson 1995). Answering this charge has been a paradigmatic challenge to Roman law and society studies (Aubert and Sirks 2002). Most Romanists and historians probably agree that Roman law reflects society and was crucial to regulating conduct and conflict. Indeed, most Western legal theory presupposes that "law is a mirror of society, which functions to maintain social order" (Tamanaha 2001).

Fifty years ago, it seemed that the differences between the lawyers' and historians' histories had faded away (Momigliano 1964). However, it has recently been observed that divergent traditions and assumptions underlying the study of Roman law and history have left "Romanists and historians inhabiting two nearly irreconcilable worlds". The Romanist approach to both law and society appears overly constrained by formal legal rules and standards, the definitive source of which are the Roman jurists' writings. It has been taken for granted, in the aftermath of Theodor Mommsen's monumental reconstruction of Roman public law, that a formal legal system backed up by state power effectively guided the behaviour of the legal apparatus and inhabitants of the Roman Empire. The historians' experience is that, in practice, state legal ordering is "weaker, less rational, and more ad hoc", and they call for a realistic picture of law informed by observed legal practice (Meyer 2004, 3; Rowe 2004). Over a hundred years ago, a similar divide opened up between legal scientists and sociologists of law.

2.2 The Legacy of the Scientific Ideal of Formally Rational Law

The history of Roman and Western law has been characterised by the development of learned juristic law with sophisticated methods of analysis and application of legal rules, and the spread of hegemonic state law over customary processes and standards of justice (Constable 1994; Whitman 1997 and 2009). The state has effectively claimed the authority to define law as rules created, recognised and applied by its officials and backed up by governmental coercion. The existence of other state and non-state sources of ordering in society is acknowledged, but these are of legal interest only upon recognition by the law of the state. Dominant positivist legal theory regards the state legal system as the most important normative order regulating conduct and conflict in society, commanding the supreme obedience of the populace by virtue of compulsory enforcement. The legitimacy of positive law rests upon internal rules of recognition, not upon moral or ethical standards external to legal system (Kelsen 1945; Hart 1961).

The practical purpose of legal science on the European continent has been to produce through systematisation and, eventually, codification, an internally coherent, gapless system of abstract legal rules and principles to guide all decision-making by legal officials (Damaska 1986, 37). Doctrine constricted legal officials to always finding rules of decision in the abstract system by means of logical legal analysis and to applying them to concrete cases according to legally relevant characteristics. Max Weber famously idealised the turn-of-the-twentieth-century continental civil-law scholarship as the highest form of legal science that produced "formally rational" law, enabling "the legal system to operate like a technically rational machine". Rational legal methods and processes are supposed to guarantee to the members of society, who are expected to know the law, stability of legal decisions and thus maximum predictability of the legal consequences of their actions (Weber 1978, 657–658, 809–831; Watson 1981, 23–38; Tamanaha 2010, 25).

As long as the legal system is perfect in theory, it is assumed that the preconditions exist for law's effective operation in practice. In order to elaborate legal rules for judges and the public, legal science has not been interested in really knowing how the law is actually applied and used in practice. Instead of systematic empirical observation, a working hypothesis sufficed that, in general, legal decision-makers apply the law in a legally logical way and that the subjects lead and organise their lives according to positive law. Continental legal culture, which has historically dominated Roman-law studies, has been characterised as profoundly anti-empirical. It has shown a kind of disdain for the legal process, which is regarded as an affair not of true lawyers but of practitioners, and of sociology of law as a discipline (Garapon and Papadopoulos 2003, 52–53; Talamanca 1991–1992, 637).

Legal sociologists have argued, since the late nineteenth century, that legal science failed to deal credibly with the social reality of law and promoted empirical methods of analysis originating from the social sciences (Arnaud and Fariñas Dulce 1998). Proponents of free law-finding insisted that the abstract system of legal rules is never gapless, because social life produces new subject matter not covered by the law and renders parts of it obsolete. Eugen Ehrlich argued that when the statute fell silent, legal propositions ought to be freely found by systematically observing the facts of living law, the rules of conduct actually recognised by the people. In the ensuing debate, Hans Kelsen pointed out that law can be approached from a normative and explanatory perspective. Legal science determines, by means of logical analysis from recognised legal sources, what rules are law (*something ought to be done*). Legal sociology determines by means of empirical analysis from observed facts regularities about law in society (*something is actually done*). Weber also duly condemned Ehrlich's confusion of law and facts, the legal and sociological analysis of law (Weber 1978, 753; Kelsen 1945; van Klink 2009).

Roman legal history has supported the scientific conception of what is law and how it translates into practice. By virtue of a narrow Roman definition, which Western legal culture has inherited, law consists only of rules that legislation and legal specialists recognise as legal. Autonomous law was the product of Roman "legal science" (Schulz 1936, 24–25, 38–39; Pugliese 1966; Lewis 2000), and Romanists as lawyers have been committed to a reconstruction of the Roman legal system from the insider perspective of "traditional" legal history (Bourdieu 1987, 814; Friedman 1991; Tamanaha 2006). Even after Roman law was surpassed in Europe by national codes, in legal science Roman law exemplified the qualities and ideals of autonomous and rational law worthy of the name for analytical and educational purposes (Stein 1980, 123; Whitman 1990, 228; Tuori 2004; 2007). It is accepted, along with Weber, that the Roman legal system achieved a "highly formal and rational character, both regarding the substantive rules and their procedural treatment", and presumed that it was the most significant normative order in Roman society (Weber 1978, 809–838, 882–889, 978; Talamanca 1990, 15).

Even today, although historical Roman law lacked many of the rational and systematic characteristics of modern law, Romanists and historians know Roman law primarily as an abstract legal system perfected by centuries of civil-law tradition. Authoritative Roman legal sources (statutes, senate's resolutions, praetor's edicts, Imperial pronouncements, jurists' replies and their authoritative commentaries) do not, however, cover the entire legal system or the phases of its development. Large areas of Roman law have actually been reconstructed from practice attested in legal and non-legal sources. It was pointed out a hundred years ago that Mommsen reconstructed Roman public law mainly from evidence of what the magistrates actually did:

> What in actual fact is Roman *Staatsrecht*? Barring the content of small number of *leges* that contain *Staatsrecht*, everything that Mommsen sets forth under this head is merely a presentation of the practice of the organs of the Roman state during the existence of the Empire. Mommsen does, indeed, arrive at general legal propositions at every point; but with very few exceptions these were the product of his own intellectual labor; they were abstracted by him from the facts; they never were the rules that regulated the facts. (Ehrlich 2002, 31, 85)

Mommsen produced an analysis mainly of the customary usages of the Roman state. He sought to abstract and fix an apparently logical and internally coherent system of *Staatsrecht* worthy of a *Rechtsstaat*. Framed as public law, this system has reinforced the expectations of legal science that Roman law as it is found in the abstract system is the same as the law as it is applied and used in practice. In addition to differentiating between historical Roman law and modern reconstructions, Roman legal historians may have to reconsider the relationship between law and the facts behind those reconstructions.

2.3 Legal Sociology and Empirical Analysis of Law

Roman legal historians have traditionally been interested in the practice of law for the purpose of reconstructing the abstract legal system rather than for the sake of understanding legal practice in its own right. Law's relation to practice is more often assumed than studied: legal practice generally unfolds, albeit with an occasional error, according to the rule book. Historians also frequently rely on this insight in reconstructing facts about society, assuming that law deals with common occurrences or that it was reasonable for the Romans to do something in light of legal expectations. Underlying the current way of thinking about Roman law and society is a tacit presumption that the law known as an abstract system, as a rule, reflects the law as it is applied and used in practice. This powerful grip of norm-centred and legally logical approach to practice is still relatively strong, and promotes the legalisation of the study of Roman history and society.

Since the late nineteenth century, legal sociology has challenged and problematised the law and society relationship. Some of the first critics of abstract legal science were Romanists, notably Rudolph von Jhering and Eugen Ehrlich, an Austrian professor of Roman law who is often recognised as the founding father of legal sociology. The Roman law tradition's allegiance to legal science is underscored by the fact that while Weber and even Jhering are regular names, Eugen Ehrlich's work has been almost forgotten. As already mentioned, Ehrlich challenged the doctrine of gaplessness of the state legal system and argued that instead of law books, rules of decision should be found by observing the practice. Despite failure in the normative theory of law, which was brought out by the controversy with Kelsen, from the sociological perspective, Ehrlich produced key insights concerning the law's relation to practice.

Ehrlich was diametrically opposed to the prevalent doctrine of the primacy of state laws as the normative order of society. His sociology of law is founded on the idea that state law represents only a small share of the normative life of society, the most important part of which consists of rules arising from the inner order of social associations. Ehrlich famously described the "living law" of society as:

> The law which dominates life itself even though it has not been posited in legal propositions. The source of our knowledge of this law is, firstly, the modern legal document; secondly, direct observation of life, of commerce, of customs and usages, and of all associations, not

only of those that the law has recognized but also of those it had overlooked and passed by, indeed even of those that it has disapproved. (Ehrlich 2002, 493)

The living law performed most of the state law's avowed function to regulate conduct and conflict, and was constantly present in life, whereas the abstract legal propositions take effect mostly in the rare instance of legal process. People may anticipate coercive legal consequences of their actions, but they normally conduct themselves "lawfully" because their social relations oblige them to do so. A good deal of state law remains "mere doctrine, norm for decision, dogma or theory" failing to become "part and parcel of life" (Ehrlich 2002, 21, 41, 61–82, 486–506).

According to Ehrlich, the living law of the society was worthy of "scientific" empirical observation irrespective of doctrinal coherence and could be shown to be frequently at variance with the expectations of the state legal propositions. Behaviour of which the law disapproved can be more or less socially acceptable, and behaviour which it permitted—for instance, recourse to the legal process—can be condemned by social associations. Moreover, state legal propositions produce a false impression of uniformity of practice in their territory of application: "In spite of the fact that the courts and other tribunals of Bohemia, Dalmatia and Galicia apply the same code, the [living] law of these countries is by no means the same" (Ehrlich 2002, 505, 501, 498). Ehrlich paved the way for scholars, whose work has undermined the standard assumption that state law mirrors society and functions effectively to maintain social order (Tamanaha 2001, 116).

With other advocates of the free law-finding, Ehrlich also challenged the scientific vision of legal decision-making. More than a logical application of abstract legal propositions to facts of cases, judging involves both discretion and a personal element (Ehrlich 2002, 13–136). This line of investigation soon found more fertile soil in the United States. In the context of judge-made case law, the so-called legal realists, whom the historians have pitted against legal formalists, undertook a coherent programme of empirical sociological analysis of what the courts will do in fact (Tamanaha 2010). The difference between theory and practice was formulated by Roscoe Pound as one between the "law in books" and the "law in action". Law in action refers to the law as it is applied by the legal decision-makers, not to popular legal practice covered more properly by Ehrlich's concept of the living law (Pound 1910; Nelken 1984).

In opposition to formalist doctrine, realists argued that law is rationally indeterminate because the precedents and statutes support more than one solution to a case. The finding of facts—a problem traditionally ignored by legal scientists—could be equally indeterminate, as the legal decision-makers could characterise them in different ways. The process of the law's application normally begins with a vague conclusion, and the legal propositions were used to justify and rationalise *post hoc*, after the facts, the decision that seemed most just. Realists concluded that abstract rules and principles cannot alone explain and predict legal decisions and undertook "the descriptive study of the causal relations between input (facts and rules of law) and outputs (judicial decisions)" (Leiter 1999). This borders more on the Roman rhetorician's than the jurist's understanding of legal process.

So far, Donald Black has advanced the most ambitious sociological theory that aims at predicting how law, courts and people behave in reality. His "pure sociology" defines law as governmental social control and a quantifiable variable, the amount of which increases and decreases in social space in inverse relation to informal social control. An important determinant of dispute resolution, litigation and adjudication is the sociological structure of the case that varies according to the relational and hierarchical distance between the legal decision-makers, the parties, and their advocates (Black 1976 and 1998). The starting-point of Black's theory, which is based on empirical findings, is entirely the opposite of that of the traditional legal science of the Weberian ideal type:

> Countless studies ... demonstrate that technically identical cases—pertaining to the same issues and supported by the same evidence—are often handled differently. People may or may not call the police or a lawyer; if they do, a prosecution or lawsuit may or may not result; some defendants lose while others win; the sentence or civil remedy imposed changes from one case to another; some losers appeal and others do not; and so on. In other words, law is variable. It differs from one case to the next. It is situational. It is relative. (Black 1989, 6)

These external observations probably resonate more with historians' rather than Romanists' experience of Roman law. Behavioural sociology of law represents the extreme end of a spectrum of empirical legal research, contrasted with interpretative analysis of legal actors' inner motives and meanings. It is argued that both legal and socio-legal positivism, focusing on formal legality, methodological rationality and empirical reality of law, tend to relegate the substance of rules and justice outside their sphere of analysis (Constable 2005).

Instead of legal systems, many socio-legal scholars study and compare legal cultures, which consist of legal attitudes and the behaviour of legal specialists, officials and the general population (Friedman 1975, 193–267; Nelken 1997). Empirical legal research seeks to produce a more realistic and multidimensional picture of law as a social phenomenon and of the operation of the legal system. It already builds on a vast amount of qualitative and quantitative empirical research by lawyers, historians, anthropologists, sociologists, and economists on law, litigation and dispute resolution in primitive, historical and modern societies (Cane and Kritzer 2010). Empirical focus unites most social legal theories of law, and distinguishes them clearly from positive and natural law traditions founded in analytical and moral philosophy (Tamanaha 2013). However, the field is characterised, as is common in social sciences and humanities (Whitley 2000), by a plurality of methods, perspectives and theoretical standpoints.

After centuries of legal and socio-legal research, the law and society relationship is going to be assessed, and perhaps modified, anew in light of research informed by evolutionary psychology and cognitive anthropology. Anthropological and historical studies show that normative ordering and dispute resolution are human universals with important similarities in general architecture (Brown 1991; Jones and Goldsmith 2005). Biolegal history suggests that, in addition to social and cultural influences, the legal ordering and behaviour of society reflect the innate structure of the human mind and shared intuitions of justice and morality (Jones 2001; Robinson, Kurzban and Jones 2007; Guttentag 2009). From this perspective, explaining the success of legal ideas and forms requires an understanding of historical and cultural contexts, as well as human species-specific cognitive capacities and epidemiology of cultural representations (Sperber 1996; Caterina 2004).

2.4 A Socio-Legal History of Roman Law

Questions concerning the relationship between legal theory and practice, prescription and description, law and fact may seem new in the field of Roman law and society studies. The same questions have been asked, and the scientific analysis of the reality of law has been called for, a long time ago concerning actual legal systems. Rather than divide the field between the Romanists and historians, trying to understand their different approaches and assumptions may help us to better appreciate the value of the other's contributions. Legally trained historians are likely to place more weight on the Roman jurists' internal perspective on the rules of law, while historians without legal training quite naturally look at law from the external perspective of facts about law. These approaches complement each other to produce a more comprehensive picture of Roman law, especially in its connection to society (du Plessis 2013).

The development of Roman law into a methodologically sophisticated system of positive law, which is analytically differentiated from the other normative orders in society, remains the starting point of inquiry into law and society in the Roman world (Frier 1985). The autonomy of law does not exclude input from, and its effect on, society. Much recent research explores how Roman legal rules worked, or were supposed to work, in practice and how external needs and interests influenced their development. In the socio-legal approach, law's relationship to society is constantly problematised and turned into empirical questions, rather than posited or presumed. The autonomy of law can be understood as relative to the degree it, as a self-referential (or autopoietic) system, "looks to itself rather than to the standards of some external social, political or ethical system for guidance in making and applying law" (Lempert 1988, 159; Luhmann 2004). It is relevant to ask to what extent, rather than whether or not, Roman law is "a mirror of prevailing customs and morals, and to what extent did it contribute to the maintenance of social order" (Tamanaha 2001, 231).

Roman legal texts represented only a narrow body of rules as law, according to which relevant legal and factual issues were framed in Roman courts, and largely ignored extra-legal rules of conduct. While formal rules and rational procedures promoted unity, legitimacy and ideology of Roman Imperial government (Ando 2000), a considerable degree of legal pluralism was maintained in the form of recognised coexistence of foreign, local and indigenous laws and customs with Roman law (Mitteis 1891; Tuori 2007b; Ando 2014). However, the construction of disputes in formally rational terms hardly conforms to lay expectations of justice (Weber 1978, 885), especially in parts of the Empire where Roman law was foreign, transplanted law. The procedural delegation of fact-finding and judgement to lay adjudicators allowed, at least to some extent, consideration of contextual extra-legal rules of conduct (Whitman 2003). Roman law's impact on regulating conduct and conflict can be properly understood only against the wide range of informal ordering and processes embedded in the social context of disputes (e.g. Ioannatou 2006; Veyne 2001; Kehoe 2007). It is to be expected that the actual role Roman law played in people's lives varied immensely between provinces, localities and groups (Humfress 2013; 2014).

Empirical legal research aims at understanding and explaining law at all levels of social life from individuals and subgroups to entire populations. In both Roman law and society studies, the quantity and quality of sources is often limited. Surviving evidence for legal attitudes and behaviour consists—in addition to ideas, rules and cases found in texts produced by the Roman jurists—of disparate and haphazard data recorded in documents and literary narratives. Anecdotal evidence is mostly given to qualitative interpretation, which has been the preferred approach of Romanists and historians. Data is usually insufficient for establishing the prevalence of legal ideas or statistics of behaviour; for instance, patterns of litigation (e.g. Kelly 1966; Bablitz 2007; Kelly 2011). This is a well-recognised obstacle to the quantitative understanding of Roman legal culture (Crook 1967, 9; Humbert 1994, 73–5).

Roman law and society studies draw increasingly on theoretical and empirical findings from better-documented societies in the interpretation of ancient legal cases and phenomena (e.g. Frier 1985; Crook 1995). The problem remains of knowing how representative the surviving manifestations are of the ideas and behaviour at the level of the entire population. Comparative data may supplement, as Keith Hopkins pointed out, "what is known from surviving sources with what was probable" (Hopkins 1983, xiii). Model life tables are commonly used to establish the probable patterns of Roman demography. Similarly, a dispute pyramid modelled on quantitative studies of litigation, and comparative litigation frequencies, can be used to estimate, for instance, the expected rates of litigation and dispute settlement in the Roman Empire (Pölönen 2008). Another potential source of population-level understanding of conduct is evolutionary psychology that seeks to explain the innate frame for human behaviour (Scheidel 2009; 2013).

Traditionally, the efforts of Roman legal historians have been aimed at understanding the internal legal culture—values, ideas and behaviour—of the Roman jurists who were responsible for the Roman law as an abstract system of rules and principles. It is important to remember, however, that law can be a poor guide to what courts and people actually do, and vice versa (Galanter 1989). Magistrates, officials, judges and advocates, mostly laymen who performed specialised tasks in the law's administration and application, have traditionally been allowed to play only marginal roles in the legal culture of the Empire, yet their ideas and decisions, rather than those of the jurists, determined how the Roman legal institutions functioned in practice and context (e.g. Metzger 2004; Fournier 2010; Kantor 2012; Bryen 2012). The least well-known area of Roman legal culture, and the most difficult to map, consists of the legal attitudes and behaviour of the general population of the Roman Empire. In a socio-legal perspective, law in books, law in action, and living law are all equally important objects of study in their own right that make up the specific legal culture of Roman society.

2.5 Conclusion

The autonomy of law and rational legal methods are considered the highest achievements of the ancient Roman civilisation, and these have also been the fount and focus of Western legal science and history. The ideals of modern juristic and positive law have guided the study of Roman law, despite the opening up, since the late nineteenth century, of societal and empirical perspectives on the study of contemporary legal systems. Whereas legal science framed society in terms of legal rules and expectations, legal sociologists framed law as a social phenomenon and set legal expectations against the reality of what courts and people actually do. Expanding inquiries into the historical and social context of Roman law, together with an influx to the field of scholars without training and commitment to legal standards, has brought old contradictions to the fore. Contemporary socio-legal scholarship, in dialogue with legal science, also provides a sound theoretical and methodological framework for the study of law and society in the Roman world.

Bibliography

Ando, C. 2000. *Imperial ideology and provincial loyalty in the Roman empire.* Berkeley.

Ando, C. (2014). "Pluralism and empire: from Rome to Robert Cover." *Critical Legal Analysis* 1: 1–22.

Arnaud, A.-J. and Fariñas Dulce, M. J. 1998. *Introduction à l'analyse sociologique des systèmes juridiques.* Brussels.

Aubert, J. J. and A. J. B. Sirks, eds. 2002. Speculum Iuris. *Roman law as a reflection of social and economic life in antiquity.* Ann Arbor.

Bablitz, L. 2007. *Actors and audience in the Roman courtroom.* London/New York.

Black, D. 1976. *The behavior of law.* San Diego.

Black, D. 1989. *Sociological justice.* New York.

Black, D. 1998. *The social structure of right and wrong.* (Revised edition.) San Diego.

Bourdieu, P. (1987). "The force of law: towards a sociology of the juridical field." *The Hastings Law Journal* 38: 805–853.

Brown, D. 1991. *Human universals.* New York.

Bryen, A. (2012). "Judging empire: courts and culture in Rome's eastern provinces." *Law and History Review* 30: 771–811.

Cairns, J. W. and du Plessis, P. J. 2007. "Introduction: themes and literature." In J. W. Cairns and P. J. du Plessis, eds., *Beyond dogmatics: law and society in the Roman world.* Edinburgh. 3–8.

Cane, P. and H. Kritzer, eds. 2010. *The Oxford handbook of empirical legal research.* Oxford.

Caterina, R. (2004). "Comparative law and the cognitive revolution." *Tulane Law Review* 78: 1501–1548.

Constable, M. 1994. *The law of the other: the mixed jury and changing conceptions of citizenship, law, and knowledge.* Chicago.

Constable, M. 2005. *Just silences: the limits and possibilities of modern law.* Princeton.

Crifò, G. 1998. *Materiali di storiografia romanistica.* Turin.

Crook, J. A. 1967. *Law and life of Rome, 90 B.C.—A.D. 212.* London.

Crook, J. A. 1995. *Legal advocacy in the Roman world.* London.

Damaska, M. 1986. *The faces of justice and state authority: a comparative approach to the legal process.* New Haven.

du Plessis, P. J. 2013. "Introduction." In P. J. du Plessis, ed., *New frontiers: law and society in the Roman world.* Edinburgh. 1–8.

Ehrlich, E. 2002. *Fundamental principles of the sociology of law.* New Brunswick.

Fournier, J. 2010. *Entre tutelle romaine et autonomie civique: l'administration judiciaire dans les provinces hellénophones de l'Empire romain (129 av. J.-C.–235 apr. J.-C.).* Athens.

Friedman, L. M. 1975. *The legal system: a social science perspective.* New York.

Friedman, L. M. 1991. "Sociology of law and legal history." In V. Ferrari, ed., *Laws and rights: proceedings of the International Congress of Sociology of Law for the Ninth Centenary of the University of Bologna (May 30—June 3, 1988)*. Milan. 123–135.

Frier B. 1985. *The rise of the Roman jurists: studies in Cicero's* Pro Caecina. Princeton.

Frier, B. (2000). "Roman law's descent into history." *Journal of Roman Archaeology* 13: 446–448.

Galanter, M. 1989. *Law and society in modern India*. New Delhi/New York.

Garapon, A. and Papadopoulos, I. 2003. *Juger en Amérique et en France: culture juridique française et common law*. Paris.

Guttentag, M. (2009). "Is there a law instinct?" *Washington University Law Review* 87: 269–316.

Hart, H. L. A. 1961. *The concept of law*. Oxford.

Hopkins, K. 1983. *Death and renewal*. Cambridge.

Humbert, M. (1994). "Le procès romain: approche sociologique." *Archives de philosophie du droit* 39: 73–86.

Humfress, C. 2013. "Law's empire: Roman universalism and legal practice." In P. J. du Plessis, ed., *New frontiers: law and society in the Roman world*. Edinburgh. 73–101.

Humfress, C. 2014. "Thinking through legal pluralism: 'forum shopping' in the later Roman empire." In J. Duindam, J. Harries, C. Humfress and N. Hurvitz, eds., *Law and empire*. Leiden. 223–250.

Ioannatou, M. 2006. *Affaires d'argent dans la correspondance de Cicéron: l'aristocratie senatoriale face à ses dettes*. Paris.

Jolowicz, H. F. and Nicholas, B. 1972. *Historical introduction to the study of Roman law*. Cambridge.

Jones, O. (2001). "Proprioception, non-law, and biolegal history." *Florida Law Review* 53: 831–874.

Jones, O. and Goldsmith, T. (2005). "Law and behavioral biology." *Columbia Law Review* 105: 405–502.

Kantor, G. 2012. "Ideas of law in hellenistic and Roman legal practice." In P. Dresch and H. Skoda, eds., *Legalism: anthropology and history*. Oxford. 55–83.

Kehoe, D. 2007. *Law and the rural economy in the Roman empire*. Ann Arbor.

Kelly, B. 2011. *Petitions, litigation, and social control in Roman Egypt*. Oxford.

Kelly, J. M. 1966. *Roman litigation*. Oxford.

Kelsen, H. 1945. *The general theory of law and state*. New York.

Leiter, B. 1999. "Legal realism." In D. Patterson, ed., *A companion to philosophy of law and legal theory*. Oxford. 261–279.

Lempert, R. 1988. "The autonomy of law: two visions compared." In G. Teubner, ed., *Autopoietic law: a new approach to law and society*. Berlin/New York. 152–190.

Lewis, A. 2000. "The autonomy of Roman law." In P. Coss, ed., *The moral world of law*. Cambridge. 37–47.

Luhmann, N. 2004. *Law as a social system*. Oxford.

Matthews, J. 2006. "Roman law and Roman history." In D. S. Potter, ed., *A companion to the Roman empire*. Oxford. 477–491.

Meyer, E. 2004. *Legitimacy and law in the Roman world:* tabulae *in Roman belief and practice*. Cambridge.

Metzger, E. (2004). "Roman judges, case law, and principles of procedure." *Law and History Review* 22: 243–275.

Mitteis, L. 1891. *Reichsrecht und Volksrecht in den östlichen Provinzen des Römischen Kaiserreichs: mit Beiträgen zur Kenntniss des griechischen Rechts und der spätrömischen Rechtsentwicklung.* Leipzig.

Momigliano, A. (1964). "The consequences of new trends in the history of ancient law." *Rivista Storica Italiana* 76: 133–149.

Nelken, D. (1984). "Law in action or living law? Back to the beginning in sociology of law." *Legal Studies* 4: 157–174.

Nelken, D., ed. 1997. *Comparing legal cultures.* Aldershot.

Orestano, R. 1987. *Introduzione allo studio del diritto romano.* Bologna.

Pölönen, J. (2008). "*Quadragesima litium*: Caligula's tax on lawsuits." *Cahiers du Centre Gustave Glotz* 19: 77–109.

Pound, R. (1910). "Law in books and law in action." *American Law Review* 44: 12–36.

Pugliese, G. 1966. "L'autonomia del diritto rispetto agli altri fenomeni e valori sociali nella giurisprudenza romana," in *La storia del diritto nel quadro delle scienze storiche.* Florence. 161–192.

Robinson, P., Kurzban, R. and Jones, O. (2007). "The origins of shared intuitions of justice." *Vanderbilt Law Review* 60: 1633–1688.

Rowe, G. (2004). [Review Meyer 2004]. *Bryn Mawr Classical Review.* Available at: http://bmcr.brynmawr.edu/2004/2004-06-22.html, accessed 30 March 2016.

Scheidel, W. 2009. "Sex and empire: a Darwinian perspective." In I. Morris and W. Scheidel, eds., *The dynamics of ancient empires: state power from Assyria to Byzantium*, Oxford. 255–324.

Scheidel, W. (2014). "Evolutionary psychology and the historian." *American Historical Review* 119: 1563–1575.

Schiavone, A. 2012. *The invention of law in the west.* Cambridge, Mass.

Schulz, F. 1936. *Principles of Roman law.* Oxford.

Sperber, D. 1996. *Explaining culture: a naturalistic approach.* Cambridge, Mass.

Stein, P. 1980. *Legal evolution: the story of an idea.* Cambridge.

Talamanca, M. 1990. *Istituzioni di diritto romano.* Milan.

Talamanca, M. (1991–1992). "Review Martin, S. D. 1989. *The Roman jurists and the organization of private building in the late republic and early empire.* Brussels." *Bullettino del'Istituto di Diritto Romano "Vittorio Scialoja"* 33–34: 631.

Tamanaha, B. Z. 2001. *A general jurisprudence of law and society.* Oxford.

Tamanaha, B. Z. (2006). "A socio-legal methodology for the internal/external distinction: Jurisprudential implications." *Fordham Law Journal* 75: 1255–1274.

Tamanaha, B. Z. 2010. *Beyond the formalist-realist divide.* Princeton.

Tamanaha, B. Z. (2013). "The third pillar of jurisprudence: social legal theory." *Washington University in St. Louis Legal Studies Research Paper* No. 13-04-01.

Treggiari, S. 2002. *Roman social history.* London/New York.

Tuori, K. 2004. "Weber and the ideal of Roman law." In A. Lewis and M. Lobban, eds., *Law and history.* Oxford. 201–214.

Tuori, K. 2007. *Ancient Roman lawyers and modern legal ideals: studies on the impact of contemporary concerns in the interpretation of ancient Roman legal history.* Frankfurt am Main.

Tuori, K. 2007b. "Legal pluralism and the Roman empires." In J. W. Cairns and P. J. du Plessis, eds., *Beyond dogmatics: law and society in the Roman world.* Edinburgh. 39–52.

van Klink, B. 2009. "Facts and norms: Eugen Ehrlich and Hans Kelsen." In M. Hertogh ed., *Living law: reconsidering Eugen Ehrlich*. Oñati. 127–155.

Veyne, P. 2001. *La société romaine*. Paris.

Watson, A. 1981. *The making of the civil law*. Cambridge, Mass.

Watson, A. 1995. *The spirit of Roman law*. Athens, Ga.

Weber, M. 1978. *Economy and society*, Vol. 2. Berkeley.

Whitley, R. 2000[2]. *The intellectual and social organization of the sciences*. Oxford.

Whitman, J. Q. 1990. *Roman law in the German romantic era*. Princeton.

Whitman, J. Q. (1997). "At the scholarly sources of Weber's melancholy." *Quaderni fiorentini per la storia del pensiero giuridico moderno* 26: 325–362.

Whitman, J. Q. (2003). "Long live the hatred of Roman law!" *Rechtsgeschichte* 2: 40–57.

Whitman, J. Q. (2009). "Western legal imperialism: thinking about the deep historical roots." *Theoretical Inquiries in Law* 10: 305–332.

PART II

READING ROMAN LAW

CHAPTER 3

MORE THAN CODES

Roman Ways of Organising and Giving Access to Legal Information

DARIO MANTOVANI
TRANSLATED BY THOMAS ROBERTS

3.1 Introduction

Adopting the "code" as a historiographical category, that is, as a point of view from which to understand and describe Roman law, provides a good example of the difficulties that confront the historical study of law. Becoming aware of interpretative challenges represents one of the principal tasks necessary in order to renew our discipline: for this reason, the example then is a matter of some interest.

There are at least three difficulties associated with the use of the legal code as a category. To begin with, the code is a phenomenon typical of modernity, which thus entails the risk of investigating the past through the prism of an anachronistic concept. What is more, even the modern concept of a legal code is not unequivocal (Canale 2009; Kroppenberg and Linder 2014). The risk, therefore, is that different answers may be obtained depending upon which conception of code, from among the available choices, is selected when investigating the past. But even assuming that it is possible to arrive at a shared definition, the past, so filtered, loses much of its interest, because if it corresponds to our categories, then the past will end up looking like nothing more than a blurred copy of today; if it does not correspond to our categories, then it will appear as an imperfect present.[1]

[1] The question put by Ankum 2001/2008 "Was Justinian's *Corpus Iuris Civilis* a codification?" is intentionally posed by stipulating a definition of "code" based on eleven characteristics. The author's negative answer is based on the failure of the *Corpus Iuris* to satisfy some of these characteristics (e.g. it did not use the language most widely spoken at the time and it did not exclude all antinomies). Along similar lines, Gaudemet 1986/1992 assessed the Roman experience in the light of "systématisation" (i.e. the internal conceptual organisation of the law, as implemented by legislators or jurists), in the form elaborated by Doneau through to the Pandectists; here too Gaudemet denied that the goal of "systématisation" had been attained, although he did acknowledge that repeated attempts at "mise en ordre" had been made, albeit according to criteria specific to Antiquity. This chapter is in fact dedicated to such attempts.

The remaining and most insidious difficulty lies in the fact that Roman law perhaps did not know genuine, fully developed codes, whilst it did nonetheless provide modernity—as often occurs—with many of the ideological building blocks with which the concept (as well as the object) of the code was constructed. Many if not all of the keywords of modern codifications[2] (and consolidations) were already enunciated by Justinian when presenting his opus in the sixth century, starting from the very name *codex*: provisions must be limited in number (C. *Haec* pr. [a. 528]: "the multitude of constitutions must be reduced"); contradictions are to be excluded (*Deo auctore* 7 [a. 530]: "no antinomy in any part of the code"); writing must be clear and concise (*Haec* 2: "precise provisions drawn up in concise language"); material must be properly ordered (*Deo auctore* 5: "distribute the entire law into specific titles"); the collection will be official and comprehensive (*Deo auctore* 11: "we order that all relations must be governed by these two codes"); normative power is concentrated in the holder of public power (*Tanta* 20 [a. 533]); its provisions are to be made public (*Summa* 5 [a. 529]: "for the awareness of the entire population") and the text must be subject to state control in order to prevent alterations (*Tanta* 22); positive law may always be changed by amendment (*Cordi* 4 [a. 534]).[3] In addition, we find already clearly enunciated the aim of reducing litigation (*Haec* pr.: "curtail the length of disputes"), namely, by increasing legal certainty and the rationalisation of justice, two goals which are typically pursued by modern codes.[4] Justinian left to posterity also the prototype of a codification in which officials and academic jurists cooperate, not to mention the underlying connection between legislation and force (*Summa* pr.: "the fundamental protection of the state originates from the root of two things, arms and laws").[5] Leaving aside the specific meaning that each of the foregoing had within the Justinianic context, these assertions, familiar to readers of the *Corpus Iuris* down the centuries, have become a repository on which the ideology of codification has drawn, with varying degrees of awareness, even prior to the Enlightenment.

The discursive link thereby established between ancient and modern experiences risks suffocating historical interpretation. In the first place, and most obviously so, the lexical as well as the ideological consonance risks concealing the (technical and political) differences between Justinian's works and modern codifications (Humfress 2012). In addition, this consonance attenuates the diversity of the modern codifications themselves, precisely due to the fact that they all draw on this Justinianic repository, whilst being dissimilar to one another. (It is sufficient to consider the gulf between post-revolutionary codes and pre-Enlightenment consolidations.)

[2] The neologism coined by Jeremy Bentham for his project *Pannomion* is understood here in the sense of a process to produce one or more codes.

[3] See e.g. Nörr 1963/2003, 275–280; Ankum 1982/2008.

[4] Although proposals for substantive reform (for example in the area of taxation) were not formulated, the *ius* was nonetheless conceived of as a fair social order, the reduction and rectification of which could have ensured greater protection for the interests of private individuals. See Rivière 2013.

[5] Some of these assertions already appear within the constitutions accompanying the *Codex Theodosianus* (CTh.1.1.5 [a. 429]; 6 [a. 435]; Nov. Theod.1 [a. 438]; see also Nov. Theod.2 [a. 447]) and in the *commonitorium* to the *Lex Romana Visigothorum* (a. 506). The introductory constitutions in turn borrow these ideas from a rhetorical repertoire (already attested in relation to law by *De rebus bellicis* 21), on which also drew the authors of literary anthologies (e.g. Macrobius).

Above all, the ideological interference just sketched has had and continues to have serious repercussions for the assessment of Roman law in the pre-Justinianic era, which is unconsciously assimilated into the European *ius commune* of the era prior to its codification. And when the Justinianic project is interpreted as a triumph of positivism and normativism (the law reduced to the will of the sovereign) the classical Republican order is, by contrast, identified almost exclusively with the law produced by jurists, disregarding the enacted law that constituted its fundamental basis, including first and foremost the *lex*, but also the praetor's edict. This was so despite the recognition of the importance of *leges* and edict expressed by contemporaries: Cicero, for example, identified them without hesitation as the two principal sources from which the *iuris disciplina* was taken (Cic. *Leg.* 1.17.). The number and above all the scope of the *leges publicae*, each of which often comprised dozens of long chapters, were without doubt greater than is currently visible: it suffices to point to the *Institutiones* of Gaius (which are transmitted separately from the Digest) to appreciate how systematically Justinian's compilers "de-legislated" the Digest (Mantovani 2012b). This phenomenon was all too easy to ascertain, although it has only been acknowledged rather late in the day. This delay was heightened precisely by an ideological element; namely, Friedrich Karl von Savigny's polemical objection in 1814 to legislation and codification, made in the name of legal science. Savigny's praise of the jurists' role had a major influence not only on the contemporary debate but also on historiography; that is, on the way in which Roman law was understood retrospectively.[6] In this case, the anti-code polemic led to an overly sharp contrast (perhaps caused more by subsequent readers than by Savigny himself) between classical law (which was taken as a model for *Rechtswissenschaft* in its "genial" stage) and Justinian's law (taken as an example of a *Gesetzbuch*, a sign of the decadence of the law).

A second negative repercussion of the parallelism established between Justinian's works and modern codifications is that legal historians tend to overlook the ways in which—long before Justinian (or even Theodosius)—the Romans dealt with the need to collect and organise the law and to make it accessible to the public at large. These were ways that do not necessarily coincide with the modern forms, and it is precisely for this reason that they need to be explored, as this chapter will attempt to do in summary form.[7]

3.2 The Republican Era

Out of the many *fils rouges* that characterise the interpretation of the history of Roman law proposed by Pomponius (*liber singularis enchiridion*, D.1.2.2), the principle of legal certainty is of particular importance. It is legal uncertainty—a void—that drives history. The initial moment, the dawn of Rome, is an age *sine lege certa, sine iure certo* (D.1.2.2.1), which reacted to this void through the means of the enactment of *leges* by the first king and his successors. Uncertainty arose again after the end of Monarchy when, according to

[6] Savigny 1814. The historicism of Savigny was reinforced by views such as evolutionism and the sociology of law: see Bretone 2004; Capogrossi Colognesi 2008.

[7] See Casavola 1998 for an analogous framing of the question, which focuses, however, on the jurisprudential literature.

Pomponius, following the repeal of the *leges*, "the Roman people set about working with vague ideas of right and with custom of a sort, rather than with legislation" (D.1.2.2.3); this led to the decision to designate the *Decemviri* to enact *leges*: they then created the XII Tables, finally providing "stability" to the legal order of the city (D.1.2.2.4).[8]

In tracing this journey towards certainty through theses and antitheses, in addition to attributing a fundamental role to statute law approved by the people (the birth of which coincided with the *iuris origo*), Pomponius stressed the importance of collection and publication. As regards the regal period, Papirius "compiled in unitary form laws passed piecemeal" (D.1.2.2.2; see also 7, 36); following a half-century crisis, the *Decemviri* "wrote out the laws in full on ivory tablets and put the tablets together in front of the *rostra*, to make the laws all the more open to inspection" (D.1.2.2.4).

Obviously, establishing the reality of historical facts is not our main interest here (that Papirius, the compiler of the *leges regiae*, lived at the time of Tarquinius Superbus is difficult to believe (Carandini 2011; Mantovani 2012a)). What truly matters, instead, is that the Romans, in a work highly representative of classical ideology of law, to wit, the history of law as written by a jurist of the Antonine era such as Pomponius, regarded the compiling of law and rendering it accessible as central issues, without which certainty is not guaranteed. Such issues are not limited in relevance to late Antiquity, and much less so only to the modern era.[9]

There is therefore a legitimate question as to how the problem was dealt with. This chapter will survey several moments that appear to be crucial and will focus precisely on the views of the ancients; that is, on their awareness of the problem and of the measures to solve it. In this way, the risk of imposing anachronistic concepts will be reduced (without, obviously, supposing that the risk can be avoided entirely).[10]

Ordinata ... erat in Duodecim tabulis tota iustitia, "the whole justice had been arranged upon twelve tables" (Flor. 1.24.1): there is a unanimous tradition of retrospectively viewing the XII Tables as the result of an endeavour aimed at documenting the full extent of the law in force (based on the principle of equality between patricians and plebeians), thereby creating *velut corpus omnis Romani iuris*, "a body, as it were, of all of Roman law".[11] In the detailed and fictionalising narrative of Dionysius of Halicarnassus, this action was motivated precisely by the lack of written and accessible sources (10.1.2): "for at that time there did not exist as yet among the Romans an equality either of laws or of rights, nor were all their principles of justice committed to writing" (transl. E. Cary). Accordingly, the

[8] The verb *fundare* expresses the idea of stability. The XII Tables, which were elaborated by *interpretatio* (§5) and implemented through *legis actiones* (§6), remain the core of this legal order, in addition to the *plebiscita* (§8), *senatus consulta* (§9), edicts of the praetor (§10) and finally the constitutions of the *princeps*, which were ultimately based on the power conferred by the people (§11): this accordingly closes the circle opened by the *leges regiae*—also approved by the people—which had constituted the *iuris origo* (pr.-§1).

[9] Before Pomponius, the nexus between *ius certum* and knowledge of the law was expressed by Quintilianus (*Inst.* 12.3.6). See Bretone 2009.

[10] The important task of assessing the actual impact that these measures had on the accessibility of the law and on the functioning of the legal order cannot here be undertaken.

[11] Liv. 3.34.7. It is from Livy that Denis Godefroy adopted the term *Corpus Iuris Civilis* in 1583. It is unclear whether public law was included in the XII Tables, despite Livy's assertion that they were "the source of all public and private law" (3.34.6).

Decemviri "should draw up the laws concerning all matters both public and private and lay them before the people; and the laws ... should be exposed in the Forum for the benefit of the magistrates who should be chosen each year and also of persons in private station, as a code defining the mutual rights of citizens" (Dion. Hal. *Ant. Rom.* 10.3.4). "Code" is the translation proposed by Earnest Cary for the Greek *horoi*; that is, "boundaries" and, metaphorically, "terms", "definitions". (The Dionysian locution was a precursor of Tacitus' renowned expression *finis aequi iuris, Ann.* 3.27.1.) The liberty taken by the translator exposes his ideological conditioning, although it was also justifiable, as in Dionysius' account the XII Tables really did have the appearance of a modern code. It is not necessary to discuss here whether or not this appearance corresponded to reality. The important point is that, in the view of the ancients (at least at the end of the Republic), the XII Tables become a symbol of the values to permanently characterise the Roman legal order: the collection and publication of the law and the derivation of its legitimacy from the operation of democratic legislative institutions.[12]

Nearly a century and a half after the XII Tables, the tale of Cnaeus Flavius points towards a new demand for access to the law. In the received account, *c.*304 BC, Flavius "stole" from the pontiffs an authoritative list of legal actions, as well as the legal-religious calendar, which he distributed to the people in book form (Rüpke 2011, 44–67). Flavius is symbolic of how publication and access exist in (dialectical) tension with the forms of social authority that seek to restrict them, here represented by the *pontifices* (Liv. 9.46.5). This polarisation embodies a crucial aspect of the Roman experience of the law overall. Roman (private) law had an accessible side, of which the XII Tables were emblematic, and an esoteric side, symbolised here by the technical skill of the *pontifices*, who interpreted the *leges* and established the forms of actions and transactions. This tension between accessibility and confidentiality will never be entirely resolved in Roman history. Or, to put it better, it will be resolved in every phase by the existence of mechanisms with a strong socio-political legitimation that enabled private individuals to be informed of the law applicable to their cases by "experts": first by the *pontifices* themselves ("one of whom was appointed each year to preside over private matters": D.1.2.2.6), followed by the "private" jurists of the late Republic. Starting from the first century AD, specific jurists were encouraged by the *princeps* to give responses to the public (D.1.2.2.49), supported (never supplanted) from at least the middle of the second century by the emperor himself with his *rescripta*. In the provinces, this system was supplemented by governors, who could instruct judges concerning questions of law, as is shown by the Egyptian papyri.[13] This mechanism ensured a balance between two poles; that is, between widespread knowledge and technical specialisation by experts. Private jurists had been legitimated to perform this role even prior to the

[12] Schiavone (2012, 85–104) regards the XII Tables as a radically democratic but failed attempt to move beyond the "sapiential character" towards a "model of statutory law". This suggestive interpretation is in my opinion a symmetrical reflex of an image of post-Decemviral Roman law that overstates its jurisprudential nature to the detriment of the legislative component.

[13] See e.g. *BGU* I 19 = *M. Chr.* 85 (11 February, 135 AD; judicial proceeding): the appointed judge Menandros consulted the *praefectus Aegypti* Petronius Mamertinus concerning the applicability of the *beneficium Hadriani* in relation to the inheritance by grandchildren of the assets of the maternal grandmother. The system is described in general by D.5.1.79.1: "governors customarily respond to judges who are in doubt about the law".

involvement of the *princeps*, both because of their socio-political prestige and because of their rational mode of argumentation, which gave them an authoritative status that placed them above political tensions. But the strength of the system was also aided by forms of publication that stifled possible attempts at manipulation.

First and foremost, the jurists did not limit themselves to giving oral opinions: they wrote them down on tablets that were sent to judges (D.1.2.2.49) and then collected them in books for wider circulation. A genuine literature was thereby born which, whilst written by private individuals, performed the function of providing a public access to the law, and its importance can only be comprehended by comparison with the Accursian *glossa* or the commentary of Bartolus de Saxoferrato. In fact, as early as the seminal work by Sextus Aelius Paetus (consul in 198 BC), the intention was to create a *book of reference*, an aggregation of (private) law as a whole. The title of his work, *Tripertita*, clearly refers to three complementary levels: (i) the rules contained in the XII Tables, on the basis of which (ii) interpretation occurred and (iii) actions were attached. The ancients considered these to be the "primary elements" of the law (*cunabula iuris*: D.1.2.2.38). One characteristic of the *Tripertita* would leave a profound mark; namely, that the presentation is laid down by a source prior and external to the jurist's writing: here, the XII Tables constitute a "framework of memory" (Wibier 2014, 64), a role subsequently to be performed by the edict (or other *leges*). In addition to reinforcing the profound link between enacted law and juristic law, the adoption of a system based on external sources entailed the deliberate rejection of a system governed by a logic based on *genus* and *species*, which is typical of modern legal science: such a rejection must be taken as characteristic of the Roman legal mentality, and not as a sign of backwardness.

We shall return (section 3.3) to the development of jurisprudential literature. Precisely at the time of Sex. Aelius, an increase in epigraphy testifies to another type of publication: the *senatus consultum de Bacchanalibus* (186 BC) requires local magistrates to publish its content on a bronze table, to be affixed in a place where it may be easily read (*AE* 2006, 21, ll. 25–27; on this practice see Ferrary 2009). This is a *habitus* that finds its model in the publication of the XII Tables and reflects also the use of bronze as a written medium, which distinguishes the practice followed in Rome and in the Western provinces from that of the Greek East, where stone was used.[14] Thus, an understanding of the Roman experience "in context" must take account of the fact that it occurred within a "written space" constituted largely of legal texts (see Beggio, ch. 4). This is an essential factor that mitigates the supposed isolation of jurisprudential law, and establishes it as but one element in a complex and interrelated communicative system (Fioretti 2012).

Some of these "writings on display" were directly relevant for private law: in addition to the *leges*, this was also the case for the praetor's edict, which was read to the people gathered in the *contio* and displayed on wooden tablets, at least from the fourth/third centuries BC. (The use of whitened boards rather than bronze for its publication emphasises the transitory duration of the edict, being formally associated with an annual magistracy.)[15]

[14] See Plin. *HN* 34.99. Eck 2015 stresses the distinction between East and West. Crawford 2011 considers whether the XII Tables were originally carved on stone.

[15] In 62 AD, an edict by the praetor L. Servenius Gallus was affixed to a column *sub porticu Iulia* in the *Forum Augustum* in front of the *tribunal* of the praetor: *T.H.* 89, I, 2, lines 2–6 (it is likely that the general jurisdictional edict was also affixed there). On the topography see Neudecker 2010. The edict of the governor was displayed in the forum of each of the Empire's *municipia: lex Irn.* 85.

Pomponius was aware that the edict performed the function of enabling access to legal information and ensuring that justice was foreseeable (D.1.2.2.10). The edict reflected the crucial role of the praetor, through his supervision of trials, not only in implementing but also in supplementing, clarifying and even correcting the law on the basis of the XII Tables, other *leges* or juristic interpretation. Over the course of a couple of centuries, edicts by magistrates holding jurisdiction (praetors in Rome; governors in the provinces; *aediles curules* in their sphere of jurisdiction, as well as *quaestores* in the public provinces) established themselves as the material and intellectual centre of gravity of the system. At the *album*, lawyers sat waiting for clients (Sen. *Ep.* 48.10); the plaintiff took his opponent there when he wanted to inform him of the action he intended to bring (D.2.13.1.1). Jurists, for their part, engaged in an intense work of interpretation of the edict, which was aimed at clarifying provisions and at recording judicial practice: their purpose was to build a repository to help magistrates and private individuals know the manner in which the edict was typically applied. Initially an object of desultory consideration, the edict was subsequently subjected to line-by-line explanation, as already reflected in Cicero's *Pro Caecina*. Commentary on the edict, as a literary form, was inaugurated by Servius Sulpicius Rufus (cos. 51 BC) with a brief work dedicated to Brutus; it was developed by Aulus Ofilius under Caesar (Mantovani 1996). This sub-genre became progressively more widespread, peaking in terms of quantity with the approximately one hundred and fifty books written by Pomponius in the middle of the second century AD, and in qualitative terms with Paul and Ulpian at the beginning of the third century. To bring to full circle the discussion of this complex system of communication, the fact that the edict was displayed at the most frequented point of each city of the Empire and that the activity of *ius dicere* was conducted in public spaces under collective control contributed to creating a premodern form of access to the law.

This system can be seen at work through contemporary eyes. In *De oratore*, written in 55 BC but set in 91, Cicero asserts that—contrary to popular belief—after shaking off its secret status the *ius civile* could easily be known:

> All its materials lie open to view, having their setting in everyday business, in the intercourse of men, and in the forum ... and they are not enclosed in so very many records or in books so very big: for identical matters were originally published by numerous authors, and afterwards, with slight variations in terms, were set down time and again even by the same writers. (1.192, transl. E. W. Sutton)

Cicero provides a dynamic representation of the communicative system whose two principal elements we have attempted to describe: part was public, under the gaze of all (due to public display and judicial and contractual practice); part was contained in the writings of jurists.

Cicero reveals that jurisprudential literature was already quite voluminous and cumulative (he also regards it as substantially repetitive). His project of creating a well-structured presentation of the law (*ars*)—reducing the disparate material to a few general principles, subject to divisions and clarified through definitions—was then taking its first steps, in the works of Quintus Mucius Scaevola and Servius Sulpicius Rufus. But it was only in the second century AD, with the *Institutiones* of Gaius, that Cicero's wish would be realised in a more complete, yet never comprehensive form. The project simply did not reflect a need felt by the public at large or by legal practitioners.[16]

What instead was felt, above all by persons active in government, was the need to create order among the *leges publicae*: a *memoria publica* was lacking; that is, an accurate record of statute law, a point stressed, again, by Cicero (*Leg.* 3.46). Looking back from the seventh century, Isidore sought to create a single narrative of Roman efforts to consolidate the law, from the XII Tables to the *Codex Theodosianus*. He describes Pompey as the first "to want to collect and establish the statutes in books", followed by Caesar.[17] There is debate as to what the purposes and objectives of these late-Republican projects were, both of which failed; there is, however, no doubt that the *leges publicae* were by then numerous and difficult to coordinate, as is confirmed in the Augustan Age by Livy, and retrospectively by Tacitus (Liv. 3.34.6; Tac. *Ann.* 3.27). Furthermore, the projects appear to be consistent with other far-reaching reforms pursued by the two leaders via legislation—first concerning criminal trials and then public and private law—that Cicero explicitly assessed as the main accomplishment of their political action (Cic. *Phil.* 1.18).[18]

The initiatives taken by Pompey and Caesar introduce us to a further aspect of the organisation of Roman law during the Republican era. Rome's constitution was unwritten, having been built up through custom over the course of generations (Cic. *Rep.* 2.2). When Polybius described the Roman *politeia* he, too, refers to this practice, giving it organic form through categories drawn from Greek political thought. However, we would be mistaken to think that the Romans had not elaborated a unitary and normative conception of the constitution or that they had to await the *De legibus* of Cicero, who pursued the task on a philosophical plane (Fontanella 2013). The need to reorganise the conquered cities, and to give laws to the colonies, had long since led them to this awareness.

This is shown by an episode involving Polybius himself. After the sack of Corinth, in 146 BC the senate sent ten commissioners to assist Lucius Mummius, who then dissolved the Achaean League and gave *politeia* and *nomoi* to each city. The commissioners eventually departed, leaving Polybius behind "with the task of travelling around to all the cities and explaining to citizens the points about which they nurtured doubts until they had grown used to the constitution and the laws" (Polyb. 39.5.2–3; for Polybius' possible involvement in

[16] Bona 1980/2003; Finazzi 2014. The 18 *libri* of Quintus Mucius appeared at least to Pomponius (D.1.2.2.41) as an accomplishment that had never previously been achieved in terms of the organisation of the *ius civile*.

[17] Isid. *Etym.* 5.1.5; Caesar's initiative is confirmed by Suet. *Iul.* 44.2. Despite both texts' use of the term *leges*, Santucci 2014, 378–379, argues that they refer to jurisprudential law. Such opinion is refuted by a scrutiny of both authors' word usage. In the *Vitae Caesarum*, Suetonius uses *lex* in the singular twenty-eight times: in twenty-four cases he refers to a *lex publica* (on eighteen occasions indicating the name or content); once to a *lex curiata*; and three times to a *lex contractus* or similar. *Leges* appears in the plural twenty-one times besides in the passage in question, always with (more or less specific) reference to *leges publicae*, not to jurisprudential law. As for Isidore, immediately after having evoked the attempts to bring together *leges*, he dedicates a series of chapters to the definition of legal terms. In chapter 5.10 he defines *quid sit lex: Lex est constitutio populi, qua maiores natu simul cum plebibus aliquid sanxerunt*; with the same propriety of language, jurisprudential law is defined in chapter 5.14: *Responsa sunt quae iurisconsulti respondere dicuntur consulentibus.*

[18] The hypothesis dates back, with some variants, to Sanio (1845, 68–76). The links between the jurist Ofilius—and his work *de legibus* (*vicensimae*?)—and the Caesarian project are uncertain.

the drafting see Polyb. 39.5.5; Paus. 8.30.9). The constitution given to the Achaeans reflected that used by Rome itself, at least as far as its timocratic structure was concerned (Pausanias 7.16.9 asserts that Mummius abolished democracy everywhere, establishing property qualifications for office). Furthermore, from a letter sent in 144 to the city of Dyme by the proconsul of Macedonia we learn that the cities enjoyed freedom, but not such as to be able to write "laws contrary to the *politeia* given back by the Romans to the Achaeans" (*RDGE* 43, ll. 9–10; Ferrary 1988, 186–199). The laws imposed by Rome were thus constitutional insofar as they incorporated socio-political principles intended to prevail over "ordinary" (so to speak) legislation. Through the glimpse these documents afford us, we see that Romans of the mid-second century BC possessed a normative conception (*nomoi*) of the constitution (*politeia*). But the conception was certainly older: in 194, after the victory at Cynoscephalae, T. Quinctius Flamininus had already given *nomoi*, again on the advice of ten legates.[19] Indeed, the practice probably dates back farther still, to the founding of colonies and the municipal organisation of Italy. For example, in 317 the senate sent patrons to Capua *ad iura statuenda*, in relation to which Livy observed that "not simply Roman arms, but also Roman laws were widely powerful".[20]

The Romans thus soon became aware of the normative nature of the constitution, through the need to regulate by enacted law the communities subjugated to them. But we do not know whether they thought of "codifying" their own public law (unless the attempt on the part of Pompey and that of Caesar aimed (also) to do this). Certainly, this capacity to formulate constitutional law was of benefit to cities within the Empire: charters granted to cities, originating as statutory enactments in Rome, regulated and so openly described to the public the structure and operation of political organs (the magistrates, the *curia* and the *comitia*), the management of common property and individual political rights (on municipal charters see also Roselaar, ch. 10). In a *municipium Latinum* such as Irni, in Baetica, at the end of the first century AD the inhabitants could read a constitutional charter of this type displayed in bronze in the forum; alongside, they would have found the *album* containing the jurisdictional edict of the provincial governor, with which municipal magistrates were also required to comply during the administration of justice. This collection of enacted legal texts, supplemented by the writings of jurists, made it possible to access all aspects of the law.[21]

[19] The *senatus consultum* speaks of the *nomoi* given by Flaminius to the Thessalians, *nomoi* which were still in force, in relation to the border dispute between Melitaia and Narthakion in *c.*140 BC (*SIG* 674, ll. 49–53, 63–64).

[20] Liv. 9.20.10. The *lex* from Bantia, written in Oscan using the Latin alphabet (ed. Crawford, *Imagines Italicae*, Vol. 3: 1437, Bantia no. 1), reflects the legal institutions and practices of Rome. Glottological considerations suggest that an earlier statute was used as a model, which Bantia had adopted *c.*300 BC, imitating in turn a municipal statute adopted by Rome. This would confirm all the more Livy's statement, because an independent city such as Bantia willingly took a Roman statute as a model, without being compelled to.

[21] The statute also provided for the publication of tenders for public contracts; of the lists of *iudices*; and of candidates for election. For an understanding of these texts some mediation by *patroni* or *iuris studiosi* will have been useful. Nevertheless, the contrivance adopted by Caligula (Suet. *Cal.* 41.1) to prevent the people from acquiring knowledge about a tax law—"He had the law posted up, but in a very narrow place and in excessively small letters, to prevent the making of a copy"—shows that public display was effective.

3.3 The Principate

With the advent of the *principes*, the situation altered, albeit slowly. The jurists continued to perform the function of "civic oracles", ensuring the consistency of the various sources of law and informing the public. However, the right to *respondere ex auctoritate princpis*—with which certain jurists were endowed starting from Augustus—indicates that the political centre of gravity had shifted, even though the techniques had not changed (see also Peachin, ch. 13). Nevertheless, legal literature gained in importance, as a consequence of territorial expansion and the democratisation of knowledge. Tellingly, the rag merchant Echion, a fictional and unlettered character in Petronius' *Satyricon*, sought to buy *aliquot libra rubricata*, "certain red-rubricked (law) books", in order to enable his son to acquire sufficient knowledge to embark upon a profitable profession (*Sat.* 46.7).[22] The adjective *rubricata* indicates that legal literature was now starting to be distinguished also by virtue of its paratext, being divided into headings that facilitated consultation and that were patterned after the layout of *leges* and *edicta*.[23] The very same demand led to an early adoption of the "code" (*codex*) format, which is alluded to already by the title *Membranae*, "Parchments", given by Neratius Priscus (cos. suff. 97) to one of his works.[24] Before becoming a keyword of modern law, the *codex*—as a book format—thus responded in a different way to the need for accessibility, which confirms the appropriateness of examining Antiquity in the light of its specific intellectual and material aspects.

A further instrument of "global" communication that overcame the increasingly large distances within the Empire was the correspondence between jurists (or with their clients), which could also end up in books: a significant example is D.3.5.33, in which the great jurist Julius Paulus, active in Rome during the Severan era, reproduced a letter sent to him by L. Nessenius Apollinaris, a jurist working in Ephesus (*AE* 1975, 793).

The growing need for legal information was also met by teaching (Cannata 2002/2012). It was Masurius Sabinus himself (along with his successor C. Cassius Longinus) who gave rise to a new figure, the "teacher of law and head of a school", one who expressed his own opinions on a number of controversial points of law, thus giving his teaching almost the flavour of a school of thought as defined by a set of doctrines, in opposition to other jurists (e.g. Nerva and Proculus). Subsequent generations coalesced around these *auctores*. This fostering of loyalty and identity was furthered also through literature: Gaius in the second century refers to Sabinus and Cassius as his *praeceptores*, though they died long before he was born. The increasing demand for legal education also led, during the second century AD, to an isagogic literature—including most prominently the *Institutiones* of Gaius—which availed itself of the methods long since exploited by Greek and Latin textbooks, including not only division of the *genera* into *species* and definitions, but also cataloguing, parallelisms and antitheses (Fuhrmann 1960). However, even in Gaius' programme the

[22] A good overview could be obtained by consulting the three books on *ius civile* by Masurius Sabinus and the *leges publicae*: see Gell. *NA* 14.2.1 and Pers. 5.90, with Nörr 2003.

[23] *P. Mich.* 456r + *P. Yale* inv. 1158r (= *CLA* Suppl. 1779) is the oldest jurisprudential papyrus that has survived (first to second century AD) and the oldest example of a *liber rubricatus*.

[24] By the fourth century AD, the parchment codex replaced the papyrus book roll (*volumen*). An early surviving example of a legal codex is provided by BPL 2589, a copy of the Pauli Sententiae.

teaching of law was based on more than a single textbook and included the customary materials; that is, large collections of cases assembled following the edictal order or other external frameworks. Gaius' programme is reflected in the study plan in use prior to the Justinianic reform (C. *Omnem*, [a. 533]; see Liebs 2008), and his own teaching manifesto has been included, in my view, in the prooemium to Justinian's Institutes (1.1.2).

The spread of law schools in the provinces not only guaranteed the training of new jurists but also helped Roman law to be applied in courts and by administrative authorities outside of Italy: legal teaching became thus a genuine instrument of government.[25] Law schools produced *iuris studiosi* who functioned as *consiliarii* or *assessores*; that is, experts who provided legal advice to magistrates and officials in their administrative and judicial activities (D.1.22.1). These trained jurists created a kind of neural network for the transmission of Roman law throughout the Empire. In the mid-fourth century, under the reign of Constantius, the *Expositio totius mundi* (25) refers to this phenomenon when describing Berytus, which hosted an important law school: "A most charming city, it has law schools that assure the stability of all the Roman legal system. Thence learned men come, who assist judges all over the world and with their knowledge of the laws protect the provinces, to which legal norms are sent."

A new sign of the attention to order and predictability is to be seen in the composition of the praetor's edict, attributed to the jurist Salvius Iulianus (*cos.* 148) during Hadrian's time. The historicity of this is a matter for discussion, although to deny it would require the refutation of clear evidence (as attempted most recently by Cancelli 2010). At least from the fourth century onward, it is described as a rearrangement (*Iulianus … in ordinem composuit*) in response to the fact that the edictal clauses were formulated differently, from year to year and from province to province, and even in a contradictory (*varie*) and disorderly (*incondite*) manner (Aurel. Vict. *Caes.* 19.1–2).

However, this was not an entirely novel concept: as early as 67 BC the tribune Cornelius secured approval for a plebiscite ordering "that the praetors administer the law in accordance with their perpetual edicts" (*ut praetores ex edictis suis perpetuis ius dicerent*) (Asc. *Corn.* 52 [p. 59C]; Dio Cass. 36.38–40, esp. 40.2–3), a provision incorporated also into the municipal statutes (e.g. *lex Irn.* 85), in such a way as to bind the jurisdiction of municipal magistrates to the edict issued by the governor of the province (or the praetor in Rome).

Hadrian's *compositio edicti* constitutes a useful case study of the interference between modern ideologies of codification and historical reconstruction. That Justinian described Julian's intervention in terms that evoked his own *ordinatio* (*Tanta* 18) led many to consider the perpetual edict as a "code", from at least the eighteenth century: it is the term used, for example, by Gibbon (Gibbon 1788/1845, 215: "this well-digested code", an expression of Justinianic flavour). After Lenel established that the *edictum perpetuum* did not possess the "systematic" order typical of a modern code, it was no longer defined by legal historians as a "code", although Julian's intervention continued to be described as a "codification": this accordingly led to a paradoxical historiographical interpretation that can

[25] In addition to Rome and Berytus, later joined by Constantinople, there is evidence of legal teaching in Salona (third century); Smyrna (third century); Augustodunum (fourth century); Carthage (fourth century); Narbona (fifth century); Lugdunum (fifth century); Caesarea in Palestine (sixth century); and Alexandria ad Aegyptum (fifth–sixth century). See Liebs 2002; Cannata 2002/2012; Jones 2007.

be labelled a "codification without a code".[26] By contrast, the true nature of the edict can only be found when modern categories are avoided: it did not amount to substantive (or procedural) "legislation"; rather, it concerned the *officium* of the magistrate who enacted it. The wording of the clauses thus left him discretion in application. The magistrate's discretion was, however, moderated by the jurists' interpretation, which was recorded in the comments *ad edictum*. *Edicta* and jurists' writings thus exemplify once again the complementarity between enacted law and case law that was typical of the Roman legal system.

During the second and third centuries, legal literature expanded in line with the need to provide a frame of reference. It has been rightly said that "classical literature was a legal consolidation in progress" (Casavola 1998, 305): in addition to commenting on legislative enactments, jurists—as Cicero had already observed—liberally cited the opinions of their predecessors, often expressing their support, though at times their disagreement, thus providing an ongoing "restatement".

However, this equilibrium was not able to withstand for long the truly new fact that characterised the Roman legal system since Augustus; namely, the ever-increasing involvement of the *principes* in lawmaking. This involvement provided a new and powerful means of disseminating the law throughout the Empire, whilst also making the retrieval of legal information more difficult.[27] A brief look into this seems in order here. Imperial *constitutiones* of general application were announced to the public by being read aloud, and therefore were often referred to as *edicta*;[28] they were also posted in public, sometimes only for a limited time, albeit with a tendency to use more durable media of display from the time of Diocletian onward.[29] The *mandata*, or instructions addressed to magistrates and officials, were not intended to be made public, except sporadically.[30] Judicial rulings also do not appear to have been recorded systematically in reports intended for circulation.[31] In quantitative terms, the *rescripta*—that is, the emperor's answers to petitions submitted to him—predominated, so much so as to lead modern scholars to define Roman Imperial rule as a reactive type of governance (Millar 1992). Questions and petitions submitted by

[26] Mantovani 1998; Bretone 2004; Tuori 2006, 185–242.

[27] The *constitutiones principis* turned into the most prolific source of law even though—ideologically—the *lex* always kept the first place, as an expression of popular sovereignty (Inst.1.2.4).

[28] Public recitation was already provided for under the *SC de Bacchanalibus* from 186 BC (*AE* 2006, 21, ll. 22–24). For additional sources, classical and late antique, Roman and provincial, see Ando 2000, 104, 108, 114–115, 181. In late-Antiquity Rome, constitutions were read aloud in the senate (e.g. CTh.8.18.1; 9.1.3 [both undated]), but also at the Pantheon (CTh.14.3.10 [a. 386/370]) and on the Palatine (CTh.10.8.3 [undated]); a constitution that prohibited priests from visiting widows and pupils for the purpose of obtaining their assets was read *in ecclesiis Romae* (CTh.16.2.20 [a. 370]). Public response to recitation in provincial cities is recorded in a lively manner by John Chrys. *Homil. In Gen.* (PG 53.112b–c).

[29] e.g. Sirm. 9; 12. On bronze: e.g. CTh.12.5.2 (a. 337); 14.4.4 (a. 367), *ad aeternam memoriam*. On painted tablets or linen sheets: CTh.11.27.1 (a. 329?). About publication methods (including also other types of *constitutiones*) see Matthews 2000; Puliatti 2008; Haensch 2009.

[30] For example, Domitian's instructions that limited the forced hiring of pack animals and the requisition of accommodations were engraved on marble in Epiphaneia (Oliver 1989, no. 40). In general see Meyer-Zwiffelhoffer 2002, 338–342; Marotta 2011.

[31] The *Decreta* (or *Imperiales sententiae in cognitionibus prolatae*), a work by Paul resulting from his direct participation in the Imperial council of Septimius Severus and Caracalla, constitutes an exception.

magistrates, officials and communities came in the diplomatic form of *epistulae*, and were not generally intended for publication, unless the recipient considered it appropriate: a renowned example being the correspondence between Pliny and Trajan; often, communities published the answers that were favourable to them. Jurists did not hesitate to include *epistulae* in their works, perhaps extracting them from archives or private records.[32] As far as private individuals were concerned, the emperor wrote his answers (*subscriptiones*) underneath the *libelli* received (which often related to legal questions) and posted them in the place where the audience had been held (*liber libellorum rescriptorum*) (see *SIG* 888, Skaptopara in Thrace; in general, Connolly 2010; Kelly 2011). Private copies were made of such texts, of which papyrus fragments survive.[33] *Subscriptiones* were then frequently cited by jurists who, however, reproduced them undated and often without the addressees, which made it problematic to cite them in court proceedings. Not much is known about the Imperial archives:[34] however, the fact that the content of *subscriptiones* is so repetitive, almost verbatim, implies, in my view, that the chancery kept repositories in which it could find precedents, which helped in simplifying work and in ensuring consistent responses. It is certain that governors kept archives (Haensch 2013), but it cannot be said whether Imperial and provincial archives were open to consultation. Although the topic awaits comprehensive study, it appears that for about three centuries the circulation of Imperial *constitutiones* remained predominantly a matter for private initiative. The *constitutiones* proliferated, but it was difficult for the public to gain complete and up-to-date knowledge of them and to incorporate them into the law in force.

3.4 Towards a Juristic Canon

In 197 AD, Tertullian,[35] addressing the *Romani imperii antistites*, “the governors of the Roman Empire”, anticipated the expressions and ideas that would pervade Justinian’s introductory constitutions (*Apol.* 4.7): “Do not you, too, prune and cut down all the wild growth of that ancient forest of law with the new axes of Imperial rescripts and edicts, as daily experience throws light upon the darkness of Antiquity?”[36] There was a widespread feeling that the end of the system of organising the law as it had been known up to that time was drawing near, now having become too dense and contradictory.

[32] An *epistula* from Severus Alexander to the *koinon* of Bithinia is preserved by *P. Oxy.* xviii 2104; *P. Oxy.* xliii 3106 and by D.49.1.25: this is an example of dissemination beyond the intended recipients (Kantor 2009, 256–258).

[33] e.g. *P. Oxy.* vii 1020 = Oliver 1989, nos. 22–222 (a. 199/200); still debated is the nature of *Aprokrimata*, see *P. Col.* 123 = Oliver 1989, nos. 226–238 (a. 200).

[34] Varvaro 2006. A large number of citations of *constitutiones* in jurists’ books, which are often interpreted as evidence for the existence and use of public archives, may, however, originate from private copies.

[35] Probably not the jurist who authored *De peculio castrensi*: Harries 2009.

[36] The emphasis is placed on substantive reform: the first example—chosen by Tertullian because it was relevant from both the Christian perspective and that of society as a whole, which had always objected to its harshness—is the Augustan marriage legislation.

The same jurists who in another way were the principal bulwark against disorder contributed to the chaos. The proliferation of disputes—that is, of very intense discussions on points of law—rendered their works repositories in which a lawyer could always hope to find an opinion favourable to his case (the drawback of jurists' disputes was already clear to Constantine: CTh.1.4.1 [a. 321]). In addition, it was difficult for jurists to keep up with the production of *constitutiones*. The last of the "literary" jurists, Arcadius Charisius and above all Hermogenianus, flourished under Diocletian; thereafter, no legal works were produced of the type written since Sextus Aelius at the beginning of the second century BC. Why this literature came to an end is one of the most difficult questions to answer about the history of Roman law. The most frequent response is that the eclipse was caused by the collapse of legal culture: no longer were there jurists with the intellectual strength of the classical jurists and who could cope with their *dissensiones*. This is not a satisfactory answer, as it disregards two fundamental aspects of late Antiquity.[37] First, in many parts of the Empire, legal culture continued to be handed down in law schools, with such prestige as to compete with rhetorical education, as Libanius in fourth-century Antioch complains (Cribiore 2007). The attraction of legal education then is shown by the rise of a bureaucratic and military class that abandoned the adherence to Greek of the previous generations and took it upon themselves to learn Latin as the language of administration and law (Rochette 2008; Eck 2009). Second, this explanation disregards the fact that, whilst jurists' works were no longer written anew, this did not in itself leave a void. The classical jurists' books continued to be copied on papyrus and parchment, as is strikingly shown by the fact that they represent almost half of Latin literary papyri from the fourth century onward (Ammirati 2010). These works were read and cited in judicial proceedings, as well as in order to interpret Imperial constitutions (as demonstrated e.g. by C.6.61.5 [a. 473]). They were also the subject of commentary in Greek (a kind of texts still largely unexplored), from which a keen understanding of classical texts is revealed: the *Scholia Sinaitica* are the most renowned although not the only example.[38]

If one recalls that after citizenship was extended to (almost) all inhabitants in 212 there was a need for a legal order that could be put in place throughout the Empire, it becomes clear why Roman law came to be frozen in the form (not modifiable, precisely for its normative character) given by the classical jurists. The jurisprudential tradition crystallised in a textual canon, which continued to be copied and interpreted, in the same manner late-Antiquity intellectuals collected and commented upon classical poetry, rhetoric, grammar or holy scriptures.

Against the backdrop of the now canonised writings of the classical jurists, the most urgent problem was how to render accessible the *constitutiones*, which continued to be issued. That is why the late-Antiquity *codices* are primarily concerned with Imperial constitutions. The *Codex Hermogenianus* was comprised almost exclusively of *subscriptiones* issued in 293 and 294, whilst the *Codex Gregorianus* brought together in at least thirteen books the *subscriptiones* (along with other types of Imperial enactments) issued by

[37] On the need to mitigate the idea of decadence see the important observations in Humfress 2012 and Ando 2013, 53–85.

[38] Coma Fort 2014b; Mantovani 2014. The editing of the writings of classical jurists in late Antiquity is covered by the research project Redhis (http://redhis.unipv.it/, accessed 28 January 2016).

Hadrian through Diocletian (the final date is uncertain). These two collections (one with a long-term focus and the other comprising updates) pursued the aim of disseminating Roman law in summary form, as a means of setting about the task of assimilating peoples with different languages and legal traditions. Since the *subscriptiones* often did nothing other than reiterate legal rules already in use, the two *codices* did not depart much in style from the jurists' book devoted to *responsa*, and even less from reference works such as *regulae* or *sententiae receptae*.[39] They therefore appear as the final expression of the old way of making law and rendering it accessible, even as they prefigure a new system.

3.5 Conclusion

In looking back at the final period of Roman legal history in the light of modern codification the temptation is strong to see it dominated by the great codes of the fifth and sixth centuries and by the ideologies extolled in their introductory constitutions: we return thus to the point from which we started. There is no need to expatiate on the characteristics of the *Codex Theodosianus* and Justinian's project, both of which have been well studied (Dovere 2013; Salway 2013; on the Theodosian textual tradition, Coma Fort 2014a; on the *Corpus Iuris Civilis,* Kaiser 2015). What is worthwhile instead is, once again, to situate them in context, whence several novel features are apparent, alongside close links with prior tradition. Concerning the *Theodosianus*, the collection known as *Constitutiones Sirmondianae* (which brought together sixteen or eighteen constitutions from between 333 and 425, focusing mainly on ecclesiastical matters; Vessey 2010) and *P. Gen.* inv. 6, containing a constitution of Honorius and Theodosius II from 423, in a version more detailed than that in the *Theodosianus* (edited by Ammirati, Fressura and Mantovani 2015), show that private and local attempts to collect and disseminate Imperial constitutions were under way at the same time that Theodosius launched his project. Moreover, evidence of the dissemination of constitutions dates back to the second and third centuries (see section 3.3). Obviously the move towards *generales leges* (i.e. enactments intended to have a general application) and the fragmentation of the formally unitary *imperium* can account for the new political importance attached to these initiatives to which the emperor wished to give his name.

On the other hand, the canonisation of classical legal literature and the continuity assured by legal teaching laid the groundwork for the Digest, an endeavour that only mistakenly can be construed as rooted in nostalgia.

In order to arrive at a more comprehensive assessment of the strands that come together in the whole Justinianic compilation, of great interest is its comparison with an anonymous anthology, likely compiled by a private individual in Italy or Gaul, probably under Constantine, which has been given the modern name of *Fragmenta Vaticana*, from the location where the manuscript preserving it is housed (*ms. Vat.* no. 5766; fourth or fifth century).

[39] "Thus the rescripts are in effect juristic *responsa* camouflaged by being issued in the names of the emperors." See Corcoran 2013, also for the dates and content of the *codices*.

Twenty-eight pages of the sylloge survive, although bibliological considerations indicate that it must have had at least two hundred and forty large-format pages, which would be equivalent to about a quarter of Justinian's Digest, and the possibility that there might have been many more pages cannot be ruled out.[40] This fourth-century collection contains a broad selection of classical literature, including six works by Ulpian, fourteen by Paul and two by Papinian (and other undetermined authors), in addition to rescripts from Severus to Constantine (thus providing textual evidence that the chancery continued to issue *rescripta* even after Diocletian).[41] The compiler perhaps drew on the *Gregorianus* and the *Hermogenianus* for the constitutions, but he undoubtedly collected others on his own initiative in the West.

A comparison of this anthology with Justinian's project reveals some points in common, such as the retention of the names of jurists and the titles of the works from which extracts were taken; reference is also made to emperors and to the date and place of publication of constitutions, information without which the *lectiones* could not have been cited in court (for Justinian, the preservation of this information becomes a show of *antiquitatis reverentia*). The nature of the collected material, including both jurisprudence and *constitutiones*, is significantly similar too. The *Fragmenta Vaticana* thus prefigure Theodosius' dream of compiling a single code fusing the *Gregorianus*, the *Hermogenianus*, the *generales leges* and the jurists' writings (according to one plausible reading of CTh.1.1.5 [a. 429]). Justinian was successful in this endeavour, though keeping separate the collections of the jurists' writings and those of the constitutions, which the Vatican anthology had already been able to unify within a single system.

What radically distinguishes the two endeavours is that Justinian's commission eliminated antinomies, repetitions and disputes between jurists. Tellingly, the *Fragmenta Vaticana* retain some of the most complex and beautiful examples of *ius controversum* to have come down to us, with a vitality entirely lacking in the *Digesta* (e.g. *Vat.* 75–89, from Ulpian's book 17 *ad Sabinum*).

To attribute this difference to less intellectual vigour on the part of the Western compiler of the Vatican collection would be ungenerous: only a legislator would have been in the legal position to modify the wording of jurists' books and of *constitutiones*. In this regard, Justinian's project marks a significant break with the past, even though it was preceded, in this respect too, by Theodosius, who had already granted his commissioners the authority to edit the *constitutiones*.[42] All in all, the *Fragmenta Vaticana* show that the Justinianic legal culture sits within a long tradition, which identified Roman law with the jurists' literature, integrated by the Imperial constitutions. It is in this regard that, also in late Antiquity, the trends towards reordering and enabling access to the law appear more complex and differentiated than a sole focus on Theodosius and Justinian's responses might suggest, under the influence of modern drives towards codification and rationalisation.

[40] Mommsen 1860, 400. In fact, the *Fr.Vat.* are comparatively more abundant, e.g. in the title *de excusationibus*.

[41] Mommsen 1860, 398–400, already rightly inferred from *Fr. Vat.* the continuation of *rescripta* after Diocletian; *contra* De Giovanni 2012. See now Puliatti 2013.

[42] From an ideological point of view, the action that comes closest is the regulation imposed by the so-called law of citations (CTh.1.4.3 [a. 426], part of a broader *generalis lex*): Fernández Cano 2000; Sirks 2014.

Bibliography

Ammirati, S. (2010). "Per una storia del libro latino antico: osservazioni paleografiche, bibliologiche e codicologiche sui manoscritti latini di argomento legale dalle origini alla tarda antichità." *Journal of Juristic Papyrology* 40: 55–110.

Ammirati, S., Fressura, M. and Mantovani, D. (2015). "*Curiales* e *cohortales* in *P. Gen. Lat.* inv. 6. Una nuova versione di una costituzione di Onorio e Teodosio II del 423." *Zeitschrift der Savigny-Stiftung für Rechtsgeschichte, romanistische Abteilung* 132: 299–323.

Ando, C. 2000. *Imperial ideology and provincial loyalty in the Roman empire*. Berkeley.

Ando, C. 2013. *L'Empire et le Droit. Invention juridique et réalités historiques à Rome*. Paris.

Ankum, H. 1982/2008. "La codification de Justinien était-elle une véritable codification?" In *Extravagantes. Scritti sparsi sul diritto romano*. Naples. 55–71.

Ankum, H. 2001/2008. "Was Justinian's *Corpus Iuris Civilis* a codification?" In *Extravagantes. Scritti sparsi sul diritto romano*. Naples. 399–412.

Bona, F. 1980/2003. "L'ideale retorico ciceroniano ed il *ius civile in artem redigere*." In F. Bona, Lectio sua, *Studi editi ed inediti di diritto romano*. Padua. Vol. 2:717–831.

Bretone, M. 2004. *Diritto e tempo nella tradizione europea*. Rome/Bari.

Bretone, M. (2009). "*Ius controversum* nella giurisprudenza classica." *Memorie Accademia Nazionale dei Lincei, Classe di Scienze Morali, Storiche e Filologiche* IX 23: 756–879.

Canale, D. 2009. "The many faces of legal codification in modern continental Europe." In D. Canale, P. Grossi and H. Hofmann, eds., *A history of the philosophy of law from the seventeenth century to 1900 in the civil-law tradition*. Berlin. 135–183.

Cancelli, F. 2010. *La codificazione dell'*edictum praetoris: *dogma romanistico*. Milan.

Cannata, C. A. 2002/2012. "Qualche considerazione sull'ambiente della giurisprudenza romana al tempo delle due scuole." In *Scritti scelti di diritto romano*. Turin. Vol. 2: 401–437.

Capogrossi Colognesi, L. 2008. *Dalla storia di Roma alle origini della società civile: un dibattito ottocentesco*. Bologna.

Carandini, A., ed. 2011. *La leggenda di Roma*, Vol. 3: *La costituzione*. Milan.

Casavola, F. P. 1998. "Verso la codificazione traverso la compilazione," in *La codificazione dall'antico al moderno. Incontri di Studio, Napoli, gennaio-novembre 1996. Atti*. Naples. 303–311.

Coma Fort, J. M. 2014a. Codex Theodosianus: *historia de un texto*. Madrid.

Coma Fort, J. M. 2014b. "La jurisprudencia de la Antigüedad Tardía: las bases culturales y textuales del Digesto." In D. Mantovani and A. Padoa Schioppa, eds., *Interpretare il Digesto: Storia e metodi*. Pavia. 23–73.

Connolly, S. 2010. *Lives behind the laws: the world of the* Codex Hermogenianus. Bloomington.

Corcoran, S. (2013). "The *Gregorianus* and *Hermogenianus* assembled and shattered." *Mélanges de l'École française de Rome—Antiquité* 125 (2). Available at: http://discovery.ucl.ac.uk/1416835/, accessed 14 February 2016.

Crawford, M. H. 2011. "From Ionia to the Twelve Tables." In K. Muscheler, ed., *Römische Jurisprudenz—Dogmatik, Überlieferung, Rezeption. Festschrift für Detlef Liebs zum 75. Geburtstag*. Berlin. 153–159.

Cribiore, R. 2007. *The school of Libanius in late antique Antioch*. Princeton.

De Giovanni, L. (2012). "Potere imperiale e forme di produzione del diritto nella Tarda Antichità." *Seminarios Complutenses de Derecho Romano* 25: 153–164.

Dovere, E. (2013). "Epifania politica del Theodosianus." *Mélanges de l'École française de Rome—Antiquité* 125 (2). Available at: https://mefra.revues.org/1742, accessed 27 June 2015.

Eck, W. 2009. "The presence, role and significance of Latin in the epigraphy and culture of the Roman Near East." In H. M. Cotton and R. G. Hoyland, eds., *From Hellenism to Islam: cultural and linguistic change in the Roman near east*. Cambridge. 15–42.

Eck, W. 2015. "Documents on bronze: a phenomenon of the Roman west?" In J. Bodel and N. Dimitrova, eds., *Ancient documents and their context*. Leiden. 127–151.

Fernández Cano, A. C. 2000. *La llamada* "ley de citas" *en su contexto histórico*. Madrid.

Ferrary J.-L. 1988. *Philhellénisme et impérialisme: aspects idéologiques de la conquête romaine du monde hellénistique*. Rome.

Ferrary, J.-L. 2009. "La gravure de documents publics de la Rome républicaine et ses motivations." In R. Haensch, ed., *Selbstdarstellung und Kommunication: die Veröffentlichung staatlicher Urkunden auf Stein und Bronze in der römischen Welt*. Munich. 59–74.

Finazzi, G. 2014. "Intorno a Pomp. Ench. 1.2.2.43." In J. Hallebeek et al., eds., Inter cives necnon peregrinos. *Essays in honour of Boudewijn Sirks*. Göttingen. 219–239.

Fioretti, P. 2012. "Gli usi della scrittura dipinta nel mondo romano." In *Storie di cultura scritta. Studi per Francesco Magistrale*. Split. 409–425.

Fontanella, F. 2013. *Politica e diritto naturale nel* De legibus *di Cicerone*. Rome.

Fuhrmann, M. 1960. *Das systematische Lehrbuch: ein Beitrag zur Geschichte der Wissenschaft in der Antike*. Göttingen.

Gaudemet J. 1986/1992. "Tentatives de systématisation du droit à Rome." In *Droit et société aux derniers siècles de l'Empire romain*. Naples. 333–350.

Gibbon, E. 1788/1845. *The history of the decline and fall of the Roman empire*, Vol. 3, ed. H. H. Milman.

Haensch, R., ed. 2009. *Selbstdarstellung und Kommunication: die Veröffentlichung staatlicher Urkunden auf Stein und Bronze in der römischen Welt*. Munich.

Haensch, R. 2013. "Die Statthalterarchive der Spätantike." In M. Faraguna, ed., *Archives and archival documents in ancient societies. Trieste 30 September–1 October 2011. Legal documents in ancient societies IV*. Trieste. 333–349.

Harries J. D. 2009. "Tertullianus & Son." In Z. Rogers, M. Daly-Denton and A. F. McKinley, eds., *A wandering Galilaean: essays in honour of Sean Freyne*. Leiden. 385–400.

Humfress, C. 2012. "Law in practice." In P. Rousseau, ed., *A companion to late antiquity*. Chichester. 377–391.

Humfress, C. 2013. "Laws' empire: Roman universalism and legal practice." In P. J. du Plessis, ed., *New frontiers: law and society in the Roman world*. Edinburgh. 73–101.

Jones, C. (2007). "Juristes romains dans l'Orient grec." *Comptes rendus des séances de l'Académie des Inscriptions et Belles-Lettres* 151: 1331–1359.

Kaiser, W. 2015. "Justinian and the *Corpus Iuris Civilis*." In D. Johnston, ed., *The Cambridge companion to Roman law*. Cambridge. 119–148.

Kantor, G. 2009. "Knowledge of law in Roman asia minor." In R. Haensch, ed., *Selbstdarstellung und Kommunication: die Veröffentlichung staatlicher Urkunden auf Stein und Bronze in der römischen Welt*. Munich. 249–265.

Kelly, B. 2011. *Petitions, litigation, and social control in Roman Egypt*. Oxford.

Kroppenberg, I. and Linder, N. 2014. "Coding the nation: codification history from a (post-) global perspective." In T. Duve, ed., *Entanglements in legal history: conceptual approaches*. Frankfurt. 67–99.

Liebs, D. 2002. "Rechtskunde im römischen Kaiserreich: Rom und die Provinzen." In M. J. Schermaier et al., eds., Iurisprudentia universalis. *Festschrift für Theo Mayer-Maly zum 70. Geburtstag*. Cologne. 383–407.

Liebs, D. 2008. "Juristenausbildung in der Spätantike." In C. Baldus et al., eds., *Juristenausbildung in Europa zwischen Tradition und Reform*. Tübingen. 31–45.

Mantovani, D. 1996. "Gli esordi del genere letterario *ad edictum*." In D. Mantovani, ed., *Per la storia del pensiero giuridico romano. Dai pontefici alla scuola di Servio. Atti del Seminario*. Turin. 60–133.

Mantovani, D. 1998. "L'editto come codice e da altri punti di vista," in *La codificazione del diritto dall'antico al moderno. Incontri di studio—Napoli, gennaio-novembre 1996. Atti*. Naples. 129–178.

Mantovani, D. 2012a. "Le due serie di *leges regiae*." In J.-L. Ferrary, ed., *Leges publicae. La legge nell'esperienza giuridica romana*. Pavia. 283–292.

Mantovani, D. 2012b. "*Legum multitudo* e diritto privato. Revisione critica della tesi di Giovanni Rotondi." In J.-L. Ferrary, ed., *Leges publicae. La legge nell'esperienza giuridica romana*. Pavia. 707–767.

Mantovani, D. 2014. "Costantinopoli non è Bologna. La nascita del Digesto fra storiografia e storia." In D. Mantovani and A. Padoa Schioppa, eds., *Interpretare il Digesto. Storia e metodi*. Pavia. 105–134.

Marotta, 2011. V. "I *mandata* nei *libri de officio proconsulis* di Ulpiano. Tecniche di governo e regole d'opportunità sociale." In E. Stolfi, ed., *Giuristi e* officium. *Regole per l'esercizio del potere fra II e III secolo d.C.* Naples. 154–193.

Matthews J. F., 2000. *Laying down the law: a study of the Theodosian Code*. New Haven.

Meyer-Zwiffelhoffer, E. 2002. Πολιτικῶς ἄρχειν. *Zum Regierungsstil der senatorischen Statthalter in den kaizerzeitlichen griechischen Provinzen*. Stuttgart.

Millar, F. 1992. *The emperor in the Roman world (31 BC–AD 337)*. London.

Mommsen, T. 1860. Codicis Vaticani n. 5766 in quo insunt iuris anteiustiniani fragmenta quae dicuntur Vaticana. Berlin.

Neudecker, R. 2010. "The forum of Augustus in Rome." In F. De Angelis, ed., *Spaces of Justice in the Roman World*. Leiden. 171–188.

Nörr, D. 1963/2003. "Zu den geistigen und sozialen Grundlagen der spätantiken Kodifikationsbewegung," in Historiae Iuris Antiqui. *Gesammelte Schriften*. Goldbach. Vol. 1: 275–306.

Nörr, D. 1996/2003. "L'esperienza giuridica di Gellio (*Noctes Atticae* XIV 2)," in Historiae Iuris Antiqui, *Gesammelte Schriften*. Goldbach. Vol. 3: 2149–2172.

Nörr, D. 2003. Historiae Iuris Antiqui. *Gesammelte Schriften*. Goldbach.

Oliver, J. H. 1989. *Greek constitutions of early Roman emperors from inscriptions and papyri*. Philadelphia.

Puliatti, S. (2008). "Le costituzioni tardo antiche: diffusione ed autenticazione." *Studia et Documenta Historiae et Iuris* 74: 99–133.

Puliatti S. 2013. "Il diritto prima e dopo Costantino," in *Costantino I. Enciclopedia costantiniana sulla figura e l'immagine dell'imperatore del cosiddetto Editto di Milano (313-2013)*. Rome. Available at: http://www.treccani.it/enciclopedia/il-diritto-prima-e-dopo-costantino_(Enciclopedia-Costantiniana)/, accessed 30 March 2016.

Rivière, Y. (2013). "Petit lexique de la 'réforme' dans l'œuvre de *codification* de Justinien." *Mélanges de l'École française de Rome—Antiquité* 125 (2). Available at: https://mefra.revues.org/1754?lang=it, accessed 27 June 2015.

Rochette, B. 2008. "L'enseignement du latin comme L² dans la Pars Orientis de l'Empire romain." In R. Ferri and F. Bellandi, eds., *Aspetti della scuola nel mondo romano*. Amsterdam. 81–109.

Rüpke, J. 2011. *The Roman calendar from Numa to Constantine: time, history, and the* Fasti. Chichester.

Salway, B. (2013). "The publication and application of the Theodosian Code." *Mélanges de l'École française de Rome—Antiquité* 125 (2). Available at: https://mefra.revues.org/1754?lang=it, accessed 27 June 2015.

Sanio, D. 1845. *Rechtshistorische Abhandlungen und Studien.* Königsberg.

Santucci, G. (2014). "*Legum inopia* e diritto privato. Riflessioni intorno ad un recente contributo." *Studia et Documenta Historiae et Iuris* 80: 373–393.

Savigny, F. K. von 1814. *Vom Beruf unsrer Zeit für Gesetzgebung und Rechtswissenschaft.* Heidelberg.

Schiavone, A. 2012. *The invention of law in the west.* Cambridge.

Sirks, A. J. B. 2014. "The Theodosian project and the *lex citandi.*" In D. Mantovani and A. Padoa Schioppa, eds., *Interpretare il Digesto. Storia e metodi.* Pavia. 75–104.

Tuori, K. 2006. *Ancient Roman Lawyers and modern legal ideals: studies on the impact of contemporary concerns in the interpretation of ancient Roman legal history.* Helsinki.

Varvaro, M. (2006). "Note sugli archivi imperiali nell'età del principato." *Annali dell'Università di Palermo* 51: 381–431.

Vessey, M. 2010. "The origins of the *Collectio Sirmondiana*: a new look at the evidence." In J. Harries and I. Wood, eds., *The Theodosian Code: studies in the imperial law of late antiquity.* London. 178–199.

Wibier, M. 2014. "The topography of the law book: common structure and modes of Reading." In L. Jansen, ed., *The Roman paratext: frame, text, readers.* Cambridge. 56–72.

CHAPTER 4

EPIGRAPHY

TOMMASO BEGGIO
TRANSLATED BY LAURENCE HOOPER

4.1 Introduction

Louis Robert once defined the Roman world as the culture of the inscription (Robert 1961, 453). Indeed, we have roughly 500,000 inscriptions in Latin alone (Millar 1983; Licandro 2002). Inscriptions contain a great variety of information on Roman society, both in the public and the private spheres, and they can certainly offer insights in the field of law. The so-called *epigraphé* (*titulus* in Latin), renamed *inscriptio* by scholars of the Humanist era, fulfilled a central communicative function in ancient Rome. Legal epigraphy in particular now represents a fundamental source for our knowledge of Roman law.[1] Indeed it is the principal, if not the only, means by which we know about certain legal documents, especially in the field of Roman public law.

Epigraphy has several significant roles in Roman legal history. First, inscriptions increase the number of legal sources available to us. Second, inscriptions sometimes give access to texts in the precise form that was held dispositive in legal proceedings. Third, they exhibit a high degree of reliability and certainly were subject to different forms of mediation than texts transmitted through a textual tradition. The access they allow can often help us grasp a provision's precise meaning and discern the intention of its author. Finally, but no less importantly, epigraphic sources can serve as a means of authentication and verification of actions or events in the history of ancient Rome.

If we were to attempt a definition of epigraphy, drawing a line to separate it from other disciplines, in particular papyrology[2] or numismatics, we might describe it as the study of texts engraved, carved, painted or in some way recorded on certain media (stone, metal, wood, plaster etc.).[3] That said, increasing awareness of the variety of media employed for

[1] I use the term "legal epigraphy" in this chapter for economy of expression, in the full knowledge that its definition is not completely settled. Rowe 2015 provides another survey of this topic, from within the field of classical epigraphy.

[2] The main distinguishing criterion here is the type of writing support used: texts marked on papyrus and parchment are grouped under papyrology. See Lepore 2010, 8.

[3] Licandro 2002, 7–8. Bruun and Edmondson 2015 provide an excellent overview of all aspects of contemporary epigraphy. For bibliographic data regarding corpora of inscriptions and venues of ongoing publication see Bérard et al. 2010; see also Cagnat 1964 and Eck 1997.

public and private writing in the ancient world, and the erosion of any meaningful distinction between permanent and perishable media or distinction between surfaces that called for formal or casual letter forms, has led some to call for a broad interdisciplinary approach to preserved forms of ancient writing (e.g. Licandro 2002, 7–8). Such reservations to one side, legal epigraphy may be defined as the branch of the discipline that studies those inscriptions that reproduce legal instruments, whether public or private (Calabi Limentani 2004, 329). It is thus a highly specialised pursuit, whose practitioner must combine the expertise of an epigraphist with that of a scholar of Roman law.

Epigraphy was a "means of communication, primary and pervasive, employed in contexts that ranged from the private and transient to the public and permanent" (Roda 2000, 242, translated). Its broad and socially diverse audience means epigraphy can contribute to our knowledge of many aspects of Roman society including religion, demography and economics, as well as, of course, issues of law and institutions. In the legal sphere, inscriptions allow us to chart the evolution of institutions, to gauge the effectiveness of laws at the moment of their application and to gain insight into the social and organisational life of *municipia* and *coloniae*. Meanwhile, agreements and contracts between private parties are particularly valuable because they preserve not only precious legal information but also people's stories, their daily lives and the role of certain individuals within the society they inhabited. Private-law inscriptions thus offer us a vivid and varied cross-section of ancient Rome in its different manifestations.

While we must not underestimate the historical insights into the Roman world that the study of epigraphic sources can bring, we must also avoid erring too far in the other direction by assuming that there will always be information of clear and indisputable sociological import in any source that contains legal material. In truth, not every inscription that records a contract, say, will also reveal the complex social reality that stands behind the agreement, while it might reveal a great deal about the shape of a certain legal institution. Again we see the specificity of the subject at hand: a legal text must always be read above all with a focus on its relations to questions of Roman law; it must therefore be interpreted according to the interpretative criteria of Roman law.

The remainder of this chapter defines briefly some very relevant types of legal instrument found in epigraphic sources. I also provide an analysis of a few particularly noteworthy and representative inscriptions.

4.2 Legal Documentation: Classification and Examples

In general, inscriptions fall into two types: *tituli* and *acta*. *Tituli* were closely connected to the monument where the inscription was displayed: an example would be a tomb inscription. *Acta*, meanwhile, comprise documents whose function was primarily public: they provided information and disseminated their content: examples include *senatus consulta*, edicts, calendars and so on.

Inscriptions with legal content can be further divided according to the public or private nature of the instrument contained and transmitted therein. Public-law inscriptions include *leges, senatus consulta, foedera* (treaties), *edicta* and *decreta magistratuum*, Imperial *constitutiones* (decisions), municipal statutes or any other instrument that can be assimilated to the latter, to wit, decrees of the *ordo decurionum* of the various *civitates*, the *fasti* and the *alba* and any other legal document directed to the attention of a relatively broad public. The nature of certain other documents remains a topic of debate; for example, the *diplomata militaria*, by which the emperor conferred specific privileges on soldiers at the moment of their honourable discharge. Finally, the overwhelming majority of private law inscriptions are *negotia*, but the category might also include, for example, fragments of Roman jurisprudence.

4.2.1 *Leges* and *Senatus Consulta*

The first example in this section is the so-called *senatus consultum de Bacchanalibus*. A bronze tablet found near Tiriolo, Calabria, in 1640,[4] today it is on display at the *Kunsthistorisches Museum* in Vienna. It bears the inscription of an *epistula* from the consuls of the year 186 BC to the magistrates of the *ager* Turano, which sets out the provisions of a senatorial decree aimed at repressing Bacchic cults.[5] The text contains some discrepancies starting from line 22, which could be the result of the consuls' having merged passages from resolutions passed in two different senatorial sessions (Liv. 39.14.6–8 and 39.18.7–9). The consuls appear to have taken it upon themselves to decide which provisions applied to the community at *ager Tauranus*. They then ordered the residents of the latter to have these rules inscribed in bronze and displayed in a public place for at least a *trinundinum* (twenty-four days).

It is worth elaborating here on the motives behind the production of this document, insofar as we can discern these from the text, as well as on the legal innovations that the document introduces. The inscription informs us that the penalty for violating the new rules would be death. Even more significantly, at the beginning of the second century BC the decree already provides for criminal proceedings against transgressors via a *quaestio extra ordinem* (Santalucia 1998, 69–102; see also Rüfner, ch. 20). The inscription is thus an important record of a new procedural system that had begun to replace the customary trial before an assembly of citizens (*comitia*). Such trials no longer fit with the needs of contemporary Rome as it underwent dramatic transformation and expansion. The text of the decree, marked at times by an archaic style, gives the impression that the senate was inspired by a moralising intent. Nonetheless, we should not completely dismiss another potential motivation for the text: the desire to prevent religious groups such as the Bacchic cults from serving as cover for political associations that could potentially conspire against the *res publica*.[6]

[4] There may in fact have been two tablets: Albanese 2001.

[5] Licandro 2002, 148. On the violent repression of the Bacchanals see also Liv. 39.18. The text of the consuls' letter can be found in *AE* 2006, 21.

[6] Such fears among the senatorial élite are recorded in Liv. 39.8–19, but see also Cic. *leg.* 2.15.37; Val. Max. 6.3.8; Tert. *Ad nat.* 1.10.16, *Apol.* 6.9.10; Firm. Mat. *Err. prof. relig.* 6.9.

The second example is the so-called *lex de imperio Vespasiani*, promulgated at some time between December 69 AD and the beginning of 70 AD. This document has been the subject of long-running scholarly debate.[7] Even the conventional name of the text is problematic, since the inscription itself does not use the word *imperium* (Mantovani 2006, 1035–1036). That this stylistically elegant document records a *lex* is no longer disputed (*RS* p. 549), because the text defines itself as such at lines 29, 34 and 36 (*RS* p. 550; Mantovani 2006, 1036 n. 4). However, the question of whether the law's promulgation by popular assembly (*comitia*) came after a pre-emptive decree of the senate remains open.[8] The law has moreover come down to us devoid of its *praescriptio* and part of the first clause. What we have is the remainder of the *rogatio* and the *sanctio*. In any case, the law in the form that we have it leaves open various interpretative possibilities regarding the range of the powers it grants to the *princeps*, not least where these concern *tribunicia potestas* and *imperium*. This ambiguity raises the question of whether the law was intended to grant more limited, complementary powers.

These important discussions notwithstanding, the peculiar nature of this inscription has led some scholars to impose on it a historical interpretation that somewhat overestimates its importance, while on the other hand ignoring some of its fundamental legal features. I refer to the problem of the so-called unprecedented clauses, which some have taken as evidence of political and institutional innovations that accompanied Vespasian's rise to power.[9] Certain interpreters of the *lex* go so far as to view it as a "constitution" of the *principatus*, the abstraction of a Latin term "Principate" to mean "rule by *princeps*": being a preeminent sign of the institutionalisation of the new system of rule.[10] It would certainly be wrong to deny the importance of this document, whose recourse to formalising the powers of the *princeps* and invocation of established precedents sought to compensate for Vespasian's obscure origins and the way in which he rose to power (Levick 1999). Nevertheless, the search for institutional, social and political innovations has often led to a misunderstanding in the interpretation of these clauses, trying to "translate" the formulation of the law "into historical argument" (Mantovani 2006, 1040, translated). Indeed, as Mantovani has shown, the disputed clauses—numbers III, IV and VIII—do not introduce innovations in the powers of the *princeps*. Indeed, far from granting Vespasian new powers, they restrict themselves to regulating the effects of certain activities already authorised and recognised in other clauses, where we do indeed find specific reference to Vespasian's predecessors (Mantovani 2006, 104–1048).

[7] The document was discovered in 1347 by Cola di Rienzo in the Basilica of San Giovanni in Laterano, Rome. The main topic of the long scholarly discussion has been the breadth of application of the so-called "unprecedented clauses". See Mantovani 2006, 1035–1055. On the *lex de imperio Vespasiani* more generally see Brunt 1977, 95–116; Hurlet 1993, 261–280.

[8] Mommsen originated this theory, which Lucrezi and Hurlet have recently accepted as plausible. According to their account, the popularly approved text of the law was based on a pre-existing *senatus consultum*. Mommsen 1887, 877; Lucrezi 1982, 146; Hurlet 1993, 265 n.14.

[9] So Brunt 1977, 103–116 and Lucrezi 1982, 161–170. Similar views are found in Hurlet 1993, 278 and Purpura 1998, 439–441, although these two scholars take much more cautious positions than Lucrezi.

[10] For a critical response see Mantovani 2006, 1039.

The problem is thus one of the correct interpretation of legal language, which cannot be glossed over in order to promote historic-political interpretations of the text that obscure its significance from the point of view of Roman law.

A third example of an inscription in this category comes under the heading *acta senatus* (verbatim records of the senate) (Volterra 1969; Talbert 1984; Buongiorno 2010): it is known as the *Aes Italicense*,[11] or at least that is the name I consider preferable (Beggio 2013, 9 n. 20). The object in question is a bronze plaque that records a *prima sententia*; that is to say, the speech given by the first senator who took the floor to give his response to the *oratio principum* by Marcus Aurelius and Lucius Commodus. The proposal in question sought to introduce price controls on gladiatorial games, with the aim of containing the costs of such displays. The document can be dated to 177 AD, or, at the latest, to the beginning of 178. Commodus attained *imperium* only at the end of 176 AD and had to wait until the beginning of the next year to acceed to the *tribunicia potestas*. The year 177 and the beginning of 178 were, moreover, a period of very intense legislative activity.[12]

What makes this text special—and we have only one tablet to work with[13]—is that it faithfully records the speech given by a single member of the senate, something that is immediately apparent in the style, which alternates between passages of high rhetoric, exalting the many gifts of the *principes* and drier, more technical, moments, which recapitulate the legal content of the *oratio principum* that had preceded it. The Latin contains some errors and grammatical imprecisions: these may be attributable to the orator himself, to the scribe working in the senate or indeed the stonecutter who made the inscription. The lapses make the document less stylistically elegant than other inscriptions we have studied, but also more immediate. Reading the tablet's text it is clear that discussion of an Imperial *oratio* by the senate involved more than passive acceptance of the emperor's proposals. Instead, senators clearly enjoyed the right to express their own opinions on the matter at hand, and sometimes even to propose amendments to motions of the emperor. The inscription therefore testifies to existence of a dialectic, however circumscribed, between emperor and senate, something surely fostered by the goodwill of Marcus Aurelius in this case.

At the beginning of the inscription, the senator reports the overjoyed reaction of the Gallic priests on hearing of this effort to contain the costs of gladiatorial events. A very vivid picture is conveyed, of a powerful social group that still had considerable political weight in Gaul at the time. We also learn that the *principes* conceded that the *damnati ad gladium*, those who had been condemned to fight in the arena and to die within a year from the sentence of death, could be sold at somewhat controlled prices to the priests themselves, in order that they could mount *trinqui* games: bloody combats that the

[11] The text was found, incomplete, by Hübner on 19 October 1888, at an excavation of the ancient city of Italica, in the Iberian province of Baetica (modern-day Andalucia). Hübner wrote the first edition of the text. See Hübner 1890; Mommsen 1890; D'Ors 1950; Oliver and Palmer 1955.

[12] For a fuller account of the reasons behind the dating given here see Beggio 2013, 11 n. 23. On Marcus Aurelius's legislative activities see Grant 1994, 39–64; Arcaria 2003, 17 and 67–68.

[13] The tablet in question contains sixty-three lines of text and is complete. It seems reasonable to suppose that the entire document comprised at least two further tablets. The first of these would have contained further introductory material, or, alternatively, the text of the *oratio principum*. The second lost tablet might have contained further provisions.

Romans disdained but which were part of an ancient Celtic tradition. The emperor clearly wished to reward these Imperial provinces, in which the gladiatorial games were especially beloved, for the crucial support they had just offered during the difficult campaigns against the *Germani*.

Other important pieces of information emerge from the text: the role of the Imperial *fiscus* in the trade in gladiators and those condemned to fight; the inclusion of these convicts in the *familia gladiatoria*; and the passing of administrative orders designating Imperial representatives to monitor adherence to the new rules. Finally, we find a detailed price catalogue subdividing the gladiatorial games and the gladiators themselves into price brackets: precious information on the costs involved in mounting such spectacles in the second century AD.[14]

4.2.2 *Constitutiones Principis*

Diocletian's *edictum de pretiis rerum venalium*, issued in 301 AD jointly with his fellow tetrarchs, is one of the most significant epigraphic sources to have come down to us.[15] The edict is important because it is a complete example of an Imperial *consititutio* transcribed as an inscription (albeit missing the *subscriptio*). The text is that of the original produced in the Imperial chancellery and therefore free from the revisions that could be made to such texts as they were copied to manuscript (Licandro 2002, 171). The ruling, which applied to the whole Empire, constituted the Imperial government's reaction to runaway inflation and price increases and was part of a wider programme of economic and fiscal reforms. (For consideration of this text as a state intervention into the economy see Koops, ch. 46.)

The first section is rhetorical and pompous, full of self-aggrandisement and biographical allusions, as the co-emperors stress their just and humane motives in putting forth this edict aimed at reining in merchants' greed. The second section comprises a catalogue of prices with over one thousand entries, subdivided into thirty-two sections, specifying a maximum allowable price for each named good or service and naming death as the penalty for overcharging.

The range of goods recorded here, together with the references to the cost of various types of rental and of hired labour, gives us a rich and nuanced portrait of Roman society and economic relations in the period. At the same time, the document bears witness to the scope of the economic crisis at the end of the third century AD, which had affected almost every economic activity in the Empire. The edict, moreover, demonstrates the ideology of Diocletian's reign: the *dirigiste* approach to the economy; the desire to reunify the Empire using a monumental project of reforms and the good name of Diocletian himself. Of course, while the emperor himself clearly believed in the necessity of his action on prices, just as he believed in the need for fiscal reform (Williams 1997), these decisions surely aimed just as much at smoothing the process of provisioning the Roman army: this

[14] See Duncan Jones 1982; Carter 2003.

[15] For a relatively complete edition see Giacchero 1974. Several new fragments have subsequently come to light.

can be deduced from the inclusion in the catalogue of many essential military supplies, while many goods in common use go unnamed.

The blinkered economic vision that underpinned the edict meant that it could not solve the problem of inflation; indeed it aggravated it by encouraging the development of a black market. Its price caps thus soon fell into disuse. Diocletian's edict was a failure, but our judgement of it, with all the benefits of our contemporary understanding of economics, must be calibrated to the times in which the decision was taken. In any case, the Imperial efforts that this epigraphic source records take on a human colour, put on display the anxieties, hopes and trepidation of a man and a world that were striving to defend a supremacy on the wane and a civilisation that remained magnificent.

4.2.3 Municipal Charters

It is difficult to choose any one document to represent this section, since the options are so many (Capogrossi Colognesi and Gabba 2006). Nonetheless, the *lex Irnitana*, the municipal charter of Irni, is undoubtedly a source worthy of note, not least for the many debates that it has provoked since its discovery in 1981 in Andalucia, formerly the Roman province of Baetica.[16]

Comprising six bronze tablets and multiple fragments of others that must at one time have accompanied them, this inscription brought to light numerous previously unknown aspects of how Roman *municipia* were organised (see also Roselaar, ch. 10). The inscription displays a high degree of proficiency both in the technique and the drafting, judging by the care with which it was prepared and its detailed structure subdivided into thematic units. These topics include the regulation of civic offices, the acquisition of Roman citizenship *per honorem*, the manumission of slaves in the presence of a *duumvir* (a municipal magistrate) and the *datio tutoris* (chs. 18–29). Next come matters including the membership of the town's *decuriones* (city councillors), municipal elections and other aspects of municipal business.[17] Chapters 84 to 93 are especially interesting: they set out much of what we know about municipal jurisdiction, supplying important pieces of information such as which magistrates had authority to rule over private disputes. Chapter 91 supplies even more important information regarding a legal fiction, introduced using the formula *siremps lex ius causaque esto*, which equates the municipal legal process to what would occur at Rome under a so-called *iudicium legitimum* (Terrinoni 2012, 159–161). This part of the text, when read in correlation with chapters 21 and 22 of the *lex Rubria* (*RS* no. 28), seems to confirm the hypothesis that a legal procedure specific to Rome could be applied outside of the metropolis and its *pomerium*, even in the absence of the criteria set down by Gaius (Inst.Gai.4.103–104).

Finally, the discovery of this inscription breathed new life into the ongoing debate on the existence of *lex Iulia municipalis* in the Augustan period: i.e. a general body of law that could serve as template for legislation in the individual *municipia* (cf. Crawford 1998;

[16] D'Ors 1982 and 1984; Gonzalez 1986; D'Ors and D'Ors 1988; Galsterer 1987 and 1988; Lamberti 1993; Wolf 2011.

[17] For example, the award of municipal contracts and the imposition of fines. A complete account of the content of the *tabulae* is in Lamberti 1993.

Talamanca 1999). The heavily tralatician character of the extant charters and the recent discovery of nearly identical texts from the second and early third century in provinces along the Danube, suggest that a common model existed that was subsequently employed for many juridically constituted communities of Latin and Roman citizens in the West (for bibliography see Roselaar, ch. 10).

4.2.4 Municipal Decrees

Recent studies, in particular those dedicated to Campania of the Roman era (Camodeca 2003 and 2008), have allowed us to reconstruct the history of many southern Italian cities, and of their ruling elites, thanks to the copious numbers of inscriptions that have been uncovered there.

The decrees made by the *ordo decurionum* (the local council) of these municipalities are undoubtedly among the most interesting of these documents (Sherk 1970; Capogrossi Colognesi and Gabba 2006). Before going any further, we should recall the caveat set out by Giuseppe Camodeca, that it is easy to overestimate the value of epigraphy in defining what we might call the "everyday business" of the *decuriones*. As Camodeca points out, epigraphic sources sometimes provide a distorted and unreliable picture of what was happening (Camodeca 2003, 173, referring specifically to the Campanian context). In essence, this is because only a few decrees were preserved as inscriptions. Nevertheless, these municipal inscriptions can still provide us with significant new information on aspects of Roman society that we would otherwise know little about.

A frequent topic of such decrees is the grant of public land for funerary monuments, sometimes on the initiative of the *decuriones*, at others on private initiative. In the latter case, once the grant was secured, the honorand, or a relative if he was already deceased, might seek to pass on the costs of the memorial to the city. One such instance is *CIL* X 1874, where a statue in honour of Gavia M. f. Marciana, a woman who died young, was paid for by the *res publica*, in this instance a synonym for the *ordo decurionum*. Other similar inscriptions contain grants of public land for funerary plots in the area immediately surrounding the town or of a public funeral paid for by the municipal treasury.

Great energy was devoted to discussion and publication of the recruitment and enrolment (*adlectiones*) of important and well-regarded citizens into the order of the *decuriones*, the granting of the *ornamenta decurionalia* and, above all, the nomination of civic office holders and magistrates, with particular regard to the *praefecti iure dicundo e lege Petronia* and the civic *legati* (cf. *CIL* X 4658). The *lex Irnitana* also describes these positions and stresses their importance (chs. 45–47). This list could go on, but it is worth concentrating our attention on the findings of recent studies of two wax tablets from Herculaneum (Camodeca 2003). The first records the authorisation by decree of the *decuriones* for the town's *duumvir* to proceed with a *datio tutelae*. Given that the document dates to *c.*40 AD, it represents the oldest of its type known to us.

The second tablet, *T.H.* 89, allows us to reconstruct the procedure for obtaining Roman citizenship by a freedman (*Latinus Iunianus*),[18] as set out in the *lex Aelia Sentia*

[18] That is to say, an individual freed before reaching 30 years of age with no applicable *causa manumissionis*.

of 4 AD, which differs from the process described by Gaius (Inst.Gai.1.29). The tablet recounts that the praetor of the city reviewed an informational report prepared by the *decuriones* of the freedman's city of origin when deciding whether full citizenship should be granted. The text thus reveals the rationale behind the rule: only the *decuriones*, with their closer acquaintance with the details of the case, were in a position to evaluate fully an individual's level of integration when considering a potential grant of citizenship.

4.3 *Negotia*

The epigraphic evidence for private agreements and contracts (*negotia*) in the Roman world covers a broad range of legal instruments.

Some of these served the essential function of publicising commercial activities (Lovato 2006, 141). For example, one inscription from Pompeii (*CIL* IV 1136) offers part of a building for rent. Other products advertised include, naturally enough, craftsmen's wares, goods of various types and even people's labour.

Numerous sources bear witness to the market in slaves. Among many possibilities, let us take the example of a text contained in the so-called tablets of Transylvania, datable to the second century AD.[19] Here we find evidence of the sale of a six-year-old girl, using a formal procedure known as a *mancipatio*, even though the parties were probably not Roman citizens.

Equally worthy of comment is the inscription known as the *Formula* (or *tabula*) *Baetica*, discovered in 1868 in Andalusia. This diptych appears to be a model contract for setting up a *fiducia cum creditore* ("loan security"), a template that could be reused every time such an agreement was negotiated.[20]

Many inscriptions of great importance exist in the area of probate. It was quite common for members of the more privileged sectors of society to have the provisions of their last will and testament inscribed on their tomb.

The corpus of epigraphic sources for private agreements was further enriched by Camodeca's new critical edition of the *Tabulae Pompeianae Sulpiciorum*.[21] This rich trove of documents, discovered in 1959 near Murecine and comprising 127 surviving inscriptions, some diptychs, some triptychs, represents a invaluable source for understanding the family origins of a prominent local family, the Sulpicii, their social role and their activities, as well as various aspects of Roman law.

The Sulpicii seem to have descended from freedmen of the noted senatorial family Sulpicii Galbae. They worked as bankers and seem to have been independent of their former patrons, since they had freedmen in their service themselves.[22] Their business must

[19] *FIRA* III^2 87. The tablets were discovered in the region of Dacia (modern-day Romania and Moldova), between 1786 and 1855.

[20] Licandro 2002, 188. Not all scholars agree, however, that the *formula Baetica* was a template rather than a single specific contract.

[21] Camodeca 1999 (and 1992). The most important studies prior to this were Wolf and Crook 1989; Gröschler 1997.

[22] Camodeca 1999, 23. See also Eck, 1996, 147–154. For the activities of freedmen see Garnsey 1981.

have generated considerable wealth—certainly banking played an important social role in ancient Rome (Andreau 1987). Among the many notable documents in this rich corpus of inscriptions, of especial legal interest are those concerning *vadimonium,* a contract between plaintiff and defendant to appear at trial or forfeit a surety, as well as *intertium,* a procedure for scheduling a trial date for the day after next.

There were two types of *vadimonium* at Rome: judicial and extrajudicial. While the legal sources almost always concentrate on the judicial type, it is extrajudicial surety contracts that we find recorded in fifteen tablets from the Sulpicii collection, as well as in some from Herculaneum (*T.H.* 6.13–15). These allow detailed study of the form of such documents, the *summa vadimonii,* as well as the steps whose completion would allow the contract to be regarded as fulfilled. In the four *vadimonia Romam*, the meeting place is always the Forum of Augustus (Camodeca 1999, 51).

Tabulae 32 and 33, meanwhile, offer further evidence for the existence of the *intertium*, a stepping stone between the trial phases of *in iure* (i.e. before a magistrate) and *apud iudicem* ("before a judge"). The *intertium* was already known from the *lex Irnitana* (chs. 90–91), as an order that could be made by the magistrate for a trial before a judge to go ahead the day after next. These two tablets add the detail that the parties would already know the identity of the judge who would rule at the point the *intertium* was issued, since individual judges are here named explicitly.

In a recent study, Elizabeth Meyer examined wax tablets and other documents of the practice of *negotia* (Meyer 2006). She proposes a largely anthropological interpretation that reimagines the legal phenomena by focusing on the question of their formalism, or even ritualism. Legal documents would thus represent the tangible signs of a reality pervaded by magic and religion. Meyer's point of view is interesting, although I still prefer an approach that sticks more closely to the interpretative principles immanent in the texts, paying attention to the legal content of the sources, in particular.

4.4 Conclusion

The selection of epigraphic material discussed here, although far from exhaustive, has aimed to represent the broad range of topics embraced by the study of legal epigraphy. Inscriptions continue to provide a more and more complete and nuanced view of the system of Roman law in all its complexity. They sometimes reveal a gap between the law as it applied on the ground and the law as it is set down in other sources. At other times, however, inscriptions provide precious confirmation of what we find in these other legal sources, helping to establish their reliability.

From the most minute aspects of private law, to the biggest questions in politics—such as the legitimation of Imperial power—epigraphic sources enrich our knowledge of legal, institutional and social realities of the Roman world.

Nevertheless, these inscriptions always remain legal documents, and the exegete who wishes to study them must always bear that in mind. Only in this way will scholars avoid traducing the most basic principles of legal epigraphy and succeed in contributing to our better understanding of Roman law.

Finally, for all the reasons given, it seems only right to hope that legal epigraphy will play an essential role in the study of Roman law and that epigraphic sources will receive full recognition for the crucial evidence they provide for the discipline.

Bibliography

Albanese, B. 2001. "Per l'interpretazione dell'iscrizione con norme del Sc. de Bacchanalibus (186 a.C.)," in Iuris Vincula, *Studi in onore di M. Talamanca*. Naples. Vol. 1: 1–34.

Andreau, J. 1987. *La vie financière dans le monde romain: les métiers de manieurs d'argent (IVe siècle av. J.-C.–IIIe siècle ap. J.-C.)*. Rome.

Arcaria, F. 2003. Oratio Marci. *Giurisdizione e processo nella normazione di Marco Aurelio*. Turin.

Beggio, T. 2013. "Riflessioni sui iuridici alla luce dell'*Aes Italicense*." In P. Buongiorno and S. Lohsse, eds., Fontes Iuris, *Atti del VI Jahrestreffen junger Romanistinnen und Romanisten (Lecce, 30–31 marzo 2012)*. Naples. 1–64.

Bérard, F. et al. 2010[4]. *Guide de l'épigraphiste: bibliographie choisie des épigraphies antiques et médiévales*. Paris.

Bruns, C. G. 1909. Fontes Iuris Romani Antiqui. Berlin.

Brunt, P. (1977). "*Lex de imperio Vespasiani*." *Journal of Roman Studies* 67: 95–116.

Bruun, C. and J. Edmondson, eds. 2015. *The Oxford handbook of Roman epigraphy*. Oxford.

Buongiorno, P. 2010. Senatus Consulta Claudianis temporibus facta. *Una palingenesi delle deliberazioni senatorie dell'età di Claudio (41–54 d.C.)*. Naples.

Cagnat, R. 1964[4]. *Cours d'épigraphie latine*. Rome.

Calabi Limentani, I. 2004[4]. *Epigrafia latina*. Milan.

Camodeca, G. 1992. *L'archivio puteolano dei Sulpicii*, Vol. 1. Naples.

Camodeca, G. (1999). Tabulae Pompeianae Sulpiciorum (TPSulp). *Edizione critica dell'archivio puteolano dei Sulpicii. I e II*. Rome.

Camodeca, G. (2003). "L'attività dell'*ordo decurionum* nelle città della Campania dalla documentazione epigrafica." *Cahiers du Centre Gustave Glotz* 14: 173–186.

Camodeca, G. 2008. *I ceti dirigenti di rango senatorio equestre e decurionale della Campania romana*. Naples.

Capogrossi Colognesi, L. and Gabba, E., eds. 2006. *Gli statuti municipali*. Pavia.

Carter, M. (2003). "Gladiatorial ranking and the *SC de Pretiis Gladiatorum Minuendis* (*CIL* II 6278 = *ILS* 5163)." *Phoenix* 57 1/2: 83–114.

Crawford, M. H. 1998. "How to create a *municipium*: Rome and Italy after the social war." In M. Austin, J. Harries and C. Smith, eds., Modus Operandi: *essays on honour of Geoffrey Rickman*. London. 31–46.

D'Ors, Á. (1950). "Observaciones al texto de la *oratio de pretiis gladiatorum minuendis*." *Emerita* 18: 311–339.

D'Ors, Á. (1982/1983). "*Litem suam facere*." *Studia et Documenta Historiae et Iuris* 48: 368–394.

D'Ors, Á. (1984). "De nuevo sobre la ley municipal." *Studia et Documenta Historiae et Iuris* 50: 179–198.

D'Ors, Á. and D'Ors, X. 1988. Lex Irnitana *(Texto bilingüe)*. Santiago de Compostela.

Duncan Jones, R. P. 1982[2]. *The economy of the Roman empire*. Cambridge.

Eck, W. 1996. "I *Sulpicii Galbae* e i *Livii Ocellae*. Due famiglie senatorie a Terracina," in *Tra epigrafia prosopografia e archeologia. Scritti scelti, rielaborati ed aggiornati*. Rome. 147–154.

Eck, W. 1997. "Lateinische Epigraphik." In F. Graf, ed., *Einleitung in die lateinische Philologie*. Stuttgart. 92–111.
Galsterer, H. (1987). "La loi municipale des Romains: chimère ou realité?" *Revue historiques de droit français et étranger* 65: 181–203.
Galsterer, H. (1988). "*Municipium Flavium Irnitanum*: a Latin town in Spain." *Journal of Roman Studies* 78: 78–90.
Garnsey, P. (1981). "Independent freedmen and the economy of Roman Italy under the principate." *Klio* 63: 359–371.
Giacchero, M. 1974. Edictum Diocletiani et Collegarum de pretiis et rerum venalium, Vol. 1: Edictum. Genoa.
Girard, P. F. and F. Senn, eds. 1978. *Les lois des romains*. Naples.
Gonzalez, J. F. (1986). "The *Lex Irnitana*: a new copy of the Flavian municipal Law." *Journal of Roman Studies* 76: 147–243.
Grant, M. 1994. *The Antonines: the Roman empire in transition*. London/New York.
Gröschler, P. 1997. *Die* tabellae-*Urkunden aus den pompejanischen und herculanensischen Urkundenfunden*. Berlin.
Hübner, E. 1890. "*Aes Italicense*." In W. Henzen, ed., Ephemeris Epigraphica. Corporis Inscriptionum Latinarum Supplementum. Berlin. Vol. 7: 385–387.
Hurlet, F. (1993). "La *lex de imperio Vespasiani* et la legitimité augustéenne." *Latomus* 52: 261–280.
Lamberti, F. 1993. "Tabulae Irnitanae. *Municipalità e* Ius Romanorum." Naples.
Lepore, P. 2010. *Introduzione allo studio dell'epigrafia giuridica latina*. Milan.
Levick, B. M. 1999. *Vespasian*. London.
Licandro, O. 2002. *Il "diritto inciso." Lineamenti di epigrafia giuridica romana*. Catania.
Lovato, A. 2006. *Elementi di epigrafia giuridica romana*. Bari.
Lucrezi, F. 1982. Leges super principem. *La "monarchia costituzionale" di Vespasiano*. Naples.
Mantovani, D. 2006. "Le clausole 'senza precedenti' della *Lex de imperio Vespasiani*." In L. Labruna, M. P. Baccari and C. Cascione, eds., *Tradizione romanistica e Costituzione*. Naples. Vol. 2: 1035–1055.
Meyer, E. A. 2006. *Legitimacy and law in the Roman world:* tabulae *in Roman belief and practice*. Cambridge.
Millar, F. 1983. "Epigraphy." In M. H. Crawford, ed. *Sources for ancient history*. Cambridge. 8–136.
Mommsen, T. 1887. *Römisches Staatsrecht*, Vol. 2.2. Leipzig.
Mommsen, T. 1890. "*Observationes Epigraphicae XLI: senatus consultum de sumptibus ludorum gladiatorum minuendis*." In T. Mommsen, O. Hirschfeld et al., eds., Ephemeris Epigraphica. Corporis Inscriptionum Latinarum Supplementum. Berlin. Vol. 7: 388–416.
Oliver, J. H. and Palmer, R. A. (1955). "Minutes of an act of the Roman senate." *Hesperia* 24: 320–349.
Purpura, G. (1998). "Sulla tavola perduta della *lex de auctoritate Vespasiani*." *Annali del Seminario giuridico dell'Università degli Studi di Palermo* 45: 413–442.
Robert, L. 1961. "Épigraphie. Les épigraphies et l'épigraphie grecque et romaine." In C. Samaran, ed., *L'histoire et ses méthodes* (*Encyclopédie de la Pléiade*). Paris. 453–497.
Roda, S. 2000². "Le fonti epigrafiche latine." In L. Cracco Ruggini, ed., *Storia antica. Come leggere le fonti*. Bologna. 241–285.
Rowe, G. 2015. "The Roman state: laws, law making, and legal documents." In C. Bruun and J. Edmondson, eds., *The Oxford handbook of Roman epigraphy*. Oxford. 299–318.

Santalucia, B. 1998². *Diritto e processo penale nell'antica Roma*. Milan.
Sherk, R. K. 1970. *The municipal decrees of the Roman west*. Buffalo.
Susini, G. C. 1973. *The Roman stonecutter*. Oxford.
Talamanca, M. 1999. "Il riordinamento augusteo del processo privato." In F. Milazzo, ed., *Gli ordinamenti giudiziari di Roma imperiale. Princeps e procedure dalle leggi giulie ad Adriano. Atti dell'VIII Convegno di Diritto romano di Copanello*. Naples. 63–261.
Talbert, R. J. A. 1984. *The senate of imperial Rome*. Princeton.
Terrinoni, A. 2012. "Sulla clausola di equiparazione 'siremps lex esto quasi'." In J.-L. Ferrary, ed., *Leges publicae. La legge nell'esperienza giuridica romana*. Pavia. 157–176.
Volterra, E. 1969. s.v. "*Senatus consulta*," in *Novissimo Digesto Italiano*. Turin. 1047–1078. Reprinted in Volterra, E. 1993. *Scritti giuridici*, Vol. 5: *Le fonti*. Naples. 193–297.
Williams, S. 1997. *Diocletian and the Roman recovery*. New York.
Wolf, J. G. 2011. *Die* lex Irnitana: *ein römisches Stadtrecht aus Spanien*. Darmstadt.
Wolf, J. G. and Crook, J. A. 1989. *Rechtsurkunden in Vulgärlatein*. Heidelberg.

CHAPTER 5

JURISTIC PAPYROLOGY AND ROMAN LAW

JOSÉ LUIS ALONSO

5.1 The Century of Papyrology

Theodor Mommsen is often quoted as predicting that the twentieth century would be the century of papyrology, just as his own had been the century of epigraphy (van Minnen 1993, 5). The dictum, whoever its author (Martin 2000; Gonis 2006), captures the enthusiasm aroused at the end of the nineteenth century by the sudden discovery of an enormous mass of new literary, legal and historical sources on papyrus.[1] The papyri, it was felt, would renew the foundations of every branch of the classical studies. In those first decades of papyrological studies, the involvement of legal historians was extremely prominent: particularly in Germany, with Otto Gradenwitz and the school of Ludwig Mitteis; in Italy, the kinship between papyrology and Roman law culminated in the figure of Vincenzo Arangio-Ruiz.[2]

Things look rather different today. The publication of papyri continues at a steady rhythm of several hundreds per year, with vast amounts waiting to be published in the future.[3] In addition to the large mass of papyri from Egypt, a non-negligible number of documents from the Near East have come to light (Cotton, Cockle and Millar 1995; Gascou 2009). Many of the texts that see the light each year are private legal instruments and acts of the Roman administration, including documents arising from legal proceedings.[4] Yet these documents rarely attract the attention of Roman law scholars.[5] Papyrology has come

[1] For a brief history of papyrology and of early papyrological finds see the chapters of Keenan and Cuvigny in Bagnall 2009: 30–78.

[2] Early juristic papyrology in Italy: Pivano 1923. On the school of Mitteis see Zimmermann 2001. Recent handbooks with extensive bibliographies include Wolff and Rupprecht 2002; Bagnall 2009; Mélèze Modrzejewski 2014; and Keenan, Manning and Yiftach-Firanko 2014.

[3] About eighty thousand texts have been published; more than a million await publication: van Minnen 2007.

[4] A useful first selection, in the "papyrological reports" regularly published by several legal history reviews: Wolff and Rupprecht 2002, 19.

[5] The most notable exception is the Babatha archive (Lewis 1989), no doubt due to the unexpected Greek translation of the *formula tutelae*.

to be regarded as a wholly separate discipline, no longer a natural province of Roman legal studies. As a result, the legal questions posed by the new documents often receive insufficient attention. Some may argue that, as far as private law is concerned, this detachment is fully justified, since the tradition preserved in the papyri is mostly not Roman, but Greek and native Egyptian. These pages aim at challenging such a position.[6]

5.2 Legal Literature and Imperial Constitutions

Copies of the books comprising the curriculum of legal studies must have existed in Egypt in late Antiquity, at least since the foundation of the law school of Alexandria.[7] Unfortunately, they seem to have suffered the general fate of papyri from the Delta, being preserved only when chance brought them to other, drier, regions of Egypt. In the case of the legal books, the loss has been almost complete: fragments of law books are extremely scarce in Egypt, although they represent almost half of all the surviving Latin literary papyri.[8] Most famous among them are *PSI* xi 1182, and *P. Oxy.* xvii 2103, the so-called "Florentine" and "Oxyrhynchite" Gaius.[9] The door is not completely closed yet: contrary to what might be expected, new fragments of legal literature still appear occasionally.[10]

The number of Imperial constitutions mentioned or more or less thoroughly reproduced in the papyri is, instead, overwhelming.[11] Here too the enormous amount of still unpublished papyri means that new material constantly appears.[12] Among this great mass of documents, some outstanding papyri deserve to be mentioned. The most famous is probably *P. Giss.* 40, our main source for the *Constitutio Antoniniana* (Buraselis 2007). Much attention has also been paid to the decisions of Septimius Severus and Caracalla during their visit to Egypt in 199–200, especially to the *apokrimata* (*responsa*) copied in *P. Col.* 123 (Haensch 2007). In general, the papyrological and epigraphic materials provide precious information about the ways in which the Imperial legislation was produced, published and preserved—a much discussed problem, particularly regarding rescripts (Coriat 1997, 322–329, 608–634).

[6] The pages that follow will be devoted mostly to private law and private legal practice. Arguably, the papyri have contributed even more decisively to our knowledge of the Roman provincial administration, but the very richness of the material makes it impossible to do it justice here. An overview may be found in Gagos and Potter 2006.

[7] Known to us only through C. *Omnem* §7, which ended its activity.

[8] *CPL* 70–101; Seider 1981; Montevecchi 1988, 238; Ammirati 2012. A list of fragments from legal codices, including those in Greek: McNamee 1995, 413.

[9] For the conjecture that links the Oxyrhynchite Gaius to the library of the family of Sarapion, an early third-century *strategos*, Houston 2014, 143–150.

[10] Most notably, *P. Haun.* 45 + *CPL* 73 A and B: Nasti 2010 and 2013. Cf. also *BKT* X 16 and *BKT* IX 201, on which see Cascione 2008.

[11] Taubenschlag 1959 II: 3–43, 45–68, 69–89; Oliver 1989; Purpura 2009.

[12] Notable, among the most recent examples, the *epistula* of Hadrian mentioned in *BGU* XX 2863, reopening a discussion initiated by Theodor Mommsen on *BGU* I 19.

A particularly relevant document is *BGU* V 1210 (159–180, Theadelphia), the so-called *Gnomon* (i.e. rule) of the *idios logos*: an epitome or supplement of the *Liber mandatorum* for the office of the procurator (*epitropos*) of the "special account" (*idios logos*). This special account had existed since Ptolemaic times and comprised most irregular, that is, non-recurrent, fiscal revenue, particularly confiscated land.[13] To the original Augustan *Gnomon*, referred to in §1, the anonymous compiler of our text added rules distilled, with variable accuracy, from later Imperial constitutions, *senatus consulta*, edicts of the prefects and decisions of previous *epitropoi*. Leaving aside its fragmentary last column, the papyrus contains 115 dispositions, including, in the aspects useful for the *idios logos*, a detailed section (§§4–54) on the law of succession, marriage, dowry and donations between spouses as applied in Egypt to the different groups of the population.[14]

The fact that these texts have come to us "directly", and not through a later codification, does not make them necessarily more reliable: depending on the public or private nature of the document, and on the intentions and skills of its author, abridgements, inaccuracies, mistakes and even manipulations are not unusual.[15]

5.3 Prefectural Edicts

The use that the provincial governors made of their *ius edicendi* is best illustrated in Egypt, where numerous papyri add to the occasional epigraphic remains. The edicts (*diatagmata*) of the prefect of Egypt that have thus survived cover the widest range of matters, both by way of general normative provisions and specific executive decisions (Katzoff 1980, Haensch 2010). Of particular relevance to private law are some of the fiscal measures in the 68 AD edict of Tiberius Iulius Alexander (*OGIS* 669; Chalon 1964); the edicts of Mettius Rufus (89 AD: *P. Oxy.* ii 237 viii 27–43), Sulpicius Similis (109 AD: *P. Oxy.* ii 237 viii 21–27) and Flavius Titianus (127 AD: *P. Oxy.* i 34), on the property record offices (*bibliothekai enkteseon*) instituted in order to keep records of private transactions on landed property

[13] The name *idios logos* is best explained by opposition to the regular revenue, i.e. taxation. The widespread translation *res privata* (Arangio-Ruiz 1957, 245; Wieacker 2006, 25) is misleading: a *res* (or *ratio*) *privata*, separate from *fiscus* and *patrimonium*, appears only in the second century (not with Severus, despite SHA *Sev.* 12.1–4, but already with Antoninus Pius: *CIL* viii 8810 and vi 41118); the *idios logos*, instead, is retained from the Ptolemaic administration since Augustus, and there is little doubt that its revenue (which included the *caduca*) belonged to the fisc, not to the *patrimonium* (Mitteis 1908, 327 and n. 24). For the office of the *epitropos*, Swarney 1970.

[14] On the *Gnomon*, Riccobono 1950; a balanced overview in Mélèze Modrzejewski 1977. Part of an earlier copy has survived in *P. Oxy.* xlii 3014.

[15] Outright falsification was common enough to elicit an Imperial reaction: Sciortino 1998. The *Gnomon* of the *idios logos* presents specific problems: here we deal with an unofficial compiler, who furthermore does not reproduce the original texts, but tries to formulate the underlying rules: striking inaccuracies have long been noticed, often resulting in confiscations that would not take place under a correct application of the Roman rule: thus, *fideicommissa* that by virtue of the *oratio Hadriani* in Inst.Gai.2.287 should merely be no longer binding, are instead confiscated (§16); confiscation is also immediate for *caduca* (§27, §30), without regard to the possible *capacitas* of other *heredes* or *legatarii* (Inst.Gai.2.207); cf. also, in §33, the outdated (Inst.Gai.1.115a) *coemptio testamenti faciendi gratia*.

(Wolff 1978, 222–255); and, on fraudulent behaviours of creditors and debtors, the edicts of Petronius Mamertinus (134 AD: *P. Fay.* 21; Wolff and Rupprecht 2002, 181 and n. 145) and Valerius Eudaemon (142 AD: *P. Oxy.* ii 237 viii 7–18; Wolff 1978, 148–150).

Remarkably, many of these edictal provisions have come to us through petitions and other trial documents that invoke them long after the issuing prefect had left office. Such is the case of the edicts of Mettius Rufus (89 AD), Sulpicius Similis (109 AD) and Valerius Eudaemon (142 AD), all incorporated into the famous petition of Dionysia, dated 186 AD. *BGU* VII 1563, a partial papyrus copy of the great edict of Tiberius Iulius Alexander, was also written decades after the original was issued. A copy of an edict of Pactumeius Magnus from 176 AD appears on the back of a petition dated 218 AD. Many sources confirm this apparent permanency of the prefectural edicts (Wilcken 1921, 14–144): a typical, often quoted example is the petition of Apollonarion in *P. Oxy.* vi 899: dated 200 AD, it relies on the argument that in 144 AD a similar case had been adjudicated in accordance with a 69 AD edict of Tiberius Iulius Alexander.

This phenomenon has often been treated as an anomaly that demands an explanation. In the provinces, as in Rome, it is argued, edicts automatically expired as soon as the issuing magistrate left office. Others argue that these later quotations, and even unequivocal instances of their application, do not necessarily imply that these edicts had binding force (Wolff and Rupprecht 2002, 106–107): they may have existed (Ando 2015) along a continuum between the normative and the merely exemplary.

The discussion stems from a questionable premise. The rule that the edictal form is intrinsically temporary is nowhere formulated in our sources: it is a modern generalisation on the basis of the jurisdictional edict of the praetor. This edict was certainly the most conspicuous, but also quite special: self-disciplining and exhaustive, therefore destined to be entirely replaced by each new praetor. For other types of resolutions, the edictal form did not by itself impose a temporal limit to their validity. The fact that it was already employed by Augustus for measures that were universally understood as permanent speaks for itself: this would not have been possible if the late Republican tradition had conceived it as necessarily ephemeral.[16]

A different question, also much debated (Mélèze Modrzejewski 2014, 286–292), is whether a general jurisdictional edict like that of the praetor was promulgated in Egypt by each prefect. An edict ordering jurisdiction in its formal and material aspects (the organisation of the *conventus*, the application of peregrine law, etc.: Lenel 1927, 4–5; Lewald 1959) seems unlikely: we would expect it to be constantly invoked in the numerous surviving petitions and trial records, where there is no trace of it; the freedom apparent in our sources regarding the organisation of the *conventus* and the application of the peregrine law also belies the existence of such edict. Since it seems evident that the formulary

[16] Despite Taubenschlag 1959 II: 65–68, the occasional Imperial confirmation of edicts of previous emperors, frequently regarding privileges, does not imply that such confirmation was necessary. Evidence to the contrary abounds: Augustan edicts are quoted as fully valid by Paul. D.48.18.8pr, *fr. de iure fisci* 8, and Plin. *Ep.* 10.79–80; an edict of Domitian by Papinian D.48.3.2.1, in spite of *damnatio memoriae*; more decisively, the explicit abrogation of an Augustan edict (*iam sublato edicto divi Augusti*) attested in D.28.2.26 = Sent.Paul.3.4b.10a, would have been inconceivable if it had expired in 14 AD. The inclusion of *edicta* among the constitutions that *legis vicem optinent* in Inst. Gai.1.5 was, therefore, fully justified. The question seems settled since Orestano 1936, 1937.

procedure was not applied in Egypt, an edict modelled on the *edictum provinciale* on which Gaius commented is even less likely. Problematic remain, however, the edictal references in the surviving third-century *agnitiones bonorum possessionis*: "polliceris" in these petitions may well be the result of thoughtless copying of an Italic original (which would seem to be confirmed by the use of consular dating, generally avoided in Egypt); yet, the subscriptions "*ex edicto. recognovi*", "*ex edicto. legi*", in *SB* I 1010 l. 11–12 and *P. Oxy.* ix 1201 l. 11, are difficult to conceive if there was no edict to refer to other than that of the Roman praetor.[17]

5.4 Roman Jurisdiction and Peregrine Law

The activity of the Roman jurisdiction in Egypt is abundantly documented by numerous surviving petitions and trial records (petitions: Kelly 2011; trial records: Anagnostou-Canas 1991). These documents provide information on the organisation of the jurisdiction and the *conventus* (*dialogismos*), on procedural practice[18] and its documentation (Coles 1966; Haensch 2008), on the discussion in the hearing itself and on the adjudication in the most diverse matters.[19]

In the context of the Eastern provinces, Egypt was singular in that there seems to have been no alternative to the Roman jurisdiction: institutions retained from the Ptolemaic order, like the *archidikastes* in Alexandria, are not an expression of an autonomous jurisdiction, but appear fully integrated in the Roman jurisdictional system.[20] Unlike the rest of the *poleis* in the Eastern Empire, neither Alexandria nor the other cities in Egypt had autonomous jurisdictional institutions. Moreover, the lack in Egypt of a municipal organisation meant that the Roman jurisdiction was mostly centralised in the person of the prefect: the *iuridicus* and the *idios logos* had their own (limited) jurisdictional power, but the numerous other officials that appear as judges in our documents seem in general to have acted by delegation of the prefect, as often explicitly stated. In practice, though, the distinction between jurisdiction and administration was not always neat, and the administrative competences of these officials could lead to autonomous decisions that were virtually jurisdictional.

[17] Wolff and Rupprecht 2002, 109, following Ankum 1970. On *katholikon diatagma* in *BGU* VII 1578 see Mélèze Modrzejewski 1982, 495; the petition concerns the revocation of a donation by ingratitude, highly unlikely for the *edictum provinciale*. The *inspectio ventris* in *P. Gen.* ii 103–104, as much as it matches the provisions of the *edictum de inspiciendo ventre*, does not require the existence of a general provincial edict. The edict mentioned by Hadrian in *BGU* I 140 could very well be the *edictum perpetuum*.

[18] Foti Talamanca 1974–1984; Haensch 1994 and 1997. For Arabia and Judaea cf., on the basis of the Babatha archive, Cotton and Eck 2005.

[19] A curiosity among the many extant trial records: in *P. Oxy.* iii 653, we witness a Roman jurist, L. Volusius Maecianus, then prefect, presiding over a trial.

[20] For an overview of jurisdiction in Roman Egypt, Mitteis 1912, 24–32, and now Jördens 2013, 60–63. Despite Seidl 1965, there is no evidence that Rome allowed for decades a wide network of Ptolemaic autonomous jurisdictional organs: Mélèze Modrzejewski 1966, 534.

In the absence of autonomous courts, peregrine private law would not have kept its hold in Egypt without the consistent endorsement of the Roman jurisdiction. The surviving court documentation confirms this assumption (Taubenschlag 1959 I: 477–493; Anagnostou-Canas 1991, 253–268). The usual term "tolerance" is insufficient here. Peregrine law was not merely tolerated but unfailingly applied by the Roman courts, even when it challenged the most basic Roman principles. Sibling marriage (Mélèze Modrzejewski 1964), and many other practices that, while they may be less shocking, were in flagrant contradiction of Roman law,[21] persisted among non-citizens under Roman rule and were accepted as fully valid by the Roman administration, as long as Romans were not involved. In the fields of status, family and inheritance, in fact, the application of Roman law to the peregrines was in general out of the question.[22] The prefect's dictum in *P. Oxy.* xlii 3015 seems in this sense programmatic: "it is best that they should judge in accordance with the laws of the Egyptians"—a claim of principle further illustrated by two prefectural decisions regarding peregrine testamentary freedom. How scrupulous the Roman jurisdiction was in this respect is shown by the frequent recourse to local legal experts (*nomikoi*) in order to ensure a proper interpretation of the peregrine rules.[23] In all our sources, in fact, we find only one unequivocal instance of peregrine law being rejected by the Roman jurisdiction (*P.Oxy.* ii 237, the famous "petition of Dionysia"): a case where, significantly, its application had been protested by one of the parties (Kreuzsaler and Urbanik 2008).

More remarkably: regarding property and contracts, Roman principles were not imposed on any transaction concluded in accordance with peregrine law, even by Romans, no matter how unthinkable under Roman law. Among these: (a) *communio pro diviso*; (b) contracts of sale with immediate real effect, dependent not on *traditio* but on the payment of the price; (c) fictitious loans as an enforceable source of obligations; (d) *contractus in favorem tertii* granting execution rights to the third party; (e) straightforward assignment of credits, in the form of a cession (*parochoresis*) of execution rights (*praxis*); (f) credit instruments enforceable directly through execution; (g) direct agency. All these practices[24] were as common under Roman rule as they had been under the Ptolemies,

[21] Un-Roman traits of the law of inheritance in the papyri: Kreller 1919, 158–164, 223–245; maternal guardianship: Gagliardi 2012.

[22] Even in these areas peregrines could of course fall under Roman law as the indirect result of its application to a Roman citizen: the Roman interdiction of soldiers' marriage, for instance, obviously affected their alien "wives" and children, in that the latter were illegitimate, and the former unable to claim back their dowries, no matter if disguised as deposits: *P. Cattaoui* I recto. A supplementary application of Roman civil law to peregrine freedmen has been conjectured in *P. Oxy.* iv 706: Mélèze Modrzejewski 2014, 264–267. The extensions of Roman law to peregrines conjectured in Taubenschlag 1955, 42 nn. 148–151 and 177 are unconvincing: Wolff and Rupprecht 2002, 135 n. 110 (*ius liberorum*), 155 n. 30 (*lex Laetoria*), 159 n. 45 (*bonorum possessio*); *SB* XX 14710 col. iii, l. 6 is insufficient to hold that *manumissio vindicta* was generally available to aliens: it is not even certain that the manumittor lacked Roman citizenship; *SB* V 7558 is not evidence of *excusatio tutelae* for peregrines: Gaius Apolinarius Niger was undoubtedly, as his son (*SB* IV 7360), *Romaios kai Antinoeus*.

[23] Taubenschlag 1959 II: 161–164; Kunkel 1967, 267–270, 354–365; updated prosopography: Jones 2007, 1354–1359.

[24] Cf. (a) Weiss 1908; (b) Pringsheim 1950, 179–232; (c) lit. in Alonso 2012, 27 n. 49; (d) Taubenschlag 1955, 401–402; (e) Wolff 1941; (f) nn. 26–27; (g) Wenger 1906.

attested for Romans[25] as well as for peregrines, and certainly recognised by the Roman administration.

Alien law was not merely applied but also adopted by the Roman jurisdiction in relevant aspects of its own organisation and procedure. The most striking instance is probably the Roman adoption of the Ptolemaic system of civil execution: well into the third century, execution is still referred to as performed according to Ptolemaic decrees (*kata ta prostetagmena* vel sim.). Although quite complex, this procedure presented the advantage of being formally presided over by the prefect but carried out mostly by officials inherited from the Ptolemaic administration.[26] Its importance is enhanced by the fact that it was the regular way to enforce debts in Egypt. For these, in fact, a court judgement seems as a rule not to have been necessary: execution upon debtors was commonly based directly on an executive document. This executive force seems to have depended less on the *praxis* clause routinely included in most debt documents[27] than on their notarisation: *cheirographa*—that is, documents drawn up without the intervention of a notary—could not be brought to execution without a previous notarisation (Wolff 1978, 129–135, 173–175).

The fact that the private legal practice persevered largely along the lines of the local traditions with the endorsement of the Roman administration does not mean that Rome left the local legal order untouched. As elsewhere in the Empire, a Roman provincial law arose from the edicts of the governor and from those Imperial constitutions or *senatus consulta* specifically intended for the province.[28] This Roman provincial law did not develop in isolation from the local peregrine institutions, but built on them, occasionally in the sense of abolition or reform, often reinforcing or developing them, as was the case with the notarial and archival system. Less discernible is the notion of a *Reichsrecht* or law of the Empire: the term is hardly suitable for the institutions of status, family and inheritance that integrate the personal law of Roman citizens (infra n. 34). Leaving these aside, there is not much that Rome imposed on citizens and peregrines alike throughout the Empire as far as private law is concerned: the limitation of *usurae* to the *centesimae* (Gnomon §105; Wolff and Rupprecht 2002, 189–190), and the opening of testaments as prescribed by *lex Iulia vicesimaria* (Kreller 1919, 395–406) are among the few instances clearly confirmed by our sources.[29]

[25] Evidence for Roman citizens in Taubenschlag 1959 I: 224–225, and 1955, 24–241 (a); 327 n. 25, 333 n. 11, 335 n. 9 (b); 339 n. 5 (c); 402 n. 4 (d); 418–419 (e); 31–312 (g). Direct execution involving Roman citizens (f): *P. Berl. Leih.* 10, *BGU* III 888, and, after the *Constitutio Antoniniana, P. Flor.* i 56, and *P. Iand.* vii 145.

[26] The most comprehensive study of this complex execution procedure, essential also for understanding how real securities worked in Egypt, is still Jörs 1915 and 1918. Cf. also Rupprecht 1997, and Rupprecht in Keenan, Manning and Yiftach-Firanko 2014, 259–265.

[27] By this clause, the debtor explicitly acknowledged the creditor's right to execute as if by virtue of judicial decision (*kathaper ek dikês*): Rodríguez Martín 2013.

[28] Kupiszewski 1964; Wolff and Rupprecht 2002, 174–200. The notion that peregrine law becomes part of Roman provincial law when endorsed by the Roman administration is better avoided if the distinction between both is to keep its utility: Mélèze Modrzejewski 2014, 284.

[29] Cf. also the extension to the provinces of *cessio bonorum ex lege Iulia* in C.7.71.4, although in *P. Ryl.* ii 75 the prefect does not seem aware of any binding legislation. On *longi temporis praescriptio* see Nörr 1969.

5.5 Peregrine Legal Practice

The alien practices that dominate private transactions in Egypt do not belong to the history of Roman law, but to that of the Greek and Egyptian legal traditions. Yet they are far from irrelevant for Roman legal studies. The influence of the Eastern provincial practice has been recognised since Mitteis as one of the driving forces behind the evolution of Roman law in late Antiquity (Mitteis 1891; cf. Kaser 1975, 7–10). Already in the second and third centuries both jurists and the Imperial chancellery had occasion to confront them: numerous third-century rescripts, particularly from the huge Diocletianic corpus, and a good part of Scaevola's *Digesta* and *Quaestiones*, cannot be studied without a proper understanding of the alien practices and conceptions that they address—even if they often do so merely in order to translate them into Roman categories or dismiss them in the name of the Roman orthodoxy (Taubenschlag 1959 I: 104–159, 505–517, 519–533). Particularly important are the contractual models associated with commerce and trade. Here, what we find in the papyri can be assumed to be in its main lines an expression of a wider Greek *koine*, with which the Roman jurisprudence was inevitably confronted. In this field, much can be gained from a combined study of the jurisprudential texts and the papyri.[30]

More generally, some attention to the Greek legal tradition documented in the papyri provides a better perspective on Roman law itself. It not only provides a fulcrum of comparison for modern scholars; it was the main source of comparison against which the Romans themselves viewed their own legal tradition: we thus gain a notion of the peculiarities of the Roman legal order that must have been apparent to the Roman jurisprudence; maybe more crucially, also a better awareness of how many elements both legal traditions have in common, despite the insistence to the contrary of much of the Roman-law literature of the twentieth century.[31]

5.6 Roman Legal Practice before the *Constitutio Antoniniana*

Before 212, Roman citizenship in Egypt, as in general in the East, was much less common than in the West. Yet despite the low number of Roman citizens in Egypt, the papyri provide ample material to reconstruct their legal life (Taubenschlag 1959 I: 194–228; Wolff and Rupprecht 2002, 149–172). Leaving aside testaments and other deeds related to inheritance,

[30] Groundbreaking, Mitteis 1898. This approach has regained presence in the last decades, in great measure due to the contributions of Éva Jakab.

[31] Possible instances of reception of Greek elements into Roman law in Mitteis 1908, 10–21, Partsch 1931, and Taubenschlag 1959 I: 421–460. Much of the detail will always remain hypothetical, but the dismissive attitude predominant in the post-war scholarship (paradigmatic Kaser 1971, 21–22, 178–179 and 1975, 7–10: "stark überschätzt") seems less the result of a dispassionate examination of the evidence than a misguided defence of the singularity of Roman law, which certainly does not depend on every Roman institution being completely free from external influences.

family and status, these "Romans", whatever their origin,[32] tend overwhelmingly to document their legal acts in Greek, and to follow the same models used by the rest of the population, even when these contravene basic principles of Roman law (nn. 24–25).

This phenomenon is not difficult to understand. Despite the lack of a legal science, the Greek legal tradition offered a well-tried framework to trade and commerce. More decisively, Egypt was endowed with a tight network of notarial institutions that for centuries had developed and refined a rich variety of contractual models. The public documents executed through these offices enjoyed a special status, further fostered by the Roman administration: property could be registered in the record office only when the acquisition had been notarised (Wolff 1978, 174–175, 227–228); and only notarised documents were accepted as a basis for direct execution against the debtor (section 5.4 ad nn. 26–27). In this context, the picture we find in the sources is hardly surprising. Roman citizenship made no difference as far as contractual practice is concerned: notarisation was as necessary for the Roman citizens as for everyone else, and contracts followed the Greek models proposed by the notaries, no matter the origin or status of the parties involved. Of course, all this would have been unthinkable if the Roman administration had had any qualms in applying peregrine law to the Roman citizens who followed it in their transactions.[33]

In Egypt, Roman citizens appear subject to Roman private law only in the fields of status, family and inheritance. Only these conform to the idea of a "personal law" that modern scholarship stubbornly attributes to Antiquity. The same holds true for non-citizens (section 5.4 ad nn. 21–22). The *Gnomon* of the *Idios Logos* is a good illustration of the care with which the personality principle was observed in these areas. The papyrological documentation in these matters is therefore, when Romans are concerned, a primary source of Roman legal practice: particularly the testaments, but also the preserved *cretiones secundum tabulas testamenti*, everything related to manumissions and the provisions of *leges Fufia Caninia* and *Aelia Sentia*, to *sponsalia*, marriage, dowry, and *leges Iulia et Papia*, to the status of children, adoption, guardianship, *ius liberorum* and *lex Iulia et Titia de tutore dando*, to *lex Laetoria* and *cura minorum*.[34] Even in these areas, where a true subjection to the personal law is the rule, we observe departures from the Roman orthodoxy: *liberi in potestate* treated as property owners,[35] guardians assisting women in transactions for which they are superfluous under Roman law, like debt collection or the granting of loans or deposits,[36] or Roman women with alien guardians.[37]

[32] Mostly freedmen, soldiers, veterans, and members of the Greek elite: Taubenschlag 1959 I: 181–193.

[33] The incorrect assumption that Roman jurisdiction adhered mechanistically to the principle of personality is not uncommon: Wieacker 2006, 160–161; Talamanca 1989, 513. More nuanced: Wieacker 1988, 516–517; Kaser 1971, 216–217.

[34] Many of them in *FIRA* III. Translated examples in Keenan, Manning and Yiftach-Firanko 2014, 118–134. An overview in Wolff and Rupprecht 2002, 153–162. For the testaments, Amelotti 1966, Migliardi Zingale 1997 and Nowak 2015. The *agnitiones bonorum possessionis* are all post-*Constitutio Antoniniana*.

[35] *P. Hamb.* i 97, *PSI* v 447, anticipating the local (mis)interpretation of *patria potestas* post-*Constitutio Antoniniana*. That a slave of Antonia Minor is registered as a cattle owner in *P. Oxy.* ii 244 is probably the result of his assimilation to an Imperial slave.

[36] *P. Lond.* ii 178 (p. 207), *BGU* I 301, *BGU* III 729.

[37] *BGU* II 472, col. ii. More disputed is the question of women acting as guardians in the papyri: cf., involving Romans, *P. Cattaoui* I verso col. i, ll.14–15, *BGU* VII 1662, *P. Lond.* iii 1164a (p. 156), *PSI* ix 1027.

Beyond these limited "personal" fields of status, family and succession, the contracts concluded by Romans in Greek are usually indistinguishable from those concluded by peregrines. Most attempts to identify "Roman" traits in these Greek contracts have been in vain.[38] Their Latin contracts, instead, which are rather scarce, do adhere to the Roman models both in form and content, even if occasionally with peregrine accretions. This prevailing conformity between language and legal tradition is the almost inevitable result of the use of notarial models.[39] The few extant Latin contracts, in fact, appear in almost all cases within a military milieu:[40] not because soldiers were particularly expected to accommodate to the Roman forms,[41] but most likely due to the availability of Latin notarial services in the army.

5.7 Legal Practice after the *Constitutio Antoniniana*

For Caracalla's momentous decision, our main source is a papyrus, the famous *P. Giss.* 40. For the consequences of the decision too, our best information comes from the papyri. The most immediately visible is the sudden proliferation of Aurelii, the *gentilicium* that the new citizens received after the emperor. The papyri provide a rich illustration of the legal practices of these new citizens after 212. The extent to which they kept faithful to their old peregrine traditions took scholars by surprise, leading to a notorious dispute between Ernst Schönbauer and Vincenzo Arangio-Ruiz (Mélèze Modrzejewski 2014, 30–301). There was no question that the old peregrine practices had survived after the *Constitutio Antoniniana*; the evidence was overwhelming. The kernel of the discussion was, instead, whether they had survived—so Arangio-Ruiz, as before him Mitteis—"*contra ius*, because of lack of interest or a certain tolerance of the Roman authorities", or, on the contrary—Schönbauer—as the expression of a law that was still fully in vigour, the Roman tolerance being conscious and official, supported perhaps by a construction of double citizenship,[42]

[38] Only a small group of sale contracts, from Egypt and the near East (*P. Hamb.* i 63, *P. Turner* 22, *BGU* III 887, *P. Mich.* ix 546, *P. Dura* 26), present convincing "Roman" elements. The cases of *acceptilatio*, stipulatory loan, and *receptum nautarum* enumerated by Taubenschlag 1959 I: 222, do not resist scrutiny. Particularly striking is how rarely Roman citizens resorted to *stipulatio* in the East: before 212, only four instances of *stipulatio* among Romans in Egypt (*P. Mich.* xv 707, *P. Hamb.* i 63, and the Latin contracts *PSI* vi 729, and *P. Mich.* vii 438), two in the near East (*P. Turner* 22, and *BGU* III 887). Even in the Latin loans *SB* XVI 12609, and *P. Fouad.* i 45, no stipulation covers the interest rate.

[39] The same correspondence was taken for granted in the Ptolemaic legislation: *P. Tebt.* 5, ll. 207–220 = *MChr.* 1 (118 BC).

[40] That is the case of the so-called soldiers' cheirographs: Arangio-Ruiz 1948, to which *SB* XVI 12609, and *P. Duk.* inv. 528 must be added. From a military milieu come also most of the preserved Latin sale contracts (cf. *CPL* 120, *PSI* vi 729, *P Oxy.* XLI 2951), and the thoroughly Roman *P. Col.* viii 221.

[41] Soldier contracts following peregrine models are not rare, cf. *BGU* I 69 and *BGU* III 741.

[42] For a discussion of the double citizenship hypothesis, Mélèze Modrzejewski 2014, 304–310. In Egypt, where for two centuries most non-Romans had been *peregrini nullius civitatis*, the hypothesis is problematic: it requires us to assume that Severus' grant of a city council (*boulê*) to the Egyptian

by an explicit safeguard clause for peregrine law in Caracalla's constitution (H. J. Wolff)[43] or aided at least merely by its recognition as *mos regionis* (Mélèze Modrzejewski).[44]

Despite the many elements of continuity, the *Constitutio Antoniniana* undoubtedly laid the basis for the true legal Romanisation of the East. The Imperial rescripts indefatigably instructed these Eastern provincials in the minutiae of Roman law: this romanisation by rescript was particularly intense under Alexander Severus, the Gordians, and, especially, Diocletian. With Diocletian, the situation changes more radically.[45] Egypt is divided into minor provinces; the local magistracies are reformed, the *curator civitatis* (*logistes*) introduced; the local calendar and the local currency are abolished; Latin is promoted as the language of the upper administration and of the courts. This time also marks the beginning of the activity of the law schools in the East, including that of Alexandria. Most decisively, the generalisation in the East of notarial offices by Imperial concession (*stationes tabellionum*) soon caused the extinction of the local notarial institutions and record offices, whose documentary traditions had been a major obstacle for the advance of Roman law in Egypt. Unfortunately, the amount of extant papyri lowers dramatically in the fourth and especially the fifth century onwards, but no history of Roman law in late Antiquity can be written without these later documents.[46]

Bibliography

Alonso, J. L. (2012). "Πίστις in loan transactions: a new interpretation of *P. Dion.* 11–12." *Journal of Juristic Papyrology* 42: 9–30.

Alonso, J. L. (2013). "The status of peregrine law in Egypt: 'customary law' and legal pluralism in the Roman empire." *Journal of Juristic Papyrology* 43: 351–404.

Amelotti, M. 1966. *Il testamento romano attraverso la prassi documentale I*. Florence.

Ammirati, S. 2012. "The Latin book of legal content: a significant type in the history of the ancient book." In P. Schubert, ed. *Actes du 26e Congrès international de papyrologie*. Geneva. 19–25.

Anagnostou-Canas, B. 1991. *Juge et sentence dans l'Égypte romaine*. Paris.

Ando, C. 2015. "*Exemplum*, analogy and precedent in Roman law." In M. Lowrie and S. Lüdemann, eds., *Between exemplarity and singularity: literature, philosophy, law*. New York. 111–122.

metropoleis in 200 AD entailed the transformation of their inhabitants into citizens, and that this condition was extended to the non-metropolitans by virtue of the doctrine referred to by Ulpian in D.50.1.30.

[43] The conjecture depends on the reconstruction of the famously bewildering *menontos*-clause in *P. Giss.* 40, ll. 8–9: Mélèze Modrzejewski 2014, 319–323.

[44] Mélèze Modrzejewski 2014, 313–318; Kaser 1971, 220. Despite Modrzejewski 2014, 7–27, 248, 257, 276, this customary law construction cannot account, two centuries earlier, for the survival of peregrine law to the Roman conquest, or for its status before the Roman jurisdiction: Alonso 2013.

[45] Bowman 2008. The changes are such that since Wilcken and Mitteis papyrologists commonly set the beginning of "Byzantine" Egypt in 284 AD.

[46] Taubenschlag 1959 I: 232–259; Wolff 1956, 1974. The papyri are crucial for our knowledge of the impact of Imperial legislation and Justinian's compilation on legal practice: Beaucamp 2007 and the many contributions of Jakub Urbanik.

Ankum, H. 1970. "La législation des préfets d'Égypte et l'edictum provinciale," in Anamnesis, *Gedenkboek E. A. Leemans*. Brugge. 63–69.

Arangio-Ruiz, V. 1948. "Chirografi di soldati," in *Studi in onore di Siro Solazzi*. Naples. 251–263.

Arangio-Ruiz, V. 1957[7]. *Storia del diritto romano*. Naples.

Bagnall, R. S., ed. 2009. *The Oxford handbook of papyrology*. New York.

Beaucamp, J. 2007. "Byzantine Egypt and imperial law." In R. Bagnall, ed., *Egypt in the Byzantine World, 300–700*. Cambridge. 271–287.

Bowman, A. K. 2008. "Egypt from Septimius Severus to the death of Constantine." In A. K. Bowman, P. Garnsey and A. Cameron, eds., *The Cambridge ancient history*. Cambridge. Vol. 12: 313–326.

Buraselis, K. 2007. Theia Dorea. *Das Göttlich-Kaiserliche Geschenk*. Vienna.

Cascione, C. (2008). "Citazione di giuristi romani in *BKT* IX 201 (*P. Berol.* inv. 21295)." *Journal of Juristic Papyrology* 38: 63–71.

Chalon, G. 1964. *L'Édit de Tiberius Julius Alexander: étude historique et exégétique*. Olten.

Coles, R. 1966. *Reports of proceedings in papyri*. Brussels.

Coriat, J.-P. 1997. *Le prince législateur*. Rome.

Cotton, H. M., Cockle, W. E. H. and Millar, F. G. B. (1995). "The papyrology of the Roman near east: a survey." *Journal of Roman Studies* 85: 214–235.

Cotton, H. M., and Eck, W. 2005. "Roman officials in Judaea and Arabia and civil jurisdiction." In R. Katzoff, and D. Schaps, eds., *Law in the documents of the Judaean desert*. Leiden. 23–44.

Foti Talamanca, G. 1974/1979/1984. *Ricerche sul processo nell'Egitto greco-romano*. Vols. 1–2: 1. Milan. 2. Naples.

Gagliardi, L. (2012). "La madre tutrice e la madre ἐπακολουθήτρια: osservazioni sul rapporto tra diritto romano e diritti delle province orientali." *Index* 40: 423–446.

Gagos, T., and Potter, D. S. 2006. "Documents." In D. S. Potter, ed., *A companion to the Roman empire*. Oxford.

Gascou, J. 2009. "The papyrology of the near east." In R. S. Bagnall, ed., *The Oxford handbook of papyrology*. New York. 473–494.

Gonis, N. (2006). "Mommsen, Grenfell, and the 'Century of Papyrology.'" *Zeitschrift für Papyrologie und Epigraphik* 156: 195–196.

Haensch, R. (1994). "Die Bearbeitungsweisen von Petitionen in der Provinz Aegyptus." *Zeitschrift für Papyrologie und Epigraphik* 100: 487–546.

Haensch, R. 1997. "Zur Konventusordnung in *Aegyptus* und den übrigen Provinzen des römischen Reiches." In B. Kramer et al., eds., *Akten des 21. Internationalen Papyrologenkongresses*. Stuttgart. 320–391.

Haensch, R. 2007. "*Apokrimata* und *Authentica*." In R. Haensch and J. Heinrichs, eds., *Herrschen und Verwalten*. Cologne. 213–233.

Haensch, R. 2008. "Typisch römisch? Die Gerichtsprotokolle der in *Aegyptus* und den übrigen östlichen Reichsprovinzen tätigen Vertreter Roms." In H. Börm, N. Erhardt and J. Wiesehöfer, eds., *Monumentum et instrumentum inscriptum*. Stuttgart. 117–125.

Haensch, R. 2010. "Quelques observations générales concernant la correspondance conservée des préfets d'Egypte." In J. Desmulliez, C. Hoët-van Cauwenberghe and J.-C. Jolivet, eds., *L'Étude des correspondences dans le monde romain de l'antiquité classique à l'antiquité tardive: permanences et mutations*. Lille. 95–113.

Houston, G. W. 2014. *Inside Roman libraries*. Chapel Hill.

Jones, C. (2007). "Juristes Romains dans l'Orient Grec." *Comptes rendus des séances de l'Académie des Inscriptions et Belles-Lettres* 151: 1331–1359.

Jördens, A. (2013) "Roms Herrschaft über Ägypten." *Journal of Juristic Papyrology* 43: 51–72.

Jörs, P. (1915 and 1918). "Erzrichten und Chrematisten." *Zeitschrift der Savigny-Stiftung für Rechtsgeschichte, romanistische Abteilung* 36: 230–339; 39: 52–118.

Kaser, M. 1971²–1975². *Das römische Privatrecht*, Vols. 1–2. Munich.

Katzoff, R. 1980. "Sources of law in Roman Egypt: the role of the prefect." In H. Temporini and W. Haase, eds., *Aufstieg und Niedergang der römischen Welt*, Vol. 3. Berlin. 807–844.

Keenan, J. G., Manning, J. G. and Yiftach-Firanko, U. 2014. *Law and legal practice in Egypt from Alexander to the Arab Conquest.* Cambridge.

Kelly, B. 2011. *Petitions, litigation, and social control in Roman Egypt.* New York.

Kreller, H. 1919. *Erbrechtliche Untersuchungen auf Grund der graeco-aegyptischen Papyrusurkunden.* Leipzig.

Kreuzsaler, C., and Urbanik, J. (2008). "Humanity and inhumanity of law: the case of Dionysia." *Journal of Juristic Papyrology* 38: 119–155.

Kunkel, W. 1967². *Herkunft und soziale Stellung der römischen Juristen.* Graz.

Kupiszewski, H. 1964. "Römisches Provinzialrecht in Ägypten." In H. Braunert, ed., *Studien F. Oertel.* Bonn. 68–80.

Lenel, O. 1927³. *Das* Edictum Perpetuum: *ein Versuch zu seiner Wiederherstellung.* Leipzig.

Lewald, H. (1959). "Conflits de lois dans le monde grec et romain." *Labeo* 5: 334–369.

Lewis, N. 1989. *The documents from the Bar Kochba Period in the cave of letters*, Vol. 1: *Greek papyri.* Jerusalem.

Martin, A. (2000). "Das Jahrhundert der Papyrologie?" *Archiv für Papyrusforschung* 46: 1–2.

McNamee, K. (1995). "Missing links in the development of *scholia*." *Greek, Roman and Byzantine Studies* 36: 399–414.

Méléze Modrzejewski, J. (1964). "Die Geschwisterehe in der hellenistische Praxis und nach römischen Recht." *Zeitschrift der Savigny-Stiftung für Rechtsgeschichte, romanistische Abteilung* 81: 69–82.

Méléze Modrzejewski, J. (1966). "Chronique papyrologique." *Revue historique de droit français et étranger* 44: 126–143; 524–541.

Méléze Modrzejewski, J. 1977. "Gnomon de l'Idiologue," in *Les Lois des Romains.* Paris. 520–557.

Méléze Modrzejewski, J. (1982). "Chronique. Droits de l'Antiquité." *Revue historique de droit français et étranger* 60: 471–500.

Méléze Modrzejewski, J. 2014. *Loi et coutume dans l'Égypte grecque et romaine.* Warsaw.

Migliardi Zingale, L. 1997³. *I testamenti romani nei papiri e nelle tavolette d'Egitto.* Turin.

Mitteis, L. 1891. *Reichsrecht und Volksrecht in den östlichen Provinzen des römischen Kaiserreichs: mit Beiträgen zur Kenntniss des griechischen Rechts und der spätrömischen Rechtsentwicklung.* Leipzig.

Mitteis, L. (1898). "Trapezitika." *Zeitschrift der Savigny-Stiftung für Rechtsgeschichte, romanistische Abteilung* 19: 198–260.

Mitteis, L. 1908. *Römisches Privatrecht bis auf die Zeit Diokletians.* Leipzig.

Mitteis, L. 1912. *Grundzüge und Chrestomathie der Papyruskunde*, Vol. 2: *Juristischer Teil I. Grundzüge.* Leipzig.

Montevecchi, O. 1988². *La Papirologia.* Milan.

Nasti, F. 201–2013. *Papyrus Hauniensis* de legatis et fideicommissis, Vols. 1–2. Naples.

Nörr, D. 1969. *Die Entstehung der* longi temporis praescriptio. Cologne.

Nowak, M. 2015. *Wills in the Roman Empire. A documentary approach.* Warsaw.
Oliver, J. H. 1989. *Greek constitutions of early Roman emperors from inscriptions and papyri.* Philadelphia.
Orestano, R. (1936). "Gli editti imperiali. Contributo alla teoria della loro validità ed efficacia nel diritto romano classico." *Bulletino dell'Istituto di Diritto Romano* 44: 219–331.
Orestano, R. 1937. *Il potere normativo degli imperatori e le costituzioni imperiali.* Rome.
Partsch, J. 1931. "Der griechische Gedanke in der Rechtswissenschaft," in *Aus Nachgelassenen und Kleineren Verstreuten Schriften.* Berlin. 346–352.
Pivano, S. (1923). "Gli studi di papirologia giuridica e la scienza italiana." *Aegyptus* 4: 245–282.
Pringsheim, F. 1950. *The Greek law of sale.* Weimar.
Purpura, G. (2009). "I papiri e le costituzioni imperiali in Egitto." *Aegyptus* 89: 155–221.
Riccobono, S. 1950. *Il Gnomon dell'Idios Logos.* Palermo.
Rodríguez Martín, J. D. (2013). "Sobre la supervivencia de la cláusula 'καθάπερ ἐκ δίκης' en los papiros romanos y bizantinos." *Revue internationale des droits de l'antiquité* 60: 243–277.
Rupprecht, H.-A. 1997. "Zwangsvollstreckung und dingliche Sicherheiten in den Papyri des ptolemäischen und römischen Zeit." In G. Thür and J. Vélissaropoulos, eds., *Symposion 1995.* Cologne. 291–302.
Sciortino, S. (1998). "Note in tema di falsificazione dei rescritti." *Annali del Seminario Giuridico dell' Università di Palermo* 45: 443–456.
Seider, R. 1981. *Paläographie der lateinischen Papyri*, Vol. 2: *Juristische und christlische Texte.* Stuttgart.
Seidl, E. (1965). "Zur Gerichtverfassung in der Provinz Aegypten bis ca. 250 n. Chr." *Labeo* 11: 316–328.
Swarney, P. R. 1970. *The Ptolemaic and Roman Idios Logos.* Toronto.
Talamanca, M. 1989. *Lineamenti di storia del diritto romano.* Milan.
Taubenschlag, R. 1955². *The law of Greco-Roman Egypt in the light of the papyri.* Warsaw.
Taubenschlag, R. 1959. *Opera Minora*, Vols. 1–2. Warsaw.
van Minnen, P. (1993). "The Century of Papyrology (1892–1992)." *Bulletin of the American Society of Papyrologists* 30: 5–18.
van Minnen, P. 2007. "The millenium of papyrology (2001–)?" In B. Palme, ed., *Akten des 23. Internationalen Papyrologenkongresses.* Vienna. 703–714.
Weiss, E. (1908). "*Communio pro diviso* und *pro indiviso* in den Papyri." *Archiv für Papyrusforschung* 4: 330–365.
Wenger, L. 1906. *Die Stellvertretung im Rechte der Papyri.* Leipzig.
Wieacker, F. 1988–2006. *Römische Rechtsgeschichte*, Vols. 1–2. Munich.
Wilcken, U. (1921). "Zu den Edikten." *Zeitschrift der Savigny-Stiftung für Rechtsgeschichte, romanistische Abteilung* 42: 124–158.
Wolff, H. J. (1941). "The *praxis*-provision in papyrus contracts." *Transactions of the American Philological Association* 72: 418–438.
Wolff, H. J. (1956). "Zur Romanisierung des Vertragsrechts der Papyri." *Zeitschrift der Savigny-Stiftung für Rechtsgeschichte, romanistische Abteilung* 73: 1–28.
Wolff, H. J. (1974). "Das Vulgarrechtsproblem und die Papyri." *Zeitschrift der Savigny-Stiftung für Rechtsgeschichte, romanistische Abteilung* 91: 54–105.
Wolff, H. J. 1978. *Das Recht der Griechischen Papyri Ägyptens*, Vol. 2. Munich.
Wolff, H. J. and Rupprecht, H.-A. 2002. *Das Recht der Griechischen Papyri Ägyptens, Vol. 1.* Munich.
Zimmermann, R. (2001). "In der Schule von Ludwig Mitteis: Ernst Rabels rechtshistorische Ursprünge." *Rabels Zeitschrift* 65: 1–38.

CHAPTER 6

ROMAN LAW AND LATIN LITERATURE

MICHÈLE LOWRIE

6.1 Introduction

Roman innovation in literature as in law was formative for these institutions' subsequent institutional history.[1] Creativity in both arenas fostered a complex interrelation that still desires systematic treatment. I start from the premise that law and literature were practices that, despite different functions and conceptualisations, shared a similar toolkit. The topics surveyed below—case studies for the field rather than comprehensive analysis—show that the Romans saw literature and the law as authoritative discourses sometimes parallel, often engaged in dynamic contest, but always as spheres for determining and disputing norms. Certain assumptions about their differences crystallised in the transition from Republic to Empire.

Law and literature were discursive practices multiple in themselves and in their interrelation at Rome during all periods in form, speech act, publication medium and their practitioners' social class. Both changed over time: their comparison offers a dizzying array of options. The umbrella of *iura* encompasses *lex* (statute), plebiscite, edicts, rescripts and judicial commentary, each with different forms and processes of authorisation—even the ancients confused the categories (Howley 2013, 14–15). Furthermore, law abuts other intellectual practices such as antiquarianism and rhetoric. Legal consulting was a different profession from arguing in court, where contestation revolved around aesthetic display as much as fairness or the rule of law.

Similarly, the standard word for literature in Cicero, *litterae* (letters), is plural. It encompasses activities distinct in genre, metre and social function. *Litteratura* originally meant writing, grammar and the elements of education. It approaches a unitary institution only in the second century AD (Marcus Aurelius *ad* Fronto, *Ep.* 2.11 [31N; 1.142 Loeb]). Legal scholarship has focused on poetry, history and philosophy as sources for Roman law and

[1] Schiavone 2012, 3: the modern conception of law as a "social and mental form" was "invented by the Romans"; Derrida 2000, 20: "literature is a Latin word."

on the regulation of "harmful" speech, including literary expression,[2] and Latin literature's interest in law has become a distinct topic.[3] Such approaches, however, assume each was a discrete discursive system and beg pressing questions: what criteria differentiate between them; how they emerged as distinct; and whether their interrelation, sometimes harmonious, sometimes uneasy, covers similar territory today.

If the argument that rhetoric and law shared discursive space still needs defence,[4] similar claims about literature meet even greater resistance. The boundaries around law are vigorously defended (Posner 2009) and challenged (Goodrich 2009). Our own commitments determine whether homologies and points of contact appear methodologically fruitful. Cicero and Gellius used law as evidence for social history; conversely, antiquarian recuperation had practical effects in court (Howley 2013). Shared features surpass law as a source for language and culture. If the law requires performative enactment, it touches rhetoric, whose aesthetics cross into literature—*pace* the defenders of each field's autonomy. Statute and verse are clarifying extremes between which ancient Rome offers a substantial grey area.

The functional differentiation between social spheres already began at Rome, but we easily retroject greater autonomy between law and literature than existed in Antiquity. These two discourses circle around the political understood as a public sphere where representation and communication affect decisions about conduct.[5] Ennius' hexameter, *moribus antiquis res stat Romana virisque* ("Roman affairs stand on ancient customs and men", *Ann.* 156 Skutsch 1985, 317), has been cited as foundational since Cicero (*Rep.* 5.1) because no other source offers a better articulation of the Roman Republican constitution.[6] It defines the *mos maiorum* (ancestral custom) as a system of performative exemplarity. A sonically crafted and formally balanced line, perhaps uttered by Manlius Torquatus who himself became exemplary, conjoins the state (*res Romana*), constitution (*stat*), political action (*viris*) and archaic legal sphere based on custom, within a hendiadys where "ancient" modifies both customs and men. Aesthetic compression gives the ideology special punch: memorability invites the internalisation of guiding values. More than mere source for pre-legal constitutional thought, the poetic medium gives the line normative force.

Crafting norms in language is the common ground between law and literature. This ranges from setting guidelines for behaviour and process, to deliberation, to broader questions of Roman identity and citizen formation. An important difference is the capacity—imagined or real—of achieving pragmatic effects: the law's force contrasts with literature's impotence, but appears formal and static beside judgement and political action; literature may not cause worldly change, but nevertheless shapes social imaginaries and transmits representations to posterity (Lowrie 2009, 327–348, 36–382). The interdisciplinary field of "law and literature" asks what form such discourses take under what social and political

[2] Crook 1967, 17 surveys literature as a source. For libel, Rives 2002; Gruen 1992, 295–296.

[3] Crook 1967, 8; Kenney 1969; Cloud 1989; Ducos 1994; Tatum 1998; McGinn 2001; Lowrie 2009, 325–382; Balsley 2010.

[4] Tellegen-Couperus and Tellegen 2013; du Plessis 2013, 3.

[5] For the public sphere, Gurd 2012; Ando 2012.

[6] Hölkeskamp 2004, 186; Wallace-Hadrill 2008, 213–231.

conditions, how they overlap and how they define themselves against each other.[7] Focus on productive ambiguities at the transition from Republic to Empire will help disentangle Roman categories for thinking about law, literature and the discursive transmission of values.

6.2 *Carmen* and the Myth of a Unified Public Sphere

When Cicero recalls learning the XII Tables as a *carmen necessarium* ("necessary song", *Leg.* 2.59) in his youth, he evokes an image of schoolchildren chanting.[8] The Republican law code is not diminished, but situated within a capacious frame. In Greek, νόμος unites custom and song (Svenbro 1993/1988, 4), categories more intuitively linked for moderns than are literature and law. Roman song, *carmen*, does not map onto custom and denotes less tuneful vocalisation than authoritative discourse oral or written (Habinek 1998; Lowrie 2009, 12–18). Poetry, archaic law, prayer, treaties and spells were all called *carmen* (Williams 1982; Meyer 2004, 44–72). Distinctive rhythms catch the attention and facilitate memorisation, but also signal generality beyond the particulars of daily speech or oratory (Habinek 2005, 1–7). The word captures the numinous efficacy of the law and poetry's link to the divine. Increasing codification and professional specialisation eventually drew law out from custom and literature out from song.

The general trend from orality to literacy also affected legal and literary expression. Although the *leges regiae* (kingly laws) and XII Tables recorded law long before literature emerged as a literate practice,[9] the canonical origins of Latin literature around 240 BC coincide to a large degree with the beginning of the pre-classical legal period (250–27 BC).[10] Custom was increasingly codified through statute, the praetor's edict and juridical commentary (du Plessis 2012, 19–20). Cicero presupposes that *lex* (statute) was formalised in writing (*Leg.* 1.19), although other legal categories (*mos*, custom; *ius*, right) were lived or thought rather than recorded.[11] Despite the etymological obscurity of *lex*, the Romans derived it from *legere* (to read).[12]

Writing became the more modern medium for both discourses. *Scribere* denotes poetic composition as early as Ennius (*Ann.* 206 Skutsch 1985, 88), while *canere* evokes the archaic

[7] For basics, consult Eden 1986 and the journals *Law and Literature, Law and Humanities, Yale Journal of Law and the Humanities*. Shakespeare is a growth area. Outside English see Steinberg 2013.

[8] Fögen 2002, 69. In non-educative contexts, legal language was also called *carmen*: Livy 1.26.6. This section condenses material from Lowrie 2009. Fögen 2007, 51–73 critiques Cicero as a source for the XII Tables.

[9] Fögen 2002, 82–84; generally, see Humbert 2005.

[10] Feeney 2005 analyses the limitations of the standard view of Latin literature's origins, but the general point stands.

[11] Cicero distinguishes written from natural law (*Leg.* 1.17).

[12] Ernout and Meillet 1939 s.v. *lex*; Maltby 1991 s.v. *lex*, including an alternative etymology from *ligare*.

past. Writing developed strong associations with satire and the literary epistle, genres oriented toward the contemporary.[13] Scenes of writing in Latin literature (e.g. Catull. 51) often depict lived experience over divine inspiration. Writing conveyed an authority grounded in the mundane and offered the advantages of literary realism, codification and an exact record. But it never entirely supplanted oral practices and the two remained intertwined.[14] The burgeoning of code and legal commentary supplemented rather than replaced custom (D.1.3.32–40). For literature, recitation became fashionable once Asinius Pollio took the practice from private into public venues, although the performance to music of polished literary works remains controversial (Lowrie 2009, 63–97). What then was to be gained from calling either law or poetry *carmen*?

Cicero's phrase marks the XII Tables as venerable, but archaic: *carmen* evokes an earlier, putatively simpler age. His recording the loss of proto-literary convivial ballads (*carmina convivalia, Brut.* 75), already lamented by Cato, is similarly nostalgic. The Augustan poets called themselves *vates* (prophet) and adopted *carmen* and *canere* (sing) as standard poetic vocabulary to appropriate the sacred aura of song (Newman 1990, 428–431). These lexical innovations claimed for literature an authoritative and traditional role at a time when the Republic's collapse eroded public speaking.

At *Ars poetica* 394–399, Horace conjures up a mythical world of overlapping social spheres: Amphion built Thebes by moving stones to the sound of the lyre and carving laws on wood. His foundational acts include the regulation of property, marriage, building towns and philosophy. Neither Horace nor his addressees, the aristocratic Pisones, could pursue the career each anticipated in the late Republic. Both Horace and young Piso turned to poetry, full or part-time, after their political "wings" were "clipped".[15] A discourse imagined as having such broad powers appealed to dispossessed poets and statesmen alike. This and similar gestures of self-authorisation compensated within literature for the foreclosure of pubic deliberative oratory. Amphion's magic divulges the phantasm, but Horace nevertheless addresses Augustan-age longing for the comparatively unified sphere of public affairs represented by Cicero's orator, already in his own time a nostalgic ideal.

6.3 *Mala Carmina* and Freedom of Speech

Law, politics and literature were never a harmonised unity and the power struggles between them fascinated writers. A major concern was freedom of speech—no universal right at Rome. Rather, social status determined who could speak in public under the Republic. Some means of censoring literature were enshrined in law and some a bare exercise of power. Legal language permeates the discussion and sets the question imaginatively under its aegis. Although poetry consistently shows itself evading legal formalities, it takes political power seriously as a threat. Three authors versed in public affairs—Horace's day

[13] Ovid's *Her.* wittily attributes writing to mythic figures.

[14] Meyer 2004, 86 n. 61, 97–101; Butler 2002. In the practice of *praeire verbis*, an officiant read aloud words before their utterance by the requisite authority, such as a magistrate, made them dispositive: Valette-Cagnac 1997, 247–302.

[15] Horace, *Ep.* 2.2.50. Lowrie 2014.

job was as a *scriba quaestorius*; Ovid abandoned legal training for poetry; Tacitus' career of public service included the consulship—offer representative examples of contestation between spheres.

Instead of subjecting his contemporaries to stinging criticism, Horace sidesteps libel in *Sermones* 2.1 by submitting censorship to critique. He stages a consultation with Trebatius Testa and mocks legal diction. The jurist warns the poet of prosecution by citing the XII Tables on *mala carmina* (bad songs).[16] Horace, however, perverts the evaluation from moral to aesthetic: so much for bad poems, but what about good ones? (2.1.83–84). The poet wins the game of wit, but higher stakes are political. The judge is Caesar, who likes Horace's poetry. Trebatius concedes: laughter dismisses the case (2.1.86). But what if Caesar's judgement tilted against him?

Ovid found out. *Tristia* 2.207 alleges a poem and a mistake as the reason for his exile: the *Ars Amatoria* encouraged adultery against Augustus' marriage legislation and the emperor reproved some transgression, whose secrecy still tantalises.[17] This epistle advances a plea that will be heard only in the court of public opinion. The legal status of Ovid's relegation depends on a *privilegium* published in an edict (2.131–138). Ovid highlights the decision's arbitrary nature and the *princeps*' failure to bring his crimes openly to court. The poem spoofs legal language throughout and undermines the law's seriousness. Ovid's exile appears cruel and illegitimate, but the joke is on Augustus, represented to posterity as exacting vengeance on a defenceless poet.

In Tacitus' *Dialogus de oratoribus*, law and literature are professional rivals. Maternus has just recited his new volume on Cato and is embarking on a tragedy about Thyestes, activities that jeopardise his security (3.2). The emperor's ability to repress elides the distinction between legal and political dangers. While the law can threaten writers, literature's appeal as an occupation lures skilled speakers away from defending clients, a socially useful endeavour. Countering criticism, Maternus declares he has sweat enough in the Forum and embraces poetry's "more august" calling (4.2). As in Horace and Ovid, literature wins from a position of vulnerability. Danger hardly deters Maternus, but enhances literature's allure. The nod to the emperor's name in *augustiorem* suggests true sovereignty exceeds the legal and political spheres.

6.4 *Theatro Populoque Romano*

If *carmen* subsumes archaic law and poetry under the same category, but law and literature rival each other in many texts, the performative dimension of the court and the theatre offers a more paradoxical model: perceived similarity brought discomfort.[18] The orator's *actio* bore a disquieting resemblance to the actor's performance on stage. While Greek actors were fully enfranchised citizens, their Roman counterparts suffered *infamia*, an increasingly official social disgrace entailing the loss of legal rights, even for the free (Edwards 1993, 123–126).

[16] Also at *Ep.* 2.1.153; XII Tables VIII 1 (*RS*), with commentary ad loc.; Rives 2002, 282; Lowrie 2009, 334.

[17] Thibault 1964. Novels: J. Williams 1972; Ransmayr 1988.

[18] For modern legal theatrics, Goodrich 2009.

Over against the plenipotentiary orator who embodied the highest Roman virtues, the actor plays his dark twin. But if the theatre is the law court's negative correlate, both are nevertheless political spaces (Wallace-Hadrill 2008, 160–169). Law, literature and their speakers vie for authority before the Roman people as ultimate arbiter.

Populus means "audience" as well as the politically constituted people (Lowrie 2014). The people were the source of Roman statute and plebiscite, from which all other law derives (Inst.Gai.1.2–7). Although Horace constructs an elite readership (*Serm.* 1.10.81–91), Ovid draws legitimation from the Roman plebs as his public when his books are banned from libraries (*Tr.* 1.1.88, 3.1.82). The acclamatory nature of Roman popular political expression aligns the people's responses across venues. They crowded the Forum to judge orators' performance as they did ludic spectacles to judge actors'. They took dramatic lines as political allegory and voiced their opinions through applause or hissing.

Cicero's *Pro Sestio* homologises popular political expression in the Forum and the theatre—the speech's performance in court adds a third venue. The applause greeting the news of his recall from exile contrasts with Clodius' malediction across Forum, theatre and arena. The *populus* (mentioned twenty-six times from 117–127!) (Kaster 2006, 115–127, 344) authorises the actors' allegorical spin on lines pro Cicero and anti Clodius. A pun on the Roman state (*theatro populoque Romano*, 116) (Parker 1999, 163) and theatrical metaphors put both politics and the law on stage (120, 123). Cicero slams his opponent as an entertainer, but his relish in relating Clodius' reversal, marked with bold alliteration and antitheses, skirts levity—the danger posed by the theatre—and he apologises to the jurors for speaking about poets, actors and games in court (119). Cicero and Quintilian both dissuade the orator from gestures overly close to theatrical performance conventions (Parker 1999, 178 n. 33). Cicero's analogy between theatre, law and politics is no game: he stands to win or lose in the theatre as a legitimate space for popular judgement, but excessive theatrics in court could jeopardise his case.

6.5 Educative Fictions

In speech act theory, fiction divides law from literature in their potential for performative fullness.[19] The legally binding vows of the marriage ceremony typify plenitude over against the theatre as privileged locus of pragmatic infelicity. For Cicero, imitation distinguishes the actor's utterances from the orator's (*De or.* 3.214) and language's capacity for fiction imperils the latter's performance. However, a strict division between reality and imitation, serious and frivolous speech cannot be maintained (Derrida 1972). Legal fiction extended Roman law beyond the original scope of any individual source of law (Ando 2015a). Conversely, fiction supplies an inadequate classificatory principle for many genres of Latin literature (Lowrie 2009: 67). Short poems (elegy, lyric, epigram) frequently addressed contemporaries, communicated specific messages, however mediated, and conveyed lived experience (Citroni 1995). Much Latin epic turned on history, and myth bears a reality beyond fact.

[19] Austin 1962, 9; Searle 1975; Lowrie 2009, 66–71.

Roman education deployed fiction for serious purposes, specifically training the youth for forensic and deliberative oratory. Declamation in the Augustan and early Imperial periods employed a stylised form of debate (Bonner 1949, 30; Bloomer 2006). Aspiring speakers tackled the pros and cons of outlandish scenarios about kidnapping, rape, loss or restitution of citizenship, that resemble comedy more than real court cases.[20] Early instruction progressed from language and literature to the more advanced topics of rhetoric and law (Bonner 1949, vi). Imagining the decision-making of historical or mythical characters in a *suasoria* taught deliberative oratory, while declaimers argued *controversiae* about stock figures (pirate, slave, priestess, free citizen defined by family position) in ethical and legal dilemmas that model, however distantly, those they would face before a jury. Such instruction emphasises moral reasoning within a system of shared norms over the cognitive skills valued in Greek rhetoric.[21]

Declamation offered yet another Roman venue for practicing situation ethics, which presented moral rules as flexible rather than universally applicable (Langlands 2011, 101). Beyond popular morality and Stoic philosophy, a variety of story types, including the collections of *exempla* in Livy and Valerius Maximus, taught how to negotiate moral challenges. The frivolous pirate stories and apparently superficial arguments (*colores*) mask the work of acculturation and demand toggling between abstraction and the details of a particular context. Such fictions educate within a ludic space (Habinek 2005, 110–157). Although the laws mentioned within declamation may not represent actual statute, many only slightly deform custom, early laws, praetorian edict or Greek law (Bonner 1949, 83–132) and hardly impede the acquisition of practical skills.

Stories whether real or made-up provide material and occasions for analysing normative limits. Quintilian's definition of the *exemplum* treats its reality as indifferent (Inst.5.11.6). The proximity of archaic Roman history to poetic fable was an obstacle to historicity, but not to teaching norms for judgement (Livy *Pr.* 6, 10). Instead of explicit comment, Livy shows his characters enacting a deliberative process as exemplary as the actions they evaluate (Chaplin 2000). While narrative details or rhetorical colour occupy our attention, social expectations are absorbed no less effectively for passing under the radar.

6.6 Typology and the *Mos Maiorum*

Lintott's observation that the stories transmitting ancestral custom were as important as statute for the Roman Republican constitution invites broader inquiry into the role narrative plays in law and politics alike.[22] The lack of a formal written constitution meant that equivalents to its various functions dwelled within other spheres. The constitution was less a system of rules than consensus about values, whose actual instantiation was subject to dispute. Stories lent substance to custom. Cicero identifies literature (books, traditional wisdom and letters) as a primary vehicle for the norms guiding his own administrative

[20] Bonner 1949, 37; Quintilian recommends studying Menander, 137.

[21] Brightbill 2015.

[22] Lintott 1999, 26; Hölkeskamp 2004, 169–198; Beard 1993.

practice (*Arch.* 14). The collected stories in Livy and Valerius Maximus preserved history, offered material for declamation and codified the *mos maiorum*.

The pertinence of story and statute alike to any situation requires interpretation. While some legal formulations supply rules, their application, like that of stories, may proceed directly from particular to particular without producing any generality.[23] Such flexibility invites the exercise of judgement. It is often unclear whether an exemplary model should be imitated or avoided and it can intertwine aspects of both. An example may not pertain in all circumstances, it can be countered with others and the same example may support opposing sides (Lowrie 1997, 46–48; Levene 2000). Such opportunities for reinterpretation explain the longevity of exemplary stories: revision guarantees continued relevance.

Narrativity inhabits law at a deep level (Brooks and Gewirtz 1996; Brooks 2006). Rather than the named heroic agents with complete story arcs canonical among Roman *exempla*, or the types of declamation's hypothetical scenarios, the law presents fragmentary narratives in typical scripts, sometimes with branching plot lines. The first of the XII Tables offers a set of potential scenes with matching prescriptions: if someone summons another, he should go; if he does not go, let a witness be called; if he flees, arrest him; if illness or age impede, give him a mule: if he refuses, do not prepare a wagon (I 1–3 *RS*). Each if-clause offers a miniature narrative easily expandable into a scene—ripe material for comedy or satire.

The dearth of pronouns in the XII Tables leaves a blank to be filled. Generic names, such as Titius (John Doe), afford greater clarity in later formulations. The jurists sometimes work toward a rule from a briefly narrated situation through increasing levels of generality. The Digest sets up an opinion by Modestinus with a story: three siblings, Titius, Maevius and Seia agreed to divide an inheritance, but Titius extracted some gold before the division (D.2.14.35). A question translates the story into more general terms ("I ask whether … an action … is available to the brother and sister against their brother"). While the proper names stand in for family relations, the family names stand in for the legal category of equal heirs. Modestinus' answer further translates the narrative into technical legal terms (defence, fraud, rejoinder, plea).

The Romans practised typological thinking across genres. Comedy, declamation and the law all turn on character types and stock scenes that illustrate social relations and the structures of power. Comedy and declamation share the law's preoccupation with family relations and questions of status, citizenship and inheritance (du Plessis 2012, 36). Canonical *exempla* record the deeds of named individuals, but the ease with which historical figures became types—"a Brutus", "a Cato"—belies the unique stature of Roman history's heroes. Horace's father points out individuals as examples of dissolute living (*Serm.* 1.4.109–110), but by identifying Albius' son by family position, Horace deploys a comic type (Leach 1971). Such paradigmatic situations inculcate Roman values and offer channels for learning deliberation.

Telling stories instead of retailing pure abstractions enhances intelligibility. Mini-narratives about Titius and company occupy the other end of the scale from the plots of epic, but they are still plots and narrative ability was prised in court. The *Ad Herennium* recommends lucidity in the *narratio* (statement of facts) and demonstrates comedy's proximity to

[23] Ando 2015c; Lowrie and Lüdemann 2015, Introduction.

trial narratives by citing iambic lines as a model of exposition (1.9.14). In declamation, one rhetorical licence was to allow slight alterations in the narrative.[24] Similarly, malleability is a defining feature of myth. In none of these cases is pure fiction in play. Hypothetical legal situations and exemplary stories are both sites for negotiating between universals and particulars, historical individuals and types, strict rule and interpretative extension.

Some techniques for closing the gap between a transmitted narrative and the demands of a specific situation were shared by literature and law, but some are proper to each. Beyond typology, where individual circumstances were slotted into a pre-existing legal mould, analogy could extend the law beyond its original scope, for example, from acorns to nuts, so as to overcome the "imperfect fit" between law and circumstance (Ando 2015b, 29–40). The formula given by the praetor mediated between the law and the case and established a framework for the law's application: if Titius were found to have extracted said gold before the inheritance's division, thus-and-such a fine would be imposed; if not, Maevius and Seia would suffer a penalty for bringing the case. While literature also engages in typology and analogy, it has no equivalent to the legal formula.

Analogy may provide the fundamental principle for the implementation of a moral, but the value of stories surpasses mere relevance (Landy 2012): the apparently useless ornamentation of literature and rhetoric arouses emotion and elicits the aesthetic response that binds communities; unmotivated detail builds the imaginative world in whose mirror society sees itself. Story and affect, over against abstraction, are the motor of Roman political thought and have made Rome interesting to political theorists sceptical about reason's role in deliberation.[25] Both law and literature reveal the inability of rules to encompass life.

6.7 Transformations in the Public Sphere

Rapid social and political change at the transition from Republic to Empire affected the conditions of and venues for public speaking. The concentration of power in the emperor and his administrators foreclosed opportunities among the elite for deliberative oratory and the *contio*'s decline realigned both law and literature in relation to politics (Morstein-Marx 2004; Dufallo 2007, 75–76). But the restriction of the field for effective political speech hardly reduced the energies poured into meaningful verbal expression, much of which was expended arguing cases or in legal counsel. The articulation of normativity previously transmitted through oratory separated. Epideictic oratory and literature absorbed its aesthetic and law its practical component. Orators who had previously spoken before the people and senate in addition to arguing cases now concentrated on the latter. The jurists, who developed law as a field of interpretation and commentary beyond a body of rules, were increasingly folded into the Imperial bureaucracy (du Plessis 2012, 22–23).

If public affairs turned to litigation, legal commentary and administration, intellectual work including philosophy, history and poetry, transformed into a way of doing politics by other means. Cicero, Sallust and the Augustan poets articulate a conception of these genres as offering appraisal and critique at the border of public life in a compensatory

[24] Brightbill 2015.

[25] Hammer 2008 and 2014; Connolly 2007 and 2014.

sphere where artful speech explored Roman identity and the moral grounding of the emerging Empire. The conspicuous withdrawal of much poetry into the private highlighted the implosion of public discursive power before Augustus' exclusive control. The poets were highly aware that their own endeavours lacked the efficacy of law and archaic song, but the emptied space of political discourse enabled their appropriation of *carmen* as a trope for poetry. Horace's mockery of those claiming the Muses dictated archaic laws and treaties (*Epist.* 2.1.23–27) contrasts the archaic meaning of *carmen* with his redefinition of literature as an institution recognisable to moderns, where aesthetic quality becomes the ground of a discursive institution definitively separate from public affairs. At the same time, law proper expanded during the classical period as the domain regulating the decisions affecting ordinary individuals. The conception of literature as highly crafted but pragmatically impotent, as watching politics from the outside, has persisted into modernity, as has the conception of law as a source of real power.

With the erosion of aristocratic authority during the late Republic, elites lost their monopoly on action and knowledge (Wallace-Hadrill 1997). Professions consequently became more specialised and differentiated (Frier 1985). The inverse correlative to the increasing power of freedmen in Imperial administration is that talented elites pursued venues of action or expression outside politics (Lowrie 2014). One direction led to the practice of law, another to writing poetry, history and philosophy. There is no Augustan equivalent to Cicero, conjoining all aspects of the public communicative sphere. His exceptional ability at law, eloquence and politics embodies an ideal that fragmented with the Republic's collapse. Horace continues part of his legacy: he speaks as a representative citizen who advanced from poor beginnings to social prominence via intellectual acuity and stylistic polish, but any hopes for a public career suffered defeat at Philippi. The Annaei advanced as Spanish provincials in Nero's Imperial court, but they combined political and literary influence without advocacy. Tacitus identifies advocates who continued the legal branch of Cicero's portfolio, but winning cases no longer required comparable eloquence.

6.8 Conclusion

Roman law and Latin literature shared an obsession with norms and transgression, with containing events in language through narrative or formula, and with negotiating the gap between individual and type. Although the myth of a unified public sphere appealed, law, politics and literature were fluid domains: always overlapping, in contest, with greater or lesser degrees of paradox. They realigned along with political change, but their interplay continued to inform the Roman social imaginary.

Bibliography

Ando, C. 2012. "Empire, state and communicative action." In C. Kuhn, ed., *Politische Kommunikation und öffentliche Meinung in der antiken Welt*. Stuttgart. 219–229.

Ando, C. 2015a. "Fact, fiction and social reality in Roman law." In M. del Mar and W. Twining, eds., *Legal fictions in theory and practice*. Cham/New York. 295–323.

Ando, C. 2015b. *Roman social imaginaries.* Toronto.

Ando, C. 2015c. "*Exemplum*, analogy, and precedent in Roman law." In M. Lowrie and S. Lüdemann, eds., *Exemplarity and singularity: thinking through particulars in philosophy, literature, and law.* London. 111–122.

Austin, J. L. 1962. *How to do things with words.* Cambridge, Mass.

Balsley, K. (2010). "Between two lives: Tiresias and the law in Ovid's *Metamorphoses.*" *Dictynna* 7: 1–29. Available at: http://dictynna.revues.org, accessed 14 February 2016.

Beard, M. 1993. "Looking (harder) for Roman myth: Dumézil, declamation and the problems of definition." In F. Graf, ed., *Mythos in mythenloser Gesellschaft: das Paradigma Roms. Coll. Rauricum* III. Stuttgart. 44–64.

Bloomer, M. 2006. "Declamation according to Quintilian and the Elder Seneca." In W. Dominik and J. Hall, eds., *Blackwell companion to Roman rhetoric.* Oxford. 297–306.

Bonner, S. F. 1949. *Roman declamation in the late republic and early empire.* Liverpool.

Brightbill, J. 2015. "Roman declamation: between creativity and constraints." PhD dissertation, University of Chicago.

Brooks, P. (2006). "Narrative transactions—does the law need a narratology?" *Yale Journal of Law and Humanities* 18: 1–28.

Brooks, P. and Gewirtz, P. 1996. *Law's stories: narrative and rhetoric in the law.* New Haven.

Butler, S. 2002. *The hand of Cicero.* London.

Chaplin, J. 2000. *Livy's exemplary history.* Oxford.

Citroni, M. 1995. *Poesia e lettori in Roma antica.* Rome.

Cloud, J. D. 1989. "Satirists and the law." In S. H. Braund, ed., *Satire and society in ancient Rome.* Exeter. 49–67.

Connolly, J. 2007. *The state of speech: rhetoric and political thought in ancient Rome.* Princeton.

Conolly, J. 2014. *The life of Roman republicanism.* Princeton.

Crook, J. A. 1967. *Law and life of Rome: 90 B.C.–A. D. 212.* Ithaca.

Derrida, J. 1972. "Signature, événement, contexte," in *Marges de la philosophie.* Paris. 365–393.

Derrida, J. 2000. *Demeure: fiction and testimony.* Stanford.

Ducos, M. (1994). "Horace et le droit." *Revue des Études Latines* 72: 79–89.

Dufallo, B. 2007. *The ghosts of the past: Latin literature, the dead, and Rome's transition to a principate.* Columbus.

du Plessis, P. J. 2012. *Studying Roman law.* London.

du Plessis, P. J. ed., 2013. *New frontiers: law and society in the Roman world.* Edinburgh.

Eden, C. 1986. *Poetic and legal fiction in the Aristotelian tradition.* Princeton.

Edwards, C. 1993. *The politics of immorality in ancient Rome.* Cambridge.

Ernout, A., and A. Meillet, eds. 1939. *Dictionnaire étymologique de la langue latine.* Paris.

Feeney, D. C. (2005). "The beginnings of a literature in Latin." *Journal of Roman Studies* 95: 226–240.

Fögen, M. T. 2002. *Römische Rechtsgeschichten. Über Ursprung und Evolution eines sozialen Systems.* Göttingen.

Fögen, M. T. 2007. *Das Lied vom Gesetz.* Munich.

Frier, B. 1985. *The rise of the Roman jurists: studies in Cicero's* Pro Caecina. Princeton.

Goodrich, P. (2009). "Screening law." *Law and Literature* 21: 1–23.

Gruen, E. 1992. *Culture and national identity in republican Rome.* Ithaca.

Gurd, S. 2012. *Work in progress: literary revision as social performance in ancient Rome.* New York/Oxford.

Habinek, T. (1998). "Singing, speaking, making, writing: classical alternatives to literature and literary studies." *Stanford Humanities Review* 6: 65–75.

Habinek, T. N. (2005) *The world of Roman song: from ritualized speech to social order.* Baltimore

Hammer, D. 2008. *Roman political thought and the modern theoretical imagination.* Norman.

Hammer, D. 2014. *Roman political thought.* Cambridge.

Hölkeskamp, K.-J. 2004. Senatus Populusque Romanus. Stuttgart.

Howley, J. A. 2013. "Why read the jurists? Aulus Gellius on reading across disciplines." In P. J. du Plessis, ed., *New frontiers: law and society in the Roman world.* Edinburgh. 9–30.

Humbert, M., ed. 2005. *Le dodici tavole: dai* decemviri *agli umanisti.* Pavia.

Kaster, R. 2006. *Cicero: speech on behalf of Publius Sestius.* Oxford.

Kenney, E. J. (1969). "Ovid and the law." *Yale Classical Studies* 21: 243–263.

Landy, J. 2012. *How to do things with fictions.* Oxford.

Langlands, R. (2011). "Roman *exempla* and situation ethics: Valerius Maximus and Cicero *de officiis.*" *Journal of Roman Studies* 101: 100–122.

Leach, E. W. (1971). "Horace's *pater optimus* and Terence's Demea: autobiographical fiction and comedy in *Sermo* 1.4." *American Journal of Philology* 92: 616–632.

Levene, D. (2000). "Sallust's 'Catiline' and Cato the Censor." *Classical Quarterly* 50: 170–191.

Lintott, A. 1999. *The constitution of the Roman Republic.* Oxford.

Lowrie, M. 1997. *Horace's narrative odes.* Oxford.

Lowrie, M. 2009. *Writing, performance, and authority in Augustan Rome.* Oxford.

Lowrie, M. 2014. "Politics by other means: Horace's *Ars Poetica.* "In A. Ferenczi and P. Hardie, eds., *New approaches to Horace's* Ars Poetica, *materiali e discussioni* 72.1: 121–142.

Lowrie, M. and S. Lüdemann, eds. 2015. *Exemplarity and singularity: thinking through particulars in philosophy, literature, and law.* London.

Maltby, R. 1991. *A lexicon of ancient Latin etymologies.* Eastbourne.

McGinn, T. A. J. (2001). "Satire and the law: the case of Horace." *Proceedings of the Cambridge Philological Society* 47: 81–102.

Meyer, E. 2004. *Legitimacy and law in the Roman world:* tabulae *in Roman belief and practice.* Cambridge.

Morstein-Marx, R. 2004. *Mass oratory and political power in the late Roman republic.* Cambridge.

Newman, J. K. 1967. *The concept of* vates *in Augustan poetry.* Brussels: Collection Latomus 89.

Newman, J. K. 1990. *Roman Catullus and the modification of the Alexandrian sensibility.* Hildesheim.

Parker, H. (1999). "The observed of all observers: spectacle, applause, and cultural poetics in the Roman theater audience." *Studies in the History of Art* 56, Symposium Papers 34: 162–179.

Posner, R. A. 2009³. *Law and literature.* Cambridge.

Ransmayr, C. 1988. *Die letzte Welt.* Nördlingen.

Rives, J. B. (2002). "Magic in the XII Tables revisited." *Classical Quarterly* 52: 270–290.

Schiavone, A. 2012. *The invention of law in the west.* Cambridge, Mass.

Searle, J. (1975). "The logical status of fictional discourse." *New Literary History* 6: 319–332.

Skutsch, O. 1985. *The annals of Q. Ennius.* Oxford.

Steinberg, J. 2013. *Dante and the limits of the law.* Chicago.

Svenbro, J. 1993/1988. Phrasikleia. *An anthropology of reading in ancient Greece,* transl. J. Lloyd. Ithaca.

Syme, R. 1958. *Tacitus*, Vol. 1. Oxford.

Tatum, W. J. (1998). "*Ultra legem*: law and literature in Horace, *Satires* II 1." *Mnemosyne* 51: 688–699.

Tellegen-Couperus, O. and Tellegen, J. W. 2013. "*Artes urbanae*: Roman law and rhetoric." In P. J. du Plessis, ed., *New frontiers: law and society in the Roman world*. Edinburgh. 31–50.

Thibault, J. C. 1964. *The mystery of Ovid's exile*. Berkeley.

Valette-Cagnac, E. 1997. *La lecture à Rome: rites et pratiques*. Paris.

Wallace-Hadrill, A. 1997. "*Mutatio morum*: the idea of a cultural revolution." In T. Habinek and A. Schiesaro, eds., *The Roman cultural revolution*. Cambridge. 3–22.

Wallace-Hadrill, A. 2008. *Rome's cultural revolution*. Cambridge.

Williams, G. 1982. "The genesis of poetry in Rome." In E. J. Kenney ed., *The Cambridge history of classical literature*. Cambridge. Vol. II.1: 53–59.

Williams, J. 1972. *Augustus*. New York.

PART III

THE CONSTITUTIONAL STRUCTURE OF THE ROMAN STATE

CHAPTER 7

SPQR
Institutions and Popular Participation in the Roman Republic

FRANCISCO PINA POLO
TRANSLATED BY MANUEL CABAL

7.1 Introduction

The Roman constitution of the Republican period was based on three pillars: the senate, the magistracies and the popular assemblies (Bleicken 1995; Lintott 1999; North 2006). The Romans never wrote down their constitution, which made it more dynamic and flexible. The Republican institutions were the result of a long process of experimentation, but they were not immutable. On the contrary, those institutions were constantly modified to adapt them to the changing circumstances of Rome's internal and foreign politics.

It seems like a paradox that the Romans justified the transformation of the Republican institutions by appealing to respect for their own traditions, symbolised by the concept of *mos maiorum*, that is, the customs of their ancestors (Pina Polo 2004). However, the concept of *mos maiorum* itself was never immutable, but rather dynamic. The concept was constantly reinterpreted to make space for new ideas and practices, according to the needs of the moment. The *mos maiorum* defined the essence of what it meant to be Roman, and was valuable to the Romans as a symbol of stability and continuity. At the same time, the Romans appealed to that concept to conceal the introduction of new customs that were indeed contrary to the traditions they claimed to defend.

Above all, the *mos maiorum* acted as an ideological "totem" for the Roman aristocracy, a protective emblem for the ruling class and, through the leadership of the rulers, to the community as well. The *mos maiorum* functioned as a symbol of identity for the Roman aristocracy, provided the backbone of the history of Rome and served as a cohesive element of the social elites that, in turn, facilitated the preservation of the *status quo*. This concept endowed the *nobilitas* with a conscience about its function in the community and kept its homogeneity.

At the same time, the *mos maiorum* implicitly supported the Republican political system by keeping the elites together, which contributed to the successful expansion of

Rome in the Mediterranean and the creation of an Empire. In turn, the success of the Republic legitimated the ruling class that led the Roman state. The underlying idea to this concept was that things should be arranged in a certain way because they had always been that way. Therefore, the *mos maiorum* supported a value system that legitimated the social hierarchy and the economic inequality, as well as their political expression.

7.2 The Formation of the Roman Constitution

Rome never had one legislator that provided a complete design of the constitution, such as Lycurgus in Sparta and Solon in Athens. Certainly, the Roman tradition attributes the institution of substantive reforms in the organisation of citizens to prominent individuals, such as the first structuring of the *civitas* to Romulus, the founder, and the introduction of popular assemblies to Servius Tullius, the sixth king. However, the Romans knew that their constitution was the result of the contributions made by several generations (Cic. *Rep.* 2.1–2; cf. Liv. 4.4.3).

The senate was considered by the Roman tradition as the only public institution to be born at the same time as the foundation of the city. Romulus created the senate as a council of the *patres* of the main families (Liv. 1.8). The ancient sources agree that, since the origins of the senate, its members were appointed for life. The senate created by Romulus supposedly had a hundred members, and this number remained the same until Tarquinius Priscus—also during the Monarchic period—added a hundred new members.

However, a text by Festus calls into question the permanent membership of the senate during the archaic period:

> There was once a time when it was not considered disgraceful for senators to be passed over, because, just as the kings by themselves used to choose (or to choose as replacements) men who would serve them as public advisers, so under the Republic the consuls (or military tribunes with consular power) used to choose for themselves their closest friends among the patricians and then from among the plebeians. This practice continued until the law of the tribune Ovinius put an end to it. Ovinius' law bound the censors by oath to enrol in the senate the best men from all ranks. The enforcement of this law had the consequence that senators who were passed over, and thus lost their place, were held in dishonour. (Festus 290 L; transl. Cornell)

Sextus Pompeius Festus was a Roman grammarian who lived in the second century AD. He wrote an epitome of the work *De verborum significatione* by Verrius Flaccus, a renowned grammarian and antiquarian of the Augustan period. The value of Festus' work resides in recovering historical information from different sources than those consulted by Livy and Dionysius of Halicarnassus, whose works had represented the culmination of the annalistic tradition of the second and first centuries BC. Although Festus' statement is so exceptional that it is not corroborated by any other ancient source, this piece of information should not be discarded (Cornell 1995).

According to Festus, the members of the senate were not originally permanent. During the Monarchy and the initial period of the Republic, the members of the senate rotated constantly and were appointed by the rulers with *imperium* from among people they trusted. Originally, the senators were advisers to the kings and, during the initial Republican phase, they were advisers to consuls or whoever were the highest magistrates in that period. This procedure lasted, according to Festus, until the Ovinian law was approved, probably in the second half of the fourth century BC. The Ovinian law granted censors the faculty to appoint the senators and to expel from the Curia those that misbehaved, which meant falling into disgrace and dishonour. If the information offered by Festus is accurate, the approval of the Ovinian law should be considered as the point of inflection after which the senate became a permanent, lifelong council, as known in the rest of the Republican period.

If the text by Festus is taken into account, it suggests that the senate only acquired significant political power when it became an autonomous institution; from the moment that the appointment of its members as counsellors stopped depending on the will of the highest magistrates. The senators only became powerful and influential after acquiring life tenure, which allowed the birth of a "political class" with a specific group identity. In addition, the permanent character of the senate facilitated the formulation of a more stable and coherent domestic and foreign policy for Rome, in a time when the Latin city was already the great power of Italy and was about to expand to the rest of the Mediterranean.

Indeed, all other ancient sources are unanimous in this respect and so undermine the credibility of Festus' exceptional claim. Nonetheless, Festus' representation of the origins and evolution of the senate—that is, an institution with a long history of change—is in fact similar to what those same sources say about the way in which the magistracies and the popular assemblies were created and developed.

According to tradition, the Roman Monarchy was abolished and substituted by a Republican regime in 509 BC. The king was replaced as supreme ruler by the consulate—two magistrates with equal power and elected by the people—which inherited the *imperium* that characterised the power of the monarch. Although the ancient sources are practically unanimous about this version and the list of consuls (*fasti consulares*) seems to confirm it, scholarship has raised doubts about it.

The existence of a double magistracy with equal powers in central Italy at such an early age is a matter of contention. The consulate of the historical period seems to be more the outcome of a long process. Its origin possibly dates back to the years 367–366 BC and the approval of the Licinio-Sextian laws, alongside the creation of the urban praetorship in that same year. The fifth century and the beginning of the fourth century BC must have been a period of experimentation, during which the highest magistracy of Republican Rome fluctuated. Ancient sources also mention the existence of the ephemeral government of the *decemviri* that drafted the Law of the XII Tables in 451–450 BC; as well as the military tribunes with consular power that alternated in office with the consuls, in the second half of the fifth century and the first third of the fourth century BC. However, it is possible that the first magistracy that substituted the Monarchy at the beginning of the Republic was a unique magistracy or a double one with a higher-ranked magistrate, maybe the *dictator* or the *praetor maximus* that Livy describes as an archaic institution (Liv. 7.3.5).

The rest of the magistracies were created during the fifth century BC: the quaestorship, the censorship, the aedileship and the tribunate of the plebs, the last two arising from the patrician–plebeian conflict. Therefore, more than a century probably took place before the Republican magistracies coexisted as we know them in the historical age: the consulate and the praetorship as the higher magistracies with *imperium*, the censorship as a higher magistracy without *imperium*, the aedileship, the tribunate of the plebs and the quaestorship—the last three as lower magistracies.

Regarding the popular assemblies, the *comitia curiata* that grouped citizens into *curiae* are traditionally believed to have existed since the beginning of the Monarchic period. The main function of these *comitia*, the tradition says, was to grant symbolically the *imperium* to the king, during the Monarchic age, and to the higher magistrates, during the Republic (*lex curiata de imperio*). The *comitia curiata* practically became irrelevant, because of the creation of the *comitia centuriata* and the *comitia tributa*. The tradition attributes to the king Servius Tullius the creation of the last two assemblies, along with the centuries and territorial tribes that were their unit of organisation, in the middle of the sixth century BC. But is this date plausible?

Servius Tullius supposedly categorised Roman citizens into five classes, according to their wealth. Each class was subdivided in centuries that, in turn, were formed by *iuniores* (men of up to 45 years old) and *seniores* (men older than 45 years). The citizens formed the army that defended the city. Every infantryman had to pay for his own equipment, subject to economic capacity. In addition, there was a cavalry formed by the richest citizens and a single century of *proletarii* formed by the poorest. This military structure was the base of the organisation of the *comitia centuriata*, where every century had a vote, which implies that the better-off classes were overrepresented given that they had a disproportionately higher number of centuries than the rest of the population.

Whether the Roman army was unlikely to have been structured in such a complex way already in the sixth century BC is debated. At that time, Rome was still a small city with little territory and population. Therefore, it seems likely that the army was structured in a much simpler way and was probably formed with those that could afford the infantry equipment (*classis*) and with the cavalry of the richest citizens. The rest of the population, the *infra classem*, remained at the margin of the army. Indeed, Rome probably had a military reform of the hoplitic type by that time, in line with similar developments in many other Mediterranean states. The military and social structure that ancient sources attribute to Servius Tullius was more likely introduced in a subsequent period, possibly in the fifth century BC. Thus, the *comitia centuriata* did not acquire its definite form until that time—the model that is known for the last centuries of the Republic.

The *comitia tributa* probably went through a similar process. According to tradition, Servius Tullius substituted territorially based tribes for the three archaic tribes of gentilician base. That is, citizens would no longer belong to a tribe by virtue of their birth, but by virtue of their home address. In this period, the four urban tribes that existed during the Republic were created, and maybe some rural tribes also appeared.

Other Mediterranean states introduced similar transformations by this time, which makes it plausible that Rome did too. Nevertheless, the more institutionally advanced Athens had these transformations introduced by Cleisthenes at the end of the sixth century BC. Therefore, if we regard as historical fact the transformations attributed to Servius Tullius, we would also need to admit that Roman society reached this institutional point before Athens, which is problematic. This is why the territorially based tribes must have been introduced in the Republican period, probably at some point in the fifth century BC. Thereafter, the number of urban tribes remained fixed at four, while the number of rural tribes gradually increased to the thirty-five tribes known to exist in the third century BC.

Given that the territorial tribes were the basic unit of the tribal assembly, the latter did not likely exist before the Republican period either. According to the ancient sources, the *concilium plebis*, the assembly exclusively formed by plebeians, was created at the beginning of the Conflict of the Orders. The tribal assembly of the whole citizenship (*populus*) and the *concilium plebis* of the plebeians evolved in parallel from the beginning of the Republic until the *lex Hortensia*, approved in 287 BC, which transformed the plebiscites of the plebeian *concilia* into mandatory law for all citizens. Since that moment, both assemblies were fused in practice, but the patricians were still excluded from the voting procedures to elect the plebeian magistrates (Develin 1975; Farrell 1986).

Although details and nuances may still be controversial, the general conclusion of this succinct analysis is that the Roman constitution resulted from a long process that lasted for centuries. The Roman constitution, as it is known in the historical age, cannot be considered finished before the fourth century, or even possibly before the beginning of third century BC, by the final phase of the conquest of Italy and the struggle between patricians and plebeians.

7.3 The Functioning of Institutions

From the moment it gained its traditionally known form, the Roman Republican constitution was remarkably stable, a feature that helped Rome to become the great Mediterranean power. However, the Romans continued introducing changes to their political institutions in order to adapt them to new realities.

A Ciceronian passage (Cic. *Leg. Man.* 60) perfectly illustrates the Roman will to adapt political institutions. As a praetor in the year 66 Cicero spoke to the people in favour of approving a law project drafted by the tribune of the plebs Manilius, with the purpose of granting Pompey an extraordinary command to fight Mithridates in the East. The orator knew that some aspects of the bill were contrary to the *mos maiorum*, as the opponents of it had already indicated. Cicero nevertheless offered an argument to get the project approved. He claimed that although their ancestors honoured tradition in times of peace, they always acted in the best interest of Rome during periods of war, implying that their decisions may have not agreed completely with the tradition. Cicero concluded his argument by pointing out that the ancestors adopted new provisions according to new circumstances. This Ciceronian passage is probably the best example of the political pragmatism that characterised the Roman Republican system.

7.3.1 Magistracies

With respect to the magistracies, the pattern of political careers (*cursus honorum*) was progressively consolidated and finally regulated by the *lex Villia annalis*, approved around the year 180 BC. This law set an order for the performance of the magistracies; in particular, a required two-year period between each one and a minimum age for the magistrates, which was confirmed by Sulla's law of the year 81 BC with some modifications. After military service, a citizen could be elected quaestor at the age of thirty, and then he could serve as aedile. Each year, there were four aediles, which were two patricians and two plebeians. These magistrates were considered inferior and were granted *potestas*. Only plebeians could aspire to be one of the ten annual tribunes of the plebs, instead of aspiring to an aedileship.

The higher magistracies were the praetorship, the consulate and the censorship. The former two had *imperium*, which meant that they could exercise military command. The minimum age to be elected a praetor was thirty-nine and to be elected a consul was forty-two. The censorship was the culmination of the political career, since it was meant for prestigious individuals that had previously served in the other magistracies. Censors were elected every five years. They were the only magistrates that remained in office for a year and a half, while the rest lasted for a year. All the magistracies were collegiate and elected by the people. To be a magistrate was an honour (*honos*) in Rome, which meant that they did not receive any remuneration. In practice, it also meant that only members of the social elite had access to them (Broughton 1951–1952, 1986; Kunkel and Wittmann 1995).

Besides these regular magistracies, Republican Rome had an extraordinary magistracy: the dictatorship (Hartfield 1982). A dictator was appointed by one of the consuls, who in turn proceeded by order of the senate. The office had an assistant with less power, the *magister equitum*. Generally, a dictatorship was established temporarily to face a military threat and, then, the dictator acted mainly as commander of the army above all the regular magistrates. However, some dictators were appointed to execute civilian activities, such as the organisation of elections. In the latter case, dictators stepped back after the specific task had been accomplished. In general, given that a dictator received absolute power, his mandate could not exceed six months in order to avoid the possibility of a tyranny. The recourse of the dictatorship was common until the end of the third century BC, as can be observed during the Hannibalic War. Since that time, the Republic abandoned the practice of appointing a dictator. Nevertheless, during the first century BC the dictatorship was revived by Sulla and Caesar.

While some magistracies remained unchanged throughout the Republic, others had changes in the number of occupants and their functions. The number of censors was always two. Their main function was to implement the census of all Roman citizens, which was used to classify them according to their wealth, as well as in the centuries and tribes that were the voting units of the popular assemblies (Suolahti 1963). The census was carried out in Rome. The citizens were summoned to appear before the censors in the Campus Martius. Each citizen had to give, upon oath, an account of himself, his family and all his property. By the end of the Republic, registers of citizens might already have been sent to the censors from colonies and *municipia* in Italy and the provinces. Nevertheless, it was only after Augustus that a systematic provincial census was developed.

The censors also conducted a review of the membership of the senate (*lectio senatus*). In the list, they typically registered the new senators that would substitute the deceased of the preceding years. But the censors could also expel those senators that had been declared guilty on trials or that had acted with dishonour (*nota censoria*). In addition, because of the prestige of this magistracy, the censors acted as moral guardians. They also awarded contracts of public works and public services, although other magistrates could perform this activity if there were not active censors at that moment. The censor's term culminated with a purification ritual for all the community (*lustrum*). Although the institution of the censorship existed until the end of the Republic, censors were not elected every five years during the first century BC, as they had been before, because of the constant Civil Wars and internal conflicts.

The consulate also remained formed by two consuls and continued to be, with the exception of the censors, the highest executive magistracy of the Republic (Giovannini 1983; Pina Polo 2011; Beck, Duplá, Jehne and Pina Polo 2011). Until the first century BC the consuls fundamentally assumed the role of *imperatores* or commanders in chief of the Roman army. Therefore, both consuls spent most of the consular year outside Rome on military campaigns, first in Italy and then in the broader Mediterranean region. Nonetheless, the consuls also had civilian functions. For example, since they were representatives of the community to the gods, they presided over expiatory sacrifices, the public games—when they were in Rome—and the Latin Festival (*Feriae Latinae*); they were the heads of the Roman diplomacy and, as such, introduced the foreign ambassadors to the senate and communicated decisions to them; they promoted laws, although not often; they managed the construction of public works, such as temples in Rome and roads in Italy; and they presided over elections.

This situation changed during the first century BC as the consuls retained their *imperium*, but only a part of those who held office assumed the command of the legions during the consular year. Those who actually did it left Rome at the very end of the year. This meant that the consuls spent most of their time in the city, whether the entirety or most of their term in office. Hence, in practice, the consuls ceased to have an important military role and the magistracy acquired a remarkably civilian character. During the first century BC the consuls stopped being generals and became above all political leaders with great visibility in Rome, both in the debates of the senate and before the people.

The praetorship is a good example of institutional adaptation to changes of historical circumstances (Brennan 2000). The urban praetor was created in 367–366 BC to assume some of the consuls' tasks, especially to substitute for them as the highest magistrates in Rome during their absence from the city. Toward the end of the First Punic War (*c*.241) a second praetor was created (*praetor peregrinus*) and, from that moment, the praetorship mainly performed two types of function: judicial in Rome and military in the provinces of the Empire. The judicial function became more visible in the first century BC. In the year 81 the dictator Sulla increased the number of permanent courts devoted to specific crimes (*quaestiones perpetuae*; see ch. 24). He mandated that a praetor preside over each court and so doubled the number of praetors elected every year. As happened with consuls, the praetors lost their military character and assumed mostly civil functions during this century.

Furthermore, as Rome progressively annexed Mediterranean territories, the number of praetors increased. In 227 BC two offices were created to assume the government of Sicilia and Corsica–Sardinia. In 197 two additional praetors were appointed to the government of the new provinces of Hispania Citerior and Hispania Ulterior. Thus, during the Roman expansion over the Mediterranean region, the conquest and the control of the territories incorporated by the Romans were the responsibility of consuls and praetors. The Roman state, however, avoided the excessive multiplication of praetors and the creation of a new magistracy to govern each province by extending the power of individuals in office (*prorogatio*). During the second and first centuries BC many consuls and praetors continued to govern their provinces as proconsuls and propraetors (that is, acting as consuls and praetors without having been elected to this purpose) after their term as consul and praetor had expired.

The latter is just one example of the sleights-of-hand legitimised by the popular will that the Romans developed in their constitution. Likewise, during the first century BC long-lasting, extraordinary commands were occasionally granted to private citizens (*privati*) that were not officially in charge of any magistracy. The extraordinary commands successively granted to Pompey represent the most relevant cases; they allowed him to fight Sertorius in Hispania, the pirates in the Mediterranean and Mithridates in the East. Once again, these commands were practical solutions to new problems. Something similar happened in the year 52 BC, when the senate appointed Pompey as unique consul (*consul sine collega*) to face the emergency caused by the assassination of Clodius. This way, the senate was able temporarily to entrust all power to one person, without officially designating him as dictator.

Indeed, Pompey had a career that was practically a series of legal frauds. In the year 70 BC he was elected as consul for the first time without having occupied any regular magistracy or having attained the minimum age. In the year 55 he was appointed as governor of the two Hispanic provinces for several years, but he never went to Hispania. He governed the provinces through legates, which anticipated the model of provincial government that Augustus implemented later.

The tribunate of the plebs lost its initial revolutionary character during the Republic and became one more stage of the political career (Bleicken 1955; Thommen 1989). To be sure, during the late Republican period, a few tribunes such as the Gracchi, Saturninus, Sulpicius and Clodius intended to introduce social and political reforms aimed at improving the well-being of the plebs or at including wider social groups into the decision-making process, against the majority in the senate. They were all accused of sedition, and were finally murdered. Indeed, those reforming tribunes were the exception and not the norm in the tribunate of the plebs, since most tribunes acted according to the will of the majority in the senate or simply went unnoticed (Cic. *Leg.* 3.23–24).

Nevertheless, the example of the reforming tribunes was considered a threat to the stability of the Republic, so that the dictator Sulla attempted to disable the institution by suppressing important functions of the tribunes. Sulla ended their capacity to propose legislation and—especially—the possibility of aspiring to higher magistracies, which turned the tribunate into a career dead end. These limitations lasted barely a decade, since the full powers of the tribunes (*tribunicia potestas*) were restored by Pompey and Crassus during their first consulship in the year 70 BC.

The tribunes did not have *potestas* because they were not magistrates proper, but they did have veto power (*intercessio*) over the decisions of all magistrates, including the higher magistrates. In addition, they assumed the function of protecting the individual rights of citizens against alleged abuses of the magistrates (*ius auxilii*). Throughout the Republic, the tribunes of the plebs were catalysts of the political life of Rome, as evidenced by the fact that they were by far the main promoters of new laws.

The aedileship was less politically compromised than the tribunate and was considered an effective platform for social exposure in Rome (Daguet-Gagey 2015). The main tasks of the aediles were to take care of the city, including the preservation of temples, street cleaning and the maintenance of aqueducts and sewers; the supervision of markets, both regarding the general provisioning of Rome and the accuracy of weights and measures; and organising the public games, to which sometimes the aediles contributed with their own money in order to gain popularity.

Finally, the quaestorship was the initial step of the political career and, after Sulla's dictatorship, this magistracy granted automatic access to the senate. The original function of the quaestors was to supervise the finances of the Roman state, in close conjunction with the consuls. Although that remained as their essential role, the number of tasks performed by them increased as Rome grew and its bureaucracy became more complex. Moreover, every year while some quaestors stayed in the city, others were assigned to the service of a provincial governor. The provincial quaestors were not only in charge of economic affairs—such as administration of the spoils, tax collection and coinage in the province—but could also sometimes replace the governor in the command of the army in spite of not being a magistracy with *imperium*, which again speaks to the typical flexibility of Roman political institutions.

Although the Roman Republican constitution was characterised by its stability, some innovations were necessary over the course of time in order to adapt the structures of government to the needs of the growing state. The prefectures (*praefecturae*) are good examples. These included the *praefecti iure dicundo*, who were appointed by the praetor to administer justice among Roman citizens living far from Rome in Italian communities in which political organisation was embryonic. A *praefectura* was both the temporary seat of the official and the legal district for which he was responsible.

7.3.2 Popular Assemblies

There were two kinds of popular assemblies: the *contiones* and the *comitia*. They can be distinguished in a number of ways. To begin with, a speech was never delivered in the *comitia*, but there was always voting to approve laws, to determine the culpability or innocence of an indicted individual, or to elect some magistrates. On the other hand, in a *contio*, there were always public speeches before the people but no voting, since this institution did not have decision-making power.

A *contio* was an official assembly convoked and presided over by a magistrate or a tribune of the plebs (Pina Polo 1989 and 1996; Morstein-Marx 2004). The president of the assembly could invite others to speak (*producere in contionem, contionem dare*), either private citizens or magistrates, but he defined the order of speakers and even the time allotted to each orator. Projects of law had to be discussed in *contiones* during a period of three market days (*trinundinum*) prior to a vote in the *comitia*. Until the institution of permanent courts in the second half of the second century BC, trials took place before the people (*iudicia populi*) and, in this case, *contiones* also had to be convoked so that various speakers argued in favour or against the defendant prior to the vote.

Additionally, there were *contiones* with the purpose of informing, of announcing edicts and with other objectives. The most frequent assemblies were the political *contiones*, in which a speaker defended his arguments and attacked those of his rivals. The *contiones* were central to Roman political life because of their role in transmitting information to people and in the creation of public opinion. The orators usually addressed the people from a platform placed between the Comitium and the Forum (*Rostra*), and sometimes from the podia of temples.

Likewise, the *comitia* had to be summoned by a magistrate. These assemblies had electoral, legislative and judicial functions (Taylor 1966; Yakobson 1999). Most of the laws were voted in the *comitia tributa*, although the *comitia centuriata* also had this prerogative. For example, the centuries voted to declare war on a foreign state. The *comitia centuriata* elected the higher magistrates—censors, consuls and praetors—while the assembly of the tribes elected the lower magistrates—aediles and quaestors. Until the institution of the permanent courts, the people voted to decide the verdict of trials: serious crimes that could go as far as the death penalty in the *comitia centuriata*, and minor crimes involving only financial penalties in the *comitia tributa*.

Since the *comitia centuriata* were originally conceived as the assemblies of the Roman people in arms, the meeting took place in the Campus Martius, outside the sacred limits of the city (*pomerium*). The *comitia tributa* originally met in the central part of Rome, either in the Forum–Comitium zone or in the Capitoline area; but in the late Republic it was common that these assemblies also met in the more extensive Campus Martius. Every male citizen voted in a unit of vote—the tribe or the century he belonged to—and, in turn, each unit cast a vote that counted to form an absolute majority.

7.3.3 Senate

The senate was always an aristocratic chamber, not only because it gathered the wealthiest families of Rome, but also because it was constituted by the former magistrates of the Republic (Bonnefond-Coudry 1989; Ryan 1998). The senate was a factor of stability in the Republic due to its social homogeneity and the long terms of service of its members. The senators usually met in the Curia, a building located at the north-western corner of the Forum, and sometimes they met in temples such as that of Jupiter Capitolinus—always on the first day of the consular year—and those of Concordia, Fides, Bellona and others.

During the Republic the senate consisted of three hundred senators, until Sulla expanded it to six hundred and Caesar to nine hundred in the first century BC. Both dictators introduced many political allies into the senate in order to secure the support of the chamber. A substantial part of those new senators had not occupied any magistracy before joining the senate, as had been the norm, and many never did thereafter.

The senate controlled Roman internal politics by issuing written recommendations as if they were decrees (*senatus consulta*) and by using magistrates as the executive arm of its decisions. The senators managed policy as regards religion, concerning both the construction of temples and the acceptance of new gods in the Roman pantheon. The senate also led diplomacy and foreign policy, and thus, the senators were the main promoters of the expansionist policy in Italy and in the Mediterranean. They allocated magistrates to each province and decided whether it should be a consul, a praetor or a promagistrate, as well as the number of soldiers that they took with them. The senate also regulated the Roman economy and set fiscal policy. In addition, the senators were the juries of the permanent courts since the last half of the second century BC, as well as the priests of the Roman civic religion. In short, the senate was effectively the governing body of the Roman Republic.

7.4 Conclusion

When he wrote his *Histories* in the second century BC, Polybius argued that Rome had the best constitution because it achieved a perfect blend of the three models to organise a state: aristocracy, democracy and monarchy. He wrote:

> So, these three types of government I mentioned ruled the constitution, and the three were ordered, administered and distributed so evenly, with such accuracy, that no one, not even the Romans, could have said with certainty whether the regime was aristocratic, democratic, or monarchical. This is logical because, by the power of the consuls we may say that the constitution is monarchical; by the power of the senate, that it is aristocratic; and if we focus on the power of the people, we would have the impression of definitely being in front of a democracy. (Polyb. 6.11.11–12).

In the past three decades, scholarship has gone through a lively and inspiring debate about the character of the Roman Republican regime: was it a democracy or an aristocracy (Jehne 1995; Millar 1998; Hölkeskamp 2010)? The distinctive features of a democracy are evident. For instance, the citizens voted freely in the assemblies. Although during centuries the oral vote risked their freedom of choice, the secret ballot instituted in the last half of the second century BC made freedom more plausible. Through the assemblies, the annual election of new magistrates and the approval of new laws depended on the popular will, although only magistrates had the faculty of proposing legislation.

Nonetheless, the limitations of this democratic system are also conspicuous. Rome progressively grew from the original small Latin city to the great power that dominated the entire Mediterranean. The initial thousands of Roman citizens became hundreds of thousands, and eventually millions scattered throughout Italy and the Mediterranean. In theory, all citizens had the same right to participate in the decision-making process, regardless of their residence. In practice, however, only those actually living in Rome or in very close territories participated in assemblies and exercised the right to vote, as it was unlikely that a citizen living hundreds of miles away would travel to do expressly that. Furthermore, the voting system allocated very unequal weight to the votes in the *comitia centuriata*, providing a disproportionally large decision power to the better-off citizens (Cic. *Rep.* 2.39; Liv. 1.43.10), although the vote in the tribal assembly seems to have been more egalitarian.

A distinctive feature of the Athenian democracy was the incentives provided by the state for citizens to participate in the public life. The main stimulus was the *misthós*, a remuneration granted by the state to citizens who performed a public service. Rome never had anything similar and no one ever proposed it: it was simply unthinkable in the Roman Republican system. Public offices—and consequently the senate—were monopolised by the ruling class, the *nobilitas*; and the names of the same families continually appeared for decades, and even centuries, at the head of the Roman state.

The *contio* was certainly a fundamental element of Roman politics in the Republican period. Politics in Rome cannot be understood without the figure of an orator trying to persuade the people or without the importance granted to public opinion. The *contio* was the point of contact between the senate and the people, through the words of the magistrates. It was the only institution in which public debate between different political positions and in front of the people was legally possible. However, in practice there were serious restrictions to being an orator, and hence to the development of the debate. The information provided by the ancient sources shows that, with very few exceptions, the speakers who addressed the people during the Roman Republic were members of the elite, mostly magistrates on duty, and the rest were former magistrates; which means that almost all the speakers at the *contiones* were senators. In short, delivering a speech before the people in Rome was never a citizen's right but a privilege of the elites.

It is not easy to define in a few words a political system that lasted for five centuries. During all that time there were enormous changes inside Rome and in the relations of the city with the world, to the point that it is plausible to talk about a sequence of different Roman Republics (Flower 2010). Yet it is possible to say that overall the Roman Republic was essentially an aristocratic regime with oligarchic tendencies, though with a limited but not negligible popular participation in the decision-making process.

Bibliography

Beck, H., A. Duplá, M. Jehne and F. Pina Polo, eds. 2011. *Consuls and* Res Publica. *High office holding in the Roman republic.* Cambridge.

Bleicken, J. 1955. *Das Volkstribunat der klassischen Republik.* Göttingen.

Bleicken, J. 1995[7]. *Die Verfassung der Römischen Republik.* Paderborn.

Bonnefond-Coudry, M. 1989. *Le Sénat de la République romaine.* Rome.

Brennan, T. C. 2000. *The Praetorship in the Roman republic.* 2 vols. Oxford.

Broughton, T. R. S. 1951–1952, 1986. *The magistrates of the Roman republic.* 3 vols. 1951–1952 New York. 1986 Atlanta.

Cornell, T. 1995. *The beginnings of Rome: Italy and Rome from the Bronze Age to the Punic wars.* London.

Daguet-Gagey, A. 2015. Splendor aedilitatum: *l'édilité à Rome (Ier s. avant J.-C.—IIIe après J.-C).* Rome.

Develin, R. (1975). "Comitia Tributa Plebis." *Athenaeum* 53: 302–337.

Farrell, J. (1986). "The distinction between *comitia* and *concilium*." *Athenaeum* 74: 407–438.

Flower, H. 2010. *Roman republics.* Princeton.

Giovannini, A. 1983. Consulare Imperium. Basel.

Hartfield, M. 1982. "The Roman dictatorship. Its character and its evolution." PhD dissertation, University of California, Berkeley.

Hölkeskamp, K.-J. 2010. *Reconstructing the Roman republic: an ancient political culture and modern research.* Princeton.

Jehne, M. ed. 1995. *Demokratie in Rom? Die Rolle des Volkes in der Politik der römischen Republik.* Stuttgart.

Kunkel, W. and Wittmann, R. 1995. *Staatsordnung und Staatspraxis der römischen Republik,* Vol. 2. *Abschnitt: Die Magistratur.* Munich.

Lintott, A. 1999. *The constitution of the Roman republic.* Oxford.

Millar, F. 1998. *The crowd in Rome in the late republic.* Ann Arbor.

Morstein-Marx, R. 2004. *Mass oratory and political power in the late Roman republic.* Cambridge.

North, J. 2006. "The constitution of the Roman republic." In N. Rosenstein and R. Morstein-Marx, eds., *A companion to the Roman republic*. Oxford. 256–277.
Pina Polo, F. 1989. *Las contiones civiles y militares en Roma*. Zaragoza.
Pina Polo, F. 1996. Contra arma verbis: *Der Redner vor dem Volk in den späten römischen Republik*. Stuttgart.
Pina Polo, F. (2004). "Die nützliche Erinnerung: Geschichtsschreibung, *mos maiorum* und die römische Identität." *Historia* 53: 147–172.
Pina Polo, F. 2011. *The consul at Rome: the civil functions of the consuls in the Roman republic*. Cambridge.
Ryan, F. 1998. *Rank and participation in the republican senate*. Stuttgart.
Suolahti, J. 1963. *The Roman censors*. Helsinki.
Taylor, L. R. 1966. *Roman voting assemblies*. Ann Arbor.
Thommen, L. 1989. *Das Volkstribunat der späten römischen Republik*. Stuttgart.
Yakobson, A. 1999. *Elections and electioneering in Rome*. Stuttgart.

CHAPTER 8

THE EMPEROR, THE LAW AND IMPERIAL ADMINISTRATION

WERNER ECK

DESPITE the importance of the army in achieving and preserving power, the Roman Empire was not, from a legal perspective, an autocracy simply acquired through and based on military power.[1] It was instead strongly founded on law, even though the law was quite often invented to achieve very specific goals and was at times violated with brutal force. A gold coin minted by Octavian in 28 BC is emblematic of this specific legal foundation; according to the legend of the coin, Octavian had restored law and public institutions: *leges et iura p(opulo) R(omano) restituit* (Rich and Williams 1999; Mantovani 2008, 5–54).

Roughly forty years later, during his last year in power, Octavian again stated in his *Res gestae* 34, that during his sixth and seventh consulate (in the years 28/27 BC) he had returned the body politic, the *res publica*, to the control and power of the senate and the people, i.e. to the "sovereign". (Of course, Augustus had continued to wield effectively autocratic power throughout.) According to his version, he had, since then, never possessed more magisterial power than had his colleagues in the individual magistracies. This formulation displays how important it was not simply for Augustus, but also for society at the time, that the norms of law and statute were held to be binding on him as *princeps*, too.

From the political reconciliation in January 27 until 23 BC, Augustus could govern, legally speaking, only on the basis of consular power: he always had an equal colleague by his side; first his closest political and military companion Agrippa, who had defeated Mark Anthony and Cleopatra at Actium, and subsequently other senators. Augustus' continuous re-election as consul between 27 and 23 BC was contrary to Republican conventions and laws; but the sequence of actions was made legally possible through specific laws, and indeed relied on Republican examples. In his position as a re-elected consul, Augustus was assigned several provinces,[2] again on the basis of senatorial decrees, but these assignments

[1] Birley 2007. See also Eck forthcoming a.

[2] Thus, he did not receive an additional proconsular *imperium*, as assumed by Kienast 2014, 87 and others, following Mommsen 1887 II, 845. For the development of Augustus' legal position and his *imperium* see Girardet 2007, 2014, as well as Cotton and Yakobson 2002, Ferrary 2001. In what follows, the differing positions are not pointed out in detail.

were temporary, at first only for a period of ten years. When Augustus resigned as a consul during the course of 23 BC he retained his command over the provinces, since not even four years out of the ten had by then elapsed. In line with Republican tradition he immediately became *proconsul* of these provinces; a specific appointment was not necessary. For many years, scholars considered the naming of Augustus as *proconsul* as an autonomous matter unlikely; but the discovery of two edicts, dated 14 and 15 February 15 BC, issued by Augustus in the province Gallia Narbonensis on behalf of a Spanish community, has since provided evidence that he did in fact hold this position (*AE* 1999, 915 = 2000, 760). According to *ius publicum*, he ranked on the same level as the other *proconsules*, who had been selected by lot to administer the other provinces after the provincial reorganisation in 27 BC. In his own provinces, Augustus had delegated these administrative duties to senators, whose legal dependence and magisterial rank was clarified by designating them as *legati Augusti pro praetore*. Everyone active in politics knew that in reality the equal rank of Augustus and the other proconsuls was suspended by the political–military power of the *provinciae Caesaris*. In public conduct, however, specific rules had to be obeyed, following the dictates of legal form.

Augustus' *imperium* as *proconsul* was legally limited to the area of *militiae*, i.e. to the provinces assigned to him. According to the rules of the Republic, an official holding prorogated power lost that power when crossing the border of the city of Rome, the *pomerium*, from the outside in. This caused political as well as practical problems, since Augustus' provincial power would have had to be renewed every time he entered Rome. As a solution, Augustus was freed from this restriction by a special law. From then on, the *pomerium* no longer deprived him of his *imperium*; it remained intact under the proviso that, formally at least, Augustus could make use of it only outside the *pomerium*. This solved one problem for Augustus but another now intervened: under this system, he had no legal power to act politically in Rome itself, especially vis-à-vis the senate. In this time of transition, when his great words about the restoration of the Republic, the *iura et leges*, were not yet forgotten, the senate had to be consulted in all important political decisions. As Augustus did not want to tarnish the gleam of the *res publica restituta*, which he had just achieved with great difficulty, so a way had to be found by which he might legally act within the *pomerium*. The solution was the bestowing of the full *tribunicia potestas*, a magisterial power detached from the plebeian tribunate. This was granted in a fashion that enabled Augustus to act politically in the city of Rome without losing his status as a patrician, which carried specific privileges, even though the patriciate and the tribunate represented opposing sides within the *populus Romanus*. Like the office of the tribune of the plebs, the *tribunicia potestas* lasted only for a period of one year; but since it was annually renewed, it came to be seen as the everlasting basis of the *princeps*' developing power.

So far, Augustus could act more or less without restriction; but he was still hampered by legal and customary barriers that he had to observe, as his politics were built on compliance with these rules. Being a consul, he could also intervene in provinces not assigned to him. After 23 BC, however, the ordinary *imperium* possessed by Augustus as proconsul no longer permitted such interventions; a situation that could have become problematic for him. We do not know at whose request this occurred, but in the same year Augustus' *imperium* was therefore redefined so that, in cases of conflict, it ranked above the *imperium* of other proconsuls. From then on, he held an *imperium maius quam*, i.e. an *imperium* that was greater than that of the other proconsul in any concrete instance. As regards its competencies, the *imperium* of Augustus did not differ from those held by other proconsuls, just as the *imperium* held by a consul and that held by a praetor were similar in content. Nonetheless, in a situation of conflict, the *imperium* of a consul prevailed over that of a praetor. It is likely that Augustus would have won any conflict with another proconsul merely because of his general position; but owing to this new rule he also held the upper hand legally speaking. It was not even necessary for him to make use of his *auctoritas*.

The legal amendment of Augustus' *imperium* was limited to his power in the provinces. Within Rome, Augustus could act only on the basis of the *tribunicia potestas*, which offered limited options, as most of the politically relevant issues had to be conducted on the basis of an *imperium* that was legally valid also within the *pomerium*. This problem affected control of the elections of the higher magistrates, the consuls in particular. Augustus was legally excluded from these elections, as his proconsular *imperium* did not extend to the area *domi*. For several years, especially between 22 and 19 BC, the consular elections in Rome were interfered with or even thwarted through turmoil. This led to a severe crisis of the new system, with some people even speaking of a controlled crisis, as it paved the way for what finally eventuated. When Augustus returned from a long journey to the eastern provinces in 19 BC, it had become clear that the elections for the highest Republican offices were stuck in a rather desperate situation; again, a special rule was enacted for Augustus. The territorial limitation of his *imperium* to the provinces was removed; with it, he could henceforth act also in Rome and Italy, which enabled him *inter alia* to conduct or directly influence the elections for the highest offices. Now, Augustus held an *imperium* that could be described as consular and proconsular at the same time, depending on where it was exercised. No conflicts concerning elections are known to have occurred thereafter. Augustus could now legally manage elections according to his aims and organise the Republic's "politics of personnel" as it suited him. For he could not appoint the traditional officeholders; they had to be elected to their socio-political position. Every magistrate elected in this way was a member of the senate for life; and the senate remained the most important political player alongside the *princeps*. Thus, it was of vital importance for Augustus to organise the composition of the senate, such that it would be a willing partner instead of a council with the potential to hamper or counteract his politics. However, in this game, both sides had to obey not just the rules of political power, but also the rules of the *ius publicum*.

Augustus adhered precisely to the rules of the *ius publicum*, and he made his adherence public. This is evident in how he handled the case of Aemilius Lepidus, his former colleague as a *triumvir*. Lepidus had been elected *pontifex maximus* after Caesar's death, a lifelong position as was the case for nearly all Roman priesthoods. In 36 BC, long before the end of the Civil Wars, after Sextus Pompeius had been neutralised in Sicily, Lepidus had tried to improve his position vis-à-vis Octavian through some kind of putsch. The putsch failed, and Lepidus was forced to withdraw from politics and held incommunicado in a villa on Cape Circei. As the holder of the highest pontificate, he could not be legally deprived of this office, and so he remained alive. In practice, therefore, the *res publica* had to proceed without the highest holder of sacerdotal power until Lepidus' death. Only when Lepidus died in 13 BC in his Italian exile, could Augustus make a play for the highest pontificate and get himself elected into this office by a public meeting attended by masses of people from throughout Italy. When he scheduled this meeting, he waited until the traditional date for the pontifical elections in March of the following year. According to Augustus, the people urged him by a vote to take over the office earlier, probably already in 36 BC; but—as he highlights in his *Res gestae*—he refused to accept the office before this date precisely because priests kept their office until their death (Scheid 2007, 45–46).

Among the senatorial elite as well as the rulers themselves the *ius publicum* was broadly taken to represent the basis of public order. This becomes particularly clear from the provisions of a *senatus consultum* dated 20 AD, which refers to a regulation from 17 AD. At this time, Germanicus, the adopted son of Tiberius, was sent to the *transmarinae provinciae*—to Syria specifically—with a special mandate. To this end, a law was passed conferring upon him the power that he was supposed to exercise as a proconsul. The *imperium* was greater than the *imperium* of every other provincial proconsul (*maius quam* ... = greater than ...), but the *senatus consultum* also makes clear that the *imperium* held by Tiberius Caesar Augustus remained greater than that of Germanicus Caesar (*AE* 1996, 885, ll. 34–35: *maius ei imperium quam ei, qui eam provinciam proco(n)s(ule) optineret, esset, dum in omni re maius imperium Ti(berio) Cae(s)ari quam Germ(anico) Caesar(i) esset*).[3] Irrespective of the political circumstances that may have led to the formulation of the *senatus consultum*, it is clear that even the relationship between the *princeps* and his son had to be spelled out legally. The specific rules of *ius publicum* stated in this popular enactment created a legally precise hierarchy of *imperia*, even though in principle the *imperium* of magistrates were construed as coequal. In this case the *princeps* stood on top, and even Germanicus was subordinate to his *imperium*; Germanicus' *imperium*, in turn, outweighed the *imperium* of the other proconsuls in case of conflict.

In 27 BC, two types of province, which differed from each other with respect to their specific administration, had been created. One type was traditionally administered by senatorial promagistrates, i.e. *proconsules*, whereas in Augustus' provinces responsibility was held by *legati* on his behalf; the appendix *pro praetore* in their official title revealed their dependence on the consular *imperium* of the *princeps*. During the reign of Claudius, provinces such as Thrace and the two provinces of Mauretania were established. These provinces were governed by so-called praesidial procurators.[4] These had never held an office in consequence of an election by the Roman people and therefore also did not have senatorial status. These offices were open to people of equestrian rank. They were assigned to their administrative functions by the emperor alone, but basically had the same functions as the senatorial governors of the existing provinces. In this way, Claudius created a new type of province. However, it is important to understand that Egypt, which had also been administered by an *eques* since the time of Augustus, did not serve as the role model, although it is not uncommonly seen that way.[5] Octavian had established Egypt as a province before the political–legal reform of 27 BC, and it had been assigned to an equestrian prefect, who—according to the Digest—had been granted an *imperium* similar to that of a proconsul by way of legislation.[6] This was necessary at that time because the prefect was initially entrusted with the command of three legions; in addition, the prefect had to dispense judgement over and for Roman citizens. During the highly uncertain situation

[3] Eck, Caballos and Fernández 1996, 40, 160–161.

[4] The term praesidial, derived from *praeses*, "governor", distinguishes procurators who functioned in the place of magistrates from others who held narrowly "financial" responsibilities.

[5] The remarks on Egypt in Tac. *Ann.* 12.60.2 refer only to the fact that legal proceedings before the prefect of this province could be conducted in the same way as before a Roman magistrate.

[6] D.1.17.1: *Praefectus Aegypti non prius deponit praefecturam et imperium, quod ad similitudinem proconsulis lege sub Augusto ei datum est, quam Alexandriam ingressus sit successor eius, licet in provinciam venerit: et ita mandatis eius continetur.* Compare Tac. *Ann.* 12.60.2: whereas Ulpian refers to the *lex* and thus to the formal legal part of the proceedings, Tacitus bases his argument on who actually initiated the law.

following the end of the Civil Wars, Octavian had to avoid the impression that he might not take the demands of the *ius publicum* seriously. For this reason, special legislation was enacted in the case of the prefect of Egypt. The specific legal competences of the prefect of Egypt thus did not derive from Augustus, but from an appropriate and authoritative institution, i.e. the people's assembly. Something similar took place under Claudius, at least as regards jurisdiction in the provinces led by praesidial procurators (Tac. *Ann.* 12.60). Presumably it was not deemed necessary to grant them a competence similar to an *imperium*, as no legions—i.e. citizen soldiers—were under the command of these equestrian officeholders. They commanded only auxiliary troops, which consisted almost exclusively of aliens at that time.

From the time of Augustus, procurators were responsible for financial matters in the provinces assigned to him, and they administered the *patrimonium principis* in the provinces run by proconsuls. Before the time of Claudius, they had also begun to administer justice. This follows from Tacitus, and it seems plausible.[7] In 53 AD, Claudius entrusted them and other procurators with extensive jurisdiction by way of a senatorial decree, at least with respect to their specific domain (Tac. *Ann.* 12.60.1). It cannot necessarily be concluded from Tacitus' report that Claudius had even granted his freedmen direct jurisdictional power (Tac. *Ann.* 12.69.4); this statement might have been made in the context of Tacitus' usual polemics against Imperial freedmen. But what matters is that even Claudius did not act alone when making a decision so essential for the Roman world; namely, granting jurisdictional power to the non-senatorial officials. Instead, he allowed it to be authorised by a senatorial decree, even though it was not the senate but Claudius and his advisers who deemed it necessary to endow officials with this power, and it was they who drafted the motion.

In fact, important decisions and reforms are quite often described in historiographic sources as if they were introduced and decreed by the emperor without consulting the senate or the people. For example, Tacitus describes Augustus as the one who endowed the prefect of Egypt with the power to conduct *legis actiones*, even though the prefect was merely an *eques* and did not hold a magisterial office. According to Ulpian, *imperium* could be transferred only by a *lex*; in Tacitus' account, on the other hand, it derives directly from Augustus (Tac. *Ann.* 12.60.2). This might be correct from a political perspective, but not from a legal point of view. Hence, in this and in other cases, one has to assume that the emperor did not simply effect legal reforms by himself, but adhered to the usual legal procedures for introducing *res novae* (Brunt 1984). Even honours like those granted to Pallas, the freedman of Claudius, who was awarded the *ornamenta praetoria* and 15 million sesterces, were not bestowed by Claudius alone but were determined in the senate (Tac. *Ann.* 12.53.2). Of course, the senate was aware of the fact that the emperor supported these decrees.

There were many potential means with which Augustus and his successors might settle problems of society or of general administration or address them for the future through

[7] See, for instance, the case of the patrimonial procurator Lucilius Capito in the province of Asia (*Ann.* 4.15.2). Tiberius stated: *quod si vim praetoris usurpasset manibusque militum usus foret, spreta in eo mandata sua.* This allows the conclusion that the jurisdiction of the procurators probably started out because the procurators—being Imperial commissioners—were taken for *de facto* officeholders and acted that way.

new legal enactments. The normal procedure of lawmaking through one of the people's assemblies, as it had been known in Republican times, was also employed by Augustus and his successors at least until the end of the first century AD, although less and less frequently as time passed. Under Augustus, laws passed by the people were relatively common. In 9 BC, for example, regulations for the protection of urban Roman aqueducts were consolidated and completed by a *lex Quinctia*; its entire text is preserved with all the formal details in the *De aquis urbis Romae* of Frontinus (Front. *Aq.* 129). The *lex Fufia Caninia* limited the possibilities for testamentary manumissions, which was also partly the aim of the *lex Aelia Sentia*; and the latter also allowed the granting of Roman citizenship upon manumission only under certain conditions (it had heretofore been unrestricted). Other *leges* were submitted to the legislative process by Augustus himself, as is evident from their being named as *lex Iulia*. This must have been of great importance to him, as he stresses it in his *Res gestae*. One of these laws was the *lex Iulia de vicesima hereditatium* of 6 AD, which introduced for the first time an inheritance tax of 5 percent (modest by modern standards). This legislation led to the creation of far-reaching regulations for the public opening of wills and their administration; but above all, it led to the creation of another public fund for the control of the money coming from this tax: the *aerarium militare*. To manage this *aerarium*, three new senatorial *praefecti* were created and Augustus was allowed to appoint them personally. At first, the inheritance tax law was widely resisted; but Augustus was able to prevail in the end because money was urgently needed for the supply of legionary veterans. The army was, after all, the vital basis of his power (RG 9; see Eck forthcoming b).

Severe resistance was also provoked by the *lex Iulia de maritandis ordinibus* of 18 BC, which *inter alia* sought to compel marriages or remarriages and the production of children; these aims were supported by privileges or disadvantages regarding applications for official positions as well as succession. Whereas the first of these laws was linked directly to Augustus through its title *lex Iulia*, the later legislation in the second half of 9 AD passed under the name of the consuls in office at that time, M. Papius Mutilus and C. Poppaeus Sabinus. That this legislation had been introduced also by Augustus, became clear quite recently through a hint in the municipal law of Troesmis, which was enacted in the later years of the reign of Marcus Aurelius (Eck 2013a and 2013b). It is stated explicitly in the municipal law that already on 28 June 5 AD, a *commentarius* had been published in Rome that laid out the basis for the regulations passed more than four years later in the *lex Papia Poppaea (commentari, ex quo lex P(apia) P(oppaea) lata est, propositi Cn(aeo) Cinna Magno Vol(eso) Val(erio) Caeso (sic!) co(n)s(ulibus) IIII kal(endas) Iulias kap(ite) XLVIIII cauta conprehensaque sunt et confirmata legis P(apiae) P(oppaeae) k(apite) XLIIII)*. The law of Troesmis provides no information as to the name of the individual who "proposed" the *commentarius*, i.e. presented it to the public, but there can be no doubt that Augustus himself stood behind it. As we know from Suetonius and especially from Cassius Dio (Cass. Dio 56.1–29; Suet. *Aug.* 34.2), the *princeps* had tried by different means and with the greatest effort to break the resistance to this law, which was clearly much greater than that to any other of his laws. To achieve his aims, Augustus granted two interim periods of several years, so that all affected persons could arrange their lives according to the provisions of the proposed law; this meant in practice that they should marry and conceive children. It is likely as well that resistance to the law lasted for such a long time because its passage was first initiated shortly before a period of internal and external difficulties, in particular the uprising in Illyricum of 6–9 AD. In the end, the law was pushed through with nearly its original scope but without mentioning Augustus, though it is likely that small functional amendments were made and reliefs granted.

As far as can be seen from what has survived, *leges* became increasingly rare after the time of Augustus. The *lex de imperio Vespasiani* is the last statute enacted by a people's assembly that has survived at least in part verbatim; it dates back to the successful Flavian usurpation in 70 AD. But as the text of the statute reveals, including the obligatory formula fixing penalties for its violation (the so-called *sanctio*), the senate had decided on the text and it was presented to the people's assembly merely *pro forma* (*ILS* 244; Capogrossi Colognesi and Tassi 2009). The last statute enacted by a people's assembly that can be linked to a specific person is the *lex Cocceia agraria*: it is very likely significant that it was moved by an emperor; namely, by Nerva himself (D.47.21.3.1).

Instead, most of the development of administrative regulations and general legal provisions were accomplished in the senate, except when it was performed by the emperor himself by other means.[8] In most cases, the acting consuls made the motion, as long as the emperors themselves did not bring the motion before the senate, probably after having discussed it with a *consilium principis* concerned with the specific issue. In most of the surviving cases, the names of the non-Imperial movers are not preserved. For example, directly after Augustus' withdrawal from his permanent consulate, a *senatus consultum* was passed that provided for the registration of *scribae* in the *aerarium*; the meeting of the senate was attended by at least 405 senators, quite a large number in relation to the usual quota. This was likely voted at the request of Cn. Piso and L. Sestius, who served as *consules suffecti* in 23 BC.[9] When the urban Roman water supply was reorganised after the death of Agrippa, the consuls of 11 BC initiated a whole series of senatorial decrees defining the tasks of the *curatores aquarum* and fixing the regulations for the operation of the *aquae*.[10] One of the suffect consuls of 42 AD initiated a *senatus consultum Largianum* regulating the succession of *Latini Iuliani* who had not made provisions for their death by drawing up a will (Inst.Gai.3.63). The last *senatus consultum* named after a senator may be traced to Servius Cornelius Scipio Salvidienus Orfitus, one of the *consules ordinarii* of 178 AD. It permitted the emancipation of slaves that were merely listed in a will as a general matter but not identified by name. If there was no doubt as to which slave the testator's order for emancipation was directed, they had to be granted their freedom (Sent.Paul.4.14.1).

Most of the senatorial decrees concerning the conduct of officials or general procedural rules seem to have been the direct result of proposals originating from the emperor. At least, this is what can be deduced from the surviving sources (Talbert 1984, 437–458). On 22 September 47 AD, for instance, the senate agreed to a proposal of Claudius stipulating that buildings in Italy could not be knocked down simply in order to make a profit. Three hundred and eighty-three senators took part in the vote (*ILS* 6043). A few years later, in 56 AD, on the basis of this decree, the *consules ordinarii* brought a request for a decision before the senate from the relatives of a certain Alliatoria Cesilla, referring to a

[8] See the catalogue in Talbert 1984, 437–458.

[9] *CIL* VI 10621 = 32272 = 37142. However, during this time the number of senators had not been reduced to 600 yet; thus, as a percentage the attendance does not seem overly impressive.

[10] Front. *Aq.* 100 f, 104, 106, 108, 111, 125, 127.

case from Mutina. The two senatorial decrees were found in Herculaneum, written on a bronze tablet; they had been made public there as a rule to be followed by the local magistrates. In 62 AD, Nero initiated a senatorial decree prohibiting provinces from sending delegations to Rome in order to give thanks to their respective governor (Tac. *Ann.* 15.22.1; Nicols 1979). In 121 AD, the senate decreed, at the request of Hadrian, that the augurs had to restore the border stones of the Roman *pomerium*. However, the decree names Hadrian as both *auctor* and *proconsul*. The latter title makes clear that he could not have presented the request to the senators himself; in fact, he had already departed on a journey to the northern provinces of the Empire (*ILS* 311; Eck 2003b). The decree must therefore have been read out in the senate as an *oratio principis*, probably through one of the two Imperial *quaestores* or through one of the consuls. A later episode provides more detailed evidence: Ulpian cites a motion put to the senate by the consuls on 14 March 129; Ulpian also specifies that they spoke concerning matters laid out by Hadrian in a *libellus*. By the time the consuls spoke, Hadrian had departed on a journey to the east; his *libellus* had been written on 3 March of that year (D.5.3.20.6): *pridie idus Martias Quintus Iulius Balbus et Publius Iuventius Celsus T{i}tius Aufidius <H>oen<i>us Severianus consules verba fecerunt de his, quae imperator Caesar Traiani Parthici filius divi Nervae nepos Hadrianus Augustus imperator maximusque princeps proposuit quinto nonas Martias, quae proximae fuerunt, libello complexus esset.*

This way of using the emperor's rights of speech in the senate, even if not by the emperor in person, obviously became more frequent as many emperors, like Trajan and Hadrian, had to leave Rome for longer periods of time (Talbert 1984, 29–302, 444–447; Musca 1985). An inscription from Miletus testifies to the fact that a request of this city, which belonged to the province of Asia, was forwarded to the senate by Marcus Aurelius together with other requests in a single *oratio*, while he himself remained in the Danubian provinces. The senate assented to the emperor's *oratio* as presented, without reformulating the individual requests as separate *senatus consulta*. What is more, the Milesians receive the answer not from the senate but from Marcus Aurelius, and he could send only the relevant excerpt of his speech rather than a specific *senatus consultum* (*AE* 1977, 801 = Oliver 1989 no. 192; *AE* 1989, 683). However, the senate did not always simply assent to requests of the emperor. About the same time, in the later years of the reign of Marcus Aurelius, an application was sent to the senate also by way of an *oratio principis*, stipulating maximum prices of gladiators. But this *oratio*, which was read out in the senate, was incorporated by a senator into his *sententia* and reformulated as a *senatus consultum*; thereby, small amendments or at least additions were obviously made to the proposal of the emperor. But the senator also emphasised that in consequence of his so acting, his *sententia* differed from what was normal at that time. And indeed, the same process is cited in an inscription from Sardis, but there only the *oratio principis* is quoted, not the senator's *sententia*, which is known from an inscription from Italica in the province of Baetica (*ILS* 9430, 5163; see also Oliver and Palmer 1955). This discrepancy can most likely be explained by supposing that the senator who submitted the *sententia* wanted to see his version or perhaps even his commitment to this issue disseminated, whereas the inscription from Sardis merely refers to the decisive *oratio* of the *princeps*. The formalities of procedure in the senate were not relevant to the reception of the text in Sardis because the political will of the emperor also stood behind the *sententia* of the senator, whose name is unknown (Eck 2000, 235–237).

Decrees of the senate, which were very numerous, either decided particular cases or created generally binding rules; increasingly, this happened only in consultation with the emperor. The emperor in turn decided legal or administrative questions more and more by himself; others could use these decisions as precedents. The most general form of such a decision was the edict. An edict was rendered first verbally and later fixed in written form. An example from Augustus' early years are the edicts mentioned above that had been issued in 15 BC at Narbo for the *castellani Paemeiobrigenses* (*AE* 1999, 915). Already Augustus could enact edicts dealing with questions brought to his attention from provinces run by proconsuls; with regard to the North African province of Cyrene, this is attested by the so-called Cyrene Edicts (*FIRA* I² no. 68.). Augustus likewise issued edicts for Italy, as is revealed by an edict concerning the aqueduct in Venafrum (*FIRA* I² no. 67; see now *AE* 1962, 92 = Capini 1999, no. 1). In 49/50, Claudius enacted rules to stop fraudulent use of the public transport system in the province of Achaia. In another edict issued at Baiae, Claudius ordered an investigation into the problems between the communities of Comenses and Bergalei in the Alpine region of northern Italy, which had been reported to him by a *delator.* This man had also informed him about members of the Alpine tribes of the Anauni, Tulliasses and Sinduni, who behaved like Roman citizens although their citizenship status was uncertain, as they were not part of the *Colonia Tridentum* but their peoples were administratively subordinated to it. Claudius himself resolved this violation of the law by affirming their citizen status, especially on the grounds that people from these Alpine tribes had already served well as soldiers in his *praetorium* for a long time (*ILS* 206). He therefore bestowed a *beneficium* on the residents of this region. Hadrian solved a similar case by an edict that was announced by him to the people's assembly in Rome on the 19 February 119 AD. More than a few praetorians, whose Roman citizenship was known to be at least uncertain or even non-existent, were thereby made Roman citizens. By the same edict Hadrian declared valid all of the legal acts these praetorians had committed up until 31 December 118 AD, as if they had been Roman citizens all along (Eck, Pangerl and Weiß 2014a and 2014b.).

In his Institutes, the jurist Gaius counted these edicts among the *constitutiones principis*, to which category—according to Gaius—the *decreta* and *epistula* also belonged.[11] Most of the surviving Imperial constitutions are decrees on citizenship that were issued in increasing numbers at least from the time of Claudius to soldiers of auxiliary troops and sailors in the navy; also extant are constitutions for soldiers of the *cohortes praetoriae* and *urbanae* who obtained as Roman citizens the right of marriage (*conubium*) with a peregrine woman.[12] Several dozen of these constitutions were issued every year, and their original versions were published at Rome on tablets made of bronze. Every soldier or veteran received an individual transcript, a so-called *instrumentum*, commonly known as military diploma. The transcripts reveal very clearly how the emperors—and, of course, the *officia* that had emerged in the emperor's entourage—reacted to changing circumstances by modifying legal norms. As a consequence, for example, from November 140 on, the children of auxiliary veterans were no longer included in grants of citizenship, at least those born during the military service of their fathers (see Weiß 2008, esp. 36); but the

[11] Inst.Gai.1.5. Collections of Imperial constitutions: Oliver 1989 with Anastasiadis and Souris 2000; for a future update of *FIRA* see Purpura 2012.

[12] See *CIL* XVI and Roxan and Holder 1975–2006; see also Eck 2003a, 2008, 2012.

children born to a veteran before he joined the army remained privileged (Eck 2011). These constitutions were released annually on a regular basis for all provinces, though they were not made public in the provinces in full. Instead, they were generally published at Rome, initially at several places on the Capitol, and from 89/90 AD *in muro post templum divi Augusti ad Minervam*. The diplomas reveal clearly that despite the great number of edicts issued each year—probably hardly less than forty or fifty—the assent of the emperor was necessary for every single constitution (Eck 2012, 33–36). The emperor himself was the immediate source of these legislative acts. The documents generated by these acts could then be cited in subsequent legal and administrative contexts, as individual diplomas could also be used by their recipients as an *instrumentum*, i.e. as a certificate proving to the provincial administration that its owner held Roman citizenship.

Numerous *epistulae* sent from the Imperial chancellery also exist. At first, they were drawn up in a single *officium ab epistulis*; later, in response to the two languages spoken in the Empire, the *officium* was divided into two departments: *ab epistulis Latinis* and *ab epistulis Graecis* (Birley 1992, 41–50). Many of the *epistulae* known to us are trivial and without legal or administrative importance; for instance, some *epistulae* only confirm that the emperor had received a document containing an honorary decree issued by a community. But other letters contain legal decisions, like an *epistula* written by Vespasian to the *IIIIviri et decuriones Saborensium* in the province of Baetica (*ILS* 6092) or another *epistula* of the same emperor sent to the community of the Vanacini in Corsica: in it, Vespasian confirmed privileges dating as early as the time of Augustus (*AE* 1993, 855). In a similar way, in a letter sent to the community of Falerio in Italy, Domitian ensured legal certainty as to the possession of *subseciva*: the matter concerned unsurveyed marginal lands that had not been allotted to anyone during some initial distribution but which had since been occupied by private persons. These letters and decisions must have been of a substantial range and variety; every administrative problem could be solved this way. The correspondence between Pliny the Younger and Trajan makes this perfectly clear. To name just one example, which had an effect on politics and administration beyond the specific case: it was by letter that Pliny asked how he should handle trials of Christians in his province of Pontus-Bithynia (Plin. *Ep.* 10.96–97). Trajan's answer, which also took the form of a letter, was of continuing effect: Tertullian at the beginning of the third century and even the ecclesiastical historian Eusebius at the beginning of the fourth century took it to be the legal basis for trials of Christians (Tert. *Apol.* 2; Euseb. *Hist. eccl.* 3.33). That said, Trajan's letter was not the only ruling on this topic. According to Ulpian, several emperors addressed the issue and thereby modified the legal landscape.

Instructions, so-called *mandata*, were given to office holders by the emperors in increasing volume, even to proconsuls, although they possessed their own *imperium*. The large mass of these instructions, however, have not survived; most of them are known only insofar as they are reflected in legal literatures. In these instructions, general rules were laid down, as well as directives related to a specific province. Such a *mandatum* by Domitian given to his procurator Claudius Athenodorus is preserved in an inscription from Syria, forbidding the unjustified use of the *cursus publicus* (*SEG* XVII 755 = Oliver 1989, no. 40). These *mandata* do not seem to have applied as a body to all provinces uniformly, even though a basic stock of them might have been in force everywhere. The *praefectus Aegypti* knew from the *mandata* given to him that he had to await the arrival of his successor before he himself could leave the province (D.1.17.1). By contrast, the customary duty of the proconsul of Asia to visit Ephesus as first city of his province is not to be found in the *mandata* of the prefect of Egypt (D.1.16.4.5). The general rules for all office holders, such as they were, were regularly amplified, if new necessities occurred or if questions about particular rules were raised frequently and thus made a general clarification necessary. Trajan, for example, added a rule to the *mandata* stipulating that all soldiers should have perfect formal freedom when making a will, after Titus, Domitian and Nerva had decided similarly but without creating a general rule applicable in all provinces (D.29.1.1pr; Marotta 1991).

Already under Marcus Aurelius, Papirius Iustus compiled the first collection of Imperial rescripts, in order to contribute to the guidance of Roman officials, but also the people in general (Lenel 1889 I, 947–952). As Ulpian clearly stresses, every proconsul had the last word in his province, as his *imperium* was stronger than the official power of everyone else working in its administration (D.1.16.8 and 1.18.4). But his *imperium* was outranked by the *imperium* of the *princeps*, in a hierarchical ordering comparable to the one revealed in the *s.c. de Cn. Pisone patre* operative between the *princeps*, Germanicus and the other proconsuls. As a result, increasing numbers of requests were sent to Rome from officials asking for legal decisions.[13] The emperors and the *officia* that developed around the emperors emerged more and more as the centre of the whole administration of the Empire, whence many things were directed and guided. The hierarchical structure of the administration in late Antiquity emerged step by step out of these countless decision-making processes (Eich 2005).

Bibliography

Anastasiades, V. I. and Souris, G. A. 2000. *An index to Roman imperial constitutions from Greek inscriptions and papyri: 27 BC to 284 AD.* Berlin.

Birley, A. R. 1992. Locus virtutibus patefactus. *Zum Beförderungssystem in der Hohen Kaiserzeit.* Opladen.

Birley, A. R. 2007. "Making emperors. Imperial instrument or independent force?" In P. Erdkamp, ed., *A companion to the Roman army.* Malden. 379–394.

Brunt, P. A. (1984). "The role of the senate in the Augustan regime." *Classical Quarterly* 34: 423–444.

Capini, S. 1999. *Molise: repertorio delle iscrizioni latine, VII: Venafrum.* Campobasso.

Capogrossi Colognesi, L. and E. Tassi Scandone, eds. 2009. *La lex de Imperio Vespasiani e la Roma dei Flavi (Atti del convegno, 20–22 novembre 2008).* Rome.

Cotton, H. M. and Yakobson, A. 2002. "*Arcanum imperii.* The powers of Augustus." In G. Clark and T. Rajak, eds., *Philosophy and power in the Graeco-Roman world: essays in honour of Miriam Griffin.* Oxford. 193–209.

dell'Oro, A. 1960. *I* libri de officio *nella giurisprudenza romana.* Milan.

[13] The *libri de officio* represent a certain counterweight against the centralisation and in support of the autonomy of the individual official position; cf., for instance, the *libri de officio proconsulis, consulis, consularium, praetoris tutelaris, quaestoris, praefecti urbis, praefecti vigilum* or *curatoris rei publicae.* See dell'Oro 1960.

Eck, W. 2000. "Emperor, senate, and magistrates." In A. K. Bowman, P. Garnsey and D. Rathbone, eds., *The Cambridge ancient history*. Cambridge. Vol. 11: 214–237.

Eck, W. 2003a. "Der Kaiser als Herr des Heeres. Militärdiplome und kaiserliche Reichsregierung." In J. Wilkes, ed., *Documenting the Roman army: essays in honour of Margaret Roxan*. London. 55–87.

Eck, W. (2003b). "Suffektkonsuln der Jahre 132–134 und Hadrians Rückkehr nach Rom im Jahr 132." *Zeitschrift für Papyrologie und Epigraphik* 143: 234–242.

Eck, W. 2008. "Militärdiplome als Inschriften der Stadt Rom." In M. L. Caldelli, G. L. Gregori and S. Orlandi, eds., *Epigrafia 2006: atti dell' XIVe Rencontre sur l'Épigraphie in onore di Silvio Panciera*. Rome. 1121–1134.

Eck, W. 2011. "Septimius Severus und die Soldaten. Das Problem der Soldatenehe und ein neues Auxiliardiplom." In B. Onken and D. Rohde, eds., In omni historia curiosus: *Studien zur Geschichte von der Antike bis zur Neuzeit. Festschrift für Helmuth Schneider zum 65. Geburtstag*. Wiesbaden. 63–77.

Eck, W. 2012. *Bürokratie und Politik in der römischen Kaiserzeit. Administrative Routine und politische Reflexe in Bürgerrechtskonstitutionen der römischen Kaiser*. Wiesbaden.

Eck, W. 2013a. "Das Leben römisch gestalten. Ein Stadtgesetz für das *Municipium Troesmis* aus den Jahren 177–180 n. Chr." In S. Benoist and G. de Kleijn, eds., *Integration in Rome and in the Roman world*. Leiden. 75–88.

Eck. W. (2013b). "La loi municipale de Troesmis: données juridiques et politiques d'une inscription récemment découverte." *Revue historique du droit français et étranger* 91: 199–213.

Eck, W. Forthcoming a. "Herrschaftssicherung und Expansion: Das römische Heer unter Augustus." In G. Negri and A. Valvo, eds. *Augusto* (in print).

Eck, W. Forthcoming b. "Das Heer im Ordnungsgefüge des augusteischen Prinzipats," in *Augusto. La costruzione del Principato, Convegno Roma, 4–5 Dicembre 2014*.

Eck, W., Caballos, A. and Fernández, F. (1996.) Das senatus consultum de Cn. Pisone patre. Munich.

Eck, W., Pangerl, A. and Weiß, P. (2014a). "Edikt Hadrians für Prätorianer mit unsicherem römischen Bürgerrecht." *Zeitschrift für Papyrologie und Epigraphik* 189: 241–253.

Eck, W., Pangerl, A. and Weiß, P. (2014b). "Ein drittes Exemplar des Edikts Hadrians zugunsten von Prätorianern vom Jahr 119 n. Chr." *Zeitschrift für Papyrologie und Epigraphik* 191: 266–268.

Eich, P. 2005. *Zur Metamorphose des politischen Systems in der römischen Kaiserzeit. Die Entstehung einer "personalen Bürokratie" im langen dritten Jahrhundert*. Berlin.

Ferrary, J.-L. (2001). "À propos des pouvoirs d'Auguste." *Cahiers du Centre Gustave Glotz* 12: 101–154.

Girardet, K. 2007. *Rom auf dem Weg von der Republik zum Prinzipat*. Bonn.

Girardet, K. 2014. "Roms Verfassungstradition und die Rechtsgrundlagen des augusteischen Prinzipats." In M. Horster and F. Schuller, eds., *Augustus. Herrscher der Zeitenwende*. Regensburg. 56–77.

Kienast, D. 2014[5]. *Augustus. Prinzeps und Monarch*. Darmstadt.

Lenel, O. 1889. Palingenesia Iuris Civilis. Leipzig.

Mantovani, D. (2008). "*Leges et iura P(opuli) R(omani) restituit*. Principe e diritto in un Aureo di Ottaviano." *Athenaeum* 96: 5–54.

Marotta, V. 1991. Mandata principum. Turin.

Mommsen, T. 1887[3]. *Römisches Staatsrecht*. Leipzig.

Musca, D. A. (1985). "*Da Traiano a Settimio Severo: senatusconsultum* o *oratio principis?*" *Labeo* 31: 7–46.

Nicols, J. (1979). "Zur Verleihung öffentlicher Ehrungen in der römischen Welt." *Chiron* 9: 243–260.

Oliver, J. H. 1989. *Greek constitutions of the early Roman emperors from inscriptions and papyri*. Philadelphia.

Oliver, J. H. and Palmer, R. E. A. (1955). "Minutes of an act of the Roman senate." *Hesperia* 24: 320–349.

Purpura, G., ed. 2012. *Revisione ed integrazione dei* Fontes Iuris Romani Anteiustiniani . Turin.

Rich, J. W. and Williams, J. H. C. (1999). "*Leges et iura P. R. restituit.* A new aureus of Octavian and his settlement of 28–27 BC." *Numismatic Chronicle* 159: 169–213.

Roxan, M. M. and Holder, P. 1975–2006. *Roman Military Diplomas*. 5 vols. London.

Scheid, J. 2007. Res gestae divi Augusti. Paris.

Talbert, R. J. A. 1984. *The senate of imperial Rome*. Princeton.

Weiß, P. (2008). "Die vorbildliche Kaiserehe. Zwei Senatsbeschlüsse beim Tod der älteren und der jüngeren Faustina, neue Paradigmen und die Herausbildung des 'antoninischen' Prinzipats." *Chiron* 38: 1–45.

CHAPTER 9

PROVINCIAL ADMINISTRATION

JOHN RICHARDSON

9.1 Introduction

The Roman Empire was a vast entity. Not only did it stretch, at its greatest extent, from the Atlantic coast of Spain to Mesopotamia and from Scotland to the Sahara, but it existed in some form from the period of the wars against Carthage in the third century BC to late Antiquity; and, indeed, could be said to continue until the fall of Constantinople to the Ottoman Turks in 1453 AD. To give an account of the administration of such an immense area over so many centuries would be a task almost as huge; but the ways in which that law was received and used across the Empire is an essential part of the understanding of its development.

This chapter will focus on the period from the beginnings of Rome's overseas Empire to the reorganisation of the provinces in the fourth century AD. These seven centuries saw great changes, not only in the extent of the Empire but also of the way that it was thought of by the Romans, and this in turn altered the way in which the provinces and their administration were regarded. They also, of course, saw major shifts in the structures of the whole state, from an oligarchic Republic to the Augustan Principate, which in turn became an increasingly obvious Monarchy in the years that followed. All this affected provincial administration and the role of Roman law and jurisdiction within it; but the initial impetus came from the military engagement of the Romans with other states outside Italy in the third century BC.

9.2 The Beginnings of Provincial Administration: The Imperial Republic

Given the origins of Rome's Empire in the wars fought against overseas powers in the third and second centuries BC, it is not surprising that it was from these military commands that the beginnings of what became provincial administration arose, and indeed much of the shape and content of the work of the governor of a province in the Republican period, including his juridical responsibilities, can be traced back to this.[1]

9.2.1 The Notion of a *Provincia* in the Third and Second Centuries BC

When used in an administrative context, the English word "province", which clearly derives from the Latin *provincia*, normally relates to a geographical area. However, although *provincia* later came to be used in this way, it did not originally carry this sense in Latin. A *provincia* was a task or responsibility assigned to a specific magistrate or promagistrate, in the fulfilment of which he would exercise the power granted to him in virtue of his election or appointment, which in the case of the higher magistracies (the consuls and the praetors) was his *imperium*. That task might consist of using his *imperium*, the executive power of the Roman people, in a military campaign within a particular geographical area, but this was not always the case. Even with military *provinciae*, the name or description of a *provincia* might not be geographical: the historian Livy several times describes a consul's *provincia* as the leadership of the army or the name of an Italian tribe, and during and after the Hannibalic War he writes of *provinciae* called "the fleet" or "the war against Hannibal".[2] Similarly in the civilian sphere, the praetor in charge of jurisdiction within the city of Rome held the *urbana provincia*. When at the beginning of each consular year the senate named the *provinciae* to be assigned to the various magistrates by lot (*sortitio*)[3] and promagistrates by senatorial decree, what they were doing was more like the allocation of portfolios than putting people in charge of geographical areas.

The significance of this for the understanding of Roman "provincial administration" is considerable. In the third century the naming of an overseas *provincia* by the senate was not the creation of what we might consider as a province of an Empire but the assignment of a military command to fight Rome's enemies in that area. Often, and indeed until the first century BC normally, a *provincia* existed only for as long as the command entrusted to the *imperium*-holder to whom it had been assigned continued. The naming of a *provincia* was not as such an act of annexation of that area to the Empire; annexation, the creation of what we might call a "province", only took place when magistrates and promagistrates were sent out to a particular *provincia* on a regular and continuous basis. It is notable that the Romans had no word for "annexation"; the creation of what is sometimes called a "permanent" *provincia* was simply a variation of the process of assigning military commands. Thus, in the case of Macedonia, it was first assigned as a *provincia* in 211 BC in the course of the Hannibalic War, after King Philip V had made an alliance with Hannibal, but ceased to be so once a treaty ended hostilities there. Through the wars against the kings of Macedonia

[1] For a fuller account of the development of the concepts of Empire and the provinces see Richardson 2008. Barrandon and Kirbihler 2010 and 2011 provide recent surveys of provincial administration under the Republic.

[2] Liv. 3.25.9 (*exercitum ducere*); 6.30.3 (*Volsci*); 27.22.2 (*Sallentini*); 44.1.3 (*classis*); 24.44.1 (*bellum cum Hannibale*).

[3] Consuls could decide which would take which *provincia* by mutual agreement (*comparatio*).

in the first half of the following century, there was again a *provincia Macedonia*, assigned to consular commanders, but there was no permanent *provincia* until 148. This was the first such *provincia* in the eastern Greek-speaking area of the Mediterranean; and indeed the use of continuous permanent *provinciae* began and for nearly a hundred years was only used in the West, where the *provinciae* of Sicily, Sardinia and Corsica were consequences of the first war against the Carthaginians and the two Spanish provinces of Hispania Citerior and Hispania Ulterior, followed the Hannibalic War.

The role of a magistrate or promagistrate in a *provincia* in the second century was essentially that of the commander of Roman troops in the area, and "provincial administration" consisted of overseeing the military and political activities of the Romans in their relations with the indigenous inhabitants, and in particular two spheres of those political relationships: taxation and jurisdiction. In the context of this chapter, it is to the second of these, the origins and development of jurisdiction, that we now turn.

9.2.2 The Origins of Roman Jurisdiction in the Provinces in the Second and First Centuries BC

Although jurisdiction became a major part of the work of a provincial governor in the last two centuries of the Republic, it is important to note that juridical activity was, as we have seen, not the primary role of the holder of a *provincia* in this period, nor indeed was it restricted to such men. The establishment of Rome's power through the Mediterranean led to appeals being made to the senate for the resolution of disputes between non-Roman communities. Thus in the mid-second century the senate authorised a praetor to deal with an appeal from the cities of Priene and Magnesia about a piece of disputed land by appointing a third city, agreeable to both parties, to act as arbitrator; or, if agreement could not be reached, to appoint one himself. The arbitrator's task was to determine which of the two disputants had been in possession of the territory when they entered into friendship (*amicitia*) with the Roman people.[4] Although this is an instance of arbitration rather than jurisdiction, the language used in the instructions to the arbitrator is clearly based on that used in the court of the urban praetor in Rome. This took place when there was no *provincia* in the region concerned, much less a "permanent" one.

Those who were in charge of a *provincia*, both of the permanent or occasional variety, were also involved in making legal decisions, taken on the basis of their own *imperium* rather than on the direct instructions of the senate. In a letter, dated probably to early 190 BC, Manlius Acilius Glabrio, consul in 191, to whom the war against King Antiochus III in Greece had been assigned, wrote to the inhabitants of Delphi, specifying the land that he had given to the god Apollo and to the city, instructing them to ensure that the allocations he had made were not altered thereafter (*SEG* XXVII 123). At almost the same moment, L. Aemilius Paullus, proconsul in charge of the *provincia* of Hispania Ulterior, issued a decree assigning land belonging to the people of the town of Hasta to "the slaves of the Hastenses who lived in the tower of Lascuta" and granting them freedom, "for so long as the people and senate of Rome see fit" (*ILLRP* no. 514). In both cases, these allocations

[4] *RDGE* no. 7. On such arbitrations see Marshall 1980.

were made without reference to the senate, though, as Paullus' decree makes clear, they could be overturned by that body.

These instances illustrate the ways in which Roman *imperium*-holders were, in the course of their military activities, also involved in actions which had legal consequences. They could not, however, be described as systematic; and, although they might, as in the case of arbitrations emanating from the senate, be couched in the legal terminology of Roman law, they did not involve provincial commanders and governors in jurisdiction as such. When that did begin to happen in areas which were repeatedly assigned as *provinciae*, more complex patterns, though bearing some similarities to what had gone before, began to emerge.

9.2.3 The Application of *Ius Civile* and of Local Law within the Provincial Communities

Passing references make it clear that, in the provinces that were regularly provided with holders of *imperium*, jurisdiction was being undertaken by these men in the second half of the second century BC. For instance, L. Calpurnius Piso Frugi, who held the *provincia* of Hispania Ulterior in the late second century and is said to have been so excessively careful in the conduct of his office that, when he wanted a gold ring made for him to replace one that had been broken, he had the gold weighed out in front of his official seat in the forum at Corduba, from which he dispensed justice, and a goldsmith made the ring there in public view (Cic. *Verr.* 2.4.56); and in Sicily the consul of 132 BC, P. Rupilius, who had put down a slave war which ravaged the island, issued a decree which laid down rules for the conduct of legal cases between members of the provincial population, between Romans and Sicilians, and between Romans (Cic. *Verr.* 2.2.32).

The provisions of Rupilius' decree, which Cicero tells us was called the *lex Rupilia* in Sicily, and the implications of Piso Frugi's public demonstration show that the jurisdiction of provincial governors at this time extended not only to Romans in their province but also to the local populations. This variety of litigants raises an important question which relates to the exercise of jurisdiction in the provinces throughout the Republican and well into the Imperial period: what was the law that the governor was applying to settle such cases? So far as disputes between Roman citizens were concerned, the answer is straightforward. The magistrates and promagistrates allocated to the provinces by the senate could use the *ius civile*, the same law as was administered by the urban praetor in Rome; but the rights of the *ius civile* were, as its name implies, available only to *cives Romani*, Roman citizens; and, though there were a considerable number of these resident in the provinces even at an early stage, much of the governor's juridical activity will have involved non-Romans, who were in Roman terms foreigners (*peregrini*), both in disputes with Romans and between themselves, especially when they belonged to different communities within the province. In the *lex Rupilia* provision is made for the governor of Sicily, in cases involving a private individual and a city, to give as judges the senate of another city, each disputant being allowed to reject a suggested body in turn; when a Roman citizen sought redress from a Sicilian, the judge was to be a Sicilian, and when a Sicilian from a Roman, the judge was to be a Roman (Cic. *Verr.* 2.2.32). This sounds similar to the process which the Roman senate employed in the case of the arbitration between Priene and Magnesia mentioned above, but it is not clear what the substantive legal basis on which such cases were to be resolved was to be.

An interesting example from the early first century can be found in the *Tabula Contrebiensis*, inscribed on a bronze tablet dated to 87 BC, which records the case of a water dispute between two peregrine communities in the Ebro valley in northern Spain, the Salluienses and the Allavonenses, about the purchase of land by the former from a third group, the Sosinestani, despite the objections of the latter. The case is embodied on the inscription in a pair of *formulae* such as would be issued by a praetor in Rome, given by the governor in the province, and which appoint the senate of a fourth local community, Contrebia Belaisca, to act of judges. The *formulae* are of considerable legal sophistication (the governor concerned, C. Valerius Flaccus, had been *praetor urbanus* in 96), and include a *fictio* which assumes the existence of the Sosinestani as a *civitas*, a community capable of taking legal decisions. It is by no means clear that the Contrebian judges understood the significance of such sophistication, since the *formulae* presented two separate issues to be decided, but the judgement is presented simply in the form of an agreement with the arguments of the Salluienses. They can be expected, however, to have understood the legal basis of the case, since it is to be judged according to local law as it applied to the Salluienses (*iure suo*) rather than according to Roman law (*iure Quiritium*), as would have been the case if the dispute had been between Roman citizens (Birks et al. 1984). Valerius Flaccus is using the process of the Roman courts to apply the local law of the area in a dispute between peregrine communities. This combination of local law and Roman legal process may well have been the way in which governors operated, using the flexibility that their *imperium* gave them, in other provinces at this early stage.

9.2.4 Limits to the Governor's Jurisdiction and Institutional Constraints on the Governor's Activities

The *imperium*, which was the reason for the allocation of a *provincia* to a particular individual magistrate or promagistrate and was the basis of all his activity including jurisdiction, made its holder effectively independent of control during his tenure of his *provincia*. He was, after all, essentially a military commander, entrusted with a specified task, and as such acted in an untrammelled fashion, especially when any distance from Rome. It was not until he returned to Rome and laid down his *imperium* on his re-entry to the city that he became answerable at law for any misdeeds he might have committed during his governorship, and it was not until 149 BC that a court, the first permanent *quaestio* to be established, was set up, the result of a law proposed by the tribune L. Calpurnius Piso Frugi, the father of the scrupulous governor of Hispania Citerior mentioned above.[5] This court was intended to deal with the recovery of monies improperly taken by holders of *imperium*, hence its name, the *quaestio de repetundis*. The details of the *lex Calpurnia* of 149 are scanty, but it is certain that by the time that the radical tribune Gaius Gracchus passed

[5] Cic. *Brut.* 106; *Verr.* 2.3.195. On the development and activity of the *quaestio de repetundis* see Lintott 1993, 98–107.

a similar law in 123, the court gave access to non-Romans in the provinces to a means of prosecuting former governors for wrongful use of their powers. Despite the political wrangles during the decades that followed, particularly over the composition of the jury which, under the presidency of a praetor, heard such cases, this *quaestio* became the main and the only formal way in which non-Roman provincials could seek recompense for misgovernment and the disgrace of an offending governor. The dictator Lucius Sulla seems to have expanded the areas covered by the law, and Julius Caesar in his consulship in 59 BC went still further, incorporating requirements from earlier laws forbidding governors from leaving their provinces except for reasons of state, specifying limits on the gifts that a governor could receive from the province and requiring every governor and his financial officer, the quaestor, to deposit a copy of their accounts in two cities in the province and another in the treasury in Rome (Cic. *Pis.* 50, 61 and 90; *Att.* 6.7.2; *Fam.* 5.20.2).

In the area of jurisdiction there were other institutional limits to the freedom that the governor enjoyed. Cicero, in a letter he wrote to his brother Quintus while the latter held the rich province of Asia in late 60 or early 59 BC, emphasised the lack of restrictions on a governor compared to an urban praetor and recommended courtesy and fairness in his juridical role (Cic. *Q. Fr.* 1.1.22), but this did not mean that he had a completely free hand. It used to be believed that each province had a statute of its own, known as the *lex provinciae*, which laid down the basic patterns by which the governor had to abide. It is now generally agreed that, although such *leges provinciae* existed for some provinces, they were usually decrees issued by individual commanders, subsequently ratified by the senate, and certainly not a law passed by the Roman popular assemblies (Lintott 1993, 28–32). The *lex Rupilia* in Sicily was one such, and some others are known; but there is no indication that these were a requisite part of the structure of a province (Rupilius' decree was made nearly a century after Sicily became a *provincia*) nor that they existed for all provinces.[6] Where there was such a *lex*, however, this would act as a constraint on the governor's jurisdiction.

The provincial governor was also constrained by the edict he himself had issued before leaving Rome to go to his province, which set out the matters on which he was prepared to hear cases and the principles on which he would make his judgements, in the same fashion as did the *praetor urbanus* and the *praetor peregrinus* in Rome. The best evidence for a provincial edict under the Republic comes from a famous letter of Cicero to his friend Atticus, written while he was governor in Cilicia in 51 BC (Cic. *Att.* 6.1.15). It appears that Cicero, like other governors, constructed his edict as he himself saw fit, rather than using a standard form taken over from his previous governors, which in Cicero's case led to an acrimonious correspondence with his predecessor. In this respect, as in others, the governor had more freedom than the praetors in Rome.

9.2.5 Provincial Jurisdiction in Practice

The governor was therefore the source of access to Roman jurisdiction within his province, and it appears that by the first century BC much of his time was taken up with this.

[6] For a recent discussion of a possible *lex provinciae* in the province of Asia see Coudry and Kirbihler 2010.

Cicero's correspondence while he was proconsul in Cilicia in 51–50 BC shows that jurisdiction took up much of his attention, and even Julius Caesar, in the midst of his military campaigns against the Gauls through the 50s BC, crossed the Alps at the end of each season to hear cases in Illyricum and Cisalpine Gaul.[7] Already in the Republican period, at least in more settled areas, a pattern had emerged of governors travelling to various parts of the province for the purpose of hearing cases, a process which, as appears from Cicero's experience, was arranged by the governor himself. To some extent he could delegate this responsibility to members of his staff; but, given that the juridical authority exercised by the governor was largely vested in himself, it was inevitable that much the greater part of work involved was done by him. In practice, governors seem to have left much jurisdiction in civil cases which involved the members of one community in the hands of that community, and this is what in Sicily was prescribed by the *lex Rupilia*; though they could intervene at any time, Cicero, writing in 50 BC from his province to his friend Atticus, reports with a certain smug self-satisfaction that he has allowed the Greek cities to use their own laws and law courts (Cic. *Att.* 6.2.4). In cases where such intervention took place, it seems to have been structured in terms of the processes of Roman law, even when the substantive law was not Roman, as can be seen in case of the dispute recorded in the *Tabula Contrebiensis* (section 9.2.3).

9.3 The Empire and the Provinces in the First Three Centuries AD: The Augustan Empire and After

The ending of the Civil War between Mark Anthony and Julius Caesar's son by adoption (soon to be called Augustus) following the battle of Actium in 31 BC led to the establishment of Augustus as the sole ruler of the Roman world, and thus to changes throughout the Empire. It is notable that the meeting of the senate in January 27 BC at which Augustus was given his new name was largely concerned with the allocation of the provinces that were henceforth to be divided into two groups: those in which substantial military forces were stationed were assigned to the emperor and known as "Caesar's", while the remainder were to be allocated by the senate and called the provinces of "the people" (Dio Cass. 53.12; Suet. *Aug.* 47; Strabo 17.3). The governors of both categories of province were to be former magistrates, either consuls or praetors, depending on the size and significance of the province, but while those in charge of the people's provinces were to be called proconsuls and to hold *imperium* in the same way as had their predecessors under the Republic, in Caesar's provinces the governors were to be *legati Augusti pro praetore*, and to function as subordinates of the emperor himself. In some areas (most importantly Egypt) the emperor appointed non-senators as *praefecti* (prefects) or as *procuratores*, a title which derived from the civil-law term for an agent. As with so many of the alterations that took place as a consequence of the change from the Republic to what was in effect a Monarchy,

[7] Caes. *B Gall.* 1.54.3; 5.1.5; 5.2.1; 6.44.3. See Marshall 1966.

the activities of the governors in the provinces were in many ways the same as they had been in the period immediately before, or at least were clearly developed from them, and this particularly applies to the juridical work of such men. The context in which they took place, however, was different, and this affected the mindset of those involved, both the governors and the governed. Among Romans the very notion of what a *provincia* was had changed: although the word was still used to describe the task allocated to a holder of *imperium*, it was used more frequently as the name of a piece of territory under Roman control, as a part of the Roman Empire; and indeed it was in the Augustan period that the Empire itself began to be referred to as the *Imperium Romanum* (Richardson 2008, 117–141). The existence of an emperor seems to have consolidated the notion of Empire.

9.3.1 The Role of the Emperor and the *Imperium*-Holders in Juridical Matters

The new structure of the provinces affected the formal context in which jurisdiction was conducted. In the people's provinces the governors functioned much as they had under the Republic and were able to delegate juridical work to *legati* as their predecessors had; but in Caesar's provinces the *legati Augusti* were themselves delegates of the emperor and thus incapable of further delegation. In some cases we hear of Imperial appointments of *legati iuridici*, made by the emperor himself in his provinces, such as Hispania Tarraconensis and Britannia. This was also the case in Egypt, where the *praefectus Aegypti* was assisted by a *iuridicus*, an official drawn from the equestrian order.[8] There also developed a parallel jurisdiction undertaken by other *procuratores* of the emperor, who were not in charge of provinces but who were responsible for the collection of taxes in the provinces of the emperor and for the management of Imperial estates. These men are recorded as conducting trials concerning public finances and with having local jurisdiction in the case of Imperial properties, and this power was formally established in 53 AD when the Emperor Claudius secured from the senate a decree to this effect (Tac. *Ann.* 12.60; see Brunt 1990, 163–187). Despite the variety of official status, these governors seem to have functioned in similar ways, and the use of major cities (*conventus*) in various parts of the province as centres for the hearing of cases became more systematic.

One limitation on the freedom of governors came about in the reign of Hadrian, when, perhaps in 131 AD, the edict of the urban praetor was standardised and made permanent by a decree of the senate, following a revision carried out by the jurist Salvius Iulianus on the emperor's instructions.[9] The edicts of other juridical magistrates, including provincial governors, were also standardised. Some twenty years later the jurist Gaius wrote a commentary on the provincial edict in thirty books, which is cited 339 times in the Digest. The content of those citations show that much of the provincial edict was the same as

[8] On *iuridici* in Tarraconensis see Alföldy 1969, 23–259; for instances in Britain see *ILS* 1011, 1015, 1123 and 1151; and for Egypt see Strabo 17.1.12 and Ulpian D.1.20, and for instances, *ILS* 1434, 1452 and 2691.

[9] C. *Tanta-Δέδωκεν* 18. The date depends on a note in Jerome, *Chron.* On Iulianus see Tuori 2007, 135–180; Bauman 1989, 235–263. Bauman argues against Jerome's dating and places the edictal reform earlier (258–260).

that of the urban praetor (hence the frequent citations in the Digest), though it must have covered other issues that would have been relevant only in a provincial setting (Lenel 1927, 4–6). This standardisation effectively removed the ability of governors to determine for themselves the cases that they intended to deal with, though it is unclear how far this was a major practical change; it may be that in practice much of the material which went into the edicts of provincial governors was by this date already on a regularly repeated pattern. That there was a considerable uniformity in the work of governors is also indicated by the appearance in the early third century of Ulpian's *De officio proconsulis*, which in ten books provided guidelines and legal material for governors of the public provinces.[10]

The greatest change from the Republican period came about through the very existence of the emperor as an overriding source of authority. Thus a series of five edicts issued by Augustus between 7 or 6 and 4 BC and surviving on an inscription from Cyrene not only dealt with the particular case of an individual sent to the emperor by the governor of the province, on the grounds that Augustus' own security might be involved, but also rules for the composition of juries in disputes delegated by the governor, and a decree of the senate, giving an alternative procedure for cases that might otherwise have been dealt with by the *quaestio de repetundis* (*SEG* IX 8). All this, it is to be noted, related to one of the people's provinces; the emperor's writ ran throughout the Empire, and was not confined to Caesar's provinces only. It was to the emperor that appeals were made, even when the governor was not involved: in 6 BC the free city of Cnidos sent an embassy to Augustus to present an accusation concerning the alleged murder of one of its citizens by another and his wife, since the accused man was dead and his widow was resident in Rome, in response to which the emperor appointed one of his "friends" (*amici*), Asinius Gallus, to investigate the matter. When Gallus concluded that the accused had suffered from harassment from the dead man and were innocent of his murder, Augustus ordered that this verdict should be entered in the public records of the city of Cnidos (*RDGE* no. 67). This was not an appeal as such as there was no prior judgement by a Roman official, but it illustrates the way in which even from the beginning of the Imperial period the emperor acted in a judicial capacity when cases were referred to him from those in the provinces.

9.3.2 Local Law and Roman Law in the Provinces

The development of provincial jurisdiction came about not only from the changes within Rome and the higher structures of the Empire, but also as a result of the interaction between governors, whether proconsuls or *legati Augusti*, and the provincial communities. These latter were, of course, as varied as the provinces in which they were situated, and the differing local legal contexts resulted in a wide range of different patterns; but in one case in particular the consequences of a decision by a Roman emperor to standardise the status of a number of peregrine communities in Spain provide the clearest picture of the way in which local jurisdiction was practiced in a Roman province in the early Imperial period.

The Emperor Vespasian, probably in 73–74 AD, granted to many Spanish communities the Latin right (*ius Latii*), and several epigraphic charters set up by these communities,

[10] Schulz 1946, 138, 243–246; Honoré 2002, 181–184, 227–228.

which as a result became *municipia Latina*, have survived (Richardson 1996, 188–210). They follow a standard form and seem to be based on a uniform model, lightly adapted for the individual communities to which they were granted. The most complete, discovered in 1981, relates to the hitherto unknown town of Irni, or, as it now became, the *municipium Flavium Irnitanum*, which received its charter in the reign of Domitian in or shortly after 91 AD.[11] The document presents details on the ordering of the life of the *municipium*, its council of sixty-three *decuriones* and its magistrates, of whom the most important were two *duoviri*. A long section just before the end (chs. 84 to 93) provides for the jurisdiction that may be undertaken by the officials of the *municipium*.

The scope of the jurisdiction of the municipal magistrates was limited, and cases which fell outside their remit were to be referred to the provincial governor, unless both parties to the dispute agreed that they might be heard locally.[12] In any case, the conduct of all cases took place in the context of the overall juridical oversight of the governor. The edict which the governor issued on his entry into his province about legal matters was to be posted, written on a whitened board, at a place in the *municipium* from which it could be read with ease (*lex Irn.* ch. 85). Nonetheless, within that general context, the *duoviri* had a considerable amount of juridical work to do. In all these matters, however, the local magistrates were enjoined to do everything as it would be done in a similar case tried in Rome; that is to say, in the court of the urban praetor. Most remarkable of all, the section on local jurisdiction ends with a catch-all clause, which states that for all matters about which members of the *municipium* shall go to law with one another and which are not specifically dealt with in the provisions of the statute, they should proceed as though the process were being carried on under Roman law and between Roman citizens (*lex Irn.* ch. 93; Johnston 1987, 63). What the local magistrates are doing is applying the provisions of Roman private law to the members of the *municipium*, the majority of whom are not Roman citizens at all, but Latins; that is to say; *peregrini*.

The evidence of the *lex Irnitana* is, of course, about what the Romans intended should happen in the Latin *municipia* in Spain, not what actually did happen. The picture it gives is, however, coherent with that which emerges from the other material already examined. The governor has overall supervision of the judicial process in the *muncipium* and justice is to be administered there according to the terms of the governor's edict; but he is only directly involved when the matter concerned is sufficiently important to merit it. There is however a fundamental difference between what was to happen at Irni and the activity of Valerius Flaccus or Cicero. In the earlier period the law that the local communities applied under the supervision of the Republican governors was the local law of the communities themselves. In the *lex Irnitana* the law to be applied was that which Roman citizens used under the *ius civile* (*lex Irn.* ch. 93). The change here is one of substantive law rather than of legal process: both the parties involved in the case recorded on the *Tabula Contrebiensis* and the Latin citizens of Irni had their disputes settled through processes which were essentially Roman in character. It is true that in neither case was the substantive law properly speaking Roman: the citizens of Irni were not for the most part *cives Romani*, and thus

[11] For the text, an English translation by Michael Crawford and a brief commentary see González 1986.

[12] *Lex Irn.* ch. 84. For the rules on reference to the governor see Burton 1996.

could not avail themselves of the *ius civile*. The careful wording of the "catch-all" clause makes clear that the Irnitani, though they were not *cives Romani* and their legal actions were under the *ius* of their own *muncipium*, were to act as though the *ius civile* applied to them. In effect, the change that has taken place is the suppression of whatever laws the community at Irni used before it became a Latin *municipium* and their replacement by another set of laws which was, so to speak, a mirage of the *ius civile*.

It must be said that the contrast between the *Tabula Contrebiensis* and the *lex Irnitana* presents almost too clear a shift towards the establishment of Roman law in the provinces. In other parts of the Empire, particularly in Egypt and the Hellenised provinces of the eastern Mediterranean, the substantive law of the local cities (or, in the case of Egypt, of the Greek and Egyptian law that had been in place in the period of the Ptolemaic kings down to 31 BC) remained in place alongside the Roman.[13] It is probable, however, that even here the drift was towards increasing use of Roman legal patterns, if only because the oversight of jurisdiction was the business of the Roman governor and, beyond him, of the emperor and his legal advisers. Even when attempts were made to retain the laws of an area, the decisions were made by men trained in Roman law.[14] The spread of Roman citizenship will also have promoted the use of Roman citizen-law, though there is evidence even after the declaration by the Emperor Caracalla in 212 AD that all free persons in the Empire were to be Roman citizens that elements of local law continued to be used, especially in Egypt.[15]

9.4 Conclusion

As we have seen, the administration of the provinces of what became the Roman Empire changed and developed as a result of shifts in the idea of what a *provincia* was; and the ways in which jurisdiction was carried out, which depended both on the governor during the Republic and on the emperor and the governor in the Imperial period and on the nature of the particular provinces themselves, was not a uniform system. Under the emperors there were moves toward more centralisation, such as Hadrian's standardisation of the provincial edict, and this increased to a considerable extent in the late third and early fourth centuries AD. Diocletian, who seized the Imperial power in 284 AD and with his co-emperor from 286, Maximian, controlled the Empire for the next three decades, radically reshaped the provinces, making them smaller and grouping them for fiscal purposes into twelve dioceses (Wilkes 2006). Though the reshaping of provinces seems to have taken place in an ad hoc rather than a systematic fashion, the result was that the governors' work was confined to civil rather than military responsibilities, and in particular to juridical matters and in a much smaller area than before. Appeals were still (and even more frequently) made to the emperors, and it was under Diocletian that collections

[13] Lintott 1993, 154–160. The classic case for the survival of local law was made by Mitteis 1891. See also Ando, ch. 22.

[14] For an example of the problems facing a governor and an emperor in attempting to reconcile different legal solutions to a situation occurring in different areas with different laws see Plin. *Ep.* 10.65–66.

[15] Briefly summarised by Lintott 1993, 157–158.

of Imperial communications to provincial governors, known as "rescripts", were put together under the title *Codex* by two officials, Gregorius (who collected rescripts from the time of Hadrian down to 291 AD) and Hermogenian (who twice updated the collection down to 295 and again to 298). These were clearly intended to provide governors with access to legal decisions which did not apply only to the province whose governor first received them but were to be relevant across the Empire.[16]

These changes originated from Diocletian's determination to reduce the danger from governors with military resources who might present a threat to the emperor, as indeed they had frequently done during the past century. This is one more example of the relationship between the military objectives of the central authorities at Rome and the nature of the provinces, and between the nature of the provinces and the way in which jurisdiction was undertaken there. Given this chain of causation which recurs regularly through the history of the administration of the Empire, it is hardly surprising that from the beginning provincial jurisdiction was not so much a system as a varying kaleidoscope of different elements, changing from period to period and from area to area. It is notable too that from the beginning it was not the substantive law of Rome which was applied, at least to those who were not Roman citizens, but rather the procedural patterns which the governors brought with them from their experience of Roman courts. Even in such an evidently Roman context as the charter issued to Irni at the end of the first century AD, the default position for cases not specifically covered by the charter is not that they should be dealt with under Roman law but in the same way as would be dealt with under Roman law: the *ius civile*, the rights of the Roman citizen, were not available even though the processes of the Roman courts were enjoined (section 9.3.2). The gradual absorption of Roman practice and, with the extension of Roman citizenship across the Empire, of the applicability of Roman law altered this imbalance, though even the extraordinary decree of Caracalla in 212 AD did not remove entirely the use of already existing local law. The very fact that it took four centuries and the remarkable and unprecedented incorporation of the free population of a vast area into the citizenship of the single city of Rome reveals clearly enough that the imposition of Roman law on the subjects of the Empire was not a policy of Roman Imperialism; the exercise of jurisdiction, like so much of Roman administration of the provinces, was rather a necessary tool for the control of the populations which Romans brought under their power, their *imperium*, and which became their Empire, *Imperium Romanum*.

Bibliography

Alföldy, G. 1969. Fasti Hispanienses: *senatorische reichsbeamte und offiziere in den Spanischen Provinzen des Römischen Reiches von Augustus bis Diokletian*. Wiesbaden.

Barrandon, N. and F. Kirbihler, eds. 2010. *Administrer les provinces de la République romaine*. Rennes.

[16] On the rescripts of the Diocletianic period and the role of the governors see Corcoran 2002, 234–253.

Barrandon, N. and F. Kirbihler, eds. 2011. *Les gouverneurs et les provinciaux sous la République romaine*. Rennes.

Bauman, R. A. 1989. *Lawyers and politics in the early Roman empire: a study of relations between the Roman jurists and the emperors from Augustus to Hadrian*. Munich.

Birks, P. B. H., Rodger, A. and Richardson, J. S. (1984). "Further aspects of the *Tabula Contrebiensis*." *Journal of Roman Studies* 74: 45–73.

Brunt, P. A. 1990. *Roman imperial themes*. Oxford.

Burton, G. P. (1996). "The *lex Irnitana*, ch. 84, the promise of *vadimonium* and the jurisdiction of proconsuls." *Classical Quarterly* 46: 217–221.

Corcoran, S. 2002[2]. *The empire of the tetrarchs: imperial pronouncements and government, AD 284–324*. Oxford.

Coudry, M. and Kirbihler, F. 2010. "La *lex Cornelia*, une *lex provinciae* de Sylla pour l'Asie." In N. Barrandon and F. Kirbihler, eds., *Administrer les provinces de la République romaine*. Rennes. 133–169.

González, J. (1986). "The *lex Irnitana*: a new Flavian municipal law." *Journal of Roman Studies* 76: 147–243.

Honoré, T. 2002. *Ulpian, pioneer of human rights*. Revised edition. Oxford.

Johnston, D. (1987). "Three thoughts on Roman private law and the *lex Irnitana*." *Journal of Roman Studies* 77: 62–77.

Lenel, O. 1927[3]. *Das* Edictum Perpetuum: *ein Versuch zu seiner Wiederherstellung*. Leipzig.

Lintott, A. 1993. Imperium Romanum: *politics and administration*. New York.

Marshall, A. J. (1966). "Governors on the move." *Phoenix* 20: 231–246.

Marshall, A. J. (1980). "The survival and development of international jurisdiction in the Greek world." *Aufstieg und Niedergang der römischen Welt* II.13: 620–661.

Mitteis, L. 1891. *Reichsrecht und Volksrecht in den östlichen Provinzen des römischen Kaiserreichs: mit Beiträgen zur Kenntniss des griechischen Rechts und der spätrömischen Rechtsentwicklung*. Leipzig.

Richardson, J. S. 1996. *The Romans in Spain*. Oxford.

Richardson, J. S. 2008. *The language of Empire: Rome and the idea of empire from the third century BC to the second century AD*. Cambridge.

Schulz, F. 1946. *History of Roman legal science*. Oxford.

Tuori, K. 2007. *Ancient Roman lawyers and modern legal ideals: studies in the impact of contemporary concerns in the interpretation of ancient Roman legal history*. Frankfurt am Main.

Wilkes, J. J. 2006. "Provincial reorganisation." In A. K. Bowman, P. Garnsey and A. Cameron, eds., *Cambridge ancient history*. Cambridge. Vol. 12: 212–264.

CHAPTER 10

LOCAL ADMINISTRATION

SASKIA T. ROSELAAR

10.1 Introduction

Local communities held an essential position in the government of the Roman Empire: most of the daily business of governing was left in the hands of magistrates of the local communities, who, as we shall see, held extensive responsibilities. For most people, the *civitas* in which they were born—which could be a town and its territory, or a group of rural communities—determined their political rights. The settlement in which they lived was the focus of their daily lives (Eck 1997, 122–123). Mobility and migration were common in the Roman Empire, leading to questions about the position of resident foreigners in these communities. Furthermore, local communities were essential in the economy of the Roman Empire: not only did towns function as markets, but they were also important property owners.

This chapter will discuss, firstly, the structure of local administration and local responsibilities with regard to jurisdiction. Secondly, it will discuss the economic assets and responsibilities of communities. Finally, we will explore the position of resident foreigners. Despite the fact that the general structures of local government are well known, there are still many uncertainties regarding the details of local administration. This chapter will indicate the main points of what we think we know, but also point to issues to be explored further in the future.

10.2 Local Government Structures

10.2.1 Legal Status

Many variations existed in the relationship of local communities to central government. Basically, they could belong to one of six categories: native (*peregrinus*) city; *municipium* with minor Latin rights; *municipium* with *ius Latii maius; municipium* of Roman citizens; Roman citizen colony; and Roman citizen colony with *ius Italicum*. The government structures varied according to the legal status of a community: peregrine towns retained their own local structures; *municipia* could do the same,[1] but many had laws based on the Roman model; *coloniae* followed Roman law (Reynolds 1988, 23–24). The difference between *municipia* and colonies gradually disappeared; indeed the laws of the *municipium* Irni and the *colonia* Urso are quite similar.[2] Even peregrine communities could voluntarily adopt many Roman institutions. Here we will examine only those communities based on the Roman model, since this was the predominant way in which communities throughout the Empire were governed. The status of a town could be changed by the favour of the emperor as a mark of honour; Hadrian, for example, granted at least eleven towns the status of colony and made twenty-one into *municipia*. Being granted the title of *municipium* or *colonia* was a great honour;[3] the title became a fixed part of the community's name and was therefore recorded in public inscriptions, in order to advertise the favour of the emperor.

The basic institutions of local government are reasonably well known, especially from five epigraphic charters: the *lex Coloniae Genetivae Iuliae* (also known as the *lex Ursonensis*) and *Tabula Heracleensis*, dated to 44 BC, and the *leges Salpensana, Malacitana* and *Irnitana*, all dating from the Flavian period.[4] Most of the evidence from the Flavian period comes from Hispania, but a fragment from Lauriacum in Noricum, dating to 212–217 AD, has the same chapter 25 as the Flavian laws; a fragment from Troesmis in Moesia Inferior (dated 177–180) also shows remarkable similarities.[5] Further similar fragments come from the *lex Villonensis* found near Sevilla, and from Duratón and Italica.[6] This suggests that the same model was in use for more than a century and across many parts of the Empire. Nevertheless, the Flavian laws vary on minor details; a "template" was found that contained blank spaces in which figures could be filled out, e.g. fines applied to certain infractions (Fernández Gómez 1991).

It has been argued that local administrators voluntarily chose to adopt Roman institutions and laws, but if this were the case one would expect much more variety in local institutions; the fact that the epigraphic laws are so similar suggests that Rome provided models for how local governments should be set up. Nevertheless, local magistracies and laws display considerable flexibility, and local variations clearly remained, so that a strictly formalistic approach is unwise.

[1] Cic. *Fam.* 13.11.3 records, for example, that the *municipium* Arpinum still had three aediles, instead of *duoviri*, as its highest magistrates.

[2] The exact nature of the Latin and Roman status of towns is complex. *Ius Latii* and municipal status did not always go together: according to Plin. *HN* 3.30 all Hispanic towns received *ius Latii* from Vespasian, but not all became *municipia*; see Galsterer 1971, 38–39, 47–48; Langhammer 1973, 7–16; García Fernández 1995, 152. The rights held by the inhabitants of communities have been debated; it has been assumed that cities as a whole (i.e. all their inhabitants) enjoyed Latin status, but it is also possible that this status only pertained to individuals; see García Fernández 1995.

[3] Gell. *NA* 16.13.1–9; SHA *Hadr.* 21.7. See Boatwright 2000, 172. For other honorific titles and names of towns, especially those derived from the emperors' names, see Galsterer-Kröll 1972; peregrine towns clearly had different honorifics than *municipia* or *coloniae*, but between the latter two there was little difference.

[4] More Republican fragments come from the *fragmentum Atestinum*, from Este in northern Italy (datable to 67 or 49 BC), and the *lex Rubria*, dated *c.*43 BC, concerning the government of Cisalpine Gaul.

[5] The Troesmis law is more detailed than other laws; see Eck 2013, 211–212.

[6] For the Spanish laws see González 1986, 242–243; Ortiz de Urbina 2013. Already in the Republic, laws were apparently created by the state for the use of towns; a secondary founder of the colony Aquileia "composed and gave laws" (*legesq(ue) composivit deditque*) in 169 BC (*AE* 1996, 685).

10.2.2 Magistrates

The Flavian laws describe the election of local magistrates and their duties in much detail. Most towns were governed by two chief magistrates, usually called *duoviri*, supported by aediles and sometimes quaestors. These men were elected by the assembly of adult male citizens of the town. Government in Rome was clearly the model for local processes: the population was divided into voting *curiae*, and the candidates with the most *curiae* behind them were elected. There were strict requirements for potential magistrates: they must be of good moral standing, without public debts, and have an honourable profession;[7] to avoid financial problems they had to name guarantors and provide securities (*lex Malac.* 59–60, 64–65; *lex Irn.* 60; see Curchin 1990, 27–29). When entering office, a *summa honoraria* was usually required; in Italy and the Spanish laws it was between 2,000 and 4,000 HS, but in Carthage 38,000 HS.[8]

The most important task of the *duoviri* was local jurisdiction—their title was usually expressly given as *duoviri i(ure) d(icundo)*. Their other tasks included presiding over elections and meetings of the local council and popular assembly; approving the manumission of slaves and appointing guardians; celebrating games and dramatic performances; arming and commanding the people; leasing out the collection of taxes and revenues; witnessing wills, et cetera.

Some debate has been caused by the fact that in some towns the highest magistrates were not called *duoviri*, but had another title. Most often we encounter *quattuorviri*, sometimes also with the qualification *i(ure) d(icundo)*. Some scholars have argued that colonies had *duoviri* and *municipia* had *quattuorviri*, or that the title *quattuorviri* was only used before a certain date. However, in Hispania most *municipia* had *duoviri* and a change over time cannot be detected. In some places both *duoviri* and *quattuorviri* are attested. The most likely solution is that, since the both *duoviri* and aediles had local jurisdiction, the term *quattuorviri (iure dicundo)* includes both *duoviri* and aediles; if the *duoviri* and aediles acted in concert, they were termed *quattuorviri*, whereas the *duoviri* on their own were indicated with the term *duoviri*.[9] Other unusual terms for local magistrates sometimes appear: *principes* are attested in second-century Hispania, while censors are known from Hispania and Bithynia in the same period (Curchin 1990, 37–40; Edmondson 2009). Even in Italy unusual titles remained, e.g. the dictator at Caere (*CIL* XI 3615). Some influence from pre-Roman institutions may have been visible: Mactar was ruled by three *sufetes* in the mid-first century AD, and by *tresviri* after it became a *municipium* (*CIL* VIII

[7] *Lex Malac.* 54; *lex Urs.* 105; *Tab. Her.* 25. See Langhammer 1973, 44–45. Usually a minimum age applied, which varied locally and could be ignored: in *lex Malac.* 54 it was 25 years; in Barcino there were 17-year-old aediles, and in the East many children were attested as magistrates (Mackie 1983, 82–83; Curchin 1990, 27, 71; Dmitriev 2005, 16–174).

[8] *Lex Urs.* 70 states that 2,000 HS should be spent by *duoviri* and aediles on gladiatorial shows or dramatic spectacles. Sometimes the difference between paying a *summa honoraria* and buying a magistracy is unclear; in Barcino offices were sold to outsiders, see Curchin 1990, 107–111. In the East, female and child benefactors were often rewarded with honorary magistrates, but this type of "payment" is not a *summa honoraria*.

[9] Galsterer 1971, 58; Curchin 1990, 33–34. Some exceptions to this rule are attested, however.

630 = 11827; VIII 23599). Some influence from Punic administration may have occurred in both Hispania as well.

Being a *duovir* brought considerable prestige and status symbols such as the *toga praetexta*, the *fasces*, two lictors and several assistants (*apparitores*). They got the best seats in the theatre and were exempt from *munera* (local duties, e.g. providing public services) during their term of office.[10] Sometimes the office was held as an honorary position by the emperor or other prominent person; in this case a local replacement (*praefectus*) carried out the actual duties.[11] Thus the office not only brought prestige to its incumbents, but also served to communicate the loyalty of the town to Rome and display the status of the town as a worthy participant in the Roman Empire.

The aediles dealt mainly with public works; they kept the streets in order, maintained public buildings, prevented violence, supervised the market, weights and measures and looked after the *vigiliae* (night watches).[12] Quaestors were charged with collecting, guarding and spending public funds, directed by the *duoviri*. In some towns they were responsible for minting coins; in the East, where local coin production continued longer than in the West, special magistrates were entrusted with this task (*lex Irn.* 20; see Mackie 1983, 59–60; Curchin 1990, 63). There were no essential differences between administration in the East and in the West; all Eastern towns had a *demos* (assembly) and *boulē* (council), but there was a larger variety of magistrates on the lower levels than in the West (Dmitriev 2005; Fuhrmann 2012).

It has been debated whether there was a strict local *cursus honorum*; usually one progressed from quaestor to aedile to *duovir*, although one of these steps could be skipped. Often the quaestorship is not mentioned at all; either it did not exist in some towns, or did not deserve mention on the epitaphs of men who had already been aedile or *duovir*.[13] However, like other magistrates, quaestors fulfilled an essential task in local government, and holding this office would have been a source of prestige for the few men in each town who occupied it; in the East, epitaphs usually mention all offices held, including those on lower levels.

It is often suggested that local office became increasingly unpopular, since it required large outlays of money in *summae honorariae*, *munera* and gifts to the population (Garnsey 1974). The *lex Malacitana* indeed provides instructions for how to elect magistrates if not enough people volunteer.[14] However, there is no reason to assume that Malaca, or any other town, experienced problems with recruiting magistrates (Garnsey 1974, 231; *contra* Galsterer 2000, 356); more likely it simply wanted to ensure that if the situation arose, it could be resolved. Nevertheless, many magistrates tried to get exemption from *munera*; for example, in 125 AD the council of Oinoanda asked the governor for a five-year exemption

[10] *Lex Urs.* 62, 125; *lex Irn.* 81. See Langhammer 1973, 62–149; Reynolds 1988, 31–33; Boatwright 2000, 44–46.

[11] *Lex Salp.* 25; *lex Irn.* 24–25. See Mackie 1983, 61–62; Curchin 1990, 34–35.

[12] *Lex Urs.* 71. See Langhammer 1973, 149–156; Reynolds 1988, 31–33.

[13] Galsterer 1971, 56; Langhammer 1973, 157–161; Curchin 1990, 29–33.

[14] *Lex Malac.* 51. The Troesmis fragment discusses the election of men to embassies, ensuring that every man took up this burdensome task; cf. D.50.7.5.5. See Garnsey 1974, 232–235.

from duties for the president of a festival.[15] However, at least until the late second century AD there is no evidence of systematic difficulty in filling local offices.[16]

Towns often approached the governor or emperor, e.g. to ask advice in a dispute with another town or in case of financial difficulties.[17] Many of these problems could easily have been solved by the cities themselves; the tendency to ask Imperial advice has often been considered an erosion of civic autonomy. Indeed, there seems to have been a development towards more direct interference; from the time of Domitian *correctores* or *curatores rei publicae* were occasionally appointed by the emperor to take charge in towns. However, their aim was not to limit the self-governing powers of the communities, but only to help out in emergency cases, at the request of the communities themselves; they restored the towns' ability to govern themselves when economic or social problems had made this impossible.[18]

Direct interference in local affairs was in fact rare; it mostly concerned *munera*, pressuring people to perform them or granting exemptions (Aelius Aristides, *Or.* 50; see Eck 1997, 125). The emperor preferred to let local government take its course, and most communities sorted out their problems themselves.[19] The government needed towns to do their job, and for the most part they did. It seems as if there was more chaos and violence in local affairs in the East than in the West, but this may be due to the fact that most of our sources refer to the East. In the West we do not have evidence for large-scale problems until the fourth century AD. Nevertheless, requests for arbitration created precedent; receiving personal attention from the emperor brought prestige, and a judgement of the emperor in a dispute could not easily be overthrown (Eck 1997, 111), so that towns became increasingly eager to approach him.

10.2.3 Town Council

The second main part of local government was the town council (*curia* or *ordo decurionum*), whose members were in function for life. The way the members were selected is not clear. Either they were selected from the ex-magistrates by the *duoviri quinquennales*, who were elected every five years to hold the census and revise the local council,[20] or alternatively, all ex-magistrates may have become members, possibly with some elected by cooption if there were not enough former magistrates.[21] It is likely that both occurred; if the number

[15] *SEG* XXXVIII 1462. Aelius Aristides often tried to get out of office holding, Burton 2001, 204–207.

[16] D.50.1.38.6. See Garnsey 1974; Reynolds 1988, 45–46; Boatwright 2000, 9–11.

[17] See Plin. *Ep.* 10.37–40. According to *lex Irn.* 80 the governor had to approve loans contracted by towns valued at over 50,000 HS per year. See Nollé 1999; Boatwright 2000, 78–80. Burton 2000 lists all epigraphically attested boundary disputes.

[18] Eck 1979, 195–205; 1997, 127–131; Jacques 1984; Boatwright 2000, 75–77. They may have appeared already in Nero's time, see Eck 1979, 191–193; Dmitriev 2005, 189–197.

[19] Reynolds 1988, 43–46; Burton 2001, 212–213; Ando 2006, 182.

[20] *Lex Urs.* 105, 124. See Shaw 1988, 811–812; Curchin 1990, 26–27, 61; Brunt 1990b.

[21] *Lex Urs.* 17 suggests that they were coopted by the existing council. *Lex Irn.* 31 states that councillors should be elected whenever there are fewer than sixty-three in office. *Tab. Her.* 22 states that when a councillor dies or is condemned, a replacement can be chosen by the *duoviri*. See Curchin 1990, 22–27.

of councillors was too low, the town could not wait for five years to receive new *decuriones*. *Adlectio* of unqualified persons, e.g. non-residents, could happen by vote of the decurions or through the emperor's patronage (Mackie 1983, 55, 79).

A councillor had to be a freeborn citizen of the town, of a minimum age and wealth; the specific criteria varied per town.[22] He had to be of good moral standing, with an honourable profession, without debts or criminal convictions. A fee was usually paid on entering the council; in Bithynia this varied between 4,000 and 8,000 HS. The number of councillors varied per town: *ordines* in Italy, Africa and the Western provinces usually consisted of fifty to a hundred members, but in the East and Africa senates could be much larger, e.g. six hundred at Tiberias and Massilia (Ausbüttel 1998, 43–44). Being a member of the council brought with it specific *munera*, but it also had advantages: decurions were exempt from physical punishment and could not be sent to the mines or be executed for homicide, and governors had to seek confirmation from the emperor for sentences of relegation imposed on decurions.[23]

The town council made decisions regarding virtually all public business: it approved public buildings, repair works, and demolition, received accounts of public business and decided on the sale, expenditure and loans of public funds and property. It set the dates for festivals and sacrifices, appointed *magistri fanorum, seviri Augustales*, ambassadors, patrons and *hospites*. It allotted seats in the theatre, called up armed men for emergencies, acted as appeal court for people fined by magistrates and advised the *duoviri*.[24] Thus the council's power was enormous, arguably more so than that of the magistrates or the people's assembly, and its members therefore enjoyed great prestige.

10.2.4 Popular Assembly

The most important task of the assembly of local citizens was the election of magistrates. In the first century AD the elections were still extremely important, as the election notices from Pompeii attest. The epigraphic charters also assume that there will be regular elections to appoint magistrates (Galsterer 2000, 355). The assembly voted on proposals suggested by the council regarding e.g. public finance, honorary duovirates and public declamations and denunciations (*lex Irn.* L; *AE* 1949, 55, *ILS* 6780; see Boatwright 2000, 47). It has been suggested that eventually councils elected magistrates among themselves, cancelling the assemblies' most important function (Mackie 1983, 55, 79), and that assemblies often ceased to meet entirely, since most issues were simply decided by the council. However, in both East and West decisions were often still taken by both council and popular assembly, even into the late Empire; the law from Troesmis gives detailed regulations on local elections, suggesting that these were still relevant in the late second century.

22 *Lex Urs.* 105. In Comum property worth 100,000 HS was required (Plin. *Ep.* 1.19), but *lex Irn.* 86 requires only 5,000; Galsterer 1999, n. 31 argues that this should read 6,000. For age *lex Malac.* 54 states twenty-five years, but the requirement in Bithynia-Pontus was twenty-two (Plin. *Ep.* 10.79); at Troesmis priests had to be at least 35 years old (Eck 2013, 204–205).

23 D.48.19.9.11–12; D.48.19.15; D.48.19.27–28. See Langhammer 1973, 189–202.

24 *ILS* 6093–6116, 6680. See Langhammer 1973, 202–277; Reynolds 1988, 25–26.

10.3 Local Jurisdiction

The most important task of the *duoviri* was the administration of justice, guided by the provincial governor's instructions (Dio Chrys. *Or.* 31.162); the title of *duovir i(ure) d(icundo)* already indicates the importance of this task. There has been some debate, however, about the legal powers of local magistrates. The *lex Irnitana* states that any lawsuit concerning a sum over 1,000 HS should be referred to the governor, as well as all matters regarding violence, liberty, partnership, trust, mandate, tutelage, fraud, theft, injury and accusation of wrongful intent, i.e. all *actiones famosae*, a conviction for which would bring the perpetrator *infamia*. Because of the importance of a good standing within the community, a decision to destroy someone's reputation should be backed up by a higher authority.

However, these matters could be dealt with locally if both parties agreed to this—which they would often have done, considering the effort and expense of taking the matter to the provincial capital or a *conventus* centre (*lex Irn.* 84; see Galsterer 1999; Metzger 2013). The aediles acted as judges in minor matters, again up to 1,000 HS at Irni, and could impose fines on a variety of matters.[25] These figures could vary considerably; in the *lex Rubria* for Cisalpine Gaul and the *fragmentum Atestinum*, 15,000 HS is the maximum value that could be judged by the local magistrates for normal civil cases, and 10,000 in cases which could lead to *infamia* (Galsterer 1999, 249). Whether local magistrates also held criminal jurisdiction is unclear; it seems unlikely that magistrates of Latin communities were allowed to condemn Roman citizens to death. Evidence from Puteoli and Cumae suggest that magistrates of Roman communities could condemn other citizens, however.[26]

If a case could not be judged locally, it was referred to the provincial governor, or, in Italy itself, to the courts at Rome. Local trial procedures, documented in the *lex Irnitana*, were very similar to those in Rome. There were two phases: one *in iure*, i.e. in the presence of the magistrate, when men were chosen as judges, arbiters and *recuperatores*, from a selection which had been made from all the *decuriones* at the beginning of the *duoviri*'s term of office (*lex Irn.* 86). Both parties could reject a certain number before the trial started. When the judges were appointed, a "notice for the third day" was granted—probably a notice to all concerned when and where the case would be judged (Inst.Gai.4.15; see González 1986, 234). After this the phase *apud iudicem* took place, in which the judge(s) would hear the case and pronounce a verdict; the trial was held in the forum or elsewhere within the community's territory. The Imperial rescripts indicate that, when one of the parties was unsatisfied with the outcome of a trial, appeals to higher authorities, e.g. the provincial governor, were available to the average citizen of the Empire. However, many people tried to go straight to the emperor, rather than to the provincial governor first, although the emperor preferred to leave as much business as possible with the governors.[27]

The powers of jurisdiction of local magistrates developed over time. With regard to the municipal laws, it has been pointed out that a grant of Latin or Roman status to a town did

[25] *Lex Irn.* 84; *lex Malac.* 66. See Mackie 1983, 59–60; Curchin 1990, 62–63; Galsterer 1999, 245; Ando 2006, 185.

[26] Fuhrmann 2012, 58; *contra* Galsterer 1999, 251–252; Ausbüttel 1998, 56. See Riggsby ch. 24 and Bryen ch. 25 in this volume.

[27] Suet. *Nero* 17 and Tac. *Ann.* 13.4 record how Corbulo admonished people to approach the governor, not the emperor; many emperors issued similar commands. See Eck 1997, 111–116.

not necessarily coincide with the creation of a law for its use; Irni, for example, already was a *municipium* before the *lex Irnitana* was granted. The purpose of such laws may therefore have been to grant the town a greater degree of juridical autonomy: its magistrates could now apply Roman law, whereas they did not have this authority before the law was passed (García Fernández 1995). *Duoviri* should follow the provincial governor's edict, which was probably very similar throughout the Empire. This meant that jurisdiction became more uniform throughout the provinces (*lex Irn.* 95; see Galsterer 1999, 252–253). Nevertheless, regulations covering local administration were not necessarily the same everywhere, as we have seen, nor was there an obligation to use Roman law (Eck 1997, 120). In peregrine communities certainly there was no obligation to use Roman law; even Roman citizens living in such a community did not have the right to *revocatio Romam*, the right to have their cases judged in Rome, although this could be granted individually (Galsterer 1999, 253).

Even if there was no obligation to use Roman law, a natural development led to more uniformity in local government. Because there were many people with different legal statuses—Roman citizen, Latin, or *peregrinus*—living in each community, it would make sense that local magistrates turned to Roman law when they had to make a decision on an issue not covered by the local laws. The *lex Irnitana* continually states that everything not covered in it is to happen "as if the case were heard in Rome". Thus a legal fiction was created that allowed local legislation to be carried out according to the *ius civile*, even if those involved were not citizens.[28] As in the case of election procedures, this shows the importance of Rome as a model for local administration. Roman magistrates arbitrating in disputes between provincial communities provided local magistrates with Roman-style laws and legal terms to use. Thus the spread of Roman law within the Empire was a consequence of the need of local communities to acquire laws covering every eventuality they might encounter (Eck 1997, 120–121; Ando 2006, 189–190); of course, that Roman law was available in the first place was the result of Roman expansion. The choice of communities to change their laws was therefore not completely free.

10.4 Public Property

Most communities consisted of an urban area with a rural territory surrounding it, often including smaller villages, though some consisted of a collection of villages.[29] Most of the land was the private property of the towns' inhabitants, but some belonged to the town collectively. The town could acquire this property in a variety of ways: when a colony was founded, some land was designated *ager publicus*, public property. This land could be rented out, as well as buildings belonging to the community; the rent from public property was usually the most important source of income.[30] A second important source of revenue were local taxes or *vectigalia*; for example, on coin exchange and the use of harbours,

[28] *Lex Irn.* 29, 91. See Thomas 1996, 1–23; Richardson (ch. 9).

[29] Villages within the territory of a larger town also enjoyed some self-government and often saw some urban development; see Nollé 1999.

[30] *Lex Urs.* 82; *lex Malac.* 63; Hyginus 82.35–84.2; Agennius Urbicus 42.28–29 (Campbell); D.6.3.1pr-1. See Ausbüttel 1998, 69–70.

roads, bridges, rivers and other public facilities.[31] Another significant source of income were fines. In the epigraphic laws, any infringement was punishable by a fine paid "to the colonists", i.e. to the public purse; these fines could be as high as 20,000 HS (*lex Urs.* 61; *lex Malac.* 66; *lex Irn.* J). A final source of income were donations by wealthy individuals, but these could usually only be applied to a specific purpose, e.g. an *alimenta* scheme.[32]

Towns spent their funds on public slaves (*lex Irn.* 72, 78), public works and maintenance, travel expenses of magistrates and to buy grain in times of scarcity. Private individuals often took over these costs, at first voluntarily, later as compulsory *summae honorariae* and *munera*, which eventually may have led to the unpopularity of local office, as we have seen. The use of public money was closely supervised: magistrates had to provide sureties for its use and present an account when the business was completed (*lex Malac.* 67–69; *lex Irn.* 67–69; *lex Urs.* 81). For decisions on public spending, three-quarters of the councillors had to be present, more than for other business (*lex Irn.* 79); public property was inspected regularly by a commission of councillors (*lex Irn.* 76). It is clear that keeping public finances in good order was important (Plin. *Ep.* 10.37–40). However, local incomes varied widely over time, so that communities could unexpectedly find themselves short of money—which might lead them to ask for Imperial assistance. Nevertheless, although towns looked toward the emperor for assistance, being reprimanded for financial failure was an embarrassment to any community.

With regard to tax obligations to the Roman state, towns were placed into one of three categories: most were *civitates stipendiariae*, obliged to pay taxes; some were *civitates foederatae*, which had a treaty with Rome regulating their rights, including their own systems of jurisdiction, although they usually paid taxes; some were *civitates liberae et immunes*, exempt from taxes and not subject to the provincial governor's jurisdiction. Federated and free towns lay mostly in the East, where such freedom had been granted during the Roman conquest; in the West, most towns were subject to tax.[33] Payment of taxes to Rome was usually the responsibility of the council or of a special committee, called *dekaprotoi* in the East and *decemprimi* in the West; if such a committee did not exist, all councillors together were responsible. If not enough tax was collected, the committee members or councillors had to supply the rest from their own money.[34] This may have been another reason why holding local office became less popular as time went on.

10.5 Citizens and Foreigners

Each town had its own citizens, people who enjoyed the full rights of citizenship in the town, such as voting in the assembly and being elected as magistrates. However, apart

[31] e.g. *OGIS* 484 (Pergamum, coin exchange); *OGIS* 4302a (Myra, tolls); *lex Irn.* J. Local officers also assisted in collecting customs taxes (*portoria*) charged on importing or exporting goods to and from the community's territory, although the revenue flowed into the coffers of the Empire. See Reynolds 1988, 34–35; Corbier 1991, 651–659; Galsterer 2000, 353–354; Ando 2006, 187.

[32] Plin. *Ep.* 4.13. There is little information about the way such trust funds were administered and how conflicts could be solved; perhaps by the *actio subsidiaria*, see Koops 2010.

[33] See Langhammer 1973, 22–24; Eck 1997, 126; Boatwright 2000, 88–93; Ando 2006, 184.

[34] D.50.4.18.26. See Brunt 1990b, 341–342; Burton 2001, 207–209; Ando 2006, 187.

from full citizens, there were also many people with other legal statuses: obviously slaves, but also resident foreigners, who were not registered as citizens of the town. These people were called *incolae*. The municipal charters describe their rights in detail: *incolae* could not run for offices or priesthoods and were not allowed to use magistrates for arrangements such as manumission and appointing guardians.[35] They were subject to the same laws as the citizens and shared the same *munera*, including paying taxes (*ius Italicum* included tax exemption, but only for citizens of the community, not for *incolae*); their voting rights were limited, since they were assigned to a single *curia*.[36] In the first century AD these *munera* were still tied to a person's hometown, so that people who moved elsewhere escaped them, but in the second they became liable to the town of domicile (Langhammer 1973, 27; Curchin 1990, 25). *Incolae* were allowed to own land and marry in the community, act as witnesses in lawsuits, shared in games, banquets and food distributions, and joined citizens in erecting honorific statues.[37] They could become members of the town council by cooption and then be elected magistrate. *Incolae* as such were therefore not seen as inferior; their existence was the result of the high level of mobility in the Roman Empire, which meant that many people lived outside the town of their birth.

A separate category of inhabitants were *adtributi* and *contributi*. There is some debate about the exact meaning of these terms, but in both cases they referred to people who were assigned to the administrative territory of a *municipium* or *colonia*. This did not mean that they received equal rights as the inhabitants of the town, however. In the case of the *adtributi*, the people concerned were of a lower legal status than the inhabitants of the dominant town, and were subjected to the jurisdiction of the town. They could not participate in the government of the town, since they retained their own administration; they held their land directly from the Roman state, so they paid taxes to the central government, not to the town. *Contributio*, on the other hand, refers to the fusion of two or more previously independent communities into one, with the same rights for all inhabitants; usually this involved two communities with Roman citizenship.[38]

Considerable debate has focused on the status of former magistrates in towns with Latin rights; the municipal charters state that they and their families became Roman citizens (*lex Salp.* 21; *lex Irn.* 21; see Galsterer 1971, 49). By the *ius Latii maius*, dated to the Hadrianic period, decurions also received Roman citizenship (Curchin 1990, 75; Boatwright 2000, 45). A problem with these grants is that the other inhabitants remained Latins, and if they did not have the rights of *commercium* and *conubium*, they could not marry, inherit from, or trade with ex-magistrates, which would seriously impede property transactions and marriages in the towns. We must conclude that former magistrates also retained full citizenship of their own towns, so that relations with their townsmen were covered by local laws.[39]

35 *Lex Irn.* 94; see Mackie 1983, 41. In general see Thomas 1996, 25–34. People could become magistrates in towns other than their home town; Aelius Aristides, for example, was asked to become *prytanis* in Smyrna (*Sacred Tales* 4.72–73; Dmitriev 2005, 159).

36 *Lex Malac.* 53; *lex Urs.* 98; D.50.15.4.2. See Mackie 1983, 40–46; Boatwright 2000, 49; Burton 2000, 198.

37 *Lex Urs.* 95, 126–127. See Mackie 1983, 41–46; Stephan 2002, 136–137.

38 For the complicated problems regarding *adtributi* and *contributi* see Gagliardi 2006, 263–328.

39 Gardner 2001, who shows that it is unlikely that *ius Latii* included *commercium* and *conubium*.

10.6 Conclusion

Literary sources make fun of small-town affairs (Iuv. 10.10–102; Hor. *Sat.* 1.5.34–36), but the magistrates themselves thought of their activities as necessary and useful. For local magistrates and priests, holding office was a source of pride and an important part of their identity, providing *dignitas* and *honos*. The town of one's birth, one's *origo*, was essential for someone's personal identity; on epitaphs and public dedications people proudly mention their hometowns (Cic. *Off.* 1.71–72; see Brunt 1990a, 273–274; Stephan 2002, 115–173). Conversely, men who made the effort to improve the prestige of their town, e.g. by petitioning the emperor for a grant of market rights or an honorary title, were honoured by their community in return (see e.g. Nollé 1999 for market rights). Even if men rose to office in Rome, they often maintained links with their own towns. Local magistrates expressed strong feelings of connection: "This is my own country; but Rome stands above all countries. I love Bordeaux (*diligo*), Rome I venerate (*colo*); in this I am a citizen, in both a consul; here was my cradle, there my curule chair" (Auson., *Ord. nob. urb.* 20.36–41). Being Roman was essentially a legal issue—as Herennius Modestinus puts it, *Roma communis nostra patria est*—but this did not necessarily mean that everyone's cultural identity was Roman; in the East especially the cultural frame of reference was predominantly Greek, although of course what it meant to be "Greek" or "Roman" changed over time (D.50.1.33; see Stephan 2002, 199–222).

The identity of most people was closely connected to the town in which they lived, whether they were born there or had chosen it for their residence as *incolae*; it was here that they fulfilled the most important civic duties and from which they gained their status as Latins or Roman citizens, and here that, by discharging their duties as magistrates and councillors, they could show themselves to be worthy citizens of the Roman Empire.

Bibliography

Ando, C. 2006. "The administration of the provinces." In D. S. Potter, ed., *A companion to the Roman empire*. Malden. 177–192.

Ausbüttel, F. M. 1998. *Die Verwaltung des römischen Kaiserreiches*. Darmstadt.

Boatwright, M. T. 2000. *Hadrian and the cities of the Roman empire*. Princeton.

Brunt, P. 1990a. "The Romanization of the local ruling classes of the Roman empire," in *Roman imperial themes*. Oxford. 267–281.

Brunt, P. 1990b. "The revenues of Rome," in *Roman imperial themes*. Oxford. 324–346.

Burton, G. P. (2000). "The resolution of territorial disputes in the provinces of the Roman empire." *Chiron* 30: 195–215.

Burton, G. P. 2001. "The imperial state and its impact on the role and status of local magistrates and councillors in the provinces of the empire." In L. de Blois, ed., *Administration, prosopography and appointment policies in the Roman empire*. Amsterdam. 202–214.

Caballos Rufino, A. 2006. *El nuevo bronce de Osuna y la política colonizadora romana*. Seville.

Campbell, B. 2000. *The writings of the Roman land surveyors: introduction, text, translation and commentary*. London.

Corbier, M. 1991. "Cité, territoire et fiscalité," in *Epigrafia: actes du colloque international d'épigraphie latine*. Rome. 629–665
Curchin, L. A. 1990. *The local magistrates of Roman Spain*. Toronto.
Dmitriev, S. 2005. *City government in Hellenistic and Roman Asia Minor*. Oxford.
Eck, W. 1979. *Die staatliche Organisation Italiens in der hohen Kaiserzeit*. Munich.
Eck, W. 1997. *Die Verwaltung des römischen Reiches in der hohen Kaiserzeit*. Basel.
Eck, W. (2013). "La loi municipale de Troesmis: données juridiques et politiques d'une inscription récemment découverte." *Revue historique de droit français et étranger* 91: 199–213.
Edmondson, J. 2009. "Les provinces hispaniques et l'impact du pouvoir romain: l'exemple de la Lusitanie." In F. Hurlet, ed., *Rome et l'Occident: gouverner l'Empire*. Rennes. 253–286.
Fernández Gómez, F. (1991). "Nuevos fragmentos de leyes municipales y otros bronces epigraficos de la Betica en el Museo Arqueologico de Sevilla." *Zeitschrift für Papyrologie und Epigraphik* 86: 121–136.
Fuhrmann, C. J. 2012. *Policing the Roman empire: soldiers, administration, and public order*. New York.
Gagliardi, L. 2006. *Mobilità e integrazione delle persone nei centri cittadini romani*. Milan.
Galsterer, H. 1971. *Untersuchungen zum römischen Städtewesen auf der iberischen Halbinsel*. Berlin.
Galsterer, H. 1999. "Statthalter und Stadt im Gerichtswesen der westlichen Provinzen." In W. Eck, ed., *Lokale Autonomie und römische Ordnungsmacht in den kaiserzeitlichen Provinzen vom 1. bis 3. Jahrhundert*. Munich. 243–256.
Galsterer, H. 2000. "Local and provincial institutions and government." In A. Bowman, P. Garnsey and D. Rathbone, eds., *Cambridge ancient history*. Cambridge. Vol. 11: 344–360.
Galsterer-Kröll, B. (1972). "Untersuchungen zu den Beinamen der Städte des *Imperium romanum*." *Epigrafische Studien* 9. Bonn. 44–145.
García Fernandez, E. (1995). "Sobre la función de la *lex municipalis*." *Gerión* 13: 141–153.
Gardner, J. F. 2001. "Making citizens: the operation of the *lex Irnitana*." In L. de Blois, ed., *Administration, prosopography and appointment policies in the Roman Empire*. Amsterdam. 215–229.
Garnsey, P. (1974). "Aspects of the decline of urban aristocracy in the empire." *Aufstieg und Niedergang der römischen Welt* II.1: 229–252.
González, J. (1986). "The *lex Irnitana*: a new copy of the Flavian municipal law." *Journal of Roman Studies* 76: 147–243.
Jacques, F. 1984. *Le privilège de liberté. Politique impériale et autonomie municipale dans les cités de l'occident romain (161–244)*. Rome.
Koops, E. 2010. *Vormen van subsidiariteit*. The Hague.
Langhammer, W. 1973. *Die rechtliche und soziale Stellung der* Magistratus municipales *und der* Decuriones *in der Übergangsphase der Städte von sich selbstverwaltenden Gemeinden zu Vollzugsorganen der spätantiken Zwangsstaates*. Wiesbaden.
Mackie, N. 1983. *Local administration in Roman Spain A.D. 14–212*. Oxford.
Metzger, E. 2013. "Agree to disagree: local jurisdiction in the *lex Irnitana*." In A. Burrows, D. Johnston and R. Zimmermann, eds., *Judge and jurist: essays in memory of Lord Rodger of Earlsferry*. Oxford. 207–225.
Nollé, J. 1999. "Marktrechte außerhalb der Stadt: lokale Autonomie zwischen Statthalter und Zentralort." In W. Eck, ed., *Lokale Autonomie und römische Ordnungsmacht in den kaiserzeitlichen Provinzen vom 1. bis 3. Jahrhundert*. Munich. 93–113.
Ortiz de Urbina, E., ed. 2013. *Magistrados locales de Hispania: aspectos históricos, jurídicos, lingüísticos*. Vitoria-Gasteiz.

Reynolds, J. 1988. "Cities." In D. C. Braund, ed., *The administration of the Roman empire (241 BC–AD 193)*. Exeter. 15–51.

Shaw, B. D. 1988. "Roman taxation." In M. Grant and R. Kitzinger, eds., *Civilization of the ancient Mediterranean*. New York. 809–827.

Sherwin-White, A. N. 1973². *The Roman citizenship*. Oxford.

Stephan, E. 2002. *Honoratioren, Griechen, Polisbürger. Kollektive Identitäten innerhalb der Oberschicht des kaiserzeitlichen Kleinasien*. Göttingen.

Thomas, Y. 1996. *"Origine" et "commune patrie." Étude de droit public romain (89 av. J.-C.–212 ap. J.C.)*. CÉFR 221. Rome.

CHAPTER 11

COLLEGIA AND THEIR IMPACT ON THE CONSTITUTIONAL STRUCTURE OF THE ROMAN STATE

JONATHAN S. PERRY

11.1 Introduction

In the spring of 1791, as the French National Assembly debated the efficacy of various means of accelerating the Revolution's pace, Parisian workers in several professions lost patience, staging strikes and demonstrations against their employers. In response, principally under the direction of Deputy Isaac-René-Guy Le Chapelier, the Assembly passed a law on 14 June banning all trade unions in the country. This law also led to the dissolution of medical and other colleges in 1792, and it would remain in force, despite the failure of the Revolution, until 1884. The driving impetus behind the law was the conviction that any limited and restricted association of individuals would pose a threat to all public institutions, as small groups would inevitably attempt to promote their selfish interests and not the interests of the entire society. The original text of the law makes it clear that, whatever workers proclaimed as their goal, it was merely a "prétexte" (Article 1) for advancing "leurs prétendus intérêts communs" ("their alleged common interests", Article 2). Workers, in short, were abusing their "liberty" to threaten "violence" and "sedition" (Articles 7 and 8), and it was thought contrary to both the spirit and the letter of the *Declaration of the Rights of Man and the Citizen* that they be permitted to assemble.

At roughly the same time, the United States Federal Constitution would guarantee the right of assembly, as one of the freedoms enshrined in its First Amendment. There is a chequered history in America in this respect, of course, as with regard to the other provisions of the First Amendment. Nevertheless, the legal principles standing behind Le Chapelier's law and the Constitutional "right of the people peaceably to assemble" shed light on the evolution of Roman associative law. This chapter could be evaluated as a case study or as an application of the "constitutional structures" of the institutional state on a less elevated level. How would the grand administrative structures of the Roman system have been perceived among the lower classes, particularly those in the municipal context? Did the state actually have an interest in promoting the "general welfare", and did this priority necessitate a further restriction of collective institutions among the sub-elite?

Although similar surveys of the development of associative law exist (see esp. Aubert 1999; Sirks 2006), this chapter will focus on a few key passages, derived principally from law codes and literary sources, in order to sketch out the legal situation of *collegia* vis-à-vis "the state". However, this material will be weighed against the rich epigraphic evidence (i.e. inscribed documents) that suggests the widespread and, in practical terms, *un*restricted nature of Roman associations. So plentiful was this material that the first monumental survey of *collegia* (Waltzing 1895–1900) compiled nearly 2,500 inscriptional references to these institutions, and this was supplemented a century later with a further ninety-one for Roman Italy alone (Mennella and Apicella 2000). As a result of Waltzing's labours, and of the subsequent investigations of twentieth-century scholars like Francesco Maria De Robertis (191–2003), a portrait of a virtually unimpeded, unencumbered *fenomeno associativo* in the first two centuries AD emerged, and this remains the overall tenor of scholarship on the matter. Perry 2006 explores the impact of nineteenth- and twentieth-century concepts on this developing notion, and one may sample from this literature, much of it produced in Fascist Italy against the backdrop of that regime's vaunted *Corporativismo*, especially with reference to De Robertis 1938.

Nonetheless, this abbreviated introduction to a highly complex and controversial subject puts forward three general conclusions, covering the span of Roman history but concentrating on the "classical period", roughly the first century BC through the second century AD. The first is that there was no appreciable state interference in Roman collegial life until the late Republic, specifically the 60s–40s BC. As a corollary point, the stories of governmental regulation of associative behaviour, especially those concerning Numa Pompilius and the Bacchanals, were retrofitted to conform to then-current debates. As these debates centred on the activities of Clodius Pulcher and Julius Caesar, I am making the further suggestions that a *lex Iulia de collegiis* was passed in 46 BC and that this law seemed to inaugurate a new stage in collegial development.

However, my second conclusion is that the appearance of governmental interference and regulation, from the late Republic throughout the Principate, was itself merely a "prétexte", as the government continued to encourage the development and proliferation of *collegia* as a means of social and political control. The well-known correspondence between Pliny the Younger and the Emperor Trajan on the dangers posed by free association and the fragmentary *s.c.* quoted on the most famous collegial inscription, concerning the *cultores* of Diana and Antinous at Lanuvium—both dating from the early second century AD—should be interpreted in this light. The central issues at stake in this investigation are whether the senate and the emperor had an interest in *actually* regulating and licensing collegial assembly, and whether legal texts can be reconciled with the inscriptional material attesting extensive collegial organisation, particularly in Italy and the Empire's Western provinces.

The third suggestion, although it will not be fully developed in this chapter, addresses the transformation of *collegia* into *corpora*, from the Severans through late Antiquity. Here, I wish to offer an alternative to Waltzing's and De Robertis' contention that associations "became stiffened and crystallised in the bureaucratic gearshifts of the state" in this period. Here again, the appearance of tighter Imperial codes for certain compulsory hereditary occupations can give the illusion that the state desired—and possessed sufficient institutional leverage—to regulate corporate assembly. As in earlier periods, it was in the best interests of governmental authorities to "licence" and "regulate" *collegia* in only the most superficial way, and the magistrates of the associations, in particular, were coopted by an elite who recognised their potential as vehicles of social control. Far from being, as Le Chapelier feared, "perturbateurs du repos public", the *collegia* were instead useful tools for controlling an aspirant class that was determined to gain prestige and recognition in a civic context.

11.2 Regulating *Collegia* and Electoral Politics in the Late Republic

The logical place to begin a survey of the position of associations in Roman law is Numa's supposed creation of *collegia*, at least as claimed in chapter 17 of Plutarch's *Life of Numa*. Plutarch observes that Numa (by tradition king from 715–673 BC) was concerned about the divisions and distinctions in society that had occasioned excessive comparisons and an actual *philoneikia* (love of strife) among the classes. In a typically moralising characterisation, Plutarch praises Numa's awareness "that hard materials which do not easily mix may be crushed and ground up and thus more easily mix on account of their smallness relative to one another". This realisation led Numa to grind down the divisions between the two groups, the haves and the have-nots, and thereby render the have-nots further divided and (perhaps counterintuitively) better able to cooperate. The multitude would be divided into sub-groups according to their trades (*technai*), which included—he specifies—musicians, goldsmiths, carpenters, dyers, leather-cutters and leather-dressers (*skutotomoi* and *skutodepsai*), coppersmiths and potters. Social gatherings were enjoined for the groups (*koinōnias* and *synodoi*), with the result that these "finely-ground" divisions gave way to a "harmonious" society in which "everyone intermingled together".

Gabba 1984 begins with this passage, noting that neither Cicero nor his contemporaries attributed the foundation of *collegia* to Numa and that there was an alternative tradition, appearing in Florus and according to which Servius Tullius formed *collegia* as a supplement to his census classes. The bulk of the article deals with the Platonic and Pythagorean elements of the remainder of Plutarch's biography, suggesting that the *collegia* were institutions already present in early Rome, but tied to Numa given his wider philosophical associations. Subsequently, Gabba circles back to the historical context of the late Republic in evaluating this material, asserting that the tradition associating Numa with *collegia* does not go back to Varro, but belongs rather to the specific political context of the mid-first century. Indeed, Numa was explicitly linked to this vocational distribution of the citizenry "in the course of the political struggles revolving around the abolition of the *collegia* in the course of the first century" BC. These struggles centred on the question of whether "they disturbed public order", and Gabba went on to cite the idea that "some of the *collegia* [perhaps from the time of Julius or Augustus Caesar] were allowed to survive on the grounds of their great antiquity" and that it was perhaps on one of these occasions that "a list of acceptable *collegia*", precisely mirroring Plutarch's list, "was drawn up".

Gabba drops this tantalising point, moving on to considerations of the selection of Numa as king by the senate and the ethnic origins of early Rome. However, more points could be made concerning the specific context of Julius or Augustus Caesar's law, one that is mentioned only briefly in Suetonius' *Life of Caesar* (ch. 42), and in an apparent doublet in his *Life of Augustus* (ch. 32). Among these is the notion that, since Caesar aimed to ban all associations except those that were "the most ancient", the action encouraged existing *collegia* to locate the licensing of their own institutions at the earliest possible stages of Roman history, and ideally within the early regal period. Gabba developed a complex political parallel between the appointment of Numa as king and the "present ... factional strife" in the first century. However, he did not amplify the precise meaning of "present factional strife" against the backdrop of, especially, Clodius' innovation in rendering *collegia* deployable agents of political pressure.

Some of this context has been explored by other scholars, most notably Accame 1942 and Linderski 1968. Here as elsewhere, Linderski draws particular attention to the phenomenon of electoral bribery that had become so pronounced in the 60s and argues that the original law may well have been Julius Caesar's, resulting from his bitter experience with Clodius' gangs before and during the so-called First Triumvirate. Yavetz 1983 followed this line of reasoning, suggesting that Caesar might have wished to prevent some of his more popular tribunes (he does not name names, but one thinks of Mark Anthony) from forming new *collegia* and turning them to similarly nefarious political purposes. In fact, one can glimpse shades of the much later law of Le Chapelier, in the conviction that narrowly defined and tightly bound groups will always be difficult to control.

One could go even further. The stories of state interference and state regulation of *collegia* before the first century BC, both under Numa and again in the suppression of the Bacchanals (as described by Livy), likely stemmed from the bitter experiences of Clodius' gangs and Caesar's need to put the genie back in the bottle. As in 1791, the regulation of associations arose from a specific political context, and the law was an attempt to restore a (notionally) more harmonious situation *ante quem*. Nevertheless, as Clodius' and Milo's clubs demonstrated, it was easy to dodge the letter of the law, ostensibly meeting for a stated religious or professional purpose and then turning their membership to the delicate art of political pressure. For the moment, though, 46 BC may mark the initiation of a process of state regulation by legal statute and subsequently, during the Principate, by senatorial decree and Imperial edict.

11.3 "Licit" and "Illicit" *Collegia* under the Principate

The transformation of the Republic into an autocracy, even if a veil was cast over its specific operations, may have made the regulation of potentially subversive groups even more desirable. But is there compelling evidence that, as the Principate evolved, there was a concerted attempt to licence *collegia*? If so, what considerations would have been employed to differentiate "licit" from "illicit" gatherings? Pressing harder, what explicit and precise *steps* would have been followed in "licensing" an organisation of this sort? Two inscriptions, evaluated against the backdrop of a chapter in the Digest and a segment of Gaius' *On the Provincial Edict*, may cast light on these questions.

An inscription discovered in 1847 (*AE* 1999, 173) records a dedication by a *collegium symphoniacorum*, to whom the senate granted permission *c.c.c.*, in accordance with the *lex Iulia*, on the authority of Augustus, for the sake of (sacred) games (*senatus c. c. c. permisit e lege Iulia ex auctoritate Aug(usti) ludorum causa*). Mommsen's expansion of the mysterious—and unique, in the inscriptional record—acronym, *coire convocari cogi*, was challenged by Berger 1947, who proposed in its place *collegium coire convenire* or *collegium constituere/celebrare/condere coire*. Introducing similar elements from other collegial inscriptions, Saumagne 1954 advocated the construction *coire convenire colligi*. While it is probably impossible to restore the abbreviated formula with certainty, it is important to note that the inscription references the involvement of both the senate *and* the emperor in the granting of "permission". Moreover, it may be significant that the stated terms of the permission, extending to *sacrae publicae* and acts performed *ludorum causa*, touch on matters of religion. This theme—and the pretexts that jurists thought might be employed along these lines—are addressed in the Digest passages below.

Four years before the discovery of the *symphoniaci* inscription, Mommsen had already dealt with the issue of senatorial and/or Imperial involvement in the licensing of *collegia*, principally on the basis of the legal compendia. However, he had also taken into account—and made a remarkable series of deductions based upon—an inscription uncovered at Lanuvium in the 1810s (*AE* 2011, 203; the fullest modern study is Bendlin 2011). This text, dated to 136 AD, contains the extensive and detailed by-laws of an organisation of *cultores* devoted to the worship of Diana and Antinous. The document is the most significant text we possess for the internal operations of *collegia*, although it should be noted that it mainly concerns the timing, funding and etiquette appropriate for the group's banquets.

An excerpt of another document, namely a "chapter of a decree of the senate of the Roman people", is quoted between lines 10 and 13 in the left-hand column of this text; unfortunately, the left edge of the stone is missing at this point. The reconstruction of the text therefore poses a number of interpretative challenges. It is impossible to determine either the number of letters lost from each line or how the quotation began. On the stone, one can read merely:

10. *vacat* KAPUT EX S C P R *vacat*
11. - c.18 -]NVENIRE COLLEGIUMQ HABERE LICEAT QUI STIPEM MENSTRUAM CONFERRE VO
12. - c. 16 -]A IN IT COLLEGIUM COEANT NEQ SUB SPECIE EIUS COLLEGI NISI SEMEL IN MEN
13. - c.16-17 -]FERENDI CAUSA UNDE DEFUNCTI SEPELIANTUR *vacat*

Even in its incomplete state, Mommsen noticed a similarity of language between this section and a paragraph in book 47 of the Digest: "But it is permitted to the *tenuiores* [more humble people] to contribute a monthly donation to a common fund, so long as they assemble only once per month, but not under such a pretext to convene an illicit *collegium*" (*Sed permittitur tenuioribus stipem menstruam conferre, dum tamen semel in mense coeant, ne sub praetextu huiusmodi illicitum collegium coeat*) (D.47.22.1.pr). The section, an excerpt from Marcian's Institutes, goes on to stipulate that, as clarified in a rescript from Septimius Severus, this restricted permission has force not only in Rome, but also in Italy and the provinces.

The striking affinity of language indicated to Mommsen's mind an affinity of subject matter, and the Lanuvians must therefore have claimed an exemption from the general ban on associations as a *collegium tenuiorum*, which could legally assemble (if only once per month) under the terms of an existing *senatus consultum*. His correlation of these materials seems all the more remarkable when one considers two further points. The members of the Lanuvian college never, in the body of a rather long inscription, label themselves *tenuiores*, nor does Marcian specify the "sepulchral" (or any other) responsibilities of licit *collegia*. Nevertheless, Mommsen created from this deduction a category of associations he termed *collegia funeraticia*, "funerary colleges", and subsequent scholars proceeded on that basis to identify and classify *collegia* according to their perceived functions, i.e. "funerary", "religious", "professional" and so on. The *De collegiis et sodaliciis Romanorum* (1843)—a work that also contains the first seeds of what would become the *CIL*—would help to establish Mommsen's reputation, but his arguments on this point have been called into doubt by many authorities over the years (and even by contemporaries like Max Conrat [né Cohn] in the 1870s). These objections would culminate in the effective dismantling of Mommsen's case in Ausbüttel 1982 (see also van Nijf 1997; Bendlin 2011 provides a rich survey of the literature).

Nonetheless, the remainder of the Digest chapter, and a similar passage in Gaius, can help clarify the legal position of *collegia*, at least in certain very specific respects. Marcian's summary of the law of association goes on to observe: "But they are not forbidden to assemble for the sake of religion (*religionis causa*) so long as this is not contrary to the decree of the senate that forbids illicit *collegia*." He continues by citing the additional specification moved by Caracalla and Geta (211–212 AD) that "it is not permitted to belong to more than one licit association" and that, if found to be a member of two, a man would have to withdraw from one and receive a refund from their common treasury. Just a few years later, Ulpian assimilated those guilty of illegal associative activity to other specific forms of disorder: "Whoever dares to found an illicit *collegium* is liable to the same penalty as those who have been convicted of occupying public places or temples by means of armed men" (D.47.22.2). One may notice here, as in the *symphoniaci* inscription, the coupling of assembly (illegal in this case) with "public" and "religious" sites. The following section (also Marcian, albeit from his work "On public trials") clarifies the legal arrangements for the division of communal property, in case of an illicit college's dissolution, and it also observes that slaves can join associations, but only with their owners' permission (D.47.22.3).

Sandwiched between these items is a revealing general pronouncement, to the effect that "In sum, unless an association or any organisation of this description convenes with the authority of an *s.c.*, or of the emperor, this association exists contrary to the provisions of the decrees of the senate and the Imperial mandates and constitutions" (D.47.22.3.1). On the surface, this provision seems clear, i.e. associations must be licensed, by a variety of specific institutions of apparently equal authority. Nevertheless, it masks a central difficulty; must *each* collegium have been *individually* licensed to be considered as acting within the bounds of the law? Could the association have claimed, as the Lanuvians may have done, to be operating under the provisions of a *general s.c.*, one that would not require a specific licence (perhaps of explicit duration) in order to be considered licit?

A layer of specificity along these lines seems to be contained in Gaius' commentary on the provincial edict:

> Permission has not been granted to anyone to form either a *societas*, a *collegium*, or a similar organisation, for this is regulated by laws, by *senatus consulta*, and by Imperial edicts. In a few situations, organisations of this kind are authorised: as, for example, the right to form organisations is permitted to those engaged as associates in tax collection, or associations of workers in the gold-mines, silver-mines and salt-mines. (D.3.4.1pr)

Gaius also noted that some groups have been "confirmed by decrees of the senate and Imperial edicts", such as bakers (*pistores*) and *navicularii* (river transport-workers) in the provinces (these were particularly numerous in the Gallic provinces, judging from inscriptional evidence). The remainder of the passage introduces further provisions on the associations' common property rights and their common liability in case of the seizure of their property. It is noteworthy that a great deal of the legal evidence hinges on the notion of collectively owned property, in terms of its collection, disbursement and dissolution. At the same time, there appears to be a vague notion of "licensing", at least in the case of "licit" *collegia*, but the precise *procedure* of registering an organisation and maintaining such a licence does not appear in this literature.

Within the substantial scholarly literature concerning *collegia* and the law, much attention has been paid to these issues, as well as to the surprising lacunae in our evidence. The best articles on the matter engage these problematic circumstances directly, and I would draw particular attention to de Ligt 2000 and 2001; Randazzo 1991–1992 and 1998; and Bendlin 2011. De Ligt makes a compelling case for the existence of a general provision regulating *collegia tenuiorum*, one that could be assumed to cover an association, provided it operated within the stipulated limits. If the organisation wished to meet more than once per month (as the Lanuvians apparently did, since their by-laws would have necessitated two meetings in August) or to assemble for a purpose other than collecting a *stips menstrua* from the membership, it would have to receive special, individual permission, from the senate or the emperor, in order to proceed. He offers the further suggestion that the original ban on holding frequent meetings was "gradually relaxed during the first half of the second century", and Randazzo similarly stresses the importance of a changing attitude, from the very top, over time. The latter draws particular attention to Hadrian's role in the general commemoration of Antinous, and this circumstance may explain "the exceptional character of such a concession" in favour of the Lanuvian cultors. Marcian's provisions, quoted in the Digest, reflect the differing priorities of the Severan age, and Randazzo is one of the few commentators on the subject who credits the individual emperors, imbued with their unique proclivities, with the scope and enforcement of this "regulation".

Nevertheless, virtually all authorities on *collegia* have underscored the seeming absence of Imperial micromanagement, or at least the light and hardly visible hand of authoritarian control in the matter of collegial assembly. Can the extensive epigraphic evidence, which contains very little indication of official "licensing" of *collegia* and apparently little concern with hiding their existence if they were in violation of the law, be reconciled with the legal citations? (For a small sample of this evidence see the recent collection of more than three hundred inscribed documents translated by Ascough, Harland and Kloppenborg 2012.) Should we imagine that there was a licensing procedure behind each attestation we discover of collegial life, or even a licence that would have to be renewed on a regular basis, by future members of each association?

11.4 "In Whatever Name they Assemble": Trajan's Directives to Pliny

It is with such considerations in mind that we should now turn to the most familiar—and the most direct—Imperial pronouncements on the regulation and the banning of associations. While serving as Trajan's specially appointed curator in Bithynia-Pontus, a position he took up in 109 AD, Pliny the Younger asked the emperor whether a *collegium fabrum*, of roughly one hundred and fifty members, should be established in Nicomedia. The reason for the request seems to have been the outbreak of a massive fire in the city, for which it was completely unprepared, lacking basic firefighting tools as well as personnel. Pliny suggests (*Ep.* 10.33) that "so few men" as those he is proposing for the service could easily be controlled, but Trajan (*Ep.* 10.34) reminds him that organisations of that sort have "left your province, and especially its cities, disturbed by factional strife". He then offers the general observation: "Under whatever name they assemble and for whatever cause we have assigned them, they soon turn into political clubs (*hetaeriae*)" (*quodcumque nomen ex quacumque causa dederimus iis qui in idem contracti fuerint hetaeriae eaeque brevi fient*). Accordingly, the emperor proposes that, instead of charging a standing fire brigade, Pliny arrange for firefighting equipment to be made available in private homes and promote self-reliance in case of a natural disaster.

Later in the correspondence (*Ep.* 10.92), Pliny again queries the implementation of Imperial policy concerning clubs. Regarding the free city of Amisus, how should he respond to a petition concerning *eranoi* (associations with common funds)? (As with *hetaeriae* above, a Greek and not a Latin term is used.) Here again, Trajan gives explicit, though multifaceted, advice (*Ep.* 10.93). The residents of Amisus should be allowed, due to their special privileges and arrangements with Rome, to form an *eranus*, especially because it is designed "for sustaining the humble people in need" (*ad sustinendam tenuiorum inopiam*). Their resources should not be used, he cautions, "for the purpose of creating disturbances and illicit assemblies" (*ad turbas et ad inlicitos coetus*), and he explicitly bans similar associations in the cities that are under his direct control. In both cases, then, it seems that Trajan is concerned that, regardless of its explicit, stated purpose, an association will always have the potential to become a nexus for political "disturbance".

However, it should be noted that he is applying this general principle in various ways, depending on the unique circumstances of the province and even the individual municipality. Moreover, van Nijf has observed that there is evidence of an association of *tektones*, the Greek equivalent of *fabri*, in Bithynia under the reign of Trajan's successor Hadrian (1997, 180). This would suggest that, even if Trajan intended a blanket provision to apply to Bithynia, this did not preclude the open acknowledgement of an association's existence in the next reign. One might suggest that the legal pronouncements made by Roman officials, including the senate and the emperor himself, had little impact on lived realities, especially in a provincial setting. Nevertheless, another explanation presents itself, if one considers the term "pretext" in a different light.

It may be the case that the emperor was here adopting a pose, threatening to disband associations while also encouraging their proliferation—provided they demonstrated a continuing loyalty to himself and to his government. I would compare Trajan's observations with an inscription that seems to record a governor's reaction to a threatened (though apparently not an actually implemented) strike among bakers in Ephesus in the late second century (*SEG* IV 512; Merkelbach 1978). The text purports to lay out the magistrate's plan of action, should a work stoppage actually take place. Among the provisions of the document are these:

> Thus it happens sometimes that the populace is plunged into tumult and uproars by the audacious assembly of the bakers in the agora. Under these circumstances they should by now have been dragged into court and have paid the penalty. But since it is necessary to put the welfare of the city ahead of the punishment of these individuals, I thought it best to bring them to their senses by an edict. Therefore, I forbid the bakers to assemble in a *hetaireia* and their officers to make inflammatory speeches, and I order them to give complete obedience to those responsible for the community and work to ensure a full supply of bread for the city. [Punishments for offenders of this edict follow, including the branding on the foot (?) with the word *decuria*.]

The tone of the magistrate's decision, and the specific punishments he threatens to mete out, indicate that he has detected a complex internal organisation in the bakers' associations, and that he is as a result deliberately targeting the groups' officers. He contrasts those who would assemble the restive bakers and stir them up with insidious speeches with those who, like himself, are charged with seeing to the "common good" of the city, appealing to the rank-and-file membership to distance themselves from their leaders. Protesting that he is personally reluctant to antagonise the bakers, the administrator claims he is only attempting to render them wiser with his actions. Thus, the opposite of wisdom would be to listen to any speeches proposing a work stoppage, which would never be in the community's, or even the bakers', best interests, especially over the long term.

By my reading, the text of this inscription deals deliberately with the notion of political speech, rather than with any economic or even social actions that might be taken by the membership. The image that has risen to the fore of the governor's mind is that of the speaker haranguing an audience of workers, whipping them up into a frenzy that could be rendered ungovernable. It is probably important, in this context, to remember that the government official is anxious to avoid unrest specifically "in the agora". Perhaps he fears disruptive speech in a part of the city accustomed to forensic exercises of a flammable type? If this were the case, then threatening the speaker who roused the more docile members of his group into action, especially in the public square, would seem a logical approach. Accordingly, then, it would have been in the governor's interest to detach the average *collegiatus* from the organisational elite. In spite of his stated reluctance, he was really targeting these dangerous speakers, and he wanted to make sure that the other bakers recognised that he was on their side and, by implication, they should be on his.

Extending this reading to the level of the emperors, one might argue that emperors actively encouraged the proliferation of *collegia* in the first two centuries AD principally in order to foster loyalty to themselves, as agents of the state but also as individuals. Thus, collegial association may have been a tool, not created but ultimately wielded by the state, in order to organise and control a potentially restive urban population, engendering loyalty, of a sort, in the process. In this light, there may have been less of a shift in the attitudes of emperors in late Antiquity, from the Severans into the third century, than has been advocated previously. In this connection, one might compare the arguments concerning collegial organisation in the towns of Intercisa (Alföldy 1958) and Solva (Schulz-Falkenthal 1966). In Alföldy's analysis, for example, Severus Alexander pursued a policy of supporting *collegia* among the poor, and these groups, in turn, demonstrated their loyalty to him, in a series of dedicatory inscriptions. This third-century emperor thereby found a way to detach associations of explicitly "needy" individuals from the town elite and to focus their aspirations on himself instead.

11.5 Conclusion

This chapter reflects important trajectories of current research on associational behaviour in the Roman world in the long century since Waltzing's *magnum opus* appeared in 1895. In its view, the *collegium* would have served as an institution of control, wielded by the elite to harness the social ambitions of the lower orders. The apparent phenomenon of regulating and licensing *collegia* would thus have been a "prétexte" on their part as well. By declaring that they possessed the power to regulate *collegia*, and then by exercising a light touch, they may have reinforced their right to regulate assembly without actually doing so. The effect would have been to encourage social mobility, to a point, while not allowing the lower classes—and especially those recently liberated from slavery—to rise so far as to threaten the elite's position. Masking their goals in the language of the "common good", the more elevated members of society, in 191 AD as in 1791, would thus ensure that the public peace was not "disturbed", at least not to an unmanageable degree.

Bibliography

Accame, S. (1942). "La legislazione romana intorno ai collegi nel I secolo a.C." *Bullettino del Museo dell'Impero Romano* 13: 13–48.

Alföldy, G. (1958). "*Collegium*-Organisationen in Intercisa." *Acta Antiqua Academiae Scientiarum Hungaricae* 6: 177–198.

Ascough, R. S., Harland, P. A. and Kloppenborg, J. S. 2012. *Associations in the Greco-Roman World: a sourcebook.* Waco.

Aubert, J.-J. (1999). "La gestion des *collegia*: Aspects juridiques, économiques et sociaux." *Cahiers du Centre Gustave Glotz* 10: 49–69.

Ausbüttel, F. M. 1982. *Untersuchungen zu den Vereinen im Westen des römischen Reiches.* Kallmünz.

Bendlin, A. 2011. "Associations, funerals, sociality, and Roman law: the *collegium* of Diana and Antinous in Lanuvium (*CIL* 14.2112) reconsidered." In M. Öhler, ed., *Aposteldekret und antikes Vereinswesen: Gemeinschaft und ihre Ordnung.* Tübingen. 207–296.

Berger, A. (1947). "C. C. C. A Contribution to the Latin terminology concerning *collegia*." *Epigraphica* 9: 44–55.

de Ligt, L. 2000. "Governmental attitudes towards markets and *collegia*." In E. Lo Cascio, ed., *Mercati permanenti e mercati periodici nel mondo romano. Atti degli Incontri capresi di storia dell'economia antica (Capri 13–15 ottobre 1997)*. Bari. 237–252.

de Ligt, L. (2001). "*D.* 47, 22, 1, pr.-1 and the formation of semi-public *collegia*." *Latomus* 60: 345–358.

De Robertis, F. M. 1938. *Il diritto associativo romano dai collegi della Repubblica alle corporazioni del Basso Impero.* Bari.

Gabba, E. (1984). "The *collegia* of Numa: problems of method and political ideas." *Journal of Roman Studies* 74: 81–86.

Linderski, J. 1968. "Der Senat und die Vereine." In M. N. Andreev, J. Irmscher, E. Pólay and W. Warkałło, eds., *Gesellschaft und Recht im griechisch-römischen Altertum*. Berlin. 94–132.

Mennella, G. and Apicella, G. 2000. *Le corporazioni professionali nell'Italia romana. Un aggiornamento al Waltzing*, Naples.

Merkelbach, R. (1978). "Ephesische Parerga (18): Der Bäckerstreik." *Zeitschrift für Papyrologie und Epigraphik* 30: 164–165.

Perry, J. S. 2006. *The Roman* collegia: *the modern evolution of an ancient concept*. Leiden.

Randazzo, S. (1991–1992). "*Senatus consultum quo illicita collegia arcentur* (*D.* 47, 22, 1, 1)." *Bullettino dell'Istituto di Diritto Romano "Vittorio Scialoja"* 94–95: 49–90.

Randazzo, S. (1998). "I *collegia tenuiorum*, fra libertà di associazione e controllo senatorio." *Studia et Documenta Historiae et Iuris* 64: 229–244.

Saumagne, C. (1954). "*Coire, Convenire, Colligi*." *Revue historique de droit français et étranger* 32: 254–263.

Schulz-Falkenthal, H. (1966). "Zur Lage der römischen Berufskollegien zu Beginn des 3. Jhs. u. Z. (die Privilegien der *centonarii* in Solva nach einem Reskript des Septimius Severus und Caracalla)." *Wissenschaftliche Zeitschrift der Martin-Luther-Universität, Halle-Wittenberg* 15: 285–294.

Sirks, A. J. B. 2006. "Die Vereine in der kaiserlichen Gesetzgebung." In A. Gutsfeld and D.-A. Koch, eds., *Vereine, Synagogen und Gemeinden im kaiserzeitlichen Kleinasien.* Tübingen. 21–40.

van Nijf, O. 1997. *The civic world of professional associations in the Roman east.* Amsterdam.

Waltzing, J.-P. 1895–1900. *Étude historique sur les corporations professionnelles chez les Romains, depuis les origines jusqu'à la chute de l'Empire d'Occident.* Leuven.

Yavetz, Z. 1983. *Julius Caesar and his public image.* London.

PART IV

LEGAL PROFESSIONALS AND LEGAL CULTURE

CHAPTER 12

LEGAL EDUCATION AND TRAINING OF LAWYERS

JILL HARRIES

12.1 Introduction

In the 260s AD, the young philosopher, Porphyry, attended the discussion seminars at Rome of the Platonist thinker and teacher, Plotinus.[1] Later he recalled Plotinus' pedagogic style, his slight speech impediment, his ability to identify the main points at issue, the question and answer structure of the discussions among the "auditors" (Gk, *akroatai*) and disciples (*zelotai*) and their canvassing of competing interpretations of master-texts. Plotinus exploited these discussions to strengthen the ideas he presented to a wider, but still restricted, public in his books;[2] ideas were tested through prolonged discussion, involving a process of identifying the right questions, excluding those that were inappropriate, and exploring alternative answers.

Legal education also began as an oral process, based on exchanges of questions and answers in a seminar context, led by a figure of authority in the discipline. After the standard periods of study of language skills and the arts of persuasion with the *grammaticus* and the *rhetor*, elite Romans followed up their legal studies informally, often with a view to professional advancement as advocates or as legal consultants and interpreters of the *ius civile*. As the Imperial administration expanded, experts in law became increasingly employed in administrative posts, rising to the heights of master of petitions (*magister libellorum*) or praetorian prefect; by the fourth century, the praetorian prefects were heads of a multilayered and hierarchical Empire-wide system of jurisdiction, and appointment as assessor to the praetorian prefect marked the first stage of an administrator's rise to the top.[3] One unintended consequence was that the "academic" professor of law became distinct from the teacher of law who derived his status from his role in Imperial government.

[1] Porphyry's *Life of Plotinus* is translated by Edwards 2000. My thanks to Gillian Clark, who pointed out the relevance of this text.

[2] Porph. *Plot.* 13.

[3] See Michael Peachin's chapter (ch. 13) in this volume.

Legal education could not lead to the creation of a "professional" body of "lawyers" in a modern sense; there was no formal body to accredit as "professionals" those who practised law. Authority could be constructed in various ways, and, while enhanced by the political or social status of some aristocratic practitioners, was also tested in the practical contexts of legal hearings before formal or informal adjudicators, or—exceptionally—the Imperial council chamber. Legal education had also a wider cultural context, in that specialist knowledge and thus training, perhaps through apprenticeships, was required for a group of disciplines (*artes, technai*), such as grammar, medicine, mathematics or architecture, along with law, which consistently advertised themselves as being useful, as well as intellectually coherent.[4] Nor was the Roman elite representative of the less well documented Empire as a whole: the law learned by the sophisticated Roman at Rome differed from the use-law, influenced by local ways of legal thinking, acquired by the humble legal scribe or advocate (*nomikos*), known from the Egyptian juristic papyri.

In what follows we shall see how the basic education shared by elite Romans affected the discourse of law; the importance of oral question and answer in advanced legal seminars; the increase in reliance on written manuals and texts based on oral teaching methods; and how previous legal master-texts were superseded by Justinian's uniquely authoritative collection.

12.2 Republic

In Rome in the first century BC, elite legal studies were embedded in the structures of patronage and power, which underpinned the *dignitas* of the Roman senator. In old age, the Roman advocate Cicero recalled how he and his friend Atticus had in their youth attended discussion groups on the law in the houses of two great political jurists, the consuls Q. Mucius Scaevola the Augur (consul in 117 BC) and his namesake the Pontifex (consul in 95 BC).[5] By inviting a select few into their homes, the quasi-public space where the meetings took place was coterminous with the private living quarters of the aristocrat and his family, the consular jurists defined their legal teaching as an act of patronage.

In Cicero's day there was no official legal syllabus at Rome, and no authority with the power to formulate or impose one. Legal problems were discussed in terms, not of principles in any abstract sense, but of cases. How those cases were organised for purposes of oral discussion is unknown. Scaevola the Pontifex' eighteen-book treatise on the Roman civil law (*De iure civili*), which was case-based, seems to have followed the arrangement of the XII Tables, still a foundation text for Roman law and routinely recited by Roman schoolboys down to the first century BC, and to have arranged his case discussions by category (*generatim*).[6] However, Cicero's project, undertaken in the 50s, to organise the *ius civile* into a structure which would allow it to be taught systematically (the *De iure civili in artem redigendo*, now lost) shows that he, for one, believed that analysis in terms of cases left much to be desired and that more could be done to make law accessible to students.[7]

[4] See Wibier 2014, 22–34.

[5] Cic. *Am.* 1.1. See also Cic. *Leg.* 1.13.

[6] Cic. *Leg.* 2.59; D.1.2.2.41.

[7] Gell. *NA* 1.22.7; see also Cic. *De or.* 1.188–189 on *genera, species* and definitions.

Legal education was not only for aspiring jurists, "men skilled or learned in the law" (*iuris periti, iuris prudentes*), but for advocates and other eminent politicians also; Cicero records disapprovingly how Rome's leading statesmen spent their leisure time reading treatises about sophisticated legal points in preference to larger philosophical questions.[8] While Cicero's jurist friend, Aquilius Gallus, observed of one case where only the facts were in dispute, that "this has nothing to do with Law, it's for Cicero",[9] Cicero the advocate never conceded that the territory of law belonged only to the *iuris prudentes*. The discourse of jurisprudence, he argued to another jurist, Trebatius, in 44 BC, was very similar to that of rhetoric and used similar devices.[10] Disciplines often borrowed from each other; thus philosophers and other non-specialists used legal terminology and ideas either metaphorically or to shape their own thinking.[11] Conversely, some jurists, such as Q. Mucius Scaevola the Pontifex and Cicero's friend Servius Sulpicius Rufus, also enjoyed high reputations as orators. Cicero's stress on the interpenetration of jurisprudence and rhetorical training was therefore not just a polemical point but based on his own observation of Roman public and elite culture.

As a teacher, Servius was credited with attempts at systematisation for teaching purposes: he divided a subject into parts, and discussed techniques of definition, explanation, the analysis of ambiguity, distinctions between truth and falsehood and modes of inference from a given proposition.[12] Servius' seminars, however, employed a less structured approach. The mode of instruction was case-based and teacher and "hearers" (*auditores*) interacted; Servius, on one occasion, found his interpretation of a case challenged by an *auditor* who cited with approval the contradictory opinion of another authority, and appears to have carried the day.[13] Servius' pupils' recording of his seminars in numerous volumes, of which he was believed by some to be the sole author, shows that seminar discussions of cases fed directly into publication, by the jurist himself or, as in Servius' case, his more socially obscure auditors.

12.3 Empire

As under the Republic, the approach to law of both teachers and auditors in advanced law seminars was conditioned by the Roman educational system. From the "grammarian", Roman schoolboys learned the basics of language and its uses, a skill which lawyers would exploit in their investigations of the meanings and derivations of words and the relationship of words to each other in sentence structure. Through exploration of canonical works of literature, such as those of Virgil and Cicero, they would have learned also of the Roman past. For these reasons, both Pomponius, in his handbook-history of Roman law and lawyers, and Gaius in his introduction to his commentary on the XII Tables, stress the importance of going back to the beginning of Rome's story to both understand and validate their discipline.[14]

[8] Cic. *Fin.* 1.12. [9] Cic. *Top.* 51. [10] Harries 2006, 126–132.

[11] On philosophy and law see Griffin 2013.

[12] Cic. *ad Brut.* 152–153. Compare Plin. *Ep.* 1.22.3 on Titius Aristo's juristic method.

[13] D.33.7.16.1. [14] D.1.2.1; D.1.2.2.

The standard curriculum also conditioned young Romans in ways of thought directly relevant to how law was taught and learned. The use of imagination provided a means of training in legal argument by distancing an issue from the operation of Roman law in the real world. The imaginary and usually dysfunctional families conjured up by the rhetors for their pupils' benefit, acquire in the writings of the jurists standard names (Titius, Seius, Maevia etc.) reflecting their familial and therefore legal relationships. Real place names, such as Rome or Capua, are used, both to give colour, and because spatial relationship (and the journey times between them) may be relevant for the case. Because this is in line with the use of "John Doe" in modern legal parlance, it is easy to forget that the practice started for its own reasons, as an educational and explanatory tool.[15]

12.3.1 Law and Declamation

While legal reasoning evolved as a distinct and specialist discourse, underlying it were assumptions about debate and argument, which derived, as Cicero had argued, from a rhetorical training. According to the Elder Seneca (37 AD), declamations, formal set speeches, categorised as *controversiae*, which encouraged exploration of arguments on both sides of a question, were a new phenomenon under the Empire (although they were not always the most effective training in the practical aspects of advocacy).[16] *Controversiae* were prepared speeches, in which the student could be expected to argue a case from opposing standpoints, on the basis of a "statement of law" formulated by the teacher. The teacher also supplied "facts", which related to a specific application of the law as stated (which did not necessarily reflect Roman or any other law). In addition to instruction in the structure and techniques of argument, young Romans learned the basics of dissecting the language of a legal text and the devices for invoking intention or spirit, when the phrasing of the law or legal document, such as a will, was inconvenient for the argument. They were also led into ethical dilemmas, such as those surrounding the use of judicial torture.[17] For such young Romans, law and legal procedure was a game played at a remarkably sophisticated level: Plutarch recorded (*c.*100 AD) that contemporaries of Cato the Younger played at trials (where Cato was always the judge), and a spoof text of a "piglet's will", deriving from perhaps the second century AD and designed for schoolboys, combines naughty jokes with scrupulous attention to correct legal terminology.[18]

Although the discussants of declamatory argument in the *Controversiae* of the Elder Seneca (37 AD) are all adults, whose contributions to the art of declamation Seneca seeks to celebrate, their approaches are in line with the conduct of "controversies" at school level.[19] Troubled relationships, for example, between fathers and sons were a staple, reflecting the many ramifications of *patria potestas* in Roman legal culture, and schoolboys were trained to think about it—but at a safe distance. In Roman law, fathers who were legally incapable

[15] Note also the use of standard names N. Negidius and A. Agerius in the praetor's formula.

[16] Sen. *Controv.* 1, Pref. 12: *Controversias nos dicimus; Cicero causas vocabat.* For criticism of declamation as an educational tool see Petron. *Sat.* 1–2; Tac. *Dial.* 31 and 35.

[17] See Bernstein 2012.

[18] Plut. *Cat. Min.* 2.5.

[19] On the relationship between standard education and legal training see Crook 1995, 163–167.

because of mental illness were classified as insane (*furiosi*); in Seneca, a father is accused by his delinquent son of madness, *dementia*.[20]

> I know that no one is granted a curator by the praetor because his father is unnatural or unjust but invariably because he is mad (*furiosus*); for the process which, in the Forum, is to petition for a curator is in rhetorical school to sue on grounds of insanity (*dementia*).

Similarly, when a husband tries to divorce his allegedly barren wife, she counter-sues for ingratitude (she had kept silent for his sake under torture); in Roman law, the only legal redress would concern the return of the dowry (*actio rei uxoriae*), but the rhetors use the case as a prompt for discussion about the conferment of *beneficia* on the husband by the wife, for which he is (allegedly) "ungrateful".[21] Questions on adultery, too, were partially distanced from Augustus' legislation on the subject, which permitted the summary execution of an adulterous wife and her lover, under restricted conditions:[22] the question of whether a husband who was physically incapable of killing his wife and her lover simultaneously could delegate the job to his son (who refuses) raises moral questions of agency (the husband's incapacity) and duty (the son's to his father, and his mother). Augustus' law, however, did not grant a son licence to kill his mother, whether or not she was caught *in flagrante* with her lover.[23]

Crucial to the process of acculturation was the choice of the right question or set of questions and therefore also the exclusion of others. Although Ulpian would claim at the start of his *Institutiones* that law (*ius*) was the (teachable) art of the good and the fair,[24] the formulation of questions concerning *aequitas*, and how values of fairness could be reconciled with awkward legal texts was also a staple of rhetorical education. On an imaginary Senecan case, where the "statement of law" is that children must nurture their parents or be put in chains, one young man finds himself renounced by both real and adoptive father for trying to support the other. "Porcius Latro" formulates the "questions" at issue:

> He divided the case into strict law (*ius*) and equity (*aequitas*), whether he could have renounced him and whether he should. If he (the father) could (legally) renounce him … was he (the son) obliged to nurture his father and in that case, he could not be renounced because of what he did because the law compelled him to.[25]

[20] Sen. *Controv.* 2.3.13

[21] Sen *Controv.* 2.5.10, where the right question to ask is disputed between Porcius Latro, Asinius Pollio and others.

[22] Cf. the formulation of "the law" at the outset of Sen. *Controv.* 1.4.pr–1: *Adulterum cum adultera qui deprehendit, dum utrumque corpus interficiat, sine fraude sit.* This, though similar in sense, differs from the wording of Augustus' text. The second clause, *Liceat adulterium in matre et filio vindicare* is not part of Augustus' law.

[23] Latro's analysis (Sen. *Controv.* 1.4.6) is that the son should have killed "the adulteress" anyway. This is contrary to Augustus' law but consistent with the rules as (mis)represented in the declamatory exercise.

[24] D.1.1.1.1.

[25] Sen. *Controv.* 1.13. On the rhetors' *abdicatio* and *mala tractatio* (ill treatment) as analogous to legal disinheritance, the *querela inofficiosi testamenti* and actions on divorce (the *actio rei uxoriae*), see Quint. *Inst.* 7.4.11.

Then chains of questions could be constructed, each following from the last. In the *dementia* case noted above, "Latro" asked: can the son sue anyone from prison? Can he sue the father from prison? Even if he has the right to do so, can he sue for an action, which the law gives the father power to take? Even if he can, should he?

How a question or series of questions is posed will automatically influence the answer(s) generated. The formulation or rejection of one question will also determine or preclude the creation of further chains of questions and thus of certain lines of argument. The rhetors knew that their methods of training, because they were not strictly "vocational", created a distinctive (and not always beneficial) culture:

> Latro appeared (Pollio said) to be acting like an advocate in the forum, to exclude inappropriate questions from consideration, but nothing shows him up more effectively as an orator of the schools.[26]

Some general discussions on moral philosophy were permissible: as in, should a son always obey his father?[27] Others, of a more speculative nature, were not. In the case of the applicant to a female priesthood with a dubious past, "Cestius" added new questions to the previous chain, only to reject them:[28]

> Do the immortal gods concern themselves with human affairs? If they do, do they worry about those of individuals? And if they do, do they concern themselves with this individual? He blamed Albucius because he had dealt with these matters not as details relevant to the question but as philosophical problems.

So when Papinian's *Responsa* designated one legal option as "kinder" or "more humane" than the other, equally plausible in legal terms, he drew in general terms on the moral teachings of the schools. However, the terms of discussion were limited by the nature of his specialist legal thinking; as a jurist, he could canvass only those options already preselected by legal discourse.[29]

12.3.2 From Oral Instruction to Written Record

Under Augustus and his successors in the first century AD, the oral mode of instruction continued, as it would for centuries to come. But increasingly, the legal educational process became dependent on the ever-expanding mass of writings of earlier jurists, and the demand for written material in accessible and organised form expanded. Simultaneously, emperors came to exert greater control over both law and legal writers; Hadrian's codification of the Praetorian Edict in *c.* 130 AD was an exercise in systematisation, which also aimed to concentrate more power over legal decision-making in the hands of the emperor and his legal advisers. Consequently, the acquisition of useful legal knowledge became more dependent on access to, and knowledge of, written collections, which combined juristic commentary with records of Imperial decisions. From this evolved the concept of a

[26] Sen. *Controv.* 2.3.13. [27] Sen. *Controv.* 2.1.20. [28] Sen. *Controv.* 1.3.8.

[29] For analysis of this in modern legal discourse see Mertz 2007, 10.

more structured legal syllabus, which would culminate in the most influential of all legal textbooks: Justinian's Digest of Roman law.

Under the early Empire, "schools" of law, like those of philosophy and other disciplines such as medicine or agriculture, were originally based on what happened between like-minded students and their teachers in the course of oral discussion. At the turn of the first and second centuries AD, Pliny the Younger referred to the former Roman residence of the jurist Cassius, "the head and father of the Cassian school"; this was also where his *auditores* would have assembled.[30] In due course, the auditors, and Cassius himself, put his views into writing and added comments of their own; Titius Aristo, for example, also a friend of Pliny, was an *auditor* of Cassius and commentated on his writing.[31] This process of oral instruction and its preservation in the written record gave rise to later analyses of relationships between lawyers (as of other disciplines) in terms of lines of "succession" between teacher (*praeceptor*) and *auditor*. While "hearers" might be expected to adhere to the doctrines of their preceptors in general, as Gaius' *Institutiones*, for example, appears to do in his frequent references to "our *praeceptores*", it should not be assumed that lawyers (or philosophers) accepted their teachers' views uncritically.[32] The legal historian Pomponius was thus probably wrong to suggest a divergence of principle between the two Roman law "schools" by differentiating between the two alleged founders as the traditionalist (Capito) versus the moderniser (Labeo).[33] In this respect, the educational practice of lawyers differed from that adopted by the second-century Christian teacher, Justin, with his pupils at Rome, although Justin, like lawyers and philosophers, did also engage directly with public discourse.[34]

Oral discussion generated text, and centuries of seminars produced multiple texts. For this, pupil pressure was partly responsible: the philosopher Plotinus' disciple, Porphyry, urged the master to record his discussions in writing, resulting in the production of twenty-four volumes over a period of six years. Plotinus' books took the form of questions and answers, "commencing his speculations from problems as they arose".[35] By the third century, texts were more prominent in seminar proceedings. Plotinus' discussions were often based on the reading of a text and then, perhaps, a "response" from a gifted student discussant; on one occasion, no initial text was forthcoming and Porphyry constructed his *responsa* from memory.[36] The seminars were essential for the formulation of Plotinus' ideas, which required strenuous testing, before they could be consigned to writing and thus wider (and less controlled) dissemination. For one student, Thamasius, uneasy that the teacher was allowing questioning on the nature of the soul (by Porphyry) to continue over a period of several days, Plotinus, perhaps playing on the words of the objection,

[30] Plin. *Ep.* 7.24.8.

[31] Contra Sherwin-White 1966, 434: "In Pliny's time, the jurists Javolenus Priscus represented the Cassians and Neratius Priscus and his friend Titius Aristo the Proculians." Priscus and Aristo did indeed correspond (D.19.2.19.2, Neratius to Aristo and D.20.3.3, Aristo to Neratius).

[32] e.g. Inst.Gai.4.78–79.

[33] D.1.2.2.47–53. Aulus Gellius identifies Labeo as a traditionalist, contra Pomponius. The best survey of law schools is Liebs 1976.

[34] Ulrich 2012, esp. 68–72 and Georges 2012. The location of Justin's teaching seems to have been in his rooms "above the Baths of Myrtinus" (*Mart. Just.* 3.2–3) and was open to all comers.

[35] Porph. *Plot.* 5.

[36] Porph. *Plot.* 15.

insisted that, if the difficulties of the questioner (Porphyry) were not resolved, there would be nothing worth consigning to a fixed text form (*biblia*) anyway.[37]

No such direct record survives of what happened in seminar discussions conducted by celebrity lawyers. The translation of the experience of teaching and learning, to the literary forms of *quaestiones* and *responsa*, however, which would be prominent in Justinian's reform of legal education in the 530s, perpetuated not only the system but a fundamental characteristic of Roman legal discourse: that a problem or question could have more than one acceptable solution and that any "question", therefore, and its (provisional) answer could be revisited by future lawyers and legal students. Questions could be posed in many forms, such as letters or private consultations on real cases,[38] but the Severan jurist Papinian's reworking of his teaching and wider legal consultancy process into written form accorded with the seminar conventions of question and answer (and further follow-up questions), with which he and his auditors were familiar.

For purposes of accessibility for consultation, Papinian's *Quaestiones* shadowed the structure of the Praetorian Edict, as fixed by Hadrian's jurists in *c.* 130, and an accepted canon of senatorial resolutions. Although Justinian's reworking of juristic texts systematically sacrificed literary form to legal content, the "question and response" structure is still visible in a minority of the 386 entries in Lenel's *Palingenesia*, through the surviving formulaic uses of *quaesitum est* or *quaero* ("it was asked" or "I ask") and *dixi* or *respondi* ("I said" or "I answered").[39] The answers could become long and complex, acquiring documentation from the opinions of earlier jurists and Imperial constitutions; there may also have been discussion of real cases, later reworked to remove the names and substitute the standard imaginary characters, Maevia, Seius and the rest. The written version did not record verbatim the responses of oral discussion; jurists, like members of the literary elite in general, would revise the content of an oral performance, be it a public reading or seminar, for purposes of publication.[40] Addressing specific questions, Papinian included statements of general juristic principle[41] and allowed one case-specific question to generate a chain of others, exploring the further implications, as a seminar dialogue may also have done. As was the case with all questions, there were at least two

[37] For problems on the exact meaning of this, see Lim 1993.

[38] For letter-style greetings in Papinian's *Quaestiones* see D.46.3.94.3: *Fabius Ianuarius Papiniano salutem* (question follows in general Titius/Seius form, perhaps an adaptation of the original for general use); D.34.9.13: *Claudius Seleucus Papiniano suo salutem* (again, general form, the adulterer Maevius' *iniustum matrimonium* with Sempronia (also accused but not convicted), which precludes the institution of either as *heres*); D.16.3.24: *Lucius Titius Sempronio salutem*, a "letter" between two "John Doe" figures, setting up a problem; D.39.5.27: a real consultation, involving the rhetor Nicostratus and the donation to him of a *cenaculum* as his residence, *defuncto Regulo* (the donor) *controversiam habitationis patiebatur Nicostratus, et cum de ea re mecum contulisset, dixi posse defendi.*

[39] e.g. D.49.1.10.3 (Ulpian): *quaeritur … Papinianus respondit*; D.12.7.5pr.; D.17.2.81: *quaesitum est … dixi*; D.26.7.37.2: *inde descendit quaestio*, within discussion of problems concerning guardianship. Papinian also inserts and answers his own questions as a means of taking forward discussion, e.g. at D.26.5.13.1: *quid ergo si non caveat*? Questions were not confined to works entitled *Quaestiones* (cf. D.26.7.7.14 [Ulpian *On the Edict* 35]).

[40] e.g. D.3.1.8; also D.45.1.115.2, citing Pegasus (late first century), (Masurius) Sabinus and Q. Mucius (Scaevola).

[41] e.g. D.6.1.62.1, specific case of disputed *fructus*, then *generaliter.*

possible answers, and Papinian occasionally canvassed both: "it could be answered", he wrote of an emancipated son's rights to the paternal estate, but, on the other hand, "the more kindly verdict" was the opposite one, which he, Papinian, favoured.[42] And, true to the spirit of controversy encouraged by oral debate, he took pains to take on and refute the opinions of his rivals.[43]

By the second century AD the increasingly unwieldy collections of records of case-discussions had been supplemented by the creation of the written textbook, laying out the basic operational principles of Roman jurisprudence. The most famous example of this, Gaius' *Institutiones*, in four books and apparently based on lecture notes, would come to dominate its field and be recognised by its incorporation, in truncated form, into Justinian's manual of the same name. Other jurists, such as Ulpian or Marcian, would follow his lead with *Institutiones* of their own, or handbooks of *Regulae* or *Sententiae*, encapsulating in a few books all that the average practitioner "needed to know" about the law.

Gaius' work provided a pocket guide to the principles underlying Roman law, beginning with his definition of the *ius civile* as the law belonging exclusively to the citizen body it served. It then covered the law of persons (one book), things (just over two books) and legal actions (just under one book). In other respects, Gaius was a traditionalist, referring frequently to the Law of the XII Tables (on which he also composed a commentary), which some contemporaries dismissed as too ancient to be relevant, and offering, as no jurist had done before him, a history of legal actions, which went back to the *legis actio* of the XII Tables and forward through the formulary procedure. How far this serves as a reliable guide to legal education as practised at Rome is uncertain, but the anecdotes of Aulus Gellius, who shared Gaius' interest in ancient Roman legal history, reveal an active and interdisciplinary culture of debate on legal—including etymological and historical—matters, conducted among groups, which congregated in the Roman Forum and elsewhere.[44]

The combination of greater reliance on the written word and the growth in a rule-based culture among Imperial administrators[45] with the longstanding tradition of Roman self-help education also encouraged private collections of reference works, such as the assemblage of Marcus Aurelius' Imperial constitutions in twenty books by Papirius Iustus.[46] Some collections, such as those used by the Collator of Mosaic and Roman law at Rome in the early fourth century or Boethius in the sixth century, for his commentary on Cicero's *Topica*,[47] were modest. The contents of the personal library of the Collator included Gaius' *Institutiones*, books 7–9 of Ulpian's *On the duties of the Proconsul* (which covered punishment of criminal behaviour), various works in one book by Papinian, Paul, Ulpian and Modestinus, the *Sententiae* ascribed to Paul, all or part of the *Codex* of Gregorius and Hermogenian (292–295 AD) and isolated books from longer works by Papinian, Paul and Ulpian.[48] The author's apparent predilection for the criminal law and the fact that, when

[42] D.37.6.8: *sed benignior est diversa sententia*. Cf. *Fr.Vat.*224, the tentative, *potest dici*, "it can be said".

[43] e.g. D.10.2.22.5; D.10.2.24pr. [44] See Howley 2013. [45] As outlined by Stein 1966.

[46] Lenel, *Pal.* Vol. 1, 947–952.

[47] Frakes 2011, on Mosaic and Roman law; Stump 1988, on Boethius.

[48] Works cited: Gaius *Institutiones*; Papinianus *Definitiones, Responsa, De adulteriis*; Paulus, *De iniuriis, De adulteriis, Responsa* (book 5), *De poenis omnium legum, de poenis paganorum*; Ulpianus

confronted with the vast complexities of the law of succession, he resorts to Gaius' basic guide[49] suggests a writer who used the law but had little interest in its further study. And Boethius, though a sophisticated legal thinker, seems to have relied largely for his law on three textbooks: the *Institutiones* of Gaius, Paul and Ulpian—a modest collection sharply contrasting with the formidable library assembled at Constantinople by his contemporary, Justinian's legal adviser, Tribonian.

12.4 Late Antiquity: Berytus and the Formalising of Legal Education

By the late second or early third century, the Roman *colonia* of Berytus (Beirut) had become a centre of legal learning and instruction, renowned for its production of judicial assessors to governors, and legal administrators.[50] Students were drawn from all parts of the Eastern Roman world, including Neocaesarea in Pontus in the 230s AD;[51] and, in the late third century, Arabia;[52] in the mid-fourth century they came from Euboea in Greece, Tarsus in Cilicia and Antioch itself, and, according to Libanius, were drawn from tradesmen and artisans as well as the local elites;[53] and by the late fifth and sixth centuries, students are known also from Armenia, Asia Minor, Egypt, Lycia and Illyricum.[54]

The law students are often recorded for reasons other than their studies of law. Severinus, from Arabia, worried that his studies would be interrupted by a premature recall to his native city; a Christian student of rhetoric and law, Appianus, from Paga in Lycia, fell victim to the Diocletianic persecution;[55] the legal studies of Anatolius of Berytus are known because of his subsequent illustrious career as praetorian prefect under Constans (r. 337–350) and Julian (r. 361–363). The sixth-century *Life of Severus* by Zacharias of Mytilene also includes incidental insights on Severus' earlier life as a law student, where he recalls that Christian observance was combined with "reading the laws" and "completing the legal readings of the teachers". This lasted all week, except for Sundays and Saturday afternoons.[56]

De officio proconsulis (books 7–9), *Ad edictum* (8 and 18), *Regulae, Institutiones*; Modestinus, *Differentiae* (2 and 6); Paulus, *Sententiae*; Gregorian Code, Hermogenian code (cited separately). Note that the Collator could have had access to the public collections at Rome, on which see Neudecker 2013.

[49] Inst.Gai.3.1–17.

[50] *Expositio totius mundi et gentium* 25 (ed. J. Rougé, Paris Éditions du Cerf 1966). For Beirut see Collinet 1925.

[51] Greg. Thaum. *Panegyric to Origen*.

[52] C.10.50.1, Diocletian and Maximian addressed to *Severino ceteris scholasticis Arabiis* (undated).

[53] Lib. *Ep.* 533; *Ep.* 1539; *Or.* 62.21 ("youths from the workshops"); *Or.* 48.22 (councillors' sons sail off to Berytus or Rome). See also Lib. *Ep.* 1375 on Hermogenus, son of Olympius, rhetor at Antioch, who studied law at Berytus and became assessor to a governor in 365. For verse epitaph for another student from Cilicia, Gilliam 1974. For full list, Hall 2004, 208–209.

[54] Zacharias of Mytilene, *Vita Severi* 55–57.

[55] Euseb. *Mart. Palest.* 4.3.5.

[56] Zacharias of Mytilene, *Vita Severi* 53.

In the early years of Justinian, law teachers from Berytus, among them the "illustrious" Dorotheus and another Anatolius, were adlected by Justinian and his legal adviser, Tribonian, onto the committees charged with the production of Justinian's *Corpus Iuris Civilis*, including his Digest, one of the primary purposes of which was educational.[57] The Digest was a concerted attempt by Justinian to reform the legal syllabus and subject both his new structure and the creation of new legal interpretations for the future to Imperial control. He aimed also to limit the cities where the new legal syllabus could lawfully be taught. The launch document of the *Corpus Iuris Civilis* declared that the "three books" (Digest, Code of Justinian and Institutes) should be sent out only to the "royal cities", Rome and Constantinople, and to "the most fair city of the people of Berytus", which "someone" had "rightly called the nurse of laws".[58] To other cities, however, such as Alexandria and Caesarea, which prided themselves on being centres of academic excellence, a warning was issued, that the emperor had been informed that certain men without legal knowledge were "wandering about and teaching false doctrine", a phrase which assimilated incompetence in law to the dissemination of heretical beliefs.[59] In future, such unauthorised teachers were to be fined ten pounds of gold and (as heretics also were) expelled from the city for teaching, while breaching the laws.[60]

In a constitution addressed to the law professors, Justinian described the Digest in terms of its role as the new definitive legal textbook. Previous attempts at a syllabus, he argued, had depended on selective and inconsistent use of a restricted number of basic texts. Aside from Gaius' *Institutiones*, students had previously studied an eccentric selection of works on a wife's property, guardianships, wills and legacies, legal proceedings, things (the law of things) and eight of the nineteen books of Papinian's *Responsa* (and those in the form of extracts), plus, independently, the *Responsa* of Paul. All this amounted, Justinian claimed, to some 60,000 lines, compared with the three million lines, from which the Digest extracts had been drawn, many of which derived from Tribonian's personal legal library.

Despite the well-advertised iniquities of the previous syllabus, Justinian's divergence from precedent was perhaps less radical than he wished it to appear. Like his predecessors, he (or rather his legal team) had been selective—but, as emperor, he could impose his selections on others. As before, the first year consisted of preliminary study, but this was now to comprise Justinian's Institutes and the first four books of the Digest. The first-year students, hitherto the "two-pounders", were to be rebranded the "New Justinians". In years two and three, students, as before, would study Legal Proceedings (D.5–11) and Things (D.12–19). In year two, as before, they would also choose special book-length subjects, by selecting four books from Digest 23–26, reserving the rest for study in the fourth year.[61] In year three, having devoted their time to what they had not yet studied from Digest 5–19, they would also look at books 20 and 21, where Papinian, the model jurist for

[57] C.1.17.2.9 (undated); C. *Tanta* 9. [58] C. *Omnem* 7.

[59] C. *Omnem 7 quia audivimus ... quosdam imperitos homines devagare et docrinam discipulus adulterinam tradere.*

[60] C. *Omnem 7 reiciantur ab ea civitate, in qua non leges docent, sed in leges committunt.*

[61] The choice was one from two on Tutelages and Curatorships (D.26–27), one from three on dowries and marriage settlements in general (D. 23–25), and the rest from the eight books on wills, legacies and trusts (D.28–36). The last fourteen books had no formal place in the syllabus but were expected to be studied in the students' own time.

previous third-year students, still featured prominently. Third-year students, who were still to be known as "Papinianists", were also encouraged to read up on his *Quaestiones* (thirty-seven books) and *Responsa* (nineteen books), precisely the problem-literature, which had been generated by students' testing of case studies in the lawyers' seminars from the late Republic onwards.[62]

12.5 Conclusion

Justinian's command-and-control model of legal education is far removed from the unstructured, ad hoc and sociable methods of instruction practised under the Republic by a Servius, or, under the Empire, by a Papinian—or, for philosophy, by a Plotinus. For centuries, Romans had operated in line with what had, customarily, worked for them. Lawyers in their seminars would not necessarily have taught "to" the order of topics present in Scaevola's treatise on the civil law (*ius civile*) (or Sabinus' abbreviated version) or to the edict, but they would have been aware of them as potential frameworks for the written outcomes of their oral discussions. As the fashion for teaching from core texts and a set syllabus took hold, discussion of written text became the central but not exclusive focus of legal instruction, and the way was open for the construction of the definitive legal syllabus by Justinian.

However, in acknowledging the central importance of Papinian, even Justinian recognised that focus on text alone could not substitute for the testing of contested concepts and interpretations. Central to both rhetoric and legal thinking, the *controversia* had trained future pleaders and jurists in the exploration of alternative questions and answers; in law, as well as other disciplines, conflicts of interpretation were explored in oral discussions frequented by the elite in seminars from Rome to Constantinople to Beirut. For those who, mistakenly, wanted certainty about "what the law was" and an end to the "ambiguities" of lawyers, this was problematic, the more so because the effective functioning of the Imperial administration required the certainties of a rule-based culture. For Justinian, therefore, one of the attractions of the *Corpus Iuris Civilis* project was that it, supposedly, removed doubt. In fact, as lawyers have demonstrated ever since, such certainty will always prove elusive.

Bibliography

Bernstein, N. W. (2012). "'Torture her until she lies': torture, testimony and social status in Roman rhetorical education." *Greece and Rome* (2nd series) 59: 165–177.

Collinet, P. 1925. *Histoire de l'école de droit de Beyrouth*. Paris.

Crook, J. A. 1995. *Legal advocacy in the Roman world*. London.

[62] Final-year students had the option of studying the *Codex Justinianus*, to be *au fait* with Imperial legislation.

Edwards, M. 2000. *Neoplatonic Saints: the lives of Plotinus and Proclus by their students.* Liverpool.

Frakes, R. 2011. *Compiling the* Collatio legum Mosaicarum et Romanarum *in late antiquity.* Oxford.

Georges, T. (2012). "Justin's school at Rome: reflections on early Christian 'schools'." *Zeitschrift für Antikes Christentum* 16: 75–87.

Gilliam, J. F. (1974). "A student at *Berytus* in an inscription from Pamphylia." *Zeitschrift für Papyrologie und Epigraphik* 13: 147–150.

Griffin, M. 2013. "Latin philosophy and Roman Law." In V. Harte and M. Lane, eds., Politeia *in Greek and Roman philosophy.* Cambridge. 96–115.

Hall, L. 2004. *Roman* Berytus: *Beirut in late antiquity.* Routledge.

Harries, J. 2006. *Cicero and the jurists: from citizens' law to the lawful state.* London.

Howley, J. 2013. "Why read the jurists? Aulus Gellius on reading across disciplines." In P. J. du Plessis, ed., *New frontiers: law and society in the Roman world.* Edinburgh. 9–30.

Liebs, D. (1976). "Rechtsschulen und Rechtunterricht im Prinzipat." *Aufstieg und Niedergang der römischen Welt,* II.15: 197–286.

Lim, R. (1993). "The *auditor* Thaumasius in the *Vita Plotini.*" *Journal of Hellenic Studies* 113: 157–160.

Mertz, E. 2007. *The language of law school: learning to "think like a lawyer".* Oxford.

Neudecker, R. 2013. "Archives, books and sacred space in Rome." In J. König, K. Oikonomopoulou and G. Woolf, eds., *Ancient Libraries.* Cambridge. 312–331.

Sherwin-White, A. N. 1966. *The letters of Pliny: a historical and social commentary.* Oxford.

Stein, P. 1966. Regulae Iuris: *from juristic rules to legal maxims.* Edinburgh.

Stump, E. 1988. *Boethius's* In Ciceronis Topica: *an annotated translation of a mediaeval dialectical text.* Ithaca.

Ulrich, J. (2012). "What do we know about Justin's 'school' in Rome." *Zeitschrift für Antikes Christentum* 16: 62–74.

Wibier, M. 2014. "Interpretandi Scientia: *an intellectual history of Roman jurisprudence in the early empire.*" PhD dissertation, University of St. Andrews.

CHAPTER 13

LAWYERS IN ADMINISTRATION

MICHAEL PEACHIN

13.1 Introduction

Ancient Rome's most prominent lawyers were often thoroughly involved in the Empire's administrative affairs. So, for example, L. Octavius Cornelius P. Salvius Iulianus Aemilianus, or simply Julian, as he is better known, held various governmental posts in the early second century AD. He was, among other things, quaestor to the emperor, tribune of the plebs, praetor, prefect of the treasury, consul and caretaker of Rome's public buildings. He also completed provincial governorships in Germany, Spain and Africa. Beyond all of that, Julian was a frequent member of the emperor's ad hoc advisory boards (*consilia*). Perhaps even more renowned than Julian are two jurists from the early third century. Domitius Ulpianus had been legal adviser (*adsessor*) to a praetor, was then the emperor's secretary for petitions (*a libellis*), prefect of the praetorian guard and prefect of Rome's food supply. Aemilius Papinianus served his nation similarly. He was an adviser to the advocate for the fisc, was also an adviser to the praetorian prefect, and was then, like Ulpian, *a libellis* and praetorian prefect. Both of these men, like Julian before them, worked steadily on the Imperial *consilia*. These three, though exceptionally successful both as lawyers and as administrators, exemplify what numerous others, albeit with varying degrees of success and prominence, also achieved.

In short, there were many Romans—and in fact, even many persons without the Roman citizenship—who in one way or another performed legal functions in an administrative context around the Empire. Therefore, if we are to portray lawyers in administration accurately, as an integral component of Roman legal culture, then our net must be cast well beyond Julian, Ulpian, Papinian and their likes. We must look far and wide geographically, then nearly everywhere in Rome's administrative structures, and finally, both up and down in the Roman social hierarchy. To accomplish all of this, however, we must face certain roadblocks raised (a) by several Roman ways of operating and (b) by the evidence available to us.[1]

[1] The best currently available account of Roman lawyers in administration is offered by Liebs 2002c. Note also Liebs 2010.

It is first crucial to realise that, at least throughout the period with which we are concerned here, the training of a legal expert was neither unified nor organised and overseen by any governing body.[2] Nor, with one potential exception (namely, the so-called *ius respondendi*), was there anything like formalised accreditation of the lawyer.[3] Thus, we simply have no stable group of formal markers which would enable us always and manifestly to identify *the* Roman lawyers. The corollary is that talk of *professional* lawyers becomes especially precarious.[4] Among the elite, those trained in law simply did not make their livings from this talent; nor did they practice law constantly, as their primary occupation on a daily basis.[5] Less well-to-do persons, on the other hand, might indeed earn their daily bread from lawyering.

A similar situation faces us with administration and administrators: "the operation of patronage rather than the application of formal procedures and rules determined the admission and promotion of administrators, who were not and never became 'professionals'."[6] This holds true, broadly speaking, for administrators of elite status. However, just as with the lawyers, sub-elite administrators came much closer to being what we would call professionals. These men received pay, which provided their livelihoods; they might remain for long periods of time in their governmental positions; and it may well be that many of these individuals amassed, in one way or another, material expertise in the substantive affairs of their administrative posts.[7] That said, it is nonetheless impossible to demonstrate that substantive legal expertise was somehow consistently or formally *required* for any given person in any given administrative post—at least during the period here under investigation.

All of this is further complicated by the fact that the Romans had no one word which could be applied universally to all those who possessed some form of legal training or expertise or who carried out some legal function—i.e. no one word equivalent to our "lawyer". Therefore, the manner in which we pinpoint Roman-era individuals who were trained legal experts, or who were actively involved with the law, must be nuanced. The available criteria are as follows.[8]

First, there are individuals who are known to have written about the law, the so-called "literary jurists". Second, those who are specifically labelled, in some fashion, by some piece of documentation (often an inscription), as lawyers, can, with properly exercised care, be presumed to have had some substantive claim to that status. And third, there are those who can be suggested as lawyers, not because there is any evidence of their having

[2] See ch. 12 by Jill Harries in this volume. For an overview, Atkinson 1970.

[3] Tuori 2004 is now the place to begin for the *ius respondendi*.

[4] With regard to Roman legal professionalism, an excellent brief discussion can be had from Crook 1995, 41–45.

[5] A higher degree of professionalism is imaginable, in that those elite individuals recognised as jurisprudents can be argued to have "possessed and exploited specific knowledge and skills which were inaccessible to laymen, and in that they also had at least rudimentary forms of regularised intercommunication, work autonomy, specialist literature, colleague 'control,' organised education, and even ethics" (Frier 1985, xiii).

[6] Garnsey and Saller 1987, 20. Cf. also Brunt 1990, 230–231, 514–515.

[7] Pay: Weaver 1972, 229. Long-time service: Cohen 1984, 41–45. Expertise: Cohen 1984, 56; Haensch 2000. Nonetheless, patronage could play a role in appointments: Purcell 1983, 138–142.

[8] This is most concisely described by Liebs 1980, 123–128, who refines the work of Kunkel 1967.

written about law, nor because we have any indication of their being called, in one form or another, "lawyer", but rather, precisely because of certain positions which they held in the government.[9] This brings us to the actual Graeco-Roman terminology for "lawyer".

Lawyers were conceived in two essential semantic categories by the Romans, and are often divided strictly into these categories by modern scholarship. First, there were those called *iuris prudentes*, or the like; such persons were generally termed *nomikoi* in the Greek-speaking East.[10] Roughly, these individuals were trained experts who provided legal counsel and/or wrote about the law.[11] Then, there were the *advocati*, generally called *syndikoi* or *synegoroi* in the East, or *rhetores* in the papyri.[12] Again speaking very roughly, these were persons trained primarily in rhetoric, rather than legal science, and who argued for clients in court.[13]

Both the most renowned jurisprudents and advocates generally came from the upper levels of society (i.e. were members of the senatorial or equestrian orders, or belonged to the local elites in the provinces), and therefore were engaged in the upper levels of the administrative system. These are the lawyers we know best—again, like Julian, or Ulpian, or Papinian. However, there were also many humble lawyers, as well as many lower-level administrative posts, in which such socially undistinguished lawyers might toil. They, too, deserve our attention.

We are often confronted, however, by perplexing evidence for all of this. So as to provide just a rough sense of the various kinds of problem, which can beset us in talking about lawyers (and especially jurisprudents) in administration, let me briefly present one document. Here is the surviving text on a fragmentary tombstone from Rome (*CIL* VI 1853):

> *[- - -]nus iuris pru/dens scr(iba) aed(ilium) cur(ulium) / v(ixit) a(nnos) LIIII m(enses) IIII d(ies) X.*
>
> [- - -]nus, the jurisprudent and clerk of the curule aediles, lived fifty-four years, four months, and ten days.

So, we have a man, whose epitaph labels him as both lawyer (*iuris prudens*) and as a clerk (*scriba*) in the office of the curule aediles.[14] The fellow will most likely have been either a freed slave or a member of the Roman plebs, and probably spent his entire life toiling away at this one occupation (NB he died at the age of fifty-four, while yet holding

[9] Extrapolating legal expertise from the fact that a man held some particular administrative post is, as we momentarily will see, a risky (often circular) procedure. But, as Liebs 1980, 126–127 points out, this can sometimes be done productively.

[10] In the Latin language, aside from *iuris prudens*, this type of expert might also be called *iuris consultus, iuris peritus, iuris magister* or *iuris studiosus*. See Tuori 2004, 307. For the Greek *nomikos* see Mason 1974, 69; and on the *nomikoi*, Kantor 2009, 262 n. 58, and Jones 2007.

[11] For what is known about the individuals who were understood as jurisprudents see especially: Kunkel 1967; Liebs 1987, 19–75; Crook 1995, 69–113; Liebs 2002a, 27–93; Liebs 2002c, 399–406 (*nomikoi*); Liebs 2005, 19–35; Jones 2007 (*nomikoi*); Liebs 2010, 15–151.

[12] For the first two Greek terms, Mason 1974, 89–90. For *rhetor*, Crook 1995, 62.

[13] For a brief exposition of the advocate–jurisconsult distinction see Crook 1995, 37–41. It is sometimes maintained that this distinction was absolute, i.e. that those recognised as *iuris prudentes* (or the like) did not argue cases in court. So, e.g. Schulz 1946, 55, 108, 119. While it is perhaps true that many jurists inclined to spurn forensic activity, it is also clear that this cannot be considered a hard and fast rule. See Kunkel 1967, 326–328.

[14] Liebs 1980, 161–162 notes that the use of *prudens*, rather than *peritus*, is here odd. That notwithstanding, the man was manifestly being labelled as an expert in the law.

the position as clerk, and lists no other administrative post). Now, had the decision not been taken by the person who fashioned the text for this tombstone to call the deceased *iuris prudens*, we would have no reason whatsoever to suppose that this man was a lawyer; for the status as jurisprudent is otherwise never attested among those who functioned as *scribae* in the Roman administrative system. The best interpretation is probably that this man had somehow acquired, in the course of his life and work, some level of legal ability, but that whoever took the decision to mark him for eternity as a jurisprudent was engaging in at least a bit of bluster.[15] Be that as it may, this man's epitaph raises two significant complexities for us.

First, what of other scribes, or at least those (let us say) who served in the office of the curule aediles? Shall we figure that all of them, or some of them, or any of them were likewise jurisprudents? Or is the present case simply anomalous? In short, on the basis of what this one tombstone reveals, are we justified in suspecting that legal expertise was in some sense, or sometimes, a *desideratum* for those who worked in this post?[16] This quandary—namely, how to know when or whether juristic skill can be presumed for the holders of particular administrative posts—is a significant problem, and has not been properly or sufficiently recognised as such.

Secondly, what are we to make of overt claims about legal expertise? Just *how much* proficiency lies behind any given assertion of status as jurisprudent? This is especially problematic for the non-literary jurists, i.e. those who are labelled as jurisprudents (again, often by inscriptions of one kind or another) but who are not attested to have written about the law. There simply are no "one size fits all" solutions to these matters. But, it must be realised that many situations of this kind lie behind much of what can be said about lawyers in administration. Caution must be a constant companion.[17]

A last issue facing us has to do with the fact that we are looking for lawyers *in* administration. Here, the problem is that a recognised legal specialist could function variously in an administrative capacity, i.e. sometimes as an office holder, other times in a more non-official or ad hoc manner. Furthermore, we must reckon with both jurisprudents and advocates in government service. Thus, for example, the man of elite (esp. equestrian or senatorial) status, who was an acknowledged jurisprudent, might at one moment hold a particular governmental office which involved him directly and principally in legal activities (say, as *a libellis*); at a second moment he might be found in an office which would frequently involve him in such activity, but did not always (say, as governor of a province);

[15] Liebs 1980, 161–162 accepts that this man was a jurist (of some level). With respect to the possible bluster here, it is worth noting that the *scribae* were reputed to lord it over their bosses, precisely because they had many years of solid experience in office, whereas their superiors did not. On this, Cohen 1984, 54.

[16] Cohen 1984, 56 does indeed, precisely because of this one inscription, assume juristic competence on the part of all *scribae* at Rome.

[17] By way of example, yet one other situation. We know of a man named Aufidius Chius, who is recorded to have given a response about a matter of usufruct (*Fr.Vat.* 77); thus, he must have been a lawyer. He was also pretty certainly, given his *cognomen* (namely, Chius), a freed slave. Liebs 1980, 147–148 thus suggests that we are not in the presence of a jurist like Pomponius or Gaius, but instead, that Chius belongs to their "Umvolk"—perhaps "orbit" in English. In short, this man's low social status might suggest a lesser degree of legal expertise, or at least, inferior stature qua jurist. As Liebs indicates, nuance in such situations is always crucial.

and at yet a third moment he might be engaged on an ad hoc basis to advise, informally or quasi-formally, another man who was holding some official post.[18] All such types of activity are best classed as being *in* administration.

13.2 Lawyers in Administration

Our approach will now be the following. For simple lack of space, we will have to function almost exclusively at the top of the social, legal and administrative realms, and also at the centre of the Empire—in short, at Rome, and with the periodically mobile Imperial court. The idea will be to cast lawyers in the emperor's ambit as broadly illustrative of what could be revealed, were we systematically to work out to the provinces, and down the hierarchies of both society and administration. In any case, at top and centre, as well as at the lower levels and periphery, one wants to ask the following questions. What sorts of men, in possession of what sorts of legal expertise, carried out what kinds of legal functions, at which levels and places in the Roman Imperial system of government?[19]

One final caveat, however, must be registered. What we will observe in the next few pages is how Roman lawyers (as we have now delimited them) *could* function in a very few areas of Roman administration. This must not be confused with a representation of how things, by virtue of some carefully organised system of formalised arrangements, along with scrupulous oversight of those arrangements, invariably *did* work.

In accord with the fact that the Roman *iuris prudens* was most essentially an expert legal adviser, we find him frequently in such a capacity in administrative contexts. Thus, right at the start of our period (in 54 BC), Cicero recommended one of the great jurists of his day, C. Trebatius Testa, to Julius Caesar, who was in need of expert legal counsel. As a result, Testa sought out Caesar in Gaul, and from all that can be discerned, remained with him until the Ides of March in 44 BC, all the while providing legal guidance to the great man. He served Caesar, however, as a friend (an *amicus*), rather than as the holder of some formally titled governmental position. Indeed, Testa remained an equestrian his entire life, and never held any state office.[20] He arguably should be perceived as a lawyer in administration; but, Trebatius Testa was never an administrator, per se.

[18] One might think here of Pliny the Younger, reminding his friend Tacitus that (*Ep.* 1.20.12): "I have frequently pleaded in court [advocate], have often functioned as judge, and have also often served on a *consilium* [legal adviser]." One man, various legal roles, and n.b., sometimes in administration, though not always. Moreover, we nowadays do not typically think of Pliny as a lawyer—or at least, he has (and indeed, had in his own day) no reputation as a jurisprudent (cf. Schulz 1946, 109 n. 3).

[19] The use of the word "men", as opposed to (say) "persons" or "individuals", is intentional, since both custom and statute prohibited Roman women from engaging in legal "professions" (and, of course, government as well). Thus, to my knowledge, we have no evidence of a woman from the Roman world ever having been called *iuris prudens*, or the like. Then, women were specifically not allowed to be *assessores* (Hitzig 1891, 44). Women were also strictly prohibited from arguing on another person's behalf in court, i.e. they could not be advocates (cf. Evans Grubbs 2002, 6–70).

[20] On Testa, and his career, see Nicolet 1974, 1043–1044, no. 350; *PIR*² T 306; Liebs 2010, 15–17.

The cooperation of Julius Caesar and Trebatius Testa harks back, on the one hand, to the earlier Republican practice of aristocratic Romans informally recruiting (legal) advisers, both for private affairs and when engaged as magistrates of the state. More importantly in the present context, this relationship prefigures the engagement of jurists in the *consilia* (advisory councils) of the Roman emperors.[21] From the time of Augustus down to that of Hadrian, emperors would sporadically enlist their friends (*amici*) and companions (*comites*)—initially senators, but later also *equites*—to provide them with advice of all sorts; among these advisers were recognised jurists, offering (especially) legal counsel. What is not so clear is just exactly how, when, and how effectively the legal expertise of these jurisprudents was actually brought into play. Still, we get glimpses. So, for example, Trebatius Testa himself, who was to Augustus as he was to Caesar an *amicus*, and thus, a *quondam* member of Augustus' board of advisers, was once summoned by the emperor, along with "the jurists" (*prudentes*), to give advice about a matter of testamentary law upon which Augustus was preparing to rule. Testa's opinion on the matter carried that day.[22]

By the time of Hadrian (if not before), an emperor apparently might, in appropriate situations, call together a "professional nucleus within the *consilium*" (Crook 1955, 59) for advice. Here, jurisprudents will have predominated. But, the details of how this core group of jurists may have functioned remain far less than clear.[23]

Then, toward the later part of the second century, we begin to hear of certain advisers to the emperor who had a proper administrative title: *consiliarii*.[24] They were not *amici*, asked to serve on an ad hoc basis, but salaried officials, of equestrian status, who apparently served for extended periods of time. In Crook's words (1955, 73–74), "small fry, humble *equites* with neither the social standing nor the influence of the great *amici* and the leading jurists, from whom they must be rigorously distinguished". Presently, there are six known *consiliarii*, and their careers span the period from about the 170s to the 220s AD. Now, of these six, three are indeed attested, in some fashion, as jurists; the other three are in no way thus labelled. It is tempting to assume that all six of these men, as well as the (surely) other *consiliarii* who have disappeared from the historical record, were jurists. However, it must be recognised that there is a fair degree of speculation involved in suppositions of this kind. Indeed, we face the same sort of problem here as we did with our

[21] Some essential literature on the Imperial *consilia*: Crook 1955; Millar 1977, 93–98, 110–122 (esp. 119–120); Amarelli 1983; Liebs 2010, 153–165.

[22] Inst.2.25pr, with Liebs 2010, 18. On the legal issue involved here (enforcement of codicils) see Johnston 1988, 25–29. On the whole issue of juristic opinion actually shaping Imperial action (or that of other magistrates) see Crook 1955, 71, 125; Peachin 2001; Liebs 2010, 9, 163 n. 755. In short, the opinions of jurists (indeed, the substantive law) did not always prevail, regardless of Testa's success in the present case.

[23] The most basic issue involves the potential existence of two strictly separate Imperial advisory boards, the one administrative, the other judicial. Crook 1955, 18, 30, 33, 58–60, 113 was of the opinion that Hadrian started giving more prominence to jurists on his advisory boards, but that there was never a formalised legal vs. administrative separation of the *consilia*; rather, there was a kind of inner circle of legal specialists from Hadrian's time on. On the other hand, Kunkel 1974, 595–601 (a review of Crook, originally *Zeitschrift der Savigny-Stiftung für Rechtsgeschichte* 72, 1955, 463–470), and 188–191 (an article originally in *Zeitschrift der Savigny-Stiftung für Rechtsgeschichte* 85, 1968) was of the opinion that there had always been separate administrative and judicial *consilia*. The issue is, to be honest, vexed. Cf. Liebs 2010, 161.

[24] See Eck 2006 and Liebs 2010, 153–159.

scriba aedilium curulium above (section 13.1). That is, does the fact that some *consiliarii* are known to have been jurists mean that all the others were too? Moreover, since some of the known *consiliarii* were jurists, shall we presume that the office itself was legal in nature, and required that its holders possess an appropriate legal training? What makes all of this even more perplexing is the fact that there is no evidence whatsoever as to exactly what a *consiliarius* did; the best guess is that he prepared legal materials for pending cases.[25]

Subsequently, between the years *c.*260 and 310, we meet three other men, all of them with the title *a consiliis*. None of these individuals is actually called a jurist. Still, it seems as if they ought to have been performing the function(s) of the earlier *consiliarii*, whatever that or those may have been, but now under a new title. Thus, one is tempted to envision the *a consiliis* as a lawyer in administration. His duty was perhaps to assist the emperor with expert legal advice whenever he was conducting trials, or generally to prepare legal business for him; but, once again, explicit evidence to such effect is entirely lacking. We are once more skating on disquietingly thin ice.

We also know of another official, working in the ambit of the emperors, who likewise may have been involved in the preparation of legal cases for the emperor's court: the *a cognitionibus*, later called *procurator/magister sacrarum cognitionum*. It seems perfectly plausible that at least some of the holders of this post, like the men who were *consiliarii* or *a consiliis*, or like our *scriba aedilium curulium*, may have possessed some legal training. If so, then they too should be included in a depiction of lawyers in administration.[26]

The last post in the emperor's orbit which must be considered is that of *a libellis*. This was an office created by Claudius. Freedmen held the position initially, until Hadrian turned it over to equestrians; and by the mid-second century, we know that trained jurists were being appointed.[27] Indeed, by the Severan period, not only did jurists hold the position as *a libellis*, but there also appear to have been individuals with legal training engaged as their subordinates in that bureau.[28] The chief point in the present context is that during the third century it can seem as if the men appointed to this office were consistently jurists, and that they played a very significant role in resolving all of the legal queries and petitions (*libelli*) which were submitted to the emperor by persons of humble status.[29]

In sum, if one considers merely the legal experts in the emperor's coterie, then we have (at least) the following administrative functionaries, who should be taken into consideration: the *amici* and *comites*, especially those attested as jurists; the *consiliarii*; the *a consiliis*; the *a cognitionibus/magister sacrarum cognitionum*; the *a libellis*; perhaps some workers in the office of the *a libellis*.[30] Just exactly how all these putative lawyers in administration

[25] See Eck 2006, 74–75.
[26] On this official see Hirschfeld 1905, 33–331.
[27] See Liebs 2010, 165–166.
[28] See Liebs 2006, 141.
[29] See: Honoré 1994; Liebs 2006; Liebs 2010. There is a problem, though, which cannot be detailed here. The usual presumption is that petitions from more important persons (whether private individuals or governmental officials) came to the emperor as letters (*epistulae*), and that these were answered by the official called *ab epistulis*. Many such *epistulae* involved legal questions. So, how did the *ab epistulis*, who is not generally presumed himself to have possessed any particular legal expertise, obtain the legal support he presumably needed to answer appropriately? We probably need to think of teamwork, both in the context of *epistulae* and of *libelli*. For some cursory suggestions along these lines see Peachin 2015.
[30] Note, furthermore, the career of P. Messius Saturninus, who served as *trecenarius a declamationibus Latinis* to Septimius Severus. He was clearly an expert *rhetor* and advocate (as is also demonstrated by his career otherwise); however, it now seems certain that he was not the jurist,

functioned together, so as to implement substantive law on a quotidian basis, is now relatively clear. That said, more work could still be done here; and there was, clearly, a very wide world beyond the Imperial court.

Given the limits of the present volume, the portrait of lawyers in administration, per se, must end here. However, a bare list of just a few other administrative positions, which could merit consideration in this regard, will provide an inkling of the broader situation. Some of these positions have a legal advisory function, while others must have entailed partially, or even entirely, advocacy or adjudication. In any case, here are some of the other administrative posts which were somehow involved with the implementation of law, and thus, whose holders might in many instances have been lawyers:[31]

assessores more broadly (again, generally called *nomikoi* in the East)
praefectus urbi
praefectus praetorio
iuridici
correctores
praetor fiscalis
advocatus fisci (there were various of these)[32]
adiutor curatoris agris emendis dividendisque
procurator ad bona damnatorum
procurator inter mancipes XL Galliarum et negotiantis
procurator ad bona cogenda in Africa
praefecti iure dicundo[33]
epistrategoi in Egypt
others of the *apparitores*?

13.3 Conclusion

When the editors of this volume asked me to discuss lawyers in administration, I blithely envisioned a concise summary of what is already well known. However, as the writing began

likewise a Messius, revealed by D.49.14.50 (see Liebs 2010, 57). Still, and just as Leiva Petersen says (*PIR*² M 527), in his position as *a declamationibus Latinis*, Messius Saturninus "surely prepared Severus' judicial speeches". Thus, we apparently have another "lawyer" working with the emperor—but now as an advocate, rather than a jurist. Cn. Cornelius Lentulus might have functioned similarly, though much earlier; namely, for Augustus. Cf. Crook 1955, 26, 160 no. 116.

[31] This list is based largely on a quick glance at the various administrative posts listed by Pflaum 1961, 1018–1019, with a few random additions. Thus, it covers only a part of the central administration, and does not consider at all exhaustively the situation in the provinces. Moreover, I have not included, for example, the various *procuratores XX hereditatium* or the various *procuratores viarum* listed by Pflaum, and about whom one might want to think in the present context. Nor are the various types of advocate engaged by local communities properly represented in this list. For just an inkling of this see Dmitriev 2005, 213–216, or Maiuro 2010, 21–212.

[32] Note also, by way of example, C. Iulius Bassus Aemilianus, *actor Caesaris ad Castor(is) et ad loricata(m)*, who, like the regular advocates of the fisc, appears to have handled fiscal trials in Rome; thus, another advocate in fiscal administration. See Maiuro 2010, 210–213. Or, note the man *electus ad causas fisci tuendas in provincia Alpium Maritimarum* (Pflaum 1961, 1046).

[33] Cf. Oliver 1963.

to take shape, the absence of anything at all like a full treatment of lawyers in the Roman administrative system became quickly apparent. John Crook, Tony Honoré, and Detlef Liebs, in particular, have brought us a very great distance; there now can be no doubt that in the circles close to the emperor, law and lawyers were ever present. Yet even with regard to this area of the Imperial administrative system, more might be eked out. For example, it seems still worth giving some thought to the ultimate ability of the lawyers to shape Imperial business according to substantive law. In any case, as we move away from Rome, or from the Imperial court, the currently available picture becomes blurry.[34] Therefore, rather than an all-encompassing resumé, this contribution has become a distressingly sketchy prolegomenon to a full study of Roman lawyers in Roman administration.

That said, one particular characteristic does seem to emerge even from this highly impressionistic portrait. With only a few exceptions, it will most likely prove quite difficult to be confident that a truly consistent and concerted effort was ever made (at least during the period here in question) to place trained legal experts in any given administrative position.[35] On the face of it, the presence, or not, of lawyers in Roman administration *seems* to have been a rather haphazard affair. Conversely, and perhaps even paradoxically, it is plain that legal expertise was indeed very widely and very often present in the Roman administrative apparatus. This makes a complete study of this phenomenon all the more urgent; for, to the extent that there are patterns, or habits, or formalised mechanisms of operation to be discovered, these should be plainly delineated.

Were such an account to be written, it might do well to follow roughly the lines of investigation set out here. It should take into its purview both jurisprudents (legal scholars and advisers) and advocates (barristers), all the while exercising caution in the identification of these lawyers, and in gauging the level of their expertise. It should seek its lawyers both among the elite administrators, and in the circles of the little people, who toiled away in the more lowly offices of the Roman government. It should pay close attention to those governmental offices in which lawyers are most likely, with some frequency, to have worked; but, it would have to retain an appropriate level of scepticism regarding the issue of mandatory and measurable legal expertise for the appointees to those positions. It should start at Rome, and at the Imperial court. It should move thence to the central administration more broadly. It should also travel through Italy, and out to all the provinces, to the innumerable local nooks and crannies where law was affecting people's lives.

What such a study would ultimately be attempting, of course, is a full portrait not even so much of lawyers in administration, but rather, of the formalised integration of legal concerns, writ large, within the Imperial administrative structures. That is, just when and just where did the Roman authorities see fit to involve legal expertise, and hence, the potentially expert application of substantive law, in their governing apparatus? And, to whose benefit, in any given instance, was this done? For in some situations, the presence of law (or lawyers) in administration must surely have been meant to serve governmental interests—think of the advocates for the fisc. In other instances, however, a service was being provided to those, who desired to use the Empire's legal system—think of the

[34] Still, for an excellent overview of lawyers in the provinces see Liebs 2002c.

[35] The potential exceptions are: the *a libellis* or the *praefectus praetorio* for a period of time in the third century; perhaps the *consiliarii* and later *a consiliis*, though as we have seen, there is speculation involved here; and probably the *assessores* to magistrates, starting in the Severan period.

emperor's legal advisers, helping to resolve his subjects' inquiries and disputes. And of course, wherever we find lawyers in play, it would be good to know, if we can, just how influential they were. That is, did the presence of lawyers generally result in the dominance of substantive law? In any case, more profound answers to these sorts of question would, in turn, represent an extremely valuable attainment for one particular reason which goes far beyond simply cataloguing lawyers active in the Roman state's administrative structures.

There can be no doubt that the basic nature of Roman Imperial rule must have played a significant role in the longevity of that regime. Indeed, one of the editors of this volume has forcefully argued that legal security, which was notionally integral to the Roman way of ruling, and which the advent of a Mediterranean-wide Roman Empire spread broadly, was a key element in Rome's staying power, precisely because this legal security materially augmented the acceptance of Rome's dominion by those living under her sway.[36] The problem for Ando, of course, as well as for all of us who wonder about such things, is that the ultimate effectiveness of a legal regime, and thus the potential benefits it brings, is horribly difficult to quantify. Ando has splendidly shown us what many residents of Rome's Empire said in this regard. They claimed, in very large part, to have been very much impressed. And there can be no doubt whatsoever that many people of many different sorts were indeed well served by, for example, the emperor in his functions as law court, and legal services department.[37] Still, it would be good to know just what lay behind the sentiments Ando has mustered. In other words, if we were to have so detailed a picture as can be painted of the Roman government's concerted efforts itself to function as a vehicle for the implementation of positive law, both as actor in this regard and as impetus for the implementation of law by others at the local level, we would thereby have gained a kind of quantitative angle on this problem, which has heretofore largely eluded us.[38] Ultimately, we need to perceive at least four related issues as parts of a whole: (1) how and what the Roman government itself invested in the implementation of positive law; (2) the extent to which the central government fostered and cooperated with local legal regimes; (3) how far both of these efforts may have succeeded; (4) what people's impressions of, and/or experiences with, these efforts were.

Such an all-embracing picture of lawyers in administration would not ultimately tell us, beyond doubt, the exact degree to which a rule of law was tangibly established by the Roman state. The extant data are simply not up to a task like that; and, most likely, no data set could be. Nevertheless, a proper synthesis, insofar as this is attainable, would yield a much better taste of what was attempted. It would provide us with one little bit of something akin to *terra firma*, from which we could then fruitfully explore further. For the time being, however, we still lack a comprehensive depiction of lawyers in administration for ancient Rome.

[36] I refer to Ando 2000.

[37] The work of Liselot Huchthausen long ago demonstrated how women, slaves, soldiers, not to mention many other "have-nots", were very well able to use the Imperial legal services. One may start with Huchthausen 1992, and thence work back to her earlier contributions.

[38] Liebs 2010, 6–7 raises precisely this issue, and then does much to resolve it in his following pages. But again, we are here in the circle of the emperor; and there was a great deal more. In particular, the interplay of Roman law and the many local legal regimes has recently been the subject of various excellent pieces of work, e.g. Kantor 2009; Fournier 2010 (with a very good review by Kantor 2011); Ando 2014; Dolganov forthcoming.

Bibliography

Ando, C. 2000. *Imperial ideology and provincial loyalty in the Roman empire.* Berkeley.

Ando, C. 2014. "Pluralisme juridique et l'intégration de l'empire." In G. de Kleijn and S. Benoist, eds., *Integration in Rome and in the Roman world.* Leiden/Boston. 5–19.

Amarelli, F. 1983. Consilia principum. Naples.

Atkinson, K. M. T. (1970). "The education of the lawyer in ancient Rome." *South African Law Journal* 87: 31–59.

Brunt, P. A. 1990. *Roman imperial themes.* Oxford.

Cohen, B. 1984. "Some neglected *ordines*: the apparitorial status-groups." In C. Nicolet, ed., *Des ordres à Rome.* Paris. 23–60.

Crook, J. A. 1955. Consilium principis: *imperial councils and counsellors from Augustus to Diocletian.* Cambridge.

Crook, J. A. 1995. *Legal advocacy in the Roman world.* Ithaca.

Dmitriev, S. 2005. *City government in Hellenistic and Roman Asia Minor.* Oxford.

Dolganov, A. Forthcoming. "*Reichsrecht* and *Volksrecht* in theory and practice: Roman law and litigation strategy in the province of Egypt." In M. Jursa and H. Täuber, eds., *Administration, law and administrative law: comparative studies in imperial bureaucracy and officialdom.* Vienna.

Eck, W. 2006. "Der Kaiser und seine Ratgeber: Überlegungen zum inneren Zusammenhang von *amici, comites* und *consiliarii* am römischen Kaiserhof." In A. Kolb, ed., *Herrschaftsstrukturen und Herrschaftspraxis: Konzepte, Prinzipien und Strategien der Administration im römischen Kaiserreich.* Berlin. 67–77.

Evans Grubbs, J. 2002. *Women and the law in the Roman empire: a sourcebook on marriage, divorce and widowhood.* London/New York.

Fournier, J. 2010. *Entre tutelle romaine et autonomie civique: l'administration judiciaire dans les provinces hellénophones de l'empire romain, 129 av. J.-C.–235 ap. J.-C.* Athens.

Frier, B. 1985. *The rise of the Roman jurists: studies in Cicero's* Pro Caecina. Princeton.

Garnsey, P. 1970. *Social status and legal privilege in the Roman empire.* Oxford.

Garnsey, P. and Saller, R. 1987. *The Roman empire: economy, society, and culture.* Berkeley.

Haensch, R. (2000). "Le rôle des *officiales* de l'administration provinciale dans les processus de décision." *Cahiers du Centre Gustave Glotz* 11: 259–276.

Honoré, T. 1982. *Ulpian.* Oxford.

Honoré, T. 1994². *Emperors and lawyers.* Oxford.

Hirschfeld, O. 1905². *Die kaiserlichen Verwaltungsbeamten bis auf Diocletian.* Berlin.

Hitzig, H. 1891. De magistratuum et judicum Romanorum assessoribus. Bern.

Huchthausen, L. 1992. *Frauen fragen den Kaiser: eine soziologische Studie über das 3. Jh. n. Chr.* Constance.

Johnston, D. 1988. *The Roman law of trusts.* Oxford.

Jones, C. (2007). "Juristes romains dans l'Orient grec." *Comptes rendus des séances de l'Académie des Inscriptions et Belles-Lettres* 151: 1331–1359.

Kantor, G. 2009. "Knowledge of law in Roman Asia Minor." In R. Haensch, ed., *Selbstdarstellung und Kommunikation: die Veröffentlichung staatlicher Urkunden auf Stein und Bronze in der römischen Welt.* Munich. 249–265.

Kantor, G. (2011). [Review Fournier 2010.] *Journal of Roman Studies* 101: 248–249.

Kunkel, W. 1967². *Herkunft und soziale Stellung der römischen Juristen.* Graz/Vienna/Cologne.

Kunkel, W. 1974. *Kleine Schriften. Zum römischen Strafverfahren und zur römischen Verfassungsgeschichte*. Weimar.

Liebs, D. 1980. "Nichtliterarische römische Juristen der Kaiserzeit." In K. Luig and D. Liebs, eds., *Das Profil des Juristen in der europäischen Tradition: Symposion aus Anlass des 70. Geburtstages von Franz Wieacker*. Ebelsbach. 123–198.

Liebs, D. 1987. *Die Jurisprudenz im spätantiken Italien (260–640 n. Chr.)*. Berlin.

Liebs, D. 2002a. *Römische Jurisprudenz in Gallien (2. bis 8. Jahrhundert)*. Berlin.

Liebs, D. 2002b. "Die vorsullanischen lateinischen Rechtstexte," "Archaische Rechtsbücher," "Die vorklassischen juristischen Fachshriften." In W. Suerbaum, ed., *Handbuch der lateinischen Literature der Antike*, Vol. 1: *Die archaische Literature von den Anfängen bis Sullas Tod*. Munich. 65–79, 56–574.

Liebs, D. 2002c. "Rechtskunde im römischen Kaiserreich: Rom und die Provinzen." In M. J. Schermaier, J. M. Rainer and L. C. Winkel, eds., Iurisprudentia universalis: *Festschrift für Theo Mayer-Maly zum 70. Geburtstag*. Cologne/Weimar/Vienna. 383–407.

Liebs, D. 2005². *Römische Jurisprudenz in Africa: mit Studien zu den pseudopaulinischen Sentenzen*. Berlin.

Liebs, D. 2006. "Reichskummerkasten: die Arbeit der kaiserlichen Libellkanzlei." In A. Kolb, ed., *Herrschaftsstrukturen und Herrschaftspraxis: Konzepte, Prinzipien und Strategien der Administration im römischen Kaiserreich*. Berlin. 137–152.

Liebs, D. 2010. *Hofjuristen der römischen Kaiser bis Justinian*. Munich.

Maiuro, M. 2010. "What was the *Forum Iulium* used for? The *fiscus* and its jurisdiction in first-century CE Rome." In F. de Angelis, ed., *Spaces of justice in the Roman world*. Leiden. 189–221.

Mason, H. 1974. *Greek terms for Roman institutions: a lexicon and analysis*. Toronto.

Millar, F. 1977. *The emperor in the Roman world (31 BC–AD 337)*. Ithaca.

Nicolet, C. 1974. *L'ordre équestre à l'époque républicaine (312–43 av. J.-C.)*, Vol. 2: *Prosopographie des chevaliers Romains*. Paris.

Oliver, J. H. (1963). "Augustan, Flavian, and Hadrianic *praefecti iure dicundo* in Asia and Greece." *American Journal of Philology* 84: 162–165.

Peachin, M. 2001. "Jurists and the law in the early Roman empire." In L. de Blois, ed., *Administration, prosopography and appointment policies in the Roman empire*. Amsterdam. 109–120.

Peachin, M. 2015. "Weitere Gedanken zum Prozess des Verfassens kaiserlicher Reskripte." In A. Kolb and U. Babusiaux, eds., *Das Recht der Soldatenkaiser—rechtliche Stabilität in Zeiten politischen Umbruchs?* Berlin. 211–224.

Pflaum, H.-G. 1961. *Les carrières procuratoriennes équestres sous le Haut-Empire romain*. Paris.

Purcell, N. (1983). "The *apparitores*: a study in social mobility." *Papers of the British School at Rome* 51: 125–173.

Schulz, F. 1946. *History of Roman legal science*. Oxford.

Tuori, K. (2004). "The *ius respondendi* and the freedom of Roman jurisprudence." *Revue internationale des droits de l'antiquité* 51: 295–337.

Weaver, P. R. C. 1972. Familia caesaris: *a social study of the emperor's freedmen and slaves*. Cambridge.

CHAPTER 14

LEGAL WRITING AND LEGAL REASONING

ULRIKE BABUSIAUX

14.1 Introduction

THE seminal influence of Roman law on posterity may be explained by the survival of a true specialist literature on law, which contains legal discourse, mainly from writings of the so-called "classical jurists" during the first to third centuries AD.[1] The transmission of these writings is due to Justinian's compilation of ancient legal sources in the sixth century AD, which is said to have preserved about 5 per cent of the existing legal literature.[2] Simultaneously, it changed the character of the texts recorded, since Justinian's compilers only collected those parts that were suitable for compilation.[3] This focus explains why they cast aside most of the literary elements, such as dedications, introductions and other information on content and style of the work.[4] Hence, in the Digest, classical Roman law is available today as a corpus of legal statements structured according to the needs and the preconceptions of Byzantine legal scholars and practitioners. This normative understanding of these texts prevailed throughout the Middle Ages until the age of codifications and is still tangible in the dogmatic research on Roman law. Yet, the fragments preserved in the Digest can be and also have been read as information on the excerpted jurists, their intellectual individuality, their different legal methods and their style.[5]

The framing of different text-types is one of the achievements linked with the name of Fritz Schulz. In his still very influential study of "Roman legal science" (1946) he

[1] On the "classical period" of Roman law see Schulz 1946, 99–101; Wieacker 1988, 19–25.

[2] C. *Tanta* (a. 533) §1.

[3] On Justinian's work see Wieacker 2006, 287–324.

[4] Little has survived, e.g. the famous introduction to Gaius' commentary on the XII Tables in D.1.2.1 (Gaius, XII Tables, book 1): "Since I am aiming to give an interpretation of the ancient laws, I have concluded … This is not because I like making excessively wordy commentaries, but because I can see that in every subject a perfect job is one whose parts hang together properly. And to be sure the most important part of anything is its beginning" (transl. ed. Watson), on this see Harris 2014, 71–72.

[5] For an overview see Santucci 2012, 150–157.

showed the Roman jurists as experts in the Weberian sense and distinguished isagogical literature, commentaries and so-called *problemata*.[6] Some of Schulz's presuppositions have been challenged by further research; Detlef Liebs' numerous works in particular have deepened the understanding of Roman legal literature. Liebs' contributions to the *Handbuch der lateinischen Literatur der Antike* present Roman legal writing within the context of the remaining Roman literature and give a detailed account of every single work of legal writing that has been transmitted by Justinian compilation.[7] Moreover, Liebs has shown that jurists unattested in the literature were nevertheless important in the legal life of Rome and stressed the distinctiveness of Roman legal writing in comparison to these jurists.[8] Another improvement fostered by Liebs' research is the acknowledgement of jurists from the Roman provinces, especially the Greek-speaking East, explaining that they drew on their cultural background also when practising the most Roman of all disciplines, namely law.[9]

One aspect that still needs further research is the analysis of the literary character (*Literarizität*) of Roman legal writing. This aspect is strongly linked to the examination of the methods employed by the Roman jurists in their works. Therefore, the present study will neither describe single works of Roman legal literature nor treat singular arguments or the weight of different arguments within legal writing and legal reasoning. In lieu thereof the internal structures of legal writing will be examined by means of a narrative analysis. The advantage of this approach lies in the fact that a narrative analysis

> does not focus on norms, foundational principles, or the policies enacted by the law, but rather attends to its narrative dimension—characters and events, how they are described, which textual and rhetorical elements serve to elaborate their content, and the communicative processes through which the lawgiver transmits the law to its audience.[10]

The narrative reading focuses on the cases ("stories") the jurists are telling, the verbal presentation of these cases and the "discourse" by which the messages are conveyed to the reader. It must be stressed that this approach is not anachronistic since the basic idea of narrative analysis was already known to the Greek philosophers, who distinguish between literature (*mimesis*) and philosophy (*logos*) and stress their coincidence in philosophical treatises.[11] Moreover, it seems that modern narrative analysis owes a great deal to ancient rhetoric, since the basic narrative structure, the story or the case, is inspired, if not taken over from the rhetorical concept of *narratio*.[12] Even if it cannot be assumed that Roman legal writing is infused with rhetorical knowledge throughout, it is evident that Roman jurists, as part of the elite, were trained in essential rhetorical techniques and therefore also used their fundamental rhetorical skills as a basis in their legal writing.[13]

[6] Schulz 1946, 141–261.

[7] See Liebs 1989, 1990, 1997 and 2002. See also the regular updates on: http://www2.jura.uni-freiburg.de/institute/rgesch1/handbuch_liebs.php, accessed 28 January 2016.

[8] Further bibliography in Liebs 2002, 560–562.

[9] Fundamental is Liebs 1976, 322–345; an overview can be found in Liebs 1997, 209–217 with further bibliography.

[10] Bartor 2012, 292–311, 293.

[11] Neschke-Hentschke 2013, 144–145.

[12] On *narratio* see Knape 2003, 98–104. On the rhetorical influence on modern narrative analysis see Deciu Ritivoi and Graff 2008, 955–957.

[13] On this see Kacprzak, ch. 16.

The programme sketched thus far necessitates a focus on writings that can be directly analysed and compared. This implies the exclusion of Republican jurists, since very little direct evidence about them has been preserved. Nor will any consideration be given to legal writing of later ages, especially that of Justinian, Byzantine and medieval study of the Roman sources. This later literature has its own problems, as well as its specific structure and style. This caveat also holds true for the so-called "epi-classical" legal writing during the period from Diocletian to Justinian: even though the legal standards are said to have been preserved within the Imperial chancellery, there is little evidence for proper legal literature, apart from isagogic writing.[14]

14.2 Different Degrees of Narrative Concentration

The first and very simple distinction that can be made when looking at Roman legal writing is the one between casuistic and non-casuistic or systematic texts. From the point of view of narrative analysis, relating a case is telling a story. But it is also obvious that cases may be more or less integrated into other structures, such as systematic presentation or argumentation. Therefore, different degrees of narrative concentration can be observed within the different types of legal writing.

Although Roman law is said to be casuistic in nature, the jurists' writings do not merely pile up cases. A very strong casuistic and therefore also narrative coinage can be observed in the "Collections of replies" (*libri responsorum*) and the "Digests" (*libri digestorum*), but also in the epistolary literature (*libri epistularum*) and in works written for the instruction of advanced students, such as writings entitled "Considerations" (*libri quaestionum*) and "Disputations" (*libri disputationum*).[15] From this point of view, the narrative analysis coincides with the literary genre of "problematic literature" coined by Schulz. But in contrast to Schulz, the narrative analysis also considers the unique work *Imperialium sententiarum in cognitionibus prolatarum ex libris sex, Decretorum libri tres* by Paul as a work of casuistic structure.[16] In this text, Paul delivers protocols of sessions before the Imperial court and gives a report of the factual background of the trial and the arguments of both sides before relating the emperor's decision (*decretum*).[17] A more indirect use of cases can be observed within the books on "rules" (*libri regularum*). In these writings the jurists try to summarise and to generalise rules by way of induction from cases.[18]

Clearly not of casuistic character are the isagogical writings[19], especially the "Small handbook" (*Liber singularis enchiridii*) written by Pomponius and the *Institutiones* by

[14] For a recent survey see Babusiaux 2015, 261–265.

[15] On different types of casuistic literature see Liebs 1997, 99–101; on *libri responsorum* and *epistulae* see Liebs 1990; on *libri quaestionum* see Babusiaux 2011, 16–18, 266–269.

[16] On this work (*libri decretorum*) see Liebs 1997, 172.

[17] Very well known is the case of Camelia Pia reported in Pal. 877 = D.37.14.24 Paul., Imperial Decisions Pronounced in Judicial Examinations on Decrees, and in Pal. 59 = D.10.2.41 Paul., Decrees, book 1, on which Peachin 1994; Wankerl 2009, 194–202.

[18] On this see Schmidlin 1976; Nörr 1972, 28–32.

[19] On isagogical writings see Liebs 1997, 187–188.

Gaius. Paul, Ulpian, Modestinus and Marcian have also written works with that title. Even if the *Institutiones* mention rescripts or replies, the corresponding cases are not narrated; the jurists only give the results obtained and try to integrate these results in their description of the existing law.[20] A more systematic approach is also found in the monographs and the commentaries on statutes.[21]

An intermediate position with a mixture of casuistic or narrative elements and a more systematic approach can be seen within the edictal commentaries (*libri ad edictum*), the commentaries on earlier jurists, the instructive works for magistrates, and in books that define themselves as *collectanea* or *epitomes* of other works.[22] Their intermediate position stems from the fact that they contain narratives of cases, but that these cases are tied back into a more systematic starting point (edictal commentaries, monographs) or integrated into a more general discussion of a legal problem (*libri ad Sabinum, notae*, instructive works). A typical example of such mixing, while coming from a systematic starting point, can be found in Ulpian's edictal commentary on *negotiorum gestio*. The passage starts with a citation of the edictal wording ("the praetor says"), which first leads to a comment on the significance of the central words of the edict and then to the presentation of different cases to which the edict applies.[23] The commentary then turns back to some central wording of the edict that the jurist defines by giving first a semasiological and then an onomasiological explication.[24] As this procedure aims at defining the application of the edict from the side of the facts, the onomasiological view is closely connected to the presentation of cases, which may be real, taken out of existing legal writing or even invented.[25]

An illustration of a general legal discussion can be coaxed out of Ulpian's argument on the sale of wine in his *Libri ad Sabinum*: The argument begins with a phrase that might be a citation of Sabinus:

> If wine which has been sold goes sour or goes off in some other way, the loss is the purchaser's, as it would be if the wine were spilled, whether through the casks being staved or for some other reason. (Transl. ed. Watson)

Ulpian then gives exceptions to this rule and cites cases, in which the vendor has to bear the risk, especially when the parties agreed upon a degustation period or had foreseen a case of *custodia*.[26] The origin of these exceptions may be called casuistic, as they can be traced back to the contractual conditions developed in contractual practice (*Kautelarpraxis*), but the jurist is systematising these exceptions under the main idea of risk allocation in a contract of sale (*periculum*).

[20] An example would be Inst.Gai.2.119–120 on the so-called pretorian testament, where Gaius cites a rescript by Antoninus Pius that prefers the pretorian heir over the civil-law heir. The best overview on the legal question is Müller-Eiselt 1982, 170–175.

[21] On the monographs see Liebs 1997, 127–128; on the commentaries on statutes see Wesel 1967, 133–137.

[22] On commentaries (*libri ad*) see Liebs 1997, 139–140; on the instructive works for magistrates see dell'Oro 1960.

[23] Pal. 347 = D.3.5.3pr.-5 Ulp., Edict, book 10.

[24] See Pal. 349 = D.3.5.3.6–11 Ulp., Edict, book 10; Pal. 350 = D.3.5.5.2 Ulp., Edict, book 10.

[25] Further details on this technique can be found in Babusiaux 2014, 34–46.

[26] Pal. 2717 = D.18.6.1pr Ulp., Sabinus, book 28, on which see Jakab, 2009,187–258.

It must be stressed that the characterisations mentioned are only approximations and that jurists felt free to define the scope of their writings differently even if they adopted the same title as another jurist. One obvious example can be taken from a comparison between two books entitled "Considerations" (*Quaestiones*), but written by two different authors, Paul and Papinian: whereas Paul pays great attention to all individual traits of the case reported, Papinian mainly uses cases in an argumentative fashion, constructing them around a larger theoretical argument.[27] Thus, Paul seems to focus on the narrative, while Papinian seems to focus on systematic questions. With regard to their respective literary genre, Paul's *Quaestiones* appear to be close to the *Libri responsorum*, with the slight difference that Paul's report of the facts is more extensive than in most *libri responsorum*. On the other hand, Papinian's *Quaestiones* are close to writings entitled "Disputations" (*disputationes*), i.e. works that even present virtual cases to develop and strengthen an argument.[28] In that respect, *disputationes* can be interpreted as insights into the process of law-finding, whereas *responsa* are the results of this process.

The differences observed in the use of narrative structures go hand in hand with divergences in the verbal representation of the cases cited by the jurists in their writings.

14.3 The Verbal Representation of the Story

Looking at the different types of casuistic literature, one can easily distinguish between different types of storytelling. The first main distinction is linked to the presentation of the case. The jurist can indeed give names, places and further details enabling the reader to identify the persons involved;[29] but in most legal works the cases will be cited without these indications, i.e. by using stock names ("Blankettname"), such as "Titius", "Maevius" and "Seius" for free men and "Stichus" and "Pamphilus" for slaves.[30] This distinction is not only linked to the differences between more or less casuistic materials in one work. That is to say that individual naming can also be found in a work like Papinian's *Quaestiones* where cases are used as arguments, whereas anonymous citing is quite often used in strictly casuistic writing such as *libri responsorum* or *digesta*.[31] This amalgamation shows that it depends upon the jurist's or his editor's[32] choices as to whether individual features

[27] For a further characterisation of Paul's work see Schmidt-Ott 1993, 58–101.

[28] On the character of *disputationes* see Lovato 2003, 3–15.

[29] A very special example is D.39.5.27 Pap., Considerations, book 29: "A young man called Aquilius Regulus wrote to the rhetor Nicostratus as follows: …" (transl. ed. Watson), on which see Babusiaux 2011, 247–249.

[30] An overview on the material can be found in Meinhart 1986, 186–197. See also ch. 12 by Harries in this volume.

[31] One can also find traces of depersonalisation before publication, e.g. Pal. 19 = D.14.3.20 Scaev., Digest, book 5: "Lucius Titius appointed a freedman to manage a moneylending business of his. The freedman issued the following *cautio* to Gaius Seius: 'Greetings to Domitius Felix from Octavius Terminalis, acting for Octavius Felix.'" (transl. ed. Watson). On the legal issues see Platschek 2013, 214–221.

[32] The edition and transmission of legal writing before Justinian constitutes a separate problem that cannot be dealt with here. See Wieacker 1975, 72–138.

of the cases are communicated or not. The use of prominent names may serve to intensify the argument, since they prove that a case really happened or that important people were involved and given some advice by the citing jurist, but it may also be that the individual features were left in the *libri responsorum* or *digesta* because the collection was edited negligently. This negligence or lack of ability could be connected with the arcane character of a work, i.e. that it was originally intended only for a restricted circle of followers of the jurist.[33]

The second and even more important distinction with regard to the verbal presentation is associated with the use of the case by the citing jurist. The author may be interested in presenting and commenting on the case, so that the case itself is the main concern of the text. But it can also be observed that cases are cited as proof, as examples (*exempla*), whose solution is widely accepted but needed in another controversial case.[34] Yet the case may also be cited or invented in order to prove the failure of another jurist; in this case, the narrative structure is a special form of *reductio ad absurdum* or part of a dialectic or topical argumentation.[35]

These features are connected with the last and most important criterion of distinction, namely the existence or use of dialogue structures within legal writing. Dialogue is the basic model for all writing in Antiquity, especially in teaching and technical argumentation.[36] Its importance in legal writing stems from the generally accepted influence of dialectics on the jurists' reasoning. At its core, dialectical reasoning consists in a dialogue between a defendant, trying to defend the widely accepted position (*endoxa*), and the offender, trying to prove the failure of the majority view. Proof is adduced whenever the defender has to accept the offender's assumptions, which are formulated in order to attack the majority view. In doing this, the offender will not adopt an openly converse position, but will try to relate his assumptions to the widely accepted position by means of a topical argument. If the assumptions are topically related to the *endoxa* position and are true, commonly accepted or acceptable, they weaken this position, and ultimately lead to its refutation. The same procedure can be used in an internal argument, where it is used to test the existing view and develop a better one. Narrative structures in dialectical reasoning serve as arguments; they are mainly demonstrations or exemplifications that are used as assumptions by the offender.[37]

While the dialogical structure can generally be found in writings that focus on the cases, such as *libri responsorum*, *digesta* and Paul's *Libri decretorum*, it can most commonly be observed in epistolary literature, commentaries on earlier jurists and the instructive writings for advanced students (*disputationes, quaestiones*). In all these writings, there is always an enquirer, which can be either a party in need of legal advice or a student. Yet, if the author attributes the role of the enquirer to an earlier jurist, he is making use of a mimetic device, since the questioning is fictitious and only serves the author's argumentation. This device is common in Paul's epitome of Labeo's "Plausible views" (*pithana*).

33 On problems of the edition of arcane works see Liebs 2008.

34 See Cic. *Top.* 44–45, on the text see Kacprzak, ch. 16, in this volume.

35 On the use of *exempla* in legal writing see Nörr 2009; further examples (for topical and dialectical use of cases) in Babusiaux 2011, 63–174.

36 See Harries, ch. 12, in this volume.

37 See Babusiaux 2011, 63–174 with further references.

Indeed, Paul often cites Labeo's legal opinion verbatim, before phrasing his severe criticism, often introduced by "on the contrary" (*immo contra*).[38] This sequence of two opposing legal opinions can be interpreted as an imitation of a dialogue, the first speaker being Labeo, the second being Paul, posthumously criticising the first. If the author addresses students, the criticism may even be harsher: In his "Considerations" Papinian constantly replies by using rhetorical questions as answers, a stylistic device that reveals the weakness of the initial question and humiliates the enquirer. On the other hand, however, the very same jurist also uses rhetorical devices that imitate dialogues whenever he wants to justify one of his legal innovations by citing an earlier jurist.[39] Even if it is evident to the audience that the previous jurist was not defending Papinian's position, the imitation of a dialogue with the predecessor lends weight to Papinian's argument.

The importance of dialogues for instruction and persuasion explains why dialogue-structures can also be found between the author and the reader of legal writing. This external dialogue can be observed in instructive works for magistrates:

> A proconsul is not absolutely obliged to decline gifts, but he should aim for a mean, neither sulkily holding completely back nor greedily going beyond a reasonable level for gifts. (Transl. ed. Watson)[40]

Even if the jurist writing does not address the magistrate directly, but only via the third person, these writings are referring to the magistrates mentioned in the title of the work. Their target audience must have been office holders wanting to learn about their responsibilities and privileges.

Aside from the aforementioned genres, there is still a wide range of legal writing without or with only few dialogical elements. The first group of writings without dialogue structures are the commentaries on statutes and the edict; the second group consists of the isagogic works, including "Sentences" (*sententiae*), *libri regularum* and "Definitions" (*definitiones*).

14.4 Discourse: The Author's Perspective

"Discourse" as the third point of comparison in narrative analysis consists of describing the process and the methods by which the story is conveyed to the addressee. In order to trace this narrative process, it is necessary to distinguish between self-presentation of the narrative voice, as a participant in the process of finding the law and as an observer.

It is evident that the jurists are presenting themselves as participants in the legislative process whenever they collect their own replies (*responsa*) or publish their letters written to a client. This perspective is therefore inherent in the *libri responsorum*, the *digesta*, the epistolary literature, but also in the instructive works for advanced students (*quaestiones*,

[38] e.g. D.33.7.5 Labeo, Plausible Views, epitomised by Paul, book 1.

[39] See Babusiaux 2011, 249–255 (rhetorical questions), 135–137 (figures of dialogue).

[40] See Pal. 2145 = D.1.16.6.3 Ulp., Duties of a proconsul, book 1.

disputationes), in which the jurists explain how to find the law. It is remarkable, however, that this attitude is also present in the instructive works for magistrates and in Paul's *Libri decretorum*. In the case of instructive literature, an example is provided by Ulpian's book on the duties of the proconsul (*De officio proconsulis libri X*).[41] In this work, Ulpian defines the rules of conduct for the provincial governor by generalising from the rescripts he cites.[42] Since he is a valued adviser in the Imperial *consilium*, Ulpian does not hesitate to interpret the Imperial rescripts with a certain authoritative pretence. This manifestation of the authorial persona is also tangible in the reports given by Paul in his *Libri decretorum*:

> Papinianus thought that he [Clodianus' heir] had repudiated the inheritance under the earlier one [testament] but could not accept under the later one [testament]. I held that he did not repudiate in that he thought that the later one was valid. He [the emperor] decided that Clodianus had died intestate. (Transl. ed. Watson)[43]

The open expression of his dissent shows that Paul thinks of himself as a protagonist within the deliberation process at court. In fact, Paul even seems to be suggesting to his reader that his legal opinion should prevail despite the Imperial decision.[44]

Displays of the jurists' influence can also be found in legal commentaries, especially the late classical commentaries on the pretorian edict. In opposition to Schulz's description of the commentary as a mere "lemmatic" interpretation of the pretorian enactment, it must be stressed that the great commentaries written by Ulpian and Paul also prescribe how to apply the edict.[45] That is to say that in these commentaries both jurists present themselves as participants in the process of finding the law, not as mere observers of the pretorian regulation. The most telling element in this respect is the use of words of personal evaluation by Ulpian (*puto*), whenever there is a debate among earlier or contemporary jurists.[46] A comparable tendency can be observed in the commentaries on Sabinus (*libri ad Sabinum*) and similiar examinations of earlier jurists. The citation of Sabinus or other earlier jurists does not constitute a report on the existing law, but serves mainly to give a pretext for the presentation of the commentator's own voice and view.[47] A similar approach is at work in the works entitled "Rules" (*libri regularum*), in which the rules are not only reported but also challenged by the author.[48]

The jurists' participation in finding the law is even more visible in writings known as "Considerations" (*quaestiones*) and "Disputations" (*disputationes*). Since they address

[41] On this work see Liebs 1997, 181–182.

[42] Fundamental is Mantovani 1993/1994, 235–267.

[43] D.29.2.97 Paul. Decrees/Imperial Judgements, book 3.

[44] On the collections see Peachin 1994, 334–338; on Paul's critical attitude see Nörr 1974, 127–130.

[45] See Babusiaux 2014, 46–54.

[46] An example for Paul is D.41.2.1.16 Paul., Edict, book 54, where he first cites the opinion of the earlier jurists (*veteres*) and then states: "The truer view (*verius*), however, is that ..." (transl. ed. Watson).

[47] A typical example is D.28.5.4pr-2 Ulp., Sabinus, book 4, where Ulpian first cites an opinion that may go back to Sabinus, before turning to Julian's opinion and giving his own viewpoint (§1): "I think that ..." and then presenting further cases as proof of his opinion (§2): "But also if, where ..., I think ...".

[48] e.g. D.28.5.52pr. Marcian., Rules, book 3. In this example a rescript issued by Marcus Aurelius contradicts the rule established by earlier jurists. Similar are *definitiones*, see Liebs 1997, 119–120.

advanced students, the argumentative procedures that are only tacitly present in other writings are here explicitly laid out or even exaggerated for didactical reasons.[49]

On the other hand, the jurists can also adopt the position of a simple observer, as can be seen in their strictly isagogical writings, especially the *Institutiones* and Pomponius' *Liber singularis enchiridii*. This perspective can also be observed in most monographs that focus on their specific subject, rather than on arguments used in law-finding.[50] An extreme example is available in Paul's sole book on "Degrees and relationships by marriage and their names" (*De gradibus et adfinibus et nominibus eorum liber singularis*), in which the jurist simply enumerates different degrees of relationship without any visible commentary, not to mention criticism.[51] This self-effacement is also common in commentaries on statutes that describe the current state of the jurists' debate on the interpretation of a certain statute, but generally do not question the legislator's intentions.[52]

14.5 Conclusion

The narrative analysis of Roman legal writing shows the coincidence of narratives and dialogues whenever jurists present themselves as participants in the process of finding the law. Therefore, the production of law seems to be strictly connected to cases and the dialogical exchange about them.

In taking the previous observations as a basis for the description of literary genres in legal writing, some existing classifications can be corroborated, while others must be challenged. The narrative analysis presented has shown that three groups of legal writing are to be distinguished: firstly, the collections of cases (*libri responsorum*, Paul's *Quaestiones*, *digesta*, *libri decretorum*, letters); secondly, the group of examination works, commentaries on the edict and on earlier jurists as well as instructive works for magistrates. The third group consists of strictly isagogical writings, commentaries on statutes and monographs. The first group is characterised by its mainly narrative nature. A typical feature of these works is that the author as a jurist is in the centre of the work and is directly involved in the process of finding the law, which in fact consists of narrating the resolution of a concrete case. In the second group of legal writing, the narrative structure is subordinated to more systematic categories, such as the edict and the *officium* of the magistrate. The third group is characterised by the almost complete absence of casuistic elements, with

[49] A typical example for a didactical presentation of the argument can be found in D.28.5.4 Ulp., Sabinus, book 4, where Ulpian first cites a decision and then develops different solutions for alternative (and even extreme) cases. An example for an amplification is D.16.3.31pr Tryph., Disputations, book 9: "The good faith that is required in contracts calls for level dealing in the highest degree; but do we assess level dealing by reference to the law of nations [*ius gentium*] only, or, in truth, in connection with the precepts of the civil and praetorian law? Suppose ..." (transl. ed. Watson).

[50] For an overview on Paulus' monographs see Liebs 1997, 162–172.

[51] See D.38.10.10 Paul., On Degrees and Relationships by Marriage and their Names, sole book.

[52] See D.23.2.44 Paul., *lex Iulia et Papia*, book 1; see also D.37.14.17 Ulp., *lex Iulia et Papia*, book 11, in which a very controversial discussion among earlier jurists is reported, but not commented on. For the legal matters see Babusiaux 2015, 250–253.

the jurists' limiting themselves to giving an account of the current state of the law without further commentary.

When comparing these groups to the existing classifications, the principal difference lies in the further integration of late classical genres into the existing literature. The most important result is that Paul's *Libri decretorum* and the instructive works for magistrates, especially Ulpian's book "On the duties of the provincial governor", can no longer be regarded as exceptional or new types of legal literature. Instead, they appear as continuations of existing legal writing. On the one hand, Paul's protocols of Imperial decisions can be seen as a further development of the collections of *responsa* given by a jurist "in private". On the other hand, Ulpian's instructive writing for magistrates is in line with the traditional genre of edictal commentary. Just as the edictal commentary prescribes how to apply the law as a praetor or provincial governor, Ulpian's *Libri de officio proconsulis* instruct the magistrate how to behave when ruling a province.

The second major result of this enquiry lies in a subdivision of various types of writing that Schulz summarises under a common heading. The first classification to be questioned is that of "problematic literature". From a narrative point of view, *libri responsorum* and *digesta* should not to be categorised together with *quaestiones* and *disputationes*, since the first group only reports, whereas the second group actually discusses the law. Even though both are based on narrative (case) and dialogue, the first group is centred on the description of the case and its solution, whereas the second group concentrates on developing the said solution, i.e. on dialogue. Therefore the writer's intentions in his contact with the reader are of a very different nature. The same objections cast doubts on the accuracy of comprising *libri ad edictum* and *ad Sabinum* with commentaries on statutes under the common heading of "Commentaries".[53] As has been shown, the commentaries on statutes differ palpably from other commentaries (*libri ad edictum/Sabinum*), since commenting on a statute (*lex*) seems to be restricted to the interpretation of the legislator's intentions, whereas commenting on the edict or earlier jurist permits the author's interference and law-finding.

The third and last result of this study is the necessity to question a well-known characterisation of Roman law as "Jurists' law". As we have seen, even the Roman jurists themselves did not pretend to be the only participants in the law-finding process as they give space to and explicitly reference the legislator (*lex*), the emperor (*rescriptum, decretum*) and tradition (*libri ad Sabinum, mos*). Similarly, the characterisation of Roman law as *ius controversum* can also be challenged. As has been shown, the jurists treat law as a matter in constant evolution. This evolutionary character in itself presupposes a solid footing in tradition and a strict control of legal opinions by the expert colleagues. This is why the jurists are constantly trying to create consensus on legal questions,[54] and indeed, the entirety of legal literature can be understood as an attempt to achieve this consensus. The publication of *reponsa* and the public disclosure of the internal discussion of the Imperial court are meant to make the arguments public; the commentaries on the edict and on books of earlier jurists can be seen as attempts to inform about existing material and overcome its

[53] On the definition of commentaries see Schulz 1946, 183–186; Liebs 1997, 139–140.

[54] On this aspect see Giaro 2007, 197–298.

weaknesses; and last, but not least, the didactical and monographical writing serves to forge a new generation of jurists that will carry on the law.

Bibliography

Babusiaux, U. 2011. *Papinians* Quaestiones: *Zur rhetorischen Methode eines spätklassischen Juristen*. Munich.

Babusiaux, U. 2014. "Der Kommentar als Haupttext." In D. Kästle and N. Jansen, eds., *Kommentare in Recht und Religion*. Tübingen. 15–55.

Babusiaux, U. 2015. "Zitate klassischer Juristen in den Reskripten der Soldatenkaiser." In U. Babusiaux and A. Kolb, eds., *Das Recht der Soldatenkaiser*. Berlin. 238–268.

Bartor, A. 2010. *Reading law as narrative*. Atlanta.

Bartor, A. (2012). "Reading biblical law as narrative." *Prooftexts* 32: 292–311.

Bretone, M. 1982[2]. *Tecniche e ideologie dei giuristi romani*. Naples.

Deciu Ritivoi, A. and Graff, R. 2008. "Rhetoric and modern literary theory." In U. Fix, A. Gardt and J. Knape, eds., *Rhetorik und Stilistik*. Berlin/New York. Vol. 1: 944–959.

dell'Oro, A. 1960. *I* libri de officio *nella giurisprudenza romana*. Milan.

Giaro, T. 2007. *Römische Rechtswahrheiten*. Frankfurt am Main.

Harries, J. 2014. "Lawyers and citizens from republic to empire: Gaius on the Twelve Tables and antonine Rome." In C. Rapp and H. A. Drake, eds., *The city in the classical and post-classical world*. New York. 62–80.

Jakab, É. 2009. *Risikomanagement beim Weinkauf*. Munich.

Knape, J. 2003. "Narratio". In G. Ueding, ed., *Historisches Wörterbuch der Rhetorik*. Vol. VI. Darmstadt. Col. 98–106.

Lenel, O. 1889. *Palingenesia Iuris Civilis*. Leipzig. (Second reprint of the 1960 Graz edition. Aalen 2000.)

Liebs, D. 1972. *Die Klagenkonkurrenz im römischen Recht*. Göttingen.

Liebs, D. (1976). "Römische Provinzialjurisprudenz." *Aufstieg und Niedergang der römischen Welt* II.15: 288–362.

Liebs, D. 1989. "Recht und Rechtsliteratur." In R. Herzog, ed., *Handbuch der Lateinischen Literatur der Antike*. Munich. Vol. 5: 55–73.

Liebs, D. 1990. "Römische Rechtsgutachten und *responsorum libri*." In G. Vogt-Spira, ed., *Strukturen der Mündlichkeit in der römischen Literatur*. Tübingen. 83–94.

Liebs, D. 1997. "Jurisprudenz." In K. Sallmann, ed., *Handbuch der Lateinischen Literatur der Antike*. Munich. Vol. 4: 83–217.

Liebs, D. 2002. "Die vorklassischen juristischen Fachschriften." In W. Suerbaum, ed., *Handbuch der Lateinischen Literatur der Antike*. Munich. Vol. 1: 560–574.

Liebs, D. 2008. "Esoterische römische Rechtsliteratur vor Justinian." In R. Lieberwirt, ed., *Akten des 36. Deutschen Rechtshistorikertages*. Baden-Baden. 40–79.

Lovato, A. 2003. *Studi sulle* disputationes *di Ulpiano*. Bari.

Mantovani, D. (1993/1994). "Il *bonus praeses* secondo Ulpiano." *Bullettino dell'Istituto di Diritto Romano "Vittorio Scialoja"* 96–97: 203–267.

Meinhart, M. 1986. "Möglichkeiten der Erfassung der Eigennamen in den Digesten." In H.-P. Benöhr et al., eds., *Festschrift für Max Kaser*. Vienna. 183–199.

Müller-Eiselt, K. P. 1982. Divus Pius constituit: *kaiserliches Erbrecht*. Berlin.

Neschke-Hentschke, A. 2013. "Literarische Form und Grenzen des Arguments in Platons Gesetzen: zu *Nomoi* 859b–864c." In M. Erler and J. E. Heßler, eds., *Argument und literarische Form in antiker Philosophie*. Berlin/Boston. 143–168.

Nörr, D. (1972). "Spruchregel und Generalisierung". *Zeitschrift der Savigny-Stiftung für Rechtsgeschichte, romanistische Abteilung* 89: 18–93.

Nörr, D. 1974. *Rechtskritik in der römischen Antike*. Munich.

Nörr, D. (2009). "Exempla nihil per se valent." *Zeitschrift der Savigny-Stiftung für Rechtsgeschichte, romanistische Abteilung* 126: 1–54.

Peachin, M. (1994). "The case of the heiress Camilia Pia." *Harvard Studies in Classical Philology* 96: 301–341.

Platschek, J. 2013. *Das Edikt* de pecunia constituta. Munich.

Santucci, G. 2012. "La scienza romanistica tedesca vista dall'Italia: il 'dogma' della fungibilità dei giuristi romani." In C. Baldus et al., eds., *Dogmengeschichte und historische Individualität der römischen Juristen*. Trento. 133–158.

Schmidlin, B. (1976). "*Horoi, pithana* und *regulae*." *Aufstieg und Niedergang der römischen Welt* 15.II: 101–130.

Schmidt-Ott, J. 1993. Pauli Quaestiones: *Eigenart und Textgeschichte einer spätklassischen Juristenschrift*. Berlin.

Schulz, F. 1946. *History of Roman legal science*. Oxford.

Stolfi, E. 2011. "Argumentum auctoritatis." In A. Lovato, ed., *Tra retorica e diritto*. Bari. 86–102.

Wankerl, V. 2009. Appello ad principem: *Urteilsstil und Urteilstechnik in kaiserlichen Berufungsentscheidungen (Augustus bis Caracalla)*. Munich.

Watson, A. ed., 1985. *The Digest of Justinian. Translation*. Philadelphia.

Wesel, U. 1967. *Rhetorische Statuslehre und Gesetzesauslegung der römischen Juristen*. Cologne.

Wieacker, F. 1975. *Textstufen klassischer Juristen*. Göttingen (reprint of the 1959 edition).

Wieacker, F. 1988. *Römische Rechtsgeschichte*, Vol. 1. Munich.

Wieacker, F. 2006. *Römische Rechtsgeschichte*, Vol. 2, edited by J. G. Wolf. Munich.

CHAPTER 15

GREEK PHILOSOPHY AND CLASSICAL ROMAN LAW
A Brief Overview

JACOB GILTAIJ

15.1 Introduction

THE relation between Greek philosophy and Roman law in the period between the second century BC and the third century AD is highly problematic.[1] For starters, there are many difficulties of textual transmission between Greece and Rome, which are otherwise outside the scope of this chapter.[2] Furthermore, rather than deriving them from Greek philosophical texts as such, the Romans in general and the jurists in particular appeared to have amalgamated Greek notions with pre-existing Roman ones, making it hard to determine in what measure references are not just a type of lip service to Greek culture. An example of such a notion might be *humanitas* (humanity), which is linked to the notions of παιδεία (education) and φιλανθρωπία (as a care for the whole of humanity) as early as the Roman Republic.[3] The main culprit in this context is Marcus Tullius Cicero, often explicitly conflating Greek and Roman terminology, making the use of his works as sources for an influence of Greek philosophy on Roman law even in later periods extremely difficult.[4] Similarly related to Cicero in particular is the problem of eclecticism and syncretism: probably adhering to a specific current in Greek philosophy himself, not only does Cicero present amalgamations of Greek and Roman terminology, even when a particularly Greek notion seems to be in play, the notion in question may very well be a compound derived from various Greek philosophical currents. The same can be said for similar notions in the texts of Roman jurists in the later Principate. Finally, a problem inherent to the state of the Roman legal sources, apart from the difficulties regarding their later transmission, is the fact that there exists a gap between the late Republic and the Principate after around 100 AD, from which only relatively few Roman

[1] See also Winkel 1997, 373–384.

[2] Merely for the difficulties regarding the revival of Aristotle in the first century BC: Barnes 1997.

[3] Schulz 1954, 128–130.

[4] “Foredoomed to failure”: Schulz 1963, 75; but Behrends 1976, 273.

legal sources have survived, making the argument for certain continuities in the influence of Greek philosophy on Roman law between those two periods once again problematic. Scholars of Roman law have used various methods and sources to help bridge that gap, such as the works of Seneca and the first century AD historians,[5] and the rhetorical sources of the late Republic and early Principate.[6]

These problems then lead to the chapter being structured as follows: on the basis of the transmitted legal sources, the piece is divided into a part on the influence of Greek philosophy on Roman law in the late Republic and one on the same influence as regards the jurists of the Principate between about a 100 AD and the third century AD. Each of these parts will then be subdivided into a part on individual Roman jurists being referred to in the sources and literature as making use of or adhering to certain aspects of Greek philosophy, and a part concerning specific Greek philosophical notions that seemingly found their way into Roman legal texts. The latter part itself will then again be subdivided into two parts: taking the problem of syncretism into account, a division according to philosophical current—Platonism, Aristotelianism, Stoicism[7]—seems to be ill-advised, and I have therefore opted for a somewhat flawed but at least philosophically sound division between logical/rhetorical subjects and more physical/ethical notions. The reader may forgive me for preferring brevity and some degree of completeness over nuance and detail in the course of this chapter.

15.2 LATE REPUBLIC

15.2.1 Individual Jurists

The first major point of contact between Roman society and Greek philosophy took place in the year 155 BC. In that year, an embassy consisting of the heads of the Athenian Peripatetic, Academic and Stoic schools of philosophy spoke before the Roman senate. Possibly in the context of the so-called Scipionic circle, from that time on the sources indicate jurists were prone to seek out a philosophical education. At first, the Stoic school seems to have garnered some popularity. Unlike the Academy and the Peripatos, this current has no central figurehead like Plato or Aristotle. Subsequent heads of the Stoic school from the third century BC on are Chrysippus, Diogenes of Babylon (speaking before the senate) and Panaetius of Rhodes. Cicero[8] and Pomponius[9] refer to M. Manilius, Quintus Mucius Scaevola *augur*, Quintus Aelius Tubero *maior* and Publius Rutilius Rufus as having been influenced by Panaetius.[10] From these jurists, only isolated fragments remain, and it is therefore impossible to assess

[5] Mantello 1979; Nörr 2003.

[6] Horak 1972, 121–141; Nörr 1972; Schmidlin 1976, 101–130; Tellegen 2003.

[7] Pythagoras will feature marginally, Epicureanism is problematic: Bund 1980, 130, 134–137.

[8] Cicero discusses the philosophical background of individual jurists on various occasions, primarily (Kübler 1934, 83 n. 5) *De or.* book 1 (for example, 45), *Tusc.* 1 (4), *Acad. Pr.* 2 (165) and *Brut.* (115).

[9] D.1.2.2.39–40.

[10] Kübler 1934, 83; Pohlenz 1948, 261; Schulz 1963, 63; Bund 1980, 131–132, 143; Wieacker 1988, 640–641.

whether they applied or employed philosophical concepts in their juristic technique. This does not, however, appear to hold true for the subsequent generation. The sources testify of both a philosophical background as well as an application of this background in the juristic works of Quintus Mucius Scaevola *pontifex*, Servius Sulpicius Rufus and Marcus Iunius Brutus in particular. Whereas Scaevola *pontifex* and Iunius Brutus[11] probably still tended towards Stoicism (or at least the Panaetian version), other schools became *en vogue* as well. Servius Sulpicius Rufus, for example, studied under the Academic Antiochus of Ascalon, who also was to become Cicero's teacher.[12] Similarly, Aquilius Gallus, Trebatius Testa,[13] Alfenus Varus and Quintus Aelius Tubero *minor* cannot be said to have an allegiance to Stoicism in particular, or any specific philosophical current at all.[14] Thus, with this generation eclecticism, picking and mixing notions and terms as they see fit, appears to have been the norm for jurists when it comes to Greek philosophy as an intellectual background to their works. The best example of an eclectic jurist in the late Republic may be Marcus Antistius Labeo, whose etymologies appear Stoic, employs Aristotle in his definition of contract,[15] and uses classifications derived from the Academy.[16] Yet, two remarks need to be made here: firstly, that the sceptic Academy, an offshoot of the Platonic current, seems to have favoured eclecticism in the sense of combining concepts derived from other currents to form new theories; and secondly, that other currents in this era tended towards including a dialogue with other currents as well, Panaetian Stoicism to name but one instance. In short, it is possible eclectic tendencies in the works of late Republican jurists can theoretically still be the result of adherence to a single philosophical current.

15.2.2 Individual Subjects

15.2.2.1 *Logic/Rhetoric*

The first and perhaps clearest influence of Greek philosophy on the works of the late Republican jurists may very well be in the sphere of the theories of language, definition and science. Even when disregarding the role of P. Mucius Scaevola, M. Iunius Brutus and M. Manilius as the "founding fathers" of the *ius civile* (law of Roman citizens),[17] Pomponius' remark that Q. Mucius Scaevola *pontifex* "first arranged the *ius civile* according to genus (type) in eighteen books"[18] is substantiated by a number of sources to a degree that it may be warranted to speak of an early treatment of law as a science as a result of the adaptation of philosophical theories.[19] The term "science" in this context means that the dialectic method enabled the late Republican jurists to organise knowledge with the purpose of suggesting legal problems that had not presented themselves yet.[20] It is, however, debatable in what measure the idea of a late Republican scientific revolution is an invented tradition.[21] In any case, Scaevola *pontifex* appears to have undertaken this ordering of the *ius civile* in two ways:

11 Yet, Kübler 1934, 92 and Bund 1980, 133, 145.
12 Kübler 1934, 83.
13 Yet, Kübler 1934, 95 and Bund 1980, 136.
14 Bund 1980, 145.
15 Συνάλλαγμα: D.50.16.19.
16 Wieacker 1988, 642.
17 D.1.2.2.39.
18 *Ius civile primus constituit generatim in libros decem et octo redigendo*: D.1.2.2.41.
19 Stein 1966, 36–48; Behrends 1976, 302–304.
20 Schulz 1963, 67–68.
21 Wieacker 1988, 639; Harries 2006, 41–45.

by defining legal notions, most prominently in a work titled the *liber* ὅρον,[22] and by dividing and subdividing these notions in genera and species (kinds).[23] An example of the latter is his division of property,[24] but it has been theorised that many of the later divisions found for example in the Institutes, the second century AD systematic teaching manual of Gaius, were formulated firstly by Scaevola *pontifex*.[25] Nor was Scaevola the only one to employ dialectic: Servius Sulpicius Rufus for instance recognised four genera of theft.[26] However, whereas a usage of dialectic by the jurists of the late Republic with the purpose of arranging the law is fairly undisputed, the situation becomes more problematic when taking the influence further, into the realms of the employment of Greek philosophical notions to decide individual cases, formulate generally applicable legal rules and principles, and even develop new legal concepts. In this, the line between arranging the law and adding novel elements to it is not always clear: take for example Scaevola's exposition of the standards of liability which were probably derived from Aristotle.[27] Is this merely arranging legal notions or introducing new elements to Roman law? An interesting problem in this regard is once again presented by Scaevola *pontifex* in the so-called *causa Curiana*, in which he seems to have opted for objective *verba* to decide cases over the subjective *voluntas* of the parties involved.[28] Perhaps in itself inspired by the Stoic theory of language,[29] the apparently principled choice of Scaevola has helped spark a debate on the Greek philosophical background of *regulae* (standards) in Roman law, their formulation as such, but also their content, scope and function with regard to the methods of the Roman jurists.[30] Already in the conception of Schulz in the dialectic discipline the composition of definitions leads to the formulation of general rules and principles, applicable to multiple similar cases.[31] Yet, as is also apparent in this debate, it is hard to separate method from content in the service of properly assessing the measure of influence of Greek philosophy when it comes to the works of the Roman jurists.

15.2.2.2 *Physics/Ethics*

With regards to the suggestion that Scaevola *pontifex* may have actually applied his stance in the *causa Curiana* also in his legal practice,[32] the problem of a lack of clear separation between method and content is compounded at the end of the Republic when more material aspects

[22] Similar to a book title of Chrysippus: Kübler 1934, 86; Pohlenz 1948, 263; Schmidlin 1976, 106–111.

[23] Aristotle, but employed by the Stoics as well: Bund 1980, 140, 144 and Wieacker 1988, 622–623 and 633–634.

[24] *Divisio possessionis*: D.41.2.3.23; Kübler 1934, 90.

[25] Schulz 1963, 64, 94–96; Behrends 1976, 295–297; Grosso 1976, 139–148; Wieacker 1988, 646–647; Winkel 2000–2001, 51–66; Tellegen 2003, 199.

[26] D.41.2.3.23: Schulz 1963, 64.

[27] D.9.2.31: Kübler 1934, 88–89; Wieacker 1988, 645–646.

[28] Initiated by Stroux 1926, elaborated upon in Stroux 1949; but see Schiller 1978, 572–577: Tellegen 2003, 197–199; Harries 2006, 100–102.

[29] Wieacker 1988, 653.

[30] Stein 1966, 65–67: with Labeo as probably the first to formulate a *regula* as such; Schmidlin 1976, 106–111; Schiller 1978, 582–584; Wieacker 1988, 633.

[31] Schulz 1963, 61.

[32] Kübler 1934, 87–88, implementing a *formula* in the province; Pohlenz 1948, 262; Behrends 1976, 297; Wieacker 1988, 644, at least derived from the Stoic theory of duties.

of Greek philosophy seem to have found their way into Roman legal practice. The problem of eclecticism, however, remained.[33] Various philosophical theories on the physical existence of material objects were used to decide individual cases.[34] If the Roman jurists of this era did apply philosophical concepts in individual cases, their purpose does not seem to be that different from how a modern-day jurist would consult scientific data to elucidate a point of law. Then again, difficulties of proof tend to arise when the consequence of the philosophical influence is stated to have led to new forms of action, such as the aforementioned creation of a novel *formula* by Scaevola *pontifex*, as well as the *actio de dolo* (legal remedy regarding fraud) and *actio quod metus causa* (legal remedy regarding duress) by Aquilius Gallus, stated in the literature to have an Aristotelian background.[35] The situation is even more problematic when the matter in question goes beyond our modern expectations of science, and relates to more ethical concepts, particularly notions with a far-reaching moral implication. In the late Republic, the influences regarding larger ethical concepts can be boiled down into two (apparently interrelated) constellations: the "law of nations" (*ius gentium*) and "nature" (*natura*).

Contact between Roman law and Greek institutions as regards to the law of nations may very well predate 155 BC: international law in Antiquity starts with the regulation of maritime commerce and treaties allowing foreigners to use domestic courts. Aristotle mentions a treaty between Etruscan city states and Carthage, encompassing matters such as personal safety.[36] As the realisation of the Aristotelian concept of δίκαιον κοινόν (common law) or the Stoic notion of a κοσμόπολις (world-city), this *ius gentium* as it appears in the Roman legal sources might have had some far-reaching consequences. Albeit partly through Cicero, a relation can be established with the development of legal protection for foreigners by the peregrine praetor, the *bonae fidei iudicia*,[37] and perhaps the *formula ficticia* of the *actio legis Aquiliae* (legal remedy regarding property damage) and the *actio furti* (legal remedy regarding theft).[38] Even more problematic is a possible philosophical background to the notion of "nature" (*natura*) in late Republican Roman law. In itself, the meaning of this term in the Roman legal sources is quite clear: the self-evident or essential character of something.[39] Yet, a degree of amalgamation with the Stoic notion of φύσις (nature) appears to have taken place in late Republican jurisprudence. The case may serve as an example of how Roman jurists made use of philosophical notions: a strict dividing line between humans and animals based on rational thought or the lack thereof is a clear, well-attested and fairly unique feature of Stoicism. A consequence of this division is that human beings are created to help other human beings on the one hand,[40] thus recognising the child of a female slave as human, i.e. belonging to the mother, rather than an object of usufruct. Iunius Brutus seems to have been the first jurist to uphold this opinion, against the common wisdom as voiced by P. Mucius Scaevola and

[33] Wieacker 1988, 640.

[34] Sulpicius Rufus/Alfenus Varus in D.5.1.76: Bund 1980, 137; Wieacker 1988, 648–649.

[35] Arist. *Eth. Nic.* III.1.4 1110 a 4: Kübler 1934, 93–94; compare Labeo in D.4.2.5. Sceptic Academy: Behrends 1976, 297.

[36] Σύμβολα περί τοῦ μή ἀδικεῖν: Arist. *Pol.* III 9–10. 1280 a 31–1280 b 17; Winkel 2009, 1455–1456.

[37] Cic. *Off.* 3.69–70: Behrends 1976, 296–297; Kaser 1993, 8, 14–16.

[38] Cic. *Verr.* 2.2.31–32; Inst.Gai.4.37: Wieacker 1988, 444–445, 642–643; Nörr 1989, 116–117; Kaser 1993, 127–128; Thomas 1995, 24–29; Winkel 2009, 1455–1456.

[39] Compare Levy 1963, 9.

[40] Pohlenz 1948, 135–137.

M. Manilius.[41] Thus, the sources suggest that a distinctly philosophical doctrine fundamentally changed an aspect of the Roman legal order. Moreover, a similar reasoning was perhaps applied to the matter of obligations towards slaves as Stoic moral duties allowed by the recognition of a shared rationality among human beings arguably already in Labeo.[42] Nonetheless, the measure in which these complexes are evidence of an influence of Greek philosophy in the works of the Roman jurists remains highly debatable.[43]

15.3 Principate

15.3.1 Individual Jurists

As previously stated, after Labeo we find ourselves dealing with a gap in the transmission of the Roman legal sources. Continuities in the influence of Greek philosophy have been argued through the Sabinian and Proculian school traditions[44] and—perhaps through Seneca—with regard to individual jurists.[45] The most obvious continuity when it comes to the influence of Greek philosophy between Roman jurisprudence in the late Republic and that in the course of the Principate from around 100 AD on is eclecticism. As much as the lack of transmitted texts allows the conclusion, the only jurist showing an adherence to a specific current is Florentinus, namely to Stoicism.[46] Also, it seems telling that both Schulz[47] and Wieacker[48] seem to estimate the influence of Greek philosophy on individual jurists as minimal compared to that in the late Republic. If we limit ourselves to the four jurists who have been transmitted to us in larger quantities, Gaius appears to have preferred Aristotle[49] and Stoicism.[50] As a member of the "circle of Julia Domna", the wife of Emperor Septimius Severus, Domitius Ulpianus may have been influenced by (neo-) Platonism,[51] but also shows knowledge of Pythagorean and Stoic notions in his works, possibly even combining them in single texts.[52] Even though Aemilius Papinianus was active under the Stoic Emperor Marcus Aurelius, this does not seem to have rubbed off on him in any significant measure, at least as regards the content of his decisions. The case of Iulius Paulus is interesting: to my knowledge, no attempt has been made to argue for a larger philosophical background to his work, which may have something to do with a lack

[41] Cic. *Off.* 1.22; Cic. *Fin.* 1.12; D.7.1.68pr.; D.22.1.28.1: Schulz 1954, 147–148; Stein 1966, 28; Behrends 1976, 282–283; Wieacker 1988, 643 n. 16; Kaser 1993, 79–80.

[42] Sen. *Ben.* 3.18.1–3.22.1; D.35.1.40.3: Mantello 1979, 334–359; Kaser 1993, 157–162.

[43] Schulz 1963, 70, 72–73, 136–137.

[44] Wieacker 1988, 649; Wieacker and Wolf 2006, 52–61, 97–106 for a discussion of the schools.

[45] Gaius Cassius Longinus: Nörr 2003, also Wieacker 1988, 649; Iavolenus Priscus: Mantello 1979, 431–451.

[46] D.1.1.3; D.1.5.4: Pohlenz 1948, 263–264; Schrage 1975, 41; Winkel 1988, 677–678; vander Waerdt 1994, 4890–4891; Wieacker and Wolf 2006, 88.

[47] Schulz 1963, 135.

[48] For example, there is no separate chapter regarding philosophical influences on Roman jurisprudence in the Principate in Wieacker and Wolf 2006.

[49] Honoré 1962, 100–110.

[50] Wagner 1978, 59–69.

[51] Crifò 1976, 734–736; Honoré 1982, 28–33; Honoré 2002, 82.

[52] For example, Winkel 1988, 678; Wieacker and Wolf 2006, 88.

of personal information on the jurist.[53] Yet, Paul is credited with relating a version of one of the essential Stoic maxims, "all wrongs are equal",[54] and providing a text containing various meanings of *ius* with a distinctly philosophical "feel" to it.[55] Moreover, the jurist gives Greek definitions and versions of the term *iniuria*,[56] suggesting a measure of interest at least in Greek culture. Then again, he is not the only jurist to employ Greek (philosophical) terms in his works: we have already mentioned Labeo's identification of contract with Aristotle's συνάλλαγμα (agreement), and to this we can certainly add Ulpian's equation of written and unwritten law with the Greek νόμοι γράφοι and ἄγραφοι (written and unwritten laws).[57] But perhaps the clearest evidence of a continuing interest in Greek philosophy may be the larger direct philosophical quotes in the legal texts. Callistratus gives us the only obvious Plato citation in the Digest.[58] Marcian, who was more generally influenced by Ulpian,[59] employs Chrysippus to define *lex* (statute).[60] Paul, finally, provides a brief citation of the function of the legislator by Theophrastus.[61] These are by no means the only Greek terms in Roman legal texts, and further research on this topic is highly desirable.

15.3.2 Individual Subjects

15.3.2.1 *Logic/Rhetoric*

By the year 100 AD, the jurists seem to have moved away from plans to arrange the law as a whole, in as far as those had ever existed. Julian's ordering of the Praetorian Edict notwithstanding, evidence of overarching efforts to systematise is limited to teaching manuals or Institutes. Yet, this does not mean that all efforts to arrange the law had ceased: divisions into genera and species were at least upheld and commented upon, probably even enhanced.[62] The same goes for general rules as formulated by the jurists, whatever their purpose or scope may have been.[63] An interesting development may be that from Aristotelian dialectic to more complicated Stoic forms of logic, particularly in Julian's work.[64] Similarly, the ordering influence of rhetoric is something that is perhaps not to be underestimated. Papinian, for example, employs rhetorical argumentation schemes in his decisions.[65] It still is a matter of debate in what measure rhetoric has had an ordering influence in any more general sense.[66] There is yet another sphere in which rhetoric may

[53] Though not specifically geared towards a philosophical background, excepting Nörr 2005.

[54] *Omnia peccata paria esse*: D.47.2.21pr, mentioning the Republican jurists Trebatius and Ofilius; Kübler 1934, 95.

[55] D.1.1.11; compare Waldstein 1976, 82–83; Maschi 1976, 694–702; Honoré 2002, 77; Nörr 2005, 540–546.

[56] Coll.2.5.1. [57] D.1.1.6.1. [58] D.50.11.2 from the *Politeia*: Winkel 1997, 377.

[59] Honoré 1982, 80, 84.

[60] D.1.3.2: Pohlenz 1948, 264; Winkel 1997, 377: orthodox according to von Arnim: *SVF* III, 314; but see Schulz 1963, 136: "pompous flourishes".

[61] D.1.3.6: Winkel 1997, 377. List in Honoré 2002, 90.

[62] See texts above and Nörr 1972, 45–53, possibly moving from an emphasis on Aristotelian *divisio* to Stoic *partitio*.

[63] For example in the *libri regularum*: Stein 1966, 79–89; Schmidlin 1976, 120–127.

[64] Miquel 1970; Nörr 1972. [65] Nörr 1972, 51; Babusiaux 2011.

[66] Horak 1972; Wieacker 1988, 669–675.

have been employed by the Roman jurists. Later Imperial regulations and decisions show a more rhetorical style, in the sense of appealing to ethical—some would say pathetic—terms and notions rather than technical–legal arguments. This change in style was effected at around the year 300 AD, in the Imperial legislation of Diocletian and Constantine.[67] However, similar terms and notions appear to have been introduced long before 300 AD, appearing both in Imperial and juristic texts by-and-large from Hadrian on. This legal decision-making style may have been introduced by the Imperial chancellery, and is seen by various scholars as the beginning of the "vulgarisation" and "Hellenisation" of Roman legal science.[68] This is caused by the fact that the notions in question seem to have been derived from Greek philosophy. A case in point is the term *aequitas* or "equity", which existed and functioned as a legal notion already in the Republic, and was probably influenced by the Aristotelian concept of ἐπιείκεια (equity). However, from the early second century AD on, the scope of *aequitas* is widened and loses some of the technical meaning it had in the Republic, ending up as a general ground for decision-making after 300 AD.[69] Other terms with arguably a rhetorical rather than a legal–technical meaning employed as the grounds for decision-making from the second century AD on include *pietas* (piety) and *humanitas*,[70] and quite possibly several of those we shall discuss below.[71]

15.3.2.2 *Physics/Ethics*

In many respects the period after 100 AD was marked by a continuation of the work of the late Republican jurists. It is an almost inherent quality of the Roman legal sources that later jurists build upon the work of earlier ones, or at least refer to it like Paul does to Scaevola's *divisio possessionis* (division of property)[72] or his division of the standards of liability.[73] In themselves, these instances need not entail a continuity in nor even knowledge of Greek philosophy in the works of the later jurist citing the text: however, additions do seem to have been made, such as Pomponius providing the Greek term for the substance of the same nature (ἡνωμένον) and giving an overview of the various types of physical material.[74] Arguably, also new theories of will and intention in Ulpian and Paul were derived from Stoic theory on the matter.[75] In itself, seeing its possible philosophical background in the late Republic and the preponderance of the term in the later sources,[76] *natura* as a legal notion could have served well to illustrate an expansion of an idea by the later jurists. Yet, in the majority of texts the meaning of *natura*, whether or not connected to φύσις in the first place, remained that of the self-evident character of the matter in question.[77] An exception to this may be once again *natura* as applied to slaves: in a distinctly Stoic fashion, Florentinus affirms the natural freedom of slaves as well as the institution of slavery as "unnatural",[78] and Ulpian refers to the natural equality of all men under natural law,

[67] Wieacker and Wolf 2006, 188. [68] Compare Schulz 1963, 296–299.

[69] Pringsheim 1932, 80–85; Wieacker 1988, 506–507; vander Waerdt 1994, 4888; Wieacker and Wolf 2006, 89.

[70] Schulz 1954, 16, 128–149; Schulz 1963, 297; Palma 1992, 4–14.

[71] Wieacker 1988, 508–510. [72] Albeit as *ineptissimum*: D.41.2.3.23. [73] D.9.2.31.

[74] Though possibly Sabinus: D.41.3.30pr; Wieacker 1988, 649.

[75] D.2.14.1.3: Kübler 1934, 91. [76] Levy 1963, 7; Waldstein 1976, 30.

[77] "That the *ius civile* cannot impair"; Inst.Gai.1.158: Levy 1963, 9, 10.

[78] *Libertas est facultas naturalis … servitus est constitutio iuris gentium qua quis dominio alieno contra naturam subicitur*: D.1.5.4pr and D.1.5.4.1; Pohlenz 1948, 264; Schrage 1975.

thus mandating regarding even slaves as persons.[79] The problem is that the value of these statements can be easily contested: only taking the *naturalis obligatio* (natural obligation) as an example, defining the obligation as natural in this context means the obligation is not legally enforceable, does not have any real consequence in law. The same could be said for the perspective of the jurists on slavery.[80]

It does, however, show that new legal thought with a philosophical background, even concerning a specific current in Greek philosophy, was developed after 100 AD. Maybe the most difficult problem in this respect is the relation between *natura* and *ius gentium*. The term *natura* is used eighteen times in the writings of the jurist Gaius,[81] but a background in Greek philosophy has primarily been assumed in the literature as regards the notion of *naturalis ratio* (natural reason).[82] In the opening text of his Institutes, Gaius defines the *ius gentium* as the law established by the *naturalis ratio* among all men.[83] A similar conception of *naturalis ratio* can be found in other places in the Institutes, indicating the ground for a universal usage of the legal notion in question.[84] However, this does not need to be a reference to either Aristotle or Stoicism in particular, but could also very well mean Gaius simply refers to Cicero.[85] In general, other texts in which knowledge of philosophical concepts is shown by the jurists might be Ciceronian in nature, or are in any case similarly eclectic. The jurist arguably the most prone to philosophical eclecticism is Ulpian, primarily considering his definition of *ius naturale* (natural law) in D.1.1.1.3, particularly when read in conjunction with his definition of *ius gentium* in D.1.1.1.4. In the texts, Ulpian begins with stating that natural law is common to all living beings, a thought comparable to the teachings of Pythagoras.[86] Then, in D.1.1.1.4, *ius gentium* is the law only all human peoples use, which, like the definition of Gaius, probably conforms most to Stoic conceptions. This is confirmed in D.1.1.4pr, where Ulpian affirms all men are born free according to natural law, and only with the *ius gentium* the institution of slavery was introduced.[87] Ulpian's definition of *iustitia* (justice) appears equally eclectic:[88] in this case, the difficulty arises from the fact this text not only seems directly reproduced from Cicero,[89] but the Stoic definition of justice itself seems to have been built on Aristotle's conception.[90] "Giving each his due" then returns as one of the *praecepta iuris* (starting points for the law), the provenance of which can be similarly attributed to either Cicero, Aristotle and/or Stoicism.[91] Finally,

[79] *Quod ad ius naturale attinet omnes homines aequales sunt*: D.50.17.32; Levy 1963, 11; Thomas 1991, 219–220; Honoré 2002, 88, with other texts.

[80] Levy 1963, 12, 15.

[81] Waldstein 1976, 30.

[82] Levy 1963, 10: Aristotle; Wagner 1978, 59–69: Stoicism; Kaser 1993, 61.

[83] Inst.Gai.1.1: Thomas 1991, 202–203; Kaser 1993, 20–22.

[84] Inst.Gai.1.189; Inst.Gai.1.154–154a: Levy 1963, 10; Kaser 1993, 87.

[85] Cic. *Off.* 3.69–70: Kaser 1993, 40–42; vander Waerdt 1994, 4883.

[86] Schulz 1963, 136; Wieacker and Wolf 2006, 88; not necessarily: Winkel 1988, 678: Theophrastus; Honoré 2002, 82: Neoplatonism; and vander Waerdt 1994, 4891–4892 for the references to Cicero texts.

[87] Levy 1963, 11–12; Honoré 2002, 79–82.

[88] *Iustitia est constans et perpetua voluntas ius suum cuique tribuendi*: D.1.1.10pr; Thomas 1991, 203–204.

[89] Cic. *Inv. rhet.* 2.160: Schulz 1963, 136; Manthe 1997 II, 11.

[90] Pohlenz 1948, 263–264; Winkel 1988, 672; Manthe 1997 II, 1–12.

[91] D.1.1.10.1: Schulz 1963, 136; Levy 1963, 15–17; Honoré 2002, 76.

iustitia and the science of law itself are expounded upon in the opening text of the Digest, stating jurists as those desiring "true philosophy",[92] which may serve as a puzzling and therefore fitting end to this chapter.

15.4 Conclusion

So what can be said about the problematic relation between Greek philosophy and classical Roman law? It seems certain Greek philosophy did play a role as an intellectual background to the works of the Roman jurists, even when taking the critical stance of Schulz into account. Moreover, on the basis of the sources, it is not far-fetched to assume an employment more or less in a scientific sense, to define, elucidate and enhance existing legal notions. This role fits well with a general trend to amalgamate Greek philosophical concepts with Roman (legal) terminology, primarily but by no means exclusively visible in Cicero. The degree to which the influence of Greek philosophy went beyond that remains problematic; namely, to decide individual cases, formulate generally applicable legal rules and principles, and even develop new legal concepts, at least partly seeing these exceed our modern understanding of the function of science vis-à-vis law, particularly when the notions in question are concepts with large implications in the realms of ethics and morality. Adding to these difficulties are the methodological problems of philosophical eclecticism and syncretism apparently prevalent in the background and works of the Roman jurists, strongly related to the dual position of Cicero as a source for Greek philosophical concepts and his own interpretation of those same concepts as possibly influencing contemporary and later jurists. Lastly, the authoritative Roman legal scholarship of the last century seems to proceed strongly from the idea that there existed a fundamental gap between the role of Greek philosophy in the late Republic and the Principate from 100 AD on. Recent research has done a lot to dispel or at least cast serious doubts on this assumption, but even more is needed to perhaps in the future come closer to the truth of the relation between Greek philosophy and Roman law.

Bibliography and Selected Further Reading

General

Barnes, J. 1997. "Roman Aristotle." In J. Barnes and M. Griffin, eds., *Philosophia togata II.* Oxford. 1–69.

Bund, E. 1980. "Rahmerwägungen zu einem Nachweis stoischer Gedanken in der römischen Jurisprudenz." In M. Harder and G. Thielmann, eds., *Festgabe für Ulrich von Lübtow.* Berlin. 127–145.

Harries, J. 2006. *Cicero and the jurists: from citizen's law to the lawful state.* London.

[92] *Vera philosophia*: D.1.1.1pr and D.1.1.1.1; Honoré 1982, 30–31; Honoré 2002, 76–79; Nörr 2005, 535, 557–561.

Kübler, B. 1934. "Griechische Einflüsse aus die Entwicklung der römischen Rechtswissenschaft gegen Ende der republikanischen Zeit," in *Atti del congresso internazionale di diritto romano I*. Pavia. 79–98.

Pohlenz, M. 1948. *Die Stoa: Geschichte einer geistigen Bewegung*. Göttingen.

Wieacker, F. 1988. *Römische Rechtsgeschichte*, Vol. 1. Munich.

Wieacker, F. and Wolf, J. G. 2006. *Römische Rechtsgeschichte*, Vol. 2. Munich.

Schulz, F. 1954. *Prinzipien des römischen Rechts*. Berlin.

Schulz, F. 1963. *History of Roman legal science*. Oxford.

Winkel, L. (1997). "Le droit romain et la philosophie grecque, quelques problèmes de méthode." *Tijdschrift voor Rechtsgeschiedenis* 65: 373–384.

Individual Jurists

Behrends, O. (1976). "Die Wissenschaftslehre im Zivilrecht des Q. Mucius Scaevola *pontifex*," *Nachrichten der Akademie der Wissenschaften in Göttingen, Philologisch-historische Klasse 7*. Göttingen. 263–304.

Crifò, G. (1976). "Ulpiano. Esperienze e responsibilità del giurista." *Aufstieg und Niedergang der römischen Welt* II.15: 708–789.

Honoré, A. M. 1962. *Gaius. A biography*. Oxford.

Honoré, A. M. 1982. *Ulpian*. Oxford.

Honoré, A. M. 2002. *Ulpian. Pioneer of human rights*. Revised edition. Oxford.

Maschi, C. A. (1976). "La conclusione della giurisprudenza classica all'età dei Severi: Iulius Paulus." *Aufstieg und Niedergang der römischen Welt* II.15: 667–707.

Nörr, D. 2003. "C. Cassius Longinus: der Jurist als Rhetor (Bemerkungen zur Tac. *Ann*. 14,42–45)." In T. J. Chiusi, W. Kaiser and H.-D. Spengler, eds., Historiae iuris antiqui, Vol. 3. Goldbach. 1585–1620.

Nörr, D. 2005. "Alla ricerca della *vera filosofia*. Valori etico-sociali in Giulio Paolo (a proposito di D. 19.1.43 S.; 1.1.11; 45.1.83; 46.3.98.8; 18.1.34.1–2)." In D. Mantovani and A. Schiavone, eds., *Testi e problemi del giusnaturalismo romano*. Pavia. 521–561.

Logic/Rhetoric

Babusiaux, U. 2011. *Papinians* Quaestiones. *Zur rhetorischen Methode eines spätklassischen Juristen*. Munich.

Grosso, G. (1976). "Influenze aristoteliche nella sistemazione delle fonti delle obbligazioni nella giurisprudenza romana," in *La filosofia greca e il diritto romano. Atti dell'Accademia dei Lincei 221*. Rome. 139–148.

Horak, F. 1972. "Die rhetorische Statuslehre und der moderne Aufbau des Verbrechensbegriffs." In F. Horak and W. Waldstein, eds., *Festgabe für Arnold Herdlitczka*. Munich/Salzburg. 121–142.

Miquel, J. (1970). "Stoische Logik und römische Jurisprudenz." *Zeitschrift der Savigny-Stiftung für Rechtsgeschichte, romanistische Abteilung* 87: 85–122.

Nörr, D. 1972. Divisio *und* Partitio. *Bemerkungen zur römischen Rechtsquellenlehre und zur antiken Wissenschaftstheorie*. Berlin.

Pringsheim, F. (1932). "Bonum et aequum." *Zeitschrift der Savigny-Stiftung für Rechtsgeschichte, romanistische Abteilung* 52: 78–155.

Schiller, A. A. 1978. *Roman law: mechanisms of development*. The Hague/Paris/New York.

Schmidlin, B. (1976). "*Horoi, pithana* und *regulae*- Zum Einfluβ der Rhetorik und Dialektik auf die juristische Regelbildung." *Aufstieg und Niedergang der römischen Welt* II.15: 101–130.

Stein, P. 1966. Regulae iuris: *from juristic rules to legal maxims*. Edinburgh.

Stroux, J. 1926. Summum ius summa iniuria: *ein Kapitel aus der Geschichte der* interpretatio iuris. Leipzig.

Stroux, J. 1949. *Römische Rechtswissenschaft und Rhetorik*. Potsdam.

Tellegen, J.-W. 2003. "The reliability of Quintilian for Roman law: on the *causa Curiana*." In O. Tellegen-Couperus, ed., *Quintilian and the law: the art of persuasion in law and politics*. Leuven. 191–200.

Winkel, L. (2000–2001). "Alcune osservazioni sulla classificazione delle obbligazioni e sui contratti nominati nel diritto romano." *Bullettino dell'Istituto di Diritto Romano IIIa serie "Vittorio Scialoja"* 103–104: 51–66.

Physics/Ethics

Kaser, M. 1993. Ius gentium. Cologne/Weimar/Vienna.

Levy, E. 1963. "Natural law in Roman thought." In W. Kunkel and M. Kaser, eds., *Gesammelte Schriften*, Vol. 1. Cologne/Graz. 3–19.

Mantello, A. 1979. Beneficium servile-debitum naturale. Milan.

Manthe, U. (1997). "Beiträge zur Entwicklung des antiken Gerechtigkeitsbegriffes II: Stoïsche Würdigkeit und die *iuris praecepta* Ulpians." *Zeitschrift der Savigny-Stiftung für Rechtsgeschichte, romanistische Abteilung* 114: 1–26.

Nörr, D. 1978. "Kausalitätsprobleme im klassischen römischen Recht, ein theoretischer Versuch Labeos." In O. Behrends, M. Dießelhorst, H. Lange, D. Liebs, J. G. Wolf and C. Wollschläger, eds., *Festschrift für Franz Wieacker zum 70. Geburtstag*. Göttingen. 115–144.

Nörr, D. 1989. *Aspekte des römischen Völkerrechts: die Bronzetafel von Alcántara*. Munich.

Palma, A. 1992. Humanior interpretatio. "*Humanitas*" *nell'interpretazione e nella normazione da Adriano ai Severi*. Turin.

Schrage, E. J. H. 1975. Libertas est facultas naturalis. *Menselijke vrijheid in een tekst van de Romeinse jurist Florentinus*. Leiden.

Thomas, Y. 1991. "*Imago naturae*: note sur l'institutionnalité de la nature à Rome," in *Théologie et droit dans la science politique de l'état moderne*. Paris. 201–227.

Thomas, Y. (1995) "*Fictio legis*: l'empire de la fiction Romaine et ses limites Médiévales." *Droits, revue française de théorie juridique* 21: 17–63.

vander Waerdt, P. A. (1994). "Philosophical influence on Roman jurisprudence? The case of stoicism and natural law." *Aufstieg und Niedergang der römischen Welt* 351.7: 4851–4900.

Wagner, H. 1978. *Studien zur allgemeinen Rechtslehre des Gaius:* ius gentium *und* ius naturale *in ihrem Verhältnis zum ius civile*. Zutphen.

Waldstein, W. (1976). "Entscheidungsgrundlagen der klassischen römischen Juristen." *Aufstieg und Niedergang der römischen Welt* II.15: 3–100.

Winkel, L. 1982. Error iuris nocet: *Rechtsdwaling als rechtsorde-probleem*. Amsterdam.

Winkel, L. (1988). "Die stoische οἰκείωσις-Lehre und Ulpians Definition der Gerechtigkeit." *Zeitschrift der Savigny-Stiftung für Rechtsgeschichte, romanistische Abteilung* 105: 669–679.

Winkel, L. 2009. "Symbola/Rechtshilfeverträge-Parallele Entwicklungen in Griechenland und Rom?" In H. Altmeppen, I. Reichard and M. J. Schermaier, eds., *Festschrift für Rolf Knütel zum 70. Geburtstag*. Heidelberg. 1449–1457.

CHAPTER 16

RHETORIC AND ROMAN LAW

AGNIESZKA KACPRZAK

16.1 Introduction

The method that the Roman jurists applied to solve various legal problems, their capacity to find pragmatic and rationally justifiable solutions, has been admired by all those studying Justinian's Digest in whatever period of time. It was only in the twentieth century, however, that the first attempts were undertaken to explain this method against the background of the broader intellectual context in which the Roman jurists operated. Given the importance of rhetoric in Roman culture and education, it seemed the perfect candidate as a possible source of inspiration for the jurists. Thus, J. Stroux in his groundbreaking article from 1926 (*Summum ius summa iniuria*) claimed that the Roman jurists borrowed from rhetoric both their reflections concerning the relationship between law and morality and their techniques of reasoning and argumentation.[1] These techniques in turn enabled them to systematise legal knowledge, thus turning it into a science.[2]

Stroux's claim applies to the period in which Roman legal knowledge began to develop into a rational discipline, i.e. from the beginning of the second until the end of the first century BC. Rhetoric in this period, together with other disciplines of Greek origin such as philosophy and studies of language and literature (*grammatica*), was a part of Greek culture that had begun to impact upon Roman society. Although it is difficult to deny that these disciplines contributed to the "scientification" of various branches of knowledge as practised by the Romans, it is impossible to establish which had the main influence.[3] This complication is due to the fact that the standard curriculum of young Roman aristocrats

[1] The final version appeared in 1949; cf. Stroux 1949, 51–52.

[2] The notion of Roman jurisprudence as a "science" was already questioned by Viehweg 1953, and more recently by Tellegen-Couperus and Tellegen 2013, 31–32. As Giaro 1994, 107 has rightly observed, the whole discussion boils down to the definition of science. Insofar as science is understood as a system of general statements from which particular conclusions are drawn, Roman jurisprudence was not a science in this sense.

[3] According to Gwynn 1926, 39, the study of philosophy in this period is even better attested than that of rhetoric.

in this period seems to have comprised all the above disciplines, as far as we can judge from historical sources.[4]

In Roman culture and education, rhetoric remained pervasive throughout the entire history of the Roman Empire. It was present both in the forum and in the courts. It provided Roman elites with an intellectual entertainment in the form of public declamations. Moreover, it was the only form of institutionalised higher education in existence until late Antiquity. Rhetoric in a sense was the air that Roman elites breathed. It is therefore inevitable that it must have shaped the minds of the jurists as well. In which areas exactly and to what extent, however, remains disputed.

The idea that ancient rhetoric may provide the clues to understanding the methods of reasoning and argumentation as applied by Roman jurists—proposed by Stroux a century ago—has been taken up and further explored in recent studies.[5] The authors of such works have focused on patterns of reasoning used by individual jurists when solving particular legal problems in an attempt to single out models of argumentation and persuasion parallel to those taught of in the schools of rhetoric. It has also been argued that such patterns of reasoning may help explain the reasons behind particular legal solutions.

If rhetoric is seriously expected to provide us with a key to understanding the legal method developed by the Roman jurists and so much admired throughout the centuries, attention should be focused on that part of rhetorical theory that concerns rational argumentation. This is what I shall concentrate on in the remainder of this chapter.

The first matter to be investigated concerns the ways in which the Roman jurists could have acquired knowledge of rhetorical methods of argumentation. Political discourses, court speeches and public declamations obviously provided an opportunity to become familiar with these methods. Such a practical familiarity would have probably sufficed if the jurists wanted to occasionally apply rhetorical arguments in their professional discourse. It could hardly provide them, however, with a deeper knowledge of the structure and functioning of the arguments in question, indispensable if they were to consciously use them as a tool for elaborating their own method. When it comes to obtaining the latter kind of knowledge—namely, methodological consciousness, rudimentary at least—schools of rhetoric seem a better suggestion.

How much time, if any, a future jurist would have spent in a school of rhetoric is nevertheless difficult to establish. The standard rhetorical curriculum lasted for three or four years.[6] Historical sources confirm, however, that future adepts of philosophy used to pass to philosophical schools after one year of rhetorical education.[7] If the analogy holds for jurists, we can surmise that the time they would have spent in a school of rhetoric did not exceed one year, provided that they did not begin the study of law directly after having accomplished their primary education. Nothing seems to compel us to dismiss the latter possibility.

[4] Cicero's intellectual curriculum is very informative in this respect; cf. Gwynn 1926, 7–71, 74–77.

[5] Babusiaux 2011; Leesen 2010; Tellegen-Couperus and Tellegen 2013.

[6] According to Bonner 1977, 137, students used to start rhetorical education around the age of 15, but could have begun rhetorical education already at 14. They would have remained at the school of rhetoric until the age of 18, and exceptionally until 19.

[7] Bonner 1977, 137.

It also has to be remembered that methods of rational argumentation were not the only subject a student of rhetoric would have learned in a school of rhetoric. Besides various means of persuasion, comprising, in addition to purely rational ones, those appealing to the emotions of the audience, he would have studied subjects such as the composition of speeches (*dispositio*), their style (*elocutio*), delivery (*actio*) and mnemonics (*memoria*). The time for learning methods of rational argumentation was thus limited, although they were considered the heart of rhetorical teaching. What was the content of this teaching?

16.2 The Principal Tools for Constructing Arguments

Quintilian's *Institutio oratoria* sets out the most complex system of devices for constructing rational arguments known from Antiquity. It gives an account of the three most important components of the art of finding arguments (rhetorical invention), i.e. *stasis* theory, *topoi* for constructing arguments and principal methods of rhetorical argumentation, namely, rhetorical syllogism and induction. It therefore provides a convenient basis for the explanation of how different rhetorical devices worked together when preparing argumentation on a given subject.

16.2.1 Methods of Argumentation (Rhetorical Syllogism and Rhetorical Induction)

Two basic methods of argumentation were commonly recognised in rhetorical theory: deductive (*syllogismos, ratiocinatio*) and inductive (*egagoge, inductio*). The division stems from Aristotle (*Rh.* 1356a–1356b, 8–10), whose revolutionary idea was to fashion rhetoric upon the model of dialectic. Accordingly, he distinguished within rhetoric two principal methods of argumentation, parallel to those of dialectic, *enthymeme* (i.e. rhetorical syllogism) and *paradeigma* (i.e. rhetorical induction).[8] Aristotle regarded rhetorical syllogism as a reasoning deductive in form (i.e. in which the conclusion necessarily follows from the premises),[9] although he recognised that its conclusions were probable rather than certain inasmuch as they were usually drawn from probable premises.[10]

The same two methods are to be found both in Hellenistic and Roman rhetoric, although the terminology has changed. The general term for rhetorical syllogism was *epicheireme* (Lat. *ratiocinatio*), instead of *enthymeme*,[11] whereas the latter term was used for particular kinds of rhetorical syllogisms (cf. *infra*).

The most frequent form of *ratiocinatio* in Latin rhetorical handbooks was, as has been convincingly argued, that of syllogism based on relations between propositions, as

[8] Kraus 2012, 19–21. [9] Kraus 2012, 21.

[10] Calboli Montefusco 1998, 11–13, following Madden 1952, 37–371, observes that only necessary signs can give rise to the valid syllogism. Cf. Kraus 2012, 22–23.

[11] Solmsen 1941, 169–170; Braet 2004, 329.

elaborated by the Stoics. However, neither its logical structure nor its deductive nature was discussed in the manuals (cf. *Auctor ad Herennium, De inventione, Institutio oratoria*). The discussion concentrated instead on the number of premises of which it typically consisted (Cic. *Inv. rhet.* 1.57–66, 1.67–75; Quint. *Inst.* 5.10.5–8, 5.14.5).

According to the prevailing opinion, the complete form of the rhetorical syllogism had five parts; i.e. two premises (major and minor), additional arguments supporting each of them and the conclusion (Cic. *Inv. rhet.* 1.58, 1.61; Quint. *Inst.* 5.14.5).[12] If one of the premises or both were evident, the confirmation could be omitted, so that the whole argument could be reduced to three parts only. Further reductions were also admissible, so that an *epicheireme* consisting of one part only was possible (Cic. *Inv. rhet.* 1.67–75). Opponents of this view have claimed that the complete *epicheireme* only had three parts; i.e. two premises and a conclusion (Cic. *Inv. rhet.* 1.59; Quint. *Inst.* 5.14.6). The nub of the debate is whether the elements that were supposed to confirm the premises were separate parts of the syllogism, as the supporters of the five-part theory claimed, or were parts of the premises themselves, as claimed by the followers of the tripartite concept of *epicheireme* (Cic. *Inv. rhet.* 1.60).[13] As the above discussion implies, *epicheireme* was an extended version of the basic syllogistic structure, containing additional elements in support of each of the premises. The additions in question could either have an argumentative or merely an embellishing function.[14] The first was the logical/dialectical type of *epicheireme,* whereas the second—the purely rhetorical type of *epicheireme*[15]—was probably dominant in the standard rhetorical tradition.[16]

If *epicheireme* was an extended version of the basic syllogistic structure, so *enthymeme* tended to be understood as an abbreviated version thereof. It usually had either one of the premises or the conclusion suppressed. The audience was supposed to supply the lacking elements on its own.[17] But the term *enthymeme* had at least one other meaning, equally or even more frequent in Latin rhetoric than the one described above. Following the tradition stemming from *Rhetorica ad Alexandrum,* the term in question denoted the type of confutative argument whereby the conclusion as postulated by the adversary was shown to have contrasted either with his own behaviour or with one of the premises (Quint. *Inst.* 5.14.2). In Cicero's interpretation the *enthymeme* so understood corresponded to the Stoic third indemonstrable [not (p and q) and p, hence not q] (Cic. *Top.* 54–55).[18] Quintilian also mentioned another meaning of *enthymeme*; i.e. a deductive argument from consequences (corresponding to the Stoic first indemonstrable: p then q, and p, hence q) (Quint. *Inst.* 5.10.1–2).[19]

Thus, the feature that distinguished rhetorical syllogism as conceived of in Hellenistic and Roman rhetoric was the fact that it contained additional elements in support of each

[12] Braet 2004, 334. [13] Solmsen 1941, 170. [14] Braet 2004, 328.

[15] Braet 2004 has shown that Cicero's *De inventione* gives an account of both types of *epicheireme* (335–336), whereas *Ad Herennium* contains only the rhetorical type (336–339). He concludes that Cicero, in his logical/dialectical account of *epicheireme,* must have drawn on philosophical rather than rhetorical sources (340).

[16] Braet 2004, 347.

[17] The abbreviation had purely rhetorical function and did not affect the logical structure of syllogism; cf. Kraus 2012, 21.

[18] Kraus 2012, 27. [19] Kraus 2012, 28.

of the premises. The additions were supposed to render the entire argument more persuasive. *Enthymeme*, on the other hand, denoted a particular form of rhetorical syllogism. Depending on which view one supported, it might refer to a syllogism with at least one of the parts suppressed (i.e. a truncated syllogism), or to one based on a specific relationship between the propositions of the major premise; namely, either that of incompatibility (more frequently) or that of necessary consequence. Other specific forms of *ratiocinatio* typically referred to in rhetorical handbooks were *dilemma* and *eliminatio,* both of which had an alternative as the major premise. Quintilian treated those forms as dependent on the *topos a divisione* (v. section 16.2.2).[20]

As for rhetorical induction, it used to be defined, in accordance with Aristotelian tradition (*Rh.* 1357 b 19), as an inference from particular cases to a particular conclusion. The dependence of this type of argument on the Socratic method, where from a series of concessions made by an interlocutor a conclusion concerning the problem under discussion was drawn, was also commonly recognised (Cic. *Top.* 42, Quint. *Inst.* 5.11.3).

It has to be stressed that syllogism and induction were considered—and actually are—two basic types of any inference.[21] As a consequence, everyone who reasons uses one of these two methods or both, no matter whether he or she has ever studied rhetoric or logic or not. The syllogistic inference, however, may have different forms, from those that are basic and intuitive to those that are more complicated. Only the latter forms may serve as an indication that a person who uses them has received some logical or rhetorical education.

16.2.2 Topoi

The common description of the *topos* found in the manuals of rhetoric is *sedes argumenti*; i.e. a place from which arguments can be drawn. They were instructions on how to build correct and convincing arguments in various types of cases. The instructions covered both the material of which arguments should be composed (material *topoi*) and the method of their composition (formal *topoi*). Both these types of *topoi* are present in Quintilian's work. To the first type belong instructions concerning the aspects of reality to be taken into consideration when looking for specific arguments. Attributes of persons, such as

[20] Rapp 2002, 62–64, holds that a common feature of rhetorical and dialectical syllogisms is found in the fact that their conclusiveness depends entirely on topical relationships. Formal *topoi* in Quintilian seem to have precisely this role.

[21] In the contemporary logic a third type of logical inference is sometimes distinguished; namely abduction, first identified by Peirce (cf. Peirce 1878). Nevertheless, the status of abduction is still discussed. Many authors classify it as a type of induction rather than a pattern of inference in its own right (Fumerton 1980, 592; Pollock 1986, 42; Ladyman 2002, 28). Some authors deny the abduction a character of logical inference altogether, interpreting it rather as a strategy of discovery (e.g. Hintikka 1998, 506). Finally there are those who, following Peirce, treat it as a third type of inference, beside induction and deduction (so called inference to the best explanation; cf. Schurz 2008). In Antiquity the phenomenon in question was not identified, although some authors claim that one specific kind of abduction, i.e. law-abduction, can be found already in Aristotle (*An. post.* 1, 34). According to this view Aristotle would have applied this type of reasoning as a means to find middle terms of syllogisms (Schurz 2008, 211–212).

their nature, characters, course of life and so forth, or of events, such as their place, time, occasion and so forth, were called *topoi* in this sense.[22]

The second type of *topoi* stem from the Aristotelian tradition.[23] They were instructions about methods of constructing arguments. They described relations either between general terms (such as genus, species, property, definition, contraries or similar terms), or between types of events (e.g. between causes and their results, between what is more and what is less likely to happen).[24] These relations justified various schemes of inference, general enough to be applied to different subject matters.[25] Thus, e.g. *topos a causis et effectis* states that whenever one event typically causes another, from the fact that the former occurred the conclusion can be drawn that also the latter did. The inference scheme based on this *topos* runs: if p then q and p, hence q, and thus corresponds to the Stoic first indemonstrable (even though in rhetoric it is never referred to as such). Moreover, if p is the necessary cause of q, then the inverse inference (q, hence p) will also be valid (Quint. *Inst.* 5.10.80–82). *Topos a genere* states that whatever belongs to a genus belongs to at least one of its species. Hence we can deny that a given thing belongs to a given genus by denying that it belongs to any of its species. Or conversely, it does belong to a given genus if it belongs to one of its species. On the other hand, if it is agreed that a thing belongs to a given genus, by showing that it cannot belong to any of its species but one, we prove that it does belong to the latter (Quint. *Inst.* 5.10.56–57). The corresponding scheme runs: A is B and B is either D, or F or G, but A is neither D nor F, hence A is G. This form of argument was known in Antiquity as the argument from elimination (*eliminatio*). It also had a version dealing with alternative propositions, which was even more widespread in rhetorical practice (cf. *infra topos a divisione*).

The most widely discussed *topos* in Quintilian is that of definition (Quint. *Inst.* 5.10.54–62, 7.3.3–27). It introduces a set of requirements for correct definitions. Knowledge of these requirements should help the speaker both to establish his own definitions and to refute those of his adversary. A correct definition should indicate the genus of the defined object, its species, the division to which it belongs, and its property. Thus, the correct definition of a horse runs: an animal (genus), mortal (species), irrational (division of species) and neighing (property). Quintilian himself admits, however, that such meticulousness is out of place in rhetoric (Quint. *Inst.* 7.3.14). Hence, the most important instructions for the speaker who wants to propose a definition are the following: it should serve the speaker's purpose well (Quint. *Inst.* 7.3.21). The property of the defined object as well as its difference from similar objects should be properly determined. Recourse to etymology and to the quality may also be helpful (Quint. *Inst.* 7.3.25). Knowledge of the proper construction of

[22] The *topoi* of this type can be described as subject matter indicators. They were already known in the pre-Aristotelian rhetoric; cf. Rubinelli 2009, 102.

[23] *Topoi* of this kind do not appear in the standard manuals of rhetoric from the Republican era, i.e. in *Rhetorica ad Herennium* and in Cicero's *De inventione*. Hence we can conclude that they did not belong to the standard rhetorical teaching of this time. It is only in *De oratore* and in *Topica* that Cicero includes them; cf. Rubinelli 2009, 111; 117–144.

[24] Cf. Ochs 1974, 197, who describes *topos* as a "pattern of relationship between classes of things". Dyke 2002, 108, defines it "as a binary relation which is used to construct if–then sentences". Its function is to warrant that the implication holds true.

[25] Implications established with the help of *topoi* could have been used as major premises of syllogisms. For the relationship between *topos* and syllogism see Dyke 2002, 109–113.

a definition, borrowed from dialecticians, seems far more useful for attacking definitions proposed by an adversary. The most efficient way to demolish a definition is to show that a feature indicated as a property of a given object belongs to other objects as well, hence the definition is too wide; or the property does not belong to an object to which a definition should apply, hence the definition is too narrow. Finally, if an object does not belong to a genus to which the species indicated in the definition does belong, the definition is false.

By the same token we can refute a definition as too wide by showing that it also covers objects lacking a generic quality that must necessarily belong to all the defined objects. Quintilian gives a very interesting example of the usage of the latter strategy: we can deny that a man, who had sexual intercourse with a married woman in a brothel, committed adultery, by arguing that his deed was not wicked (i.e. it does not belong to the class of wicked deeds to which a deed must necessarily belong to be qualified as adultery): in this case the definition of adultery as sexual intercourse with another's wife has been refuted as too wide, on the grounds that it comprised a deed which does not belong to the class of wicked deeds. The corresponding scheme of inference runs as follows: some A is not C, all B is C, hence some A is not B, where A stands for sexual intercourse with another's wife, C for the class of wicked deeds and B for adultery (Quint. *Inst.* 7.3.6).

Property (*proprietas*), which is a part of the definition, could be used as the independent basis for an interesting type of argument; namely, as a proof that someone either had, or had not, committed a deed of which he was accused. Since certain deeds are compatible with certain qualities, but not with their contraries, we can argue in the following way: since X is an honest man, and being honest is contrary to injuring people, it is unbelievable that X has injured anyone (Quint. *Inst.* 5.10.64). The corresponding scheme of inference runs: if A is B, and B is contrary to C, then A is not C.

Topos a divisione (Quint. *Inst.* 5.10.65–70) is worth mentioning insofar as two forms of argument that were very popular in ancient rhetoric depended on it. They are elimination and dilemma, both based on the alternative between various possibilities. They are valid, provided that the alternative is exhaustive. By eliminating all possibilities of something to happen one can prove that it did not happen at all (e.g. if he is a citizen, either he was born as such, or made one; if neither is the case, he is not a citizen, Quint. *Inst.* 5.10.65), or granted that something did happen, and having excluded all but one way in which it could have happened, one proves that it actually happened in that way: if p then either q or r or s, but p and neither q nor r, hence s (e.g. if the slave is in your house, then either he was born there, or was given to you, or was captured by enemies, or he is another's slave. But if he was neither born in your house, nor given to you, nor bought, nor captured by enemies, then he is another's slave, Quint. *Inst.* 5.10.67). Dilemma is a kind of argument in which each term of the alternative leads to a conclusion desired by the speaker. Provided that the alternative is exhaustive, at least one of these conclusions must be true: (p or q) and (p then r), and (q then s) hence r or s (Quint. *Inst.* 5.10.69). A particular form of this argument is the one in which the conclusion to which each term of the alternative leads is the same (Quint. *Inst.* 5.10.70). Hence the conclusion is proven, provided that the alternative is exhaustive: (p or q) and (p then r) and (q then r), hence r.[26]

[26] Cf. Calboli Montefusco 2010, 366–371.

From a logical point of view, both forms of argument in question are simple and intuitive. However, to formulate an alternative that is truly exhaustive is a very difficult task, as Quintilian remarked (Quint. *Inst.* 5.10.67). Therefore, the majority of arguments of these kinds, as used in rhetorical practice, do not comply with the above requirement and are as such fallacious. Nevertheless, they are an efficient rhetorical tool of persuasion, if formulated in such a way as to conceal their logical deficiency. Quintilian's main suggestion is to put them in the form of a rhetorical question. Thus, in the case of the argument from elimination, instead of enumerating all the possible terms of the alternative in order to eliminate all but one, it is better to confront the adversary directly with the latter and ask if he can think of any other possibility (Quint. *Inst.* 5.10.68); e.g. "if you have not stolen this thing, how did it come to be in your possession?" Dilemma should also be put in the form of a question whereby the adversary is constrained to choose one of the alternative possibilities, each of which is equally unfavourable to him (Quint. *Inst.* 5.10.69). In formulating the question, the speaker makes an assumption that the alternative is exhaustive, although in the majority of cases it is not. As a consequence, rhetorical usage of dilemma in the majority of cases boils down to begging the question.[27]

What makes the above-mentioned schemes of inference efficient tools of rhetorical argumentation are the strategies of their application. As a consequence, it is not the logical schemes themselves but rather the way they are used in order to obtain a given result that informs us of the rhetorical skills of the person who uses them.

16.2.3 Status

The doctrine of status was thoroughly elaborated and turned into a system of rhetorical invention by Hermagoras of Temnos in the middle of the second century BC. It has developed in the context of judicial oratory.[28]

Status defined the central issue under debate, i.e. the one on which the disputing parties disagreed. The subsequent strategy of argumentation depended on its identification, since both parties focused on the arguments relevant thereto.

Status was identified as a result of the first exchange of standpoints between the prosecutor and the defendant, i.e. the prosecutor's charge and the defendant's answer. For example, if the prosecutor claimed that x killed his mother, and the defendant answered that x was justified in doing so, then the central issue under debate boiled down to the question "whether x was justified in killing his mother". The term "status" sometimes referred to the first exchange of claims between the parties, sometimes to the defendant's answer only, and sometimes to the question that arose from the above exchange. It was agreed, however, that the defendant's role was crucial for determining the status of the case, since it was his task to decide which aspects of the prosecutor's charge he could deny and which he had to admit given the circumstances of the case.[29] The defendant could deny the fact itself, claiming either that the deed in question was not committed at all, or not by the

[27] Cf. Craig 1993, 63: "The very use of dilemma seems to confer legitimacy on the assumptions that inform it."

[28] Braet 1987, 79; Braet 1989, 239.

[29] Braet 1987, 81–83.

person accused thereof. If that was not possible, he could deny the legal qualification of a deed. If the latter was also unquestionable, he could adduce exonerating or justifying circumstances. Finally, if none of the previous strategies were possible, he could deny the competence of the court. Accordingly, all possible statuses were classified according to the following genera:[30] questions concerning facts (*coniectura*), questions concerning definition of facts (*definitio*), questions concerning quality of facts (*qualitas*), questions concerning competence of the court (*translatio*).[31]

Apart from the four general statuses described above, Hermagoras also distinguished four types of legal questions (*quaestiones legales*) that concerned the interpretation of written texts, laws especially. They were subsidiary to general status, insofar as an interpretation of a text might have been useful for establishing both definition and quality of a deed committed by the accused, as well as the competence of the court. Hence, it was generally agreed that legal questions could have been raised within all the general statuses except conjecture.[32] It was also a decision of each of the disputing parties which legal status to choose, i.e. what basis for interpretation of relevant laws to adopt so that they best support their respective claims.

To settle on a status was a decision crucial for further debate, insofar as it determined the choice of arguments to be used. It is not surprising therefore that in Hermagoras' system instructions on how to find relevant arguments were grouped according to the different kinds of status. Quintilian in *Institutio oratoria* partly follows this systematisation (i.e. having described rhetorical devices useful for all types of questions [Quint. *Inst.* 5.8.4–5.14.26], he gives specific instructions for each status separately [Quint. *Inst.* 7.1.4–7.10.6]). Also in this respect (i.e. as far as strategies of argumentation are concerned), legal statuses were related to general ones. Hence, it was generally agreed that strategies appropriate for the conjectural status could have been applied in cases of the conflict between the letter and the intent of a law (*scriptum et voluntas*), of ambiguous laws (*ambiguitas*), as well as in those concerning conflicting laws (*leges contrariae*). The strategies appropriate for the status of quality were regarded useful in all types of legal questions.

Whether the status doctrine applied to non-judicial oratory or even to questions belonging to other fields of knowledge, such as philosophy, is disputed.[33] Even though such a possibility was generally recognised, no account was given on how the doctrine in question would have functioned in those other fields.[34]

[30] Quintilian, probably following Theodore of Gadara, defined status as the genus of a question as arising from the first exchange of contrasting claims between the disputing parties; cf. Braet 1987, 82.

[31] The distinction was questioned in post-Hermagorean rhetoric; cf. Lausberg 1998, 59.

[32] In many post-Hermagorean classifications legal questions were as a matter of fact not at all qualified as a separate genus, but were distributed among different rational statuses. Thus e.g. Quintilian qualifies questions of ambiguity of laws as belonging to conjecture, those concerning extensive interpretation of a law as belonging to quality, and those regarding conflict between the letter and intent and contradictory laws either as cases of conjecture or of quality, according to circumstances of a case; cf. Holtsmark 1968, 367.

[33] Although the status doctrine is best adapted to judicial oratory, it could have been applied, by analogy, to other types of oratory as well; cf. Lausberg 1998, 47.

[34] The idea that the status theory could be applied to non-rhetorical questions as well, e.g. to philosophical ones, was generally accepted in Latin rhetoric (Lausberg 1998, 47). How this theory would have functioned outside the rhetoric is unclear. The only one to have attempted to actually apply it to ethical and philosophical questions was Cicero (cf. Ochs 1989, 225–227). Braet 1989,

Applying the status doctrine meant something more than simply discussing such questions as whether something had happened or not; what the definition of a certain thing was; what qualities it had or what a written text really meant. Rather, it meant choosing a strategy for further debate, i.e. formulating the question to be disputed as concerning facts, definitions or qualities. It is impossible therefore to establish whether someone applied the status doctrine exclusively on the grounds that he was dealing with a question of one of the above types. To conclude that he did, some information about his decision-making process, i.e. the motives that led him to formulate the question in given terms, would be needed. Applying the status doctrine also implied choosing one of the well-defined strategies of argumentation, suggested in rhetorical handbooks for the relevant status.[35] Hence, an application of one of such standard strategies can also serve as an indication that a person using it had knowledge of and consciously applied the doctrine in question.

16.3 RHETORIC OF THE JURISTS

16.3.1 Some Methodological Remarks

Long before rhetorical theory had developed, oratory in the sense of the art of speaking convincingly already existed. No rhetorical theory existed when the great Attic orators composed their famous speeches, often cited by successive rhetoricians as a model of good oratory. As Quintilian himself remarked, many rhetorical devices had been successfully applied by early speakers, to be described in manuals of rhetoric only afterwards. It was a common practice of Attic orators, e.g. to argue against the letter of the law and in favour of its supposed intent, long before Hermagoras identified and described this type of controversy (*scriptum et voluntas*). Syllogism and induction are two basic forms of reasoning people normally use, even if they had never learned them, nor could identify them as such. According to Quintilian, rhetorical theory described and classified (rather than invented) means of argumentation and persuasion that people intuitively use. It follows that to qualify a piece of reasoning applied by a jurist as one of the devices described in manuals of rhetoric (e.g. as a syllogism or induction, or as an argument against the literal meaning of a law), cannot be used to conclude that he knew rhetorical theory, let alone purposely applied it. More data would be required to reach such conclusions. Information that a Roman jurist actually had some rhetorical education would certainly be helpful. The consistency in usage of certain means of argumentation, possibly those more sophisticated rather than the basic ones, would be another possible indication. As far as the status doctrine is concerned, the fact that someone followed a sequence of arguments typically advised for issues of a given kind could serve as a hint that he had some knowledge of rhetoric. Unfortunately, it is very rarely the case that legal sources provide us with information of this sort.

253–254, however, convincingly argues that the status doctrine, due to its dialogic nature, hardly applies outside of the field of oratory.

[35] Carter 1988, 99.

16.3.2 Rhetoric in Legal Sources?

I have chosen a fragment from the Digest, containing a piece of reasoning attributed to Marcus Antistius Labeo, a famous jurist from the early Principate, to demonstrate some of the complications that modern scholars are likely to encounter when trying to establish rhetorical impact on juridical thinking. Labeo's interest in branches of knowledge other than jurisprudence such as *grammatica* (theory of language and literary criticism) and rhetoric is directly confirmed by historical sources. Scholars of Roman law have long since admired the logical consistency of his legal thought. He has been credited with using a refined version of the Stoic hypothetical syllogism. The argumentative strategy transmitted in the text I have chosen contains some elements that may seem to have been taken from rhetorical teaching.

The text in question (D.30.36pr) contains Labeo's interpretation of a will. The problem consists of the interpretation of the following two interconnected bequests: "I bequeath to Titia all my slaves who are weavers, except those whom I have bequeathed to another by this will. I bequeath to Plotia all my slaves, born in my house, except those whom I have bequeathed to another." Since some of the slaves belonging to the testator were both weavers and were born in the testator's house, the question arose to which of the two bequests, if any, they belonged. Labeo decides that they were owed by Titia and Plotia in common. As Horak has remarked, the case in question is almost certainly a fictitious one, insofar as it seems too unlikely to have ever happened in real life.[36] Labeo is dealing with the problem of the interpretation of a text written in an ambiguous manner. So far his strategy may seem similar to that applied by teachers of rhetoric: inventing cases, often completely unlikely ones, in order to teach students how to resolve particular kinds of problems was their common practice. Moreover, dealing with ambiguities in written texts (both laws and private documents), was one of the standard types of rhetorical issues (*constitutio legalis ex ambiguitate, cf. supra*, section 16.2.3). Unfortunately, Labeo's solution, as transmitted in the Digest, lacks a complex justification (which is the case in the overwhelming majority of the Digest texts). It does contain, however, some hints that enable us to reconstruct the reasoning behind the solution. Labeo stresses the fact that it is impossible to determine which slaves were exempted from which bequest. As a matter of fact, house-born weavers would have been exempted from Titia's bequest, only if they did belong to Plotia's bequest, inasmuch as they were house-born. There is no way to ascertain that they were. It might also have been the case that they were exempted from Plotia's bequest on the grounds that they were bequeathed to Titia, inasmuch as they were weavers. The formulation of both bequests leads to a vicious circle. It is worth noting, however, that in given circumstances Labeo's solution, that weavers born in-house belonged to Titia and Plotia in common, is the only logically possible one. Since it is impossible to determine whether they were exempt from Titia's bequest, or from Plotia's bequest, they must belong to both. To support his solution Labeo is contrasting his case with a similar, simpler one (D.30.36.1). If the bequests ran as follows: "All my slaves who are weavers except those born in my house", and "All the slaves born in my house except the weavers", then the weavers born in the house would have belonged to none of the legatees in question (they would remain

[36] Horak 1969, 92.

with the heir). In the initial case, however, such a solution would contradict the wording of the bequests. The conclusion that the weavers born in the house should be exempted both from Titia's and from Plotia's bequest would indeed contradict the premise, i.e. the testator's statement to the effect that only the slaves effectively bequeathed to one of the legatees were to be excepted from the bequests of another.[37]

Inventing fictitious cases in order to illustrate problems related to the interpretation of ambiguous texts was a common practice among teachers of rhetoric. Considering both this fact and the pieces of Labeo's reasoning as transmitted in the text, are we entitled to conclude that he knew and consciously applied the status doctrine?

For a speaker, applying a status meant finding out what aspect of the adversary's claim was the easiest to question. On these grounds he would choose the strategy of argumentation best fitting his own demands. If he considered the text on which his adversary's plea relied ambiguous enough to admit an interpretation sustaining his own claim, he would apply the status *ex ambiguitate*. Hence he would probably choose one of the strategies of argumentation typically suggested in manuals of rhetoric for these types of cases, i.e. he would consider the context in which an ambiguous sentence has been used, he would try to restore to the author's intent, and finally he would argue that his interpretation was either more useful or more honest than the one proposed by his adversary (cf. Cic. *Inv. rhet.* 2.116–122). If we are to rely on Cicero's testimony, Crassus in the *causa Curiana* systematically applied all the above strategies.

Labeo did not apply any of them—at least the Digest text contains no indication that he did. Rather, he seems to have relied entirely on his logical skills: his interpretation is the only possible result that does not lead to an open contradiction between the ambiguous sentences of the will. As a matter of fact there is no place for controversy, since any other interpretation would plainly contradict the wording of the will. Hence, the fact that the case Labeo considers seems a fictitious one (which is highly probable but by no means certain) remains the only basis for believing that he applied the status doctrine. However, even if the case actually was fictitious, it might have been invented in order to demonstrate the usefulness of logic for legal interpretation, rather than Labeo's penchant for rhetorical argumentation.

16.4 Conclusion

Rhetorical theory provided the speaker with tools of persuasion that would enable him to justify any solution of a given problem that he happened to defend. However, it would not instruct him on the way to arrive at the solution in question, inasmuch as the latter depended on the interests either of those whom he represented or his own. Roman jurists did sometimes undertake the task of defending private people in courts and then their

[37] An objection may be raised that this solution is also not entirely consistent with the wording of the bequests, insofar as the slaves belonging to both bequests in common are not entirely exempt from either of them. Nevertheless, the solution can be defended on the grounds that from each bequest the ideal part of "common" slaves, precisely the one ascribed to another bequest, is exempted.

function was similar to that of the speaker. The Digest texts, however, present them in a different role, of those able to discover correct solutions of juridical problems—i.e. not only conforming to the law but also objectively reasonable, and corresponding to the moral standards of the day. To the extent that we want to understand the reasons behind their decisions, as well as the methods by which they reached them, rhetorical theory seems not extremely helpful: as a matter of fact, rather than teaching how to arrive at correct solutions, it provided instructions on how to defend solutions already taken and dependent on personal preferences. It is true that the objective correctness of a given solution can sometimes serve as a justification thereof: to that extent, rhetoric could have been relevant for the technical juridical discourse, i.e. insofar as it taught methods of construing and refuting rational arguments. Teachers of rhetoric, however, used to warn their students that rational arguments were not always the best to convince the audience. Hence methods of rational argumentation formed only a part, albeit a very important part, of rhetorical theory. Nor were rhetorical schools the only place in which methods of rational argumentation were taught. They were mastered and deeply analysed rather by philosophers and dialecticians than by rhetoricians. Rhetoric certainly was an extremely important art in Antiquity, which provides us with cultural context indispensable for understanding both the mentality of the jurists and the ways in which law functioned in reality. Using rhetoric as a tool for understanding the methods of communication of the jurists with society and among themselves is a very promising direction of studies (cf. the contribution by Ulrike Babusiaux in this Handbook). However, to what extent it might have influenced the method of technical juridical discourse as elaborated by Roman jurists remains a still open question that calls for further research.

Bibliography

Babusiaux, U. 2011. *Papinians* Quaestiones: *zur rhetorische Methode eines Spätklassische Juristen*. Munich.

Bonner, S. F. 1977. *Education in ancient Rome: from the elder Cato to the younger Pliny*. London.

Braet, A. C. (1987). "The classical doctrine of *status* and the rhetorical theory of argumentation." *Philosophy and Rhetoric* 20: 79–93.

Braet, A. C. (1989). "Variationen zur Statuslehre von Hermagoras bei Cicero." *Rhetorica* 7: 239–259.

Braet, A. C. (2004). "Hermagoras and the *Epicheireme*." *Rhetorica* 22: 327–347.

Calboli Montefusco, L. (1998). "*Omnis autem argumentatio ... aut probabilis aut necessaria esse debebit* (Cic. *Inv.* 1,44)." *Rhetorica* 16: 1–24.

Calboli Montefusco, L. (2010). "Rhetorical use of dilemmatic arguments." *Rhetorica* 28: 363–383.

Carter, M. (1988). "*Stasis* and *kairos*: principles of social construction in classical rhetoric." *Rhetoric Review* 7: 97–112.

Craig, C. O. 1993. *Form as argument in Cicero's speeches: a study of dilemma*. Atlanta.

Dyke, E. (2002). "*Topos* and *Enthymeme*." *Rhetorica* 20: 105–117.

Fumerton, F. A. (1980). "Induction and reasoning to the best explanation." *Philosophy of Science* 47: 589–600.

Giaro, T. (1994). "Die Illusion der Wissenschaftlichkeit." *Index* 22: 107–134.
Gwynn, A. 1926. *Roman education from Cicero to Quintilian*. Oxford.
Hintikka, J. (1998). "What is abduction? The fundamental problem of modern epistemology." *Transactions of the Charles S. Peirce Society* 34: 503–533.
Holtsmark, E. B. (1968). "Quintilian on *status*: a *progymnasma*." *Hermes* 96: 356–368.
Horak, F. 1969. Rationes decidendi: *Entscheidungsbegründungen bei deb älteren römischen Juristen bis Labeo*. Innsbruck.
Kraus, M. (2012). "Teorie dell'entimema nell'antichità." *Pan* 1: 17–30.
Ladyman, J. 2002. *Understanding philosophy of science*. London.
Lausberg, H. 1998. *Handbook of literary rhetoric: a foundation for literary study*. Leiden.
Leesen, T. 2010. *Gaius meets Cicero: law and rhetoric in the school controversies*. Leiden.
Madden, E. H. (1952). "Crossroads of logic, rhetoric and metaphysics." *The Philosophical Review* 61: 368–376.
Ochs, D. 1974. "Aristotle's concept of formal topics." In K. V. Erickson, ed., *Aristotle: the classical heritage of rhetoric*. Metuchen N.J. 194–204.
Ochs, D. (1989). "Cicero and philosophic *inventio*." *Rhetoric Society Quarterly* 19: 217–227.
Peirce, C. S. 1878. "Deduction, induction and *hypothesis*," in *Collected papers*, 1932 Cambridge. Vol. 2: 619–644.
Pollock, J. 1986. *Contemporary theories of knowledge*. Totowa.
Rapp, C. (2002). *Aristoteles: Rhetorik*, Vol. 2. Berlin.
Rubinelli, S. 2009. Ars Topica: *the classical technique of constructing arguments from Aristotle to Cicero*. Lugano.
Schurz, G. (2008). "Patterns of abduction." *Synthese* 164: 201–234.
Solmsen, F. (1941). "The Aristotelian tradition in ancient rhetoric II." *The American Journal of Philology* 62: 169–190.
Stroux, J. 1949. "Summum ius summa iniuria: *Ein Kapitel aus der Geschichte der* interpretatio iuris," in *Römische Rechtswissentschaft und Rhetorik*. Potsdam
Tellegen-Couperus, O. and J. W. Tellegen. 2013. "*Artes Urbanae*: Roman law and rhetoric." In P. J. du Plessis, ed., *New frontiers: law and society in the Roman world*. Edinburgh. 31–50.
Viehweg, T. 1953. *Topik und Jurisprudenz: ein Beitrag zur rechtswissentschaftlichen Grundlagenforschung*. First edition. Munich.

PART V

SETTLING DISPUTES

Civil Actions and Civil Procedure

CHAPTER 17

MAGISTRATES WHO MADE AND APPLIED THE LAW

FREDERIK J. VERVAET

17.1 Introduction

ALTHOUGH legal historians of ancient Rome distinguish between the Archaic (753–250) and Pre-classical (250–27) periods, this chapter takes a political approach and is concerned with what is commonly known as the Roman Republic, spanning the period from 509 to 27. More specifically, the focus is on what could be termed the classical Republic: the Roman polity as it emerged from the so-called "struggle of the orders" and that one could define as a plutocratic democracy, dominated by the patricio-plebeian consular nobility, from roughly 350 to 50, when the rise of Julius Caesar and the ensuing Civil Wars would result in the establishment of Monarchical rule. This scope is warranted in that these three centuries represent the flowering of (pro)active magisterial involvement in the creation and application of Roman law. Before this period, Roman law was mostly customary, with strong religious associations (Bujuklić 1998, 90–140; Watson 1999, 71–83), whereas the early Empire saw the decline of the involvement of Rome's urban magistrates in the production and application of law, a function rapidly absorbed by the emperor and his sprawling officialdom as well as a highly professionalised body of jurisprudents. Since the administration of the provinces is discussed elsewhere in this volume, this survey is mostly concerned with the city of Rome and, to a lesser extent, Italy.

In *Topica* 5.28, M. Tullius Cicero (cos. 63) produces a striking précis of what he considered to be the foremost sources of Roman civil law; namely, statutes, decrees of the senate, judicial decisions, opinions of those learned in the law, edicts of magistrates, custom and equity.[1] In other words, since the magistrates of people and plebs played a vital role in the drafting and implementation of laws, *senatus consulta*, the issuing of judicial decisions and edicts, they were indispensable actors in the production, dissemination and upholding of

[1] For the fairly similar situation under the early Empire see Inst.Gai.1.2. On the sources of Roman law see Robinson 1997, 25–53; Alexander 2010, 238–240. On jurisprudence and jurisconsults see Wieacker 1988, 519–617; Frier 1985; Alexander 2010, 246–252.

Roman law. Before discussing their involvement in law-making, it is important to observe that the term *lex*, law, can be used with varying degrees of strictness. In its strictest sense, the word signifies statute law as magisterial bills ratified by vote of the popular assemblies; namely, the *comitia centuriata* and the *comitia tributa*. As from the *lex Hortensia* of 287, this connotation also came to include tribunician bills passed by the *concilium plebis*, the assembly of the Roman *plebs* (Gell. *NA* 10.20). In its broader sense, however, *lex* can also denote customary law (such as the *leges regiae*, the "royal laws", or the Laws of the XII Tables); the procedural *formula* that marks the beginning of the lawsuit; or the magisterial edict outlining a set of *formulae* and administrative rules of engagement. Although this chapter will be chiefly concerned with statute law and edicts as those sources of law mostly produced by the magistrates of people and plebs, these qualifiers have ramifications for the second component concerning the role of magistrates in the application of the law.

17.2 MAGISTRATES MAKING THE LAW

17.2.1 Statute Laws

Since the Republican polity essentially was a plutocratic outfit that served the conservative interests of Rome's landed aristocracy, it should not surprise that legislation could only be drafted, promulgated and put to the vote by a limited number of ranking magistrates.[2] Amongst the annually elected magistrates of the people, only the college of the consuls and the praetors held the *ius agendi cum populo patribusque*, the right to call and preside over meetings of the people and the senate. In addition, this key prerogative was also held by a small number of non-annual *curule* magistracies; namely, the dictator and his *magister equitum*, the *interreges*, as well as such special commissions who held it by virtue of extraordinary privilege, like the *decemviri legibus scribundis* (450/449) and the *triumviri rei publicae constituendae* (43–27).[3] All of these magistrates were able to convene any type of popular assembly (on which see ch. 7, this volume), and they all invariably held the highest patrician auspices (the *auspicia maxima*), indispensable for the conduct of any state business, as well as some form of full *imperium* (*dictatorium*, *consulare* or *praetorium*). Characteristically of the aristocracy's sense of honour and hierarchy, there was a well-defined pecking order in terms of what magistrate(s) enjoyed the prior right of initiative in dealing with senate and people: dictators would outrank consuls, consuls enjoyed precedence over praetors, while amongst the consuls, priority and initiative rested with that consul holding the *fasces* (and thus the high command) in any particular month. Similarly, the *praetor urbanus* enjoyed some form of precedence over all other praetors and traditionally assumed the consuls' responsibilities in their absence.[4] By contrast, the

[2] On law-making in the Republic see Watson 1974; Kunkel and Wittmann 1995, 319–321 and 607–626; Crawford 1996, 1–38; Williamson 2005, 62–128.

[3] See e.g. Cic. *Leg.* 3.10; Gell. *NA* 14.7.5; Vervaet 2010. For the differences between annual and non-annual magistracies see Coli 1953.

[4] Gell. *NA* 14.7.4–5 and 8; Vervaet 2014, 3–53. On the primacy of the *praetor urbanus* see e.g. Festus, ed. Lindsay 1913, 154; Cic. *Mur.* 41, *Fam.* 10.12.3. For debates and voting in the senate also being governed by rank and hierarchy see Gell. *NA* 14.7.9; Ryan 1998; Pina Polo 2013.

tribunes of the plebs were the only plebeian magistrates that held the *ius agendi cum plebe*, the capacity to call assemblies of the plebs.

This prerogative to call popular assemblies was strictly reserved, as neither senate nor individual citizens were able to do so, however significant their collective or individual clout. Private citizens (or, for that matter, other magistrates) could only hope to express their opinions in *contiones*, either collectively or individually, the latter only by invitation from the magistrate calling the assembly (Mommsen 1887, 1:201; Linderski 1986, 2209–2210.). The number of venues was equally restricted: while the *comitia centuriata* could only convene on the Campus Martius, for historical reasons, the other full assemblies of people and plebs had to be called within the one-mile periphery around the *pomerium*. An essential feature of the Republican polity was that even soldiers *sub sacramento* enjoyed the right of appeal (*ius provocationis*) within this specific zone, in order to allow them, too, a free vote in all electoral and legislative assemblies (Liv. 3.20; Gell. *NA* 15.27.5; Giovannini 1983, 19–26.). Nonetheless, the democratic process was significantly constrained by a number of other constitutional checks. First, there is the fact that the centuriate organisation and voting procedures strongly favoured the wealthy and senior segment of the male citizen body, while the tribal assemblies gave massive numerical advantage to rural voting districts (thirty-one in total) and their landowning elites. They also discriminated against the growing numbers of freedmen, since these were typically enrolled in the urban districts (numbering only four). Second, the College of the Pontiffs as well as the Augural College continued to hold significant sway over the comitial process under the classical Republic. The Pontiffs controlled the calendar, whilst the Augurs could render null and void the results of any popular vote at different stages by declaring flaws of procedure. Since both Colleges were dominated by the inner core of the consular nobility, they acted as powerful conduits of the most ranking and senior elements in the senatorial aristocracy. In light of these considerations, it is fair to conclude that both the production and application of statute law very much remained an elite affair under the Republic.

In the relative political calm of the heyday of the classical Republic (*c.*300 to *c.*133), the process of lawmaking normally involved all three key components of what Polybius (6.11–18) represents as an exemplary mixed constitution; namely, the magisterial executive, the senatorial aristocracy, and the popular assemblies—a balanced machinery of state that proved extraordinarily effective in times of war. Until the Civil War of 88, consuls and, occasionally, praetors generally sponsored laws as directed by the senate (Williamson 2005, 14–16). Although any consular or praetorian bill could be presented to either the centuriate or tribal assembly, the choice of assembly would be dictated by tradition and expediency (Pina Polo 2011, 100–107; *contra* Sandberg 2001, 105–113, 119–131, advocating a more rigorous division of comitial spheres of competence).

The fact that the consuls of the pre-Gracchan era spent much of their tenure in the field put significant constraints on their legislative capability, especially as they had a very busy agenda in first months of the year. Nonetheless, consular laws concerned issues of paramount importance such as the right of appeal of Roman citizens,[5] formal

[5] Regardless of ongoing scholarly division as to the origins and enforcement of the right of appeal (the *ius provocationis*), most consider the *lex Valeria* of 300 to be historical: see, e.g. Kunkel and Wittmann 1995, 166–169, 169; Pina Polo 2011, 111.

treaties, declarations of war against major foreign entities, the organisation of the military, the organisation of judicial courts, grants of citizenship, the calendar, and the fight against excessive luxury, corruption and political violence. After the violent upheavals of the Gracchan tribunates (133 and 123/22), the consuls tended to stay in Rome longer and were increasingly relied on by the senate to pass politically significant legislation (Pina Polo 2011, 99–121). From 70 however, a coalition of dynasts comprising Cn. Pompeius Magnus, M. Licinius Crassus and C. Iulius Caesar increasingly relied on a mixture of military manpower and support amongst the vastly increased urban plebs to push through consequential legislation as consuls, overwhelmingly against the will of the senate. As a consular *lex Pompeia Licinia* in 70 rescinded Sulla's restrictions on *tribunicia potestas*, this "untraditional" consular legislation was complemented by equally contested legislative activity on the part of friendly tribunes of the plebs (cf. also further in this section). Paradoxically, this *popularis* strategy to ramp up the use of statute law in order to subvert the traditional primacy of the senate in a growing number of major public affairs, often in favour of a small number of legally privileged (pro) consuls, eventually resulted in the demise of public law and the establishment of imperatorial autocracy (Williamson 2005, 367–414; Vervaet 2014, 214–292). Although the *praetor urbanus* is often attested as calling *contiones* to discuss public business, including proposed legislation, there is every indication that praetorian laws were quite rare, especially in the pre-Gracchan period. This suggests that in the absence of both consuls, the senate would have turned to the tribunes of plebs to enact any legislation they saw fit, probably through the ranking praetor. Interestingly, however, the senate regularly charged the *praetor urbanus* with the task of convening the *comitia tributa* for the appointment of special, non-annual magisterial commissions (especially those concerned with agrarian and colonial business), even when one or both consuls were present in Rome (Brennan 2000, 119–121).

Although the office ranked below that of praetor or consul and was generally held by aspiring junior aristocrats, the tribunes of the plebs were responsible for the bulk of comitial legislation under the Republic (Bleicken 1955, 43–73; Thommen 1989, 42–129). This can be explained in terms of their wide political responsibility and special powers, the legal requirement for tribunes to remain in Rome, and their numbers—no less than ten as from 457. As for the scope of tribunician lawmaking, one can roughly distinguish between three historical stages. Before the conclusion of the "struggle of the orders" around 300, the plebeian tribunes, created in 494 for this very purpose, would persistently champion plebeian causes. On the level of public law, the tribunes played a critical role in the struggle to obtain regular and mandated plebeian access to the higher magistracies as well as key priesthoods. This was matched by their role as protectors of individual and collective plebeian civil rights vis-à-vis the coercive powers of the overwhelmingly patrician higher magistrates. With a few exceptions, this was followed by a long period of synergy and conformity, when the office came to be incorporated in the senatorial *cursus honorum* and tribunician legislation became an additional conduit for codifying the will of the senate. In this period, the senate would regularly ask (one of) the consuls (or the urban praetor) to have (one of) the tribunes of the *plebs* put a certain issue to the vote in the *concilium plebis*—a procedure that was also used to resolve political stalemates within the senatorial aristocracy (e.g. Liv. 30.27.1–5).

The wide scope of tribunician policy interests, given their role as advocates of the popular interest (Polyb. 6.16), and their continuous presence in Rome account for the sheer breadth and regularity of tribunician legislation, covering such issues as prorogation, creation and transferal of military commands, peace treaties and alliances, conferment of citizenship on individuals or communities, festivals, colonial foundations, weights, measures and currency denominations, electoral measures, and the dispensation of justice and special courts (Sandberg 2001). However, ever since the divisive agrarian and political programmes of Tiberius and Gaius Gracchus (133 and 123/122) had shattered the relative consensus amongst the senatorial aristocracy, the tribunate of the plebs increasingly became one of the spearheads in the struggle between *populares*, aristocrats advocating measures to alleviate the plight of the masses, and *optimates*, those nobles favouring the status quo. Resultantly, the intensity, scope and ambition of tribunician legislative activity significantly increased, a development facilitated by roughly contemporary tribunician legislation on the secret ballot.[6] Aspiring tribunes now moved into departments that traditionally were the reserve of senate and consuls, such as taxation and foreign policy, mostly against senatorial sentiment. Having learned the lesson from the demise of the Gracchans, L. Appuleius Saturninus in 103 and 100 was the first tribune to enter into a political alliance with a military strongman, C. Marius. The final decades of the Republic would witness the massive use of furloughed or retired legionaries to force through the *popularis* consular and tribunician legislation that would destroy the traditional balance of power, especially in the years 70, 59, 58 and 55.[7]

The bulk of legislation carried by non-annual *curule* magistrates, such as dictators or extraordinary legislative commissions, comes from the peripheral periods of the classical Republic. Equally notable is the fact that the historic significance of their lawmaking was disproportionate to their ephemeral appearance in the historical record. Roman tradition has it that in 451/450 a special magisterial board with consular authority and the power to issue edicts with the force of law—the *decemviri consulari imperio legibus scribundis*—set about compiling previously unwritten rules into twelve tables of laws as a means to mitigate patrician domination of the law (Broughton *MRR* 1: 45–48). This so-called Law of the XII Tables, inscribed on bronze tables and displayed on the Forum, was much concerned with such key areas as property and family law and became widely considered by the Romans as the foundation of their civil law (ch. 3, this volume). Discontinued after 202, the dictatorship is also credited with a critical role in the resolution of the "struggle of the orders" and the emergence of the new plebeio-patrician consular nobility that would dominate the classical Republic. Paradoxically, the very magistracy that had often provided a tool for patrician suppression of plebeian demands (in the form of the *dictatura seditionis sedandae causa*: the dictatorship to quell seditions) was repeatedly used to push through laws that gradually opened up the major magistracies and priesthoods to the plebeian elite and gave plebiscites the same universal force as *leges populi*. As such, these laws complemented a parallel legislative effort on the part of a number of tribunes of the plebs.

[6] In 139, a *lex Gabinia* first introduced voting by ballot in the election of magistrates: Broughton *MRR* 1: 482. As Cicero indicates with marked hostility (*Leg.* 3.35–39), three more such laws would follow in 137, 131 and 107, respectively extending the ballot to trials before the people (*iudicia populi*), the adoption or rejection of laws, and, finally, trials for treason, omitted from the law of 137.

[7] See Broughton *MRR* 2: 126, 187–188, 190, 193–196, 214–215 and 217; Thommen 1989, 140–147.

Importantly, much of this combined legislative drive towards a relative democratisation of the Roman polity also tackled major socio-economic problems, alleviating the issue of debt-slavery (*nexum*), attempts at capping the amount of public land any citizen could hold (in *possessio*) or opening market days for legal business.

The troubled final decades of the Republic witnessed two more legislative magistracies. L. Cornelius Sulla used his unprecedented *dictatura rei publicae constituendae et legibus scribundis* (82–79) to enforce a reactionary and restrictive legislative programme meant to restore and fortify the senate's supremacy. The main aim of the triumvirate *rei publicae constituendae* (43–27), formalising the alliance between M. Antonius, M. Aemilius Lepidus and C. Iulius Caesar Octavi(an)us, was to rid the Republic of their opponents and secure their own predominance (Vervaet 2004 and 2010). Whereas several Cornelian Laws continued as cornerstones of Roman public and criminal law for centuries to come, often in the form of updated Julian Laws (passed by both Caesar and Augustus), the bulk of triumviral *edicta* were meant as temporary devices and rescinded by Octavian himself in 28 (Rich and Williams 1999, 194–199, 212–213; Vervaet 2010, 137–139; Dalla Rosa 2015).

Although the censors, reportedly established as a higher magistracy in 443 to relieve the work of the consuls, could not convene the people, their mandate gave them enormous legal influence. It was by virtue of the *census*, the official registration of the personalia (full *nomina*, age, spouse and children) and property of adult citizens (Kunkel and Wittmann 1995, 427–429), that individual Roman males were assigned to a certain class/voting unit in the *comitia centuriata* as well as a certain position in the army, the most affluent Romans being assigned to the cavalry (hence their collective denomination: *equites publici*). As supervisors of public morals, censors also had the power to issue *notae censoriae* to individual citizens on account of dereliction of civil duties. Citizens who had their names marked suffered exclusion from their existing tribal registration and their right to vote, whilst any senators or *equites* who received a censorial blame were stripped of their respective ranks. As Lintott notes, this moral censure "appears to be an extraordinary, and arbitrary, supplement to the jurisdiction of the courts". Until Sulla, who passed dictatorial legislation making the quaestorship the formal qualification for entry to the senate, the censors also managed the membership of the senate (through *lectio senatus*). Last but not least, they were responsible for the regulation of the *tributum* (property tax) and the superintendence of all other forms of public revenue (*vectigalia*), for leasing public property and letting out the rights to undertake the construction of roads and other public infrastructure as well as the collection of customs and provincial taxes (Kunkel and Wittmann 1995, 391–471; Lintott 1999, 115–120).

No appraisal of magisterial lawmaking could be complete without brief but emphatic acknowledgment of the role of magisterial and pontifical *scribae*.[8] Their historical importance as experts in legalistic jargon and ritualistic *formulae* is disproportionate to their record in our overwhelmingly aristocratic sources. One striking anecdote may suffice to corroborate this observation. In the older system of *legis actionis*, the first stage of proceedings before the magistrate (termed *in iure*) required the presence of a pontiff who would recite highly ritualistic *formulae* for solemn repetition by plaintiff and defendant.

[8] On the *scribae* see Kunkel and Wittmann 1995, 116–119. On magisterial *apparitores* see Purcell 1983; Cohen 1984.

These *formulae* were the domain of the pontifical college, whose members alone could use and interpret them. Late in the fourth century, Gnaeus Flavius, son of a freedman and one of the scribes of the maverick patrician censor Appius Claudius Caecus (cos. 307, *II* 296; censor in contested circumstances from 312 to 308), made the bold move of publishing these *formulae/actiones* after his boss had organised them in book form. In doing so, he democratised the *ius civile* and hastened the decline of pontifical jurisprudence. Possibly (again?) with the support of his patron Caecus, himself one of the earliest Republican jurists, he also erected a calendar in the Forum indicating the *dies fasti*, days on which legal business was permissible, another blow to pontifical power.[9]

17.2.2 Edicts

All magistrates of people and plebs had the *ius edicendi*, the right to issue official edicts valid for the duration of their tenure, and these constitute the second foremost instrument of direct magisterial involvement in the production and application of law. Consular edicts were mainly concerned with public affairs and major administrative, socio-economic or military issues of an ad hoc nature, sometimes also involving Italy and the provinces. As regards domestic matters, consular edicts mostly communicated senatorial votes to the people assembled *in contione* and were displayed in frequented places such as the *Forum Romanum* (Pina Polo 2011, 83–98).

Gaius' statement (Inst.Gai.1.6) that very extensive law (*amplissimum ius*) resides in the edicts of the *praetor urbanus* and the *praetor peregrinus*, whose jurisdiction was also exercised by the governors in the provinces, as well as in the edicts of the *curule aediles*, holds largely true for the Republic. The edict annually issued by the incoming urban praetor played a crucial role in the development of Roman civil law. As with other such *edicta*, the intent was for the praetor publicly to communicate the legal principles and procedures he intended to follow when administering justice amongst citizens during his year in office, and what civil actions he would accommodate in his court. As the procedure *per formulas* mostly replaced the system of *legis actionis* (by c.200, Brennan 2000, 132; see also Gell. *NA* 16.10.8 and Inst.Gai.4.30; Watson 1974, 111; Wieacker 1988, 450), this edict would also define the necessary *formula* for each action. Whilst much of the content rapidly became tralatician, newly appointed praetors could make amendments, allowing for welcome innovation.[10] Together with the annual edict of the *praetor peregrinus*, responsible for jurisdiction involving non-Romans, this edict also provided an important model for the jurisdictional edicts issued by (pro)magistrates in the provinces at the start of their tenure. In several provinces, these again largely tralatician gubernatorial edicts would complement the so-called *lex provinciae*, really a constitutive edict typically laid down by the imperator who had overseen the annexation and drafted in close consultation with senior senatorial commissioners (Hoyos 1973). At all events, the praetorian

[9] Liv. 9.46.5–6 recounts that Flavius published the *civile ius* and the Fasti as aedile in 304, but Cicero *Att.* 6.1.8 (compare *De or.* 1.186) and Pliny *HN* 33.17 are adamant he did so as a *scriba*. On the historic importance of the so-called *ius civile Flavianum* see also D.1.2.2.7.

[10] This inspired the jurist Aelius Marcianus to describe the edict as *viva vox iuris civilis*, "the living voice of the civil law" (D.1.1.8).

edict became so influential that Cicero talked of the *ius praetoris* (*Verr.* 2.1.109) and observed that this had overwhelmingly replaced the XII Tables as the chief source of Roman legal science (*Leg.*1.19), while he conceived of the praetor himself as the *iuris civilis custos* (*Leg.* 3.8). As explained by the famous jurist Papinian (*c.*148–211) in D.1.1.7.1, "praetorian law" (*ius praetorium*) thus came to substantiate, supplement or improve the *ius civile*, and was eventually also termed magisterial law (*ius honorarium*) after the high office (*honor*) of the praetor.

In their edict (first attested in Plautus *Merc.* 419, *Capt.* 813–24 and Cato in Gell. *NA* 17.6.2; reconstructed in Lenel 1927, 554–568), the *curule aediles* publicised the principles for the exercise of their jurisdiction over the markets in Rome as well as their other supervisory functions (see section 17.3). Some of its best-known provisions ordered the seller's warranty for latent defects of slaves or beasts of burden. Already around 150, jurists were extending the implied warranty of the aedilician edict to all sales, and even under the early Empire its central provisions remained unaltered (Lenel 1927; see also du Plessis 2010, 270–272).

Foremost amongst the censorial *edicta* with wide legal and criminal ramifications are the so-called *leges censui censendo* and the *leges censoriae*. The first, also termed the *formula census*, was a mostly tralatician edict, published in the *Forum Romanum* as well as the fora and *conciliabula* of the *ager Romanus* (Roman public land), stipulating who was to participate in the census and the timeframe, what kinds of property were subject to the census and the way in which their value was to be estimated, as well as the terms of the individual oath and the penalties. The *leges censoriae* defined the specific terms on which taxes (*tributa*), other public revenues (*vectigalia*) and public works were let (to the highest bidder for a *lustrum*, a period of five years), together with the rights and duties of the purchasers, published in every case before the start of the auction. Insofar as these *leges* concerned similar matters, many clauses would again have been of a tralatician nature (Kunkel and Wittmann 1995, 422–435, 446–461).

17.3 Magistrates Applying the Law

Before we survey those magistracies involved in the application of the law, it is useful to set the stage with a few introductory observations. Although Cicero attests that all magistrates had juridical authority (*iudicium*, *Leg.* 3.10), the nature and extent of magisterial involvement in the application of the law differed for each category of magistrate. Only magistrates *cum imperio* (dictators, consuls, praetors), for example, held the right to coerce reluctant citizens (as well as non-Romans) to obey their orders and decrees (*coercitio*), if need be by inflicting corporal punishment (either flogging or decapitation). This same category of magistrates also had the power of summons (*vocatio*) and arrest (*prensio*), while the tribunes of the plebs and certain other magistrates only had the power to arrest. By the late Republic, however, the tribunes of the *plebs*, too, appear to have acquired the power to summon. The quaestors, by contrast, could neither summon nor arrest (Gell. *NA* 13.12–13; Kunkel and Wittmann 1995, 123–124). The sources indicate that criminal investigations (*quaestiones*), too, were the exclusive reserve of magistrates with *imperium* (Pina Polo 2011, 128), which begs the thorny question as to the operational scope of magisterial jurisdiction and law enforcement and the social reach of Roman courts (Pölönen 2006).

At any rate, there is every indication that the higher magistrates and even the tribunes of the plebs were mostly concerned with big-ticket prosecutions or major issues of law enforcement. It has already been stated that the consuls and the tribunes of the plebs played a far more important role in the production of statute law as compared to the praetors, or, for that matter, any other magistracies with the *ius agendi cum populo*. However, when it comes to the routine application of the law in the classical Republic, much the opposite is true, as that field was consistently dominated by the praetors, as well as the tribunes of the plebs, the aediles and a number of minor magistracies. For the sake of convenience, we will first consider the responsibilities and roles of the annual magistracies of people and plebs, followed by an assessment of the involvement of the non-annual magistracies. Within both categories, the so-called major magistracies will be discussed first.

In addition to their role as supreme commanders in Rome's major wars, the consuls' overall domestic responsibility was to safeguard the ancestral Republic, i.e. the profoundly stratified social order with its very uneven distribution of wealth and the traditional balance of power. Whereas they always played an important legislative role, the consuls were much less involved with the city's routine civil jurisdiction. In exceptional circumstances, the senate would entrust them with judicial inquiries (*quaestiones*) of the highest importance. The suppression of the Bacchanalia in 186 is a well-known example (Liv. 39.18.1–3). Apart from conspiracies, the consuls were also entrusted with inquiries regarding corruption, the expulsion of non-Romans or illegal actions of Roman magistrates (Pina Polo 2011, 122–134). From the mass killing of Gaius Gracchus and his associates in 121 until 40, the senate occasionally put (one of) the consuls in the position akin to that of the legendary dictators *seditionis sedandae causa*. By virtue of a discretionary decree they received *carte blanche* to take any measures necessary "to ensure that the Republic suffers no harm"—a measure of last resort that often resulted in summary executions of Roman citizens. This empowerment continued to be a festering issue in the escalating struggle between *optimates* and *populares*, the latter maintaining that such violated a citizen's age-long legal right of *provocatio*—appeal to the people or the tribunes of the plebs against the threat of corporal punishment by one of the magistrates *cum imperio*.

On the one hand, as the minor colleagues of the consuls and holders of a lesser *imperium* but identical auspices, the praetors could exercise most of the consuls' official prerogatives. Just like the consuls, they could conduct major military operations. In the absence of the consuls or by their command, they were equally capable of conducting criminal investigations. Though the praetors were unable to organise consular and praetorian elections (Gell. *NA* 13.15.4), their legislative activity was no different from that of the consuls in both scope and constitutional process. On the other hand, the praetors played a vastly more important role than the consuls in the application of the law and civil jurisdiction. Although there remains debate as to the original rationale for the creation of a distinct *praetura* in 367 and initial praetorian authority and responsibilities (Brennan 2000, 58–78), the jurisdiction amongst citizens rapidly became one of the main briefs of the *praetor urbanus*.[11] The Roman expansion in Italy and the corresponding increase of foreigners in Rome resulted in the creation of a second praetorship in 246, the *praetor peregrinus*.

[11] Cf. Festus ed. Lindsay 1913, 468: *praetor qui inter cives ius dicet*.

Whereas the higher magistrates had probably served as judges themselves in the early Republic, the classical Republic indeed saw two important developments. Although civil jurisdiction ultimately derived from the consuls' *imperium*, their military role meant that the routine dispensation of justice overwhelmingly became the realm of the praetors. Until the rise of autocracy, the praetors continued to be indispensable for the conduct of Roman trials (*iudicia*) of all sorts.[12] Second, their involvement took a distinct form. In the *legis actio*, the oldest known form of Roman procedure, the praetor would play a particularly important role throughout the first stage of proceedings and at the start of the second. The first stage took place *in iure*, the locality where a magistrate held court (usually the *Comitium*) (D.1.1.11). In a private suit, this stage consisted of a hearing before the praetor, where he decided between the requests of the plaintiff and the defendant. In a criminal case, however, this involved a complicated series of actions to decide if the accused should become a formal defendant (*reus*) and who should have the right to prosecute him/her. The second stage, termed *apud iudicem*, constituted the actual trial (*iudicium*) and commenced with the praetor's appointment of one or more private person(s) who took on the role of *iudex* or *arbiter* (*addicere* or *dare iudicem*) and eventually pronounced a verdict (*sententia*) on the basis of the factual evidence deemed relevant in the preliminary stage.

In the formulary system that came into use around the close of the third century BC and eventually mostly replaced the *legis actiones*, the praetor also provided the juror(s) during the proceedings *in iure* with the *formula* defining rules for litigation and the terms for requiring the defendant to pay damages. This judge, much like the praetor himself, invariably was a male of suitable social and moral standing. Before the emergence of permanent criminal courts (neatly termed *quaestiones perpetuae* in Cic. *Brut.* 106), magistrates *cum imperio* and sometimes tribunes of the plebs also acted as prosecutors in *iudicia populi*, public trials before the assembly of prominent men accused of serious criminal offences against the Republic such as electoral bribery (*ambitus*), violence and public disorder (*vis publica*) or political treason (*perduellio*). These elaborate trials consisted of several separate investigations (*anquisitiones*), and the verdict was rendered by vote in the *comitia centuriata* or *tributa*. The penalty varied from a fine to capital punishment and the consecration of one's estate, exile offering an alternative to members of the elite.[13]

In 149, however, the tribune L. Calpurnius Piso Frugi (cos. 133) passed a law establishing the first ever standing criminal court (*quaestio*) for cases of extortion (*de pecuniis repetundis*—"for the recovery of moneys"), a matter previously handled by ad hoc *quaestiones* established by the senate in reaction to specific allegations. This law represents a genuine milestone, as it heralded the gradual demise of the rather unwieldy *iudicia populi*.[14] Although ad hoc *quaestiones* would continue to be created for special offences until the very end of the Republic, the following decades saw the establishment of additional standing courts. In 81, Sulla as dictator institutionalised the new system by setting up some seven standing courts (assault, homicide, electoral bribery, violence, extortion and

[12] Leifer 1914, 206–224, revising Mommsen 1887, 2:101–125, 207–238; Kunkel and Wittmann 1995, 326–328; Brennan 2000, 63, 125–135. On consular supremacy in respect to praetors see Brennan 2000, 445 and 454–455.

[13] On praetor and *iudex* see Kaser 1964. On civil procedure see chs. 18–22; on Roman criminal justice see chs. 23–26.

[14] Broughton *MRR* 1: 459; Lintott 1981; Kunkel and Wittmann 1995, 385.

treason). Each of these was presided over by a praetor or a (mostly aedilician) *iudex quaestionis* (Kunkel and Wittmann 1995, 708).

Whereas judges were initially chosen by free agreement of the parties involved, the system of standing *quaestiones* mandated selection from a list (the *album iudicum selectorum*), at first exclusively manned by senators, later also by equestrians and a third category (the *tribunii aerarii*), closely aligned with the latter. From the tribunate of C. Gracchus down to the Civil Wars of the 40s, the composition of these juries remained an issue of fierce legal and political contention between *optimates* and *populares*, especially as regards *quaestiones* concerned with allegations of provincial maladministration such as treason (*de maiestate*) and extortion (*de pecuniis repetundis*). The root cause of this conflict was the increasing politicisation of prosecutions of ranking senators fuelled by the aristocracy's internal struggles and the growing tension between senatorial governors and equestrian tax farmers and loan sharks active in their provinces.

As opposed to *iudicia populi* and ad hoc *quaestiones*, the magistrates in charge of the standing courts did not initiate prosecutions themselves. Initially, charges were brought by the wronged individual, a family member or his chosen representative. Later, any private citizen could request authorisation from a presiding magistrate to prosecute before his court. In the case of competing petitions, the presiding magistrate organised a pretrial hearing (*divinatio*) in which a panel of jurors decided on the accuser, whilst the others could still act as *subscriptores* by signing the indictment. All these characteristics easily explain why, more often than not, the verdict depended on the political constellation of the moment rather than the actual degree of guilt (Gruen 1968 and 1974). After the jury rendered a verdict by majority vote (a tie meant acquittal), the magistrate passed judgement and sentence, which under the Republic was final. The sentence invariably was a hefty fine or exile, the equivalent of capital punishment for the elites. Magistrates *cum imperio* and men absent on public business could not be prosecuted in a *quaestio*. That all these *iudicia/quaestiones*, including tribunician trials, usually took place in an open space where spectators were free to stand around and watch (hence defined as the *corona*, crown) further contributed to the publicity and political ramifications of these trials.[15]

As the guardians of plebeian interests, the tribunes of the plebs also made a significant contribution to the application of the law. First and foremost, they held the *ius auxilii*, the right to come to the assistance of individual citizens and even colleagues against the coercive power of the magistrates with *imperium* by virtue of a personal intercession to protect their physical integrity.[16] In times of political tension, this prerogative could also be exercised on behalf of entire groups. Second, tribunes also regularly assumed the role of prosecutor, (in)directly initiating trials against those perceived to be breaking criminal law, be it customary or statutory, the penalty being a fine, imprisonment or exile. *Abrogationes* (impeachments) no doubt represent some of the most extreme tribunician actions, and only occurred from the tribunate of Ti. Gracchus.[17]

[15] On the so-called *quaestiones perpetuae* see Jones 1972; Lintott 2007, 68–77; Harries 2007.

[16] See Kunkel and Wittmann 1995, 10; 136; 158; 168–170; 176; 206; 587–594. The *ius auxilii* was not identical to and yet closely associated with the tribunician *ius intercessionis*, the latter prerogative being associated with the tribunician *ius prohibendi* (veto-power) against magisterial edicts, rogations and *senatus consulta*.

[17] See Bauman 1968 for the fact that *abrogatio imperii* (impeachment) could only be decided by popular vote and was meant to clear the path for further criminal prosecution (*de maiestate*) by first stripping the defendant of his immunity.

Although incapable of convening people or plebs, and often ignored or poorly documented, a number of other colleges, both major (i.e. holding some category of the highest auspices) and minor (i.e. holding lesser auspices), also played a very important role in the application of the law. Foremost among the former category were a number of non-annual magistracies (i.e. those magistracies created for specific purposes) such as the censors and those ad hoc colleges commissioned with the execution of (consular, praetorian or tribunician) agrarian and colonial legislation (Gargola 1995, chs. 3, 5; Dart 2011; *ILS* 46). Given their enormous economic responsibilities, the censors exercised significant investigative and jurisdictional prerogatives—predominantly concerned with controlling private leaseholders of public works (termed *cognoscere et iudicare de sartis tectis*) and the *probatio* of new infrastructure. The censors' jurisdiction also comprised the power to clear unauthorised buildings in public spaces and the regulation of urban water consumption, departments where they held *potestas* superior to that of the aediles (Kunkel and Wittmann 1995, 462–466).

A number of minor magistracies (without the *ius agendi cum populo/plebe*) also significantly contributed to the dispensation of justice and law enforcement. The aediles stand out in this category as responsible for the *cura urbis*, a vast mandate that comprised supervision of markets and corn-supply, public infrastructure and public venues, hygiene and funerals, temples (*aedes*) and other religious buildings and the supply and consumption of water. Both the *cura annonae* and the *cura aquarum* projected their authority well beyond the city. Unsurprisingly, both pairs of aediles also undertook prosecutorial duties and public trials against transgressors of criminal and administrative laws regulating the city's infrastructure, commercial life and agrarian activity. Like tribunician prosecutions, these trials took place before the people, who voted either in the *comitia tributa* or in the *concilium plebis*. If found guilty, the aedile in charge of the prosecution would impose a hefty fine, if need be through confiscation. The aediles could also prosecute (groups of) individual citizens for acts of indecency and immorality or publicly scandalous behaviour (Kunkel and Wittmann 1995, 481–505; Lintott 1999, 131–133).

Finally, there remain a number of junior magistracies ranked at the bottom of the *cursus honorum*. Worth mentioning here are the *tresviri capitales*, the four *praefecti Capuam Cumas* and the *decemviri stlitibus iudicandis*. Together with the *tresviri a(ere) a(rgento) a(uro) f(lando) f(eriundo)*, they formed the Vigintisexvirate ("the board of twenty-six"), a group of minor magistracies with mostly juridical and administrative competencies and elected under the presidency of the urban praetor in the *comitia tributa* (as opposed to the *curule aediles* and the quaestors, chosen in the same assembly under consular presidency) (Kunkel and Wittmann 1995, 532–51; Lintott 1999, 131, 137–143). Originating in the third century, the *tresviri capitales* probably started as aides to the *praetor urbanus*. As their title suggests, they were charged with the criminal jurisdiction of slaves and the lower strata of the urban *plebs*, as well as supervising the state prison and executions. At the helm of a small band of public slaves, they also had to watch for fires, keep order and arrest lowly malefactors (thieves, runaway slaves, etc.), duties they probably exercised under the aediles' supervision. While the *praefecti Capuam Cumas* performed praetorian jurisdiction and more general administration in Campania from 211, the *decemviri stlitibus iudicandis*, first recorded around 150, judged actions initiated by *sacramentum* (i.e. by one of the ancient *legis actiones*) in disputes over *libertas*, the status of being free.

17.4 Conclusion

The emergence of the Augustan Monarchy also meant the demise of proactive magisterial involvement in making and applying the law. Although Augustus still bothered to enact key legislation through the consuls or by virtue of his tribunician power (*Res Gestae* 6.2), Imperial edicts, *mandata, rescripta* and *constitutiones* as well as *senatus consulta* gradually replaced comitial legislation as a source for statute law.[18] He also initiated a number of reforms that firmly placed the (application of the) law under Imperial control. Most importantly, he introduced the *ius respondendi*, the privilege granted to certain jurists to provide litigants and lay judges with legally binding advice, as well as the *cognitio* procedure (Bauman 1989, 235–315). Although first used for claims not enforceable by the praetors, this procedure eventually replaced the formulary procedure in both civil and criminal trials (Turpin 1999 and Metzger 2013, 26–28). These *cognitiones* were mostly presided over by salaried Imperial officials who rendered verdicts themselves, and allowed for appeal. Meanwhile, serious political crimes such as treason now became a matter for the senate. Resultantly, the system of standing *quaestiones*, though intended by Augustus to continue, became completely obsolete during the third century AD. Finally, he also allowed both individuals and communities directly to petition the emperor for a legal ruling (Millar 1977, 203–272).

Bibliography

Alexander, M. C. 2010. "Law in the Roman republic." In N. Rosenstein and R. Morstein-Marx, eds., *A Companion to the Roman republic*. Oxford. 236–255.

Bauman, R. A. (1968). "The abrogation of *Imperium*, some cases and a principle." *Rheinisches Museum* 111: 37–50.

Bauman, R. A. 1989. *Lawyers and politics in the early Roman empire: a study of relations between the Roman jurists and the emperors from Augustus to Hadrian*. Munich.

Bleicken, J. 1955. *Das Volkstribunat der klassischen Republik. Studien zu seiner Entwicklung zwischen 287 und 133 v. Chr.* Munich.

Brennan, T. C. 2000. *The praetorship in the Roman republic*. Oxford.

Broughton *MRR* = Broughton, T.R.S. 1951/52, *The magistrates of the Roman republic*, Vols. 1–2. Cleveland.

Bujuklić, Z. (1998). "The *leges regiae: pro et contra.*" *Revue internationale des droits de l'antiquité* 45: 90–140.

Cohen, B. 1984. "Some neglected *ordines*: the apparitorial status-groups." In C. Nicolet, ed., *Des ordres à Rome*. Paris. 23–60.

Coli, U. 1953. "Sui limiti di durata delle magistrature romane," in *Studi in onore di Vincenzo Arangio-Ruiz nel XLV anno del suo insegnamento*. Naples. 395–418.

Crawford, M. H., ed. 1996. *Roman statutes*. 2 vols. London.

[18] See Tac. *Ann.* 4.16; Inst.Gai.1.2, 1.4–5. Ironically, Cicero's wish for *senatus consulta* to obtain the force of law (*Leg.* 3.10 and 27–28), intended as a measure to strengthen a Republic besieged by dynasts, became reality only under the Monarchy he so sought to avoid.

Dalla Rosa, A. 2015. "L'*aureus* del 28 a.C. e i poteri triumvirali di Ottaviano." In T. M. Luchelli, ed., Viri militares, *Rappresentazione e propaganda tra Repubblica e Pricipato. Atti del Convegno Venezia, 15 ottobre 2013*. Venice. 171–200.

Dart, C. J. (2011). "The impact of the Gracchian land commission and the *dandis* power of the Triumvirs." *Hermes* 139: 337–357.

du Plessis, P. J. 2010⁴. Borkowski's textbook on Roman law. Oxford.

Frier, B. W. 1985. *The Rise of the Roman jurists: studies in Cicero's* Pro Caecina. Princeton.

Gargola, D. J. 1995. *Lands, laws, and gods: magistrates and ceremony in the regulation of public lands in republican Rome*. Chapel Hill.

Giovannini, A. 1983. Consulare imperium. Basel.

Gruen, E. S. 1968. *Roman politics and the criminal courts 149–78 BC*. Cambridge, Mass.

Gruen, E. S. 1974. *The last generation of the Roman republic*. Berkeley.

Harries, J. 2007. *Law and crime in the Roman world*. Cambridge.

Hoyos, D. (1973). "*Lex provinciae* and governor's edict." *Antichton* 7: 47–53.

Jones, A. H. M. 1972. *The criminal courts of the Roman republic and Principate*. Totowa.

Jolowicz, H. F. and Nicholas, B. 1972³. *Historical introduction to the study of Roman Law*. London.

Kaser, M. (1964). "Prätor und Judex im römischen Zivilprozess." *Tijdschrift voor Rechtsgeschiedenis* 32: 329–362.

Kaser, M. and Hackl, K. 1996². *Das römische Zivilprozeßrecht*. Munich.

Kunkel, W. 1962. *Untersuchungen zur Entwicklung des römischen Kriminalverfahrens in vorsullanischer Zeit*. Munich.

Kunkel. W. and Wittmann, R. 1995. *Staatsordnung und Staatspraxis der römischen Republik. Zweiter Abschnitt. Die Magistratur*. Munich.

Leifer, F. 1914. *Die Einheit des Gewaltgedankens im römischen Staatsrecht*. Munich.

Lenel, O. 1927³. *Das* Edictum perpetuum: *ein Versuch zu seiner Wiederherstellung*. Leipzig.

Linderski, J. (1986). "The augural law." *Aufstieg und Niedergang der römischen Welt* II 16: 2146–2312.

Lintott, A. 1981. "The *leges de repetundis* and associate measures under the republic." *Zeitschrift der Savigny-Stiftung für Rechtsgeschichte, romanistische Abteilung* 98: 162–212.

Lintott, A. 1999. *The constitution of the Roman republic*. Oxford.

Lintott, A. 2007. "Legal procedure in Cicero's time." In J. Powell and J. Paterson, eds., *Cicero the Advocate*. Oxford. 61–78.

Metzger, E. 2005. *Litigation in Roman law*. Oxford.

Metzger, E. 2013. "An outline of Roman civil procedure." *Roman Legal Tradition* 9: 1–30.

Millar, F. 1977. *The Emperor in the Roman World (31 BC–AD 337)*. Ithaca.

Mommsen, T. 1887. *Römisches Staatsrecht*. 3 vols. Leipzig.

Mommsen, T. 1899. *Römisches Strafrecht*. Leipzig.

Pina Polo, F. 2011. *The consul at Rome: the civil functions of the consuls in the Roman republic*. Cambridge.

Pina Polo, F. (2013). "The political role of the *consules designati* at Rome." *Historia* 62: 420–452.

Pölönen, J. 2006. "The case for a sociology of Roman law." In M. Freeman, ed., *Law and sociology: current legal issues*. Oxford. 398–408

Purcell, N. 1983. "The *apparitores*: a study in social mobility." *Papers of the British School at Rome* 51: 125–173.

Rich, J. W. and Williams, J. H. C. (1999). "*Leges et Iura P.R. Restituit*: A new *aureus* of Octavian and the settlement of 28–27 BC." *Numismatic Chronicle* 159: 169–213.

Robinson, O. F. 1997. *The sources of Roman law: problems and methods for ancient historians.* London/New York.

Ryan, F. X. 1998. *Rank and participation in the republican senate.* Stuttgart.

Sandberg, K. 2001. *Magistrates and assemblies: a study of legislative practice in republican Rome.* Rome.

Thommen, L. 1989. *Das Volkstribunat der späten römischen Republik.* Stuttgart.

Turpin, W. (1999). "*Formula, cognitio* and proceedings *extra ordinem.*" *Revue internationale des droits de l'antiquité* 46: 499–574.

Vervaet, F. J. (2004). "The *lex Valeria* and Sulla's empowerment as dictator (82–79 BCE)." *Cahiers du Centre Gustave Glotz* 15: 37–84.

Vervaet, F. J. (2010). "The secret history: the official position of *Imperator Caesar Diui filius* from 31 to 27 BCE." *Ancient Society* 40: 79–152.

Vervaet, F. J. 2014. *The high command in the Roman republic: the principle of the* summum imperium auspiciumque *from 509 to 19 BCE.* Stuttgart.

Watson, A. 1974. *Law making in the later Roman republic.* Oxford.

Watson, A. 1999. *Ancient Roman law and modern understanding: at the edges.* Athens, Ga.

Wieacker, F. 1988. *Römische Rechtsgeschichte. Erster Abschnitt. Einleitung, Quellenkunde. Frühzeit und Republik.* Munich.

Williamson, C. 2005. *The laws of the Roman people: public law in the expansion and decline of the Roman republic.* Ann Arbor.

CHAPTER 18

ROMAN COURTS AND PRIVATE ARBITRATION

LEANNE BABLITZ

18.1 Introduction

In the modern world many identify taxes, the dentist and the courtroom as evils to avoid at all costs, but sometimes they cannot. The ancient Romans seem to have felt the same. They, too, felt that they had neither the time nor the money to take a dispute to court and hope that "justice" would be served—whoever's justice that might be. But, like us, sometimes they found themselves there, wondering how things had gotten to that point. This contribution sketches the methods available to a Roman citizen to resolve a dispute with another individual.[1] Two further specifications are necessary: I focus on the norm rather than the exception and on civil disputes between individuals.[2] Being a predominantly agrarian society, the most common disputes likely involved property (e.g. boundary lines, ownership). A close second in frequency probably were disputes over broken contracts; loans not repaid, products not delivered or a substandard product offered (Kelly 1976, 71–92). The available resolution methods cover a spectrum from those that functioned completely outside the legal system (asking a mutual friend to mediate) to those that utilised the system (taking the matter before a magistrate). Available options also varied depending on where one lived—in Rome or elsewhere in Italy or in the provinces. The chronological focus is on the classical period of Roman law, the second century BC to the second century AD. An individual contemplating litigation likely weighed several factors when deciding whether to act at all and then to determine which method best suited the circumstances. The second part of the chapter briefly explores several of these factors. Ultimately it is suggested that a highly varied and sophisticated machinery existed in Roman society by means of which individuals could (seek to) resolve disputes.

[1] For an introduction to Roman law regarding non-Roman citizens see Richardson 2015, as well as Alonso, ch. 5 and Ando, ch. 22.

[2] On criminal law and disputes involving violence see chs. 24–25.

The ancient sources on this topic are various but not plentiful. Ancient archives of wax tablets, such as the *Tabulae Herculanenses* and the *Tabulae Sulpiciorum*, and various papyri, mostly from Egypt, provide the most direct evidence of how people resolved their disputes on a daily basis.[3] Ancient literary texts, ranging from Plautus to Pliny the Younger, present useful information, though scattered. Litigants talk of matters they had to take to court, individuals talk of occasions when they served to help others resolve their disputes as mediators, arbitrators or judges, or advocates talk (sometimes quite a bit) about the speeches they made on behalf of a client, sometimes even publishing their speeches.[4] Various normative texts, from the XII Tables to the *lex Irnitana* to Gaius' Institutes, tell us what ought to have happened.[5] The evidence we have suggests, however, that affairs rarely unfolded accordingly. This is also often a problem with the classical jurists, who inform us on a wide variety of topics such as the rules regarding the appointment of judges. However, finding beauty in the intricacies of the law, they sometimes focus on norms or hypotheticals at some remove from the real experience of conflict resolution.

18.2 Methods of Conflict Resolution

Legal anthropologists have created various typologies of how different societies address disputes. Three of these categories are relevant for this discussion as they engage a third party to aid the resolution: 1) mediation, which finds the two parties calling upon a third party to help them, through discussion, to reach a compromise solution; 2) arbitration, in which the two parties ask a third party to hear their sides and make a decision which they will obey; and 3) adjudication, in which one party places the dispute before a third party, usually a state agent, who then, using the power of the state, calls the second party before him and renders a decision.[6] Evidence of Romans using all three of these methods can be found across the Empire.[7] However, while the likelihood of some sort of written record emanating from the resolution process increases as one moves from mediation to

[3] The Herculaneum tablets were originally published in very mediocre editions by G. Carratelli and V. Arangio-Ruiz beginning in 1946; Giuseppe Camodeca has been gradually re-editing the entire corpus. The critical edition of the *Tabulae Sulpiciorum* is Camodeca 1999. For a helpful brief discussion of the four most important collections of wax tablets see Wolf 2015. On dispute resolution in Egypt see Kelly 2011. An archive of documents of a Nabatean Jewish woman, Babatha, discovered in a cave by the Dead Sea that date to the time of the Bar Kokhba revolt, shows her involvement with the Roman legal system. See Lewis 1989; Cotton 1993, 1997; Nörr 1995.

[4] See Bablitz 2007 for an introduction to the ancient literary evidence and further bibliography. The classic work is Crook 1967.

[5] Most recently see the overview provided by Metzger 2013b, esp. 3–7. For the text of the *lex Irnitana* see González 1986 and Lamberti 1993. Metzger 2013a provides a brief description and bibliography.

[6] Nader and Todd 1978, 9–11; Gulliver 1979, 1–24; Roberts 1979, 53–79; Rouland 1994, 262–266; Roebuck and Fumichon 2004, 12–14; Kelly 2011, 246–247.

[7] These categories are the stuff of academics. Rarely does reality sort itself so neatly. In practice what is often found is an "entanglement of dispute resolution" (Kelly 2011, 245): a dispute may move back and forth between these categories and occupy interstitial spaces many times before its ultimate resolution.

adjudication, the surviving documentation is never anything more than meagre. In this discussion, we will move in order from methods that completely exclude the state to the method in which the case is heard by an officially appointed judge.

Two individuals seeking to resolve a quarrel may turn to someone to mediate their dispute. This individual could be anyone they liked. Living in a highly socially stratified society, they may turn to a patron, a local magistrate, or (if they live in the country) perhaps a senator who has a villa nearby (e.g. Plin. *Ep.* 7.30; Bablitz 2007, 105). Clearly, this individual would have to be respected by them both as they must agree to the selection. They may likewise ask a mutual friend. This person helps them to negotiate a satisfactory resolution. This was a process in which the two parties talked the matter out, and the mediator worked mostly to keep lines of communication open and everyone calm. Once they found a resolution, no authority would hold them to abide by their agreement other than the social pressure exerted by the mediator and the community.

Another option, while quite close to mediation, moves into a different category of conflict resolution; that of arbitration, the subject of D.4.8.[8] Although issues of social prestige no doubt regularly intervened, disputants could ask an individual of any rank to serve as an arbitrator (D.4.8.7pr; see also D.4.8.3.3). The arbitrator is described in ancient texts as bound by honour to decide between the disputing parties on the ideals of fairness and good sense, and indeed the role of the arbitrator became subject to legal regulation along various lines, including the possibility of being compelled to render a decision. Having selected someone to serve as arbitrator, the disputants presented their sides to him, and he was charged to reach a decision based on what he felt was fair and good common sense. These criteria gave him a fair degree of discretion. Again, no authority compelled the parties to abide by the ruling of the arbitrator other than the social pressure exerted by the arbitrator and the community (Roebuck and Fumichon 2004, 64). After the ruling of the arbitrator, one of the parties might refuse to be bound by the arbitrator's decision because they felt the arbitrator did not act as a *vir bonus* would have. This meant that everyone had wasted their time, and another method would need to be undertaken to resolve the dispute.

The differences between mediation and arbitration are slight but salient. The arbitrator is put in a position far closer to judging than the mediator, who might push the two parties towards a middle ground. In arbitration, the two parties do not move to a common ground during the process; instead, they present their positions. That done, they leave the matter to the arbitrator, who then decides. The arbitrator is granted autonomy to determine what is fair. With a mediator, by contrast, the parties retain considerable agency and the mediator aids in shaping the conversation.

A further option sees the disputants again select an arbitrator, but now they employ a procedure that has the potential to involve the state. After selecting an arbitrator, the parties make a *compromissum*, a mutual contract, in which they set out the details of the dispute and agree to set it before their named arbitrator, cooperate in the proceedings and abide by the decision. The contract also specifies a penalty that a plaintiff will pay if he breaches the terms of the contract; the penalty is usually monetary, an amount high enough to serve as an incentive.

[8] For what is given see Broggini 1957; Roebuck and Fumichon 2004, 46–66; Humbert 1994.

How is the state involved here (Roebuck and Fumichon 2004, 94–134)? By making the *compromissum*, the disputants commit themselves to the arbitrator's decision by contract. Whatever the status of their initial dispute, the new dispute has a form that involves state interest. If one party refuses to accept the arbitrator's decision, the other can go to the state authorities and sue for breach of contract.

If mediation and arbitration were unacceptable to either disputant, the only option was adjudication. Where the disputants lived within the Roman world determined the available judicial machinery. This was not an issue for either mediation or arbitration since both procedures functioned, for the most part, outside the state legal system. Numerous jurisdictions existed in the Roman world, too many to discuss here, so we will focus on the two jurisdictions in which the most Roman citizens of the classical period lived: the city of Rome and *municipia* in Italy.

If the disputants lived in a *municipium*, one party would notify the other that he or she was going to approach the state for resolution. Ideally, they would then appear together before one of the two *duoviri*, the chief magistrates of the *municipium*. The instigator describes the nature of the dispute; the other party might speak also. The magistrate then draws up a formula, following model clauses, in which he lays out the nature of the dispute, its various features, and poses a question or a cascading series of questions, whose answer(s) then determines the decision. It inheres in the nature of the questions posed by Roman *formulae* that options for judgements were binary. Where necessary, the magistrate would also attach a penalty to one outcome.[9] The *duovir* then asks the litigants whom they wish to serve as their *iudex*. They, again, may choose the same individual they would have considered as a mediator or arbitrator. However, the fact that the litigants are now before the *duovir* suggests that they could not agree on using either mediation or arbitration, which in turn suggests that their relationship is such that agreeing upon a mutual acquaintance to serve is unlikely. If the litigants cannot suggest a name, the *duovir* has a list of potential *iudices* from which they select.[10]

At this point, the *duovir* appoints the *iudex* and the *iudex* sets the time and place for the hearing of the full case. At this hearing the litigants put their interpretation of events before the *iudex*; they call witnesses; they provide evidence; and finally, the *iudex* renders his judgement (a monetary award) according to the parameters of the formula provided by the *duovir*. The ruling is final. One caveat exists. Not all cases could be dealt with by the *duovir*. Limitations included the financial value involved in the dispute, the nature of the case itself, and the agreement of both disputants to have the matter heard locally.[11]

[9] For a useful overview of the current understanding of the civil procedure see Metzger 2013b and 2015. Our main source for the formulary procedure is Inst.Gai.4.30–187. See also Kaser 1996², 220–382; Metzger 1997, ch. 5.

[10] We infer the procedure used in Rome for the selection of judges from the *lex Irnitana*, a city charter for the town of Irni in Spain, which we believe was modelled on the practice in Rome. See Birks 1988; Lebek 1993; Kaser 1996², 192–196; Metzger 2013b, 24.

[11] *Lex Irn*. ch. 84. See Rodger 1990 and 1996; Metzger 2013a. The office of *iuridicus* with jurisdiction in Italy was created in the last decades of the period covered in this article. Introduced by Hadrian, the *iuridici* (there were four in Italy) did not become permanent until the reign of Marcus Aurelius. See Simshäuser 1973; Eck 1995, 315–326 and 1999, 253–275.

If the disputants lived in Rome, they had a greater variety of magistrates to approach in the first instance. The *praetor urbanus* would likely be their choice. With the emergence of the position of the emperor and the creation of the office of the *praefectus urbi*, two new options appeared for such cases, though it seems that the emperor's court, at least in its early years, dealt more with cases in which the litigants felt the need for the extra speed and protection offered by his court (Kaser 1996², 445–451; Millar 1977, 516–537). Before the praetor, the procedure would be the same as that before the *duovir*. The emperor, too, might hear disputes, although it is doubtful his courts served as a court of the first instance with any regularity (fairy tales of emperor replacing magistrates in court for a day notwithstanding). Whatever the case, the emperor generally did not delegate cases but rather heard cases and rendered judgement himself. The city prefect seems also to have heard cases himself rather than assigning them to others.[12]

How did adjudication differ from arbitration? Cicero can best answer this question:

> A proceeding before a magistrate (*iudicium*) is for a certain sum; arbitration for an uncertain one. We come before the *iudicium* with the expectation that we shall either win or lose the whole amount in question; we go to arbitration on the understanding that we shall end up neither with nothing nor as much as we asked for. The very words of the formula are proof of this. What is the formula before a *iudex*? Direct, hard, simple: "If it appears that 50,000 sesterces are due." Unless the claimant can prove that 50,000 sesterces are due, to the penny, he loses the case. What is it in an arbitration? Mild, moderate: "As much should be awarded as is the more fair and proper." That man admits he is asking for more than is owed to him but says that he will be more than satisfied with whatever he gets from the arbitrator. So one has confidence in his case; the other, not. (Cic. *Rosc. Com.* 4.10–11)

Arbitration thus means that potentially everyone will be slightly unhappy, whereas adjudication means one side will be very happy and the other side very unhappy. This disadvantage stems from the narrowness of the formula, the nature of description given to the dispute by the praetor, with the preset penalty. The hearing before a *iudex* was very narrowly defined and the ruling could only go one way or the other. The *iudex* had no authority to alter or adjust anything based on his own common sense; he must rule within the boundaries established by the *formula*. Arbitration gave much more power to the arbitrator to determine what was fair and right, drawing on his own judgement.

Adjudication also suggests the impossibility of negotiation between the claimants. If the disputants could talk and reason with each other, there would be no need to turn to a magistrate. Negotiations with a mediator or even the agreement to present the matter to an arbitrator could move the matter along. But if one party flatly refused to enter mediation or arbitration, the only option available to the other party was to turn to the state. Cicero describes the law regarding arbitration this way: "I admire the elegance not only of the substance of the law but of its very language. It says: 'If they dispute' (*si iurgant*). By *iurgum* is meant a controversy between people of goodwill, not a lawsuit, *lis*, between enemies. Therefore the law is thinking of neighbours disagreeing but not litigating" (*Rep.* 4.8). If either party dug in, or got their back up, little could be done without resorting to the state-appointed judge.

[12] Vitucci 1956; Garnsey 1970, 90–98; Jones 1972, 90–118.

18.3 Additional Factors in Selecting a Method of Resolution

These then were the options for conflict resolution available to Roman citizens in Rome and *municipia* within Italy. The discussion thus far has presented these based solely in terms of the degree of willingness of the disputants to reach an agreement. Thus at the extremes, mediation suggests great willingness to compromise, and adjudication assumes the refusal of at least one of the parties to entertain any other option. However, many other factors could influence the resolution method used. The second half of this chapter presents several of these factors.

Wealth and social prestige were important factors in influencing how a conflict was resolved in Roman society (see Meyer, ch. 21). It is fair to say that as one moves from mediation to adjudication, the monetary cost to one or both disputants rises greatly. These costs come primarily in the form of time lost from one's livelihood to take the dispute to the authorities and payment for legal support, either for a secretary/scribe or an advocate, though indirectly. On the other hand, both mediation and arbitration might allow the disputants to keep the matter near their homes, perhaps even holding the hearing in one of their homes, and to set meeting times with the mediator or arbitrator that fit their individual schedules. If the matter went before the *duovir* or one of the magistrates in Rome, at least a half-day was probably consumed. Typically, magistrates opened their courts in the morning hours, the business hours of the Roman day, and since scheduling appointments with the magistrate was not possible, all who had business before the magistrate had to appear and wait their turn. Once a *iudex* had been appointed, it was possible for the parties to arrange that hearing to their schedule, but the initial appearance had to be done during business hours.

Costs rose exponentially, of course, if one's case had to go to Rome because it could not be heard locally.[13] In this regard, the inhabitants of Rome had a decided advantage. If a dispute went to Rome, both disputants would be faced with additional costs. Either they or their representatives/agents had to travel from their *municipium* to Rome, unless they were so lucky as to have someone in Rome who could deal with the matter for them.[14] Once in Rome, they approached the praetor. The never-ending workload of the praetor suggests that his court opened at the beginning of the business day and for the entire day a steady flow of petitioners passed before him.[15] However, the praetor did not hold court every day. It was possible, then, that disputants (equally both those who lived in Rome and those who did not) might have to wait some days to see the praetor. Even if he were hearing petitions on the first day they arrived, they would have to wait in line. We do not

[13] The jurisdictional limit for local magistrates varies widely in the evidence we have. A limit of 1,000 sesterces is found in the *lex Irnitana* (ch. 84); 10,000 in the *Fragmentum Atestinum* (l. 6) and 15,000 in the *lex de Gallia Cisalpina* (chs. 21–22). These amounts seem to refer to the same type of situation. See Rodger 1996; Metzger 2013a.

[14] See Inst.Gai.4.83, 86–87; *TPSulp* 27; Kaser 1996², 21–213; Metzger 2007, 19–192 and 2015, 285.

[15] For the court hours and workload of the praetors and other magistrates see Bablitz 2007, 182–184.

know if the praetor regularly succeeded in dealing with all those who appeared before his court on any given day. It is quite possible he did not do so, and some may have to return again the next day, only to wait again.[16] For out-of-town disputants, lodgings would have to be found in Rome. Once the praetor had created the *formula* and the *iudex* had been appointed, the parties might seek a rapid timetable. Certainly in the case of disputants from outside Rome, most parties would be eager for a short interval between the appointment of the *iudex* and the hearing proper.

No matter what one's wealth, potential litigants would weigh the value of a ruling in their favour against the costs that would be incurred before choosing adjudication instead of mediation or arbitration. The financial implications of legal activity would encourage most people to try first to resolve their disputes through mediation and arbitration. For many residents of the Empire, adjudication required time away from work; for some, travel to a distant city was wholly impracticable. Also, equity was most easily achieved if the two parties to a dispute were similar in social position (see also Meyer, ch. 21). If two poor farmers disputed the boundary between their farms, both would operate under similar constraints, feel similar reluctance to go to court, and agree to mediation or arbitration. If one party were much wealthier than the other, he might refuse mediation and arbitration with the goal of forcing the poorer party to let the matter drop. What could the weaker party do? He (or she)[17] might have access to someone of influence who could work on his behalf, but reliance on such methods meant that justice must have very often been denied.[18] Such problems were compounded when one confronted someone with the energy, resources and will to exploit the courts to the point of harassment (Kelly 2011, 287–326).

The methodologies of conflict resolution discussed here involved varying degrees of publicity. Mediation and arbitration involved little more than a third party to serve as mediator/arbitrator, and the discussions could be held anywhere, most likely someone's home. As such, no one beyond those immediately involved may have known much. However, adjudication commencing before the *duovir* or praetor was very public. The disputants had to state the nature of their dispute in the public space in which the magistrate was working, probably before several others seeking the magistrate's ear.[19] Once a *iudex* had been appointed, one might regain some privacy. While the evidence is slight and difficult to interpret, it appears that no limits were placed on the location where the *iudex* and disputants met. It is possible, and perhaps likely, that the hearing took place within a home rather than in a public structure like the city's forum. We must not forget, however, that a Roman home also served public functions, and thus moving a hearing to this environment may not exclude all the interested public. At a minimum, though, it would probably exclude tired construction workers, for example, from using the hearing as their lunchtime entertainment—a possibility if the hearing took place in a forum (Bablitz 2015).

[16] See Bablitz 2007, 24–27 for the logistical issues of the praetors' courts within the Forum of Augustus.

[17] On women before the law see Halbwachs, ch. 34; see also Cantarella, ch. 32 and Perry, ch. 33.

[18] Kelly 1966, 1–84; Garnsey 1970, 207–218; Bablitz 2007, 77–81.

[19] For an introduction to the spaces of justice in Rome see Bablitz 2007, 13–50. For publicity of the courts in Roman Egypt see Kelly 2011, 170–177.

While the three methodologies of conflict resolution involved varying degrees of publicity, the participants could extend that publicity in either direction. One party might insist on a very public location, even for arbitration. The law does not specify who determined the location of the hearing. We do not know what would happen if the parties disagreed. It is likely that the arbitrator or *iudex*, once appointed, had authority to fix the location. Moreover, a *iudex* might have his own agenda too regarding publicity. Serving as a judge was a public honour as well as a duty, and a *iudex* might wish to be seen fulfilling the function (Bablitz 2007, 11–115).

Five documents from Puteoli provide perhaps our only written evidence of a specific location for a hearing of a civil case that was in its judgement stage, as opposed to the preliminary stage before a magistrate (*TPSulp* 35–39; Camodeca 1999, 106–11). All five record the setting of hearings before an arbiter *ex compromisso* for a specific time, date and location. Of the five, this is the only complete one (*TPSulp* 36):

> Marcus Barbatius Ephaphroditus arbiter *ex compromisso* between Caius Sulpicius Cinnamus and Caius Julius Prudens in the presence of them both fixed the date of hearing and ordered them to attend on 15 March next in Puteoli, in the Hordionian Chalcidicum, from 3pm to 4pm. Done at Puteoli on 14 December in the consulate of Gnaeus Lentulus Gaetulicus and Titus Curtilius Mancia (55 AD).

Arbitration in which the parties used a *compromissum* to bind themselves to the arbitrator's decision can perhaps be viewed as occupying a middle position among the methods of conflict resolution regarding the degree of privacy possible. It could provide privacy equal to that of mediation, unless one of the parties broke the *compromissum*. If this occurred, then the other party had to take the matter before the magistrate for enforcement, thus shifting into a more public arena.[20] While nothing demanded that the hearing be either out of the public eye or in it, Cinnamus and Prudens are scheduled to appear before the arbiter Ephaphroditus in a public location—the Hordionian *Chalcidicum*. In another of these documents (*TPSulp* 35) the same arbitrator set a hearing for between 3 pm and 5 pm in the Octavian *Chalcidicum* instead of the Hordionian. In the other three documents, which clearly follow the same pattern and thus must address arbitration hearings, the location is specific—the Octavian *Chalcidicum*.

Modern scholars tend to reveal their own biases when discussing privacy issues and litigation. In 1976, when describing the *unus iudex*, J. M. Kelly argued that the institution of the *unus iudex* worked to avoid a public airing of a litigant's business (Kelly 1976, 112–133). In 2004, Roebuck and Fumichon stated that the hearing before an arbiter *ex compromisso* "was in private and not open to the public" (Roebuck and Fumichon 2004, 173). Others have made equally unequivocal statements on this issue. The Puteoli documents urge caution. Our only evidence for the location of hearings before an arbitrator, which, moreover, seems to be standard in form, specifies a location that we would deem public. The sample size is small, of course.

[20] For a detailed examination of arbitration *ex compromisso* see Roebuck and Fumichon 2004, 94–134.

18.4 Conclusion

This chapter has surveyed the methods available to Roman citizens to resolve their disputes and also considered some social and economic factors that probably influenced an individual's thinking about those methods. One's location, whether in Rome, Italy or the provinces, in a city with magistrates holding jurisdiction or another type of community, further shaped one's options and weighting of them. Basic similarities in systems of social differentiation within the Empire probably produced considerable similarity in the operation of non-official means of dispute resolution throughout the Empire. Wealth, status and publicity, so important to so many aspects of Roman society, must have loomed large in any disputant's mind when pondering a remedy. What is more, these practices and institutions could also be used in bad faith. In this way, the resolution system could be both part of the solution and part of the problem.

Appendix on Terminology: *Iudex* and *Arbiter*

The study of Roman means of conflict resolution is bedevilled by problems of terminology (Roebuck and Fumichon 2004, 14–17). The terms most often used in the ancient sources of all genres to describe the third party who aids the disputants are *arbiter* and *iudex*. In Republican texts, the term *iudex* tends to be used of individuals appointed by the praetors to serve as a single *iudex* in an adjudication, while the term *arbiter* refers to the individual chosen by disputants to serve as mediator or arbitrator. The *iudex* had to follow the *formula* given him in reaching his judgement, while the arbiter had greater personal discretion. But as early as the very beginning of the Imperial period, usage ceased to respect this distinction, and it may never have been hard and fast. Festus, writing in the second century AD, uses the word *iudex* in the definition he provides for the word "arbiter": "a *iudex* who has arbitration and control of the whole matter is called an arbiter." Ulpian, writing in the decade after 212, quotes Sextus Pedius, a jurist of the late first century AD, as using the terms *arbiter* and *iudex* very nearly interchangeably: "a person is held to have undertaken arbitration [*recepisse autem arbitrium videtur*] who has taken the role of *iudex* and promised to put an end to their disputes by means of his pronouncement" (D.4.8.13.2). Other texts do not help resolve this issue. Pliny the Younger complains of the work that follows him from Rome to his country house: "Town business chases after me even here. There are some who would make me their *iudex* or *arbiter*" (Plin. *Ep.* 7.30.2: *qui me iudicem aut arbitrum faciant*). This could be simple hendiadys but, since the role of an arbiter *ex compromisso* existed, he may distinguish between that role and serving as a lay *iudex*. The municipal law from Irni seems to use the terms interchangeably. Chapter 86 describes who is eligible to be a *iudex* and how the city magistrates will formulate a list of potential *iudices* for litigants to choose from if they cannot agree on a friend or acquaintance. At the very end of the chapter, it is specified how magistrates are to appoint the *iudex* selected by the litigants: "he is to order the person from among those *iudices*, who is appropriate under this statute, to be granted and assigned as *iudex* or arbiter and to judge." Here, hendiadys seems likely. The rubric for chapter 89 also suggests strong equality between *iudices* and *arbitri*: "In which cases single iudices or arbiters and in which cases recuperatores are to be granted and how many" (*De qu[ibus rebu]s singuli iudices arbitriue et de quibus re[cipera]tores dentur et quod dentur*; transl. Crawford).

Where does this leave the student of Roman law? This fluidity of terminology perhaps is best interpreted as evidence of a legal system that contained a number of methods for conflict resolution, ranging from mediator to judge with much in between. The overlapping terminology gestures at the near-identical function of these many alternatives.

Bibliography

Bablitz, L. 2007. *Actors and audience in the Roman courtroom*. London.

Bablitz, L. 2015. "Bringing the law home: the Roman house as courtroom." In K. Tuori and L. Nissin, eds., *Public and private in the Roman house, Journal of Roman Archaeology*, Supplement Series. Portsmouth. 63–76.

Birks, P. (1988). "New light on the Roman legal system: the appointment of judges." *Cambridge Law Journal* 47: 36–60.

Broggini, G. 1957. Iudex Arbiterve: *Prolegomena zum* Officium *des Römischen Privatrichters*. Cologne.

Camodeca, G. 1999. Tabulae Pompeianae Sulpiciorum (TPSulp.). *Edizione critica dell'archivio puleolano dei Sulpicii*. Rome.

Cotton, H. M. (1993). "The guardianship of Jesus Son of Babatha: Roman and local law in the province of Arabia." *Journal of Roman Studies* 83: 94–108.

Cotton, H. M. 1997. "Deeds of gift and the law of succession in the documents from the Judaean desert." *Akten des 21. Internationalen Papyrologenkongresses, Berlin 1995* (= *Archiv für Papyrusforschung*, Beihelt 3). Stuttgart-Leipzig. 179–186.

Crook, J. A. 1967. *Law and life of Rome: 90 B.C.–A.D. 212*. New York.

Eck, W. 1995. *Die Verwaltung des Römischen Reiches in der Hohen Kaiserzeit: ausgewählte und erweiterte Beiträge*. Basel.

Eck, W. 1999[2]. *L'Italia nell'Impero Romano. Stato e amministrazione in epoca imperiale*. Bari.

Garnsey, P. 1970. *Social status and legal privilege in the Roman empire*. Oxford.

González, J. (1986). "The *lex Irnitana*: a new copy of the Flavian municipal Law." *Journal of Roman Studies* 76: 147–243.

Gulliver, P. H. 1979. *Disputes and negotiations: a cross-cultural perspective*. Orlando.

Humbert, M. (1994). "Arbitrage et Jugement à Rome." *Droit et cultures* 28: 47–63.

Johnston, D. ed. 2015. *The Cambridge companion to Roman law*. Cambridge.

Jones, A. H. M. 1972. *The criminal courts of the Roman republic and principate*. Oxford.

Kaser, M and Hackl, K. 1996[2]. *Das römische Zivilprozeßrecht*. Munich.

Kelly, B. 2011. *Petitions, litigation, and social control in Roman Egypt*. Oxford.

Kelly, J. M. 1966. *Roman litigation*. Oxford.

Kelly, J. M. 1976. *Studies in the civil judicature of the Roman republic*. Oxford.

Lamberti, F. 1993. Tabulae Irnitanae: *municipalità e* ius Romanorum. Naples.

Lebek, W. D. (1993). "La *Lex Lati* di Domiziano (*lex Irnitana*): le strutture giuridiche dei capitoli 84 e 86." *Zeitschrift für Papyrologie und Epigraphik* 97: 159–178.

Lewis, N. ed. 1989. *The documents from the Bar Kokhba period in the cave of letters: Greek papyri*. Jerusalem.

Metzger, E. 1997. *A new outline of the Roman civil trial*. Oxford.

Metzger, E. 2007. "Lawsuits in context." In J. W. Cairns and P. J. du Plessis, eds., *Beyond dogmatics: law and society in the Roman world*. Edinburgh. 187–205.
Metzger, E. 2013a. "Agree to disagree: local jurisdiction in the *lex Irnitana*." In A. Burrows, et al., eds., *Judge and jurist: essays in memory of Lord Rodger of Earlsferry*. Oxford. 207–226.
Metzger, E. (2013b). "An outline of Roman civil procedure." *Roman Legal Tradition* 9: 1–30.
Metzger, E. 2015. "Litigation." In D. Johnston, ed., *The Cambridge companion to Roman law*. Cambridge. 272–298.
Millar, F. 1977. *The emperor in the Roman world (31 BC–AD 337)*. Oxford.
Nader, L. and Todd, H. F. 1978. "Introduction: the disputing process." In L. Nader and H. F. Todd, eds., *The disputing process—law in ten societies*. New York. 1–40.
Nörr, D. (1995). "The *xenokritai* in Babatha's Archive (*Pap. Yadin* 28–30)." *Israel Law Review* 29: 83–94.
Richardson, J. 2015. "Roman law in the provinces." In. D. Johnston, ed., *The Cambridge companion to Roman law*. Cambridge. 45–58.
Roberts, S. 1979. *Order and dispute: an introduction to legal anthropology*. Oxford.
Roebuck, D. and de Loynes de Fumichon, B. 2004. *Roman arbitration*. Oxford.
Rodger, A. (1990). "The jurisdiction of local magistrates: chapter 84 of the *lex Irnitana*." *Zeitschrift für Papyrologie und Epigraphik* 84: 147–161.
Rodger, A. (1996). "Jurisdictional limits in the *lex Irnitana* and the *lex de Gallia Cisalpina*." *Zeitschrift für Papyrologie und Epigraphik* 110: 189–206.
Rouland, N. 1994. *Legal anthropology*, transl. P. G. Planel. London.
Simshaüser, W. 1973. Iuridici *und Munizipalgerichtsbarkeit in Italien*. Munich.
Vitucci, G. 1956. *Ricerche sulla* praefectura urbi *in età imperiale (sec. I–III)*. Rome.
Wolf, J. G. 2015. "Documents in Roman practice." In D. Johnston, ed., *The Cambridge companion to Roman law*. Cambridge. 61–84.

CHAPTER 19

REPUBLICAN CIVIL PROCEDURE

Sanctioning Reluctant Defendants

ERNEST METZGER

19.1 Introduction

THOSE who study classical civil procedure tend to follow a divided methodology: by necessity they favour traditional doctrinal research until forced abruptly to turn to social behaviour and the non-traditional sources that record it. The failure of past scholars to recognise the right instant and make the turn was a common cause of error. The demands of the field are perhaps unusual, and the discussion in section 19.2 defends the divided methodology and illustrates with a single example: litigants who are reluctant to be sued.

19.2 Divided Methodology

Doctrine and formal sources of law are the first objects of research in Roman civil procedure. This is simply because the order and character of forensic events is governed in the first instance by positive law: edict, statute, constitution. The inescapable structure of litigation is in these sources, supplemented by juristic commentary. A second reason is that civil procedure is dominated by formulas—positive law at second hand—and these formulas dictate the behaviour of the participants and channel the development of the law. Generally, a formula is a prescribed scheme of words, adapted to a specific affair and then spoken or written, allowing a person to affect his or her legal position, whether privately or in litigation.[1] In litigation we think first of the written formulas passed from magistrate to judge under the formulary procedure. But they reached much further than this; there were formulas for oaths, for settlement, for avoiding vexation litigation, for promising or

[1] On *forma* and *formula* see especially Mantovani 1999, 15–16; Talamanca 1990, 307–308. For a discussion of formulas as expressions of style and archaism see Meyer 2004, 44–63.

attesting an appearance, for securing interdicts, and many more.[2] Roman jurists were in part responsible for their creation, and they comment directly upon them or acknowledge them implicitly in their commentary.[3] But the key point is that formulas give us the fine details of actual litigation, and this means their study is a priority.

Perhaps predictably for a field so dominated by edict and enactment, most aspects of what we call autonomy are largely missing.[4] Procedure figures in a supportive role, as an aid to the autonomy of private law (Schulz 1936, 32–33; Lewis 2000, 41–45), but is not itself noticeably autonomous. Rules of procedure were reformed bluntly by statute, most famously by a *lex Aebutia* (perhaps late second century BC) and a *lex Iulia de iudiciis privatis* (17 BC) (Metzger 2012, 18–19), and also by overtly political acts such as the *lex Cornelia de iurisdictione* (67 BC), which attempted to curb abuses by praetors[5] who did not always administer justice according to the edicts they themselves had published.[6] Some early statutes on procedure, moreover, were rooted in experience,[7] designed to reduce litigation and curb overeager litigants.[8] In a similar manner successive praetors, and the jurists who assisted them, reformed the edicts on procedure having likely been witness to the very problems needing remedial action.[9]

Formal sources of law are nevertheless exhausted very quickly and give way to literary sources, documents, monumentalism, sculpture, architecture, painting, clothing and

[2] The question-and-answer *sponsio* was frequently modified for different purposes. Each praetorian stipulation, for example, had its own formula, as did the various *sponsiones* used for obtaining security in litigation, discouraging vexatious litigation, initiating a lawsuit by wager, and so on. For a sample of these formulas see Mantovani 1999, 103–108, and the sources cited at 16 n. 5. An under-remarked fact is that there was sometimes a wholly different formula used for writing the formula down. See the useful excursus ("Die Formen der Stipulation in den Urkunden der klassischen Zeit") in Nelson and Manthe 1999, 469–485.

[3] For sources on the growth of cautelary jurisprudence and the use of formulas in the Republic see Schulz 1946, 49–52; Schiller 1978, 272–274. On the diminishing importance of formulas as vehicles of legal development under Augustus see Schulz 1946, 111–112.

[4] The exception is the underlying understanding (or conceit) that procedure operates apart from the usual power relations. On this aspect of autonomy see Schiavone 2012, 288–292, 335–337, 374–378. In discussions of procedure, this is customarily described as the "Grundsatz der Unparteilichkeit" ("principle of impartiality") and is most evident in the two-stage, public/private division in litigation (Kaser and Hackl 1996², 8–9).

[5] On the question whether this effort affected both urban and peregrine praetors see Brennan 2000, 2: 464.

[6] For the political atmosphere in which the reforms took place see Metro 1969; Frier 1985, 73–74; Frier 1983, 23–231. For the sources see Rotondi 1962, 371.

[7] On autonomy and the genesis of laws see Schulz 1936, 24–25.

[8] The introduction of the *legis actio per condictionem* via two statutes *c.*200 BC introduced an interval of thirty days which (it is believed) allowed for reflection and possibly settlement: Inst. Gai.4.17b–20; Pugliese 1962, 352–354. A *lex Pinaria* of unknown date did the same for the earlier *legis actio per sacramentum*, perhaps for the same purpose: Metzger 1997, 58–59.

[9] See Metzger 2012, 158. There are some good examples at D.2.11.2.6–8 (floods and storms preventing a court appearance); D.2.1.7pr (defacing the published law); D.4.6.26.4 (lazy or unavailable municipal magistrates forcing litigants to seek revival of their lost actions). In spite of the evident practicality of civil procedure, the nineteenth century found a way to intrude Pandectism, in the form of broad "principles of procedure" which purported to guide the Romans in their procedural law-making but in fact serve only as rough descriptors for the benefit of modern scholars (Metzger 2004).

coinage.[10] These are secondary to the formal sources for the reasons given, but they are also indispensable. The scarcity of sources on procedure is one reason (Metzger 2005, 1–4); the more important reasons are in the character of the law.

Classical procedural law never covered the full range of events that modern procedural law considers necessary. The edict as redacted by Salvius Iulianus in the early second century AD gives the clearest picture of the law's limited range.[11] The titles on procedure describe a small number of single events, with events at the beginning and end of the lawsuit heavily represented.[12] This is at the expense of, for example, rules for the conduct of trials, which are largely left to rhetorical conventions (Crook 1995, ch. 1), and which, in turn, send us to sources on oratory and architecture. Rules on evidence are also mostly lacking; we know for example that parties were required to disclose early in litigation the evidence they would rely on at trial (D.2.13.1.3; see also section 19.5) and that there could be no judicial disposition on a will without production of that will (D.29.3.1.1), but for genuine examples of the duty to disclose, and details of what is disclosed, we rely heavily on documentary evidence, in particular a selection of documents from Herculaneum.[13]

Areas governed by the law, moreover, are sometimes governed incompletely and leave the litigants room to order their affairs in ways which are permitted but not determined by any rule. The first-century wax tablets that came to light in such numbers in the last century give many examples of these—for lack of a better term—"underprescribed acts". There are promises to appear, in which the first statement obeys the edict and the second statement adds a clause on which the edict was (apparently) silent (Metzger 2005, ch. 5). There is a written formula with a preface (*praescriptio*) that neither contradicts the rules on prefaces, nor matches what those rules lead us to expect (*TPSulp* 31 = Camodeca 1999, 1:97–99). There is an agreement on terminating litigation, which contains all manner of familiar formulas, but assembled together in a model unknown to us (*TPSulp* 27 = Camodeca 1999, 1:88–92). These are not examples of theory versus practice, but of parties finding their own way in a system with an evident light touch. As subjects of research, they give us the opportunity to reconcile (or not) traditional and non-traditional sources.

[10] More than a sample of relevant literature is not possible. Bablitz gives a study of platforms, including those depicting legal scenes, based on relief sculpture and coinage: Bablitz 2008, esp. figs. 6 and 12; on the *paenulae* that Maternus, in Tac. *Dial.* 39.1, criticises as inappropriate for advocates see Frier 2010, 73–74; on the significance of certain statuary as meeting places for litigants see Neudecker 2010, 166–169; on papyri as sources for advocacy see Crook 1995; on wax tablets and Roman procedure see Meyer 2004, 79–86, 216–249; on the physical space in which justice was administered see Kondratieff 2010; Carnabuci 1996, 19–43; Bablitz 2007, 51–70.

[11] The references are to Lenel 1927. The two opening titles are also reconstructed by Domingo 1995, 121–122, but the discrepancies do not affect the discussion here.

[12] The titles properly on procedure, reconstructed in Lenel 1927, are I and II (municipal jurisdiction, including recalcitrant litigants and the exaction of promises to appear in Rome), III (notice of the suit), IV (settlement), V (summons), VI (formal request for suit), VII (postponements *in iure*), VIII (representation), XII (security for judgement), XIII (pretrial hearings), XLIV (defences), and XLV (praetorian stipulations). For a short, descriptive overview of the entire edict, and the relationship of its parts, see Lenel 1927, 31–48.

[13] See Bürge 1995, 29–31; Metzger 2005, 161–163. Naturally there may be other surviving documents that were disclosed in a similar way; this corpus happens to give us enough context to make the determination.

19.3 Summoning Reluctant Opponents

Roman civil procedure directed relations between the litigants and a tribunal, but also relations between the litigants themselves. These latter, "horizontal" relations were represented in a large number of publicly enforced, but privately executed, transactions. For example, there were ordinary, ultimately private contracts that were nevertheless ordered by decree; interdicts were left to the petitioners to carry out; and face-to-face oaths were sometimes compulsory. Because there were so many horizontal relations like these, litigants did much of the heavy lifting: evidence-gathering, record-keeping, execution and (the subject below) getting one's opponent to physically appear before a magistrate.

Under the classical law, a civil lawsuit would begin with two events, not necessarily in this order:[14] the claimant would (1) inform his opponent of the action he intended to bring, and (2) summon him to the place where justice was administered. Both were private acts that took place without the intervention of the magistrate unless, in the latter case, the claimant wished to sue one of a class of restricted persons (Inst.Gai.4.183). The summons (*in ius vocatio*) has a very long history in the civil procedure of Rome and Roman Italy, beginning with the XII Tables of the middle fifth century BC and continuing to (perhaps) the early third century AD.[15] The general features of the institution are known, but the most obvious question has no simple answer: what is the sanction for failing to come when summoned?

A very cynical answer was given by John Kelly fifty years ago: until the early Empire the ability of a plaintiff to bring his defendant to court depended, in the last resort, on superior physical strength (Kelly 1966a, ch. 1). Kelly dismissed all of the current theories, which in his view attempted to patch over a difficult issue with hope and guesswork. He suggested that only social institutions could ultimately coax the defendant or temper the plaintiff. The opposite view is set out by Kaser and Hackl: with the formulary procedure "the Praetor now enforced the suit by direct coercion" (Kaser and Hackl 1996^2, 222). They relied on two edicts which, though not addressed to summons specifically, nevertheless were capable of bringing the defendant to heel in all manner of circumstances.

The discussion below suggests a solution by reconsidering the question. Summons by *in ius vocatio* is a very ancient institution, and with the development of new ways of litigating, its character changed. It began as a means to introduce a lawsuit, but with the addition of ever more pretrial activity, it soon became—with the basic mechanics unaltered—a means of bringing about a litigant's presence for the conduct of negotiation within the presence, or threatened presence, of the magistrate administering justice. A reluctant defendant is not simply, or even primarily, "resisting summons", but showing an unwillingness to engage with his opponent. It is this unwillingness to engage that required a remedy.

[14] Cf. Lenel 1927, 31, who concludes from the order of titles in the edict—*editio* before *in ius vocatio*—that the first duty of a claimant was to inform his opponent of the forthcoming action.

[15] The edicts on summons continue to be the subject of edictal commentary into the early third century; see Lenel 1889: Paul nos. 113–119 and Ulpian nos. 227–239. A different form of summons, the *litis denuntiatio*, is attested from the first century AD in Egypt, and may well have been the usual form of summons by 322; see Lévy 1998, 25–251 n. 13, 247–257.

19.4 Summons and Remedies for Recalcitrance

The reconstructed fragments of the XII Tables include a series of provisions on *in ius vocatio* and preserve many details that were to remain into the classical law. A modern reconstruction presents the relevant fragments as follows (*RS* 2:584–590; see also Agnati 2002, 29–59).

1.1. *si in ius uocat,?ito;? ni it, antestamino; igitur <im> capito.*
1.2. *si caluitur pedemue struit, manum endo iacito.*
1.3. *si morbus aeuitasue escit, iumentum dato; si nolet, arceram ne sternito.*
1.4. *adsiduo uindex adsiduus esto. proletario?ciui? quis uolet uindex esto.*

1.1. If he (i.e. anyone) summons to a pre-trial,?he (the defendant) is to go;? If he does not go, he (the plaintiff) is to call to witness; then he is to take him.
1.2. If he (the defendant) delays or drags his feet, he (the plaintiff) is to lay a hand on.
1.3. If there is illness or age, he (the plaintiff) is to provide a yoked beast of burden; if he shall be unwilling, he is not to prepare a carriage.
1.4. For an *assiduus* an *assiduus* is to be guarantor. For a *proletarius*?citizen? whoever shall wish is to be guarantor.

The events described in these provisions are of course contested, but the summary in Kaser and Hackl (with a few additions) will serve the present purposes (Kaser and Hackl 1996^{2}, 64–68). A claimant without assistance or formality summons his opponent to come before the magistrate. If the opponent does not come, the claimant may bring him *in ius* against his will, so long as the claimant first calls witnesses; these witnesses probably forestall a charge of *iniuria* against the claimant (Masi Doria 2001, 332–336). The application of force against an opponent who physically resists is permitted in XII Tab. 1.2. It is some variant of *manus inectio*—usually a severe method of enforcing judgement debts—but judgement and execution are unthinkable in this context, where no claims have even been examined. Provision for disability in XII Tab. 1.3 is highly ambiguous; it appears to suggests that the claimant need not provide a carriage if the *vocatus* is unwilling to accept a beast, though the matter may turn instead on the claimant's unwillingness to provide a carriage (*RS* 2:588, relying on Varro *Sat. Men.* 188). The two negatives in the clause, moreover, are capable of conveying precisely the opposite: that if the *vocatus* is unwilling to accept a beast, the claimant should provide a carriage (Bürge 1993, 61–74). The *vindex* described in XII Tab. 1.4 is believed to be responsible for ensuring the appearance of the *vocatus* at a later date.[16]

Nothing in these rules suggests there was any legal remedy against a defendant who failed to follow. The rules are concerned instead with removing whatever obstacles the

[16] The role of the *vindex* is contested; Kaser and Hackl support the view that the *vindex* was responsible for ensuring the defendant's appearance at a later date, while later scholars suggests that the *vindex* was a true substitute—a *defensor*—for the defendant. See Kaser and Hackl 1996^{2}, 67; cf. Albanese 1998, 28–29; Trisciuoglio 2007, 288 and n. 6

claimant might confront in bringing his opponent *in ius*. Legal remedies, such as they were, were the product of the urban praetor's edictal powers and came long after the XII Tables. The dating of individual edicts is notoriously difficult and no less so in this case; the first of the remedies mentioned belongs to the formulary procedure, but the second could be earlier, particularly on the hypothesis that the urban praetor directed his earliest edicts to the enforcement of the civil law (Kelly 1966b, 348–349).

The first remedy was a penal action created by the praetor and given against a *vocatus* who neither comes *in ius* nor gives a *vindex*.[17] The penalty is unknown, though actions of this type often condemned the defendant in the amount of the plaintiff's loss (Kaser and Hackl 1996^{2}, 224 n. 40). That the action existed, and that it was directed at persons who disobeyed summons, is not in doubt. Its effectiveness, however, is very uncertain, given that proceedings on the action would require, again, the defendant's cooperation. Possibly it was not designed to command obedience, but to perpetuate claims that were in danger of being unactionable by limitation, or extending property rights in danger of being lost by prescription (Metzger 2012, 16–162).

A second remedy shows more promise. This is the edict or edicts that allowed the seizure (*missio*) and forced sale of goods of a person who, under some configuration of clauses, concealed himself fraudulently, was undefended, and (perhaps) was absent (Lenel 1927, §§ 205, 206). The remedy was used in diverse circumstances, perhaps most frequently against judgement debtors and, according to Kaser and Hackl, against *vocati* (Kaser and Hackl 1996^{2}, 222–223). Evidence that the remedy was specifically used against *vocati* resisting summons is poor,[18] but the edictal language, so far as we can reconstruct it, is "unparticularised".

This remedy has recently been examined very thoroughly by Johannes Platschek as part of his study of the *Pro Quinctio* (Platschek 2005). Older studies had assumed that the urban praetor issued two edicts on recalcitrance, one under the rubric *Qui absens iudicio defensus non fuerit*, and the other under *Qui fraudationis causa latitabit*. The first is the controversial one: the main source is *Pro Quinctio* 60, introduced as part of Cicero's argument that his client's goods were not possessed according to the terms of the edict. Unfortunately no extant manuscript gives the words *Qui absens* etc. They are included in many modern editions on the faith of two Humanist scholars who claimed to have read them.[19] Naturally this edict, on its terms, would apply seamlessly to defendants resisting summons, and even more so on the common assumption that "absence" in the supposed edict refers to "absence *in iure*" (Kaser and Hackl 1996^{2}, 223 n. 24; Buti 1984, 275). Platschek's study, which can only be sketched here, brings considerable light to these issues. His main aim is to

[17] See Inst.Gai.4.46, 4.184; D.2.6 (interpolated rubric); Platschek 2005, 161–162. Cf. D.2.5.2.1 (summons before municipal magistrate in Italy enforced by *multa*, not penal *actio in factum*).

[18] The *missio* described in Cicero's speech *pro Quinctio* is presumed to be an example of the praetor's edictal powers to punish the non-appearance of a litigant, but the course of events suggests the remedy was in fact directed against a failure to meet a compulsory order to appear. See Metzger 2005, 34–39; cf. Lintott 2008, 49–50 n. 23. See also D.42.4.2, allowing *missio* against a litigant who conceals himself after putting forward another to make an appearance in his place.

[19] See Platschek 2005, 159–160; Lenel 1927, 415 n. 13. Notably, the most recent edition of the *Pro Quinctio* does not print the disputed words, even as a supplement, a decision the editor explains at length: Reeve 1992, xliv–liv.

show that we lack evidence for a self-standing edict on "absence" and that, to the contrary, the notion of absence is collapsed into the other, far better attested edict *Qui fraudationis* etc. Gaius gives us a notion of how the edict worked: "Either the living or dead may have their goods sold: those of the living, for example, *who fraudulently conceal themselves and are not defended in their absence*" (Inst.Gai. 3.78). The apparent redundancy in "conceal" and "absence" has suggested to many that either Gaius has conflated two edicts, or the text is corrupt. But the text makes reasonable sense on the understanding—supported in the sources—that every *latitans* is thereby *absens*, and that to be otherwise *absens* is to be, not "absent *in iure*", but outside the *continentia urbis*.[20] This would explain why Gaius uses two clauses to express what is basically a single idea: a person is within the words of the edict if he conceals himself fraudulently *without it being the case that* he is absent from Rome and defended.[21] This fits well with the words of the edict *Qui fraudationis* etc., preserved by Ulpian: "I will order the possession and sale of the goods of one who conceals himself for the sake of fraud, if he is undefended in the opinion of a good man" (D.42.4.7.1).

In short: the evidence is poor that there existed an edict punishing a person for being "absent *in iure* and undefended". This is unfortunate, because such an edict would be ideal against a *vocatus* resisting summons. Instead, we have an unparticularised remedy: an edict directed against a person—not necessarily a *vocatus*—who conceals himself fraudulently in order to put his opponent to some disadvantage. This would have been a clumsy and indirect remedy in the earlier system of procedure. That it is the ideal remedy for the developed system of procedure is the argument below.

19.5 Pretrial Activity

To understand the value of the edict *Qui fraudationis* etc. in the developed system of procedure requires considering first how a lawsuit typically progressed from summons to the final act *in iure*, the "joinder of issue" (*litis contestatio*). Unfortunately, imagining the course of a typical lawsuit is notoriously difficult to do with only traditional legal sources. They tell us what a Roman litigant needed to know, not what he already knew. Wolfgang Kunkel wrote in 1973:

> Jurists cared little for what was purely factual. This is particularly true where problems of proof were concerned, and truer still for legal business that was openly conducted, business that the jurists could assume was familiar to their readers, since it took place daily in the Forum for all to see, though to us this living picture is utterly foreclosed. Our perspective suffers its keenest loss where classical procedure is concerned, where, moreover, the

[20] Platschek builds this from several sources, but particularly important are D.50.16.173.1 (on absence and the *continentia urbis*) and D.50.16.199pr (a person within the *continentia* is not regarded as absent unless he is concealing himself).

[21] See Platschek 2005, 193–205. The "single edict theory", one should note, is not perfectly proven. See Rüfner 2008, 774. There is a text of Ulpian citing the opinion of Celsus, who appears to distinguish the case of *latitare* from *abesse*: D.42.4.7.17. Also worth weighing is the suggestion of Gómez-Iglesias that the praetor, for purposes of a forced sale, would treat a fraudulent absence differently from a simple one (Gómez-Iglesias 1989/1990, 36–37).

> [J]ustinianic sources have left us only traces, more or less faded, and whose treatment in book four of Gaius' Institutes is largely limited to the technical aspects of the "formulary procedure." Today it is a painstaking process, using literary sources, to form a picture of a legal dispute's actual course in its individual stages, and of the character of "litis contestatio" with which the preliminary proceedings before the magistrate concluded; this picture must in many respects remain entirely hypothetical and disputed. (Kunkel 1973, 197; transl. Metzger)

The observation is accurate, though modern scholars are less pessimistic. Kunkel was writing about a corpus of wax tablets from Puteoli; they were then recently discovered but badly restored. This valuable find is now more accessible, and with these and other documents, together with studies since Kunkel's time, a living picture of litigation is now much more within reach.

The provisions of the XII Tables quoted above depict a straightforward course of events: the defendant is brought *in ius*, and an exchange of words follows. Over time, however, the interval between the summons and disposition by joinder of issue became more crowded with events. This was the natural result of a system becoming more sophisticated in weeding out unnecessary actions and issues, and also a reflection of the new freedom enjoyed by litigants in ordering the details of their lawsuit under the formulary procedure. But the key point is that the prolongation of this early stage will have affected profoundly the importance of summons in any single lawsuit.

The change may have begun as early as the introduction of the *legis actio per condictionem*, mentioned above,[22] but the formulary procedure, used by Roman citizens from some unknown time in the third or second century BC,[23] created strong incentives for the litigants to slow themselves and consider their course. The defendant now had his own side of the story to tell: the new procedure allowed affirmative defences,[24] and no plaintiff could rush into a lawsuit in ignorance of his opponent's facts. Defendants themselves had new reasons to be wary, from *praescriptiones* that might extend their liability[25] to *clausulae arbitrariae* which might place on them an impossible burden of restoring the plaintiff's property.[26] The whole of this deliberative interval is captured in the institution of *editio*: the requirement that the litigants disclose to one another their claims and evidence before requesting a formula and trial (Kaser 1996^2, §30(I); Lenel 1927, 59–64). The leading study is by Alfons Bürge; his immediate aim was to disprove the dominant opinion,

[22] See section 19.2. Possibly around that time (200 BC), litigants were invited to avoid debt litigation by making an exchange of oaths. See Liebs 1986, 164–165; Kaser and Hackl 1996^2, 112 n. 17. The performance of the oaths would take place *in iure*, see Plaut. *Rud.* 14, but prior discussion would be desirable.

[23] The history of its introduction is unknown. The most recent explanation is Talamanca's (1999, esp. 74–76, 199–203): the urban praetor began granting formulary actions to Roman citizens at some time after the peregrine praetor, whose office was created perhaps 242 BC, began doing so, but those actions lacked civil-law effects (e.g. precluding future litigation on the same claim) until the *lex Aebutia* (perhaps late second century).

[24] For a theory of how they were introduced see Lenel 1876, 44–46.

[25] Inst.Gai.4.130–133. The leading modern work is Pellecchi 2003.

[26] See Inst.Gai.4.114; cf. Inst.4.17.2. For examples see Mantovani 1999, nos. 2, 46.

according to which "disclosure" played the role of a contractual offer, acceptance of which led to joinder of issue.[27] Central to his argument was a quantity of evidence—juristic, literary, documentary—that tended to show that, to the contrary, *editio* was an opportunity for latitude ("Spielraum") in the formation of claims and defences.[28] A passage from Cicero's *Partitiones oratoriae* nicely describes the scene; Cicero is here explaining to Cicero *filius* the various occasions for judicial oratory:

> And even before the lawsuit there is usually an argument about the composition of the lawsuit itself, where the issue is whether the action belongs to the person who is suing, or if he still has it or ceased to have it, or whether the action will proceed under that law or with these words. (Cicero *Part. or.* 99)

Bürge suggests that jurists will have been active during this fraught period of negotiation. We imagine workaday professionals, preparing the litigants for the irreversible step of receiving an action from the praetor.

Other laws, besides *editio*, draw attention to this period of negotiation. When Gaius introduces the matter of postponements, he gives us the unsurprising fact that the parties' business may take more than one day: "When an opponent has been called *in ius* but business (*negotium*) cannot be completed on that day ..." (Inst.Gai.4.184). The practice of coming to "court" for negotiation is also nicely illustrated in several wooden *tabulae*, which variously attest promises to appear (*vadimonia*), or proofs of appearance (*testationes sistendi*), at locations *near but not at* the magistrate's tribunal.[29] This very detail suggests the parties will have an opportunity to enter into a conversation about their potential suit.[30] A particularly good example is from Puteoli and dated AD 49: the parties wish to settle their ongoing litigation by oath; they meet according to a prearranged *vadimonium*; an oath is then tendered *in foro apud statuam Matris Idaeae Magnae*.[31] In short, this early

[27] Bürge 1995. For the theory's origins see Wlassak 1924, 72–104, and for its reception in modern scholarship see the discussion and literature cited in Metzger 2010, 31–33.

[28] Bürge 1995, 4–17. Among the juristic evidence see e.g. D.2.13.1pr (*editio* is an opportunity for a defendant to decide whether to fight or concede); D.5.1.21 (a debtor "buys time" after *editio* if he admits the debt); D.43.3.2.4 (avoiding an interdict after *editio* by accepting a *cautio*); D.43.3.1.4 (when the choice of action is uncertain, it is the usual practice for both to be disclosed to the opponent). Among the literary evidence, he cites Cicero's speeches *Quinct.* and *Caec.* as illustrating a painstaking negotiation on the details of the respective suits. Among the documentary evidence, he cites the many first-century records of promises to appear (*vadimonia*) which name a meeting place near but not at the tribunal; this would indicate an intention to converse privately.

[29] For the Puteoli tablets see *TPSulp* 1–19 = Camodeca 1999, 1:49–72. For the Herculaneum tablets see *T.H.* 6, 13, 14 (*ante tribunal praetoris urbani*), 15, summarised in Metzger 2005, 19–191. For the proposition that divine presence via statues and altars gave force to legal acts conducted within their sight see Neudecker 2010, 161–170. This very detail—the place of appearance—suggests to some that these documents attest voluntary, private acts, on the argument that compulsory *vadimonia* (and accompanying proofs of appearance) would name the magistrate's tribunal as the place of appearance. See Cloud 2002, 159–160; Donadio 2009, 244–245. Compare Rodger 1997, 162 (arguing that the place of appearance does not have this significance). For the proposition that the place of appearance should not be read to indicate voluntary, private acts, see Metzger 2005, 53–55.

[30] See Bürge 1995, 5, but with the caveat that the tribunal itself—a small, raised platform—is an unsuitable place for crowds of litigants to meet, whatever the purpose.

[31] *TPSulp* 28 = Camodeca 1999, 1: 93–95. Note that the place of the tendering of the oath, but not the meeting place, is recited in the document.

phase of litigation is now prolonged by events, and the simplicity of the XII Tables—where the *vocatus* is summoned to the magistrate—is gone. A much-discussed juristic fragment shows the new reality:[32]

> One who is called *in ius* is released in two cases: if someone will defend him, and if the matter shall have been settled before [the litigants] arrive *in iure*.[33]

The options are no longer "come or give a *vindex*", but "come, give a *vindex*, or settle before arriving".[34]

19.6 Overcoming Reluctance

Von Bethmann-Hollweg, one of the earliest of the great modern writers on Roman civil procedure, noticed that Cicero's speeches contained only one reference to *in ius vocatio* (von Bethmann-Hollweg 1865, 2, 199 n. 17). This is an important observation, but not for the reason he offered. He believed that, in practice, private summons was discarded in favour of a voluntary contract to appear. The better explanation is that bringing one's opponent to the praetor was secondary to engaging that opponent in the pre-litigation give-and-take, made necessary by the new complexities of the formulary procedure. For the same reason—and this is the principal thesis here—a claimant would have little use for a particularised remedy directed at resistance to summons, of the kind Kelly sought and Kaser and Hackl "found". The *in ius vocatio*, by Cicero's time, was so reduced in importance that the question "how was it was enforced?" no longer had any urgency. The claimant is concerned not with whether his opponent "follows", but more generally whether his opponent will negotiate, refine, defend, settle and ultimately be willing to litigate if necessary. What he requires is a broad remedy that dissuades his opponent from withdrawing, a remedy covering all the various ways an opponent might choose not to engage, including, but not limited to, resisting summons. The remedy is well attested: the edict on fraudulent concealment was actionable against a person who put himself beyond reach, however he effected this, so long as he did so fraudulently, and in order to put his opponent to some disadvantage. Disobedience could lead to the seizure and sale of the person's property. The judicial machinery needed nothing more.

[32] See most recently Trisciuoglio 2007, 294–300 (with literature).

[33] D.2.4.22.1: *Qui in ius vocatus est, duobus casibus dimittendus est: si quis eius personam defendet, et si, dum in ius venitur, de re transactum fuerit*. The fragment, though from a commentary on the XII Tables, probably refers to contemporary procedure. Compare Albanese 1998, 27–28 (the fragment refers only to the *legis actio* procedure, on the argument that a *vocatus*, in contemporary procedure, could not be forced to follow, and only on that assumption would *dimittendus* make sense) with Tafaro 1976, 237–238 (*si … defendet* drawn broadly to cover both the old and new procedure). Lenel (1927, 66–68) treats the passage as relevant to contemporary procedure.

[34] On *dum in ius venitur* see Trisciuoglio 2007, 299.

Bibliography

Agnati, U. 2002. Leges duodecim tabularum: *Le tradizioni letteraria e giuridica. Tabulae I–VI*. Cagliari.

Albanese, B. (1998). "Osservazioni su XII Tab. 1.4: il *vindex* per *adsidui* e *proletari*." *Index* 26: 15–40.

Bablitz, L. 2007. *Actors and audience in the Roman courtroom*. London.

Bablitz, L. (2008). "The platform in Roman art, 30 BC–AD 180: forms and functions." *Studies in Latin Literature and Roman History* 14: 235–282.

Brennan, T. C. 2000. *The praetorship in the Roman republic*. New York.

Bürge, A. 1993. "*Si nolet arceram ne sternito/Ne minore aut si volet maiore vincito*: Positives zu zwei Negationen in den Zwölf Tafeln," in *Mélanges Felix Wubbe*. Fribourg. 61–81.

Bürge, A. (1995). "Zum Edikt *de edendo*." *Zeitschrift der Savigny-Stiftung für Rechtsgeschichte, romanistische Abteilung* 112: 1–50.

Buti, I. 1984. *Il* Praetor *e le formalità introduttive del processo formulare*. Camerino.

Camodeca, G. 1999. Tabulae Pompeianae Sulpiciorum (TPSulp.). *Edizione critica dell'archivio Puteolano dei Sulpicii*. Rome.

Carnabuci, E. 1996. *I luoghi dell'amministrazione della giustizia nel foro di Augusto*. Naples.

Cloud, D. (2002). "Some thoughts on *vadimonium*." *Zeitschrift der Savigny-Stiftung für Rechtsgeschichte, romanistische Abteilung* 119: 143–176.

Crook, J. A. 1995. *Legal advocacy in the Roman world*. London.

Domingo, R. 1995. *Estudios sobre el primer título del edicto pretorio*, Vol. 3: *Palingenesia y reconstrucción*. Santiago de Compostela.

Donadio, N. 2009. "La funzione della *stipulatio 'certo loco sisti'* rispetto alla ricerca del *vocandus* e alla reintegrazione del danno per l'assenza impeditiva dell'*in ius vocatio*." In H. Altmeppen, I. Reichard and M. Schermaier, eds., *Festschrift für Rolf Knütel zum 70. Geburtstag*. Heidelberg. 239–270.

Frier, B. 1983. "Urban praetors and rural violence: the legal background of Cicero's *pro Caecina*." *Transactions of the American Philological Association* 113: 221–241.

Frier, B. 1985. *The rise of the Roman jurists: studies in Cicero's* Pro Caecina. Princeton.

Frier, B. 2010. "Finding a place for law in the high empire: Tacitus, *Dialogus* 39.1–4." In F. de Angelis, ed., *Spaces of justice in the Roman world*. Leiden. 67–87.

Gómez-Iglesias Casal, A. (1989/1990). "Las sanciones pretorias en la fase inicial del proceso." *Revista de Estudios Histórico-Jurídicos* 13: 17–38.

Kaser, M. and Hackl, K. 1996². *Das römische Zivilprozeßrecht*. Munich.

Kelly, J. M. 1966a. *Roman litigation*. Oxford.

Kelly, J. M. (1966b). "The growth pattern of the praetor's edict." *Irish Jurist (New Series)* 1: 341–355.

Kondratieff, E. 2010. "The urban praetor's tribunal in the Roman republic." In F. de Angelis, ed., *Spaces of justice in the Roman world*. Leiden. 89–126.

Kunkel, W. (1973). "Epigraphik und Geschichte des römischen Privatrechts." *Vestigia. Beiträge zur alten Geschichte* 17: 193–242.

Lenel, O. 1876. *Über Ursprung und Wirkung der Exceptionen*. Heidelberg.

Lenel, O. 1889. Palingenesia iuris civilis. Lepizig.

Lenel, O. 1927³. *Das* Edictum Perpetuum: *ein Versuch zu seiner Wiederherstellung*. Leipzig.

Lévy, J.-P. 1998. "La *litis denuntiatio* et sa place dans l'évolution de la procédure extraordinaire," in *Mélanges de droit Romain et d'histoire ancienne: hommage à la mémoire de André Magdelain*. Paris. 247–257.

Lewis, A. 2000. "The autonomy of Roman law." In P. Coss, ed., *The moral world of the law.* Cambridge. 37–47.

Liebs, D. 1986. "The history of the Roman *condictio* up to Justinian." In N. MacCormick and P. Birks, eds., *The legal mind.* Oxford. 163–183.

Lintott, A. 2008. *Cicero as evidence: a historian's companion.* Oxford.

Mantovani, D. 1999². *Le formule del processo privato Romano: per la didattica delle istituzioni di diritto Romano.* Padua.

Masi Doria, C. 2001. *"Aurem vellere,"* in Iuris Vincula. *Studi in onore di Mario Talamanca.* Naples. 5:315–342.

Metro, A. (1969). "La *lex Cornelia de iurisdictione* alla luce di Dio Cass. 36. 40. 1–2." *Iura* 20: 500–524.

Metzger, E. 1997. *A new outline of the Roman civil trial.* Oxford.

Metzger, E. (2004). "Roman judges, case law, and principles of procedure." *Law and History Review* 22: 243–275.

Metzger, E. 2005. *Litigation in Roman law.* Oxford.

Metzger, E. 2010. "Civil procedure in classical Rome: having an audience with the magistrate." In F. de Angelis, ed., *Spaces of justice in the Roman world.* Leiden. 27–41.

Metzger, E. 2012. "Obligations in classical procedure." In T. A. J. McGinn, ed., *Obligations in Roman law: past, present, and future.* Ann Arbor. 158–173.

Metzger, E. (2013). "An outline of Roman civil procedure." *Roman Legal Tradition* 9: 1–30.

Meyer, E. A. 2004. *Legitimacy and law in the Roman world:* tabulae *in Roman belief and practice.* Cambridge.

Nelson, H. L. W. and Manthe, U. 1999. Gai Institutiones *III.* 88–181: *die Kontraktsobligationen. Text und Kommentar.* Berlin.

Neudecker, R. 2010. "The forum of Augustus in Rome: law and order in sacred spaces." In F. de Angelis, ed., *Spaces of justice in the Roman world.* Leiden. 161–188.

Pellecchi, L. 2003. *La* praescriptio: *processo, diritto sostanziale, modelli espositivi.* Padua.

Platschek, J. 2005. *Studien zu Ciceros Rede für P. Quintius.* Munich.

Pugliese, G. 1962. *Il processo civile Romano,* Vol. 1: *Le* legis actiones. Milan.

Reeve, M. D. 1992. Oratio pro Quinctio. Leipzig.

Rodger, A. (1997). "*Vadimonium* to Rome (and elsewhere)." *Zeitschrift der Savigny-Stiftung für Rechtsgeschichte, romanistische Abteilung* 114: 160–196.

Rotondi, G. 1962. Leges publicae populi Romani. Hildesheim.

Rüfner, T. (2008). Review of Platschek, Studien zu Ciceros Rede für P. Quinctius. *Zeitschrift der Savigny-Stiftung für Rechtsgeschichte, romanistische Abteilung* 125: 766–774.

Schiavone, A. 2012. *The invention of law in the west.* Cambridge, Mass.

Schiller, A. A. 1978. *Roman law: mechanisms of development.* The Hague.

Schulz, F. 1936. *Principles of Roman law.* Oxford.

Schulz, F. 1946. *History of Roman legal science.* Oxford.

Tafaro, S. (1976). "Fideiussor iudicio sistendi causa." *Labeo* 22: 232–252.

Talamanca, M. 1990. *Istituzioni di diritto Romano.* Milan.

Talamanca, M. 1999. "Il riordinamento Augusteo del processo privato." In F. Milazzo, ed., *Gli ordinamenti giudiziari di Roma imperiale: princeps e procedura dalle leggi Giulie ad Adriano.* Naples. 63–260.

Trisciuoglio, A. 2007. "Sul *vindex* della *in ius vocatio* in età decemvirale: in margine a XII Tab. 1.4," in *Studi per Giovanni Nicosia.* Milan. Vol. 8: 285–304.

von Bethmann-Hollweg, M. A. 1865. *Der römische Civilprozess,* Vol. 3. Bonn.

Wlassak, M. 1924. *Die klassische Prozeßformel.* Vienna.

CHAPTER 20

IMPERIAL *COGNITIO* PROCESS

THOMAS RÜFNER

20.1 Introduction

The term *cognitio* process is used by legal historians to denote a new form of procedure that evolved within the Roman legal system from the reign of Augustus onward. Scholars use the term with reference both to civil and to criminal procedure. This chapter will focus on civil procedure.[1]

The new form of civil procedure was distinguished by the absence of the division of proceedings into two phases, the first one before a Republican magistrate or provincial governor (*in iure*) and the second before a judge (*iudex*) or panel of judges who were appointed ad hoc for the trial (*apud iudicem*). Proceedings in the new form were heard by the presiding official from beginning to end. The abandonment of the two-phased model entailed the end of the use of the *formulae*, which gave the formulary procedure its name.

The new form derives its name from the fact that the verb *cognosco* and the noun *cognitio* refer to the judicial examination and disposition of a case (Mancuso 1997, 389–390). A few sources suggest that *cognosco* and *cognitio* were used during the early Empire to refer to proceedings in which no *iudex* was appointed (D.1.18.8, 9; Suet. *Claud.* 15). However, it is far from certain that *cognitio* ever had the technical meaning that modern scholars attach to it.

Modern scholars also use the words *extra ordinem* with reference to the new procedure. Like *cognitio*, these words occur in the sources, but they probably did not have the character of a technical term referring to the procedural model that superseded the traditional formulary procedure (Turpin 1999, 544–573).

Various other innovations of civil procedure emerged during the Imperial period. They concerned the summons mechanism, the law of proof, execution of judgement, costs, and the introduction of an appeals process. Many of these innovations are portrayed in modern scholarly literature as features of the *cognitio* process. However, there is no necessary link

[1] On the emergence of the criminal *cognitio* process see Santalucia 1998, 213–215.

between these innovations and the disappearance of the two-phased model. Many of these new features may have been present in proceedings that were still divided into two phases in accordance with the formulary system.

After a long transitional period, the various procedural innovations consolidated into a coherent set of rules, which completely replaced the formulary process. The new system emerged from about the mid-fourth century, and many of its characteristics can be traced to modern procedure. Where Roman law influenced modern procedural law, this influence did not come from the formulary process, but from the *cognitio* process, which is enshrined in Justinian's codes.

20.2 Procedural Innovations of the Imperial Epoch

20.2.1 The Single-Phased Procedure

Three factors may have contributed to the demise of the traditional procedure. Firstly, in some cases no pertinent action existed under the formulary system; the emperors introduced a new remedy outside the formulary system and entrusted certain officials with the adjudication of these cases. Secondly, emperors from Augustus onward asserted the right to adjudicate in person claims of various kinds outside the traditional system.[2] Finally, provincial governors found the formalities of judge selection impracticable in their province and decided cases themselves.[3] Originally, the single-phased procedure was confined to these three areas. Later, its scope of application expanded until it became the new standard procedure and completely supplanted the traditional system.

20.2.1.1 *New Remedies*

The earliest and probably the most prominent example of the creation of a new remedy outside the system of the formulary process is the legal recognition of *fideicommissa* by the first emperor, Augustus.

Fideicommissa were trust-like arrangements for the purpose of making gifts upon death (bequests) (see Jakab, ch. 38). The traditional device to make such gifts was the legacy (*legatum*), which required compliance with certain formalities and was subject to various legal restrictions. In order to circumvent these restrictions, Roman citizens resorted to the *fideicommissum*. Rather than making a direct testamentary gift in the form of a *legatum*, the testator would ask one of the persons who were to take parts of the estate as heirs or legatees to act as trustee and pass on all or part of what they were to receive to the intended beneficiary (Johnston 1988, 9–10).

[2] On the legal bases of the emperors' judicial activity see Buti 1982, 35; Kaser and Hackl 1996, 446–447; see also the innovative theory of Spagnuolo Vigorita 2007, 542.

[3] Sirks 2009, 51–52; Kaser and Hackl 1996, 438; Buti 1982, 14–15 and 43.

Before Augustus, *fideicommissa* were not enforceable and depended entirely on the trustee's readiness to comply with the wishes of the deceased. According to the narrative offered by Justinian's Institutes, Augustus entrusted the consuls with enforcing the claims of beneficiaries against recalcitrant trustees. Later, a post for an additional praetor (*praetor fideicommissarius*) was created for the handling of lawsuits based on *fideicommissa*.[4] In the provinces, *fideicommissa* fell under the jurisdiction of the provincial governor (Inst.Gai.2.278).

A similar development took place with regard to claims for family support (*alimenta*). The Romans had long recognised a moral duty to support one's parents or children in case of need.[5] However, there was no formulary *actio* that the party in need could bring against wealthier blood relatives. At some point, perhaps under the reign of Antoninus Pius (138–168),[6] the mutual obligation of parents and children to support each other was legally recognised. Again, the consuls were given the task to hear and enforce claims for family support. In the provinces, jurisdiction was granted to the governors.[7]

The remuneration of various types of professional services is a third area in which the emperors created a new remedy outside the traditional system of the formulary process (Buti 1982, 38; Kaser and Hackl 1996, 456). Advocates are the most prominent example. For a long time the Romans perceived advocacy as an aristocratic profession that could not be exercised for money. The *lex Cincia* of 204 BC contained a prohibition of payments for legal services (Dimopoulou 1999, 152–157). In the course of the Imperial age, this prohibition was relaxed. On the initiative of Emperor Claudius, in 47 AD the senate permitted payments of up to 10,000 sesterces provided that the fee was not agreed upon or paid before the end of the case.[8] Claudius legalised the payment of fees, but he did not give the advocate a legal claim against his client. Specifically, the advocate was unable to bring a claim on the basis of a contract of *locatio conductio*.[9] During the reign of the Antonine dynasty (96–192) it became possible for advocates to bring a claim for their fees.[10] In the provinces, the provincial governors were competent to hear such cases. It is unclear who heard them in Rome (Kaser and Hackl 1996, 456). Similar remedies were created for other professions.[11]

In all the cases discussed so far and in a couple of other areas (cf. Kaser and Hackl 1996, 453–460), the emperors bypassed the formulary system. The officials entrusted with the enforcement of the new claims were authorised to decide the cases themselves[12] and did not issue a *formula* (Inst.Gai.2.278, on *fideicommissum*). It was possible for the magistrate or official who presided over the case to charge another person with some part of the

[4] Inst.2.23.1; cf. Johnston 1988, 22–23; Giodice Sabbatelli 2001, 83–153.

[5] See de Francesco 2001, 47–58 on indirect means making it possible to enforce this obligation even within the traditional procedural framework.

[6] The first Imperial rescripts on pertinent issues are ascribed to Antoninus Pius: D.25.5.5–7; C.5.25.1 (undated); cf. Kaser and Hackl 1996, 455 n. 38.

[7] Buti 1982, 38; Kaser and Hackl 1996, 455. Some doubts are expressed by de Francesco 2001, 37–38.

[8] Tac. *Hist.* 11.7; Plin. *Ep.* 5.9.4; cf. Dimopoulou 1999, 216–221; Buongiorno 2010, 219–227.

[9] Cf. Dimopoulou 1999, 474–479; du Plessis 2012, 101.

[10] Dimopoulou 1999, 453; Wieling 1996, 442 ascribes the introduction of the new remedy to Antoninus Pius.

[11] Cf. du Plessis 2012, 94–115; on medical doctors see du Plessis 2012, 96–98 and Wacke 1996, 416.

[12] D.31.29pr (on *fideicommissum*); on the importance of this text for the early history of the so-called *cognitio* process see Giodice Sabbatelli 2007, 2277 n. 6 and the references therein; for an extensive treatment of the substance of D.31.29pr see Giodice Sabbatelli 2006, 93–128.

judicial business. So, for example, the praetor who had jurisdiction over *fideicommissa* might commission someone to act as arbitrator (*arbiter*) and calculate the worth of the estate's assets and liabilities and determine whether the *fideicommissum* could be complied with.[13] If the final decision was left to an arbitrator or judge (*iudex*) appointed ad hoc, proceedings were divided into two phases in a similar way as under the traditional formulary process.

20.2.1.2 *The Emperor as Judge*

The emperors often acted as judges themselves. Suetonius reports that Augustus heard cases until late in the night (Suet. *Aug.* 33). In their judicial activity, the emperors were not bound by the traditional rules of the formulary process.

It is not clear to what extent the emperors exercised original jurisdiction in civil cases. Very few sources clearly support the assumption that the emperors acted as judges of the first instance.[14] In most texts, it is evident or at least possible that the emperor decided on appeal.

The exact character of Roman appellate procedure cannot be determined with a satisfactory degree of certainty. It was in itself a procedural innovation which developed from Augustan times onward. Appeals were possible against judgements rendered under both the traditional and the new system (Casavola 1998, 97).

Apparently, the appellate court was free to set a judgement apart for any factual or legal error (Litewski 1966, 312). It is not clear, though, to what extent the parties were allowed to introduce new factual allegations or new evidence that had not been proffered during the trial. A constitution by Emperor Diocletian from 294 takes a liberal approach to the admission of new material (C.7.62.6.1[undated]), but the sources do not contain much information on the situation in earlier times. Although there are some indications that Diocletian's approach was in line with earlier practice,[15] it is impossible to decide whether the emerging appellate procedure was in substance a trial *de novo* or a mere review of the proceedings in the court below (cf. Pergami 2000, 29; Pergami 2007, 4148). It would seem that the emperor's appellate activity would be much more likely to have favoured the transition to a one-phased trial if the former were the case.

Neither the extent of the emperors' activity as civil judges of the first instance nor the nature of the appellate process as a new trial rather than a review can be established with certainty. It remains an open question if the personal exercise of judicial functions by the emperors was as important for the development of the *cognitio* process as is traditionally assumed.

[13] D.42.2.7; on this text and some other sources attesting the activity of *arbitri* in the context of the adjudication of claims under a *fideicommissum* see Giodice Sabbatelli 2001, 265–270; Giodice Sabbatelli 2002, 639–644.

[14] See the discussion by Kelly 1957, 79–90; cf. also the overview of texts from the Digest in Rizzi 2012, 134–138.

[15] See Litewski 1968, 228–229 and Pergami 2007, 4148 (both citing D.49.1.3.3).

20.2.1.3 *The Provinces*

It appears from the sources that there were huge differences in the procedural models followed in the provinces at different times and in different parts of the Empire: Cicero's Verrine speeches show that in the first century BC the formulary procedure was in use in Roman Sicily (cf. Cic. *Verr.* 2.2.31; 2.3.152). In Egypt, for which there is a wealth of evidence in the papyri, the Roman governor (*praefectus Aegypti*) employed a procedure that was single-phased in principle from the beginning of the Roman rule (Kaser and Hackl 1996, 469). Yet, even for Egypt, a few sources suggest that the formulary procedure was not completely unknown.[16]

The existence of a standard provincial edict based on the formulary procedure and of a commentary on this edict by the classical jurist Gaius proves that Egypt was an exception. It is difficult to tell, though, for how long and to what extent the formulary procedure was followed in several provinces.

The Babatha archive found in the Jordan desert contains a formula for the *actio tutelae* translated into Greek and adapted to local circumstances (*P. Yadin* 28–30). While this is strong evidence that the formulary procedure was known in the Roman province of Arabia at the beginning of the second century AD,[17] it is no proof that the use of the two-phased system was universal or that the procedural rules applied were exactly the same as in the capital. Likewise, the fact that the *lex rivi Hiberiensis*, which dates to the reign of Emperor Hadrian and comes from the Roman province of Hispania Tarraconensis, refers to proceedings *extra ordinem* (*Lex Rivi Hiberiensis* III 35; on this passage Torrent 2013, 449) does not prove that the single-phased model had already become prevalent in Roman Spain at the time: the two-phased procedure was certainly still in use in the neighbouring province of Baetica a few decennia earlier, when the *lex Irnitana* was drafted (cf. Hackl 1997, 148–150). There is a Greek inscription from Ephesus that indicates that the formulary procedure was still in use in the Eastern province of Asia under Hadrian (*I.Ephesos* no. 21486, cf. Fournier 2010, 33, 376–378).

On the balance of the evidence, it seems that the formulary procedure was introduced in most, if not all, provinces. Even so, it has to be assumed that provincial governors were able to exercise greater influence on the final disposition of cases than were the magistrates in the capital because they were able (or even forced by the circumstances) to appoint members of their own staff as judges for the second phase of proceedings.[18] It seems also likely that provincial governors at times chose to bypass the formalities of the formulary procedure and decided cases themselves at a time when the appointment of a judge and the issuance of a formula were still considered indispensable by the jurists in the capital.

When a governor would follow the formulary procedure and when he would prefer to depart from it were probably determined by considerations of practicability rather than by strict legal rules (Lemosse 1998, 245). There are also examples where the provincial governor does not appoint a *iudex* or issue a *formula* in keeping with the traditional procedure,

[16] *P. Oxy.* xlii 3016 (cf. Fournier 2010, 32); *PSI* vii 743r frag. e (cf. Nörr 2000, 213–214).

[17] Nörr 1998a, 322; Nörr 1998b, 86; more cautious Lemosse 1998, 244.

[18] The way in which Verres dealt with a lawsuit brought by a certain Heraclius (Cic. *Verr.* 2.2.41) may provide an early example in point, cf. Torrent 2013, 453–454; Genovese 2009, 265; Platschek 2001, 255–256.

but instructs a subaltern official to continue proceedings begun before the governor. In theory, this way of leaving some part of judicial business to a subordinate was fundamentally different from the old formulary procedure, because this delegation was discretionary (Merola 2012, 58) whereas the magistrate was obliged to appoint a judge under the traditional system. In practice, such cases likely rendered the transition from the old two-phased model to the new system where the magistrate was free to make the final decision himself almost imperceptible to the public.[19]

It is hardly surprising that there is no evidence for the formulary procedure in the provinces from the third century AD. The two-phased procedure seems to have completely disappeared from provincial practice in the second half of the second century (Fournier 2010, 33).

20.2.1.4 *Suppression of the Formulae*

When did the formulary procedure become obsolete in the entire Empire including the capital? Gaius bases his account of Roman civil procedure in the middle of the second century AD entirely on the formulary procedure, but by 226, a quarrel about rent payments due from the corporation of *fullones* in the city of Rome was apparently handled in a single-phased procedure by the *praefectus vigilum* (*CIL* VI, 266). By this time, the scope of application of the traditional formulary procedure and the jurisdiction of the praetors must have been considerably diminished.

Traditionally, a constitution from 342 AD has been interpreted as definitely abolishing the formulary procedure.[20] Recently, it has been argued that an earlier enactment from 294 that limits the capacity of provincial governors to appoint inferior judges (*iudices pedanei*) should be read as a legislative suppression of the traditional two-phased system (Liva 2007, 168; cf. Merola 2012, 59 n. 49). Even if the latter hypothesis is true, the Imperial constitution probably did little more than to formalise the abolition of a procedure which was no longer in use in legal practice: while the jurists of the early third century still seem to be basing their reasoning on the traditional procedural model, it had all but disappeared by the middle of the century (Kaser and Hackl 1996, 517).

20.3 Court Hierarchy

The new procedural model entailed a reorganisation of the court system—or rather, it forced the Romans to create a stable court system for the first time.

When the *cognitio* process became the standard procedure, the court of the urban prefects (*praefecti Urbi*) of Rome and Constantinople emerged as the courts of first instance for the two capital cities of the Empire (Kaser and Hackl 1996, 536–537). The praetors retained a minor judicial role (Kaser and Hackl 1996, 539; Russo Ruggeri 1998, 104). In the

[19] Kaser and Hackl 1996, 461; cf. Ando 2012, 87 who aptly speaks of a process which "mimicked that of the so-called formulary system".

[20] C.2.57.1 (a. 342); cf. Kaser and Hackl 1996, 171; Guarino 1999.

provinces, the courts of the provincial governors functioned as courts of first instance (Kaser and Hackl 1996, 532–533).

With the introduction of appellate review, a complicated system of appellate courts was created.[21] At the top of the hierarchy of the courts were the emperor himself and his highest officials, the praetorian prefects (*praefecti praetorio*), against whose decisions no appeal was available (Pergami 2000, 413–416, 44–447).

20.4 Summons Procedure

Under the traditional rules, proceedings were initiated through a private summons: the claimant asked the defendant orally to accompany him immediately to the place where the competent magistrate sat (*in ius vocare*—to call to court) (see Metzger, ch. 19). During the Empire, summons by means of *in ius vocare* was gradually replaced by a new summons procedure characterised by the use of written documents and by the involvement of the authorities. The chronology of this development is difficult to reconstruct due to the confusing terminology of the sources: non-technical terms that may or may not indicate a substantial change were used for the summons procedure as early as the first century AD.[22] On the other hand, the term *in ius vocare* was still used in legal and non-legal texts when it had long lost its technical meaning and the private oral summons procedure was clearly obsolete (Cascione 2012, 242).

It seems plausible that the new official summons procedure developed in connection with the new single-phased trial, because both were innovations that enhanced the importance of the official presiding over the proceedings. However, there are indications that proceedings following the traditional two-phased model were sometimes initiated by a semi-official summons[23] and that *in ius vocare* may have been used to initiate proceedings which were otherwise not governed by the rules of the formulary procedure (Torrent 2013, 449).

The new summons procedure was referred to as *denuntiatio* (notice). It was (still) an order issued by the claimant to the defendant asking him to appear in court, but it was usually recorded in a witnessed deed (*testatio*) and could be reinforced by an order of the court (*denuntiatio ex auctoritate*). This procedure is attested by documents in the Babatha archive (*P. Yadin* 23–26; cf. Guasco 2013, 413–414). It may have been legally prescribed as the standard method of initiating proceedings by Emperor Antoninus Caracalla.[24] A constitution by the Emperor Constantine changed the legal framework significantly: it required all summonses to be made with the assistance of the authorities.[25] The presence

[21] For details see Pergami 2000, 402–469.

[22] On Seneca, *Ben.* 3.7.1 and other texts containing the expression *ad iudicem vocare* cf. Pavese 2009; see also Valiño 2000 on the terminology used in D.5.1.79pr.

[23] Nörr 1998a, 340–341; the *denuntiatio* mentioned in *TPSulp* 25 = *AE* 1973, no. 146 is not a summons: Camodeca 1999, 86 *contra* Arcaria 2003, 105 n. 193.

[24] Cf. Metzger 2005, 172–173, who assumes that Aurelius Victor *Caes.* 16.11 refers to Caracalla; but see Lemosse 1990, 14 and Arcaria 2003, 95–106, who accept the text as it stands according to the manuscript tradition and ascribe the reform to Marcus Aurelius.

[25] CTh.2.4.2 (undated); cf. Lévy 1998; Agnati 2012; Guasco 2013.

of witnesses and the production of a *testatio* were no longer sufficient. Constantine's legislative intervention may have eased the transition from summons by (*litis*) *denuntiatio* (notice [of claim])[26] to the so-called *libellus* procedure that was in use from the mid-fifth century AD onward (Lévy 1998, 255–256.). Under this procedure, the claimant sent a written statement of his claim (*libellus*) to the court. The court served the defendant with the *libellus* and issued a summons (Kaser and Hackl 1996, 57–572).

The emergence of the default judgement as an effective means to sanction the defendant's failure to appear is linked to the development of the new summons procedure.[27] There was no practicable default procedure under the traditional system: the only sanction in the case of non-compliance with an *in ius vocare* was the initiation of bankruptcy proceedings against the debtor.[28] This mechanism was too clumsy to serve the claimant's interests and it was too harsh on the defendant, especially if the defendant had failed to appear in proceedings concerning a small claim.

In the context of the new forms of summons, it became possible to give judgement against a defendant who did not appear. This simple and effective mechanism appears well established as early as the middle of the second century AD.[29]

20.5 Evidence

Under the traditional procedural system, no rules of evidence law existed (Metro 2001, 109). In late Antiquity, a body of evidence law developed. The judge assumed a more active role during the trial, and at the same time he became subject to stricter rules guiding his fact-finding (Puliatti 2010, 121–122, 128).

The general tendency of the emerging evidence law was to favour written documents over the testimony of witnesses (Fernández de Buján 2003, 21–22). One such rule was, "One witness is no witness" (*unus testis, nullus testis*): according to a constitution of the Emperor Constantine, the testimony of one man which was not corroborated by another witness had no legal value.[30] The extensive provisions on the evidentiary value of documents enacted by Emperor Justinian in 538 AD constitute the final point of this development (Nov.73; cf. Fernández de Buján 2003, 24–25).

It should be noted, though, that ancient Roman law never developed a rigid system of evidentiary rules like that of the European *ius commune*. Even in late Antiquity, the judge remained free in his evaluation of the evidence. The applicable provisions declared

[26] The term *litis denuntiatio* is used by modern historians for the post-classical summons procedure, whereas *denuntiatio* alone usually refers to the procedure in earlier periods. There is no basis in the sources for this terminological distinction; cf. Lévy 1998, 255.

[27] On the connection between the form of summons and the default procedure see Buti 1982, 44; Guasco 2013, 420.

[28] Kaser and Hackl 1996, 224; Obarrio Moreno 2009, 25–52; see Bellodi Ansaloni 1998, 54 with n. 6 on the sanction for failure to appear at the second stage of proceedings.

[29] D.4.1.7pr; C.7.43.1 (undated); cf. Bellodi Ansaloni 1998, 59 and 61; see also Obarrio Moreno 2009, 53–99.

[30] C.4.20.9 (a. 334) = CTh.11.39.3; on the novelty of this rule see Metro 2001, 113.

certain evidence inadmissible (like the testimony of a single witness). They usually did not regulate the relative value of different means of proof (Simon 1969, 349). The fact that Constantine's constitution, which introduces the rule *unus testis, nullus testis*, also provides that the testimony of witnesses from the upper classes should be given more weight than that of other people constitutes a notable exception.

20.6 Execution

The means of enforcement for civil judgements under the traditional system were limited in two important ways. There was no way to obtain specific performance of non-monetary claims, and there was no efficient way to enforce a single claim (Inst.Gai.4.48; D.42.1.13.1; cf. Winkel 2010, 482–483). If the debtor did not comply with a judgement, the standard way to enforce the judgement was the commencement of a bankruptcy-like procedure that aimed at the (partial) satisfaction of all claims against the debtor.[31] These limitations were removed—or at least relaxed—during the Imperial age.

The situation concerning the availability of specific performance is not entirely clear. A much-discussed text from the Digest mentions the possibility to enforce a claim for the surrender of a corporeal thing specifically by forcibly taking away the chattel from its possessor. The text is ascribed to the late classical jurist Ulpian (D.6.1.68). It appears to prove that Ulpian accepted the specific enforcement of claims *in rem* within the context of the traditional (formulary) procedure. It seems likely, however, that the text as it stands is the result of subsequent changes to Ulpian's original statement. Perhaps the interpolation was made when the Roman currency collapsed in the late third century (Winkel 2010, 485, 488). In times of monetary crisis, specific performance becomes crucial.

Later sources confirm that specific performance was available in some cases. A bailiff (*exsecutor*) would assist the judgement creditor in the process of forcible execution.[32] Even so, the old rule against specific performance was not completely abandoned even in Justinianic law (Winkel 2010, 488).

The isolated execution of single claims without the need to initiate insolvency proceedings became possible when the device of *pignus in causa iudicati captum* (pledge taken to satisfy a judgement) was introduced. The bailiff (Díaz-Bautista Cremades 2013, 85–93) seized property from the debtor that served as security for the judgement claim (cf. C.8.22.1 [a. 213] with von der Fecht 1996, 53) and could eventually be sold to satisfy a monetary claim.[33]

Emperor Antoninus Pius probably introduced the new method of execution in the second century AD (von der Fecht 1996, 49). Most scholars assume that it was only available within the context of the single-phased *cognitio* process, yet there is at least one text that points to the possibility of executing on a judgement given after a two-phased trial in this way.[34]

[31] See Kaser and Hackl 1996, 388–401; on debt bondage as an alternative means of execution see Klinck 2013; Kaser and Hackl 1996, 387–388.

[32] C.7.4.17 (a. 530) (cf. Winkel 2010, 485–487); CTh.11.36.25 = C.7.65.5.1 (undated) (cf. Kaser and Hackl 1996, 626).

[33] Cf. Díaz-Bautista Cremades 2013, 26 for an overview of the main sources.

[34] D.42.1.15pr. Cf. von der Fecht 1996, 51; Díaz-Bautista Cremades 2013, 47–50.

20.7 Conclusion

It is obvious that the development of civil procedure during the Empire mirrors the constitutional development of the Roman state. The new organisation of the courts shifted power to the members of the Imperial administration (Robles Reyes 2009, 87). The appellate process and the stricter rules of evidence served further to enhance the emperor's control over the administration of justice throughout the Empire.

Even though many of the procedural innovations helped to strengthen the emperor's power, the new system also made Roman courts more accessible: the old summons mechanism had effectively left it to the claimants if they had the means and sophistication to bring their opponents to court. With the new system, the claimant was able to rely on the help of the authorities. The enhanced effectiveness of the execution process made it easier for creditors to pursue and enforce their claims.

The evolution of a hierarchy of courts and the introduction of legal remedies for the claiming of *honoraria* favoured the emergence of a legal profession (cf. Bablitz 2007, 142). This, in turn, must have made access to justice easier for those who were not in the position to have friends and relatives who would represent them in court. In this context, the introduction of an obligation of the losing party to compensate the costs of the winner may also have encouraged parties with lesser means to go to court (Valiño 2003, 404–405).

The results of our survey are thus highly ambivalent. Roman civil procedure in late Antiquity paradoxically became at the same time more bureaucratic and more accessible, at once more Monarchical and more citizen-friendly.

Bibliography

Agnati, U. (2012). "Costantino abolisce la privata testatio (C.Th. 2.4.2)." *Teoria e storia del diritto privato* 5. Available at: http://www.teoriaestoriadeldirittoprivato.com/index.php?com=statics&option=index&cID=255, accessed 8 June 2015.

Ando, C. 2012. *Imperial Rome AD 193 to 286: the critical century.* Edinburgh.

Arcaria, F. 2003. Oratio Marci: *Giurisdizione e processo nella normazione di Marco Aurelio.* Turin.

Bablitz, L. 2007. *Actors and audience in the Roman courtroom.* London.

Bellodi Ansaloni, A. 1998. *Ricerche sulla* contumacia *nelle* cognitiones extra ordinem. Milan.

Buongiorno, P. 2010. Senatus consulta Claudianis temporibus facta: *una palingenesi delle deliberazioni senatorie dell'età di Claudio (41–54 d.C.).* Naples.

Buti, I. (1982). "La *cognitio extra ordinem* da Augusto a Diocleziano." *Aufstieg und Niedergang der römischen Welt* II.4: 29–59.

Camodeca, G. 1999. Tabulae Pompeianae Supliciorum (TPSulp.): *edizione critica dell'archivio puteano de Sulpicii*, Vol. 1. Rome.

Casavola, F. P. (1998). "Gli ordinamenti giudiziari nella Roma imperiale: *princeps* e procedure dalle leggi Giulie ad Adriano." *Index* 26: 89–98.

Cascione, C. (2012). "Matrone *vocatae in ius* tra antico e tardoantico." *Index* 40: 238–243.

de Francesco, A. (2001). "Il diritto agli alimenti tra genitori e figli: un'ipotesi ricostruttiva." *Labeo* 47: 28–62.

Díaz-Bautista Cremades, A. 2013. *El embargo ejecutivo en el proceso cognitorio romano.* Madrid.

Dimopoulou, A. 1999. *La rémuneration de l'assistance en justice: étude sur la relation avocat-plaideur à Rome.* Athens.

du Plessis, P. J. 2012. *Letting and hiring in Roman legal thought:* 27 BCE–284 CE. Leiden.

Fernández de Buján, A. (2003). "Testigos y documentos en la practica negocial y judicial romana." *Iura* 54: 21–47.

Fournier, J. 2010. *Entre tutelle romaine et autonomie civique: l'administration judiciaire dans les provinces hellénophones de l'empire romain (129 av. J.-C.–235 apr. J.-C.).* Athens.

Genovese, M. 2009. "*Qui cives romani erant, si siculi essent ... Qui siculi, si cives romani essent* (Cic. *Verr.* 2.2.12.31): nuovi spunti interpretativi e riflessi sulla valutazione dell' esercizio della *iurisdictio* nel corso delle *praetura siciliensis* di Verre," in *Studi in onore di Remo Martini.* Milan. Vol. 2: 215–255.

Giodice Sabbatelli, V. 2001. Fideicommissorum Persecutio. *Contributo allo studio delle cognizioni straordinarie.* Bari.

Giodice Sabbatelli, V. 2002. "*Iurisdictio de fideicommissis e poteri dati.*" In C. Masi Doria and C. Cascione, eds., *Diritto e giustizia nel processo.* Naples. 609–645.

Giodice Sabbatelli, V. 2006. *Studi sull'officio del console.* Bari.

Giodice Sabbatelli, V. 2007. "Un 'affare di cuore'." In C. Masi Doria and C. Cascione, eds., Fides Humanitas Ius: *Studi in onore di Luigi Labruna.* Vol. 4. Naples. 2275–2303.

Guarino, A. 1999. "*Aucupatio Syllabarum.*" In R. Ruedin, ed., *Mélanges en l'honneur de Carlo Augusto Cannata.* Basel. 167–169.

Guasco, A. (2013). "CTh. 2.4.2. Un provvedimento imperiale sul processo civile tra principato e tardoantico." *Studia et Documenta Historiae et Iuris* 79: 405–421.

Hackl, K. (1997). "Der Zivilprozeß des frühen Prinzipats in den Provinzen." *Zeitschrift der Savigny-Stiftung für Rechtsgeschichte, romanistische Abteilung* 114: 141–159.

Johnston, D. 1988. *The Roman law of trusts.* Oxford.

Kaser, M. and Hackl, K. 1996². *Das römische Zivilprozeßrecht.* Munich.

Kelly, J. M. 1957. Princeps ivdex: *eine Untersuchung zur Entwicklung und zu den Grundlagen der kaiserlichen Gerichtsbarkeit.* Weimar.

Klinck, F. (2013). "Die vorklassische Personalvollstreckung wegen Darlehensschulden nach der *lex Poetelia.*" *Zeitschrift der Savigny-Stiftung für Rechtsgeschichte, romanistische Abteilung* 130: 393–404.

Lemosse, M. (1990). "Les réformes procedurales de Marc-Aurèle." *Labeo* 36: 5–18.

Lemosse, M. 1998. "Le procès provincial classique," in *Mélanges de droit romain et d'histoire ancienne: hommage à la mémoire de André Magdelain.* Paris. 239–246.

Lévy, J.-P. 1998. "La *litis denuntiatio* et sa place dans l'évolution de la procédure extraordinaire," in *Mélanges de droit romain et d'histoire ancienne: hommage à la mémoire de André Magdelain.* Paris. 247–257.

Litewski, W. (1966). "Die römische Appellation in Zivilsachen (IV)." *Revue internationale des droits de l'antiquité* 15: 143–351.

Litewski, W. (1968). "Die römische Appellation in Zivilsachen (II)." *Revue internationale des droits de l'antiquité* 13: 231–323.

Liva, S. (2007). "Ricerche sul *iudex pedaneus*: organizzazione giudiziaria e processo." *Studia et Documenta Historiae et Iuris* 73: 159–196.

Mancuso, G. (1997). "*Decretum Praetoris.*" *Studia et Documenta Historiae et Iuris* 63: 343–400.

Merola, G. D. 2012. *Per la storia del processo provinciale romano. I papiri del medio Eufrate.* Naples.

Metro, A. 2001. "*Unus Testis, Nullus Testis.*" In J. W. Cairns and O. F. Robinson, eds., *Critical studies in ancient law, comparative law and legal history: essays in honour of Alan Watson.* Oxford/Portland. 109–116.

Metzger, E. 2005. *Litigation in Roman law.* Oxford.

Nörr, D. 1998a. "Prozessuales aus dem Babatha-Archiv," in *Mélanges de droit romain et d'histoire ancienne: hommage à la mémoire de André Magdelain.* Paris. 317–341.

Nörr, D. (1998b). "Römisches Zivilprozeßrecht nach Max Kaser. Prozeßrecht in der Provinz Arabia." *Zeitschrift der Savigny-Stiftung für Rechtsgeschichte, romanistische Abteilung* 115: 80–98.

Nörr, D. (2000). "PSI VII 743r fr. e: Fragment einer römischen Prozeßformel. Bemerkungen zum vorhadrianischen Edikt und zu den *Hermeneumata Pseudodositheana.*" *Zeitschrift der Savigny-Stiftung für Rechtsgeschichte, romanistische Abteilung* 117: 179–215.

Obarrio Moreno, J. A. 2009. *El proceso por* contumacia: *origen, pervivencia y recepción.* Madrid.

Pavese, M. P. 2009. "*Ad iudicem vocare,*" in *Studi in onore di Remo Martini.* Milan. Vol. 3: 55–68.

Pergami, F. 2000. *L'appello nella legislazione del tardo impero.* Milan.

Pergami, F. 2007. "Effetto devolutorio e *ius novorum* nel processo romano della *cognitio extra ordinem.*" In C. Masi Doria and C. Cascione, eds., Fides Humanitas Ius: *Studi in onore di Luigi Labruna.* Vol. 6. Naples. 4145–4161.

Platschek, J. (2001). "Das *ius Verrinum* im Fall des Heraclius von Syrakus." *Zeitschrift der Savigny-Stiftung für Rechtsgeschichte, romanistische Abteilung* 118: 134–263.

Puliatti, S. 2010. "Accertamento della *veritas rei* e principio dispositivo nel processo postclassico romano." In S. Puliatti and U. Agnati, eds., *Principi generali e tecniche operative del processo civile romano nei secoli iv-vi d. C.* Parma. 103–128.

Rizzi, M. 2012. *Imperator cognoscens decrevit.* Milan.

Robles Reyes, J. R. 2009. *Magistrados, jueces y árbitros en Roma.* Madrid.

Russo Ruggeri, C. 1998. "Nota minima sulla competenza del pretore in età giustinianea." *Index* 26: 99–108.

Santalucia, B. 1998[2]. *Diritto e processo penale nell'antica Roma.* Milan.

Simon, D. 1969. *Untersuchungen zum justinianischen Zivilprozeß.* Munich.

Sirks, A. J. B. 2009. "*Cognitio* and imperial and bureaucratic courts." In S. N. Katz, ed., *The Oxford international encyclopedia of legal history.* Oxford. Vol. 2: 51–54.

Spagnuolo Vigorita, T. 2007. "La repubblica restaurata e il prestigio di Augusto. Diversioni sulle origini della *cognitio* imperiale," in *Studi per Giovanni Nicosia.* Milan. Vol. 7: 521–543.

Torrent, A. (2013). "*Lex rivi Hiberiensis* desde el processo formulario a la *cognitio extra ordinem.*" *Index* 41: 437–454.

Turpin, W. (1999). "*Formula, cognitio,* and proceedings *extra ordinem.*" *Revue internationale des droits de l'antiquité* 46: 499–574.

Valiño, A. (2000). "En torno a la adscripción al procedimento formulario de D. 5, 1, 79 pr. (Ulp. 5 de off. Procons.)." *Iura* 51: 87–105.

Valiño, A. (2003). "A proposito de la condena en costas en el derecho justinianeo." *Revue internationale des droits de l'antiquité* 50: 401–441.

von der Fecht, W.-R. 1996. *Die Forderungspfändung im römischen Recht.* Cologne.

Wacke, A. (1996). "Die Anerkennung der Medizin als *ars liberalis* und der Honoraranspruch des Arztes." *Zeitschrift der Savigny-Stiftung für Rechtsgeschichte, romanistische Abteilung* 113: 382–421.

Wieling, H. 1996. "Advokaten im spätantiken Rom," in *Atti dell'Accademia romanistica Costantiniana. XI. Convegno Internazionale.* Naples. 419–463.

Winkel, L. 2010. "L'exécution réelle dans le droit romain classique et postclassique." In C. Russo Ruggeri, ed., *Studi in onore di Antonio Metro.* Milan. Vol. 6: 481–488.

CHAPTER 21

EVIDENCE AND ARGUMENT

The Truth of Prestige and its Performance

ELIZABETH A. MEYER

21.1 Introduction

"What is truth?" Pilate is, famously, alleged to have asked Jesus (John 18:38). This question, at least phrased this way, was awkward for a Roman court, and indeed modern commentators debate whether truth had any place in the Roman courts at all. For although Cicero called the court "a place for truth" (*Clu.* 202) and the centrality of truth as an aim of the Roman courts has recently been stressed (Riggsby 1999; Masi Doria 2013, 21–28), this emphasis was in response both to an energetic and well-founded claim that the courts functioned primarily as an agonistic venue that pitted the status ("reputation and place") of plaintiff and defendant against each other (Swarney 1993, 155) and to a challenge that juries rewarded outstanding performance with victory regardless of the facts (Zetzel 1994). It is in the context of this larger debate that the observable lack of emphasis given to the deployment of evidence (at least as we would understand evidence) and the notable obsession with argumentation (including attention lavished on arguments that we would consider unfair or irrelevant) gain significance. For the subordination of evidence *to* argumentation is not a Roman perversion of justice and truth, but a clue that helps to illuminate the physics of the Roman courts, what forces governed their matter and motion.

Roman legal regulation did not control the use of evidence or the forms of argumentation (Powell and Paterson 2004, 33); here, as Aquilius Gallus once tartly remarked in another legal matter, "*nihil … ad ius; ad Ciceronem*" ("nothing involving the law; [it's a matter] for Cicero", Cic. *Top.* 51). Evidence and argument were elements of the rhetorical art of persuasion, and persuasion, Cicero argued emphatically, was based on "what fellow-citizens … think, feel, believe, and hope" (*De or.* 1.223). So success in the courts, the Roman speaker's aim, depended on shared Roman expectations, and these proved remarkably stable from the middle Republic through (at least) the third century AD. Such expectations admitted truth as a desirable goal—Cicero stated that the role of the judge was "always to follow the truth"—but in practice preferred graspable verisimilitude in the presentation of a case.[1] This therefore meant that truth and its methods of demonstration—arguments and evidence—received their warmest welcome when conveyed by people radiating social prestige, *dignitas* and *auctoritas*. For Romans in court, truth and social status were not matter and anti-matter, destined to destroy each other. Rather, while truth was constructed out of arguments and evidence, as matter is of atoms, the sub-atomic particles—the participants displaying the many worthy and status-related qualities, both internal and external, esteemed in Roman society—were bound together into atoms and molecules by the force of prestige. Moreover, like matter in nature, truth upon investigation was not static: the courts, setting participants into motion, observed and measured their behaviour, for in a trial a man's worthy qualities were not just stressed but, necessarily, performed, and performance under stress proved an individual's worth and thereby demonstrated the truth of his claims. This is why the most eventful revelations in the Roman courts took the form of loss of self-control or of rhetorical fluency, not surprise eyewitnesses or newly discovered incriminating documents—and why trials were dramatic and entertaining. Explosions of expectations could occur.

21.2 Evidence, Argument and Prestige

Types of evidence ("materials for the proving", *materies ad probandum*) are listed and discussed in several rhetorical treatises. Cicero (*De or.* 2.100, 116) mentioned *tabulae* ("tablet-documents"), witness-testimony, pacts, agreements, stipulations, laws, *senatus consulta*, agreements, legal decisions, blood-kin, relatives by marriage, decrees, juristic responses, the lives of the participants; Quintilian (*Inst.* 5.1.2, borrowing in part from Aristotle) added evidence obtained under torture, previous judgements, rumours, and oaths. Already it is clear that this universe is not our universe: for us, rumours, our relations, and our lives are not "evidence" (May 2002), and forensic science has transformed how our courts can think about facts and evidence. Many of the types of proof listed by Cicero and Quintilian that correspond more closely to our idea of evidence are not seen in action very often,[2] and indeed only two seem to be referred to with any frequency in actual cases, *tabulae* and witnesses or written witness-testimony. And only *tabulae* seem to have independent weight, i.e. impact that comes from the fact of their existence rather than from who made them (for the reasons see Meyer 2004, 218–225). The value of the contribution of the other types is deeply enmeshed in the quasi-gravitational force field of prestige, where the weight of witnesses and testimony or of written documents such as archives or letters was affected by the perceived prestige of their authors (Meyer 2004, 229–232). Thus all of the letters (*litterae*) that Verres and his friends adduce at trial in 70 BC are proof only (in Cicero's nimble reinterpretation) of Verres' wickedness—because Verres' villainy, the major argument, Cicero has already established.[3] Similarly, because Apuleius' opponents in his trial

[1] *Off.* 2.51 (where, also, a client's acts must be depicted as *veri simile* even if a speaker must depart from truth); Quint. *Inst.* 4.2.31–32, 34 and 6.2.5 (job of the orator can be to "wrench the minds of the jury away from the contemplation of truth"). See Gotoff 1993, 290, 297; Riggsby 1999, 1–11.

[2] Although Powell 2010 rightly points out that the procedures of the courts (there was an "evidentiary phase" that generated no published speeches) and the intent of an author in publishing a speech combine to reduce the profile of evidence in what survives; but if evidence were crucially important to how a case was conceived this would have been reflected in the speeches, and is not.

[3] Cic. *Verr.* 2.1.83; 2.3.92; 2.3.122–128; 2.3.154–157; 2.3.167–168.

for magic of 158–159 AD are stupid and uneducated rustics, the letters they bring in as proof have clearly been misread (stupid!) or forged (bad Greek!), although these opponents no doubt intended that, once they had established that Apuleius was a shady character, the letters would prove that he was a magician (*Apol.* 78–83, 87). No surviving speech, in short, ever gives the impression that it was built around external proofs. Rather, argument was a coherent and joyous masterpiece and itself a type of proof (Cic. *De or.* 2.116), its component parts and techniques borrowed from the overflowing toolbox of the Greek rhetorical tradition, studied, taught, adapted to a Roman context, and practiced. Most students of rhetoric knew the six or seven parts of a speech (*digressio* was optional), the thirty or so types of argument (*topoi*), the commonplaces, the rhetorical figures, the collections of exemplary anecdotes, the interpretations of the situation (*colores*) so beloved of practice declamation: these were configured, practiced, and second nature to speakers and listeners alike. Argumentation mattered above all: "to a good judge", said Cicero, "arguments are more powerful than witnesses" (*Rep.* 1.59). Argument incorporated, but preceded and dominated, proof (Broggini 1964, 243, 271; Pugliese 1964, 282; Crook 1995, 18–21).

But what were arguments used *for*—what did speakers use them to *say*? When one looks for repeated, and therefore widely successful, argumentation, one does not need to look far to see a pattern. No matter the type of case or court, however lofty or humble,[4] prestige underpinned any argument a Roman advocate had, and aspects of its preeminence were eventually enshrined in high- and late-Imperial law.[5] Sometimes identified as "character-" or "*ethos*-based" argument (May 1988; Wisse 1989; Riggsby 2004), arguments employing prestige actually depended on a wider and more socially significant set of characteristics than "character" alone implies (*Rhet. Her.* 3.10–15; Cic. *Off.* 2.44–51; Lendon 1997, 34–43). Known qualities of prestige included bloodline, financial resources, legal status (often deducible from clothing), magistracies currently or formerly held, achievements, social importance (were crowds of clients present? important friends?), moral character (both rumoured and judgeable through public deportment) and education. The nouns used to indicate prestige were similarly various (estimation, brightness, reputation, glory, weightiness; and especially *dignitas* and *auctoritas*, "worthiness" and "authority"), the adjectives tending towards superlatives and evocations of weight and visual brilliance (Garnsey 1970, 223–233; Lendon 1997, 58–63, 272–276).

Roman treatises on rhetoric therefore devote much time to the central task of establishing a protagonist's abundant prestige, and the denial of this to the adversary: most of the atom's mass is in its nucleus. The earliest, the pseudo-Ciceronian *Rhetorica ad Herennium*, encourages laudation of a protagonist, especially for duties (*officia*), along with vilification of an adversary (1.8; 2.5), and outstanding deeds, excellence, and good birth are all grounds (if need be) for pardon (2.25). Cicero expands this (*Inv. rhet.* 2.32–37), noting also that the

[4] We know less about smaller civil cases with one judge or cases heard in front of "rustic" judges in the cities of Italy, but Quintilian's *Institutio oratoria* is self-consciously addressed to *all* would-be speakers at *all* levels (e.g. 8.3.14; 11.1.42, 44–48; 12.10.53), and although he recommends adjusting rhetorical tone downwards for lesser courts, the dependence of arguments on prestige remains the same.

[5] Greenidge 1901, 272–275, 481–482; Lévy 1959, 192–197; Garnsey 1970; Honoré 1981, 174–175; Burton 1987, 431–434; Fiori 2013 examines the origins and continued (but declining, he argues) influence of what he calls "hierarchy" on proof in court.

protagonist's *dignitas* is the heart of a credible narration (*Inv. rhet.* 1.29), that it is especially effective to stress, also, other "external" excellences (money, blood-kin, family, friends, homeland, *Inv. rhet.* 2.177), and that diminution of a protagonist's *honor* and *auctoritas* will diminish, also, his defence (*Inv. rhet.* 2.33). *Dignitas*, deeds, and an "estimation of life" establish "habits, intentions, deeds": they create the presumption that the story the orator tells is true (*De or.* 2.182–183). Quintilian agrees, noting the importance of stressing the *dignitas* of the client (*Inst.* 2.15.6; 4.1.13). "Character" (*animus* or *persona*) is part of what is stressed, but character was defined in terms of Roman prestige, not an internal or ethical standard of goodness, and was measured by achievement and deportment that correlated with social standing.[6] Poverty, for example, both deformed character and was an external sign of deformed character, while wealth (properly acquired and wisely deployed) was an external sign of internal excellence. In sum, the establishment of prestigious qualities had "a miraculous effect", and in openings, in stating the case, or in the peroration was "so strong … that it was often worth more than the case itself", as Cicero has Antonius say in the *De oratore* (2.184). Quintilian must, indeed, warn the neophyte that the "fortune" (the powerful or humble position) of the protagonist does not *alone* make the case just or unjust (*Inst.* 12.7.6).

This reliance on the prestige of the protagonists was not merely hypothetical, a matter of learned discussion passed on from handbook to handbook. Its importance to Romans in judging a case explains indignation when it is not effective (e.g. Cic. *Clu.* 95), as well as the odd fact, long known, that most Roman court cases took place between approximate social equals. The small did not attack the great in court. Why? Because they knew they could not win: most aspects of a person's prestige were public knowledge and could be estimated before a court case was even undertaken. And the great did not attack the small in court either, because this was seen as both unnecessary and poor form. Magistrates, whose official *potestas* increased their personal prestige and powers of prosecution (Cic. *Clu.* 154), could themselves bring cases against The Great, but risked terrible and public failure. When summoned, by a tribune, on a charge of encouraging allies to rebel in 90 BC, M. Aemilius Scaurus (cos. 115 BC) arrived in the forum, supported (because of illness and great age) by "certain young *nobiles*", and said, " 'Q. Varius asserts that M. Scaurus, *princeps senatus*, called upon the allies to resort to war; M. Scaurus, *princeps senatus*, denies the accusation; there is no witness; Quirites, which of us do you choose to believe?' "—that is, a tribune or (as he twice repeated) the *princeps senatus*? "With these words he transformed everyone's attitude, and the tribune of the *plebs* himself let him go."[7] This preliminary skirmish of prestige proved the parties too unequal. No trial occurred, although other Varian witch-hunts in this first year of the Social War did convict three men—of lower status (Gruen 1965, 68).

So estimates were made even before a case was brought. Once a case began, prestige also shaped the strategies followed. The appeal of prestige-arguments was universal, a kind of lowest-common-denominator argument that all juries, even the least well-educated, could grasp (Cic. *Fin.* 4.74 on Murena's trial, with May 1988, 59). So protagonists and

[6] Cic. *Leg.* 1.27, facial expression (*vultus*) reveals habits (*mores*), and *mores* and moral virtues are part of *dignitas* (Cic. *Off.* 1.45–46). See Garnsey 1970, 208, 210, 223, 258–259; Lendon 1997, 40–41.

[7] Asc. *Scaur.* 22C; Val. Max. 3.7.8; Quint. *Inst.* 5.12.10.

their relatives are all described in sparkling and superlative prestige-terms by Cicero.[8] Opponents, on the other hand, are massively and memorably vilified: as, for example, gladiators and gladiatorial trainers, and as men of bad moral character or inappropriately lavish lifestyle or reprehensible personal appearance (including wearing non-Roman clothing).[9] Verres alone is depicted as a robber, a pirate, a pestilence; adulterous and impious; poorly educated and ignorant of Greek; ungrateful and disloyal; greedy; a violator of guardianship (*tutela*); a practitioner of bribery and extortion in the past, and intent on them in the future.[10] In sum, "he is a man of no *auctoritas*" (*Verr.* 2.3.19). Two hundred years later, Apuleius can denigrate his opponents in many of the same ways, with an added emphasis on how stupid and uneducated they are: audacious, rapacious, and avaricious; rustic, ugly, greedy and drunken, ungrateful; and mocking of the divine.[11] It was, therefore, perfectly appropriate to build a case on prestige and prestige alone. Appius Annius Atilius Bradua, attired in patrician sandals and bringing a murder charge (after having waited three years, so he could accuse while holding the consulship) against his brother-in-law L. Vibullius Hipparchus Tiberius Claudius Atticus Herodes, offered no evidence, preferring only to praise himself, his family and his benefaction to an Italian city. This strategy gave Herodes Atticus the opportunity to say in response, with a meaningful look at Bradua's footwear, "you have your good birth in your toe-joints". Herodes himself was equally distinguished (if more Greek) in descent but a man famous for his education and far richer, and had provided benefactions throughout the Empire (as he pointed out). He was acquitted—in a case summarised by Philostratus as "the truth prevailed" (*VS* 555–556). To remind listeners of a protagonist's great prestige was usually successful.[12] Bradua's unfortunate problem was that Herodes' prestige, when all was summed up, was just a nanogram greater than his own.

Speaking of your own wonderfulness, as in this case, was also perfectly acceptable. Cato the Elder too had praised himself, reading out a list of the good deeds of his ancestors as well as his own (*ORF*³ 173), and Pompey had been "an exceptionally eloquent narrator of his own exploits" (Quint. *Inst.* 11.1.36); perhaps most spectacularly, Apuleius defending himself on a charge of magic stressed that he was rich and a *duumvir* (joint-mayor) from a "most splendid" (Roman) colony (*Apol.* 24); oppressively well-educated, a theme

[8] *Rosc. Amer.* 24; *Q. Rosc.* 17–19; *Caecin.* 104; *Font.* 37, 40–41; *Clu.* 11, 196; *Rab. perd.* 2; *Mur.* 15–54; *Sull.* 69–82; *Flacc.* 8, 24–25, 100–101, 104–106; *Sest.* 5–17; *Cael.* 1, and see also Ramage 1985 on metaphors of brilliance for Caelius and his supporters; *Planc.* 3 (life of greatest integrity, the most modest habits, the highest trustworthiness—"all the qualities to be expected from good men"), 32, 60–62, 67; *Scaur.* 13, 46–50; *Deiot.* 16, 26.

[9] *Rosc. Amer.* 17, 109–118, 133–135; *Q. Rosc.* 20; *Sest.* 18–26; *Mil.* 73–78, 87 (Clodius). See McClintock 1975; May 1988; Craig 2004.

[10] Merely a selection: robber, 1.11; pirate and pestilence, 1.2; adulterous, 1.14; impious, 2.1.6–7; poorly educated, 2.1.47, 2.4.126–127 (Verres knows no Greek!); ungrateful and disloyal, 2.1.39–40; greed, 1.42; violator of *tutela*, 2.1.153; bribery, 1.16–25; extortion, 2.2.165.

[11] 1 (audacious), 34, 53 (stupid), 5, 9, 17, 38 (uneducated), with 30 (no knowledge of Greek); 91, 99 (rapacious and avaricious); 9, 10, 16, 53, 66 (rustic); 16 (ugly), 222 (greedy and drunken, of a witness), 98, 85–86 (ungrateful, of a witness), and 56 (mocking divine).

[12] Success from prestige, e.g. Cic. *Div. Caec.* 64; Val. Max. 8.1. abs. 10; *P. Oxy.* 1408 lines 9–10 (21–214 AD), Tryphon *axiologotatos* and he wins; Lieberman 1944–1945, 24–25 gives examples from rabbinic sources.

throughout the entire speech; and possessed of many high-status friends (*Apol.* 57–58, 61–62, 72). In rolling one's credits, one only had to avoid *exceptionally* arrogant immodesty (Cic. *De or.* 2.209), although even here, as Quintilian put it, "there is a form of eloquence that is becoming in the greatest men, but inadmissable in others" (*Inst.* 11.1.36; also 8.2.1).

The evocation of the prestige of a protagonist thus applied a kind of gravitational constant, always giving weight to arguments used in any Roman court—although the force prestige exerted was more powerful than gravity, and closer to the orders-of-magnitude-greater "strong interaction" of particle physics. The character-argument—"my client is this type of person, therefore he could not have done this"—is a universal argument, identified as such by Apuleius himself (*Apol.* 90), and still employed today (Powell and Paterson 2004, 36). Both worked together in the Roman court.

21.3 Witnesses

Supporting this fundamental and forceful argument was the prestige of witnesses. As handbooks exhorted, prestigious witnesses added to the prestige of the litigant;[13] it was the work of the wise judge "to weigh each [witness] according to his force (*momentum*)", said Cicero (*Font.* 21). More witnesses were always better, since their weight accumulated, and only one might eventually be claimed to be insufficient, "even were he Cato", men said (Plut. *Cat. Min.* 19.4), which makes clear that it was *auctoritas* of precisely Cato's sort that was most desirable.[14] Indeed, although the seeming independence of witnesses was important (Powell 2010, 28–29)—so that they would truly add their own weight—it sometimes seemed that witnesses were also called only to praise the defendant. Asconius (*Scaur.* 28C) noted that Scaurus in 54 BC had been praised by nine consulars, and such so-called *laudatores* were customarily (said Cicero) at least ten in number (*Verr.* 2.5.57). This was a practice that Pompey tried but failed to curb in 52 BC (Dio Cass. 40.52.2), because prestige had to have its say, because *laudatores* and witnesses could so rarely be distinguished, and because numbers increased the weight of an advocate's case. Quintilian found it easy to commend *honesti* as witnesses to the court (*Inst.* 5.7.24).

Witnesses were chosen carefully, not only for the contribution of their weight but because a witness's contribution was given weight by his own personal standing: his life was *his* "witness" (Cic. *Sull.* 79). As Cicero explained in the *Topica* (73):

> it is not every person who is worth consideration as a witness. To establish credibility (*fides*), prestige (*auctoritas*) is sought; but *auctoritas* is given by one's nature or circumstances. *Auctoritas* from one's nature depends largely on excellence (*virtus*); in circumstances there are many things that lend *auctoritas*, such as talent, wealth, age, [good luck,] skill, experience, necessity, and even at times a concurrence of fortuitous events. For it is common belief that the talented (*ingeniosi*), the wealthy, and those proved worthy (*digni*) by long life are credible. This may not be correct, but the opinion of the common people

[13] e.g. *Rhet. Her.* 2.9; at 4.2, even historical *exempla* are to be chosen from only "most approved" (*probatissimi*) authors; Quint. *Inst.* 5.7.23–34.

[14] This became a legal principle, CTh.11.39.3 = C.4.20.9 (a. 337).

> can hardly be changed, and both those who make judicial decisions and those who judge reputations (*existimant*) steer their course by that.

Judges of court cases and reputations believe that prestige creates credibility: convincing truth is the possession of those who are prestigious. Cicero claimed that "everyone knows that *auctoritas* helps in proving the truth, not backing a lie" (*Quinct.* 75), and Apuleius noted that because one of his own witnesses was "weighty" and "upstanding" his testimony was "most convincing and truthful" (*Apol.* 61–62). Prestige and truth go hand in hand because the first is the foundation of the second. Hadrian wrote, in the high Empire, that judges were free to judge as they wished, since judges knew "what [witnesses'] *dignitas* and 'estimation' are", and "sometimes the number of witnesses, sometimes their *dignitas* and *auctoritas*, at others common knowledge settles the truth ... you must judge from your own conviction what you believe and what you find not proved" (D.22.5.3.1–2).[15]

A successful case was, then, buttressed by witnesses whose prestige confirmed the truth of what they said and added to that of the defendant. This emphasis on witnesses' prestige could be so strong that it could even obscure the factual relevance of witnesses' evidence. An extreme example of this in the late Republic: P. Servilius Isauricus happened to be passing by the forum when a trial was taking place, and recognising the defendant, he stepped forward as an impromptu witness and said (Val. Max. 8.5.6):

> "Judges, I know nothing about the man on trial—where he comes from, or what sort of a life he has led, or whether the charge is brought deservedly or out of malice. *This*, however, I know: that when he encountered me making a journey on the Via Laurentina in a rather narrow place, he refused to dismount from his horse. You yourselves will judge whether this has any relevance to your scrupulosity (*religio*); I thought it should not be suppressed." The jurors, hardly listening to all the other witnesses, found the defendant guilty. For among them was valued both the greatness (*amplitudo*) of the man [Servilius Isauricus] and his serious indignation at his neglected *dignitas*, and they believed that he who did not know how to respect 'first men' (*principes*) would rush into any sort of crime.

A consular and former censor with *amplitudo* speaks about an important character trait in a man he does not know, and of no direct factual relevance to the issue at trial; the man is instantly condemned. Thus you can see, concluded Dio (45.16.1–2), "how the Romans of that period respected men who were prominent through worth (*axiōma*) and hated those who behaved insolently, even in the smallest matters". Cicero also acted in accordance with the assumption that prestige and praise mattered most, certainly more than direct knowledge of the facts (see esp. *Q. Rosc.* 42–44).[16]

The branding of opposing witnesses as "light" or insignificant (*leves*) was also, therefore, one aim of the energetic advocate. Sometimes it was easy: women and boys were light by definition, as were provincials, especially Greeks ("scruple and trustworthiness in the giving of testimony that nation has never cherished", Cic. *Flacc.* 9); others, even citizens, could be denounced for poverty, bad moral character, general lack of *auctoritas*, or for

[15] Judges should also look for *fides*, D.22.5.1, *dignitas, fides, mores, gravitas* (D.22.5.2), and social status (*condicio*; D.22.5.3pr).

[16] See Schmitz 1985 and 1989.

simply being "unknown".[17] Confronted with distinguished witnesses, on the other hand, one must either cross-examine them closely or (a dangerous tactic) damage their prestige. When Cicero faced such a situation—five "first men also powerful in the senate" who were "most brilliant"—Asconius (*Corn.* 60–61C) claims that he was very careful indeed, arguing only against their *interpretation* of events. He "did not do violence to the *dignitas* of these most distinguished citizens", displaying "moderation" in the "very difficult task" of not allowing their *auctoritas* to damage his client.

21.4 Advocates

Protagonists must be, or be depicted as, outstandingly prestigious—to the greatest extent that reality and artfulness would allow; witnesses too, whose standing added to that of the protagonist and acted as a guarantee of the truth of their testimony, even if it was often only praise. But the demiurge in this universe of excellence was the advocate himself, who not only set the electrons spinning around the nucleus but added himself to this cloud of particles in motion. For the prestige of the advocate contributed to the case he was arguing too. "Lucius Philippus will fight for me, most flourishing man of the polity in eloquence, weight, and honour; Hortensius, excelling in talent, nobility, estimation, will speak; noble men support me", Naevius is imagined gloating in the *Pro Quinctio* (72).[18] The Athenians in the second century AD appealed to two massively splendid consular brothers to bring their oppression by a "tyrant" (Herodes Atticus) to the attention of the emperor (Philostr. *VS* 559). But persons of lower prestige, like Christians or men out of favour with the emperor, had to soldier on with no advocate at all, or with second-choice replacements—for as Cicero noted in another context, the most difficult cases got only the worst and most obscure advocates, "perhaps because ... orators must also offer up their *auctoritas*" (*Clu.* 57).[19]

Since prestige was necessary in an advocate, it (like that of protagonists and witnesses) had to be advertised. Cicero began his career circumspectly, but during and after his consulship, he would be less delicate—his friends, his achievements, his talents, and his reputation all figure in speeches ostensibly made on behalf of other people.[20] This deeply satisfying strutting was, and was intended, to assist the client, as again the handbooks

[17] Women: Cic. *Flacc.* 90–93. Provincials and Greeks: Cic. *Flacc.* 9–10, 36, 64–66; *Font.* 14–16, 27–33, 44–46 (Gauls); *Scaur.* 38–45 (Sardinians); *Rab. post.* 34–36 (Alexandrian Greeks). See Vasaly 1993, 192–218; Riggsby 1999, 130–136. Others "lessened": Cic. *Flacc.* 6–24, 34–36, 40 (an "unknown"), 42–53 ("a man poor, sordid, without honour, without estimation, without money"). Apuleius' accuser was also dismissed as "through rustication, unknown" (*Apol.* 16).

[18] Philippus can "choose" to plead, so perhaps was there as a character-witness (Cic. *Quinct.* 80).

[19] Advocates for Christians start in the mid-third century: *Act. Pion.* 5.2–3, 6; *Act. Max.* 1.1; *Act. Phil.* (Greek) col. XII lines 196–197 and (Latin) 1.3, 4.1, 5.5, 6.2 and 4, 8.1 (all in Musurillo 1972). Those out of Imperial favour, e.g. M. Scribonius Libo (Tac. *Ann.* 2.29: none of his wife's relatives would help him) and Calpurnius Piso (Tac. *Ann.* 3.11: five refused before three others stepped up). Mart. 2.32 complained that patrons too often made excuses to clients, refusing to speak.

[20] May 1981 and esp. 1988, 51, 89–90, 163–169; Paterson 2004.

make clear.[21] This could work in three ways. The advocate was physically present, so this added to his client's weight. Torquatus when consul in 65 BC acted as Catiline's *advocatus* and was depicted (perhaps not only metaphorically) as bringing his *sella curulis* and *ornamenta* (Cic. *Sull.* 81–82) to bear on the case. He was successful—as was Cicero in a trial of *his* consular year, when he lectured the jury, "listen, listen to the consul!" (Cic. *Mur.* 78; also 86 and 90). More distinction in an advocate was always better, and a great effect could also be achieved by the multiplication of distinguished advocates (Crook 1995, 127–129).

Moreover, Cicero often emphasised similarities between himself and his client, so that his prestige would bolster that of his client even more directly,[22] and he and other advocates would extend the force of this strategy by emphasising similarities between protagonist, speaker and judge or jury. "I have appeared as the prosecutor" of Verres, Cicero cries, "by the greatest desire and with the greatest expectation of the Roman people, not to increase the ill-will felt for the [senatorial] *ordo*, but to help in ameliorating *our* common dishonour!" (*Verr.* 1.2). Apuleius referred repeatedly to the common bonds of education and philosophy he shared with the judge in his case (*Apol.* 1, 11, 25, 36, 38, and so on). In 216 AD, a very distinguished Roman speaking for Gohariene peasants (imagine!) before Caracalla intoned: "To the peasants, the contest (*agōn*) is over piety (*eusebeia*), and to you [Caracalla] nothing is more important than piety. So now they have confidence in the present instance contesting a case before a most pious king and judge."[23] We are like you; we are sure, therefore, that you will find in our favour.

Finally, the speaker's *auctoritas* undergirds the credibility of the claims he is making on his own, or his client's, behalf. What Cicero is in effect saying is, I—Cicero!—believe in him (for he is like me); I—Cicero!—believe in what I am saying; therefore you should believe me and him. And Cicero lost very rarely; there was so much *auctoritas* "in everything he said", said Quintilian (*Inst.* 10.1.111–112), that people were ashamed to disagree with him. As Quintilian summarised, a worthy advocate displays the *auctoritas* of the *vir bonus et gravis*, thereby adding his own distinction to the case he is representing; and the *auctoritas* of the speaker, derived from his life and his manner of speaking, imparts *fides* or trustworthiness to his narration of the case (Quint. *Inst.* 11.3.184, 4.2.125). If the advocate was believed to be a "good man", then this would be of the utmost weight at every point; indeed, he would thereby add to the case "not the diligence of the advocate but very nearly the credibility of the witness" (*Inst.* 4.1.7), and in turn the credibility he had shown when a witness, if he had ever been one, enhanced (said Cicero) his *auctoritas* as an advocate (*Sull.* 9–10 with *Schol. Bob.* 7).

Opponents also did not hesitate to take cruel advantage of an advocate's low prestige. Cicero in defending Roscius of Ameria pitied Erucius (the opposing speaker) his questionable paternity and his overconfident deportment (*Rosc. Amer.* 46, 59–61). Torquatus in prosecuting Sulla called Cicero a *peregrinus* (since he was, after all, from Arpinum; Cic. *Sull.* 22–23), and Asinius when defending Urbina's heirs argued openly that the choice of Labienus as plaintiff's advocate was proof that the plaintiff had a poor case (Quint. *Inst.*

[21] Cic. *De or.* 2.182, 3.211; Quint. *Inst.* 6.2.18 (*bonitas* of speaker especially beneficial to client in any case).

[22] e.g. in *Mur.* 3, *Sull.* 2 and 35, *Flacc.* 101; at *Mil.* 100 Cicero stresses what he has done *for* Milo; *Deiot.* 39 (*amicitia* with Deiotarus); see May 1988, 59–60.

[23] Gohariene: *SEG* XVII 759 col. II.35–37. Other direct appeals to similarity or bonds, e.g. Strabo 14.5.674; Sen. *Ben.* 5.24.1–3; Quint. *Inst.* 3.7.25; Dio Cass. 54.21.8.

4.1.11). Even Ulpian later noted the problem created by advocates without any *dignitas* (D.1.16.9.4). *Auctoritas* in the speaker was, in short, crucial, as it had been, also, for witnesses and protagonists: for the same reasons, and in many of the same ways.

Merely *being* prestigious was not, however, enough. To win through, the particular participants in a trial had to move according to laws of the Roman universe: all—protagonist, witnesses, advocates—had to *demonstrate* their *auctoritas*, behave in ways appropriate to, and commensurate with, their prestige. Acting and speaking with the dignity and weight attributed to you were necessary, and it was particularly important for those with prestige to show it by revering it in others. Thus, "I know what is due to your weightiness, to this assistance [the *assessores*], that gathering of citizens, what the *dignitas* of P. Sestius, the greatness of his danger, my age, and my high position demand", rhapsodised Cicero to the jury (*Sest.* 119): prestige places many demands upon the speaker, but above all the proper observance of what is due to judge or judges, audience, client and to the advocate himself, and when displayed identifies and binds all parties to each other into molecules of truth, excluding opponents.[24] The blind man is not even allowed to approach the praetor, because "he cannot see and respect the magistrate's insignia" (D.3.1.1.5). One demonstrates one's own prestige through style and delivery of speech, which "depicts, as it were, the *mores* of the speaker" (Cic. *De or.* 2.184), but one shows a fine discrimination and understanding of the judge's prestige by varying one's style of address depending on the judge to whom one was speaking (Quint. *Inst.* 11.1.43–45).

Everyone understood the concept; but mistakes could be made. A distinguished person (or his advocate) could pursue a misguided strategy or bring disgrace upon himself.[25] Hectoring, inappropriate joking, impertinent interruption, improper tone, intransigence, indecorous walking or gesturing, or even the wrong clothes—all of which showed a lack of deference to the judges—identified you as the Wrong Sort of Person, as did loss of control. They made you less dignified than people had thought; they made you unlike your (dignified) judges; they made you less worthy of deference, less credible, and more likely to have behaved in the ways opponents said you had. Rutilius Rufus in 92 BC spoke "not as a suppliant or a defendant, but rather as [the jury's] teacher and master" (*magister et dominus*; Cic. *De or.* 1.231), and—shockingly—lost. Isidorus before Claudius, the Alexandrians before Gaius, Appian before Commodus, Christians before provincial governors in martyr-acts, all behave with a ghastly impudence that—from a Roman point of view—made their eventual failure, even execution, all but inevitable.[26] Their demeanour alone made their essential

[24] Cic. *Rosc. Amer.* 10; Cic. *Q. Rosc.* 15; *Planc.* 2; *Rab. post.* 6; *Mil.* 99 (the jury has always esteemed Cicero); Quint. *Inst.* 4.1.16–22.

[25] See *Rhet. Her.* 4.60, the prestigious man who proves he lacks *virtus*.

[26] Isidorus: at *Act. Alex.* no. 4 iii.5–51 (Musurillo 1954, 19) accuses Claudius of being the Jewess Salome's son; he is condemned. Alexandrians: before Gaius their "great laughter" showed "disrespect to the emperor, for whom even a measured smile is unsafe", Philo *Leg.* 361; at *Act. Alex.* no. 8 iii.4–42 (Musurillo 1954, 45) Trajan says to Alexandrians, "you must be eager to die, having such contempt for death as to answer even me with insolence." Appian: *Act. Alex.* no. 11 iv.82–84 (Musurillo 1954, 67), Commodus calls Appian "one who has lost all sense of shame" in Philostr. *VA* 8.4 Apollonius is accused of lack of respect because he refuses even to look at the Emperor. Christians: *Act. Scill. Mart.* 14 (Musurillo 1972, 88 no. 6), obstinacy to be punished; *Act. Crisp.* 5 (Musurillo 1972, 304 no. 24), accused is "hard and contemptuous". Refusing to answer is contumacy, cf. D.11.1.11.4; see Sherwin-White 1952, 21–211, along with Johnson 1927, 23–24 on proper behaviour before tribunal.

wrongness patent: so Pliny drew character-lessons, and diagnosed guilt, from the "pertinaciousness" and "inflexible obstinacy" of the Christians who came before him (*Ep.* 10.96.3), and Apuleius encouraged Maximus the judge to view Apuleius' persistently *pertinax* opponent in the same light (*Apol.* 2–3). Judges quite properly paid attention to appearance (and dress, especially the toga)[27] and to deportment, and self-control was important as well. When in dispute with the Athenians in 173 or 174 AD, Herodes Atticus' great prestige barely prevailed against the pressure of Marcus Aurelius' wife and daughter, the standing of the Athenians, and his own grief-crazed invective against the emperor—a shocking loss of control. "With an aggressive and unguarded tongue ... he cried, 'This is what I get for showing hospitality to Lucius [Verus] ...! These are the grounds on which you judge men, and you sacrifice me to the whim of a woman and a three-year-old child!'" (Philostr. *VS* 56–561). Emotional outbursts lowered high prestige or were clear signs of low prestige, for they contravened standards of appropriate behaviour in the great or confirmed a capacity for immoderation and untruth in the lesser (cf. Quint. *Inst.* 11.1.29). An opponent's lunge or stumble into impropriety was the hope of every ambitious advocate, as was the judicious, tempered, dignified and effective demonstration of his own protagonist's prestige.

Witnesses could make mistakes as well. Proper—careful—behaviour had to be observed, for witnesses too could bring harm to themselves (and the case) by losing control, by haranguing rather than testifying. "Remember, when any of *you* gives testimony", Cicero said, addressing a jury, "how you are accustomed to be careful ... even in the words you use, lest any word seem to be immoderate, or to have slipped out because of some passion!" (*Font.* 28). The demeanour of the witness must be respectful; he must take his task seriously; he must watch his words; he must not contradict himself; he must display no animus. Being Roman, he is of course incapable of lying (unlike Greeks: Cic. *Flacc.* 9–12), even when righteously incensed. But being pushy or eager to do damage is a mistake and made even prestigious witnesses "light" (Cicero *Sull* 79; Valerius Maximus 8.5.3, 4). The Right Sort of witnesses, behaving properly, were allowed to pose very polite challenges to "good men", but others were not, and passion and anger were to be avoided at all cost.

The Roman court therefore could, despite its orderly and perceptible mechanics, be a place of surprising events, of unpredictable detonations. Even bystanders, in a kind of Roman "observer effect", could affect the outcome with *their* prestige: as Cicero said when defending Publius Sulla, "all those who are present, who make an effort, who want the defendant acquitted, defend him to the extent of their participation and *auctoritas*" (*Sull.* 4). The *corona*, the circle of spectators at a trial, itself had *auctoritas* and *dignitas* (Cic. *Rosc. Amer.* 1–2),[28] sometimes chanted its opinions,[29] and when important people adorned it, their particular prestige vibrated invisibly through the area as well. Augustus himself appeared, unsummoned, at two trials, and merely by answering a question swung the verdicts in the directions he wanted (Dio Cass. 54.3.2–3, 54.30.4). Such Imperial interventions from the *corona* could be very disruptive to expectations, since emperors' prestige (and therefore their claims to truth and deference) was greatest: when Tiberius sat at the

[27] Deportment, Cic. *Orat.* 25.86; Quint. *Inst.* 6.3.29–35, 11.3.68–136. Toga, Quint. *Inst.* 11.3.137–149; as sign of respect, Heskel 1994, 134; also Dyck 2001.

[28] *Corona*, Cic. *Verr.* 2.5.143–144 (and its valuation like that of experts, *Brut.* 184–193); importance, Millar 1998, 13, 41, 71–72, 217.

[29] Cic. *Verr.* 2.2.188, *Rab. Perd.* 18, *Flacc.* 66, *Brut.* 88; in trials of Christians, Potter 1993, 141.

edge of the praetor's tribunal and by his presence caused "the lobbying and petitions of the powerful" to be ignored, the result, said the unreconciled Tacitus, was "taking the truth into account, but undermining liberty" (*Ann.* 1.75.2). Other emperors did understand the force of prestige: neither Antoninus Pius nor Marcus Aurelius convicted the great Herodes Atticus (on charges of wife-murder and tyrannising the Athenians, respectively), but rather than offend the almost equally prestigious prosecutors, in both cases condemned Herodes' freedmen instead.

21.5 Conclusion

Truth in a Roman court could thus not be identified and imposed, contrary to argument and evidence, even by an emperor—for truth was awkward, unconvincing, insulting and never enough on its own. Even Cicero, who claimed that courts sought truth and judges followed it, observed that truth simply asserted without support "was not sufficiently accommodated to popular approval" (*Brut.* 114, with Crook 1995, 173). Both sides of the modern controversy are therefore in fact correct: truth was the aim, the major matter of the Roman courts, but had to be constructed with arguments and evidence held together by the force of prestige that people recognised and expected. In these courts, parties had to move according to the mechanics of the Roman universe, performing by their qualities, their appearance, their actions and their speeches their own prestige, the fundamental argument, the fundamental evidence and the fundamental force of the Roman court.

Bibliography

Broggini, G. 1964. "La preuve dans l'ancien droit romain," in *La preuve Iᵉ partie: antiquité.* Brussels. 223–276.

Burton, G. P. 1987. "Government and the provinces." In J. Wacher, ed., *The Roman world.* London. 423–439.

Craig, C. 2004. "Audience expectations, invective, and proof." In J. G. F. Powell and J. Paterson, eds., *Cicero the advocate.* Oxford. 187–214.

Crook, J. A. 1995. *Legal advocacy in the Roman world.* Ithaca.

Dyck, A. R. (2001). "Dressing to kill: attire as a proof and means of characterization in Cicero's speeches." *Arethusa* 34: 119–130.

Fiori, R. 2013. "La gerarchia come criterio di verità. *Boni* e *mali* nel processo romano arcaico." In C. Cascione and C. Masi Doria, eds., Quid est veritas? *Un seminario su verità e forme giuridiche.* Naples. 169–249.

Garnsey, P. 1970. *Social status and legal privilege in the Roman empire.* Cambridge.

Gotoff, H. C. 1993. *Cicero's Caesarian speeches: a stylistic commentary.* Chapel Hill.

Greenidge, A. H. J. 1901. *The legal procedure of Cicero's time.* Oxford.

Gruen, E. S. (1965). "The *lex Varia.*" *Journal of Roman Studies* 55: 59–73.

Heskel, J. 1994. "Cicero as evidence for attitudes to dress in the late republic." In J. L. Sebesta and L. Bonfante, eds., *The world of Roman costume.* Madison. 133–145.

Honoré, T. 1981. "The primacy of oral evidence?" In C. F. H. Tapper, ed., *Proof and punishment: essays in memory of Sir Rupert Cross.* London. 172–192.

Johnson, H. D. 1927. *The Roman tribunal*. Baltimore.

Lendon, J. E. 1997. *Empire of honour: the art of government in the Roman world*. Oxford.

Lévy, J.-P. 1959. "Ciceron et la preuve judiciaire," in *Droits de l'antiquité et sociologie juridique: mélanges Henri Lévy-Bruhl*. Paris. 187–197.

Lieberman, S. (1944–1945). "Roman legal institutions in early rabbinics in the *Acta martyrum*." *Jewish Quarterly Review* 35: 1–55.

Masi Doria, C. 2013. "Linee per una storia della *veritas* nell'esperienza giuridica romana 1. Dalle basi culturali al diritto classico." In C. Cascione and C. Masi Doria, eds., Quid est veritas? *Un seminario su verità e forme giuridiche*. Naples. 1–64.

May, J. M. (1981). "The rhetoric of advocacy and patron-client identification: variation on a theme." *American Journal of Philology* 102: 308–315.

May, J. M. 1988. *Trials of character: the eloquence of Ciceronian* ethos. Chapel Hill.

May, J. M. 2002. "Ciceronian oratory in context." In J. M. May, ed., *Brill's Companion to Cicero: oratory and rhetoric*. Leiden. 49–70.

McClintock, R. C. 1975. "Cicero's narrative techniques in the judicial speeches." PhD dissertation, University of North Carolina, Chapel Hill.

Meyer, E. A. 2004. *Legitimacy and law in the Roman world:* tabulae *in Roman belief and practice*. Cambridge.

Millar, F. G. B. 1998. *The crowd in Rome in the late republic*. Ann Arbor.

Musurillo, H. 1954. *The acts of the pagan martyrs*. Acta Alexandrinorum. Oxford.

Musurillo, H. 1972. *The acts of the Christian martyrs*. Oxford.

Paterson, J. 2004. "Self-reference in Cicero's forensic speeches." In J. G. F. Powell and J. Paterson, eds., *Cicero the advocate*. Oxford. 79–96.

Potter, D. S. 1993. "Performance, power and justice in the high empire." In W. S. Slater, ed., *Roman theater and society*. Ann Arbor. 129–159.

Powell, J. G. F. 2010. "Court procedure and rhetorical strategy in Cicero." In D. H. Berry and A. Erskine, eds., *Form and function in Roman oratory*. Cambridge. 21–36 and 309–328.

Powell, J. G. F. and J. Paterson 2004. "Introduction." In. J. G. F. Powell and J. Paterson, eds., *Cicero the advocate*. Oxford. 1–57.

Pugliese, G. 1964. "La preuve dans le process romain de l'époque classique," in *La preuve Ie partie: antiquité*. Brussels. 277–348.

Ramage, E. S. (1985). "Strategy and methods in Cicero's *pro Caelio*." *Atene e Roma* 30: 1–8.

Riggsby, A. M. 1999. *Crime and community in Ciceronian Rome*. Austin.

Riggsby, A. M. 2004. "The rhetoric of character in the Roman courts." In J. G. F. Powell and J. Paterson, eds., *Cicero the advocate*. Oxford. 165–186.

Schmitz, D. 1985. *Zeugen des Prozeßgegners in Gerichtsreden Ciceros*. Frankfurt.

Schmitz, D. (1989). "Zeugen im Verres-Prozeß nach Ciceros Darstellung." *Gymnasium* 96: 521–531.

Sherwin-White, A. N. (1952). "The extortion procedure again." *Journal of Roman Studies* 42: 43–55.

Swarney, P. R. 1993. "Social status and social behaviour as criteria in judicial proceedings in the late republic." In B. Halpern and D. W. Hobson, eds., *Laws, politics and society in the ancient Mediterranean world*. Sheffield. 137–155.

Vasaly, A. C. 1993. *Representations: images of the world in Ciceronian oratory*. Berkeley.

Wisse, J. 1989. Ethos *and* pathos *from Aristotle to Cicero*. Amsterdam.

Zetzel, J. (1994). Review of C. P. Craig, 1993. *Form as argument in Cicero's speeches*. http://bmcr.brynmawr.edu/1994/94.01.05.html, accessed 13 February 2016.

CHAPTER 22

LEGAL PLURALISM IN PRACTICE

CLIFFORD ANDO

22.1 Introduction

The Roman Empire was legally pluralist. That is to say, in any given political space, multiple bodies of law, deriving from discrete sources, and multiple institutions of dispute resolution, potentially held authority over any given issue. The nature of the situation naturally varied from case to case. At Rome, the situation took a specific form, as the various sources of law (legislative assembly, praetor, senate and emperor) were understood to derive their legislative authority and jurisdiction from the same source. In provincial contexts, by contrast, some body of law, derived from a local legislative institution recognised by Rome, nominally held sway, even as Rome claimed the right to impose legislation in matters of interest to itself and Roman courts came increasingly to function as courts of the first or second instance.

This chapter explores how Roman courts accommodated alien subjects and foreign law. By "Roman courts" is intended courts supervised by Roman magistrates, either those elected or appointment at Rome or dispatched or delegated by such. Jurisdiction in autonomous communities of Roman citizens, so-called "municipalities", will be considered only in passing (on their governance see Roselaar, ch. 10). Although a socio-legal study of non-Roman courts in the Roman period is a major desideratum, outside Egypt it is scarcely possible to sketch even an institutional history of local legal systems.[1] Section 22.2 outlines aspects of Roman jurisdiction among foreigners under the Republic, such as appear to explain significant aspects of Roman practice and theory in the better attested conditions of the Principate. Section 22.3 considers procedural mechanisms available in Roman courts to accommodate persons not nominally entitled to appear in them. Section 22.4 considers briefly an important corollary; namely, the situation of newly enfranchised Romans resident in alien communities. Section 22.5

[1] Courts outside Egypt: Fournier 2010; Kantor 2013, 2015. Egypt: extensive bibliographies are available in Alonso 2013, Keenan, Manning and Yiftach-Firanko 2014 and Alonso, ch. 5.

turns to Roman rules regarding the law to be applied in courts in provincial contexts, as are known from the high Empire.

22.2 Republican History and Later Theory

The XII Tables countenance the appearance of foreigners in Roman courts (XII Tab. II 2 (*RS*); Kaser 1984, 16–17), and Polybius affirms commercial relations to have been covered in the first treaty between Rome and Carthage, which he dates to the first year of the Republic. What is more, the text as Polybius understood it allowed each party access to local courts under equal rights with the indigenous population, and implies that a rule of territoriality governed choice of law (Polybius 3.22, esp. 8–9). By contrast, sources in the classical period note that certain legal actions were unavailable to foreigners, even at Rome, and specific forms of commercial and social relations were disallowed between Romans and aliens. On this basis, ancients and moderns hypothesise that aliens were somehow excluded from Roman courts wholesale, and in particular were not allowed use of the *legis actiones*. There can be no doubt that the Emperor Augustus enacted restrictions as regards both personality and territoriality in the use of Roman legal forms (Inst.Gai.4.104–105; *SEG* IX 8, 5th edict), and in my view it is likely that his actions have too often been interpreted as continuous with, rather than reactionary against, earlier practice. That said, it is possible to read the surviving evidence for public law statutes of the second century BC such that it appears special accommodation was made (and perhaps needed) for the presence of foreign participants in the prosecution of Roman magistrates (Richardson 1987).

Scholars who endorse strong versions of the exclusion of foreigners from private law relations with Roman often cite the exceedingly late testimony of Pomponius (second century AD; D.1.2.2.28) and John the Lydian (sixth century AD; *De mag.* 1.38, 45), to the effect the Romans first created a *praetor inter peregrinos c.*241 BC, in the immediate aftermath of the First Punic War. Corey Brennan, however, has argued that the new praetor was first created as a magistrate for (and thus to hold jurisdiction in) the new province of Sicily (Brennan 2000, 85–89). The suggestion is attractive, and could be strengthened. As Brennan observes, it makes better sense of the titles of the two praetors as they are attested in the earliest sources, *praetor urbanus* and *praetor qui inter peregrinos ius dicit*: they are differentiated not according to a rule of personality but by location. In any event, this is just the period when Rome developed significant new institutions to administer law among conquered populations, including the so-called *praefectus iure dicundo*, a magistrate dispatched to places where Rome had dissolved institutions of public authority but acknowledged the need to supervise ongoing private law relations (Liv. 26.1.7–10).

In the event, three trends that impinge on the topic of this chapter are broadly visible in Republican sources. First, although in Roman historical memory, Rome had once regularly imposed citizenship on conquered populations as a means to integrate persons and territory into the Roman state, by the later mid-Republic, Rome was insisting on stronger forms of a citizen–alien distinction (Ando 2016).

Second, by the late second century BC, Rome had a clear practice of conceding so-called "autonomy" to conquered populations. In Greek and Roman practice, "autonomy" consisted in the right of a politically constituted community "to use its own laws" (*utere suis legibus*) in regulating private-law affairs among those dwelling in its territory (Ando 2011a, 7–71). Thus in 104 BC, Lucius Caesius, a Roman general in Spain, accepted the surrender of a Spanish people and then "ordered them to be free, and the buildings, laws and all other things that had been theirs on the day before they surrendered themselves, he ordered them to retain so long as the people and senate of Rome shall wish" (*ELRH* U2). It is extraordinarily likely that, as with the new mechanisms developed by Rome for governing Sicily, the practice of conceding autonomy responded at least in part to the weak infrastructural power of the Imperial state. Rome could not have imposed its legal system *tout court*, even if it had wanted to. But the developed practice of conceding local autonomy had important political consequences, conducing stability in the system as a whole (Ando 2014).

Third, the Roman state, and dynasts in the late Republic, issued both jurisdictional rules for provincial landscapes (the best known is that for Sicily, Cicero *Verr.* 2.2.32; Kantor 2010) as well as ad hoc grants of privilege to favoured individuals, who were in essence granted the power to select the fora that would hear any dispute in which they were involved (*SEG* LI 1427; *SEG* LIV 1625; Raggi 2006, 109–172). (Late Republican jurisdictional rules issued for peninsular Italy and Transpadana are to a point distinct: on these see Ando 2011b, 25–27.) Such grants to individuals demonstrate not only a practical awareness of the value of forum-shopping, but also a willingness to resort to a rule of personality rather than territoriality in determining choice of law. That said, it is also clear that these grants destabilised the rule of law and produced considerable resentment in the communities where such individuals operated; it seems likewise clear that the edicts of Augustus and decree of the senate from 7/6 BC preserved at Cyrene were intended to impose order and remove exceptions to jurisdictional rules across the Empire now that the chaos of the Civil Wars was ended (*SEG* IX 8).

A final set of related principles visible in the late Republic shaped practice in our topic in the classical period. First, grants of autonomy to one side, Rome claimed for itself the power to impose its laws on others "where it concerns our *res publica*, our *imperium*, our wars, our victory, our safety" (Cicero *Balb.* 20–22). Second, Rome claimed authority over most matters it deemed related to public order, including areas of what we now term criminal law; and even where it granted power to local authorities, it gradually imposed its own procedural norms on their operation (Fuhrmann, ch. 23; Bryen, ch. 25).

22.3 Fictions in Roman Procedure

Although choice of law and conflict of laws problems must have arisen in courts at Rome, the evidence that survives is highly imperfect. Most importantly, extant codifications of both Imperial constitutions and classical jurisprudence were produced long after the existence of separate bodies of civil law was nominally terminated by the universalisation of Roman citizenship. Theory and precedents in regard to what we might term international private law had long ceased to have strong salience to legal practice.[2] That said, texts of

[2] Sullivan 2016 offers a survey of scholarship regarding the nature (and existence) of international private law in Roman Antiquity.

the classical period whose wording is preserved, not least Gaius' Institutes and numerous inscribed statutes, lay out solutions to relevant problems. What is more, the jurists do reflect on conflicts among sources of law at Rome, and it may well be that their reflections on these problems, focusing as they do on the pursuit of substantive justice while respecting the legitimacy of the many sources of law, can help us to appreciate the evidence for Roman practice in non-Roman contexts, where the evidence is more fragmentary and less subject to discursive elaboration and theoretical reflection.

In Roman texts, and those surviving from the western Mediterranean, the major tool for accommodating foreigners in Roman courts was procedural. It consisted in the application of fictions, by which persons above all, but also things and actions, were translated across some boundary and the case thereby rendered justiciable by Roman courts using Roman procedure.[3] Such fictions are massively attested not simply in jurisprudence but also in statute. This is crucial: fiction is not simply a tool of legal analysis, by which academic lawyers explain the operations of procedure to each other (any more than is analogy or substitution); rather, the use of fictions was ordained by statute and is attested in surviving legal instruments.

The most extended reflection on the use of fictions to accommodate aliens in Roman courts survives in bk. 4 of Gaius' Institutes, in a section whose overall subject is not aliens or pluralism but rather the procedural mechanisms available for overcoming some injustice in the conventional operation of statute law. The section on the so-called *fictio civitatis* runs as follows:

> Again, if a peregrine sues or is sued on a cause for which an action has been established by Roman statutes, there is a fiction that he is a Roman citizen (*civitas Romana peregrino fingitur*), provided that it is equitable that the action should be extended to a peregrine (*si modo iustum sit eam actionem etiam ad peregrinum extendi*), for example, if a peregrine sues or is sued by the *actio furti*. Thus, if he is being sued by that action, the formula is framed as follows: "Be *X iudex*. If it appears that a golden cup has been stolen from Lucius Titius by Dio the son of Hermaeus or by his aid and counsel, on which account, if he were a Roman citizen, he would be bound to compound for the wrong as a thief," etc. ... And again, in some cases we sue with the fiction that our opponent has not undergone a *capitis deminutio*. (Inst.Gai.4.37–38; transl. de Zulueta)

Here, the background condition necessitating the fiction is that aliens were excluded from the relevant private (civil-)law action. Not as a matter of course, but if substantive justice is served by transgressing the norm of exclusion, a fiction is available, according to which an alien is contingently treated as if he were a citizen. The hypothetical situations imagined by Gaius therefore concern suits in which one litigant is Roman and another alien, and the law to be applied by the Roman court is Roman. Note, too, the specification of the subsequent chapter, whose first sentence is quoted above: the fiction is also available in cases where one litigant has undergone a change of status, even where the person has suffered a punishment that deprived him of Roman citizenship. It would not be just if the exclusion of that person from access to Roman law rendered him immune to actions

[3] The most recent survey of fictions in Roman law is Ando 2015a; see also Ando 2011a, 1–18, 115–131. The topic cries out for monographic study.

arising from conduct before the loss of citizenship. In such cases, he can be treated as if the punishment had not yet occurred.

Fictions of this kind, which is to say, those that treat some non-Roman person or thing as if it were Roman, are visible in at least five areas throughout the classical period of Roman law: (i) in legislation treating situations wherein an alien might be involved in actions involving Roman persons or public land; (ii) in legislation directed at non-Italian landscapes, where it is conceded that Roman language might not account for the totality of social reality; (iii) in specifications regarding procedure, directed at populations in areas being annexed (in some way) to the Roman state; (iv) in *omnibus* clauses, to wit, attempts to capture for legal regulation all situations not specifically addressed in the legislation; and (v) in legislation and legal instruments treating aliens who conducted themselves as if they were Roman. Let me provide examples of these in turn.

(i) In the *lex agraria* of 111 BC, it is specified that for cases involving Italian land owned by the Roman state, to which one party is either Latin or alien, a trial is to be granted and judge(s) appointed as if the party in question were a Roman citizen (*RS* no. 2, ll. 29–31). (ii) In the same law, it is provided that communities in Africa that are neither colonies nor municipalities may be treated as if they were; provision is also made for persons who were not colonists but were enrolled as such nevertheless (*RS* no. 2, l. 31; see also ll. 55, 58–51, 66–67). (iii) In a statute passed at Rome concerning jurisdiction in Gallia Cisalpina, perhaps *c.*42 BC, in a chapter specifying the procedure to be followed locally in cases involving loans of less than 15,000 HS, it is laid down that "the law, the issue, the right of action and the suit shall be the same for all persons in every respect as they would apply, or as it would be appropriate for them to apply if that person ... had confessed concerning these matters before the praetor at Rome or before the person who in Rome had jurisdiction over these matters" (*RS* no. 28, ch. XXII, col. II, ll. 29–43; translation *RS*). (iv) A late chapter in the generic municipal charter attested in both the Spanish provinces and along the Danube requires adherence in detailed matters of procedure to the Augustan *lex Iulia* on judicial affairs, even though that law had in several matters restricted access to Roman law and use of Roman forms to citizens and the city of Rome. There then follows an *omnibus* clause: "On whatever matters there is no explicit provision or rule in this statute ... the municipal citizens ... should deal with each other ... under the civil law under which Roman citizens deal or will deal with each other." Elsewhere in the charter, it is more directly stated that "the statute and law and position is to be as if a praetor of the Roman people had ordered judgement to take place between Roman citizens ... under whatever statute ... it is appropriate for *iudicia privata* to take place in the city of Rome" (*lex Flavia municipalis* chs. 93, 91; translation Crawford; on this text see Roselaar, ch. 10).

(v) Over time, Roman courts repeatedly confronted instances in which individuals had been mistaken about their status and had conducted themselves as if they were Roman citizens, partaking not simply of the privileges but also the duties of citizenship, including sitting on juries and serving in the legions. Edicts of both Claudius and Hadrian survive dealing specifically with aliens who had served in the praetorian guard, a service open only to citizens. In both cases a fiction is employed: the relevant parties are granted citizenship, and all the relevant actions that they had conducted prior to the grant of citizenship are granted legal validity as if they had been citizens all along (Cicero *Off.* 3.47; *ILS* 206; Eck, Pangerl and Weiss 2014; Ando 2015b, 92).

Not for naught did Velleius Paterculus describe the effort of Quintilius Varus to pacify and civilise Germany as having occurred through the imposition of the rule of law. More particularly, he describes the Germans as having perceived and exploited the Roman conceit, with the result that it was Varus who was confused:

> But the Germans, in a fashion scarcely credible to one who has no experience of them, are extraordinarily crafty and terribly savage all at once—a race born to lying. By feigning a series of made-up lawsuits, now summoning each other to disputes, now giving thanks that Roman justice was settling them and that their savagery was being rendered mild by this unknown and novel discipline and that quarrels that were customarily settled by arms were now being settled by law, they brought Quintilius to such a degree of negligence that he came to think of himself as if he were the urban praetor administering justice in the forum and not as commanding an army in the middle of Germany. (Velleius 2.118.1; Ando 2011b, 47)

Although Velleius aligns himself with Augustan and Tiberian propaganda in denouncing both the Germans and Varus alike for the slaughter of his army by Arminius, we have seen that the procedural fiction, according to which law should be administered among aliens in provincial landscapes even as it is administered by the praetor among citizens at Rome, was standard in Roman legislation long before, and long after, this event.

One last observation is crucial at this juncture. The use of Roman private-law procedure, and even of legal fictions, could be wholly divorced from the choice of substantive law. This appears to be true in respect of some private-law disputes in Gallia Cisalpina, where a hypothetical in the *lex de Gallia Cisalpina* specifies that the formula to be applied is that of the "[the praetor] who holds jurisdiction among foreigners at Rome" (*is quei Romae inter peregreinos ius deicet; RS* no. 28, ch. XX, col. I, ll. 22–31 at 24–25). It is certainly the case in the famed *Tabula Contrebiensis*, which records the Roman arrangement of a third-party arbitration in early first-century BC Spain. In that case, the Roman magistrate employs a Roman private-law, two-stage formulary process, including a fiction, in order to announce both choice of law and frame the questions of fact to be considered by the judges.[4]

22.4 Choice of Law across Life Histories

Problems of jurisdiction and choice of law must consistently have presented themselves also in the cases of individuals who underwent a change of citizenship. This occurred as a regular matter in several contexts: certain Roman judicial punishments entailed a loss of status, including loss of citizenship; Romans who enrolled in colonies of Latin

[4] Cf. the hugely insightful observation by Birks, Rodger and Richardson (1984, 60): "Nowadays we easily think of pleading and procedure as matters separable from the substance of the law. But under the formulary system, the texts of the formulae were the foundations of substantive law, and innovation in their wording was the principal means by which that substantive law was changed."

status became juridically Latin; aliens elected to magistracies in a wide range of provincial communities received Roman citizenship upon completion of their term of office (Gardner 2001); aliens who completed a full term of service as a soldier in an auxiliary unit received Roman citizenship with their honourable discharge; and, increasingly, children of marriages of parents of discrepant status could be elevated to the higher status, including Roman citizenship, rather than automatically classed in the lowest relevant status (Gardner 1996). The problems that arose in theory for such persons are much discussed in the sources, and may be simply sketched. In the present context, it is clear that any solution to these issues entailed specific difficulties for adjudication of disputes at law, but extant evidence allows us only to gesture at the framework within which solutions were likely crafted.

The problem as described by Roman sources is as follows: some legal regulations governing social, economic and contractual relations among persons differed between Roman and other bodies of law. (It is in the nature of our sources that they assert the distinctiveness of Roman law from *ius gentium* qua undifferentiated aggregate of practice among other peoples, rather than offering a point-by-point comparison between Roman law and any other single body of law.) Loss of citizenship sundered the continuation of Roman-law relations among persons. For example, the power of a father over his children was broken if he lost Roman citizenship, "as reason does not permit that a person of alien status should have a Roman citizen in his *potestas*" (Inst.Gai.1.128), and likewise a son who lost citizenship through punishment or voluntarily relinquished it by enrolling in a Latin colony ceased to be in his father's power (Inst.Gai.1.128, 131). As the Romans believed that they were unique in their adherence to agnation as principle for determining juridical status (and other legal relations), so they believed cognation to be "natural": thus, change of civil law status affected a Roman citizen's civil law relations, to wit, his agnatic ties, but cognate ties remained unaffected, "because considerations of civil law can destroy civil law rights, but not natural ones" (Inst.Gai.1.158). Among the issues potentially implicated in a person's change of status were numbered *patria potestas, manus* (for wives in *manus* marriage), *mancipium*, guardianship and rights over freedmen (*lex Flavia municipalis* chs. 21–23), as well as testamentary succession and rights of marriage.

Alongside the presence of resident aliens of whatever citizenship, families that underwent a change of citizenship via a systematic grant of citizenship must have been a frequent cause of conflicts of law problems in Roman courts. At a most basic level, Roman legislation attempted to resolve these difficulties in three steps. First, issues of personal status and intersubjective relations implicated in Roman notions of the *familia* and personal power were to be adjudged according to Roman law, a rule perhaps easier to state in theory than vindicate in practice (*lex Flavia municipalis* chs. 21–23). Second, civil law relations not implicated in legally protected aspects of social dependency were to be resolved according to local law (D.50.17.34; see also D.50.1.27.1, 50.1.29, 50.1.34, and section 22.5). Finally, as regards fiscal and liturgical obligations, high Imperial grants of citizenship (including the universal grant by Caracalla) contain a savings clause to the effect that "rights [and obligations] at local law being preserved" (*salvo iure gentis*), which is commonly interpreted as sustaining the obligations of newly enfranchised Romans toward their (former) communities (*IAM* II 94; *P. Giss.* 40, ll. 8–9).

22.5 Pluralism in Practice

Two fundamental aspects of practice deserve mention but cannot be treated in this context. In provincial contexts, Roman courts served as courts of both the first and second instance. The evidence does not permit us to say whether attitudes toward the use of local norms or dissonance between Roman and local norms varied with the status of the court. In addition, Roman courts in the provincial contexts are often described as having employed a procedure different from that employed for civil trials at Rome; namely, the so-called *cognitio* procedure, in which the presiding magistrate settled questions of law and also investigated issues of fact and issued judgement (see Rüfner, ch. 20). However, it is clear that magistrates in provincial contexts also regularly delegated supervision of courts and, indeed, employed a two-stage process. More importantly, although magistrates might invite the advice of experts in local law, or cities holding assizes might make such experts available, we are not in a position to say whether their use was tied to any particular procedural form.

In developed Roman theory of the second century AD, local polities recognised by Rome as legislative authorities over particular landscapes generated their own codes of law (Inst. Gai.1.1; Ando 2014, 7–11). In matters other than those related to the Roman *familia*, practice in the high Empire largely observed a principle of territoriality in choice of law. (The problem can be difficult to untangle not simply because practice might diverge from this norm for many reasons, but also because of the tight circularity of Roman vocabulary: as *civitas* means both "citizenship" and "juridically constituted community, sovereign over a particular space", a rule specifying that choice of law should be determined by *civitas* must be parsed before its import can be understood.) Statements of principle to this effect emerge from Gaius' commentary on the standardised edict on jurisdiction issued by provincial governors on their arrival in their provinces, regarding sale of land and eviction (D.21.2.6), as well as multiple instances in Trajan's correspondence with Pliny (e.g. *Ep.* 10.109, 10.113: "I think, then, that the safest course, as always, is to follow the law of each *civitas*" [transl. Radice]), as well as the opening lines of a papyrus record of judicial proceedings from the reign of Trajan: "It is best that they give judgements according to the law of the Egyptians" (*P. Oxy.* xlii 3015).

Adhering to such principles raised two additional problems of considerable historical and comparative importance (Ando 2015c). How were the Romans to know—how did anyone know—what local law was (Kantor 2009)? What authorities or technologies of memory existed or were brought into being by the superimposition of Roman courts and their standards of evidence?

By the high Empire, numerous individuals are attested on inscriptions and papyri as experts in local law, sometimes as advocates assisting private litigants, sometimes as experts adduced by supervising magistrates (Jones 2007; Kantor 2013). It is noteworthy that such experts, as well as citations of local law, are much more common in the high Empire than earlier. This might be consequent upon patterns of survival in the evidence; it might follow from their citation in that period in Roman rather than local courts, proceedings and actions of Roman courts being better attested. But the possibility cannot be excluded that "local law" was occasionally consolidated and local experts produced by the demands of Imperial knowledge systems and the distorting effects of Imperial power, a pattern well attested in the comparative study of colonial law.

As a corollary, even under the high Empire, in spite of the presence of a principled commitment to the use of local norms and the historical attestation of (a limited number) of experts in local law, Roman jurists also produced cascading hierarchies of norms to which a judge should have recourse. What is notable is the concession that there might be no relevant written law, nor can the possibility be excluded that the law is simply not written:

> What ought to be held to in those cases where we have no applicable written law is the practice established by customs and usage. And if this is in some way deficient, we should hold to what is most nearly analogical to and entailed by such practice. If even this is obscure, then we ought to apply law as it is in use in the city of Rome. (D.1.3.32pr)

More crucially, although in some cases it appears that Roman magistrates employed experts to inform them what local law was (*P. Oxy.* ii 237, col. VII, ll. 29–38, col. VIII, 2–7, is a famous instance), it also seems clear that in many contexts the content of local law was settled adversarially, even as the facts of the case were debated (Ando 2015c). This produced the paradoxical result that when the technologies of memory failed to guarantee secure and stable knowledge of local norms, Roman magistrates were advised to confirm the content of local law by verifying that the norm as cited to them had been upheld in earlier proceedings:

> When it appears that somebody is relying upon a custom either of a *civitas* or of a province, the very first issue which ought to be explored, according to my opinion, is whether the custom has ever been upheld in contentious proceedings. (D.1.3.34)

The result is paradoxical because a context that lacked a communally endorsed source of knowledge of law might seem likely also to have lacked disinterested mechanisms for recording judgements in prior cases, especially at a level of detail that made the norms cited in those cases available for inspection. But the optimism (or solipsism) of Roman jurists in respect of the nature of knowledge in the practice of law persisted, nonetheless. What is more, it lay in the nature of Roman power that Roman norms as regards the inscription of legal proceedings were gradually taken up, as well as imposed, in many areas around the Empire (Ando 2000, 117–130, 363–364; Keenan, Manning and Yiftach-Firanko 2014, *passim*, but esp. 482–502).

22.6 Conclusion

Both political considerations and limitations on state infrastructural power urged the Romans to allow the use of local norms in local courts. The evidence for the pre-classical period is faulty, and the situation in the late Republic was chaotic, but the early Principate witnesses a strong tendency toward a stable regime of respecting territoriality as a principle in choice of law as regards private law issues. Numerous situations, not least human mobility, trade and contract across jurisdictional boundaries and changes of personal status, tested the limits of this regime. In conclusion, it must also be observed that, just as Rome claimed the power to impose law on alien communities in matters that affected its power and security, so Roman magistrates were unconstrained in their power to reject the application of local law in pursuit of substantive justice (*P. Oxy.* ii 237 is again a case in point; Sullivan 2016). In doing so, they were no doubt applying their notion of substantive justice. It perhaps merits observation that in so proceeding, they were applying in alien contexts a principle first visible in Roman argument as regards conflicts among sources of law at Rome: a common justification for praetorian "emendation" of statute law was the correction of injustice (Inst.Gai.3.25–26).

Bibliography

Alonso, J. L. (2013). "The status of peregrine law in Egypt: 'customary law' and legal pluralism in the Roman Empire." *Journal of Juristic Papyrology* 43: 351–404.

Ando, C. 2000. *Imperial ideology and provincial loyalty in the Roman empire.* Berkeley.

Ando, C. 2011a. *Law, language, and empire in the Roman tradition*. Philadelphia.

Ando, C. 2011b. "Law and the landscape of empire." In S. Benoist, A. Daguey-Gagey and C. Hoët-van Cauwenberghe, eds., *Figures d'empire, fragments de mémoire: pouvoirs et identités dans le monde romain impérial (IIe s. av. n.è.—VIe s. de n.è.).* Paris. 25–47

Ando, C. (2014). "Pluralism and empire, from Rome to Robert Cover." *Critical Analysis of Law: An International & Interdisciplinary Law Review* 1: 1–22. Available at: http://cal.library.utoronto.ca/index.php/cal/article/view/20917, accessed 18 August 2015.

Ando, C. 2015a. "Fact, fiction and social reality in Roman law." In M. del Mar and W. Twining, eds., *Legal fictions in theory and practice.* Boston. 295–323.

Ando, C. 2015b. *Roman social imaginaries: language and thought in contexts of empire.* Toronto.

Ando, C. 2015c. "*Exemplum*, analogy and precedent in Roman law." In M. Lowrie and S. Lüdemann, eds., *Between exemplarity and singularity: literature, philosophy, law.* New York. 111–122.

Ando, C. 2016. "Making Romans: democracy and social differentiation under Rome." In M. Lavan, R. and J. Weisweiler, eds., *Imperial cosmopolitanisms: global identities and imperial cultures in ancient Eurasia.* Oxford.

Birks, P., Rodger, A. and Richardson, J. S., (1984). "Further aspects of the *Tabula Contrebiensis.*" *Journal of Roman Studies* 74: 45–73.

Brennan, T. C. 2000. *The praetorship in the Roman republic.* New York.

Eck, W., Pangerl, A. and Weiß, P. (2014). "Edikt Hadrians für Prätorianer mit unsicherem römischem Bürgerrecht." *Zeitschrift für Papyrologie und Epigraphik* 189: 241–253.

Fournier, J. 2010. *Entre tutelle romaine et autonomie civique: l'administration judiciaire dans les provinces hellénophones de l'Empire romain (129 av. J.-C.– 235 apr. J.-C.).* Athens.

Gardner, J. F. (1996). "Hadrian and the social legacy of Augustus." *Labeo* 42: 83–110.

Gardner, J. F. 2001. "Making citizens: the operation of the *Lex Irnitana.*" In L. de Blois, ed., *Administration, prosopography and appointment policies in the Roman empire: proceedings of the First Workshop of the international network Impact of Empire. Roman Empire, 27 B.C.–A.D. 406, Leiden, June 28–July 1, 2000.* Amsterdam. 215–229.

Jones, C. P. (2007, publ. 2009). "Juristes romains dans l'Orient grec." *Comptes Rendus de l'Académie des Inscriptions et Belles-lettres* 2007: 1331–1359.

Kantor, G. (2009). "Knowledge of law in Roman Asia Minor." In R. Haensch, ed., *Selbstdarstellung und Kommunikation: die Veröffentlichung staatlicher Urkunden auf Stein und Bronze in der römischer Zeit*. Munich. 249–265.

Kantor, G. (2010). "*Siculus cum Siculo non eiusdem ciuitatis*: litigation between citizens of different communities in the Verrines." *Cahiers du Centre Gustave Glotz* 19: 187–204.

Kantor, G. 2013. "Law in Roman Phrygia: rules and jurisdictions." In P. Thonemann, ed., *Roman Phrygia: culture and society*. Cambridge. 143–167.

Kantor, G. 2015. "Local law in Asia Minor after the *Constitutio Antoniniana*." In C. Ando, ed., *Citizenship and empire in Europe, 200–1900: the Antonine Constitution after 1800 years*. Stuttgart. In production.

Kaser, M. (1984). "*Ius honorarium* und *ius civile*." *Zeitschrift der Savigny-Stiftung für Rechtsgeschichte, romanistische Abteilung* 101: 1–114.

Keenan, J. G., Manning, J. G. and Yiftach-Firanko, U. eds. 2014. *Law and legal practice in Egypt from Alexander to the Arab conquest: a selection of papyrological sources in translation, with introductions and commentary*. Cambridge.

Raggi, A. 2006. *Seleuco di Rhosos. Cittadinanza et privilegi nell'oriente greco in età tardo-repubblicana*. Pisa.

Richardson, J. (1987). "The purpose of the *lex Calpurnia de repetundis*." *Journal of Roman Studies* 77: 1–12.

Sullivan, W. (2016). "Substantive justice and choice of law in classical Roman law." *Critical Analysis of Law* 3.1: 157–174.

Criminal Law and Social Order

CHAPTER 23

POLICE FUNCTIONS AND PUBLIC ORDER

CHRISTOPHER J. FUHRMANN

23.1 Introduction

Because Rome had neither public prosecutors nor modern-style police departments, law enforcement in the Roman world largely depended on private initiative, self-help and other non-institutional mechanisms. This fact is discernible through every stage of Rome's legal history, beginning with the XII Tables. Where today we might expect a police officer to arrest a suspected criminal, Rome's earliest written laws describe a public process in which victims themselves identified, arrested and hauled accused malefactors to court, or sometimes punished them in the act.[1]

In Rome and the provinces alike, private denunciation (*delatio*) was fundamental in punishing crime (Rivière 2002, esp. 274–285 on provincial delation). Individuals were expected to protect themselves and their own interests, and Roman society at all levels drew on a rich variety of means to counter threats and uphold public order. Relevant factors include fear of supernatural punishment, threat of social opprobrium, clear familial and social hierarchies and the use of collateral and securities to enforce agreements. For the upper class, private security was the norm, in the form of attendants, doormen (*ianitores, ostiarii*), estate guards (*circatores, saltuarii*) and other slaves; a big man could expect further help from his retinue of clients, if needs be. Property owners used door-locks adapted from the Greeks, and Romans seem to have invented the padlock. Brazenly carrying weapons in town was frowned on, but anyone travelling through the countryside would go armed to ward off attackers. Poor people were not without effective defences, such as guard dogs, and popular literature preached vigilance against the thief in the night.[2]

The legal right of self-defence is evident throughout Roman law and literature, whereas no single text or literary genre clearly describes institutional policing. Indeed, late-twentieth-century scholarship on ancient public order tended to stress "self-help" and other

[1] *XII Tab.*1.1, 2.3, 8.12–14 (*FIRA*); see also Bryen, ch. 25, this volume.

[2] For references on the preceding see Fuhrmann 2012, 46–52.

non-institutional aspects of community self-regulation. This scholarship is sound, if partial in its scope, and provided a valuable corrective to modernist assumptions (e.g. Nippel 1995; Lintott 1999). Yet casual readers might form the impression that Rome was completely without police, and rarely intervened in matters of public order. A generation of undergraduate students has absorbed the same message from the lecture hall: Rome had no police. This claim is untrue, and recent work on ancient policing is hopefully beginning to correct that misconception. For our purposes, the working definition of police covers any group of men armed or organised by the state, who compelled civilians to obey laws, or otherwise imposed the state's will, including official guards, market inspectors, arrest parties, prison staff and Roman soldiers tasked with temporary security duties in civilian areas.

Police institutions typically were not planned out as such, but evolved from the accrual of ad hoc administrative innovations. Policing measures were normally motivated by the cynical interests of the state, its rulers and society's elites, but this unsurprising fact does not preclude incidental benefits to others; in fact, we have some explicit evidence for governmental concern towards ordinary people and their safety. The scattered nature of the evidence, and the unsystematic development of the relevant institutions, makes understanding Roman policing difficult; the effort is rewarding nonetheless for shedding light on an underappreciated aspect of ancient state activity in general, and the practicalities of Roman law and order in particular.

The discussion that follows is roughly chronological, from less complex forms of security and law enforcement to a focus on the fuller police institutions of the Principate. We conclude with extremely brief comments on policing in the later Roman Empire, a topic which deserves its own separate study. My fundamental goal here is to establish and explain the reality of policing in the Roman Empire, and the state's involvement in public order. I will not argue that policing was necessary, or good, or somehow more "evolved"; yet we have enough evidence to show that institutional policing was a widely appreciated option that power-holders frequently resorted to during the Principate. This tendency is somewhat surprising, given the significant imperfections of policing, well known at the time, ranging from corruption and abuse to simple ineffectiveness.

23.2 Policing by Civilian Officials

23.2.1 Magisterial Power in Republican Rome

While there was nothing akin to modern police in archaic Rome, state processes loom in the world of the XII Tables. For example, the common-sense self-defence tactic of screaming for help during a home invasion, mandated in *Tabula* VIII 13 *FIRA* = I.18 *RS*, would also have the effect of securing witnesses for a trial later. In Republican Rome, key police functions were essentially carried out by the magistrates themselves, and by their underlings (attendants or *apparitores*, and public slaves). Later Romans thought of their ancestors as people who were taught to "fear the magistrate".[3] In Republican Rome, censors

[3] *Disticha Catonis* 12. On the following see also Kelly, ch. 29.

regulated public morals, consuls used lictors to impose their will, praetors issued legal regulations, aediles policed markets and other public spaces and tribunes of the plebs could arrest threatening people.

Republican Rome even had a trio of specialised police officials, the *tresviri capitales*. These junior magistrates oversaw the jail and executions, operated some kind of night patrol (hence their nickname *nocturni*), exercised jurisdiction over petty crimes and low-class offenders, and dispensed summary justice in the Forum. The modern minimisers of Roman policing object that three junior officials would have little impact in a city of thousands; perhaps, but their very existence means we cannot say Rome had *no* police. Nor should we assume their effect was negligible. Already c.200 BC, Plautus' audience clearly understood the fear felt toward the *tresviri* by a lonely slave on an innocent night errand for his master:

> What am I to do now, if the *tresviri* lock me up in jail? Tomorrow I'll be dragged out from that meat-locker of a cell to be whipped. I won't be allowed to argue my case, no one will come from my master, and everyone will assume I'm getting the evil I deserve. So eight brawny blokes will hammer on miserable me like an anvil.

Plautus' "eight brawny blokes" remind us that the *tresviri* had some kind of subaltern staff who performed floggings and executions for them.[4]

We should also note that the Romans did not relegate the punishment of crime to their city's periphery as modern states tend to today. Instead, the moans of prisoners in the Tullianum mingled with the cries of criminals being flogged just yards away in the Forum itself; close by were sites where the community's perceived enemies might meet a spectacular end from the Tarpeian Rock, or (looking ahead) humiliation on the Gemonian Steps, not to mention all the criminal blood shed in the nearby Colosseum. In other words, the state's punishment of crime and disorder was a public highlight of Rome's most central topography.[5]

Moreover, the constitution of the Roman Republic, in practice, proved flexible enough to deal with unexpected threats to public order, such as the growth of Bacchic cults in 186 BC. According to Livy (39.8–19), the senate, consuls, aediles and *tresviri capitales* acted on informants' testimony to repress the cult throughout Italy, arrest some of its priests, and organise extra watches against arson and illegal nocturnal meetings. Subsequent strictures on the cult (*ILS* 18) were so strict that some might argue they were meant to legislate it out of existence.

23.2.2 Local Security and Civilian Policing outside of Rome

Civilian security arrangements in the West outside of Rome are obscure, even with the fuller epigraphic record of the early Imperial period. Just as an individual was permitted—indeed, expected—to defend himself, and might kill an assailant with impunity, so communities under Roman rule enjoyed the autonomy and flexibility to counter a critical threat with organised force "whenever the need might arise", as the *lex Irnitana* put it

[4] Plaut. *Amphit.* 155–160; cf. *Aul.* 416; *Asin.* 131; Cascione 1999.

[5] Robinson 1992, 150–182; Nippel 1995, 4–26; Cadoux 2008.

(ch. 19; cf. Urso's charter, 103). Magistrates' oaths from other municipal charters include "elastic" clauses, authorising any legal action the town requires.[6] The same attitude prevailed in the Greek East, where the town council (*boulê*) shared responsibility with the magistrates to maintain basic security in the town and its territory.

While the word "bandit" can be a slanted term in our sources, there is a strong tone of uncomplicated celebration for local forces who bravely fought bandits, killing some in the fray, and arresting others; this praise comes from sources as diverse as a novel, popular acclamations and the emperor himself.[7] These instances evaded restrictions on local authorities' power to exact the death penalty, which seem most operative following a proper arrest. Closed communities such as the Qumran sectarians probably got away with wholly ignoring Roman law and executing community members for transgressing its religious codes. Meanwhile, Western sources hint of search parties for missing persons and posses who swept bandits from the countryside, yet it remains unclear if these were officially sanctioned in some way.[8] Jesus' rebuke to his arresters ("You've come out as though against a bandit, with swords and clubs, to arrest me?") shows how posses armed themselves (Mark 14:48 = Matt. 26:55).

In communities that shared Rome's style of magistracies, town mayors (*duoviri*) routinely used lictors to arrest people, while aediles inspected weights and measures (as did a variety of specialised officials in eastern cities). *Servi publici*, slaves owned by the community they served, watched over public buildings, took part in arrest parties and served as prison guards throughout the Empire. Especially in the Gallic provinces and other northern areas, about twenty suggestive inscriptions point to specialised security officials in some areas, bearing titles such as "prefect of the watch" or "anti-banditry prefect". Apuleius (*Met.* 3.3) may allude to such a figure when he has a character describe himself as a diligent *praefectus nocturnae custodiae* who "went around the whole town, door by door" on his nightly rounds.[9]

Civilian police institutions were more advanced in Eastern areas such as Egypt, the Levant, Asia Minor and Greece, where a longer history of state development gave rise to some pre-Roman policing experiments. Rabbinic sources show Jews adapting their own traditions of guards and inspectors to life under Roman rule. In many Greek communities, members of the local elite took turns serving as guardians of the peace, with titles such as *eirênarchês* or *paraphylax*. Often these officials commanded a force of mounted *diôgmitai* ("pursuers"), who helped the city control its hinterland (Sperber 1998, esp. 32–43; Brélaz 2005).

Egyptian papyri amply illustrate the great variety of civilian guards and police arrangements, which were mostly performed as temporary compulsory public services. Many liturgical guard assignments reiterate the centrality of irrigation and grain in this unusual province, such as sluice guards, river guards, harbour guards, crop guards, estate guards and guards of the threshing floors. Not all of these figures were very imposing or effective. Some watchtower guards were mere children (e.g. *O.Florida* 2). In one case, thieves

[6] e.g. *lex Salp.* 26.45.5–7; *lex Malac.* 59; cf. *lex Irn.* 19.17–22, 20.32–37 and 26.43–46.

[7] Xenophon *Ephesiaca* 2.13 (cf. 3.95); *SEG* XLIX 1866 = Brélaz 2005, 423–431; *AE* 1979, 624 (= *IB* 5, Commodus to Boubôn).

[8] e.g. Appian *B Civ.* 4.120; Pliny *Ep.* 6.25; cf. Iuv. 3.306–308.

[9] Riess 2001, 174–236; Fuhrmann 2012, 52–66; cf. Roselaar, ch. 10.

beat and tied up two pedestrian victims *and* the nearby watchtower guard (*P. Fay.* 108; the purpose of such a feeble lookout was presumably to alert others in case of trouble; compare Dio Cass. 54.4 on guards using bells to raise an alarm).

Egyptian civilian policing distinguished between two security roles that are usually not clearly delineated elsewhere: guard duty versus summoning or arresting suspects. One measure of this distinction is a papyrus from 392 AD (*P. Oxy.* vii 1033) in which two Oxyrhynchite night guards vehemently complained that they were being forced to carry out arrests *and* attend to the city watch without support, with the result that they feared for their lives. In addition to limited resources, jurisdictional boundaries could be a real problem. In one first-century example (*P. Mich.* vi 421), a victim of a donkey theft and his local policeman (*archephodos*) tracked the thieves to a neighbouring town, but the police there beat them both and detained them for three days, giving the donkey thieves time to get away. While such details are both alluring and invaluable, papyri remain imperfect sources. Fragmentary letters, non-contextualised summonses and one-sided petitions swelling with *topoi* cannot be treated as clean data. Even in Egypt where the sources are incomparably rich, the development and interrelation of different police arrangements remains unclear, and a full analysis of police in Roman Egypt has yet to be written.[10]

23.3 Emperors and Military Policing

Henceforth we will focus on police duties performed by soldiers serving emperors, governors and other Roman authorities. Military policing became increasingly pervasive over the course of the Principate, but not necessarily at the expense of the civilian police arrangements described above.

23.3.1 Republican Precedents for Military Policing

The roots of Roman military policing are traceable to the late Republic. Amid that era's crises, the state occasionally granted sweeping powers to particular leaders to enforce some kind of order. Soldiers played a role in many of these episodes, such as the Cretan mercenaries who helped eliminate Gaius Gracchus' partisans in 121 BC. Catiline's revolutionaries in 63 BC were countered by a mixture of private informants, ad hoc guard posting, and ultimately troops in the field. The Republic frequently and flexibly used the praetor's military authority to counter piracy, slave insurrections and other pressing security challenges that were deemed inferior to a consul's dignity (Brennan 2000). Pompey and Caesar each violated Republican tradition by using soldiers for routine policing within the *pomerium*, in Rome itself.[11] When Mark Anthony, Octavian and Lepidus proscribed their enemies during the Second Triumvirate, it was soldiers who hunted down many of their prey.

[10] Bagnall 1993, 134–135. Partial treatments include Torallas Tovar 2000 and Homoth-Kuhs 2005.

[11] Cic. *Mil.* 37.101; Caes. *B Civ.* 3.1; Dio Cass. 40.50–54; Suet. *Iul.* 43.

23.3.2 Early Emperors and Military Policing, especially in Rome and the West

Augustus was most responsible for setting military policing on a growth trajectory during the Principate. Major disorders in Italy, left over from the Civil Wars, prompted the first experiments. Specifically, slave flight, rampant banditry and freemen being kidnapped into slavery all threatened to undermine the legitimacy of the new regime. Augustus, assisted by his stepson Tiberius, distributed military posts (*stationes militum*) as needed in Italy. Tiberius created more of these stations after he succeeded Augustus in 14 AD.[12] Augustus' Principate saw an unprecedented expansion of police institutions in Rome itself, where at least 10,000 armed men (including praetorians, urban cohorts, *vigiles*) patrolled the streets. By the late first century AD, there were at least 20,000 military police in Rome. With a possible ratio of police-to-civilian inhabitant of 1:50, few modern cities are as thickly policed as Rome c.100 AD. Political stability was the prime motivation behind Rome's policing personnel, but this does not preclude incidental security benefits to ordinary people. Augustus even posted extra guards in the city during major spectacles, lest burglars take advantage of the emptiness of residences whose dwellers were out enjoying the show (Suet. *Aug.* 43).[13] By the Severan era, the prefect of the *vigiles*, urban prefect and praetorian prefects had accrued considerable criminal jurisdiction in Rome and Italy (D.1.11–12, 1.15). Troops in Rome were imperfect state agents, as their presence often offended civilians (Juv. 16, for instance), and fickle praetorians notoriously intruded into Imperial succession. As early as the second century BC, authorities sometimes moved to expel unpopular groups from Rome, such as Jews, astrologers and certain philosophers. Such expulsions were never effectively implemented, and often amounted to little more than ploys for popularity.[14] "Bad" emperors tried to use soldiers and other agents to monitor the populace for dissent.[15] But Rome was nothing like a modern "police state".

While the capital city was a special case, early emperors did expand military policing in Italy and the provinces.[16] Over the course of the first century AD, branches of the Rome-based urban cohorts were stationed in Carthage and at the important mint in Lyon (*ILS* 2130: *mil. coh. Lugudunensis ad monetam*). The ports of Ostia and Puteoli in Italy received extensions of Rome's *vigiles* (though fire-fighting was the *vigiles*' primary role, their duties crossed over into policing in various ways). Soldiers were a growing presence in the Empire's main cities throughout the early and later Roman Empire. Emperors and governors sometimes used these troops to put down riots, but this was not always a politic choice, and some authorities chose instead just to let popular agitation flare up and burn itself out.[17]

[12] *RGDA* 25 (with Dio Cass. 49.12); App. *B Civ.* 5.132.547; Suet. *Aug.* 32, *Tib.* 8 and 37.

[13] Sablayrolles 1996; Coulston 2000; Ricci 2011; Fuhrmann 2012, 113–145; Bingham 2013, esp. 81–114; Kelly 2013.

[14] See Fuhrmann 2012, 120–121 and 142–143 for references.

[15] e.g. Epict. *Diss.* 4.13.5 (probably Epictetus' *bête noir* Domitian); Dio Cass. 78.17 (Loeb; Caracalla); cf. Tac. *Ann.* 4.67–69. Even Hadrian is censured: SHA *Hadr.* 11.

[16] e.g. Suet. *Claud.* 25; SHA *Hadr.* 18.10, and Tertullian *Apol.* 2.8. For further references on the following see Fuhrmann 2012, 123–238.

[17] e.g. the proconsul Gallio in Corinth, Acts 18; see Kelly ch. 29, this volume.

At the broader level of managing public order in the Empire as a whole, emperors actively involved themselves in disorders and disputes in provincial communities throughout the Roman world. Augustus enslaved the people of Cyzicus for flogging and killing Roman citizens during some kind of disorder (*stasis*, Dio Cass. 54.7); this is but one of several examples of the Augustus' interfering in provincial disputes, which he indulged in without manifest partiality towards any particular community or social class, and regardless of a province's supposed "senatorial" status (Crete–Cyrenaica and the Cyrene edicts: *SEG* IX 8) or a city's "free" status (e.g. Cnidos: *ARS* 147). Others followed Augustus' example: Tiberius answered scandalous mistreatment of a centurion's corpse in Pollentia with troops, who seized the town and held most of its inhabitants "in chains for life" (*vincula perpetua*, Suet. *Tib.* 37; also a reminder that long-term detention or imprisonment existed in the Roman world) (Krause 1996; Rivière 2004). In 59 AD, Nero worked with the senate to punish Pompeii for a bloody amphitheatre riot there, exiling individuals responsible for the disorder, banning future gladiator shows for ten years, and dissolving illegal clubs (*collegia*, Tac. *Ann.* 14.17; on *collegia* see Perry, ch. 11.). Emperors' direct engagement in public order outside Rome was commonplace.

Emperors certainly used praetorians and other specially appointed soldiers to defend their interests, assassinate their enemies, and squelch particular flare-ups of crime or banditry. In the early second century the *frumentarii* soldiers appear as specialists in the sensitive work of administrative communication, domestic espionage and assassination. They had a headquarters on the Caelian Hill in Rome, but also circulated throughout the provinces (most of our information on *frumentarii* in fact comes from Eastern sources). Concern over intelligence and control was nothing new, of course; Augustus, after all, had instituted the so-called "Imperial post" or *cursus publicus* to know more quickly what was going on in each province, according to Suetonius (*Aug.* 49). Soldiers on various types of missions used the state transport system, and frequently abused civilians through phony "requisitions" of their pack animals and supplies. Emperors and other authorities promulgated several condemnations of this kind of mistreatment and other elements of police corruption, and the jurists humanely reiterate proper standards of conduct (e.g. D.1.18.6, esp. 5). Modern scholars tend to focus too negatively on Rome's failure to stamp out official malfeasance, but against this high bar it is only fair to note the government's continual energy in correcting abuse, and the faith in the system on the part of civilians who took the trouble to file complaints about corrupt police.[18]

23.4 Governors and Military Policing

Roman provincial governors were key agents of policing and public order in the Empire. Several passages of the Digest highlight their law-and-order role, for instance:

> It is fitting that a good and serious governor (*praeses*) should see to it that the province he rules remains pacified and quiet (*pacata atque quieta*). He will achieve this without difficulty if he earnestly pursues evil men and clears them from his province. For he must hunt

[18] Mitchell 1976; Ando 2000, 363–382; Kolb 2000; see now *AE* 2009, 1428.

> out committers of sacrilege, bandits, kidnappers and thieves, punishing each in proportion to the crimes committed. He must also repress their abettors, without whom a bandit cannot hide for long.[19]

When Fronto was preparing to govern Mauretania at the behest of Antoninus Pius, he was eager to secure the services of one friend for his military experience fighting bandits. Governors' subjects expected them to provide security and suppress crime.[20]

Every governor would have at least a few hundred soldiers at his disposal, and these men were one of a governor's most important means for successfully ruling his province. These soldiers were temporarily seconded from their larger military units and attached to the staffs (*officia*) of each governor. Governors routinely used these soldiers for police work. In fact, provincials viewed the governor and his entourage as islands of security in a dangerous world.[21]

Christian texts pertaining to persecution specifically detail police work done by the governors' men. Even discounting exaggeration and other problems of these sources, third-century martyr *acta*, letters and biographies reveal a keen awareness of policing jargon as different types of soldiers on governors' staff hunt for Christian leaders, arrest and hold them, take part in their trials and eventually execute them. The spectacle of punishment literally became the stuff of nightmares, and not just on the part of Christians.[22] These lasting images of dread in people's imagination fulfilled the very goal of many governors' approach to law and order. While Ulpian noted (D.1.16.8) that a governor had "greater authority than anyone in the province, after the emperor", in fact many factors constrained his sway on the ground. A governor certainly did not have enough troops to secure every part of the province at all times (Apul. *Met.* 2.18). So instead, when it was necessary to make a strong statement against criminality, he sometimes resorted to a certain economy of violence by showy public executions of outlaws. Accounts of Jesus' death highlight the cruelty of Pilate's Roman soldiers as they flog and crucify him. But in other ways the most famous crucifixion was atypical, particularly the respectful treatment eventually accorded to Jesus' corpse. The jurist Callistratus pointed out (D.48.19.28.15) that most governors tried to crucify bandits and leave their bodies exposed exactly where they had committed their crimes. Callistratus specified two judicious reasons for this practice: first, so that the horrible sight might deter others from crime; second, so that the manifest and lasting punishment would provide some solace for the families victimised by the bandit. This pervasive punishment by exposure shows up in a number of gallows-humour expressions and popular stories.[23]

The correspondence between Trajan and Pliny, when the latter was governor of Bithynia-Pontus in the early 110s, provides the material for a telling case study of Roman law and order in one place at one time. Here we see top-level concern over several

[19] D.1.18.13pr. Cf. D.1.18.3 and D.11.4.3. *Praeses* is a generic term covering all types of provincial governors: D.1.18.1; on governors, note Richardson, ch. 9, this volume.

[20] Fronto *ad Anton. Pium.* 8.1 (Loeb I, 236); 1 Peter 2:13–14; Apul. *Florida* 9.36.

[21] Haensch 1997, esp. 710–726; Epict. *Diss.* 4.1.91; Apul. *Met.* 2.18.

[22] Christian sources: Shaw 2003; non-Christian nightmares: Artem. *Oneir.* 1.35, 1.39–40, 1.48, 1.70, 1.77, 2.49–54.

[23] e.g. Hor. *Ep.* 1.16.48; Iuv. 14.77; Phaedrus *App.* 15; Petron. *Sat.* 111–12; cf. pseudo-Quintilian *Declamationes minores* 274.13. See now Cook 2014.

matters, large and small: fraudulent city accounts, staffing of prison guards, movements of small numbers of soldiers, meetings and associations, employment and status of condemned criminals, legal status of other individuals, proper use of the state transport system and religious crimes. This file of letters is often misread; on the grand scale, they are typically forced into a narrow petition-and-response reading that does not do justice to the rich, sometimes proactive state procedures in the background of Roman governance (note Ando 2016). As for policing by Roman soldiers, Pliny repeatedly asked Trajan for permission to use soldiers in various policing roles. Trajan almost always said no, which has misled some scholars into claiming that Rome exercised a consistent policy against using soldiers as police. I argue for the opposite conclusion. Pliny's requests show just the kind of tasks governors and other power-holders were tempted to use soldiers for, from shoring up dodgy prison staffs and escorting travelling officials, to requisition missions and providing security in communities that needed their help (Pliny *Ep.* 10.19–22, 10.27–28, 10.77–78.). Not all governors and emperors were as conscientious and careful as Pliny and Trajan depict themselves in their letters, and Pliny's reaction to problems in Bithynia suggests why policing by Roman soldiers increased in the second and third centuries AD.

Although all soldiers in the provinces were notionally under the command of a governor, not all soldier-police can be clearly tied to traditional modes of military command. Imperial procurators, for example, sometimes had soldiers at their disposal, helping to guard mines or Imperial estates. In one telling example (Frend 1956), peasants from two discordant villages on an Imperial estate in Phrygia specifically asked for a military policeman (*stationarius*) to be posted among them, to ensure fair resolution of a dispute over what each village owed to the state transport system. *Stationarii* appear in second- and third-century sources as low-ranking soldiers performing temporary guard duty, often among civilians. *Stationarius* can be a casual label describing a single day's assignment policing spectacles in Rome or controlling road traffic, or it can refer to longer-duration postings as a policeman in certain communities for a year or two. *Stationarii* are not to be confused with higher-ranking soldiers such as *beneficiarii consulares* (bureaucrats who only occasionally engaged in police work) or out-posted *regionarii* centurions who exercised broader responsibility for an area's security. These various types of out-posted soldiers received petitions from victims of crime who were eager for the attention of any state authority, but such soldiers were not intended to be a "police judiciaire". They were posted according to the state's regulatory and security needs in each area, and some received decrees of official gratitude from local authorities. Others generated complaints by taking advantage of their authority, committing acts of violence and extortion and otherwise abusing civilians.[24] Many out-posted soldier-police seem to have been acting with little supervision from governors or other commanders, but largely they must have performed their duties adequately enough not to enter the source record for good or ill.

[24] Fuhrmann 2012, 197–238, 249–252; France and Nelis-Clément 2014; and Peachin's commentary on *P. Sijp.* 15.

23.5 Coordination of Police Authorities in the Roman Empire

The types of policing described above can be divided between different levels of authority: private security, civilian magistrates, the emperor, governors and military police who were not closely supervised by traditional power-holders. One question that remains is how effectively these different levels of authority cooperated with each other. There was fundamental coordination between the emperor and governors, especially those of "Imperial" provinces whom he selected, at least in the emperor's initial choice and instructions (*mandata*) he gave to a governor (Eck, ch. 8). Subsequent interactions would vary depending on the personalities of each man and circumstances in the province.

The most routine coordination of police authority was between governors and the civilian authorities who did most of the real work of arresting and trying local troublemakers. To oversimplify: if these were petty, low-status and manifestly guilty offenders, most communities should have little trouble handling the matter themselves. But anything more complicated (capital cases, higher-status disputants who might appeal the local court's verdict, conflicts between communities or ones that aggravated deep local rifts) was likely to need the governor's attention. But here again much depended on individual inclination. Crooked governors, who were not rare, sought opportunities for extortion and bribery. Hearing cases was a significant part of a governor's duties, but many were not particularly conscientious; they would make the easy choice to do just what local assessors wanted them to do.[25] Some more careful, pro-active governors rejected local policing practices they deemed unsatisfactory. Pliny (*Ep.* 10.19) felt so uneasy about the use of public slaves as prison guards that he supplemented them with soldiers. Antoninus Pius, as governor of Asia under Hadrian, disliked the way civilian police (*eirênarchai*) interrogated suspects and sometimes wrote malicious reports that would unfairly ensure their condemnation. In this case, Hadrian and Antoninus Pius reiterated much more stringent standards of interrogation, documentation and court procedure, threatening exemplary punishment if any *eirênarch* submitted dishonest reports thenceforth (D.48.3.6pr-1).

Other than the general patterns and examples noted above, the four main levels of police authority in the Roman Empire (civilian, Imperial, gubernatorial, military) were not particularly well coordinated. There are some exceptions, and Decius and Valerian's harassment of Christians in the 250s constitute an ambitious attempt to coordinate police authorities. On the surface, it is easy to dismiss these emperors' unsuccessful religious policies, which were out of step with previous emperors' typical approach to religion and law enforcement alike. They remind us of how erratic the Imperial will can be, and their edicts were unevenly enforced. On the other hand, the third-century persecutions suggest a top-down confidence in the state and its mechanisms of enforcement, a level of ambition unlike the "reactive", "petition-and-response" minimalist model of Roman governance. In some places, the decrees of distant emperors set into motion a police apparatus with interlocking types of authority, from the emperor to out-posted

[25] e.g. Philostrat. *VA* 5.36; cf. depictions of Pilate's trial of Jesus.

soldiers, with civilian magistrates working alongside the governors' men to track and arrest Christian leaders.[26]

The clearest instance of police coordination, however, is Romans' desperation to prevent slave flight, which led to especially ambitious police efforts to find, recapture, detain and return fugitive slaves. A wide range of sources reflects these procedures, which are also listed concisely in a single title of the Digest (11.4, "On runaway slaves"). Emperors decreed that any slave-owner could obtain a letter from the governor, and a gubernatorial attendant if needed, to search for a missing slave. In Italy, even senators and procurators of Imperial estates had to open their estates for such searches. *Stationarii*, harbour guards, local magistrates, estate bailiffs (*vilici*) and other authorities had to hold recaptured slaves diligently to ensure they would not escape. Abettors of runaways are likewise threatened with serious punishments. Slave flight was not merely an economic problem for individual masters; the sheer illegality of slaves absconding was an affront to Roman order, but even more than that, it also disturbed Romans' dichotomous belief that each person is either a slave or free (Inst.Gai.1.9). With that fundamental distinction in mind, Romans warily tried to manage their slave population and prevent possible uprisings (Fuhrmann 2012, 21–43).

23.6 Conclusion

While different forms of security coexisted in the eras treated above, military policing was a mainstay of public order and state control during the first, second and early third centuries. Policing changed considerably from the time of Diocletian and Constantine, with the disappearance of certain military police (including the *frumentarii* and almost all of Rome's police complement), and emerging forms of civilian police such as *agentes in rebus*, and *riparioi* in Egypt. As Roman power collapsed in the West, the Byzantine state continued developing its own mix of traditional Roman policing (such as soldiers policing some cities) and policing novelties (particularly new types of high officials and royal guards).

So from the second century BC onwards, we can detect a wide array of Roman experiments with police institutions. Policing is a fact of Roman history, so let us dispense with the hackneyed refrain that the Roman world was a police-less society. In provinces East and West, civilians of all ranks seemed familiar with police, and sometimes valued their presence despite the real threat of police brutality and corruption.

Policing, again, was not inevitable or even necessarily effective, but it was what state officials opted to use to address a range of ad hoc challenges. The prevalent use of soldiers for routine policing during the Principate is explained by the basic fact of Rome having a large, expensive, professional army, in which most men never saw combat in a full-scale war. Without anything like ancient China's bureaucracy, where else could Roman authorities turn when they needed disciplined agents of the state to help the Empire function? Using soldiers as police was one answer. Whether dealing with civilian police or

[26] Fuhrmann 2016, arguing the primacy of governors and their *officia* in these episodes.

military ones, they were all imperfect, yet state authorities kept using them, and ordinary people thought it worthwhile to bring their problems to their attention. These facts show that Rome's rulers and subjects alike had faith in institutional policing as a worthy state activity.

Bibliography

Ando, C. 2000. *Imperial ideology and provincial loyalty in the Roman empire*. Berkeley.

Ando, C. 2016. "Petition and response, order and obey: contemporary models of Roman government." In H. D. Baker et al., eds., *Governing ancient empires*. Vienna.

Bagnall, R. 1993. *Egypt in late antiquity*. Princeton.

Bingham, S. 2013. *The praetorian guard: a history of Rome's elite special forces*. London.

Brélaz, C. 2005. *La sécurité publique en Asie Mineure sous le Principat*. Basel.

Brennan, T. C. 2000. *The praetorship in the Roman Republic*. 2 vols. Oxford.

Cadoux, T. J. (2008). "The Roman *carcer* and its adjuncts." *Greece & Rome* 55: 202–221.

Cascione, C. 1999. Tresviri capitales: *storia di una magistratura minore*. Naples.

Cook, J. G. 2014. *Crucifixion in the Mediterranean world*. Tübingen.

Coulston, J. 2000. "'Armed and belted men': the soldiery in imperial Rome." In J. Coulston and H. Dodge, eds., *Ancient Rome: the archaeology of the eternal city*. Oxford. 76–118.

France, J., and J. Nelis-Clément, eds. 2014. *La* statio: *archéologie d'un lieu de pouvoir dans l'empire romain*. Bordeaux.

Frend, W. H. C. (1956). "A third-century inscription relating to *angareia* in Phrygia." *Journal of Roman Studies* 46: 46–56.

Fuhrmann, C. 2012. *Policing the Roman empire: soldiers, administration, and public order*. Oxford.

Fuhrmann, C. 2016. "How to kill a bishop: organs of Christian persecution in the third century." In R. Haensch, ed., *Recht haben und Recht bekommen im* Imperium Romanum: *das Gerichtswesen der Römischen Kaiserzeit und seine dokumentarische Evidenz. JJP* Suppl. 24. Warsaw. 241–261.

Haensch, R. 1997. Capita provinciarum: *Statthaltersitze und Provinzialverwaltung in der römischen Kaiserzeit*. Mainz.

Homoth-Kuhs, C. 2005. Phylakes *und* Phylakon-*steuer im Griechisch-römischen Ägypten: ein Beitrag zur Geschichte des antiken Sicherheitswesens*. Munich.

Kelly, B. 2013. "Policing and security." In P. Erdkamp, ed., *The Cambridge companion to ancient Rome*. Cambridge. 410–424.

Kolb, A. 2000. *Transport und Nachrichtentransfer im Römischen Reich*. Berlin.

Krause, J.-U. 1996. *Gefängnisse im Römischen Reich*. Stuttgart.

Lintott, A. 1999². *Violence in republican Rome*. Oxford.

Mitchell, S. (1976). "Requisitioned transport in the Roman Empire: a new inscription from Pisidia." *Journal of Roman Studies* 66: 106–131.

Nippel, W. 1995. *Public order in ancient Rome*. Cambridge.

Peachin, M. (2007). "Petition to a centurion from the NYU papyrus collection and the question of informal adjudication performed by soldiers (*P. Sijp.* 15)." In A. J. B. Sirks and K. A. Worp, eds., *Papyri in Memory of P. J. Sijpesteijn*. Chippenham. 79–97.

Ricci, C. (2011). "*In custodiam urbis*: notes on the *cohortes urbanae* (1968–2010)." *Historia* 60: 484–508.

Riess, W. 2001. *Apuleius und die Räuber: ein Beitrag zur historischen Kriminalitätsforschung.* Stuttgart.

Rivière, Y. 2002. *Les délateurs sous l'Empire romain.* Rome.

Rivière, Y. 2004. *Le cachot et les fers: détention et coercition à Rome.* Paris.

Robinson, O. 1992. *Ancient Rome: city planning and administration.* London/New York.

Sablayrolles, R. 1996. Libertinus miles: *les cohortes de vigiles.* Rome.

Shaw, B. (2003). "Judicial nightmares and Christian memory." *Journal of Early Christian Studies* 11: 533–63.

Sperber, D. 1998. *The city in Roman Palestine.* Oxford.

Torallas Tovar, S. 2000. "The police in Byzantine Egypt: the hierarchy in the papyri from the fourth to the seventh centuries." In A. McDonald and C. Riggs, eds., *Current research in Egyptology.* Oxford. 115–123.

CHAPTER 24

PUBLIC AND PRIVATE CRIMINAL LAW

ANDREW RIGGSBY

24.1 Introduction

It is not clear what this chapter is about. What Roman "criminal law" comprises has varied significantly, if quietly, in the literature. While there are of course handbooks and treatises with such titles (or "Straf-/Kriminalrecht", "diritto penale", "droit pénal" etc.), scholars often show little interest in defining their subject matter.[1] There are perhaps three typical approaches, though one often finds a combination of them in practice. The first approach is to offer a theoretical definition. Thus, Mommsen 1899 simply asserts (literally on page one) that "The criminal law ["Strafrecht"] is based on the moral concept of duty as far as the state has determined to enforce it", regardless of Roman categories. A second approach is more concrete. It accepts as criminal a stipulated list of subject matters, typically ones treated as "criminal" in one or more modern legal systems, whatever their status in Roman law. So, for instance, Robinson's 1995 handbook does not explain its list of chapters on "Theft and Related Offences", "Violence against the Person", "Sexual Offences" etc. Third, some scholars take one or more Roman categories together and equate them to "criminal" law (e.g Falchi 1937 on, in essence, *crimina*). Typically, this last approach at least tacitly draws on one or the other of the first two to give some guidance of what Roman categories are to be included.[2]

As I have already hinted, the root of these differences lies in the fact that the terms in the title beg an important question. Is there such a thing as Roman "criminal" law at all? Not only is there the potential for mismatch between cultures alluded to above, but even

[1] Exceptions are typically essayistic, as Cascione 2012.

[2] Kunkel 1962 is hard to fit into this scheme because his theories are set against the background of an implausibly expansive, essentially extra-legal, "police jurisdiction".

modern understandings of the term are fragmented in many of the same ways as the treatments of Roman law, so there is uncertainty on both sides of the comparison.

The goal of this chapter will be to assess the utility of the terminology of "crime" and "criminal" to the Roman legal world. It might be objected immediately that this project unduly imposes modern categories on the ancient evidence, but that view is impossible to sustain for both specific and general reasons. First, the use of modern terms like "crime" is extremely widespread, and to ignore the possible problems itself does more violence to the ancient evidence than addressing them. Second, in practice my method (for which see the next paragraph) will require considerable attention to the organisation of native Roman categories. And that is especially important because, finally, determining exactly what those native categories are is not nearly as straightforward as is often imagined.

I propose, then, that the historical inquiry into the nature of supposed Roman criminal law can usefully be treated as a version of the linguistic problem colloquially described with the phrase "is there a word for it?" It has long been observed both by scholars and ordinary speakers that individual words can lack an exact equivalent in other languages. Yet, as both linguists and philosophers of language have pointed out, translation (broadly construed as a process) nonetheless normally results in communication of meaning.[3] Most things turn out eventually to be sayable in the target language, if only at greater length and, implicitly or explicitly, as part of a broader exchange. My method, then, will be to compare a variety of categories on either side (that is, ancient and modern) and consider how they do and do not correspond. Even if (perhaps especially if) there is no good Roman equivalent for the criminal, mapping the articulations of the general topic tell us important things about the Roman legal imaginary.

A few preliminary warnings about terminology will be in order. First, and most generally, English terms should *not* be taken as glosses for their Latin cognates. In part, the separation is meant to avoid prejudicing questions about the original vocabulary, and in part it is meant to allow capture of ideas that do not necessarily correspond to any single Roman category. This will be particularly important for three words. By "action" I mean any legal proceeding, whatever the venue (so, wider than Latin *actio*). By "prosecutor" I mean the person who initiates an action, even if we would sometimes refer to that person as, for instance, the "plaintiff". And by "offence" I will mean the real-world behaviour that the law aims to prevent or control, again, even if the conventional term might be something else like "tort" or "breach". I will also collapse the distinctions between certain similar offences in both ancient and modern contexts.[4]

[3] Philosophy: Davidson 1973. Linguistics: "'No word for X' archive" (http://languagelog.ldc.upenn.edu/nll/?p=1081, accessed 13 April 2015).

[4] I offer the following conventional cover terms: theft = *furtum, rapina, arbores furtim caesae, vi bona rapta*, etc. (D.47.1, 6–9, 14–18); dropping objects = *deiecta et effusa, posita et suspensa* (9.3); property damage = Aquilian actions, *pauperies, pastus pecoris* (D.9.1, 9.2, 19.5.14.3); guardianship = *tutor suspectus* (D.26.10), *rationibus distrahendis* (D.27.3); deviant legal process = the several actions at D.2.2–11 plus *calumnia* (D.3.6)

24.2 Roman Formal Categories

While the focus of this section will be on Roman categories, we still need some preliminary notion of what, for us, constitutes the criminal to give some idea of where to start looking. One might proceed either by theoretical, abstract definition or by listing a number of "typical" crimes. Theoretical definitions tend to focus on notions like punishment, protection of public or collective interests and a pervasive role for the state in proceedings.[5] A list of offences would probably include, among others, homicide, theft, assault, treason, rape, forgery and arson. I will have much more to say about this in sections 24.2 and 24.3, but for now a loose combination of the two ideas will suffice to organise the discussion. What parts of Roman law, then, look "criminal"?

Iudicia publica. The late Republic (particularly the period 149–81) saw the establishment of courts often today called "criminal"; in Latin these can be called both *quaestiones perpetuae* (institutionally "standing inquiries") and *iudicia publica* (substantively "public courts"). Originally, any person could offer to prosecute any offence, and cases were heard before large elite juries. A few additional offences were introduced under Augustus (and perhaps Julius Caesar), but the original procedure went out of use, perhaps quickly, under the Empire (on the history of procedure under the Principate see section 24.3 and ch. 20). Still, the offences they responded to remained a standing category of Roman law (D.48.1.1; see the Table in section 24.3 for a full list). Book 48 of the Digest treats essentially the same list of offences plus *plagium* (cf. Inst.4.18.10). On its own terms, this set is fairly well defined, but that is because the entire membership is stipulated (based on, essentially, historical accident).[6] Substantively all of these offences have been criminal in at least some modern systems. They do not, however, include some acts that are broadly treated as criminal today (principally thefts and simple assaults; also, at least originally, arson, forgery of most private documents, blackmail and defamation) nor many "moral" offences that are treated as criminal more sporadically (e.g. intoxicants, gambling, prostitution). Moreover, although the term *publicum* is itself suggestive of one criterion for the criminal, it is never defined or given an explanatory value.

Delictum.[7] As a result, many discussions of Roman "criminal" law also take in the category of *delictum*, which encompasses some classic types of criminal behaviour, especially theft and assault. We will return to this, but first I note that *delictum* is a harder category to pin down than *publicum*. In the Digest the word itself has a variety of senses. Sometimes, it explicitly includes public offences to which is it often opposed today (D.48.2.20pr [note *ceteris*]; 48.15.7pr; 48.19.1pr, 5.2; especially for soldiers, e.g. 28.3.6.6). In its broadest sense, it seems to encompass bad behaviour that is not in itself subject to legal penalty (D.4.4.47.1; 12.7.5pr; 21.1.1.8, 17.6; 24.3.39pr; 25.2.21.5; 38.17.2.34). Only occasionally does it seem to refer

[5] For a review of different views see Antony Duff, "Theories of criminal law", *The Stanford Encyclopedia of Philosophy* (http://plato.stanford.edu/archives/sum2013/entries/criminal-law/, accessed 13 April 2015).

[6] The *lex Cornelia de iniuriis* (D.47.10.5pr) has features that some take as characteristically public, but are perhaps better taken as simply statutory. *Concussio* (extortion by fraudulent threat of public authority) rises to the level of a public offence if the threat is of criminal prosecution (D.47.13.2).

[7] See Descheemaeker 2009, 52–67 for an attempt at a diachronic account.

to a legal category that can be contrasted with both private/civil actions (D.4.4.9.2; 5.1.57pr; 14.5.4.2; 44.7.49pr) and public ones (D.21.1.17.18; 47.8.2.24). Moreover, whatever the term may have meant abstractly, it is also unclear which specific actions it is taken to comprise. Gaius offers two slightly different approaches. In the Institutes (Inst.Gai.3.88, 182) *delictum* covers any obligation not arising from contract: his examples are *furtum, bona vi rapta, damnum iniuria datum* and *iniuria*. In a series of passages excerpted from *Res cottidianae*, we see a similar typology, but with the term *maleficium* instead of *delictum* (D.44.7.1pr), followed by the same examples (D.44.7.4).[8] Here, however, Gaius adds three other examples which are "like" (*quasi*) the delicts: a judge "making the case his own"; throwing material from windows; operators of ships, etc. liable for loss at the hands of their staff (D.44.7.5.4–6; cf. Inst.Gai.4.1–5). As yet another alternative, we may observe the actions grouped together in book 47 of the Digest in the title *de privatis delictis*. This includes thefts, *iniuria*, violation of tombs and a few minor items,[9] but not actions for property damage, treated in earlier books. Since Gaius' lists are both explicitly exemplary, and since the organisation of the Digest is not highly theorised, it is hard to tell even whether the omissions or distinctions between versions are significant.

At the same time, however, there are acts never named *delicta*, but whose treatment is typologically similar. The category includes description as *poenalis*, penalty in the form of a multiple of the prosecutor's *interesse*, availability to the heirs of the victim, non-availability against the heirs of the wrong-doer and a one-year time limit. Among the actions matching most of these criteria are those against a surveyor who gives faulty measurements (D.11.6), a vexatious prosecutor (D.3.6), a person who illegitimately summons a parent or patron to court (D.2.4), a person who does not obey the orders of a presiding magistrate (D.2.3), a person who prevents another from appearing in court (D.2.7), and (sometimes) a tutor who has not done his duty (D.26.10.1.6). In what follows I will use *delictum* conventionally to refer to non-public penal offences, but it must be remembered that the category is not so clear-cut.

Actiones populares. If the *iudica publica* attracts attention at least in part because of the importance of the "public" to some notions of criminality, the same might be true for the cognate *actiones populares*, which may be pursued by any citizen (specially interested persons have priority in some cases). As with *delicta*, a number of actions are explicitly described in our sources as *popularis*, while others (most in epigraphically attested statutes) have no formal categorisation but share the key features of open prosecution and set fines. Actions attested in juristic sources include those against violation of tombs (D.47.12), dropping objects (D.9.3), keeping dangerous animals insecurely (D.21.1.40, 42), damaging the praetor's album (D.2.1.7), moving boundary stones (D.47.21), damaging a public road (D.43.8.2.34), and prematurely opening a will (D.29.5.25.2). Epigraphic statutes typically

[8] Like *delictum* and *crimen*, *maleficium* potentially covers any wrongdoing, though it tends (like *delictum*) to more private matters. I am not impressed by attempts to find precise but evolving differences in usage between this term and *delictum* and/or *crimen*, *pace* Albertario 1936, Honoré 1962, 102; Descheemacker 2009, 53 is sound, though I am less certain of the broader argument.

[9] The final title (*de popularibus actionibus*) can be read as sitting as a distinct category between the delicts proper in this book and the public crimes in the next book. I would also observe that, given the residual status of *stellionatus* (D.47.20), all three of the final titles could be seen as only marginally attached to the list.

foresee prosecution against a person (usually a magistrate) who does not administer the individual law (citations at *RS* I:11). The relation of this category to the *iudicia publica* and *delicta* is complex. On the one hand, there is some substantive overlap with the latter. Violation of a tomb is grouped with the delicts in book 47 of the Digest, and, in fact, the general rules for the *actiones populares* are the last title in that book (D.47.23). Dropping objects is one of Gaius' examples of quasi-delict. On the other, there is more procedural similarity to the public. Beyond open prosecution, their penalty is typically fixed, they do not permit the prosecutor to appoint a procurator, and their rights do not form part of the prosecutor's estate before *litis contestatio*. Occasionally such actions are even described as "public" (*RS* I:11).

Crimen/criminalis.[10] Frequently, Latin *crimen* seems to refer to offences either within the jurisdictional area of the notional *iudicia publica*, or at least assimilated to those (e.g. D.47.2.93 theft treated *criminaliter*). And, indeed, an explicit opposition between *crimen* and *delictum* is sometimes made (D.21.1.17.18; 47.2.83pr; 47.20.3.1). Yet elsewhere *crimen* extends more broadly to include at least *delicta*, and perhaps other bad behaviour (D.48.1.7; 48.15.6pr; 48.16.3; 48.19.1.3). In still other instances, *crimina* are explicitly contrasted with "pecuniary" matters (D.3.6.1.1; 22.5.1.1; 49.9.1), even though several public offences are monetary in one way or another (e.g. D.47.21.3pr, 48.15.7pr). This category, like that of *delicta*, is not stable, but on any interpretation it is likely to be narrower than modern "crime".

Poena/poenalis. Though not as common as *crimen* or *delictum*, *poenalis* seems to represent an important category insofar as it is used in explanatory fashion. That is, jurists report that a given *actio* has certain procedural features *because* it is a penal action (e.g. D.9.3.5.13; 11.3.13.1; 40.12.21pr-1). Yet the term seems almost never to be applied to the *iudicia publica*. The evidence for the categorisation of delicts as *poenalis* is better, though still not substantial. Most instances refer either to *actiones populares* or to various forms of interference with the exercise of jurisdiction. *Poena* is more common and clearly can refer to the result of a conviction by the *iudicia publica*, but even so the more common uses seem to be those just mentioned for the adjectival form. If we can discern a technical sense, it is not broad enough to accommodate the bulk of the criminal.

If none of these categories, at least in their seemingly technical senses, are as broad as "crime", perhaps we should look for a composite? In fact, it has long been conventional to lump together the *delicta* and offences of the *iudicia publica* for roughly these reasons, and the formal features suggest including popular actions as well. Then, however, we start to encounter excessive breadth instead, comprising actions not clearly criminal in any sense. Many of these issues revolve around content and will be treated in section 24.3, but there are formal ones as well.

An obvious problem is the Aquilian action for wrongful damage. As has been pointed out, it is not clear how to justify the Roman claim that this is a penal action (Inst.Gai.4.9; cf. Inst.4.3.9; D.9.2.23.8). Condemnation for *duplum* could be avoided by confession and payment of *simplum*; that is, any penalty was for the denial, not the underlying offence (seemingly confirmed by D.46.3.7). It is logically possible that the same payment was

[10] For present purposes, I ignore the well-known ambiguities inherent in this term between "accusation" (the earlier sense) and "thing of which one is accused", and (within the latter sense) between conceptual/general criminal *offences* and actual/specific criminal *acts*.

conceived of as both penalty and compensation (Zimmermann 1996, 974), but it is also possible that the (very ancient) Aquilian action came to be assimilated to other, genuinely penal actions because it did not arise from contract or other previous relationship. Also, unlike most *delicta* and public offences, the *lex Aquilia* does not require the prosecutor to show *dolus* on the part of the defendant.

Another problem lies in the extension of liability for theft or damage to the operators of ships, inns and stables for the acts of their employees (D.44.7.5.6). First, this includes essentially Aquilian liability and so is suspect on all the above grounds. Then it removes the requirement of *dolus* (at least on the part of the owner being sued) to establish the operator's liability for thefts as well. Whatever the status of theft and property damage, this action is designed to ensure good management, at least a step away from whatever the underlying policy concerns on damage and theft.

The seeming minor *delicta* and *actiones populares* are mostly penal, but do not otherwise seem criminal (and the *actio suspecti tutoris* is not even penal, D.26.10.3). The public character of actions regulating guardians (D.26.10.3 and D.27.3.1.19–24) and against corrupting slaves (D.11.3) can be conjectured, but are not secure. The question is more acute in the case of the action against surveyors (D.11.6). This is explicitly in the place of a contractual action on *locatio conductio* (surveyors are one of the "liberal" professions who are not hired), and though explicitly *poenalis*, the action in practice provides only compensation (D.11.6.3pr, 3; 5.1). That is, both the penal nature of the action and its non-contractual status seem to be all but fictional (the action does require *dolus*, a higher standard of responsibility than a normal contract). In addition to issues of their substance, several *actiones populares* (dropping objects, perhaps damaging roads) do not require a showing of *dolus*.

One could in theory make further adjustments. For instance, one could eliminate the quasi-delicts (though the very existence of this set is weakly attested) or the *actiones populares* (though their public/penal form makes that hard). However, such operations would further weaken the claim of the resulting category to being a native Roman one. Moreover, such an attempt glosses over problems with even the "basic" notions of public and delictual offences. However, this is not our only option. The above discussion has focused on formal features with minimal and crude attention to the subject matter of the offences. Section 24.3 will consider whether a more substantive approach would be more productive.

24.3 Substance of the Offences

The following chart lays out most of the public, delictual and popular actions according to a conventional view of the divisions (and compressing some actions as described in n. 4, marked here by *). For public offences I give both the Latin name of the court and an English translation. It should be kept in mind, however, that the English-language categories are hardly natural themselves, and in some cases are potentially misleading. For instance, the offence of *plagium* has a different focus than "kidnapping" (or "sequestro di persona" or "Freiheitsberaubung"). I will address this and some other significant differences below:

Delicta	*Actiones Populares*	"Public"
theft*	*album corruptum*	*de sicariis* homicide
property damage*	dropping objects*	*Vis* Violence
Insult	desecrating a tomb	*Ambitus* electoral bribery
corrupting a slave	wild beasts	*Falsum* counterfeiting/forgery
[hiding assets]	damaging public roads	*Repetundae* extortion by official authority
Dolus	prematurely opening will	*Peculatus* theft of state property
reporting false survey measures	moving boundary stones	*Maiestas* insult to the Republic
calumnia		*plagium?* kidnapping?
unlawful summons to court		
disobeying the court		*Annona* interfering with grain supply
preventing appearance in court		*Adulterium* Adultery
malfeasance as guardian		jailbreak?
Dolus	sanctions for interfering with various statutes	*stellionatus*

I have argued elsewhere that the offences tried by the *iudicia publica* were originally understood as affecting the community as a whole (Riggsby 1999, 151–71). In most instances (*ambitus, vis, repetundae, peculatus, falsum, maiestas*) this takes the form of grave public disorder or interference with the operations of the organs of state.[11] Note particularly, that *vis* at this period appears to be restricted to acts *contra rem publicam*, primarily riot and sedition. Thus it contrasts neatly with violence between individuals, which is a form of the delict *iniuria*. Similarly, most thefts are delicts, but taking state property is the public offence *peculatus*.

The two seeming exceptions to this pattern are homicide and *plagium*. Absent special circumstances, however, homicide in general was not a public offence until 81 BC or slightly before.[12] Those special circumstances included murder by a near relative (which had collective implications for religious pollution), abuse of capital process and killing in the context of gang violence and banditry, all dangers to the community as a whole. The extension of public status to all forms of intentional homicide, taken along with other restrictions on

[11] A partly overlapping set of offences (poisoning, counterfeiting, forgery and perhaps adultery) involves "invisible" acts. I have suggested these are therefore perceived to exist everywhere (and so are a collective problem) so long as criminals are on the loose.

[12] Cloud 1969; Riggsby 1999, 50–55; Gaughan 2009.

weapons and on the use of violence in dispute resolution, suggests an attempt to shift the legitimate use of violence increasingly from private hands to the state's, as part of a broader trend towards a more powerful and more centralised state during the late Republic and early Empire. While objections to the Weberian cast of that argument can and have been raised, pointing to gaps in the law (self-defence; violence against one's own slaves), the point is not a fully extensive or effective state monopoly, but rather a move in that general direction.

The *lex Fabia de plagariis* prohibited treating a person as your slave who was either free or not yours, and the sources stress the role of concealment (D.48.15; Buckland 1908, 32). This could fall under my category of "invisible" crimes (n. 11), but more important is its marginal status as a public offence. Not only does it not appear in Macer's canonical list, but the original penalty of a set fine (D.48.15.7) is more typical of an *actio popularis* than a public offence.

I now suggest that if public offences are those that threaten harm to collective interests, then delictual offences threaten individual interests, and popular offences threaten generic ones. "Individual" refers here to an interest whose violation in the case of one person does not imply collateral damage to anyone else's interests. My taking your car, for instance, does not typically threaten the notion of private property in general. "Generic" interests, by contrast, are ones that are threatened *en masse*, even if not universally, by individual acts. Your driving drunk threatens an indefinitely large group. Note two things about this typology. First, strictly speaking, it is not the interests but the violations that are individual, generic or collective. Theft by title fraud, for instance, might be thought to jeopardise more property than just what is actually stolen, and thus fall into a different category than, say, shoplifting. This example also illustrates the second point. These categories, and any like them, are socially constructed in the strongest sense. They depend on how this or that offence was viewed by (some group of) Romans; there is no objective matter of fact.

A theft, a libel or a slip of a careless barber's razor (all *delicta*) harm only particular persons. Throwing things out windows into a crowded street or keeping lions, tigers and bears (popular offences) endanger the whole neighbourhood. Note in particular the following distinction. A tree-cutter is liable (delictually) to an individual harmed by a branch dropped too carelessly (D.9.2.31). But there is popular liability if something is thrown from a house into a place *quo vulgo iter fiet* (D.9.3.1pr). The act inherently threatens many even if in particular cases it harms only one. The justification for preventing "violation" of tombs is apparently religious, and so has collective implications (D.47.12.4).

There are cases of possible overlap between public and popular offences, but none turn out to be clear problems. The various statutory *actiones populares* could have been construed as injury to the whole by abuse of state apparatus (as in the regulatory use eventually adopted for *repetundae* [Riggsby 1999, 123–126]), but we may note both that those offences are relatively late to appear in the public courts and that the popular actions are generally directed at non-, not mal-feasance; many individual citizens may suffer, but the collective sovereignty is not expressly challenged (I reiterate the necessarily constructed nature of this). One could imagine road damage as a public offence like *peculatus*, but the focus of the former is actually on hindering transit (the prosecutor gets his own *interesse*), not the loss to the state. That said, the public/popular distinction may be blurred by other factors. The *actiones populares* clearly predate the *iudicia publica* and are naturally not replaced even when the latter are introduced. They also appear principally in municipal statutes and so are marginal to the legal system as a whole and in particular are not readily replaced by *iudicia publica*.

The sketch I have just given is based on the late Republican situation, but the facts change thereafter. The general trends of the Imperial period are simple to describe: the expansion of public jurisdiction (without abolition of any delictual or popular actions) and less clear articulation of the system as a whole. First, there are a few new criminal statutes. Under Caesar and/or Augustus new laws bring more violence under the jurisdiction of the public courts. The forms that had been public offences all along were governed by a *lex Iulia de vi publica* (D.48.6), while non-political forms involving gathering a mob (D.48.7.2, 4pr, 5, 8) were tried as *vis privata* (D.48.7). Courts were also established to try adultery and harm to the grain supply (D.48.5, 12). The latter fits the "public" easily enough. The former would require us to imagine a substantial reassignment of authority over reproduction to the state, parallel to the transfer of violence.

Second, other offences are assimilated to the existing statutory categories, often by *senatus consultum*. So, for instance, the homicide statute also came to cover castration, taking up arms to gain possession of property, concealing a shipwreck or instigating sedition (D.48.8.3.4). *Falsum* is extended to private documents beyond wills (D.48.10.1.4, 9.3). As we have them in the Digest, there is enormous overlap between *maiestas* and *vis publica*, which seems to be a late development, though we do not always know in which statute a given provision originated. Also, the *actio popularis* against violating tombs was taken (at least in part) into the law on *vis publica* (D.47.12.8) and the delict of *concussio* into the homicide law (D.47.13.2).

Third, a number of the *delicta* come to give rise to dual liability. They could be prosecuted in the original way or "criminally" by the *cognitio* of the official with jurisdiction: *iniuria* (D.47.10.45), thefts (D.47.2.93, 47.9.1.1, cf. 47.14.2), *praevaricatio* (D.47.15.2), *expilata hereditas* (D.47.19.3), jailbreak (D.47.18.1pr). These offences, then, never went before a *iudicium publicum*. They are assimilated to the public in that (a) the "new" procedure is explicitly attested as such, not as a modification of the old, (b) this new procedure is often described with the language of *crimina*, and/or (c) the outcome is now typically a punishment of the sort normally restricted to the world of the *iudicia publica*.

Lastly, we see the creation of the new hybrid offence of *stellionatus*, a type of fraud. This is treated in book 47 of the Digest, and is there said not to be a public offence (D.47.20.1, cf. 47.11.3). But the same passage also says that it is not private. Furthermore, Ulpian says that as the *actio de dolo* relates to private matters, so *stellionatus* does to public ones, and it has penalties that seem characteristically public (D.47.20.3.1–2). In substance, the comparison to *dolus* means that it is residual but expansive. Ulpian and Modestinus list a number of specific frauds and conspiracies, but in principle it seems to criminalise any behaviour the state wishes (D.47.20.3–4).

In its own terms, the late Republican system of public offences, *actiones populares* and *delicta* has a passably clear parallel articulation in terms of both form and substance, but all three categories show some fuzziness on both counts. Moreover, there are a number of other operative categories of varying explicitness and importance (e.g. *poena*, *dolus*, pre-existing relationship). Later developments tend to reduce the clarity of this system further.

In comparison to modern notions of crime, the earlier Roman categories are individually narrow, but collectively rather broad. Moreover, the very existence of sub-articulations is a distinctive feature. In some senses the later expansion of the public offences and "criminalisation" of delict seems to produce a category more like modern crime. On the other hand, the Roman version still omits important parts of the modern category (broadly speaking, offences against the environment, economy, privacy and morals). Moreover, the composite is actually very ill defined in Roman terms, corresponding to no particular term, procedure or juristic typology. The overlap with the modern category is, I will now argue, largely an accident due to historical forces that have little to do with the specific subject matter of the law in question.

24.4 What Is to Be Done?

The account above of the original *iudica publica* claimed that they were political in a subjective sense. Limitation of offences to the collective interests of the community is by definition a more or less self-conscious decision about the distribution of power within and by that community. But discussion of any version of the "criminal" will be political in an objective sense. It, too, involves choices about how and where state power is brought to bear, even if the surrounding rhetoric is framed in terms of individual rights or (more often?) dangers. This invites us to consider the broader political context of the evolution just traced.

The rise of the Imperial state, both in terms of its scope and its increasingly centralised and authoritarian character had both direct and indirect effects on this body of law. Directly, to the extent that the public courts and their successor procedures continued to be the venue in which to hear cases of wrong-doing against collective and particularly state interest, the expansion of public jurisdiction is hardly surprising. More and more of life became the business of the state and so naturally changed its status. The creation of *stellionatus* is perhaps the ultimate expression of this tendency. That which is not specifically permitted is as least potentially criminal. Indirectly, the desire to bring all the apparatus of power under the supervision of the emperor helped create the *cognitio*. The mere fact of the transition made it somewhat easier to move substantive matters into the replacement procedure. As civil cases also made their way more slowly into *cognitio*, it became that much easier for the public jurisdiction to absorb more subject material as procedural differences were effaced. The time lag, incidentally, is perhaps not surprising. To the extent that the criminal is especially bound up with the political, the former is more easily subject to changes in the broader political order.

Yet the (quite broad) sense of the "political" just used is not exclusive. That is, the criminal law is simultaneously a political institution and a legal one, and so is subject to the normal internal forces of the partly autonomous legal sphere. The conventional practices of the jurists are certainly relevant here, such as their generally casuistic style and their failure to fully normalise a restricted technical vocabulary (as we have seen with most of the key terms used here). I would, however, draw attention to two other factors. On the one hand, there was enough flexibility in the system to privilege reform over revolution. Without, for instance, the possibility of separate rules for the reipersecutory use of principally penal actions (D.9.2.23.8; 47.8.2.27, 9.2.2, 20.1.6), a more radical rethinking of categories might have been necessary. Perhaps most important for the present question is the tendency of the jurists to think in terms of types, rather than typologies. The "penal" and the "popular" (and to a lesser extent the "public") are each reasonably well-defined types, but that definition is almost entirely by way of a list of properties. Most jurists are not interested in systematic relational comparison. Hence, no one ever really confronts the "division of labour".

At the same time, this area of law is different from others in being less juristic. All of the *iudicia publica* are statutory, both in conception and origin, as are some *delicta* and many of the *actiones populares*. Moreover, the overtly political nature of many criminal offences seems to have discouraged juristic attention until relatively late (e.g. Cascione 2012, 288–90). Paradoxically, the effects of this history seem to have been largely disruptive. In general, of course, there is the fact that laws are drafted by relatively few individuals and are subject to a single vote, not the discipline of juristic back-and-forth, potentially over generations. The formulaic character of much statutory language cautions us not to make too strong a distinction in this respect, but the potential for greater diversity is there. One of the greatest examples of this is perhaps the creation over a fairly short time of the new institution of the *iudicia publica*. Moreover, even statutes that are perhaps unexceptionable in their own time are locked in place in a way that juristic discourse is not. Consider, for instance, the distinctions among kinds of theft which were locked in from the days of the XII Tables and the evolution of *actiones populares* in an environment that largely predated the *iudicia publica*. In a few moments, principally the reigns of Sulla and Augustus, the single mind of the guiding legislator might have created some unity. This helps account for the relative coherence of the late Republican/early Imperial situation, but at the same time it allows for certain kinds of idiosyncrasy. It is not clear, for instance, why Sulla wished to "promote" a few types of *iniuria* to a different kind of procedure or even exactly what he thought that procedure amounted to (n. 6). Yet that special status remains locked in even in the Digest.

If, then, the late Republican situation is configured according to a different logic than contemporary criminal law, and the Imperial law is increasingly shaped by factors that have little to do with any particular conceptualisation of its subject matter, are the modern terms hopelessly anachronistic? Not all uses are equally problematic. There is, of course, no difficulty in legal analysis of individual Roman categories that sometimes happen to be called "criminal", e.g. *furtum* or the *iudicia publica*. Moreover, "crime" as a general phenomenon in the modern sense was a real and significant thing in the Roman world. There was taking and killing and so forth, and it makes perfect sense to study those phenomena if we wish, as well as the various societal responses to them. Those could involve policing, familial strategies like vendetta and production of narratives or tropes, and there is no reason not to study juristic production from this historical point of view as well.[13] This much, I take it, is like studying the Roman "economy" even though there was no such ancient concept (but also keeping in mind that that conceptual difference certainly had real world effects). As a legal matter, however, it may be best to avoid the term altogether.

Bibliography

Albertario, E. 1936. "Maleficium," in *Studi di diritto romano*. Milan. Vol. 3: 197–208.

Bryen, A. 2013. *Violence in Roman Egypt: a study in legal interpretation*. Philadelphia.

Buckland, W. W. 1908. *The Roman law of slavery: the condition of the slave in private law from Augustus to Justinian*. Cambridge.

[13] See, for instance, Bryen 2013 and ch. 25 or, on the largest scale, Harries 2007.

Cascione, C. 2012. "Roman delicts and criminal law: theory and practice." In T. A. J. McGinn, ed., *Obligations in Roman law: past, present, and future*. Ann Arbor. 267–295.
Cloud, D. (1969). "The primary purpose of the *lex Cornelia de Sicariis*." *Zeitschrift der Savigny-Stiftung für Rechtsgeschichte, romanistische Abteilung* 86: 258–286.
Davidson, D. (1973). "Radical interpretation." *Dialectica* 27: 314–28.
Descheemaeker, E. 2009. *The division of wrongs: a historical comparative study*. Oxford.
Duff, A. 2013. "Theories of criminal law." *The Stanford Encyclopedia of Philosophy*. First published 14 October 2002; substantive revision 14 May 2013. http://plato.stanford.edu/archives/sum2013/entries/criminal-law/, accessed 13 April 2015.
Falchi, G. 1930–1937. *Diritto penale romano*. 3 vols. Treviso.
Gaughan, J. 2009. *Murder was not a crime*. Austin.
Harries, J. 2007. *Law and crime in the Roman world*. Cambridge.
Honoré, A. 1962. *Gaius*. Oxford.
Kunkel, W. 1962. *Untersuchungen zur Entwicklung des römischen Kriminalverfahrens in vorsullanischer Zeit*. Munich.
Mommsen, T. 1899. *Römisches Strafrecht*. Leipzig.
Riggsby, A. 1999. *Crime and community in Ciceronian Rome*. Austin.
Robinson, O. 1995. *The criminal law of ancient Rome*. Baltimore.
Zimmermann, R. 1996. *The law of obligations: Roman foundations of the civilian tradition*. Oxford.

CHAPTER 25

CRIMES AGAINST THE INDIVIDUAL

Violence and Sexual Crimes

ARI Z. BRYEN

25.1 Introduction

One of the great joys of paging through Justinian's Digest is the wealth of detail it provides on the Roman world at work, in towns, cities and countryside; like a Juvenalian satire, the jurists provide us with precious descriptions of bustle, shipping and building; of buying, selling and deal-making; and of the world of characters (some well-intentioned, others not) who populated this busy landscape.[1] The corollary of this frenzy of activity was that the potential for harm abounded. At a particular horizon in Roman history, however, a distinct class of harmful acts began to emerge. These acts were understood not to inflict loss, but rather to wound a person's *existimatio*—his public face.[2] The term alerts us that these special types of harm were held to affect more than a person's private subjectivity, but affected rather a person's place in society; if left unavenged or at least without rectification, they were understood to degrade not the perpetrator but the victim. It is therefore unsurprising that, in a society in which slavery was endemic, these were harms that could be felt primarily by free people; slaves and the slavish were generally denied the "ordinary luxury of negative reciprocity"—the ability to avenge these offences and mark themselves as being redeemed from degradation (the phrase comes from Scott 1992, 23).

Intentional, degrading treatment of the person and his household (especially in the form of adultery or illicit sexual liaisons with members of his family) emerged as an intellectual and political problem in Roman legal thought starting at the end of the Republic, *pari passu* with the crises of sovereignty that paralysed the Roman state. Starting in this

[1] Acknowledgements: I would like to thank the editors and the participants at the Edinburgh planning meeting for their feedback. This manuscript was completed in residence at the American Bar Foundation; I thank the ABF for its hospitality.

[2] *Existimatio*: Callistratus, D.50.13.5pr. I use the masculine pronoun on purpose: these concepts were gendered in the Roman world.

period, Romans of the literate class took a new interest in personal harms and the concepts of citizenship and membership that underwrote them, producing a view of the citizen that in some aspects very much resembled his sovereign, and vice-versa: an intact representative of his household, one who was both peculiarly vulnerable but also capable of avenging himself and his dependents; one who was capable of great violence but who possessed sufficient self-control to wield it only against criminals, slaves or the slavish.

The purpose of this chapter is to excavate this understanding of the relation between the ideal citizen and his family, violence and "crime".[3] This involves linking law and society in two ways: by locating the emergence of these ideas within their historical context; and by explaining how juristic understandings of violation of the person were part of a denser network of signs and symbols that Roman intellectuals adapted to analyse the end of the Republic and the transition to one-man rule. To link law and its context in this manner requires more than looking at the history of procedures for dealing with the valuation or classification of injuries, or reading the relevant sections of the Digest (though this is indispensable). It involves looking also at the ways in which ideas about law's relations to interpersonal violence were put to work in narrative texts that sought to explain the peculiar nature of the Roman citizen body (in both senses of the term), political change and sovereignty.

25.2 From Debtors to Citizens

The integrity of the person was not of especial interest to the earliest Roman legislators. In the XII Tables, three provisions alone deal with injuries: one with broken bones, one with a *membrum* that has been *ruptum*, a third with "injury"—either an injury done to someone (*iniuria<m>*), or treating another injuriously (*iniuriā*). Scholars differ as to the proper reconstruction and interpretation of each of these provisions, as well as their relationships to one another and to the procedures subsequently devised for dealing with interpersonal violence (the *actio iniuriarum*) or for pricing damage to slaves, chattels and objects (*damnum iniuria datum*).[4] So far as ideas about personhood are concerned, however, earliest Roman law was in general less interested in acts that were per se degrading, but rather with acts having the potential for ensnaring their victim in webs of debt and dependence.[5]

[3] I use the term "crime" in accordance with normal English usage to designate a particular class of acts marked as somehow exceptionally problematic and deserving of punishment. Useful recent surveys of Roman criminal law in English include Bauman 1996; Robinson 1996; Harries 2007; Riggsby (ch. 24, this volume).

[4] On the XII Tables see Watson 1975; on links to subsequent law, Birks 1969; Cursi 2002; Cursi (ch. 45, this volume).

[5] Implicitly I am rejecting the idea that ancient law finds its origins in managing an "honour society" in which individuals violently avenge threats to their persons. For the historiography of that of that idea and important critiques see Whitman 1995–1996. The XII Tables and the texts quoting them are cited according to the edition of *RS*.

The XII Tables used two modes to establish the value of compensation for harms. The first was to treat compensation as a fixed sum. In the case of felling a productive tree, the penalty was 25 asses (I.16). A tree and a man were treated in the same way: injury (*iniuria/*<*m*>) to another was also priced at 25 asses (I.15). In the case of broken bones, the penalty was 300 asses for the bone of a free man, 150 for that of a slave (I.14), paid specifically as a penalty (*poena*<*e*>). The second was to provide compensation by forcing the harmer to hand over the culpable object or pay the price demanded by the victim. Thus damage by animals was urged towards settlement by threatening the owner with loss of his animal in *noxa* (VIII.2). In cases of accidental harm, animals were substituted for compensation (VIII.13). A similar line of thinking may lie behind the perplexing case of a destroyed limb, for which the XII Tables held out the possibility of painful and disfiguring retaliation to push parties to settlement (I.13, with Miller 2006). Only in a single case might compensation have been priced to market rates: for double value in the case of a non-manifest theft by an underage party, who was also to be flogged at the judgement of the magistrate (VIII.5); the text, however, is hard to reconstruct.[6]

By contrast, when we look to the acts that the XII Tables marked as especially problematic ("crimes", in my sense), the harshest penalties seem designed not to prevent intentional acts of degradation, but rather to punish acts that are likely to drive someone into a state of debt or dependence. So-called "manifest" thieves could be killed if caught at night (I.17); manifest thieves could also be flogged and "handed over" (*transque dato, addicere*: Inst.Gai.3.189) unless they convinced their captor to accept a more favourable settlement (I.19 with *RS* II 614–615). The victim of theft never relinquished his right to the stolen object, presumably even if he had to enter into debt to offset its loss (I.22). Theft of foodstuffs was treated with particular ire: whoever cut crops at night would be "hanged for Ceres", unless underage (VIII.4). The penalty for the man who enchants crops or "attracts" the harvest of another (*qui fruges excantasset*, VIII.4) is not preserved, nor is the penalty for the one who "sings a wicked song" (*malum carmen incantasset*, VIII.1). But it was likely a harsh punishment, probably death.[7] This "wicked song" might be understood as a particular kind of curse on another's crops (killing them out of spite—*invidia*—rather than trying to "attract" them as one's own property), or it might be understood as public declarations that someone acted inappropriately, impugning their reputation and hence their creditworthiness (cf. Lintott 1999, 6–21). Lastly, the arsonist who burnt a pile of grain, thus threatening the basic subsistence of the family, was to be beaten and burned alive, if he did it on purpose (VIII.6).

The leitmotif in the cases with the harshest punishments is not harm to honour or personhood. What links them instead is that they are the sorts of things in consequence of which a previously independent person might find himself driven to a neighbour to have to borrow to repair. Stealing, and particularly stealing or destroying crops or stored foodstuffs (that is, the following year's subsistence), or ruining credit, might force victims to borrow, potentially from hostile parties. Accordingly, harsh punishments were also directed against corrupt acts from those who provided social insurance against being

[6] The provision is attested in Plin. *HN* 18.12: *impubem praetoris arbitratu verberari noxiamve duplionemve decerni*. Crawford emends to <<*verberato duplioneque damnum decidito*>>, on the basis of Festus, *Pauli Exc.* 181L.

[7] August. *De civ. D.* 2.9 = Cic. *Rep.* 4.12; cf. Porph. ad Hor. *Epist.* 2.1.152–155.

indebted to hostile parties. Patrons were declared *sacer*—able to be killed at will—if they harmed clients (VIII.10), those who bore false witness were thrown from a rock (VIII.12); and whoever lied about the formal transmission of property was held to be "unacceptable" (*inprobus*) and barred as a witness (*intestabilis*; VIII.11).[8]

This analysis has limits. The preserved evidence is biased in complex ways, and mediated through juristic and antiquarian traditions that were themselves developing. It is nonetheless telling that the preserved material tends to be organised around questions of compensation for specific acts, on the one hand, and the exclusion of malefactors who might ensnare their victims in debt, on the other. Nonetheless, we might venture to say that the concern for the civic community that animates this legislation is with who is legitimately to be kept "in" and who cast "out": when a likely consequence of debt was enslavement and exclusion from the community, the treatment of those who caused people to enter into debt illegitimately was to exclude them in turn, by applying to them some form or other of capital punishment or formal denaturalisation (declaring them *sacer*, for instance).

25.3 Citizens, Sovereigns, Degradation

If the XII Tables were interested in the circumstances under which a person might be legitimately excluded from the civic community, later law worried instead about the possibility that a person might be degraded but nonetheless included. This came to be a problem with political stakes, in two senses. First, living with degraded citizens became a problem of political community in the late Republic, for the possibility that the man serving with you in battle or making decisions in the assembly had been forced to suffer degradation and had been unable to redeem himself was incompatible with the notion that Roman citizens were a privileged community deserving of ruling a vast Empire. Second, the possibility of violation and degradation became something of a problem of sovereignty in an age that was characterised by an increasingly close, indeed almost totemic, relationship between the person of the successful general/warlord and political leadership.[9] To be sure, such bald statements do scant justice to what were complex relationships between ideas of citizenship, bodies, politics and leadership; nonetheless, some broad patterns can be detected.

The earliest part of this history exists primarily in traces of legislation and procedural innovations: debt slavery (*nexum*) was abolished by a *lex Poetelia* of 326 BC; harms to property (slaves, chattels and inanimate objects) were regulated by a *lex Aquilia* of the third century BC; probably around the same time the praetor began to develop an *actio iniuriarum* that changed the procedure for evaluating injuries, moving from a fixed price to an individualised evaluation of a penalty and trial of the facts of the case before *recuperatores*. *Iniuria* emerges from the Republican period onwards to comprise most acts of interpersonal violence, short of murder. Three broad categories were included in the

[8] VIII.9, on guardians, may be an exception here; unfortunately the original wording of the provision is nowhere attested.

[9] Cf. Thomas 1984; on degradation cf. Richlin 1992. On *iniuria* generally, Hagemann 1998.

praetorian edict: intentional, degrading, direct contact with another person (such as beating him "with a fist or a stick"); intentional, degrading words, spoken or shouted in public (*convicium*); or acts that challenged the *pudicitia* of the victim or his family members (D.47.10.1.2). These were treated primarily as private delicts, and, though over the course of the first centuries AD they were increasingly prosecuted *extra ordinem*, at the level of juristic theory they remained private acts that generated relationships of obligation between two individuals, where the violator was forced to redeem, through a monetary penalty, "the pain of having one's liberty infringed".[10]

Starting in the first century BC, the scope of the category began to expand. In 81 BC Sulla's *lex Cornelia de iniuriis* added a criminal action to the praetorian action, forbidding "beating, thrashing or entering (another's) home with force" (D.47.10.5pr). Probably in the early first century AD, the praetor forbade any act treating a person like one who suffered civic disenfranchisement (*infamia*), or an act that caused him to be treated in such a way (Daube 1951/1991). By the second century, actionable acts could include exploiting legal procedures to make that person seem vile or unworthy of credit (Inst.Gai.3.220), preventing someone from casting nets into the sea (D.47.10.13.7), or trying to smooth-talk a woman such that one offended against good morals (*adversus bonos mores adtemptare*: D.47.10.15.20). In short, by the period of the high Empire, *iniuria* had come to be a broad category through which citizens were offered the possibility to redress any degradation of their body or their *dignitas*, or any threat to their civic personhood (D.47.10.1.2).

To be actionable, the harms had to be deliberately inflicted, and the violator had to be counted as having a particular type of intentionality. Harm by animals, children and madmen was not capable of prosecution as *iniuria*, since these members of society lacked the requisite capacity to do wilful harm (*doli capax*: D.47.10.3.1). *Iniuria* was therefore an offence perpetrated primarily by adult men, always potential social equals (though actual differences in wealth and status will complicate this presumption). It need not, however, be an offence always perpetrated *against* an equal: *iniuria* could be done against one's dependants: one's children, wife or slaves. The difference here is that the person able to sue for the *iniuria* was not the injured person, but rather the head of the household (at least in praetorian law). Thus, for an act of violence against a son, the father would sue; in intentional, degrading violence against a slave (that was intended to reflect badly upon the master), the master would have the lawsuit. A *pater familias* was responsible for his dependants, slaves and freedmen included. With these lines of responsibility came a series of limitations on one's dependants; not only would they not be responsible for suing offenders, they were barred from suing the *pater familias* himself for his violence against them, save in extraordinarily limited circumstances in which the *pater* could no longer be held to protect his dependants *as* dependants—such as when he treated a freedman as a slave (D.47.10.7.2).

In contrast to the XII Tables, the praetorian law of *iniuria* does not regulate property or define the terms under which someone is legitimately excluded from society. It produces instead a vision of the citizen as someone who is not willingly dominated at all by another citizen (for this would taint him with slavishness), one who is also the protector

[10] Cf. Daube 1951/1991, 481, discussing Cic. *Caecin.* 12.35 (*actio enim iniuriarum ... dolorem imminutae libertatis iudicio poenaque mitigat*).

of his household and his dependants. What is more, this body of law posits a version of the social contract, agreed to by independent male members, that divides a public realm from a private one. In public, the guarantee of personal inviolability makes interaction with other male citizens possible by creating an ideal of reciprocal recognition between violator and violated, such that harms might be avenged and the victim might recover his place in society (while taking account, to be sure, of *actual* differences in status and dignity). In private, the ideal citizen both dominates and protects his subordinates, keeping them off limits from others, but leaving them without a remedy for his own violence. As far as his family is concerned, every citizen becomes a little sovereign.

By analogy, this vision of the citizen worked to justify the political transformations of the late first century: as the citizen is to his family, so the emperor is to his community. The honorific language bestowing "fatherhood" on the politically powerful who exercised extra-constitutional violence on their citizen "families" made the link easy (*pater* or *parens patriae*, bestowed on Marius, Sulla, Caesar and Augustus, as well as upon Cicero when he executed the Catilinarian conspirators). Accordingly, much of the early elaboration of the position of the emperor in the Roman state was articulated through the category of *maiestas* (harm to the sovereign/Roman state)—a concept reinvented in the early Principate along the lines of the *lex Cornelia de iniuriis*. The new concept of *maiestas* tracked almost precisely the categories included under the crime/delict of *iniuria*, including physical harm to the person of the emperor (or the images that represented it); defamation of the character of both the emperor (and, initially, the senatorial elite); and violation of the "house" (*domus*) of the emperor. Descriptions of *maiestas* are indeed so deeply coloured by the language of *iniuria* that it is at times impossible to distinguish when a source—either juristic or literary—draws primarily from one or the other.[11]

Because of the ways in which violence came to be conceptually linked, in the early Principate, to ideas of politics and citizenship, the problem of violent degradation provided fertile space for jurists, poets and commentators of other sorts to think about the perils of political community. One example will have to suffice, though it is of particular interest since it is told by the Augustan-era jurist, Labeo. Presumably excised from the Digest by Justinianic compilers, it is preserved as a tiny fragment by Aulus Gellius, who sets it within a dialogue about the relation between law and philosophy. Favorinus, the philosopher, makes his case for philosophy by poking fun at the bizarre mismatch between the harshest and the most lenient punishments in the XII Tables. To further demonstrate the inadequacies of law, Favorinus musters an incidence of absurdity documented by Labeo:

> And therefore your friend Labeo also, in the work which he wrote *On the Twelve Tables*, expressing his disapproval of that law, says: "One Lucius Veratius was an exceedingly wicked man and of cruel brutality. He used to amuse himself by striking free men in the face with his open hand. A slave followed him with a purse full of *asses*; as often as he had buffeted anyone, he ordered 25 *asses* to be counted out at once, according to the provision of the Twelve Tables." Therefore, he continued, the praetors afterwards decided that this law was obsolete and invalid and declared that they would appoint arbiters to appraise damages. (Gell. *NA* 20.1.13, transl. Loeb)

[11] Cf. Bauman 1974, 117–118 and *passim*. Notable is *s.c. de Pisone Patre*, l.33, in which the *neglecta maiestate domus Augustae* is contrasted to the *neglecto etiam iure publico*.

This story is often cited as an instance of praetorian "correction" of the *ius civile*: because the original legislators failed to link the pricing of harms to inflation (a problem in an expanding Empire), the wealthy were placed in a position to take advantage of the weak. But to read this little juristic narrative as mere history is to miss Labeo's more interesting exploration of the relationship between violence and the pitfalls of a political community in which notional equality in the eyes of private law was in tension with actual differences in power. To think about this problem, Labeo conjures a particular kind of agent, Lucius Veratius, who does his damage *pro delectamento*—purely for fun, to enjoy the pain of others, and then to deprive them of the opportunity to assess, on their own, what sum might seem sufficient to compensate them for their pain. Veratius' fun is only partly in the harming of others; the remainder comes from the joy of tossing coin at them, of treating his fun with their bodies as a purchasable commodity. For Labeo, the problem is alleviated only when jurisprudential reasoning is substituted for a defective statute, such that it can mediate this tension between the formal equality of citizens and the vicious desires that are produced by the concentration of (economic) power in the hands of a single person. Labeo's logic can be extended, for this link between power, desire and violation is critical for understanding the law related to sexual crimes as well.

25.4 The Citizen and his Household

As with *iniuria*, crimes related to sex were connected not only to the integrity of the household, but also to a politicised discourse prevalent among late Republican and early Imperial aristocrats regarding the proper attitude towards pleasures and appetites. This discourse about pleasure and appetite, in turn, was connected to developing ideas about political behaviour and civic membership.

Much of what we know about the earliest history of sexual crimes is shrouded in obscurity. The tradition of antiquarian writing claims that the *pater familias* would have dealt with harms to the "personhood" of any of his charges by his domestic jurisdiction (e.g. Dion. Hal. *Ant. Rom.* 2.25.5–6). Suggestions in later writers that censors had the power to disenfranchise "degraded" persons are perhaps suggestive, but evidence for the historicity of a *lex Sca(n)tinia* that enabled the withdrawal of civic rights from males penetrated by other males is slim indeed (Richlin 1993). Later writers (such as Valerius Maximus) record Republican-era trials of people for various sexual offences, though how much of his might be coloured by anachronism is an open question (cf. Fantham 1991). It is likely that broad consensus prevailed about proper sexual etiquette, and thus legislative declarations regarding the regulation of sexual behaviour were never mandated. This is not to say that accusations of inappropriate sexual behaviour (lewdness, incest etc.) did not figure prominently on the judicial or forensic stage, only that they resisted elaboration in a legislative idiom.

Until, that is, the reign of Augustus. In 18 BC Augustus introduced the *lex Iulia de adulteriis coercendis*, which criminalised *stuprum* and *adulterium* (D.48.5.13(12)). Both *stuprum* and *adulterium* occupied a common intellectual space with *iniuria*, in the sense that sexual advances might be understood to offend the father or the husband or both. *Stuprum* might be defined as "proscribed sexual conduct", and in the writings of the jurists referred in particular to acts compromising the chastity of unmarried women or boys. Just as the rules on *iniuria* outlined who was an illegitimate target of male violence, *stuprum* outlined who was an illegitimate object of male desire. The "aggressor" was the active partner, though his assault need not have been violent; indeed, both partners may have been willing participants. Willingness, however, was no bar to the degradation of the victim: the male who agreed to be penetrated orally or anally was agreed to be a degraded creature; if he was a Roman citizen, he had additionally engaged in *stuprum*, as had his penetrator. In the case of *struprum* against women, the test was that the woman be potentially marriageable: sex with prostitutes and one's own slaves was acceptable, as was sex with non-citizens. Sex with someone else's slaves might still be considered *iniuria*, if it was felt to offend the master; the praetor also offered an action for "corrupting a slave". Sex with degraded citizen women was not *stuprum* if their degradation barred them from marriage; namely, if they had engaged in prostitution, acted on stage or been condemned in a public trial or for adultery (Tit.Ulp. 13.2).[12]

Augustus' legislation treated both *stuprum* and *adulterium*, terms it used seemingly interchangeably. The jurists were more precise. *Adulterium* had a more narrow range. If *stuprum* could only be committed against those capable of marriage, at the centre of adultery law was the protection of those who *were* married, wives and husbands in particular. The *lex Iulia* criminalised both the married woman who had sex with men other than her husband, as well as the person who had sex with her. It further penalised the husband if he failed to divorce his wife, on the grounds that, by failing to divorce her, he had engaged in pimping (*lenocinium*).

Augustus' legislation went further than a praetor would have gone: in its attempts to hearken back to an anachronistic ideal of domestic jurisdiction, it allowed the enraged father or husband, under certain conditions, to kill the adulterer, and in some cases, the adulterous daughter too. Outlining the conditions for these killings provided much work for the jurists (who wrote a number of books on the *lex Iulia* in particular).[13] According to Augustus' legislation, fathers could kill their adulterous daughters along with the adulterers themselves provided that they were caught in the act, that the daughter was in her father's *potestas*, that the father was *sui iuris*, and that the adultery took place in the father's house or in the house of his son-in-law (D.48.5.21(20)–23(22)). Lest we jump to the conclusion that Roman fathers (or the jurists who imagined them) were axe-wielding, daughter-slicing maniacs, it is worth considering the ways in which the jurists processed the requirements of this strange provision: to defang somewhat this severe provision they read it with a cold literalism. Says Ulpian:

> The words of the statute, "shall have caught the adulterer *in his daughter* (*in filia*)" do not appear to be otiose; for the intention was that this power should be available to the father if and only if he should catch his daughter actually engaged in the crime of adultery. Labeo approves [this interpretation], and Pomponius has written that a person caught in the actual act of love (*in ipsis rebus veneris*) is killed. This is also what Solon and Draco say: ἔν ἔργῳ, "in the act". (D.48.5.24[23]pr, transl. ed. Watson, emphasis added).

[12] The best introduction in English is Treggiari 1991, 261–319.

[13] *Libri de adulteriis*, as recorded by Lenel: Papinian (*De adulteriis libri II* and a *liber singularis*), Paulus (*De adulteriis libri III* and a *De adulteriis liber singularis*), and Ulpian (*Ad legem Juliam de adulteriis libri V*); compare to a single *Liber de iniuriis* by Paulus.

The literalism and the appeal to tradition perhaps made the jurists blush just slightly; this does not mean, of course, that, in the above conditions, they did not intend the aggrieved party to be angry: adulterers who were not killed could certainly be abused, for instance, and without recourse to a prosecution for *iniuria* (D.48.5.23[22].3).

Augustus extended the right to kill to husbands too, but under more limited circumstances; namely, if the adulterer was a degraded person. Says Macer:

> it is permitted by this statute that a husband is permitted to kill a man whom he catches in adultery with his wife in his own house ... if the [paramour] is a pimp or if he was previously an actor or performed on the stage as a dancer or singer or if he has been condemned in criminal proceedings and is not yet restored to his previous status, or if he is a freedman of the husband or wife or of the father, mother, son, or daughter of any of them ... or if he is a slave. (D.48.5.25[24]pr, transl. ed. Watson)

How this would be ascertained, in the heat of the moment, is unclear, and poses a conundrum that renders the law almost impossible to apply. The *lex Iulia* only allowed husbands to kill in the heat of anger; stopping to contemplate the status of the victim might be imagined to be a case of planning or lying in wait, which the jurists made clear was *not* allowed in the punishment of an adulterer. Perhaps the legislator imagined that, if, in the heat of the moment, the husband killed the adulterer, then he might subsequently be *excused* if the dead man fell under one of the enumerated conditions. Suffice to say, however, that the jurists made certain to conceive the law in such a way that it did not incentivise marital rage, and that husbands had to be on warning. For the jurists this burden upon the angry husband was probably a good thing.

Of course, an unauthorised murder might be hard to prove later, and what these strict penalties seem to have created is an incentive for the adulterer to settle with the husband or father to avoid either criminal charges or on-the-spot violence. But precisely because settlement would have created profit for the husband or father, all acceptance of settlements was classed as *lenocinium*, too. Even the giving up of a dowry (that is, through a divorce that was legally the wife's fault) would have fallen under this heading (D.48.5.12[11].3).

Like *iniuria*, sexual crimes were a fruitful locus for thinking about the nature of civic community, and they are highlighted as stories that explain historical changes, much in the same way that Labeo's story about Lucius Veratius explains praetorian "correction" of the civil law. One example from the same historical period will suffice: the story is drawn from the third book of Livy's *Ab Urbe Condita*. It details the consequences of first an act of *iniuria*, then a threatened act of *stuprum*. The story begins in the period of Appius Claudius the *decemvir*, whose *libido stuprandae* causes him to hatch a plot against Lucius Verginius, a *vir exempli recti domi militiaeque* (3.44.2); that is, precisely the sort of idealised Roman citizen that was outlined by the praetorian rules on *iniuria*.

In Livy's telling, Verginius had betrothed his daughter, Verginia, to Lucius Icilius, a former tribune.[14] While Verginius is away, Appius suborns one of his dependants to claim the girl as a slave; once so claimed, she could be delivered into the possession of the dependant to be enjoyed by Appius. Accordingly, Appius' dependant seizes Verginia, drags her to court, and claims her as his own; Appius accordingly awards him possession. Both

[14] Transl. Loeb. On this episode see the analysis of Fögen 2002.

of these acts—the false claim and the knowingly incorrect use of the award of possession—are, in Livy's telling, themselves acts of *iniuria* (3.44.7; 3.45.4). And they provoke a popular outcry in the city of Rome. Icilius, Verginia's husband-to-be, protests, and demands that the proceedings be delayed. His threats to rally the crowd prevail over Appius' formally correct but shocking decision. His appeals succeed, and the proceedings are delayed. Verginius is summoned from the army, and conflict looms in Rome.

The two men later meet in Rome, Appius on his tribunal, and Verginius clad in rags. Verginius announces to Appius that he had given his daughter "to Icilius, to marry, and not to you, Appius, to violate" (*non ad stuprum educavi*: 3.47.7). Nevertheless, Appius judges that the girl is in fact a slave, and he awards possession of Verginia to his dependant, threatening the use of state violence against whoever would stand in his way. At this, Verginius grabs Verginia, and offers Appius "proof" that she was indeed his daughter, and free: he stabs her in the throat, thereby asserting his domestic jurisdiction over his dependants.

The story is grisly, but operates upon a series of contrasting images similar to the ones used by Labeo: the continent man is contrasted to the one animated by desires both for goods and the degradation of others. Similarly, it invokes the categories of private law to think about the difference between a whole person who "counts" in society and one who is a slave. In the case of Veratius, the thrill of violence comes in the cheapness with which a citizen's body can be purchased, and the civic community thus undermined; in the case of Verginius, the narrative turns on the attempt, under colour of law, to treat a free person as a slave, and subject her to *stuprum*. Thus, in Verginius' attempt, back in the army camp, to defend his actions, he explains to his fellow soldiers that "to him the life of his daughter had been dearer than his own, if she had been permitted to live pure and chaste; when he saw her being carried off like a slave to be dishonoured (*cum velut servam ad stuprum rapi videret*), thinking it better to lose his children by death rather than by outrage (*contumelia*) he had been compelled by pity to a seeming act of cruelty ..." (3.50.5–6). Lastly, both of these stories use violations of personhood to explain key moments of historical change, and in particular, historical changes that shift the role of political institutions. In the story of Labeo, the acts of praetorian correction; in the case of Verginius, the re-establishment of the tribunate in wake of the *decemviri*.

25.5 Conclusion

Jurisprudence is not political theory, but it is not innocent of it either. Nor are violence and degradation abiding concerns of all human societies; rather, these categories emerge historically, and come to be linked to one another in ways that explain consequential shifts in politics. In the case of "crimes against the individual", the violation of a citizen's body came to be an important locus wherein jurists and writers could think about what it meant to be a citizen, and what, similarly, it meant to be a sovereign.

Bibliography

Bauman, R. A. 1974. Impietas in principem: *a study of treason against the Roman emperor with special reference to the first century A.D.* Munich.

Bauman, R. A. 1996. *Crime and punishment in ancient Rome*. New York.

Birks, P. (1969). "The early history of *iniuria*." *Tijdschrift voor Rechtsgeschiedenis* 37: 163–208.

Cursi, M. F. 2002. Iniuria cum damno: *antigiuridicità e colpevolezza nella storia del danno aquiliano*. Milan.

Daube, D. 1951/1991. "*Ne quid infamandi causa fiat*: the Roman law of defamation." In D. Cohen and D. Simon, eds., *Collected studies in Roman law*. Frankfurt. Vol. 1: 465–500.

Fantham, E. (1991). "*Stuprum*: public attitudes and penalties for sexual offences in Republican Rome." *Echos du Monde Classique/Classical Views* 35: 267–291.

Fögen, M.-T. 2002. *Römische Rechtsgeschichten: über Ursprung und Evolution eines sozialen Systems*. Göttingen.

Hagemann, M. 1998. Iniuria: *von den XII-Tafeln bis zur justinianischen Kodifikation*. Cologne.

Harries, J. 2007. *Law and crime in the Roman world*. Cambridge.

Lintott, A. W. 1999². *Violence in republican Rome*. Oxford.

Miller, W. I. 2006. *Eye for an eye*. Cambridge.

Richlin, A. 1992. *The garden of Priapus: sexuality and aggression in Roman humor*. New York.

Richlin, A. (1993). "Not before homosexuality: the materiality of the *cinaedus* and the Roman law against love between men." *Journal of the History of Sexuality* 3: 523–573.

Robinson, O. F. 1996. *The criminal law of ancient Rome*. Baltimore.

Scott, J. C. 1992. *Domination and the arts of resistance: hidden transcripts*. New Haven.

Thomas, Y. 1984. "Se venger au forum: Solidarité familiale et procès criminel à Rome (premier siècle av.–deuxième siecle ap. J.C.)." In R. Verdier and J. P. Poly, eds., *La Vengeance: études d'ethnologie, d'histoire, et de philosophie*. Paris. 65–100.

Treggiari, S. 1991. *Roman marriage:* iusti coniuges *from the time of Cicero to the time of Ulpian*. Oxford.

Watson, A. (1975). "Personal injuries in the XII Tables." *Tijdschrift voor Rechtsgeschiedenis* 43: 213–222.

Whitman, J. Q. (1995–1996). "At the origins of law and the state: supervision of violence, mutilation of bodies, or setting of prices?" *Chicago-Kent Law Review* 71: 41–84.

CHAPTER 26

CRIMES AGAINST THE STATE

CALLIE WILLIAMSON

26.1 Introduction

During most of the Republic, the Romans relatively slowly identified and criminalised actions viewed as threats to state security or the existence of the state. Instead, they employed institutional mechanisms to determine a specific response to specific actions deemed threatening. The interaction between the consul and the senate in 186 BC to suppress the cult of Bacchus was typical. On the consul's information the senate established a court of inquiry whose findings initiated a sequence of actions resulting ultimately in the execution of cult members (Liv. 39.8–19). If there was no unanimity in dealing with crisis, the Romans resorted to their unique public lawmaking process as a means for developing community consensus, resolving potentially disruptive issues that could not be bindingly resolved by the senate or magistrates. It was not until roughly 100 BC that the Romans saw the need for a public lawmaking assembly to criminalise offences that "diminished the superiority of the Roman people" (*maiestas populi Romani minuta*), for the first time identifying by statute a serious crime against the state.[1] *Maiestas*, fundamentally an attack on the collective authority of the people, and later, under the Empire, on the emperor, continued in use for the next 600 years, during which conceptions of the state and the identification of offences threatening to the security or the existence of the state underwent significant change.

26.2 Republic

26.2.1 Early and Middle Republic, 509–134 BC

Before the formal emergence of a Roman state, the Romans seem to have reacted to disturbances by removing threats to fundamental relationships underlying the community

[1] Ferrary 1983, 2009. Following Rowe 2014, 305, I use "superiority" instead of "greaterness" to translate the term.

that eventually constituted the state. This way of thinking is reflected in the written laws known as the XII Tables, enacted in the mid-fifth century BC and posted in the centre of Rome, whose few surviving literary fragments preserve some of these threats: a son's killing of his parent (parricide) (superseded by D.48.9), a patron harming his client (VIII 10 [*RS*]), bearing false witness (VIII 11–12, and see VI 2) and stealing crops (VIII 4–5). These acts were punishable by death. While the Romans appear to have moved only slowly beyond such a rudimentary community to a state, it is a unique feature of that move over the centuries that they institutionalised mechanisms of stability in their political structure. Critical among the mechanisms were the lawmaking assemblies that enabled the Romans to resolve internal differences before they rose to the level of threats to the existence of a state in a continual process of formation (Williamson 2005).

From early in the Republic, the Romans used the public lawmaking process as a means of negotiating community consensus to resolve potentially disruptive issues which could not otherwise be peaceably resolved. The lawmaking process made possible the gradual creation of Rome's characteristic bipartite political structure, the Roman senate and Roman people, mediated by annually elected magistrates, in a series of compromises that were initiated by the publication of the XII Tables, and like them were enacted in lawmaking assemblies. In this way the Romans resolved the roughly two-hundred-year struggle for political dominance between plebeians and patricians that threatened to split the state apart.

Accompanying the growing pains of a young state were the distinct threats Rome faced from external enemies in Italy, and by the third century BC beyond Italy. Romans who aided an enemy of Rome in time of war committed the offence of *perduellio*, the most serious crime against the state over the entire period. A recognisable offence from the earliest Republic, *perduellio* comprised a range of actions perceived as directly hostile to the state. *Perduellio* appears to have been a capital offence from the beginning, like parricide, whether or not the death penalty was specified in the XII Tables.[2] Initially, *perduellio* appears to have been adjudicated by a special two-man panel, the *duumviri perduellionis*. With the creation of the office of tribune and the statutory regulation of the right of appeal to the people (*provocatio*), a decision of guilty by the *duumviri* may have initiated further proceedings on the penalty in a judicial assembly (*iudicium populi*) convened by a tribune. Alternatively the *duumviri* may have determined an actionable case for *perduellio*, which was then adjudicated in an *iudicium populi*. Many questions remain open: the origin and the basis of authority of the *duumviri*; whether or not a man found guilty of *perduellio* could avail himself of *provocatio; damnatio memoriae* following conviction for *perduellio*; and procedure in general (Santalucia 1994, 35–48).

The nature of the crime is more certain. By examining known trials, Brecht demonstrated that *perduellio* was restricted in meaning to actions that put the security or existence of the Roman state at risk from an external enemy, successfully countering the prevailing view of *perduellio* as vaguely all-encompassing (Brecht 1938). This fundamental component of *perduellio*, actions hostile to the state in wartime, seems to have persisted until 107 or 106 BC, the date of the latest reliable trial for *perduellio* in its traditional sense

[2] D.48.4.3, disputed in *RS* 2:703.

during the Republic (Alexander 1990, 30). Although *perduellio* disappears from literary reference for almost a hundred years, it was not forgotten (Cloud 1963, 231).

When the stability in Rome's political structure began to weaken in the mid-second century BC, the Romans no longer viewed persons and groups external to Rome as the only threats to state security. The stability of the state was also at risk from wayward action by, and increasingly aggressive competition among, members of the Roman elite. The existence of the state faced its most serious threat from actions that "diminished the superiority of the Roman people". In the last century of the Republic these were criminalised in four statutes: *leges maiestatis*. The final *lex maiestatis*, enacted either by Julius Caesar or by Augustus, remained the law of the land for the next six centuries.

26.2.2 Late Republic, 133–44 BC

Understanding the first *lex maiestatis*, the *lex Appuleia* of the tribune Saturninus, *c.*100 BC, is critical to understanding the legal construct generally. This work must begin by investigating the underlying concept, "the superiority of the Roman people" (*maiestas populi Romani*). There is no firm agreement about the etymology of Latin *maiestas*, though its relation to the comparative adjective *maior* ("greater") seems clear enough, and its pattern of usage also suggests some religious connotation.[3] Moreover, it is not now possible to determine the initial appearance of the formula *maiestas populi Romani* in a juridical context. In later theorisations of Roman foreign relations, and later accounts of legal instruments from the Republic, relations between Rome and outside states are constructed such that foreign allies are obliged to uphold "the superiority of the Roman people" (see esp. D.49.15.7.1). It may have been current by the mid-third century BC, and it might have been articulated as a term of art in trials before the people (Ferrary 1983, 556–557). Intrinsic to the formula is the superiority of Rome over external states and peoples. The statutory crime of "diminishing the superiority of the Roman people", however, inverts the idea. Directed inwards instead of out, *maiestas* dealt with Roman threats to the superiority of the Roman people. A product of the last century of the Republic, *maiestas* belongs to a cluster of sometimes competing efforts, some in lawmaking assemblies and others in the senate, to stabilise a wavering political system.

As conceived by Saturninus, *maiestas* was a crime committed by magistrates who interfered with lawmaking procedures or disregarded the commands of the people. The immediate circumstances of the *lex Appuleia* are believed to involve either the misappropriation of booty and military failure of the proconsul Servilius Caepio in 105 BC, or the opposition of a related Servilius Caepio as quaestor in 103 BC to a land distribution proposal of Saturninus (Ferrary 2009). Viewed against the backdrop of the momentous changes and political innovations of the preceding decades, the *lex Appuleia* represents a logical development in the "century of revolution". This period witnessed the establishment, by vote of the people, of permanent courts to control elite competition as it was manifested in identifiable offences: in

[3] Etymology: Gundel 1963; Thomas 1991. On Thomas see Lanfranchi 2013, who sees *maiestas* as a construct in the sociology of power, not law, drawing on the perspectives of the Italian philosopher Giorgio Agamben.

addition to *maiestas*, these included extortion (*repetundae*), electoral bribery (*ambitus*), embezzlement (*peculatus*), forgery of documents or counterfeiting coins (*falsum*), assault (*vis*) and murder by stabbing or poison (*sicariis et veneficiis*).[4] Thus, in a legal context, *maiestas* was one of many legal steps taken to stabilise Rome in the face of increasing tension by recognising and regulating crime. *Maiestas*, however, had the most far-reaching effect.

This period also witnessed the creation of novel, extra-legal mechanisms directed against elite competition, the cause of destabilisation. Most notable is the extraordinary senate decree, called by modern scholars the *senatus consultum ultimum* (*SCU*), prompted by opposition to the tribune Gracchus in 121 BC. The decree called the people to defend the state against enemies identified by the senate, specifically Gracchus. In response to the decree, Roman senators instigated an armed confrontation that resulted in Gracchus's death by suicide and the deaths of many supporters. Saturninus's efforts when tribune, twenty years later, to associate himself with Gracchus provide grounds to think these events could well be a proximate cause of the *lex Appuleia*.

Where once scholars posited that the *lex Appuleia* extended or included magistrates in the *maiestas populi Romani*, it is more generally believed that the statute aimed to secure the decisions of lawmaking assemblies. Inherent in the "superiority of the community" is the authority of the Roman people to negotiate consensus through the public lawmaking process in which the people voiced their commands through their tribal vote. No matter how Romans voted in each tribe, it was understood on a deep level that community consensus was expressed through the majority vote of the tribes (Williamson 2005, 10–128). As defined in a handbook on rhetoric, *c.*80s BC, " he diminishes the superiority of the state who destroys the things constituting the greatness of the community" ([*m*]*aiestatem is minuit qui ea tollit ex quibus rebus civitatis amplitudo constat*) where the superiority of the state is "that which comprises the dignity and greatness of the community" (*in qua continetur dignitas et amplitudo civitatis*) (*Rhet. Her.* 2.11.17; 4.25.35).

It remains to clarify the identity of the Roman people whose superiority the statute sought to defend. Contemporary scholarship understands Roman orators to have praised or condemned various constructions of the "people" according to their personal politics: for example, the *populus* is good and its actions legitimate when it follows the lead of the senate; the *populus* is bad when it enacts proposals by lawmakers from the side of the *populares* like Saturninus (Ferrary 1983, 564). Yet after the enactment of the statute, and following the senate-directed murder of Saturninus, the first men tried in the newly established *quaestio maiestatis* were supporters and associates of Saturninus. Of his opponents, apparently only one, Caepio, was tried unsuccessfully under the *lex Appuleia*. The legal enactment having established a conceptual and institutional framework for (political) action, it was henceforth available to all parties. Instances of application to one side, the legitimacy of the framework derived from acceptance of the notion that the law had expressed the will of the Roman people.

There were at least three more *leges maiestatis*. In 90 BC, the *lex Varia* addressed aristocrats accused of lending aid to the Italians during the Social War. Believed to have been of limited application, the *lex Varia* seems to have treated aiding the enemy, in this case Latin and Italian allies of Rome, as *maiestas* not *perduellio*. In 81 BC, the *lex Cornelia*

[4] Elite competition: Williamson 2005, 301–314.

addressed provincial governors who acted without authorisation of the Roman people or the senate. The final and historically most important statute was a *lex Iulia* of Julius Caesar or Augustus, on which more later. To what extent the three statutes incorporated new provisions with the old or replaced provisions in the previous statute or the entire statute is unclear. What is clear is the common thread running through all four: the conduct of elected leaders with respect in particular to the commands of the people.

The *leges maiestatis* also share common if superficial characteristics with other contemporary statutes, especially the *leges repetundarum*. These include similarities in procedure and penalties as well as a shared focus on misconduct of provincial officials. Hence, the many efforts to identify surviving fragments of laws engraved on bronze tablets with enactions of the period known from literary sources rarely achieve consensus (see, e.g. *RS* nos. 7, 8). Due in part to such similarities, the modern investigator is sometimes confronted by a seemingly inexplicable resort to different courts for what appear to be the same offence: *quaestio maiestatis* or *quaestio de vi*—the latter said to be the court of choice for Romans of lesser status—or *quaestio repetundarum*. On occasion, the Romans resorted to other mechanisms entirely. One example is the extralegal *SCU*, and another is the practice of declaring (by statute or decree) Romans on the losing side *hostes* (enemies) in the years of Civil War after 89 BC. Other statutes were enacted, too, addressing specific wrongdoings by Roman leaders, e.g. the *lex Clodia* exiling Cicero for the murder of Romans without trial following his issuance as consul of the *SCU* against Catiline and his supporters in 63 BC. Sometimes former procedures were revived, as was the case when the senator Rabirius was accused of *perduellio* in 63 BC for the murder of Saturninus in 100 BC following the issuance of another *SCU*. This unsuccessful trial before a *iudicium populi* is considered an anomaly. What must have been obvious reasons to Romans for the choice of one over another crime or court, or something else altogether, is often a mystery to modern investigators. The problem continues beyond the Republic and into the Empire.

26.3 *Maiestas* under the Empire

26.3.1 Augustus to Hadrian, 27 BC–138 AD

The usual approach taken by scholars attempting to refine the meaning of *maiestas* in both Republic and Empire is resolutely empiricist: one identifies the trials, the accused, the accusations and the penalties imposed. Like Brecht's study on *perduellio*, almost all studies of *maiestas* from the late Republic to the later Roman Empire include a listing of trials.[5] To understand the scope of the crime we rely on details of process, from accusation to penalty. While the trial-listing method of investigation is essential, it often elides and hence effaces from consideration occasions when activities that appear very similar to modern eyes were handled differently by Romans. The method is also useful nearly exclusively in periods where literary sources are strong. The most concrete result these efforts

[5] These include Ferrary 2009 (Republic); Bauman 1967 and Peachin 2015 (Republic and Augustus); Rogers 1935, 1960; and Demicheli 1984–1985 (Empire).

have yielded is the observation that accusations and trials under the *lex maiestatis* were products of political and social tensions of the day.

To be sure, those tensions rested on conceptions of the state and threats to the security of the state that changed over time. With the fall of the Republic came the establishment by Augustus of the position of emperor. From now on, the Roman emperor spoke for the Roman people as the primary agent in maintaining the remarkable cohesion of Roman society. The emperor came to embody the superiority of the Roman people, and through him, as the chief lawmaker of Rome, were channelled the commands of the people (Williamson 2005, 427). In effect, the people bestowed their collective voice on the emperor. The *maiestas principis* (superiority of the emperor) was rapidly established as equivalent to the superiority of the Roman people. Our ability to write a history of this process has been dramatically enhanced by discovery of the *senatus consultum de Cn. Pisone patre* of 20 AD (*s.c. de Pisone*), which records a conviction for *maiestas*, citing both the *maiestas domus Augustae* ("the superiority of the Imperial house") in conjunction with *ius publicum* (*AE* 1996, 885, ll. 32–33; commentary in Eck, Caballos and Fernández Gomez 1996). As Ando writes, "[a]llowing disrespect to Augustus and later to Tiberius to be understood as a slight against the *maiestas* of the Roman people forms part of a conceptual and social revolution ..." (Ando 2011, 105).

Under the Empire, the concentration of political authority in the person of the emperor meant that *maiestas* rapidly came to embrace many more actions than it had earlier. Literary sources during the Julio-Claudian and Flavian dynasties report accusations leading to indictments on actions that threaten the emperor's person, his position and his dynasty, from casting the emperor's horoscope to defamation, from adultery with women in the Imperial family to conspiracy to assassinate. Accusations of *repetundae* and other crimes were sometimes accompanied by an accusation of *maiestas*. *Maiestas* also transcended the person of the emperor. Perceived offences against the Imperial cult, the bulwark of dynasty, were offences against the emperor. The importance of the Imperial cult is clear in the fragments of a statute from the reign of Vespasian regarding the Imperial cult in the province of Narbonese Gaul. Recording in precise detail the ritual requirements of the *flamen provinciae*, it was engraved on bronze and publicly displayed, a monument to *maiestas principis*.[6] The scope of *maiestas* might extend to offences that were crimes in their own right, magic or astrology. It was a fine line between the practice of astrology and casting the emperor's horoscope, the latter a threat to the emperor's person (Sánchez-Moreno Ellart 2009). Whether these offences were actually found in the *lex maiestatis* is uncertain. It is clear that the *lex maiestatis* was applied to a wider range of generally high-ranking individuals both public and private, the latter including senators, equestrians and women, progeny or descendants of old Republican families, whose actions threatened the emperor or his dynasty. What emerges from studies of *maiestas* during the first and early second centuries of the Empire is a view of emperors, senators, equestrians and the Roman people striving for accommodation in a new system that on the one hand hearkens to the political institutions of the democratic Republic, in particular the stature of the senate,

[6] *Lex de flamonio provinciae Narbonensis*: Williamson 1987b. Monumental uses of bronze: Williamson 1987a.

and on the other hand enshrines the primacy of the emperor atop the reconfigured institutions of the Republican Monarchy.

With this change in the form and boundaries of politics, a new type of political actor emerged: the informer (*delator*), who might arise from any status class. *Delatores* were much maligned in literary sources of the period, like Tacitus, for whom they were greedy participants in the emperors' despotism. Nonetheless, *delatores* had a recognised function in the new order, were rewarded monetarily by the Imperial treasury from the confiscated estates of the condemned, and were sometimes rewarded with Imperial honours. *Delatores* from lower orders could gain sufficient local standing to merit public acknowledgment, attested in a document preserved on a wax tablet from Herculaneum (Camodeca 2009). The importance of informants to the emperor and his administrators, over time, is reflected in the comments of the early-third-century-AD jurist Modestinus that even people who hitherto could not make accusations—people who suffered *infamia*, slaves, women and soldiers—could do so under the *lex Iulia maiestatis* (D.48.4.7pr-2; D.48.4.8).

Various emperors, among them Domitian, Nerva and Hadrian, are said to have publicly disavowed the *lex maiestatis* because of the resentment its use by their predecessors or even themselves had engendered among Roman senators. Whether or not the *lex maiestatis* was ever formally disavowed, it never disappeared. Emperors both utilised the *lex maiestatis* and refuted it, but they seem never to have abolished it (Brunt 1984). Its scope was altered or expanded to adapt to changing ideas of the state, but the central idea of *maiestas* as a crime against the state persisted.

26.3.2 The *lex Iulia maiestatis*

The statute under which indictments for *maiestas* fell in the first century AD, and in all subsequent centuries, was the *lex Iulia maiestatis*. There are sound reasons for assigning the statute to either of two sponsors, Julius Caesar, *c.*46 BC, or Augustus, *c.*19–18 BC (Ferrary 2009, 223). Regardless of sponsorship, this is the statute under which accusations were brought and penalties levied henceforth. Information about the provisions of the *lex Iulia* is sparse. The single most important ancient literary record is the selection of juristic commentary collected in chapter 48.4, *Ad legem Iuliam maiestatis*, of Justinian's Digest. Here is found a legal definition of *maiestas*; reflection on the now much wider range of actions that do and do not constitute it; consideration of the many individuals who may bring accusations; as well as penalties for conviction. However, Digest 48.4 only presents the *lex Iulia* as known to and annotated by the jurists of the late second and third centuries AD whose writings are included.

Regrettably, there are few reliable pointers as to what was in the statute as originally enacted, and information from classical historians writing about the first century may well be tendentious. Some matters that jurists say directly were embraced by the *lex Iulia* included instances of *falsum*, for example (D.48.4.2, on which see Cloud 1963, 213). Other concepts appeared to have remained autonomous, especially *perduellio* (Cloud 1963, 231). Exactly how the scope of the concept changed is not known. Beyond interpretative and contextual change, we do not know if the statute was ever emended, whether by statute, decree of the senate or Imperial rescript. The most important analysis of D.48.4 was published fifty years ago (Cloud 1963). Doubtless, scholars in future will have more to say about the literary *lex Iulia*. In the meantime, the providential discovery in Hispania of the bronze tablets engraved with the *s.c. de Pisone* of 20 AD has allowed us to inquire into the understanding of the *lex Iulia* within forty to sixty-five years of its enactment.

The *s.c. de Pisone* records the proceedings and outcome of the prosecution of Calpurnius Piso, governor of Syria, for *maiestas*. Accused of poisoning Tiberius' heir, Germanicus, according to Tacitus, Piso was actually indicted on the charge of *maiestas* because he moved his troops out of his province to wage war without authorisation. His subordinates were so charged and prosecuted. Procedurally, the decree confirms the continued use of a *quaestio maiestatis*, chaired by a praetor, which heard the cases of Piso's subordinates. Piso himself had committed suicide before coming to trial. His trial went forward nonetheless in the senate, with the emperor bringing the indictment and the senate arguing the case.

The decree confirms that the penalty under the *lex Iulia* was still *aquae et ignis interdictio* (interdiction of fire and water)—which Cicero reported in *Phil.* 1.9.23 for the *lex maiestatis*—effectively barring the condemned person from community life and exercise of Roman citizenship and entailing loss of property as well as *damnatio memoriae*.[7] The penalty was set for Piso's two subordinates by the praetor presiding over the *quaestio* on instructions from the senate, relaying the wishes of Tiberius. Since Piso himself had pre-empted the trial, and thus the penalties, by suicide, the senate per Tiberius's wishes forbids the women in his family from mourning him, calls for the destruction of statues and other structures erected by him and confiscates his property. In sum, the *s.c. de Pisone* confirms that in the reign of Tiberius at least, the *lex Iulia maiestatis* established (or carried over from the *lex Cornelia*) the unauthorised movement of legions as grounds for indictment; it provided for (or continued) a *quaestio* under a praetor; it prosecuted the defendant even when deceased; and it set the penalty as interdiction with all its collateral consequences (ll. 121–123). With the exception of the *quaestio*, these provisions among many others are also found in the late classical reflections on *lex Iulia* contained in Digest 48.4.

Incidental to the original *lex Iulia*, but nonetheless important, the *s.c. de Pisone* also represents a stage in the transition from the standing courts of the Republic to the *cognitio* process (on which see Rüfner, ch. 20). The functioning of emperor and senate as a court is here on display, opening a window onto the emerging judicial powers of the emperor, as well as the judicial functions of the senate (Richardson 1997; Peachin 2015; see also Eck, ch. 8). These changes would have an impact on all criminal matters, including *maiestas*.

26.3.3 Second and Third Centuries AD

Maiestas in the second century continued to reflect the changing concepts of state and threats to the state. The state, still called *res publica*, was seen more as a totality of provinces ruled by a central authority whose power was dependent on the support of people from every province, not merely Italy. The suggestion that Caracalla's edict in 212 AD extending Roman citizenship to nearly all inhabitants of the Empire thereby strengthened the concept of *maiestas populi Romani* is not improbable (Sherwin-White 1973, 283). Crimes against the state could now be committed against the state as a political organism

[7] See Flower 1998 for a listing of penalties in her analysis of *damnatio memoriae*, a much-studied aspect of *maiestas* and *perduellio*.

as well as against the emperor. In the definition of Ulpian, lawyer and *magister libellorum* to Septimius Severus from 202 to 209 AD, the people were paramount: the crime of *maiestas* is that "which is committed against the Roman people or against their security" (*quod adversus populum Romanum vel adversus securitatem eius committitur*) (D.48.4.1.1).

Coinciding perhaps with more serious threats from external enemies along the borders of the Empire, *perduellio* again appears in the literary record in the second century. As evidence, the lawyer Neratius Priscus, suffect consul in 97 AD under Trajan and later on Hadrian's council, addressed the ramifications of conviction for *perduellio* for remarriage (D.3.2.11.3). Later second- and third-century jurists addressed the implications of *perduellio* for inheritance and bequests and rights of patrons (D.29.2.86.1; D.31.1.76.9; D.39.5.31.4; D.38.16.1.3; D.37.14.4). No later than the reign of Marcus Aurelius, *perduellio* was included in the *lex Iulia* (D.48.4.4pr). Precision on this point is difficult, for it is obvious that the severity of penalties exacted for *perduellio* had long since laid demands on the Roman civil law. Ulpian regarded *perduellio* as the most serious form of *maiestas* in that death before prosecution for *perduellio*, unlike other forms of *maiestas*, did not extinguish the collateral consequences of conviction; namely; loss of status and confiscation of estate, both of great consequence for heirs (D.48.4.11). Conversely, all forms of *maiestas* were equal with respect to eliciting testimony. Romans of high station as well as low were, by the third century, subject to torture to confirm evidence, because the emperor's person was involved (D.48.18.10.1).

Of greater long-term significance, perceived threats to the Imperial cult from new religions now began to further expand the compass of *maiestas*. As long as the Imperial cult was a foundation of dynasty and concord, its rituals and accoutrements were a routine part of everyday life. For the most part, small-scale cults in the first and second centuries raised no flags to provincial Roman administrators, unless cult practice included criminalised acts like magic. Administrators did require cult adherents to observe the common ritual practices of the Imperial cult, and Christians often refused. The resulting confusion on the part of administrators during much of the second century about what kinds of acts rose to the level of *maiestas* is obvious in the literary record. A personal exchange between Pliny and Trajan and the formal rescripts by Septimius Severus and Caracalla settling questions of law about when perceived injuries to statues of the emperor constituted *maiestas* under the *lex maiestatis* are merely the tip of the iceberg (Plin. *Ep.* 10.96–97; D.48.4.5.1–2; Pekáry 1985). The legal advisers of every emperor in the second and third centuries doubtless received hundreds of similar questions from administrators holding court in distant provinces. It was not until the later third century that emperors linked state security more directly to the proper observance of the rituals of the Imperial cult. This was the period of large-scale official persecutions of Christians, Manichaeans and Jews. But whether the legal grounds for persecution were *maiestas* or something else, such as sacrilege (*sacrilegium*), is unclear; the offences constituting *sacrilegium* could also fall under the scope of *maiestas*. The similarity may help to explain why Ulpian opens his comments on the *lex Iulia maiestatis* with the observation that "closest to *sacrilegium* is the crime called *maiestas*" (D.48.4.1pr).

In practical terms, with emperor and dynasty now a fact of life, it appears that fracturing the provincial base of the emperor's power had become the biggest threat to state security. Maybe for this reason, by early in the third century at latest, soldiers were gradually included among the individuals who could bring accusations of *maiestas* (D.48.4.7.1). But *maiestas* could be a dangerous indictment when strong regional loyalties were involved. Perhaps in part for this reason, the emperor Marcus Aurelius refused to condemn Avidius Cassius, governor of Syria, for *maiestas*, following the governor's misguided usurpation in 175 AD, despite the senate's call to indict him and his senatorial supporters. A native of Syria, Avidius Cassius had strong support among Syrians and had additional support in Egypt before his assassination (Dio Cass. 72.22–30).

26.4 *Maiestas* in the Later Roman Empire

Maiestas both changes and stays the same as the fundamental crime against the state in the later period. Known trials for *maiestas* in the fourth century, recorded by Ammianus Marcellinus, are based on offences familiar from the earlier Empire, though by now the process is different (Demicheli 1984–1985). That the Emperors Arcadius and Honorius, in 397 AD, found it necessary to issue a constitution expanding the offences constituting *maiestas* and consequent penalties suggests that the *lex Iulia* was now outdated (CTh.9.14.3 [a. 397]). When Christianity became the official religion of the state, *maiestas* and *sacrilegium* continue to intersect. Now, the Roman state was committed to suppressing heretical Christian sects through legislation. A constitution of Theodosius I in 380 AD (CTh.16.1.2pr, 16.1.2.1) was an initial step: Theodosius desires all Romans to convert to Christianity, specifically to the Catholic creed mandated by the council of Nicea in 325 AD. All other creeds were heretical, and Christians believing in them committed *sacrilegium* (heresy). First collected in the Theodosian Code of AD 438, such Imperial enactments continued in the Code of Justinian in the sixth century.

During the period, the distinction between *maiestas* and heresy grew, but so, too, did the similarities. On the one hand, the definitions of heretical acts were "precisely defined and doctrinal in nature" whereas *maiestas* was "vaguely defined and political or military in nature" (Barnard 1995). But on the other, suicide in anticipation of prosecution for heresy, as for *maiestas*, was no deterrent to accusation, trial or sanction. The unique correspondences between heresy and *maiestas* suggest that heresy was perceived as equally threatening to state security. And yet, not all offences against religion constituted heresy. Some cases were prosecuted "as for" *maiestas*. In AD 409, a constitution of Theodosius ruled that the crime of *superstitio* by "god-fearers, Jews and those who profaned Sundays" would be punished as for *maiestas* (CTh.16.8.19 … *sciat, se ad maiestatis crimen esse retinendum*). Other actions—for example, refusing sanctuary in a church to fugitives—were similarly punished as for *maiestas* (C.1.12.2 [a. 409]). The latter, and cases like it, are distinguishable both from heresy and on the surface from *maiestas*, falling in a yet-to-be-explored grey area.

26.5 Conclusion

Maiestas lasted throughout the Empire and beyond, shaped to fix changing perceptions of the Roman state across centuries and then taken up in the legal systems of the Germanic kingdoms that seized the reins of authority following the collapse of Roman power in the

West (Lear 1929). As a crime whose meaning was intuitive and evolving, from the time it was first identified as such in the late Republic, *maiestas* reflected Roman conceptions of their state and what constituted threats to their state over hundreds of years. Throughout, the *lex maiestatis* was a legal mechanism employed, rightly or wrongly in the eyes of contemporary Romans, to ensure the continued existence of Rome. That *maiestas* remained for so long one of the most significant criminal-law constructs of ancient Rome underscores its value as a window, as yet not fully opened, onto the Romans' changing perception of their world from earliest times.

Bibliography

Alexander, M. 1990. *Trials in the late Roman republic, 149 BC to 50 BC*. Toronto.

Ando, C. 2011. *Law, language, and empire in the Roman tradition*. Philadelphia.

Barnard, L. (1995). "The criminalisation of heresy in the later Roman empire: a sociopolitical device?" *Journal of Legal History* 16: 121–146.

Bauman, R. A. 1967. *The* crimen maiestatis *in the Roman republic and Augustan principate*. Johannesburg.

Brecht, C. H. 1938. Perduellio: *eine Studie zu ihrer begrifflichen Abgrenzung im römischen Strafrecht bis zum Ausgang der Republik*. Munich.

Brunt, P. A. 1984. "Did emperors ever suspend the law of *maiestas*?" in Sodalitas: *scritti in onore di Antonio Guarino*. Naples. 469–480.

Camodeca, G. (2009). "*Delatores, praemia* e processo senatorio *maiestatis* in una inedita tabula Herculanensis di età Neroniana." *Studia et Documenta Historiae et Iuris* 75: 381–402.

Cloud, J. D. (1963). "The text of Digest XLVIII.4, *Ad Legem Iuliam Maiestatis*." *Zeitschrift der Savigny-Stiftung für Rechtsgeschichte, romanistische Abteilung* 80: 206–232.

Demicheli, A. M. (1984–1985). "I processi di lesa maestà in Ammiano Marcellino." *Annali della Facoltà di Giurisprudenza di Genova* 20: 95–126.

Eck, W., Caballos, A. and Fernández Gomez, F. 1996. *Das* senatus consultum de Cn. Pisone Patre. Munich.

Ferrary, J.-L. (1983). "Les origins de la loi de majesté à Rome." *Comptes rendus de l'Académie des Inscriptions et Belles-lettres* 127: 556–572.

Ferrary, J.-L. 2009. "Lois et procès *maiestatis* dans la Rome républicaine." In B. Santalucia, ed., *La repressione criminale nella roma repubblicana fra norma e persuasione*. Pavia. 223–249.

Flower, H. (1998). "Rethinking *damnatio memoriae*: the Case of Cn. Calpurnius Piso Pater in CE 20." *Classical Antiquity* 17: 155–187.

Gundel, H. G. (1963). "Der Begriff *Maiestas* im politischen Denken der römischen Republik." *Historia* 12: 283–320.

Lanfranchi, T. 2013. "La majesté: l'autre nom de la souveraineté?" Lectures 2 (28 March 2013) and 3 (6 April 2013). Seminaires des membres de l'école française de Rome. Available at: http://semefr.hypotheses.org/886 and http://semefr.hypotheses.org/907, accessed 14 February 2016.

Lear, F. S. (1929). "*Crimen laesae maiestatis* in the *lex Romana Wisigothorum*." *Speculum* 4: 73–87.

Levick, B. M. 1976. *Tiberius the politician*. London.

Peachin, M. 2015. "Augustus' emergent judicial powers, the *crimen maiestatis*, and the Second Cyrene Edict." In J.-L. Ferrary and J. Scheid, eds., *Il princeps romano: autocrate o magistrato? Fattori giuridici e fattori sociali del potere imperiale da Augusto a Commodo*. Pavia. 3–59.

Pekáry, T. 1985. *Das römische Kaiserbildnis in Staat, Kult und Gesellschaft dargestellt Anhand der Schriftquellen*. Berlin.

Plescia, J. (1971). "On the persecution of Christians in the Roman empire." *Latomus* 30: 120–132.

Richardson, J. S. (1997). "The senate, the courts, and the *SC de Cn. Pisone patre*." *Classical Quarterly* 47: 510–518.

Rogers, R. S. 1935. *Criminal trials and criminal legislation under Tiberius*. Middletown.

Rogers, R. S. (1960). "A group of Domitianic treason trials." *Classical Philology* 55: 19–23.

Rowe, G. 2014. "The Roman state: laws, lawmaking and legal documents." In C. Bruun and J. Edmondson, eds., *The Oxford handbook of Roman epigraphy*. Oxford. 299–318.

Sánchez-Moreno Ellart, C. (2009). "Ulpian and the stars. The *actio iniuriarum* against the astrologer: some reflections about Dig. 47.10.15.13 (Ulp. Lib. 77 *Ad Edictum*)." *Iuris antiqui historia: an international journal on Roman law* 1:195–222.

Santalucia, B. 1994. *Studi di diritto penale romano*. Rome.

Sherwin-White, A. N. 1973[2]. *The Roman citizenship*. Oxford.

Thomas, Y. (1991). "L'institution de la majesté." *Revue de synthèse* 112: 331–386.

Williamson, C. (1987a). "Monuments of bronze: Roman legal documents on bronze tablets." *Classical Antiquity* 6: 160–183.

Williamson, C. (1987b). "A Roman Law from Narbonne." *Athenaeum* 65: 173–189.

Williamson, C. 2005. *The laws of the Roman people: public law in the expansion and decline of the Roman republic*. Ann Arbor.

PART VI

PERSONS BEFORE THE LAW

Status

CHAPTER 27

SOCIAL STATUS, LEGAL STATUS AND LEGAL PRIVILEGE

TRISTAN S. TAYLOR

27.1 Introduction

In the early second century AD, the Roman senator Pliny congratulated the governor of Baetica, Calestrius Tiro, on his administration of justice. Pliny lauds Tiro for being both loved by the lesser people (*minores*), and esteemed by the province's leading men (*principes*). In particular, Pliny praises Tiro for preserving the distinctions of rank and dignity (*discrimina ordinum dignitatumque*) in his judicial activities, as once such distinctions are confused, nothing is more unequal than the resulting equality (*nihil est ipsa aequalitate inaequalius*) (*Ep.* 9.5). Pliny's brief missive reveals much about elite ideas on the relationship between social status and the administration of justice; in particular, the belief that equality did not lie in treating all as equal before the law, but rather in respecting distinctions of rank and status. In this regard, Pliny refers to two broad hierarchical categories: the leading (*principes*) or powerful people (*potentes*), and the lesser folk (*minores*). Pliny also states that some governors do not respect such distinctions appropriately, obtaining a bad reputation through deciding too often for the *minores* from their fear of seeming to yield excessively to the *potentes*. This implies that respect for rank and status flowed from the governor's discretion, rather than strict application of legal rules. Pliny's epistle neatly encapsulates the issues for inquiry here: what was the relationship between legal and social status in Roman law, and to what extent did legal or social status distinctions grant legal privilege?

27.2 The Law of Persons

Legal status under Roman law receives its most systematic discussion in the law of persons. This body of law outlines distinctions that define a person's ability to interact with both the Roman civic community and Roman legal institutions, and his or her position within the *familia* or Roman household, particularly in relation to an individual's control of property (Frier 2012, 1398–1399).

A person's legal status depended on his or her *caput*, or legal personality. *Caput* comprised three hierarchical components: freedom (*libertas*), citizenship (*civitas*) and *familia*, or position within a Roman household (Inst.Gai.1.159–163; D.4.5.11). A Roman citizen possessed all three elements, a provincial (*peregrinus*) only *libertas* (although possessing citizenship in a provincial community) and a slave none. As *libertas* distinguished free from slave it was "the primary division in the law of persons" (Inst.Gai.1.9). Slaves, although invested with a complex legal capacity, were *res* (things), items of property (Inst.Gai.1.52) (see ch. 30).

Although limited by gender and rank—women were excluded from political participation, and the opportunities of those of low rank or social status restricted—Roman citizenship enabled participation in the Roman political community. Citizenship also enabled full interaction with Roman private law, again divided on gender lines (see Inst.Gai.1.32–34; on women see chs. 32–34); in particular; citizenship provided rights of *commercium*, allowing participation in legal processes and transactions, the right to make a will (*testamenti factio*) and the right to enter a Roman marriage (*conubium*), necessary for the begetting of citizen children. In addition, citizens possessed public-law rights, including service in the Roman legions, exemption from arbitrary corporal punishment and a right to appeal the death sentence to the people (du Plessis 2015, 102). Various subordinate statuses existed, such as Latin rights, that enabled the partial enjoyment of a citizen's private law rights (Crook 1967, 43–44). Non-citizens could enter legal transactions with citizens, but had only limited access to Roman legal institutions (Inst.Gai.1.19).

Citizens were further subdivided into freeborn people (*ingenui*) or freed slaves (*libertini*) (Inst.Gai.1.10–11). *Libertini* were part of their manumitting *familia* and were subject to a number of legal requirements towards their manumitting patron: the performance of services (*operae*), the provision of gifts (*munera*) and the display of respect (*obsequium*) (du Plessis 2015, 105–107). Freedmen also suffered some public-law disabilities, including exclusion from public offices and the legions,[1] although their children generally enjoyed full citizen rights (Inst.Gai.1.29–30; see further on freedmen ch. 31).

Roman law also created a variety of statuses that limited a citizen's legal capacity to control property within a *familia*. Full property rights were limited to those who were *sui iuris* (legally independent)—generally speaking those without a living ascendant in the male line (*pater familias*). Women married under *manus* marriage (uncommon by the late Republic), and individuals with a living *pater familias* and slaves were said to be *alieni iuris* (under another's power or *potestas*) (Inst.Gai.1.48–49) and as such had a limited private law capacity and no property rights. However, this status was irrelevant to political participation (D.1.6.9). To further protect the property of the *familia*, those considered vulnerable to exploitation were under curatorship or *tutela: sui iuris* children under the age of puberty, women, minors, spendthrifts and the insane. These institutions required either

[1] Two other categories of freedmen lacked full citizenship: Latins and *dediticii*: du Plessis 2015, 92–93, 101 and 109–110.

the administration of a ward's property, such as for a minor, or the guardian's authorisation for certain legal transactions, as for adult women (Inst.Gai.1.142–143). Roman family law is discussed fully elsewhere (chs. 35–38).

As important as these legal statuses were in delimiting someone's interaction with Roman law, they do not convey the complexities of Pliny's distinctions of rank and dignity: e.g. although institutions such as *tutela* or *patria potestas* greatly affected rights under Roman law, they applied equally to all citizens, regardless of their *ordo* or *dignitas*.

27.3 Roman Society: Orders and Status

Distinctions of *ordo* and *dignitas* in Roman society may be understood via the concept of social status, whether through the analytical framework of Roman conceptions, Weberian ideas of social status or ideas of class—whether in a Marxist sense or in a broader sense of self-contained economic groups sharing similar values (see, e.g. Garnsey and Saller 2015, 132–133, 147; Harris 1988; Morley 2004, ch. 4; Mayer 2012, ch. 1; Wallace-Hadrill 2013). All these paradigms have their merits, and the most appropriate framework depends upon the question asked. Here, it is best to adopt the framework expressed by Romans themselves. Although this paradigm largely represents the perspective of the elite, such people both made and administered the laws. Something of this framework can be gleaned from Tacitus' description of the reaction of various groups of Roman society to Nero's death: the senate, *equites*, the army, respectable free people and *liberti* were delighted, in contrast to the sordid urban poor (*plebs sordida*) and worst of the slaves (*deterrimi servorum*) (*Hist.* 1.4). Thus, to Tacitus, society comprised a number of distinct, hierarchical, groups—hence his pejorative language for the urban poor (Morley 2004, 77). Roman society can perhaps be best conceptualised as a pyramid, at the apex of which sat the elite ranks, in terms both of social status and of power, political and legal (Alföldy 1985, 146). The basis for the hierarchy of these groups lay in Pliny's *ordo* and *dignitas*, which, respectively, are analogous to modern concepts of rank and social status. "Ranks" or "orders" are social categories defined by rules (Garnsey and Saller 2015, 136), and their clearly defined nature enabled them to be both the subjects of legal restrictions and beneficiaries of legal privileges, akin to a legal status. The best defined ranks were the elite *ordines*: the senate, *equites* and decurions or local elites, who held a near monopoly on political and legal power. Social status varies to a greater degree than rank and is the valuation of a person's social esteem based on a range of status indicators (Garnsey and Saller 2015, 136, 14–141; Morley 2004, 77–78). There was a significant overlap in Roman elite thinking between rank and social status as the key markers of social esteem: character, birth, office and wealth (Garnsey 1970, 234) also delimited eligibility for the elite orders, membership of which was, itself, a marker of social status (Alföldy 1985, 106).

27.3.1 The Elite

Aside from the Imperial family, the highest rank in all periods was the senatorial order, which included the most important magistrates (chs. 7–9 and 17), and whose members held the highest social status through the social esteem attached to rank and office. Initially the preserve of a small group of aristocratic, patrician families, the so-called "struggle of the orders" (*c.*fifth to third centuries BC) expanded senatorial membership such that it became delimited by key markers of social esteem: wealth, birth, conduct and office. Thus, in the Republic before Sulla, the censors chose as senators those who had held the highest offices or were from families who had done so, possessed the equestrian census of 400,000 sesterces, and were of good character (Lintott 1999, 68–71). After Sulla (82–80 BC), election to the junior magistracy (questorship) became the basis of membership (Lintott 1999, 70). Here, markers of social esteem, like character, wealth and family, affected someone's electoral chances. Augustus (31 BC–14 AD) made further efforts to enhance the order's prestige through further regulating the entry and conduct of members: the property qualification was increased to 1 million sesterces, roughly 250,000 times a labourer's daily wage (MacMullen 1974, 89–90). Admission also became concentrated in the emperor's hands, shifting the focus of elite competition from elections to the emperor's patronage (Talbert 1984, 9–16). Augustus' marriage legislation (18 BC and 9 AD) prohibited marriage between senators and their descendants through to the third generation (great grandchildren) and freedpersons or disreputable partners: actors and their daughters, prostitutes, procurers and women condemned in a criminal court (Tit.Ulp.13; D.23.2.44pr; McGinn 2002). These prohibitions reflect a belief that conduct was a key criterion of rank and social status. Related to this, a senatorial decree of 19 AD banned senators and their descendants through to the third generation from participating in public spectacles (Levick 1983, 98–100). Within the senatorial *ordo* itself there was a hierarchy of social status: for example, those whose families had long held senatorial rank claimed more prestige than the "new men" (*novi homines*) who were their families' first senator.

Below senatorial rank was the larger, more amorphous, equestrian order or *equites*, the precise boundaries of which are disputed. Originally one of the Republican census categories, membership required property of 400,000 sesterces, citizenship and free birth, increased under Tiberius (14–37 AD) to two prior generations of free birth (Plin. *HN* 33.32). It is unclear whether it was also necessary to have been admitted to the order by Imperial grant (Garnsey and Saller 2015, 137). This order had similar behavioural restrictions to senators, such as the prohibition on participation in public spectacles (Levick 1983, 98–100), and had always been politically important as a source of individuals commencing a political career. Under the Principate, *equites* gained more responsibilities in Imperial administration, including the governorship of provinces, from which they derived prestige. By the late second century AD a titulary hierarchy had evolved for them, ranging from *egregius* (excellent) for procurators, to *eminentissimus* (most renowned) for praetorian prefects (Garnsey and Saller 2015, 137). While there were distinctions of social status between the two top *ordines*, movement and intermarriage between them was frequent (Morley 2004, 79).

The third elite *ordo* was the curial order, comprising decurions or town councillors (ch. 10). Membership usually required holding a local magistracy, eligibility for which was regulated by requirements of birth, wealth and conduct. While free birth was often required, sons of freedmen could enter this rank. Wealth qualifications varied between communities, but were generally less than for the other elite orders: in Imperial-era Comum in northern Italy it was 100,000 sesterces, as opposed to the equestrian minimum of 400,000

(Plin. *Ep.* 1.19; Garnsey and Saller 2015, 137–138). The standards of conduct expected are clear from the so-called *Tabula Heracleensis*, a late Republican inscription containing the preconditions for local office (Crawford 1996, I, 355–391). An erstwhile decurion could be excluded for, *inter alia*, being an actor, gladiator or gladiatorial trainer, insolvency, dishonourable discharge from the army, running a brothel, engaging in demeaning occupations such as being an undertaker, auctioneer or town crier and condemnation for various delicts (*Tab. Her.* ll. 108–125).

These elites were distinguished by various visible markers, the usurpation of which was illegal, including clothing—such as the broad purple stripe (*latus clavus*) worn by senators and their sons and the gold ring and narrow purple stripe of the *equites*—and privileged seats at public spectacles (Garnsey and Saller 2015, 139–140).

While elite women were excluded from political positions, they gained social prestige from birth, wealth and conduct, and held a social status commensurate with that of their *familia*.

At least until the *Constitutio Antoniniana* of 212 AD that, although its precise effects remain uncertain (e.g. Tuori 2007, 41–43), extended Roman citizenship to many of the Empire's free inhabitants, a provincial elite had existed, holding citizenship of their local communities rather than Roman citizenship. Although they did not enjoy the political and legal benefits of Roman citizenship, their social status within their own communities depended upon similar markers of social esteem to the Roman elite (on law in the provinces see also ch. 22).

27.3.2 The Sub-Elite

The elite comprised a minuscule proportion of the Roman Empire (Alföldy 1985, 146). The majority appear to us only in half-glimpses in the sources, obscuring the relationship of social status to legal status among them (Knapp 2011; ch. 28). Nonetheless, just as stratification occurred within the elite, so, too, among humbler citizens. Alföldy has argued that, in addition to distinctions between rural and urban populations, legal distinctions—in particular between freeborn, freed and slaves—were significant demarcations among the non-elite. However, these strata reflected the different relationships of dependency each group had on the elite, as opposed to their hierarchical relations to each other (Alföldy 1985, 133, 147). This contrasts the elite view that the significant status division among non-elite citizens was the legal distinction between freeborn and freed. This view was a product of the elite prejudice against *libertini* based on their servile origin, and was reflected both in the legal requirement of free-birth for admission to the elite orders (Mouritsen 2011, ch. 6) and in the Augustan marriage laws, which prohibited prostitutes, procurers, actors or those condemned in public trials from marriage to freeborn people, but not to freedmen (Tit.Ulp.13.2; Kehoe 2011, 149).

While the majority of the population were at subsistence level, there nonetheless existed "middling" income groups between the elite and the poor (Scheidel and Friesen 2009; Garnsey and Saller 2015, 147), who might also possess elite aspirations. The possibility of social mobility is reflected in stories of upward movement into the elite, such as a humble labourer who eventually became a town councillor (*CIL* VIII 11824; MacMullen 1974,

43–44). Similarly, those among the non-elite with sufficient means to do so made claims to status through display such as funerary epitaphs or decorated houses, although whether such display also indicates a distinctive "middle class", with a coherent set of values, remains controversial (Mayer 2012; Wallace-Hadrill 1994, 173–174; Wallace-Hadrill 2013). Some claimed status through advertising their role in collegial groups, such as membership by freedmen of the *Augustales*, an Imperial cult, in various *municipia*, which is analogous to elite claims to status through office-holding (Alföldy 1985, 131; ch. 11). However, there are numerous non-elite epitaphs proudly advertising both freed status and trades frowned upon by the elite, suggesting that the markers of social esteem among the non-elite differed from those central to elite ideology (Knapp 2011, 181–182; Morley 2004, 79; Joshel 1992, 166–169).

As social status depended on several criteria of social esteem, "status dissonance" could arise when people accumulated wealth and influence that surpassed the limits suggested by their rank and legal status (Mouritsen 2011, 111). This was particularly true of freedmen of the Imperial household (*familia Caesaris*) in the early Principate, who enjoyed influence through their proximity to the emperor, roles in the Imperial administration and their wealth. Their status is illustrated by their relatively high rates of marriage to freeborn women (Weaver 1972, 193), and by the hostility that their success provoked in the elite (e.g. Plin. *Ep.* 7.29.3; Garnsey and Saller 2015, 142–143). The increased use of *equites* in the Imperial administration over the first and second centuries AD instead of freedmen can be seen as a reaction to this phenomenon that attempted to limit the access of freedmen to social status (Mouritsen 2011, 96–97).

27.3.3 Citizenship and Status

Civitas was a fundamental determinant of how someone interacted with Roman law and was required for elite rank and social status. Its privileges continued to be valued at least until the *Constitutio Antoniniana* and remained a reward for those who served in Rome's auxiliary forces and for local elites (Sherwin-White 1973, 313). There was also continued reliance on its privileges in relation to criminal punishment: in the early second century, Pliny, while governing Bithynia, sent Roman citizens professing Christianity to Rome, whereas he summarily punished provincials for the same crime (Plin. *Ep.* 10.96).

Status distinctions based on elite criteria were also given effect in the application of the law, particularly criminal penalties, despite the theoretical privileges of citizens, such that the elite received more favourable treatment than others. The origins of this distinction are unclear due to poor evidence on how low-status defendants were generally dealt with, but it may perhaps be associated with a movement away from the use of permanent jury courts, *quaestiones perpetuae*, with set penalties, to the general use of *cognitio*, trial by magistrate alone, which gave penal flexibility to the judge (D.48.19.13). By the time we have evidence under Hadrian (117–138 AD), this discretion was being exercised in such a way, reinforced by Imperial constitutions and juristic writing, that a "dual-penalty" system had evolved, pursuant to which those of higher social status, or *honestiores*, were subject to lighter penalties than those of lower social status or *humiliores* (e.g. D.48.19.28.13–14; Garnsey 1970, 103–104). Thus, *honestiores* were rarely executed for capital offences, instead undergoing exile. *Humiliores*, in contrast, suffered aggravated forms of the death penalty or condemnation to public works or the mines, which had formerly been servile penalties, although a distinction was still usually maintained between free *humiliores* and slaves (Garnsey 1970, Part II; Aubert 2002, 129–130; Millar 2004). Although Imperial constitutions usually draw the baseline for the *honestiores* at the level of decurions and veterans (e.g. D.49.18.3; Garnsey 1970, 245–251), who comprised the *honestiores* and *humiliores* was not clearly defined, but rather depended on the judge's determination of a person's rank and social status: Pliny's *ordo* and *dignitas*.

27.3.4 Status and Dishonour

Certain actions, whether it be conviction of a crime or becoming an actor, could render someone ineligible for certain *ordines*. Such behaviour also had legal ramifications for citizens, which reflected a longstanding desire on the part of the state, encapsulated even by the Republican censors, to define rank and social status on the basis of a "community of honour" (Kehoe 2011, 149–151; on marginalised people see also ch. 28).

Thus, conduct, as well as delimiting social status and rank, impacted upon legal status. This principle receives systematic expression in the late-second-century jurist Callistratus' discussion of *existimatio* (esteem, reputation), which he defines as a state of "uninjured *dignitas*, established by law and custom, that can be reduced or removed under the authority of the law by our misdeed" (D.50.13.5.1). *Existimatio* was connected with *caput* and thus, when a person underwent *capitis deminutio maxima* and lost all three elements of *caput*—freedom, citizenship and *familia*—that person's *existimatio* was removed. However, it was only reduced by non-capital penalties, such as exclusion from public office (*honores*) or exile, or when a person's conduct resulted in inclusion among those listed under the praetorian edict as undergoing *infamia*. This last group included most of those discussed above as barred from municipal office for disreputable conduct (D.3.2.1; Kaser 1956; Gardner 1993, ch. 5). *Infamia* embraced a variety of legal disabilities that were initially of separate origin. Later jurists use the term for many different types of legal disgrace (Kaser 1956). In addition to exclusion from public office and restrictions on legal representation, persons whose *existimatio* had been reduced (*infames, ignominiosi* or *famosi*) underwent, like *humiliores*, harsher penalties than those with intact reputations (*integra fama*: D.48.19.28.16). Dishonour could also a limit someone's ability to accuse (D.48.2.16) or to be a witness (an *intestabilis*) (e.g. Coll.9.2.2; D.22.5.2 and 22.5.3.5). Persons with diminished *existimatio*, under elite values, had little social status, although the legal limitations imposed would have "had little impact on the ordinary lives of most citizens" (Gardner 1993, 154).

27.3.5 Slaves

Slaves were both viewed as the lowest rung of the social hierarchy by elites, and placed at the bottom of the hierarchy of legal status as mere things. Nonetheless, differences in social status could appear among slaves (ch. 30), who ranged from manual labourers in wretched conditions to comparatively better-placed urban household slaves, including those in the emperor's household. Like their freedmen counterparts, Imperial slaves might accumulate wealth in their *peculium* as well as influence due to proximity to the *princeps* (Garnsey and Saller 2015, 142). The *s.c. Claudianum* of 52 AD, which enslaved free women who persisted in cohabiting with slaves, can be seen as a response to the social dissonance created by wealthy slaves who could attract free women as partners despite their lack of legal status (Kehoe 2011, 148).

27.4 Access to Justice: Legal Privilege and Legal Advantage

Equal access to justice in the Roman legal system was distorted by features that granted either explicit legal privileges or structural legal advantage to certain people, both procedurally and in certain transactions, and through the application of the law in the administration of justice (Garnsey 1970, 2).

A mid-second-century-AD papyrus conveys clearly the difficulties that could confront a weaker party:

> [the opponent is] a former Exegete of the town of Arsinoe, who possesses a great deal of influence in the villages through his arrogance and violence; and I shall be unable to oppose him before a jury, for he is very influential ... he relies on the prestige of his office, enjoying great power in the villages. (*P. Fouad.* 26, transl. MacMullen 1974)

Wealth, office and rank, hallmarks of social status, combined with violence and intimidation are claimed to yield juristic advantage (MacMullen 1974, 11–12). Such claims form a rhetorical *topos*; thus, evaluating their literal truth in individual cases is difficult (Kelly 2011, 61–62, 125); nevertheless, their frequent occurrence suggests their inherent plausibility.

27.4.1 Structural Advantage

In all Roman legal procedures, wealth conferred legal advantage. It might be used illicitly for bribery, about which there was much complaint (Kelly 1966, 33–42). In terms of licit advantage, however, simply accessing the courts had costs: travel expenses, lost income and securing an advocate and legal advice. For example, with regards to legal representation, by Diocletian (284–305 AD) 250 denarii could be charged for opening a case, and 1,000 for pleading it—far exceeding a contemporary farm labourer's maximum daily wage of 25 denarii (Connolly 2010, 18). Those of lower status were not completely excluded; for example, *tabelliones* could draw up legal documents and charged only 10 denarii per hundred lines in Diocletian's reign (Connolly 2010, 18). By the Empire, further assistance might be available through the governor himself, who had a basic duty to ensure that people could find advocates, particularly when disadvantaged (D.1.16.9.4–5; Kehoe 2011, 156). Nevertheless, a status imbalance between the parties could have led an advocate to decline the case of the lower-status party (Bablitz 2007, 165–167). In addition, a member of the elite may have had greater personal knowledge of the legal system through personal experience with litigation either as a party or as a judge, and through the standard elite education (Johnston 1999, 123).

A further structural advantage for the elite was the degree to which Roman legal procedures relied on the parties taking the initiative. Thus, in the main Republican form of civil procedure, the formulary system (ch. 19; Kaser and Hackl 1996, 151–434), the plaintiff had responsibility for both compelling the defendant's attendance and for executing any favourable judgement, even by force. (Kelly 1966, 12–14; Garnsey 1970, 204). This could present difficulties for a plaintiff facing a stronger defendant. Nevertheless, the emphasis on observing correct behaviour, critical to social status, may have compelled a Roman to attend a court or respect a judgement (Kelly 1966, 21–23; Garnsey 1970, 189). There were also legal remedies. The presiding magistrate could grant *missio in possessionem*, which theoretically allowed the plaintiff to take possession of the defendant's property for sale (Johnston 1999, 123–124), although this also could have been physically resisted (Kelly 1966, 11). By Augustus' reign, however, it became an offence to forcefully resist a summons (D.48.7.4pr; Garnsey 1970, 192–193; cf. Kelly 1966, 12). The shift in the Imperial period to a litigation system, *cognitio*, where proceedings were controlled by an official who had the power to enforce both attendance and judgement, ameliorated this structural disadvantage (ch. 20; Kelly 1966, 29–30; du Plessis 2015, 79–82; Johnston 1999, 121–122; Kaser and Hackl 1996, 435–516).

27.4.2 Prejudice

Responsibility for administering the legal system was concentrated in the hands of the social elite. Not only did the application of elite judicial discretion contribute to a systematic distinction in judicial penalties between *honestiores* and *humiliores*, but this prejudice can be seen in other aspects of the trial process too. Thus, in evaluating the *fides* (trustworthiness) of witnesses, jurists say that the judge ought to consider the witnesses' *condicio* (status), including their rank (a decurion or plebeian?), conduct (have they led a blameless life?) and their financial status (well off or needy?) (D.22.5.3pr; ch. 21).

In the formulary system the praetor, a senator, could affect a case by granting or refusing an action or remedy (Johnston 1999, 124–126). It would not be surprising that he would favour those who possessed a similar social status to himself, both for his own political advantage and out of class prejudice. For example, as a rule, praetors would not grant actions to lower-status persons against those of higher status for fraud (*dolus*), as it might entail *infamia* for the liable party (D.4.3.11.1). It is probable that this discretion was exercised in similar circumstances with reference to other delicts involving *infamia*, such as *furtum* (theft), *vi bonorum raptorum* (robbery with violence) or *iniuria* (insult) (Inst.Gai.4.182; Garnsey 1970, 185–186). Furthermore, all the members of the *album iudicum* (list of judges), from whom the *iudex* (judge) was chosen in the formulary system, were from the elite, either with a minimum qualification of 200,000 sesterces in Rome, or drawn from the curial class locally (Johnston 1999, 127; Bablitz 2007, 92–100). The *album iudicum* also supplied the jurors for the permanent criminal courts (Robinson 1995, 2–6; Jones 1972, ch. 2). Such courts appear to have exercised some favouritism towards the elite. Thus Tacitus claims that justice in the court for *repetundae* (provincial extortion), which dealt almost exclusively with senators, was thought to be distorted by, *inter alia*, influence (Tac. *Ann.* 2.2). Similarly, when the senate developed a criminal jurisdiction under the Principate, particularly for *maiestas* (treason) and extortion (Garnsey 1970, chs. 1–2; Jones 1972, ch. 3; Robinson 1995, 7–9; Talbert 1984, ch. 16) prosecutions of senators before it often "resulted in unjustified acquittals or in penalties unduly light or soon remitted, of little deterrent force" (Brunt 1961, 220; cf. Talbert 1984, 486). However, those of lower social status whom the senate tried were more frequently convicted and with heavier penalties (Garnsey 1970, 35). Once the *cognitio* system dominated both civil and criminal jurisdiction in the Imperial period, the Imperial official hearing the case also would generally have come from the elite (ch. 17).

These aspects of legal advantage had less impact in the absence of status imbalance, where the social esteem of the two parties was roughly equal (Peachin 1996, 70). How often balance or imbalance would have existed is difficult to determine. For example, in petitions, claims of status imbalance have all the hallmarks of being rhetorical *topoi*, rather than necessarily reflecting actual inequality (Kelly 2011, 61–62). There is some tentative evidence from the literary sources that the parties were often of equal status, at least in cases involving the elite (Kelly 1966, 28, 65). Further down the social hiearchy, the evidence, including legal petitions and records of cases, suggests that individuals from a wide range of social and legal statuses attempted litigation, indicating that they were not deterred by their opponent's status, whether because there was no imbalance, or whether the system was thought to correct such imbalances. However, all disputants generally possessed at least some means: in addition to the money required for travel, legal advice and so on, disputes about property, whether in relation to succession, contract or property law, required the existence of some property to be subject to dispute. Indeed, most cases recorded in papyri and petitions involve disputes concerning property (Bablitz 2007, 74; Kelly 2011, 163; Connolly 2010, 139). Most cases in the Digest concern succession and family law (Kelly 1976, 71–96). Although firm conclusions are difficult as the Digest contains more material on succession than other topics, a not insignificant proportion of such cases could involve members of the same *familia* and social status, although succession disputes could also involve, for example, imbalanced contests between freedmen and their deceased patron's relatives.

Even where a status imbalance did exist, it did not totally blind or bind those who administered the legal system. Thus Aulus Gellius, while acting as a *iudex* in a private case, was unable to render judgement for either party in a claim by a man considered of good character against one with a poor reputation: unable to decide for the former due to a lack of evidence, or absolve the the latter due to his poor character (Gell. *NA* 14.2; Garnsey 1970, 210). While Gellius' failure to dismiss the case in the absence of evidence "speaks volumes" as to the potential potency of status (Johnston 1999, 129), neither did it result in the condemnation of the defendant, and, notably, Gellius' *consilium* of advisers recommended deciding on the basis of evidence rather than status. Similarly, status did not prove determinative when a judge gave a freedman, unable to produce decisive evidence at trial, extra time to prove his case against a *gymnasiarch* (a municipal official), rather than simply dismissing his case (*P. Mil. Vogl.* I.25). In criminal proceedings, not only was an Alexandrian town councillor condemned to be executed for his murder of a prostitute, despite the remonstrations of fellow councillors, but part of his property was confiscated for his victim's impoverished mother (*BGU* IV 1024).

27.4.3 Addressing Imbalance: Patronage and Petition

Two potential ways of addressing imbalance in litigation were patronage and petition. Patronage was an important aspect of Roman society whereby a patron, generally of higher status, would aid a client, including assisting with legal advice and litigation (Dion. Hal. *Ant. Rom.* 2.10.1; Kelly 1966, 27; Kelly 2011, 213–219). In those aspects of the formulary system reliant on the plaintiff's initiative, a patron could assist in enforcing attendance or executing judgement against a recalcitrant defendant. However, patronage could also be utilised to resist a better legal claim (Kelly 1966, 27).

A further avenue for assistance was to petition an official, even the emperor—the Empire's ultimate patron (on the emperor see further ch. 8), whose authority and legal position gave his view great influence over the presiding judicial officer (Kehoe 2011, 155; Connolly 2010 23–24). Such petitions would present a set of facts and request an opinion on them. When answered, such petitions could be used in a variety of ways: to resolve the issue, pressure a person to settle or to assist in an actual trial (Connolly 2010, 25–26). Analyses of the petitioners in Egyptian papyri and the third-century-AD collection the *Codex Hermogenianus* reveal an array of people from "the middling sort", usually those with some property well above the subsistence level (Connolly 2010, 139; Kelly 2011, 124, 166). However, petitions could also be used by those of greater status and resources to gain legal advantage (Kelly 2011, 244, 286).

27.5 Conclusion

Legal status bore a complex relationship to social status in the Roman world. For the elite, social status was defined in part by membership of various ranks or *ordines*, membership of which was in turn delimited by possession of various marks of social esteem, including specific legal statuses, particularly free birth and citizenship. The law was also utilised to regulate the conduct of this elite, in particular to create a "community of honour": those whose conduct, as well as wealth and birth, determined them worthy of privilege and advantage. The fact that the holding of public office granted social prestige and a significant role in the administration of the judicial system allowed the elite to infuse the system with their own values, in both the making and application of the law, creating distinctions between the advantaged and disadvantaged beyond those categories enumerated in Roman law of persons. In this process, the emperor played a dual role: both enforcing and enhancing the status of the elite and simultaneously acting through the petition system as the ultimate patron to check disadvantage.[2]

[2] The author wishes to acknowledge the MacMillan Center and Classics Library, Yale University, the UNE Partnerships Fund, the volume editors, Alethea Desrosiers, Sarah-Jane Ripa, Jakub Urbanik, José Luis Alonso, Ben Kelly, Thomas Rüfner and Sarah Lawrence.

Bibliography

Alföldy, G. 1985. *The social history of Rome*. London.

Aubert, J.-J. 2002. "A double standard in Roman criminal law? The death penalty and social structure in late republican and early imperial Rome." In J.-J. Aubert and A. J. B. Sirks, eds., Speculum iuris: *Roman law as a reflection of social and economic life in antiquity*. Ann Arbor. 94–133.

Bablitz, L. 2007. *Actors and audience in the Roman courtroom*. London.

Brunt, P. A. 1961. "Charges of provincial maladministration under the early principate." *Historia* 10: 189–227.

Connolly, S. 2010. *Lives behind the laws: the world of the* Codex Hermogenianus. Bloomington.

Crawford, M. H. ed. 1996. *Roman statutes*. 2 vols. London.

Crook, J. A. 1967. *Law and life of Rome: 90 B.C.–A.D. 212*. London.

du Plessis, P. J. 2015[5]. *Borkowski's textbook of Roman law*. Oxford.

Frier, B. 2012. "Status, legal and social." In S. Hornblower and A. Spawforth, eds., *Oxford classical dictionary*. Oxford. 1398–1399.

Gardner, J. 1993. *Being a Roman citizen*. London.

Garnsey, P. 1970. *Social status and legal privilege in the Roman empire*. Oxford.

Garnsey, P. and Saller, R. 2015[2]. *The Roman empire: economy, society, and culture*. Berkeley.

Harris, W. V. 1988. "On the applicability of the concept of class in antiquity." In T. Yuge and M. Doi, eds., *Forms of control and subordination in antiquity*. Leiden. 598–610.

Johnston, D. 1999. *Roman law in context*. Cambridge.

Jones, A. H. M. 1972. *The criminal courts of the Roman republic and principate*. Oxford.

Joshel, S. 1992. *Work, identity and legal status: a study of the occupational inscriptions*. Norman.

Kaser, M. (1956). "*Infamia* und *Ignominia* in den römischen Rechtsquellen." *Zeitschrift der Savigny-Stiftung für Rechtsgeschichte, Romanistische Abteilung* 73: 22–278.

Kaser, M. and Hackl, K. 1996[2]. *Das römische Zivilprozeßrecht*. Munich.

Kehoe, D. P. 2011. "Law and social formation in the Roman empire." In M. Peachin, ed., *The Oxford handbook of social relations in the Roman world*. Oxford. 144–163.

Kelly, B. 2011. *Petition, litigation, and social control in Roman Egypt*. Oxford.

Kelly, J. M. 1966. *Roman litigation*. Oxford.

Kelly, J. M. 1976. *Studies in the civil judicature of the Roman republic*. Oxford.

Knapp, R. C. 2011. *Invisible Romans*. Cambridge, Mass.

Levick, B. (1983). "The *Senatus Consultum* from Larinum." *Journal of Roman Studies* 73: 97–115.

Lintott, A. 1999. *The constitution of the Roman republic*. Oxford.

MacMullen, R. 1974. *Roman social relations 50 B.C. to A.D. 284*. New Haven.

Mayer, E. 2012. *The ancient middle classes: urban life and aesthetics in the Roman empire, 100 BCE–250 CE*. Cambridge, Mass.

McGinn, T. A. J. 2002. "The Augustan marriage legislation and social practice: elite endogamy versus male 'marrying down'." In J.-J. Aubert and A. J. B. Sirks, eds., Speculum iuris: *Roman law as a reflection of social and economic life in antiquity*. Ann Arbor. 46–93.

Millar, F. 2004. "Condemnation to hard labour in the Roman empire from the Julio-Claudians to Constantine." In H. Laton and G. Rogers, eds., *Government, society, and culture in the Roman empire*. Chapel Hill. Vol. 2: 120–150.

Morley, N. 2004. *Theories, models and concepts in ancient history*. London.

Mouritsen, H. 2011. *The freedman in the Roman world*. Cambridge.

Peachin, M. 1996. Iudex vice Caesaris. Stuttgart.

Robinson, O. F. 1995. *The criminal law of ancient Rome*. London.

Scheidel, W. and Friesen, S. J. (2009). "The size of the economy and the distribution of income in the Roman empire." *Journal of Roman Studies* 99: 61–91.

Sherwin-White, A. N. 1973². *The Roman citizenship*. Oxford.

Talbert, R. J. A. 1984. *The senate of imperial Rome*. Princeton.

Tuori, K. 2007. "Legal pluralism and the Roman empires." In J. W. Cairns and P. J. du Plessis, eds., *Beyond dogmatics: law and society in the Roman world*. Edinburgh. 39–52.

Wallace-Hadrill, A. 1994. *Houses and society in Pompeii and Herculaneum*. Princeton.

Wallace-Hadrill, A. (2013). "Trying to define and identify the Roman 'middle classes'. Review: Emanuel Mayer, *The ancient middle classes: Urban life and aesthetics in the Roman empire, 100 BCE–250 CE* (Harvard University Press, Cambridge, MA 2012)." *Journal of Roman Archaeology* 26: 605–609.

Weaver, P. R. C. 1972. Familia caesaris: *a study of the emperor's freedmen and slaves*. Cambridge.

CHAPTER 28

LEGALLY MARGINALISED GROUPS—THE EMPIRE

ROBERT KNAPP

28.1 Introduction

Marginalisation means removing persons or groups of persons to the edge of a society's central acts and functions. This can be done overtly by laws and judicial procedures, or simply by habit and custom, or, as is most usual, by a combination of all of these social actions. Discussion of marginalisation quickly becomes entangled in the question of what criteria to apply in seeking out marginalised groups. On the one hand, the culture itself has internal perceptions of who and what is marginalised. On the other, outside observers, as historians must always be, most usually impose their own values in determining and then assessing marginalised elements. Take one example: the role of women in ancient Rome. Historians, looking in from the outside, might consider them marginalised—socially differentiated and often excluded from many important political, economic and cultural aspects of society. Thinking from contemporary perspectives on the appropriate role of women in society, the historian would likely judge if not outright assume that women were repressed and oppressed in Roman society. To an elite Roman male, however, and perhaps even to most elite females, women were not socially excluded or limited. Rather, their role in their inclusion was just different from men's role. From a Roman's perspective, women were not marginalised at all—they had an important, even central role in society. That role was just not political and economic, i.e. not public. Like distributive justice, distributive social value emphasises that each person's place is important, but important does not mean same, or even equal in a modern sense. We can discuss the marginalisation of women in ancient Rome, but it is essential to understand how much of that concept, with all its judgemental power, is our own, not that of Roman culture in general. I take into consideration both the modern and the Roman perspectives on marginalisation.

The high Empire to about 300 AD is the focus. Roman legal evidence from the Republic reflects a different social and political situation, as does the period from, roughly, Constantine forward. The legal evidence itself largely comes from the post-Constantinian period in the form of the *Codex Theodosianus* (438 AD) and the *Digesta* of Justinian (formulated in the mid-sixth century AD). This situation presents evidential challenges for the earlier period(s). In general, there is little earlier than the time of Hadrian, whence the earliest Code material comes, while the Digest contains only a few pre-Hadrianic entries (Garnsey 1970, 8).

The core concern of Roman law was property and family. Private issues are the main topic of laws, edicts and rulings of the legal system; administrative law or sacred law get much less attention. This is especially true of the Digest, where only four books in fifty focus on administrative law, just one does on criminal law and sacred law is almost entirely absent. The Code has a bit more non-private law but Gaius, too, focuses his instruction on private law (Robinson 1997, 103–104). Thus huge swaths of life were never touched by either the processes or principles of the legal system, either for the core group most interested, or for sporadic users. For a full picture of marginalisation in all aspects of life a much broader picture would be needed, employing literary, epigraphic and archaeological material. But the project at hand is to describe what role the legal system played in marginalising certain people and actions.

While historians would consider women, slaves (Joshel 2010), children (Krause 2011), sons-in-power and freedmen as legally marginalised, Romans would see them as socially crucial, merely differently legally situated from Roman adult males. On the other hand, Roman law did purposefully marginalise one group. The system gradually moved common people (*humiliores*) more and more to the edge of society, while the elite solidified its hold on the centre. The legal system also targeted people engaging in socially reprehensible activities. *Infamia*, an extra-legal, marginalising moral black mark, accrued both from engaging in some specific profession (e.g. actor, gladiator, mortician) as well as from conviction for a large number of crimes (e.g. fraud, theft). Finally, the legal system clearly and specifically set three other groups to the side of normal social life: soldiers, the handicapped and, most completely of all, outlaws along with, eventually, Christians.

This matrix of marginalisations is most often imposed by extra-legal methods. In ancient Rome, there were no laws against specific groups based on bias against geographic origin, education (or lack thereof), personal appearance, religious activities, economic activity or political affiliations. Of course, particular harmful actions (real or perceived) resulting from particular religious outlooks or political designs could and did draw legal ire. But there was no sweeping legislation. Rather, a complex network of social prejudices and realities worked to marginalise people with little education, wealth and claim to good birth, or with weird religious habits, or dedicated to odd economic or political arrangements in their personal lives. Law and the legal processes came into play in various ways to define and enshrine specific responses, but given the apparent lack of organised policing and of a state prosecutorial system, the enforcement of measures relied on the cooperation of fellow citizens in adhering to and, when necessary, enforcing accepted behaviour.

There were laws and processes, however. The legal structure disabled many groups in some fashion from full participation in society. For example, attitudes toward the poor or toward the proper role of women, minors or slaves effectively placed them (and they self-placed as well) at the margins of central political, economic and social activities in which free adult males always played the dominant role. So as important as extra-legal factors were, the legal structure was nevertheless a key element in regulating social relations as it favoured some and disadvantaged others.

28.2 Roman, Non-Romans and the Law

The Roman legal system affected first and foremost Romans (Sherwin-White 1979). Even in theory, perhaps only 10–15 per cent of the inhabitants of the Empire were Roman citizens before the grant of universal (with exceptions) citizenship in 212 AD. A reasonable guess (which is all that is possible) places the overall population of the Empire at 60–70 million, with around 7–8 million Roman citizens, the majority of whom (4.5–5.5 million) lived in the Italian heartland (Scheidel 2007). In addition, Latins of whatever stripe seem to have used Roman law and to have had access to Roman courts (Sherwin-White 1979, 116). There are numerous traces of the assimilation of Roman procedures to those of the Latins. For all intents and purposes, the two categories, Roman and Latin, can be treated as one (Sherwin-White 1979, 268).

Non-Romans, however, were denied the basic elements of the citizenship. But non-Roman citizens were not in general required by Rome to use the system. They resolved issues by their own local laws and customs. There was no appeal from them to Roman courts. There is a clear distinction between access to formal legal procedures, civil or criminal, and access to Roman authorities as final adjudicators. Since the sources are full of provincial non-Romans appealing to Roman officials or the emperor, it is important to make clear the difference between the formal use of Roman legal procedure and the exercise of overall jurisdiction by provincial governors, and, *a fortiori*, by emperors. Fundamentally, an emperor could deal with non-citizens as he wished. He could take appeals from local jurisdictions, but this was entirely discretionary. Once he took such appeals, it would be natural, but not required, to use the habits and mentalities of Roman law to decide the case. As to a person in charge of a province, he, too, had wide discretion, although he needed to be aware (or made aware) of Imperial decrees or other constraints specifically relevant to a case at hand. What an "appeal" could mean was a "retrial" by a Roman who actually reheard the case on his (a Roman's) own terms and procedures. Or it could mean a swift decision based upon a personal assessment, with no regard for technicalities of Roman procedure. So a non-Roman (person, community) had direct access to Roman justice, but did not have a right to the procedures of Roman law. The reality is that, except in limited circumstances, the Roman legal system almost totally marginalises the vast preponderance of the population of the Empire, generally without distinction as to ethnic group or political entity. Only a small number of non-citizens were direct, active participants in the legal system, and these were almost always the elite because of the time and cost necessary to pursue issues before a Roman official. Roman law was never seen as a "Romanising" institution. It existed to serve Roman citizens, even in their interactions with *peregrini*, and protected Roman interests. The result of the relatively small number of citizens and the laissez-faire attitude of Roman overlords toward provincial communities was that the vast majority of persons' legal issues were decided outside the Roman legal system, marginalised from the perspective of that system.

Leaving aside the non-citizens, within the citizen body the scope and rules of the Roman legal system were formulated by free, male, adult, *sui iuris* citizens with the interests of the active participants in mind; that is, their own interests. These males were, *in toto*, no more than 20 per cent of the entire citizen population (free, slave, both sexes, all ages). Within that potentially active citizenry, 1–2 per cent of the male population essentially controlled most aspects of life. This would be a mere 0.1–.2 of the entire citizen population of ~8 million, perhaps around 30,000 individuals. Another perhaps 20 per cent of that male population were potential but seldom active players in the drama of the dominant, another ~300,000 persons. So, to be generous, perhaps these 300,000 free adult males could see the legal system as both accessible and effective in dealing with their concerns—a mere 4 per cent of the entire citizen body and only ~0.5 per cent of the Empire's entire population. If it is assumed that only the elite 1–2 per cent of the citizenry actually accessed the system regularly, then only a tenth of that number were regularly engaged in legal processes. Everyone else was marginalised—that is, their social, economic and political concerns were dealt with only as they were congruent with or impinged on some interest of these few adult citizen males.

There was some recognition that a large portion of the citizenry was being left out of the system, both citizen and, sometimes, non-citizen. In D.1.16.9.4 we read that *dignitas* should not dictate outcome: "Accordingly, he [the judicial official] is duty bound to watch that he has some system of ranking applications, and in fact to make sure that everyone's request gets a hearing and that it does not turn out that while the high rank of some applicants gets its due and unscrupulousness gets concessions, middling people do not put their requests, either having quite failed to find advocates or having instructed less well-known ones, whose position is not one of any standing" (transl. ed. Watson). D.1.16.9.5 adds: "But if someone should represent himself as being unable to find an advocate because of his opponent's power, it is just as much incumbent on the proconsul to give him one. But it is wrong for anyone to be oppressed by the sheer power of his opponent; in fact, it tends to harm the reputation of the person who has charge of the province, if someone gets away with such overpowering behaviour that everyone is afraid to take instructions as an advocate against him" (transl. ed. Watson). D.1.16.9.6 extends this principle to citizens in the provinces: "The foregoing remarks apply in common to all colonial governors and should be taken to heart by them too" (transl. ed. Watson). Apparently it merited repeating to provincial governors: "The provincial governor should be religiously zealous in preventing more influential people from inflicting wrongs on those of lower station and in seeing that those who defend the latter are not framed up on charges of infamous crime when they are innocent" (transl. ed. Watson) (D.1.18.6.2; cf. D.1.18.6.4; D.1.18.19pr).

In the legal material there is scant evidence that these admonitions were followed regularly, or even sporadically. Certainly, the mere possession of citizenship was far from an assurance of just treatment. While citizenship supplies certain formal rights, these rights were no guarantee against arbitrary actions by magistrates, or worse (Garnsey 1970, 266, 280). In other words, citizenship spared the citizen the radical marginalisation visited upon peregrines, but did not ensure access to the full scope of legal protections theoretically afforded by laws and legal procedures.

28.3 Marginalised Groups

Let us assume the position of the citizens who controlled not only the legal but also the political, economic and social aspects of life for the inhabitants of the Empire, and look at the groups they push to the edges of power in their world. The law treated core elements of elite society extensively. Although marginalised from the perspective of public power and authority, legal material views issues involving the family, women, children, slaves and freedmen as integral parts of the core concerns of private and even, although to a lesser extent, public life. The system dealt with these groups in a non-hostile, practical way. Their disabilities are fairly well known, and can be summarised briefly here.

"In many articles of our law, the condition of females is worse than that of males" (D.1.5.9; Gardner 1991). The legal system assumes an inherent disability in women that prevents them from doing manly things in society (Milnor 2011). As an example, D.2.13.12, states: "Women are held to be excluded from the office of banker since this is a masculine type of work" (transl. ed. Watson). They suffer a lengthy series of disabilities because except in a few special cases they are not *sui iuris*; that is, they are in the legal power of some male and cannot operate independently at law, as a male can. The key to their disabilities is the fact that they are *in potestate* to another. They cannot vote, bring prosecutions or sit on juries, or hold *potestas* over any free citizen; they are subject to *tutela* in legal transactions and financial doings. In fact their marginality is very similar to that of *infames*, who will be discussed shortly (Gardner 1993, 85–87, 152). Yet, about one in four of the 114 attested cases in literary sources are brought by women, and these women represent the full social range from senatorial rank to freedmen (Bablitz 2007, 221–223 for list). Children, sons-in-power and slaves also suffer from being in someone else's *potestas*, and their disabilities in all their variety derive from this fact.

Freedmen are a little different (Mouritsen 2011; Knapp 2012). They are full citizens, and the adult males are *sui iuris*, with the same caveats that apply to any other adult males. Their issues derive from the fact that they were once slaves, but are now free citizens. As slaves, they were the possession of their owner. As freed slaves, they are as though born again, with the former master now their patron, their new father. Slave-not-slave, not-free-now-free creates a complicated relationship to the patron and to the patron's familial situation, including his property, and to his immediate family, for example with regard to an inheritance the freedman might gain, or an inheritance the freedman might leave. Requirements regarding *operae* (a way of recouping some of the value of the once-slave), *obsequium* (duties like those expected of an emancipated child) and inheritance make this clear (Gardner 1993, 20, 43, 51). However, freedmen had the same general package of civil rights as other citizens. Specific disabilities are often mentioned: senators could not marry women of slave origins; freedmen could not hold magistracies or most priesthoods; they could not vote, serve in most of the armed forces, be decurions or equestrians; in criminal law they were subject to greater penalties or punishments. These disabilities had, however, little consequence in the lives of almost all freedmen and represent an elite irritated at the uppitiness of a few über-successful freedmen in and around senatorial and Imperial families. This elite bias produces a greatly exaggerated picture of the marginalised social situation of freedmen in general.

These groups' marginalisation is related to their social positions and roles in the *familia*. Two other classes of marginalised people need to be briefly mentioned. Soldiers under the Augustan system were organised into a military family based upon procreational celibacy and loyalty to the emperor. They suffered some disabilities regarding inheritance, and had some special privileges such as being able to use their private funds (*peculium*) without their father's permission (Knapp 2012). But their condition is so special that it is hardly correct to think of them as marginalised. The other group is persons with physical handicaps.

Deaf, mute or blind persons had some restrictions put on their abilities to be active in legal processes, mostly because, given the oral and visual nature of those processes, their disabilities inhibited full participation (Gardner 1993, 155; Stahl 2011). A good example is Reg.Ulp.20.13, "The dumb man cannot make a will, because he cannot utter the words of the nuncupation; the deaf man, because he cannot hear the words of the *familiae emptor*" (transl. Gardner). Laws deal with the repercussions of these disablements, not with accommodating or intentionally marginalising handicapped persons. Those with mental illness (*furiosi*) were likewise circumscribed both in their legal abilities and in regard to the results of their actions while insane. They are assimilated to the capacity of children. So, for example, idiots cannot participate in the praetor's court (D.3.1.2) and "nothing is understood to be done in the presence of a lunatic (*furiosus*)" (D.4.8.49pr) (transl. ed. Watson).

28.4 Marginalising Moral Behaviour

Persons whom the law stigmatised because of moral shortcomings deserve more extensive treatment. *Infamia* rendered a person an *infamis* (Buckland and Stein 1963, 91–92; McGinn 2011). But there was no law of infamy to be broken. Rather, anti-social actions, as defined by the culture, create a social and legal condition. It is a by-product of legal action, not the precipitator of it (Crook 1967, 84–85). This originated in Republican legal habits and decisions, for *infamia* goes back to black marks (*notae*) awarded by the censors. Then the praetors' decisions became the source of precedent and action in awarding *infamia*. A legal decision could include deprivation of rights (e.g. to hold public office) associated with *infamia*, but it bears repeating that no one is ever convicted of *infamia*; per se. D.3.1.1.5 prohibited those *notabilis in turpitudine* (an exceptionally disreputable person) from representing others in court. Conviction of a range of crimes such as theft or outrage (*iniuria*) brought *infamia* in tow, as did dishonourable discharge from the armed forces, fraud and losers in certain civil suits (Crook 1967, 84). Simply practice of certain professions, themselves not illegal, also brought *infamia*. Examples are morticians, ushers(!), auctioneers, actors, persons intimately involved in arena games (gladiators, *bestiarii* and *lanistae*), pimps and prostitutes, the latter having actual legal disabilities as well (McGinn 1998, 46). In the case of professions, a combination of moral abhorrence and of being a paid endeavour created the problem (Gardner 1993, 152). There were other serious disabilities for various reasons (Greenidge 1894 gives forty!). Misconduct of various sorts in family relations engendered *infamia* as well. It is hard to give a general description of what brought on *infamia*, but certainly irresponsible, frivolous and/or morally disreputable behaviour was often targeted (Gardner 1993, 152). The legal repercussions were extensive, but far from debilitating. An *infamis* could not prefer a charge in court, nor could he represent others in court, bring an accusation in a criminal case, or hold public office or positions. The restrictions were potentially severe for *honestiores*, since they reified social ostracism and a diminution of *dignitas*. However, a glance at this list assures that common folk were not much affected by *infamia*. Although the restrictions were potentially severe for elites, they are, at best, of little consequence in the lives of plebs, the vast majority of the population. Prostitutes (McGinn 2011), actors, gladiators and *bestiarii* (Leppin 2011) would have cared little about being designated as *infames*.

Marginalisation through *infamia* is the result of legal reification of social discrimination based upon social displeasure. Legal discrimination could also be based upon wealth and its concomitants in Roman society: power and status (*dignitas*).

28.5 Marginalising Ordinary Romans

The term *humiliores*, "the lesser sort", is used to designate persons of lesser status than the ruling class. This and its various stand-ins such as *plebei, homines mediocres* and *tenuiores* encompass a distinct social category, persons and groups of lesser status than that of the *honestiores*, "the better sort". Men are categorised in this way, and treated at law according to these categories, but the actual terminology is never standardised, and the Digest never offers definitions or lists of attributes defining the terms (Crook 1967, 95–97; Garnsey 1970). Administrative attitudes and decisions are actually more active in creating and enforcing the marginalisation of *humiliores* than laws themselves, or any legal theory. It was not so much the laws as the people who made, interpreted and enforced them that created the marginalisation of the less well-off. The process is in full swing as early as the first century AD, and simply carries to official extremes the innate prejudice of the higher orders for the common folk. As time went on, courts with overlapping jurisdictions, a flexible structure for determining punishments and the power of authorities to act without much control in judicial decisions, meant that the gap between high-status groups and the common people, whether citizens or non-citizens, widened (Garnsey 1970, 269–270).

It hardly needs repeating that Roman law and procedures favoured those with much *dignitas*. The elite philosophically did not believe in equality in the modern Western sense at all. Whenever they made legal decisions, their fundamental sense of "we are the ones who count" served to marginalise actions of others and to treat the marginalised differently from themselves. Thus there is little on labour or on the problems of the small tenant in the law codes and decisions (Crook 1967, 282). But it would be wrong to say that such common people do not figure in the legal material at all. D.9.1.3 notes that if an animal harms a free man, "account can be taken of the expenses of medical treatment and the loss of employment and of the opportunity of taking a job which were caused by the party being disabled" (*factus inutilis*). D.9.2.5.3 notes that it is actionable if a shoemaker knocks out the eye of a freeman apprentice boy as punishment for doing a job poorly, and D.9.2.6 says much the same thing: *praeceptoris enim nimia saevitia culpae adsignatur* ("for excessive brutality on the part of a teacher is blameworthy"). The *lex Aquilia* seems quite often to involve ordinary people in examples of lawsuits for damages arising from harm suffered.

In addition, although the difference in rank and awareness might cause hesitation, there are examples of simple people asking for legal help, strongly indicating that such people could and did on occasion use the legal system. In one case, a shopkeeper asks a famous jurist for an opinion:

> One night a shopkeeper had placed a lantern above his display counter that adjoined the footpath, but some passer-by took it down and carried it off. The shopkeeper pursued him, calling for his lantern, and caught hold of him; but in order to escape from his grasp, the thief began to hit the shopkeeper with the whip that he was carrying on which there was a spike. From this encounter, a real brawl developed in which the shopkeeper put out the eye of the lantern-stealer, and he asked my opinion as to whether he had inflicted wrongful damage, bearing in mind that he had been hit with the whip first. My opinion was that unless he had poked out the eye intentionally, he would not appear to have incurred liability, as the damage was really the lantern-stealer's own fault for hitting him first with the whip; on the other hand, if he had not been provoked by the beating, but had started the brawl when trying to snatch back his lantern, the shopkeeper would appear to be accountable for the loss of the eye. (D.9.2.52.1, transl. ed. Watson)

In another case, a workman (*faber*) purchases a slave for a modest amount, ten *aurei*, and teaches him his trade. He then sells the trained slave for twenty *aurei*. The purchaser subsequently sues him in court on the grounds that the slave was unsound. Surely such a workman was a person of relatively modest means (D.17.1.26.8).

And at times the situation of a *humilior* comes up:

> If the deceased was a tenant farmer or lodger and there is no money to pay for his funeral, Pomponius writes that the funeral expenses should be met from his movable property, and if any surplus remains, that should be retained to cover any arrears of rent. (D.11.7.14.1, transl. ed. Watson)

Or a *homo mediocris* is left the right to use a large house in an inheritance, and has the legal right to rent out some of it (D.7.8.4pr).

It can be argued from these and other examples that the legal material shows that "people outside the elite viewed the petitioning process as effective in settling issues in family law", and the petition process to emperor also indicates that "people in the Empire expected ... their government ... would serve to defend the rights of all the oppressed and dispense justice" (Kehoe 2011, 155). The Egyptian material, in particular, shows that many petitions were given to local officials and to the governor. However optimistic the minds of *humiliores* regarding these petitions, the reality was much different. Just as petitioning the king in England, or a duke of an estate, the powerful used the image of *noblesse oblige* to perpetuate the ideal that the humble had a disinterested partner among the powerful; someone who would listen and help. While an official might render something like justice in cases between those of equal status, even involving humble folk, any action of a *humilior* against an *honestior* would have been a different situation. Just as a king was unlikely to favour the interests of a peasant over those of a knight, powerful Roman officials, steeped in the values of distributive justice that underpinned their outlook on the world, were unlikely champions of the humble, even though in some specific instances it appears that they did act in that way.

But more often, when ordinary folk are mentioned in the legal material, their basic interests are not what is really at stake. For example, seamen (the manager of a ship, not the common seaman), innkeepers and stable keepers are singled out not because they are poor, disadvantaged or anything like that, but because they are entrusted with property and need to be held accountable (D.4.9.1pr-8). There is also the case of a wealthy man bringing a suit against a shopkeeper for fouling the air of his dwelling above the shop: "Aristo holds that the man who leased a cheese shop from the authorities of Minturnae, can be prevented from discharging smoke by the owner of the building above it" (transl. ed. Watson) (D. 8.5.8.5).

The vast preponderance of material treats the *humiliores* as lesser beings. This is done both overtly through a few laws and many judicial decisions, and indirectly, for the whole system allowed the unlimited amassing of wealth and property which was then used to maintain the status of an elite at the expense of others. The legal minds recognised what was going on: "we cannot be in an equal position vis-à-vis a person of greater influence and resources" (D.4.7.3pr) (transl. ed. Watson). In one of Seneca's *Controversiae* (10.1.2) an *honestior* is dealing with a *humilior*: "The rich man says, 'Bring me to court'" The poor man says, "Could I, a poor man, bring charge against a rich man?" Lesser beings knew their situation.

One might imagine that the marginalisation would be ameliorated, if not prevented, by the rights and privileges common to all Romans citizens. This does not occur, however. The status of citizen does not seem to have ensured access to the legal system, or equal treatment once within it. It is the *dignitas*/position of the person, not the status as citizen that counts. In some cases, for example regarding the status and privileges of non-citizen decurions in provincial towns, the non-citizen had greater protection than a *humilior* citizen. Citizenship as an element in the judicial system fails utterly to compensate for/level out/oppose the attitudes, power, wealth and *dignitas* of the elites running the system. Rather, *humiliores* had very restricted access to the legal system because, among other things, the cost and the travel necessary to pursue cases worked against them. Then there was the double standard in making decisions once within the system, and especially the scale of penalties vis-à-vis the *honestiores* when they were involved. The prejudice gradually took greater and greater hold in judicial and administrative actions, the distinction between *humiliores* and *honestiores* gaining full recognition by Hadrian's time. After that, procedures became increasingly formulated, applied and severe as time went on. There was a gradual decline in rights and status of *humiliores* until they were almost on the level of the common folk among non-citizens.

28.6 Completely Marginal: Outlaws

Outlaws operated beyond the Pale of the law, Roman or otherwise, but not necessarily beyond its reach. One type of outlaw, the robber, fraudster or cutpurse, operates more or less within lawful society, taking advantage of its weaknesses in legal procedure or enforcement of law and order. These people are held to the laws and at least sometimes punished through formal legal channels. They are "outlaws within the law", so to speak. As such, they are not marginalised but treated as aberrant participants in the system, and punished accordingly when caught—and punished with less savagery than those who operate externally to society in general, who are truly outside the law. These outlaws seemed to threaten the very structure of society. They had not even the minimal legal options afforded criminal defendants. When caught, they could be treated *pro damnatis*, as if already found guilty, without any legal niceties or protections (D.48.3.6.1). Whether brought before a local magistrate or a Roman official, their summary treatment was pretty much guaranteed. As outcasts, they were cast out; as outlaws, the laws offered no protection. Their marginalisation was complete, as the managers of the legal system gave them no quarter. All legal processes were directed toward their control or annihilation.

The distinction between internal and external outlaws is indistinct, of course, in practice. Actions against both types of outlaw were, at least in the provinces, based on the decision-making and coercive powers of a local magistrate, governor or someone with delegated authority. In Rome the old Republican courts soon disappeared during the Empire, to be replaced with tribunals or individual magistrates. Beyond Rome, all dealing with criminals, including outlaws, was *extra ordinem*; that is, without a tribunal and at the discretion of a magistrate (D.48.19.13: "These days it is allowed to him who tries a crime *extra ordinem* to levy what sentence he wishes, either quite severe or quite lenient, provided that in either case he does so with moderation."). Thus how a criminal was punished could vary greatly from place to place and situation to situation. Small-time thieves could be punished quickly and savagely, but society and its legal representatives acted in a frenzy against external outlaws: the bandits and pirates. A governor, or even his subordinate, could and did often make summary judgement on the mere charge of banditry. Even more than this, private citizens were authorised to act unilaterally to kill bandits. C.9.16.3 (a. 265) states: "Decree of the Emperor Gallienus. If, as you claim, you killed an outlaw, there is no doubt that he who had wilfully premeditated killing you was himself justly killed." Lucius, protagonist of Apuleius' *Metamorphoses*, claims he should be honoured for having slaughtered bandits breaking into a home (*Met.* 3.6). Savage executions of bandits by burning, crucifixion or in the jaws of wild beasts "set a good example" and served to rebalance in some way by showing that society could continue even in the face of such dastardly people. ("*Nonnumquam evenit, ut aliquorum maleficiorum supplicia exacerbentur, quotiens nimium multis personis grassantibus exemplo opus sit*" D.48.19.16.10.) Outlaws were the most marginalised people in the Empire (Shaw 1984, 1993; Knapp 2012).

Very much like outlaws, legal procedures came to consider Christians as beyond the accepted margins of society. Their "hatred of the human race", as Tacitus (*Ann.* 15.44) succinctly put it, meant that Christians were outside the protections not only of the *ius civile*, but of the *ius gentium*, perhaps even of the *ius naturale*. Hostile legal action was therefore, as in the case of other outlaws, required in order to maintain good order within the "human race". But unlike outlaws per se, Christians had done no physical damage to those within lawful society. Because their deeds had been directly harmful, criminals needed to be punished as examples and deterrents, even if they promised never to commit crimes again. But if the object of punishment was to repair the damage done by a deed and prevent its recurrence in the acts of others, the act of repudiating the rejection of ancestral custom was a victory for the society, affirmation that acceptance of the ancestral ways was the *sine qua non* for membership in that society. Christians, as they had done no one any actual harm, merely needed to rejoin the human race. They could come back into the fold simply by rejecting their aberrant behaviour. Confession and repentance could not buy an acquittal for theft, as the act of thievery could not be taken back. The attitude of defiance and hostility toward ancestral, accepted habits could be reversed. In addition, the repentant then became a living example of the correctness of ancestral, polytheistic behaviour. Because the one who repented was reintegrated into lawful society, he also became a deterrent to aberrant activity, proclaiming at once the rightness of the ancestral ways and the ease with which trouble could be avoided. As such, he was much more valuable living than dead—and so the willingness to accept recantation as the end of the affair in the case of accusations against Christians. Their self-marginalisation could be reversed by self-reintegration.

28.7 Conclusion

The Roman legal system reflected its cultural matrix. The legally imposed seating at public spectacles brought the law into the business of encompassing in a single place the marginalisations it spread throughout its workings. As a mechanism for marginalisation, the system favoured some and disadvantaged others. Exactly how and to whom this happened varied greatly. Although to a Roman elite the situation would take on a very different hue, to modern Westerners some were disadvantaged to greater or lesser extent within the core of the society—people such as women, children, slaves and freedmen—while others were marginalised in the eyes of both ancients and moderns, such as the *infames* and outlaws. While it is easy to pick apart the legal system and point to its shortcomings from a modern perspective, it is important to remember that a legal system is more than a sum of its parts. However historians may parse it, persons of all sorts, from the poor to the wealthy and powerful, probably had some confidence that their needs could be met within the system. This might be in formal proceedings, or, more often, it could be met by following the precepts and rules of the legal system in such situations as inheritance law, without ever actually coming into the legal system itself in terms of criminal or civil actions (Kehoe 2011, 155–156). It is not a small thing for a legal system to be able to provide guidance in a wide range of life's activities, without active involvement on a day-to-day basis. Even in an environment of discrimination and marginalisation, the legal system held the basic Roman social fabric together for centuries.[1]

Bibliography

Ando, C. 1996. *Citizen and alien in Roman law*. Los Angeles.

Bablitz, L. 2007. *Actors and audience in the Roman courtroom*. London.

Bablitz, L. 2011. "Roman society in the courtroom." In M. Peachin, ed., *The Oxford handbook of social relations in the Roman world*. Oxford. 317–334.

[1] Suggested reading: careful reading of the chapters on marginalised persons in Peachin 2011 and Knapp 2012 provide basic information. Gardner 1993 is a judicious look at the life of a Roman citizen, with a bent toward legal sources.

Buckland, W. W. and Stein, P. 1963³. *A text-book of Roman law: from Augustus to Justinian.* Cambridge.
Crook, J. A. 1967. *Law and life of Rome: 90 B.C.–A.D. 212.* London.
De Ste.-Croix, G. E. M. 1981. *The class struggle in the ancient Greek world: from the archaic age to the Arab conquests.* Ithaca.
Gardner, J. F. 1991. *Women in Roman law and society.* Bloomington.
Gardner, J. F. 1993. *Being a Roman citizen.* London.
Gardner, J. F. 1998. *Family and* familia *in Roman law and life.* Oxford.
Garnsey, P. 1970. *Social status and legal privilege in the Roman empire.* Oxford.
Greenidge, A. H. J. 1894. Infamia: *its place in Roman public and private law.* Oxford.
Joshel, S. 2010. *Slavery in the Roman world.* Cambridge.
Kehoe, D. 2011. "Law and social formation in the Roman empire." In M. Peachin, ed., *The Oxford handbook of social relations in the Roman world.* Oxford. 144–163.
Knapp, R. C. 2012. *Invisible Romans.* Cambridge, Mass.
Krause, J.-U. 2011. "Children in the Roman family and beyond." In M. Peachin, ed., *The Oxford handbook of social relations in the Roman world.* Oxford. 623–642.
Leppin, H. 2011. "Between marginality and celebrity: entertainers and entertainments in Roman society." In M. Peachin, ed., *The Oxford handbook of social relations in the Roman world.* Oxford. 660–678.
McGinn, T. A. J. 1998. *Prostitution, sexuality, and the law in ancient Rome.* Oxford.
McGinn, T. A. J. 2011. "Roman prostitutes and marginalisation." In M. Peachin, ed., *The Oxford handbook of social relations in the Roman world.* Oxford. 643–659.
Metzger, E. 2005. *Litigation in Roman law.* Oxford.
Milnor, K. 2011. "Women in Roman society." In M. Peachin, ed., *The Oxford handbook of social relations in the Roman world.* Oxford. 609–622.
Mouritsen, H. 2011. *The freedman in the Roman world.* Cambridge.
Peachin, M. ed. 2011. *The Oxford handbook of social relations in the Roman world.* Oxford.
Robinson, O. F. 1997. *The sources of Roman law: problems and methods for ancient historians.* London.
Scheidel, W. (2007). "Roman population size: the logic of the debate." *Princeton/Stanford Working Papers in Classics* version 2.0: 20 July 2007, Available at: http://www.princeton.edu/~pswpc/pdfs/scheidel/070706.pdf, accessed 14 February 2016.
Scheidel, W. 2008. "Roman population size: the logic of the debate," in L. de Ligt and S. Northwood eds., *People, land and politics. Demographic developments and the transformation of Roman Italy, 300 BC–AD 14.* Leiden. 17–70.
Shaw, B. D. (1984). "Bandits in the Roman empire." *Past and Present* 105: 3–52.
Shaw, B. D. 1993. "The bandit." In A. Giardina, ed., L. G. Cochrane, transl., *The Romans.* Chicago. 300–341.
Sherwin-White, A. N. 1979². *The Roman citizenship.* Oxford.
Stahl, J. 2011. "Physically deformed and disabled people." In M. Peachin, ed., *The Oxford handbook of social relations in the Roman world.* Oxford. 715–733.

CHAPTER 29

REPRESSION, RESISTANCE AND REBELLION

BENJAMIN KELLY

29.1 Introduction

This chapter is about the extreme outer limits of law's Empire, the borderlands where the rule of law ends, and the primal need to defend the political order begins. In other words, it is concerned with the legal and ethical issues connected with the repression of serious threats from within to the Roman political order, specifically sedition, conspiracies, riots and provincial revolts. On occasions, of course, the repression of such threats took place entirely outside law's realm. The real or perceived gravity of the situation would unleash the state's capacity for overwhelming violence, and order would be restored by massacres, mass enslavements and beatings—apparently without serious challenges to the legal (or ethical) propriety of the response. But on other occasions, law was very relevant. Judicial institutions and legal categories were employed to legitimate repressive action; conversely, legal rights and conventions were invoked to limit and critique such crackdowns.

Two concerns therefore run through this chapter. The first is to reconstruct the legal underpinnings of repressive responses to fundamental threats to the political order, insofar as such underpinnings existed. This involves consideration of substantive rules of criminal law, of judicial processes and of coercive powers inherent in certain offices. A second concern is to outline the various types of limitations on state power that were routinely invoked in relation to acts of repression. Some of these limitations were embedded in positive law; for instance, the right of appeal (*provocatio*) and citizen immunity from torture. Others were more the product of custom and practice, such as the expectations of a public trial and of a clearly formulated charge. It is also important to notice various ethical discourses that were used to try to restrain the full force of the law, discourses including those of *clementia* ("mercy"), *crudelitas* ("cruelty") and *saevitia* ("harshness"). Such discourses were instances of wider Roman society—especially aristocratic society—attempting to influence the uses to which legal powers and processes were put.

29.2 Sedition in the Republic

During the Republic, the senate and magistrates faced three fundamental problems in dealing with sedition in the city of Rome. The first related to manpower: there was no standing army, and in any case the exercise of military command was prohibited within the *pomerium*.[1] A second problem emerged from the rights of *provocatio* and tribunician intercession. Certainly from 300 BC, and perhaps earlier, citizens in civilian life had a legal right to appeal to the people against a magistrate's decision to execute or scourge them using his powers of summary discipline (*coercitio*)—at least in political cases.[2] There was also a separate but possibly related right; namely, the *ius auxilii*: the right of the tribune of the plebs to intervene and protect a citizen from harsh treatment by a magistrate. Thirdly, whilst the *iudicium populi* and (in the late Republic) the *quaestiones de vi* and *maiestatis* provided judicial fora in which charges of rioting and sedition could be brought, they were not always sufficiently expeditious to deal with serious threats, and could be coerced or entirely shut down by a hostile crowd.

At least according to the Romans' own traditions about their early history, an initial response to such problems was to use the office of dictator. Dictators were reportedly appointed to deal with sedition on occasion during the early Republic.[3] If these reports are true, the dictatorship was probably attractive for this purpose because the office was immune from *provocatio* (Liv. 2.29, 4.13, 8.33–35; Festus 198M). There were also the facts that dictators had no colleagues to interfere with their work, and that they were apparently immune from tribunician *auxilium* (Liv. 2.18.8; Plut. *Fabius Maximus* 9, with Drogula 2007, 446). But there are no reports of the dictatorship being used to deal with domestic unrest in the third century BC or later. The *lex Valeria* of 300 BC is reported to have removed dictators' immunity from *provocatio*;[4] if this is correct, then the utility of the dictatorship for repressing sedition would have henceforth been limited.

The legal issues involved with repressing sedition came to the fore again thanks to the activities of Ti. Gracchus and his supporters in 133–132 BC. The initial crackdown on Gracchus was little more than a lynching, with only some very vague appeals to legal principle. But then an inquiry involving the consuls of 132 AD and a *consilium* was established following a decree of the senate—although the legality of this was very questionable too.[5] The *lex Sempronia* of 123 AD, passed by Tiberius' brother Gaius, put this question beyond doubt by requiring a vote of the people before a capital sentence could be pronounced.[6] Henceforth,

[1] Drogula 2007, 435–442 with earlier literature.

[2] On the *leges de provocatione* and the historicity of those reported for the early Republic see von Ungern-Sternberg 1970, 31, n. 32; Lintott 1972; Bauman 1973b. On *coercitio* see Drogula 2007, 428–430 with further literature.

[3] Dion. Hal. *Ant. Rom.* 5.70.2–3; Liv. 4.13–16; 6.11–17; *Inscr. Ital.* 13.1 (368 BC).

[4] Festus 198 M; cf. Bauman 1973b.

[5] Cic. *Amic.* 37; Val. Max. 4.7.1; Plut. *Ti. Gracch.* 20. See von Ungern-Sternberg 1970, 38–43 and Lintott 1999b, 162–3 on its legality (or lack thereof).

[6] Cic. *Rab. perd.* 12; cf. Plut. *C. Gracch.* 4, with discussion by von Ungern-Sternberg 1970, 48–54. The law did not prevent courts set up by a vote of the people from pronouncing capital sentences: Lintott 1999a, 163.

quaestiones extraordinariae of the sort used in 132 (and also perhaps in the Bacchanalian affair of 186 BC) were not legally possible.[7]

In 121 BC, therefore, the senate devised a new solution to deal with what it perceived to be another emergency situation created by C. Gracchus and his supporters: the so-called *senatus consultum ultimum* (*SCU*).[8] The senate decreed "that L. Opimius the consul should see to it that the *res publica* suffer no harm".[9] Relying on this decree, Opimius availed himself of a military force and led a lethal crackdown on Gracchus and his supporters in which several thousand people allegedly died (Plut. *C. Gracch.* 16–17). This same decree was used in a variety of other emergency situations to authorise action against those who found themselves on the wrong side of the majority of senators (Golden 2013, 104–149 for references).

Whilst various modern scholars have made quite categorical statements about the legality of the *SCU*,[10] the better view is that its legality was arguable, but that not everyone accepted the arguments. Several separate (quasi-)legal justifications are visible in the sources. First, the very wording of the decree shows that it was presented as a measure to avert harm to the Republic. When L. Opimius was prosecuted (and acquitted) in 120 BC for repressing the Gracchans, the defence was that ignoring the *lex Sempronia* had been legally justified by considerations of public safety (Cic. *De or.* 2.106, 2.132, 2.134, 2.165). One can perhaps see in this argument a version of a principle that is expressed in Cicero's *De legibus*: "Let the safety of the people be the highest law" (3.8: *salus populi suprema lex esto*). Secondly, Sallust refers to the *SCU* as conferring power on magistrates "in accordance with Roman custom" (*more Romano*). Since custom was viewed as the bedrock of constitutional propriety (cf. Pina Polo, ch. 7), Sallust may be reflecting an argument that, by the late Republic, the decree had been employed often enough and for long enough to legitimate it.[11]

Whatever arguments were made in support of the legality of the *SCU*, it is evident that not everyone accepted them. Opimius' prosecutors in 120 BC obviously did not. Furthermore, in 63 BC an elderly senator, C. Rabirius, was tried for *perduellio* ("treason") for his role in the repression of Saturninus in 100 BC. Both the surviving version of Cicero's speech in defence of Rabirius and also Cassius Dio's account of the incident treat it as a partisan attempt to impugn the legality of the *SCU*, an impression that is accepted by most modern scholars.[12]

Aside from the *SCU*, several mechanisms were used during the late Republic to deal with political emergencies. The *tumultus* declaration was repurposed for such ends. Originally,

[7] von Ungern-Sternberg 1970, 53–54. Bacchanalian affair and aftermath: Liv. 39.8–19; *FIRA* I.30; cf. von Ungern-Sternberg 1970, 29–38; Lintott 1999b, 161–162.

[8] The decree is called this by Caes. *B Civ.* 1.5 and Liv. 3.4 (anachronistic), although the title was not a technical term in Antiquity.

[9] Cic. *Cat.* 1.4: *uti L. Opimius consul videret ne quid res publica detrimenti caperet*, cf. Cic. *Phil.* 8.14.

[10] e.g. Golden 2013, 148.

[11] Sall. *Cat.* 29; cf. Cic. *Mil.* 70. Note too Drogula 2007, esp. 447–451.

[12] Cic. *Rab. perd.*; Dio Cass. 37.26–28; Suet. *Iul.* 12; cf. Lintott 1999b, 168–169; von Ungern-Sternberg 1970, 83–85.

this declaration was made in response to a pressing threat from a foreign enemy. It empowered the responsible magistrates to raise an army quickly, and to ignore the usual exemptions from military service that some citizens enjoyed on the grounds of age, occupation or priestly service.[13] In the late Republic, this decree came to be used on occasion to raise armies to deal with incidents of armed sedition.[14]

A final kind of emergency decree was the so-called *hostis* declaration.[15] This was used first in 88 BC, when C. Marius and eleven of his supporters were declared enemies (*hostes*) in a senatorial decree and a statute passed by an assembly.[16] As the death throes of the Republic continued, the senate passed *hostis* decrees during other crises,[17] although there is no evidence of other occasions on which matching statutes were passed.[18]

The purported legal effect of the *hostis* decree was to declare that the targets had, at some point in the past, become *hostes* and thus had already forfeited their Roman citizenship. This meant that they had lost their right of *provocatio* and could be killed without offending the *lex Sempronia*: arguably no capital sentence on citizens had been pronounced, but rather the loss of citizens' civil rights was being declared (Bauman 1973a, 279–282). Unlike the *SCU*, the *hostis* decree expressly named the individuals at which it was directed; it also allowed them to be killed by anyone with impunity after the initial emergency had abated (Bauman 1973a, 277). The targets of the decree had almost always fled Rome by the time it was passed, thus putting them—as a practical matter—outside the reach of the magistrates and the courts in Rome.[19]

As with the *SCU*, the *hostis* declaration was controversial. We hear from Valerius Maximus that in 88 BC the aged augur Q. Mucius Scaevola refused in the senate to vote Marius a *hostis*; to judge from the fact that Sulla surrounded the *curia* with troops, Scaevola was not the only senator with misgivings (Bauman 1973a, 273). In response to the Catilinarian conspiracy of 63 BC, Cicero attempted to extend the legal analysis implicit in the *hostis* declaration and argue that the ringleaders of the conspiracy who had been apprehended in Rome (and against whom no *hostis* declaration had been passed) by their very actions were enemies of the state, and therefore had lost their citizenship automatically.[20] We learn, however, that several senators of a *popularis* persuasion stayed away from the sitting of the senate in which these conspirators were sentenced to death "lest they vote on a capital matter concerning a citizen" (Cic. *Cat.* 4.10). Moreover, after the execution of the conspirators, Cicero was immediately attacked by two tribunes for executing citizens without trial (Cic. *Fam.* 5.2.8; Cass. Dio 37.42.1), and this charge was implicit in the legislation that Clodius used to secure Cicero's exile in 58 BC (Vell. Pat. 2.45.1; Dio Cass. 38.14.4; Livy, *Per.* 103).

[13] Golden 2013, 44–45.

[14] For references and discussion see Lintott 1999b, 153–155; Golden 2013, 42–103, 189–199.

[15] Fundamental on this decree is Bauman 1973a. See too von Ungern-Sternberg 1970, 111–122; Lintott 1999b, 155–156.

[16] Livy, *Per.* 77; Vell. Pat. 2.19; cf. App. *B Civ.* 1.60–61; Cic. *Brut.* 45.168; Val. Max. 3.8.5.

[17] For references see Lintott 1999b, 155–156.

[18] Although note D.4.5.5.1, and the discussion of Bauman 1973a, 283–285, 291–292.

[19] Lintott 1999b, 156; cf. Bauman 1973a, 278.

[20] Cic. *Cat.* 4.10; cf. Cic. *Sest.* 39.

29.3 Conspiracies against the Emperor

The coming of the Principate brought with it a new kind of fundamental threat to the political order in the form of conspiracies to assassinate the emperor and to usurp the purple. When such plots were discovered (or allegedly discovered) before anything had happened to the emperor, the praetorian guard could now in theory and (mostly) in practice be used to apprehend conspirators who were in the immediate vicinity of the emperor himself. In these cases, there was therefore no need to legitimate the creation of an informal posse by passing the *SCU*. The *hostis* declaration was, however, still used in the Principate on a few occasions when it was not possible to apprehend immediately a rebel or an emperor who had been toppled.[21]

Once conspirators were in custody, the charges they faced were obvious enough: conspiring to kill a magistrate or a holder of *imperium* or *potestas* fell within the definition of *maiestas* (D.48.4.1.1). Moreover, from the time of Augustus onwards, acts (and sometimes words) that diminished the majesty of the emperor and his family were interpreted as amounting to treason as well (see Williamson, ch. 26). There are some reports from the early Principate of conspirators being tried by jury courts (e.g. Suet. *Tib.* 8.1; Dio Cass. 54.3.5–6) or before an emperor exercising his judicial powers (e.g. Tac. *Ann.* 15.58). Once the senate was fully established as a court, conspirators were sometimes tried before it (e.g. *Inscr. Ital.* 13.1, p. 205, cf. SHA *Ant. Pius* 7.4). Certain emperors attempted to make a virtue of the fact that they left such trials to the senate (e.g. SHA *Hadr.* 7).

The process of repressing alleged conspiracies against the emperor prompted heated debate. While some authors admit that the punishment of people who plotted against the emperor was at times warranted,[22] it is frequently claimed that emperors punished alleged conspirators out of paranoia and with inadequate evidence of guilt,[23] or that they did so for ulterior motives or having been duped by devious informers or courtiers.[24] Moreover, there were often concerns that the emperor and his supporters had transgressed certain expectations about proper legal process. The concerns centred less on the denial of *provocatio*, which would not have helped conspirators much, since ultimate appeal was now to the emperor—the very target of the conspiracy and, quite often, the leader of the repression.[25] There were, however, other, more relevant rights. In the wake of some conspiracies, Roman citizens—even high-status ones—were tortured, in spite of the traditional prohibition on torturing free people; such cases are generally reported with shock by our sources for the Principate.[26] Some emperors are criticised for executing putative conspirators without charge or proper trial.[27] On other occasions, the complaint was that the

[21] e.g. Suet. *Tib.* 54; *Calig.* 7 (Nero Julius Caesar and Drusus Julius Caesar, 29 and 30 AD); Suet. *Ner.* 49; Dio Cass. 63.27.2b (Nero, 68 AD); SHA *Marc.* 24.9, *Avid.Cass.* 7.6 (Avidius Cassius, 175 AD); Dio Cass. 74(73).8.5 (Falco, 193 AD). See too D.4.5.5.1.

[22] Amm. Marc. 19.12.17; Dio Cass. 55.18.1.

[23] e.g. Amm. Marc. 29.1.18; Tac. *Ann.* 15.73; cf. Dio Cass. 55.19; Sen. *Clem.* 1.20.

[24] Ulterior motives: Dio Cass. 55.18.5, 59.21.4, 69.2.5; SHA *Hadr.* 4.3; Tac. *Ann.* 15.73. Courtiers and informers: Dio Cass. 55.18.6, 61(60).29.4–6a; Tac. *Ann.* 2.27–28, 11.1–3, 16.18; Suet. *Claud.* 37.

[25] Appeal under the Empire: Santalucia 1998, 219–221, 270, 275–276; Garnsey 1966.

[26] e.g. Dio Cass. 57.19.2, 60.15.6; Sen. *Ira* 3.18, cf. Dio Cass. 59.25.5b. See too Garnsey 1970, 141–147, 213–216.

[27] e.g. Iuv. 10.69–72; Tac. *Ann.* 15.69, 16.18; cf. Dio Cass. 55.19.2.

accused was condemned in a secret hearing, which offended the convention that trials should be held in public.[28]

As the Imperial period progressed and the emperors' autocracy became more absolute, legal limitations (both formal and conventional) on the process of repressing conspiracies were eroded. The expectation of publicity in trials faded around the turn of the second century AD.[29] Moreover, by the early fourth century, citizens were no longer legally immune from torture in treason cases.[30] Ammianus Marcellinus, writing in the second half of the century, assumes that it is entirely reasonable to torture people of all statuses if a conspiracy against the emperor is being investigated.[31]

Not all the restraints advocated by the elite on the emperor's handling of conspiracies related to process: some fell more into the category of internal, ethical limitations. Repressive actions against political conspiracies that were regarded as in some sense excessive or too widely directed are condemned as examples of *crudelitas* and *saevitia*.[32] On the other hand, *clementia* towards conspirators is loudly praised. In the *De clementia*, Seneca recommends that the young Nero should show mercy to conspirators and other wrongdoers partly for utilitarian reasons, claiming that it will increase the popularity of the *princeps*, and hence his ultimate security. He also argues that extenuating circumstances often reduce conspirators' culpability and that some are capable of reform (Sen. *Clem.* 2.7). In the third century, this issue was still sufficiently important to prompt Cassius Dio to use a tradition about Augustus' mild response to a particular conspiracy as an opportunity to invent a lengthy dialogue between Augustus and Livia in which the latter successfully advocates the benefits of *clementia* (Dio Cass. 55.14–22; cf. Sen. *Clem.* 1.9–10). Later still, Ammianus Marcellinus also forcefully expressed the view that it is preferable for an emperor to find reasons for pardoning conspirators, not opportunities for punishing them (Amm. Marc. 19.12.17).[33]

29.4 Riots in the Imperial Period

During the Principate, the authorities in the city of Rome had far greater resources to cope with rioting than their Republican counterparts, since there were now permanent military forces in the form of the praetorian guard and urban cohort. There were also permanent military forces available to put down riots in several of the other large cities of the Empire.[34] If the need arose, soldiers were dispatched to smaller cities in which order

[28] e.g. Tac. *Ann.* 11.2; cf. Tac. *Ann.* 13.4. For publicity and criminal trials see generally Crook 1955, 106; Lintott 1972, 253–254.

[29] Santalucia 1998, 218–219.

[30] D.48.18.10.1; cf. CTh.9.5.1pr = C.9.8.3 (a. 314); CTh.9.35.1 = C.9.8.4 (a. 369); Sent.Paul.5.29.2; cf. Garnsey 1970, 141–147, 213–216.

[31] Amm. Marc. 19.12.17, with Garnsey 1970, 143.

[32] e.g. Sen. *Ira* 3.18–19; Suet. *Tib.* 61.

[33] For other statements about clemency for conspirators see Dio Cass. 59.26.4; SHA *Marc.* 24–25; *Avid. Cass.* 7–14; Tac. *Ann.* 2.31.

[34] For a classic discussion of urban unrest see MacMullen 1966, 163–191. Sünskes Thompson provides a list of disturbances, including riots, in the Severan period (1990, 21–44), with analysis (1990, 95–166). Aldrete 2013 provides a recent treatment of riots in Rome, with bibliography. Kelly 2007 discusses source problems and the process of repressing riots.

had broken down.[35] In the later Empire, the standing military presences in Rome and the new capital of Constantinople were somewhat limited, which made riot repression more difficult, although troops could still be brought in (Nippel 1995, 98–100).

When troops were unleashed, this could result in the beating and killing of rioters (sometimes a few, sometimes a large number) until the disturbance stopped.[36] On other occasions, the arrest of at least some rioters is mentioned.[37] This was done with a view to punishing them, either summarily or after a trial. There are also a few clear references to people being tried for participation in a riot.[38]

The juristic sources make clear the legal underpinnings of the prosecution of rioters before courts. Rioting was an offence under both the *lex Iulia de vi* and the *lex Iulia maiestatis*, so rioters in Rome could be prosecuted before the courts established by these statutes.[39] A charge could also be brought before a magistrate or governor exercising *cognitio* using the offence categories of these statutes. By the Severan age, there was also a legal regime in place relating to the repression of urban youth violence: according to Callistratus, governors should initially deal with the turbulent behaviour of those commonly called the *iuvenes* ("the youths") with admonishments and beatings; recidivists, however, must be exiled or even punished capitally, especially if they too often behaved seditiously and riotously (*seditiose et turbulente*).[40]

From various juristic sources we learn that the rights of people convicted of rioting were somewhat abridged. According to the *Sententiae Pauli*, the penalties that governors and other officials faced for ignoring a citizen's attempt to appeal to the emperor did not apply if the convicted person had been imprisoned for committing a crime against public order (*disciplina publica*) (Sent.Paul.5.26.1–2). In usual criminal cases, the governor could refuse to allow the accused to appeal to the emperor, but was required to write to the emperor to confirm this decision before the punishment could be carried out. But by a pronouncement of Marcus Aurelius, this requirement was waived in cases of sedition and bloody factional strife (*factio cruenta*) to avert an imminent threat (D.28.3.6.9; cf. D.49.1.16pr).

When it came to the more direct repression of rioters by troops, a detailed legal justification would in many cases have been unnecessary. The governor had a general duty to maintain the peace in his province (D.1.18.13pr). Prior to 212 AD, riots in provincial cities would have mostly involved peregrines who did not enjoy the right to appeal to the emperor, and would have been repressed by governors with *imperium* who could punish crimes quite summarily and with few restraints.[41] Of course, rioting

[35] e.g. Suet. *Tib.* 37; Tac. *Ann.* 13.48.

[36] e.g. Tac. *Ann.* 14.61; Sen. *Oct.* 846–850 (Rome, 62 AD); Joseph. *BJ* 2.494–498 (Alexandria, *c.*66–68 AD); Hdn. 1.12.6–9 and Dio Cass. 73(72).13.4–5 (Rome, 190 AD); Euseb. *Hist. eccl.* 8.14.3 (Rome, 311 AD). In other cases, it is clear that soldiers were at least used to cow the crowd into submission: Tac. *Ann.* 12.43 (Rome, 51 AD); Tac. *Ann.* 14.45 (Rome, 62 AD).

[37] e.g. Vett. Val. 5.6.120–121 [ed. Pingree].

[38] *CPJ* 158 a & b, 435; Joseph. *AJ* 20.118–136; Joseph. *BJ* 2.232–246; *P. Oxy.* xxii 2339; Tac. *Ann.* 14.17; Vett. Val. 5.6.120–121 [ed. Pingree]; cf. *IEph.* 2.215 = *IMagn.* 114; Cic. *Verr.* 2.1.73–85.

[39] D.48.4.1.1; D.48.6.3pr–48.6.3.3; D.48.6.5pr; D.48.6.10pr.

[40] D.48.19.28.3; cf. Rodriguez 2012 on the relevance of this legal regime to Caracalla's massacre of the Alexandrians in 216 AD.

[41] On the governor's *imperium* see Richardson ch. 9. In practice, governors often opted to try peregrines for crimes using procedures that were quite similar to those used with Roman citizens. Furthermore, there is the complication that the magistrates of some cities might have retained some level of local criminal jurisdiction; see Roselaar ch. 10.

crowds in Rome or Italy would have contained many Roman citizens; so too with any rioting crowd elsewhere in the Empire after 212 AD. In these instances, killings carried out by troops who had been commanded directly by the emperor would be unproblematic. In other cases, one imagines that soldiers could claim that they had beaten or killed rioters in self-defence. But the fact that rioters in the Imperial period (unlike some during the late Republic) were mostly lower class probably meant that nobody enquired into these questions too closely. Our surviving sources are certainly rather uninterested in them.

This lack of interest in legal niceties does not mean, however, that our Imperial authors thought that there should be no restraints on the actions of emperors, magistrates and governors faced with riotous situations. But the restraints that they urged were more of an internal, ethical nature.[42] There was often a feeling that authority figures (and especially emperors) should avoid responding to riots punitively, and instead show mercy. Libanius enunciates this in relation to a riot in Antioch in 387 AD: rioters are demented, and the appropriate way to treat the insane is with medicine, not punishment; it is incumbent on the emperor to show clemency towards them (Lib. *Or.* 19.8–24).

This is not to say that violent and punitive repression of riots was ruled out altogether: this was sometimes thought to be a sad necessity. In some reports of riots, however, authority figures of whom the author basically approves are presented as trying other methods of defusing the situation first before finally resorting to military force. When military repression was used, there was often (albeit not invariably) a feeling that only tyrannical emperors would repress non-violent crowds for verbal unruliness at the chariot races, gladiatorial games or other spectacles. Thus, for example, disapproving accounts survive about Caligula's summary execution of members of a crowd who protested verbally in the Circus Maximus against his tax regime (Joseph. *AJ* 19.24–26; cf. Dio Cass. 59.28.11). As Josephus notes in his account, the people of Rome generally expected emperors to respond positively to shouted petitions at spectacles. The general aversion to responding with massacres to verbal protests and requests is encapsulated in Libanius' anecdote about how Constantine I judged it as "appropriate to a ruler" (βασιλικός) to tolerate verbal unruliness from a crowd (Lib. *Or.* 19.19).

29.5 Provincial Revolts

If the ancient sources show minimal interest in the legalities of riot repression, this observation applies *a fortiori* to provincial revolts.[43] Presumably, those guilty of rebelling against Roman rule in a province could have been brought before the relevant

[42] For a fuller treatment of the arguments in this and the following paragraph see Kelly 2007, 16–167 with further references.

[43] On the causes of provincial revolts see Dyson 1971 and 1974, now to be read with Woolf 2011. Pekáry 1987 and Sünskes Thompson 1990, 21–44, 176–190 provide catalogues of revolts and some analysis. Gambash (2009, 2012 and 2013) focuses on the Roman responses to the revolt of Boudica and the Jewish revolt of 66–73/4 AD. MacMullen 1966, 192–241 discusses provincial revolts, *inter alia*.

provincial governor and (at least from the late Republic) charged with *maeistas* or *vis*. Reports of such judicial responses to provincial revolts are, however, exceedingly rare.[44]

The reasons for this rarity are not difficult to fathom. Provincial revolts were generally serious military emergencies, and as such provoked the sort of large-scale retributive measures that the Romans often visited on defeated foreign enemies. Thus, once the rebels were worsted in pitched battle, a number of unpleasant fates could await them and their people. Men of fighting age, and sometimes whole communities, were massacred.[45] In the case of other revolts against Roman rule, mass enslavements are reported, as is the destruction of rebel settlements and crops.[46] There is scant sign in the surviving sources of any legal qualms concerning the massacre or enslavement of populations, or the incineration of crops and settlements. The reasons are doubtless similar to those suggested in relation to riots: before 212 AD the vast majority of rebels were peregrines and hence subject to unlimited gubernatorial *coercitio*; and even in the late Empire, most rebels were of low socio-economic status.

This is not to say that more subtle and constructive responses to the problem of revolts by subject people were impossible, either in the wake of revolts, or even in anticipation of them. In some cases, populations who had revolted or had tendencies in this direction were disarmed by the Roman authorities.[47] When revolts did break out and were repressed, hostages were sometimes then taken to ensure future good behaviour.[48] Some lucky rebels were given land on which to start a new, more prosperous, and—in theory—less disruptive life.[49] The same perceived connection between landscape and rebelliousness is also visible in M. Vipsanius Agrippa's policy of relocating populations from the mountains to the plains following the Cantabrian revolt of 19 BC—although not before he massacred the men of military age and disarmed everyone else (Dio Cass. 54.11.5). It has also recently been suggested that in the aftermath of the Boudican revolt, the initial slaughter gave way to a rather nuanced Roman policy of mollifying local resentment, designed to prevent another flare-up in Britain.[50] Since oppressive behaviour by Roman provincial administrators was often seen as a factor in provoking revolts, the *quaestio repetundarum* (cf. Richardson, ch. 9) was regarded by some as restraining riots and rebellions, since it gave outraged provincials a non-violent means of redress (Cic. *Verr.* 2.1.82).

These more nuanced responses to the problem of provincial revolts were no doubt partly the result of pragmatism, but ideology probably had a role. There are traces in the sources of ethical reservations about the harsh treatment of rebellious populations: such treatment was, after all, not especially congruent with the claim that the Romans ruled their Empire

[44] The few examples of such reports include App. *Hisp.* 38, Caes. *B Gall.* 6.44, Joseph. *BJ* 2.77 (cf. *AJ* 17.298), and Tac. *Hist.* 4.13.

[45] e.g. App. *Hisp.* 68; Tac. *Ann.* 14.37.

[46] e.g. Enslavements, App. *Hisp.* 68, 98; Dio Cass. 54.31.3, 54.34.7; Liv. 34.21. Destruction of settlements and crops, App. *Hisp.* 71, 87, 98; Flor. 1.33.9; Liv. 34.9.

[47] *Chrest. Wilck.* 13 (with Philo *In Flacc.* 92–93; cf. 86–91, 94); Dio Cass. 54.31.3; 60.21.4; Tac. *Ann.* 12.31.

[48] e.g. App. *Hisp.* 38, 41.

[49] App. *Hisp.* 43–44, 75; Livy *Per.* 55.

[50] Gambash 2012; cf. Gambash 2013, 182–183.

for the benefit of their subjects. Occasionally, one even sees such a beneficent ideology at work in cases in which defeated rebels were afforded *clementia*.[51]

More often, though, ancient authors were forced to grapple with the ideologically inconvenient truth that rebellions were repressed with merciless brutality. One response to this awkward reality was to emphasise the rebels' bad faith and trickery toward their Roman overlords and allege that they had committed lurid atrocities during the revolt.[52] Sometimes, too, provincial revolts (and also slave rebellions) were assimilated with *latrocinium* ("banditry") (Grünewald 2004, 33–71), an activity whose perpetrators by definition forfeited many conventional protections afforded by morality and law. Another discursive strategy was to treat the provincial rebels not as pacified *peregrini* but rather as foreign *hostes*. This is perhaps most clearly seen with the Jewish revolt of 66–73/4 AD, in the wake of which a triumphal procession was held in Rome and coins were struck with the legend "Judaea captured" (*Judaea capta*)—responses usually reserved for victories over foreign enemies.[53] One can see a similar tendency in narratives of other revolts. Rebels are routinely called *hostes*, and the authors' labelling of particular uprisings slides between the language of rebellion (e.g. *rebello*, ἀφίστημι) and that of war (*bellum*/πόλεμος).[54] In some narratives of military action, standard ethnographic stereotypes attached to particular barbarian groups are stressed to emphasise the otherness of the rebels—and hence their exclusion from the Romans' moral realm.[55]

29.6 Conclusion

The threats to the Roman political order with which this chapter has been concerned were quite diverse, as were the Roman authorities' repressive responses to them. But a number of connecting themes have emerged. One is the ongoing tension during all periods of Roman civilisation between, on the one hand, ideas about the appropriate legal and ethical limitations on the exercise of state violence against the individual, and, on the other hand, the perceived need to deal with fundamental political threats efficiently. Another theme relates to status: the sources, perhaps unsurprisingly, show a great deal more concern about the propriety of repressive acts against high-status individuals—both in the sense of those enjoying higher civic status, and also in the more general sense of those with higher socio-economic status. Furthermore, status was in some senses malleable, since there were attempts to declare—either legally or discursively—the seditious or the rebellious to be *hostes*, thereby excising them from the citizen body or the peregrine population of the Empire. A final point relates to the impact of autocracy. While both legal and ethical discourses about the limits of state repression exist in all periods of Roman history, the

[51] Caes. *B Gall.* 7.41; Suet. *Tib.* 20 (cf. Dio Cass. 56.16; Vell. Pat. 2.114); Tac. *Ann.*1.57.

[52] Bad faith and trickery: Liv. 28.24, 28.32; Polyb. 11.29, 11.31, 3.40, 3.67; Vell. Pat. 2.118–119; Tac. *Ann.* 1.58. Atrocities: App. *Hisp.* 96; Dio Cass. 62.7; Tac. *Ann.* 14.33; Val. Max. 7.6 ext. 2.

[53] Gambash 2013, 183–187.

[54] e.g. Dio Cass. 56.18–25, 62.2.2–3, cf. 62.9.2; Suet. *Tib.* 16; Tac. *Ann.* 1.57; cf. Tac. *Ann.* 2.88, 14.29–39; Tac. *Agr.* 14–16; Vell. Pat. 2.11–112, 2.118–119.

[55] e.g. Dio Cass. 62.11; Liv. 35.5.

increasingly autocratic system of the later Empire prompted a stronger focus on the ruler's ethical response to various threats, especially on his exercise of *clementia* and avoidance of *crudelitas*. This preoccupation was very different from the fierce emphasis on citizens' rights in the late Republic.

Bibliography

Aldrete, G. 2013. "Riots." In P. Erdkamp, ed., *The Cambridge companion to ancient Rome*. Cambridge. 425–440.

Bauman, R. A. (1973a). "The *hostis* declarations of 88 and 87 BC." *Athenaeum* 51: 27–293.

Bauman, R. A. (1973b). "The *lex Valeria de provocatione* of 300 BC." *Historia* 22: 34–47.

Crook, J. A. 1955. Consilium principis: *imperial councils and counsellors from Augustus to Diocletian*. Cambridge.

Drogula, F. K. (2007). "*Imperium, potestas*, and the *pomerium* in the Roman Republic." *Historia* 56: 419–452.

Dyson, S. L. (1971). "Native revolts in the Roman Empire." *Historia* 20: 239–274.

Dyson, S. L. (1974). "Native revolt patterns in the Roman empire." *Aufstieg und Niedergang der römischen Welt* II.3: 138–175.

Gambash, G. 2009. "The Roman state's response to local resistance." PhD dissertation, Princeton.

Gambash, G. (2012). "To rule a ferocious province: Roman policy and the aftermath of the Boudican revolt." *Britannia* 43: 1–15.

Gambash, G. (2013). "Foreign enemies of the Empire: the great Jewish revolt and Roman perceptions of the Jews." *Scripta classica israelica* 32: 173–194.

Garnsey, P. D. A. (1966). "*The lex Julia* and appeal under the Empire." *Journal of Roman Studies* 56: 167–189.

Garnsey, P. D. A. 1970. *Social status and legal privilege in the Roman empire*. Oxford.

Golden, G. K. 2013. *Crisis management during the Roman republic: the role of political institutions in emergencies*. Cambridge.

Grünewald, T. 2004. *Bandits in the Roman empire: myth and reality*, transl. J. Drinkwater. London/New York.

Kelly, B. (2007). "Riot control and imperial ideology in the Roman Empire." *Phoenix* 61: 150–176.

Lintott, A. W. (1972). "*Provocatio*: from the struggle of the orders to the principate." *Aufstieg und Niedergang der römischen Welt* I.2: 226–267.

Lintott. A. W. 1999a. *The constitution of the Roman republic*. Oxford.

Lintott, A. W. 1999b². *Violence in republican Rome*. Oxford.

MacMullen, R. 1966. *Enemies of the Roman order: treason, unrest, and alienation in the Empire*. Cambridge, Mass.

Nippel, W. 1995. *Public order in ancient Rome*. Cambridge.

Pekáry, T. (1987). "*Seditio*: Unruhen und Revolten im römischen Reich von Augustus bis Commodus." *Ancient Society* 18: 133–150.

Rodriguez, C. (2012). "Caracalla et les Alexandrins: Coup de folie ou sanction legale?" *Journal of Juristic Papyrology* 42: 229–172.

Santalucia, B. 1998². *Diritto e processo penale nell'antica Roma*. Milan.

Sünskes Thompson, J. 1990. *Aufstände und Protestaktionen im* Imperium Romanum: *die severischen Kaiser im Spannungsfeld innenpolitischer Konflikte*. Bonn.

von Ungern-Sternberg, J. 1970. *Untersuchungen zum spätrepublikanischen Notstandsrecht:* Senatusconsultum ultimum *und* hostis-*Erklärung*. Munich.

Woolf, G. 2011. "Provincial revolts in the early Roman empire." In M. Popović, ed., *The Jewish revolt against Rome: interdisciplinary perspectives*. Leiden/Boston. 27–44.

CHAPTER 30

SLAVERY
Social Position and Legal Capacity

RICHARD GAMAUF

30.1 Introduction: Slavery and "Social Death"

The approach of the classical Roman jurists to slavery was ambiguous and pragmatic.[1] Unlike Aristotle, who postulated the existence of slaves by nature,[2] the late classical jurists acknowledged that slavery violated natural law (D.1.5.4.1), but at the same time accepted it as an institution of the *ius gentium* (D.1.1.4). They presented capture in war (even if no longer the main source of the slave supply; Scheidel 2011) as the paradigm of enslavement, thereby providing both the historical foundation of the institution as well as some justification. The term *mancipium* (slave)[3] was associated with capture by force (*manu capere*); its synonym *servus* was etymologically distorted in order to create the flimsy excuse that enslavement in fact benefited an enemy by saving (*servare*) him from death (D.1.5.4.2–3; D.50.16.239.1).[4]

The enslaved person lost social or familial affiliations, became a thing—a *res mancipi*[5]—and could be owned, sold, rented, mortgaged etc. As the Harvard sociologist Orlando Patterson famously framed it—borrowing from Ulpian (D.35.1.59.2; D.50.17.209)—slavery amounted to "social death" (Patterson 1982). Legal texts reflect this aspect whenever slaves appear as no more than mere examples of valuable movable property. But legal discourse equally reveals

[1] On the "legal character" of Roman slavery see Honoré 2012; comprehensive treatments of slave law: Buckland 1908; Robleda 1976; Boulvert and Morabito 1982; Watson 1987; Melluso 2000; Gardner 2011; the *Corpus der römischen Rechtsquellen zur antiken Sklaverei* (*CRRS*, since 1999) and the respective articles in the *Handwörterbuch der antiken Sklaverei* (since 2006). Bibliographies: Boulvert and Morabito 1982, 166–182; Rainer and Herrmann-Otto 1999, 31–43; Bellen and Heinen 2003, 481–565 and online at: http://www.adwmainz.de/index.php?id=1584, accessed 8 August 2014.

[2] Garnsey 1996, 35–38; Hunt 2011, 41–44. The jurists did not imply intellectual inferiority in slaves (e.g. D.5.1.12.2), but expected average abilities (D.21.1.18pr).

[3] Mostly used for slaves as objects; Morabito 1981, 29–30.

[4] Literature in McClintock 2010, 127–128, n. 15; similar Auson. *Biss.* 3.3–4.

[5] On *res mancipi* see ch. 40.

slaves' potential for autonomous actions—legal and unauthorised alike—because the jurists were consulted regarding the consequences of slaves' lawful actions as well as when these had transgressed limits. Therefore their writings present a unique documentation of violations of status boundaries. Some were rather harmless, such as attending games, looking at paintings, taking part in religious practices etc. instead of concentrating on one's duties (D.11.3.1.5; D.21.1.65pr; D.21.1.1.9–10). Then one finds a broad range of acts of resistance, from shirking work (D.21.1.17.14), showing disrespect (D.9.4.4pr; D.11.3.15) or acting rebellious (*seditiosus*—D.11.3.1.5) to assassinating the master (D.29.5). In addition, there are further instances of slaves challenging the system, in ways different from resistance, by ignoring their place in society and blending—not always unnoticed—into the free population.[6] Some established long-term relationships with free women,[7] others were accepted as "son-in-law" by a Roman *pater familias* (D.16.3.27) or for some time completely inverted the established order, as did the fugitive slave Barbarius Philippus, who became praetor and issued edicts and decrees (D.1.14.3).[8]

30.2 Legal Capacity

30.2.1 Personal Status of Slaves

The mid-second-century jurist Gaius regarded the distinction between free persons and slaves as basic for the law of persons (Inst.Gai.1.9 = D.1.5.3). In a large slave-holding society the legal consequences of the lack of freedom (*status libertatis*) were only too self-evident; so neither Gaius in his legal primer nor any other Roman jurist ever compiled a comprehensive list of the ensuing disabilities. Slaves were, by definition, at the very bottom of the hierarchy of persons,[9] unable to hold any rights; in modern terms,[10] they lacked legal capacity.[11] This explains why slavery as an institution received little attention in Gaius'

[6] Slaves and free were almost impossible to distinguish: D.18.1.5.

[7] The *senatus consultum Claudianum* sanctioned a woman who wanted to remain in such a union with the loss of freedom; Harper 2010; Willvonseder 2010; Sirks 2011; on marriage between mistress and former slave see Weber 2008 and Liebs 2014.

[8] On this and similar cases see Knütel 1989.

[9] Some texts declare that all slaves were in an identical legal position, which therefore could not deteriorate (D.1.5.5pr; D.4.5.3.1). Generalisations of this kind are potentially misleading. There were privileged as well as disadvantaged groups of slaves: *Servi publici* owned by the state or a municipality had a better legal position (Weiß 2004), whereas that of *servi poenae*/slaves of punishment (persons awaiting execution: McClintock 2010) was considerably harder. Different treatment could result from general enactments (e.g. the *lex Aelia Sentia* of 4 AD restricting manumission; Buckland 1908, 539–540; Watson 1987, 29–31) as well as private-law acts (testaments, contracts; on provisions for better or stricter treatment in contracts of sale see McGinn 1998, 289–291). On the variability of slaves' social status cf. Schumacher 2011.

[10] Modern legal concepts cannot adequately capture slavery, because treatment of a human being as a thing is excluded by definition (see for example § 285 of the Austrian Civil Code). Having capacity to act but no legal capacity, as was the case with Roman slaves, would be equally contradictory in terms nowadays.

[11] However, during the Principate slaves could bring complaints of mistreatment (*infra* 3.2.) or when a promise of manumission for payment (*suis nummis*) was not kept (D.40.1.4; Heinemeyer 2013, 281–286).

Institutiones,[12] even though slaves were ubiquitous in Roman legal literature,[13] both as objects and as actors (Morabito 1981). For Gaius, the right of life and death and the claim to all acquisitions embraced the legal essence of the master's power (*dominica potestas*—Inst. Gai.1.52 = D.1.6.1.1).

30.2.2 Business Activities

By the latter effect of *dominica potestas* the law allowed owners to exploit not just the physical powers or personal services of slaves, but also to employ them as business agents. Due to their lack of legal capacity, the master (*dominus*) could become possessor and owner of everything they purchased;[14] a result that free agents could not effectuate.[15] Consequently, slaves were active on every level and in all areas of Roman business.[16]

30.2.2.1 *Acquisition of Property through Slaves*

When using slaves in agriculture or manufacture the master wanted to own the results of their work, which required his possession; i.e. the establishment of his intentional physical control over a thing.[17] He could express his intention to possess (*animus possidendi*) either in advance by an order (*iussum*) to a slave or by the later approval of an acquisition (*ratihabitio*); to exercise physical control (*corpus possidendi*) almost any slave was suitable.[18] With a *peculium*[19]

[12] Gaius dealt with it in three paragraphs (Inst.Gai.1.52–54), less than half a percent of the surviving text. On slavery in the *Institutiones* see Morabito 1987.

[13] According to Morabito 1981, 33–34, slaves appear in approximately 25 per cent of the Digest texts and 28 per cent of the Imperial constitutions.

[14] He then had possessory remedies (*interdicta*), the *rei vindicatio* (ownership claim) (see chs. 41 and 40) and protection against wrongful damage (on the *lex Aquilia* see ch. 45)

[15] Inst.Gai.2.95. No direct agency existed in classical Roman law. A free agent became possessor and owner (D.41.1.59), and if he transferred ownership to a third party the defrauded principal only had a claim for damages against his disloyal agent.

[16] Free work was of limited importance (Kehoe 2012); workers hiring out their services under a labour contract (*locatio conductio operarum*) were predominantly slaves (Bürge 1993).

[17] On *possessio* see ch. 41; on the acquisition of possession (and ownership) through slaves see Klinck 2004, 40–188.

[18] Mentally ill slaves were excluded. Maturity was no requirement; only the ability to follow orders (D.41.2.1.9–13). Jurists assumed that average slaves worked since the age of 5 (D.7.7.6.1). Furthermore, the slave had to be in his master's possession, but for practical reasons possession and the ensuing ability to acquire for the master were, at least by some jurists, regarded intact even during a slave's flight, until he was captured by a third party (D.41.2.1.14; Klinck 2004, 118–136; Klingenberg 2005, 121; Ankum 2010, 15–16).

[19] The term could encompass all kinds of property (see Buti 1976, 13–14 on its origin). In legal language, *peculium* denotes funds administered by persons-in-power (children, wife *in manu*, slaves). Slaves' *peculia* are taken for granted as early as the fifth century BC in the XII Tables (Tab. 7.12); many examples are documented in Plautus' plays (late third, early second century BC). A *peculium* was given by the master (*concessio peculii*); the grant of free administration (*libera administratio*) enabled the slave to alienate the property; see Wacke 2006 and Heinemeyer 2013, 125–131. It might be revoked at any time (*ademptio*); however, this was seemingly not common; cf. Buchwitz 2012, 229. On *peculia*: Buckland 1908, 187–238; Żeber 1981; Kirschenbaum 1987, 31–88; Watson 1987, 9–101; Pesaresi 2008 and 2012; Bürge 2010; Fleckner 2010; Aubert 2013.

slaves could act independently[20] and acquire without the master's direct orders or knowledge, even in far-away provinces (D.41.2.44.1; D.41.2.1.14). The *peculium* manifested the master's general intention to possess whatever slaves would lawfully acquire,[21] which was implemented by the slaves' decisions (*animo servorum*—D.41.2.3.12).

30.2.2.2 *The Master's Liability for Debts*

A large-scale use of slaves in business required protection for their commercial partners in case of default as well. Slaves could conclude binding contracts, but due to the doctrine, that a legal tie (*vinculum iuris*) existed only between the contracting persons themselves,[22] the master was not immediately liable for a slave's obligations. A slave's debt was no *obligatio civilis,*[23] because the slave lacked legal standing in court (D.50.17.107; Metzger 2014) and the *dominus* was not party to the contract. While the master obtained all rights and could sue his slave's debtors, a slave's creditor could not do so in reverse. This asymmetry would have blocked slaves' access to credit; full responsibility of the owner, on the other hand, might have had equally chilling effects, when *domini* had to reckon with uncontrollable losses or even bankruptcy due to commercial misfortune, miscalculations and even slaves' malevolence.[24]

The praetorian *actiones adiecticiae qualitatis*[25] balanced these divergent interests. In addition to the non-actionable claim against the slave, an action lay against the *dominus* (D.15.1.44) which "redirected" a contractual claim against the material beneficiary. The extent of liability corresponded to the master's direct influence on a transaction. He became fully liable under an *actio quod iussu* as far as he had personally authorised the creditor to contract with his slave.[26] In case of a *peculium*, his liability could not exceed its value in the *actio de peculio* or of any (additional) benefit (*versum*) from a transaction in the *actio de in rem verso.*[27] A *ratihabitio* (approval) of an earlier transaction could give rise

[20] Slaves were expected to work more willingly and effectively when they made their own decisions (Columella, *Rust.* 1.8.15). Plaut. *Rud.* 915–919 even satirises a slave's self-exploitation; on the risky uses of a *peculium* see n. 42.

[21] The *peculium* could neither be restricted to certain transactions nor did an explicit prohibition to contract with a slave release the master from liability; cf. D.15.1.29.1; D.15.1.74pr. For the establishment of *corpus possidendi* cf. in n. 19.

[22] On privity of contract cf. ch. 43.

[23] It obligated the slave, thus performance did not lead to unjustified enrichment. On "natural" obligations see Zimmermann 1990, 7–10.

[24] A slave should only improve the master's position (D.50.17.133); noxal surrender (see ch. 45) ensured that delictual liability never exceeded the slave's value (Inst.Gai.4.75; D.47.2.62(61).5). The significance of economic sabotage is unclear: compare Finley 1998, 179 with the position of Bradley 1990, 150.

[25] Dating: Wacke 1994 and de Ligt 1999 and 2002. The term was coined in the Middle Ages on the basis of D.14.1.5.1 and emphasises the additional character: the *intentio* (the part of the *formula* containing the plaintiff's claim) of the respective contractual *actio* names the slave as contracting party; the *condemnatio* orders to sentence or acquit the *dominus.* On the *actiones adiecticiae qualitatis*: Wacke 1994; de Ligt 1999; Miceli 2001; Johnston 2007; formulas in Mantovani 1999, 79–82.

[26] Inst.Gai.4.70; D.15.4; de Ligt 2002.

[27] D.15.1–3. Though both were contained in one *formula* (*actio de peculio vel de in rem verso*), the jurists treat them separately; literature on *peculium* in n. 20; on the *actio de in rem verso* Chiusi 2001.

to responsibility *quod iussu* or *de in rem verso*.[28] Additional actions (*institoria, exercitoria*) were granted if a slave had been appointed business manager (*institor*) or ship captain (*magister navis*).[29] If the claim exceeded the limits of one action, the creditor could resort to further *actiones adiecticiae* (C.4.25.2 [a. 222]).

For the sentencing in an *actio de peculio* the *iudex* had to establish the *peculium*'s value. To the goods registered as *peculium* the master's "debts" to his slave, fraudulent reductions and intentionally tolerated losses were added;[30] conversely, a slave's "debts" to his master[31] or other household members were deducted. For these reasons, legal texts document the importance of *peculia* for the internal and external economic relationships of a Roman household and business life at large (Gamauf 2009).

30.2.2.3 *The Economic Functions of a Peculium*

A *peculium* could contain all kinds of assets (money, land, under-slaves/*vicarii*[32] D.15.1.7.4).[33] With the right of free administration (*libera administratio*) a slave could dispose of its funds almost like an owner.[34] It was of course always owned by the master, but kept separately in accounting from his further estate or other *peculia*.[35] Periodically the slave reported to the master (or a slave managing his financial affairs); then it was decided which acquisitions would be transferred to the master's immediate patrimony and which remained with the slave.[36] In the first case, the slave was reimbursed;[37] in the second, a bad bargain burdened the *peculium*.

In an *actio de peculio* the master's potential liability could never go beyond the *peculium*'s value. (In this regard, it resembled a modern limited liability corporation.)[38] But by leasing means of production or loaning money to the slave, instead of transferring such assets to the *peculium* the *dominus* facilitated the use of extra goods without raising his liability (D.15.3.16; D.33.7.20.1; D.15.3.10.8).[39] (Another important limitation of risk was owed to the fact, that as far as a *peculium* had been assembled by the slave's own efforts,[40] the

[28] The decisive factor was whether the *ratihabitio* had been directed at the creditor (*actio quod iussu*—D.15.4.1.6) or at the slave (*actio de in rem verso*—D.15.3.5.2).

[29] Kirschenbaum 1987, 89–121; Aubert 1994; de Ligt 1999.

[30] D.15.1.21pr; Grotkamp 2005; Johnston 2007, 177–179; Aubert 2013.

[31] Because creditors were satisfied in the order in which they filed their claims, the master's privilege was based on the assumption that he would always be first (D.15.1.9.2).

[32] On *vicarii* Reduzzi Merola 1990.

[33] See also Aubert 2013, 197–198.

[34] The jurists excluded transactions to which the master would never have consented (D.15.1.46) and gifts (D.24.1.3.8; D.47.2.52.26). Roman literature (Petron. *Sat.* 30) and inscriptions (Bradley 1984, 109–110; Schumacher 2001, 269) show slaves with probably extended powers.

[35] For the allocation of a thing to the *dominus* or the *peculium* the registration in the accounts was decisive (D.2.13.4.3; D.15.1.4pr; D.15.1.5.4); the same applied between slave and his *vicarius* (D.15.1.4.6.).

[36] Petron. *Sat.* 53; Gamauf 2009, 335–336. Acquisitions became permanently part of a *peculium* when the master, having been informed, did not withdraw them (D.15.1.7.1, D.15.1.3.4).

[37] If the slave did not receive compensation, the creditor could at least claim the value of the thing as *versum*.

[38] See Zwalve 2002.

[39] Actual delivery was required; a *peculium* could not be created or increased through a mere act of accounting (D.15.1.8).

[40] The basis for a *peculium* could consist of savings or gifts (D.15.1.39; D.15.1.57.2); the ability to "acquire a *peculium*" raised his value (D.21.1.18pr). The *peculium* could remain with the slave in a

dominus, economically speaking, did not risk "his money".)[41] But an inadequate *peculium* might deter potential business partners, who measured the slave's creditworthiness by it.[42] Beside their *peculia*, slaves could do additional businesses under orders for the master's direct account (D.15.3.3.5; D.40.7.39.2; D.46.3.35.), as his partners (D.33.8.22.1), and as *institores* or *magistri navium*.

30.3 Social Position

30.3.1 Determining Factors

It is commonplace that the conditions of a slave's life primarily depended on his master's attitudes (Finley 1998, 161). Nevertheless, legal texts reveal various factors that defined the daily existence and social position within and outside the household. Often the same factor could prove beneficial and detrimental alike, depending on the circumstances. Of relevance were gender, education, training, monetary value, a *peculium*, the kind of job etc. The character of life was further affected by the location of the household—urban or rural (*familia urbana/rustica*), its size and a slave's function, the intensity of personal contact to the owner or other free persons, whether a slave lived rather independently,[43] in the same household as the *dominus*, or subordinate to a (in most cases unfree) superior.[44]

30.3.2 Treatment of Slaves and Legal Restrictions on the Master's Powers

Essentials for a slave's life were the sufficient supply of food and clothes, decent treatment and tolerable work etc. The master's right to freely decide in such matters was expressly restated in second-century legislative enactments that admitted some restrictions (Coll.3.3.2 = D.1.6.2 = Inst.1.8.2). Starting in the first century AD, physically mistreated, sexually abused slaves, or slaves lacking the necessities of life, could seek asylum at an Imperial statue (*ad statuas confugere*) or, in the Eastern provinces, also in some temples. After that, or if directly asked for protection, an officer (*praefectus*

sale (D.15.1.32.2; D.19.1.13.4; D.21.1.18.2; Sent.Paul.2.17.6); after manumission *inter vivos* it belonged typically to the slave, unless the master had explicitly ordered otherwise (Wacke 1991).

[41] If a master was sentenced on the slave's behalf, the amount was deducted from the *peculium*; cf. D.33.8.16pr. The recklessness of Trimalchio in the pursuit of his business career (Petron. *Sat.* 76) may shed light on the way slaves administered their *peculia* in order to maximise profits (and their chances of buying their freedom); see Gamauf 2009, 336; on the volatility of *peculia* Aubert 2013, 199.

[42] D.15.1.32pr. and Inst.Gai.4.74. Bürge 1999, 183–184 regards the *actio de peculio* as an indirect means of the creditor to lay his hands on the *peculium*.

[43] D.33.7.19.1 mentions a slave artisan, whose duties were probably reduced to paying an annual sum to his owner.

[44] On such situations cf. Edmondson 2011.

urbi, provincial governor) heard the complaints and could order their sale as a relief (less for humanitarian reasons than to safeguard the caste of slave owners against the consequences of excesses; Gamauf 1999). In addition, certain punishments or uses of slaves were officially controlled.[45] But there was also support by the authorities for the *domini*, e.g. in the search for fugitive slaves (Fuhrmann 2012, 21–43); municipalities offered the services of public slaves for rent to help with the torture or execution of slaves (*AE* 1971, 88).

30.3.3 Personal Contacts and Relationships with the Master

With the master present a slave might expect rewards for his loyalty, such as promotions and gifts (Plaut. *Mostell.* 253–254; Plaut. *Pers.* 192; D.41.1.37.1) or even manumission.[46] Factors such as personal ties from childhood (to wet-nurses, teachers, foster siblings—D.40.2.13), contact to friends[47] and the chance of controlling access to him were beneficial.[48] Among the disadvantages was the master's supervision in matters of the *peculium*,[49] the risk of harsh punishment[50] or fits of temper.[51] While the master held overseers responsible (Collumella, *Rust.* 1.8.16–18; D.21.1.17.5), the legal sanctions he himself had to face for mistreatment were hardly deterring. At most, a successful complaint led to a sale and he was compensated with

[45] A master needed to prove reasonable cause (D.48.8.11.2) before he could send slaves to fight (against wild beasts) in the arena; Hadrian is credited with banning the sale of slaves to brothel-keepers, the use of slave-prisons/*ergastula* and executions without court decision (SHA *Hadr.* 18.7–10). The unreasonable killing of one's slave was treated as murder from the middle of the second century (Inst.Gai.1.53). The punishment dictated by the *lex Cornelia de sicariis et veneficis* applied also to the castration of slaves (D.48.8.3.4; D.48.8.4.2); slaves abandoned in sickness (on the Tiber island) became free upon recovery (Suet. *Claud.* 25.2; D.40.8.2). On the various measures see Buckland 1908, 36–38; Watson 1987, 115–133.

[46] Mouritsen 2011, 141–159.

[47] A friend could aid in the purchase of liberty (*suis nummis*: Heinemeyer 2013) or plead in favour of a slave awaiting punishment (D.21.1.17.4; D.21.1.43.1; D.11.3.5pr); unauthorised interference with disciplinary measures might be sanctioned irrespective of humanitarian motives (D.4.3.7.7). Free friends often made gifts to slaves (D.41.1.37.1) or appointed slaves as heirs or legatees (Buchwitz 2012). D.3.5.5.8(6) mentions friendship (*amicitia*) with another's slave, which was also a motive to act as a slave's mandatary (D.46.2.34pr); on friendship with other people's freedmen cf. Mouritsen 2011, 49–50.

[48] On the contacts of slaves with clients and visitors see Joshel 2010, 185; on gifts (or bribes) to slaves see Buchwitz 2010, 40–401, 406.

[49] If the *dominus* knowingly tolerated the mismanagement of a *peculium*, losses did not reduce his liability (D.15.1.21pr). This rule presupposes some duty to supervise a slave, when possible; for the same reason the master was not privileged vis-à-vis outside creditors in the *actio tributoria*, when he knew that a slave was trading with (parts of) his *peculium* (D.14.4.1pr).

[50] Supervisors had limited disciplinary powers; for estate managers (*vilici*) Cato, *Agr.* 5.1; Varro, *Rust.* 1.16.5; Columella, *Rust.* 1.8.10 and 11.1.25. Petron. *Sat.* 53 indicates that overseers sometimes even ordered executions. Teachers or instructors might use physical punishment within certain limits only (D.9.2.5.3–7pr; D.21.1.17.3 and D.21.1.17.5). The language of an epitaph in which agricultural slaves commemorate an estate manager for his moderation (*CIL* IX 3028 = *ILS* 7367: *quibus imperavit modeste*) resembles that of Imperial constitutions or jurists' writings on the treatment of slaves (Coll.3.3.5; D.21.1.17.3), which indicates that masters and slaves applied comparable standards; for similar American examples cf. Patterson 1982, 12.

[51] D.21.1.17.4 mentions a slave hiding to evade the violent temper of his master; satirists blame women for ill-treating maids on a "bad hair day"; cf. Gamauf 2012, 254.

the price.[52] Punishment for sadistic owners was more of a theoretical than real threat (Liebs 2012, ch. 12).

For rural slaves even such protection was out of reach; furthermore, brutality of supervisors was not a reason for complaints.[53] The overall severity of farm life is also demonstrated by the custom of exiling (*relegare*) urban slaves to the countryside by way of punishment.[54] Life was markedly less tiring for many in urban upper-class households, because tasks were easier and some leisure was granted (Gamauf 2014). But these were "privileges" under the sword of Damocles of the *senatus consultum Silanianum*. In case the master or family members were assassinated it mandated the torture of all slaves under the same roof (*sub eodem tecto*) with the victim and the execution of those who had not provided utmost support.[55] There was no mercy for slaves who had put their own life before their master's (D.29.5.1.28); therefore, all slaves, but especially those in higher positions, were well advised to watch their comrades,[56] because the *s.c.* allowed for no exemptions based on rank or the like.

30.3.4 Sexuality: Exploitation, Prostitution and Familial Relationships

In the owner's presence it was unavoidable for many slaves to provide sexual services, regularly requested from slaves of both sexes and all ages.[57] Legal restrictions existed only insofar as excesses might cause violent resistance (Coll.3.3.1–3; D.1.12.1.8; Sen. *Q Nat.* 1.16.1; Plin. *Ep.* 3.14). Compliance, on the other hand, could bring rewards, e.g. better education or jobs for "pets" (*delicati/deliciae*),[58] manumission, an inheritance, or marriage for a concubine.[59] Children fathered by the master were—like all progeny

[52] Inst.Gai.1.53; D.1.6.1.2; Inst.1.8.2; Coll.3.3; D.1.6.2; see Gamauf 1999.

[53] Gamauf 1999, 55. On the other hand, the *s.c. Silanianum* was not applied if an overseer had been assassinated.

[54] D.7.1.15.1; D.28.5.35.3; Petron. *Sat.* 53 and 69.

[55] D.29.5; C.6.35; Sent.Paul.3.5. On the *s.c. Silanianum* recently Harries 2013. The most conspicuous example of its application was the execution of four hundred household slaves after the murder of Pedanius Secundus in 61 AD (Tac. *Ann.* 14.42–45).

[56] Collective actions by slaves were especially feared. D.42.4.7.4 mentions domestic seditions (*seditiones domesticae*), probably by slaves.

[57] Petron. *Sat.* 75; Sen. *Controv.* 4 praef. 10; slaves could not refuse any of their master's wishes (Sen. *Ben.* 3.19.1; Publilius Syrus 616 Q64). On slavery and sexuality see Kolendo 1981; Morabito 1986 and Harper 2013, 26–28, 44–46. The eighteenth-century example in Patterson 2012, 326–327, is instructive as to the potential frequency of such demands. The Jamaican planter Th. Thistlewood recorded 3,852 sexual acts with 138 slave women over a period of thirty-seven years in his diary (on average he drew on fourteen different women per year).

[58] Petron. *Sat.* 46, 75. Trimalchio brags that sexual services virtually made him master of the household (Petron. *Sat.* 76.1: *dominus in domo factus sum*; cf. also Publilius Syrus 596 Q44); on *deliciae* see Laes 2003. The jurists denied such slaves preferential treatment (D.40.2.16pr).

[59] Manumissions in order to marry the master were exempted from the *lex Aelia Sentia* (Inst. Gai.1.19; Wacke 2001; Mouritsen 2011, 43); concubines were tacitly excluded from the property to be sold when someone had mortgaged all his belongings (D.20.1.8; Sent.Paul.5.6.16). Literature on marriage of *patrona* and *libertus* in n. 7.

of an unfree mother (*partus ancillae*)—slaves and his property (Herrmann-Otto 1994). Even though they were sometimes raised together with the legitimate offspring (Inst. Gai.1.19) the jurists refused to acknowledge fatherly emotions.[60] Biological family and *familia servorum* could overlap in other ways as well:[61] Freedmen sometimes inherited their unfree "wives" (*contubernales*),[62] children (D.32.41.2), siblings (D.40.2.11) and even parents (Inst.Gai.1.39; Epit.Gai.1.1.7; Inst.1.6.5)! Separation of slave children from their mothers was apparently common,[63] but "family members" might stay in contact even after (D.21.1.17.5).

Prostitution of slave women was widespread (McGinn 1998 and 2004; Rainer 2014), and it has been suggested that pimps were the most frequent purchasers of *ancillae* (Treggiari 1975, 341), though there are indications of some state control in these matters (SHA *Hadr.* 18.8). Rich Romans participated without risking the legal stigma (*infamia*) attached to pimping by running brothels through slaves (D.3.2.4.3) or renting properties out to pimps (D.5.3.27.1). In contrast, the seller of an *ancilla* could prohibit her prostitution by a *ne serva prostituatur* clause, which bound all later owners (McGinn 1998, 288–319).[64]

30.3.5 The Social Consequences of Slaves' Education, Skills or Value

Better education, special skills or talents raised a slave's value, which resulted in better treatment and easier manumission. Digest texts and other sources suggest that learning a trade at least doubled a slave's price; training as painters, librarians, actors or charioteers could lead to almost unpredictable increases (D.6.1.28; D.9.2.23.3; D.19.1.43; Gamauf 2012, 236–243).[65] The protection afforded by the jurists to such exquisite property occasioned legal "privileges" for luxury slaves. A usufructuary was banned from assigning menial tasks to exceptional slaves or spoiling their skills (D.7.1.15.1). They were entitled to food and clothes befitting their "rank and dignity" (D.7.1.15.2; Knoch 2005, 26–29), and legal protection against assaults (D.47.10.15.44). Since not the slaves' welfare but pecuniary interests were preserved, the owner could revoke such "privileges" at will, unless third-party interests suffered (cf. D.19.1.54pr). Certain slaves might turn out to be "irreplaceable", which reduced their prospect of manumission during their master's lifetime (but brought privileges; section 30.3.6).[66]

[60] Their sentimental value was not compensated for in Roman law (D.9.2.33pr; D.35.2.63pr; D.19.5.5pr; Wacke 2009; Kindler 2012).

[61] On slave families see Mouritsen 2010 and Willvonseder 2010.

[62] For epigraphic evidence of women owning their "husbands" see Evans Grubbs 1993, 131, n. 25.

[63] Knoch 2005, 144–145.

[64] Harper 2013, 49 motivates this with the "frequency of biological relations between master and slave".

[65] Charioteers or actors were sometimes able to pay enormous sums for manumission (Plin. *HN* 7.128–129; Meijer 2010, 86–87).

[66] In this category were a *dispensator* (household superintendent) or *vilicus* (bailiff): Carlsen 1995, 151; Herrmann-Otto 1994, 386–391; Schumacher 2001, 292–293; Schumacher 2010, 36.

30.3.6 The Social Repercussions of a *peculium*

A *peculium* could improve a slave's daily life in many ways, firstly because it usually meant release from constant supervision and an improvement of his social standing (Zwalve 2002, 121). In exceptional cases, such slaves even led a life of luxury, like the *dispensator* Musicus Scurranus, who belonged to the emperor Tiberius and was able to travel in senatorial style with the impressive entourage of sixteen *vicarii* to Rome.[67] More common were less flamboyant uses, such as financing small personal items,[68] extra food,[69] leisure (circus, theatre, baths, wine, gambling, prostitutes etc.)[70] or religious activities.[71] The financial means of the *peculium* permitted a slave to enter into a relationship with a free woman (D.11.3.16), to impress a Roman father so as to be given his daughter in "matrimony" (D.16.3.27) or an *ancilla* to provide her slave "husband" with a "dowry" (D.23.3.39pr).[72] If a slave was intentionally drawn to squander it, the master could recover twice his losses from the instigator (*actio servi corrupti*—action for the moral corruption of a slave; D.11.3.2).[73]

From a social perspective, the *peculium*, regardless of the master's ownership, was widely treated as if belonging to the slave.[74] Slaves paid for freedom with "their money" (*suis nummis*: Heinemeyer 2013; Mouritsen 2011, 159–180) made gifts to their masters (Buchwitz 2010, 254; D.15.3.7pr) or bequests to other household slaves.[75] It furthermore supported social control[76] by punishing wrongdoing by its withdrawal or by compensating losses or damages inflicted upon other household members (and thereby reducing the prospect of financing manumission).

30.4 Conclusion

Among the sources on Roman slavery, legal texts stand out for their quantity and the vast range of information available. Yet the majority of the unfree population lived outside the jurists' attention, because they were neither involved in economic interactions in public nor so valuable as to receive the sort of attention that caused the discussions about physical and mental defects, which turn D.21.1, according to Keith Bradley, into "one of the most realistic collections of slave experiences available for classical Antiquity" (Bradley 1994, 52). And

[67] *CIL* VI 5197; epigraphic evidence for similar cases in Schumacher 2001, 270–274.

[68] In Petron. *Sat.* 75.4 a slave boy bought toys and trinkets.

[69] Roth 2005.

[70] Hor. *Epist.* 1.14.15; Columella, *Rust.* 1.8.1; D.11.3.1.5; D.21.1.4.2; D.21.1.25.6; D.21.1.65; D.50.16.225; Plaut. *Stich.* 426–428, *Poen.* 843–844.

[71] Columella, *Rust.* 1.8.6 warns of superstitious slaves' money-wasting; on dedications to the gods by slaves see Schumacher 2001, 269 and Buchwitz 2010, 407–408.

[72] On *peculium* and family see Buchwitz 2010, 409–410.

[73] Harke 2013, 11–15.

[74] D.15.1.47.6; D.15.1.32pr; D.50.16.182; Isid. *Etym.* 5.25.5. On the slave's *de facto* "ownership" see Buti 1976, 13–70 and Knoch 2005, 178 with further references.

[75] Plin. *Ep.* 8.14; Petron. *Sat.* 53. The master's "generosity", which was necessary in this case, might also serve as a means of subtle exploitation; cf. Gamauf 2009, 340.

[76] On *peculium* and social control see Bradley 1984, 108–110; see also Kehoe 2013, 182–183.

slaves whose lives were exhausted in gruelling occupations (e.g. Apul. *Met.* 9.12) had little opportunity to break rules in a manner necessitating expert legal opinions.[77]

Therefore, the legal record tells more about the experiences of exceptional slaves, those "rich" and able to buy their freedom, those who were skilled and valuable enough as to be "pampered" or who had a "family". But they were "socially dead" as well, insofar as the master (or mistress) could at any time retract a *peculium*, command a librarian to the quarries and an athlete to clean the latrines (D.7.1.15.1), break up a slave family by sale[78] and—since "there is nothing dishonourable if the master orders it" (Petron. *Sat.* 75)—exploit any slave for his (or sometimes her) sexual pleasure. The master's *ius vitae necisque* meant, furthermore, that he was not asked too many questions when punishment had resulted in death (C.9.14.1pr and 1 [a. 319]) and that the prospects of success for complaints about ill-treatment were limited.[79]

Many longstanding discussions regarding slaves' legal and social status, such as whether a slave was more a "person" or a "thing",[80] or whether slavery as such had ameliorated during the Principate, and if so, whether for humanitarian or pragmatic reasons,[81] will probably never reach consensus. But expecting humanitarian concerns in a system deeply marked by the social fault lines of slavery on every level is in itself a form of bias that can easily become misleading. The rules of *iniuria* (defamation),[82] which were designed to reflect social status and honour (*existimatio*), offer such an example. The creation of an *actio iniuriarum servi nomine* (in the slave's name)[83] has been sometimes taken as signifying the "recognition of his human character" (Buckland 1908, 79).[84] The details, however, support a less "humanitarian" reading as well. The action depended on a *causae cognitio* (preliminary examination) by the *praetor* who himself selected the cases worthy of consideration by a regular judge. There was little chance to be accorded an action unless the victim was a well-behaving slave (of the "best quality"/*bonae frugi*)[85] or in an important position (D.47.10.15.43 and 44). No protection whatsoever was granted in case of verbal abuse or light beatings (D.47.10.15.44; Inst.Gai.3.222; Inst.4.4.3). Whipping by magistrates for showing signs of disrespect (D.47.10.15.39) or private individuals who thrashed slaves in order to correct their *mores* (*corrigendi/emendandi animo*—D.47.10.15.38) was not regarded by the judge as a violation of *boni mores*.[86] This regime invited the citizen collective to stamp out "unslavish" behaviour[87] instead of protecting slaves' dignity or "human

[77] Such are of course mentioned when jurists try to define terms such as *instrumentum* (tools, equipment) but with no hints as to the circumstances of their lives.

[78] Mart. 10.31 scorns a *dominus* for selling a slave, only to purchase luxury food with the price.

[79] Watson 1987, 124–128; Gamauf 1999, 54–56.

[80] Cf. e.g. Harrington 1994; Birks 1989; Knoch 2005, 20–40.

[81] See, e.g. Gamauf 1999, 117–135; Knoch 2005; McClintock 2010, 13–20; Gardner 2011, 432.

[82] See ch. 25.

[83] Mantovani 1999, 76; Hagemann 1998, 81–87.

[84] Similar Buchwitz 2010, 397–399; see also Fusco 2010, 432, n. 19. Knoch 2005, 220 even assumes that the slave had a right to complain; for economic reasons see Harries 2013, 52; for an indirect protection of the master see Fusco 2010.

[85] Jakab 1997, 190–195.

[86] Whipping was typical as a punishment for slaves and was therefore inappropriate for free; cf. Gell. *NA* 10.3.17; Hdt. 4.1–4 with Finley 1989, 186–187 and Saller 1994, 133–153. Beating another's slave *corrigendi animo* did not justify the causation of injuries (cf. D.9.2.5.3–7pr).

[87] See the anecdote in Plin. *Ep.* 3.14.7.

nature".[88] Considering how finely tuned the classical law of *iniuria* was with regard to social status, honour etc., it was hardly by accident that not even Musicus Scurranus[89] and his like should feel safe in public, because at any time someone might take offence at their ostentations and react with verbal abuse, or even a few slaps, in order to remind them of their place in Roman society, because there was little protection of the *actio iniuriarum* in such cases.[90] So, even in the case of the most "privileged" of slaves the law reinforced social displacement and paid little respect to their human nature.

Bibliography

Ankum, H. 2010. "The functions of expressions with *utilitatis causa* in the works of the classical Roman lawyers." In R. van den Bergh and G. van Niekerk, eds., L. Wildenboer, co-ed., Libellus ad Thomasium: *essays in Roman law, Roman-Dutch law and legal history in honour of Ph. J. Thomas (Fundamina. Editio specialis).* Pretoria. 5–22.

Aubert, J.-J. 1994. *Business managers in ancient Rome: a social and cconomic study of* Institores, *200 B.C.–A.D. 250.* Leiden.

Aubert, J.-J. 2013. "*Dumtaxtat de peculio*: What's in a peculium, or establishing the extent of the principal's liability." In P. J. du Plessis, ed., *New frontiers: law and society in the Roman world.* Edinburgh. 192–206.

Bellen, H. and H. Heinen, eds. 2003. *Bibliographie zur antiken Sklaverei I (Neu bearbeitet von D. Schäfer und J. Deissler auf Grundlage der von E. Herrmann in Verbindung mit N. Brockmeyer erstellten Ausgabe, Bochum 1983).* Stuttgart.

Birks, P. 1989. "An unacceptable face of human property." In P. Birks, ed., *New perspectives in the Roman law of property: essays for B. Nicholas.* Oxford. 61–73.

Boulvert, G. and Morabito, M. (1982). "Le droit de l'esclavage sous le Haut-Empire." *Aufstieg und Niedergang der römischen Welt* II.14: 98–182.

Bradley, K. R. 1984. *Slaves and masters in the Roman empire: a study in social control.* Brussels.

Bradley, K. R. (1990). "*Servus onerosus*: Roman law and the troublesome slave." *Slavery & Abolition* 11: 135–157.

Bradley, K. 1994. *Slavery and society at Rome.* Cambridge.

Buchwitz, W. 2010. "Fremde Sklaven als Erben: Sozialer Aufstieg durch Dritte." In A. Corbino et. al., eds., Homo, caput, persona. *La costruzione giuridica dell'identità nell'esperienza romana: Dall'epoca di Plauto a Ulpiano.* Pavia. 393–425.

Buchwitz, W. 2012. Servus alienus heres: *die Erbeinsetzung fremder Sklaven im klassischen römischen Recht.* Vienna.

Buckland, W. W. 1908 (repr. 1970). *The Roman law of slavery: the condition of the slave in private law from Augustus to Justinian.* Cambridge.

Bürge, A. 1993. "*Cibaria.* Indiz für die soziale Stellung des römischen Arbeitnehmers?" In M. J. Schermaier and Z. Vegh, eds., Ars boni et aequi: *Festschrift für W. Waldstein zum 65. Geburtstag.* Stuttgart. 63–78.

[88] Cf. Saller 1994, 145: "[N]one (of the Roman authors) argued that slaves possessed a sense of honour that made corporal punishment wholly inappropriate."

[89] See n. 68.

[90] Excluded was the *actio iniuriarum servi nomine*, not an action on behalf of the *dominus* if an insult was directed at him (D.47.10.15.35), nor, of course, the *actio legis Aquiliae* if the slave sustained injuries.

Bürge, A. 1999. *Römisches Privatrecht: Rechtsdenken und gesellschaftliche Verankerung. Eine Einführung*. Darmstadt.

Bürge, A. 2010. "Lo schiavo (in)dipendente e il suo patrimonio." In A. Corbino et al., eds., Homo, caput, persona. *La costruzione giuridica dell'identità nell'esperienza romana: Dall'epoca di Plauto a Ulpiano*. Pavia. 369–391.

Buti, I. 1976. *Studi sulla capacità patrimoniale dei* servi. Naples.

Carlsen, J. 1995/2001. Vilici *and Roman estate managers until AD 284*. Rome.

Chiusi, T. 2001. *Die* actio de in rem verso *im römischen Recht*. Munich.

de Ligt, L. (1999). "Legal history and economic history: the case of the *actiones adiecticiae qualitatis*." *Tijdschrift voor Rechtsgeschiedenis* 67: 205–226.

de Ligt, L. 2002. "D. 15,1,1,1 and the early history of the *actio quod iussu*." In L. de Ligt et al., eds., Viva vox iuris Romani: *essays in honour of J. E. Spruit*. Amsterdam. 197–204.

Edmondson, J. 2011. "Slavery and the Roman family." In K. Bradley and P. Cartledge, eds., *The Cambridge world history of slavery*, Vol. 1: *The ancient Mediterranean world*. Cambridge. 337–361.

Evans Grubbs, J. (1993). "'Marriage more shameful than adultery': slave-mistress relationships, 'mixed marriages' and late Roman law." *Phoenix* 47: 125–154.

Finley, M. I. 1998. *Ancient slavery and modern ideology*. Expanded edition edited by B. D. Shaw. Princeton.

Fleckner, A. M. 2010. *Antike Kapitalvereinigungen: ein Beitrag zu den konzeptuellen und historischen Grundlagen der Aktiengesellschaft*. Cologne.

Fuhrmann, C. J. 2012. *Policing the Roman empire: soldiers, administration, and public order*. Oxford.

Fusco, S. 2010. "*De iniuriis quae servis fiunt*. Un caso di rilevanza giuridica della *persona servi*?" In A. Corbino et al., eds., Homo, caput, persona. *La costruzione giuridica dell'identità nell'esperienza romana: Dall'epoca di Plauto a Ulpiano*. Pavia. 427–433.

Gamauf, R. 1999. Ad statuam licet confugere: *Untersuchungen zum Asylrecht im römischen Prinzipat*. Frankfurt.

Gamauf, R. 2001. "Zur Frage 'Sklaverei und Humanität' anhand von Quellen des römischen Rechts." In H. Bellen and H. Heinen, eds., *Fünfzig Jahre Forschungen zur antiken Sklaverei an der Mainzer Akademie 1950–2000*. Stuttgart. 51–72.

Gamauf, R. 2007. "*Cum aliter nulla domus tuta esse possit* ...: fear of slaves and Roman law." In A. Serghidou, ed., *Fear of slaves—fear of enslavement in the ancient Mediterranean. Peur de l'esclave—Peur de l'esclavage en Mediterranee ancienne (Discours, représentations, pratiques). Actes du XXIXe Colloque du Groupe International de Recherche sur l'Esclavage dans l'Antiquité (GIREA). Rethymnon 4–7 Novembre 2004*. Franche-Comté. 145–164.

Gamauf, R. (2009). "Slaves doing business: the role of Roman law in the economy of a Roman household." *European Review of History—Revue européenne d'histoire* 16: 331–346.

Gamauf, R. 2012. "Kindersklaven in klassischen römischen Rechtsquellen." In H. Heinen, ed., *Kindersklaven—Sklavenkinder. Schicksale zwischen Zuneigung und Ausbeutung in der Antike und im interkulturellen Vergleich: Beiträge zur Tagung des Akademievorhabens Forschungen zur antiken Sklaverei (Mainz, 14. Oktober 2008)*. Stuttgart. 231–260.

Gamauf, R. 2014. "*Erro*: Suche nach einem verschwundenen Sklaven. Eine Skizze zur Interpretationsgeschichte des ädilizischen Edikts." In J. Hallebeek et al., eds., Inter cives necnon peregrinos: *essays in honour of Boudewijn Sirks*. Göttingen. 269–287.

Gardner, J. F. 2011. "Slavery and Roman law." In K. Bradley and P. Cartledge, eds., *The Cambridge world history of slavery*, Vol. 1: *The ancient Mediterranean world*. Cambridge. 414–437.

Garnsey, P. 1996. *Ideas of slavery from Aristotle to Augustin*. Cambridge.

Grotkamp, N. (2005). "Missbrauch und Gebrauch des *peculium*." *Münstersche Beiträge zur antiken Handelsgeschichte* 24: 125–145.

Hagemann, M. 1998. Iniuria: *von den XII-Tafeln bis zur Justinianischen Kodifikation*. Cologne.

Harke, J. D. 2013. *Corpus römischer Rechtsquellen zur Sklaverei, III. Die Rechtspositionen am Sklaven*, Vol. 2: *Ansprüche aus Delikten am Sklaven*. Stuttgart.

Harper, K. (2010). "The *SC Claudianum* in the *Codex Theodosianus*: social history and legal texts." *Classical Quarterly* 60: 610–638.

Harper, K. 2013. *From shame to sin: the Christian transformation of sexual morality in late antiquity*. Cambridge, Mass.

Harrington, J. D. (1994). "*Res* or *persona*: Roman civil law's influence on southern slave law." *Labeo* 40: 236–245.

Harries, J. 2013. "The *Senatus Consultum Silanianum*: court decisions and judicial severity in the early Roman empire." In P. J. du Plessis, ed., *New frontiers: law and society in the Roman world*. Edinburgh. 51–70.

Heinemeyer, S. 2013. *Der Freikauf des Sklaven mit eigenem Geld*—Redemptio suis nummis. Berlin.

Heinen, H., ed. 2006. *Handwörterbuch der antiken Sklaverei*. [CD-ROM]. Stuttgart.

Herrmann-Otto, E. 1994. Ex ancilla natus. *Untersuchungen zu den "hausgeborenen" Sklaven und Sklavinnen im Westen des römischen Kaiserreiches*. Stuttgart.

Honoré, A. 2012. "The nature of slavery." In J. Allain, ed., *The legal understanding of slavery: from the historical to the contemporary*. Oxford. 9–16.

Hunt, P. 2011. "Slaves in Greek literary culture". In K. Bradley and P. Cartledge, eds., *The Cambridge world history of slavery*, Vol. 1: *The ancient Mediterranean world*. Cambridge. 22–47.

Jakab, É. 1997. Praedicere *und* cavere *beim Marktkauf: Sachmängel im griechischen und römischen Recht*. Munich.

Johnston, D. 2007. "Suing the *Paterfamilias*: theory and practice." In J. W. Cairns and P. J. du Plessis, eds., *Beyond dogmatics: law and society in the Roman world*. Edinburgh. 173–184.

Joshel, S. R. 2010. *Slavery in the Roman world*. Cambridge.

Kehoe, D. 2012. "Contract labour." In W. Scheidel, ed., *The Cambridge companion to the Roman economy*. Cambridge. 114–130.

Kehoe, D. 2013. "Law, agency and growth in the Roman economy." In P. J. du Plessis, ed., *New frontiers: law and society in the Roman world*. Edinburgh. 177–191.

Kindler, M. 2012. Affectionis aestimatio: *Vom Ursprung des Affektionsinteresses im römischen Recht und seiner Rezeption*. Berlin.

Kirschenbaum, A. 1987. *Sons, slaves, and freedmen in Roman commerce*. Jerusalem/Washington, DC.

Klinck, F. 2004. *Erwerb durch Übergabe an Dritte nach klassischem römischen Recht*. Berlin.

Klingenberg, G. 2005. *Corpus der römischen Rechtsquellen zur antiken Sklaverei (CRRS). Teil X: Juristisch speziell definierte Sklavengruppen, 6:* Servus fugitivus. Stuttgart.

Knoch, S. 2005. *Sklavenfürsorge im Römischen Reich: Formen und Motive*. Hildesheim.

Knütel, R. 1989. "Barbatius Philippus und seine Spuren (*Falsus praetor, parochus putativus*, Scheinbeamter)." In D. Schwab et al., eds., *Staat, Kirche, Wissenschaft in einer pluralistischen Gesellschaft: Festschrift zum 65. Geburtstag von P. Mikat*. Berlin. 345–365.

Kolendo, J. (1981). "L'esclavage et la vie sexuelle des hommes libres à Rome." *Index* 10: 288–297.

Laes, C. 2003. "Desperately different? *Delicia* children in the Roman household." In D. L. Balch and C. Osiek, eds., *Early Christian families in context: an interdisciplinary dialogue.* Grand Rapids/Cambridge. 298–324.

Liebs, D. 2012. *Summoned to the Roman courts: famous trials from Antiquity*, transl. L. R. Garber and C. Gustley Cürten. Berkeley/Los Angeles.

Liebs, D. 2014. "Sie liebte ihren Sklaven." In J. Hallebeek et al., eds., Inter cives necnon peregrinos: *essays in honour of Boudewijn Sirks.* Göttingen. 409–428.

Mantovani, D. 1999². *Le formule del processo privato romano: Per la didattica delle Istituzioni di diritto romano.* Padua.

McClintock, A. 2010. *Servi della pena: Condannati a morte nella Roma imperiale.* Naples.

McGinn, T. A. J. 1998. *Prostitution, sexuality, and the law in Ancient Rome.* New York/Oxford.

McGinn, T. A. J. 2004. *The economy of prostitution in the Roman world: a study of social history and the brothel.* Ann Arbor.

Meijer, F. 2010. *Chariot racing in the Roman empire*, transl. L. Waters. Baltimore.

Melluso, M. 2000. *La schiavitù nell'età giustinianea: Disciplina giuridica e rilevanza sociale.* Paris.

Metzger, E. 2014. "*Cum servo agere.*" In J. Hallebeek et al., eds., Inter cives necnon peregrinos: *essays in honour of Boudewijn Sirks.* Göttingen. 533–543.

Miceli, M. 2001. *Sulla struttura formulare delle* actiones adiecticiae qualitiatis. Turin.

Morabito, M. 1981. *Les réalités de l'esclavage d'après le Digeste.* Paris.

Morabito, M. (1986). "Droit romain et réalités sociales de la sexualité servile." *Dialogues d'histoire ancienne* 12: 371–387.

Morabito, M. (1987). "Esclavage et enseignement du droit: les Institutes de Gaius." *Index* 15: 51–61.

Mouritsen, H. 2010. "The Families of Roman slaves and freedmen." In B. Rawson, ed,. *A companion to families in the Greek and Roman worlds.* Oxford. 129–144.

Mouritsen, H. 2011. *The freedman in the Roman world.* Cambridge.

Patterson, O. 1982. *Slavery and social death: a comparative study.* Cambridge, Mass./London.

Patterson, O. 2012. "Trafficking, gender, and slavery: past and present." In J. Allain, ed., *The legal understanding of slavery: from the historical to the contemporary.* Oxford. 322–359.

Pesaresi, R. 2008. *Ricerche sul* peculium *imprenditoriale.* Bari.

Pesaresi, R. 2012. *Studi sull'*actio de peculio. Bari.

Rainer, M. 2014. "Zur Prostitution von Sklavinnen in Rom." In J. Hallebeek et al., eds., Inter cives necnon peregrinos: *essays in honour of Boudewijn Sirks.* Göttingen. 627–64.

Rainer, M. and E. Herrmann-Otto. 1999. *Corpus der römischen Rechtsquellen zur antiken Sklaverei (CRRS): Prolegomena.* Stuttgart.

Reduzzi Merola, F. 1990. Servo parere. *Studi sulla condizione giuridica degli schiavi vicari e dei sottoposti a schiavi nelle esperienze greca e romana.* Naples.

Robleda, O. 1976. *Il diritto degli schiavi nell'antica Roma.* Rome.

Roth, U. (2005). "Food, status, and the *peculium* of agricultural slaves." *Journal of Roman Archaeology* 18: 278–292.

Scheidel, W. 2011. "The Roman slave supply." In K. Bradley and P. Cartledge, eds., *The Cambridge world history of slavery*, Vol. 1: *The ancient Mediterranean world.* Cambridge. 287–310.

Schumacher, L. 2001. *Sklaverei in der Antike: Alltag und Schicksal der Unfreien.* Munich.

Schumacher, L. 2010. "On the status of private *actores, dispensatores* and *vilici*." In U. Roth, ed., *By the sweat of your brow: Roman slavery in its socio-economic setting*. London. 31–47.

Schumacher, L. 2011. "Slaves in Roman society." In M. Peachin, ed., *The Oxford handbook of social relations in the Roman world*. Oxford. 589–608.

Sirks, A. J. B. 2011. "The *Senatus Consultum Claudianum* in 438 and after in the west." In K. Muscheler, ed., *Römische Jurisprudenz—Dogmatik, Überlieferung, Rezeption: Festschrift für D. Liebs zum 75. Geburtstag*. Berlin. 623–636.

Treggiari, S. (1975). "Family life among the staff of the Volusii." *Transactions of the American Philological Association* 105: 393–401.

Wacke, A. (1991). "*Peculium non ademptum videtur tacite donatum*. Zum Schicksal des Sonderguts nach der Gewaltentlassung." *Iura* 42: 43–95.

Wacke, A. (1994). "Die adjektizischen Klagen im Überblick. Erster Teil: Von der Reeder- und der Betriebsleiterklage zur direkten Stellvertretung." *Zeitschrift der Savigny-Stiftung für Rechtsgeschichte, romanistische Abteilung* 111: 280–362.

Wacke, A. 2001. "*Manumissio matrimonii causa*: die Freilassung zwecks Heirat nach den Ehegesetzen des Augustus." In H. Bellen and H. Heinen, eds., *Fünfzig Jahre Forschungen zur antiken Sklaverei an der Mainzer Akademie 1950–2000*. Stuttgart. 133–158.

Wacke, A. 2006. "Die *libera administratio peculii*: Zur Verfügungsmacht von Hauskindern und Sklaven über ihr Sondergut." In T. Finkenauer, ed., *Sklaverei und Freilassung im römischen Recht. Symposion für H. J. Wieling zum 70. Geburtstag*. Berlin. 251–316.

Wacke, A. 2009. "Das Affektionsinteresse: heute und in römischen Rechtsquellen." In M. Avenarius et al., eds., Ars Iuris: *Festschrift für O. Behrends zum 70. Geburtstag*. Göttingen. 555–588.

Watson, A. 1987. *Roman slave law*. Baltimore/London.

Weber, E. 2008. "*Libertus et coniunx*." In P. Mauritsch et al., eds., *Antike Lebenswelten: Konstanz—Wandel—Wirkungskraft: Festschrift für I. Weiler zum 70. Geburtstag*. Wiesbaden. 367–380.

Weiß, A. 2004. *Sklave der Stadt: Untersuchungen zur öffentlichen Sklaverei in den Städten des Römischen Reiches*. Stuttgart.

Willvonseder, R. 2010. *Corpus der römischen Rechtsquellen zur antiken Sklaverei (CRRS). Teil IV: Stellung des Sklaven im Privatrecht, 1: Eheähnliche Verbindungen und verwandtschaftliche Beziehungen*. Stuttgart.

Żeber, I. 1981. *A study of the* peculium *of a slave in pre-classical and classical Roman law*. Wrocław.

Zimmermann, R. 1990. *The law of obligations: Roman foundations of the civilian tradition*. Cape Town.

Zwalve, W. J. 2002. "Callistus' case: some legal aspects of Roman business activities." In L. de Blois and J. Rich, eds., *The transformation of economic life under the Roman empire. Proceedings of the Second Workshop of the International Network Impact of Empire (Roman Empire, c. 200 B.C.–A.D. 476), Nottingham, July 4–7*. Amsterdam. 116–127.

CHAPTER 31

MANUMISSION

HENRIK MOURITSEN

31.1 Introduction

A chapter on manumission in Roman law requires little justification given the striking popularity and sheer scale of this practice. The Romans appear to have freed their slaves more often and in greater numbers than any other slave-based society in history.[1] The alienation of human property—with the attendant creation of a free person with recognised rights and obligations—required a legal framework not just in order to regulate the manumission process itself but also to define the status of the ex-slave as well as his/her relationship with the former owner.[2] Since manumission essentially was an economic transaction with important social implications, the rules and regulations that evolved inevitably reflected wider societal structures that will have to be taken into account whenever we try to understand the legal framework.

A brief survey of this kind can merely scratch the surface of a phenomenon as complex and multifaceted as manumission, and in this chapter we will therefore focus on those areas where Roman manumission, right from the outset, stood out as historically unique and then trace the later developments that sprang from these early foundations. Three main areas will be considered. Firstly, the most striking aspect of Roman manumission was probably the ancient custom of enfranchising former slaves, and to understand this feature we will have to look at the specific social context of early Rome where it first emerged. Secondly, the question of citizenship takes us directly to the most important caesura in the legal history of slave emancipation: the Augustan manumission laws. These measures appear to have been concerned above all with the enfranchisement of former slaves, and the outcome was a new framework that was to endure with few changes into late Antiquity. Finally, the Imperial period saw a steady refinement in the rules regulating manumission, subject as it was to the enduring attention of the jurists. It is not always clear, however, whether this interest was driven by actual social pressures or a tendency

[1] For general accounts of Roman manumission see Treggiari 1969; Hopkins 1978; Fabre 1981; Bradley 1994; Weiler 2003; Mouritsen 2011; Perry 2014.

[2] The fundamental discussion is Buckland 1908. See also Watson 1987.

towards ever-greater fine-tuning of the legal framework inherent in the juristic discourse. As such, manumission offers an instructive case study of the relationship between "law" and "life" in the Roman Empire.

31.2 Citizenship and Familial Integration

As far back as records survive, the Romans appear to have granted citizenship to former slaves. The practice has few parallels in the history of slavery and caused surprise among contemporary observers in Greece, where ex-slaves were excluded from the citizen body and classified as metics, resident aliens.[3] Contrary to common assumptions, the Roman citizenship of former slaves was not of a defective, lower type but essentially complete and endowed with all basic rights. Most crucially it secured their newly gained freedom by offering them personal protection on a par with other citizens. In addition, it gave them the right to own property, dispose of it by will and receive bequests in the form of inheritances and legacies. It also guaranteed basic entitlements in the public sphere, including the right to vote and appear in court.

Although former slaves carried certain disabilities, that did not make their citizenship "second-class", since these were shared by substantial sections of the Roman population, in some cases even the large majority. The disadvantages they suffered were above all related to the citizen's public roles, and in particular those associated with the exercise of authority. Freedmen were barred from magistracies, state priesthoods and the highest orders; that is, the senatorial, the equestrian and the local *curiae*.[4] Their exclusion was probably never formalised in law, at least during the Republic, since it was considered a given that persons who had been dishonoured by slavery—and hence carried the indelible stigma of *macula servitutis*—could never attain equal worth to those who had not.[5] The freedman's past would therefore always prevent him from exercising power over *ingenui*. Still, in this respect he was far from alone, since similar disabilities prevented the poor (formally defined as those who had little or no property to register at the census) from reaching positions of authority, partly because of their lack of resources but also because of the dishonour and immorality widely associated with poverty. The perceived similarities between the two categories are further illustrated by their common relegation to the four urban units in the tribally organised assemblies and to the lowest-ranking centuries in the *comitia centuriata*. The latter was justified by their *de facto* exclusion from military service, one of the key elements of Roman citizenship and identity under the Republic. During national emergencies they might be called up for garrison duties or as rowers for the navy, but they were never put on the front line.[6] The reluctance to exploit valuable manpower resources is a telling testimony to the depth of concern caused by the admission of

[3] Cf. *SIG*³ 543. On Greek manumission see Weiler 2003, 180–189; Zelnick-Abramovitz 2005.

[4] Membership of the two highest orders was policed by the censors. At municipal level the *lex Visellia*, 24 AD (C.9.21.1), formally barred freedmen from the *ordo decurionum*, although in practice they had probably always been excluded.

[5] For a discussion of the stigma attached to former slaves see Mouritsen 2011, 10–35.

[6] Mouritsen 2011, 71–72.

former slaves into free society, which raised troubling questions about their moral fibre and reliability.

The well-attested concerns about the "servility" and dishonour of former slaves make the practice of enfranchising freedmen so much more intriguing, not least when one considers the complete nature of their citizenship. To gain a better understanding of the origins and rationale of this custom we will have to consider the particular conditions that obtained in early Roman society, where it first took hold. There are obvious difficulties involved in any attempt of this nature, but it may still be possible to reconstruct, in broad outline, a social and legal environment where the enfranchisement of freedmen was not just feasible but made perfect sense. A key factor would seem to be the extraordinary role of the *pater familias*, who exercised unlimited power over all members of his household as well as the entire familial property. It would seem that what has historically been the primary prerogative of the state, namely its monopoly of legitimate violence, in early Rome was partly delegated to the heads of households, who were given the power to punish, execute or sell those under his *potestas* and *dominium*, creating, as the ancients themselves noted, a remarkable similarity between the status of children and slaves. Leaving aside the complex issue of the nature of the *res publica*, which clearly did not correspond to the modern concept of "state", this delegation of domestic power would seem to reflect a relatively "primitive" society with a poorly developed central authority.[7] A further result of this "decentralisation" of state functions was the ability of private citizens to perform actions that had real and substantive implications for society as a whole. Thus individual *domini* could free slaves with a minimum of "state" involvement, since officials merely oversaw the manumission rather than effected it. The freeing of a slave essentially remained a private act in which the collective in principle took no interest, despite its public repercussions.

Through the unilateral decision of the *dominus* the slave was turned into a Roman citizen, but as crucially he also became a free member of the domestic unit, and it is that process which represents the other unique strand of Roman manumission. The freedman's newly gained freedom was accompanied by his formal integration into the *familia*. This happened through the freedman's assumption of the *nomen gentilicium* of the master, who in turn would take on the official role as *patronus*, which conferred both moral and to some extent legal authority over the freedman. The kinless status of the slave meant that after manumission the patron could without difficulty assume a pseudo-paternal position in relation to the freedman.[8] This fiction was partly enshrined in law; freedmen were, for example, listed alongside natural relatives in the context of prosecution and the ability to give legal evidence, and according to the *lex Pompeia* they could even be tried for *parricidium* if they killed their patron.[9] They may not formally have entered the patron's *gens*, presumably because that might entitle them to a share of his estate (Cic. *Top.* 29), but the fact that they took the familial *nomen* carried great symbolic weight and could also have practical implications, e.g. in the context of funerary and other testamentary provisions which often defined recipients as those who shared the *nomen*.[10]

[7] The role of the *patres familias* in the early Republic has been explored by Linke 2005 and 2014.

[8] Mouritsen 2011, 68–70. On the definition of slaves as kinless see Patterson 1982.

[9] *Lex coloniae genitivae* 95.15–19 (*RS* 407, 426); D.22.5.4; *lex Pompeia*, D.48.9.1.

[10] Mouritsen 2011, 38–39.

Implicit in this conceptualisation of the freedman–patron relationship lay an expectation of familial continuity, the former slave remaining in his patron's service and under his authority—indeed often under his roof. Viewed from this perspective, manumission emerged as a legal act by which an owner redefined the status of a person under his control, a process not dissimilar to filial emancipation, and it could be argued that as the living outcome of this action the new freedman logically received the same civic status as the pseudo-paternal patron who had "created" him.[11] The semi-familial aspect might explain why congruence between the status of *libertus* and *patronus* remained the default rule, and any departure from this principle, e.g. caused by exile, was treated as a matter of concern.[12] Viewed from this perspective the enfranchisement of freedmen becomes part of the wider legacy of the distinct world of early Rome, when it first became customary for slave owners to "reproduce" themselves socially—with limited "state" involvement or oversight—and expand their free household through a legal procedure that as a by-product also created a new citizen.

While these factors may possibly explain the citizen status of former slaves, there were of course public implications of these private acts, above all in the political sphere. The prospect of freedmen wielding political power was an anathema to Roman sensibilities, but the risk of that happening could be easily neutralised through the particular structure of the assemblies, which allowed the weight of individual votes to be calibrated. The transparent inequalities of influence were accepted because Roman citizenship, in contrast to that of the Greek city-states, was not defined primarily in terms of political power.[13] Thus, public proceedings from the very beginning had a strong ritual character, suggesting a largely acclamatory function. Moreover, the practice of block voting, unparalleled in the ancient world, lent all political participation an abstract quality, which rendered the vote of individual citizens secondary to that of the largely artificial voting units. Therefore, while Roman citizenship guaranteed individual freedom and personal protection, it was largely detached from the active exercise of political power. It was this particular feature that enabled Rome to expand its citizen body to such a remarkable extent, internally through manumission and externally through conquest, territorial integration and the enfranchisement of subject peoples. If Roman citizenship had been defined and articulated in conventional political terms, that would not have been possible without jeopardising internal stability.

The relegation of freedmen to the unarmed centuries and the urban *tribus* ensured that their voting potential was never realised; nevertheless, their very existence presented a temptation for politicians eager to expand their support base and *clientelae*. It is therefore in this particular context that we hear most often of legislative initiatives relating to freedmen during the free Republic. A number of attempts were made, often in quick succession, to redistribute freedmen, which either failed or were quickly reversed. The attention paid to the freedman vote is unsurprising, especially when one considers their likely numbers, which may have been substantial already under the Republic. But that does not, of course, allow us to describe them as a separate constituency with distinct interests, as much as an untapped political resource.

[11] Volterra 1955 is fundamental to this understanding of the enfranchisement of freedmen.

[12] e.g. *lex Irn.* 23, 97; cf. Plin. *Ep.* 10.11.2.

[13] Gauthier 1974 and 1981; Meier 1997.

31.3 The Augustan Reform of Manumission

During the Republic, several different forms of manumission developed, which modern scholarship tends to divide into "formal" and "informal", the important distinction being that the former led to enfranchisement while the latter did not. "Formal" manumission included the freeing of slaves *vindicta*, "by the rod", through registration in the census and by testament, while slaves could be freed informally *inter amicos* and *per litteras*. Informal manumission carried no official recognition, although the liberty of those freed in that way enjoyed the protection of the urban praetor. As a result, they lived as free but died as slaves, implying that any possessions they had automatically reverted to the master/patron, as did presumably the children they left behind.[14] The patronal benefits were therefore evident, which undoubtedly explains the existence of "informal" manumission.

The most important reforms of manumission belong to the reign of the first emperor, when a number of laws were passed that dealt with a range of different aspects. Their fundamental aims and implication are debated, but most likely they were a response to changes to the Roman citizenship during the late Republic. As the Empire expanded and came to encompass the entire Mediterranean, Roman citizenship was transformed from a local status held by free members of the community into a widely coveted "virtual" citizenship which carried with it a number of privileges and opportunities that could be enjoyed irrespective of domicile. Provincial subjects could now aspire to becoming Roman citizens without giving up their local citizenship, which had previously not been possible because of Rome's refusal to accept "double citizenship".[15] But as her citizenship evolved into a "supra-national" status detached from soil and residency, the issue effectively vanished, although the principle may never have been formally abandoned. Crucially, as the Roman citizenship evolved into a higher, universally desirable status, the ancient practice of enfranchising former slaves began to appear increasingly anomalous; it is against this background the Augustan efforts to create a new legal framework may be viewed.

It has long been assumed that Augustus' primary aim was to limit the scale of manumission, but closer scrutiny of the measures themselves suggests they had little impact on the overall number of freedmen in Roman society. More likely, the overriding concern was to restrict access to the Roman citizenship; for what the reforms did do was to create a multi-tiered system of personal statuses intended to reflect the age and behaviour of the former slaves. Related to these concerns were measures to ensure that masters selected—and were capable of selecting—the members of their *familiae* who were best suited for freedom/citizenship. The first step was to regulate the "untidy" practice of informal manumission, which effectively left the freedman in a legal limbo, being neither entirely free nor unfree. The size of this group may also have been growing along with the expansion of Rome, which made it increasingly difficult to carry out formal *manumissio vindicta* that required the presence of a Roman magistrate. After the passing of the *lex Iunia* these freedmen

[14] Cic. *Top.* 2.10; Reg.Ulp.1.10; Inst.Gai.1.22, 3.56; Frg. Dosith. 4–8 (*FIRA*).

[15] Sherwin-White 1973, 296–299.

became so-called *Latini Iuniani*, a new status that somehow associated them with the *Latini Coloniarii*.[16] Since the freedom of these former slaves was now recognised in law, the Augustan initiative in effect increased rather than reduced the number of freedmen in Roman society.

Building on this reform the *lex Aelia Sentia* in 4 AD laid down a set of criteria defining who qualified for which status. Most importantly it prescribed that slaves freed below the age of thirty would no longer receive citizenship but become *Latini*. This marked a significant restriction on the access to citizenship, but it also offered the opportunity to "upgrade" to full citizen status through child-rearing. A complex procedure known as *probatio anniculi causa*, well documented in the records of Herculaneum, granted citizenship to Latins who had been freed below the age of thirty, entered into legal marriage and recorded the birth and first birthday of a child.[17] Later, in 75 AD, the so-called *senatus consultum Pegasianum* extended this right to *Latini Iuniani* freed above the age of thirty.[18] Another means of gaining full citizen status was through *iteratio*, a process by which the patron repeated the manumission at a time when the freedman had become eligible. Augustus further introduced the novel status of *libertus dediticius* for freed slaves, who had been disgraced and punished by their masters. The name associated them with defeated enemies and offered only the merest recognition of their free status while restricting their liberty in various ways.

The result of these reforms was a hierarchy of civic statuses to which former slaves in principle would be allocated according to individual merit. But although the automatic enfranchisement of freedmen was now a thing of the past, there are few signs of any serious attempt to ensure that only "good" slaves would be freed and/or enfranchised; in fact the measures in several respects come across as rather half-hearted. The requirement that slave owners select only "worthy" slaves—and were fit to do so—may have been little more than a gesture reminding owners of their social responsibilities. Although it was now prescribed that masters had to be of sound mind and minors could not free slaves without the express consent of a *consilium*, the impact on manumission rates is likely to have been modest, since young owners probably never had freed many slaves in the first place—and in any case could do as they wished as soon as they came of age. It is also worth noting that no attempt was made to restrict the rights of, for example, *infames* or freedmen to free slaves despite their dishonour.

Testamentary manumission was the subject of a separate law, the *lex Fufia Caninia* (2 BC), which stipulated the number of slaves a master could free by will, according to a scale that gradually reduced the proportion permitted the larger the household was.[19] The law once again emphasised the importance of selection and discrimination in the manumission process, but the practical consequences may have been limited. Large-scale testamentary manumission had probably always been a rarity, certainly of entire households. The occasions where it did happen undoubtedly attracted considerable attention as well as a

[16] Inst.Gai.3.56; Frg. Dosith. 6. The date of the *lex Iunia* is disputed, but Balestri Fumigalli 1985 convincingly showed that it must predate the *lex Aelia Sentia*. For *Latini Iuniani* see Sirks 1981, 1983; Weaver 1990, 1997; Lopez 1998.

[17] See the detailed dossier recording the enfranchisement of Venidius Ennychus, Camodeca 2006.

[18] Inst.Gai.1.31; Reg.Ulp.3.4; *Schol. Iuv.* 4.77 (Wessner/Teubner).

[19] Inst.Gai.2.224, 2.228, cf. Gardner 1991; Mouritsen 2011.

degree of opprobrium, since it ignored the testator's obligations towards the heirs in favour of personal ostentation.[20]

A primary aim was to ensure that the majority of new freedmen did not move directly from servile to citizen status. Manumission may always have raised concerns about the crossing of boundaries and the transition between supposedly essential categories, but following the changes to Roman citizenship it became paramount that the new citizens, just like enfranchised provincials, such as auxiliary veterans, be seen to meet certain "standards" in terms of maturity, good behaviour and services to Rome.[21] Among the latter counted contributions to the growth of the Roman population. As we saw, procreation was rewarded with citizenship, and further incentives to child-rearing were offered in the shape of greater control over the freedman's own estate and personal independence for *libertae*.[22] Thus the patron's share of the freedman's estate was reduced the more offspring the latter reared, and freedwomen could gain *ius trium liberorum* if they raised four children, as opposed to the three normally required. Again these rules would seem to contradict common notions that the first *princeps* sought to contain the "servile" element within the Roman population.

The Augustan laws reveal some preoccupation about the behaviour of freedmen. A poorly documented section of the *lex Aelia Sentia* dealt with patronal complaints about disobedient and ungrateful freedmen,[23] and the *lex Fufia Caninia*, which at least formally restricted testamentary manumission, may also have reflected anxieties about *liberti orcini*; that is, freedmen whose patron resided in the underworld. This type would for obvious reasons not have been subject to the same kind of pseudo-paternal control as "normal" freedmen who had a living patron; for although the patronal role would then pass to one of the heirs, the personal ties would inevitably have been weaker and the crucial bonds of *officium* and *pietas* largely absent.

The new status of *dediticius*, reserved for disgraced freedmen, is perhaps best understood as a political statement about civic restoration and social "purity".[24] Roman slave owners could free any slave they wished, potentially allowing "unworthy" individuals to enter free society. Most likely, however, that was an ideological rather than an actual problem, as the ineffectual nature of the Augustan measures also suggests; for unless the slave in question carried obvious marks of punishment and degradation, such as scars and tattoos, masters were free to continue as before. No effective state oversight of manumission was put in place and, as before, no official authority checked the "quality" of the slaves who were being freed. This part of the reform may therefore be interpreted as a response to deep-seated fears about social "pollution", as also indicated by the relegation of the *dediticii* beyond the hundredth milestone from Rome, both physically and symbolically keeping them apart from the main citizen body.

[20] Dion. Hal. *Ant. Rom.* 4.24.6 famously railed against the practice in his outburst against contemporary manumission.

[21] Cf. Suet. *Aug.* 40.3–4. Atkinson 1966.

[22] *lex Papia Poppaea* 9 AD, cf. e.g. Gardner 1998, 60f. The *lex Iulia et Papia* also provided exemption from promised services to freedmen with two children *in potestate* (or one five-year-old), D.38.1.37pr, 1–3.

[23] D.50.16.70, cf. Wilinski 1971.

[24] Inst.Gai.1.27: cf. Reg.Ulp.1.11; cf. Mouritsen 2011, 33–34, 83.

In sum, it is difficult to perceive these measures as attempts to address specific social problems caused by manumission and the freed population. They do, in fact, make better sense when situated in the wider context of what has become known as Augustus' "moral" legislation; that is, his laws on issues such as adultery, marriage and procreation and unions across social boundaries. Among their most striking and novel features was the fact that the "state" entered so directly into the domestic sphere and intervened in the established rights and powers of the *patres familias*. Such radical steps were justified by the manifest social breakdown and prolonged civil wars that seemed to call for drastic action in order to restore ancient *mores*. Viewed from this perspective the Augustan manumission laws emerge as part of the new regime's response to contemporary anxieties about societal decline, naturally heightened in times of civil war and political breakdown. Still, the form they took also reflects more fundamental concerns generated by the Roman freedman as a social category; for while society expected the freedman to behave in a certain—respectful—manner towards his patron, these norms were only to a relatively limited extent enshrined in law. Thus when a *dominus* decided to redefine his authority over the slave and relinquish his ownership, the latter acquired a position in the early Roman household comparable to that of an emancipated son. The surrender of formal power meant that there were narrow limits to the obligations that could be imposed, and that created one of the main tensions in the Roman system of manumission, between, on the one hand, the ideal role of the freedman and, on the other hand, the legally defined means by which that could be enforced. Since the authority of the patron was rooted in *pietas* and *mos* rather than law, the correct behaviour of freedmen automatically became a moral issue and the focus for more generalised concerns about the health of society. It therefore comes as no surprise that Augustus included freedmen in his programme of national renewal. However, since these concerns about manumission in principle were timeless and irresolvable, they would resurface at regular intervals during the Imperial period. Most prominently, the thorny question of re-enslavement of *liberti ingrati* would recur, e.g. Tac. *Ann.* 13.26–7. Emperors long shied away from that radical option, and preferred other sanctions, including domestic chastisement. Commodus made it possible for a freedman to lose his liberty if he attacked his patron, but not until Constantine was the taboo fully broken and manumission revoked if the freedman showed himself ungrateful.[25]

What was the lasting impact of the Augustan reforms? The most important outcome was undoubtedly the creation of a new legal category: the *Latini Iuniani*. We cannot tell precisely how common they were: no particular markers allow us to identify them in, for example, the epigraphic record, where they feature with normal *tria nomina* despite their lack of citizenship. There are good reasons to assume they were numerous, however, not least the relatively frequent manumission of younger slaves as indicated by epitaphs.[26] A range of factors would have helped in boosting their numbers. The new age restrictions represented the most serious limitation on the enfranchisement of former slaves, and since child-rearing would not always have been feasible, many Junian Latins would have been permanently stuck in that position. Moreover, until 75 AD that option was available only for those freed below the age of thirty. *Iteratio* may have been a possibility, but that

[25] D.25.3.6.1, cf. Watson 1987, 17–18; CTh.4.10.1 = C.6.7.2 (a. 326), cf. Harper 2011, ch. 12.

[26] See e.g. Mouritsen 2013 on aristocratic *columbaria*.

procedure evidently required the patron's consent, which may not have been forthcoming. Many patrons probably preferred their *liberti* to have Latin status, which ensured their full entitlement to the freedman's estate. But perhaps as importantly there would often have been insurmountable practical obstacles to formal manumission, whose associated rituals and procedures were all rooted in the small and intimate world of early Rome. As her territory expanded it would somewhat paradoxically have become more and more difficult to carry out formal manumission; only in the core regions of Italy, in Latium and Campania, would it still have been relatively easy to track down a Roman magistrate to preside over the procedure.[27] This combination of economic and logistical factors makes it likely that at any given time a very substantial proportion of Roman freedmen, perhaps even the majority, held Latin rather than citizen status. The new status of *Latinus Iunianus* therefore remains the central legacy of the Augustan manumission reforms; and it was to last over five centuries, until Justinian finally abolished it in 531 AD.[28] Incidentally, that also meant that it is conspicuously absent from the Digest, leaving the work of the second-century AD jurist Gaius as our primary, indeed almost sole, source on the legal details of this status.

31.4 The Digest and the Practice of Manumission under the Empire

Although the following centuries saw no major changes to Roman manumission, the legal framework was continuously being refined through the steady accumulation of Imperial edicts and rescripts and above all the writings of the *iuris prudentes*, much of which was later incorporated into Justinian's Digest. This vast body of legal texts provides a hugely detailed record of Roman manumission, offering invaluable insights into the practice as well as the wider social concerns it gave rise to. But despite the richness of the material, or perhaps rather because of it, we are sometimes forced to consider the relationship between the regal record and the lived reality. For while it would seem plausible to assume that the *iuris prudentes* generally concentrated on issues likely to cause legal disputes, it is not always evident that the amount of attention devoted to certain topics necessarily reflected the scale of the problem itself. From a legal perspective the place of former slaves in free society presented a host of complex issues for jurists to explore, often through quite hypothetical examples, but we may suspect that many of these potential conflicts in reality were resolved informally through negotiation and the application of social pressure.

The Digest covers a wide range of technical problems relating to freedmen and, as one would expect, among the issues that seem to have generated most dispute was testamentary manumission, which often hinged on the interpretation of single words and clauses in wills. A particular form of testamentary manumission was by *fideicommissum*, by which the heir was instructed to free a slave when certain conditions had been fulfilled, in effect creating a form of suspended freedom, D.40.5. The freedman could be required to perform specific tasks for the heir, serve him for a stipulated period or pay a certain amount of

[27] Plin. *Ep.* 7.16.4, 7.32.1 illustrate the problems involved in performing formal manumission.

[28] See Corcoran 2011.

money. The scope for disputes was ample, especially if the slave became a so-called *statuliber* and occupied an ambiguous position between slavery and freedom during the period he was working to fulfil the conditions.[29] Perhaps surprisingly, Roman lawyers applied the principle of *favor libertatis* in cases where the status of the slave was in doubt.[30] That, however, should not be taken as indicative of a central policy to promote manumission; in general it was of no concern to the Roman authorities whether a slave owner chose to manumit or not, and the rule was invoked only when the intentions of the master were unclear and open to interpretation.

Judging from the legal sources Roman wills often included special provisions for freedmen, which provides an important clue to the workings of manumission. Annuities and other means of securing the future of the household after the patron's death appear to have been both common and uncontroversial, as suggested by the fact that freedmen often feature in case studies where the status of the beneficiary is irrelevant.[31] Testamentary provisions served as reward for continued service and hard work after freedom had been granted, which reminds us that in Rome manumission normally did not mark the end of a process of promotion but was part of a complex system of incentives—albeit, of course, a very important one—that covered the whole life span of the slave/freedman, and at different stages included improved work conditions, the right to a family, training and education, *peculium, vicarii*, investments and finally legacies and inheritances. The freedman counted as member of the patron's extended *familia* and was as such naturally included among those benefiting from his duty of care. The prospect of continued patronage and material security would have been a powerful spur for freedmen to conform and submit to the authority of their patron. Roman lawyers even envisaged an element of reciprocity to this pseudo-familial relationship, requiring the freedman to provide assistance should his former master fall on hard times.

While this vision of continuity and familial integration of freedmen finds wide support in the legal sources, other parts of the Digest might suggest a far more detached, even independent role of former slaves in relation to their patrons. Most obviously the existence of payment for freedom would seem to question the picture just outlined, adding as it does a transactional element, which would have qualified the fundamental debt and obligation that formed the basis for the Roman "construction" of manumission. The question is, however, how widespread this practice really was. Given its presumed frequency, references to payment are surprisingly rare in the Digest. It could of course be argued that since the slave had no legal personality, any disputes about payment for freedom would never reach the courts and therefore not feature in the legal literature. Still, the absence of the manumission contracts, which are so common in the Greek and Hellenistic world, is notable. The legally enforceable *paramonē* agreements which continued to dominate in Greek-speaking parts of the Empire seem to have no equivalent in Roman law.[32] The notion of common "self-purchase" therefore tends to be inferred from the Roman institution of *peculium*, the set-aside which slaves (and dependants *in potestate*) could keep with their masters' (or *pater familias*') permission. However, the existence of these funds does not in itself indicate that they were used as payment for freedom. Certainly, there is no

[29] D.40.7: "*De statuliberis*"; Buckland 1908, 286–291. [30] Ankum 2005.

[31] e.g. D.32.35.2; Champlin 1991, 131–136; Frier 1993; Mouritsen 2011, 154–158.

[32] On *paramonē* see e.g. Hopkins 1978; Zelnick-Abramovitz 2005.

suggestion in the Digest that it functioned as a "savings account" which would be converted into freedom as soon as it reached the slave's market value.[33] Most tellingly, it appears that former slaves normally were allowed to keep their *peculia* after manumission.[34]

"Self-purchase" would also have raised ideological concerns, since it clashed with the treasured ideal of selection and discrimination in the manumission process, which in principle should be determined only by the personal qualities of the slave rather than his ability to pay. Furthermore, the transfer of funds in return for freedom clearly undermined the role of the patron and the moral bond that was supposed to tie the freedman to his former master. These concerns are vividly illustrated by the unique procedure associated with the *servus suis nummis emptus*, "the slave bought with his own money".[35] This peculiar method of manumission involved the purchase of the slave by a third party with the slave's "own" money, i.e. *peculium*, followed by the immediate freeing of the slave by his new owner. The rationale behind this complex procedure has been debated, but the key to understanding it probably lies in the outcome, which was a freedman who had no relationship whatsoever with his former master, familial, moral or legal. The new *libertus* was to all intents and purposes independent, owing his "pro-forma" patron only the most basic respect. The *servus suis nummis emptus* therefore marked a radical departure from the conventional ideal of the dependent freedman, and the contrived separation of the freedman from his former owner may have been an attempt to negotiate the disconcerting weakening of the patronal role which payment invariably involved. Rather than a diminished patronal authority it seems that a clean break between the parties was preferred, which further suggests that payment was considered the exception rather than the norm.

Discontinuity of service could also be organised contractually in the form of *operae*, services defined as one day's work.[36] In those cases the slave would, before his emancipation, make a formal pledge to perform a certain amount of *operae* and then repeat the promise after manumission had taken place. *Operae* feature regularly in the Digest, where jurists engage in extended discussions about what kind of *operae* could be demanded and how they should be performed. Scholars have therefore assumed that the institution was not just prone to frequent disputes but was also a common way of regulating libertine obligations. *Operae* are, however, virtually absent from non-legal sources, which makes one wonder whether the extensive coverage they receive in the Digest may be a product of a particular type of legal discourse, which naturally zoomed in on socially sensitive issues, of which the quasi-contractual nature of *operae* agreements would have been a prime example. For there can be no denying that this regulation of the patron–freedman relationship would have sat uncomfortably with the traditional ideal of a bond based purely on *pietas*, gratitude and moral debt. *Operae* in effect formalised discontinuity and a break in relations, and they therefore invited continuous legal elaboration, which particularly explored situations where the interests of patron and freedman might come into conflict with each other, e.g. as competitors engaged in the same type of business. Despite the frequency with which *operae* appear in the Digest their use may have been quite restricted. Thus a closer look at the legal case studies indicates that *operae* typically were applied

[33] See the important discussion in Andreau 2004.

[34] Cf. Mouritsen 2011, 176f, with further references.

[35] Mouritsen 2011, 172–174.

[36] The fullest treatment of this institution remains Waldstein 1986.

in very specific circumstances where the slave/freedman had a particular expertise and talent, e.g. as a doctor, artist or actor, which allowed him to earn a living independently of his patron. In those cases the owner may occasionally have allowed the slave to leave his household, while retaining the option of calling on his services should he wish so.

In tricky legal areas such as *operae* the lawyers essentially grappled with a basic problem intrinsic to the freedman's status in Roman society, being at the same time legally independent as well as morally tied. This tension raised a host of questions focusing on the kind and amount of obligations that could be imposed on the freedman without undermining his free status. Formalised services like *operae* brought these issues to the fore precisely because they represented an attempt at formalising what was fundamentally a matter of *mos* and object of informal negotiation. For as suggested above, in reality the balance of power between the parties, morally, socially and economically, would generally have ensured that such "domestic" disputes were settled without recourse to the law. In the *Hadriani Sententia* the emperor even reminds the litigants to apply their *sensus communis*, "community spirit", and resolve the matter among themselves.[37] The law dealt with those rare instances where the relationship was regulated in more formal terms, e.g. through *operae*, and it follows that a purely legal perspective is likely to distort our picture of how manumission functioned in practice. The most powerful indication that it generally worked to the patrons' advantage and satisfaction is the enduring popularity of the practice throughout the history of the Roman Empire. If that had not been the case, manumission would presumably have declined in scale and frequency. The fact that this did not happen is testament to the fact that manumission had become a vital element of a uniquely complex and highly profitable system for the exploitation of unfree labour.

Bibliography

Andreau, J. 2004. "Les esclaves 'hommes d'affaires' et la gestion des ateliers et commerces." In J. Andreau, J. France and S. Pittia, eds., *Mentalités et choix économique des Romains.* Paris. 111–126.

Ankum, H. 2005. "Der Ausdruck *favor libertatis* und das klassische römische Freilassungsrecht." In E. Herrmann-Otto, ed., *Unfreie Arbeits- und Lebensverhältnisse von der Antike bis in die Gegenwart.* Hildesheim. 82–10.

Atkinson, K. M. T. (1966). "The purpose of the manumission laws of Augustus." *The Irish Jurist* 1: 356–374.

Balestri Fumagalli, M. 1985. Lex Iunia de manumissionibus. Milan.

Bradley, K. R. 1994. *Slavery and society at Rome.* Cambridge.

Buckland, W. W. 1908. *The Roman law of slavery: the condition of the slave in private law from Augustus to Justinian.* Cambridge.

Camodeca, G. (2006). "Per una riedizione dell'archivio ercolanese di L. Venidius Ennychus II." *Cronache ercolanesi* 36: 189–211.

Champlin, E. 1991. *Final judgments: duty and emotion in Roman wills, 200 B.C.–A.D. 250.* Berkeley.

[37] *Hadr. Sent.* 8 (Corp.Gloss.Lat. III.37–34.5, cf. Flaminini/Teubner 1814–1827), cf. Mouritsen 2011, 222–223.

Corcoran, S. 2011. "'Softly and suddenly vanished away': the Junian Latins from Caracalla to the Carolingians." In K. Muschler, ed., *Römische Jurisprudenz—Dogmatik, Überlieferung, Rezeption. Festschrift für Detlef Liebs zum 75. Geburtstag*. Berlin. 129–152.

Fabre, G. 1981. Libertus. *recherches sur les rapports patron-affranchi à la fin de la République romaine.* Rome.

Frier, B. W. (1993). "Subsistence annuities and per capita income in the early Roman Empire." *Classical Philology* 88: 222–230.

Gardner, J. F. (1991). "The purpose of the *Lex Fufia Caninia*." *Classical Views* 35: 21–39.

Gardner, J. F. 1998. *Family and* Familia *in Roman law and life*. Oxford.

Gauthier, P. 1974. "'Générosité' romaine et 'avarice' greque: sur l'octroi du droit de cité," in *Mélanges W. Seston*. Paris. 207–216.

Gauthier, P. (1981). "La citoyenneté en Grèce et à Rome: participation et intégration." *Ktèma* 6: 167–179.

Harper, K. 2011. *Slavery in the late Roman world, A.D. 275–425*. Cambridge.

Hopkins, K. 1978. *Conquerors and slaves.* Cambridge.

Linke, B. 2005. "Bürger ohne Staat? Die Integration der Landbevölkerung in der römischen Republik." In J. Oebbecke, ed., *Nicht-normative Steuerung in dezentralen Systemen.* Stuttgart. 121–150.

Linke, B. 2014. "Die Väter und der Staat: die Grundlagen der aggressiven Subsidiarität in der römischen Gesellschaft." In C. Lundgreen, ed., *Staatlichkeit in Rom? Discurse und Praxis (in) der römischen Republik*. Stuttgart. 65–90.

López Barja de Quiroga, P. (1998). "Junian Latins: status and number." *Athenaeum* 86: 133–163.

Meier, C. 1997. "Der griechische und der römische Bürger: Gemeinsamkeiten und Unterschiede im Ensemble gesellschaftlicher Bedingungen." In E. G. Schmidt, ed., *Griechenland und Rom: Vergleichende Untersuchungen zu Entwicklungstendenzen und -höhepunkten der antiken Geschichte, Kunst und Literatur*. Erlangen/Jena. 41–66.

Mouritsen, H. 2011. *The freedman in the Roman world.* Cambridge.

Mouritsen, H. 2013. "Slavery and manumission in the Roman elite: a study of the columbaria of the Volusii Saturnini and the Statilii Tauri." In M. George, ed., *Roman slavery and Roman material culture*. Toronto. 43–68.

Patterson, O. 1982. *Slavery and social death: a comparative study*. Cambridge, Mass.

Perry, M. J. 2014. *Gender, manumission and the Roman freedwoman*. Cambridge.

Sherwin-White, A. N. 1973². *The Roman citizenship*. Oxford.

Sirks, A. J. B. (1981). "Informal manumission and the *lex Iunia*." *Revue internationale des droits de l'antiquité* 28: 247–276.

Sirks, A. J. B. (1983). "The *lex Iunia* and the effects of informal manumission and iteration." *Revue internationale des droits de l'antiquité* 30: 211–292.

Treggiari, S. 1969. *Roman freedmen during the late Republic*. Oxford.

Volterra, E. 1955. "Manomissione e cittadinanza," in *Studi in onore di U. E. Paoli*. Florence. 695–716.

Waldstein, W. 1986. Operae Libertorum: *Untersuchungen zur Dienstpflicht freigelassener Sklaven*. Stuttgart.

Watson, A. 1987. *Roman slave law*. Baltimore/London.

Weaver, P. R. C. (1990). "Where have all the Junian Latins gone? Nomenclature and status in the early Empire." *Chiron* 20: 275–305.

Weaver, P. R. C. 1997. "Children of Junian Latins." In B. Rawson and P. Weaver, eds., *The Roman family in Italy: status, sentiment, space*. Oxford. 55–72.

Weiler, I. 2003. *Die Beendigung des Sklavenstatus im Altertum: ein Beitrag zur vergleichenden Sozialgeschichte*. Stuttgart.

Wilinski, A. 1971. "Intorno all'*accusatio* e *revocatio in servitutem* del liberto ingrato," in *Studi in onore di Edoardo Volterra*. Milan. Vol. 2: 559–569.

Zelnick-Abramovitz, R. 2005. *Not wholly free: the concept of manumission and the status of manumitted slaves in the ancient Greek world.* Leiden.

Gender

CHAPTER 32

WOMEN AND PATRIARCHY IN ROMAN LAW

EVA CANTARELLA

32.1 Introduction

During the long centuries between the date of the mythical founding of Rome (753 BC) and the first decades of the sixth century AD, when Justinian's *Corpus Iuris Civilis* was enacted, the legal condition of women underwent substantial transformation.[1] In order to understand this process, it is necessary to recall that during the first centuries of its history Rome was a quintessentially patriarchal society (Inst.Gai.1.55: *Fere nulli alii sunt homines qui talem in filios suos potestatem habent qualem nos habemus*), where only *patres familias* (i.e. male citizens who were the head of a family) enjoyed full civil and political rights. The other members of the family enjoyed only certain rights, and some did not enjoy any at all. The Roman *familia* was very different from the one we define as a family today.[2] According to the jurist Ulpian (third century AD) (D.50.16.195.1–2) *familia* was a group of persons subjected to the authority of the head of the family *natura aut iure*, that is both by virtue of "nature" (*natura*) and "law" (*iure*). The persons subjected to the *pater familias* "by nature" were his children (male and female) and the descendants of male children; the persons subjected "by law" were his wife, the wives of his male descendants, and his slaves. The power of the *pater familias*, originally supposedly called *mancipium*, in historical times came to be called *patria potestas* over children, *manus* over wives and *dominica potestas* over slaves. According to this description of the family, Roman law defined as *sui iuris* ("of his own right"), only the *pater familias*. All the others (descendants and wives *in manu*: see later) were considered *alieni iuris* ("of another person's right"). Over the centuries paternal authority underwent important changes, which in different ways limited it. Both the status of slaves and of free persons (daughters or wives) changed. Rome had grown from a small village of peasants and shepherds to a metropolis that ruled the world.

[1] Cf. Pomeroy 1975; Gardner 1986; Cantarella 1993; Thomas 1997, 103–176; Cantarella 2006.

[2] Cf. Dixon, ch. 35. A useful and brief survey of the scholarship in English is in Garnsey and Saller 2014, 170–171. On the need of integration with European scholarship see McClintock 2009; Capogrossi Colognesi 2010 and Cantarella 2014.

Political, social and economic conditions (not to say mentalities and religious beliefs and practices) changed the way of thinking of the Romans, their way of life and their attitude and behaviour towards women. For these reasons, we will divide the following exposition into two periods: the Monarchy and the Republic; the Principate and the Empire.

32.2 The Monarchy and the Republic

Any discussion of this topic must start with slave women. Considered by the law not as persons but as property of their owner (exactly as male slaves) they were bound to work in the house and for the family, grinding grain and cultivating the fields. Their duties also included being sexually available to the male members of the family. They did not have the possibility to form sentimental relations and to build a family of their own. If a female slave formed a relationship with a man (a slave, as well), this relationship (called *contubernium*) could be interrupted by the master, who could sell one or both of them to different buyers. The children born from a *contubernium* belonged, as slaves, to the owner of the slave woman. The best indication of female slaves' legal condition is a question that divided the jurists: is the child of a female slave to be considered *fructus* (fruit)? Roman law provided that the term "*fructus*" not only meant natural fruits but all the autonomous products of a thing or animals, such as wood, wool, milk and so on. As a rule, they belonged to the owner of the "mother-thing". But if the thing had been given in usufruct, they belonged to the holder of the usufruct. Let us return to the female slave, who, as an object, could be given in usufruct: what if she gave birth to a child during this period? According to the law the child belonged to the holder of the usufruct, but children of a slave were "fruits" too valuable to the owner of the "mother-thing" to be lost. For this reason, in the interest of the owners of slaves, in the second century BC the jurist Brutus decided that the children of a slave were not to be classified legally as fruit (D.7.1.68pr). But his opinion was so controversial that the debate was still mentioned by the jurist Gaius (Inst.Gai.2.50; D.22.1.28) in the second century AD.[3]

What about women who were free? Even if their position could not be compared to that of female slaves, their subjection to the *pater familias* was extensive. At birth, if accepted by the *pater familias* within the family, they fell under his *patria potestas*. If the father did not accept the newborn he could expose it to the elements. The ceremony of acceptance depended on the sex of the baby: the male new born was deposited at the feet of the *pater*, who, in case and as sign of acceptance raised it in his arms, in a solemn gesture called *tollere* or *suscipere liberos* (to raise children). If it was a female the rite was reduced to the order to feed the baby (*alere iubere*). The symbolic value of the different forms of acceptance reserved to female and to male deserves reflection.

Patria potestas also included the right of killing (*ius vitae ac necis*: Dion. Hal. *Ant. Rom.* 2.26–27).[4] A woman whose sexual behaviour had been deemed reproachable could be put

[3] Cantarella 1993.

[4] The extent of the powers of the *pater familias* still gives rise to great discussion. See Saller 1987, 22–34; Saller 1994. More recently see the history of scholarship sketched by Capogrossi Colognesi 2010, 147–174.

to death. Fathers who did not exercise this right could oblige the daughter to abort her child; or, they could expose it at birth should they choose to do so. They had the right to decide when and to whom the daughter had to be given in marriage. Usually a Roman woman was betrothed when she was between eight and ten years old in a solemn ceremony called *sponsalia*. On that occasion she was given a ring to put on the fourth finger of her left hand, from where the Romans believed a nerve originated that stretched to the heart. From that moment she was a *sponsa* and was bound to fidelity to her future husband. Marriage was celebrated when she reached majority, at 12, and upon celebration she left her original family and joined the family of her husband.

The most ancient nuptial rite was *confarreatio*, a solemn religious ceremony which took its name from a *panis farreus*, a loaf of spelt (*farrus*) that the bride and the groom had to share as a symbol of the beginning of their common life. It consisted of a solemn sacrifice to Jupiter before the *Pontifex Maximus*, the *Flamen Dialis* (one of the most important priests) and ten witnesses. It was reserved for patricians, and according to Gaius (Inst.Gai.1.112) in the second century AD was still in use for the marriage of the *Flamen Dialis*. Much more widespread was *coemptio* (perhaps in origin reserved for plebeians), an application of the old form of sale and purchase (called *mancipatio*), in the course of which the object was sold to the buyer in the presence of a *libripens*; that is to say, a person who held a scale on which the buyer had placed the price of the object. Even if in the case of *coemptio* the price of the bride was symbolic, it is highly likely that originally the wife was bought in reality, as suggested also by the fact that in the second century AD Gaius (Inst.Gai.1.113) writes that during *coemptio* the husband "buys the woman" (*emit mulierem*). A further element to support this hypothesis consists of a unique institution called *usus*. In Roman law ownership could be acquired by *usucapio*, i.e. the use of an object for a certain period of time, indicated by the XII Tables as one year for movable goods and two years for immovable ones (XII Tab. 6.3 [*FIRA*], *apud* Cic. *Top.* 4.23). *Usus* was *usucapio* of a woman in cases where *coemptio* had not been celebrated or had been technically unsuccessful (e.g. for an error in the ritual words that had to be pronounced). As a consequence of *usus* the wife, after one year of cohabitation (the same term employed for movable goods) joined the family of the husband, who acquired *manus* over her (see later), and by virtue of this power obtained the right to put her to death for adultery and for drinking wine (Dion. Hal. *Ant. Rom.* 2.25.6). Finally we must recall that upon marriage women were given a dowry, i.e. a certain amount of goods (ownership of which belonged to the husband) that compensated them for the loss of inheritance within the group of origin, and represented a contribution to their life in the new one.

The disciplinary power of the husband over the wife included the power to put her to death in case of adultery (Dion. Hal. *Ant. Rom.* 2.25.6). Some centuries later, Cato commented on this law: "if you [i.e. the husband] catch your wife in adultery, you can kill her; if she catches you, she cannot even touch you with a finger" (Gell. *NA* 10.23.5). According to the same law, the husband could kill the wife also when she had been caught drinking wine (prohibited to women in the first centuries of the city). A further law, supposedly enacted by Romulus, stated that a marriage could be interrupted (apart from the case of death of one of the spouses) only by the husband (Plut. *Rom.* 22). The husband could repudiate his wife without paying any penalties in three cases: if she had committed adultery, if she had taken the keys of the cellar (where wine was kept) and if she had aborted her child without his consent (Plut. *Rom.* 22.3). If none of these reasons existed he had to pay a pecuniary penalty.

In 450 BC the XII Tables confirmed these rules. Perhaps following that code, perhaps later, in case of divorce the husband pronounced the famous order directed to his wife: "take back your things" (*tuas res tibi habeto*), "res" here meaning the wife's personal belongings such as dresses and jewels (Plaut. *Amph.* 3.2.47, *Trin.* 2.1.49; Cic. *Phil.* 2.69). Originally, these words were only a social custom and did not have legal effect. Of course, if the husband was still subject to *patria potestas*, the power to interrupt the marriage belonged to his *pater familias*.

Women's economic rights, in the first century of Rome, were in some way contradictory: they were able to possess a patrimony, but they were in part excluded from the possibility to acquire it, and even when they could acquire it they could not freely dispose of it (XII Tab. 5.2 [*FIRA*], *apud* Inst.Gai.2.47).

The most ancient form of testament (*testamentum calatis comitiis*) was celebrated before the *comitia curiata*, where women were not allowed. Thus, originally women could not make a will nor could they be nominated as heirs. During the third and second centuries BC, however, a new form of testament was introduced that eventually replaced the old one. It was called *testamentum per aes et libram* and was available to women (both as testators and as heirs).[5] Since the time of XII Tables, in the absence of testamentary dispositions (which in Roman law took precedence on intestate succession), the order of successors was the following. The first line of heirs were the *sui* (sons and descendants in the male line who, at the death of the *pater familias*, became *sui iuris*). In the absence of *sui* the patrimony passed to the *adgnati proximi*, the nearest collateral relatives in the male line (XII Tab. 5.4 [*FIRA*]). Women were included both in the category of *sui* and of *adgnati*: they formed part of the category of *sui* as daughters, as daughters of a deceased son of the *de cuius*, and as wives *in manu* (given the fact that according to the law wives *in manu* were *loco filiae*; that is to say, "as daughters" of their husband); they were also included in the category of *adgnatae* in relation to their paternal uncle, if their father had died.

As far as intestate succession was concerned, therefore, women enjoyed inheritance rights as men. Given the extent of the discrimination that they suffered in other fields of the law, scholars have discussed the possible origin of this rule at length. In light of the composition of the original Roman population, was it, perhaps, an influence of the Sabine civilisation? Or was it due to the influence of the Etruscan period of domination? Etruscan influence is usually considered the most probable explanation, but even if so, it was altered by the Roman idea that women had to be subject to male power. To achieve this aim, the Romans set a rule that in fact, for some centuries, nullified women's legal capacity in this field. This rule imposed the guardianship of a *tutor* (guardian) on women *sui iuris* (who did not have a male having *patria potestas* or *manus* over them) (XII Tab. 5.1 [*FIRA*], *apud* Inst.Gai.1.144–145; Inst.Gai.1.190).

Guardians were persons (usually the nearest relative in the male line) in charge of *sui iuris* individuals who had the capacity to be holders of rights (legal capacity), but not the capacity to exercise them (capacity to act), because they were considered incapable of understanding and of free will. According to the XII Tables these persons were: 1) women for

[5] Peppe 1984, 55–62.

their entire lives; 2) men up to fourteen years old (when, upon reaching puberty, they were considered "capable"). According to the XII Tables, at the basis of this was the belief that women "because of the frivolity of their spirit" (*propter levitatem animi*: according to one reconstruction of XII Tab. 5.1 [*FIRA*]) were never capable of taking care of themselves. As a consequence they could not dispose of their patrimony, neither *inter vivos* nor *mortis causa*, without the authorisation of a person (the guardian), usually a relative who at their death would be their heir. Soon enough, however, women found legal ways to circumvent the guardianship of a tutor (see section 32.3).

How did women react to their status? During the first centuries of the Republic a series of events showed a certain tension in the relation between sexes. In 331 BC a number of important persons died mysteriously and many *matronae* were tried for poisoning: *venena* (poisons) had been found in the houses of some of them. The women pleaded not guilty: they claimed that the *venena* were *venena bona* (medicaments), and when challenged to drink the liquids they accepted, but died as a result. The trial ended with 160 women condemned (Val. Max. 2.5.3; Liv. 8.18). In 215 BC, in a politically and economically difficult moment, a *lex Oppia*[6] (Val. Max. 9.1.3; Liv. 34.1.3; Tac. *Ann.* 3.33–34; Gell. *NA* 10.23 and 17.6; Oros. 4.20.14; Zonar. 9.17.1) forbade women from wearing excessively coloured clothing and an excessive quantity of jewels (Liv. 34.1.3). Women's discontent was such that twenty years later, in 195, a great number of them invaded the streets, calling for the cancellation of the law. For Cato, such behaviour was beyond belief and so dangerous as to be unacceptable: we cannot surrender to women's will, he said, "as soon as they will start to be equal to us, they will be [our] superiors" (Liv. 34.3.2). But the two magistrates in charge of the question defended the women's position and the law was cancelled. In the same years, however, a further unjust law for women was passed. In 169 BC, the *lex Voconia* (Cic. *Rep.* 3.17; Inst.Gai.2.226 and 2.274) established that women could not be instituted as heirs of citizens who had a patrimony larger than 100,000 asses and that a legacy to them could not exceed half of the estate.[7] This meant, combining the two provisions, that women could receive at most half of the inheritance of a citizen of the first class. Needless to say, Cato was in favour of the law. In his opinion women, when rich, became independent and arrogant (Gell. *NA* 17.6). Finally, some ten years later a further disquieting episode happened. Between 184 and 180 a strange epidemic caused many deaths, and a great number of women were accused and sentenced to death (Liv. 40.37.4–5).

However one interprets these disturbing episodes, they indicate the definite existence of a tension between genders. What were the reasons for this situation? Let us consider women's social role. Given their indispensability in order to reproduce families and citizens, women who accepted that role, behaving as perfect wives and mothers, were accorded great formal respect and social esteem. Some were celebrated as examples of behaviour. The legendary case of Lucretia, wife of Collatinus, raped by Sextus, son of Tarquinius Superbus, last king of Rome (Cic. *Fin.* 2.20.66; Val. Max. 6.1.1; Liv. 1.58.5–1.59.3; Ov. *Fast.* 2.685–856; Dion. Hal. *Ant. Rom.* 4.66–77; August. *De civ. D.* 1.19) is a case in point. Though innocent, Lucretia decided to commit suicide, asking her father and her husband to avenge her. Their attempt to convince her to abandon her purpose was useless: she had to die, she

[6] Desideri 1984, 63–73.

[7] For a new reading of *lex Voconia* see McClintock 2013, 183–200ff.

said, in order to prevent other women from enduring a similar fate. Such was the intolerability of the offence to a woman who symbolised all the feminine virtues, according to legend, that the people rose against the foreign kings and Rome became a Republic.

Many *exempla* that celebrated women of that kind can be found. *Exempla* were stories repeated as instruction to Roman citizens, which played an important role as a means to persuade and induce them to respect Roman virtues. But if a person did not behave according to the *exempla*, a strong social penalty in the form of shame befell this person. If a woman was less perfect than Lucretia or any other women of that kind, if her behaviour engendered suspicion, social blame was as strong and effective as the celebration of the perfect *matronae*, as demonstrated by the famous case of Clodia, the woman deeply loved and celebrated under the name of Lesbia by Catullus.[8] Clodia lived in the first century BC when the condition of women had changed profoundly (as we will see) and women, or at least some of them, had emancipated themselves. She was a young and beautiful woman who refused to play the role of desperate widow dictated by tradition. She had a passionate love affair with Catullus, younger than her (a quite unusual thing at the time), and left him for Caelius (even younger than Catullus). According to Cicero, who defended Caelius in a trial that pitted the two ex-lovers against one another (Cic. *Cael.* 3–31; Plut. *Cic.* 29), she had to be considered as a prostitute of the lowest level.

32.3 From Augustus to Justinian

In the age of Augustus, women's lives were incomparably different from that of the first centuries. Modern scholarship has therefore described it as their "emancipation".[9] As is well known, many *caveats* are necessary when applying a modern term to an ancient situation. Nonetheless, in this case the level of personal and economic freedom achieved by the female part of the population really seems to justify the use of the word.

In order to understand the circumstances that allowed such a legal and cultural evolution it is necessary to start by examining the new legal rules. Originally the only kinship recognised by law was kinship in the male line (*adgnatio*). The law did not even recognise the relation between mother and her children. At the end of the Republic these principles began to change, and women started to be considered capable of obtaining custody of their children if the magistrate in charge of it (the *praetor*) acknowledged the shameful conduct of the father. At the time of Ulpian (third century AD) it was stated that children had to respect their father and their mother equally (D.37.15.1). Under Hadrian, the *senatus consultum Tertullianum* established that a mother of three children was granted the *ius trium liberorum*; that is to say; she was exempt from guardianship and could inherit from her offspring, albeit after the children's children, their father and certain *adgnati* (D.38.17). In 178 AD a *senatus consultum Orfitianum* established that children could inherit from their mother ahead of her brother and other *adgnati* (D.38.17; Inst.3.4; C.6.56–57). Finally, under Justinian a mother could inherit from her children even without the *ius liberorum* (C.3.3 and 4).

[8] Cantarella 2006, 113–126.

[9] Vigneron and Gerkens 2000, 107–121.

The institution that underwent the biggest transformation was marriage. Over time, the transfer of the wife to the husband's family was considered with increasing disfavour. Marriage started to be viewed as a relationship between two persons who decided to live together in order to produce a family. Ancient marriage ceremonies ceased to be considered necessary for the existence of the conjugal bond.[10] A union started to be considered a marriage whenever two persons (both of them having *conubium*, i.e. legal capacity to marry, based on citizenship and age) began to cohabit with *affectio maritalis*, i.e. the will to be husband and wife.[11] Ceremonies that accompanied the beginning of their conjugal life were still celebrated but they were only social indicators of the existence of *affectio maritalis*. Just as the beginning, the end of marriage also did not require legal acts. *Affectio maritalis* had to persist during the marriage, and the conjugal bond ended when this affection failed in one or in both the spouses and the couple ceased to live together (*Nuptiae sunt coniunctio maris et feminae et consortium omnis vitae, divini et humani iuris communicatio*: D.23.2.1). A truly revolutionary change occurred in the nature and rules concerning marriage and divorce. Both these institutions had become so simple and so free that it is not easy to find a comparable conception in Western history. A notable fact, finally, is that divorce had become available also to women.

Important changes occurred also in the economic regulation between the families of the spouses. When the new marriage (called by modern scholars *sine manu*) replaced the old one (usually defined *cum manu*) the dowry continued to be seen as a contribution by the wife to support the expenses of conjugal life (D.23.3.56.1). In Augustan times, however, new provisions began to limit the right of the husband to dispose of it. In 18 AD a *lex Iulia de fundo dotali* forbade the husband from selling dotal lands located in Italic territory, in post-classical times the prohibition was extended to all the immovable goods, and Justinian decided that the consent of the wife to alienation of such goods was ineffective. At the same time, a legal rule was introduced that, in case of the dissolution of the marriage, the dowry had to return to the wife. Where the former husband refused, the wife could use a legal action called the *actio rei uxoriae* (Inst.Gai.4.62; Tit.Ulp.6.6 and 7; Lenel 2010, 302–310). The husband, however, was allowed to withhold part of it on account of the "immorality" of the wife.

Another institution that underwent important transformations was guardianship. The first rule aimed at improving the position of women was to give them the possibility to change the legitimate *tutor* (as we know, a relative), and to replace him with a person of their choice, whom they trusted. Originally this involved a *coemptio fiduciae causa*, a very complicated and presumably very rare legal act, but under the Principate women were allowed to address the magistrate against the tutors who had denied them authorisation to act, and during the Empire the rules became more and more favourable. A provision included in an Augustan law (*lex Iulia and Papia Poppea*) stated that freeborn women (*ingenuae*) with three children and freedwomen (*libertae*) with four were freed from guardianship (Inst.Gai.1.194). Under Claudius, *ingenuae* were freed from legitimate guardianship. Finally even the ancient rule prohibiting women from acting as guardians was abolished. In 224 AD Alexander Severus reconfirmed it (CTh.5.35.1), but in 390 widows were allowed to

[10] Cantarella 1993, 116–121; Capogrossi Colognesi 2005, 63–81.

[11] Astolfi 2014; Fiori 2011, 197–253.

be guardian of their children and grandchildren, albeit only upon promise that they would never remarry (CTh.5.35.2). And in 530 Justinian extended, to natural mothers, the right to be guardians.

In addition to the above-mentioned civil-law rules, the *praetor*, from the third century BC, had intervened using his jurisdiction and his decisions to create a new system of succession (called *bonorum possessio*) which allowed women to receive *mortis causa* from their original *pater familias* also if married *cum manu*, and to receive from their husband even if they had not entered into his family. It could happen, and it happened, then, that women received money from two families. Furthermore, the *praetor* extended the right to participate in the succession also to the *adgnati*, as we know the relatives in the female line.

These main legal innovations were inevitably tied to the change of the way of life of the Romans, the forms of government, the contact with other countries and, above all, of the territorial expansion of the city. By conquering more and more territories and countries Rome had become the centre of an Empire. It would be an error to underestimate the effect of Roman Imperialism on gender relationships. Not only had the economy changed, but as a consequence mentalities had also changed, and with them the relations between genders. The last two centuries of the Republic had been centuries of wars, among which was the devastating second Punic War. The male population had been decimated, many women had lost their father and their husbands, they had become *sui iuris*. Guardianship existed only formally: guardians did not have the possibility to control their wards, they had their own problems. Even women who still had a father or a husband were in fact free: bound to participate in a long military campaign, men had to stay abroad for long periods. The only persons that they could (and were obliged to) trust were their wives or daughters, who had to take care of their affairs and their patrimony. In addition, men often died in war and their heirs were often women (or orphans). Women had become economically independent, and this helped them to acquire a new psychological and social consciousness of their capabilities and their right to be free from the necessity to obey men's will. The archaeological evidence from Pompeii demonstrates the involvement of women in everyday professions and shows the extent to which the free behaviour of the upper classes also rubbed off on the lower ones. The legal contracts in which women appear as shrewd businesswomen (for example, *TPSulp* 60)[12] or the graffiti with female appreciation of gladiators are but a few examples.

The relation between genders became complicated. Roman men found it difficult to accept the new reality. For centuries they had been convinced that the unity of the family and the respect of its values was the basis of the force of the state, and they still believed it. Women had to behave as they had always done: paraphrasing Plato, Scipio (in Cic. *Rep.* 1.43) says that when women and slaves do not obey, anarchy ensues. The majority of men, including Augustus, agreed. His concern about a substantial decrease in the birth rate, and thinking that this was due to Romans' reluctance to marry, caused him to pass two laws, the *lex Iulia de maritandis ordinibus* (18 BC) and the *lex Papia Poppea nuptialis* (9 BC), which later merged into a single text (*lex Iulia et Papia*). The two laws established that men between 25 and 60 and women between 25 and 50 were obliged to marry or remarry persons of the appropriate groups. If the marriages did not produce offspring,

[12] Camodeca 1999, 152–154.

limitations on the rights of succession applied (Inst.Gai.2.286). By contrast, rewards were given to fertile couples (we have already cited the *ius liberorum*, i.e. liberation from guardianship, for especially fertile women) (Tit.Ulp.16.1 and 14).

The most interesting rules, however, were those included in the *lex Iulia de adulteriis* (D.48.5; C.9.9),[13] the object of which was to ensure that family life followed rigorous ancestral principles. Conjugal fidelity of women had always been at the centre of family organisation and ideology, and the Augustan legislation confirmed it, punishing as adultery not only the violation of the conjugal faith by a wife, but any sexual intercourse of a woman (even if unmarried) with a man who was not her husband. But in confirming the ancient principles, the law introduced a radically new principle. Until then, sexual crimes were considered a family matter, punished by husbands and fathers.[14] With Augustus they became a *crimen*; that is to say, a behaviour that had to be prosecuted in a public trial and punished (with *relegatio in insulam*, exile on an island) upon denunciation by any citizen. The ancient *ius occidendi* remained, but with some limits, providing a highly detailed list of cases to establish the circumstances under which it could be exercised. The husband no longer had the right to kill the adulterous wife, but was bound to repudiate her. If he did not, he could be accused of pandering. He retained the right to kill the accomplice caught *in flagrante delicto* in his house or if he was a slave or an "infamous" person such as a gladiator, a dancer or even a freedman.

The law was a total failure (Sen. *Helv.* 16.3; Suet. *Tib.* 35; Tac. *Ann.* 3.25.2; Iuv. 2.37, 6.115–135, 6.183–190, 6.224–240, 6.347–349). In a century, trials for adultery numbered just over twenty. Of course, that did not mean that Roman women had decided to obey the law. On the contrary, they protested against it in a most extraordinary manner. As the law excluded from punishment prostitutes and pimps, Roman *matronae* started to register themselves as prostitutes: an act of civil disobedience (the first female act of that kind registered by the sources) that clearly shows a change in women's attitude toward masculine power, in public and private. The reason why the Augustan law on adultery was not applied, then, was not tied to women's acceptance of the rules. It was due to the male opposition to the transfer into the public space of a private question: the sexual behaviour of the women of the group.

The period of "emancipation" was destined to be followed by the restoration of the old familiar and of civic values and customs. With the changing of political, economic and social conditions, the bureaucratisation of power and the militarisation of the state, the conditions that had allowed and favoured emancipation no longer existed.

The decline of the state was accelerating. In the second century AD the decrease in the birth rate had reached its peak. The Roman ruling class was decimated, and its replacement was ensured only due to the mass of new citizens, many of whom were enfranchised former slaves. The refusal of women to accept the burden of motherhood was identified as the main cause of this decline. Women's practice of interrupting voluntary pregnancies without men's consent worried the authorities. In Rome, abortion[15] was not disapproved per se. If the master of a slave or the husband or the father of a free woman decided so,

[13] Daube 1972, 373–380; Cohen 1991, 109–126; McGinn 1998, 140–247; Rizzelli 2014, 145–322.

[14] Cantarella 1996, 1296–147 [2005, 105–120].

[15] On abortion in the Greek and Roman world see Nardi 1971.

it was a normal practice: as the jurist Papinian writes, an unborn child "*homo non recte dicitur*": it cannot be correctly defined as a person (D.35.2.9.1). It was only a *spes animantis*, the hope of a living being (D.11.8.2). But the Romans could not admit that women deprived the men of the right to decide. Under Marcus Aurelius and Lucius Verus a certain Rutilius Severus asked the emperors to solve a problem: his wife who he was in the process of divorcing denied being pregnant, while he maintained that she was. The emperors decided that the wife had to be examined by three midwives and, if she was pregnant, a guardian should be appointed to ensure that she did not abort (D.25.4.1). A new legal institution was born: as a pregnant woman was called *venter*, her guardian was called a *curator ventris* (about the *missio ventris in possessionem* and its *curator* see D.37.9).[16]

Men did not trust women: since they had "emancipated" themselves, they were suspected of aborting for superficial reasons. Toward the middle of the second century, Plutarch denounces "dissolute women who use expulsive and abortives only to be impregnated anew and find pleasure" (*Mor.* 134–135), and the philosopher Favorinus, taking up an accusation already made against women by Ovid (*Am.* 2.14) and Seneca (*Helv.* 16.3), speaks of the madness of women who abort their children in order not to disfigure their bellies (Gell. *NA* 12.1.8–9). In their opinion the fall of the birth rate was women's fault, as well as the troubles created by their greed for luxury and pleasures: silk from China, perfumes from Arabia, jewels from the Eastern countries etc.

Abortion was a threat both to men's authority and to society. It had to be counteracted with special new rules. As adultery it had been a private matter for centuries, but under Septimius Severus and Caracalla (198–211 AD) this principle changed (D.48.19.39; D.48.8.8; D.47.11.4). A woman had aborted after divorce because she did not want to give an offspring to her former husband, who had become an "enemy". The emperors condemned her to be exiled. For the first time in Roman history an abortion was punished with a public penalty. The reason was not the tendency (visible in other fields) to imbue the legislation with Christian principles. The offence punished was the violation of a fundamental male right. Commenting on a rescript of Septimius Severus and Caracalla, the jurist Marcian (D.47.11.4) is explicit: it was indecent that a woman could with impunity deprive her husband of his right to a progeny.

The field where the most important interventions were necessary—through the authorities—was the family: old values and virtues had to be restored. The *lex Iulia de adulteriis*, as we have seen, established that female adultery represented a danger to society as a whole and could be punished at the request of any citizen. Subsequent legislation harshened the penalties. In 339, Constantius and Constans established that the adulteress and her accomplice had to be put to death with the terrible *poena cullei*, which until that moment had been reserved for parricide and consisted of the placing of the condemned person in a bag (*culleus*) with a dog, a monkey, a rooster and a viper and throwing them into a river (CTh.11.36.4).[17]

Antoninus Pius established that the man who had killed his adulterous wife would not be punished as a murderer, but would be punished less severely according to his social class. If he belonged to a low class he would be sentenced to forced labour for life;

[16] Thomas 1986, 211–236; Cantarella 2002, 269–282.

[17] Cantarella 1996, 264–289 [2005, 215–235].

if he belonged to a higher class he would be exiled to an island. Marcus Aurelius and Commodus confirmed this law and established less severe penalties for the husband who had killed his wife outside the conditions under which the *lex Iulia* justified the killing of the lover (D.48.5.39(38).8). Alexander Severus established that this penalty should be exile (C.9.9.4[undated]).

Finally, the situation went back to the rule in force before the *lex Iulia*; that is to say, impunity for the husband who had killed his wife (Sent.Paul.2.27.1). In 506 AD the *lex Romana Visigothorum*, aimed at the Romans who lived under the Visigoths, established that the husband should not be punished for killing either the lover or the wife. Only under Justinian were the limits of impunity again tightened: in *Novella* 117.15 he stated that the impunity covered only the killing of the lover, not of the wife, and established that the husband enjoyed impunity only if he killed his wife's steady lover and not only an occasional one.

Finally, in 556 Justinian established that a guilty wife could avoid the death penalty: she would be shut up in a convent and would be allowed to leave only if the husband forgave her within two years. If not, or if the husband died during that period, she would spend the rest of her life in the convent (Nov. 134.10). Thus female adultery was punished with a sort of life imprisonment. As at the beginning of Roman history, women's sexual fidelity was considered the fundamental and absolute duty of women.[18]

But it would be impossible to end this chapter without some reference to the profound effects of Christian ideology on the relationship between genders: according to Christ's teaching, husbands also had to be sexually faithful to their wives. According to Jesus, men and women had equal dignity in marriage: "The husband must give the wife what is due to her—wrote Paul (*Cor.* 7.3–5)—and the wife equally has to give the husband his due. The wife cannot claim her body as her own; it is her husband's. Equally, the husband cannot claim his body as his own; it is his wife's." The new rule reflected the idea that, as the same Paul writes in *Gal.* 3.28, there should be "neither Jew nor Greek, nor slave nor free man, nor woman nor man". Genders were equal; an idea that contributed to teach men to respect women and to give women more consciousness. It is true is that, albeit in principle equal, women had to be subordinate to men: after describing marriage as an equal partnership, Paul writes: "Women's heads are men … Men are the image of God and the mirror of his glory, whereas women reflect the glory of men" (*Cor.* 11.3, 11.7).

Certainly, Christianity as a whole helped overcome the negative image that women had carried for centuries: despite their gender identity they were baptised equally with men. They were persons. But it did not help to cancel discrimination and subordination inscribed in the laws concerning marriage and divorce. According to Christ's teaching, marriage could not be dissolved.[19] The Christian emperors tried to impose this principle, totally opposite to the Roman ideology and tradition, dividing divorces in three types: 1) *Ex iusta causa*, "a just cause", behaviour claimed by one of the spouses, corresponding to a fault of the other. These behaviours were different according the sex of the spouse. Husbands' faults included, for example, attempting to prostitute their wives, or keeping notoriously a concubine. Wives' faults were, instead (of course besides adultery), having attended a banquet or

[18] On the further history of adultery as a crime of honour see Cantarella 1991, 229–244.

[19] Evans Grubbs 1995, 65–73.

the baths without their husband's consent. The only fault common to husbands and wives was in to trying to kill the spouse. 2) *Sine ulla causa* were divorces initiated by one or both the spouses outside the cases that allowed divorce. 3) *Communi consensu*, finally, were divorces initiated by both parties without a "just cause". As well as the persons who had asked for a divorce *sine ulla causa*, those who had initiated the procedure *communi consensu* suffered some punishments. But the social discontent for these rules was such that the sanctions for who had initiated a *communi consensu* procedure were cancelled by Justinian's successor, Emperor Justin.

Bibliography

Astolfi, R. 2014. *Il matrimonio nel diritto romano classico*. Padua.

Camodeca, G. 1999. Tabulae Pompeianae Sulpiciorum (TPSulp.), *Edizione critica dell'archivio puteolano dei Sulpici*. Rome.

Cantarella, E. 1991. "Homicides of honor: the development of Italian adultery law over two Millennia." In D. I. Kertzer and R. P. Saller, eds., *The family in Italy*. New Haven/London. 229–244.

Cantarella, E. 1993. *Pandora's daughters: the role and status of women in Greek and Roman antiquity*. London.

Cantarella, E. 1996 [2005]. *I supplizi capitali in Grecia e a Roma*. Milan.

Cantarella, E. 2002, "Marriage and sexuality in republican Rome: a Roman conjugal love story." In M. C. Nussbaum and J. Sihvola, eds., *The sleep of reason: erotic experience and sexual ethics in ancient Greece and Rome*. Chicago/London. 269–282. [= *Diritto e società in Grecia e a Roma. Scritti Scelti*. Milan 2012. 631–646.]

Cantarella, E. 2006. *Passato prossimo. Donne romane da Tacita a Sulpicia*. Milan.

Cantarella, E. 2014. "La famiglia romana tra demografia sociale, antropologia e diritto." In F. Milazzo, ed., Ubi tu Gaius ego Gaia. *Modelli familiari, pratiche sociali e diritti delle persone nell'età de principato*. Milan. 3–21.

Capogrossi Colognesi, L. 2005. "*Matrimonium, manus* e *trinoctium*," in *Marriage: Ideal-Law-Practice. Proceedings of a conference held in memory of H. Kupiszewski*. Warsaw. 63–81. [= *Scritti scelti* II. Naples 2010. 843–863.]

Capogrossi Colognesi, L. 2010. "La famiglia romana, la sua storia e la sua storiografia." *Les Mélanges de l'École française de Rome* 122: 147–174.

Cohen, D. 1991. "The Augustan law on adultery: the social and cultural context." In D. I. Kertzer and R. P. Saller, eds., *The family in Italy*. New Haven/London. 109–126.

Daube, D. (1972). "*Lex Iulia* concerning adultery." *Irish Jurist* 7: 373–38. [= *Collected Studies* Vol. 2 (1991) 1267–1276.]

Desideri, P. (1984). "Catone e le donne. (Il dibattito liviano sull'abrogazione della *lex Oppia* e la condizione giuridica della donna romana.)" *Opus* 3: 63–73.

Evans Grubbs, J. 1995. *Law and family in late antiquity*. Oxford/New York.

Fiori, R. 2011. "La struttura del matrimonio romano," *Bullettino dell'Istituto di Diritto Romano "Vittorio Scialoja"* 105: 197–233. [= Ubi tu Gaius ego Gaia: *Modelli familiari, pratiche sociali e diritti delle persone nell'età del principato*. Milan. 323–366.]

Gardner, J. F. 1986. *Women in Roman law and society*. Bloomington.

Garnsey, P. and Saller, R. 2014. *The Roman empire: economy, society and culture*. London.

Lenel, O. 2010. *Das* Edictum Perpetuum. Amsterdam.

McGinn, T. A. J. 1998. *Prostitution, sexuality, and the law in ancient Rome*. Oxford.

McClintock, A. 2009. "Review of Michele George (ed.), The Roman family in the Empire: Rome, Italy, and beyond, Oxford 2005." *Bryn Mawr Classical Review* 38: 1–5. Available at: http://bmcr.brynmawr.edu/2009/2009-01-38.html, accessed 31 March 2016.

McClintock, A. (2013). "The *Lex Voconia* and Cornelia's jewels." *Revue internationale des droits de l'antiquité* 60: 183–200.

Nardi, E. 1971. *Procurato aborto nel mondo greco romano*. Milan.

Peppe, L. 1984. *Posizione giuridica e ruolo sociale della donna romana in età repubblicana*. Milan.

Pomeroy, S. 1975. *Goddesses, whores, wives, and slaves: women in classical Antiquity*. New York.

Rizzelli, G. 2014. "*Adulterium*. Immagini, etica, diritto," in Ubi tu Gaius ego Gaia. *Modelli familiari, pratiche sociali e diritti delle persone nell'età del principato*. Milan. 145–322.

Saller, R. P. (1987). "Men's age at marriage and its consequences in the Roman family." *Classical Philology* 82: 21–34.

Saller, R. P. 1994. *Patriarchy, property and death in the Roman family*. Cambridge.

Saller, R. P. (1999). "*Pater familias, mater familias*, and the gendered semantics of the Roman household." *Classical Philology* 94: 182–197.

Thomas, Y. (1986). "Le 'ventre': corps maternel, droit paternel." *Le genre humain* 14: 211–236.

Thomas, Y. 1997. "La divisione dei sessi nel diritto romano." In P. Schmitt Pantel, ed., *Storia delle donne. L'antichità*. Rome. 103–176.

Vigneron, R. and Gerkens, J.-F. (2000). "The emancipation of women in ancient Rome." *Revue internationale des droits de l'antiquité* 47: 107–121.

CHAPTER 33

DEFINING GENDER

MATTHEW J. PERRY

33.1 Introduction

MODERN scholars use the term "gender" to refer to the assumptions, beliefs and norms that society attributes to men and women, which are grounded in the concepts of masculinity and femininity. Often juxtaposed with the phrase "biological sex", which references the anatomical and genetic traits that characterise (and distinguish) men and women, gender is understood to be "constructed" within a culture. Gender is real, but it is not stable, since it is constantly being reinterpreted and redefined within societies. Moreover, gender as an identity does not exist in a vacuum; it intersects and combines with other categorising systems, such as race, class, legal status and age in order to produce distinct sets of norms. In other words, an aristocratic Roman citizen would have experienced, and identified himself/herself in accordance with, a different set of gender norms than a poor slave living in the same community.

The study of gender in relationship to Roman law is a relatively new field of inquiry whose emergence was not uncontested among legal scholars. Gender, as a subject of academic analysis, first developed within socio-historical scholarship in the 1960s and became firmly established only in the 1980s (Scott 1986; Zinsser 1993; Downs 2010; Bartlett 2012).[1] In addition, as Janne Pölönen has shown in chapter 2, the integration of an interdisciplinary "law and society"-style approach with more formal legal scholarship has been a protracted and debated process. Gender-based studies often embody many of the key attributes that traditional scholars, who favoured internalist legal analysis, critiqued about sociological alternatives: it focused on actors and issues that were underrepresented in the source material—and thus of minor significance—or else produced decontextualised or distorted conclusions. Nonetheless, historians and lawyers have begun to incorporate aspects of gender theory into their work, expanding the study of Roman law and society.

Scholars have emphasised gender's significance as a category of analysis because it permeates all aspects of a culture, and serves to both establish and reinforce social distinctions.

[1] The study of gender was grounded in both feminist scholarship and the socio-political women's movements taking place in early- and mid-twentieth-century Europe and North America.

In a seminal article for the field of gender history, Joan Scott explained: “gender is a constitutive element of social relationships based on perceived differences between the sexes, and gender is a primary way of signifying relationships of power” (Scott 1986, 1067). Gender shapes the way that all individuals view and experience their world. As legal authorities in ancient Rome sought to delineate the structure and hierarchy of their society, gender would factor heavily into the discussion.

This chapter will examine how law contributed to the definition and establishment of gender in the Roman world and several of the important ways that gender shaped the law. To begin, it will explore how jurists explicitly and deliberately addressed the issues of gender and biological sex (which were largely conflated in pre-modern thinking). There was a recognised difference between men and women, which resulted in different statuses under the law. Jurists needed to delineate these categories and justify their distinction. The chapter will then examine a few significant areas of law where the more subtle elements of gender are visible. Even when not deliberately defining gender to clarify law or legislating overtly gendered matters, legal sources can illuminate gendered consciousness and premises. Law-and-society scholars have ardently stressed that there was a nuanced and multifaceted relationship between the strict doctrine of the law and the evolving culture and exigencies of the community. In establishing the specific rules governing Roman society, legal authorities drew upon and reproduced prevalent and entrenched assumptions about the nature of men and women and their place in the world.

The final section, section 33.4, investigates the regulation of sexuality in Roman law. In its broadest sense, sexuality refers to sexual desire and behaviour, *and* popular interpretation of such desire and behaviour. The proper performance of sexual conduct was an important element of gender archetypes; those individuals who deviated from established norms were deemed problematic and potentially dangerous. Scholars of gender and sexuality have argued that ancient societies conceptualised “abnormal” sexual activity, such as men allowing themselves to be sexually penetrated, less as a sexual orientation in the modern sense and more as a sign of gender deviance (Halperin 1989; Williams 2010).

33.2 Law Defines Gender

Jurists distinguished the legal position of women from that of men, recognising that women possessed a limited and inferior status (D.1.5.9). Every individual had to be categorised as either male or female. In regards to intersex individuals (*hermaphroditi*), Ulpian declared that they should be classed within the sex that was most physically prevalent (D.1.5.10). Thus, the law established that male physical traits (*virilia*) were the features that rendered an individual a man (with superior male rights) (D.28.2.6.2). The key determining factor almost certainly would have been the visible presence of a penis. In one example, Paul used the capacity for sexual arousal (*sexus incalescens*)—presumably meaning penile erection—as the indicator of whether or not an intersex individual should be classified as male (D.22.5.15.1).[2] Moreover, the law deemed the gendered body to be essentially

[2] This specific example concerned the ability to witness a will, which was denied to both women and children (D.28.1.20.6; Inst.2.10.6).

static, recognising the physical characteristics at birth to be a critical factor in establishing a person's status. This meant that if the male sex organs were altered in some way (e.g. castration, injury, impotency), the individual was still considered male under the law. This is evidenced by the fact that, up until the time of Justinian, both castrated men (*castrati*) and sexually impotent men (*spadones*) could exercise the male prerogative of adoption (Gardner 1998).[3]

A related aspect of this legal differentiation between men and women was the need to distinguish between childhood and adulthood. The gender of children was, for the most part, elided in favour of their status as minors; it was only upon reaching adulthood that gender began to have significant legal meaning. Definitely by the time of Augustus (and most likely earlier), Roman law deemed girls to be adults at the age of twelve, regardless of whether or not they had reached puberty. There was a difference in opinion regarding males, as some jurists believed that boys should automatically be recognised as men at the age of fourteen, whereas others argued that the onset of puberty was the preferred marker (Treggiari 1991, 39–43; Gardner 1998; see also Vuolanto, ch. 37).

Roman law was androcentric in that it treated the case of the freeborn, adult, male citizen as the norm and default, establishing privilege and patriarchy as the ensuing order. This male subjectivity stemmed from gendered notions of production, politics and household management ultimately rooted in assumptions about natural capabilities. Men had traditionally occupied a more significant role in public and private life, which warranted (and necessitated) increased legal attention. Women, children and (to a slightly lesser extent) freedmen appeared as special entities who only warranted mention when their legal situation deviated from the "norm". Nonetheless, women still possessed a significant presence in the body of classical law, largely due to their considerable economic rights.

These distinct legal statuses not only built but also responded to assessments of the competency and capability of women, and thus their capacity for individual agency. An important contributing factor to this discussion was the perceived bodily weakness of women, which encompassed both a physical and an intellectual deficiency. Several scholars have traced the influence and efficacy of this appraisal in various aspects of Roman law and society (Beaucamp 1976; Dixon 1984; Crook 1986; Gardner 1993, 87–89; Arjava 1996, 23–256; Halbwachs 1999; see also Cantarella, ch. 32 and Halbwachs, ch. 34). Among the key legal responses to this "womanly weakness" were the mandatory financial guardianship imposed upon women over the course of their lives and the barring of women from certain professions and social roles. The latter condition effectively delineated categories of men's and women's work. For example, Hermogenian noted that a woman's sex prevented her from performing tangible civic duties (*corporalia munera*, D.50.4.3.3; cf. Feldner 2000). In another striking, and rather unique, example, Callistratus declared that women were not allowed to hold the position of banker (*officium argentarii*), since this was "men's work" (*opera virilis*, D.2.13.12, cf. Frier and McGinn 2004, 461; Benke 2011; Benke 2012a).[4]

What is perhaps most interesting is the fact that at least some jurists recognised the fallacy of these claims, and yet continued to uphold the legal restrictions. Gaius argued that

[3] Justinian's Institutes allowed *spadones* to adopt, but not *castrati* (Inst.1.11.9).

[4] Jurists also explicitly labelled serving as a tutor as men's work (D.26.1.16pr; D.26.1.18).

there was no substance to claims of feminine inability and no reason why adult women should remain in perpetual guardianship (Inst.Gai.1.190). Similarly, when explaining women's inability to serve as judges, Paul attributed this exclusion not to a lack of good sense (*iudicium*), but rather to custom (*mores*)—women simply did not perform civic duties (*civiles officii*, D.5.1.12.2). Suzanne Dixon has argued that the concept of "womanly weakness" did not actually originate in early Rome, but rather was imported in the later Republic in order to rationalise the continued existence of *tutela mulierum*. She concludes, then, the idea of female helplessness did not represent a true belief in the intellectual deficiency of women, but rather an attempt to exclude women from traditional masculine spheres (1984).

The androcentric foundation of Roman law was also reflected in and reinforced by the Latin language, where masculine nouns could indicate both a male and female object, and the masculine plural was used to represent mixed-gender groups. Jurists noted that, for the most part, the masculine terms applied to individuals of both sexes (e.g. Inst.Gai.1.72; D.3.5.3.1; D.50.16.152; D.50.16.195pr). Given the disparate statuses of men and women, there was often a need to clarify, which would lead to female subjectivity in legal opinions. In these cases, the feminine terms only applied to women; men were explicitly excluded (D.31.45pr). The need to make clear linguistic ambiguities extended beyond simple divisions between male and female. For example, jurists needed to explain that in certain cases the term "woman" (*mulier*) might refer to all members of the female sex (*quaecumque sexus feminini sunt*, D.34.2.25.9) rather than the more standard understanding of a sexually mature individual (*virgo viripotens*, D.50.16.13pr).

An additional complicating factor was that slaves and livestock—living entities with a clear biological sex—were valuable commodities, whose testation or transfer of ownership commonly required documentation. Jurists needed to clarify the potential ambiguity that could result from a written will. In one case, a testator bequeathed two *muli* to his heir, but only left behind two *mulae*. Servius replied that "the legacy was owed, since *mulae* are included under the term *muli*, in the same way that *servae* are largely included under the term *servi*. This comes from the fact that the masculine gender always includes the feminine." (D.32.62).

While this opinion reveals the potential for masculine-normative titles such as "*muli*" or "*servi*" to obscure a person's or animal's gender, it also indicates that jurists understood there to have been important differences between men and women. Here, Servius's qualification about female slaves being "largely" (*plerumque*) included under the term *servi* is significant. Whereas the title *muli* always included female mules, the title *servi* included female slaves only "most of the time". This suggests that the perceived distinction between female and male slaves was greater than that between female and male mules. On the one hand, this example speaks to the significance of reproduction to Roman beliefs about gender. The opinion implies that since mules are sterile, there is little need to distinguish males from females.

Servius's statement also infers an assumption that gender was a more important category for classifying humans than for animals. Ulpian wrote elsewhere that if a buyer purchased a female slave thinking that she was male, then the sale was automatically void. Such an error did not have to result from deceit or misinformation; the simple fact that a mistake had been made was enough to nullify the sale. In contrast, if an individual purchased a mature woman thinking that she was a virgin, the sale was not invalid unless the seller had let the buyer knowingly persist in the error (D.18.1.11.1; D.19.1.11.5). The latter example speaks to significance and depth of the perceived distinction between men and women; in this case, the law considered a female slave not simply as an inferior or defective body, but rather as wholly different entity altogether.

Even in cases where the law was supposed to apply uniformly to both men and women, language nonetheless elided female activity and reinforced a male superiority. In addition to explicitly separating men and women into different (and unequal) legal categories, it, by linguistic convention, also reinforced the notion of a male-normative and patriarchal experience. Accordingly, feminist legal theory encourages scholars to ask "the woman question"—"to identify the gender implications of rules and practices which might otherwise appear to be neutral or objective" (Bartlett 1990, 837).

33.3 Tracing Gender in Roman Law

Modern scholars have begun to study how gender norms may have shaped the law and legal practice in general, and how, in turn, these gendered laws may have impacted the lives of women and men throughout the Roman world (Gardner 1995; Herrmann-Otto 2002; Benke 2012a). Legal texts have been fruitful sources for exploring the assumptions and beliefs ingrained in Roman society. Indeed, many of the common stereotypes about men and women appear frequently: men are practical and restrained whereas women are ornamental and extravagant; husbands are the productive estate owners providing for, and safeguarding, their households, whereas women are subordinate dependants in need of guardianship and protection (Gardner 1995).

One of the most interesting arenas for tracing the interplay between gender and law are the concepts of *potestas, pater familias* and *mater familias*, which illuminate how gender assumptions both obscured and limited the legal agency of women. *Potestas* was the power that a head of household (*pater familias*) possessed over his dependants. By law, all the property and possessions of a household belonged to the *pater familias*; his descendants (and possibly his wife) could own nothing in their own right. But while the term *pater familias* may have evoked the patriarchal image of an elder male in charge of a family, its strict legal meaning was that of "estate owner" and the title could be applied equally to unmarried men, women, children—anyone who was not under the *potestas* of another (Saller 1999; Benke 2005). This became increasingly relevant during the late Republic when marriages *sine manu* grew more popular and wives were less frequently in the *potestas* of their husbands. Nonetheless, the existence of the masculine term *pater familias*, which was at the foundation of the law of property, still literally gendered ownership as male.

Gendered notions of *potestas* effectively limited the power of the female *pater familias* by denying her the same rights and opportunities as her male counterparts. Any children produced in a marriage were in the *potestas* of their father, and upon his death, became independent themselves. Therefore, even though women married *sine manu* would have become independent estate owners upon the death of their fathers, they could never have their own dependents (D. 50.16.195.5). Since a female *pater familias* could ever be the only member of her *familia*, she was excluded from the full range of legal rights held by the estate owner, and thus was effectively marginalised under the law (Gardner 1995, 377).

In comparison, Roman authors and jurists used the term *mater familias*, the linguistic parallel to *pater familias*, much more informally—and imprecisely—in ancient texts. Modern scholars have demonstrated how the term enjoyed several different meanings, ranging from a wife in the *manus* of her husband, to any married woman, to any woman *sui iuris*, to any morally upright woman (Kunkel 1930; Fiori 1993–1994). During the Augustan era, legal authorities began to use the term more specifically to identify the class of women liable under the *lex Iulia de adulteriis coercendis* (McGinn 1998, 147–156; Saller 1999). Thus a Roman woman might have been concurrently both a *mater familias*, by virtue of being respectable, and a *pater familias*, by virtue of being legally independent. Nonetheless, the seeming parallelism of the two terms essentially reinforced the common gender stereotype of a male head of house and his wife, despite not always being accurate.

Another fruitful arena for exploring gender norms is the law of *iniuria*, which considered harm inflicted upon a free individual, including damage to one's personal rights or reputation (what might be described as "insult"). Specific examples of *iniuria* mentioned by Gaius include striking the victim with a fist, stick or whip, verbally berating him/her, falsely depicting him/her as a debtor or writing defamatory words (Inst.Gai.3.220). Since the level of injury or insult was derived from the context of the interaction and the status of the recipient, similar acts did not always yield the same outcomes, nor were all injurious actions of equal consequence. Accordingly, Andrew Riggsby noted that "*iniuria* reflects a wider variety of cultural values" and "makes explicit" kinds of social hierarchy (Riggsby 2010, 194). It is significant that the standard injuries to women mentioned in Roman law were infringements on their sexual integrity and repute. In contrast, the standard insults to men focused on physical blows and forcible entry into another's *domus* (Gardner 1995; Saller 1999, 196). Jurists recognised that individuals might suffer *iniuria* indirectly through actions directed against others. However, while men were frequently discussed as having suffered because of their female relatives, there is no mention of the reverse.

Juristic consideration of the corruption of slaves (*corruptio servi*) similarly illuminates how gendered assumptions and expectations even permeated the line between slave and free. The Praetor's Edict broadly defined "corruption" as persuading a slave to do something with the intention of "making him or her worse" (*facere deteriorem*), which Ulpian interpreted to mean compelling a slave to do or to consider something immoral or improper (D.11.3.1). In a lengthy excerpt on the applicability of multiple charges, Ulpian provided six examples of incidents where offenders could be prosecuted for a combination of the theft, injury or corruption of a slave (D.47.1.2). In each case, he referred to the masculine *servus*, except in the one example involving theft and sexual corruption, where an *ancilla* was the subject (D.47.1.2.5). Even if this exception was grounded in reality—Ulpian was referencing six actual cases, and just one happened to involve a female slave—this single exception among a body of similar examples highlights the gendered dimensions of Roman law.

Perhaps the most interesting example highlighting the complexities of gender in Roman law is the case of the "cross-dressing" senator. A key point of debate regarding the execution of wills was the extent to which considerations of a testator's intent might challenge or redefine the literal wording of the document. According to Pomponius,

Quintus Mucius Scaevola had once addressed this issue by referencing the existence of a senator who was accustomed to wearing women's dining clothes (*scire se quendam senatorem muliebribus cenatoriis uti solitum*, D.34.2.33). Scaevola hypothetically remarked that, if this man had left a legacy of "women's clothing", it would not include the aforementioned dining clothes, since the senator himself had considered them to be "men's clothing" (as evidenced by his personal use of the garments). One the one hand, this comment speaks to the gendered nature of clothing in Roman society and the social meanings imbued upon garments. Yet it is particularly notable in that it contains none of the vitriol or moral undertones associated with references to cross-dressing appearing in various didactic accounts or the political propaganda of Cicero. Scaevola seems to have been concerned only with how non-standard practices impacted the execution of Roman law, and passes over the potentially transgressive nature of the behaviour (Tuori 2009).

33.4 Legal Regulation of Sexuality

Arguably the most visible and most powerful juncture of gender and the law was the regulation of sexual conduct. According to Roman social norms, free women were supposed to avoid all forms of extra-marital sexual activity and to produce legitimate children with their husband. So long as they did not endanger the chastity of these women, men had licence to engage in extra-marital intercourse with appropriate companions, such as slaves or prostitutes. This licence extended to partners of either sex, so long as the Roman man was the penetrating (as opposed to the penetrated) partner. The standard legal term for sexual misconduct was *stuprum*, which customarily denoted the sexual penetration of any Roman citizen, male or female. Adultery (*adulterium*) was a specific form of *stuprum* that involved the sexual penetration of a married female citizen.[5] The regulation of sexual conduct was one of the few areas of Roman law where the female experience was "normative", even to the extent of obscuring male activity.

During the Republic, the standard means of redressing sexual misconduct appears to have been the family council, wherein the *pater familias* of the offender, and other senior family members, were responsible for curtailing and punishing undesirable behaviour. The seriousness of the transgression is indicated by the prevalent belief that, in certain cases, death was an appropriate punishment—as was technically the prerogative of the *pater familias*. In addition, there is also some evidence—albeit very scant—that presents sexual misconduct treated in a more public setting. Livy recorded several instances from the mid-Republic when the people of Rome supposedly investigated and settled cases of adultery by *iudicium populi*, which consisted of a series of community hearings concluded by a vote taken in the popular assembly (Liv. 8.22.2–4, 10.31.9, 25.2.9). Since this procedure

[5] After the passage of the *lex Iulia de adulteriis coercendis*, which ostensibly focused on this particular form of *stuprum*, jurists often juxtaposed the terms *adulterium* and *stuprum*, with the later denoting sex with an unmarried female citizen.

was created ostensibly to adjudicate offences against the entire Roman people, it speaks to the perceived danger posed by sexual misconduct—and the deviation from gender norms these acts represented.

Whether or not there was legislation that explicitly addressed adultery in the Republic is debatable. There are references to the "marriage laws" introduced by the Dictator Sulla in the first century BC and the "many earlier laws" that the *lex Iulia de adulteriis coercendis* (*c.*18 BC) abrogated (Plut. *Comp. Lys. et Sul.* 3.2; Coll.4.2.2, Paul). The most concrete example is the infamous, yet poorly attested, *lex Scantinia* from the Republican era. This law definitely addressed *stuprum* committed against citizen males, and almost certainly all other forms of *stuprum* as well, and clearly suggests a mounting desire to publicly regulate sexual misconduct through legal mechanisms (Fantham 1991; Ryan 1994; Williams 2010, 13–136).

Legislation passed during the reign of Augustus, which remained the basis for the regulation of sexual conduct throughout the rest of the Empire, codified the belief that sexual property was not only a part of individual and familial honour, but also the hallmark of a Roman citizen (McGinn 1998, 7–247; Milnor 2005, 14–185). A critical premise embedded in Augustus's social agenda was that sexuality was linked to the stability and safety of the Roman state (Joshel 1997; Walters 1997; Cantarella 2002, 97–210; Severy 2003; Williams 2010).[6] The *lex Iulia de maritandis ordinibus* (18 BC), together with the *lex Papia Poppaea* (9 AD), penalised individuals who did not marry and produce children by denying them the ability to claim legacies.[7] These laws essentially defined procreation as a significant, if not necessary, element of being a Roman man or woman.

The *lex Iulia de adulteriis coercendis* significantly altered the way that sexual offences was handled in Roman law and society, most notably by establishing a standing jury court (*quaestio perpetua*) to try adultery cases. In this regard, the *lex Iulia* effectively classified adultery and other forms of sexual misconduct as criminal—and hence public—offences (Cantarella 1991; Cohen 1991; McGinn 1991). Roman lawmakers expected, and even compelled, men to avoid unchaste women as potential wives and to divorce adulterous spouses. Penalties for sexual misconduct included fines, exile and execution, with the severest punishments seemingly reserved for male citizens who allowed themselves to be penetrated.[8] In this case, offenders not only failed to adhere to established gender norms, but actually inverted them, taking on what jurists (and non-legal authors) characterised as the womanly role (Gardner 1998). Women convicted under the law were required to wear a toga, thus associating them with prostitutes, and were excluded from the category of *matres familias* (McGinn 1998, 156–171).

The figure of the prostitute provides a useful example of how gender intersected with other categories/identities to produce unique sets of norms within Roman law. Prostitutes

[6] According to Tacitus, Augustus went so far as to call sexual misconduct "sacrilege and treason", even though, as the historian noted, this classification surpassed the strict letter of his laws (*Ann.* 3.24).

[7] There is some evidence that individuals who were physically unable to produce children were exempted from the penalties (Gardner 1998).

[8] Although the *lex Iulia* explicitly preserved (in an attempt to increasingly constrain) a father's right to kill his adulterous daughter (see Cantarella 1991; Treggiari 1991, 262–319; Shaw 2001; Benke 2012b).

(and pimps) suffered a diminished legal status characterised by a wide range of civic disabilities. Not only did female prostitutes lose a package of rights, they were also compelled, first by custom and then by law, to adopt the toga—traditional male garb—in order to highlight their degraded standing (McGinn 1998). Both legally and symbolically, Roman law excluded female prostitutes from the category of women.

33.5 Conclusion

It was an unimpeachable fact for lawmakers and jurists in ancient Rome that men and women were physiologically different; the key issue was the extent to which this difference should—or must—be reflected in the law. Starting with the male citizen as the normative foundation, legal authorities either subsumed women into this category or else explicitly denoted how their standing under the law deviated. Overwhelmingly, the exceptionality of women resulted in an inferior status. It is also possible to see Roman law defining gender in more subtle ways. Foundational concepts such as the *pater familias* were gendered as male, notwithstanding the fact that women were included in the category. The continued existence of the *tutela mulierum*—despite its shrinking efficacy and relevance—nonetheless reinforced the existence a "womanly weakness", even as some jurists unequivocally disavowed it. All of this demonstrates the influence that custom and social inertia had upon gender in the law. In turn, the authority bestowed by law bolstered these assumptions and beliefs within Roman society.

Bibliography

Arjava, A. 1996. *Women and law in late antiquity*. Oxford.

Bartlett, K. T. (1990). "Feminist legal methods." *Harvard Law Review* 103: 829–888.

Bartlett, K. T. (2012). "Feminist legal scholarship: a history through the lens of the *California Law Review*." *California Law Review* 100: 381–430.

Beaucamp, J. (1976). "Le vocabulaire de la faiblesse féminine dans les textes juridiques romains du IIIe au VIe siècle." *Revue historique de droit français et étranger* 54: 485–508.

Benke, N. 2005. "Aemilia Pudentilla—a landowning lady." In R. van den Bergh, ed., Ex iusta causa traditum: *essays in honour of Eric H. Pool*. Pretoria. 19–31.

Benke, N. 2011. "Why should the law protect Roman women? Some remarks on the *Senatus Consultum Velleianum* (ca. 50 A.D.)." In K. Børresen, S. Cabbibo and E. Specht, eds., *Gender and religion in Europe: European studies*. Rome. 41–56.

Benke, N. 2012a. "Gender and the Roman law of obligations." In T. A. J. McGinn, ed., *Obligations in Roman law: past, present, and future*. Ann Arbor. 215–246.

Benke, N. (2012b). "On the Roman father's right to kill his adulterous daughter." *The History of the Family* 17: 284–308.

Cantarella, E. 1991. "Homicides of honor: the development of Italian adultery law over two millennia." In D. I. Kertzer and R. P. Saller, eds., *The family in Italy from antiquity to the present*. New Haven. 229–244.

Cantarella, E. 2002[2]. *Bisexuality in the ancient world.* New Haven.
Cohen, D. 1991. "The Augustan law on adultery: the social and cultural context." In D. I. Kertzer and R. P. Saller, eds., *The family in Italy from antiquity to the present.* New Haven. 109–126.
Crook, J. A. 1986. "Feminine inadequacy and the *Senatusconsultum Velleianum*." In B. Rawson, ed., *The family in ancient Rome.* Ithaca. 83–92.
Dixon, S. (1984). "*Infirmitas sexus*: womanly weakness in Roman law." *Tijdschrift voor Rechtsgeschiedenis* 52: 343–371. [Reprinted in S. Dixon, ed. 2001. *Reading Roman women.* London. 73–88.]
Downs, L. L. 2010[2]. *Writing gender history.* London.
Fantham, E. (1991). "*Stuprum*: public attitudes and penalties for sexual offences in republican Rome." *Echos du Monde Classique/Classical Views* 35: 267–291.
Feldner, B. (2000). "Zum Ausschluss der Frau vom römischen *officium*." *Revue internationale des droits de l'antiquité* 47: 381–396
Fiori, R. (1993–1994). "*Materfamilias*." *Bullettino dell'Istituto di Diritto Romano "Vittorio Scialoja"* 96–97: 455–498.
Frier, B. W. and McGinn, T. A. J. 2004. *A casebook on Roman family law.* Oxford.
Gardner, J. F. 1986. *Women in Roman law and society.* Bloomington.
Gardner, J. F. 1993. *Being a Roman citizen.* London.
Gardner, J. F. (1995). "Gender-role assumptions in Roman law." *Echos du Monde Classique/ Classical Views* 39: 377–400.
Gardner, J. F. 1998. "Sexing a Roman: imperfect men in Roman law." In L. Foxhall and J. Salmon, eds., *When men were men: masculinity, power and identity in classical antiquity.* London. 136–152.
Halbwachs, V. T. 1999. "*Ipsae sibi negotia tractant*: Zur Frau als Geschäftpartnerin im Spiegelrömischrechtlicher Quellen." In I. Piro, ed., *Regle et pratique du droit dans les réalités juridiquesde l'antiquité.* Catanzaro. 349–363.
Halperin, D. M. 1989. *One hundred years of homosexuality and other essays on Greek love.* London.
Herrmann-Otto, E. 2002. "Frauen im Römischen Recht: mit einem Ausblick auf Gender Studies in der Alten Geschichte und der antiken Rechtsgeschichte." In B. Feichtinger and G. Wöhrle, eds., *Gender Studies in den Altertumswissenschaften: Möglichkeiten und Grenzen.* Trier. Vol. 1: 25–40.
Joshel, S. 1997. "Female desire and the discourse of empire." In J. P. Hallet and M. B. Skinner, eds., *Roman sexualities.* Princeton. 221–254.
Kunkel, W. 1930. "*Mater familias*," in *Realencyclopädie der classischen Altertumswissenschaft.* Stuttgart. Vol. 14: 2183–2184.
McGinn, T. A. J. (1991). "Concubinage and the *lex Iulia* on adultery." *Transactions of the American Philological Association* 121: 335–375.
McGinn, T. A. J. 1998. *Prostitution, sexuality, and the law in ancient Rome.* Oxford.
Milnor, K. 2005. *Gender, domesticity, and the age of Augustus: inventing private life.* Oxford.
Riggsby, A. M. 2010. *Roman law and the legal world of the Romans.* Cambridge.
Ryan, F. X. (1994). "The *lex Scantinia* and the prosecution of censors and aediles." *Classical Philology* 89: 159–162.
Saller, R. P. (1999). "*Pater familias, mater familias*, and the gendered semantics of the Roman household." *Classical Philology* 94: 182–197.
Severy, B. 2003. *Augustus and the family at the birth of the Roman Empire.* London.

Scott, J. W. (1986). "Gender: a useful category of historical analysis." *The American Historical Review* 91: 1053–1075.
Shaw, B. (2001). "Raising and killing children: two Roman myths." *Mnemosyne* 54: 31–77.
Treggiari, S. 1991. *Roman marriage:* iusti coniuges *from the time of Cicero to the time of Ulpian.* Oxford.
Tuori, K. (2009). "*Dig.* 34,2,33: the return of the cross-dressing senator." *Arctos* 43: 191–200.
Walters, J. 1997. "Invading the Roman body: manliness and impenetrability in Roman thought." In J. P. Hallet and M. B. Skinner, eds., *Roman sexualities*. Princeton. 29–43.
Williams, C. A. 2010². *Roman homosexuality*. Oxford.
Zinsser, J. 1993. *History and feminism: a glass half full.* New York.

CHAPTER 34

WOMEN AS LEGAL ACTORS

VERENA HALBWACHS

34.1 Introduction

"*Mulieres enim quae perfectae aetatis sunt, ipse sibi negotia tractant* ..." ("For women of full age deal with their affairs for themselves ..."),[1] writes the Roman jurist Gaius in the middle of the second century AD in relation to the institution of *tutela mulieris*. In his words, this institution had at that time already become an empty formality, envisaging as it did the approval of the tutor for particular legal transactions undertaken by women. According to Gaius, women ran their affairs themselves, and the fact that they required the (controlling) support of a tutor on account of their oft-cited *levitas animi*[2] was, according to Gaius, "*magis speciosa quam vera*"—more appearance than reality.

This text, often quoted primarily since the expansion of research activity in the field of women in Antiquity in general over the last few decades, as well as in the field of female agency in the social and legal dimension in particular, serves as a starting point. It allows exploring issues such as the fact of female legal–contractual agency, of formally existing restrictions, but also of the mutation of these in the context of judicial practice.

Women as legal actors appear (as men do) across diverse fields of action, and the spectrum covered by the term is broad. To begin with, a distinction may be drawn between the public and private spheres as locations of legal agency. If the aim is to highlight the actions of women against the backdrop of the Roman social order, however, such a distinction cannot merely replicate the normatively determined framework with reference to "private law" or "public law". Rather, the focus should be on the scope of action available to women within what is generally understood as agency under private law, and how they utilised these opportunities and/or were in fact able to utilise them at all. Thus the task must be to separate a narrower, private realm—for example, matters concerning inheritance, family and dowry—from a broader one, such as, for example, participation in public business transactions. Moreover, the capacity of women under procedural law to enforce or defend

[1] Inst.Gai.1.190, transl. Gordon and Robinson 1988.

[2] Inst.Gai.1.190. See Dixon 1984; Höbenreich and Rizzelli 2003, 40–55.

the claims they had won through their actions in the contractual–legal sphere must also be considered.

In a chapter devoted specifically to the subject of women as "legal actors", it is on the one hand necessary to describe in the abstract the generally prevailing legal conditions, together with their deviations from and inequalities with the legal position of men. However, areas of equality should also be emphasised and, in my view, stressed in particular, because it is precisely these areas of equality which may to some degree surprise us in our perception of the Roman social order that was, without doubt, characterised by patriarchy, not least on account of later legal developments specifically relevant to the legal capacity of (especially married) women.

Furthermore, concrete examples from legal practice can and should illustrate our knowledge of quasi-abstract legal regulations, but they should also correct and expand them. Despite the extremely fragmentary nature of the available documents relevant to the present question, a range of finds nonetheless furnishes us with a vivid image of women as legal actors.

34.2 Sources

How can we track down concrete evidence of the abstract legal capacities of women and how they exercised those capacities? First, legal documents, such as papyri, give us feminine names of persons involved in the action. However, the vast majority of jurist writings in the Digest are very general or abstract in formulation and the actual cases which may have prefaced the legal discussion can no longer be identified.[3] The place, time and other historical elements such as the names of the persons involved have been eliminated in the process of transformation into the general/abstract form. (The Roman jurist Ulpian refers to the fact that the formulation "*si quis*" ("if anyone") may refer either to a man or a woman, a text that the compilers placed right at the front of the title "*De verborum significatione*", "On the significance of words"). Thus the participation of women is barely recognisable, either quantitatively or qualitatively, in such a design. Only where deviations in the legal treatment of female and male genders emerge, do women become visible. In this context, the Digest is therefore above all a source for the aspect of difference; that is, of the legal inequality between man and woman.

By contrast, the Imperial rescripts, which have primarily come down to us through the *Codex Iustinianus*, are regarded in this respect as a virtual counterpart to the Digest. Imperial rescripts are authoritative legal answers relating to individual legal disputes or attendant legal processes, issued in response to petitions submitted to the Imperial chancellery.[4] The *Codex* contains approximately 4,600 constitutions, of which over 2,500 concern private individuals. This group mainly covers the period 117 to 305 AD. Because the preserved rescripts indicate to whom they are addressed, under which emperor they were issued, and generally also when and sometimes where they were issued, they are not simply

[3] On this problem see most recently the contributions in Depauw and Coussement 2014.

[4] Nörr 1981; Honoré 1992; Connolly 2010.

legal sources; they are also valuable historical artefacts, which allow us to gain a concrete, practical insight into the legal actions of the petitioning parties and their legal conflicts. For the purposes of our enquiry it is pivotal that almost a quarter of these—approximately 650—are addressed to women, providing us with an astonishingly rich seam of material relating to their participation in social, economic and legal processes.[5] Moreover, it is possible to determine whether the fact that a woman submitted the petition had any impact on the outcome of her legal problem. Thus the *Codex* texts, in contrast to the juristic writing from the Digest, through the nature of their selection—which was certainly not determined on the basis of the gender of the person seeking the answer—almost by chance offer evidence in the first instance for equality in the treatment of men and women.

In addition to these legal sources, in a narrower, conventional sense, legal–historical research has in recent times devoted itself increasingly to studying documents from legal practice in Antiquity, with a focus on the participation of women in legal transactions.[6] Here, purely by way of example, we might cite the finds from the Babatha archive, the commercial deeds from the Sulpicii archive, the legal dispute between a certain Dionysia and her father or the lawsuit of Petronia Justa concerning her status. These sources, preserved on papyrus or wax tablets (*tabulae*), guide us through the everyday legal life of the Roman Empire, even in regions far removed from the Imperial centre, and thereby provide us with insights into the legal and contractual practice of the time, and the relationship between local and Roman law.[7]

34.3 "*In multis iuris nostri articulis deterior est condicio feminarum quam masculorum*"

This succinct statement[8] by the late classical jurist Papinian (early third century) must be considered in greater depth from the point of view of the legal scope of action of women, particularly as it continues to define our image of the female role in Roman Antiquity up to the present day.

Without doubt, the capacity of women in the public–legal realm was fundamentally different from that of men. Women were prohibited from holding public office:[9]

> *Feminae ab omnibus officiis civilibus vel publicis remotae sunt et ideo nec iudices esse possunt nec magistratum gerere nec postulare nec pro alio intervenire nec procuratores existere.* (D.50.17.2pr)

[5] Huchthausen 1974 and 1976; Sternberg 1985; Halbwachs 1999; Connolly 2010.

[6] Jakab 2013; Reduzzi Merola 2012.

[7] For an introduction see Tuori 2007.

[8] D.1.5.9: "There are many points in our law in which the condition of females is inferior to that of males." (All translations from the Digest are from Watson et al.)

[9] Forgó-Feldner 2000; Peppe 1984; Bauman 1992 gives an overview of the opportunities which—particularly "prominent"—women nonetheless took advantage of in order to exert influence in the public/political realm.

> Women are debarred from all civil and public functions and therefore cannot be judges or hold a magistracy or bring a lawsuit or intervene on behalf of anyone else or act as procurators.

This fact is frequently mentioned in the sources and in various contexts. Women could neither accede to the office of *magistratus*, nor serve as *iudex*. The jurist Paul observed that the exclusion of women from public office was not because of any lack of judgemental capacity (*iudicium*) arising from nature, as was the case in respect of the deaf, mentally ill or under-age, but because it was in accordance with the *mores*.[10]

To a certain extent this closes the circle of argument that we find with the Roman jurists. Gaius, quoted at the start of this chapter, opines that the generally assumed *levitas animi* was more appearance than reality, thus also denying that women were not in a position to transact business (absolutely) on their own account, on the basis of their natural aptitudes. If, from this point of view, one reads for example the rescripts to Dionysia[11] and Octacilia,[12] where the advocacy for the son of Dionysia for her part and the assumption of the *tutela impuberum* or guardianship by Octacilia is at issue, and where it is described in the rescript as a *munus/officium virile* (a male duty or office) and *ultra sexum muliebrum/ultra sexum feminae infirmitatis*, the following conclusion is reached. The *infirmitas, levitas* or *imbecillitas* of the female sex was considered even by the Roman jurists as a construct of the *mores*, and was often tied in with the *topos* and postulate of the female *pudicitia*, the virtue of modesty.[13]

The fact that women, according to these rules, could not assume guardianship over their under-age children (*tutela impuberis*) undoubtedly represented a significant interference in their scope of action, as management of—frequently not inconsiderable—assets was a core area of legal competence as evidenced by the large number of sources on the subject of the *tutela impuberis*. It is notable, however, that although the ban was not relaxed *de iure* until the late classical period, and then finally abolished,[14] a range of sources provide evidence of a *de facto* administration of the assets of under-age children by their mother before this point.[15] Moreover, we find configurations in which the mother releases the child's tutor by means of a stipulation from responsibility under the *actio tutelae* with respect to the ward by issuing a guarantee herself. Of course, this resulted in legal consequences with regard to the (non-)applicability of the *senatus consultum Velleianum*.[16] Furthermore, a surprisingly detailed case report has come down to us in the Digest, from which it emerges that a grandmother had managed the business affairs of her grandson and had granted him maintenance payments, which were now being claimed by the grandson's successors in the context of the settlement of a non-contractual obligation (*negotiorum gestio*).[17] The jurist Paul argued here with reference to a number of applicable

[10] Cf. D.5.1.12.2; see Benke 1995. [11] C.2.12.18 (a. 294). [12] C.5.35.1 (a. 224).

[13] On epigraphic and literary sources that emphasise this ideal picture of the Roman woman see most recently Lamberti 2014, 61–77.

[14] Kaser 1975, 227–228.

[15] On these sources and on the relationship and potential mutual influence of Roman law and Greek legal practice in the provinces see Chiusi 1994; Giunti 2012, 366–379; Gagliardi 2012 with a comprehensive literature overview on the topic of the woman as guardian.

[16] C.4.29.6pr (a. 228); on the *senatus consultum Velleianum* see later in this section.

[17] D.3.5.33; see Halbwachs 2014 with additional evidence.

rescripts that dealt with similar sets of circumstances. Thus we see that despite the formal bar on the assumption of a *tutela impuberis* by a woman, with the justification that this was a *munus virile* and not suited to women due to the female *infirmitas*, the jurists firstly accepted the practical agency on the part of women and, secondly, sought and found legal solutions in order to take account of the conflicts emerging from this fact.

The aforementioned papyri from the so-called Archive of Babatha also provide evidence of the entanglements of women in matters of guardianship and in recent years have provided the basis for enquiries into the relationship between local law in the newly created province of Arabia and Roman law. In the early 1960s, a range of documents from the years 97–132 AD were found on the west coast of the Dead Sea. They provide us with information on the legal relationships of a woman of Jewish extraction named Babatha.[18] Babatha pursues a case against the tutors of her son Jesus from her first marriage in which she argued that the maintenance payments for him were too low. She wished to take over the administration of the assets of her son personally, as she was of the opinion that this would produce higher yields, and consequently a more fitting allowance for him. Unfortunately, the outcome of the legal dispute is unknown, as the relevant documents are missing.

Let us now return to Ulpian's statement in D.50.17.2pr. Women were also prohibited from representing others before a court; in other words to file petitions (*postulare*) or to intervene for the liabilities of other persons (*intervenire*). The prohibition on postulation leads us to the story of a certain Carfania, who is named by Ulpian[19] as a cause of the prohibition:[20]

> Next comes an edict against those who are not to make applications on behalf of others. In this edict the praetor debarred on grounds of sex and disability. He also blacklisted persons tainted with disrepute. On grounds of sex, now he forbids women to make applications on behalf of others. The reason for this is to prevent that they involve themselves in the case of other people contrary to the modesty in keeping with their sex—that women fulfil male offices. Originally, this was in fact brought about by a most disapproved woman—Carfania—who by brazenly making applications and disturbing the magistrate gave rise to the edict.

Turning to the question of the legal opportunities and consequently also to the actual recourse of women to legal transactions in the field of private law (be it in the "purely private" sphere, be it in the framework of "extra-domestic" participation in business life), the question of the competence of women in contractual and property matters is a central one. Contractual competence is the precondition of any (legally effective) business activity, while the legal right to own property is presumably a key motivation for making legal transactions. Whereas in modern legal systems this topic is largely governed in a unified manner for every person, in Roman Antiquity a differentiation according to

[18] For details and an extensive bibliography see Oudshoorn 2007; also Katzoff and Schaps 2005; Meyer 2007; Grzimek 2001, 23–40.

[19] D.3.1.1.5.

[20] On the case of Carfania and her reception in the contemporary literature from the point of view of the supposed *pudicitia* of female participants in public life see Chiusi 2013; Lamberti 2014, 78–79; Benke 1995; Höbenreich and Rizzelli 2003, 61–72.

specific groups of people is required, due to the pronounced stratification of the Roman social order.

An initial differentiation between the free and unfree (slaves) strata must be made. Although slaves lacked legal competence to the extent that they could also be the objects of legal transactions, they were, however, *utilitatis causa* viewed as legally competent when it was expedient for the *dominus* or *domina* to utilise them for the conclusion of legal transactions. At this lowest rung of the social hierarchy, a differentiation by gender is not discernible, and female slaves acted more or less as independently as male slaves within the context of their *peculia*.[21]

In the case of free persons (*ingenui*—persons born free, and *liberti*—freed slaves) a distinction must again be made between those subject to authority (*alieni iuris*) and others (*sui iuris*). Free women were either *sui iuris* (in which case their legal capacity was largely equal to that of men, with the exception of the restrictions to be discussed here such as the *tutela mulieris*), or they stood—entirely independent of their age—under the *patria potestas* of their father (a fact which nonetheless did not distinguish them from their male relatives assembled within the same agnatic family unit) or under the *manus* of their husband (*filiae loco*), and were thereby not competent to own property.[22] It remains to be pointed out that a free woman not subject to authority, even if she was married (without entering into a *manus* marriage), was in a position (from the age of 12 onwards) to engage in legal transactions independently to a large degree, and to assign the profit from these transactions to her own assets. At this point it should also be stressed that in the *manus*-free Roman marriage a strict separation of property was maintained and the woman remained the owner of her estate. Even gifts between spouses were forbidden, and legally enforceable mutual maintenance rights did not exist, only the moral obligation of the husband to support his wife from the fruits of the *dos*.[23] All these facts greatly distinguish Roman law from many successive European legal systems up to the beginning of the twentieth century. Yet these are barely mentioned in the theories relating to the reception of Roman law; indeed, they have been more or less consciously suppressed, and to the present day only surface in specific areas of research, including conceptualisations of living conditions in Antiquity. Furthermore, *conventio in manum* in the course of a marriage becomes ever rarer as early as the late Republic, and by the time of the Principate represents only an "isolated exception".[24]

The institution of *tutor mulieris*,[25] too, who had to give his *auctoritas* (approval) for certain business transactions of *sui iuris* women, lost its practical significance in social life

[21] By *peculium* is understood a special asset, which is given over by the *dominus* to his male and female slaves (or by the *pater familias* to the children-in-power) to be independently managed by them; the holder of authority also remains the owner of the asset. On the economic activities of persons subject to authority see e.g. Gamauf 2009; on the legal implications and/or on the so-called adiectitious liability of the holder of authority benefiting economically from the business dealings see Kaser and Knütel 2014, 292–295.

[22] For an overview of the structure of the Roman *familia* see Kaser and Knütel 2014, 86–96. On literary sources on the position of married women see, for example, Höbenreich and Rizzelli 2003, 112–166.

[23] Cf. Halbwachs 2010.

[24] See Kaser 1971, 323–325.

[25] See Kaser and Knütel 2014, 369–370; Gardner 1986, 5–29; Holthöfer 1997 (with extensive literature overview).

as early as the classical period (to a large extent also due to legal changes relating to the appointment or selection of the actual tutor). The type and form of transactions requiring *auctoritas tutoris* become fewer in number due to the increase in formless transactions. The type *tutor legitimus* (*tutor* is the closest agnatic relative) was abolished in the first half of the first century AD; the self-interest of the *tutela* was no longer a relevant characteristic for a party who was no longer an intestate heir. Women gained ever more influence over the selection of their tutor. The causes and motivations for these changes were probably multilayered—not least the waning of agnatic ties and of the role of exercising control as a tutor, regarded as onerous, particularly in cases where the woman had already achieved a high degree of personal autonomy within the existing social structure. Yet the final disappearance of this legal institution, which had already been superseded, did not occur until the early fourth century, on the basis of a Constantinian constitution.[26]

This is a good example of a long-term *de iure* adherence to a situation that cannot have had any *de facto* significance for a long period of time.[27] The fact that traditional arguments for the institution of *tutela mulierum* based on the feminine *levitas* and *infirmitas animi* were "*magis speciosa ... quam vera*", as Gaius says, was also demonstrated by the *ius trium vel quattuor liberorum* provided for in Augustus' statutes relating to marriage law.[28] Through this "right of three children" for women who were born free, or the "right of four children" for freed women following the birth of a corresponding number of children, they were freed not only from certain (disadvantageous) provisions of marriage law (for example, the duty to marry, on pain of sanctions in matters of inheritance),[29] but also from the dictate of *tutela mulierum*.[30]

This right was later granted as a privilege to certain persons independent of the birth of children, in order to obtain certain advantages. In our specific context, a report by Suetonius in the *Vita divi Claudii*[31] is of interest. In order to secure the food supply to a sufficient extent, persons working in grain transport were to receive particular motivation through the granting of certain privileges. Among such *magna commoda* for the manufacturers of trade ships, in addition to the granting of citizenship to *Latini* and the liberation of citizens from the regulations of the *lex Papia Poppaea*, Suetonius also lists the granting of *ius quattuor liberorum* to women.[32] The text may in fact also reveal something about the engagement of women in this industry. In any case, it becomes clear that the notion that women needed protection from the dangers posed to their assets through economic transactions by way of the institution of *tutela mulierum* was no longer current;

[26] C.2.44.2.1 (undated).

[27] Jakab 2013 has investigated the wax tablets from the Sulpicii archive, commercial documents from the first century AD found in Pompeii in 1959, from the point of view of the participation of women in financial transactions; she comes to the conclusion that the fact that tutors are barely mentioned in these documents from legal practice may lie in the fact that women had their business transactions carried out by slaves and freed persons to a particularly large extent (Jakab 2013, 148–149).

[28] Treggiari 1991, 60–80.

[29] To this extent this right also applied to men after the begetting of three or four children and released them, for example, from the obligation of taking on a *tutela*.

[30] Inst.Gai.1.145.

[31] Cf. Suet. *Claud.* 18–19.

[32] On the question of why explicitly only the right of four children of freed persons is mentioned here see Sirks 1980 and Höbenreich 1997, 77–79.

it would most likely have been entirely absurd to rob them of this protection through the granting of privileges.

If one considers the legal capacity of women in business and contractual life from the point of view of the difference with that of men, we must of course mention the *senatus consultum Velleianum*.[33] This *s.c.*, dated around the middle of the first century AD, forbade women from obligating themselves through intercessions. Classical Roman law understood the term intercession as the assumption of an external debt and the liability for such a debt—whether the woman stood as guarantor or third-party pledgor alongside the indebted third party, or whether she assumed the liability instead of the (indebted) third party. Ulpian justified this measure with the familiar *topoi*, namely that women must be given assistance due to their *imbecillitas sexus*, that they must be protected from themselves.[34] Paul in turn opined that, because women were traditionally excluded from *officia civilia*, this should be the case where not only their own affairs were at stake, but also the assets of the whole family.[35] To what extent the actual intention of the *s.c.* was the protection of women, or in fact their exclusion from a highly relevant segment of the Roman economy, is a controversial topic within the literature.[36] On the one hand, the effect of the *s.c.* was not in the form of an absolute, strict invalidation of intercession transactions; rather, it was enforced through an *exceptio senatus consulti Velleiani* of the female respondent that could also be waived. Moreover, the woman could not, for example, dispose of her liability if her creditor did not know that she had become his debtor through intercession.[37] This hardly accords with the postulated goal of protection. In the pronounced casuistry of the sources, it is in any case clear that a high degree of legal uncertainty existed as to whether a specific set of facts was to be subsumed under the elements of the *s.c.* or not. Thus under certain circumstances a woman appeared less attractive as a potential intercession debtor than a man.[38]

34.4 "*Parvi autem refert … masculus sit an mulier*"

This statement[39] by the jurist Ulpian is admittedly taken from a specific context; namely, the question of the adiectitious liability of a ship owner for business transactions concluded by his captain (*magister navis*). Nevertheless, it seems as if the same applies to all

[33] The multiplicity of records which have come down to us and the broad casuistry on this topic in any case provide evidence of the real relevance for women and/or their business partners and also give an insight into the highly complex tripartite legal relationships in which women were involved.

[34] D.16.1.2.2. [35] D.16.1.1.1. [36] See most recently Benke 2001 and Finkenauer 2013.

[37] D.16.1.4pr.

[38] This eventuality was also recognised absolutely by the jurists: Cf. D.16.1.11: "*Si mulier tamquam in usus suos pecuniam acceperit alii creditura, non est locus senatus consulto: alioquin nemo cum feminis contrahet, quia ignorari potest, quid acturae sint.*" (If a woman receives money for her own use, but with the intention of lending it to another, there is no place for the *senatus consultum*; for otherwise no person will contract with women because he cannot know what they might do.) On the possibility for women to waive protection by providing surety see Finkenauer 2013.

[39] D.14.1.1.16: "It is immaterial whether [the shipowner] be male or female".

areas of legal transactions that do not explicitly provide for unequal treatment of the sexes. Ulpian's sentence, that whenever "*si quis*" is written it "*masculos quam feminas complectitur*",[40] suggests such a conclusion, and we hardly find any further indications of explicit differentiation in the legal sources, with the exception of the few restrictions referred to above. The fact that in the *Corpus Iuris* we often find quasi-modern gender-neutral formulations must not (cf. Ulpian) lead to the misapprehension that women were excluded where they were not specifically mentioned. The reason for this is more likely due to the fact that these clarifications on the part of the jurists appear where apparent legal uncertainty reigned due to the concrete legal configuration in that instance. This can be established particularly clearly in the field of adiectitious liability.[41] Here, the legal relationships between three parties are always at issue, and the person cited as liable must vouch for an obligation which she herself did not contractually give rise to. Thus the situation is not dissimilar to an intercession transaction, and interceding was (in principle) prohibited for women by the *s.c. Velleianum*. As abstract as these sources may be in their writing, they do however provide very good evidence of the actual participation of women in specific fields of economic life.[42] Thanks to recent research, which increasingly tackles the role of women outside the family and "purely private" sphere, independent female action has also—to a certain extent—found its way into the relevant textbooks on Roman law.[43] Through earlier, all-too-abstract modes of representation that were primarily focused on those points at which the legal status of women differed from that of men, this received too little attention—indeed, it was actually concealed. The *topoi* of *levitas, infirmitas* or *imbecillitas* of the female sex created by the Roman jurists, in this way, shaped the image of the legal, social and economic competence of women in their time up to the present day.

In the rescripts mentioned at the start of this chapter, legal themes relating to all areas of life appeared. Of course, questions relating to inheritance or dowry are well represented here, as are, for example, the consequences of the prohibition on marital gifts. With regard to dowry and the prohibition on marital gifts, the participation of the woman is of course inherent to the topic. To this extent, the multiplicity of juristic writing on this topic in the Digest demonstrate that women did not seek to avoid legal conflicts resulting from such legal relationships, which were in the narrower sense "private", but rather were concerned to pursue their claims in a consistent manner.[44] If these disputes within the family are not

[40] D.50.16.1: "*Verbum hoc 'si quis' tam masculos quam feminas complectitur*". (This expression "If anyone" covers both men and women.) On the semantic absurdity of this statement, as "si (ali) quis" in any case encompasses both the feminine and the masculine form see Benke 2000. Whereas such "general clauses" today—allegedly—aid the better readability of texts, it was important for the compilers themselves to stress that both genders were indeed encompassed by the masculine form as well as the feminine.

[41] Cf. e.g. also D.14.3.7.1.

[42] The fact that Ulpian in D.14.3.7.1 does not employ merely theoretical statements can be seen in a rescript to a certain Antigona from the year 293: C.4.25.4 *Impp. Diocletianus et Maximianus AA. et CC. Antigonae: Et si a muliere magister navis praepositus fuerit, ex contractibus eius ea exercitoria actione ad similitudinem institoriae tenetur.* (Even if the *magister navis* is employed by a woman, she has liability arising from its contracts in accordance with the example of *actio institoria*.)

[43] Cf. e.g. Kaser and Knütel 2014, 95–96.

[44] Papyri, although extant in large numbers almost exclusively in the area of Graeco-Roman Egypt, also provide information on the way the authorities there responded to the fact that different legal

comparable with a businesswoman acting in the public realm, one recognises here the self-confident action of (married) women all the more. Alongside these (often, legally speaking, extremely demanding) configurations of the family nexus, we also see that women brought a large number of petitions relating to sales contracts, rental agreements and primarily also loan transactions. In the latter case, women are above all present as providers of credit. The demand for the considerable wealth in the hands of women becomes as visible here as the organisational structures as many people availed themselves of their capital through both free and unfree administrators.[45] In the context of lending activities the involvement of women in *fenus nauticum* (shipping loans) is particularly striking,[46] whereby women actually appear overrepresented in the few preserved texts.[47] And also the many sources which are extant in the *s.c. Velleianum* provide evidence of the active participation of women in financial transactions.

We can only briefly refer here to the spectrum of professionally active women, in other words those who fitted into legal processes other than through economic activity with capital available to them through inheritance, for example, as was thoroughly customary for the Roman upper class.[48] The available material on this subject consists, besides literary material, primarily of archaeological sources. Here we do admittedly find job titles, although these provide little information on the legal relationships, working conditions, organisational–operational structures etc.[49] In today's terminology, most of these occupations would be described as being in the service industry. As with men, the majority were slaves and freed women, who were employed as subordinate workers or as specialists with specific technical skills.[50] Women who introduce their own capital in order to achieve a

circles came into contact with one another. These sources, too, confirm both the presence of women as well as their readiness to engage in conflict in the course of their legal transactions. On the legal dispute of a certain Dionysia, who in 186 AD brought a petition to the *praefectus Aegypti* to defend herself against financial claims brought by her father, see Kreuzsaler 2008 and Kreuzsaler and Urbanik 2008.

[45] To this extent this is congruent with the observations of Jakab 2013 in the documents of the Sulpicii archive. It should be mentioned here that the late classical jurist Callistratus declares that women could not practice the profession of *argentarius* (see Gardner 1986, 235–237). The justification for this again follows the familiar model: the business of the *argentarii* is a profession reserved to the male sex (D.2.13.12: "*Feminae remotae videntur ab officio argentarii, cum ea opera virilis sit*"—women are held to be excluded from the office of banker since this is a masculine type of work.) On the profession of an *argentarius*, who probably provided various financial transactions such as custody or money-changing transactions to a modest degree (though effected in the public realm), see Bürge 1987.

[46] The *fenus nauticum* is granted by the lender for the financing of the transportation of goods across the sea. Capital plus interest are only to be repaid if the ship and/or the goods reach their destination safely, which means that the creditor assumes the *periculum*, in other words the risk of loss caused by *vis maior.* To compensate for this, it was possible in the case of this type of credit business (which at the end of the day represents a type of insurance contract unknown to Roman law) to demand interest rates that exceeded the maximum permissible rate of interest.

[47] On the rescripts to Aurelia Iuliana (C.4.33.4 [undated]) and Aurelia Cosmiana (C.4.33.3 [a. 286]) see Halbwachs 1999.

[48] See also Eichenauer 1988; Kampen 1981; Gardner 1986, 233–255; Höbenreich and Rizzelli 2003, 167–177.

[49] However, papyri have come down to us from Roman Egypt that do show detailed agreements with *nutrices* (wet-nurses) (Eichenauer 1988, 270).

[50] Joshel 1992.

return and to increase their assets are not covered by the occupational designations found in the sources.

34.5 Conclusion

Women as legal actors rather than as only passively affected individuals are to be found in the classical sources more often than is generally assumed. This is borne out by literary reports as well as in documents from legal practice, whereby the latter—in relation to later periods—have unfortunately (hitherto) only come down to us to a limited extent and have only recently been the subject of evaluation and review from the point of view of the participation of women. But the juristic writings—and this is surely coincidental and not programmatic—provide us with a range of cases in which women are involved, in which they take a stand for their claims (and in doing so act successfully) and where an unequal treatment in the legal opinion is not discernible. Here the task is to direct our focus onto these configurations, while of course taking into account the Roman social order, and not to allow the issue to be clouded by subsequent measures which limited the autonomy of (above all, married) women.

Bibliography

Bauman, R. 1992. *Women and politics in ancient Rome*. London/New York.

Benke, N. (1995). "Women in the courts: an old thorn in men's sides." *Michigan Journal of Gender & Law* 3: 195–256.

Benke, N. 2000. "*In sola prudentium interpretatione*: Zu Methodik und Methodologie römischer Juristen." In B. Feldner and N. Forgó, eds., *Norm und Entscheidung: Prolegomena zu einer Theorie des Falls*. Vienna/New York. 1–85.

Benke, N. 2001. "Why should the law protect Roman women? Some remarks on the *Senatus Consultum Velleianum* (ca. 50 A.D.)." In K. Børresen, S. Cabibbo and E. Specht, eds., *Gender and religion in Europe: European studies*. Rome. 41–56.

Bürge, A. (1987). "Fiktion und Wirklichkeit: Soziale und rechtliche Strukturen des römischen Bankwesens." *Zeitschrift der Savigny-Stiftung für Rechtsgeschichte, romanistische Abteilung* 104: 465–558.

Chiusi, T. (1994). "Zur Vormundschaft der Mutter." *Zeitschrift der Savigny-Stiftung für Rechtsgeschichte, romanistische Abteilung* 111: 155–196.

Chiusi, T. 2013. "*Fama* and *infamia* in the Roman legal system: the cases of Afrania and Lucretia." In A. Burrows, D. Johnston and R. Zimmermann, eds., *Judge and jurist: essays in memory of Lord Rodger of Earlsferry*. Oxford. 143–165.

Connolly, S. 2010. *Lives behind the laws: the world of the* Codex Hermogenianus. Bloomington.

Depauw, M. and S. Coussement, eds. 2014. *Identifiers and identification methods in the ancient world: legal documents in ancient societies*, Vol. 3 (Orientalia Lovaniensa Analecta 229). Leuven.

Dixon, S. (1984). "*Infirmitas sexus*: womanly weakness in Roman law." *Tijdschrift voor Rechtsgeschiedenis* 52: 343–371.

Eichenauer, M. 1988. *Untersuchungen zur Arbeitswelt der Frau in der römischen Antike*. Frankfurt.

Finkenauer, T. (2013). "Der Verzicht auf die *exceptio SCti Velleiani* im klassischen Recht." *Tijdschrift voor Rechtsgeschiedenis* 81: 17–49.

Forgó-Feldner, B. (2000). "Zum Ausschluss der Frau vom römischen officium." *Revue internationale des droits de l'antiquité* 47: 381–396.

Gagliardi, L. (2012). "La madre tutrice e la madre *epakolouthetria*: osservazioni sul rapporto tra diritto romano e diritti delle province orientali." *Index* 40: 423–446.

Gamauf, R. (2009). "Slaves doing business: the role of Roman law in the economy of a Roman household." *European Review of History—Revue européenne d'histoire* 16: 331–346.

Gardner, J. F. 1986. *Women in Roman law and society*. Kent. [= Gardner, J. F. 1995. *Frauen im antiken Rom: Familie, Alltag, Recht*. Munich.]

Giunti, P. (2012). "Il ruolo sociale della donna romana di età imperiale: tra discriminazione e riconoscimento." *Index* 40: 342–379.

Grzimek, P. 2001. *Studien zur* taxatio. Munich.

Halbwachs, V. 1999. "*Ipsae sibi negotia tractant*: Zur Frau als Geschäftpartnerin im Spiegel römischrechtlicher Quellen." In I. Piro, ed., *Règle et pratique du droit dans les réalités juridiques de l'antiquité*. Catanzaro. 349–363.

Halbwachs, V. 2010. "*Non enim donat, qui necessariis oneribus succurrit*: Überlegungen zum Verhältnis von Schenkungsverbot und Unterhaltsleistungen zwischen Ehepartnern." In R. van den Bergh and G. van Niekerk, eds., Libellus ad Thomasium: *essays in Roman law, Roman-Dutch law and legal history in honour of Philipp J. Thomas*. Pretoria. 13–141.

Halbwachs, V. (2014). "*Haec disceptatio in factum constitit*: Bemerkungen zur *pietas* im römischen Unterhaltsrecht." In R. van den Bergh et al., eds., Meditationes de iure et historia: *essays in honour of Laurens Winkel*. Pretoria. 371–382.

Höbenreich, E. 1997. Annona: *Juristische Aspekte der stadtrömischen Lebensmittelversorgung im Prinzipat*. Graz.

Höbenreich, E. and Rizzelli, G. 2003. Scylla: *Fragmente einer juristischen Geschichte der Frauen im antiken Rom*. Vienna/Cologne/Weimar.

Holthöfer, E. 1997. "Die Geschlechtsvormundschaft: Ein Überblick von der Antike bis ins 19. Jahrhundert." In U. Gerhard, ed., *Frauen in der Geschichte des Rechts*. Munich. 390–451.

Honoré, T. 1992. *Emperors and lawyers: with a palingenesia of third-century imperial rescripts 193–305 AD*. Oxford.

Huchthausen, L. (1974). "Herkunft und Stellung weiblicher Adressaten von Reskripten des *Codex Iustinianus* (2. und 3. Jh. u.Z.)." *Klio* 56: 199–228.

Huchthausen, L. (1976). "Zu kaiserlichen Reskripten an weibliche Adressaten aus der Zeit Diokletians (284–305 u.Z.)." *Klio* 58: 55–85.

Jakab, É. 2013. "Financial transactions by women in Puteoli." In P. J. du Plessis, ed., *New frontiers: law and society in the Roman world*. Edinburgh. 123–15.

Joshel, S. 1992. *Work, identity, and legal status at Rome*. Norman Okla.

Kampen, N. 1981. *Image and status: Roman working women in Ostia*. Berlin.

Kaser, M. 1971. *Das römische Privatrecht*, Vol. 1. Munich.

Kaser, M. 1975. *Das römische Privatrecht*, Vol. 2. Munich.

Kaser, M. and Knütel, R. 2014. *Römisches Privatrecht*. Munich.

Katzoff, R. and D. Schaps, eds. 2005. *Law in the documents of the Judaean desert* (Supplements to the *Journal for the Study of Judaism* 96). Leiden/Boston.

Kreuzsaler, C. 2008. "Dionysia vs. Chairemon: Ein Rechtsstreit aus dem römischen Ägypten." In U. Falk, M. Luminati and M. Schmoekel, eds., *Fälle aus der Rechtsgeschichte*. Munich. 1–13.

Kreuzsaler, C. and Urbanik, J. (2008). "Humanity and inhumanity of law: the case of Dionysia." *The Journal of Juristic Papyrology* 38: 119–155.

Lamberti, F. (2014). "Donne romane fra Idealtypus e realtà sociale: Dal *domum servare* e *lanam facere* al *meretricio more vivere.*" *Quaderni Lupiensi di Storia e Diritto* 4: 61–84.

Meyer, E. A. 2007. "Diplomatics, law and romanisation in the documents from the Judean desert." In J. W. Cairns and P. J. du Plessis, eds., *Beyond dogmatics: law and society in the Roman world.* Edinburgh. 53–82.

Nörr, D. (1981). "Zur Reskriptenpraxis in der hohen Prinzipatszeit." *Zeitschrift der Savigny-Stiftung für Rechtsgeschichte, romanistische Abteilung* 98: 1–46.

Oudshoorn, J. G. 2007. *The relationship between Roman and local law in the Babatha and Salome Komaise archives: general analysis and three case studies on law of succession, guardianship and marriage.* Leiden/Boston.

Peppe, L. 1984. *Posizione giuridica e ruolo sociale della donna romana in età repubblicana.* Milan.

Reduzzi Merola, F. (2012). "Le donne nei documenti della prassi campana." *Index* 40: 380–386.

Sirks, A. J. B. (1980). "A favour to rich freed women (*libertinae*) in 51 A.D. On Sue. *Cl.* 19 and the *Lex Papia.*" *Revue internationale des droits de l'antiquité* 27: 283–293.

Sternberg, T. (1985). "Reskripte des Kaisers Alexander Severus an weibliche Adressaten." *Klio* 67: 507–527.

Treggiari, S. 1991. *Roman marriage:* iusti coniuges *from the time of Cicero to the time of Ulpian.* Oxford.

Tuori, K. 2007. "Legal pluralism and the Roman empires." In J. W. Cairns and P. J. du Plessis, eds., *Beyond dogmatics: law and society in the Roman world.* Edinburgh. 39–52.

PART VII

LEGAL RELATIONS

Persons and Family

CHAPTER 35

FAMILY

SUZANNE DIXON

35.1 Introduction

The striking feature of the Roman family—striking even to observers from classical Antiquity—was the unique power, including "the right of life and death", *ius vitae necisque*, accorded for life to the (senior) Roman father, *pater familias*, over his legitimate children and his sons' children, all of whom remained in his paternal power (*patria potestas*) even as adults, unless specific legal steps were taken to remove them from the father's power and, technically, from the family of their birth.[1]

This archetypically patriarchal system, granting such formidable power over persons and property to the senior male and defining family membership in "agnatic" terms, through the male line, might have suited the relatively simple pastoral/agrarian society of the seven hills in the distant past, but it continued its legal life throughout the many centuries of Roman expansion first into Latium, then peninsular Italy and far beyond.[2] When Roman citizenship was effectively extended to nearly all free inhabitants of the vast Empire of the early third century AD, families previously governed by varied traditions legally became Roman families.

In the meantime, Rome itself had changed, many laws had changed and the very sources of law had changed from the time of its traditional founding in the eighth century BC. More changes still were to come (the Christianisation of the Empire; the split between East and West; and the influence of Greek language and custom in the Eastern Mediterranean). Other "rationalisations" of the Roman legal corpus had taken place before the sixth-century Christian emperor Justinian ordered a new, authoritative edition to be formed from the cumulative statutes and rulings of centuries and adapted to current law, yet *patria potestas* continued to figure in the volumes that bore his name: the Justinianic Digest, Institutes and Code.

If this process assisted contemporaries, it has posed problems for successive generations of modern legal scholars but—rather like Roman law itself—the teaching and scholarship

[1] Aulus Gellius, *NA* 1.12; Sachers 1953; Westbrook 1999.

[2] See Saller 1994, 155; 1999 for over-reading of the role of the *pater familias*.

of Roman law has tended to change in piecemeal fashion, influenced by national and disciplinary perspectives.[3] Wherever Roman law is still studied by undergraduates, textbooks continue to present an enviably straightforward précis of the law under helpful sub-headings not unlike those used by the great second-century Lebanese jurist Gaius for students of his own day. Thus "persons", property, succession can be reviewed, memorised and duly reproduced in twenty-minute blocks for end-of-year examinations with some token consideration of such lawyerly issues as remedies, liabilities and status as if they are more or less unproblematic. Of course, there are more sophisticated and specialised works available to students. My point is that the focus is on systematising the material and on the law as a distinct category for students being trained for a modern career practising law.[4]

The term "legal historian" can now be applied to scholars in slightly different ways. Traditional *Rechtshistoriker* are, happily, still applying to the texts of the Digest their finely honed philological and philosophical skills. To them we owe the painstaking collation from the Digest of scattered quotes from Gaius and their reconstruction into the more accessible book-form of his Institutes.[5] To them we continue to look for insight into the extent to which Digest references to allegedly classical statutes and judgements have been interpolated with post-classical terminology and concepts.

Increasingly, studies of issues related to what might be termed "Roman law of the family" have drawn on but moved away from such traditions. The earlier tendency to treat Roman law as a block of rational principles conveniently summarised in the Digest or its more compact and accessible companion version, the Institutes of Justinian, has largely given way to a daunting appreciation of the difficulties of reconstructing the law of the Republic or the early Imperial period from the heavily interpolated and redacted later versions. The response of these neo-*Rechtshistoriker* is neither wholly legalistic nor wholly philological. Classically trained, they acquire the relevant expertise in Roman law and in such dynamic and complex specialist areas as inheritance strategy, close-kin prohibitions, intergenerational conflict and gender relations, depending on their focus. They have also widened the range of sources they use to include epigraphic, literary and theological texts.[6] Being human, they soon find they cannot do everything. They typically focus on specific regions and historical periods in order to contextualise their legal findings and to determine the impact of major changes—the mandated celibacy of the Roman Imperial army, the Christianisation of the Empire, changes in the legal status of wives and therefore of the legal relationship between mother and child, and the perennially productive area of paternal power (Thomas 1986/1996).

[3] Dixon 1992, 39–45. Cf. Vuolanto, ch. 37 in this volume.

[4] Thus Corbett 1930; Jolowicz 1932/1965; Watson 1967 and Gardner 1986 have provided thoughtful, solid approaches to legal issues relevant to the family, but still within the textbook tradition.

[5] e.g. de Zulueta 1946 and 1953 or Bruns 1909, *Fontes*, and Riccobono et al. 1940–1943 (*FIRA* II) for collections of the sources used by legal historians of the late Republic and early Empire.

[6] To me, the use of the Babatha archive by scholars such as Naphtali Lewis, Evans Grubbs and now Oudshoorn was a revelation, with the illustration of a Roman subject using Jewish and Roman law by turn. Yet it is not so different from the juristic papyrology, with which I had been long familiar, in which "Romans" of ethnically and culturally Greek, Egyptian or Jewish origins approached the authorities of Egypt, which from 31 BC had been under the delegated personal rule of the emperor.

Earlier studies reflected a Darwinian confidence in social evolution and a strict distinction between primitive and civilised systems, which was often bolstered by an overly literal reading of legal and kinship terms. Crook's 1967 *Law and Life of Rome* used the law as a source—modified by reference to other sources—to illuminate the lives and institutions of Romans particularly in the late Republican and early Imperial periods. It launched a new generation of scholars with an empirical approach to Roman family relations.[7] This approach has since spread to studies of the family and gender in late Antiquity.[8] Scepticism characterises the work of such scholars. They test long-held truisms—such as the effective legal acknowledgement of paternal power, whether those individuals ceremonially released from their family (such as Vestals or adopted children) were judged to be wholly separate from it for all legal purposes, or the impact of Christianity on laws governing children and marriage.[9]

I found it exciting to be part of that shift towards legal sociology, which owed much to the intellectual and social upheavals of the 1970s. The new Roman lawyers, like their nineteenth-century precursors, drew enthusiastically on cross-disciplinary and cross-cultural studies of social institutions and legal systems.[10] I was therefore both amused and suitably humbled to see its rather patronising characterisation in a recent work:

> We can now see that anthropologists, writing in the 1980s, were symptomatic of a shift in research that affected more than one discipline. At the same time, historians began to reconceptualise the study of the family in the west by boldly—or perhaps naively—taking up the concept of 'kinship' just as anthropologists were losing heart. (Sabean and Teuscher 2013, 2)

Such is the fate of all scholarly innovators.

35.2 *Pater Familias*, *Patria Potestas* and Definitions of "Family" Roles

"Given the social importance of family and kinship, it is surprising that Roman society never settled on definitive concepts of kinship and family, but rather developed several concepts of each. The resulting variety makes it difficult for modern historians to define *the* Roman family or the larger Roman kinship group" (Harders 2013, 20).

Roman concepts of family and kinship—whether nuclear or extended, whether defined legally, ritually or socially—stress the corporate unit over the individual. Yet there is no Latin word for "family" as such. Meanings teased out by Roman jurists for the Latin

[7] Names such as Corbier, Peppe, Rawson, Saller, (Y.) Thomas, Treggiari and Weaver recur in bibliographies of Roman family and law.

[8] Such as Beaucamp 1990, Evans Grubbs 1995 and Arjava 1998a and 1998b.

[9] Saller 1994; Shaw 2001; Westbrook 1999 (paternal power); Dixon 1992 e.g. 58–60, Lindsay 2011 (separation from family); Evans Grubbs 1995 (Christianity and the law on family).

[10] Engels' classic pamphlet on the family encapsulates the universalising tendencies of nineteenth-century scholarship. Many twentieth-century studies of Roman law and the family like those of Westrup 1934 (and, indeed de Zulueta 1953) reflect similar ethnographically-based beliefs in universal or recurrent trends, such as bride-sale and the joint patriarchal household.

"*familia*" included a household (both free and slave inhabitants), the slaves connected to a particular household or a business operated by slaves and freed slaves with a common original owner.[11] None of its many usages carried the connotations of its etymological descendants ("family", "famille", "familje" and so on). The Latin term also appears in legal compounds like *pater familias* (as one word or two), literally "father of the *familia*"; a word that is used now as shorthand for a particular kind of patriarchal rule.[12] Certainly the *pater familias* was at the core of the Roman family. The term signified a legally independent Roman male citizen holding supreme—indeed, sole—rights of property ownership within a defined circle (which we shall explore) as well as extreme powers over the persons of others within that unit by virtue of his paternal power (*patria potestas*).[13] This distinctively Roman combination of personal and real powers exceeded that commonly associated with "head of household" status in other contemporaneous societies, as famously expressed by the jurist Gaius:

> *Item in potestate nostra sunt liberi nostri, quos iustis nuptiis procreavimus. quod ius proprium civium Romanorum est. fere enim nulli alii sunt homines qui talem in filios suos habent potestatem, qualem nos habemus.*
>
> Similarly, those children whom we have produced in legitimate marriage are in our power. This is a distinctive right of Roman citizens, for hardly any other peoples have the kind of power we hold over our children. (Inst.Gai.1.55 (second century AD, citing the emperor Hadrian, in response to petitioners))

Gaius clearly included himself in that "we", as if the implications were active in his day (mid- to late second century AD). The Roman father's (or grandfather's) right of life and death (*ius vitae necisque*) over his children was similar to that he exercised over his slaves (*dominium*), as owner (*dominus*).[14] His powers over his wife depended in part on their form of marriage, which determined whether she was deemed legally a member of his family and was in her husband's (or father-in-law's) "hand" (*manus*) or remained in the family of her birth, and therefore within her own father's power (*potestas*) until his death.

Legal terms such as *pater familias, mater familias, filius familias, filia familias* throw light on the Roman family and its members, but they cannot be translated as "father/mother/son/daughter of the family". As stated above, "*familia*" seldom denoted "family". Compounds such as *pater familias, filia familias* refer not so much to family relationship as to the individual's standing within the estate, although the connection between the two is evident (Saller 1999). Thus an unmarried and childless fifteen-year-old Roman boy whose father had died was at law a *pater familias* because he was independent (*sui iuris*) of paternal authority and therefore had the capacity to own property and the potential to become a "head of the family" in every legal sense. By the same token, a forty-five-year-old

[11] Dixon 1988, 1–3; D.50.16.195.1, 3.

[12] In English, "Victorian *paterfamilias*" is a standard term, e.g. Himmelfarb 1968, 199 of a literary Victorian father (based on Virginia Woolf's own father); or more generally, http://sentence.yourdictionary.com/paterfamilias, accessed 20 February 2014.

[13] Dixon 1988, xiv, 268. See also Saller 1999, 182, who also critiques the authoritative *RE* 1949 entry by Sachers, esp. 2138.

[14] Authors, notably Saller 1999, 133–153, have cautioned against over-arguing this analogy. See also Gardner 1993, 12–14; McDonnell 2006, 174; Westbrook 1999.

Roman consul with a living father was at law a *filius familias* even if he was himself a grandfather.

Roman society was not gender-neutral but there was a certain symmetry in some areas. The position of *filius familias* and *filia familias* is a case in point. While in the power of their father (*in patria potestate*) the *filius familias* and *filia familias* had the rights of equal heirs to the paternal estate, and they were both subject to the extreme limitations of their personal rights dealt with in section 35.3.[15] In this sense, they were defined not as members of the "family" so much as by their location in the ongoing collective construct of the family holdings. Consider the modern farmers and aristocrats who describe themselves as "holding the land in trust for my children/future generations".[16] The Roman family estate was enshrined in law as a unit in which all members had some stake and which was part of the family's history and future, but legally the unit was owned and managed by the *pater familias* for life. A son's money was termed *peculium* (the same term applied to that of a slave)—something he could own and administer, but subject to the control of the *pater familias*.[17]

35.3 Rights and Obligations of Individual Family Members

This financial control involved obligations, especially the obligation of the father to feed his children. It also affected other powers, such as the children's freedom to marry or divorce. A valid Roman marriage required the consent of the fathers of the bride and groom.[18] The social reality was more nuanced: the women of the family played a key role in arranging matches, and older sons and daughters remarrying were more likely to make their own decisions, but legally and socially the father's situation was powerful, not least because he alone could authorise a dowry for his daughter or provide a son with the means to establish and maintain a conjugal household. Paternal authority was not all that it has been held to be by scholars, but by the standards of twenty-first-century Western culture, it was extraordinary.

It was long assumed that this economically conservative institution reflected the values of an agrarian society in Latium in the regal and early Republican period, from the eighth to the third centuries BC, in which multigenerational households probably worked subsistence farms.[19] Leaving aside the issue of whether this joint patriarchal household ever existed, it is a fact that over time—let us say, from about the eighth century BC to the

[15] Saller 1999; McDonnell 2006, 174.

[16] This aristocratic commonplace has been extended to national heritage (Harris 1994, 886) and become a generalised environmental statement: "We do not inherit the land from our ancestors, we borrow it from our children". Sometimes represented as a Native American saying (e.g. http://www.theclimategroup.org/blogs/changhua-wu-the-clean-revolution-in-china/caring-for-the-earth-that-is-borrowed-from-our-children/ (accessed 17 March, 2016)), the trope has been used e.g. by Kofi Annan (http://en.wikiquote.org/wiki/Kofi_Annan, last accessed 15 February 2014) and is likely to be of more general origin.

[17] Thomas 1982.

[18] This was slightly modified over time, Treggiari 1982, 1991.

[19] e.g. Westrup 1934. This longstanding proposition, first challenged by Crook 1967a and regularly contested by Saller esp. 1994, has recently been upheld with the usual literary examples by

sixth century AD—Roman political power extended not only over the Italian peninsula but throughout the Mediterranean and beyond. Roman rule extended to great masses of slaves, former slaves, freeborn citizens of subject states and—increasingly—a broad range of ethnically and culturally diverse Roman citizens who came under the umbrella of Roman law. Gaius' observation about the special powers of the Roman *pater familias* goes on to refer to the emperor Hadrian's (117–138 AD) response to the implications for a petitioning citizen. The effective extension of Roman citizenship in 212 AD to nearly all free subjects of the Empire arguably had its greatest impact in the transfer of this uniquely Roman institution.[20]

Standard Roman textbooks list the powers of the *pater familias* over his wife and children, and scholars have examined all the elements to test their limits and changes over time or across different regions.[21] The list includes the power to decide whether to rear a newborn and the power to kill an adult child for justifiable causes—such as the adultery of a married daughter or treasonable behaviour by a son.[22] Over time, such decisions were hedged about by legal and social expectations and qualifications. A Roman *pater familias* could sell his sons and pay off debts with his children's labour, but the law eventually determined that if he bonded his son, the son was emancipated from his power (*potestas*) when he had served the due time. The strongest checks on paternal power were applied under Imperial rule, eventually prohibiting a father from ending a daughter's happy marriage against her will. This list is necessarily a summary version.[23]

35.4 Agnatic and Cognate Relations: The Framework of Inheritance and Legal Kinship

The term *proximus agnatus* ("nearest agnate") occurred in the XII Tables formulated in the fifth century BC.[24] Agnatic relations in Roman law were determined through the male line. If a Roman man *sui iuris* married lawfully and had legitimate children they became his heirs (*sui heredes*), as did his sons' legitimate children. If he had no children and died intestate, his closest agnate (*proximus agnatus*) was his own brother or sister or, failing them, the children of his brothers. The agnatic line governed succession to material goods, but also to the family name and to sacral and other obligations. A minor whose father died succeeded to the inheritance in equal shares but fell into the guardianship (*tutela*) of his closest adult male agnate until the age of majority (14 for a boy originally, but this was later extended to 25, in the lesser form of *curatela*). Thus property itself passed equally to siblings of both

McDonnell 2006, 174. Cf. Dixon 1992, 3–5, which briefly locates the traditional view in its scholarly context.

[20] Taubenschlag 1916, now superseded by the detailed analysis of Arjava 1998a.

[21] e.g. Jolowicz 1932/1965, 248–249; Thomas 1976, 413–418; Kaser 1955, 290–299.

[22] Corbier 1993; Westbrook 1999; Benke 2012.

[23] Jolowicz 1932/1965, 248–249; McDonnell 2006.

[24] Jolowicz 1932/1965, 122; Bruns 1969, 15–40.

sexes, but responsibility for administering the estates of others—including those mentally incapable of managing their own share, by reason of their age (*minores*), gender, insanity or prodigality (*furiosi* and *prodigi*)—was held by the closest adult, legally independent male relation(s) through the male line, such as a paternal uncle(s) or older brother.

The closest agnates of an unmarried, fatherless Roman man were his brother or sister (*consanguinei*, "blood connections") and they were his heirs if he died without having made a will. If after marrying by *iustum matrimonium* ("proper marriage") that man had legitimate children, those children became his closest agnates and his heirs (*sui heredes*). Originally, there was no gender distinction between agnates but gradually female agnates beyond the immediate level of sibling (*consanguineus*) or child (*suus heres*) were eliminated—that is, your sister or legitimate daughter were very close in the line of intestate succession, but nieces were not on an equal footing with nephews, nor were female cousins reckoned the same as male cousins.

The term *proximus agnatus* continued to figure in praetorian decisions assigning an estate awarded on intestacy. In practical terms, though, *agnati* tended to be used of those beyond the immediate level of proximity—just as in common English usage "relatives" is generally used of those *beyond* the immediate nuclear family. *Agnati* was essentially confined to legal contexts, whereas the general term *cognati* (relatives), which embraced all family relationships, appeared in literary and epigraphic sources.

As well as material goods, Roman family members inherited the family (gentile) name from their father. They also inherited the family *sacra*, the obligation to honour ancestors at regular festivals for the dead. There was a general rule of thumb that a universal heir should pay for the proper funeral of the deceased person out of the estate. Patrician or plebeian rank, which had become socially meaningless by the late Republic, was also inherited from the father but nobility had to be earned by each generation.

Quite apart from inheritance, Romans always had a good understanding of their kin connections.[25] Brothers and sisters saw themselves as closely related, even if a sister was legally a member of her husband's family, even if a brother had for some reason been released from their father's power (*potestas*).[26] The law, too, acknowledged this "blood" connection in certain contexts, as in deeming brother–sister sexual connections unlawful even between slaves, who technically had no legal family.[27] Prohibitions against lavish gifts, designed to avoid the erosion of estates, allowed for exceptions on the grounds of (biological) kinship, and these, too, extended beyond technical definitions of family.[28]

The overwhelming issue in Roman law of the family stemmed from a change in marriage preference, in consequence of which there was, strictly speaking, little legal relationship between husband and wife and therefore between mother and child. By the late Republic (first century BC) it was unusual for a wife to be in her husband's "hand" (*manus*, analogous to *potestas*). She therefore legally remained a member of her family and was in her father's power (*potestas*), and on his death became "independent" (*sui iuris*). If a

[25] Dixon 1992, 140 on the tendency to maintain and extend kinship (e.g. to in-law connections) rather than reduce it. Cf. D.22.5.5.

[26] e.g. through adoption by a new *pater familias*; see Lindsay 2011.

[27] On slave and soldier families see Dixon 1988, 53–58.

[28] The exceptions to the *lex Cincia* of 204 BC were primarily based on family relationship, including cognate relationships (*Fr.Vat.* 266–316, Rotondi 1912/1966, 262).

married woman *sui iuris* died intestate, her own immediate family (brothers and sisters, then brothers' male children) inherited her estate as being her closest relatives at law. There was no strong expectation that husbands and wives would name each other in the first instance as heirs, so that was not seen as a problem. It is apparent, however, that by this time it was deemed proper that her children should be her heirs.

This anomaly could be addressed in practice by making a will. In principle a Roman will had few limitations or restrictions. A Roman woman *sui iuris* could therefore—with the authorisation of her *tutor/es*—institute her children as heirs. This seems to have happened regularly and was generally approved by society at large, which saw the mother–child bond as significant, whatever the legal position. Interestingly, such a development must have been facilitated by the married woman's own male relatives, since they were most likely to exercise *tutela* ("guardianship") over her financial and legal dealings or to have passed that on to other men.[29] Roman family and inheritance law was traditionally based on checks against the erosion of family property.

By late Republican and early Imperial times, the mother–child bond was acknowledged socially. Its legal recognition through praetorian and Imperial judgements, then Imperial legislation, was slower.[30] The process is mapped in summary form by a Byzantine preamble:

> So rigorously did the law of the XII Tables observe the rigid rule of giving preference to issue by males and of rejecting those who were related to a person through the female line that there was no mutual right of taking each other's inheritance even between a mother and her son or daughter, save insofar as the praetors would summon such persons to the succession, through the closeness of their cognatic relationship, by the possession of the estate styled 'as cognates' (*unde cognati*). (Inst.3.3pr *On the Tertullian senatus consultum*)
>
> Conversely, the Orfitian senatus consult was passed to allow children to succeed their intestate mothers, being introduced in the consulate of Orfitus and Rufus in the reign of the divine Marcus. Both son and daughter succeed at law, even though they be in the power of another; and they take precedence over blood brothers and agnates of their deceased mother. (Inst.3.4pr *On the Orfitian senatus consultum*)[31]

By the same token, some concessions were eventually made to the possibility of widowed mothers acting effectively as *tutores*—financial administrators—for their minor children. This was a great departure from the hardwired principle that *tutores* were male monitors of family estates. It, too, had ramifications for the later, Christian Empire.[32]

In fact, the impact of Christianity on Roman law of the family is still being teased out. Scholars have argued that the Church had a vested interest in reshaping kin presumptions

[29] A Roman father could nominate a *tutor* in his will. Otherwise *tutela legitima* would pass on the rules of intestacy to a woman's brother(s) or, failing brothers, a paternal uncle. A *tutor legitimus* could decline the duty and nominate a *tutor*, e.g. a freed slave with financial skills, as long as he was a male Roman citizen. Dixon 1984 on the changes to the concept of lifelong female *tutela* and its eventual disappearance.

[30] Dixon 1988, 44–47. Crucial developments in the second century AD include the Hadrianic *senatus consultum Tertullianum* acknowledging a bereaved mother's (limited) right to succeed to her child, and the *senatus consultum Orfitianum* 178 AD giving children a limited right of succession to their mothers' estate on her intestate death.

[31] Translation Thomas 1975.

[32] Vuolanto 2002.

and attitudes to marriage—especially remarriage—and reproduction and the disposition of property.[33] The penalties Augustan legislation imposed on childless widows and widowers virtually enforced remarriage, a practice frowned on in early Christianity. This trend, and the favouritism towards parents of three children, were eased out of the Imperial legal system.[34]

Others, however, have seen more evidence of continuity than radical change to the law of family and marriage following the Emperor Constantine's momentous decision to bring Christianity officially inside the Imperial tent in the fourth century AD.[35] The relationship was not clear-cut. The great mass of ethnically diverse Roman subjects had, after all, always operated under a potentially dual (or more) system, especially if they were Roman citizens—like the apostle Paul or the inhabitants of Roman Egypt. The widowed Jewish businesswoman Babatha showed a readiness to "cherry pick" the legal means most useful to her. We are still determining the extent to which kinship and related legal concepts were shaped by this kind of interaction over the centuries.[36]

Ambiguity and contradiction were embedded in law of the family and drove change. But piecemeal. Slaves had no family at law, yet they formed families and sometimes, painfully, achieved freedom for key members to ensure a family future through manipulating the possibility for status mobility that remained in Roman law until the social hardening of late Antiquity.[37] Soldiers, forbidden marriage under Augustus' legislation, also formed unions and were slowly granted concessions for their sons, who did have the legal rights of legitimate Roman children.[38]

35.5 Conclusion

Family is universally a significant concept, frequently presented in moral and emotional terms among others. This essay, in legal handbook format, has focused on issues of power and property within the family, such as legitimacy, ownership, marriage, inheritance and legal definitions of family membership and obligations. It has necessarily taken a reductive approach to the Roman family, summarising complex scholarly issues, and merely touching on the impact of the regional differences and massive economic changes arising from Imperial expansion. The impact of Christianity on the law and practice of Roman institutions such as marriage and the family continues to be the subject of intense debate.

Insofar as there is a consistent historical thread in the law of the Roman family over the period from regal Rome to the Christian Empire of Justinian's Digest, it is in the intermittent accommodation by the legal system of social imperatives. The change in marriage preference within Roman Italy by the late Republic involved a shift in legal family relations, not least between mother and child, which forced change to rules governing

[33] The most radical thesis is that of Goody 1983.

[34] McGinn 2008. On remarriage, see Humbert 1972.

[35] Beaucamp 1990; Evans Grubbs 1995.

[36] Lewis 1983 and 1994; Kraemer 2003; Oudshoorn 2007.

[37] Rawson 1966; Martin 2003. Garnsey 1970a on the change in status access.

[38] Dixon 1992, 53–58; Garnsey 1970b; Phang 2001.

inheritance and maternal "guardianship". But change which did not cause conflict and therefore recourse to the law tends to go unnoticed by historians, since it leaves fewer traces in the record. The effective impact of *patria potestas* played out differentially throughout the multi-ethnic Empire and the traditional Roman institution of "perpetual guardianship of women" simply petered out, as "*manus* marriage" had done before it.

Scholars of Roman law and the family are themselves subject to historical change. They are less inclined these days to look for universal, racially based origins or for simplistic connections between Christianity and attitudes to marriage or children. Whether they focus on the ideas within the surviving legal *corpus* or choose to move beyond the traditional sources and regional boundaries of earlier generations of scholars, they are sure to challenge existing notions and to enhance our understanding of the Roman family and its legal manifestations. Like the family, their task is dynamic.

Bibliography

Arjava, A. (1998a). "Paternal power in late antiquity." *Journal of Roman Studies* 88: 147–165.

Arjava, A. 1998b. *Women and law in late antiquity.* Oxford.

Balch D. and C. Osiek, eds. 2003. *Early Christian families in context.* Grand Rapids.

Beaucamp, J. 1990. *Le statut de la femme à Byzance (4e–7e siècle), I (Le droit impérial).* Paris.

Benke, N. (2012). "On the Roman father's right to kill his adulterous daughter." *The History of the Family* 17: 284–308.

Bruns, C. G. 1909. Fontes Iuris Romani Antiqui. Tübingen (Aalen, single-volume 1969 reprint).

Corbett, P. E. 1930. *The Roman law of marriage.* Oxford.

Corbier, M. 1993. "Constructing kinship in Rome: marriage, divorce, filiation, and adoption." In D. Kertzer and R. Saller eds., *The family in Italy from antiquity to the present.* New Haven. 127–144.

Corbier, M. 2001. "Child exposure and abandonment." In S. Dixon, ed., *Childhood, class and kin in the Roman world.* London/New York. 52–73.

Crook, J. A. (1967a). "*Patria Potestas.*" *The Classical Quarterly* 17: 113–122.

Crook, J. A. 1967b. *Law and life of Rome.* London.

de Zulueta, F. 1946. *The Institutes of Gaius.* Part I Text with Critical Notes and Translation. Oxford.

de Zulueta, F. 1953. *The Institutes of Gaius.* Part II Commentary. Oxford.

Dixon, S. (1984). "*Infirmitas sexus*: womanly weakness in Roman law." *The Legal History Review/Tijdschrift voor Rechtsgeschiedenis* 52: 343–371.

Dixon, S. 1988. *The Roman mother.* London.

Dixon, S. 1992. *The Roman family.* Baltimore/London.

Engels, F. 1884. *The origins of the family, private property and the state, in light of the researches of Lewis H. Morgan.* Moscow.

Evans Grubbs, J. 1995. *Law and family in late antiquity: the emperor Constantine's marriage legislation.* Oxford.

Gardner, J. F. 1986. *Women in Roman law and society.* London.

Gardner, J. F. 1993. *Being a Roman citizen.* Beckenham.

Garnsey, P. 1970a. *Social status and legal privilege in the Roman empire.* Oxford.

Garnsey, P. (1970b). "Septimius Severus and the marriage of soldiers." *California Studies in Classical Antiquity* 3: 45–53.

Goody, J. 1983. *The development of the family and marriage in Europe.* Cambridge.

Harders, A.-C. 2013. "*Agnatio, cognatio, consanguinitas*: kinship and blood in Ancient Rome." In C. H. Johnson, et al. eds., *Blood and kinship: matter for metaphor from ancient Rome to the present.* New York. 18–39.

Harris, R. E. 1994. *From Essex England to the sunny southern U.S.A.: a Harris family journey.* Atlanta.

Himmelfarb, G. 1968. *Victorian minds* (1995 Elephant paperback, Chicago; from 1968 original, Knopf, New York).

Humbert, M. 1972. *Le remariage à Rome: étude d'histoire juridique et sociale.* Milan.

Jolowicz, H. F. 1932/1965. *A historical introduction to the study of Roman law.* Cambridge.

Kaser, M. 1955. *Das römische Privatrecht I.* Munich.

Kraemer, R. S. 2003. "Typical and atypical family dynamics: the cases of Babatha and Berenice." In D. Balch and C. Osiek eds., *Early Christian families in context.* Grand Rapids. 13–157.

Lewis, N. 1983. *Life in Egypt under Roman rule.* Oxford.

Lewis, N. 1989. "The documents from the Bar Kokhba Period in the cave of letters: Greek Papyri." Jerusalem.

Lewis, N. (1994). "The Babatha archive: a response." *Israel Exploration Journal* 44: 243–246.

Lindsay, H. 2011. "Adoption and heirship in Greece and Rome." In B. Rawson, ed., *A companion to families in the Greek and Roman worlds.* Oxford/Malden. 346–360.

Martin, D. 2003. "Slave families and slaves in families." In D. Balch and C. Osiek eds., *Early Christian families in context.* Grand Rapids. 207–230.

McDonnell, M. 2006. *Roman manliness:* 'virtus' *and the Roman republic.* Cambridge.

McGinn, T. A. J. (2008). "Something old, something new: Augustan legislation and the challenge of social control." *Ancient History Bulletin* 22:1–32.

Oudshoorn, J. C. 2007. *The relationship between Roman law and local law in the Babatha and Salome Komaise archives: general analysis and three case studies on law of succession, guardianship and marriage.* Leiden.

Phang, S. E. 2001. *The marriage of Roman soldiers (13 B.C.–A.D. 235): law and family in the imperial army.* Leiden.

Rawson, B. (1966). "Family life among the lower classes at Rome in the first two centuries of the Empire." *Classical Philology* 61: 71–83.

Riccobono, S., et al. eds. 194–1943, Fontes Iuris Romani Anteiustiniani (FIRA). Florence.

Rotondi, G. 1912/1966. Leges Publicae Populi Romani. Milan/Hildesheim.

Sabean, D. W. and Teuscher, S. 2013. "Introduction." In C. H. Johnson, et al. eds., *Blood and kinship: matter for metaphor from ancient Rome to the present.* New York. 1–17.

Sachers, E. 1949. "*Pater familias.*" In *Realencyclopädie der classischen Altertumswissenschaft* 18.4, 212–2157. Stuttgart.

Sachers, E. 1953. "*Potestas patria.*" In *Realencyclopädie der classischen Altertumswissenschaft* 22.1, 1046–1175. Stuttgart.

Saller, R. P. 1994. *Patriarchy, property and death in the Roman family.* Cambridge.

Saller, R. P. (1999). "*Pater familias, mater familias*, and the gendered semantics of the Roman household." *Classical Philology* 94: 182–198.

Shaw, B. C. (2001). "Raising and killing children: two Roman myths." *Mnemosyne* 54: 131–177.

Taubenschlag, R. (1916). "Die *patria potestas* im Recht der Papyri." *Zeitschrift der Savigny-Stiftung für Rechtsgeschichte, romanistische Abteilung*, VII, 37: 177–230.

Thomas, J. A. C. 1975. *The Institutes of Justinian: text, translation and commentary*. Amsterdam/Oxford/New York.

Thomas, J. A. C. 1976. *Textbook of Roman law*. Amsterdam/Oxford/New York.

Thomas, Y. (1982). "Droit domestique et droit politique à Rome: remarques sur le pécule et les honores des fils de famille." *Mélanges d'archéologie et d'histoire de l'école française de Rome: Antiquité* 94: 528–580.

Thomas, Y. 1986/1996. "Fathers as citizens of Rome, Rome as a city of fathers (second century BC–second century AD)." In A. Burguière et al. eds., *A history of the family*. Vol. 1: *Distant worlds, ancient worlds*. Oxford. 228–269 (French original, Paris, 1986).

Treggiari, S. (1982). "Consent to Roman marriage: some aspects of law and reality." *Échos du Monde Classique/Classical Views* 26: 24–34.

Treggiari, S. 1991. *Roman marriage:* iusti coniuges *from the time of Cicero to the time of Ulpian*. Oxford.

Vuolanto, V. 2002. "Women and the property of fatherless children in the Roman Empire." In P. Setälä et al., eds., *Women, wealth and power in the Roman empire*. Rome. 203–243.

Watson, A. 1967. *The law of persons in the later Roman republic*. Oxford.

Westbrook, R. 1999. "*Vitae necisque potestas*." *Historia* 48: 203–223.

Westrup, C.W. 1934. *Introduction to early Roman law: comparative sociological studies. The patriarchal joint family*. Copenhagen.

CHAPTER 36

HUSBAND AND WIFE

JAKUB URBANIK

36.1 Introduction

The fact that the Roman law of marriage has been subjected to extensive study in contemporary scholarship is in itself noteworthy.[1] And yet there is seemingly nothing so alien to marriage in the modern world than the specific way in which the Roman jurists treated marriage. Moreover, there seems to have been quite a gap between what the Roman lawyers thought and what the average person in Rome considered as marriage. Last but not least, the law seems to have been concerned much more with the economic consequences of marriage than with the marriage itself. A number of the sources, therefore, deal primarily with the issue of the creation and return of dowry and nuptial donations; the fact of the marriage was only of secondary interest. Yet these texts are crucial in reconstructing the legal nature of Roman marriage. In this chapter I will first consider the tension between marriage-in-law and marriage-in-society. I will thereafter examine the (modern) theories on the legal construct of marriage, analyse the same dichotomy in ancient sources, and finally I will attempt to explain the unusual way the Roman marriage was constructed.[2] In this chapter I will deal solely with the construct of marriage proper, leaving aside all the economic issues connected to it such as the dowry and the principles governing its return via *actio rei uxoriae*; the system of matrimonial property (depending on whether the wife passed under the power (*manus*) of her husband or his *pater familias* or remained in her family of origin or independent); and the vexed question of the ban on donations between spouses.

[1] For a comprehensive treatment of the subject see e.g. Volterra 1991, and recently Astolfi 1996–2012. For a social perspective see Treggiari 1991.

[2] See section 36.2 and section 36.6; the "oddness" of the Roman construct is visible not only when compared to modern perspectives on marriage, which are still strongly influenced by canon law, but also when contrasted to its contemporaries within the Mediterranean; cf. e.g. Mélèze Modrzejewski 1979 for Greek marriage.

36.2 Consorts in Law

A useful collection of the notable legal principles ascribed to Ulpian and put together around the end of the classical period offers a comprehensive description of marriage in law: [3]

> A legitimate marriage is made when there is *conubium* between the contracting parties, and if the man is an adult and the woman is able to procreate, and if both of them agree—if they are legally independent—or also their parents, if they are still in their power. (Tit. Ulp.5.2; cf. D.23.2.2)

Three conditions have to be met in order to constitute a union recognised as marriage by law (or perhaps, phrased differently, for a marriage to have legal effect). Marriage is contracted between two people of legal age (i), having the capacity to marry (*conubium*) in relation to one another (ii), and through their agreement to marry (iii).

(i) *Age*. The author does not specify what the exact legal age for marriage is. Following the Sabinian tradition he prefers an individual decision in each case. One becomes adult as soon as one is able to procreate. This rule was not uncontested: the Proculians favoured fixing the moment of coming of age—fourteen for boys, twelve for girls—the solution adopted by Justinian, and through him the canonical legal order. Nevertheless, its invocation in the classical period demonstrates one of the most important features of Roman marriage: its procreative goal. Marriage was contracted *liberorum quaerendorum/procreandorum causa*[4] (for the same reason any kind of a legally recognised union between people of the same sex in Roman Antiquity was clearly not a marriage in the legal sense).[5] This aspect, intrinsic to Roman marriage as early as the archaic period, is clearly visible in the myth of the "first" Roman divorce—of Publius Carvilius Ruga on the grounds of his wife's sterility (Watson 1965). It was reinforced even further in the Augustan legislation

[3] With Volterra (cf. Volterra 1972, 442–444 [= 179–180]), against J. Gaudemet (1949, 321) and others, I assume that even if the passage in question may not be classical itself, it transmits a genuinely classical idea (compare Avenarius 2005). It is much more revealing than the renowned fragment from the works of Modestinus: D.23.2.1: Marriage is a joining of a husband and a wife, a partnership in all aspects of life, a communication under divine and human law. Cf. also, *inter alia*, Volterra 1991, 230.

[4] See Péter 1991, *passim*, esp. s. iii 3, for a study of the history of the formula, which is predominately known from literary sources and from evidence of legal practice (see *P. Mich.* vii 434 + *P. Ryl.* iv 612 = *ChLA* iv 249 = *SB* V 8011 = *FIRA* III 17 = *CPL* 208–209, http://www.papyri.info/ddbdp/chla;4;249/ (accessed 8 April 2016), second half of the second century AD) and only rarely found in dogmatic texts (cf. C.5.4.9 [a. 276–282] and D.50.16.220.3), a fact possibly due to the Justinianic adjustment of these texts. See also Volterra 1991, 236–238, n. 30.

[5] The notices of the supposed "marriages" of Nero (cf. Suet. *Ner.* 28–29, Dio Cass. 62.29, 63.13) and Elagabalus (SHA *Heliogab.* 10; Dio Cass. 80.15), being everything that a Roman marriage *was not*, prove it sufficiently. On the legal existence of homosexual partnerships (e.g. the disputed tomb of the co-free-women Fonteia Helena and Fonteia Eleusis, *CIL* VI 18524, Augustan period?), see literature at http://www.britishmuseum.org/research/collection_online/collection_object_details.aspx?assetId=391042&objectId=394264&partId=1, accessed 29 January 2016; on the subject see also Hersch 2010, 33–38.

promoting marriage and procreation, hence the appearance of legal debates as to whether a sterile man may marry at all.[6] Even if we admit that the laws passed during the reign of the first *princeps* had little, if any, effect on the actual growth of the Roman population, they still expressed the social and legislative ideal of marriage, an idea, also mirrored in legal practice.[7]

(ii) *Conubium* corresponds to the positive ability to contract a lawful marriage with a specified person (Roselaar 2013). Some factors indicate the general marriageability of an individual, yet it always needs to be assessed in a particular case, and it is therefore a relative quality. This quality is first and foremost linked to Roman citizenship. Roman marriage was an institution of political life, its main functions being the strengthening of the civic community and the increase of the citizen body. Yet, as is well known, the Roman concept of citizenship differed greatly from the politic attitude of any of the Greek *poleis*. With the rise of the Republic and later under the Principate, alongside the extensive expansion of Roman territory in the Mediterranean and beyond, it became more inclusive. The *ius conubii* was gradually extended to new groups of non-citizens, starting with the Latins. This comes as no great surprise, since the inhabitants of Latium would be—in the eyes of the Romans themselves—the closest kin to the inhabitants of Rome. In 4 AD the *lex Aelia Sentia*, while limiting manumissions, provided that a person freed contrary to its provisions could still gain citizenship status if he fathered a year-old child in a relationship with another Latin or Roman. Thus such non-citizens obtained *conubium* with Romans as long as it had been done in order to produce children. [8] Interestingly, especially in view of the considerations of section 36.4, even if their marriage did not produce all the legal effects of a union between citizens (the father did not acquire *patria potestas* over his children) it was still termed a lawful marriage (*matrimonium iustum: T.H.* 89, l. 5 [63 AD], *legitimae nuptiae: Lex Irnitana* par. 2A).

In some cases *conubium* would be excluded entirely for specified groups of people. An often-cited case is the lack of *conubium* between patricians and plebeians prior to *lex Canuleia*, seemingly because of religious reasons, though in reality it was also an attempt to consolidate the patrician order (Linderski 2005, esp. 23–231; Liv. 4.6.2). Until a change of the law by Septimius Severus in 197 AD, soldiers were divested of *conubium* during their service, and yet they kept informal unions, which to all social effects seem to have been treated like true marriages,[9] and which would be recognised as such upon an honourable discharge. Officials sent from the capital to the provinces could not marry local women because of the Imperial mandates (see n. 12). Augustus withdrew[10] *conubium* between people of senatorial rank of either sex and freedmen as well as free-born persons involved

[6] See D.28.2.6pr and D. 23.3.39.1; see also Val. Max. 7.7.4.

[7] See *P. Mich.* vii 434 + *P. Ryl.* iv 612, *PSI* vi 730, but also Greek contracts of divorce and marriage from the epoch post-dating the *Constitutio Antoniniana*, e.g. *P. Cair. Masp.* i 67006v (Antinoopolis, 566–570 AD, marriage) and *P. Lond.* v 1712 (Antinoopolis, 569 AD, divorce).

[8] See Camodeca 2006, 189–211, esp. 200–201 for the description of the privilege granted by *lex Aelia Sentia*.

[9] A telling example is *P. Tiberianus* 11 (= *P. Mich.* vii 475, beginning of the second century AD, APIS record: michigan.apis.2451), a letter from a recruit Cl. Terentianus sent to his mentor Cl. Tiberanius (not father; see Strassi 2008, 113–123).

[10] Rather than confirm the earlier Republican principles in the field. For a discussion of the problem see, among others, McGinn 1998, ch. 3 and esp. 85–102 with literature.

in disreputable trades (first and foremost prostitutes and procurers but also actors and others who dedicated themselves to theatric arts).

Blood relation in the direct line excluded *conubium* entirely, in the lateral line marriage was allowed between first cousins, and since the time of Claudius and the notorious case of his marriage with Agrippina Iunior, an uncle could marry his fraternal niece. And yet, one has to stress, the Romans tolerated marriages of siblings or half-siblings among the Egyptians, at least until they were turned into Roman citizens by *Constitutio Antoniniana*.[11]

(iii) *Affectio*. The final aspect of the "Ulpianic" definition, agreement, seems *prima facie* self-evident. In order to marry one has to agree, if a party were in power of another, this person would have to grant his consent to the marriage as well. Numerous sources confirm this foundational principle of Roman marriage: formless consent is enough to constitute marriage, provided that other preliminary requirements have been satisfied:

> If anything has been bequeathed [to a woman] under the condition "should she marry into a family", the condition is taken to have been fulfilled as soon as the wife had been led [to the marital home], even if she has not yet entered the bedroom of the husband. For marriage is made not by sleeping together but by consent (*consensus*). (D.35.1.15 = 50.17.30 [Ulpian])

Notice that the celebration of a nuptial procession is not decisive; it simply makes the consent to marriage, by itself formless, evident (D.24.1.66pr; Volterra 1991, 238–240). This is also visible in other texts: an attempted marriage, the beginning of which was visibly celebrated yet was void because of some impediment, comes into being as soon as this impediment ceases to exist, provided the parties still want to be married.[12] Another text containing the same principle reveals possibly the most bizarre—compared to what we think marriage is—aspect of the Roman marriage:

> If the wife and the husband have lived apart for a long time, yet they have a mutual regard for the marriage (which as we know happens even between people of consular rank), I deem the donations to be void, since the marriage continued; it is indeed not intercourse that makes marriage, but marital affection (*maritalis affectio*). (D.24.1.32.13; see also D.39.5.31pr, to the effect that marriage is created by *affectio*, and not by its documentation, *tabulae*)

The jurist discusses a donation made between husband and wife; a transaction prohibited by law. Its validity will naturally depend on the (non-)existence of the marriage. The couple in question apparently lived apart, yet they regarded one another as their spouse,

[11] A provocative hypothesis of Hübner, that the endogamic marriages were practiced between adopted siblings and not blood ones, has met fierce criticism (Hübner 2007; Remijsen and Clarysse 2008; Rowlandson and Takahashi 2009, see also Mélèze-Modrzejewski 1964). It is interesting to notice how the former spouses become in the documentary practice just "siblings" post 212 AD (cf. the archive of Theognostos, and a recently published *P. Pintaudi* 42 preserving a wet-nurse contract for a baby born to a brother–sister union after the *Constitutio Antoniniana*).

[12] D. 23.2.4: a girl younger than twelve becomes a lawful wife the day she comes of age; D. 23.2.65.1: a marriage of a provincial official to a local woman becomes valid the day he demits his office, as long as he "persists in the same will (i.e. still wants to be married)" (*si in eadem voluntate perseverat*); cf. also a citation of Paul's statement in a similar case dealt with by Gordian in his response to Valeria, C.5.4.6 (a. 239).

hence the donation was considered void. Notice that in order to draw this conclusion, Ulpian needs to assume that during the entire time of the marriage both spouses mutually fostered the idea of being married.

The creation of a marriage relies on the agreement of the spouses, but so also, it seems, does its continued existence. A number of sources in which the classical jurists discuss whether or not a marriage may have survived, notwithstanding a desertion on the part of one of the spouses, strengthen this hypothesis. I will deal with them in more detail in sections 36.4 and 36.5, as they constitute the nucleus of the modern debate on the formation of marriage in Rome. Before I can deal with this matter, though, I wish to draw attention to the discrepancy between the legal theory presented above and social reality.

36.3 Consorts in Life

A modest yet elegant Roman marble gravestone for the freedwoman Statilia Hilara provides the following:

> To Statilia Hilara, freedwoman of Titius. Amarantus the polisher and Philologus, the steward have erected (this monument) for the wife. You rest well, Hilara, and if the souls of the dead know it, remember our (names?), we shall never forget (yours). (*CIL* VI.2 625)

The inscription is one of thousands dedicated to the memory of a good wife, and it follows a typical pattern. Yet, as Treggiari and Dorken have noticed, this example stands out (Treggiari and Dorken 1981). Two men bid farewell to Hilaria, swearing not to forget her name. Both are slaves, and yet this seemingly does not prevent them from describing her as *coniunx*, "a wife". Hilara's tomb is one of over twenty collected by Treggiari and Dorken from among inscriptions from the city of Rome that provide evidence of a curious phenomenon: a woman with two living husbands who jointly erected her tombstone (Treggiari and Dorken 1981, 271–272). In many of these onomastics suggesting lower origins, they are often slaves or freedmen; sometimes one of the "husbands" is freeborn, the other of servile status.[13] The term *fidelissima coniu(n)x* (*CIL* VI.2 9366) is clearly not a legal term. Even if we discount the hypothesis that these people lived in a polyandrous union (Treggiari and Dorken suggest that the men may have been consecutive partners of the same woman, the first relationship possibly interrupted by a manumission of one the "spouses"), we are still left with ample epigraphic evidence of a legally impossible marriage between a slave and a free person.

Quadrato pointed out that this is not uncommon in the legal sources either (Quadrato 2010).[14] In a number of legal texts the terms that normally should refer to a marriage proper

[13] There is one Imperial slave (*CIL* VI.2 4370), and three monuments are dedicated to slave-women, one of them erected jointly by a citizen and slave. The inscriptions follow in great majority the same pattern. A notable exception stipulates that the tomb would be designed for the woman, the men who erect it and their children and freedmen (*CIL* VI.2 13268); in *CIL* VI.2 4370 the two husbands stress that they act together (*concordi*).

[14] While supporting his view in general, I am more sceptical about the attribution of the same idea to the term "marriage" in Ulpian's D.1.1.1.3. The jurist juxtaposes there the state of nature, as seen

(*uxor, vir, uxorem ducere, dos, dotem dare, nubo etc.*) actually denote attempted, yet void, marriages. A significant example is to be found in a famous case discussed by Paul:

> Lucius Titius when he had under his power a daughter Seia, gave her in marriage to Pamphilus, a slave belonging to someone else. He also gave him a dowry, which was documented as a deposit. The (slave's) master did not denounce the whole affair and the father died, and so did soon afterwards Pamphilus. I ask by what action Seia may demand the money, since she became the father's heiress. Paul answered, since he (the father) could not constitute a dowry, the money should be demanded on deposit with regards to the *peculium* (of the slave). (D.16.3.27; see Quadrato 2010, 235; Watson 1991)

Without going into the contractual nature of the agreement, note the following two points. First, the parties were conscious that the union in question could not be regarded as a marriage, and yet they intended it to be one and they made an effort to provide it with the best legal protection possible, (dis)simulating a marriage under a contract of deposit. In doing so they were not alone. Although the names of the persons in this text are standard in legal hypotheticals, this situation has close echoes in real life. Legal practice from Egypt provides cases of attempted marriage of soldiers, with dowries hidden, just like in this instance, under the pretext of a deposit. A telling example is visible in a pair of documents from Alexandria, *BGU* III 729 (a. 144 AD)—a contract of deposit, but actually a hidden dowry, and *P. Lond.* ii 178 (a. 145 AD), a declaration of the same woman that she has received her dowry back, having divorced the soldier.

In second place, the jurist does not seem to have been troubled by the apparent action of the parties in contravention of the law (think of the consequences of *s.c. Claudianum*!). Asked for legal advice for the woman, he carefully expounds his answer, pointing out that the legal remedy in question would have to consider the benefit of a praetorian action *de peculio*, otherwise the deposit could not be considered enforceable in the eyes of the civil law. This should not surprise. After all, a union of Seia and Pamphilus did not constitute a threat to the public order (and safety), unlike the attempted marriages of soldiers. In the latter case, which constituted a clear illegality, Roman officials were not so keen on granting legal protection (see *P. Catt.i*; Phang 2001, 33–34 and Appendix 1). However, again, once the threat to public order had been removed the well-disposed lawmaker would be likely to accept the legal effects of these non-legal situations. Hence, honourable discharge was regularly followed by a grant of citizenship and *conubium* with the wives (*sic*!: *uxores*) the soldiers had had by that time, as well as paternal power over any children that may already have been born (see, e.g. *CIL* XVI 24, ll. 11–16; a similar retroactive grant of *conubium* appears in other awards of citizenship, e.g. *Tabula Banasitana, IAM* 94). The reasons for the Hadrianic grant of *bonorum possessio* in the class of *liberi* to the illegitimate children of deceased soldiers were similar.[15]

by him, to human affairs. He seems therefore more likely to have used the term in its proper legal meaning (see further Urbanik 2014a).

[15] *BGU* I 140 (= *FIRA* I 78 = *MChr.* 373 = *Sel. Pap.* ii 213, 119 AD), ll. 1–28. Among other, noteworthy examples of the soldiers unions, on which see Phang 2001, *passim*, cf. also *P. Mich.* iii 203 (= *SB* IV 7356, Pselkis and Karanis 114–116 AD): a letter of a soldier Satornilos to his mother, announcing that "another male child has been born to me, whose name is Agathos Daimon" (http://papyri.info/ddbdp/p.mich;3;203, accessed 29 January 2016).

One needs to keep in mind, of course, that the law tried to draw a firm line between marriage and concubinage, seemingly reserving the latter for a situation in which a marriage would not be legally possible or socially acceptable,[16] in real life—as the examples above show—this distinction faded.[17] Moreover, every now and then, the law also seemed to have ceded before social reality.[18]

36.4 Modern Theories on Roman Law of Marriage

The legal nature of Roman marriage has been a source of debate within Romanist studies during the course of the last century.[19] In brief, the older view now defended only in a very few recent studies (Robleda 1970, ch. 3; Robleda 1980 and 1982; Huber 1977) held that Roman marriage was created by the initial consent of the spouses and that it persisted until one of the parties decided to end it through divorce. The now generally accepted view, on the other hand, regards the continuous agreement of the spouse to be married as the cornerstone of the marriage. In other words, a marriage ceases to exist as soon as either party loses the will to remain married. This theory, already put forward by Bonfante and Orestano, found its most fierce advocate in Edoardo Volterra. Two of his arguments deserve special mention.

The first was that divorce in Rome needed no form to take effect. In fact, in a number of passages, various jurists discuss the effectiveness of a divorce caused by a unilateral desertion (and hence the legal consequences of the validity of a donation or a duty to restore the dowry to the former wife). Take one picturesque example. D.24.1.64, a fragment of Labeo's works epitomised by Javolenus, presents an issue of nullity of a donation made by a now deserted husband to his ex-wife, should she thereafter return to her former spouse. In such a case, there could be doubt whether the separation was a real one (and thus the gift was valid) or a simulated one (and thus the gift was void). Labeo reports that the original case was presented to Trebatius and concerned an actual couple well known for their tortured

[16] Note also a very accurate statement by M. Humbert (Humbert 1990, 189) that concubinage was meant to "fill in the gaps left wanting by the law". See, e.g., D.24.1.3.1 with Quadrato 2010, 230–232. It remains doubtful whether a marriage could coexist with a concubinage: according to Sent.Paul. 2.20.1 having wife and a concubine at the same time was not permitted, yet a careful examination of other sources seem to demonstrate the contrary: Cristaldi 2014, 171–177 (see especially the epigraphic evidence, 173).

[17] Cf., e.g., *CIL* I.2 2527a (Rome, Republican period) a joint tomb of Publius Quinctius, freedman of Titius, a copyist, his wife and co-freedwoman Quinctia and Quinctia Agatea, his own freedwoman and concubine. It is not clear whether Quinctia (the wife) and Quinctia Agatea (the concubine) shared the life of Publius at the same time, but quite clearly it was not the social standing of either of them that made one *uxor* and the other concubine.

[18] See D.48.5.14.1 with Quadrato 2010, 233–235 and Rizzelli 1997, 187. See also a striking case of Flavia Tertulla married by her own grandmother to her maternal uncle. The emperors Marcus Aurelius and Lucius Verus recognised the legality of the issue of this union (D.23.2.57a).

[19] See also n. 1.

relationship, Maecenas and Terentia,[20] and that the original solution was based on whether or not the divorce was a real one. Javolenus adds that Proculus and Caecilius put forward some conditions to establish whether the divorce was real, a new marriage of the ex-partners or a lengthy separation, so long as there "would be no doubt the second marriage (of the people) was a new one". It is obvious from the context that the wife did not bother with any formalities when leaving her husband; the mere desertion—and thus an instantaneous lack of marital affection—was enough to break the marital bond. Other sources corroborate this idea.[21]

This position is not undermined by an apparent contradiction posed by D.24.2.9.[22] Solazzi suggested some time ago that the passage should be read in its original context, i.e. a study on adulteries, and thus most probably initially[23] referred to the procedure introduced only for divorce involving the infidelity of the wife. Volterra followed this reasoning.[24] The chief argument of the supporters of the initial consent theory, namely that in all of the sources discussing unilateral separations the parties complied with this procedure, and the jurists dispensed with mentioning that fact as an obvious one, clearly results in a vicious circle.[25] Contrariwise: if in all these instances the seven-witnesses procedure had been actually followed, the jurists would have taken care to explain that the real will of the parties was not what it seemed to be: and yet they do not (as is the case D. 24.2.3 cited in section 36.5).[26]

The other argument, closely related to the first one, consists in a statement that the classical Roman law did not know bigamy. The contracting of a new marriage simply dissolved the previous one, as it was impossible to have marital affection for two persons at the same time. This becomes evident from even a cursory reading of D.24.1.64 and D.23.2.33, where the "veracity of divorce" is established, among others, by the fact that one of the ex-partners remarried.[27]

[20] Guarino 1992, 146, suggests it may very well have been Augustus who, in his capacity as Maecenas' heir, posed the question to his "court-lawyer" seeking to recover what had been expended by his testator.

[21] The other relevant sources, presenting, *mutatis mutandis*, similar problems, are D. 23.2.33, *Fr. Vat.* 106–107. See also D.25.2.11pr, citing Marcellus' 8 book of the *Digest* which grants *actio rerum amotarum* should either of the spouses expel the other from home.

[22] D.24.2.9: "no repudiation shall be ratified unless it happens in the presence of seven adult Roman citizens not including a freedman of the divorcing party."

[23] It is possible that this fragment was placed in the title 24.2 *De divortiis et repudiis* in order to expand the mandatory application of the procedure, in harmony with Justinian's attempt to limit (and finally abolish) free divorce altogether.

[24] Solazzi 1960, 33–39, esp. 34–35 and n. 4; summary of Volterra's argumentation in Volterra 196–1961, 302. Other authors suggested that the procedure might be obligatory for all the unilateral divorces (Longo 1953, 93–95), a thesis, however unattainable in the light of the sources analysed above. See also Yaron 1963, *passim*, esp. 59–60, who thought the procedure would be necessary for a divorce between absent spouses, an interesting yet ultimately unprovable theory.

[25] Huber 1977, 151–152; Robleda 1982, 374–375; cf. also recently Astolfi 2004, 314–315.

[26] Three sources making explicit references to the "law" or "legal procedure" in regards to divorce are usually interpreted to favour the general application of the principle expressed in D.24.2.4. These are D.24.1.35, D.38.11.1.1 and D.48.5.44 (43). The two latter ones could possibly be dismissed as they concern, respectively, a particular case of a freedwoman's marriage to her patron and either Julian law on adulteries or the Law of XII Tables. The mention of a "*legitima observatio*" in D. 24.1.35 seems to constitute an obstacle to what has been said so far, yet its evidence clearly contradicts the majority view of D.24.1.64, D.23.2.33, *Fr. Vat.* 106–107 and D.25.2.11, so it may have originally had limited application as well; see further Volterra 196–1961, 304–305; Volterra 1999, 415–416 [= 235–236].

[27] See further Volterra 1999, *passim*. Read also D.24.2.11.2 where the jurist considers the cases in which a woman freed in order to marry her master retrieves *conubium* once she has divorced him. Again a number of circumstances make it evident that the patron had wanted to divorce her too.

Recently Astolfi tried to combine the two theories, arguing that to form a marriage according to Roman law, two forms of consent were necessary: the initial one to create and the continuous one to keep the marriage going (Astolfi 2004, esp. 26–43, 44–45). This idea stems from an ingenious construction of D.20.1.4, where Gaius compares mortgage to marriage to the extent that both are contracted and created *consensu*. I do not support this interpretation: matrimony (or rather its creation) is merely used here to explain that a hypothec is also contracted by a formless consent (so the passage does not regard the nature of marriage itself). Yet, this theory demonstrates an important fact about the nature of the studies on Roman marriage: the (pre)modern application of strict legal categories results in the overlegalisation of Roman marriage.

36.5 Between Law and Social Reality

The jurists seemed to be conscious of the problematic nature of their construction of marriage. They accordingly tried to mitigate the uncertainty brought about by this intrinsically dissoluble character of marriage by establishing two complementary principles. On the one hand, the dissolution of marriage once created was only effective if the parties showed their perseverance in the decision. This is best shown by a passage from Paul's commentary to the *Edict*:

> A true divorce only takes place if it occurs in the spirit of a permanent disjunction. Therefore whatever is done or said in heat of anger, shall not be ratified before persistence shows that it was the judgement of the spirit. And hence a wife who came shortly back having sent a bill of divorce (*misso repudio*) in the heat of the moment (*per calorem*) is not considered to have divorced. (D.24.2.3; see also D.24.1.32.12)

A *iudicium animi* manifested by a firm keeping of one's decision not to be married any more was therefore necessary for a divorce. This view is corroborated by a number of sources presenting the lack of any divorce formalities (discussed in section 36.4). The fact that a jurist might have asked whether a return of the same spouses constitutes a new marriage or continues the former state proves that for practical reasons the *affectio maritalis* formula cannot have been strictly applied in everyday life. On the other hand, the classical jurists seem to have created a sort of a presumption[28] of marriage in case of cohabitation of a man and a woman together. One of the *Rules* of Modestinus is the most evident proof of it:

> Companionship with a free woman should be interpreted as marriage not concubinage, unless she has made a trade of her body. (D.23.2.24)

This presumption was so strong that another late classical jurist, Marcian, instructed that if one wanted to keep a woman who would normally be considered marriageable as

[28] A Byzantine scholion to Bas.28.4.14 in fact employs the term πρόληψις (Scheltema—Holwerda b v 1818).

a concubine one should provide evidence of this fact by a written document (D.25.7.3pr, on which see McGinn 1991, 359–362; on its post-classical interpretation see Urbanik 2011, 129–130, n. 12).

Some certainty about the existence of a marriage was added through the institution of dowry. On the one hand, it made marriage more likely to have occurred. On the other, its restitution could help to assert the truth, rather than simulation of divorce.[29] Last but not least the social aspect of marriage, its importance for Roman society as such, often stressed in the sources, doubtlessly contributed to the formulation in favour of marriage as the guiding principle in the interpretation of other legal relations. An excerpt from the *Questions* of Paul is a clear proof:

> [O]ne has to adopt this solution for the benefit of the marriage (*favore nuptiarium*) and especially because of the sentiment of the persons. (D.24.3.45)

So formulated, the principle allows the jurist to overcome the rule excluding a stipulation made in favour of a third party and to grant a divorced spouse an *actio utilis* on the basis of a stipulation through which her maternal grandfather wanted to secure a restitution of the dowry to her upon the dissolution of marriage. Additionally in this case, this marriage-favourable interpretation seems to have been aimed at safeguarding the position of the woman who had posed the legal question. The same considerations may be drawn from the famous Ulpianic statement "marriage is created by an agreement and not by an intercourse". In the original case a woman sought a payment of a bequest left to her under a condition that she should marry. The marriage was contracted between absentees, a *ductio in domum mariti* followed, and then the husband most probably died. The decision that marriage indeed took place rendered the woman's standing much more beneficial (D.35.1.15, on which see Volterra 1991, 239 n. 34).

36.6 *Cui Bono?*

Why was such an impractical principle created? Why did the Roman jurists support a model of legally recognised unions that necessarily included a formless way to dissolve them? Why was a freely undertaken agreement not to dissolve one's marriage, or to pay a penalty should it happen, considered against *boni mores*, as we learn from a constitution of Alexander Severus?

> It has been established since time immemorial that marriages are free. And therefore neither agreements excluding divorce are valid, nor stipulations imposing pecuniary penalties on the one who divorces are to be ratified. (C.8.38.2 [a. 223])

A tentative answer—given the silence of the sources—may be sought via the identification of the beneficiaries of such a solution. Over sixty years ago Fritz Schulz stated:

[29] Even if in some cases the problem discussed in our sources is the fact that a valid marriage did not follow. See D.16.3.27 interpreted above or D.23.3.21 on efficacy of a dowry stipulation should eventually marriage not be contracted.

> The classical law of marriage is an imposing, perhaps the most imposing, achievement of the Roman legal genius. For the first time in the history of civilization there appeared a purely humanistic law of marriage, viz. a law founded on a purely humanistic idea of marriage as being a free and freely dissoluble union of two equal partners for life. (Schulz 1951, 103)

Who is favoured by a freely dissoluble marriage? Roman tradition imagined that in the early history a marriage was not dissoluble. The tenor of Plutarch's account of Romulus' mythical ban on divorce clearly shows whose benefit lay behind this decision (Plut. *Rom.* 9). The fact that half of the husband's estate goes to the woman illegally divorced clearly shows that her interest was at stake. Divorced, left alone, a woman who at marriage had been expected to legally leave her family of origin, was a non-entity in a patriarchal society. The gradual emancipation of women, both social and legal, and the decline of *conventio in manu mariti*, as well as the steady development of a legal duty on the part of the husband to restore the dowry (the praetorian *actio rei uxoriae*) went some distance to ameliorate the situation. Roman women gained a voice through these measures.[30] They did not need a husband any more in order to manage their affairs efficiently. And yet this radical legal and economic change did not alter the vision of the role of a wife in Roman society, which remained very much the same: adorned with *pudicitas*, devoted to wool-weaving, a faithful companion to her husband.[31]

Schulz's idea seems to be verified, *à rebours*, by Constantine's ban on unilateral divorces (CTh.3.16.1, a. 331). It is true that the law was addressed to both sexes, yet the consequences of the illicit divorce (as well the cases in which it was admitted) clearly show that the target of his enactment was the depraved cupidity (*prava cupiditas*) of freely divorcing wives. Should they dare desert their husbands and remarry, they would lose all their things up to the tiniest hairpin, an instrument by which the lawmaker literally pricked the bubble of overblown matrimonial freedom (see further Urbanik 2007 and 2014b).

I think we may add to Schulz's explanation yet another category of people for whom a free marriage would be advantageous, formally recognising their autonomy: adult children-in-power. The pseudo-Ulpianic text cited at the start of this chapter reminds us firmly that the consent of family superiors was necessary for marriage, but it was only secondary to the consent of the spouses. Moreover, by a provision of the *lex Iulia de maritandis ordinibus*, a *pater familias* who does not grant his consent could be made do so by a magistrate, and a Severan constitution compelled a father to provide a dowry (D.23.2.19). Other sources firmly restate that no father may impose marriage (or its rupture) on his child of whatever sex, no matter whether he/she is still under *potestas* or not.[32] The famous case of Dionysia (*P. Oxy.* ii 237, 189 AD, yet citing cases almost a century earlier) clearly

[30] Cf. e.g. one of many texts in which one presumes daughter's will by the fact she does not oppose her father: D.23.1.12: The one who does not reject father's will is understood to agree to it.

[31] As attested by copious epigraphic evidence, of which probably one of the most significant examples is the *Laudatio Murdiae* (*ILS* 8394), ll. 26–30; see further Lindsay 2004. Note, however, that the dedicatee must have been quite an independent woman herself, even if married twice and being mother to adult son(s). On a vision of women, oscillating between wool-weaving matron and prostitute see, most recently, Lamberti 2014 (64–65 on Murdia).

[32] See, e.g., D.23.2.21: A son-in-power ought not be compelled to marry. For impossibility to divorce one's child against his/her will see D.45.30.1.5, Sent.Paul.5.6.15, and C.5.17.5pr (a. 294). On the issue see further detailed discussion in Urbanik 2002.

shows that this principle, forming the Roman public order, was to correct the "inhumanity" of the local legal orders under Roman rule (Kreuzsaler and Urbanik 2008). Yet it also shows how far the social reality may have been from the legal ideal.

36.7 Conclusion

The gist of the legal view of Roman marriage is that no one may constrain another person to marry or stay married. We are reminded of it by yet another fragment of Marcian's Institutes:

> A patron cannot marry (his) unwilling freedwoman. (D.23.2.28)

Marriage remains the free choice of an individual, and in this sense it protects his or her autonomy. The jurists put forward this solution, which would by no means be widely socially accepted. The unanswerable question remains what prompted them to do so: in the light of the misogyny of our literary sources, the explanation offered above still puzzles us and calls out for revolutionary spirit among the jurists.[33]

To conclude, let us return to *CIL* VI 18524. The effigy contains two persons whose right hands are joined: obviously a married couple. Only later, reading the inscription, do we realise that cannot be the case, as both of them are women. We have been misled by appearances and preconceptions. This seems very often to be the case in modern studies of Roman marriage. Scholars of ancient history tend to underesteem the legal aspect of marriage. Modern legal historians, in turn, tend to "overlegalise" social reality. And both perceive Roman marriage through the lens of modernity, seeking to recognise the known traces, and sometimes trying to draw lessons from the past for the future (Urbanik 2014b).

Bibliography

Astolfi, R. 1996⁴. *La* lex Iulia et Papia. Padua.

Astolfi, R. 2000. *Il matrimonio nel diritto romano preclassico*. Padua.

Astolfi, R. 2004. *Il matrimonio nel diritto romano classico*. Padua.

Astolfi, R. 2012. *Studi sul matrimonio nel diritto romano postclassico e giustinianeo*. Naples.

Avenarius, M. 2005. *Der pseudo-ulpianische* liber singularis regularum: *Entstehung, Eigenart und Überlieferung einer hochklassischen Juristenschrift*. Göttingen.

Bonfante, P. 1963. *Corso di diritto romano, Vol. 1. Diritto di Famiglia*, ed. G. Bonfante and G. Crifò. Milan.

Camodeca, G. (2006). "Per una riedizione dell'archivio ercolanese di L. Venidius Ennychus. II. Il dossier sull'acquisto della civitas Romana mediante anniculi causae probatio *ex lege Aelia Sentia.*" *Cronache Ercolanesi* 36: 189–211.

[33] Suffice it to recall how Apuleius always impugns women for their divorces: "In either case it is the woman to be blamed, who either has been so unbearable that she had to be sent away, or so audacious to divorce herself" *(Apol.* 92).

Corbett, P. M. 1930. *The Roman law of marriage*. Oxford.

Cristaldi, S. A. 2014. "Unioni non matrimoniali a Roma." In F. Romeo, ed., *Le relazioni affettive non matrimoniali*. Milan. 141–200.

Gaudemet, J. (1949). "*Iustum matrimonium*." *Revue internationale des droits de l'antiquité* 2 (1949 = *Mélanges F. De Visscher* I), 309-366.

Guarino, A. (1992). "Mecenate e Terenzia." *Labeo* 38: 137–146.

Hersch, K. 2010. *The Roman wedding: ritual and meaning in Antiquity*. Cambridge.

Huber, J. 1977. *Der Ehekonsens im römischen Recht*. Rome.

Hübner, S. (2007). "'Brother–sister' marriage in Roman Egypt: a curiosity of humankind or widespread family strategy." *Journal of Roman Studies* 97: 21–49.

Humbert. M. 1990. "L'individu, l'état: quelle stratégie pour le mariage classique?" in *Parenté et stratégies familiales dans l'Antiquité romaine. Actes de la table ronde des 2-4 octobre 1986* (Paris). (Collection de l'École française de Rome, 129). Rome. 173–198.

Kreuzsaler, C. and Urbanik, J. (2008). "Humanity and inhumanity of law: the case of Dionysia." *The Journal of Juristic Papyrology* 38: 119–155.

Lamberti, F. (2014). "Donne romane fra Idealtypus e realtà sociale. Dal *domum servare* e *lanam facere* al *meretricio more vivere*." *Quaderni Lupiensi di storia e diritto* 4: 61–84.

Linderski, J. 2005. "Religious aspects of the conflict of the orders: the case of *confarreatio*." In K. A. Raaflaub, ed., *Social struggles in archaic Rome: new perspectives on the conflict of the orders*. Oxford. 223–238.

Lindsay, H. (2004). "The *Laudatio Murdiae*: its content and significance." *Latomus* 63: 88–97.

Longo, G. 1953[2]. *Diritto romano: Diritto di famiglia*. Rome.

McGinn, T. A. J. (1991). "Concubinage and the *Lex Julia* on adultery." *Transactions of the American Philological Association* 121: 335–375.

McGinn, T. A. J. 1998. *Prostitution, sexuality, and the law in ancient Rome*. Oxford.

Mélèze-Modrzejewski, J. (1964). "Die Geschwisterehe in der hellenistischen Praxis und nach römischem Recht." *Zeitschrift der Savigny-Stiftung für Rechtsgeschichte, romanistische Abteilung* 81: 52–82 (reprinted in *Statut personnel et liens de famille*, Aldershot 1993, no. VII).

Mélèze-Modrzejewski, J. (1981). "La structure juridique du mariage grec." *Symposion* (1979): 37–72. (= 1981. *Scritti in onore di Orsolina Montevecchi*. Bologna. 231–268), reprinted in *Statut personnel et liens de famille*, Aldershot 1993, no. V.

Péter, O. (1991). "*Liberorum quaerendorum causa*—L'image ideale du mariage et de la filiation a Rome." *Revue internationale des droits de l'antiquité* 38: 285–331.

Phang, S. E. 2001. *The marriage of Roman soldiers, 13 B.C.–A.D. 235: law and family in the imperial army*. Leiden.

Quadrato, R. (2010). "*Maris atque eminae coniunctio: matrimonium* e unioni di fatto." *Index* 38: 223–252.

Remijsen, S. and Clarysse, W. (2008). "Incest or adoption? Brother–sister marriage in Roman Egypt revisited." *Journal of Roman Studies* 98: 53–61.

Rizelli, G. 1997. Lex Iulia de adulteriis: *Studi sulla disciplina di* adulterium, lenocinium, stuprum. Lecce.

Robleda, O. 1970. *El matrimonio en derecho romano*. Rome.

Robleda, O. (1980). "Il consenso matrimoniale presso i Romani. Il mio punto di vista alla luce delle fonti." *Conferenze storico-giuridiche*: 101–151.

Robleda, O. (1982). "Il divorzio a Roma prima di Costantino." *Aufstieg und Niedergang der römischen Welt* II.14: 347–390.

Rowlandson, J. and Takahashi, R. (2009). "Brother–sister marriage and inheritance strategies in Greco-Roman Egypt." *Journal of Roman Studies* 99: 104–139.

Schulz, F. 1951. *Classical Roman law*. Oxford.

Solazzi, S. (1960). "Studi sul divorzio. III Il divorzio senza forme." *Scritti sul diritto romano* III. Naples. 1–38 [= (1925) *Bullettino dell'Istituto di Diritto Romano "Vittorio Scialoja"* 34: 295–319].

Strassi, S. 2008. *L'Archivio di Claudius Tiberianus da Karanis*. Berlin.

Treggiari, S. 1991. *Roman marriage:* iusti coniuges *from the time of Cicero to the time of Ulpian*. Oxford.

Treggiari, S. and Dorken, S. (1981). "Women with two living husbands in CIL 6." *Liverpool Classical Monthly* 6: 269–272.

Urbanik, J. 2002. "D. 24.2.4: ... *Pater tamen eius nuntium mittere posse*: l'influsso della volontà del padre sul divorzio dei sottoposti." In T. Derda, J. Urbanik and M. Węcowski, eds., Ἐυεργεσίας χάριν: *studies presented to Benedetto Bravo and Ewa Wipszycka by their disciples, Warsaw* [*The Journal of Juristic Papyrology Supplement*, no 1]: 293–336.

Urbanik, J. 2007. "La repressione constantiniana dei divorzi: La libertà dei matrimoni trafitta con una forcina." In Fides. Humanitas. Ius: *Studi in onore di Luigi Labruna*. Vol. 7. Naples. 5705–5726.

Urbanik, J. (2011). "Broken marriage promise and Justinian as a lover of chastity: on *Novela* 74 and *P. Cairo Masp.* i 67092 (553)." *Journal of Juristic Papyrology* 41: 123–151.

Urbanik, J. 2014a. "4.2 Divorce." In J. Keenan, J. Manning and U. Yiftach-Firanko, eds., *Law and legal practice in Egypt from Alexander to the Arab conquest: a selection of papyrological sources in translation, with introductions and commentary*. Cambridge. 154–174.

Urbanik, J. (2014b). "On the uselessness of it all: the Roman law of marriage and modern times." *Fundamina* 20: 946–960.

Volterra, E. 1960–1961. *Lezioni di diritto romano. Il matrimonio romano*. Rome.

Volterra, E. 1972. "*Iniustum matrimonium*," in *Studi in onore G. Schierillo* II. Milan. 441–470 [= 1991 *Scritti giuridici* III. Naples. 177–206].

Volterra, E. 1991. "*Matrimonio (diritto romano)*," in *Enciclopedia del diritto* xxv [= 1991 *Scritti giuridici* III. Naples. 22–303.]

Volterra, E. 1991–2002. *Scritti giuridici i–viii*. Naples.

Volterra, E. 1999. "Per la storia di reato di bigamia in diritto romano," in [= 1934 *Scritti giuridici* VII. Naples] [originally published in *Studi in memoria di Umberto Ratti*. Milan. 1934. 387–447].

Watson, A. (1965). "The divorce of Carvilius Ruga." *Tijdschrift voor Rechtsgeschiedenis* 33: 38–50.

Watson, A. (1991). "A slave's marriage: dowry or deposit." *Journal of Legal History* 12: 132–139.

Yaron, R. (1963). "*Divortium inter absentes*." *Tijdschrift voor Rechtsgeschiedenis* 31: 54–68.

CHAPTER 37

CHILD AND PARENT IN ROMAN LAW

VILLE VUOLANTO

37.1 Introduction

Roman society was a society of young people: at any one time, some one third of the population was younger than fifteen years of age (Parkin 2010, 105–107). The importance of children for the ordinary Roman without a pension system, living directly from agriculture and depending on physical labour, lay in the fact that children meant welfare, especially in old age. Children were crucial also for the elites: they stood for the continuity of family wealth, name and honour—and of the Empire itself (Vuolanto 2015, 30–34, 202–203). Moreover, it seems that at any given point, one sixth of all property was in the hands of fatherless children under fourteen, and up to one third was owned by young people under twenty-five.[1] Still, "child and parent" was not a category of its own in Roman law.

In studies on Roman law, parents and children appear most often in connection with particular points of law, as accidental subject matter in cases when the main interest is on themes like parental authority, status of an individual or changes in Roman legislation during the early Empire. Since the 1980s social historians have also begun to use legal material to study family economy, parent–child relationship and child exposure.[2] These two research traditions have interacted only sparingly, and only the recent boom of handbooks and companions has led to studies tackling children and law in the context of the Roman family in a more comprehensive manner: Judith Evans Grubbs (2011a) has shown how the legal understanding of relationships between children and parents was used to propagate Roman family values, especially *pietas*, among the less Romanised population. Thomas McGinn (2013) has argued, in turn, that (later) Roman legislation specifically favoured children.

[1] Saller 1994, 190, 203; see Holleran and Pudsey 2011 on demographic models and their limitations.

[2] See the bibliography at the end of the chapter. For social historical research see esp. Dixon 1988 and 1992; Saller 1994 and 1999, with e.g. Arjava 1998 on paternal power; Rousselle 1998, 168–178 on pederasty; Vuolanto 2003 on selling of children; Evans Grubbs 2009, 2011b on abandonment.

In the following I will study the main points where Roman lawgivers of the Empire tried to intervene in the relationships between parents and their (minor) children, and to seek reasons for their interest in these cases. The texts discussed in this chapter can be divided roughly into two categories: firstly, those dealing with the property of children and the consequences of their legal incapacity; questions of guardianship are at the centre of this part of the discussion. The second theme is parental power over the person of the child, with discussions on *patria potestas*, maternal authority and personal status at its core; exposure, killing and selling of children are the main topics here. The third section deals with the reciprocal obligations between parents and children.

37.2 Wealth, Parents and Guardianship: The Economic Incapacity of Children

The use and protection of family property played a central role in Roman law. In these considerations the status of the children was more important than their age. In principle the *pater familias*, the eldest *sui iuris* ascendant in the male line of the *familia*, not only had complete ownership of the family's assets, but also legal liability for his dependants and for contracts involving them. Thus, children (or grandchildren) under the *pater familias* could, as a rule, not own the property they had accrued by way of gifts or testamentary bequests.[3]

Still, children *in potestate* could be given financial assets to use: the *peculium*. By the early Empire, activities based on the *peculium* had become a common part of Roman economic life, offering a means for offspring to undertake independent financial actions—especially if given "free administration" (*libera administratio*) of the fund, as was often the case—while at the same time providing limited legal responsibility for the fathers involved. Complex legislation was enacted to regulate the relationships between the owners, the users of the *peculium* and third parties; the exact legal nature of the *peculium* remains a matter of scholarly debate in modern literature.[4] A father could, if he so wished, release his children under his power by *emancipatio*. The children then became independent, *sui iuris*, and capable of owning and managing property. Unfortunately, there is little information on the scale of or motivations for emancipation before late Antiquity, when children seem to have been set free from the paternal power on reaching adulthood as a matter of course.[5]

When a minor child was emancipated, the situation was the same as when the father had died: a guardian was required. As the principal task of the guardian was to take care of the economic arrangements of his ward's maintenance and to be the spokesman in legal matters, *tutela* included the administration of their running expenses, authorisation of contracts,

[3] See e.g. Inst.Gai.2.86–90; 2.123–124 with Benke 2012, 287; Frier and McGinn 2004, 291–296; Saller 1999; and Matthew J. Perry, ch. 33. It has to be noted that a *pater familias* might have been himself a minor—or a woman.

[4] Kirschenbaum 1987; Frier and McGinn 2004, 263–289; and Gamauf, ch. 30.

[5] Gardner 1998, 10–24 and 104–113. For late Antiquity, Arjava 1998, 161–162.

paying debts and investing profits. Extensive legislation developed to regulate different aspects of *tutela*: there were detailed rules for applying to act as guardians, for the administration of their duties, like selling of landed property, and for giving reports during and at the end of the guardianship.[6] The troubles and burdens of guardianship (both for *tutores* and for the wards) became a *topos* in Roman law and literature. On the other hand, to exercise *tutela* was almost as a sacred *officium*: the way one administered guardianship revealed one's virtue or moral weakness.[7] The legislation left some scope for independent action for the ward, however, if old enough: *infantes* were not able to administer their own affairs at all, whereas *impuberes*, which later legislation defined starting at the age of seven, could administer their own affairs to some extent, but needed the authorisation of their guardians.[8]

Upon reaching the age of puberty a person *sui iuris* attained their full legal capacity. *Tutela* ceased, and it was possible to administer one's property and to contract a marriage. There was discussion in the legal literature whether puberty should be determined individually or set at fourteen for boys: Gaius in the second century AD presented both alternatives for determining majority, but in the Justinianic legislation the formal age of majority for boys was fixed at fourteen. In general, the age in years probably had less relevance than the individually and locally changing notions of majority.[9] In the city of Rome, for example, adulthood for boys began with the ceremony of the taking of the *toga virilis*. In the Roman Republic, this meant being subject to military service and having the right to vote in the *comitia*. The age for this depended on individual circumstances (family situation and traditions, the actual puberty), with considerable variation between thirteen and nineteen years of age (*toga virilis*: Harlow and Laurence 2002, 67; Rawson 2003, 142–144). For girls, the marriageable age was twelve, but here also the actual age of puberty and subsequent marriage often seem to have been more important factors for social majority (Harlow and Laurence 2002, 13–19; Dixon 1992, 101).

Still, even persons no longer regarded *impuberes* could not achieve full economic independence if they were less than twenty-five years old. These *minores* were considered to lack judgement and continued to need guidance. Therefore, special protection was afforded them, first from the early second century BC by their ability to plead under the *lex Plaetoria* if defrauded, and later in the pretorian edict, by the right of *restitutio in integrum* ("restoration to original condition"). In order that *minores* could still do business, it was possible for them to apply for the appointment of a *curator*: without his approval any transaction was not binding. To have a *curator* became mandatory during the reign of Marcus Aurelius.[10] Consequently, *cura minorum* and *tutela*, which had intermingled

[6] Inst.Gai.1.142–196, D.26 *passim* with e.g. D.3.5.28–37 *passim, P. Oxy.* iv 727 (154 AD); McGinn 2013, 354–355; Vuolanto 2002, 211–218; Gardner 1998, 244–249; Krause 1995, 97–103.

[7] Responsibility: D.26.7.5.10; C.5.51.9 (a. 293) and C.5.46.2 (a. 246). Securities: e.g. C.5.42 *passim*; (Imagined) troubles for wards: D.22.1.3.3; Lib. *or.* 1.4 with Krause 1995, 13–145, 173–175; on moral weight of guardianship see Cicero on Verres as a *tutor*: Cic. *Verr.* 2.1.9–94. See also Cic. *Clu.* 41; Juv. 8.79 and Gell. *NA* 5.13.2.5 with Saller 1994, 19–192, 199–202.

[8] C.6.30.18, esp. pr. and 4 (a. 426) with McGinn 2013, 354–355.

[9] Inst.Gai.1.196; Inst.1.22pr.; C.5.60.3 (a. 529); Tit.Ulp.11.28 (in *FIRA* II, 276) with Parkin 2010, esp. 102, and Gardner 1998, 146–148.

[10] D.4.4.1pr.-3 and Inst.1.23pr., with Fayer 1994, 593–611 and Saller 1994, 188–189. Originally, women were under *tutela mulieris* after their *tutela minorum* had ended, but when this institution dissolved they also received a *curator* (e.g. D.26.5.13.2).

in some contexts already by the early second century AD, began to merge and by the end of the fourth century there was but one institution, even if a formal difference can still be seen in Justinian's Code.[11] Guardianship was only one, albeit probably the most usual, way of organising or manipulating the financial strategies. For the wealthy, Roman law also offered other instruments such as adoption, usufruct and *fideicommissum*.[12]

It has been estimated that during the early Roman Empire between 37 per cent and 50 per cent of the population still had fathers living at the age of twenty-five (Saller 1994, 189; on demographic models see n. 1). For them, if they were not emancipated, legal majority (or marriage) did not mean any change—all property remained under the management of the father. For daughters this situation was due to the change in the forms of marriage. By the late Republic most marriages were contracted *sine manu*, meaning that the bride remained under her own father's power. In these marriages there was no hereditary relationship between a mother and her children until, under Hadrian, the *senatus consultum Tertullianum* enabled mothers who had the *ius liberorum* to inherit from her children, and then, in 178, the *senatus consultum Orphitianum* gave children (both legitimate and illegitimate) first claim to inherit from their mother upon intestacy (Gardner 1998, 228–233; McGinn 2013, 346–348).

Mothers could not legally intervene in the property management of their children. While legislation gave mothers the obligation to find a guardian for the child if there were none appointed in their father's will (*tutor testamentarius*), or there were no older paternal male relatives available to act as *tutor legitimus*, she could not serve as a guardian herself. Not only did widowed mothers belong to another line, but they could also remarry and thus be more inclined to act against the best interest of their children and their paternal relatives. Still, reality was different, and even Roman legislation acknowledged the strong role mothers had in the lives of their children. Thus, magistrates were obliged to obey the will of the mother in nominating guardians, and the mother had the duty to oversee them. Mothers also often acted as (unofficial) guardians and advisers to their children. Mothers' guardianship was institutionalised in the late fourth century AD, even if only on condition that they did not remarry.[13]

In all, how the property of children was used and protected was a major concern to Roman lawgivers. Legislation concerning the property of minors was based on two principles: firstly, childhood was a separate, vulnerable life phase during which children's property needed protection. Secondly, being in *tutela* was a special threat to the patrimony. Roman law on guardianship was very detailed, and for no other issue in the legislation dealing with minor children is there as much contemporary discussion and legislation preserved for us. The spread of guardianship through *cura minorum* extended the period of vulnerability even to ages over twelve or fourteen. Moreover, it seems that a change took place in the late Republic as the idea of seeing guardians primarily as protecting

[11] D.27.1.13pr; D.4.4.34.1; D.4.1.8 with e.g. Apul. *Apol.* 68; no difference in *Leg. saec.* 8 (=*Librum iuris syro-romanum* 8) and Nov.89.14, but difference still indicated in Inst.1.23 and Nov.72. See also Saller 1994, 188 and Beaucamp 1990, 101 and 319.

[12] Usufruct: Johnston 1989; Dixon 1988, 47–48; Adoption: Lindsay 2011; *Fideicommissum*: Dixon 1988, 47–51.

[13] For different categories of *tutela* see e.g. Inst.Gai.1.144–186 and D.26.2–5 with Fayer 1994, 403–428. For guardianship and mothers see Vuolanto 2002 and Beaucamp 1990, 314–319 and 325–337.

the property and the interests of the agnatic kin group was supplanted by the idea that guardians were to be chosen for the benefit of their wards and also for their upbringing. Children's way of life (*mores*), character and living circumstances were to be taken into account in decisions concerning guardianship.[14] Still, guardianship was a means of protecting not only the children, but also the interests of the family line and the *res publica*.

37.3 Authority in Person: *Pater Familias* and Parental Power

As far as children's property is concerned, *patria potestas* was not in any way a peculiar system during the minority of the children and while they remained in their father's household. However, the Roman father's extensive powers over the persons of children have generated much debate among scholars of the Roman world—especially as the powers given to the *pater familias* were seen as a peculiar feature of the Roman legal system even by the Romans themselves (see esp. Inst.Gai.1.55). The basic principle is clear: the *pater familias* had total power over the person of his dependants. In its most simple form, this meant that a father had an unlimited authority, unequalled by others, to discipline and punish (McGinn 2013, 257; Saller 1994, 114–120, 142).

But the power of the father was linked to social expectations, balanced by the requirement of *pietas* between parents and children—an affectionate relationship characterised by reciprocal responsibilities across the generations: parents were to take care of their offspring during their minority, and children were expected to honour their parents and take care of them in old age.[15] Still, the Roman father seemingly possessed the right to sell or even kill his children. In particularly, Roman fathers' right to kill (*ius vitae necisque*) was perpetuated in the literature of the late Republic and Roman Empire, thereby creating an idealised vision of Republican times as a paradise of paternal power, moral strength and *gravitas*, with just fathers putting the interest and continuity of *res publica* ahead of their own lineage. However, there are no historically documented cases known to us in which a father killed his child legally.[16] However, in the Augustan legislation, fathers were given a right to kill their daughter in cases of adultery, albeit within such narrowly defined limits that it is often assumed the condition would hinder any actual action under the law (D.48.5.23–24 with Benke 2012, 292–293). These "faint echoes" of the right to kill show that the extensive rights connected with *patria potestas* had relevance as a part of the Roman identity—if not in everyday Rome. The position and power of the *pater familias* over his household were

[14] For the emphasis on property see D.50.17.73. Late Republic see e.g. Cic. *Off.* 1.25.85; D.26.1.1. For the early third century see D.26.7.12.3 with D.27.4. On the claimed shift in the purpose of guardianship see McGinn 2013, 354–355; Rawson 2003, 71–73; Krause 1995, 86–87.

[15] Evans Grubbs 2011a; Gardner 1998, 268–270 and Saller 1994, 105–114, 130–131, 151–153.

[16] *Ius vitae necisque:* Westbrook 1999 (dead letter) vs. Shaw 2001 (myth) vs. McGinn 2013, 356–357 (symbol of authority) vs. Benke 2012 (marginal application). For the literary tradition see Gaughan 2010, 23–52 and Westbrook 1999, 206–207. See also a Hadrianic case with a father having appealed this right in vain: D.48.9.5 with McGinn 2013, 356 and Frier and McGinn 2004, 196–203. In D.48.8.2 and C.9.17.1 (a. 319) the killing of one's children is self-evidently prohibited.

crystallised in the *ius vitae necisque* in a way that made it impossible to expressly abolish it, even if in practice the legislation left no place for it to be realised (quotation: Westbrook 1999, 221; see also Benke 2012, 288–289, 293).

Cicero, for example, thought that *patria potestas* had "originally" included some kind of a right to sell one's children,[17] but for the period for which we have sources, the selling of freeborn children or pledging them *loco servi* were understood as offences—but with no punishment to parents. The situation reflects two tendencies in Roman family legislation of the Imperial period: firstly, honouring the (imagined) *mos maiorum* made it impossible to explicitly restrict the powers of the *pater familias*, and secondly, losing one's freedom was ideologically regarded as a fate worse than death: "Liberty was of such value for our ancestors (*a maioribus*) that fathers, who had *ius vitae necisque* towards their children, were not allowed to take away their liberty." However, in legislation no distinction was made between fathers and mothers here, and there is no trace of any *ius vendendi* as a father's legal right to sell his children into slavery during or after the late Roman Republic.[18]

Even if it seems that there was no special ritual with legal content by which the father accepted the newborn child (Shaw 2001, 56–77), Roman law seems to have viewed newborn children differently than it did older ones. This is evident in the selling of children: the selling of older freeborn children was disapproved of, and yet parents had the right to sell their newborns.[19] Nor were there any legal prohibitions against children being exposed or killed at birth by their parents before 374 AD (CTh.9.14.1 [infanticide] and C.8.51.2 pr.-1 [exposure]). Still, there are no sources that would give a Roman father any legally sanctioned right to kill, reject or abandon his newborn children or to give them away, and no Roman text links these acts to *patria potestas*.[20] Indeed, when newborn children are discussed in legislation, the parents are discussed together—there is no indication that the principal actor would be or should be the father.[21] Thus, the attitude towards the newborn child depended on the social and legal status of the baby, as a creature in the marginal, only in the process of becoming a member of the society (Laes 2014), rather than about *patria potestas*. It was a question of parental, not paternal authority.

Whereas the idea of *patria potestas* remained the leading principle in organising the economical relationships between fathers and children during the Roman Empire, it had very little relevance in relation to matters of the person. The lack of evidence makes it impossible to conclude if there were any actual changes to the Republican regime. Still,

[17] See Cic. *De or.* 1.40.181.9 (*memoria sic esset proditum*); Dion. Hal. *Ant. Rom.* 2.27; Inst.Gai.1.132 and 4.79 with Vuolanto 2003, 179–188 (Empire) and Fayer 1994, 215–231 (Republic).

[18] Quote: CTh.4.8.6 (a. 323). See also e.g. D.21.2.39.3; C.7.16.1 (Caracalla, no date); 4.43.1 (a. 294); Sent.Paul.5.1.1 and Nov.Val.33 (a. 451) with Vuolanto 2003, 180–182, 188.

[19] Explicitly at least from early fourth century onward: *Fr.Vat.*34 (*FIRA* II, 469; a. 313) and CTh.5.10.1 (a. 329) with Vuolanto 2003, 182–185.

[20] See e.g. D.28.2.11, which refers to infanticide as being permitted to fathers "once" (in the past). For exposure and rejection of children see Westbrook 1999, 208–209. Moreover, the father did not need to be a *pater familias*. This against e.g. Benke 2012, 288 and Dixon 1992, 40, 122; see also Evans Grubbs 2011b, 22–24.

[21] See e.g. C.8.51.1–3.3; CTh.3.3.1 (there is a reference to fathers but only in the later *interpretatio*); CTh.5.10.1 with Vuolanto 2003, 184–185 on selling of children.

ideologically, *patria potestas* was an important tool in propagating Romanness and proper family relationships.

37.4 Mutual Duties and Obligations: The Best Interest of the Child?

How far were parents expected to support their children, and what were children's obligations towards their elderly parents? Filial *pietas* required children to respect and obey the parents, and, consequently, support a father and other relatives in need. Indeed, the obligation also concerned mothers and maternal relatives, based on an estimation on fairness and affection for kin. The traditional notion of *pietas* was interpreted as a legal principle: what *pietas* demanded should also be the law. Law regulated the financial side of the parent–child relationship with the aim of safeguarding the rights and safety of the parents also in their old age.[22]

On the other hand, *pietas* required parents to behave dutifully towards their children. In this sense, the principle of *pietas* was above *patria potestas*—parents, even fathers, could not act entirely as they wished. Thus, for example, children had the possibility of bringing an action of undutifulness (*querela inofficiosi*) if mistreated or disinherited in their parents' will (Frier and McGinn 2004, 377–383; Champlin 1989, 204–205, 209). More generally, the sustenance of minor children was self-evidently part of the parental *pietas*—nobody could deny his children, leaving them without support. Even if this emerged as a legal obligation only in mid-second century AD, it had a long history as "a moral obligation and social expectation". A person who denied material support to newly born (*partum*) children was deemed to have killed them. Furthermore, a mother could not seek compensation for the upbringing of her own children; this was her duty. That the protection of children's interests was at play can be also deduced to the degree that it was legal for the husband to make it a condition of a *legatum* that a widow should not remarry as long as she had underage children.[23] A case in the Digest about a father's obligation to support his adult son, a craftsman unable to provide for himself because of illness, without any reference to their legal relationship (emancipated or not), also indicates that *patria potestas* had here no significant role (D.25.3.5.7 with Evans Grubbs 2011a, 383). These obligations would go against a father's right to abandon his offspring—leading to the conclusion that exposure was seen to take place only in exceptional circumstances and before the child's integration in the family.

In case of divorce the principal rule was that children followed their father as members of his *familia*. Still, there were disputes about children, and sometimes the mother

[22] Evans Grubbs 2011a, 38–383; with McGinn 2013, 352–353, 356. On old age support see Parkin 2003, 213–216.

[23] D.25.3.5.1-17; C.8.46.9 (a. 294); C.8.51.2pr (a. 374) with McGinn 2013, 352–353 (quotation), 357; *Partum*: D.25.3.4; *Pietas* of the mother see e.g. C.5.31.6 (a. 224) and D.26.10.1.7 with Evans Grubbs 2011a, 384; Condition for *legatum*: D.35.1.62.2.

challenged the father's will and even obtained *custodia* of her children. However, the father did not lose his *potestas*, and was obliged to pay for maintenance.[24]

Because of the obligation of support and matters of inheritance, children born after divorce or after the death of the father were given special attention in legislation. Indeed, decisions regarding children's status had to be done as soon as possible so that there would be no disadvantage for the child: the law ordered notification of the pregnancy and possible inspections to determine paternity.[25] An unborn child is to receive maintenance since he or she is born for the benefit of both the ascendant male (*parenti*) and for the community (*rei publicae*); similarly, an abortion was seen as violating the rights of the father—there was no "right to life" specifically for the foetus.[26]

On the other hand, many legal texts use the argument of a child's best interest. For example, a failure to notify early enough of the pregnancy could not harm the best interest of the child (even if it could harm the parents'), and an unborn child could be given a special guardian, *curator ventris*. Still, only in the fifth century AD and with the (Christian) aim of trying to make divorces more difficult, an idea appears that divorce itself could be harmful for the children.[27] In all, "the interest of children is defined in a manner at least potentially distinct from those of other members of the family" (McGinn 2013, 354). Still, when the advantages for children are referred to, also the benefits for the Roman Empire are paid attention (e.g. in D.37.9.1.15; 24.3.1; Nov.Maior.6.9 [a. 458]).

On the whole, the well-being and protection of children cannot be considered as self-evident starting points while discussing children in pre-modern legislation. Thomas McGinn has, however, argued that the Augustan laws were a starting point for the favouring of the children in Roman law.[28] Whereas there is a general consensus that the legal position of children indeed enhanced during the early Empire, it seems that this was an unintended development in Roman law aiming rather at favouring the interests of (elite) lineages, and the inviolability of the freeborn status in slave society. The changes in second-century-AD legislation, which reorganised inheritance patterns, could also be explained as indications of the strengthened importance of agnatic lineage, rather than specifically aiming at protecting the financial interests of children. Moreover, the status of individuals was central to the legal discussion. Freeborn children were to be returned to their original condition, and, for example, parents selling their children were not punished. The concept of "child labour" did not exist, and parents were free to lease out work of their children as they wished as far as it did not endanger the child's freeborn status.[29] Children were discussed in the context of their families, especially parents, and it was not so much the children themselves, but rather their wealth and status that the Roman legislation protected.

[24] e.g. D.43.30.1.3; D.43.30.3.5–6 with C.5.24.1 (a. 294); Evans Grubbs 2005, 36–41.

[25] D.37.10.1.11 and 37.10.3.5 with McGinn 2013, 349–350. Evans Grubbs 2005, 43–45, on the edict *de inspiciendo ventre* and *s.c. Plancianum*.

[26] D.37.9.1.15, also D.24.3.1. For abortion see D.47.11.4 and 48.19.39 with Harries 2007, 87–88.

[27] D.25.3.1.1–16; D.37.9.1.21–26 with McGinn 2013, 35–352; Divorce: Nov.Theod.12 (a. 439) with Evans Grubbs 2005, 46–47.

[28] McGinn 2013, 342–348. But, for example, how are children favoured by D.24.3.1, which urges that women need to have dowries so that the community might be "replenished with children?"

[29] Child labour: Laes 2011, 148–152, 165–221; selling and leasing out children: Vuolanto 2003, esp. 187–188.

Indeed, the Roman legal system seems to have used children's status as an important way to influence society and proclaim proper values. One example of this was that, traditionally, soldiers could not enter into a marriage. The only *familia* military men should have was their legion. Even if soldiers freely formed permanent relationships with women in places where they were serving, a child born from such union was not legitimate and followed the mother's status. These children were officially fatherless (*sine patris*), like all illegitimate children. In the mid-second century, a soldier could name his children and their mother in his will, but only at some time during the reign of Septimius Severus were soldiers in service allowed to marry (Phang 2001, 89–114, 379–389). The rights of these "natural" (*naturales*) children caused much debate in late Antiquity, and the policy on illegitimate children fluctuated; Constantine, for example, prohibited fathers of illegitimate children from leaving anything to them, while Valentinian I allowed some inheritance to be given to them, and Theodosius II was even more "liberal".[30] More generally, no legitimate children could be born from unions between free and slave: all children of slave women were slaves and legally belonged to masters.[31] The free and respectable were to be kept strictly separate from the servile and lowly.

37.5 Conclusion

Roman legislation, or rather, the culture that produced it, recognised childhood as a separate period of life, but one which had no clearly differentiated age limits—its end was a gradual process starting at the age of twelve (girls) or fourteen (boys) and puberty, furthered by marrying and having children, and concluding with full legal independence at the age of twenty-five. During this period these individuals needed special care and protection. Children were to be constantly under someone else's authority. This meant not only restrictions—in managing property, and in incapacity to represent oneself or others—but also some privileges; children before puberty, for instance, were legally incapable of committing a crime.[32] There were also legal remedies to which children could appeal, like *restitutio in integrum*. Moreover, the best interests of children were invoked in legislation, and, in all, "the second-century emperors took a particular interest in the welfare of the children and in fostering parent–child links".[33] Still, because the second century also marks the earliest high point of our knowledge of the Roman legal sources, it is arguable whether the actual sentiment towards children was any more positive or favourable than it had been earlier in the Roman world,[34] or whether the motivation of legislation was to yield any special favours for children; the changes in legislation may be seen as natural responses to

[30] Evans Grubbs 2014; see her n. 7 for scholarship on illegitimacy and Constantine's legislation.

[31] See e.g. Inst.Gai.1.82 and 89, with Weaver 1991, and CTh.12.1.6 (a. 319).

[32] D.47.2.22pr and 23, with Rawson 2003, 74–75, 138–139 and Thomas 1975. The condition of being *doli incapax* could end at the age of ten if the children in question could be shown to have understood the nature of their deed.

[33] Evans Grubbs 2005, 46. Also Rawson 2003, 69–71; McGinn 2013, 355–356. For an attempt to track "children's rights" in Antiquity see Tafaro 2009.

[34] See, however, Evans Grubbs 2011a, 382. On the caveats of identifying change for Roman family see Dixon 1997.

the issue that much of the wealth was in the hands of minors. A complex society needed to ensure that its financial life functioned.

In all, children were not by any means marginal to the concerns of Roman legal authorities.[35] Roman law tried to promote familial *pietas*, protect the economic interests of family lineages and defend freeborn status. Even if these aims do not as such refer to any specific favouring of children, this certainly shows an understanding of childhood as a distinctive phase of life, to be dealt with through specific legislative measures.

Bibliography

Arjava, A. (1998). "Paternal power in late antiquity." *Journal of Roman Studies* 88: 147–165.

Beaucamp, J. 1990. *Le statut de la femme à Byzance (4e–7e siècle)*, Vol. 1: *Le droit impérial*. Paris.

Benke, N. (2012). "On the Roman father's right to kill his adulterous daughter." *History of the Family* 17: 284–308.

Bradley, K. R. 2013. "Images of childhood in classical antiquity." In P. S. Fass, ed., *The Routledge history of childhood in the western world*. London/New York. 17–38.

Champlin, E. (1989). "*Creditur vulgo testamenta hominum speculum esse morum*: why the Romans made wills." *Classical Philology* 84: 198–215.

Dixon, S. 1988. *The Roman mother*. London.

Dixon, S. 1992. *The Roman family*. Baltimore/London.

Dixon, S. 1997. "Continuity and change in Roman social history: retrieving 'family feeling(s)' from Roman law and literature." In M. Golden and P. Toohey, eds., *Inventing ancient culture: historicism, periodization and the ancient world*. London/New York. 79–90.

Evans Grubbs, J. 2005. "Children and divorce in Roman law." In K. Mustakallio et al., eds., *Hoping for continuity: childhood, education and death in antiquity and the middle ages*. Rome. 33–47.

Evans Grubbs, J. 2009. "Church, state, and children: Christian and imperial attitudes toward infant exposure in late antiquity." In A. Cain and N. E. Lenski, eds., *The power of religion in late antiquity*. Farnham/Burlington. 119–132.

Evans Grubbs, J. 2011a. "Promoting *pietas* through Roman law." In B. Rawson, ed., *A companion to families in the Greek and Roman worlds*. Oxford/Malden, Mass. 377–392.

Evans Grubbs, J. 2011b. "The dynamics of infant abandonment: motives, attitudes and (un-intended) consequences." In K. Mustakallio and C. Laes, eds., *The dark side of childhood in late antiquity and the middle ages*. Oxford. 21–36.

Evans Grubbs, J. 2014. "Illegitimacy and inheritance disputes in the late Roman Empire." In B. Caseau and S. Hübner, eds., *Inheritance, law and religions in the ancient and mediaeval worlds*. Paris. 25–50.

Fayer, C. 1994. *La familia romana: aspetti giuridici ed antiquari. Parte I*. Rome.

Frier, B and McGinn, T. A. J. 2004. *A casebook of Roman family law*. Oxford.

Gardner, J. F. 1998. *Family and* familia *in Roman law and life*. Oxford.

Gaughan, J. E. 2010. *Murder was not a crime: homicide and power in the Roman republic*. Austin.

[35] See also McGinn 2013, 258; more generally Bradley 2013, esp. 34.

Harlow, M. and Laurence, R. 2002. *Growing up and growing old in ancient Rome: a life course approach*. London/New York.
Harries, J. 2007. *Law and crime in the Roman world*. Cambridge.
Holleran, C. and Pudsey, A. 2011. "Introduction: ancient historical demography." In C. Holleran and A. Pudsey, eds., *Demography and the Graeco-Roman world: new insights and approaches*. Cambridge/New York. 1–13.
Johnston, D. 1989. "Successive rights and successful remedies: life interests in Roman law." In P. Birks, ed., *New perspectives in the Roman law of property: essays for Barry Nicholas*. Oxford. 153–167.
Kirschenbaum, A. 1987. *Sons, slaves, and freedmen in Roman commerce*. Jerusalem/Washington, D.C.
Krause, J.-U. 1995. *Witwen und Waisen im Römischen Reich*, Vol. 3: *Rechtliche und soziale Stellung von Waisen*. Stuttgart.
Laes, C. 2011. *Children in the Roman empire: outsiders within*. Cambridge.
Laes, C. (2014). "Infant between biological and social birth in antiquity: a phenomenon of the *longue durée*." *Historia* 63: 364–383.
Lindsay, H. 2011. "Adoption and heirship in Greece and Rome." In B. Rawson, ed., *A companion to families in the Greek and Roman worlds*. Oxford/Malden, Mass. 346–360.
McGinn, T. A. J. 2013. "Roman children and the law." In J. Evans Grubbs, T. Parkin and R. Bell, eds., *The Oxford handbook of childhood and education in the classical world*. New York. 341–364.
Parkin, T. 2003. *Old age in the Roman world: a cultural and social history*. Baltimore/London.
Parkin, T. 2010. "Life cycle." In M. Harlow and R. Laurence, eds., *A cultural history of childhood and the family: i: antiquity*. Oxford. 97–114, 199–201.
Phang, S. E. 2001. *The marriage of Roman soldiers (13 B.C.–A.D. 235): law and family in the imperial army*. Leiden.
Rawson, B. 2003. *Children and childhood in Roman Italy*. Oxford.
Rousselle, A. 1998. *La contamination spirituelle, science, droit et religion dans l'antiquité*. Paris.
Saller, R. P. 1994. *Patriarchy, property and death in the Roman family*. Cambridge.
Saller, R. P. (1999). "*Pater familias*, *mater familias*, and the gendered semantics of the Roman household." *Classical Philology* 94: 182–197.
Shaw, B. D. (2001). "Raising and killing children: two Roman myths." *Mnemosyne* 54: 131–177.
Tafaro, S. (2009). "Los derechos de los niños en la experiencia jurídica romana (The rights of children in the Roman legal experience)." *Revista de Derecho Privado* 17: 177–202.
Thomas, J. A. C. (1975). "Delictal and criminal liability of the young in Roman law." *Recueils de la Société Jean Bodin* 38: 9–31.
Vuolanto, V. 2002. "Women and the property of fatherless children in the Roman Empire." In P. Setälä et al., *Women, wealth and power in the Roman Empire*. Rome. 203–243.
Vuolanto, V. (2003). "Selling a freeborn child: rhetoric and social realities in the late Roman world." *Ancient Society* 33: 169–207.
Vuolanto, V. 2015. *Children and asceticism in late antiquity: continuity, family dynamics and the rise of Christianity*. Aldershot.
Weaver, P. 1991. "Children of freedmen (and freedwomen)." In B. Rawson, ed., *Marriage, divorce and children in ancient Rome*. Canberra. 166–190.
Westbrook, R. (1999). "*Vitae necisque potestas*." *Historia* 48: 203–223.

CHAPTER 38

INHERITANCE

ÉVA JAKAB

38.1 Introduction

"If we become heirs to a certain person … that person's assets pass to us" (Inst.Gai.2.97–98). With these words Gaius explains how things are acquired in bulk (*per universitatem*). In book 2 and 3 of his *Institutiones* he deals with the acquisition of ownership; inheritance forms a considerable part of it: 279 passages, compared to contract law discussed in just 93. This generates a ratio of roughly three to one. Similarly, out of the fifty books of the Digest, eleven are occupied with the law of succession (Crook 1967, 118). Modern scholars have calculated that some 60 or 70 per cent of all Roman litigation arose over problems connected with inheritance (Kelly 1976, 71–92; also Frier 1985, 37–38).

Roman society was based on rigid family structures with a powerful father (*pater familias*) at the top, the very embodiment of patriarchal authority, who ruled over his children, wife and slaves (Saller 1994, 102; Evans Grubbs 2002, 20–22). But death put an end to all legal capacity—with his last breath the deceased lost all his rights and assets. Law, religion and morals interacted in shaping the rules that governed the passing of the family property to the next generation. The family *sacra*, future sacrifices for paternal kinship and piety (*pietas*) were of great relevance in bequeathing one's assets. The social environment expected a strong family sentiment to exist on both sides: a testator should think of his closest relatives and should furnish them with adequate financial means for their future life, while heirs should care for the memory of the deceased.

According to recent research, Rome had far higher birth and death rates than those of modern European countries: approximately thirty-five births and deaths per 1,000 per year compared with ten today (Saller 1994, 12). The average life expectancy at birth for the Romans stood at twenty to thirty years.[1] Roman society was a rather dynamic one, with a high mortality rate and a quick change of generations. War, epidemic, poor nourishment and a low standard of health care often led to early death (Scheidel 2007, 38–41). A good *pater familias* had to be aware of this risk and had to arrange his affairs in a timely manner.

[1] Scheidel 2007, 38–39 with a critical approach and Saller 1994, 13. Cf. also the life table of Ulpian D.35.2.68, although it is not real demographic information; Frier 2000, 790–792.

According to Plutarch, Cato the Elder was anxious lest he should be left intestate for a single day (Plut. *Cat. Mai.* 9.6).

Following a law and society approach it seems useful to leave to one side the traditional narratives of textbooks. Indeed, intestate succession represented the first stage of inheritance in legal history, yet in the period with which we are concerned (90 BC–200 AD), testamentary succession was the first choice in legal life. Sir Henry Maine went so far as to declare that the Romans had "a horror of intestacy" (Champlin 1991, 6–8). Reading the works of Cicero, Pliny, Seneca, Lucian or Augustine one gets the impression that wealthy citizens made their wills already at a young age and remade them several times during their lives. Pliny stated that a person's will was the mirror of his character (Plin. *Ep.* 8.18). "The Romans tell the truth only once in their lives, in their will", declared Lucian, criticising the contemporary elite (Lucian, *Nigr.* 30). There can be no doubt that wills mattered more for "the propertied and the educated" of Roman society. They were "obsessed with the making of wills, both their own and others, to a degree and for reasons which may be hard to grasp today"—as Champlin has pointed out (Champlin 1991, 6).

38.2 A Case Study

"Finally, there is the illustrious case of Manius Curius and Marcus Coponius, which was recently heard before the Court of a Hundred—what a crowd of people, what anticipation!"[2] In a dramatic way Cicero reports of a hearing before the Court of a Hundred, the *Centumviri*, who were in charge of inheritance cases (Harries 2006, 10–101). The trial took place around 90 BC and became widely known as the *causa Curiana*.[3] The facts are simple: Marcus Coponius, a wealthy Roman citizen, made a will in which he instituted his son as sole heir. In case his son died before reaching puberty he provided in the will that Curius should be his heir. At the moment of Coponius' death no son had been born. Referring to the will, Curius took possession of the estate. However, Marcus Coponius, the brother of the deceased, brought an action against him demanding possession of the estate as intestate heir.

It is worth mentioning that testamentary and intestate succession excluded one another in Roman law. It could never happen that there was one heir for an estate under the will and a different one under the law, thereby sharing the estate (a few exceptions will be mentioned below). It was widely accepted in Cicero's time that a testator could provide for the eventuality that his instituted heir should die before reaching puberty, i.e. before being capable of making his own will. The only problem was that Coponius relied on having a legitimate son (conceived in a valid Roman marriage) at the time of his death, but his hopes had clearly been dashed. A posthumous child born after the testator's death (but conceived before) had the same right to inherit in Rome.

[2] Cic. *De orat.*1.180; transl. Frier and McGinn 2004, 349. Cicero dealt with the case several times; cf. *Caecin.* 18.51–53; *Brut.* 39.145; *Top.* 10.44, 52.194–53.199; *Inv. rhet.* 2.122 etc.

[3] The dating varies from 90 BC to 93 BC; cf. Wieacker 1967, 151. For reasoning in inheritance cases see recently Harries 2006, 97–99.

Two respectable and skilled lawyers were involved in the trial: Q. Mucius Scaevola for the claimant and M. Licinius Crassus for the plaintiff. The legal problem was whether the testament remained valid if the first *heredis institutio* failed. Could Curius replace the son who did not exist?[4] Generally, if the *heredis institutio* failed, the testament was null and void—and possession of the estate passed under the law (i.e. intestate).

The case of Curius became a test between the old conception of the civil law based on formal, strict norms and the new conception of praetorian law based on flexible categories of equity. In fact, it became a test case measuring the limits of private autonomy in family property matters. Furthermore, the Court's decision signified a common desire in Roman society to repress the old system of agnatic family control over private property issues. The *causa Curiana* became a *topos* for the changing values in interpreting legal documents, the controversy between *verba* and *voluntas*—strict wording versus explicit or maybe hypothetical will. Cicero reminds us several times that the famous Quintus Mucius Scaevola lost the case. The Court of Hundred dismissed Coponius' claim: Curius could retain possession of the estate.[5] The main argument was that obviously Coponius made his testament in order to avoid passing his property intestate.

38.3 Roman Wills

A will (*testamentum*) was a legal document with archaic roots, a solemn declaration manifested in a prescribed (oral or written) form by which a testator nominated one or more successors on whom his property rights and liabilities should be transferred. The word *testamentum* implies that the declaration of free will (*mens*) of the testator was made before trustworthy witnesses (*testes*), providing for publicity and transparency (Meyer 2004, 113–115).

According to Gaius, there were two kinds of will in use in archaic Rome: one made solemnly in the assembly of the Roman people (in the *comitia calata*) and the other among soldiers in arming for a battle (*in procinctu*, "with togas girded up") (Inst.Gai.2.101; cf. Rüfner 2011, 3). The first was a rather complicated affair under strict social control; the second was less formal but restricted to a very specific context. Indeed, the Romans soon introduced a third way to make a will, based on the formalities of the ancient form of sale, *mancipatio*.[6] It was called *testamentum per aes et libram*, a legal act carried out through "copper and scales", in the presence of both parties and (at least) five adult Roman citizens as witnesses. It was a fictitious sale with the purpose of transferring the entire estate of the testator into the possession of a trustee, a *familiae emptor* (purchaser of the family estate), tasked with distributing it after the testator's death to the heirs he had named (Inst. Gai.2.102; cf. Rüfner 2011, 4–6; Watson 1971, 8–21).

[4] Slightly different, Thomas 2014, 730 asked whether a *substitutio pupillaris* included a *substitutio vulgaris*.

[5] Wieacker 1967, 164 argued that the Court decided wrongly.

[6] Inst.Gai.2.104; transl. Francis de Zulueta. For the formalities of the *mancipatio* cf. Watson 1971, 11.

Surprisingly, this rather formal type of will remained popular for centuries. The formalities changed slightly, the role of the trustee became fictitious, while the dispositions of the will were treated as valid and followed as a matter of law (Rüfner 2011, 5). Suetonius reports that even Julius Caesar and Augustus used this type of will for disposing of their political and pecuniary legacy (Suet. *Tib.* 23; *Claud.* 4.7; *Ner.* 4.). Pliny the Younger reports on wills made *per aes et libram* by the Roman elite at the beginning of the second century AD (Plin. *Ep.* 8.18; cf. Tellegen 1982, 160). As for ordinary people, epigraphic evidence shows the popularity of disposing through "copper and scales". A good example is the soldier Antonius Silvanus, who served in Egypt and chose the old formula even in 142 AD: "Purchaser of the estate for the purpose of testation: Nemonius, corporal of the troop of Valerius ..." (*FIRA* III nr. 47). It is not clear if the formalities of the old *mancipatio*—as known in the XII Tables from the fifth century BC—were carried out precisely even by Augustus in Rome or by Antonius Silvanus in Roman Egypt. It seems more likely that the *mancipatio* lost its original significance, but the solemn wording was carefully retained in notary practice as a special kind of deed, a unique ritual formula for drafting wills.

According to praetorian law, the old formula was in no way obligatory any more. Probably as early as the second century BC, the edict specified only the requirement that a will must be sealed with the seals of seven witnesses (Inst.Gai.2.119). Either using the old pattern "through copper and scales" or just sealed on wax tablets, wills had to be drafted in a written text and fashioned in a special style, as described by Gaius:

> before everything else it must be ascertained whether there has been an institution of an heir made in solemn form ... (117) "Be thou Titius my heir"; but the form: "I order that Titius be my heir" seems now also to be approved; not approved is the form: "I wish Titius to be my heir"; also disapproved by most authorities are the forms: "I institute Titius my heir" and "I make Titius my heir". (Inst.Gai.2.116–117; translation de Zulueta)

Even in the classical period, Roman wills follow strict formal requirements. Gaius explains both social and legal expectation as he dwells on every detail. He tries to teach his readers to avoid typical failures and to prepare them for their visit to a notary's office.

Not only the proper wording but also the material on which to write was fixed by custom or often by law. The Romans drew up testaments mostly on *tabulae*, writing tablets made of wood, of which one side was slightly deepened and covered with wax or shellac as a writing surface (Wolf and Crook 1989, 1–40). For legal purposes, they devised means to bind tablets together, such that one copy of the contents was visible on the outside, while another was sealed and protected on the inside. The whole could be opened if need arose to confirm the external text. The form may have had sacral roots (Meyer 2004, 44–63). According to Cicero, Coponius also declared his last will on such *tabulae*, albeit he seems to have chosen an incorrect formula (Thomas 2014, 730 argues that Coponius was ill served by his legal advisers).

In 61 AD a *senatus consultum Neronianum* ruled how such *tabulae* should be produced: the tablets should be pierced, witnesses should be present for the sealing of the text to save the *fides* of the inner text (*scriptura interior*) on the first two *tabulae* of a triptych, and the seals should be placed over a string. Indeed, epigraphic evidence and literary sources demonstrate that Roman wills were drafted in this fashion (cf. Meyer 2004, 112–120). More likely, wills of Romans were valid only if they followed the formalities depicted above. This is clearly a concern in the Gnomon of *Idios logos* (§§8 and 34), and in Imperial constitutions regarding Roman and provincial practice (Inst.Gai.2.281).

There thus existed a remarkable tension between the freedom of testation and the strict formalities set by public power for drafting Roman wills. On the one hand the private autonomy of fathers to dispose of their estates was fully recognised by Roman law. On the other hand strong social and family expectations led to severe formal requirements in order to control testators and to protect the financial basis of traditional family structures. Without doubt, since the time of the XII Tables, every *pater familias* could dispose of his family estate in case of his death as he wished. However, the state interfered in this "freedom of testation" by fixing rules concerning the form of a valid will. The use of *tabulae* and solemn words, the requirement of a notary and witnesses served to avoid high-handed, despotic actions. The free will of the *pater familias* therefore stood under some control of public policy. The testator had to face the disapproval of his community, of his social environment, if he deviated from social expectations (cf. Zimmermann 2007, 27–28). The general approach of the courts was determined by traditional family models and represented rather conservative social expectations.

38.4 Testators, Heirs and Legatees

Only Roman citizens could make a valid Roman will and could be instituted as an heir in terms of one (on citizenship and access to law see Ando 2011, 1–4). Only Romans had the right to dispose of their possessions *mortis causa*, i.e. to institute heir(s) or legacies according to Roman law. To be concerned with "testamentary affairs"—of one's own or others—was a very Roman business.

Succession was strictly forbidden between Romans and peregrines. Indeed, not every Roman could make a valid will, because it required full legal capacity (*testamenti factio activa*). As the paternal fortune belonged only to the *pater familias*, only persons *sui iuris* (persons not in *potestas*) were entitled to dispose of the entire family estate. However, in the classical period, a son in *potestas* could dispose of certain funds earned in military or administrative service (*peculium castrense* and *quasi castrense*). Furthermore, there were many other restrictions as regards who could make a will or who could inherit under a will. For example, persons under penalty or mentally disabled were excluded.

From the time of Hadrian, women could make a will with the consent of their guardian. Earlier, women (even if *sui iuris*) could only make a valid will if they underwent a fictitious "selling" (*coemptio*) and submitted to a new guardianship for this purpose (Inst.Gai.2.118, 122). In legal life, as reported from Roman Egypt, women had to suffer under further restrictions: for example, a legacy left by a Roman woman to a female infant was forfeited (cf. Crook 1967, 120).

Generally, even a carefully prepared will was not certain to secure the passage of an estate to the persons specified in it. Capacity lost after its writing—for example, as a consequence of exile or adoption—automatically led to testamentary incapacity; any testament made prior became void.

On the other hand, there were several limitations on the capacity to inherit as well (*testamenti factio passiva*). New and strict rules were introduced in the legislation of Augustus, too. Generally, uncertain persons (*incertae personae*) could not be instituted as heir or be given legacies. According to this rule, neither future generations (children or grandchildren not yet born or conceived at the time the will was made) nor corporations (for example, a community) could inherit at all (Crook 1967, 121). However, in legal life such limitations could be surmounted. Pliny the Younger asked the emperor by letter how to act when a certain Julius Largus from Pontus, whom he had never met nor even heard of, asked him in his will to be his heir and then to transfer the whole estate—less a legacy to himself of 50,000 sesterces—to the cities of Heraclea and Tyana (Plin. *Ep.*10.75; for the context cf. Tellegen 1982, 165–167).

Epigraphic evidence informs us about the physical appearance of Roman wills. Let us return to the will of Antonius Silvanus, dated 142 AD:[7] it was drawn up on wooden tablets (*tabulae*), as was usual in Rome, although it was produced in a military camp close to Alexandria. The text was written in Latin, albeit with a Greek subscription by the testator; obviously it was drafted by a scribe and not by the testator himself. Wills commonly contained a great deal of information about social status and the professional career of the deceased: Antonius Silvanus documented his full name, troop and military rank. First, he appointed his son, Antonius Saturninus, as whole heir; he then explicitly disinherited all other possible claimants (ll. 8–9). He also set a fixed time limit for entering the inheritance, one hundred days, exactly the limit specified in the praetor's edict at Rome (ll. 9–10). In the second place he named his brother, Antonius R[...], as heir, ensuring that one of his near relatives entered into responsibility and carried out his dispositions. To institute a second possible heir was a common type of substitution (*substitutio pupillaris*), as we have seen already in the will of Coponius. It is remarkable that Antonius Silvanus explicitly disinherits his son unless he enters into the estate within a hundred days. The testator might have been advised to avoid usual tricks as recorded in the Digest: sometimes the appointed testamentary heir (if he was heir under law as well) sought to evade the will, in order to avoid the duty of paying out high legacies. Refusing to be heir under the will, the will became void; yet the same person might later try to enter the estate under law (intestate), free of inconvenient legacies and trusts (cf. Crook 1967, 124).

When one compares the instructions of Antonius Silvanus with the law on intestate succession it is clear that he followed the mainstream rules of intestacy. Usually freedom of testation did not lead to a high-handed squandering of family possessions. A reasonable father had a strong family sentiment and disposed responsibly (Saller 1994, 155–160). Pliny the Younger might have thought along these lines when he wrote to Rufinus that "men's wills are the mirror of their character". He had an example in mind: that of Domitius Tullus, previously a wasteful fellow, who named his daughter as heir and bestowed on his grandchildren extremely gratifying legacies, too (Plin. *Ep.* 8.18).

Antonius Silvanus also left several legacies (ll. 16–37): for his brother, for his concubine and for a comrade Hierax, who is appointed as agent (*procurator*) to clear his military account and transfer it to Antonia Thermutha, the mother of his son. According to old custom, a legacy had to be left using prescribed, solemn words: "To him I give and legate" (l. 27). Antonius Silvanus followed this pattern, even though it is very likely that his

[7] *FIRA* III nr. 47; further wills of Roman soldiers are *FIRA* III 50 (= *BGU* I 326); *P. Lugd. Bat.* XIII 14; *BGU* VII 1662; *P. Wisconsin* I 14; *SB* X 10530; cf. Phang 2001, 217–221.

Antonia Thermutha (probably a freedwoman),[8] whom he obviously could not marry, did not have any legal capacity in Roman law.

From a legacy arose the right to acquire ownership of single items (*activa*) without being responsible for any debt of the deceased. Depending on the form, the legatee acquired ownership immediately or could petition the heir to deliver the objects bequeathed to him (Inst.Gai.2.194–205; du Plessis 2010, 228–229). If the heir or legatee lacked legal capacity (e.g. a peregrine or a community as an uncertain person), he could not inherit. For such cases, a new type of bequest was created, called a trust (*fideicommissum*) (Johnston 1988, 21–29). Initially, trusts were "not part of the established legal order" and therefore they were free from limitations and restrictions (Johnston 1988, 21). If a trustee were asked to carry out wishes of the testator, their fulfilment depended entirely on his *fides*. Soon, however, trusts became enforceable and a special magistrate called the *praetor fideicommissarius* took care of it. A *fideicommissum* might be of single items such as a slave or a piece of land or of the entire estate or a certain part of it. Benefiting through *fideicommissa* might be conditional; conditions might be specified in the will itself or in a separate informal document called a codicil (D.36.1.23[22]pr).

Beside the appointment of heirs or bequeathing of legacies a will might contain a number of minor provisions such as the appointment of guardians or manumission of slaves. Indeed, the will of Antonius also disposed of the manumission of his slave Cronio, if he behaves properly and gives an account to his heir or to his agent (ll. 31–35). The last order concerns household accounts or his *peculium*, if the slave ran his own business. Through manumission, testators generally rewarded long and honest service and loyalty to the family (Mouritsen 2011, 182; see also ch. 31, this volume). Manumissions were often combined with legacies or other forms of gratuitous allotments.[9] It is difficult to estimate the volume of testamentary manumissions in Roman society; recent scholarly literature fixed it approximately at 5–8 per cent (Champlin 1991, 140–142). Commencing in the first century BC, various laws limited testamentary manumissions. It is commonly supposed that the legal restrictions tried to curb the "irresponsible generosity" of testators (Mouritsen 2011, 184). However, the limitations might also have aimed to protect heirs from a bequest overwhelmed with manumissions, reducing the estate to nil or even to indebtedness. In some cases, the manumission of a slave was combined with his appointment as heir for less than humanitarian purposes, as it might free near relatives from an indebted bequest. Crook called such orders a "particularly rotten trick"; it was, however, a solution recognised by the legal system.

38.5 Intestate Succession

The Digest commences its discussion of the praetorian rules of intestate inheritance under the heading: "If there shall be no will (*tabulae*)" (D.38.6). The entire law of intestacy is

[8] Phang 2001, 219–220; Evans Grubbs 2002, 156–161 and 323; Campbell 1994, 154–156.

[9] e.g. *CIL* XIII 5708 from Gaul or *CIL* VI 10229, the so-called "will of Damusius", cf. Mouritsen 2011, 182–183.

discussed in just fourteen titles, occupying a thin set of fourteen pages in the modern printed version. Intestacy was not only a "horror of Romans", but seems to have been also of slight relevance in legal life. In the classical period, the rules of intestate inheritance became effective only as a supplement, if there was no valid will (no will at all or one which lacked legal effect) (cf. du Plessis 2010, 207). For such cases, the praetor elaborated a system which partly preserved and partly changed the archaic rules of *ius civile*. His aim was to pay more attention to near relatives apart from the old agnatic family ties. Therefore he "split succession on intestacy into several parts by constructing different classes: the first is that of children, the second of statutory heirs, the third of cognate relatives and finally that of husband and wife" (D.38.6.1.1–2).

For a better understanding of the praetor's invention, let us take a look at the archaic rules of the *ius civile* as reported by Gaius: "By the law of the Twelve Tables, the inheritances of those who die intestate go first to their *sui heredes* … if there be no *suus heres* … the inheritance goes to the agnates … if there be no agnate, the same law … calls the *gentiles* (fellow clansmen) to the inheritance" (Inst.Gai.3.1, 9, 17; translation de Zulueta). As *sui heredes* were considered all children (sons and daughters with equal share) who stood in *potestas* of the deceased *pater familias* at the moment of his death, further his adoptive children and his wife if she was in *manus* (legally in the position of a daughter). A posthumous child was also a *suus heres* if he would have been in the *potestas* of the deceased had he been born before his death. *Sui heredes* inherited in equal share; one's children or grandchildren took the share that their deceased father would have taken (stirpital representation). Excluded were all the persons who ceased to be in *potestas* through emancipation or other types of *capitis deminutio* (for example, through marriage of a daughter into *manus*). In the second class, the nearest agnates were taken into account: as a practical matter, this meant the brother or sister of the deceased. As to the third class, in the classical period, clansmen were no longer of relevance. Intestate succession in the XII Tables reveals the family structure of archaic times. *Potestas,* power over children, wife, daughter-in-law and grandchildren, represented the only legally relevant tie between relatives. This principle might seem rigid for modern readers but it met the expectations of its social and economic environment. The family was the only unit that really mattered, not individuals bound by affection. Social life and economic existence were run under the command and protection of the *pater familias* (see Dixon, ch. 35 in this volume).

Changing social values required new legal solutions. In inheritance law, innovation was realised through the praetor's edict. As the magistrate in charge for the administration of justice, the praetor was able to grant *bonorum possessio* (possession of property) upon proof of a reasonable *causa*. This extra-procedural tool entitled the claimant to hold possession of an estate unless an heir under the *ius civile* brought an action against him. Through a confusing set of rules, step by step, the praetor erected a new system that allowed a certain group of successors to obtain possession of an estate. Sometimes the praetor granted absolute protection against claims by an heir under *ius civile* (*bonorum possessio cum re*), in other cases against everybody but an heir under *ius civile* (*bonorum possessio sine re*) (Buckland 1925, 234).

According to the edict, in the first class were all children (descendants) and children's children, according to the principle of stirpital representation. Apart from archaic agnatic family ties, an emancipated son (or his children) or a married daughter could be included here, too. Nevertheless, tensions could arise, because emancipated children usually received their share of the family estate when the agnatic ties were severed, for example, in the form of a donation or dowry. To maintain the principle of equal shares, those individuals were obliged to take their previous acquisition into account (*collatio bonorum*). Ulpian reports such a case (D.37.6.5pr): a *pater familias* emancipated his son long before his death, but kept one of his grandsons in his *potestas*. Under the rules of the *ius civile*, as a *suus heres* the grandchild should have inherited the entire estate. However, in classical law, thanks to the flexible equity of the praetorian edict, the father of the grandson, although he left agnatic family ties long before, was invited to be joint heir with his son. In this case of legally reconstituted family relations, stirpital representation did not apply, because the grandson had his own claim as the only *suus*. However, his father, the emancipated son of the deceased, was obliged to take account of his possessions and share the inheritance with his son (*collatio*). Ulpian's decision demonstrates how considerable changes were produced by praetorian interference.

According to the edict, the second class named in the old rules of intestacy was retained. If there were no descendants of the first class, in the second class the praetor invited the *legitimi*, to wit, *sui* and *proximi agnati* according to archaic rules. However, significant innovations were introduced in the third class, that of *cognati*. Here, all nearest cognates were taken into consideration: descendants, ascendants and blood relations up to the sixth grade of relationship. Two or more on the same grade shared the estate equally; the nearest excluded the farther and there was no stirpital representation.

Finally, only in the fourth class—if there were no *liberi*, nor *legitimi*, nor *cognati*—the praetor invited the married partner who outlived the deceased. It might seem unjust, but the bad position of the spouse is a clear result of the model of marriage without *manus*, based on a strict separation of financial affairs. Strictly speaking, there could be no family tie between husband and wife if the marriage was one without *manus*.

Even more confusing was the lack of intestate succession between a mother and her children. Two late decrees of the senate tried to improve this situation. The *s.c. Tertullianum* applied to mothers with three or more children: if the child died intestate, the mother could take in the third class (if there were no descendants and ascendants), with a sister in equal share. The *s.c. Orfitianum* enacted the right of children (whether legitimate or illegitimate) to succeed on their mother's estate on the first class (cf. du Plessis 2010, 211–212). These two decrees of the senate are puzzling because they applied rules devised for blood relationships in a radically new way, to a special context, before solutions using those principles had developed in practice. Obviously, the senate paid attention to relevant changes in family structures, which had had an impact on legal culture. As marriages with *manus* became scarce, the legal incapacity of women lost much of its rigidity. The wills of mothers and children might regularly have named the other, according to mutual affection and obligation as understood in social life. What is remarkable is the application of rules for blood relations to illegitimate ties. A similar progress can be observed in constitutions and administrative norms regarding intestate succession in military context.

38.6 Risk in Succession

Succession to someone's estate as universal heir involved an acquisition in bulk, a so-called *universalis successio*. The heir stepped into the possessions of the deceased as his successor in a broad sense. He inherited not only assets or property rights but was also responsible for all the debts of the deceased. Whether under will or under law, becoming an heir was a business with a high financial risk: generally, responsibility for debts of the deceased was not limited to the inheritance but also affected the personal estate of the heir (or that of the heirs, if there were more, according to their share). Foresight and careful calculation were necessary before entering into an inheritance. Persons belonging to the group of *sui heredes* could not even think over their chances: they inevitably became heirs, without any formal or informal act of entry (Inst.Gai.2.156–157). To other heirs the praetor granted some time for careful deliberation, usually a hundred days. In legal life, testators could also set individual deadlines, as we have seen in the will of Antonius Silvanus. Once entered, the heir was liable for all debts, even if they exceeded the inheritance: in extreme cases, an heir might face insolvency or bankruptcy, and all his possession were put up for auction.

This situation required legal help. First the praetor interfered to separate the estate of the deceased from that of the heir(s), as regards creditors. Any creditor could apply within a reasonable time. The matter was important because a refused inheritance caused considerable damage to legatees and trustees: without an heir, the entire will was void (D.36.1.4pr). To avoid such cases and to protect heirs from bankruptcy, the praetor announced (for the *sui heredes*) the possibility of abstaining from the succession. To all other heirs, the praetor granted the power of deliberation (*potestas deliberandi*) within a certain deadline (usually a hundred days) (Inst.Gai.2.161–162). "But if an heir who has the power of abstaining meddles with hereditary property, or if one who is allowed to deliberate ... enters on, he has thereafter no power of abandoning the inheritance, except he be under the age of twenty-five" (Inst.Gai.2.163). Generally, persons *sui iuris* under the age of twenty-five were protected by the praetor against disadvantageous or deceptive business. Also, in cases of an insolvent inheritance, the praetor could grant them an *in integrum restitutio* (restoration to the status quo) (Crook 1967, 117).

38.7 Conclusion

The freedom of wills and the importance of rich legacies in social and political networking might lead to an uncommon phenomenon too. The testator might have distributed a great deal of legacies and excluded the heir from any actual benefit. The instituted heir might then refuse an overextended (to wit, overdepleted) inheritance: but that made the whole will forfeit. To avoid this situation, a new law, the *lex Falcidia*, was issued under Augustus: "Any Roman citizen who ... wishes to make a will giving and bequeathing his money and property to whomever he chooses, shall have right and power ... to bequeath as much money as he wishes to any Roman citizen, so long as the amount bestowed as legacy is such that the heirs take under the will no less than a quarter of the estate" (D.35.2.1pr). D.35.2 contains complicated discussions about how to calculate the "Falcidian quarter" in cases of complex estates.

Social control over the power of testation can also be seen in the legal rules for restraining disinheritance. Without doubt, already in the XII Tables, *sui heredes* could have been disinherited if explicitly excluded (*nominatim*). However, there was a strong social expectation in every period of Roman history that one should leave his fortune to one's children, grandchildren and near relatives. Testators neglecting family feelings were scorned. Pliny recounts the story of an old Roman who had fallen in love and had disinherited his daughter after just eleven days (Plin. *Ep.* 6.33). Valerius Maximus reports with embarrassment that Aebutia, mother of two daughters, made only one of them her heir, without the other having done her any injury (Val. Max.7.8.2). In the case of such "insane" wills, the praetor had the right to interfere; although the praetor was not able to issue a completely new inheritance law, he could give some kind of protection to such persons in the form of a *bonorum possessio contra tabulas*, a grant of title to property to unjustly omitted close relatives.

A similar restriction was the possibility to appeal an unjust will, one in which the testator excluded near relatives and bequeathed the family estate to others without serious reason. The claim described the will as contrary to natural duty (*inofficiosum*). If proved, the testator was declared "insane" for excluding his near relatives and the will forfeited in this part. In classical law, unjustly disinherited descendants, ascendants or brothers and sisters had a claim for the quarter of the family estate (*debita portio*). However, generally the children had to provide proof that they had constantly rendered respectful obedience to their parents, as proper family sentiment demanded (C.3.28.28pr, quoting a constitution from 321 AD).

Bibliography

Ando, C. 2011. *Law, language and empire in the Roman tradition.* Philadelphia.

Buckland, W. W. 1925. *A manual of Roman private law.* Cambridge.

Campbell, B. 1994. *The Roman army, 31 BC–AD 235: a sourcebook.* London.

Champlin, E. 1991. *Final judgments: duty and emotion in Roman wills, 200 B.C.–A.D. 250.* Berkeley.

Crook, J. A. 1967. *Law and life of Rome: 90 B.C.–A.D.212.* Ithaca.

du Plessis, P. J. 2010[4]. *Borkowski's textbook on Roman law.* Oxford.

Evans Grubbs, J. 2002. *Women and the law in the Roman Empire: a sourcebook on marriage and widowhood.* London.

Frier, B. W. 1985. *The rise of the Roman jurists: studies in Cicero's* Pro Caecina. Princeton.

Frier, B. W. 2000. "Demography." In A. Bowman, P. Garnsey and D. Rathbone, eds., *The Cambridge ancient history.* Cambridge. Vol. 11: 787–816.

Frier, B. W. and McGinn, T. A. J. 2004. *A casebook on Roman family law.* Oxford.

Gardner, J. F. and Wiedemann, T. 2000. *The Roman household: a sourcebook.* London/New York.

Harries, J. 2006. *Cicero and the jurists: from citizen's law to the lawful state.* London.

Johnston, D. 1988. *The Roman law of trusts.* Oxford.

Kelly, J. M. 1976. *Studies in the civil judicature of the Roman republic.* Oxford.

Manthe, U. 1997. "Ein Sieg der Rhetorik über die Jurisprudenz: der Erbschaftsstreit des Manius Curius—eine vertane Chance der Rechtspolitik." In U. Manthe and J. von Ungern-Sternberg, eds., *Große Prozesse der römischen Antike.* Munich. 74–84.

Meyer, E. A. 2004. *Legitimacy and law in the Roman world:* tabulae *in Roman belief and practice.* Cambridge.

Mouritsen, H. 2011. *The freedman in the Roman world.* Cambridge.

Phang, S. E. 2001. *The marriage of Roman soldiers 13 B.C.—A.D. 235: law and family in the imperial army*. Leiden.

Rüfner, T. 2011. "Testamentary formalities in Roman law." In K. G. C. Reid, M. J. de Waal and R. Zimmermann, eds., *Comparative succession law, I: Testamentary formalities*. Oxford. 1–26.

Saller, R. P. 1994. *Patriarchy, property and death in the Roman family*. Cambridge.

Scheidel, W. 2007. "Demography." In W. Scheidel, I. Morris and R. P. Saller, eds., *The Cambridge economic history of the Greco-Roman world*. Cambridge. 38–86.

Tellegen, O. E. 1982. *The Roman law of succession in the letters of Pliny the Younger*. Zutphen.

Thomas, P. 2014. "The intention of the testator: from the *causa Curiana* to modern South African law." In J. Hallebeek et al., eds., Inter cives necnon peregrinos: *essays in honour of Boudewijn Sirks*. Göttingen. 727–740.

Watson, A. 1971. *The law of succession in the later Roman republic*. Oxford.

Wieacker, F. (1967). "The *causa Curiana* and contemporary Roman jurisprudence." *The Irish Jurist* 2: 151–164.

Wolf, J. G. and Crook, J. A. 1989. *Rechtsurkunden in Vulgärlatein*. Heidelberg.

Zimmermann, R. 2007. "Compulsory heirship in Roman law." In K. G. C. Reid, M. J. de Waal and R. Zimmermann, eds., *Exploring the law of succession: studies national, historical and comparative*. Edinburgh. 27–48.

Property

CHAPTER 39

THE ECONOMIC STRUCTURE OF ROMAN PROPERTY LAW

RICHARD A. EPSTEIN

39.1 Introduction

My task in this volume is to summarise within a short space the salient features of Roman property law. I approach this topic not as a classicist steeped in the niceties of Roman culture and the Latin language, but as a lawyer who has examined elsewhere the basic structure and design of systems of property rights with an eye to understanding their internal coherence and economic efficiency. Taking on this task requires, of course, an appreciation of the peculiarities of ancient Rome and Roman law. Surprisingly, however, these play a relatively modest part in the overall analysis. The Romans had to address challenges fundamental to all legal systems. Their legal rules had to be resilient enough to serve in good times as in bad, both in Rome and throughout the Empire. The many excellent studies on the productivity of agricultural land or the overall Roman market economy are thus orthogonal to the problems raised here (e.g. Finley 1999; Temin 2012), which involve the internal mechanics of the Roman system. The durability of Roman solutions over centuries and across continents offers strong evidence that their choices were sound notwithstanding their shaky and uncritical reliance on *ratio naturalis*, or natural reason, to buttress their conclusions. Filling that foundational gap requires a more systematic approach, based on the twentieth-century transactions cost approach of Ronald Coase (Coase 1960). Ironically, that approach does not undermine the Roman approach but illustrates the soundness of its critical features.

To defend this thesis in a decidedly Roman fashion, I ask these questions in order (Nicholas 1962). First, how is property acquired? Second, what is the property so acquired? Third, how is that property protected? Fourth, how is that property transferred? Fifth, how are divided interests created in property? Sixth, how are unintended mergers of property sorted out?

39.2 Acquisition of Property

Property rights in land, chattels or animals could be acquired by transfer from the emperor or from some prior owner. They could also be acquired by taking first possession of land, chattels (movables) or animals. In all cases, the initial possession yielded *dominium*, or ownership rights good against the rest of the world. These rules on *occupatio* did not apply to *res communes*, which as Justinian noted (Inst.2.1), included rivers, beaches and the air. This durable distinction between common and private property reflected a recurrent trade-off between costs of exclusion and costs of coordination (Epstein 1994). Common ownership facilitates effective transportation and communications, but precludes extensive development. Rivers, lakes, seas and beaches have their greatest value as open-access resources that no one may reduce to private possession. But land, which requires extensive cultivation and construction, must be subject to exclusive ownership to allow for a return from the investment of labour.

The first possession doctrine therefore never allowed one to take ownership of a river or lake, even if riparians might take limited quantities of water for domestic purposes, or build huts on the beach in storms. In contrast, ordinary movables (*mobiles*) were reduced to ownership by taking them into possession. The rules for animals were more difficult because of a running dispute over whether hot pursuit, wounding or actual capture was needed to reduce the animal to private ownership,[1] a Roman debate that carried over into modern times.[2] Land poses a greater challenge because it can never be grasped in hand. Accordingly, the initial possessor (turned owner) had to give notice to the rest of the world by demarcating its boundaries with stones or other markers. The Roman system rightly discussed only how possession was either acquired or lost. The individual owner was presumed to retain possession of any land or chattels until it was transferred or abandoned. Possessory remedies were available when his home or goods were seized while away, thereby promoting the stability of possession, which in Roman times and today is one hallmark of a mature system of property.

39.3 Extent of Property

The second task of Roman law was to determine the scope and duration of property interests created by first possession or voluntary transfer. Two basic rules contributed to the efficiency of that system. The first is associated with the maxim, *Cuius est solum, eius est usque ad coelum et ad inferos*, whosoever owns the soil owns from the depths of the earth to the tops of the heaven. Somewhat surprisingly, this rule was only formally

[1] See e.g. Inst.Gai. 2.66–70; Inst. 2.1.12. Gaius examines the first possession rules after delivery, while Justinian reverses the order. Gaius put Roman-law rules first, natural-law rules second. Justinian adopted the natural temporal sequence—acquisition before transfer—after the forms disappeared.

[2] See, Pierson v. Post, 3 Cai. R. 175 (N.Y. Sup. Ct. 1805).

articulated by the glossator Accursius in the twelfth century (Bouvé 1930, 246–248). But the rule surely represents Roman legal practice, given the unquestioned ability of a landowner to open mines or prevent overhangs, which only ran into trouble with the advent of air travel. This rule effectively reduced the resources needed for acquiring and defining property rights. The right to go below the surface guarantees that the owner has support for his own structures. The exclusive access to mineral rights allows for efficient extraction, either by the owner or by a licensee. The vertical rights above the land permit a single owner to build without having to gain the permission of others. The clarity of the rule also gives public notice of ownership in three dimensions once the surface boundaries are marked off.

The clear delineation of these ownership rights also establishes the correlative duties of everyone else. The primary duty of strangers is to forbear entrance upon the land (*transgressio*), or physical invasions by smell, filth and the like (*nocumentum*). The content of these duties follows from general legal principles, and does not vary with context to the case. Others can fulfil that duty regardless of their wealth; and the forbearance requirement works equally well in small and large communities alike (Epstein 2011).

39.4 Loss and Recovery of Property

While these property rights are good against the world, rights of action are granted to an owner only against a person who takes or damages the land in question. Given the instability of title in ancient times, Roman law had to decide who could sue whom when possession changed. Usually, the suit could be brought by the party dispossessed against the dispossessor. But endless complications could arise whenever either the initial possessor or the dispossessor died before the property could be recovered, or whenever the dispossessor sold, gave or left the land to a third person who may not have had knowledge that the property was stolen. In these cases, Roman law provided that the *rei vindicatio* was technically brought against the property, so ultimately it did not matter whether any rival claimant was an initial dispossessor or a subsequent taker. The law of familial descent meant that on the death of the original owner, the next in line within the family could maintain the suit.

In unstable times, an initial dispossession from land could be followed by a second or a third. The Romans developed two rules to respond to that challenge, both of which are in use today. The first rule is *prior in tempore, potior in iure*, which translates "prior in time is higher in right" *not* "first in time is highest in right". The difference here is critical. A protective rule restricted only to the first possessor is of no use in disputes between the first and second dispossessors. That lapse in turn entails that on initial dispossession, property remains forever unprotected and thus reverts to the state of nature, which again contributes to massive social instability. Hence the rule of *relative* title works between any two claimants to the property. Necessarily, the correlative rule is the *ius tertii* (which has no explicit articulation in the Roman texts), whereby no one is entitled to defend his present possession against a rival claimant by setting up the higher title of a third person—whose rights are left untouched by the outcome of any particular dispute.

The next piece of this puzzle asks how any dispossessor or his successor in title perfects title against any prior owner, including the first possessor. The Roman rules of *usucapio* (taking by use) address that problem by allowing a party whose initial possession is wrongful to obtain good title against an owner by passage of time, which converts a wrong to a right. It does so to encourage quick resolution of title disputes, with the analogous rules of adverse possession in English law. Clear title thus allows the new owner to develop, mortgage or sell the property, without fear that these investments will be snatched away by some unknown party. The Roman decision to allow longer periods of usucaption against total strangers than prior owners nicely balances the equities in these title disputes. More controversial is the Roman decision to deny *usucapio* for any property taken by theft or violence, even when in the hands of an innocent purchaser. This rule lets victims of deliberate wrongs recover their property, but denies full value of clear title to a good faith purchaser.

39.5 Voluntary Transfers of Property

Romans jurists well understood that in a commercial society parties obtained mutual gains by sale of all forms of property. Roman transfer rules, however, rightly varied by type of property. Thus, in the classical period Roman law used consensual contracts for the sale of goods, which required no particular formalities to be fully enforceable by both buyer and seller, even if no earnest money had been paid over. It also understood that the physical delivery of a chattel (*traditio*) with the intention to transfer property transferred ownership without any further formalities. The intent element was strictly required, in order to distinguish between transfers of ownership from bailments, where the transferee had an obligation to return the thing to the transferor. In sales both title and hence risk of loss (*res perit domino*) passed to the buyer on delivery. Risk allocation under bailments was more complex and often depended on for whose benefit the bailment was made, as discussed later. The highest standard of care (*custodia*) applied for bailment made for the benefit of the bailee; an intermediate standard (ordinary care) applied for bailments for mutual benefit; and the lowest standard of care (*bona fides*) for those made for the benefit of the bailor.[3]

The outright transfer of more durable and valuable forms of property required greater formality. Thus classical Roman law drew a distinction between *res mancipi*, which were subject to formalities, and *res nec mancipi*, which were not. The former class included land, large draught animals that were capital assets in Roman times, slaves and all children both male and female. Mancipation was often used for the marriage of a daughter (Inst.Gai.1.116–123). The extensive formalities for *mancipatio* (a scale bearer and six witnesses) served two functions. First, it signalled to the parties (as a deed does today) that this ceremony was no preliminary negotiation, but a completed transfer. Second, it offered a convenient way to give notice to the world, especially in small communities, that the transfer had taken place. One key difficulty with land was that its alienability

[3] See section 39.6.

was often in doubt because of the potential claims of the heirs to the property after the death of the *pater familias*. One view, therefore, was that any taker from the head of the family could be forced to return the property at the demand of the new *pater familias*. That system would yield only divided interests in land, which imposed an effective constraint against heavy investments in land, which could then be coopted by the family of the original seller. The efficient solution in these cases is to allow for the sale and to impose, if need be, restrictions on the ability of the head of the family to consume the proceeds. In English law this is achieved by using a family trust, a more robust institution than the Roman *fiducia*, which offered less protection against the misconduct of the fiduciary. To achieve the sale, the Romans resorted (as did the English in later times) to a fictitious judgement. The real seller was sued by the real buyer, who claimed that the title was always his, so that no transfer was needed at all. The formal ceremony gave hint of both the origin and transformation of the practice: "This man I claim as belonging to me by right quiritary and be he purchased to me by this ingot and this scale of bronze" (Inst.Gai.1.119). The reference to quiritary title is the highest in Roman law, but the "be he purchased" indicates that the real purpose of the transaction was to transfer title to the buyer. Once the fictional lawsuit was accepted, the second phrase was added to eliminate any residual ambiguity.

39.6 Divided Interests

Any legal system works most effortlessly when a single owner has rights that are good against the rest of the world, because the problems with divided control do not arise. In many instances, however, the retention or transfer of the entire interest in property comes at a real cost, if the best use of the property requires the division of control among two or more individuals. The dominant economic inquiry is whether the gains from the division of a single property into multiple interests exceed the transaction costs needed to effectuate the division. Obviously, in many settings that proposition is false, in which case no deal takes place. Nonetheless, it is as true today as in Roman times that in some settings divided ownership increases value. Such divisions are found with bailments, leases, mortgages, covenants, easements and life estates (or usufructs in Roman law).

No legal set of rules can indicate when these property divisions should take place; that choice depends on economic factors of which the transactors have the best knowledge. But what every legal system can do is reduce the costs of creating divided interests in property, so as to increase the velocity of these transactions. Two formidable complications can stand in the path of creating divided interests. First, these divided interests make it difficult to determine which (or both) of the two (or more) parties should hold the rights to sue for the loss of or damage to the property, or to enter into voluntary transactions with third parties. Second, principled rules must be developed to police the boundary lines between the two interests, so that neither party can undermine the arrangement by taking more than its allocated portion of rights. Necessarily, however, each additional fractionalisation of rights over discrete assets adds new burdens, both with respect to the outside world and among the parties.

The initial question is whether the legal system should tolerate these divided interests at all, given the systematic burdens. The answer yields a split verdict. Virtually every legal system imposes some limitation on the types of divided interests it will recognise. In dealing with chattels or animals, the most common form of division is that of a bailment or a loan, which are relatively simple transactions. But with land, the variations are more numerous because its permanence and great value increase the potential gains from creating multiple interests, even though they complicate the state of the title. In modern systems, the law keeps orderly account of multiple interests in land through a comprehensive recordation system, especially in those systems that can be computer-organised. But Roman law had no public index to allow anyone to determine who owned what partial interest in a given plot of land. The lack of secure title thus complicated routine purchases, leases and sales of land.

This one key feature has two dramatic consequences. The first is that it forced the Romans to resort to other means to assure potential transactors of who was in a position to deal with the property and to what extent. Second, following from the first, is that the Romans slimmed down the types and numbers of interests that could be created in any parcel of land, which reduced the stress on the notice function. These limitations often go under the name *numerus clausus*, or "closed number", of interests in land, which, as its name suggests, originated in Roman law (see Rudden 1987; Merrill and Smith 2000). Note how these principles play out with different divisions of property.

39.6.1 Bailments of Personal Property

A bailment is a voluntary transaction whereby A delivers property to B with the understanding that it shall be returned at some future time. Before A bails personal property to B, the parties must first develop rules that indicate what the bailee may and may not do with the property.[4] Generally, principles of freedom of contract apply to these deals, but in practice most people do not negotiate terms, instead relying on standard background terms to resolve these issues. The basic principle matches the risk of loss of a chattel with the distribution of its benefits (Epstein 2009). In both Roman and English law,[5] a bailment is for safekeeping (and thus for the bailor), while the usual rule exempts the bailee from liability except in cases of gross neglect. Where it is for the benefit of the bailee, as in use, the liability is strict, except in cases of robbery or natural destruction. Where the use is for the joint benefit of both parties, usually a standard of reasonable care is required.

In dealing with third parties, the Romans were reluctant to allow each party to sue for the extent of his interest because of the difficulty of developing joinder rules. Accordingly, their basic rule assigned the right of action to the party that bore the ultimate loss, which meant that the creditor could sue for the loss or damage of property in his possession. In contrast, the owner could sue if the property was in the hands of a bailee who held it for safekeeping, because as between the two parties the risk of loss was on the depositor, except in cases of bad faith or gross neglect. The basic point of the Roman classification

[4] Inst.Gai. 3.195–208, discussing the interaction between the law of bailment and *furtum*.

[5] *Coggs v. Bernard*, 92 Eng. Rep. 107 (K.B. 1703) (Holt, J.).

was to reduce the complexity and circuity of actions needed to sort matters out in regimes of divided property rights.

39.6.2 Divided Interests in Land

The situation with land was more complicated, as the division could be by way of *usufruct*, licence, mortgage, trust or servitude.

Usufruct. The owner of the property (sometimes called, misleadingly, the bare proprietor, or the reversioner or remainderman in English law) allowed a second person the right to use the land and to collect the fruits, both for life. The closest English analogy is the life estate in possession, with which there are instructive differences and parallels. In Roman law the usufruct was only a possessory interest, such that only one such interest could be created at any one time. There could not, as it were, be a usufruct on a usufruct. That practice contrasts sharply with the English recognition of life estates in remainder, which vastly complicated title for any piece of land, potentially reducing the effectiveness of its management. In addition, the Roman usufruct could not be alienated without the consent of the owner, a sensible rule that precluded the possibility that a friendly usufructuary would dispose his interest to a stranger hostile to the bare proprietor. This need for interest alignment is an important safeguard because even the best legal rules regulating the respective rights of the usufructuary and the bare owner are subject to slippage, which the commonality of interest, such as that between relatives, can help to stabilise.

Setting the boundaries between the usufructuary and the bare owner occupies many pages in the Digest because of the interdependence of the two interests in land over a wide range of possible uses. In modern times, elaborate provisions in deeds often specify what a life tenant can do with the property, but the Roman system relied very heavily on standardised default terms that could not be (or at least were not) varied by contract. Indeed, one reason why Roman classifications had to be so accurate was that it was too costly to vary them by contract. In practice, therefore, the standard "default" terms became binding on all parties who entered into that relationship. The economic risk is that the usufruct, while in control, could take actions that benefited himself but hurt the bare proprietor, because their interests were not separable. Worse still, the duration of the usufruct was highly uncertain. Perhaps usufructuaries should be able to move walls if their life lasted twenty-five years; but not if they were expected to live for only two. So the texts are filled with sensible categorical rules that by definition ignore these vital individual variations (D.7.1.9; D.7.1.13.4). The usufructuary may redecorate the walls of a house, but not alter its basic floor plan or walls. The usufructuary may operate existing mines, and also open new ones (under certain conditions, see D.7.1.13.5).

Yet difficulties lurk below the surface. At what rate can the valuable ore be removed? The accommodations are always flawed. Deny the right to open and the potential gains can be unnecessarily deferred for decades. Allow the mines to be opened, and they may be worked out too quickly during the usufructuary's life. Modern estate plans usually deal with these conflicts by separating the business decision on how best to mine from the distributional question of who gets what from the net profits. Putting the net proceeds of sale into a trust allows for dividend distributions on an annual basis. Unfortunately, the

Romans had neither the liquid assets nor the strong trusts that undergird modern capital markets. They could not separate, therefore, decisions on use from those on distribution. Imperfect accommodations of what constitute proper use and improper waste were thus inescapable in their legal system.

Licence and leases. The second form of property relationship is the licence or lease, whereby one person holds land and uses it for a defined period of time, after which it returns to its original owner. Today these leases are rightly classified as strong property interests because the tenant in possession has the right to recover possession for his term of years from any third person. He also has the right to prevent the landlord from entering the premises during the lease term so long as the tenant is not in breach of any of its covenants, such as those to pay rent or to maintain the premises in good order. Nonetheless the Romans did not regard the lease as a property interest in the robust sense because the tenant enjoyed neither of the two forms of protection just mentioned. Instead the tenant was restricted to a damage action against the landlord for breach of contract, including any covenant of quiet enjoyment.

This result followed because the tenant's remedy was treated as an action on the contract of hire (*locatio conductio*), perhaps the most ubiquitous of the Roman contract forms. But the term "hire" should not come as a surprise, for it is possible today to hire a car, hire a driver or hire a car with a driver. Essentially, the contract of hire covered any case in which one person had for a fee the temporary use of the labour or thing, real or personal, of another person, as is reflected in its modern usage. As leases became longer, and their value increased, the need for stronger protection grew. The English law transformed a lease from a simple contract of hire to a protected estate by manipulating the forms of action (Maitland, Chaytor and Whittaker 1936). But the evolution of leasehold arrangements in civil-law countries took place after the decline of Roman law.

Mortgages. The third form of divided interest is the mortgage. Modern law with recordation allows the creation of multiple mortgages on a single piece of property, whose priorities can be recorded. But Roman law had only two ways to divide the interest. One party could control the title papers to the property, and the other could remain in possession. The implicit understanding is that the outsider who deals with the property wants to see both before dealing. Nonetheless, the risk of double dealing was acute because the law did not give the borrower any clear action against a lender who took the property from him, so the use of real security was only of limited importance in Roman law, relative to personal guarantees, which received extensive attention and elaboration in the classical law. Security of personal property required that the lender take possession of the goods under *pignus*, or pawn, which meant that the property held as security could not be put to productive use so long as the loan remained unpaid. It was only when English law let a borrower of property remain in possession of land during the life of the loan that real property became a major source of financing.

Fiducia. The fourth class of divided interests is *fiducia*, or the early form of a trust arrangement, which is reflected in the modern use of the term "fiduciary" duties. Here, the property is transferred from one person to another, but for the purpose of management and protection, not for the purpose of a loan. In these cases the relationship usually could be terminated at the request of the creator of the arrangement, but its utility was limited, for the beneficiary had no strong protection if the trustee transferred the *res* to a third party free of trust. It was also unclear how many separate beneficial interests could be created under the arrangement. The modern trust arrangement overcomes these conveyance difficulties by separating legal ownership (with powers of management and disposition) from equitable ownership (with rights to either the use or proceeds of the property) in both common and civil-law countries, where legislation has narrowed any earlier differences between the two systems. Most trusts hold liquid assets, but trusts of land are not uncommon. These usually allow the current tenant in possession to veto sale of the property by the trustee.

Servitudes. The last class of divided interest in Roman law covers servitudes, which includes what are termed today both easements and restrictive covenants (Nicholas 1962). By the first, the holder of the dominant tenement has the right to enter the land of the servient tenement. The scope of the easement determines whether this right extends only to passage on foot, or by animals, or carts and the like. By the second, the law imposes restrictions on what an owner can do with his own property, to the benefit of a neighbour. A height restriction that protects views or allows for the passage of light and air is perhaps the most common restrictive covenant, whose value is far greater in urban than in rural settings. The interests here are of sufficient importance that their transfer is subject to the usual formalities of *mancipatio*, to insure clarity between the parties and to give notice to the rest of the world. To prevent undue complication of the title, the general law restricts the scope of servitudes. It is not possible to place a servitude on a servitude, or subject them to time limitations or specific conditions. Similarly, servitudes can only bind adjacent properties, thus reducing the difficulty of detecting who is in breach, and facilitating (by reducing the number of parties) the renegotiation or termination of the servitude. These restrictions on freedom of contract give greater clarity to third persons without imposing serious economic disadvantages on the initial parties or their successors in title. The practices that are barred are ones that generally do not make economic sense. The added clarity to the relationship allows servitudes to hold their value over time.

Consistent with the general theme, neither type of servitudes may require any positive actions by the owner of the servient tenement. Both only give limited rights of use to the holder of the dominant tenement. The servitude created, moreover, binds the land. Unlike personal covenants, for example, to cut the grass, both its benefit and burden work for the benefit of subsequent takers. All these rules work in tandem to maximise the combined value of the plots in question. Rights of way can often be observed by potential buyers, which is why they were probably more common than restrictive covenants, for which visual inspection is less reliable. Once potential buyers or lenders are on notice that a neighbour holds a dominant tenement, further inquiry can reveal the scope of that servitude. The prohibition against service obligations makes sense because service relationships are personal, and unlike liquidated debt obligations are not freely assignable or delegable under the conventional contract law. A contract to cut hair, or even a lawn, will not clutter a land transaction. Keeping the duties in their negative form thus standardises the obligation and thereby encourages the alienability of the land on both sides. Having servitudes bind the land also removes any risk of holdout because the holder of the servient tenement cannot force the buyer of the dominant tenement to repurchase his access right at a price that reflects his higher intensity of use.

39.7 *Accessio, Confusio* and *Specificatio*

The last distinctive Roman institution arises when the property of two parties, whether land or movables, are combined together into a new whole. These rules are of immense sophistication. First, whenever the return of the two things to their original condition is possible, restoration of the status quo ante is the dominant solution. Where the combination of the two things is indissoluble, any party who in bad faith combined the two properties has no claim to the combined product. That loss of title was a sensible way to make illicit combination a no-win proposition for the party that undertook it.

The difficult situations arose when there was an innocent union of the property of two parties, either by virtue of a mistake or the actions of an independent third party. These rules could apply to land where one party built a structure on property that belonged to another, thinking that he was its owner. Similar situations could occur when one person made a statue out of marble that was owned by another. Any effort to return to the status quo ante would result in the destruction of the added value that would serve the interests of neither side. By the same token, it would have been a mistake to treat the two parties as co-owners, i.e. partners, of the property to the extent of their respective contributions. Partnership is a *bona fide* contract, which can only work between two or more persons that have high levels of trust with each other, which is rarely the case when mistake or chance throws two parties together at random.

To meet this challenge, Roman law introduced a system of forced exchanges, which brings the so-called "just compensation" principle into high relief. Its application takes place in two stages. By the first, the law has to decide *which* of the two parties should be entitled to keep the thing. One per se rule is that the owner of the land (which can only be conveyed by *mancipatio*) is entitled to the land with its improvement. When the good faith improver is in possession of the land, the owner may recover the property only upon payment of, roughly speaking, the fair market value of the materials and labour that the mistaken party put into the object. Procedurally, this usually took place by subjecting the *vindicatio* of the owner to an *exceptio doli*, unless the money in fact was paid. Where the original owner was back in possession, later Roman law allowed an "equitable action" to recover the value added. In both cases, this creditor/debtor relationship eliminated mutual fiduciary duties and created an easy way for the two parties to go their separate ways. In using this system, the Roman law set the debt equal to the benefit provided, which eliminated haggling over the two respective contributions. It thereby left the subjective value of the combination, which is far harder to measure, to the landowner.

With a statue, the usual solution was to give the statue to the sculptor on the ground that it was far more difficult to establish the subjective value of the distinctive statue than it was to assign the value to a fungible chunk of marble. Notwithstanding the controversies over some of the particular cases, the overall framework continues to endure today where organised markets are not available. Technically, the cases of *accessio, confusio* and *specificatio* create bilateral monopoly situations where there is only one buyer and one seller, and thus no unique price at which the property can exchange hands with voluntary trade. The just compensation formula creates additional burdens on valuation, but eliminates the ability of either side to hold out. That solution is still in standard use today for any such cases, which arise with both private necessity and the vastly large subject of takings for public use, with just compensation under the modern law of eminent domain.

39.8 Conclusion

The beauty in the Roman system lies both in the fashioning of the individual pieces and in fitting them together. A great Empire rested on great law.

Bibliography

Bouvé, C. (1930). "Private ownership of airspace." *Air Law Review* 1: 232–258.

Coase, R. H. (1960). "The problem of social cost." *Journal of Law and Economics* 3 1–44.

Epstein, R. A. (1994). "On the optimal mix of common and private property." *Social Philosophy and Policy* 11: 17–41.

Epstein, R. A. (2009). "The many faces of fault in contract law: or how to do economics right, without really trying." *Michigan Law Review* 107: 1461–1477.

Epstein, R. A. 2011. *Design for liberty: private property, public administration and the rule of law*. Cambridge.

Finley, M. I. 1999. *The ancient economy*. Berkeley.

Maitland, F. W., Chaytor, A. H. and Whittaker, W. J. 1936. *The forms of action at common law: a course of lectures*. Cambridge.

Merrill, T. W. and Smith, H. E. (2000). "Optimal standardization in the law of property: the *numerus clausus* principle." *Yale Law Journal* 110: 1–70.

Nicholas, B. 1962. *An introduction to Roman law*. Oxford.

Rudden, B. 1987. "Economic theory v. property law: the *numerus clausus* problem." In J. Eekelaar and J. Bell, eds., *Oxford essays in jurisprudence: third series*. Oxford. 239–263.

Temin, P. 2012. *The Roman market economy*. Princeton.

CHAPTER 40

OWNERSHIP AND POWER IN ROMAN LAW

LUIGI CAPOGROSSI COLOGNESI
TRANSLATED BY THOMAS ROBERTS

DOMINIUM *ex iure Quiritium*,[1] which exercised such a lasting and varied influence on the legal tradition of medieval and modern Europe, is the keystone not only of the Roman legal system, but also of the entire Roman social framework (Bonfante 1926; Kaser 1956; Capogrossi Colognesi 1969; Diòsdi 1970; Cannata 2001, 151–163, 459–473; see also Pennitz 1991; Dubouloz 2011). The strict hierarchical structure of the family, centred on its *pater familias*, was securely rooted in his absolute freedom to make independent choices regarding the disposal and usage of the entire family estate. As in many pre-capitalist societies, land played a central role in Roman society, even during the most pronounced stage of its economic development. Landed wealth determined the scope of one's ability to participate in government, as the political status of citizens was related to land owned, either directly or by his *pater familias*. Even in the Imperial age, despite social changes and the progressive integration of Italian and provincial elites, the power of the aristocracy continued to be based on the unitary nature of the wealth of major property owners, power over which was nominally vested in the *pater* alone.

Throughout the classical period, Roman law drew a fundamental distinction between *res mancipi* and *nec mancipi*. This reflected a difference in value between the two categories of property within an economy that was essentially agrarian. It also gave rise to differences in the way ownership of such property could be transferred. In the words of Gaius, *res mancipi* were *res pretiosiores*: urban and rural property, working and transport animals and slaves. *Res nec mancipi* covered all other forms of movable property.

In order to obtain ownership over *res mancipi*, a solemn and complex ritual involving *mancipatio* was required. This required the pronouncement of a fixed formula, the presence of at least five Roman citizens as witnesses, and a "scale holder", with a set of scales, to symbolise the full and accurate payment of the purchase price by weighing uncoined bronze. At some point, likely in connection with developments in coinage, the transaction

[1] The Romans referred to Roman ownership as *dominium ex iure Quiritium* from the archaic name for the Romans, the *Quirites*.

lost its original meaning as an actual sale consisting of the formal exchange of an object in return for a price. In many cases the transaction became a formality; its only effect being the transfer of ownership of *res mancipi*.[2] Beyond this, however, under *mancipatio*, the buyer also received from the seller a formal guarantee, the *auctoritas*, against any possible interference by other persons with his new property. By the *actio auctoritatis*, the buyer was thus able to demand from the seller twice the purchase price, should he be lawfully deprived of his right of ownership. But such *auctoritas* only applied in instances where *mancipatio* retained its ancient function as a real sale, which did in fact occur into the Imperial era (Arangio-Ruiz 1956, 193; Gallo 1960, 21–38).

Both the simpler *traditio*, which was used for *res nec mancipi*, and the other common procedure for transfer of ownership, *in iure cessio*, were unilateral. The first involved the mere delivery of the item (even though jurists subsequently imposed a further requirement of a legal foundation [*iusta causa*] for the transaction and intention). *In iure cessio* was an early instance of the systematic use of *fictiones* in order to achieve new results. The buyer claimed ownership over the property, and the *dominus* deliberately declined to react. The (former) owner was thus unsuccessful in the process and yielded the right claimed by the other party.

Ownership could also be acquired by the mere fact of possessing an item for a certain period of time. This was relevant in conditions when documentation of title were poor; it was also relevant when the procedure of sale was in some respect deficient. Possession produced ownership when one's material relationship with the item—the *usus* of the thing—persisted for one (movable items) or two years (immovable ones).[3]

At least until the third century BC, ownership in Roman law was expressed through factual control of a corporeal object more than by the idea of an abstract right over it. The person acquiring an object by *mancipatio* or asserting ownership by *legis actio sacramento in rem*—the two fundamental mechanisms of ancient Roman law—accompanied their solemn assertion with material apprehension of the *res*. *Usus* likewise emphasised physical control of a corporeal object as a vehicle for securing ownership.

From the beginning, the ultimate nature of ownership as a special kind of right was evident. The other legal powers that could be vested in a Roman citizen (other than the personal rights over his family) had a specific content and addressee: the right to claim payment of money or a certain service from a third party etc. By contrast, the content of ownership rights could not be determined in advance since they were only limited by the duty to enjoy that right without unfairly harming other parties. Furthermore, the claim vested in the holder of such a right was essentially negative: he could require other citizens not to make any attempt to interfere with his full enjoyment of the object under his ownership. More than all other rights, it essentially became evident only when a third party interfered with the owner's peaceful enjoyment of the object.

From the XII Tables on, legal instruments were honed or even created from scratch to extend the protection of private property. Rules of this period suggest a relatively compact

[2] In its abstract form involving mere fictitious sale, this act was used to achieve widely varying legal effects: from the establishment of the husband's power over his wife (*coemptio*), through the subjection of a free man to a condition of semi-slavery by another *pater*, to the formal release from a debt obligation or the drafting of a will (*mancipatio familiae* and *testamentum per aes et libram*).

[3] On the modes of acquisition of property see Watson 1968; Romeo 2010.

world made up of small-scale owners, whose utmost autonomy was stressed, while also being required to cooperate in matters of intersubjective interest. Plots of land were regulated by very visible boundaries, which were protected also by religious sanctions. They appear to have been linked within a network of agricultural pathways, which were often shared between various owners. In addition, the conduct of individual owners was regulated in order to prevent their causing harm to their neighbours.[4]

The body of rules governing the relations between neighbours, the use of rural roads (or the *viae vicinales*: from *vici*, the smaller rural settlement) and the regulations applicable to flood defences contributed to the creation of a patchwork of small-scale rural districts. These districts then constituted the base unit for the Roman territorial system. In addition, from the time of the XII Tables, it is likely that it was possible to use *mancipatio* to transfer ownership (or joint ownership) of very limited plots of land intended for highly specific uses, such as paths or live springs supplying water to people and animals in the countryside. In this way, the scarcity of natural resources was at least in part dealt with by maximising their usage.

Following the Samnite Wars and the definitive subjugation of the Latin League in 338 BC, an entirely novel institutional experiment was launched, with the aim of integrating the various Italic peoples through different forms of political dependence. Colonies (of Roman and Latin status) and *municipia* (of full Roman citizens as well as citizens *sine suffragio,* without political rights) were the main instruments of Roman hegemony over Italy. Taking the *ius civile* as a model, new forms of ownership proliferated under the various legal and territorial systems spread throughout Italy, all of which fell under the full sovereignty of Rome. Both the statutes of the individual Latin colonies and, at least in part, those of the *municipia sine suffragio* provided for forms of private ownership that were distinct from the *dominium* of the Roman *ius civile*, even though they were also based on Roman sovereignty. It was only the legal unification of the peninsula after the Social War that put an end to that singular experiment. In any case, the growth of Roman direct and indirect control of Italian territory allowed for an enormous process of redistribution of both the rural population and agricultural wealth.

Roman law also came to acknowledge ways, unknown to the *ius civile*, whereby something could belong to someone. These included first and foremost forms of possession that had evolved in parallel to Rome's expansion throughout Italy. They resulted from the allocation to private individuals of areas of *ager publicus,* which were formally owned by the *civitas* (Roselaar 2010). The violent disputes concerning these lands that occurred in various periods of Roman history are the best evidence of their importance. Although these *possessiones* were different from the *dominium* of the *ius civile*, they did have a direct

[4] One particular procedural instrument introduced at the time of XII Tables is prominent within this context, also due to its broad scope: the *actio aquae pluviae arcendae*. This action, which was progressively extended and became more complex, subjected the full powers available to the *dominus* over his property to a superior and more general interest to curb losses, allocating them in the least unfair manner between all owners affected by outflowing rainwater. The direct but inevitable result of this rule was a drive towards coordination between various interested parties, with the aim of cooperating mutually in flood defence works against rainwater—which was and remains one of the scourges affecting the Italian territory. It thereby transformed individual works into a—much more effective—common effort, often under the oversight of local authorities.

impact on the economic relevance of Roman landownership over the last few centuries of the Republic. During that period, patterns of agricultural landholdings changed as Roman oligarchs acquired control of large areas of public land. In all likelihood, the possession of the *ager publicus* also gave rise to a new idea of private possession separate from ownership.

This seems to have occurred relatively early, during the Second Punic War if not earlier. At that time the praetor undertook to provide legal protection to the possessor of land owned by another private party in the form of a new procedural mechanism, the interdict *uti possidetis*.[5] By this means, the praetor issued an order preventing interference by any citizen with the peaceful enjoyment of possession. Another interdict, *utrubi,* was later issued to protect possession of movable property. From that time onwards, therefore, possession must have been regarded as a legal concept distinct from the *dominium* of the *ius civile*. In this way, an important step was made in the process of "dematerialising" Roman property, which came to be conceived as a "right" independent of physical control of the object. Indeed, such an early distinction between the material enjoyment of a property and legal entitlement was by no means easy. Some legal systems, including relatively well-developed systems, have never fully realised such a distinction.

On the other hand, not all holders of possession were protected by these prohibitions. They were only available to possessors who had not obtained the item through violence or bad faith and had not received it on a temporary basis.[6] It is likely that the praetor initially sought to forestall the use of violence. However, a secondary effect proved to be much more significant over the longer term, impinging directly on substantive law. The recognition of the self-standing significance of possession changed the position of litigants in disputes relating to ownership. So long as the material condition of the object in dispute was not yet significant, the opposing parties were placed on the same level. Now it was possible to distinguish between the procedural claim made by a person asserting ownership but without possession, and that of a defendant who, by contrast, possessed the object. Only the claimant was required to prove the legal foundation of his claim. The defendant could limit himself to passive conduct and win the case even without furnishing positive proof of his right: it was sufficient that the claimant be unable to demonstrate his own. This change in the procedural logic became fully apparent with the shift from the archaic *legis actiones* to the formulary procedure, which had already started in the second century BC.

Henceforth, possession had a preliminary importance for any dispute *de proprietate* (Inst.Gai.4.148). Not only were disputes over possession preliminary to the *vindicatio* of ownership; their outcome often conditioned future developments. In many cases it was not easy for the claimant to give strong evidence of his property right.

It was subsequently almost inevitable that jurists took the further step of identifying a stronger possessory scenario under which possession had been acquired through legitimate mechanisms. Relying on the concept of *iusta causa*, "legitimate cause", for possession, they defined types of possession that were based on some form of legitimate title (acquisition, donation etc.), out of the larger class comprised of the forms of possession

[5] On the date: the comedies of Plautus refer to the wording of the interdict *uti possidetis*, specifically the clause *nec vi nec clam nec precario*. On interdicts see in general Kaser and Hackl 1996, 408–421.

[6] Schulz 1951, 428–433; Labruna 1971; Falcone 1996; Solidoro Maruotti 1998; Cannata 2001, 179–252.

protected by interdicts. These were then treated as within the scope of the archaic institute of *usus*. Possession that gave rise to ownership was thus transformed into the more "modern" figure of *usucapio*. Under *usucapio*, as under *usus*, a right of ownership could be acquired through a period of unbroken possession, upon condition that there was a *iusta causa* for the possession and good faith on the part of the usucaptor.[7] A further requirement later specified that actual control must be accompanied by *voluntas*: the intention to keep it for oneself as a genuine *dominus*.

The granting of legal salience to possession constituted only the first part of a broader transformation of the ancient form of property rights. Until that time, *dominium* had been the only legal instrument capable of ensuring the power of enjoyment of an object. Some developments had been possible: by requiring the person vested with that right to limit his ownership in time or to given contexts (e.g. *mancipatio fiduciae causa*),[8] or by applying it to objects intended for highly specific usages, such as trails or springs in the countryside. However, it was a cumbersome instrument, precisely due to its scope and the power vested in the *dominus*.

Here arose another fundamental innovation, which was to have considerable and lasting effects. During the period marked by the major transformations of the Punic Wars, the ancient form of marriage *cum manu*, under which the wife became entirely subject to the husband *loco filiae*, was less and less widely used. From at least the time of the XII Tables, the fiction of the *trinoctium* had rendered marriage compatible with the total independence of the woman from her husband and her family. This, however, gave rise to a new problem: that of ensuring economic protection to the wife in the (not uncommon) eventuality that the husband died first, without, however, impoverishing their children.[9]

The turning point came with the invention of a new legal relationship rigorously subject to a time limit. No single name is associated with the invention of usufruct, and yet this legal mechanism, which enabled enjoyment of property—esp. real estate—to be vested in a person other than its *dominus*, proved to be of enormous importance.[10] The unitary content of full enjoyment of an object, which had previously been connatural with ownership, was thus divided: *dominium* was "compressed" by the existence of another right intended to apply for a predetermined time (no longer than a human life) and which could not be

[7] This reference to *iusta causa* is made by mentioning *usucapio* as *pro emptore, pro herede, pro donato, pro legato, pro soluto*. On the other hand, *possessio pro suo* indicates the position of a possessor who intends to keep the object for himself and not on behalf of another. On *usus* and *usucapio* see Kaser 1988; Hausmaninger 1964 and Nörr 1969.

[8] A peculiar application of *mancipatio* was based on the inclusion of a clause in the agreement according to which the buyer undertook to transfer the object by *mancipatio* back to the *mancipio dans*; for example, when a *res mancipi* served as guarantee for the payment of a debt.

[9] This was a contradictory result due to the legal structure of the Roman family and to the rules of succession that restricted the lawful succession of the widow (who, as a woman, was unable to make a valid will independently at that time) to her male relatives, *agnati*, which did not include her own children. Thus, if her husband had bequeathed his property to her in his will, it would never accrue to the legitimate children. Consequently, his property would ultimately be transferred to the wife's family of origin, to which the husband was not related. The old *ius civile* thus proved to be incapable of achieving two different yet legitimate results: that of ensuring adequate economic security for the widow whilst also conserving the family wealth within the legitimate lineage.

[10] On usufruct see Grosso 1958; Bretone 1962; Giuffrè 1992.

transferred. From the original bundle of powers of the owner were hived off those that constituted what we might call "ordinary enjoyment" of the object. A holder of a usufruct could use a house or cultivate land, or even lease them out, but not alter them in substantial ways. This is because, upon expiry of the usufruct, the *dominus* was to reacquire the object in the condition in which he had temporarily transferred it. The importance of usufruct to structuring control of property and passage of wealth between generations can scarcely be overstated.

During approximately the same period, another right over the property of another powerfully increased the forms of exploitation of Roman property; to wit, praedial servitudes, rights vested in a person as the owner of land to make a certain use of another's land, in the service of exploitation of his own. This gave rise to the idea that one property "served" another, the so-called "dominant" property (Capogrossi Colognesi 1966 and 1976; Grosso 1969; Rodger 1972; Corbino 1979; Bannon 2009; Tuccillo 2009; Möller 2010; Basile 2012). Later, Roman jurists introduced the distinction between *iura praediorum rusticorum et urbanorum*, rural and urban praedial servitudes. These were subject to different regulations, depending upon historical but also structural circumstances. It is also likely that the core of rustic servitudes, the *iura aquarum et itinerum*, was much older, dating back even to the forms of ownership of private paths and waterway courses considered in relation to the period of the XII Tables (p. 626). The fact that the *iura aquarum et itinerum*, and only then, continued to be classified as *res mancipi*, in contrast to usufruct and urban servitudes, demonstrates their antiquity. Moreover, dedicated interdicts were introduced in the praetor's edict for these figures only, to protect one's *quasi possessio* of them,[11] clearly under inspiration from the possessory interdict par excellence, the *uti possidetis*.

Thanks to the creative force of juristic interpretation, both usufruct and praedial servitudes were adopted by the *ius civile* and were protected by civil-law actions. While property remained the supreme expression of legal power of the *res privatae*, it was now possible that more circumscribed rights over an object could be awarded to a person other than the owner. For this reason, these were called *iura in re aliena*.

Between the end of the third and the start of the second centuries BC, as a consequence of new building techniques and the growth of urban populations, the old Roman–Italic *domus* occupying one or more floors and closed to the outside was replaced by multistorey buildings receiving light and air from the outside, the antecedent of the early Imperial *insulae*. This resulted in a reduction in the autonomy of each dwelling, whilst situations characterised by reciprocal interference and disturbance proliferated. In many cases, relationships of this kind were organised by the Roman jurists in the form of new servitudes, to which no form of property was applicable.[12] This massive innovation also affected the

[11] *Possessio iuris* is referred to by Ulpian (D.43.26.2) and previously by Labeo as cited by Ulpian (D.37.1.3.1, despite Cannata 2001, 251 n. 232). *Quasi possessio iuris* is found in Inst.Gai.4.139, and in Papinian as cited by Ulpian (D.4.6.23.2). See in general Capogrossi Colognesi 1976 and now Basile 2012.

[12] e.g. to the right to prevent one's neighbour from increasing the height of his building or to lean one's own building and scaffolding onto the neighbour's walls, or to drain rainwater from one's own roof onto that of one's neighbour. Here there was no "possession" of a place or a space: there was only the intangible element of a benefit for oneself and a harm or tolerance imposed on the neighbour involving a "right to do" or an obligation "not to do or to acquiesce".

ancient rustic servitudes, which the jurists attempted to reconfigure as *iura*. They accordingly attempted to preserve certain characteristics of the previous system, but without its rigidity and breadth of ownership, thus guaranteeing greater efficiency throughout the entire Roman agricultural system.

The benefit created for a property by these new rights was referred to as the *utilitas fundi*. However, its definition was not left to the subjective judgement of the interested parties. It was the jurists, and ultimately the praetor, who hammered out the general and objective criteria of utility in rural and urban contexts.[13] The strict interpretation of *utilitas* thereby imposed limited the parties' ability to create new servitudes, though it did consistently increase the value of urban and agrarian property. The rights were attached to the property, and entitlements established by servitudes could only, and of necessity, be transferred along with the properties in favour of which they were created.

However, in contrast to usufruct, and in an analogous manner to ownership, these *iura praediorum* were permanent in nature: the possibility of a temporary servitude was excluded. Nonetheless, these servitudes could come to an end, either by the objective disappearance of the *utilitas fundi* or the simple *non usus* on the part of the holder of the right (loss on the grounds of *non usus* could also occur in relation to usufruct).[14] In keeping with the new economic dynamism of late Republican society, these new figures only remained valid for as long as they were effectively deemed to be useful and were in fact used by their holders. This is in contrast to ownership, which was never subordinated to considerations of its utility to its holder. [15]

This new system of rights over material objects in turn contributed to effecting a clearer configuration of ownership itself. It is this period that witnessed the first representation of the right of ownership in abstract terms. *Dominium* appears for the first time in a passage by Alfenus, the pupil of Servius (D.8.3.30). This was an important symptom of conceptual refinement, operating in parallel with a gradual assertion of abstract terms in Latin.

At the same time, the praetor enriched the already effective protections afforded ownership and possession with a series of procedural innovations. A few in particular should be noted, many of which have been inherited in full or in part by modern continental legal systems. From the *operis novi nuntiatio* to the *cautio damni infecti*, from the *interdictum quod vi aut clam* to an extensive use of the *actio negatoria*, in addition to the formidable enhancement of the longstanding *actio aquae pluviae arcendae*: a broad range of interventions enriched the original core developed in the early Republic (Bonfante 1926, 289–453).

The creative work of the late Republic also refined a guarantee for compliance with an obligation, which was added to the older *mancipatio fiduciae causa*; namely, the pledge. It was accepted that the creditor could have an effective power over certain assets of the debtor until the obligation was honoured. In the early second century, Cato had already

[13] For a long time, a servitude of leading water (*aquaeductus*) was only permitted in order to irrigate another property or to supply water for the needs of people and livestock, and not also to increase the aesthetic quality of the *villa*, thus operating only *ad amoenitatem*.

[14] On the other hand, urban servitudes were extinguished not by *non usus*, but by a positive action brought by the owner of the servient property that did not allow the exercise of that right, referred to by the Romans as *usucapio libertatis*.

[15] The principles governing usufruct are accurately interpreted by Crook 1967, 152 as evidence of the lack of interest of the Roman jurists in the economic impact of their rules.

suggested that farming equipment brought onto the property by a tenant could be withheld by the *dominus* as guarantee for his debt. This situation was protected by a dedicated interdict, although it was only when the praetor introduced an *actio Serviana* during the first century BC that the pledge became relevant under the *ius civile*.

Contextual change over the centuries now impelled another substantial change. The form of publicity provided by *mancipatio* now appeared obsolete, [16] as did the distinctions that had undergirded the taxonomy of *res mancipi* and *nec mancipi*. This was the premise for a considerable innovation of the systems for transferring ownership, on which another factor also exerted an influence.

As early as the second century BC, jurists and the praetor had recognised the consensual contract of sale as a source of reciprocal obligations between the parties protected by actions under civil law. Its typical content stipulated as the main obligation incumbent upon the seller the requirement to transfer only the material availability of the object sold, not full ownership. Modern scholars generally explain this aspect by ascribing the origin of this form of contract to a context of international commercial relations, under which foreigners could not use the forms available under the *ius civile* or acquire civil-law *dominium*. The new rules played a decisive role in favouring a new system for the circulation of goods (Arangio-Ruiz 1956, 178; Vacca 1988, 54–74).

Formerly, in situations involving a *res mancipi* transferred without *mancipatio* or *in iure cessio*, the buyer acquired only possession. Now the praetor granted him protection, even against the owner. He introduced a specific procedural exception against any claims by the transferor who might formally have retained the *dominium*. In the meantime, the buyer's protection was further extended by an *actio ficticia*; namely, the *actio Publiciana*. By this mechanism it was assumed (fictitiously) that possession had lasted for the period of time necessary for usucapion and that therefore the person bringing the claim had already become *dominus ex iure Quiritium*.

According to the jurists, Roman law thereby came to recognise the existence of *duplex dominium*, two forms of property:[17] one merely civilian, yet without effect; the other created by the jurisdiction of the praetor, the *in bonis habere* (Ankum et al. 1987–1990; Vacca 1988; Thielmann 1994; Capogrossi Colognesi 1999, 153–157). The first cases of *in bonis* protected by the praetor were precisely those that were the result of the fulfilment of a contract of sale.[18] Due to the strict logical and chronological sequence operative between the

[16] It was at this time in fact, as noted by Gaius (Inst.Gai.2.16), that their number remained unchanged, leaving out the new types of *res pretiosiores* that had emerged at the time of the great economic boom of the late Republican era. Gaius cites camels as animals that continued to be *nec mancipi* yet nonetheless *qui collo dorsove domantur*; however, it would be more appropriate to cite merchant ships, which had been important since at least the third century BC.

[17] Gaius (Inst.Gai.2.40) writes that at one time, for the Romans too, *unum esse dominium*, such that "a man had either quiritary dominion or none at all". However, subsequently they "decomposed dominion so that one person might have quiritary ownership of an object of which another person had bonitary ownership".

[18] The formula of the *actio* in question has been approximately reconstituted according to the following pattern: "if that slave that Aulus Agerius bought in good faith and which has been given to him", thus referring to the substantive relationship underlying the *traditio*: exchange of an object against payment of a price, thereby overcoming the formally unilateral nature of property transfer transactions *iure civili*.

new contract and praetorian ownership, it is likely that the latter was established no later than the first century BC.

However, praetorian ownership did not entail the disappearance of the *mancipatio*, which was widely practised throughout the Imperial era, as documentary evidence confirms. In effect, there existed two concurrent systems within the sphere of economic exchange controlled by the Romans. However—and this is crucial—the two systems were also largely convergent since, at least in relations between citizens, *usucapio* enabled the *in bonis* possessor rapidly to obtain full quiritary dominion.

Towards the end of the Republic the system governing the sale of property and the forms of transfer of ownership had thus been extraordinarily enriched. Alongside the old and never abandoned use of *mancipatio* for real sales, with effective payment of the price (*supra*, p. 525), the new obligation-form of sale expanded the range of solutions available to private parties, enabling payment of the agreed price and transfer of the object to occur after conclusion of the contract, perhaps even at a different location. Moreover, the mere obligation to transfer possession and not also *dominium* under the Roman *ius civile* made this new relationship accessible also to foreigners, exponentially expanding the class of potential users. It must be borne in mind that, at that time, increasingly numerous business relations tied Romans to *peregrini*, who still accounted for the majority of inhabitants throughout the Empire.[19]

On the other hand, this new dynamism, which affected the forms of transfer of ownership, had only partial effect on the regime of *iura in re aliena*, which did not have inbuilt the ownership–possession distinction, which was precisely what permitted innovation in the realm of transfer. Consequently, not only could praedial servitudes and usufructs not be the object of *traditio* or be acquired through usucapion, but it was also impossible to subject them to the *exceptio rei venditae et traditae* in order to protect their "possession", as they could not be merely possessed. Furthermore, they could not be subject to the *fictio* of the *actio Publiciana*, which was premised on something that was structurally or legally impossible; namely, their acquisition through usucapion.

The rigidity of the *ius civile* with regard to these rights therefore remained unchanged, in a context that saw formidable liberalisation of the system of land ownership. A paradox thus persisted, resolved by praetor's jurisdiction.

To understand the resolution crafted by the Romans, it is necessary to attend to the close relationship between the obligation incumbent upon the seller under *emptio venditio* and the protection granted by the praetor for purchases of *res mancipi* by simple *traditio*. Recall, too, that the contract of sale did not cover exclusively transfers of ownership. It was also used to create praedial servitudes. (The situation was different for usufruct on account of its primary, if not unique, goal of providing a source of maintenance to widows, granted principally through a testamentary will). The establishment of those rights and obligations was very often founded on a preliminary agreement within which an appropriate financial consideration was to be stipulated. It is precisely this that had to be formalised within a regular *emptio venditio*.[20] However, how was it then possible to maintain also

[19] Similarly, it was necessary to extend to such people praetorian protection for property over which possession only had been acquired, even if this was not remedied by usucapion and could not be protected by the fiction of the *actio Publiciana*.

[20] Traces of preliminary contracts of sale relating to servitudes may be found in many passages of the Digest: D.8.1.20 and 18.1.80.1; D.8.5.16; D.19.1.3.2 and D.8.6.19pr; D.21.2.10; D.21.2.46.1; and

in these cases the typical effect of sale, consisting in the obligation not simply to transfer the right but also to transfer the object? How was it possible to transfer this right physically to the disposal of the buyer?

However, these are not the only reasons that call for reflection. Another difficulty arises out of the prohibition on usucapion for praedial servitudes. In fact, the efficacy of personal obligations and the enjoyment of usufruct itself were temporally circumscribed, while servitudes, like ownership, were not so circumscribed and could have permanent effect. The result was that the fundamental mechanism intended to provide certainty within legal relationships, namely usucapion, was wholly ineffective even for the most insignificant of praedial servitudes. Since it was impossible to apply usucapion to these situations, it was always necessary to produce the original title establishing the right, to wit, the tangible evidence of the *mancipatio* or the *in iure cessio*, which might have occurred two or three generations before. Absent that proof, no remedy was available for these minor rights, with the result that it was possible to call into question the formal validity of a transaction concluded many years before, which the passage of time could (in this case) not alter.

The greatest jurist of the Augustan era, Labeo, clearly raises the problem of *emptio venditio* of a servitude. For Labeo, it is clear that a right of this kind could not be freely disposed of by the buyer, and yet a contract of sale did not entail an obligation to establish a servitude under civil law (D.8.1.20). He concluded that the seller should be obliged to allow the buyer peaceful *de facto* enjoyment of the servitude. The same solution was proposed by Javolenus, who describes the situation as surrogate possession: *pro traditione possessionis*. The road was thereby opened to the informal manner of establishing servitudes referred to as *traditio vel patientia*.[21]

The same scheme was also applied to the eligibility of *iura in re aliena* for usucapion. Here too, the corrective function of Roman jurisprudence intervened, confirmed by the praetor's edict and the authority of Imperial constitutions. It was allowed that proof of the *vetustas* of the exercise of individual legal rights could be furnished in place of a missing deed of purchase. Antiquity of usage was thus granted genuine constitutive value, irrespective of the original title (D.39.2.26.4; D.43.20.3.4 and above all D.8.5.10pr; D.39.3.1.23 and D.43.19.5.3). However, these solutions did not alter the principles and limits that had become established within the *ius civile* itself.

The endpoint of this process in the classical period was the extension of the protection provided by the *actio Publiciana* to usufruct and to servitudes (D.6.2.11.1; Mannino 1996 and 2007). This was achieved by a legal fiction, effacing the clear incompatibility of those rights with usucapion. Roman jurisprudence thereby recuperated praedial servitudes and usufruct within a regime largely analogous to that of ownership between the second and first centuries BC. The system moved beyond—abandoned, even—the exclusive application of civil-law forms, while reunifying and extending the system of real rights.

D.8.4.10, 11.7.10 and D.8.4.13pr. Paul expressly refers to the sale of a usufruct, including by a *dominus* (D.18.6.8.2). In two renowned passages on water servitudes, Paulus refers to *venditio* (D.8.3.30 and 18.1.40.1).

[21] Cf. D.8.5.14pr., D.6.2.11.1. The clear formulation by Ulpian in D.8.3.1.2 is only found towards the end of the classical period.

This was made possible precisely by drawing on the different registers of the *ius civile* and the *ius honorarium.*

In this way, the evolutionary process that characterised this sector of Roman law followed a logic completely different from that which has characterised the history of modern legal systems, with their strong focus on establishing regimes of *iura in re* in as unitary a manner as possible: ownership and real rights. By contrast, the coexistence of the *ius civile* and *ius honorarium* made it possible for the Romans to allow partial solutions founded on contradicting dynamics to coexist side by side, each of which was associated with a different regulatory mechanism.

Occasionally, these partial solutions in their different domains affected one another, as when the crafting of rights within the *ius honorarium* led to the recognition of rights in *ius civile*, through the operation of *usucapio.* This characteristic of the system can easily be underestimated, which caused much difficulty for modern Romanists, with their tendency to resort to a contrived *reductio ad unum.*

The jurists contributed to this difficulty. Their articulation of a kind of *dominium* in relation to the *in bonis* possessor further added to an ambiguity concerning the very concept of ownership, which was at times construed as a *ius* and at others seen as practically a *res.* This ambiguity contributed to much confusion regarding Roman concepts of ownership in the twentieth century (Garnsey 2007, ch. 7). The history of this ambiguity illuminates the process of catachresis that affected all Roman legal categories, which operated alongside a recurrent tendency to conflate the factual control of a corporeal thing and the property right.

Alongside the original *iura in re aliena*, the Imperial age witnessed the gradual emergence of a new figure, *superficies*, which amounted to a right to build on land belonging to another. (Public concessions of land for the construction of commercial *tabernae* had already been granted during the Republican period.) This ran contrary to the very rules of Roman law. Nevertheless, starting from the third century AD the procedural position of the holder of this right, known as the *superficiarius*, was similar to that of the effective owner. The configuration of *emphyteusis*, which occurred at an even later date, was even more complex, reflecting principally new forms of agrarian exploitation and the presence of large properties.

Among many changes in the legal system, Diocletian effectively stipulated equivalent treatment for provincial and Italian land, which had theretofore been exempt from taxation. Almost a century after Roman citizenship, and thus Roman law had been extended to almost all free residents of the Empire, the regime governing the ownership of land was now also unified. This accelerated the marginalisation and subsequent disappearance of the distinction between *res mancipi* and *nec mancipi*, which was definitively enshrined by Justinian. This process was driven by the need of Roman law to account for provincial landownership. This is visible also on a terminological level. Terms relating to possession and those relating to ownership were confused: *possidere* and *possessio* were widely used to refer to ownership, at times even specifying that this amounted to a *firma possessio.* This was a "vulgar" use, pushed by subjects operating on the margins of the "cultivated" law of the jurists. Thus, a direct relationship with the object as the essence of ownership, which was never entirely superseded, was expressed to the full in the impoverished language of new generations.

Bibliography

Ankum, H., van Gessel-de Roo, M. and Pool, E. (1987–1990). "Die verschiedenen Bedeutungen des Ausdrucks 'in bonis alicuius esse/in bonis habere' im klassischen römischen Recht." (Part 1) *Zeitschrift der Savigny-Stiftung für Rechtsgeschichte, romanistische Abteilung* 104: 238–436; 105: 334–435; 107: 155–215.

Arangio-Ruiz, V. 1956. *La compravendita in diritto romano,* Vol. 1. Naples.

Bannon, C. J. 2009. *Gardens and neighbors: private water rights in Roman Italy*. Ann Arbor.

Basile, R. 2012. Usus servitutis *e tutela interdittale*. Padua.

Bonfante, P. 1926. *Corso di diritto romano*, Vol. 2.1. Rome.

Bretone, M. 1962. *La nozione romana di usufrutto dalle origini a Diocleziano*, Vol. 1. Naples.

Cannata, C. A. 2001. *Corso di istituzioni di diritto romano*, Vol. 1. Turin.

Capogrossi Colognesi, L. 1966. *Ricerche sulla struttura delle servitù d'acqua in diritto romano*. Milan.

Capogrossi Colognesi, L. 1969. *La struttura della proprietà e la formazione dei* iura praediorum *nell'età repubblicana*, Vol. 1. Milan.

Capogrossi Colognesi, L. 1976. *La struttura della proprietà e la formazione dei* iura praediorum *nell'età repubblicana*, Vol. 2. Milan.

Capogrossi Colognesi, L. 1999. *Proprietà e diritti reali: usi e tutela della proprietà fondiaria nel diritto romano*. Rome.

Corbino, A. 1979. *Ricerche sulla configurazione originaria delle servitù*, Vol. 1. Catania.

Crook, J. A. 1967. *Law and life in Rome: 90 B.C.–A.D. 212*. London.

Diòsdi, G. 1970. *Ownership in ancient and pre-classical Roman law*. Budapest.

Dubouloz, J. 2011. *La propriété immobilière à Rome et en Italie. Ier–Ve siècles: organisation et transmission des* praedia urbana. Rome.

Falcone, G. 1996. *Ricerche sull'origine dell'interdetto* uti possidetis. Palermo.

Gallo, F. 1960. *Il principio* emptione dominium transfertur *nel diritto pregiustinianeo*. Milan.

Garnsey, P. 2007. *Thinking about property: from antiquity to the age of revolution*. Cambridge.

Giuffrè, V. 1992. *L'emersione dei* iura in re aliena *ed il dogma del "numero chiuso"*. Naples.

Grosso, G. 1958². *Usufrutto e figure affini nel diritto romano*. Turin.

Grosso, G. 1969. *Le servitù prediali nel diritto romano.* Turin.

Hausmaninger, H. 1964. *Die* bona fides *des Ersitzungsbesitzers im klassischen römischen Recht*. Vienna/Munich.

Kaser, M. 1956². *Eigentum und Besitz im älteren römischen Recht*. Cologne.

Kaser, M. (1988). "Altrömisches Recht und *usucapio*." *Zeitschrift der Savigny-Stiftung für Rechtsgeschichte, romanistische Abteilung* 105: 122–164.

Kaser, M. and Hackl, K. 1996². *Das römische Zivilprozeßrecht*. Munich.

Labruna, L. 1971. Vim fieri veto: *alle radici di una ideologia*. Naples.

Mannino, V. 1996. *La tolleranza dell'*usus servitutis *nell'esperienza giuridica romana*. Turin.

Mannino, V. 2007. "Il possesso dei diritti nell'esperienza romana e secondo alcune 'soluzioni' codicistiche." In *Studi in honore di Luigi Labruna*. Vol. 5. Naples. 3163–3179.

Möller, C. 2010. *Die Servituten*. Göttingen.

Nörr, D. 1969. *Die Entstehung der* longi temporis praescriptio. Cologne.

Pennitz, M. 1991. *Der "Enteignungsfall" im römischen Recht der Republik und des Pinzipats*. Cologne/Weimar.

Rainer, J. M. (1987). "Nochmals zu den Gründen und der Datierung der *lex Scribonia*." *Zeitschrift der Savigny-Stiftung für Rechtsgeschichte, romanistische Abteilung* 104: 631–638.

Rodger, A. 1972. *Owners and neighbours in Roman law*. Oxford.
Romeo, S. 2010. *L'appartenenza e l'alienazione in diritto romano*. Milan.
Roselaar, S. 2010. *Public land in the Roman republic: a social and economic history of* ager publicus *in Italy, 396–89* BC. Oxford.
Schulz, F. 1951. *Classical Roman law*. Oxford.
Solazzi, S. 1947. *Requisiti e modi di costituzione delle servitù prediali*. Naples.
Solidoro Maruotti, L. 1998. *La tutela del possesso in età constantiniana*. Naples.
Thielmann, G. (1994). "Nochmals: Doppelveräusserung durch Nichtberechtigte—D. 19, 1, 31, 2 und D. 6, 2, 9, 4—." *Zeitschrift der Savigny-Stiftung für Rechtsgeschichte, romanistische Abteilung* 111:197–241.
Tuccillo, F. 2009. *Studi su costituzione ed estinzione delle servitù prediali:* usus, scientia, patientia. Naples.
Vacca, L. 1988. "Il c.d. *duplex dominium* e l'*actio Publiciana*." In E. Cortese, ed., *La proprietà e le proprietà*. Milan. 39–74.
Watson, A. 1968. *The law of property in the later Roman republic*. Oxford.

CHAPTER 41

POSSESSION IN ROMAN LAW

CHRISTIAN BALDUS
TRANSLATED BY DAVID KERR

41.1 Introduction: Law and "Reality"

Possession is a prime example of the complexities of interaction between law as a normative order and the non-normative contingencies in the world it seeks both to describe and to regulate. In a nutshell, the concept refers to effective control over objects to which the legal system ascribes a specific meaning. When the legal system does so, it has to engage in non-legal facts. It can still define the objects—usually just as they are defined for the purposes of legal control, i.e. above all, ownership. But what is effective control?

Possession therefore presents a dual problem. If the law makes normative effects dependent on a fact, coordination with the rules on legal control is necessary, e.g. ownership. The fact—i.e. an element from outside the system—must firstly have its relevance determined and secondly have a value placed on it through the assignment of legal consequences. Both are normative acts. Time and again, this has produced two tendencies, already visible in Roman law: the tendency to load effective control with normative elements and to leave evaluative judgements to the judge. Roman law does not "teach" us what a diachronically correct solution to the problem could be. It maps out conceivable solutions and demonstrates their consequences under certain socio-economic conditions.

It is not possible to present the multiplicity of individual problems and solutions, and certainly not their economic and social context, in an introductory account. At best, one may trace how the Roman jurists themselves understood the functions of what we call "possession". In what follows, only legal sources from Rome itself have been used, as they are key and follow a legal logic unique to the Romans. The occasionally differing use of *possidere, possessio* etc. in literary sources (particularly in the case of Livy) also colours legal discourses, but has not been tackled due to lack of space. The legal situation in the provinces adds another element of complexity (see Jördens, ch. 42). Finally, post-classical law is only mentioned in passing. The sources from this period regard ownership and possession as more closely related than the classical sources, and they continue classical discussions, at best, in a changed way. Justinian, however, restores that classical separation between effective and legal control. Given the current state of the literature, we certainly cannot say how

Roman society dealt with possession as a legal phenomenon and legal concept. A coherent reappraisal of all the relevant sources (legal and otherwise) remains wanting.

41.2 Visions of Possession

41.2.1 The Roman Sources at a Glance

Roman law does not have a unified doctrine of possession. This is not owing to the presence or absence of "doctrine" in Rome, but because of the purposes for which Roman jurists addressed effective control: usually in the context of cases and from two or three essential perspectives. It is not completely clear how these connected with civil procedure in a court of law (section 41.3). However, we can observe how they eventually converged and how different concepts evolved (sections 41.4 and 41.5).

We refer to "possession" and "possessor" in this chapter, but these are of course modern concepts and anything but neutral terms. Most contemporary legal systems treat possession as a unified concept containing two or three elements: *corpus* (physical control), *animus* (mental intent) and possibly *causa/titulus* (right to possess). These systems also freely ascribe different functions to possession, which go back to various Roman roots. We have to distinguish three functions of the modern concept referred to as "possession", each considered from the point of view of court procedure. We also find these three elements in Roman law, but not configured in the same way as today.

41.2.1.1 *Functions of Possession*

First, effective control is sometimes protected from disturbances by means of praetorian orders (*interdicta*). The main source is book 43 of the *Digesta Iustiniani* (*de interdictis*) (see section 41.3.1 for details). Second, the possessor is a suitable defendant in the vindication procedure (see D.6.1 and also section 41.3.2). This is in practice a key function. Third, and equally important in ownership actions, certain situations of effective control can give rise to acquisitive prescription (*usucapio*) and therefore to the acquisition of ownership (archaic: *meum esse*; later: *dominium; proprietas*, see Capogrossi Colognesi, ch. 40).

These relationships cannot be traced to a textually unified root. In particular, the edict, insofar as it is possible to ascribe an external system in the modern sense to it, only contains *bonorum possessio*, the right of possession of the property of a deceased person (Title XXV) and that is something different (see section 41.4.3). The term *possessio* (etc.) alone does not appear in the formula of the *rei vindicatio* (but in the related case law), but it does in formulas of the interdict (see section 41.3.1). Roman jurists therefore did not yet have to use this term in all discussions for linguistic reasons, but did of course deal with the question as to whether it promoted the application of law. Its historical genesis may go back to the physical occupation of land and therefore the differentiation of spheres of dominance within the archaic *gentes* (for etymology see D.41.2.1pr).

We find other statements in certain legal sources preserved independently from the Justinianic project and also in non-legal literature. Admittedly, in the latter case (e.g. in Livy), the proportion of non-technical or transferred uses of the word is very high, so that the legal sources are also more important for the social context of the law of possession. Moreover, it is the case law of the Digest that enables us to keep track of the way understanding of possession changed.

It is usual today to describe the first function of possession (in modern terms) as *possessio ad interdicta* and the third as *possessio ad usucapionem*. (It is a matter of dispute whether *possessio civilis*, occasionally mentioned in the sources, can be equated to the modern concept of *possessio ad usucapionem*). The terminology and scope of the second function remain problematic. If an object (originally land) is taken away from someone, the interdict will restore that person to the position of possessor and the counterparty must institute an action against him to recover it (*rei vindicatio*). According to general rules, it was the claimant (or plaintiff) who bore the burden of proof. For this reason, the interdict was regularly applied for first. It was only during the next stage, if the matter progressed that far, that the question arose as to the type of physical control required for a *rei vindicatio* action to be brought. Procedurally, this physical control could not be equated to interdictal possession, as a vindication of a thing could also be brought against people who had not previously initiated the interdict procedure, nor to usucapion possession, as the possession of people who could not acquire by usucapion also disturbed the exercise of ownership.

41.2.1.2 *Elements of Possession*

Since the Romans did not have a unified concept it would be impossible to distinguish *in abstracto* between the above functions. We usually only know through exegesis what the focus of an individual source is. We have to reconstruct the context by making an intellectual effort to combine various exegeses. However, it is probably safe to say (details in section 41.4.4.1) that each possessory action requires a moment of physical control. When problems arise, this moment is initially supplemented by the intent to own (*animus*), which subsequently becomes (at least for Paul) a prerequisite for *possessio*, and, as far as usucapion possession is concerned, a title must also exist that legally justifies the possession (*causa, titulus*)—usually, but not always, a right. In post-Roman times these three elements were enshrined in doctrine and now determine the discussion of possession in Europe. This brings us to the images that shape our view.

41.2.2 Modern Retrospectives

As a matter of method, it is best to be self-aware about the understanding one brings to the study of the Roman material. The German and English systems (the German being comparatively Roman) both ascribe legal character to effective control, as does the French. The key differences lie in the way the normative element is combined with the factual. English law categorises normatively, and in specific ways shaped by history, whereby effective control situations confer rights. French law requires the existence of a subjective right to possess in order to qualify the possessory act as *possession*. German law textually does not regard normative elements as constitutive for possession, but legal practice and doctrine do use para-normative elements (the so-called *Verkehrsanschauung*) where the *corpus* is weak. None of these three models is entirely Roman or entirely un-Roman, and this is the very reason why the danger of anachronism is so high.

41.2.3 An Archaeology of Possession?

41.2.3.1 *Needs of an Archaic Society*

The development of early Rome was based on ownership and not possession. Individual ownership, together with the other powers of the *pater familias,* emerged only gradually from older ties to the *gens.* This is still evident—as a relic—from the special requirements that applied to the transfer of ownership of particularly important agricultural objects, *res mancipi,* especially Italian estates. We may assume that these objects had been withdrawn from individual disposal for longer than the others (the *res nec mancipi*) (see Capogrossi Colognesi, ch. 40). Moreover, individual ownership remained—like all legal positions—practically limited by social norms (*mores, decorum,* and so on). Yet clarity about ownership was required, both among the living and in cases of succession. This is reflected above all in the institution of *usucapio,* which is based on *usus.* Ownership had to be determined quickly so that individual objects as well as entire collections of assets were not left ownerless.

41.2.3.2 *Usus: Traces, Conjectures, Developments*

According to Cic. *Top.* 4.23 (see also Inst.Gai.2.42), the XII Tables contain the much-debated sentence *usus auctoritas fundi biennium, ceterarum rerum omnium annu(u)s* (XII Tab. (*RS*) VI 3, adapted: "For an estate, *auctoritas* of usage is two years; for other things, it is one year"). The debate about this phrase can be summarised as follows: *usus* was significant in the development of two institutions: that of usufruct (*ususfructus*) and that of usucapion. Subsequently, the latter became conditional upon *possessio,* i.e. *possessio* based on a possessory title (see section 41.4.4.2). An essentially identical catalogue of *causae possessionis* and *usucapionis,* grounds for acquiring ownership under *ius civile,* was created. When a *res nec mancipi* was delivered, classical law deemed that a transfer of ownership had also taken place, but only if a *causa,* e.g. a purchase, was also involved. This meant that the purchase was both *causa possessionis* for the acquirer and *causa traditionis* for the two parties and had the effect of also creating ownership in the person of the acquirer. If it was ineffective, however, ownership (subject to further preconditions described in section 41.3.3) could nevertheless arise at a later date because the idea of purchasing was the *causa usucapionis.* We do not know exactly how factual the *usus* was initially, but we can in any event say that it was for the first time placed on a legal footing. In any case, it is useful to look at the roots of "use".

41.3 Uses of "Possession" in Roman Civil Procedure

41.3.1 Protection of *de facto* Situations by *Interdicta*

Interdictal possession arises in a situation in which ownership is of no assistance, because it does not exist—at least, according to the prevailing reconstruction. In the third and second centuries BC, the Republican authorities had ceded captured land (*ager publicus*) to private individuals who had passed some of it on to other private individuals. Conflicts of use between these smallholders could not be resolved under the law on ownership (compare section 41.4.2), because the users only "possessed" the land subject to revocation at any time and did not actually have a *meum esse* or, as formulated in classical legal terms, a *dominium ex iure Quiritium*.

The praetor used his procedural freedom of action, rooted in his *imperium*, to introduce urgent legal remedies to combat trespass: *interdicta*. It prohibited (*interdicere*) the disturbance of *de facto* physical control by another, initially over immovable property and then also over movable property. There is not space to describe the variety of these remedies (the significance of which cannot be overestimated for Roman practice): the Digest contains thirty-two titles (in book 43) on individual interdicts.

Only specific groups of people were interdictal possessors: the usucapion possessors (see section 41.3.3); the smallholders already mentioned, and the *vectigalis* tenant (we do not have space to discuss the nature of the rental relationship here, cf. D. 39.4.11.1: *Agri publici, qui in perpetuum locantur* ... ; an idea of the complexity of late classical notions is provided in D.2.8.15.1); also mortgagees; that is, those creditors holding a security, whose right did not entitle them to *usucapio*, but who wished to defend their possession of the object. Despite a weak textual basis, the prevailing view also classifies the sequester as an interdictal possessor, a construction particularly in the interest of the party who is found to be in the right at the end of the dispute.

The basic structure of the interdicts is based on a *veto* or a different type of order to the defendant (*restituas, exhibeas*). Some of the interdict *formulae* handed down contain the term *possessio*, as for example in D.43.2.1pr, the so-called *interdictum quorum bonorum*: "possession of those goods is granted to him on the basis of my edict."

In their attempts to sort the various interdicts into groups, the Roman jurists' main criterion was whether the possession was to be newly acquired, reacquired or defended (see, for example, D.43.1.2.3). They focused both on the uniqueness of interdict protection and on its functional interplay with the protection of ownership in a matter-of-fact way. (cf. D.43.1.2.2).

Many of those who applied for interdicts wanted to force their adversary to make an ownership claim and consequently to bear the burden of proof incumbent on the claimant (or plaintiff):

> Anyone who contemplates suing for a thing ought to consider whether he can obtain possession of it by some interdict. For it is far more convenient for him to be in possession himself and put the burden of being plaintiff on his opponent than for him to sue with his opponent in possession. (D.6.1.24)

If we wish to understand what interested the Romans themselves about *possessio*, we have to take a closer look at the procedure. For procedural and then consequently also for "substantive" purposes, the classical jurists made a precise distinction between possession and ownership (see D.41.2.12.1; D.41.2.17.1). The idea that ownership arose from (*naturalis*) *possessio* (compare section 41.4.6) is only mentioned as a historical reminiscence: D.41.2.1.1.

41.3.2 Standing in *vindicatio* Procedures

41.3.2.1 *On vindicationes*

Today, legal scholars from continental Europe understand "vindication" to mean a claim or action for the restitution of a thing based on ownership. Of the various *vindicationes* of Roman law, the *rei vindicatio* has remained the paradigm for an action *in rem*. This becomes particularly clear in metaphorical use in many languages (e.g. "revendication" in French can be a political or social claim). Under Roman law, however, it was possible to vindicate everything that was the object of absolute rights (historically speaking, what we used to call absolute rights stems from vindication procedures), e.g. rights of lien, usufruct and servitudes. This is clearly shown, for example, in the vindication of a person into slavery or freedom.

In what follows, we will concentrate on vindications of things and leave aside both the problem of the so-called property rights in servitudes and the problem of a unified "legal nature" of positions that were summarised as *iura in re aliena* and are today conceived as limited rights *in rem*, i.e. encumbrances on property. Finally, we leave aside the question of whether or not a "vindication model" explains the entire history of early Roman law, since it cannot be decided on the basis of the sources. In any case, it must always be borne in mind that a text mentioned by Justinian's compilers as forming part of the law of possession (namely in D.41 or D.43) may have originated within the context of a specific action, e.g. for vindication of a thing or an action for the restitution of an inheritance, and can only be understood in this connection.

41.3.2.2 *legis actio sacramento in rem*

In early Roman legal proceedings, possession was not a precondition for the capacity of the defendant to be sued, but a relationship awarded by sovereign power for the duration of the proceedings to one of the two parties who claim ownership: "The praetor declared *vindiciae* in favour of one of the two parties, that is, he established one as interim possessor" (Inst.Gai.4.16). In this sense, possession was therefore something that has been legally constituted and not something that constituted rights (above all procedural positions).

41.3.2.3 *rei vindicatio: per sponsionem and per formulam petitoriam*

This changed with the advent of the formulary procedure to the extent that ownership actions were permitted *per formulam petitoriam*. The *sponsio* formula which existed at the same time only named the *ex iure Quiritium meum esse* of one of the parties (Inst.Gai.4.93) and was therefore very similar to the old *legis actiones* procedure (Inst.Gai.4.94); it may be understood as a transitional form.

Although the *formula petitoria* does not mention "possession" either, but only (*actoris*) *esse* of the *res qua de agitur*, it does contain an element indirectly linked to the factual control of the object: the *clausula arbitraria* or restitution clause *neque ea res arbitrio iudicis Aulo Agerio restituetur* (cf. Inst.Gai.4.16). It is a matter of dispute whether the person who may have had to provide restitution by order of the *iudex* was expressly mentioned here too.

At any rate, the restitution clause ignited the debate as to who was capable of being sued in a vindication of a thing. It was clear to the jurists of Antiquity that it was not only *possessores* on the day of the judgement that had to be considered. It was also possible on the basis of the *rei vindicatio* to convict anyone who fraudulently gave up possession or fraudulently pretended to be the possessor (in order to shield the real possessor). This was possible in practice because the judgement was handed down according to general rules, that is, based on the monetary value of the thing, and restitution *in natura* was not enforced. For this reason, no strict connection was required between the capacity to be sued in the vindication procedure and possession, and consequently there was no procedural need for the Roman jurists to systematise the doctrine of possession.

If it was also possible for non-possessors to be sued, the question remains whether all possessors were capable of being sued. It is no longer possible to establish with certainty the chronological order of the jurists' debate, as each quotation cited in the Digest under a particular name can also contain material that refers back to older authors not identified as such. It is, however, clear that usucapion possessors (see section 41.3.3.2) were always regarded as being capable of being sued. This is in keeping with the main function of a vindication: to prevent the acquisition in good faith of third parties (by acquisitive prescription). Indeed, some interdictal possessors (see section 41.3.1.) could not acquire by prescription. Nevertheless, their capacity to be sued was discussed, which can be explained by the objective of having them assume the role of the defendant which is favourable in terms of providing evidence (see again D.6.1.24). At the end of the classical period, Ulpian went beyond this discussion by only requiring *facultas restituendi* instead of a *possessio*, and it is a matter of dispute whether he meant only the factual possibility of restitution or also the legal possibility (D.6.1.9, concluding: "however, I think a suit can be brought against all those who hold things and have the power to return them").

41.3.3 Acquisition of Ownership

Possession is relevant to the acquisition of ownership (see ch. 40 by Luigi Capogrossi Colognesi) if the thing is to be acquired through *traditio* or *usucapio*, but not in the case of acquisition through the two older forms of acquisition, the *mancipatio* (in the case of *res mancipi*) and the *in iure cessio* (in the case of *res mancipi* or *nec mancipi*). Functionally, *traditio* is therefore understood to be a preliminary stage of usucapion at the same time, which is why the sources sometimes use *tradere* and *capere* binomially. If the thing has been delivered, but there is no justification on the part of the transferring party, *causa*, good faith and the passage of time can nevertheless lead to the transfer of ownership. This means that such objects as can also be delivered can be usucaped, even when *res mancipi* are involved.

41.3.3.1 *Traditio*

The object must be corporeal (D.41.1.43.1) and delimited (D.41.2.26), i.e. capable of being possessed. The sources usually refer to *tradere* of the thing and sometimes also *possessionem tradere*. As a rule, this is corporeal delivery.

41.3.3.2 *Usucapio*

Usucapion is mentioned here only with a view to identifying the features that exist in individual possessory titles as these demonstrate the regulatory aims of the institution. According to the prevailing view, the possessory titles are at the same time also grounds for acquisition. A catalogue of these *causae* is effectively provided by the title headings of book 41 of the Digest: *pro emptore* (D.41.4), *pro donato* (D.41.6), *pro derelicto* (D.41.7), *pro legato* (D.41.8), *pro dote* (D.41.9), *pro herede, pro possessore* (D.41.5), *pro suo* (D.41.10). The first five *causae* do not present any particular difficulties: anyone who believes, and has reason to believe, that he owns a thing on the basis of purchase, donation, surrender of ownership by a third party, (vindication) legacy (except for a legacy by damnation, which is merely obligatory, and could not of course give such a position) or marriage portion, acquires it by prescription.

On the other hand, the existence of the other titles shows even more clearly than in the other *causae* the effort made to prevent objects from becoming ownerless wherever possible. A party who takes things from an estate held in abeyance acquires them if necessary *pro herede*, even without good faith (for the case of reaching beyond the estate see D.41.5.3). Whether, in addition, a title encroaches in favour of a party who possesses it without a specific notion of a ground for acquisition or presents it before a court has been hotly disputed. The connection between the grounds for acquisition *pro herede* and *pro possessore* seems to be based on the action for the restitution of an inheritance, as in this case it has to be decided whether the potential defendant is the possessor of the inheritance or whether only individual actions are considered (cf. Jakab, ch. 38).

Debate continues about the relevance of merely imaginary *causae* (putative titles), probably only to be affirmed in the case of the ground for usucapion *pro solute* (by the non-creditor in good faith). In principle, a possessory title created without authorisation was irrelevant (except in the situations where possession *pro suo/pro possessore* had been accepted), because the rule *nemo sibi ipsi causam possessionis mutare potest* restricted acquisition *pro herede*.

41.4 Towards a Coherent Use and Concept of *Possessio*?

41.4.1 Necessities of the Imperial Roman Experience

Roman law never advanced to a stage where it became a system capable of subsumption in the modern sense, mainly because the jurists did not require it. However, the density and complexity of decisions increased during the course of the Principate to such an extent that it became essential from the end of the second century AD to collect and arrange the material so that it could be further developed in an orderly manner. Paul is a key figure in this area, especially as far as *possessio* is concerned. After a brief explanation of the relationship between *possessio* and the concept of *bonorum possessio* in inheritance law (section 41.4.3), we outline how Paul made the element of the *animus* independent and how the catalogue of possessory *causae* eventually looked (section 41.4.4). The situation later referred to as *detentio*, where a possessory *causa* is missing, could already be objectively identified at this time (section 41.4.6). We have therefore reached the stage of doctrinal development (section 41.4.5), which was to encourage modern jurists to make various attempts to construct from the Roman sources a closed objective and notional system, mainly by abstracting the procedural peculiarities of the law of Antiquity.

41.4.2 Key Topics in D.41.1–41.3

Central elements of the first three titles of Digest book 41 originate in book 54 of Paul's "commentary on the edict", where Paul engaged in a major effort at systematisation. For his part, Paul essentially relied on late Republican and early classical jurists, including some, of whom hardly any other texts are known. For this reason, Justinian's selection of texts gives the impression of a debate that was already old and stale by Paul's time.

41.4.3 *Possessio* and *Bonorum Possessio*

The existence of a title on usucapion *pro herede* does not mean that each heir is necessarily the possessor under property law. The jurists stress the opposite (D.41.2.23pr). Traditionally, *bonorum possessio* was a concept chosen by the praetor for the allocation of assets on death, which he effected *iure honorario* in order to avoid the concepts of *ius civile*, but this allocation was not qualified as *possessio*.

The scenario in the mid-second century AD is reflected in the institutional works handed down independently of Justinian, especially by Gaius. Gaius addresses questions concerning the law of possession both from the aspect of the acquisition of ownership (*traditio, usucapio*: Inst.Gai.2.12–28, 41–79) and in the event of interdicts (Inst.Gai.4.143–155). It is not yet possible to identify a systematic integration of the two aspects in this case, or indeed an ordering of the *causae possessionis*. This changes roughly a generation later (see section 41.4.4). But even in the pseudo-Ulpianic *Liber singularis regularum*, *possessio* only appears in the margin in 19.8 in a definition: *usucapio est autem dominii adeptio per continuationem possessionis anni vel biennii.*

41.4.4 Iulius Paulus and his Time

Exactly why Paul went on to study possession in detail is as yet unexplained. Most questions were, as shown, already quite old, as were the first attempts to systematise the *possessio(nes)* (cf. D.41.2.3.21–23). Paul's teacher, Scaevola, also dealt with questions concerning possession, but a doctrinal profile on him to this effect has not yet been found. It is conceivable that Papinian, who was only a little older and got to the heart of more than one problem relating to the law of possession, exerted an influence, but there is not yet sufficient evidence of this. Paul's main achievement is that he restructured the two elements *corpus* and *animus* independently of *titulus/causa.*

14.4.4.1 *corpus and animus*

Probably the most frequently quoted passage on possession is:

> We take possession physically and mentally, not mentally alone or physically alone. But when we say that we must take possession both physically and mentally, that should not be taken to mean that one seeking to possess an estate must go round every part of it; suffice it that he enters some part of the estate, but with the intent and awareness that thereby he seeks to possess the entire estate to its boundaries. D.41.2.3.1 (Paul. 54 ad ed.) (See also D.41.2.41)

What is required, therefore, is the simultaneous presence of both elements. Paul does not interpret *corpore* always in the corporeal sense we know from the interpretation of the *lex Aquilia* (*damnum corpore corpori datum*). The *corpus* can also be obtained, e.g. through slaves (D.41.2.3.12). Conversely, *possessio* is lost through *acta contraria* of both elements (D.41.2.8).

Employing conceptual experiments visible already in the early classical period (see, for example, D.41.2.51), the binomial *corpus-animus* becomes comprehensible to us in the second half of the second century AD, e.g. in Marcellus (D.41.2.19.1; cf. D.41.2.34pr). However, it is in subsequent writers that the difficulties of the concepts are most clearly flagged: for example, how are the two categories to be applied when a slave loses physical control of a thing (D.41.2.44–46). Under such circumstances, how long would the master's *animus* retain possession? It appears from these debates that it was through Paul that the binomial *corpore et animo* became foundational to work on possession, however difficult the doctrine proved in practice.

41.4.4.2 *causa/titulus*

As explained above, the doctrine of *causa* did not undergo a comparable structuring. It did not become a unified principle, nor did the doctrine of *possessio pro suo/pro possessore* reach a point which would have made it possible to renounce the *causae* accepted individually. After all, interdict possession also remained entangled in its limitation to the cases that had grown up historically, with the result that even usucapion possession did not dissolve into a basic unified institute of "possession".

The consequences for subsequent development of law are obvious (see section 41.2.2). There are no legal systems that regard possession as purely corporeal or purely due to mental intent. In this respect, almost all Western legal systems construe *corpore et animo* and concede only relaxations of the *corpus* requirement. On the other hand, numerous models of causal and non-causal possession compete in the—still distinct—functions of the acquisition of ownership and the maintenance of *de facto* physical control.

41.4.5 Types and Concepts of Possession

Another consequence of the above-mentioned limits of systematisation was that the terminology used in the sources remained unclear. In the passages quoted it is often impossible—or only possible through exegetic conjecture—to determine whether the reference point was an interdict procedure, a dispute in which ownership was to be decided, or whether it referred to a specific case at all. The latter group of passages was attractive to future generations striving for legitimation and abstraction. Roman law could be used for a wide variety of concepts of possession. Conversely, historical knowledge of Roman practice is more difficult to come by where the reference to the case is unclear. In any case, the conclusion that Paul wanted to express himself generally through a unified institution would also be questionable for the general-sounding passages. It may be that a few of his texts could be related both to interdictal possession and to usucapion possession. Furthermore, it may be that he regarded the relationship between *corpus* and *animus* as the same for both of these applications. What is certain is that he required the *causa* as a distinguishing feature between them, with the uncertainties outlined above.

41.4.6 Feeble Roots, Late Career: *Detentio*

Detentio is not a word used in Roman legal terminology but a post-Roman expression for physical control without possessory *causa*. Sometimes (but not consistently), this phenomenon in Rome is referred to as *naturalis possessio*. The modern Romanist in a codified civilian system may ask categorically, in terms of their national Code of Law, whether detention is covered by the rules on possession; detention is *merely* having the thing, i.e. essentially a negative concept. The Roman jurist mentions "natural" possession only occasionally and then usually in a negative sense as well, where he wanted to exclude or modify individual possessory rules (see, for example, D.41.2.24 for the slave, D.41.5.2.2 for the *filius in potestate*, D.41.2.12pr for the usufructuary); occasionally an extension is also involved (D.41.5.2.1). The description of a *possessio* as *naturalis* can moreover serve purposes other than differentiating a *possessio* from the regular situation; that is, *possessio* that produces legal consequences. In particular, it can underline the "natural" character of physical control, e.g. of children (see, for example, D.41.1.11; D.41.1.53). D.41.2.3.3 concerns a preliminary stage in the acquisition of possession *solo animo*.

All of this centres on juristic patterns of argumentation, from which an "institution" should not be construed unthinkingly, at any rate not with the assistance of non-legal elements, especially those from philosophy.

41.5 [Provincial Uses and Post-Classical Developments

Classical law therefore resembles a torso. However, this torso also underwent substantial changes in post-classical times. Recent research rightly takes care not to regard post-classical history as a story of decline. It should be noted, however, that the dominant elements of the post-classical law of possession abandon key elements of classical law.

Influences, which were already emanating from provincial law in the classical period, could have played a part in this.

41.5.1 Republican Grass Roots

Like the whole "system" of provincial government by Rome, the models of control and use were not unified, particularly in terms of immovable property. No standardisation can be observed in the Roman-law tradition in this regard. This would have been unwise politically and in terms of practical administration. The universal transfer of accepted institutions of the *ius civile*, such as *dominium*, to non-Romans was out of the question from the outset. The comparatively recent *possessio*, whose creation coincided approximately with the acquisition of the first provinces, was certainly not suitable for universal export. The views of the provincials themselves can, if any, also be distilled from literary sources, at all events with great care.

41.5.2 *Possessio vel Ususfructus*

A specifically provincial form of control (see Inst.Gai.2.7), *possessio vel ususfructus*, is neither possession nor usufruct in classical terms, as the two institutions had been strictly separated as shown, for example, in D.41.2.52pr:

> *Permisceri causas possessionis et usus fructus non oportet, quemadmodum nec possessio et proprietas misceri debent: nam neque impediri possessionem, si alius fruatur, neque alterius fructum amputari, si alter possideat.*

In post-classical semantics, *possessio(nes)* refers more often than previously to the specific object being controlled, e.g. a piece of land. On the other hand, *possessio vel ususfructus* describes—as was the case in classical law—a comprehensive right of dominion over provincial land, i.e. neither purely *de facto* control nor a *ius in re aliena*. This institution increased in importance during the post-classical period. This reflects the increasing contamination of legal and *de facto* control, already furthered in the provinces by the fact that the institutions of the *ius civile* were not generally open to provincials. Even the *Constitutio Antoniniana* (212 AD) did not—as far as can be ascertained from the sources—result in a universal expansion of the *ius civile*. To what extent the new citizens were aware of their new status and their new private law and to what extent they were interested in them anyway, has to be determined for individual areas of the law and provinces (for Egypt compare ch. 42 by Jördens). For the history of what we refer to retrospectively as the law of possession, we can therefore subordinate *possessio vel ususfructus*. At best, it would be interesting to know—but in doctrinal detail—what aspect of it represents a specific continuance of the classical *possessio*.

41.5.3 *Longi Temporis Praescriptio*

There were attempts to resolve uncertainty about different possessory relationships in the late classical (Sept. Sev. and Caracalla a. 199, *FIRA* I 437, 438) and above all in the post-classical period (Hon./Theod. C. 7.39.3, [a. 424]; C. 7.31.1.3, [a. 531]) with an institution established in addition to *usucapio*, to protect specific parties acting in good faith: the twenty-year and, subsequently, thirty-year *longi temporis praescriptio*. This was supplemented with a *longissimi temporis praescriptio*, which also protects those of bad faith (cf. *FIRA* III, 318, 32–323). Without the corrective of *bona fides*, possession therefore gains the upper hand over ownership.

41.6 Conclusions and Perspectives

In conclusion, "the" Roman possession proves to be a side effect, a mere shadow of ownership. Certainly, this is not in Jhering's sense that it is the "outer side" of ownership. Rather, interdictal protection arose in a historically contingent way because jurists did not want specific persons, who have actual control of a thing, to be owners. At the same time, they did not want to leave them without protection either, and usucapion possession is only one element in the acquisition of ownership which was normatively controlled by determining the *causa*.

The actual practical value of assigning *possessio* lay in allocating roles to the parties in the vindication procedure. We can therefore observe a reversal of processes during the Republican period. In the *legis actiones* procedure the assignment of possession was a component of an ownership dispute. In the *formula petitoria* the assignment of possession by interdict became one of several possible preliminary procedures, with the probably intentional side-effect that if the evidence available was unclear, it was often the case that this preliminary procedure was no longer followed by a vindication procedure. Even if the possessor did not have a *causa* for usucapion, his position was still procedurally unassailable and that was sufficient for practical purposes. In the classical period, however, the dependency of the vindication procedure on *possessio* decreased still further. No coherent doctrine came into being. It is impossible to judge with certainty the extent to which late classical use of concepts and notions from the law of possession were at the centre of the development of legal doctrine or legal policy.

This appears slight compared to the varied reception of the concept of *possessio* in the later history of private law. When people say or think "possess", they are necessarily thinking of their own tradition and have in their mind's eye explanatory models that promise to overcome the lack of sources, especially with regard to the legal position in the provinces. It is a serious temptation to join together the fragments of ancient law with theoretical glue. Yet it is so important to identify one's own patterns of perception *ex negativo* as any positive conclusion explaining the past has no legitimacy without a basis of reliable sources. For example, it may be the case that time and again throughout history conquerors only permitted "possession" in the lands they conquered in order to avoid "ownership", whatever these terms may have meant at the time. On whether such phenomena are evidence of an ancient matrix, however, we cannot reach a serious conclusion on the basis of the current state of knowledge of the sources, and it is, when all is said and done, the *ars nesciendi* in connection with detailed work on the sources and thorough knowledge of the literature that marks out the (legal) historian.

Bibliography

Albanese, B. 1985. *Le situazioni possessorie nel diritto privato romano*. Palermo.

Albanese, B. (2003). "Il possesso del sequestratario." *Annali del seminario giuridico della università di Palermo* 48: 45–69.

Andrés Santos, F. J. Forthcoming. "*Die Erbschaftsklage (hereditatis petitio).*" In U. Babusiaux et al. eds., *Handbuch Römisches Privatrecht*. Tübingen.

Aricò Anselmo, G. (1988). "Il sequestro *omittendae possessionis causa*." *Annali del seminario giuridico della università di Palermo* 40: 217–341.

Babusiaux, U. et al. eds. Forthcoming. *Handbuch Römisches Privatrecht*. Tübingen.

Baldus, C. (2006). "Die systematische Funktion der sogenannten Verkehrsauffassung beim Verlust des Besitzes: Portugiesisches, deutsches und römisches Modell." *Zeitschrift für europäisches Privatrecht* 14: 766–784.

Baldus, C. 2011. "Anspruch und Verjährung: geschichtlich und systematisch." In O. Remien, ed., *Verjährungsrecht in Europa—zwischen Bewährung und Reform*. Tübingen. 5–28.

Baldus, C. 2012. "Estudio Preliminar" on M. F. C. de Savigny [*sic*], *Tratado de la posesión según los principios del derecho romano* [reprint of a Spanish translation of "Das Recht des Besitzes"], Buenos Aires. 7–13.

Baldus, C. 2015. "Interkulturalität und *ius gentium*: Erbrecht in den Juristentexten?" In F. Lamberti et al., ed. 2015. *Il diritto romano e le culture straniere. Influenze e dipendenze interculturali nell'antichità*. Lecce. 167–197.

Baldus, C. Forthcoming. "Die Herausgabeklage des Eigentümers (*rei vindicatio*)"; "Die Vorlegungsklage (*actio ad exhibendum*) und Interdikte auf Vorlegung." In U. Babusiaux et al., eds., *Handbuch Römisches Privatrecht*. Tübingen.

Basile, R. 2006. "Onere della prova, possesso e procedimento interdittale. Profili storici e comparatistici." In C. Cascione, ed., *Parti e giudici nel processo. Dai diritti antichi all'attualità*. Naples. 493–530.

Biavaschi, P. 2006. *Ricerche sul "precarium"*. Milan.

Böhr, R. 2002. *Das Verbot der eigenmächtigen Besitzumwandlung im römischen Privatrecht. Ein Beitrag zur rechtshistorischen Spruchregelforschung*. Munich/Leipzig.

Briguglio, F. 2007. "'Tantum de possessione quaeritur'. Gai. 2, 95 e l'acquisto del possesso 'per procuratorem'. Nuove indagini paleografiche sulla lacuna contenuta nel folium 86v del manoscritto veronese 'Codex XV (13)'," in *Studi per Giovanni Nicosia*, Vol. 1. Milan. 107–140.

Briguglio, F. 2007. *Studi sul* procurator, Vol. 1: *L'acquisto del possesso e della proprietà*. Milan.

Capogrossi Colognesi L. 1999. *Proprietà e diritti reali. Usi e tutela della proprietà fondiaria nel Diritto Romano*. Rome.

D'Angelo, G. 2007. *La perdita della possessio animo retenta nei casi di occupazione*. Palermo.

Dalla Massara, T. (2011). "Diritti dominicali e situazioni possessorie tra vecchio e nuovo diritto europeo". *Teoria e storia del diritto privato* 4:1–124.

Dedek, H. (1997). "Der Besitzschutz im römischen, deutschen und französischen Recht. Gesellschaftliche Gründe dogmatischen Wandels." *Zeitschrift für europäisches Privatrecht* 5: 342–365.

Ernst, W. 1992. *Eigenbesitz und Mobiliarerwerb*. Tübingen.

Falcone, G. (2012). "Osservazioni su Gai. 2.14 e le *res incorporales*." *Annali del seminario giuridico della università di Palermo* 55: 125–170.

González Roldán, Y. 2012. "*Interdicta* y pérdida dolosa de la posesión." In P.-I. Carvajal and M. Miglietta, eds., *Estudios jurídicos en homenaje al Profesor Alejandro Guzmán Brito*, Vol. 2, Alessandria. 651–675.

Jhering, R. 1869². *Über den Grund des Besitzesschutzes: eine Revision der Lehre vom Besitz*. Jena. [reprint Aalen 1968].

Jhering, R. 1889. *Der Besitzwille: Zugleich eine Kritik der herrschenden juristischen Methode*. Jena. [reprint Aalen 1968].

Kaser, M. 1956². *Eigentum und Besitz im älteren römischen Recht*. Cologne/Graz.

Kaser, M. (1981). "Nochmals über Besitz und Verschulden bei den *actiones in rem*." *Zeitschrift der Savigny-Stiftung für Rechtsgeschichte, romanistische Abteilung* 98: 77–146.

Kaser, M. 1982. "'Pro herede vel pro possessore'," in *Studi in onore di Arnaldo Biscardi*, Vol. 2. Milan. 221–260.

Klinck, F. 2004. *Erwerb durch Übergabe an Dritte im klassischen römischen Recht*. Berlin.

Klinck, F. Forthcoming. "Der zivile Besitz (*civilis possessio*)"; "Die Ersitzung (*usucapio*)." In Babusiaux et al., eds., *Handbuch Römisches Privatrecht*. Tübingen.

Lambrini, P. 1998. *L'elemento soggettivo nelle situazioni possessorie del diritto romano classico*. Padua.

Marrone, M. 1989. "Rivendicazione (Diritto romano)." In *Enciclopedia del Diritto*. Milan. Vol. 41: 1–29. (Reprint: 2003. *Scritti giuridici I* (ed. G. Falcone). Palermo. 383–413.)

Migliardi Zingale, L. (1999). "Diritto romano e diritti locali nei documenti del Vicino Oriente." *Studia et Documenta Historiae et Iuris* 65: 217–231.

Nicosia, G. 2008². *Il possesso. I., Dalle lezioni del corso di diritto romano 1995–96*. Catania.

Nicosia, G. (2013). "*Possessio* e *res incorporales*." *Annali del seminario giuridico della università di Palermo* 56: 275–283.

Nitsch, A. Forthcoming. "Sonstige Interdikte." In U. Babusiaux et al. eds., *Handbuch Römisches Privatrecht*. Tübingen.

Nörr, D. 1969. *Die Entstehung der* longi temporis praescriptio: *Studien zum Einfluß der Zeit im Recht und zur Rechtspolitik in der Kaiserzeit*. Cologne/Opladen.

Pool, E. H. (2013). "D. 41, 2, 3, 21: Titulierte Besitzarten, Erwerbsgründe und das *unum genus possidendi*." *Tijdschrift voor Rechtsgeschiedenis/The Legal History Review* 81: 527–559.

Rodríguez Martín, J.-D. (2007–2008). "Sobre la posesión del *sequester*." *Seminarios Complutenses de Derecho Romano* 20–21: 361–387.

Roselaar, S. T. 2010. *Public land in the Roman republic: a social and economic history of* ager publicus *in Italy, 396–89 BC*. Oxford 2010.

Savigny, F. K. von. 1865⁷. *Das Recht des Besitzes: eine zivilistische Abhandlung*. 7th ed. prepared by A. F. Rudorff. Vienna. [reprint Aalen 1990.]

Schiavo, S. 2012. "Il prefetto Eustazio, Giustiniano e la *vacua possessio absentium*," in *Coniectanea iuris. Studi sul diritto in transizione*. Bologna. 137–157.

Sirks, A. J. B. 2009. "Einiges zum prekarischen Besitz." In H. Altmeppen et al., eds., *Festschrift für Rolf Knütel zum 70. Geburtstag*. Heidelberg. 1135–1146.

Sirks, A. J. B. (2014). "*Causae adquirendi eius quod nostrum non sit* (D. 41,2,3,21): 'rechtmäßiger Eigenbesitz'?" *Tijdschrift voor Rechtsgeschiedenis/The Legal History Review* 82: 209–239.

Solidoro Maruotti, L. 1998. *La tutela del possesso in età costantiniana*. Naples.

Vacca, L., ed. 2012. *Possessio e tempo nell'acquisto della proprietà. Saggi romanistici*. Milan.

Vandendriessche, S. 2006. Possessio *und* dominium *im postklassischen römischen Recht: eine Überprüfung von Levy's Vulgarrechtstheorie anhand der Quellen des Codex Theodosianus und der posttheodosianischen Novellen*. Hamburg.

Various authors 1974. "Atti del convegno internazionale sul tema: I diritti locali nelle province romane con particolare riguardo alle condizioni giuridiche del suolo." Accademia Nazionale dei Lincei. Rome, 26–28 October 1971.

Varvaro, M. 2008. *Ricerche sulla* praescriptio. Turin.

Varvaro, M. (2012). "Gai 4.163 e la struttura della *formula arbitraria nell'agere ex interdicto sine poena.*" *Annali del seminario giuridico della università di Palermo* 55: 705–734.

Varvaro, M. 2016. "La definizione della *possessio* nel Festo Farnesiano fra tradizione manoscritta, edizioni e interpretazione storiografica," in *Scritti per Alessandro Corbino*. Lecce.

Wimmer, M. 1995. *Besitz und Haftung des Vindikationsbeklagten*. Cologne.

Zamorani, P. 1977. Possessio *e* animus, Vol. 1. Milan.

CHAPTER 42

POSSESSION AND PROVINCIAL PRACTICE

ANDREA JÖRDENS
TRANSLATED BY JULIAN WAGSTAFF
AND CURATED BY DENNIS P. KEHOE

42.1 Introduction

In Adolf Berger's definition, according to Roman law "[t]he factual, physical control of a corporeal thing (*possessio* or *possidere corpore*) combined with the possessor's intention to hold it under physical control, normally as the owner" is to be distinguished both "from the mere physical holding of a thing (*tenere, in possessione esse*)" as well as "from ownership (*proprietas, dominium*), since at times one person may be the owner and another the possessor of the same thing" (Berger 1953, 636). To what extent these distinctions held sway in the provinces remains an open question. Even after Roman law, at least in theory, became universally binding on nearly all free inhabitants following the *Constitutio Antoniniana* in 212, definitive conclusions on this point are difficult if not impossible to reach. The following observations must therefore be content to limit themselves to the questions of ownership and possession in purely general terms, at least as far as the sources provide any information at all on the relationships pertaining to them.

Certainly formal Roman law, the *ius Quiritium*, only applied in the provinces to the extent that it concerned transactions between Roman citizens. Thus in the provinces, private property in land could not be acquired in the Roman sense, in accordance with Gaius's famous statement *in provinciali … solo dominium populi Romani est vel Caesaris* (Inst.Gai.2.7). The particular forms of property acquisition and property protection associated with the *dominium ex iure Quiritium* were only applicable to Italian land. The specific problems arising from Augustus' demobilising the armies recruited for the Civil Wars were overcome through the construct of the *ius Italicum*, whose bestowal on colonies founded by Roman citizens led to the emergence—or creation, if you will—of Italian soil even beyond the Apennine Peninsula (Bleicken 1974). Provincial property relations remained essentially unaffected by this development, as Rome respected the local legal systems and largely refrained from intervening in them; new regulations mostly supplemented or clarified existing legal traditions. This principle could also apply in certain circumstances to the property of Roman citizens located in the provinces, provided it had been acquired in the forms customary in that location, whereby it was subject to the same legal and tax system applicable to that of the peregrine population.

42.2 The Province of *Aegyptus* as a Case Study

Even if the Roman distinction between *dominium* and *possessio* did not have any equivalent in other legal systems, the notion of private ownership of land and soil certainly existed there as well, although differing conceptions are to be expected, depending on the tradition of various legal groups and cultures. In view of the often meagre evidence, it is only with great difficulty that provincial definitions of landownership can be pursued in any degree of detail, and so it is hardly possible to develop a consistent picture. Nonetheless, several recent works address the changes that Roman rule brought to provincial land, particularly in terms of economic relationships (for example, Corsten 2005 on Asia Minor; Hoffmann-Salz 2011 on Hispania Tarraconensis, Africa Proconsularis, Syria; Blei 2013 on Raetia; and in general Kehoe 2007).

The sole exception to lack of evidence is the province of *Aegyptus*, which to some extent represents the proverbial exception that proves the rule. This is because, as is well known, tens of thousands of texts on papyrus remained preserved in the arid areas of the Nile Valley, providing a great deal of evidence for questions about legal definitions of land in a provincial setting. For this reason, it makes sense to focus primarily on a single province, and to use it as a case study to illustrate broader legal issues, bearing in mind, of course, that conditions in the Roman Empire as a whole cannot necessarily be extrapolated directly from insights based on the Egyptian material. This is not because of the presumed "special position" often accorded to Egypt by scholars—especially as there is no such thing as the typical province in that sense, since each is atypical in its own way—but rather because of the multiplicity of legal systems that existed side by side throughout the period of Roman rule.

Therefore, if the following observations are based upon the rich seam of source material from Imperial Egypt, the aim is primarily to understand the social and economic conditions in which the attested conceptions of ownership and corresponding property relations manifested themselves. A detailed discussion of the treatment of this property in the context of private law—one need only mention the keywords inheritance, purchase/sale, rent/lease, transfer of security etc.—is, however, impossible. The same applies to the question as to how Roman administrative bodies and courts—which were not infrequently identical with one another—treated the legal concepts relating to property that they found in the provinces, intervened in a regulatory capacity or even established new laws. Both of these questions would exceed the boundaries of this chapter to a very great extent, particularly as individual cases would require extensive discussion. At the same time, regulatory institutions, which underwent considerable expansion under the Romans, must not be overlooked. This applies in particular to the so-called "property archive", a treatment of which is indispensable in the light of its central importance to the questions under discussion here.

We certainly cannot glean from the Egyptian material any general insight into the concept of property and possession in provincial legal systems. Nonetheless, it should be possible to draw inferences both about the flexibility of Roman authorities in the treatment of local legal traditions, including in response to their possible evolution, as well as about Roman administrative needs. Egypt thus represents a useful case study for the way in which new legal traditions evolved in each province as products of the transformational processes set in motion for the reasons outlined.

42.3 Terms and Concepts

Despite the centuries-long endurance of Roman rule, Latin was never able to establish itself universally either as an official or everyday language in the Greek East, and its use generally remained limited to the upper echelons of the administration and the army. When communication with the provincial population was necessary, it was generally conducted in Greek. At the same time, a distinct problem emerged in the realm of law. One basic issue was that legal terminology was very seldom congruent across Greek and Latin cultures. Magie (1905; cf. also Mason 1974: ix) identified three possible ways to render Roman legal terminology in Greek. The first is *per comparationem*, by which a Greek institution that exhibits the greatest degree of overlap is identified as the equivalent of the Roman institution. In rendering *per translationem*, by contrast, one endeavours to capture the meaning of the Latin term as exactly as possible using linguistic means, in some cases including a literal translation. Finally, *per transcriptionem* involved directly reproducing a Latin term in Greek letters. In the case of Egypt, one generally encounters the first two means of translating Roman concepts.

The equating of *possessio* with διακατοχή, as observed by Mason (1974, 36), follows the second principle. Its root διακατέχω is occasionally to be found earlier, along with the noun διακάτοχος that is derived from it (e.g. *P. Tor. Choach.* 12 [11.12.117 BC] with Pestman 1992, 196), although διακατέχω initially seems to have possessed a "pre-Roman *allgemeine Bedeutung*" (Cotton and Yardeni 1997, 243 n. 19). The situation was different—perhaps from the very beginning—for the abstract term διακατοχή, which was presumably specified as a standard translation by Rome itself, as the use of this term in the *agnitiones bonorum possessionis* emerging after the *Constitutio Antoniniana* in Egypt suggests (see most recently Gagos and Heilporn 2001). The rendering attested once previously by means of the simple κατοχή (*M. Chr.* 373, 24 [4. - 29.8.119 AD] = Oliver 1989, no. 70) was not, however, continued, presumably not least because there was a risk of confusing it with the institution of contractually agreed or statutorily imposed limitation of disposal of property—the so-called "distraint" (*Verfangenschaft*)—which the term usually connoted.

Throughout all periods Greek legal terminology was retained, which again confirms the general validity of the first principle: "The designation of κράτησις and κυριεία is common, whereby the first characterises the mastery of the object and the authority for physical access to the object, and as such is to a certain extent comparable with possession, while the second entails the entitlement to actual and legal disposal of the object. In the Roman period one occasionally encounters the equation of κυριεία with *dominium* and κράτησις with *possessio*; ultimately this applies to the expression alone. In addition, Byzantine legal terminology also employs δεσποτεία together with κυριεία and νομή together with κράτησις" (Rupprecht 1994a, 132). Occasionally one also encounters the less technical κτῆσις, particularly for assets in land and thus later with the narrower meaning of "estate" or even the name of a territory. Private assets as a whole, both movable and immovable, were called τὰ ὑπάρχοντα or—less frequently—διαφέροντα. One Egyptian peculiarity is represented by potential limits on the full right of disposal, in that there might exist a legitimate claim by a third party to the property or parts of it. As the edict of M. Mettius Rufus on the so-called "property archive" indicates in particular, such a lien under indigenous law ensured not least the claims of wives and children arising from a dowry or a bequest of grandparents, which, as was customary, had passed into the husband's assets and so into his authority to dispose of them. Under certain circumstances appropriate restrictions could be added in the form of the so-called κατοχή, including by order of the state, apparently as a pre-emptive step in connection with the nomination to liturgical service (most recently Jördens 2010b, 282). Those assets designated with a notice of distraint were thereby protected from any other form of use, whereby with respect to the first restriction even the privileged status of the state as creditor, πρωτοπραξία, granted as a matter of principle, was relegated to second place.

42.4 Land

Just as in the law of persons, in which the multiplicity of status groups which had existed hitherto was replaced by a simple tripartite division into *cives Romani*, citizens of a Greek *polis* and finally the majority *peregrini* population—the last referred to without distinction in this case as Egyptians—the Romans also undertook a far-reaching reform of land law, whereby they classified all arable land as either *ager publicus* or *ager privatus*. Available arable land was thus subsumed into one or other of these two categories, under whose umbrella, however, the complex system of different land categories persisted with varying rates of tax, which also varied from *nome* (district) to *nome*, generally retaining their traditional designations.

A common characteristic of *ager publicus* was a significantly higher taxation rate as well as the hereditary and unalterable obligation of state cultivators. At the same time there were many discrepancies between the general formulation of the law and its specific application, resulting in an overall picture that was not always free of contradictions, particularly with regard to this dichotomy in classifying land employed by the Romans. This has given rise to frequent misunderstandings and misinterpretations in the scholarly literature, which have been magnified by the lack of correspondence between the Egyptian definitions of rights to land and familiar concepts of Roman law. Only in recent times has it been possible to portray in detail the fundamental reorganisation of the Egyptian agricultural sector effected by the Romans (cf. in particular Rowlandson 1996 and 2005 and most recently Monson 2012).

Central elements of the Ptolemaic agrarian system were adopted during this process, and in particular the external forms remained to a large extent untouched. At the same time, however, the Romans implemented a range of measures that were to erode the structures from within and eventually to transform them fundamentally. Here let us merely mention changes to the methods for determining tax liability; the granting of privileges and benefits and, in particular, the generous promotion of private investment, as a result of which the pressure towards privatisation engendered by the growth in population, particularly in the Nile valley, continually increased. The problems that emerged increasingly and eventually on a regular basis as a result of this trend, were in turn countered by the Romans always in a conservative manner. The Romans tended to promote stability and where necessary made selective concessions, while avoiding wholehearted and thoroughgoing reforms. Deviations from the classification of land as state or private, once it had been established, remained rare and were therefore hardly relevant, while the allocation of deserted arable land to entire village communities in the form of so-called ἐπιμερισμός or ἐπιβολή (the assignment of uncultivated land to the *proximi possessores*) led to further tensions.

The *de iure* and *de facto* configuration of property relations therefore increasingly diverged, a fact that was not officially recognised until the final abolition under Diocletian of δημοσία γῆ—former state land eventually reduced to being a mere land category of privately occupied land. At the same time, the parcels of land that had hitherto been state land were handed over as private land to the people who worked it, although admittedly still without the due adjustment of tax payments.

42.4.1 State Land

All land for which tax was previously paid directly to the crown was taken by the Romans as *ager publicus* or δημόσια ἐδάφη. This affected in the first instance land that had hitherto been royal land (βασιλικὴ γῆ), but also less common categories of land such as the so-called πρόσοδος, which was particularly highly taxed and therefore presumably more lucrative, shoreland (αἰγιαλός), which was only occasionally utilisable as agricultural land, as well as portions of former temple land (ἱερὰ γῆ). We cannot speak of large-scale confiscations of temple land in its entirety, in contrast to earlier assumptions. In the Nile Valley and even in Upper Egypt, where during the Ptolemaic period a large proportion of arable land was in the hands of temples or sanctuaries, state land only accounted for one third of cultivable land area. In Fayyum, by contrast, the proportion approached 50 per cent. These ratios remained remarkably stable despite occasional fluctuations in the allocation of land during the first three centuries, which again underscores the ossification of the system prior to the Diocletian land reform.

The cultivation of state land was the responsibility of state farmers previously called βασιλικοὶ γεωργοί, but now known as δημόσιοι γεωργοί. Rich sources of information on this subject survive primarily from the river oasis of the Fayyum west of the Nile, thanks to both the extremely high quality of papyrological sources that have come down to us, as well as the large scale of public landholding there. In Fayyum, the state farmers were incorporated into associations, which were established for the most part at village level. Comparable to these were the πιττάκια in Theadelpheia and the κληρουχίαι in Karanis, although these latter organisations had fewer members and were for this reason probably a peculiarity of larger localities (Geremek 1969, cf. also Rowlandson 2005, 190–191). In the Nile Valley, by contrast, the relatively small proportion of state land seems to have fostered a mixed cultivation of private and public lands. This situation, coupled with the loss of status that occurred under the Romans for those farmers who had previously enjoyed the special protection of the king, soon led to the disappearance of the corresponding status designations (Rowlandson 2005, 188).

The rights and obligations of state farmers were nominally determined by custom, albeit ones that had not necessarily applied since time immemorial. According to recent research, even Hellenistic concepts are discernible (Rowlandson 2005, 174–175, cf. also Rathbone 2003 on the corresponding phenomenon in Rome). The establishment of farmers' rights and obligations did not take place via written means; instead, sons or other closely related persons took the place of the previous holder by means of an oath. Oaths appear to have been recorded in written form mainly in cases of acquisition by more distant relatives (Rowlandson 2005, 187). Contracts under private law are only documented in subleases (Herrmann 1958, 82; cf. also *P. Bingen* 59 [22.?9.33]: a lease for ninety-three years), as well as in occasional internal agreements between holders of cultivation rights, such as when they exchanged parcels allocated to themselves (Hagedorn 1986). The cultivation of the land, or the land itself—the latter in particular for grazing—could also be given over to third parties for a limited period of time in a so-called *epichoresis*, taking into account the fact that in the case of state land, it was always only the right (and duty) of cultivation and not ownership that was transferrable (Rupprecht 1984, 373–374, 384). For this reason, successors to cultivation rights were designated under private law as mere διάδοχοι, but not, however, as heirs, κληρονόμοι (Rupprecht 1994b, 235).

Leasing of land by the state appears to have taken place (contrary to earlier assumptions) only in the case of land with reduced yield, so-called ὑπόλογος γῆ, which was assigned and sometimes even sold to the highest bidder at advantageous terms by means of an auction (Jördens 2009, 468–485). The occasionally occurring term διαμίσθωσις probably refers to the redistribution of the parcels of land (at irregular intervals?) among the cultivators in a community by means of drawing lots (κλήρωσις). This process (in contrast to what was long supposed) was not carried out by state institutions, but remained within the purview of local functionaries (Rowlandson 2005, 182–183, 191–192; Monson 2012, 15–151). Responsibility for this, as for all other tasks associated with the administration of state land, resided with the councils of so-called elders or πρεσβύτεροι consisting of up to ten (elected?) members under the leadership of a ἡγούμενος, and sometimes assisted by a scribe. In addition to all aspects of distributing public land—the aforementioned general redistribution as well as the reallocation of individual plots of land due to the death or unavailability for other reasons of the previous incumbent—the councils also undertook the regular distribution of the seed loans that were traditionally granted, and above all the organisation of customary community duties; for example, those connected with water usage or guard duty. As representatives of the state peasants at village level, and thus forming the actual hinge between the peasants and the state institutions, the πρεσβύτεροι were increasingly entrusted with other types of duties, acquiring responsibility (for example) for representing the village scribe and for all payments due from the village as a whole, whether for in-kind requisitions or other levies, on a more or less liturgical basis.

42.4.2 Private Land

Ager privatus, or ἰδιωτικὰ ἐδάφη, included not only private land (ἰδιόκτητος γῆ), which was already recognised as such under the Ptolemies, but also former state lands that had often been privately cultivated for generations. This again affected some temple land (Monson 2012, 131–141, 219), but above all the κληρουχικὴ or κατοικικὴ γῆ formed from the *kleroi* of the Ptolemaic military settlers, the *klerouchoi* or *katoikoi* (cf. now Scheuble-Reiter 2012, 142–194 with important nuances), which at least in the Fayyum constituted the most significant portion of private land. In both cases, a *de facto* private ownership had evolved over the course of the centuries, which was finally also recognised *de iure* by the Romans. This special aetiology led in this case also to a situation where, due to the once precarious position of katoikic land, a transfer of ownership was only possible, or in any case customary, in the specific form of the so-called *parachoresis*, but not as a true sale in return for payment of a purchase price (Rupprecht 1984).

Private land was distinguished from the δημόσια ἐδάφη primarily through their significantly lower tax rate. Private land was taxed at the rate of only one, or at the very most two, *artabai* of wheat per *aroura*, in addition to a few smaller levies, such as transport costs for the grain paid as tax in the form of the ναύβιον κατοίκων. In total, the annual rate on private land was on average only a third of the rate normally applicable to state land, which could in some cases rise as high as five *artabai* per *aroura*. To this extent, the principle of fixed tax rates favoured by the Romans, which replaced the variable harvest tax that had existed previously (Monson 2012, 184–191), represented a particular benefit for the low-taxed private land. Under certain circumstances, the reduced rates were also extended to the purchasers of state land, and often even tied to a tax holiday of several years, particularly if they declared themselves prepared to undertake improvements on the land, henceforth categorised as ἐωνημένη γῆ (Jördens 2009, 486–489).

42.4.3 Imperial Domains

One category of nominally private land finally emerged with the estates or οὐσιακὰ ἐδάφη handed over to members of the Imperial family or close associates of the court since the reign of Augustus. This land came into Imperial ownership as οὐσιακὴ γῆ towards the end of the Julio-Claudian dynasty. The cultivation of these estates, generally consisting of scattered parcels of land, was carried out by οὐσιακοὶ γεωργοί, who resembled state farmers in their form of organisation, but in the early Imperial period came to enjoy particular privileges. Initially, it is clear that members of the Imperial *familia*, or also freed slaves dispatched from Rome, were preferred for the coordination of the units managed by local stewards, into whose shoes indigenous large-scale leaseholders increasingly stepped (Kehoe 1992, 18–35). The declining interest in large-scale leaseholds of this kind, which even appeals by governors failed to alter (*IHibis* 4, 11–15 para 3 [6.7.68], with Jördens 2009, 506–511), tended to promote assimilation within the *patrimonium*. Under the Flavians this land was finally equated with state land, but received its own administration with the creation of a new department, the οὐσιακὸς λόγος (Monson 2012, 103).

42.5 Priesthoods

The rights denoted by κυριεία καὶ κράτησις were also assigned to priesthoods or, more precisely, to the holdings in temple assets associated with them in each case. These holdings had formed a significant source of income in Egypt since time immemorial. In principle hereditary, the rights and obligations associated with priesthoods could also be assigned to third parties and the incomes drawn from them leased or pledged as security. The extent of the holdings was a function of the individual priesthoods, and particular payments, services or investments could lead to an accumulation that was in certain circumstances also inherited. The holding of multiple priesthoods at the same time was in principle possible (Monson 2012, 212–227). The state reserved for itself, apparently as early as the pre-Hellenistic period, the awarding of particularly lucrative leadership functions such as the office of prophet. The auctions conducted under the Romans of course removed nearly any hope that an office together with all its rights and privileges would remain in the family, as one bidder for an office as prophet might still have hoped for in the high Imperial period (*P. Tebt.* ii 294, 17–19 [5.1.147], with Talamanca 1954, 20–210).

42.6 Other Types of Asset

In addition to private land as well as houses and parts of houses, real estate assets also included workshops, oil mills, stables, warehouses and other productive areas. Joint and/or part ownership was possible, and both in the form of real and notional division among co-owners. As in the case of land, in principle a co-owner was free to dispose of his or her share in the property, although in the second century AD tendencies towards a pre-emptive right of purchase on the part of the other co-owners emerged (Rupprecht 1981 and 1983). It is hard to imagine this in the case of places of burial, which were evidently also counted as real estate, according to entries on the personal declarations in the property archive (e.g. *P. Oxy.* ii 274, 27 [28.8.97]: one half of a common grave with the father's sister). This also explains the regulations in regard to burial plots in the so-called *Gnomon* of the *Idios Logos*, the handbook of the financial procurator responsible for certain receipts to the Imperial treasury, according to which the burial sites of state debtors, along with all their other assets, with the exception of the headstones, were liable to confiscation since the time of Trajan (*BGU* V 1210, 8–20 paras. 1–2 [around 150], with Kramer 1998). Slaves, too, represented an asset to this extent, for which a declaration and entry in the property archive was customary. In their case, as a consequence of the custody resulting from confiscation pending final sale, much greater problems could arise for the authorities (Jördens 2009, 322–324). Other valuables, however, were not recorded herein, as, for example, livestock, although they could play a considerable role in inheritance disputes (cf. e.g. *BGU* II 388 [157–159]).

There were also some noteworthy changes regarding the disposition of property belonging to women. First, the property given to them at the time of their marriage no longer passed in its entirety to the husband's power to dispose. In addition, the traditional form of dowry (φερνή) underwent a significant change. In its traditional form, the wife, in the event of divorce, in principle only had a claim for the return of the dowry's appraised value. The dowry was now supplemented first by specification of personal objects such as jewellery and clothes, referred to as παράφερνα, and second by an additional contribution consisting of land and slaves, the so-called προσφορά. Since they were part of the everyday configuration of married life, and in the case of παράφερνα, subject to the usual wear and tear, the husband possessed only a right of use of these additional contributions for the duration of the marriage. Accordingly, this made dispensable in both their cases the declaration of the appraised value customary in the case of the dowry (Yiftach-Firanko 2003, 129–140).

42.7 Regulatory Authorities

The regulatory bodies created during the Ptolemaic period were again greatly expanded under the Romans. This led to declarations being required across a range of areas, although admittedly these often had only a supplementary function. Special inspection procedures were also introduced, of which the best known are certainly the various forms of *epikrisis* for privileged groups of people, such as members of the *gymnasion* or veterans. In the present context, of special interest is the *anakrisis*, which slaves had to undergo since at least the time of Commodus (Wolff 1978, 255–260; Straus 1997). Probably the most important innovations related to the public archives, which underwent continuous expansion from the earliest days of Roman rule, both in the *nomes* as well as in the capital itself (Jördens 2010a). Particular attention must be given here to the property archive, established to ensure the functioning of private transactions.

42.7.1 Systems for Declaration

Even if the system of declarations in Imperial Egypt underwent a significant expansion, it only played a subsidiary role in the recording of assets (in contrast to the Roman census procedure), because traditionally other ways and means were available for this purpose. The few declarations in which people are recorded along with their assets were regularly made by Roman citizens, in the context of the Empire-wide census of Roman citizens (Rathbone 2001). In contrast to the much more common declarations, which served as the basis for tax assessment and were therefore to be submitted to the *strategos* and βασιλικὸς γραμματεύς as the highest financial authorities of the *nome*, these evidently went directly to the governor's office in Alexandria, which doubtless also explains their rarity.

The most common type of declarations in Egypt were the so-called κατ' οἰκίαν ἀπογραφαί, which were made every fourteen years. In these, the head of the household (who was normally identical with the house owner) had to account for the people making up each household, including free people and slaves (Bagnall and Frier 2006). Its main purpose, if not its only purpose, appears to have been the registration of peregrines assessed for capitation tax. However, since the declarations also recorded empty houses, information could simultaneously be obtained from them regarding current real estate ownership. This latter purpose may have been of relevance in establishing the so-called πόρος, which measured qualifications for the allocation of liturgical offices (Lewis 1997, 73–75). Here again, however, there was a preference to rely on local authorities, such as the village scribe and the files that he maintained (cf. *P. Petaus* 10 and 11 [both 2.5.184]).

Similarly, land ownership was also recorded, if only indirectly, by means of the land registers drawn up by the same local authorities; declarations of this type are first documented under Diocletian. The declarations that were to be submitted to the property archive, of course, do not fall into this category, as is made clear by their being addressed to the *bibliophylakes*, who were clearly entrusted with the direction of this archive as a liturgy. Livestock declarations, on the other hand, are in evidence from early on. They initially probably only represented a supplement to the already existing livestock census, but they became mandatory for camels, beginning with the Hadrianic period. Occasional declarations regarding other movable assets such as ships or grain are always attributable to special circumstances (Jördens 2009, 95–134).

42.7.2 The So-called "Property Archive"

Probably the most idiosyncratic creation of the regulatory bodies promoted by the Romans in the province of *Aegyptus* was the so-called βιβλιοθήκη ἐγκτήσεων, which was split off from the general *nome* archive in the third quarter of the first century, although the reason for this and, indeed, the precise chronology remain unclear. As the name alone suggests, this "archive of acquisitions" recorded the status of private landownership and probably also slave ownership, with a focus on recording any changes in ownership status (such as liens imposed by creditors, or, in certain circumstances, family members). In light of the lack of a general principle of registration, however, it does not seem to have been a form of cadastre, contrary to earlier assumptions. Apart from a large number of declarations submitted to it, we are primarily dependent for information regarding its mode of operation on an edict of the governor M. Mettius Rufus from the year 89. This edict addressed recurring problems in relation to the implementation of provisions locally, and thus again provides detailed information on the processes of the archive (*P. Oxy.* ii 237 col. VIII, 27–43 = *FIRA* I 60 [1 or 31.10.89]; see in particular Wolff 1978, 222–255).

Accordingly, all κτήτορες—in other words, private owners of all kinds of real estate as well as (apparently) slaves—were required to declare all private property and rights of pledge to the property archive, along with other possessory titles, within six months of their acquisition, with an indication of their origin. On this basis, summary sheets, so-called διαστρώματα, were compiled for each private individual under his ὄνομα, under which these titles were to be recorded according to place and object. The procedure for the property of women and children, when the power to disposal had temporarily passed to the husband or parents, is also regulated. In the event of changes to the status of property, the issuing notaries had to obtain beforehand a corresponding ἐπίσταλμα from the archive, which provided information on the right to dispose of the property. Penalties applied in the case of non-compliance. Notations concerning legally recognised restrictions, resulting, for example, from rights of pledge declared for the first time, or κατοχαί (liens) imposed by the state, were entered in the form of παράθεσις next to each affected object in the margin of the διάστρωμα (according to *P. Oxy.* ii 274 [28.8.97, with a host of dates mentioned therein between 88 and 97]; Wolff 1978, 235–238). All of these files—declarations as well as διαστρώματα—were to be carefully retained as a matter of principle, and to be updated at regular intervals, thus ensuring that the institution was always current.

The declarations submitted concerning the newly acquired possessory titles were known by the familiar term ἀπογραφή, whereas for *katoikic* land a specific term, in this case μετεπιγραφή, was current for the reasons described above. Ordinarily the registers were to be kept up to date by this means alone—that is, with the aid of so-called regular or special *apographai*, which were to be submitted following each change of ownership. If necessary, however, so-called general *apographai*—that is, declarations by all κτήτορες in relation to their entire property—could be required at the special instigation of the prefect, although this evidently did not take place at regular intervals, as was previously assumed. The purpose of this institution must necessarily be seen in the "protection of private legal business for its own sake", as expressly stated by the governor himself (Jördens 2010b, with reference to Wolff 1978, 253). Parallels from other provinces, such as the (fragmentary) edict from Sibidunda in Pisidia and in particular the decree of Q. Veranius from Myra in Lycia, point to the general concern of Rome in this area (cf. *SEG* XIX 854 [2nd century] = Oliver 1989, no. 186; *SEG* XXXIII 1177 [43 AD]; see in particular Wörrle 1975 on this question).

Bibliography

Bagnall, R. S. and Frier, B. W. 2006². *The demography of Roman Egypt*. Revised edition. Cambridge.

Berger, A. (1953). "Encyclopedic dictionary of Roman law." *Transactions of the American Philosophical Society, N.S.* 43/2: 333–808.

Blei, J. 2013. Dominium populi Romani vel Caesaris *und* causa dominica: *römische Rechtstradition und Fiskalsukzession im bairischen Dukat der Agilolfinger*. Berlin.

Bleicken, J. (1974). "*In provinciali solo dominium populi Romani est vel Caesaris*: zur Kolonisationspolitik der ausgehenden Republik und frühen Kaiserzeit." *Chiron* 4: 359–414.

Corsten, T. 2005. "Estates in Roman Asia Minor: the case of Kibyratis." In S. Mitchell, C. Katsari, and D. Braund, eds., *Patterns in the economy of Roman Asia Minor*. Swansea. 1–51.

Cotton, H. M. and Yardeni, A. 1997. *Aramaic, Hebrew, and Greek documentary texts from Naḥal Ḥever and other sites*. Oxford.

Gagos, T. and Heilporn, P. 2001. "20. A new *agnitio bonorum possessionis*." In T. Gagos and R. S. Bagnall, eds., *Essays and texts in honor of J. David Thomas*. Oakville. 175–185.

Geremek, H. 1969. *Karanis: communauté rurale de l'Égypte romaine au IIe–IIIe siècle de notre ère*. Wrocław/Warsaw/Kraków.

Hagedorn, D. (1986). "Flurbereinigung in Theadelpheia?" *Zeitschrift für Papyrologie und Epigraphik* 65: 93–100.

Herrmann, J. 1958. *Studien zur Bodenpacht im Recht der graeco-aegyptischen Papyri*. Munich.

Hoffmann-Salz, J. 2011. *Die wirtschaftlichen Auswirkungen der römischen Eroberung: vergleichende Untersuchungen der Provinzen Hispania Tarraconensis, Africa Proconsularis und Syria*. Stuttgart.

Jördens, A. 2009. *Statthalterliche Verwaltung in der römischen Kaiserzeit: Studien zum* praefectus Aegypti. Stuttgart.

Jördens, A. 2010a. "Öffentliche Archive und römische Rechtspolitik." In K. Lembke, M. Minas-Nerpel and S. Pfeiffer, eds., *Tradition and transformation: Egypt under Roman rule (Hildesheim, 3–6. 7. 2008)*. Leiden/Boston. 159–179.

Jördens, A. 2010b. "Nochmals zur Bibliotheke Enkteseon." In G. Thür, ed., *Symposion 2009: Vorträge zur griechischen und hellenistischen Rechtsgeschichte (Seggau, 25–30, 8. 2009)*. Vienna. 277–29.

Kehoe, D. P. 1992. *Management and investment on estates in Roman Egypt during the early empire*. Bonn.

Kehoe, D. P. 2007. *Law and the rural economy in the Roman empire*. Ann Arbor.

Kramer, B. (1998). "Zum Gnomon des Idios Logos §1, 15." *Archiv für Papyrusforschung* 44: 253–254.

Lewis, N. 1997[2]. *The compulsory public services of Roman Egypt*. Florence.

Magie, D. 1905. De Romanorum iuris publici sacrique vocabulis sollemnibus in Graecum sermonem conversis. Leipzig.

Mason, H. J. 1974. *Greek terms for Roman institutions: a lexicon and analysis*. Toronto.

Monson, A. 2012. *From the Ptolemies to the Romans: political and economic change in Egypt*. Cambridge.

Oliver, J. H. 1989. *Greek constitutions of early Roman emperors from inscriptions and papyri*. Philadelphia.

Pestman, P. W. 1992. *Il processo di Hermias e altri documenti dell'archivio dei choachiti (P. Tor. Choachiti)*. Turin.

Rathbone, D. 2001. "6. *PSI* XI 1183: record of a Roman census declaration of A.D. 47/8." In T. Gagos and R. S. Bagnall, eds., *Essays and texts in honor of J. David Thomas*. Cincinnati. 99–113.

Rathbone, D. W. 2003. "The control and exploitation of *ager publicus* in Italy under the Roman republic." In J.-J. Aubert, ed., *Tâches publiques et entreprise privée dans le monde romain*. Geneva. 135–178.

Rowlandson, J. 1996. *Landowners and tenants in Roman Egypt: the social relations of agriculture in the Oxyrhynchite nome*. Oxford.

Rowlandson, J. 2005. "The organisation of public land in Roman Egypt." In J. C. Moreno García, ed., *L'agriculture institutionelle en Égypte ancienne: état de la question et perspectives interdisciplinaires*. Lille = *CRIPEL* 25: 173–196.

Rupprecht, H.-A. 1981. "Zum Vorkaufsrecht der Gemeinschafter nach den Papyri." In E. Bresciani, ed., *Scritti in onore di Orsolina Montevecchi*. Bologna. 335–342.

Rupprecht, H.-A. 1983. "Zu Voraussetzungen, Umfang und Herkunft des Vorkaufrechts der Gemeinschafter nach den Papyri." In *Symposion 1979: Vorträge zur griechischen und hellenistischen Rechtsgeschichte (Ägina, 3–7, 9. 1979)*. Cologne/Vienna. 287–301.

Rupprecht, H.-A. 1984. "Rechtsübertragung in den Papyri. Zur Entwicklung von Parachoresis und Ekchoresis." In D. Nörr and D. Simon, eds., *Gedächtnisschrift für Wolfgang Kunkel*. Frankfurt am Main. 365–39.

Rupprecht, H.-A. 1994a. *Kleine Einführung in die Papyruskunde*. Darmstadt.

Rupprecht, H.-A. 1994b. "Die Vererblichkeit von Grund und Boden im ptolemäischen Ägypten." In G. Thür, ed., *Symposion 1993: Vorträge zur griechischen und hellenistischen Rechtsgeschichte (Graz-Andritz, 12–16. 9. 1993)*. Cologne/Weimar/Vienna. 225–238.

Scheuble-Reiter, S. 2012. *Die Katökenreiter im ptolemäischen Ägypten*. Munich.

Straus, J. A. (1997). "Les autorités responsables de l'ἀνάκρισις des esclaves dans l'Égypte romaine." *Chronique d'Égypte* 72: 332–340.

Talamanca, M. 1954. "Contributi allo studio delle vendite all'asta nel mondo classico." *Memorie, Accademia Nazionale dei Lincei, Classe di Scienze Morali, Storiche e Filologiche* 8.6.2: 35–251. Rome.

Wörrle, M. 1975. "Zwei neue griechische Inschriften aus Myra zur Verwaltung Lykiens in der Kaiserzeit." In J. Borchhardt, ed., *Myra: eine lykische Metropole in antiker und byzantinischer Zeit*. Berlin. 254–30.

Wolff, H. J. 1978. *Das Recht der griechischen Papyri Ägyptens in der Zeit der Ptolemaeer und des Prinzipats*, Vol. 2: *Organisation und Kontrolle des privaten Rechtsverkehrs*. Munich.

Yiftach-Firanko, U. 2003. *Marriage and marital agreements: a history of the Greek marriage document in Egypt, 4th century* BCE–*4th century* CE. Munich.

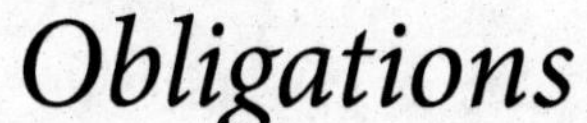

Obligations

CHAPTER 43

OBLIGATIO IN ROMAN LAW AND SOCIETY

DAVID IBBETSON

43.1 Introduction

Four centuries ago, in his commentaries on the civil law, Donellus analysed the nature of *obligatio* in Roman law.[1] Subsequent scholars by the score have continued his work and continue to do so.[2] It would be impossible in a short piece to engage with all of this literature, so the purpose of the present discussion is simply to outline what is known and to locate it within the Roman world.

Lawyers today rather take it for granted that there is a branch of the law called the law of obligations, including at the very least contract and tort, and that there is something called an obligation, designating the situation where one person is legally constrained to do or abstain from doing something to another. But neither of these is obvious, and it is highly likely that both are the products of Roman jurisprudence (Gaudemet 2000). It is true that in his treatment of justice in the *Nicomachean Ethics* Aristotle linked together contract and wrongdoing, the voluntary and involuntary types of *sunallagmata*—transactions or interactions—that might generate a requirement of corrective justice (*Eth. Nic.* V.2, 1131a2–9), but it goes too far to identify Aristotle's *sunallagma* with the Romans' *obligatio*: the former is an interaction that gives rise to corrective justice, the latter the abstract consequence of such a transaction (Biscardi 1982, 133–135).

To understand the nature of *obligatio* we should begin with the verb form, *obligare*, and see its etymology and meaning. Its core meaning, already by the time of Plautus (*Truc.* 5.1.64), is to bind, tie up or fasten, with its root *ligare* derived from the Greek λυγόω, with the same sense (Ernout and Meillet 1959, 521). Its secondary, abstract meaning of putting a person under a duty, which is found by the end of the Republic, maintains its link with this concrete meaning of binding or tying. In addition, it could refer to the binding of a thing, as where its owner pledged it to another (Plaut. *Truc.* 2.1.6).

[1] *Commentariorum de Iure Civili* 12.1.4–10 (in *Opera Omnia* [Florence 1841], 3-427-431).

[2] Cf. Arangio-Ruiz 1960, 283 n. 1: "La Letteratura è infinita". It has not shrunk.

It is from here that we get, at the latest by the time of Cicero, the noun *obligatio* (*Ad Brut.* 1.18.3).

Related to it is *nexum*. We need not enter into the controversy about the institution, abolished in the fourth century BC (Buckland and Stein 1963, 429–431), but may observe that it too is linguistically related to tying, the verb *nectere* being effectively a synonym of *ligare* (Ernout and Meillet 1959, 630). It involved one person falling into the bondage of another by a formal transaction *per aes et libram*, and perhaps encapsulated an idea or image of being bound and led off into captivity. By the time of the classical jurists it seems to have been practically synonymous with *obligatio* (D.46.4.1; D.10.2.33).

But we should remain with the verb *obligare* for the moment. In the active voice it referred to the momentary act of binding or constraining, and once that momentary act had passed no additional meaning could be given to it. The perfect *obligavi*, that is, did no more than refer back to the event that had already occurred. This focus of the verb placed the active participant centre stage: he was the person who bound the other. It follows from this that as we move into the abstract, legal domain it was the act of obliging that lay at the core of the word in the active voice. It was possible to use a reflexive form of the verb, where it was the active party who came under the duty. According to Quintus Mucius, a borrower who misused the thing lent was liable as a thief, *furti se obligavit* (Gell. *NA* 6.15.2); again the stress is on the way in which the liability had been created, not on the continuing state.

The passive voice was rather different, since it could refer both to the momentary act of becoming bound and the continuing state of being bound. Hence, a person might be *obligatus*; that is to say, he might have become obliged and still be obliged. The *lex de Gallia Cisalpina* (*terminus ante quem* of 42 BC), for example, deals with the situation where someone has confessed himself to be obliged, "*obligatum se … esse confessus erit*", using the past participle (*RS* no. 28, ch. XXII, ll. 33–34).

The juristic texts in the Digest reflect this usage. When the active voice is used in the present tense it is normally to make a general statement, such as that an *institor* binds his principal or that a slave obliges someone to his master (D.14.3.7.2; D.45.1.62), and in the perfect tense it looks back to an act of obliging that has occurred in the past, as where a landowner has obliged himself to compensate for *damnum infectum* or to make a gift (D.36.4.5.1; D.39.5.12). In the passive, the usage is similar. In the present tense it makes a general statement, such as that we are obliged in some circumstances (D.44.7.52pr, 1, 2, 3, 5, 6, 8), and in the perfect tense it refers to something which has happened in the past which has consequences for the present. The person who has dug a pit where he should not do so, with the result that an animal has fallen into it and been injured, has thereby become obliged—*obligatus est*—under the *lex Aquilia* (D.9.2.28pr).

Verbs precede abstract nouns. David Daube has shown that in many situations the Roman jurists never got as far as creating abstract nouns, using instead verbal forms, or that they clearly preferred verbal forms to nominal (Daube 1969, 2–63). *Obligatio*, however, is a frequent occurrence in the texts, hardly less frequent in the Digest than the various forms of the verb.[3] We can say that the development of the noun presupposes a sophistication of thought about the institution, an ability to treat an active relationship as a thing,

[3] I calculate that the verb outnumbers the noun roughly in the proportion 4:3. Contrast *occupare* and *occupatio*, roughly 20:1.

and that at least by the time of Labeo, the first jurist known to have used the noun, Roman law had taken that step.[4]

As a noun, *obligatio* has none of the imbalance of the verb, for it can refer both to the act and to the state of obliging, from both the active and passive standpoint. That said, there is probably a slant towards the passive end: it makes perfect sense to speak of a person being obliged without specifying who it is that is doing or has done the obliging, whereas we cannot so easily speak of the active party to the obligation without saying or implying who it is that is being or has been obliged. Perhaps more to the point, though, the noun carries with it a greater sense of the relationship between two persons than does the verb. It is this that accounts for its function in the institutional structure of Roman law.

It is noteworthy that, despite the fact that the etymology of *obligatio* lies in lay usage, the word itself is very unusual in classical Latin outside the legal context; it seems not to be found before Tertullian around 200 AD (*Apol.* 28.1). The bilaterality, which was so useful in the law in expressing the relationship between two people, was out of place in an ethical context where what was important was the duty under which one person found him- or herself. Here it was only when the word had developed sufficiently that it could refer simply to the duty without any connotation of a correlative right that it could be applied freely in the field of ethics.

43.2 Obligations: The Institutional Structure

The place of obligations in the Institutes of Gaius and Justinian can be easily described. According to Gaius, all law relates to persons, things or actions (Inst.Gai.1.8). Obligations are seen as forming part of the law of things.[5] In this category Gaius deals first with the law of property, the relations between persons and things, and then moves on to obligations. The transition occurs at Inst.Gai.3.88:

> *Nunc transeamus ad obligationes. Quarum summa divisio in duas species deducitur: omnis enim obligatio vel ex contractu nascitur vel ex delicto.*
> Let us proceed to obligations. Their basic division is into two species: for every obligation arises either from contract or from delict.

This then provides the shape for Gaius' treatment of personal obligations: first contracts, then delicts or wrongs. The same duality is found in Gaius' treatment of personal

[4] D.50.16.19 (Ulpian, 11 *ad ed.*): *Labeo libro primo praetoris urbani definit, quod quaedam "agantur", quaedam "gerantur", quaedam "contrahantur": et actum quidem generale verbum esse, sive verbis sive re quid agatur, ut in stipulatione vel numeratione: contractum autem ultro citroque obligationem, quod graeci sunallagma vocant, veluti emptionem venditionem, locationem conductionem, societatem: gestum rem significare sine verbis factam.* The reference to *sunallagma* may suggest a link with Aristotle, but Labeo's use of the word is more in line with its normal Greek sense of contract than with Aristotle's wider meaning.

[5] Though there was an earlier view, not without merit, that obligations were really part of the law of actions in Gaius' framework: Jolowicz 1952, 471–476.

actions: these, he says, seek to enforce an obligation imposed by contract or delict (Inst. Gai.4.2; see section 43.6); though we should observe that already in the Institutes he has referred to the personal action to enforce a legacy *per damnationem* (Inst.Gai.2.213). In truth, contract and wrongdoing are merely the two principal sources of *obligatio*, and in the Digest Gaius is seen to be giving a slightly expanded categorisation, adding an additional residuary group:

> *Obligationes aut ex contractu nascuntur aut ex maleficio aut proprio quodam iure ex variis causarum figuris.*
>
> Obligations arise either from contract or from wrongdoing or by some special right from various types of causes. (D.44.7.1pr)

Noteworthily, although the sources of obligations are given in the Institutes, Gaius gives nothing like a definition of *obligatio* (for discussion see Falcone 2011, 17). We might say that his primary reason for introducing the category of obligations into the institutional framework at this point has nothing to do with obligations themselves, but serves rather to provide a peg on which to hang the discussion of contracts and delicts.

Justinian's Institutes 3.13pr-2 are more forthcoming, though perhaps little more revealing:

> *Nunc transeamus ad obligationes …*
>
> *Omnium autem obligationum summa divisio in duo genera deducitur: namque aut civiles sunt aut praetoriae. Civiles sunt, quae aut legibus constitutae aut certe iure civili comprobatae sunt. Praetoriae sunt, quas praetor ex sua iurisdictione constituit, quae etiam honorariae vocantur.*
>
> *Sequens divisio in quattuor species deducitur: aut enim ex contractu sunt aut quasi ex contractu aut ex maleficio aut quasi ex maleficio.*
>
> Let us proceed to obligations …
>
> The basic division of all obligations is into two genera: for they are either civil or praetorian. Civil are those which are constituted by statutes or at least recognised by the *ius civile*. Praetorian are those which the praetor has established out of his own authority, which are also called honorary.
>
> The next division is into four species; for they arise from contract, or as if from contract, or from wrongdoing, or as if from wrongdoing.

The transition is the same as in Gaius' Institutes, from property to obligations, but we now have two *divisiones* of the sources of obligations, one formal and one substantive. It is the latter on which we should concentrate. Four types are given—from contract, as if from contract, from wrongdoing and as if from wrongdoing—adopting the same structural approach as Gaius but expanding the content. It is this fourfold classification that shapes Justinian's Institutes' subsequent treatment of the substance of personal obligations. Notwithstanding this expanded classification, however, in book IV of the Institutes personal actions are still treated as being derived from either contract or delict (Inst.4.6.1).

43.3 Definitions of *Obligatio*

As well as expanding the sources of *obligationes*, Justinian's Institutes (3.13pr) includes what we might take to be a definition of *obligatio*:

Obligatio est iuris vinculum, quo necessitate adstringimur alicuius solvendae rei, secundum nostrae civitatis iura.

An *obligatio* is a tie of law by which we are of necessity constrained to pay some thing according to the laws of our *civitas*.

As a workable definition of *obligatio* this looks less than ideal (Guarino 2000, 263). First of all, there appears to be some redundancy in the use of both *necessitate* and *adstringimur*: if we are constrained to do something, then we cannot but be constrained to do it of necessity. It may, however, be that the correct translation of the Latin is something like "An *obligatio* is a tie of law, whereby we are constrained by the necessity of paying some thing, according to the laws of our *civitas*", which would avoid this problem.[6] Secondly, taking the Latin at face value, the only thing that is described as the object of the *obligatio* is a payment, a handing over; there is no consideration that there might be an obligation to do something, an *obligatio faciendi*. Thirdly, the constraint is by the laws of our *civitas*, hardly the phrase to be used when describing the law of a world Empire. Moreover, since we have just learned that the *summa divisio* of *obligationes* is between those which arise from the *ius civile* and those which derive from the *ius honorarium*, the reference to the laws of our *civitas* cannot be a reference simply to the Roman *ius civile*, though it may reflect an earlier understanding according to which the term *obligatio* was only appropriate to relationships arising under the *ius civile* (Arangio-Ruiz 1960, 290). And fourthly, the focus on constraint or enforceability is too narrow to deal with the class of unenforceable natural obligations, something of which we know from elsewhere in the Roman legal corpus (see section 43.6). The definition, if we can call it that, has all the marks of having been lifted from a classical or immediately post-classical source, possibly from Papinian (to whom all but two of the Digest's uses of *vinculum* in the sense of an abstract bond are attributed) (see in particular Albanese 1984, 167), or possibly from Gaius' *Res Cottidianae*.[7] The latter is perhaps more likely; even leaving out stylistic considerations, it is easier to imagine Justinian's compilers having turned to the Gaian text than to Papinian to find their "definition". In any event, whatever its source, it has probably been decontextualised without much thought for its generality or its appropriateness to the sixth century rather than the second or third. If what was to follow was an analysis of the nature of *obligationes*, a definition of this sort would have been near disastrous, but as a preliminary to the discussion of the different *causae* it does no harm. It stresses the personal nature of contractual and delictual obligations and their associates, contrasting with the relationship between person and thing which characterised the law of property.

Of central importance to this definition, though, is the description of the *obligatio* bond as a tie *of law*. Other relationships dependent on trust, *fides*, might generate a bond between two people, but that bond was not a tie of law. It was not an *obligatio*. For the original author of the definition, be it Gaius or Papinian, it may be that the reflexive relationship

[6] Falcone 2003, 173.

[7] Falcone 2003, 3–71 (summarised conveniently in Falcone 2005, 67 available at http://www.dirittoestoria.it/iusantiquum/articles/Falcone-Officium-vincolo-origini-definizione-obligatio.htm, accessed 29 January 2016). Attributions to Florentinus or Modestinus lack solid grounding, and the suggestion of Arangio-Ruiz that it is a post-classical gloss on Gaius' Institutes (Arangio-Ruiz 1945, 2.56) has not found favour.

between *obligatio* and *actio* may have been essential. If this were so, *obligatio* might perhaps then have referred exclusively to an enforceable relationship and hence have excluded any idea of natural obligation.[8] It does not absolutely follow that the *vinculum iuris* necessitated an *actionable* obligation, though; so long as the bond was one which had legal ramifications it could be described as a tie of law.

A rather different definition, or description, is attributed in the Digest to Paul:

> *Obligationum substantia non in eo consistit, ut aliquod corpus nostrum aut servitutem nostram faciat, sed ut alium nobis obstringat ad dandum aliquid vel faciendum vel praestandum.*
>
> The substance of obligations does not consist in that it makes some property or servitude ours, but it binds another person to us to give, do or be responsible for something. (D.44.7.3pr)

The contrast with property is here made absolutely explicit. The *obligatio* does not make something ours, but constrains another person; it is therefore personal rather than real. It does not have as its object only a payment, but a transfer, a doing or a standing responsible for something, thereby avoiding the narrowness of the definition in the Institutes. The localism inherent in the reference to *civitas* in the Institutional definition is absent, and there is no verbal redundancy as may have occurred with the inclusion of *necessitate*. Most importantly, though, while the definition in the Institutes has a very firm focus on the person who is obliged, Paul's approach is more two-sided: another person is bound *to us* to give or do something.

This double aspect of the noun *obligatio* is fundamental. It can be seen from the standpoint of the beneficiary of the obligation, the person who is under the obligation, or both. Moreover, it has the capacity to be reified, so that the relationship between person and person can be seen as a thing, an asset of the beneficiary and a liability of the person obliged.

43.4 *Obligatio* as Relationship

Although the *obligatio* connotes a relationship between persons, in a specific context it might refer to that relationship from the standpoint of the person bound. This is clear, for example, in D.39.2.18.5. One person makes a *stipulatio* with his neighbour that his eaves might project over the neighbour's land, and then buys a second property. It is said that the original *stipulatio* (probably) does not apply to the second house, lest the *obligatio promissionis* be increased.[9] When the *senatus consultum Velleianum* regulated *obligationes* of women, it was transparently referring to their being bound (D.16.1.2.1). Similarly, a transfer of a slave to be freed by the transferee after the death of the transferor is said to create an *obligatio*, i.e. an obligation on the transferee to free the slave (D.17.1.27.1); and a *fideiussor* can fall under an *obligatio* (e.g. D.13.4.8). On entry into a *hereditas*, the heir

[8] Natural obligations are discussed in section 43.6.

[9] The text deals with the slightly more complex application of this, to the case where a *stipulatio* is made to two co-owners.

takes on (*suscipit*) the *obligationes* of an inheritance (D.4.2.17), a procurator may take on the *obligationes* of his principal (D.3.3.67), a son or slave should be relieved of an *obligatio* (D.15.1.11.2), and more generally a person may be freed from an *obligatio* (e.g. D.23.3.58.1). An *obligatio* could be transferred from *fideiussor* to freedman (D.4.3.7.8), or from a solvent to an insolvent debtor (D.4.4.27.3), or a noxal *obligatio* can be transferred where another person confesses that he or she is the owner of a slave whose wrong is the basis of a claim (D.11.1.4pr). When it is said that an *obligatio* would be made more burdensome, it cannot be anything but the burden to the person who is under the obligation that can be meant (D.45.1.99pr). Finally, although it is a new relationship that is created when an *obligatio* is novated, the focus is on the new liability that comes into existence rather than on the new right (e.g. D.12.1.21).

Equally, the *obligatio* can be seen from the standpoint of the beneficiary. A *stipulatio*, for example, could be described as an act to obtain an *obligatio* (*actus ad obligationem comparandam*) (D.12.1.2.5); it is something from which the stipulator acquires an *obligatio* (D.45.1.95), though where the name of one's son is added as an alternative payee no *obligatio* is created for him thereby (D.45.1.56.2). There are frequent references in the Digest to the acquisition of an *obligatio*;[10] a slave acquires *obligationes* for his master,[11] an *obligatio* of mortgage cannot be acquired through a free person (D.13.7.11.6), where one person lends money in the name of another an *obligatio* is acquired by the person in whose name the money is lent (D.12.1.9.8). An *obligatio* of the ancestor accrues to the heir (D.21.2.51.3), and if there are co-heirs the *obligatio* must be divided between them (D.38.1.15.1). Should the heir sell the *hereditas* he must transfer any *obligationes* he has created to the purchaser (D.18.4.2.8). That it was the beneficiary's side of the *obligatio* that was being referred to could be stressed by describing it as a *ius obligationis*, as something that could be sold (D.20.6.5.2).

Although references to *obligatio* normally refer primarily to one side of the relationship or the other, they might refer to the relationship itself. Hence, Ulpian (following Labeo) describes a contract as *ultro citroque obligatio* (D.50.16.19), stressing the bilaterality of the *obligatio*, and more specifically in the context of the contract of *commodatum* Paul writes of the *obligatio inter dandum accipiendumque* (D.13.6.17.3), thereby bringing into the foreground that the *obligatio* is a link between the two parties and not something that adheres to one of them or the other.

43.5 *Obligatio* as Thing

Although the *obligatio* was at its core a relationship between two parties, as a noun it was reified so that it was seen as an asset in the hands of the beneficiary. In his Institutes, Gaius places *obligationes* in his list of incorporeal things, alongside inheritances, usufructs and servitudes; something that is repeated by Justinian (Inst.Gai.2.14; Inst. 2.2.2; similarly D.1.8.1.1). An *obligatio* therefore had a duration; it could be said to be born (D.16.3.26.2)

[10] e.g. D.45.1.126.2; D.45.1.141.3; D.45.3.1.2; D.46.3.22; D.22.1.11.1.

[11] D.45.3.28pr; D.13.5.5.10; D.45.3.2; D.23.3.46pr.

and to be extinguished or brought to an end.[12] It could endure or remain,[13] or it could be perpetuated (D.12.2.9.3). If a transaction was undone so that there was *restitutio in integrum*, a former *obligatio* could be restored (D.19.5.9). When a novation occurred it could be said that the *obligatio* had been changed (D.17.1.45.2), and as a thing it could be sold or transferred (D.20.6.5.2; D.45.1.76pr). Indeed, so proprietary was the *obligatio* that both Ulpian and Julian say that it can be made the subject of a *condictio*; where a promise had been made without a *causa* the promisor could bring a *condictio* to reclaim the *obligatio* itself, not the sum of money that had been promised (D.12.7.1pr; D.12.7.3).

As well, since it could be conceived of as a thing, an *obligatio* could be split into parts or divided up (D.46.8.17; D.46.1.26; D.46.1.27.4). It followed therefore that part of an *obligatio* could be released, leaving the remainder of the *obligatio* intact (D.32.37.4; D.34.3.7pr). It was easy to deal with co-heirs, since it could be said that an *obligatio* owed by or to the testator could be divided between them, each having or being liable for a share.[14] Exactly the same applied to co-ownership; when a promise was made to a co-owned slave, for example, the *obligatio* could be divided up among the co-owners (D.46.3.29). It is at this point that we can see the flexibility that is achieved by the use of the noun rather than the verb. No doubt it would have been possible to have reached the same results solely by using the verb, but it would hardly have been linguistically economical to do so (Daube 1969, 43–44).

Further than this, the use of the noun made it possible to formulate more sophisticated legal rules than would have been possible without it. Suppose Titius enters a contract to pay 100 to Maevius; there is now an *obligatio* for the 100. Subsequently he undertakes to pay the 100, a *constitutum debiti*; there is now a further *obligatio* to pay the 100, so that there are two *obligationes* to pay the same sum. Payment of the 100 will discharge both *obligationes*, but it is held by Ulpian that *litis contestatio* in an action on the initial contract did not destroy the *obligatio* arising under the *constitutum debiti* and vice versa (D.13.5.18.3). The two *obligationes* to pay the same sum of money can to that extent be treated as independent of each other. In the same way, a person could have a right under a will and under a *stipulatio* against the same person for the same thing: here again it could be said that there were two *obligationes*, each independent of the other (D.44.7.18).

43.6 *Obligatio* and *Actio*

The rather rough and ready definition of *obligatio* as a *vinculum iuris* found in Justinian's Institutes, a tie of law by which we are of necessity constrained to pay some thing according to the laws of our *civitas*, brings into the foreground the relationship between *obligatio* and *actio*. If the effect of the *obligatio* was that one person could be forced to pay (or do) something by the beneficiary, this would be achieved by the beneficiary bringing an action against the person under the *obligatio*. To that extent, therefore, there was an intimate connection between *obligatio* and *actio*, the one being a corollary of the other.

[12] D.20.6.6pr; D.34.3.21.1; D.45.1.140.2; D.42.6.3pr; D.23.3.76.

[13] D.17.1.26pr, D.23.3.68; D.12.6.26.4 (and many other examples).

[14] D.7.1.5; D.10.2.25.10; D.10.2.25.13; D.38.1.15.1; D.45.1.2.3.

So intimate was this link that book 44.7 of the Digest has as its title *De Obligationibus et Actionibus.*

Yet it is not quite accurate to say simply that *obligatio* is the correlative of *actio.* As Gaius states, the connection is between obligations and *personal* actions:

> *In personam actio est, qua agimus, quotiens litigamus cum aliquo, qui nobis vel ex contractu vel ex delicto obligatus est, id est, cum intendimus dare facere praestare oportere.*
>
> An action *in personam* is one in which we proceed against someone who is obliged to us either from contract or delict, an action, that is, in which we claim that he ought to give, do, or be responsible for something. (Inst.Gai.4.2)

Moreover, it is only an intimate relationship, not an equivalence. The *obligatio* gives rise to the *actio*, the *actio* is grounded on the *obligatio.* There is, therefore, a separation in time between the two; the purpose of the *actio* is to obtain performance of the *obligatio* and thereby to dissolve it. This is an important aspect of the relationship between the two ideas. While the *obligatio* exists, as well as the legal relationship between the parties there is a social relationship of dominance and subordination. The inevitable period of time between the creation of the *obligatio* and its dissolution (whether it be by *actio* or by performance) marks the continuance of this social relationship (cf. Mauss 2002, 45–47). The *obligatio* might continue indefinitely, it might never be dissolved, thereby stretching the duration of the power relationship. It may even be the case that the debtor might sometimes be expected *not* to perform, since it might not be appropriate for the person in the subordinate position to determine when the relationship should end (Veyne 1987, 146).

The establishment of this distinction between *actio* and *obligatio* was significant, for it enabled the Romans to develop a type of obligation that was not actionable; the so-called natural obligation, *obligatio naturalis.* Although no action lay to enforce the obligation it was nonetheless owed, so that no *condictio indebiti* lay to recover it back if it was in fact performed. Though the language of natural obligation might have been applicable to situations actionable under the *ius gentium* rather than the *ius civile* (D.45.1.126.2; D.50.17.84.1), its importance for our present purposes lies in its applicability to situations where there was only a social duty. Hence a freedman who performed day labour for his patron in the erroneous belief that he was under a legal liability to do so could not bring an action for the value of the services: although there was no liability at law there was a social duty—*officium*—to perform (D.12.6.26.12). A woman erroneously believing herself liable to give a dowry does so; she may not recover it back since there was an underlying motive of *pietas* which still existed even when the mistaken belief was removed (D.12.6.32.2). A person who borrowed money could not reclaim it if he was sued for it and paid after *litis contestatio* but before judgement, since even if he was absolved in the action the natural obligation would have remained.[15] Although there are insufficient texts to enable us to delimit the concept with precision, the idea of *obligatio naturalis* meant that it was possible for the Roman jurists to construct a non-legal sense of *obligatio*, giving secondary legal effect to such Roman virtues as *fides, honor* and *pietas.*

[15] D.12.6.60. For the classicality of these passages, all referring to the views of Julian, see Landolt 2000.

43.7 *Obligatio* and Contract

As has been seen, the words *obligatio* and *obligare* were derived from the root *ligare*, meaning to bind. In classical law the binding might stem from any source that generated a claim *in personam*. Its breadth and lack of focus are indicated in passing by Ulpian in D.5.1.19.1:

> *Si quis tutelam vel curam vel negotia vel argentariam vel quid aliud, unde obligatio oritur, certo loci administravit: etsi ibi domicilium non habuit, ibi se debebit defendere et, si non defendat neque ibi domicilium habeat, bona possideri patietur.*
>
> If a person has administered a tutelage, a curacy, business activities, banking, or anything else from which an *obligatio* arises, in a certain place, he will have to defend himself there even if he did not have his home there, and if he neither defends nor has his home there his goods will be seized.

More specifically it might flow from a delict (e.g. D.4.5.7.1; D.9.4.19pr; D.44.7.4), from the giving of a dowry (D.4.2.21.3; D.23.5.10; D.24.3.66.5), from a will (D.34.1.22.2), from a legacy (D.30.82pr) or from a judgement (D.15.1.3.11).

Above all, an *obligatio* might flow from a contract, so much so that it could sometimes be treated as synonymous with contract. This is clearest in Ulpian's description of the nature of contract as something which stemmed from an agreement:

> *Conventionis nomen generale est, ut eleganter dicat Pedius nullum esse contractum, nullam obligationem, quae non habeat in se conventionem, sive re sive verbis fiat: nam et stipulatio, quae verbis fit, nisi habeat consensum, nulla est.*
>
> The term agreement (*conventio*) is general, so that Pedius elegantly says that there is no contract, no *obligatio*, that does not have an agreement within it, whether it arises by delivery or words: for even the *stipulatio*, which arises by words, is void unless there is agreement. (D.2.14.1.3)

Here, unequivocally, there is an identification of *obligatio* with contract; and even if the reference to *obligatio* is interpolated (and there is no strong reason to think that it is), the text shows that someone at some time believed them to be equivalent, and that this was not so outlandish that it was excised by Justinian's compilers. While it is, of course, nonsense within the institutional structure to say that every *obligatio* is based on agreement—most obviously those obligations which arise out of delict have no element at all of *agreement* within them—there is nonetheless a close connection between *obligatio* and contract. Tryphoninus, for example, in the context of a sale, writes of liability having arisen out of a contract or an *obligatio* of whatever sort (*ex contractu et qualiquali obligatione a debitore interposita*) on the part of the debtor (D.20.5.12.1). And when it is said that a slave acquires an *obligatio* for his master (section 43.4) it must be a contract which is at the forefront of the mind; in other situations where a master might become the beneficiary of an obligation through the involvement of a slave—for example, where the slave was injured and the master thereby had a claim under the third chapter of the *lex Aquilia*—it would not really be appropriate to speak of the slave acquiring an *obligatio* at all. Moreover, it is not uncommon to find an *obligatio* identified with the contract which underlies it, as where Pomponius writes of an *obligatio empti et venditi* (D.18.1.6.1), or an obligation arising out of a loan is called an *obligatio mutui* (D.12.1.2.2), an obligation arising out of a mandate an *obligatio mandati.*[16] Most common is the *obligatio pignoris*;[17] so much so that *obligatio* standing alone might refer to a mortgage, where it is the land that is bound rather than just the person.[18] The similitude is implicitly visible when *obligationes* round off a list of contracts: *ab emptione venditione, locatione conductione ceterisque similibus obligationibus* (D.2.14.58). In other words, we can point here to an equivalence between *contractus* and *obligatio contracta* (Fiori 2013, 40, 47).

43.8 Conclusion

This apparently close link between *obligatio* and contract may be more than an accident flowing from the survival of sources. In Akkadian and Hittite, for example, the abstract nouns cognate with the verb denoting the act of binding refer specifically to contracts or treaties;[19] and in Hittite the active sense implicit in the verb form is carried across into the noun to the extent that it might refer to a treaty imposed on a vassal state and not (or not only) to one founded on an agreement (Bryce 1999, 51). It may be, then, that in Latin too there was originally a focal sense of active binding behind the use of the noun, and hence an association with the voluntary act of contracting. Whether or not this is so—and it is no more than speculation—it remains the case that the Roman's development of the *obligatio* in the sense of any legal bond between persons represents a major development in legal thought—one which survives almost unthinkingly into present-day legal discourse.

Bibliography

Albanese, B. (1984). "Papiniano e la definizione di *obligatio* in I.3.13.pr." *Studia et Documenta Historiae Iuris* 50: 167–187.

Arangio-Ruiz, V. 1945. "Noterelle Gaiane," in *Festschrift für Leopold Wenger zu seinem 70. Geburtstag*. Munich. 2.56

Arangio-Ruiz, V. 1960[14]. *Istituzioni di diritto romano*. Naples.

Biscardi, A. 1982. *Diritto greco antico*. Milan.

Bryce, T. 1999. *The kingdom of the Hittites*. Oxford.

Buckland, W. W. and Stein, P. 1963[3]. *A Text-book of Roman law: from Augustus to Justinian*. Cambridge.

Daube, D. 1969. *Roman law: linguistic, social and philosophical aspects*. Edinburgh.

Ernout, A. and Meillet, A. 1959[4]. *Dictionnaire étymologique de la langue Latine*. Paris.

Falcone, G. 2003. Obligatio est iuris vinculum. Turin.

[16] D.17.1.1pr; D.17.1.22.4; D.17.1.32; D.17.1.59.5; D.19.2.52.

[17] e.g. D.13.7.11.6; D.13.7.24pr; D.15.4.3; D.20.1.23.1; D.20.1.29pr; D.20.1.34.1; D.20.3.4, D.20.4.21pr; D.20.6.11.1 (note the contrast with *actio personalis*); D.24.1.7.6; D.27.9.3pr; D.39.5.35.1; D.46.3.38.5; D.46.3.69; D.48.10.28. Already in the first century AD: *lex municipii Malacitani* (*CIL* II 1964).

[18] D.20.1.6; D.20.1.8; D.20.1.26.1; D.27.9.3.1; D.27.9.5.10; D.27.9.5.13.

[19] *Chicago Assyrian Dictionary*, s.v. riksu; *Hittite Etymological Dictionary*, s.v. ishiyal-, ishiul-.

Falcone, G. (2005). "*Officium* e vincolo giuridico: alle origini della definizione classica delle'*obligatio*" *Ius Antiquum* 16: 67, available at http://www.dirittoestoria.it/iusantiquum/articles/Falcone-Officium-vincolo-origini-definizione-obligatio.htm, accessed 19 March 2016.

Falcone, G. 2011. "Sistematiche Gaiane e definizione di *obligatio*." In L. Capogrossi Colognesi and M. F. Cursi, eds., Obligatio-*obbligazione: un confronto interdisciplinare*. Naples. 17–52.

Fiori, R. 2013. "The Roman conception of contract." In T. A. J. McGinn ed., *Obligations in Roman law: past, present, and future*. Michigan. 4–75.

Gaudemet, J. (2000). "Naissance d'une notion juridique: les débuts de l''Obligation' dans le droit de la Rome antique." *Archives de philosophie du droit* 44: 19–32. (also published in Iuris Vincula: *Studi in Onore di Mario Talamanca* (Naples 2001), 4.135).

Guarino, A. (2000). "*Obligatio est iuris vinculum*." *Studia et Documenta Historiae et Iuris* 66: 263–268.

Jolowicz, H. F. (1952). "*Obligatio* and *actio*." *Law Quarterly Review* 68: 469–480.

Landolt, P. L. 2000. Naturalis obligatio *and bare social duty*. Cologne.

Mauss, M. 2002. *The gift: the form and reason for exchange in archaic societies*, transl. W. D. Halls. London.

Veyne, P. ed. 1987. *A History of private life: from pagan Rome to Byzantium*, transl. A. Goldhammer. Cambridge.

CHAPTER 44

CONTRACTS, COMMERCE AND ROMAN SOCIETY

ROBERTO FIORI

44.1 Introduction: A Leading Case between the Second and First Century BC

In his *De officiis*, Cicero recalls a trial of the second–first century BC dealing with the disclosure of information in the sale of a house. According to the XII Tables, the seller was held liable to a double penalty for false statements pronounced during the formal act of conveyance (*mancipatio*). A certain T. Claudius Centumalus, having received from the augurs an order to demolish those parts of his house that hindered their observations, put the house up for sale without informing the purchaser about said order. The buyer P. Calpurnius Lanarius, having concluded the sale, then received the same notice from the priests, and having discovered that the buyer had been aware of the order before the offer for sale, summoned him to court. M. Porcius Cato (trib. pl. 99 BC) was appointed as the judge and decided that, according to good faith, the seller should make good the loss to the buyer (Cic. *Off.* 3.66–67; Fiori 2011b, 319–323).

This was clearly a leading case. With the passage of time, the jurists apparently established that the seller was liable not only for false declarations, as provided for in the XII Tables, but also for mere non-disclosure, because such behaviour was against good faith, and the duties of the parties in a sale were supposed to comply with fair conduct.

What is interesting to us is that Cicero recognises a continuous progress from the rules of archaic law to the more modern principles of the contract of sale. What is more, the duties of the parties were not constructed on the basis of an abstract and theoretical structure, but rather taking into account the principle of good faith—a legal concept intimately linked to the social and ethical values of Roman culture.

To understand the Roman idea of contract, one must therefore consider at least three major factors: the dependence of classical law on the archaic legal system; the connection between law, society and culture; and finally the role of the jurists' personalities in the development of law. These factors are often underestimated in textbooks that concentrate more on illustrating the contractual "system" than on its "history" (see e.g. the excellent work by Grosso 1963).

44.2 Before Contract: Archaic Society, Farming and Early Commerce (Eighth–Fourth Century BC)

We must start from the Roman idea of law, which was not positivistic. The Romans inherited from their Indo-European past the idea of an order of the universe that permeated both nature and the relationship between gods and men. This order simultaneously had both a religious and a juridical meaning, so that the priests who studied it did not have the perception that they were creating something anew, but rather discovering its rules. The legal system of the city was a mere fragment of this order. The Romans had their own internal rules, but this did not mean that the rules of other peoples were not perceived as "law". The main difference was, however, that foreign law had no effect within the system set for the *Quirites*, the *ius Quiritium*, and was not protected by the judicial organisation of the city, based on the so-called *legis actiones*. Alongside the *ius Quiritium* there were a number of legal institutions available to foreigners, called *ius gentium*, which were "law", but were not protected by the city authorities.[1]

Within the *ius Quiritium*, an economic transaction could be legally effective only when taking certain specific forms. First, there were acts that did not take the formation and the performance of the transaction into account, but only its final result, when coincidental with a transfer of property. When the object was of no particular value (*res nec mancipi*), simple delivery (*traditio*) could let ownership of the property pass from one party to another (on this point see also Capogrossi Colognesi, ch. 40). Although we have no proof in our sources, it is highly probable that conveyance had to be justified by a transaction of some kind, even if it was not enforceable. Another way to transfer ownership was to start a fictitious litigation before the magistrate, the acquirer declaring his right of property without being contradicted by the other party (*in iure cessio*): this form of conveyance was applicable also to the most valuable items (*res mancipi*) and took no account of the agreement between the parties.

In the second place there were acts that, although formal, were adaptable to a much larger number of arrangements than the simple transfer of property. The first of these acts was called *mancipatio*, and consisted in the weighing of the copper or bronze (*aes*) agreed as price for the acquiring of power over a valuable thing (*res mancipi*) or a person, performed in the presence of (at least) five witnesses and of a man holding the scales (Inst. Gai.1.119). The second was a formal promise to give or do something, called *sponsio*. This act created a duty to perform only on the promisor, but the act needed the participation of

[1] I have tried to demonstrate this assumption in many works: see particularly Fiori 2011b, 97–120. The common idea that the *ius gentium* is a development of the *ius honorarium* has no justification in the sources and is the product of the positivistic culture of modern scholars: Fiori 1998–1999, 165–197.

the promisee, since it was structured as a question and an answer—e.g. "do you promise to give?" (*dari spondes?*), "I promise" (*spondeo*) (Inst.Gai.3.92).

Both acts seem very ancient. As for the *mancipatio*, the use of metal as exchange tool can be traced back, in Italy, to the Early Bronze Age (2300–1700 BC; Peroni 1996, 109–110). As far as *sponsio* is concerned, it is considered to be one of the most original creations of Roman law (Kaser 1971, 538), but it was quite similar to (and maybe historically derived from) an oath (acknowledged by Kaser 1971, 168), that is, to one of the most widespread institutions of ancient law, which in Roman law preserves traces of its Indo-European past (Benveniste 1969, 2:111–122, 209–215).

The formality of these acts has often been linked to religious reasons and to a supposed rigidity of the system. But it should instead be explained with reference to specific features of archaic society; namely, a small number of transactions, an economy based on agriculture and livestock farming, a lack of written records and oral forms of transmission of memory. The more solemn an act, the more easily it could be remembered by witnesses, who had to be present in a *mancipatio* to ensure its validity, but who were certainly also asked by the parties to assist them in a *sponsio* in order to provide future proof. The enforcement of the duties created by these acts could in fact rely only on the *fides* of the parties and of the witnesses, their "credit", on the extent of their trustworthiness within society. This had very serious consequences, since the proven breach of *fides* deprived the guilty of every reliability and therefore substantially, if not formally, of every right (Fiori 2011a, 104–106).

Mancipatio and *sponsio* were formal but not rigid, being adaptable to a variety of purposes. This is evident for the *sponsio*, which could be filled with every kind of content, from the giving of things to the performance of activities. It could even give rise to a substantially bilateral relation through the mutual exchange of promises.[2] This is true also for the *mancipatio*. Owing to the utterances (*nuncupationes*) pronounced during the ceremony, the parties could clarify the specific purpose of the act (Corbino 1994, 16–37): such as to confer to the husband the power over his wife (*coemptio*) (Inst.Gai.1.123; Boeth. on Cic. *Top*. 3.14), to let the *pater* appoint an heir (*testamentum per aes et libram*) (Inst.Gai.2.104) or to surrender the guilty slave or son to the victim of a delict as a form of compensation (*noxae deditio*) (Inst.Gai.1.140, 4.79). Moreover—what is more important for us—this act could grant legal value to transactions that classical law will define as "contracts". For example, if the act was aimed to confer the power over a thing or a slave for an indefinite time, it created an effect similar to the classical sale (Inst.Gai.1.119). If, on the other hand, the power was given only for a fixed time—for example, when the *pater* gave his son in exchange for price for some time,[3] or bound himself to work for the *accipiens* to guarantee a loan until the debt was paid (*nexum*)[4]—the effect was similar to the classical lease or loan.

In other words, economic transactions were already roughly differentiated—in the XII Tables we find verbs like *vendere, emere, locare*[5]—but their specific features could be relevant only if made explicit during the ritual through formal utterances. The will of the

[2] It is doubtful (and not attested in the sources) whether the parties could link the promises to each other by making one promise conditional upon the fulfilment of the other. For criticisms of this view see Arangio-Ruiz 1954, 60.

[3] XII Tab. 4.2 (*FIRA*). [4] XII Tab. 6.1.

[5] Cf. XII Tab. 12.1 (*emere, vendere, locare*). See also Tab. 4.2b (*vendere*), 7.11, and 7.12.

parties was important, but of secondary concern: what mattered in the end was the effect of the formal act. And if in the *mancipatio*, the effect was the bestowing of a power on a party, in the *sponsio* the promise of a future activity created an *obligatio*, a duty to perform arose.

We said above that alongside the *ius Quiritium* was the *ius gentium*, open to foreigners. It is likely that this part of the law had already found a protection outside the tribunal of the magistrate at a very ancient time. In the markets held in Rome, a role was played by a subject who acted as broker, witness, adviser, and arbitrator, and was named *arbiter* maybe after a Punic loan, already during the Etruscan Monarchy (Martino 1986). He was probably asked by the litigants to settle their disputes on the basis of commercial practices, and this developed a corpus of precedents which formed for each type of bargain a set of rules that was felt dutiful for the parties to respect.

44.3 The New Roman Economy and the Development of the Formulary Procedure (Fourth–Second Centuries BC)

The new context established by Roman Imperial action in Italy significantly changed the horizon of Roman economy and society. The institutions of archaic law and their reliance on the personal *fides* of the parties and of their witnesses were no longer suitable for a city that was becoming the centre of the world and was involved in international trade where members of different communities had no awareness of each other's "credit". The formalism of the *ius Quiritium*, the *raison d'être* of which lay in the need to preserve the memory of the transaction, lost its utility, while the increase in international trade, which is to say, commerce between citizens and non-citizens, brought to the fore issues unresolvable using pre-existing forms.

Magisterial protection was granted by means of a new form of civil procedure called *per formulas*. There is no general agreement on how it came into being: in my opinion, the praetor followed two different paths.[6] On the one hand, he created judicial protection for the institutions that had nothing to do with the *ius*. At the beginning of his annual term of office, he issued an edict where he promised to grant protection to certain cases listed in the document alongside the corresponding remedies. Since the claims of the parties were not based on *ius*, the judge was not required to "reveal the law" (*iudicare*) as in the archaic procedure, but only to confirm the promise of the defendant to pay the plaintiff a sum of money corresponding to the value of the litigation if the facts submitted by the plaintiff appeared to be true (*condemnare*); or on the contrary to confirm the commitment of the plaintiff to consider the defendant freed from his promise if the facts appeared not to be

[6] See Fiori 2003. It is generally held that only one model of procedure existed, but according to some authors it came into existence from the development of the *legis actiones*, and to others from the *formulae in factum conceptae* created by the praetor in his edict. For an overview of these doctrines see Talamanca 1987, 25–28; Kaser and Hackl 1996, 153–161.

true (*absolvere*). This set of remedies created by the praetor had the effect of giving rise to an entire new section of "law" that was called "law (based on the power) of the magistrate" (*ius honorarium, ius praetorium*) because it left untouched the "true" law of the city, called *ius civile*.

On the other hand, the praetor created judicial protection for the institutions of *ius gentium*. Since these were also perceived as part of the *ius civile*, the judge could also in this case theoretically "reveal the law" (*iudicare*). However, being not part of the *ius Quiritium*, these claims could not be introduced in a trial *per legis actiones*. The praetor therefore asked the defendant to fictitiously confess his debt, agreeing to choose an *arbiter* to determine what was due to the plaintiff. The confession was conditioned to the test of the claims of the plaintiff or of the justifications of the defendant. If the test resulted in favour of the defendant, his confession could not be taken into account by the judge and he was therefore freed from the claims of the plaintiff. Otherwise, he was bound to his confession and, having confessed a debt relevant in the *ius civile*, the procedure had the same civil effects of the *legis actiones*. By this means, the institutions of *ius gentium* received the protection of the institutions of *ius Quiritium*.

These different procedures had different grounds. The claims of *ius gentium* were based on "law", and the protection in any case was granted by a magistrate. By contrast, the claims of *ius honorarium* could be admitted only if the magistrate granted a trial for that specific case (normally, by virtue of having promised to do so in his edict). While the latter were listed one by one in the edict, so that the claim should perfectly fit with the description of the promised protection, the former were granted without any specific promise. In other words, the honorary actions had to be shaped as "typical", while the civil ones could be treated generally as claims based on a civil *obligatio*.

44.4 The Origins of the Contractual System: An Undifferentiated Protection?

As far as we know, the classical contracts were all part of the *ius civile*. Since at the beginning typicality was a specific feature of the *ius honorarium*, and since a discussion about the typicality of contracts can be found in the works of the jurists only starting from the second century AD, it is probable that, until the end of the Republic, contracts were differentiated from one another only on an economical level, but that from the juristic point of view they were generically *obligationes contractae*—that is, were *obligationes* whose specific feature was to be based on an agreement. This being granted, it becomes probable that until the end of the Republic contracts were protected by means of two general civil actions, both derived from the archaic procedure *per legis actiones*. We can try to reconstruct their structure from the classical actions derived from them.

The first was an *actio certi* called *condictio*, which was used to claim a fixed sum of money or a determined thing (*certum*). The second was an *actio incerti*, used for claims undefined in quantity. The two actions were granted by the praetor according to different *causae*, which corresponded to the various contracts. The *actio certi* did not change according to the claims involved; the *actio incerti* could take two forms. The judge could be asked to condemn or absolve the defendant according to what he owed to the plaintiff (*oportere*), or to what he owed to the plaintiff in relation to good faith (*oportere ex fide bona*). Good faith was a novelty, having arisen in the commercial practice of the new Roman economy, and was quite different from the notion of *fides*. The latter, referring to the specific "credit" of the subject, could operate in a narrow community, where everyone had his status and could lose it after the breach of the *fides*. The former, on the other hand, was a fictitious and conventional *fides*, based on the behavioural paradigm of the respectable, "good" people (*boni*): in the confusing and ever-changing world of international trade, an objective and abstract parameter was needed, one that could be applied to and used by people who belonged to different communities and came in contact only occasionally. "Good faith" was not, however, an ethical principle opposed to the law, but instead a standard of economic rationality in the formation and performance of the contract. Therefore it helped in the judicial reconstruction of the content of the obligation, taking into consideration all the implied terms of the contract as arisen in the international markets, even if they were not made explicit by the parties in the agreement or in the trial (D.19.1.11.1; Fiori 2011a).

Around the second century BC, a *lex Aebutia* stated that all trials could have civil effects when taking place at Rome, between Romans, and with a Roman *iudex unus*. After this reform, the fiction that the second type of formulary procedure (described in section 44.3) rested on became unnecessary. The first type of trial could indeed at this point also have civil effects, and the Romans chose to use it to protect claims under *ius civile* that were formerly protected by the *legis actiones*. Gradually, the one and only civil procedure became the first type of formulary procedure described above (section 44.3), which is to say, the procedure that requested "typical" actions (Fiori 2003). This is probably what shaped the Roman contractual system as "typical".

44.5 The "Typical" Contractual System (Second–First Centuries BC)

Owing to a general lack of evidence, we know very little about the work of the jurists of the third–second centuries BC. From scattered references in the Digest and the evidence from the literary sources, we are led to believe that at this time a great amount of work was already being done.

The sources give us examples of the activity of the jurists in answering legal questions (*respondere*) and in giving assistance, particularly in drafting documents (*cavere*). In both cases, the work of the jurists is already very complex (Talamanca 1981, 15–39, 304–354). As for *respondere*, Sextus Aelius Paetus Catus (cos. 198 BC) asserted that in the sale of a slave, if the delay in delivery was due to the buyer, the seller was entitled to claim expenses for food before an *arbiter* (D.19.1.38.1). M. Porcius Cato Licinianus (192–152 BC) faced the problem of what happens in the case of the death of the debtor who had promised to pay a penalty if the obligation was not performed, and where one of his co-heirs had violated the promise (D.45.1.4.1). M. Iunius Brutus (praet. 142 BC) dealt with the right assigned to the vendor not to sell the object if he received a better offer within a given time (D.18.2.13pr).

As for cautelary jurisprudence, we have some formulas reproduced by M. Porcius Cato the Elder (234–149 BC) and by M. Terentius Varro in their works "On agriculture", some of them taken from the *Libri actionum* written by the jurist Manius Manilius (cos. 149 BC). In these we find examples of letting and hiring aimed at the completion of a specific task or at the simple provision of services, and examples of the sale of the produce of the land for grazing, of wine and of livestock, often connected with the use of *stipulationes* as forms of warranty.[7]

Until the end of the second and the beginning of the first century BC, we find no evidence of what could be called a "system". It is only in the work of Q. Mucius Scaevola (*d.*82 BC) that we find the first classification of the *obligationes contractae*, according to the way they arise: pronouncing specific words (*verbis*); performing acts that do not require words (*re*); or on the basis of the sole agreement (*consensu*).[8] This is a very important scheme: it is adopted first by Gaius as a didactic classification of contracts and later by the Justinianic *Institutiones*.[9]

At this point, we are able to supply a brief picture of the "system". There were two different types of loan, both coming into being by the delivery of a thing (*re*). The first was called *mutuum*, and concerned the lending of money and other fungible things to be consumed by the borrower, who became their owner, and who was obliged to return items of the same type, quantity and quality. The second was called *commodatum*, and was the loan of a thing—generally non-fungible—for use: the borrower was a mere *detentor* and should return the very same thing received by the lender (Pastori 1954). The other *obligationes re contractae* were *depositum*, where a thing was delivered to be kept in custody (Gandolfi 1976); *fiducia*, which obliged the person who had received a thing by *mancipatio* or *in iure cessio* for fiduciary reasons, to convey it back according to the agreement (Noordraven 1999; Fercia 2012); *pignus*, which created a debt for the creditor who had received a thing as pledge, namely the obligation to give back the thing after the guaranteed obligation expired.

The *obligationes verbis contractae* pivoted around *stipulatio*, which was the *verborum obligatio* par excellence. It was identical to the archaic *sponsio* but could be performed also by foreigners, who were allowed to pronounce verbs other than *spondeo*. The *obligatio* arose from the words of the promisor (*verbis*), and this latter was the only one bound to it. For this reason, the content of the obligation was determined in strict adherence to the pronounced *verba*, and therefore facts concerning the underlying will of the parties could be taken into consideration only by means of an express judicial defence (*exceptio*).[10] The other contracts—the promise of the freedman to work for his *patronus* (*promissio*

[7] Cat. *Agr.* 146–150; Varro *Rust.* 2.2.5–6; 2.3.5; 2.4.5; 2.5.10–11. On these see Cardilli 1995, 63–133 and Fiori 1999, 24–45, both with bibliography.

[8] D.46.3.80. On the fragment and its problems see especially Cannata 1970, 213–235. We know that Mucius was the first to order the subject matter of *ius civile* according to genera (D.1.2.2.41), but since, in this fragment, his attention was concentrated more on the *solvere* than on the *contrahere obligationem* (Fiori 2007, 1955–1974), it is possible that the distinction was even earlier.

[9] Gaius also includes *obligationes litteris contractae*: these were probably already in Mucius' text, but were likely deleted by the compilers of the Digest.

[10] The problem of the relevance of the *conventio* in the *stipulatio* is much more complex: see Talamanca 1978, 195–266.

iurata liberti), and the promise to give a dowry (*dotis dictio*)—were merely variations of the *stipulatio*.

Owing to the general lack of importance of written documents in Roman law, the *obligationes litteris contractae* were simple annotations on the *pater familias'* account book of an already existent debt, that gave rise to an obligation in favour of a creditor (*nomina transcripticia*): in this way, a non-literal contract might be transformed into a literal one (*transcriptio a re in personam*), or a substitution might be effected in respect of the parties to a contract (*transcriptio a persona in personam*).

The *obligationes consensu contractae* were both very complex and important. *Emptio venditio* (sale) was the exchange of a thing and a price (*pretium*), usually consisting in money; it is, however, probable that during the Republic the mutual exchange of things (*permutatio*, barter) was also considered a form of sale. *Emptio venditio* did not transfer civil-law ownership: *dominium* could pass only by means of a separate act of conveyance that coincided with the archaic institutions of *mancipatio, traditio* or *in iure cessio*. Rather, in keeping with the nature of the Roman contract as *obligatio contracta*, sale had effect only in the law of obligations: when the buyer was a citizen, it created the duty to convey civil-law ownership of the thing (*dominium ex iure Quiritium*); when conducted with a foreigner, it created only the duty to deliver the thing (*tradere possessionem*).[11]

Locatio conductio is usually translated as letting and hiring, but the name of the contract should not mislead the modern reader. It was the only bilateral long-term contract the Romans knew, so that it comprised all transactions involving the exchange between the enjoyment of a thing or of a personal activity, and a price (*merces*) usually consisting in money—but, once again, it is probable that during the Republic also the mutual exchange of enjoyments was considered as a form of letting and hiring (Fiori 1999, 228–241). Therefore the Romans spoke of *locare conducere* every time they were dealing with transactions where a price was paid for the use of a thing, for the performance of daily work, for the construction of a house, for the transportation of goods or persons etc.[12]

In the contract of *societas* (partnership) the performances of the parties were not reciprocal, but consisted in the cooperation of all the *socii*. The partnership could be "general", concerning the whole estates of the partners (*societas omnium bonorum*) or all their future earnings (*societas omnium quae ex quaestu veniunt*), or be aimed at a specific purpose (*societas unius negotiationis*). Since it created obligations only for the parties of the contract, partnership had no relevance to the outside world: it had therefore nothing to do with the modern institution of "company", which is a legal subject created by the partnership of the parties.[13]

Mandatum (mandate) created on one party the obligation to carry out an activity asked by the other party. The origin of this contract lies in the aristocratic values of the Roman culture, which compelled a citizen to help his friends without any personal gain.

[11] On this duty see Pugliese 1991, 25–70. This theory must be preferred to the other according to which the duty of the vendor was only to deliver the thing (see particularly Arangio-Ruiz 1954, 162–181). It has recently been argued that the seller had the duty to allow the buyer the protection *in rem* granted to the owner in the different forms of civil, honorary and provincial property: Cristaldi 2007. On this contract see generally Talamanca 1993.

[12] On this contract see recently Mayer-Maly 1956; Fiori 1999; du Plessis 2012.

[13] On this contract see Wieacker 1936; Arangio-Ruiz 1950; Bona 1973; Santucci 1997.

It was therefore a gratuitous contract, as opposed to the contract of employment that—being reciprocal and onerous—took the form of a *locatio conductio* of the activity (*opera*) (Arangio-Ruiz 1949; Watson 1961; Nörr and Nishimura 1993).

As we said before, all these contracts were protected by a *condictio* when the claim concerned a *certum* (*mutuum, obligationes verbis*[14] or *litteris*[15] *contractae*), or by an *actio incerti* that often involved good faith (*stipulatio incerti, obligationes re contractae* other than *mutuum, obligationes consensu contractae*). It is particularly in this second field that Mucius' contribution is important. He deals with the problem of equality in exchange in partnership (Inst.Gai.3.149; Inst. 3.25.2; D.17.2.30) and sale (D. 18.1.66.1), and with good faith in transactions (Cic. *Off.* 3.70) also from the point of view of judicial defence (Cic. *Att.* 6.1.15).

This interest in the internal rules of contracts was shared by the most important personality of the following generation, Servius Sulpicius Rufus (*d.*43 BC). Servius concentrated his work on the structure of the contracts, stressing the value of contractual balance, which is one of the most prominent features of good faith.[16] Of particular interest are his positions on partnership—where he took a different view from Mucius about the shares of profits and losses, having however in mind the same idea of equality[17]—and on letting and hiring, where he formulated a rule, that would be repeated for centuries, according to which the decrease in value of a performance must be balanced by a corresponding reduction in the counter performance.[18]

44.6 The Innominate Contracts (First–Second Centuries AD)

As we have seen, the *prudentes* of the first century BC focused on the internal structure of contracts, and do not seem to have been concerned with the need to distinguish them from one another. In light of the common idea that one of the most characteristic features of classical contract law is its typicality—that is, that an agreement becomes a "contract" only when it corresponds to a specific type or form—this should seem quite strange. But if we consider that the sources of the third–second centuries BC do not draw a clear distinction

[14] The *actio operarum* was a form of *condictio*; we are not informed about the action for the *dotis dictio*: for the plausibility of the *condictio* see Talamanca 1990, 564.

[15] Cf. Cic. *Rosc. com.* 4, 13 and 5, 14, on which the literature cited by Kaser 1971, 525 n. 27, 544 n. 19 see more recently Saccoccio 2002, 141–153.

[16] On good faith and contractual balance see Fiori 2011a. For a quite different reconstruction of the notion of *bona fides* as "keeping one's word" see Talamanca 2003.

[17] Inst.Gai.3.149 (cf. Inst.2.25.2). According to Servius, the different allocation of *lucrum* and *damnum* did not involve a disparity between gains and losses, but between gains and costs. For this interpretation see Wieacker 1936, 361; Bona 1973, 24–34; Fiori 2011a, 209–215.

[18] D.19.2.15.2. On this rule (*remissio mercedis*) in the lease of things see du Plessis 2003 and Capogrossi Colognesi 2005. On its relevance in all forms of *locatio conductio* see Fiori 2011a, 148–159. On its importance for the general problem of unforeseen circumstances and good faith see Cardilli 2003, 20–28.

between the different types nor face the problem of atypical agreements, we may surmise that the general action that we assumed as the original protection for all claims of *incertum* was only slowly replaced by the typical actions, and therefore that typicality was not yet important in the Roman law of contracts. This is confirmed by the fact that we find discussions about the protection of innominate (i.e. atypical) contracts only from the second century AD onwards.

It is often said that the M. Antistius Labeo (*d.*10/11 AD) was the first jurist to propose such a protection and it has been suggested that he did so in connection with a new theory of contract as agreement (Santoro 1983; Gallo 1992–1995). However, as far as we can see, Labeo did not formulate any theory of contract, but instead reaffirmed the traditional view that concluding a contract was merely a way to create an obligation, to the extent that the obligation "is" the contract, and not merely its effect (D.50.16.19, on which Fiori 2012a). Moreover, he never dealt with atypical contracts, but instead with the atypical protection of typical contracts.

This is an important point. In some cases it was difficult to ascertain the position of the parties. For example, carriage-by-sea contracts could be so complex that it was impossible to determine whether the merchant was the *locator* or the *conductor*, and therefore which *actio* was to be used. In other cases, the primary obligations of a contract could be ineffective until a fact assumed as condition occurred. In this instance, the typical actions of the contract could not be used, but this did not mean that there was no contract or obligation. When, for example, the occurrence of the condition depended partially on the behaviour of one of the parties, who then did not fulfil the obligation according to good faith, that party was liable. In such circumstances, the general *actio incerti* that we have postulated for the pre-Aebutian period would have helped, because it protected the parties notwithstanding their position, and was not linked to a specific type. However, by the time of Labeo it had apparently disappeared. He therefore proposed another similar, general action, whose formula contained no reference to a contractual type but only to a generic duty, and the description of the case was outside and before the formula (*praescripta verba*): thus the judge was not bound to the position of the parties or to the proposed qualification of the transaction, and could take into account the generic claim of the plaintiff (Cursi and Fiori 2011, 145–160, 180–183).

The two law schools of the second–third century AD, the Sabinians and Proculians, concentrated instead on the distinction between reciprocal contracts. On the one side, a clear line was drawn between sale and lease, denying the possibility of a lease whenever a transfer of property occurred. On the other side, the difference was stressed between those transactions where the positions of the parties were clearly distinguishable, and those where it was not: in the exchange of two things or of two enjoyments, one could not say who was the seller or the hirer, whereas when the exchange was between a thing and money, or enjoyment and money, the roles of the parties were clear, and that allowed choosing between the *actio empti* or *venditi*, and between the *actio locati* or *conducti*.[19]

When it was impossible to use the typical actions, the jurists denied the existence of a typical contract. But they did not deny that there was an obligation, at least when one of

[19] On the emergence of the "limiting definitions" in the jurisprudence of the second century AD cf. Fiori 1999, 183–259.

the parties had suffered a detriment (*causa*) of some kind, having performed his duty, or having received damages. And since there was an obligation based on an agreement, they admitted that there was a contract, although atypical or "innominate", and that therefore an action should be granted.[20] Thus they proposed to use the atypical actions of their time: the *condictio* for claims of *certum*, and Labeo's *agere praescriptis verbis* for claims of *incertum*.

44.7 The Blurring of the Distinctions between Contracts and the Loss of Some of their Typical Features in the Late Classical Period (Third–Fourth Century AD)

The formation of the classical contractual system was largely influenced by the formulary procedure. One of its most prominent features, typicality, was achieved only gradually: the discussions about the boundaries of each type can be found only from the second century onwards, and is closely dependent on the issue of their protection. We have postulated, for the previous period, the existence of general civil actions for claims of *certum* or of *incertum*, alongside typical praetorian actions, and the existence of two different formulary procedures—a praetorian and a civil one. It was probably after the merger of these two forms of litigation, and because of the more subtle reflection conducted by the late Republican jurists on the internal hallmarks of each transaction, that typicality became foundational also for the civil law. However, we have also seen that the "closure" of the contractual system was immediately followed by the rise of a general protection for the atypical contracts: economy and society could not tolerate the denial of protection to some transactions only because they did not fit perfectly with the schemes of the typical system.

During the third and fourth centuries AD, some changes occurred in law and society that contributed to modify this picture. To begin with, the aristocratic ideals at the basis of the gratuitousness of many Roman contracts became outdated. This led to a more difficult distinction between the activity performed within a *locatio conductio* and other contracts such as *mandatum* and *depositum*: it was no longer felt as socially disqualifying to accept money for acting as mandatary or depositary (Fiori 1999, 263–277). This process was helped by the development, during the Principate, of a procedure called *extraordinaria cognitio*, which was used also to protect the onerous forms of "gratuitous" contracts, and particularly the obligation to pay a salary within a mandate.[21]

The same happened to *mutuum*, but for different reasons. Since it had always been protected by a *condictio* that permitted the lender to claim the exact sum he had given to the borrower, interest on the loan was promised by an ancillary *stipulatio*. However, from the

[20] D.2.14.7pr-2. For this interpretation of the much-debated notion of *causa* in the fragment see Fiori 2012b, 52. For an overview of the different interpretations see Dalla Massara 2004, 132–133.

[21] On the relevant texts see Arangio-Ruiz 1965, 115–116 and the other literature cited in Fiori 1999, 266–267.

third century on, interests were considered as part of the *mutuum* when involving produce or when the money was given by a *civitas*.

Also the classical features of Roman *stipulatio* underwent substantial changes, probably because of the influence of Greek law: the oral form of the contract was gradually replaced by written documents, and the underlying reason (*causa*) of the promise became more and more relevant.

These are processes that would lead to the post-classical degeneration of the classical contractual system, before its partial restoration promoted by Justinian—but we cannot deal with them here (Levy 1956).

44.8 Conclusion: The Centrality of the *Obligatio*

As we have seen, the Roman conception of contract was "objective". Agreement between the parties was always necessary, but it was not enough to create a "contract". To qualify for enforcement at law, the agreement either had to correspond to a "type", or had to cause a detriment to at least one of the parties. These rules ensured that nearly every agreement that had had some kind of performance received protection. It is important to note, however, that this result was not achieved by the simple granting of legal effects to the will of the parties, but rather because the need to compensate the detriment was seen as an *obligatio*.

When we speak of *contractus* in Roman law we should therefore remember that it was a concise expression to mean the *obligatio contracta*. The idea of "duty" is at the centre of the Roman conception, probably because this developed from the most ancient "contract", the *sponsio*, which—as we have seen—did not create a power over something or someone, but a duty of conduct. The idea of *contrahere* is important only to differentiate the *obligatio contracta* from the other forms of obligation that did not imply an agreement of the parties.

This possible origin also explains another aspect of the idea of *obligatio*. We know that the *sponsio* was used not only to promise a conduct but also to create personal security: a *sponsio* could oblige the promisor not only to give a thing (*dare*) or to perform an activity (*facere*), but also to act as guarantor (*praestare*). When we think that this is exactly the content of the *obligatio* and of its procedural remedies (*actiones in personam*) as pictured by the classical jurists (D.44.7.3pr; Inst.Gai.4.2), we understand that we cannot translate *obligatio* merely as "duty to perform", as we are used to doing following the modern categories of civil law, which strongly distinguish between "debt" and "liability" (*Schuld und Haftung*).[22] With the exception of the claims for *certum*—which of course are related only to the precise performance—we must refer to the *obligatio* as the duties derived from the agreement: the duties to perform, but also the duties of compensation arising from the non-performance of the contract, for which the debtor is—so to speak—"guarantor" (*praes*), be it ascribable to him or not.[23] All this is expressed by the

[22] On these problems, and particularly on the meaning of *praestare*, see Cardilli 1995.

[23] This has been observed by Cannata 1992, 70–71 and Cardilli 1995, 233–241.

wording of the procedural *formulae*: every claim is intended to a condemnation to "all that is due" (*quidquid oportet*), making no difference that the requested sum corresponds to the fulfilment of the contract, to the allocation of risk or to damages for liability (Fiori 2011b, 15–151).

The centrality of the *obligatio* within the conception of contract confirms once more a characteristic feature of Roman law—that is, a constant change in continuity—and is probably the reflection of a more general *Weltanschauung* inherited from the archaic culture, that does not place the human will at the centre of the universe, but rather the web of duties on which the cosmic balance expressed by the *ius* is based.

Bibliography

Arangio-Ruiz, V. 1949. *Il mandato in diritto romano*. Naples.

Arangio-Ruiz, V. 1950. *La società in diritto romano*. Naples.

Arangio-Ruiz, V. 1954². *La compravendita in diritto romano*, Vols. 1–2. Naples.

Arangio-Ruiz, V. 1965. *Il mandato in diritto romano*. Naples.

Benveniste, E. 1969. *Le vocabulaire des institutions indo-européennes*, Vol. 2. *Pouvoir, droit, religion*. Paris.

Bona, F. 1973. *Studi sulla società consensuale in diritto romano*. Milan.

Cannata, C. A. 1970. "La distinctio *re-verbis-litteris-consensu* et les problèmes de la pratique," in *Sein und Werden im Recht. Festgabe U. von Lübtow*. Berlin. 431–455 (= 2011 *Scritti scelti di diritto romano*, Vol. 1. Turin. 213–235).

Cannata, C. A. (1992). "Sul problema della responsabilità nel diritto privato romano." *Iura* 43: 1–82.

Capogrossi Colognesi, L. 2005. Remissio mercedis: *una storia tra logiche di sistema e autorità della norma*. Naples.

Cardilli, R. 1995. *L'obbligazione di* praestare *e la responsabilità contrattuale in diritto romano (II sec. a.C.–II sec. d.C.)*. Milan.

Cardilli, R. 2003. "Sopravvenienza e pericoli contrattuali." In *Modelli teorici e metodologici nella storia del diritto privato: obbligazioni e diritti reali*. Naples. 1–37.

Corbino, A. 1994. *Il formalismo negoziale nell'esperienza romana*. Turin.

Cristaldi, S. A. 2007. *Il contenuto dell'obbligazione del venditore nel pensiero dei giuristi dell'età imperiale*. Milan.

Cursi, M. F. and Fiori, R. (2011). "Le azioni generali di buona fede e di dolo nel pensiero di Labeone." *Bullettino dell'Istituto di Diritto Romano "Vittorio Scialoja"* 105: 145–184.

Dalla Massara, T. 2004. *Alle origini della causa del contratto: elaborazione di un concetto nella giurisprudenza classica*. Padua.

du Plessis, P. J. 2003. *A history of* remissio mercedis *and related legal institutions*. Rotterdam/Deventer.

du Plessis, P. J. 2012. *Letting and hiring in Roman legal thought: 27 BCE–284 CE*. Leiden/Boston.

Fercia, R. 2012. Fiduciam contrahere *e* contractus fiduciae: *prospettive di diritto romano ed europeo*. Naples.

Fiori, R. (1998–1999). "*Ius civile, ius gentium, ius honorarium*: il problema della 'recezione' dei *iudicia bonae fidei*." *Bullettino dell'Istituto di Diritto Romano "Vittorio Scialoja"* 101–102: 165–197.

Fiori, R. 1999. *La definizione della* locatio conductio: *giurisprudenza romana e tradizione romanistica*. Naples.

Fiori, R. 2003. Ea res agatur: *i due modelli del processo formulare repubblicano*. Milan.

Fiori, R. 2007. "*Contrahere* e *solvere obligationem* in Q. Mucio Scevola." In Fides humanitas ius: *Studi in onore di Luigi Labruna*. Vol. 3. Naples. 1955–1974.

Fiori, R. 2011a. "*Bona fides*: formazione, esecuzione e interpretazione del contratto nella tradizione civilistica (Parte seconda)." In R. Fiori, ed., *Modelli teorici e metodologici nella storia del diritto privato*, Vol. 4. Naples. 97–242.

Fiori, R. 2011b. *Bonus vir: politica filosofia retorica e diritto nel* de officiis *di Cicerone*. Naples.

Fiori, R. 2012a. "*Contrahere* in Labeone." In E. Chevreau, D. Kremer and A. Laquerrière-Lacroix, eds., Carmina iuris: *mélanges en l'honneur de Michel Humbert*. Paris. 311–331.

Fiori, R. 2012b. "The Roman conception of contract." In T. A. J. McGinn, ed., *Obligations in Roman law: past, present, and future*. Ann Arbor. 40–75.

Gallo, F. 1992–1995. Synallagma *e* conventio *nel contratto*, Vols. 1–2. Turin.

Gandolfi, G. 1976. *Il deposito nella problematica della giurisprudenza romana*. Milan.

Grosso, G. 1963³. *Il sistema romano dei contratti*. Turin.

Kaser, M. 1971². *Das römische Privatrecht*, Vol. 1: *Das altrömische, das vorklassische und klassische Recht*. Munich.

Kaser, M. and Hackl, K. 1996². *Das römische Zivilprozeßrecht*. Munich.

Levy, E. 1956. *Weströmisches Vulgarrecht, Das Obligationenrecht*. Weimar.

Martino, P. 1986. *Arbiter*. Rome.

Mayer-Maly, T. 1956. Locatio-conductio: *eine Untersuchung zum klassischen römischen Recht*. Vienna/Munich.

Nörr, D. and S. Nishimura eds. 1993. Mandatum *und Verwandtes: Beiträge zum römischen und modernen Recht*. Berlin/Heidelberg/New York.

Noordraven, B. 1999. *Die Fiduzia im römischen Recht*. Amsterdam.

Pastori, F. 1954. *Il commodato nel diritto romano*. Milan.

Peroni, R. 1996. *L'Italia alle soglie della storia*. Rome-Bari.

Pugliese, G. 1991. "Compravendita e trasferimento della proprietà in diritto romano." In L. Vacca, ed., *Vendita e trasferimento della proprietà nella prospettiva storico-comparatistica*. Milan. 25–70.

Saccoccio, A. 2002. Si certum petetur: *dalla* condictio *dei veteres alle* condictiones *giustinianee*. Milan.

Santoro, R. 1983. *Il contratto nel pensiero di Labeone*. Palermo.

Santucci, G. 1997. *Il socio d'opera in diritto romano: conferimenti e responsabilità*. Padua.

Talamanca, M. 1978. "*Conventio* e *stipulatio* nel sistema dei contratti romani." In H. Kupiszewski and W. Wołodkiewicz, eds., *Le droit romain et sa réception en Europe*. Warsaw. 195–266.

Talamanca, M. 1981. "Costruzione giuridica e strutture sociali fino a Quinto Mucio." In A. Giardina and A. Schiavone, eds., *Società romana e produzione schiavistica*, Vol. 3: *Modelli etici, diritto e trasformazioni sociali*. Rome/Bari. 15–39, 304–354.

Talamanca, M. 1987. "Processo civile (diritto romano)." *Enciclopedia del diritto*. Milan. Vol. 36: 1–80.

Talamanca, M. 1990. *Istituzioni di diritto romano*. Milan.

Talamanca, M. 1993. "Vendita (diritto romano)." *Enciclopedia del diritto*. Milan. Vol. 66: 303–475.

Talamanca, M. 2003. "La *bona fides* nei giuristi romani: 'Leerformeln' e valori dell'ordinamento." In L. Garofalo, ed., *Il ruolo della buona fede oggettiva nell'esperienza giuridica storica e contemporanea*, Vol. 4. Padua. 1–312.
Watson, A. 1961. *Contract of mandate in Roman law*. Oxford.
Wieacker, F. 1936. Societas: *Hausgemeinschaft und Erwerbsgesellschaft*. Weimar.

CHAPTER 45

THE SCOPE AND FUNCTION OF CIVIL WRONGS IN ROMAN SOCIETY

M. FLORIANA CURSI

45.1 Introduction

The chapter is divided into two sections broadly reflecting the different historical periods and social contexts in which certain legal phenomena emerged and developed. The first deals with the evidence from the XII Tables (mid-fifth century BC) in which the first types of delict and the first forms of obligation—the prototypes of the classic *poenae obligatio*—were introduced. The second focuses on subsequent developments in Republican and classical law during which the praetor modified the last remaining physical penalties of the XII Tables into *poenae obligationes*, and during which time the notion of the ancient delicts were transformed through the Republican and classical *interpretatio prudentium*. Afterwards, in the third century BC, the *lex Aquilia de damno* was enacted, and finally, in the first century BC, during the violent fall of the Republic, the praetor introduced the *actio vi bonorum raptorum*, dealing with robbery. Simultaneously, during the late Republican period, the increase in international trade and reasons of public policy created the need to ensure the reparation of damage in some new cases. Several of these new, praetorian delicts were later included in the quasi-delict category by Justinian. Ultimately, though, the system of delicts and quasi-delicts, being constructed through enumeration, was too narrow to ensure the total reparation of the private damages deriving from unlawful conduct. To this end, a new type of action, the *actio de dolo*, was introduced to repair the loss caused by *dolus*, in the absence of any specific delictual action.

45.2 The XII Tables and the Origins of Delictual Obligations

It is well known that an act that constitutes a wrong against an individual and his interests is called a delict, while an act that constitutes a wrong against the public interest is called a crime. In the XII Tables, the distinction between crime and delict was not clear. The same case could constitute both a delict and a crime. When Gaius, quoting a provision from the XII Tables (D.47.9.9 = XII Tab. 8.10), describes situations involving setting fire to a building or sheaves of wheat beside a house, he distinguishes between a case of intentional action and one of unintentional action: in the first instance, criminal liability arises, while in the second, in which the act is carried out *casu, id est negligentia* (by chance, that is, through negligence), compensation for damages is prescribed in terms of delict (*noxiam sarcire*).

In other provisions, the case is clearly a delict, as where damage was caused to the patrimony of an individual taking away a movable thing belonging to another (*furtum*) or destroying it (*rupitiae*), or where the victim's bodily integrity was compromised. In all these cases, the unlawful conduct may be said to be a civil wrong, a delict, because a person has injured a private interest and they become liable to the victim of the wrong, not to the community at large.

The main interest of the Roman lawgivers who created the XII Tables was to establish a set of rules based on a variety of cases, avoiding any generalisations or abstract definitions. The law of delict in the XII Tables is not a systematic construct, but is based on different cases of damages against the patrimony or against the person collated in a way that is not easy to reconstruct. The supposed influence of Greek lawgivers or, more probably, the logic of the ancient codes of the Near East, built on concrete interests, can be considered key to understanding the seemingly haphazard "system" of delicts (Diliberto 1992, 416). Because of the introduction of the XII Tables, the original system of private vengeance changed to one in which the victim at first had the right to inflict the same form of harm he had suffered (*lex talionis*) or had the power to seize the wrongdoer (*manus iniectio*). Later, the victim had to accept compensation instead of taking vengeance. Originally, it was a compromise between the victim and the wrongdoer, but latterly the sum was fixed by the law either as a specific sum or as multiples of said sum. This last form of pecuniary compensation for the wrong was the prototype[1] of the classical obligation preserved in the Justinianic Institutes as a *iuris vinculum* (*poenae obligatio*), a duty which binds the wrongdoer to the victim and from which a liability arises (Inst.3.13pr). This *vinculum* to pay a pecuniary composition of the wrong is the pressure applied by the rule, in the case of delicts, to avoid the wrong. In all likelihood, the notion of *obligatio* was the same both in delicts and in contracts, but, while different *genera obligationum* (*re, verbis, litteris, consensu*) arose from contracts, the *obligatio* arising from delicts was *unius generis*, consisting in the performance of the wrongful act (*re*) (D.44.7.4).

The rise of the ancient obligations is linked to the history of the delicts. The oldest ones are personal injuries (in the sense of bodily injuries) and *furtum*. The XII Tables contain three provisions about personal injuries (XII Tab. 8.2, 3, 4, *FIRA*): the first is *membrum ruptum* (XII Tab. 8.2). If a man broke another's limb, the victim could inflict the same injury upon the wrongdoer (*talio*), but only if no settlement had been agreed upon. The second was *os fractum* (XII Tab. 8.3). When a man broke another's bone, the wrongdoer

[1] Following the suggestion of Kaser 1971, 474, it would be more correct to use the expression *Haftungsverhältnisse*—literally, "relations of liability"—when referring to these first obligations, thereby avoiding their identification with the later notion of *obligatio*. However that may be, the classical obligation must be considered a notional reference to the shape of the oldest one.

was obliged to compensate the wrong by paying a specific sum of money, fixed as 300 asses for a free man, 150 asses for a slave. The final one dealt with *iniuria facere* and established that if a man acted in a wrongful way to another, the penalty was 25 asses (XII Tab. 8.4).

The configuration of the first two delicts is clear enough: mutilation or damage of a limb and breaking of a bone.[2] It is more difficult to identify the subject of the last rule, as it depends on which version of the text one follows. One version is handed down by Gellius while the other contains modern emendations. In the first case—the choice that I prefer (Cursi 2002, 223–237; Cursi 2010, 7–10, 13–19)—there is a delict of *iniuria facere* (Albanese 1991 [1980] 2, 1535–1550; Völkl 1984, 4–207); in the other, a delict of *iniuria* (Pugliese 1940, 1–38). (Some scholars even remove the text from the XII Tables entirely: Birks 1969, 163–193, especially 189–193; Manfredini 1977, 15–166.) The text of the law deals with the conduct (i.e. to act in a wrongful way) and not with the effect of this conduct—the wounding of the victim's bodily integrity like in *membrum ruptum* and *os fractum*. The nature of this conduct has to be linked with the two other provisions and it must have covered less severe physical assaults, without the visible consequences of the other ones: for example, a slap in the face as in the case handed down by Gellius of Lucius Veratius (Gell. *NA* 20.1.13). Veratius amused himself by slapping the faces of people he met. A slave followed him and immediately paid 25 asses to the victim. The penalty of 25 asses, in comparison to the more serious penalties of the first two provisions, should be seen as a guide to the seriousness of the three delicts and makes it likely that less severe physical assaults were the subject of the *iniuria facere*.

The treatment of *iniuria* in the XII Tables shows a state of transition from a system of private vengeance to one in which the law allows (*membrum ruptum*) or obliges (*os fractum* and *iniuria facere*) the victim to accept compensation for the wrong by fixing its amount. Only in the provisions about the *os fractum* and *iniuria facere* did the notion of obligation arise. Neither in the crude *talio*—which is a physical penalty—nor in the compensation offered by the wrongdoer can an obligation from the delict be said to have arisen. In fact the compensation can be interpreted in two different ways: either it is immediately effective, without any form of *vinculum*, or it creates a duty arising from the transaction and thus the obligation does not arise from the delict, but from the transaction itself, like any contractual obligation (Cursi 2011b, 145–150). The victims of the *iniuria* are free men and slaves. This distinction is evident in the second provision about the *os fractum*. But neither in the first nor in the third provision are there any indications of the *status* of the victim. It can be supposed that the law about *membrum ruptum* was applicable to both, because the compensation offered by the wrongdoer allowed two different penalties, depending on the *status* of the victim. In contrast, the law on the *iniuria facere* provides only for the free man, because there is only a penalty (25 asses). In this case, the wrongdoing was so slight that the lawgivers decided to repair only the wrong done to the free man.

The ancient notion of theft is much discussed. For some scholars it consists in taking away another's goods with the aim of profiting from them (Albanese 1991 [1969] 1, 573)—the

[2] Huvelin 1903, 378; Pugliese 1940, 33; Wittmann 1972, 4–6; Watson 1975, 218–219; Pólay 1986, 17; Hagemann 1998, 40–41.

choice I prefer;[3] for others, it also includes some forms of damage (Fenocchio 2008). In the XII Tables there is no definition of *furtum*, merely certain provisions about different penalties depending on different types of theft. In case of *furtum manifestum*, when the thief was caught *in flagrante delicto*, if he was caught at night—*fur nocturnus* (XII Tab. 8.12)—or during the day and he defended himself with a weapon—*fur qui se telo defendit* (XII Tab. 8.13)—the victim could lawfully kill the thief. In other cases of *furtum manifestum* (theft during the day without weapons), the thief, if he was a free man, was first scourged and then assigned to the victim of the theft (*addictio*). But a thieving slave, after the *verberatio*, was hurled from the Tarpeian rock (*praecipitatio e saxo*) (Gell. *NA* 11.18.8 = XII Tab. 8.14). In a case of *furtum manifestum* the physical penalty was combined with a pecuniary penalty: the manifest theft without weapons committed by an *impubes* was punished with *verberatio* and compensation of the damage (*noxiam sarcire*). But for *furtum nec manifestum* the XII Tables recognised only a pecuniary penalty for double the value of the stolen thing (XII Tab. 8.16). Similarly, for *furtum conceptum et oblatum*—when the stolen goods were found in the premises of an occupier against whom the *actio* was brought—the punishment was a penalty triple that of the damage (Inst.Gai.3.191 = XII Tab. 8.15*a*).

The different penalties presume different levels of seriousness and different periods of elaboration of the concept of theft. *Furtum manifestum* was more serious than *furtum nec manifestum* and its penalty reveals an archaic form of self-redress that the XII Tables have recognised, probably deriving from similar provisions of the laws of Solon (Pepe 2004). In contrast, the pecuniary penalty of *furtum nec manifestum* reflects the most recent stage in which the liability of the delict began to be redeemable by payment of a sum of money. As in the history of the personal injuries, only in the pecuniary penalty of *furtum* can the first form of obligation from theft be found.

The provisions about wrongful damage to property in the XII Tables are very fragmentary and contain various penalties (cf. Cursi 2010, 3–6, 12–13). The law about the lighting of a fire has been already cited: it is a delict, with the compensation of damage (*noxiam sarcire*), and also a crime depending on the unintentional or intentional conduct of the wrongdoer. Similarly, the law on the depasturisation of another person's land provides two different penalties: against the *pubes* the death penalty (*suspensio Cereris*), against the *impubes* the compensation of damage (Plin. *HN* 18, 3, 12 = XII Tab. 8, 9). For the damage done by animals (*pauperies*) the penalty is the reparation of damage too (D.9.1.1pr = XII Tab. 8.6). The other cases of wrongful damage are expressive of a definitive distinction between crimes and delicts and are punished with a pecuniary reparation of the wrong: like the damage caused by a public aqueduct to private property (D.43.8.5 = XII Tab. 7.8*b*); the damage made by the unlawful cutting of another's trees (Plin. *HN* 17.7 = XII Tab. 8.11); the case of the *consecratio* of a *res litigiosa* (D.44.6.3 = XII Tab. 12.4); the *actio in duplum* against the embezzlements of the *tutor* (D.26.7.55.1 = XII Tab. 8.20) that the scholars identify with the *actio rationibus distrahendis*; the *actio in duplum* in the *tignum furtivum iunctum* (D.47.3.1pr = XII Tab. 6.8), with similar requirements and penalty of the *furtum nec manifestum*; and finally the *actio in duplum* granted in case of embezzlement (Coll.10.7.11 = XII Tab. 8.19).

3 The provisions on *furtum conceptum et oblatum* present evidence for the first theory, because someone has carried off the stolen things.

45.3 Developments in Republican and Classical Roman Law

During the Roman Republic, the development of the delicts of *furtum* and personal injuries consisted of the change of the physical penalties (*talio, addictio*) into pecuniary penalties. Also, the fixed pecuniary penalties (for example, 25 asses for *iniuria facere*) changed into a sum that appeared to a court of *recuperatores* to be equitable under the circumstances. In reality, the fixed penalties of the XII Tables became obsolete: in the course of the following centuries they became so depreciated that their statutory penalty became derisory, as shown in the case of Veratius.

Around the fourth and third centuries BC, the praetor introduced an *edictum de iniuriis aestimandis* that provided an *actio iniuriarum aestimatoria* in which the pecuniary penalty was commensurate to whatever is *bonum et aequum* (Gell. *NA* 20.1.13); and an *actio furti manifesti* with a *poena quadrupli* (fourfold the value of the stolen *res*). In both cases the praetor probably developed the idea of a pecuniary penalty already contained in certain provisions of the XII Tables concerning the two delicts and extended its application proportionate to the seriousness of the wrong.

The provision of the *actio iniuriarum* presupposes the development of the notion of *iniuria*. The XII Tables dealt with three different forms of personal injury, in the absence of a unitary concept of *iniuria*. In my view, the earliest elaboration of *iniuria*-delict is traceable to Plautus' comedies at the end of the third century BC (Cursi 2002, 248–268). In the *Poenulus* the *actio iniuriarum* is mentioned with reference to the protection of the reputation of a father whose daughters have been treated like slaves by a merchant who had imprisoned them. In this case the *iniuria* was not a physical assault but a defamation, an insulting behaviour. Starting from the personal injuries the jurists built the *iniuria*-delict including the personal injuries and the disregarding of another's personality: *iniuria* in the sense of *contumelia*.

It must be highlighted that the defamation in the *Poenulus* is suffered not only by the daughters being treated like slaves, but also by their father, according to a form of indirect insult that the Romans called *iniuria per alias personas*. This form of *iniuria* was introduced by a praetorian revision of the original "system" of the XII Tables, but it was not a radical innovation: some of the features of the ancient delict presumably survived unchanged, but are attested like juridical category in a later period. That was because the *pater* had *potestas* over his sons and daughters, who were *alieni iuris*, so that every event of legal significance affected the *pater*, and not only the sons. In my view this form of indirect insult (*iniuria per alias personas*) was also based on the criterion of reparation of damage in the *lex Aquilia* (Cursi 2012a, 255–288).

During the same period of the elaboration of the *iniuria-contumelia*, probably in the third century BC, the *lex Aquilia* concerning wrongful damage to property was enacted (date: Cursi 2002, 147–165; Serrao 2009, 561–564). It superseded all earlier laws that had dealt with unlawful damage to property—XII Tables and others alike. The *lex Aquilia* contained three chapters (Cursi 2002, 167–180; Cursi 2010, 26–32, 44–50; Valditara 2005; Corbino 2008): the first one provided that the person whose slave or four-footed animal classed as *pecus* was wrongfully killed should receive the highest value that the thing had

had in the previous year (D.9.2.2pr); the second chapter—no longer in use in classical Roman law because the *actio mandati* was available too—concerned the *adstipulator*. The *adstipulator* was a person whom a *stipulator* asked to act as a kind of trustee and to recover what he, the *stipulator*, was owed by the *promissor*. An *adstipulator* who released the debtor from his obligation by *acceptilatio* was understood by this clause to cause damage to the *stipulator* with intentional fault and so was condemned to give so much money to the *stipulator* (Inst.Gai.3.215). The third chapter provided that where property was wrongfully "burnt, smashed or maimed" the owner should receive "how much it was worth in the nearest thirty days" (D.9.2.27.5).

It is highly likely that the first two *capita* were the more ancient parts of the law, and that the original version of chapter 1 only dealt with the killing of a slave (Cursi 2002, 208–212). We also know that the case of the wounding of the slave would be developed only later by the *prudentes* through the interpretation of the third *caput* of the *lex* (Cursi 2002, 197–208). So, at the time the law was passed, injury against a slave was regulated differently, depending on the nature of the offence: when he was killed, the case fell under the *lex Aquilia*; when he was wounded, it was a matter of *iniuria*. The *iniuria* against a *servus* was not only conceived of as an offence to the slave, but above all as a *contumelia* against the *dominus*: a form of *iniuria per alias personas* (Cursi 2002, 248–268). The *dominus* had *potestas* over the slave, who was *alieni iuris*, so that every offence to a slave was an insult to the master. It is difficult to believe that the rule set out by the *lex Aquilia* followed a different logic: on the contrary, in my view the killing of a slave—just like his wounding—amounted not only to a prejudice against the patrimony of the *dominus*, but also to an *iniuria-contumelia* against the owner's *potestas*, the power of life and death of the master over his slaves, because in killing the slave the offender usurped a *potestas* that was not his to wield, depriving the legitimate possessor of that power. In other words, the expression *occidere iniuria* in the first chapter of the Aquilian law reproduced the same legal mechanism of the delict of *iniuria-contumelia*. This may seem like an obvious point, but the interesting fact is that the Romans in both cases (and in a way that is completely novel compared to the system of damages prevailing before the *lex Aquilia*) defined this offence as *iniuria*.

It is clear, however, that the decision to borrow the notion of *iniuria* from the delict of the same name could only lead to its "comprehensive" adoption (Cursi 2002; Cursi 2011a, 16–29; *contra* Schipani 1969). The legislator of the *lex Aquilia* could not omit an essential element of that delict (and one that was especially prominent in its new praetorian form); namely, the requirement of intentional fault (*dolus*). The two delicts *iniuria* and *damnum iniuria datum* were at the beginning perfectly complementary: the first dealt with physical offences, other than killing, against the slave and moral offences against his *dominus*; and the second dealt with the killing of the slave and moral offences against his *dominus*. The subsequent extension of the first *caput* to *pecus quadrupes*—by virtue of the essential similarity between men and animals, the only ones that can be killed—and the introduction of the third *caput*, which widens the protection for damage to inanimate *res*, are without doubt significant additions to the content. The extension of the protection to the inanimate *res* also introduced a substantial novelty. For the first time, an explicit reference to *damnum* appears in the text of the law. Perhaps the reference to the slave (and subsequently to the *pecus quadrupes*) was still too closely linked to the logic of *iniuria* to be able to talk of *damnum*. By including inanimate *res*, a new notion of damage was introduced, laying the foundations for distinguishing between *iniuria* and *damnum iniuria datum*.

This phenomenon is a reflection, both socially and legally, of the progressive reification of the slave: the case derived from the delict of *iniuria*, in the first chapter of the law, belongs to domestic slavery—where, even if there are differences in the money payments, the injured slave is placed on the same level as a free man—but in commercial slavery, the slave is equated with inanimate objects in the common case of *damnum*. It is at this point that the emphasis on the property aspect of Aquilian damage is supported by the introduction of fault as a subjective criterion that can justify compensation in all cases where damage is not deliberately done. It must also be pointed out that this is not only a temporal coincidence linked to the jurisprudential interpretation of the Aquilian cases, specifically where the application of the statute initially may have seemed doubtful. Such well-known cases include the resort to self-defence in a manner deemed excessive (D.9.2.5pr): the abuse of an instructor's disciplinary authority that results in permanent physical damage to a student (D.9.2.5.3, 7pr = D.19.2.13.4); injury to passers-by inflicted by careless tree-trimmers (D.9.2.31); and the intentional infliction of harm upon an animal grazing illegally on one's property (D.9.2.39pr). It is my view that the two innovations are connected: the need to compensate damage, understood not only as an offence to the *dominus* but as a real loss of property, led to the extension of cases of application of protection by means of the subjective requirement of *culpa*, which did not allow the involuntary conduct of the agent to go unpunished (Cursi 2012b, 296–319). This innovation, moreover, has the effect of extending Aquilian protection to cases that up to that point had not been included in the application of the law. Originally, the intentional injuring of a slave was covered by the delict of *iniuria*, and it was therefore pointless to have a legal provision that punished such a case as *damnum iniuria datum*. When the Aquilian *iniuria*, originally equal to intentional fault, was transformed into *culpa*, the protection *ex lege Aquilia* became subjectively wider than that guaranteed by the delict of *iniuria*; at this point, the *prudentes* decided to insert also the cases of unintentional injury of a *servus* and *pecus quadrupes* among the *ceterae res* of the third *caput*.

A transformation of this kind could only lead to a coherent modification of the nature of Aquilian action from penal to mixed, by adding a specific compensatory feature to the original penal intent. At the end of the Republic, the *lex Aquilia* was extended and adapted in many ways: from killing through a direct act that caused the death of a slave or animal, according to the original meaning of the verb *occidere*, the application of the first chapter of the law was extended to all manner of causing death (also through an indirect act). Similarly, in the third chapter, *urere, frangere, rumpere* ("burning, smashing or maiming") were superseded by the wider term, *corrumpere* ("spoiling"). In consequence, praetorian actions were granted not only in cases of direct causation of the damage, as in the original application of the statute (*Aquilian actio directa*), but also in cases of indirect causation (*actio utilis*) even without physical destruction: loss that does not derive from physical damage was recoverable through an *actio in factum* (Zimmermann 1990, 1022 on pure economic loss).

The *actio directa* could be brought where the defendant had injured the plaintiff *corpore corpori*, by the body to the body, meaning that harm had to be physically inflicted by the defendant. For example, the defendant would be liable if he had struck and broken something that belonged to the plaintiff. The plaintiff was allowed to use the *actio utilis* for harm that was *corpori* but not *corpore*, to the body but not by the body, as, for example, if the defendant locked up the plaintiff's slave in a room where he starved: the harm was not done physically but the slave had died, causing a loss to the plaintiff. The plaintiff was allowed to use the *actio in factum* for harm that was neither *a corpore* nor *in corpus*, neither by the body nor to the body, as, for example, if the defendant untied the plaintiff's slave so he could run away; the slave was now beyond reach, but this time the defendant himself had not physically moved him.

Moreover, the injured party could recover his full *quod interest*: in this context, the term did not refer to the full value of the object that had been damaged, as in the first application of the *lex*, but to the actual damage suffered by the plaintiff (i.e. the mere difference between the full value and the reduced value after interference). The introduction of this criterion to evaluate the damage permitted the extension of the role of plaintiff to the non-owner: usufructuaries and pledgees were counted among those who could avail themselves of the Aquilian remedy (in particular, *actio utilis*). Although the personal injury to a free person could not be compensated under the *lex Aquilia*, the introduction of the *quod interest* criterion allowed for the recovery of the pecuniary loss when a member of one's family had been injured and the actual damage suffered and the medical expenses had been incurred as a result (Cursi 2010, 61–66, 69–72).

Notwithstanding the provision of *actiones utiles* and *in factum legis Aquiliae* that completed the protection provided by the direct action, the Republican jurists developed some types of damage that were not recoverable by the *Aquilian* actions. In these cases, if the damage was produced by the other people's deception and no typical actions were available, the praetor ensured the reparation of the damage through the *actio de dolo* (D.4.3.1.1). This action filled a gap in the Roman typology of actions, introducing a corrective. Cicero testifies that the remedy was introduced by Aquilius Gallus to punish the disconnect between what is simulated and what is real when no other actions were available. By the *actio de dolo* the pecuniary loss that neither by the body nor to the body was caused, and furthermore without a material behaviour, was compensated. In the previous case of the slave set free by the defendant, the harm was neither by the body nor to the body but the defendant's behaviour was material. On the contrary, when the economic loss was caused by false information, it is clear that the behaviour of the defendant was immaterial. The *actio de dolo* was only used in the case when the loss had been caused with *dolus* (Cursi 2008).

By the time of Justinian, the gradual decline of the praetorian system of actions and the tendency to use general actions led to indifference towards the *actio de dolo*. On the other side, the marginalisation of the remedy is highlighted by the wider application of the *actio in factum legis Aquiliae*. A straightforward reading of Justinianic Institutes points to the inescapable conclusion that an *actio in factum* could be used, in the absence of any other remedy, when a loss had been wrongfully caused, notwithstanding that there had been no damage suffered to any property (Inst.4.3.16).

The mood of violence in the final period of Republican history led the praetor to introduce two actions in the *edictum* against particularly serious forms of *damnum* and *furtum* with a penalty *in quadruplum*. The first action was against *dolo malo vi hominibus armatis coactisve damnum datum*; the second one was against people who had stolen another person's thing by use of violence (*bona vi rapta*). The link with the *furtum* makes robbery one of the four delicts quoted by Gaius among the sources of the *obligationes ex delicto* (Inst.Gai.3.182). It is probable that the robbery, before the enactment of the praetorian *edictum*, was punished like a case of *furtum nec manifestum* with a penalty *in duplum* (cf. Vacca 1972, 145–148). The seriousness of the robbery in comparison to the *furtum nec manifestum* could have pushed the praetor to introduce the action, shaped on the more serious type of *furtum manifestum* with the penalty *in quadruplum*.

In the late Republican period the increase of international trade on the one hand, and for reasons of public policy arising from the new architectural configuration of the city on the other, led to the need to ensure the reparation of damage originating from the lack of surveillance or supervision by the person responsible for such. In the case of the *actio de effusis vel deiectis* the *habitator* he was held responsible if something had been thrown out or poured down from his house, irrespective of whether he himself, a member of his family, one of his slaves, or anybody else from his house had actually thrown out or poured anything down. A similar case was the position of the *nauta, caupo* and *stabularius* in the *actio furti* and *actio damni*: sea carriers, innkeepers and stable-keepers were liable if their customer's goods were damaged or stolen by their employees. The Roman jurists called this form of vicarious liability *culpa in eligendo et in vigilando* and invented it directly from the adaptation of known cases to the new ones that the praetor was beginning to address (Cursi 2012b, 303–314). The *actio ex lege Aquilia* obviously provided the main reference model regarding the subjective criterion of liability (*culpa*). The adaptation of Aquilian negligence to these scenarios was, however, not entirely innocuous. To presume culpability on the part of a person who may be different from the actual author of the wrong, means perverting such a criterion through the introduction of a form of strict liability. Vicarious (strict) liability was a novelty introduced by the praetor, ensuring a positive compensation of the damage in such cases.

These cases, together with the case of the liability of the judge for making wrong decisions (*iudex qui litem suam fecit*), are included by Justinian under the quasi-delicts (Inst.4.5), as opposed to delicts. What separates these two categories is a matter of contention. Some scholars argue that delictual liability arises from an intentional inflicting of harm, whereas quasi-delictual liability is characterised by negligence. But the case of the *iudex qui litem suam fecit*, based on the intentional conduct of the judge, as well as Aquilian *culpa*, contradict this hypothesis. Other scholars maintain that the distinction is based on the civilian origin of the delicts and the praetorian introduction of the quasi-delicts. But this last criterion does not explain the choice of including the *rapina* in the delicts, despite its praetorian origin (although in Inst.Gai. 3.209 the *rapina* is a form of *furtum*). Above all that, the Justinianic choice of including only several cases in the quasi-delict category leaves open the problem of the completeness of the category. Regardless of the criterion chosen to distinguish the delicts and the quasi-delicts, it is well known that some cases, like the damage repaired by the praetorian *actio de pauperie*, do not fall under either category. Historical investigation should seek to distinguish the gradual elaboration of the typological system of civil wrongs from the Justinianic classification, which sought to efface historical specificities and uses the category of quasi-delicts, in contrast to the four types of delict handed down by Gaius without a specific criterion of distinction.

45.4 Conclusion

The Roman jurists focused their attention on creating and defining specific wrongs, rather than drafting a general law or theory of wrong. This enumerative system developed from the legal rules in the XII Tables concerning *furtum*, personal injuries and wrongful damage to property into a more complex system of delicts by increasing the scope of *damnum iniuria datum* and by adding the delict of robbery.

The jurists, the lawgivers and the praetor then modified the ancient framework of wrongs: sometimes new types of delict linked with the previous ones were created—like *damnum iniuria datum*, which was at the beginning perfectly complementary with the *iniuria-contumelia*, or the robbery like a form of *furtum*—sometimes the subject of the wrongs were changed, according to the transformation of the social and economical context, adapting the actions to always cover different cases—the *actio de effusis vel deiectis*, the *actio damni et furti adversus nautas, caupones, stabularios* that Justinian would include in the quasi-delict category.

Despite that, some wrongs were left without penalty. So the *actio de dolo* was introduced as a subsidiary remedy to fill the gaps of the typical system of actions. It was a type of action too, but its subsidiarity makes it a general remedy that crossed the boundaries of the Roman typical system of actions. The system paved the way for the introduction of a general action: the Justinianic *actio in factum generalis* that applied to all types of loss and became the nucleus of the modern generalised law of delict.

Bibliography

Albanese, B. 1991. "Una congettura sul significato di *iniuria* in XII Tab. 8.4," In *Scritti Giuridici*. 2 vols. Palermo. 1535–1550.

Birks, P. B. H. (1969). "The early history of *iniuria*." *The Legal History Review* 37: 163–208.

Corbino, A. 2008². *Il danno qualificato e la* lex Aquilia: *corso di diritto romano*. Padua.

Cursi, M. F. 2002. Iniuria cum damno: *antigiuridicità e colpevolezza nella storia del danno aquiliano*. Milan.

Cursi, M. F. 2008. *L'eredità dell'actio de dolo e il problema del danno meramente patrimoniale*. Naples.

Cursi, M. F. 2010. *Danno e responsabilità extracontrattuale nella storia del diritto privato*. Naples.

Cursi, M. F. (2011a). "What did *occidere iniuria* in the *lex Aquilia* actually mean?" *Roman Legal Tradition* 7: 16–29.

Cursi, M. F. (2011b). "La formazione delle obbligazioni *ex delicto*." *Revue internationale des droits de l'antiquité* 58: 143–173.

Cursi, M. F. (2012a). "*Pati iniuriam per alios* (Gai. 3, 221–222)." *Bullettino dell'Istituto di Diritto Romano "Vittorio Scialoja"* 2: 255–288.

Cursi, M. F. (2012b). "Roman delicts and the construction of fault." In T. A. J. McGinn, ed., *Obligations in Roman law: past, present, and future*. Ann Arbor. 296–319.

Diliberto, O. 1992. *Materiali per la palingenesi delle XII tavole*, Vol. 1. Cagliari.

Fenocchio, M. A. 2008. *Sulle tracce del delitto di* furtum: *genesi sviluppi vicende*. Naples.

Hagemann, M. 1998. Iniuria: *von den XII-Tafeln bis zur Justinianischen Kodification*. Cologne/Weimar/Vienna.

Huvelin, P. 1903. *La notion de l'iniuria dans le tres ancien droit romain*. Paris.

Kaser, M. 1971². *Das Römische Privatrecht*, Vol. 1. Munich.

Manfredini, A. D. 1977. *Contributi allo studio dell'*iniuria *in età repubblicana*. Milan.

Pepe, L. 2004. *Ricerche sul furto nelle XII Tavole e nel diritto attico*. Milan.

Pólay, E. 1986. Iniuria *types in Roman law*. Budapest.

Pugliese, G. 1940. *Studi sull'*iniuria. Milan.

Riccobono, S. ed. 19412. Fontes iuris Romani Anteiustiniani, Vol. 1. Florence.

Schipani, S. 1969. *Responsabilità* ex lege Aquilia: *criteri di imputazione e problema della* culpa. Turin.

Serrao, F. 2009. "Uomini d'affari, *adstipulatores*, *lex Aquilia* alla fine del III secolo a.C.," in *Studi in onore di Remo Martini*. Milan. Vol. 3: 559–582.

Vacca, L. 1972. *Ricerche in tema di* actio vi bonorum raptorum. Milan.

Valditara, G. 2005². Damnum iniuria datum. Turin.

Völkl, A. 1984. *Die Verfolgung der Körperverletzung im frühen römischen Recht: studien zum Verhältnis von Tötungsverbrechen und Injuriendelikt*. Vienna/Cologne/Graz.

Watson, A. (1975). "Personal injuries in the XII tables." *The Legal History Review* 43: 213–222.

Wittmann, R. 1972. *Die Körperverletzung an Freien im klassischen Römischen Recht*. Munich.

Zimmermann, R. 1990. *The law of obligations: Roman foundations of the civilian tradition*. Cape Town.

Economics

CHAPTER 46

PRICE SETTING AND OTHER ATTEMPTS TO CONTROL THE ECONOMY

EGBERT KOOPS

46.1 Introduction

Aulus Gellius tells the story of a certain Lucius Veratius who struck people across the face to amuse himself and would afterwards order a slave to count out the 25 asses prescribed as penalty by the Law of the Twelve Tables (Gell. *NA* 20.1.12; XII Tab. 1.15 [*RS* no. 40]). It is doubtful whether that price reflects the circumstances of 451–450 BC, since Roman coinage only became common in the context of the Pyrrhic War. After several weight reductions and a devaluation, asses were replaced as the unit of accounting by the denarius and sesterce in 211 BC, and subsequently further reduced in weight (Wassink 1991, 469–470; Crawford 1985, 25–31, 55–60). Gellius borrowed the story from the Augustan-era jurist Labeo, and by this time the as had little value at all: "who could be so poor, that he would be deterred from the desire to commit personal injury by 25 asses" (Gell. *NA* 20.1.12; cf. Plin. *NH* 17.7)?

There are two reasons to introduce this story. The first is that Gellius/Labeo notes that the praetors responded by issuing an edict on the appraisal of damages in claims for personal injury (in the sense of bodily injury) (*de iniuriis aestimandis*). Roman law was moving away from a schedule of fixed payments to ward off revenge, a system prevalent in many ancient legal cultures, and toward a flexible estimate depending on the circumstances of the case. Around the same time, the fixed penalty of 15–300 for breaking the bones of a slave or free man was replaced by the *lex Aquilia* of *c.*287 BC, leading to a flexible assessment of damage to goods.[1] Over the course of time, the Roman jurists developed criteria to assign value as objectively as possible, and their concepts provide a legal and perhaps also social view on ideals of price formation; for instance, by distinguishing the *verum pretium* from actual market prices. This will be treated later (section 46.4), after

[1] XII Tab. 1.14 (*RS* no. 40). Zimmermann 1990, 955–958 and 1050–1052.

some remarks on the formation of market prices and ways in which the Roman state intervened in the price-setting mechanism (section 46.3), to be followed by some notes on Diocletian's Edict on Maximum Prices of 301 AD (section 46.5).

46.2 Scope of This Chapter

The second reason to introduce Veratius' story is that it raises an obvious question. What is to be considered an "attempt to control the economy"? Every statutory price attempts to control behaviour through economic (dis)incentives enshrined in law, even if a functioning market for personal insults can hardly be said to exist. Veratius' behaviour was that of a rational agent who weighed private delectation against a public penalty, and in this sense the Roman state attempted and eventually failed to control the economy of personal injury. Meanwhile, a different attempt at control is lurking in the background of this story. As a result of a policy of weight reduction of the as during the Republic and reduction of the silver content of the denarius under the Empire, fixed prices became illusory in the long term, because "bad money drives out good money" (Gresham's law), leading to payment in bad new coins while old coins were hoarded or melted down for their metal content (Wassink 1991, 469–485). The fixed fines mentioned in grave inscriptions or in the Flavian municipal laws serve as examples: even a fine of 20,000 sesterces became modest during the hyperinflation of the late third century AD. And so monetary policy takes precedence among the ways in which the Roman state influenced the economy, even if debasement of the coinage was effected through the Imperial mints rather than by enactment. Thus, some price schedules enshrined in statute bear little relation to the economy *stricto sensu*, while some interventions with major economic impact were the result of policy considerations rather than enactment or interpretation by the jurists. A similar problem exists with regard to the sumptuary laws of the late Republic. Reissued several times but rarely enforced,[2] these laws privileged the domestic economy over luxury foodstuffs bought at market, by setting a maximum spending allowance for luxury items. Such rules were not intended to direct the economy, even if they incidentally had an economic impact; their purpose was rather to encourage self-regulation by the Roman elite to keep the social peace (Rosivach 2006). Other examples, to be multiplied at will, are the senatorial and equestrian property requirements, maximum amounts for guarantees per year, fixed prices for the acquisition of citizenship by Junian Latins, or the maximum value of locally adjudged suits under the Flavian municipal laws.[3]

The problem, then, is one of definition. Here, the concept of "the Roman economy" covers the production, distribution and consumption of scarce goods and services in the Roman Empire during the long classical period. It would be impossible to discuss all measures of state or private actors that tried to bend this economy to political or private

[2] *Lex Fannia* (163 BC) and *lex Licinia* (103 BC): Gell. *NA* 2.24.1–15; Plut. *Sull.* 8.2; Suet. *Caes.* 43.2; *Aug.* 34.1; *Tib.* 34.1; Tac. *Ann.* 3.52.

[3] Property requirements: see Szaivert and Wolters 2005, 32–34 and 314. *Lex Cornelia de sponsu* (81 BC): Inst.Gai.3.124. Buying citizenship: Inst.Gai.1.32b–34; Epit.Ulp. 3, 5–6. Maximum value of local suits: *lex Irn.* 84.

gains. Instead, the focus is on measures that were *intended* to *structurally* influence price formation *in the market*, other than by affecting supply and demand, and on legal interpretations that presuppose such price formation. “Intention” is an awkward term, but it excludes the effects of government spending on infrastructure, the state apparatus and the army. Such spending influenced price formation, but not intentionally. “Structural” is a problematic notion as well, but it serves to exclude incidental largesse or emergency relief, as well as windfalls from proscriptions and *bona caduca*. By implication, some economic interventions cannot be considered either, such as Caesar’s debt restructuring of 48 BC or his rent remission of 47 BC,[4] since interventions under such circumstances were not supposed to have any permanency, even if they occurred intermittently. The “market”, finally, is taken as the notional place where supply and demand meet to exchange commodities for a value expressed in prices. The regulation of physical markets is the subject of another chapter (de Ligt, ch. 50) in this volume.

46.3 Formation of Market Prices

A developed economic theory was absent in the classical world, but it should come as no surprise that more than a basic awareness of market operations existed, even if rising prices were often blamed on profligates and profiteers for moral reasons (Finley 1985, 19–23). Tacitus’ analysis of the financial crisis of 33 AD may serve as an example (Tac. *Ann.* 6.16–17; see also Dio Cass. 58.21.4–5). Some moneylenders had supplied money at usurious rates, in defiance of a law issued by Caesar to regulate moneylending and property-owning in Italy. They were denounced to the senate, which decided to enforce Caesar’s law but give the moneylenders—many of them senators—an eighteen-month indulgence to set their affairs in order. The result was a credit crunch (*hinc inopia rei nummariae*). Hoping to restore the flow of money, the senate decreed that every creditor had to invest two thirds of his currently outstanding claims in Italian land. But fearing that defaulting debtors would leave them unable to meet this obligation, creditors called in the full amount of debt to buy land. This led to a general panic, court cases and foreclosures, leading in turn to too much land and not enough money on the market, falling land prices, and further defaults and ejectments. In the end, Tiberius had to assuage the crisis by slashing interest rates to 0 per cent for the next three years and injecting 100 million sesterces into the economy, which slowly restored trust until private lenders reappeared (the story is not without earlier or later parallels). Trial and error led Augustus and subsequent Roman emperors to arrive at an almost Keynesian approach to economic crises, by a mix of currency depreciation (the classical equivalent to deficit spending) and increased government expenditure (Wassink 1991, 473). Less complex examples may be found as well. According to Dio, so much money entered the city following Augustus’ conquest of Egypt in 30 BC that prices soared and loans were taken at a third of the usual interest rate (Dio Cass. 51.21.5). And the agronomists stress the importance of nearby markets and means of transportation in

[4] Debt remission: Caes., *BC* 3.1.2–3; Suet., *Caes.* 42.2; Dio Cass. 42.51.1–3 (also see 42.50.4). Rent remission: Dio Cass. 48.9.5.

the selection of crops and farm localities, as well as the effects of cyclical price fluctuations (Varro, *Rust.* 1.16.2–3, 1.69.1; Columella, *Rust.* 3.2.1), which in turn led the Roman jurists to produce complicated agricultural contracts, selling or pledging the produce in advance.[5]

Local markets were producers' primary destination, but transportable goods and manufactures such as olive oil, pottery and textiles were produced for consumers throughout the Empire, as the archaeological record demonstrates. Whether such production for remoter markets occurred with any regularity is difficult to say. The "embedded" nature of the essentially regional Roman economy, whether embedded in "overriding values" or the "networks of the Bazaar", is commonly set against the fluidity of capital, labour and (some) transportable goods, as well as the degree of monetisation and the institutional flexibility offered by Roman law, to argue either for or against the existence of integrated markets and a market economy.[6] At least for high-value, transportable commodities such as slaves, most interpretations favour the existence of an integrated market (Harper 2010, 214; Scheidel 2005, 9–11). In this context, it should be noted that the Roman state directed traffic through a differentiated structure of tariffs and customs, even going so far as to encourage integration with the Italian market by abolishing customs dues on goods coming into Italy (Nicolet 2000, 109–114). Tacitus indicates that transaction costs were indeed passed on, stating that Nero remitted the sales tax on slaves in name alone, as it was now imposed on the vendors who raised their prices accordingly (Tac. *Ann.* 13.31).

Prices were generally not set by state intervention but by the forces of supply and demand. Apart from Diocletian's Edict on Maximum Prices (section 46.5), by far the best price series come from the papyri uncovered in Roman Egypt (prices from literary authors: Szaivert and Wolters 2005). As Rathbone notes, "the prices in private sales seem, on the whole, to be 'real' prices arrived at individually by market bargaining rather than being standardised, customary or notional prices" (Rathbone 1997, 211). This is, of course, not to say that all bargaining happened on equal terms. Asymmetrical information and differences in status influenced bargaining power, as always, and so the jurist Paul warns that it is "naturally" allowed to buy what is worth more for less, and sell what is worth less for more, and generally for parties to a transaction to run rings around one another (D.19.2.22.3: *naturaliter*; see also D.4.4.16.4). As a legal norm, the *bona fides* coloured the performance of contractual duties rather than the formation of the contract, and as long as two capable and consenting parties bargained for a licit end, in proper form and in the absence of mistake, fraud or duress, the contract would be upheld (Zimmermann 1990, 255–259, 577; Kaser 1971, 227–252). Cicero's treatment of the case of a merchant who sold wheat to famished Rhodes, knowing that a relief fleet would arrive the next day, shows that a moral duty was recognised to refrain from profiteering; but it also presupposes that the contract itself was valid at law (Cic. *Off.* 3.50; Zimmermann 1990, 257). Rather than by Cicero, practice is perhaps better shown by the example of Italian merchants who sold cheap wine to alcoholic Gauls and counted their blessings (Diod. Sic. 5.26.3).

Fair dealings in the market place were supervised by the aediles (see de Ligt, ch. 50), who checked measures and weights and had jurisdiction over complaints concerning slaves and cattle. They could offer rescission or price reductions in case of defects, the

[5] Cato *Agr.* 144.1 and 147; D.18.1.39.1; D.19.1.25; D.47.2.62.8. Erdkamp 2005, 120–134.

[6] Overriding values: Finley 1985. Networks: Bang 2008. Integrated markets: Temin 2006 and 2013.

latter of which involved an appraisal of the value of the defect thing and a comparison to the notional value of the same thing without this particular defect. The aediles were particularly suited to such appraisals because of their knowledge of the prices regularly realised at market. No evidence has come to light, but they (or the *agoranomoi*) may have kept lists of current prices, as suggested by an edict of Hadrian that forbade sellers at Ephesus from charging soldiers on official duty more than the market price of ten days ago (Hauken and Malay 2009).

Similar to the provisioning of the army but politically even more important was the constant and adequate supply of grain to Rome.[7] The existence of grain distribution, for free after the *lex Clodia* (58 BC), was a major attempt to control the economy, as well as a major strain on state resources. Considering most of Roman history, the political reasons for this intervention speak for itself. The state's default position appears to have been that it acquired most of its grain from Imperial estates and through taxation in kind, and bought additional grain from private suppliers at current prices (Temin 2013, 32–35, 101; see also Erdkamp 2005, 240–306). The state did not maintain large public grain fleets, with concomitant expenses and risks, preferring to offer private transporters citizenship, subsidies or immunities as an incentive.[8] In general, it seems that the emperors trusted market forces to supplement and transport the public supply, and took incidental action through subsidies or maximum prices. At the local level, this is mirrored by rulings that city councillors should not be forced to provide grain at fixed low prices (D.48.12.3.1; D.50.1.8; D.50.8.7(5)pr).

Price-gouging and price-fixing by cartels or private individuals may or may not have been problematic. The avarice of profiteering and stockpiling merchants is a common literary topic, and the Flavian municipal law of Irni explicitly forbids such practices and threatens it with a fine of 10,000 sesterces per infraction (*lex Irn.* 75; see also D.5.1.53; D.47.11.6pr). In practice, though some stockpiling is necessary in any agrarian economy to cushion against crop failure, it seems likely that most farmers followed the annual production cycle, preferring certainty to speculation (Erdkamp 2005, 155–164). The Roman state stockpiled grain for political reasons, so that Germanicus could lower prices in a time of need by opening the granaries, while Nero restored confidence during a panic by throwing spoiled grain into the Tiber, signalling that the state had stocked enough to waste a little (Germanicus: Tac. *Ann.* 2.59. Nero: Tac. *Ann.* 15.18).

Some private price-fixing was sanctioned by the state, since the regular way of pricing state contracts was to auction them for a set period of time to the highest (taxes, goods) or lowest (construction) bidding company (Malmendier 2002, 91–222). Tax collectors would become so inflamed with bidding frenzy, according to Paulus, that they should only be allowed the contract if they provided sufficient security (Sent.Paul. 5,1a, 1). Other monopolies were lucrative as well. Pliny mentions red lead from Hispania and balsam oil from Judea, with prices fixed under the auction contract (*statuta lege*) (Plin. *NH* 33.118, 54.123). The *societas* made its profit by adulterating the product and reselling it for over three times the amount paid to the state. One may wonder whether the publicity of the auction process

[7] In addition to the dole, Severus is said to have initiated a daily handout of oil: SHA *Sept. Sev.* 18.3.

[8] Citizenship: Inst.Gai.1.32c. Subsidies: Suet. *Claud.* 18.2. Immunities: D.50.5.3; D. 50.6.6(5).5.3; D.50.6.6(5).5.

always led to the best price. Caesar mentions that the Gaul Dumnorix won tax contracts for a low price because no one dared to bid against him, and the triumvirs used a similar strategy of intimidation after their victory in the Civil War (Caes. *BG* 1.18; Cassius Dio 47.14.4–5, 47.17.3). Yet the auctions were announced and transacted publicly, as the dossier of the Pompeian auctioneer Caecilius Iucundus shows (Andreau 1974), and they appear to have been a popular method of arriving at reasonably transparent and efficient prices (Malmendier 2002, 221–222).

The choice to auction state contracts was hardly influenced by such notions though, but rather by the fact that the Roman state initially had neither the manpower nor the inclination to oversee operations. This changed over the course of the Empire. The growth of an Imperial administrative service pushed out some forms of tax-farming (Günther 2008, 102–115; Malmendier 2002, 61–62), and as more and more economic power fell into the hands of Imperial agents, the state and the Imperial *fiscus* increasingly took an interventionist approach. This process was no doubt hastened from the outset of the Antonine plague by a succession of misfortunes that is loosely described as the crisis of the third century (Wassink 1991, 477–486). Under such circumstances, interventions by benevolent emperors came to be regarded as a positive stabilising influence. An example is a story told of Alexander Severus in the late-fourth-century *Historia Augusta*, which may carry an echo of Diocletian's Price Edict. When petitioned to lower the price of pork and beef, the child-emperor purportedly refused, but forbade the slaughter of sows, suckling pigs, cows and calves until so many had been born that oversupply corrected the issue (SHA *Alex.* 22,7–8). In contrast, around 110 AD Trajan forbade Pliny to force unused state funds upon lenders unwilling to accept a 12 per cent interest rate because they could borrow privately on better terms, but insisted that Pliny should lower the interest rate until enough borrowers were found (Plin. *Ep.* 10.54–55). Similarly, Hadrian stated that government leaseholders should not be forced to take up unprofitable contracts that remained unsold at auction (D.49.14.3.6). In all, barring exceptional cases of expropriation or the forced sale of maltreated slaves (Pennitz 1991; Matthews 1921, 252–255), the Roman state seldom intervened in the freedom to enter—or not to enter—into a contract for a certain price (C.4.10.5 [a. 530]: *initio libera potestas unicuique est habendi vel non habendi contractus*).

46.4 Value Assessments at Law

As noted, the mechanism of price formation was well understood, if only as a lesson learned from experience. For legal purposes, however, it was necessary to further interpret the prices realised at market. A plaintiff could have a larger interest in destroyed property than its mere replacement value or its purchase cost minus depreciation. The market for certain goods could be volatile, dysfunctional or even non-existent: a division of the non-transferable right of *usus* comes to mind (D.10.3.10.1). In both examples, the private judge tasked with assessing damages (*litis aestimatio*) was instructed by the writ (*formula*) specific to the case to consider other factors (Kaser and Hackl 1996, 372; Kaser 1971, 499–502). In consequence, legal estimates of "true" (*verum*) or "just" (*iustum*) prices, though based on "real" prices and possibly in accordance with them, could as well go beyond or below the market price, which itself was rarely used as the standard of valuation.

In cases involving specific goods (*certa*) other than money,[9] notional buyers and sellers had to be invented to arrive at "true" prices that assumed normal market operations. Paul notes that olive oil is not valued the same in oil-producing Hispania and Rome, nor in times of scarcity and plenitude—which is normal—but then adds that the valuation should nevertheless leave out price shocks (D.35.2.63.2). Similarly, a slave owner is considered enriched to the extent of the replacement price for unnecessary goods purchased for him by his slave as if they were necessary, but only to the "true" value of necessary expenditures (D.15.3.5pr). These examples show that the immediately realisable cash value was distinguished from the regular or "true" price that was the standard in claims for "whatever the thing is worth" (*quanti ea res est*) (Kaser 1971, 499; Matthews 1921, 241–244). The former was used in tax matters, plausibly, for instance, when calculating the manumission tax on slaves (Günther 2008, 121–125). The "true" price, on the other hand, was an estimate of the value that a proverbial regular person would place on the goods under normal circumstances. Compared to actual market prices, the "true" price represented an attempt to objectify valuation by filtering out the influence of price shocks and market failures, as well as that of personal sentiment and interest (D.9.2.33pr and D.35.2.63pr).

Sentiment did not lend itself to estimation by a court of law, though its influence on personal behaviour was recognised.[10] A slave son held special value to his natural father, but this *affectio* was not taken into account when the son was part of an inheritance, or was injured, or if the father had bargained for his manumission, or when valuing a legacy of the services of a slave.[11] Ulpian is instructive as to the reason. Regarding freedman fraud (which touched on the patron's right to inherit), he explains that a patron cannot rescind the alienation of land with the mere argument that he grew up there, or that his ancestors are buried there, "because it is accepted that the fraud has to pertain to damage in money" (D.38.5.1.15: *fraus enim in damno accipitur pecuniario*). Sentiment could not be reduced objectively to a price: a fact that was all the more important because the Roman law of civil procedure required all judgements to be expressed in monetary terms (*condemnatio pecuniaria*) (Kaser and Hackl 1996, 372; Pennitz 1991, 249–324), adding to the importance of valuation matters in general. That sentimental value was ignored, though, does not mean that all personal interest fell by the wayside. An action for an *incertum*, where the judge was instructed to assess "whatever ought to be given or done" (*quidquid ... dare facere oportet*), allowed room to award damages for consequential loss and lost profits in addition to the value of the object lost.[12] If a mule were damaged, the depreciation of the other mule in the team would be taken into account (D.9.2.22.1). And so, if capable of valuation, the subjective interest (*id quod*

[9] Kaser and Hackl 1996, 316–317; Zimmermann 1990, 825; Kaser 1971, 492–493.

[10] A slave owner was presumed not to have wanted to charge his favourite or necessary slaves under a general hypothec: D.20.1.6.

[11] Inheritance: D.35.2.63pr. Damage to property: D.9.2.33pr. Manumission: D.19.5.5pr. and 5. Legacy of services: D.7.7.6.2. Matthews 1921, 247–249.

[12] Kaser and Hackl 1996, 318; Zimmermann 1990, 826–827; Kaser 1971, 493–494 and 500–501. The same holds true for actions aimed at *quanti ea res erit* or *quanti interest*.

interest) in e.g. a *bona fide* contract or in cases of damage to property was certainly considered. As Zimmermann notes, this represents a shift in the judicial assessment of damages "from an objective, standardized point of view to a more sophisticated and equitable approach, characterized by individualizing and, on the whole, subjective criteria" (Zimmermann 1990, 826).

Except in the peculiar case of estimation on oath (*iusiurandum in litem*) (in cases of *contumacia*: Kaser and Hackl 1996, 339–340), the value of the condemnation was set by the private judge, who may have had little experience or training in assaying. Parties offered evidence to support their valuations and doubtlessly called in expert witnesses, yet very few sources provide information about the assaying profession or the standards it employed. Some rules can be discerned from the writings of the jurists though, particularly on the *lex Falcidia* (see ch. 38).[13] Appraisals were made at the present normal value, with no regard to book values or possible future sales, because, as Paulus notes, "it would be preposterous to be called enriched before we have acquired."[14] Nevertheless, this was precisely what was needed when valuing legacies under a condition precedent, which requires an assessment of the odds of future fulfilment of the condition. The jurists suggested the use of the market value (*quanti id venire potest*) in such cases (D.35.2.45.1; D.35.2.73.1; Matthews 1921, 250), but it is important to note this was an *estimated* market value for lack of any true market in conditionally owned goods. The same held for annuities.[15] Some argued that the rule ought to apply to legacies of conditional claims as well, assigning to each party the odds that the event would or would not occur, but it appears that the invention of a fictive market in conditional claims went too far for the practical minds of the Roman jurists. The problem was better solved by giving mutual guarantees and settling once matters became clear (D.35.2.45.1; D.35.2.73.1; see also D.35.3.1pr). Legacies for maintenance payments (*alimenta*), finally, were valued at current price by a rather more refined yardstick; namely, the life expectancy of the recipient. This is the context of Ulpian's famous life table (D.35.2.68pr).

The legal ingenuity and mental acrobatics displayed by the jurists is impressive. They show an awareness of most factors that still influence valuation in modern courtrooms, including such abstract concepts as the opportunity cost of loans and delayed profits (D.35.2.45pr.; D.35.2.66pr.; D.35.2.73.4). Rather than any pressing social need, system-internal considerations seem to be the reason why different standards applied in different cases, acquiring their own momentum by being fitted into the "seamless web" of the law. It does appear that the jurists tended towards valuation at (adjusted and estimated) present market prices when confronted with e.g. conditional legacies, while making an effort to establish the present value of future claims more precisely by the use of life tables; but this warrants no speculation about the difference between volatile prices and calculable death. *Aestimatio* was up to the judge, and the jurists merely provided forensic techniques for establishing credible valuations in a

[13] On valuations under the *lex Falcidia* see Rüfner forthcoming.

[14] D.35.2.63pr.: *esse autem praeposterum ante nos locupletes dici, quam adquisierimus.* Also see D.35.2.42; D.35.2.62.1; D.47.8.4.11; Matthews 1921, 249.

[15] D.35.2.55. A perpetual annuity to a city was valued at twenty-five times the annual amount, assuming a fictitious 4 per cent interest: D.35.2.3.2. A perpetual usufruct to a city was valued at thirty years: D.35.2.68pr.

courtroom. However, such techniques could only be persuasive if they reflected widely held views; and in this sense the notion of "true" or even "just" prices is illuminating.

46.5 Diocletian's Interventions

The jurists left the question of *unjust* prices to the orators because, absent fraud, questions of commutative justice had little relevance to the validity of the contract (Zimmermann 1990, 255). However, once the aedilician remedies were expanded to include contracts other than the sale of slaves and cattle (see de Ligt, ch. 50), what constituted fraud became increasingly important. It is perhaps in this context that Diocletian's chancellery issued the famous constitution on *iustum pretium* of 285 AD,[16] containing two innovations, about which, countless words have been written since the reception of Roman law. First, the seller of land (and only he!) could ask for additional payment (or rescission) in case of grave disadvantage; second, the constitution established a standard of proof for unjust prices, which were presumed to start at less than half the "true" price. Since it threatened all buyers of land for less than this *minimum* with an obligation to pay the remainder, the constitution forms an attempt to nudge the price of land by influencing private negotiations. Perhaps such indirect control was possible in 285 AD, when "true" prices could still be ascertained and inflation stood at roughly 5 per cent. But only a few years later, inflation levels had spiralled to 23 per cent per year for the period 293–301 AD, owing to a poisonous mix of monetary reform and lavish government spending (Wassink 1991, 486–492). Under these circumstances, minimum "just" prices made no sense and other measures were in order.

The result was an ambitious (but less influential) effort to put an immediate stop to inflation by fixing *maximum* prices through public law. The *edictum de pretiis rerum venalium*[17] of 301 AD constitutes an attempt to restructure all of economic life by decree, by providing a list of close to 1,500 things which carry a maximum price varying from 2 to 150,000 denarii. Of course, it failed. No complete copy survives, but both Latin and Greek fragments (Latin being the primary language) have been recovered from forty-five different sites in the Eastern half of the Empire, allowing for near-complete reconstruction. The lengthy edict was posted in public places, sometimes with an accompanying proclamation by the provincial governor, as in Aezani; non-compliance with its provisions was punishable as a capital crime.[18] There is no direct evidence for promulgation in the West, but absence of proof is certainly not proof of absence, and a section on transportation prices to maritime destinations in the West seems to assume a broader validity. In any case, the price lists have attracted considerable attention from economic historians, although much remains unclear about how the prices were established or their internal relation (Rathbone 2009, 317–321).

[16] C.4.44.2 (a. 285). Also see C.4.44.8 (a. 293). The text has been charged with major interpolations, but its tenor fits well with other legislation by Diocletian: Platschek 2011 against Zimmermann 1990, 259–261.

[17] Editions: Giacchero 1974; Lauffer 1971. Discussion of recent finds in Salway 2010; Crawford 2002. A new edition is sorely lacking.

[18] Aezani proclamation: *AE* 1997, 1443. Capital crime: praef. 18. Speidel 2009, 493–496.

Lactantius described the consequences of the edict: the collapse of markets, the scarcity of goods, violence and bloodshed (Lactant. *De mort. pers.* 7). Even allowing for the exaggerations of a Christian partisan, it is clear that the edict failed spectacularly and was rescinded no later than 305 AD. According to the preamble, the edict was issued to protect the purchasing power of the military from profiteers, but from the variety of affected services and goods it is evident that its scope was broader. In fact, the edict was probably intended to curb inflation and restore the buying power of gold, working in conjunction with a monetary reform edict found at Aphrodisias that was prepared simultaneously (*AE* 1973, 526a; Speidel 2009, 496–502). It was a drastic break with the favour that Diocletian and other emperors had shown to party autonomy; but nevertheless it was not the first attempt to intervene by way of price ceilings. Earlier emperors had imposed ceilings on various goods as an emergency measure, or had regulated the prices of eunuchs, lawyers' fees and gladiatorial games for political reasons.[19] Sometimes such enactments were enforced (Lawyers: Plin. *Ep.* 5.9.3–4), more often not. What they have in common is their intent to signal an Imperial policy to combat excesses, rather than any attempt to permanently control particular prices. As such, they may be compared to the earlier sumptuary laws (see section 46.2). In this regard and in spite of its draconic punishments, Diocletian's edict appears as a conservative measure that, by its increase in scale, turned into a revolutionary overhaul of the entire economy.

46.6 Conclusion

Everything in Rome had its price (Iuv. 3.183–184: *omnia Romae cum pretio*), and this price was regularly formed by the operation of free market forces in a process of negotiation. Awareness of (the causes of) price fluctuations was more widespread than is often granted. The freedom to enter or refuse a contract was enshrined in the Roman legal system, reflecting its "core features of economic liberalism" (Zimmermann 1990, 258). Market prices influenced valuations for legal purposes, but they were not the only standard of value, since more refined tools were often required. The Roman jurists showed great finesse in developing such tools, particularly in their discussions of the value of future or conditional goods under the *lex Falcidia*.

Interventions mostly occurred in times of perceived market failure and crisis, but the Roman state generally left price formation to the forces of supply and demand. In any case, most interventions were not intended to have any permanence, but rather served to signal the involvement of an active and principled government. The economic policy of the Roman state, if these words are not too strong, consisted of attempts to influence supply and demand, through government spending and monetary controls as well as selective taxation and production incentives, while accepting the resulting prices as a necessary outcome. In all, price setting was largely absent from the Roman economy: not because the mechanism was unheard of, but because it went against a deeply ingrained belief in the primacy of party autonomy.

[19] Shortage: Dio Cass. 60.17.8. Eunuchs: Suet. *Dom.* 7.1. Lawyers: Tac. *Ann.* 11.5–7. Games: *CIL* II 6278.

Bibliography

Andreau, J. 1974. *Les affaires de Monsieur Jucundus*. Rome.

Bang, P. F. 2008. *The Roman bazaar: a comparative study of trade and trade markets in a tributary empire*. Cambridge.

Crawford, M. H. 1985. *Coinage and money under the Roman republic: Italy and the Mediterranean economy*. Berkeley.

Crawford, M. H. ed. 1996. *Roman statutes*. 2 vols. London.

Crawford, M. H. 2002. "Discovery, autopsy and progress: Diocletian's jigsaw puzzles." In T. P. Wiseman, ed., *Classics in progress: essays on ancient Greece and Rome*. Oxford. 145–163.

Erdkamp, P. 2005. *The grain market in the Roman empire: a social, political and economic study*. Cambridge.

Finley, M. I. 1985. *The ancient economy*. Berkeley.

Giacchero, M. 1974. Edictum Diocletiani et Collegarum de pretiis rerum venalium in integrum fere restitutum e latinis graecisque fragmentis, Vol. 1: Edictum and Vol. 2: Imagines. Genoa.

Günther, S. 2008. Vectigalia nervos esse rei publicae: *die indirekten Steuern in der römischen Kaiserzeit von Augustus bis Diokletian*. Wiesbaden.

Harper, K. (2010). "Slave prices in late antiquity (and in the very long term)." *Historia* 59: 206–238.

Hauken, T. and Malay, H. 2009. "A new edict of Hadrian from the province of Asia, setting regulations for requisitioned transport." In R. Haensch, ed., *Selbstdarstellung und Kommunikation: die Veröffentlichung staatlicher Urkunde auf Stein und Bronze in der römischen Welt*. Munich. 327–348.

Kaser, M. 1971. *Das römische Privatrecht*. Munich.

Kaser, M. and Hackl, K. 1996[2]. *Das römische Zivilprozeßrecht*. Munich.

Lauffer, S. 1971. Edictum Diocletiani de pretiis: *Diokletians Preisedikt*. Berlin.

Malmendier, U. 2002. Societas publicanorum: *staatliche Wirtschaftsaktivitäten in den Händen privater Unternehmer*. Cologne.

Matthews, N. (1921). "The valuation of property in the Roman law." *Harvard Law Review* 34: 229–259.

Nicolet, C. 2000. *Censeurs et publicains: économie et fiscalité dans la Rome antique*. Paris.

Pennitz, M. 1991. *Der "Enteignungsfall" im römischen Recht der Republik und des Prinzipats: eine funktional-rechtsvergleichende Problemstellung*. Vienna.

Platschek, J. (2011). "Bemerkungen zur Datierung der *laesio enormis*." *Zeitschrift der Savigny-Stiftung für Rechtsgeschichte, romanistische Abteilung* 128: 406–409.

Rathbone, D. 1997. "Prices and price formation in Roman Egypt." In J. Andreau, P. Briant and R. Descat, eds., *Économie antique: prix et formation des prix dans les économies antiques*. Saint-Bertrand-de-Comminges. 183–244.

Rathbone, D. 2009. "Earnings and costs: living standards and the Roman economy (first to third centuries AD)." In A. Bowman and A. Wilson, eds., *Quantifying the Roman economy: methods and problems*. Oxford. 299–326.

Rosivach, V. J. (2006). "The *lex Fannia Sumptuaria* of 161 BC." *The Classical Journal* 102: 1–15.

Salway, B. 2010. "*Mancipivm rvsticvm sive vrbanvm*: the slave chapter of Diocletian's edict on maximum prices." In U. Roth, ed., *By the sweat of your brow: Roman slavery in its socio-economic setting*. London. 1–20.

Scheidel, W. (2005). "Real slave prices and the relative cost of slave labor in the Greco-Roman world." *Ancient Society* 35: 1–17.

Speidel, M. A. (2009). "Wirtschaft und Moral im Urteil Diokletians: Zu den kaiserlichen Argumenten für Höchstpreise." *Historia* 58: 486–505.

Szaivert, W. and Wolters, R. 2005. *Löhne, Preise, Werte: Quellen zur römischen Geldwirtschaft*. Darmstadt.

Temin, P. 2006. "The economy of the early Roman empire." *The Journal of Economic Perspectives* 20: 133–151.

Temin, P. 2013. *The Roman market economy*. Princeton.

Wassink, A. (1991). "Inflation and financial policy under the Roman empire to the Price Edict of 301 A.D." *Historia* 40: 465–493.

Zimmermann, R. 1990. *The law of obligations: Roman foundations of the civilian tradition*. Cape Town.

CHAPTER 47

LAW, BUSINESS VENTURES AND TRADE

JEAN-JACQUES AUBERT

47.1 Introduction

TRADE and business life seem to have been regulated by law at a rather late date in Roman history. Admittedly, some early evidence for legal provisions related to economic activities is extant, in the form of international treaties with Carthage (509 BC) and with neighbouring communities, such as the so-called *Foedus Cassianum* (493 BC), all of them recorded by later historians, such as Polybius (second century BC), Dionysius of Halicarnassus, and Livy (first century BC and AD). The XII Tables (traditionally dated to the mid-fifth century BC) and scattered pieces of legislation dated to the mid-Republican period and dealing with money-lending (e.g. *lex Genucia de foeneratione* of 342 BC, *lex Sempronia de pecunia credita* of 193 BC) and debt-bondage (e.g. *lex Poetelia Papiria de nexis* of 326/313 BC) brought only modest changes to the legal framework in which trade was to develop (Aubert 2014a[2]). During the last two centuries of the Republican period, trade and consumption were the target of a series of sumptuary laws bearing mostly on food, but also on other luxury items.[1] Even though the impact of *leges publicae* bearing on private law may be significantly underestimated (Mantovani 2012), it is clear that statute law was not the way legal issues arising from business activities were addressed and solved.

By the time Rome became a Mediterranean power with global commercial interests, in the late third century BC, edictal (i.e. praetorian and aedilician) law was the venue of choice to provide the business community with adequate legal remedies in order to protect traders involved in litigation (Aubert 2015). With the creation and timely grant of legal actions pertaining to contracts and delicts, praetors and aediles presided over the making of a sophisticated system available to Romans and non-Romans, free and non-free economic actors. Little is known about the circumstances surrounding the elaboration of edictal law. On the basis of what remains of classical juristic opinions, it seems that the system was rather stable over the early Imperial period. The Roman law of barter

[1] Coudry 2004, 2012. On the economic aspects of sumptuary legislation, Aubert forthcoming.

(*permutatio*) (Aubert 2014b, possibly a late classical development), sale (*emptio venditio*), lease and hire (*locatio conductio*), mandate (*mandatum*), partnership (*societas*), loan for consumption (*mutuum*) or use (*commodatum*), deposit (*depositum*) and pledge (*pignus*), supplemented by more generic verbal commitments (such as *stipulationes*) or more specific written ones (*nomina transcripticia, syngraphai, chirographa*), and eventually by all kinds of agreements referred to as *pacta* and *conventiones*, covered most contractual situations encountered in the conduct of business activities from production to consumption, including storage and distribution (Zimmermann 1990; Johnston 1999). To those should be added various forms of agency and liabilities based on inadequate behaviour such as fraud (*dolus*), negligence (*negligentia*) and ignorance (*ignorantia*) (Aubert 1994; Petrucci 2002; Miceli 2008).

The production and distribution of goods and the provision of services were carried out by both private and public economic actors using their and/or others' capital and/or human resources, directly or through intermediaries, partners, employees or dependants. From each scheme arose diverse, though comparable, legal problems. The remedies devised by magistrates and enforced by judges within the twofold formulary procedure (*ordo*) called for adjustments and interpretations offered by Roman jurists and practitioners. Their opinions and the solutions they promoted are reflected in both classical jurisprudence and in some rather scarce documentary evidence, such as inscriptions, graffiti, tablets and papyri.

Actual cases of business ventures are not so commonly attested in extant texts. In addition, the documentary evidence is by nature limited in scope, allowing for a partial view of possibly exceptional situations. Take, for instance, the so-called Muziris papyrus, a famous second-century-AD document from Roman Egypt (*SB* XVIII 13167) recording a contract of freight, only a fragment of which is preserved.[2] It provides for unidentified goods to be transported on camels by an unidentified private entrepreneur from an unidentified harbour on the Red Sea over the desert to the upper-Egypt town of Koptos, to be consigned there in a public warehouse (*demosiai lemptikai apothekai*) before being loaded on river-boats and shipped downstream to Alexandria, ultimately to be delivered there at the custom house. The goods were assumedly imported from India across the Indian Ocean to be consumed in an unidentified place. The transportation and storage over the short stretch to which the papyrus refers involved cameleers (*kamelitai*), guards (*paraphylakes*), agents (*epitropoi*) and managers (*phrontistai*).

The lack of expected detail and specific information is often combined with accidental or intentional opacity. Take the curious letter of Augustan date sent by one Syneros to Chion, a member of the Imperial household, about the shady business of the slave Epaphras at Oxyrhynchus:

> (*recto*) From Syneros to his friend Chion, many greetings. If you are well, it is good. Theon brought me Ohapis, the royal banker from Oxyrhynchus, who told me about Epaphras' shamelessness. Therefore I'll say nothing more than that: do not accept to incur any loss on account of them! Believe me, excessive kindness injures people, and how! He will show you what it is all about when you convoke him, but hold on: whoever makes such a large profit from such a petty sum will kill his master! Then I'll scream if I see something, by gods and

[2] Rathbone 2000; Morelli 2011; Harris forthcoming.

mankind [*crossed out*: if you ... these, not to anybody?]. You will be able to take revenge lest someone else decides to do so. [*verso*] To Chion, of Caesar. (*P. Oxy.* xliv 3208; see also *CPL* 246, 247)

In spite of the large amount of known and published papyri, the evidence for business ventures is remarkably scarce in Roman Egypt and elsewhere, outside agriculture.[3] The same is true of the less numerous wax (or wooden) tablets from Campania, Transylvania, Britain or elsewhere.[4]

Actual cases of business ventures may lurk behind classical juristic opinions collected in Justinian's Digest. Classical jurists are known to have adopted a casuistic approach, traces of which are sometimes perceptible in the sixth-century compilation. An excerpt from the first book of the *Decreta* by the early-third-century jurist Iulius Paulus (D. 14.5.8) discusses the appointment by one Titianus Primus of a slave in charge of lending money and taking pledges (*mutuis pecuniis dandis et pignoribus accipiendis*). Incidentally, the slave was notorious for making cash advances to barley traders and conducting other business activities not specifically included in the implied charter of appointment (*lex praepositionis*, possibly limited to an oral or even implicit agreement); for instance, by taking a lease on storage spaces, obviously to keep pledges in nature. As it happened, the slave eventually ran away and Titianus Primus was sued over his (i.e. the slave's) actions. Obviously, the principal insisted on a strict interpretation of the scope of the appointment, a position shared by Paul. His opponent pushed for a wider interpretation and mustered the support of no less an authority than the prefect of the food supply, whose decision was eventually backed on appeal by the emperor himself (Jakab 2014, 347).

47.2 A Case Study of Business Venture: The Management of Storage Space

What the Muziris papyrus and Paul's opinion have in common is the explicit, unavoidable reliance on storage facilities for trade, no matter whether it was local, regional, or long-distance trade. Storage was a key element of business life, because of the geographical and/or time gap between production and consumption, often implying processing, packaging and transportation. Like, or even more than, any other aspect of ancient economic activity, the process of storing goods involved significant risks for all parties, connected with title of property, contracts, damage and theft, and therefore generated various kinds of litigation. This ubiquitous activity left many traces in both textual and material remains.[5]

[3] This is true, too, of the Classical and Hellenistic Greek world; cf. Chandezon 2011.

[4] See later on the Sulpicii archive (*TPSulp*); cf. also the Iucundus archive from Pompeii (*T. Jucundus*); the Vindolanda tablets from Hadrian's Wall (*T.Vindol.*, late first and early second century AD); the Transylvanian tablets from Alburnus Maior (*T.Dacia*, second century AD); or the Albertini tablets (*T.Alb.*) from North Africa in the late fifth century.

[5] Rickman 1971, 164–209; Wacke 1980/1996; Rickman 1998; Virlouvet 2006, 2007; du Plessis 2012, 173–189; Jakab 2014.

Three Roman inscriptions usually identified as *leges horreorum* document the legal aspects of storage management in Imperial times (*FIRA* III^2 145a–c). To make sense, they must be read as a group, even though they were set up quite independently from one another and may not even be contemporary. Two of them were discovered in the late nineteenth and early twentieth centuries, at a time when Latin epigraphists often doubled as legal scholars as well. As a result, the third text, as fragmentary as it is, was initially published with many conjectures based on what was previously known through the earlier material. However, all reconstructions remained at best hypothetical and triggered counterpropositions, the philological and legal nature of which blurred the debate about the meaning of what was actually legible. Consequently, this material can still yield some interesting information about the management of storage spaces.

The first inscription[6] was published in 1885. It is a large marble slab found in the vicinity of Porta Salaria, north of Rome, and preserved in the Capitol Museum. The left part of the stone is badly damaged, although all other sides seem to be intact.[7] The first four lines are engraved in larger size than the rest of the inscription and thus advertise the type of business: these are storage spaces (*horrea*), evidently Imperial property.

The legible letters in line 2 (LOC, from *locare* or *locatio*, as confirmed by the rest of the inscription) suggest that spaces of various types, such as closets (*armaria*) and open areas (*loca*), went for rent for a limited though renewable period of time. By contrast, lines 6–12 spell out the conditions under which individual sections were rented out, in the form of a *lex contractus* or job description, as stated by the words *lex horreorum* in line 5. Let us note the strange disposition of the text in that line, the left part of which must have included the end of the previous sentence ("*ex hac die et ex* …"), be it the kalends, *nonae* or ides of a specific though unknown month.

The regulation section (ll. 6–12) starts with the modalities for cancellation of the lease (*renuntiare*) with advanced notice on December 13 and full payment of the rent. The loss of the beginning of lines 7 and 8 hides the content of the next provision, which may have dealt with tacit renewal of the lease with the same conditions and for the same rent. The use of *hedera* leaves in ll. 8–10 signals a strong mark of punctuation, each leaf introducing a new provision. The lessee of the space, whatever its nature (*armaria, loca* etc.), may have been interested in subletting (*elocare*) part(s)—or all—of the space, but the damage to the beginning of line 9 makes it uncertain whether or not he was entitled to do so, and if so, under what conditions. The extant text suggests, however, that under specific, though unknown, circumstances, no standard of liability for safekeeping (*custodia*) was imposed upon the lessee (as opposed to the sublessee?). The next provision bears on the goods (*invecta inlata*) stored in the premises, to be explained by the third inscription (cf. n. 13). The meaning of the *venia* and *chirographum* mentioned in ll. 1–11 is unclear. The last provision frees the landlord or manager (*horrearius*) from any liability for deposits not assigned to a keeper (*custos*), supposedly in cases when the goods were lost, stolen or damaged in the absence of proper registration.

Whatever the meaning of this hocus pocus, nothing in the above analysis rests upon reconstructions or conjectures, other than [*cu*]*stodia* in line 9, a fairly safe bet. The

[6] *FIRA* III^2 145a = *ILS* 5914. Rickman 1971, 198–200; du Plessis 2012, 177, with translation.

[7] *Supplementa Italica. Roma (CIL VI). 1. Musei Capitolini*, Rome 1999, 435, no. 1512. Huelsen's remark in *CIL* VI, iv.ii.3462, ad 33747 is ambiguous, but Silvio Panciera confirms (personal communication) that only the left part was damaged, so that the regulation did not extend over line 12.

inscription is undoubtedly dealing with the management of storage spaces (*horrea*) belonging to the Roman emperor and entrusted to an employee or contractor (*horrearius*) in charge of letting out sections (either *armaria* or *loca*, i.e. equipped or not) of the building for a limited but renewable period, against payment of a rent (*pensio*). The manager (*horrearius*) is to be held liable for safekeeping insofar as the tenants (and subtenants) follow specific rules. The business involves three levels: the emperor as landlord (*dominus*), the *horrearius* as manager and the tenants/subtenants (*quisquis in his horreis conductum habet*) as customers. The purpose of the inscription is twofold: advertisement (ll. 1–4) and regulation (ll. 5–12).

The second text[8] was read on an inscription found in the Chiesa S. Martino on the Esquiline Hill in 1654, and copied in a manuscript (cod. Barbarini 30, 92, fol. 162) in the seventeenth century, before becoming permanently lost. Only the upper part of the text was then extant or legible. What is left corresponds to the advertising section of the inscription from Porta Salaria:

> In these *horrea*, property of Quintus Tineius Sacerdos Clemens . . . , for rent: the whole building (*horrea*), rooms (*apothecae*), sections (*compendiaria*), closets (*armaria*), halls (*intercolumnia*), closet spaces (*loca armaris*), as of today and starting on the first of July.

Lines 4 and 5 seem to be intact and list in a decreasing order various options offered to potential tenants. Remarkably, the whole building (*horrea*) is for rent, in bulk or in parts, in the latter case with immediate vacancies and projected ones. This detail suggests that the *lex horreorum*, if this is what we are dealing with,[9] was issued by the landlord, not by the manager, in order to define the types of services (and places) to be offered for rent to potential customers. Some words, such as *compendiaria* and *loca armaris*, are found only in those two or three inscriptions identified as *leges horreorum*, with no parallel in extant Latin juristic texts.[10] These inscriptions constitute a small cluster of documents of similar nature, and their respective function is clarified by the comparison and extrapolation of what is preserved in each of them. As for the Esquiline text, nothing suggests that the initial advertisement was followed with a set of regulations. The landlord may very well have been a public figure or at least a member of a known family:[11] One Quintus Tineius Sacerdos Clemens was ordinary consul in 158, and the name is attested in several inscriptions, most noticeably on a lead pipe discovered in Praenestum (*CIL* XIV 3038), where he appears in the position of *dominus* (in the genitive case) with regard to the *officinator* Lucius Marius Valens:

a) K TI SACERDOTIS KLM *(to be read from right to left)*
b) L MARIVS VALENS FECIT *(with reverse final Ss)*

[8] *FIRA* III² 145b = *ILS* 5913 (Rome, Esquiline, second or early third century AD). Rickman 1971, 197–198, with an explanation of various technical terms.

[9] Rickman 1971, 197: "not a *lex horreorum*, but a notice of lease."

[10] Cf. *Vocabularium Iurisprudentiae Romanae. Compendiarium*, cf. *TLL* 3 (1906–1912) 2036.36–39, is attested only in *CIL* VI 33747 and 33860, as 37795 was published too late to be taken into account. *OLD* s.v. translates "a fitment in a granary" but cites no other instance.

[11] *PIR* III 323, no. 172. Cf. also nos. 165 (cos. ord. a. 195), 170 (cos. suff. under Commodus), 171 (cos. II a. 219), also attested on a *fistula plumbea*, cf. *Lancianium syll. aq.* n. 114 (*praeterea Sacerdos*).

One point is clear: the management of *horrea* seems to be standardised, no matter whether the landlord was the emperor or some private individual(s). The similarities between private and public sectors in other economic activities are well documented, be it in water management and tile or brick production. In all cases, letting out the facilities alternates with direct or indirect management. In this regard, the management of Roman storage spaces looks similar to that of clay-beds (*figlinae*), starting as private establishments to be taken over by the senatorial elite and eventually by the Imperial administration. The interest of the latter in a variety of economic activities may lie in elected or imposed public policies. The fourth-century-AD author of the *Historia Augusta* records that Severus Alexander played a significant part in the process:

> He built public storage buildings in all neighbourhoods and all those who had no private facilities (*custodiae*) brought their goods there. (SHA *Alex.* 39.3)

In that case, like in the *lex horreorum* from Porta Salaria (*CIL* VI 33747), public *horrea* were made available to private customers. Consequently, such facilities were not limited to public or military use,[12] and insofar as the few extant *leges horreorum* seem to indicate, their management was not necessarily affected by the nature of their purpose.

The third and last inscription traditionally identified as a *lex horreorum* is described by the editor in *CIL* as "a fragment of a marble slab with elegant lettering" and was discovered in 1910 in the Chiesa S. Saba on the Aventine Hill.[13] The text is damaged on the left, right and lower margins, and displays just enough letters to secure its identification as a *lex horreorum*, although there is no way to specify the public or private function of the facilities. The restitution [*Horr*]*ea Umm*[*idiana*], or possibly [*Horr*]*ea Umm*[*idiana* | *Cornificia*]*na*, in connection with Marcus Aurelius' younger sister, Annia Cornificia Faustina, and her husband M. Ummidius Quadratus, cos. 167, is plausible and clever, but remains highly hypothetical. In that case, as in the previous ones, the enterprise would have been controlled by members of the senatorial aristocracy or of the Imperial family, and its management would have been necessarily entrusted to agents or (chief-)tenants. Line 5 opens the regulation section, with a provision concerning stored goods, possibly to be regarded as a pledge (l. 6: [*pig?*]*nori erunt*) to enforce payment of the rent ([*pensi?*]*o solvatur*), while the next provision may refer to the spatial organisation within the facilities (*horrea*) and the eventual restoration of the place upon cancellation of the lease. Some clue to understanding the words "*inaedificaverit*" and "*refigere*" may be found in Ulpian's opinion on usufruct:

> If he [= the *usufructuarius*] has internally rearranged the premises, (in my opinion) he is not entitled to take down nor dismantle what has been built in, but he can claim back exactly what has been dismantled. (D.7.1.15pr)

The analysis and comparison of all three inscriptions (*FIRA* III² 145a–c) raise more questions than they provide answers. The management of storage buildings and spaces

[12] This should not be taken for granted; cf. CTh.12.6.16 (a. 375). Cf. also Rickman 1971, 180, 191, and 195.

[13] *FIRA* III² 145c = *CIL* VI 37795 (of uncertain date). Rickman 1971, 200–201; du Plessis 2012, 187, with translation.

calls for hire and lease (*locatio conductio*), deposit (*depositum*), safekeeping (*custodia*) and pledge (*pignus*), within diverse and complex contractual relationships between owners, managers, staff and customers (Dubouloz 2008; France 2008). Indirect agency is implied. While the main purpose of storage spaces lies in the safekeeping of goods, sometimes with high value, litigation connected with such economic activities stems from a variety of obligations based on contracts and delicts. The very existence of *leges horreorum* implies some degree of sophistication resulting from—or justified by—the known diversity of commercial practices.

The *lex horreorum* from Porta Salaria explicitly refers to several parties: the owner of the building (*Caesar Augustus*), its manager (*horrearius*), possibly concurrently lessee and lessor, a member of the staff (*custos*) and the customer or lessee (*quisquis in his horreis conductum habet*). The advertising part (lines 1–4) proposes a contract of hire and lease between two parties: one represents any potential customer interested in renting storage space in this specific location; the other party to the contract is harder to identify, either the owner of the premises or the manager—the nature of the legal relationship between the former two apparently falling outside the scope of the *lex*.

Two documents from Pompeii shed light upon this ambiguity. They are painted wall inscriptions concerning the rental of commercial facilities. The first shows Gnaeus Alleius Nigidius Maius, the owner of an *insula*, or apartment building, named Arriana Polliana, renting out various sections of the building, such as shops (*tabernae*), stalls (*pergulae*), a dining room (*cenacula equestria*?) and a house (*domus*), as of next 15 July (*CIL* IV 138 = *ILS* 6035; Dubouloz 2011, 183–86). The owner invites all interested parties to call on his slave Primus, who presumably would finalise the contract on behalf of his master. The inscription records the *lex praepositionis* (job description or charter of appointment), enabling the slave to act as business manager (*institor*), along the lines of a legal arrangement described by Servius Sulpicius Rufus, back in Cicero's time, and quoted by Ulpian:

> Servius, too, in the first book of his commentary *Ad Brutum*, states that when a transaction was made with an *insularius* or with a person appointed as the manager of a building or to be in charge of the wholesale purchase of grain, the principal is fully liable. (D.14.3.5.1; Dubouloz 2011, 180–183)

According to both Servius and Ulpian, Primus is a slave manager whose legal transactions make his master fully liable for any damage resulting from verified breach of the contract, the tenant availing himself of an *actio* (*conducti*?) *institoria*, featuring different names in *intentio* (Primus) and *condemnatio* (Cn. Alleius Nigidius Maius). Let us suggest that Servius' reference to an *aedificio praepositus* ("*quem qui aedificio praeposuit*") may pertain to an *horrearius* or a *vilicus horreorum*. As it happens, Roman jurists were familiar with the analogy between *insulae* and *horrea* in view of the legal issues raised in the context of their respective management.

The other painted wall inscription from Pompeii shows similarities with Primus' *lex praepositionis*, but features a female (land)owner renting out various facilities (*tabernae, pergulae, cenacula*), first and foremost a bathing establishment (*balneum*), located on her estate (*praedia*) (*ILS* 5723 = *FIRA* III², 143b; Dubouloz 2011, 168, n. 34). The duration of the lease, five years starting on 13 August, is standard in Rome (*lustrum*). The meaning of the abbreviations SQDLENC in the last line of the inscription is uncertain: it is likely to have had an administrative rather than legal purpose, any *lex contractus* being bent on providing clarification rather than creating puzzlement. Thus Mommsen's *s(i) q(uis) d(esiderabit) l(ocatricem) e(o) n(omine) c(onvenito)* (would-be tenants should contact the landlady!) sounds closer to the truth than Rosini's *s(i) q(uis) d(omi) l(enocinium) e(xerceat) n(e) c(onducito)* (pimps should abstain!). As a landlady, Iulia Felix could be her own *locatrix* or else could rely on a business manager like Primus. The higher the social status of the owner, the more likely he or she was to resort to the latter solution.

Landlords (*locatores*), whether they were *domini, insularii* or *horrearii* (and their female counterparts), were bound to make contracts with tenants (*conductores*), whether they were middlemen or residents/customers. Thanks to the first-century-AD so-called Sulpicii archive from Puteoli, we are in a position to get a closer look at the kind of transactions they were involved in. On 2 July 37, one Diognetus, the slave of Gaius Novius Cypaerus, wrote a *chirographum*[14] in front of his master and upon his explicit order (*iussum*), stipulating that one Hesychus, the slave of an Imperial freedman named Tiberius Iulius Evenus (Primianus), had taken a lease on two separate sections of the *Horrea Bassiana* located in Puteoli, where specific quantities of grain and legumes were stored as security for a loan made to Hesychus by one Gaius Novius Eunus, himself the freedman of Cypaerus. While Eunus appears in several documents in the archive,[15] the big shot seems to have been Cypaerus, also attested as a grain merchant (*mercator frumentarius*) in Puteoli, which may explain the symbolic rent of one sestertius a month for two sections (*horreum* et *intercolumnia*) of the *horrea*.

Diognetus acts as the manager of public storage facilities (*Horrea Bassiana publica Puteolanorum*), either in his own capacity, as *servus cum peculio*, whose credit may occasionally be bolstered by the explicit and punctual backing of his master in the form of a *iussum*, or as an agent (*praepositus*) of the actual *horrearius*, who would be in the present case Caius Novius Cypaerus.[16] Either way, it is necessary to clarify the nature of the legal relationship between the owner of the facilities, be it the colony of Puteoli, the emperor, or a private individual, and the entrepreneur running the business (*horrearius*). This can be done on the basis of both epigraphic and juristic evidence.

Some Latin inscriptions record *vilici horreorum*, Imperial or private slaves in charge of storage facilities, either individually or collectively.[17] Recent studies have established the primary function of *vilici* as business managers in various sectors of the economy and public/Imperial administration.[18] However, not all managers are listed as *vilici*, and some did hide under a wide variety of titles. This is why any *horrearius* can reveal either an

[14] *TPSulp* 45.III.5 (*scriptura exterior*). For the nature of the contract (written as *chirographum*; consensual as *locatio conductio*; and oral as *stipulatio*) cf. Meyer 2004.

[15] Caius Novius Eunus is attested in *TPSulp* 45, 51–52 and 67–68 (37–39 AD). His case is to be compared with that of Lucius Marius Iucundus, *mercator frumentarius*, whose creditor, Gaius Sulpicius Faustus, is dealing with Nardus, the slave of Publius Annius Seleucus, for the lease—at 100 sestertii a month—of a section of the *Horrea Barbatiana*; cf. *TPSulp* 46, 53 and 79 (a. 40).

[16] I am not convinced by the editor's suggestion that "*me locasse*" should be corrected into "*eum locasse*" on the ground that *TPSulp* 45.I.2.6, 45.III.5.5, 46.I.2.6, and 46.III.5.5 would have been recorded upon dictation and the mistake repeatedly and mechanically copied (Camodeca 1999, 123–125).

[17] *ILS* 1620 (Rome, Columbarium Liviae, time of Claudius or Nero); *ILS* 1621 (Rome, Aventine Hill, first century AD?); *AE* 1912, no. 36 (Rome), cf. Carlsen 1995, 36, fig. 5.

[18] Aubert 1994, chs. 3–5; Carlsen 1995; France 2001.

independent entrepreneur, or a business manager acting on behalf of an absentee owner, or even a mere employee (*ILS* 3663, Rome, 75 AD).

Such an ambiguity of status would have been a source of concern for many an ancient economic actor contracting with *horrearii* and taking substantial risks in doing so. The jurists picked up on this uncertainty: before anyone would entrust strangers, even professionals, with the safekeeping of his property, he would be wise to enquire about their reliability and credentials. The mission is sensitive, as the stakes, financial and other, may be high. Caution is required and should be reciprocal: both the owner of the facilities and the entrepreneur or manager must clarify every party's liability. Likewise, both customers and managers have to know for a fact who will eventually be responsible for any loss or damage, whether it is the manager acting on his own account, the owner of the facility acting as his principal or employer, or some middleman, like a chief tenant. The *lex praepositionis* was supposed to set things straight. When the situation was unambiguous, as in the painted wall inscription set up by Gnaeus Alleius Nigidius Maius (above), there was no need dwelling on it, the conditions being implicitly agreed upon, based on common sense and usage. Any divergence, on the other hand, should be expressly notified: Ulpian recalls that the appearance of an appointment (*praepositio*) could be dispelled by the posting of a *proscriptio*, the effect of which was to limit, or nix altogether, the liability of the principal. Consequently, the employee would be considered not an agent, but a mere watchman (*custos*) (D.14.3.11.2–4, 6).

Long ago, scholars sifted through Justinian's Digest and Code and gathered a small corpus of texts that shed light upon the legal relationship between owner and *horrearius*. Surprisingly, these texts are usually read as illustrating a single system, to the exclusion of all others, even though recent studies on business management show the coexistence of models accommodating a wide variety of economic and social factors, such as investment, profit, manpower, local customs and so on, all likely to change over time and space.

These juristic writings are now thematically arranged in titles bearing on specific subjects. They had been culled out of scholarly monographs and commentaries that contributed to devising a wide spectrum of legal solutions to various problems arising from actual or fictitious situations. There is no reason why a collection of texts belonging to one and the same title should represent a unified perspective. The compilers were undoubtedly bent on eliminating blatant contradictions. They were not always successful in producing a smooth and homogeneous sequence of texts, the original context of which often lurks in the background and conditions the meaning of each excerpt.

In the matter of commercial storage, several titles of the Digest are of interest: mostly 16.3 on deposit (*depositi vel contra*), 19.2 on hire and lease (*locati conducti*) and, to some extent, 4.9 on custody (*nautae caupones stabularii ut recepta restituant*). Let us dwell for a moment on hire and lease and those specific provisions governing the management of storage spaces. In an excerpt from a posthumous work edited by Iavolenus in the time of Trajan or Hadrian, the Augustan jurist Labeo discusses the case of a lessor (*locator horrei*) who imposes a disclaimer denying any liability on his part for some categories of pricy items (gold, silver, precious stones) that some lessees would have kept in the premises. Some lessee ignores the disclaimer and nevertheless stores such items, with the lessor's passive knowledge. Labeo considers that in spite of the disclaimer, the lessor is fully liable, his lack of reaction being understood as approval of the lessee's attitude and cancellation of the announced restriction (*propositum*) (D.19.2.60.6; Rickman 1971, 201).

All commentators note that the end of the text as it was transmitted makes no sense. Mommsen proposed a solution involving a typical jump from and to an identical word (*propositum*). Besides, the phrase "*suo periculo*" sounds unnecessary and may be the result of a gloss. Be that as it may, it appears that the *locator horrei*, based on the singular of the genitive (*horrei* rather than *horreorum*), is a manager, the issue of ownership of the premises being irrelevant to the case in point. Labeo's opinion may sound paradoxical, since it tends to deny the validity of the *lex horreorum*, more specifically the validity of the provision regarding the storing of pricy items. A natural objection would be that such a provision runs against the very definition of *horrea*, where, Paul recalls, private individuals store their most precious belongings (D.1.15.3.2). A change of doctrine may have occurred between the Augustan and the Severan periods: Gaius states in his commentary to the provincial edict that anyone who is paid to watch over other people's belongings is fully liable (D.19.2.40). In that regard, the identified exception of the damaged *lex horreorum* from Porta Salaria may provide a *terminus post quem* for the shift, in the first half of the second century AD.

The same Labeo has a different scheme in mind in another excerpt (D.19.2.60.9), where a *horrearius* is opposed to a *locator totorum horreorum* on the one hand and *conductores* on the other. It seems logical to identify them as respectively the manager, the owner, and the customers renting space inside the *horrea*. This interpretation fits the situation revealed in the *lex horreorum* from Porta Salaria. According to Labeo, the liability for safekeeping (*custodia*) falls upon the manager, not upon the owner(s). Modern commentators usually reject the phrase starting with *nisi* as interpolated. Then, Labeo would be stating the obvious. The provision "*nisi si in locando aliter convenerit*" specifically recalls the purpose of the *lex locationis* or *lex horreorum*. In the legal relationship between owner (*locator totorum horreorum*) and manager (*conductor totorum horreorum*), the contract bears on the unrestricted enjoyment of the premises. In the legal relationship between manager (*locator horrei, apothecae, cellae, compendiariorum* etc.) and customers (*conductores horrei, apothecae, cellae, compendiariorum* etc.), the object of the contract is more complex and the rules are specific to a *locatio horreorum*. The contract provides for the enjoyment of some space and a guarantee for safekeeping of whatever is stored in there, in exchange for the payment of rent (*merces, pensio*). Therefore, there is no reason why the owner/*locator totorum horreorum* should be held liable for the safekeeping of those belongings entrusted to the *horrearius*, unless the legal relationship between them provides for a substitute or additional liability. This would occur if the owner had agreed to stand surety for the manager or if the latter was the duly appointed agent of the former, to be in charge of the *horrea*.

Let us focus on this latter arrangement: appointment (*praepositio*) was not conditioned by the nature of the legal relationship between principal and agent, be it based on some contract (hire, mandate, procuratorship, or unsolicited, though subsequently ratified, management) or dependency. The last sentence of Labeo's excerpt explicitly refers to an alternative arrangement with the contract of hire and lease, possibly including a *lex praepositionis* within the *lex locationis horreorum*, thus changing the standard of liability of the owner, then acting in the capacity of principal.

A similar situation is evoked in a text excerpted from the *Sententiae Pauli*: the owner (*dominus horreorum*) is exempted from any liability in case of robbery, unless, we are told, he has (explicitly?) accepted the responsibility for *custodia* of the premises (implying also their content) (D.19.2.55pr = Sent.Paul.2.18.3; on the text see Rickman 1971, 201). If the liability was not his, whose was it? The customers'? Or the manager's, with whom the customers contracted for safekeeping, the one who gets paid for it and whose slaves *custodes* were to be tortured in the course of the investigation? Paul, in a text quoted earlier (D.1.15.3.2), records an Imperial rescript of Antoninus Pius or, more likely, Caracalla, addressed to one Erucius Clarus, authorising the questioning under torture of slaves employed as *custodes*, including Imperial slaves, perhaps an indication that *horrea* could be under joint management (public/Imperial-private), not unlike the administration of the water supply.

A possible echo of this rescript is found both in Justinian's Code and in the late-fourth-century *Mosaicarum et Romanarum legum collatio* (C.4.65.1 [a. 213]; Coll.10.9). Dated to 213 and addressed by Caracalla to Iulius Agrippinus, the rescript exempts the owners (*domini/locatores horreorum*) from any liability in case of robbery and burglary. There is no hint there that the liability remains with a manager, the point being that no entrepreneur should be held accountable for an act of God (*vis maior*).

It is not the place to discuss all the subtleties of the Roman law of safekeeping (Alzon 1965; Robaye 1987). Ulpian rightly underlines that criteria of liability can vary from one case to another, according to the nature of the contract (D.50.17.23). Fraud (*dolus*) is always taken into account, fault (*culpa*) and negligence (*negligentia*) only occasionally. In some cases, special care (*diligentia*) is required (Voci 1990; MacCormack 1994). In addition, the parties to the contract had the opportunity to change the standards of liability from one case to the other (*nominatim*) by using special agreements that could add, lessen or strengthen usual conditions, as long as these agreements were made in good faith.[19] According to Ulpian, such agreements presuppose the existence of a *lex contractus*. Some circumstances are clearly identified as acts of God: banditry, piracy, civil war, fire and flooding give rise to no liability. Burglary is, however, negotiable, and a special agreement to this effect could be entered into the *lex contractus* or be, even subsequently, added to it. In 222 AD, Severus Alexander issued a rescript imposing judicial torture on the staff of *horrea* in exchange for exemption from liability on the part of their owners, and recognising the validity of special arrangements (C.4.65.4 [a. 222]).

47.3 Conclusion

Epigraphic and legal sources supplement each other to shed light upon many aspects of the management of storage facilities. The conditions were specified by the parties within a *lex contractus* or *lex locationis*, once labelled *lex horreorum*, where idiosyncratic arrangements had to be spelled out in order to define the extent of the liability of each party, owners, entrepreneurs or managers, and customers, for damages resulting from breach of contract or faulty behaviour by one side or the other. The sheer number of storage facilities across the Empire, from the archaic period to late Antiquity and beyond, suggests that the management of *horrea* must have been rather standard and that explicit, written and

[19] Giffard and Villers 1970, 117–20.

posted *leges horreorum* must have been exceptional for that reason. Similar conclusions have been reached in connection with other would-be ubiquitous, though rarely attested, *leges contractus*, such as the job descriptions of those companies of undertakers, whose universal business of death is well documented in first-century BC/AD Puteoli and Cumae, but actually nowhere else. It may serve as a reminder that the three Roman inscriptions that were used as a starting point provide evidence for departure from the norm rather than for well-established practices. The same may be true, to some extent, of the writings of the classical jurists whose interest was often triggered by marginal and/or unusual situations.

Bibliography

Alzon, C. 1965. *Problèmes relatifs à la location des entrepôts en droit romain*. Paris.

Aubert, J.-J. 1994. *Business managers in ancient Rome: a social and economic study of* institores, *200 B.C.–A.D. 250*. Leiden.

Aubert, J.-J. 2003. "Contrats publics et cahiers des charges (en guise d'introduction)," in *Tâches publiques et entreprise privée*. Neuchâtel/Geneva. 1–25.

Aubert, J.-J. 2005. "Corpse disposal in the Roman colony of Puteoli." In W. V. Harris and E. Lo Cascio, eds., Noctes Campanae: *studi di storia antica ed archeologia dell'Italia preromana e romana in memoria di Martin W. Frederiksen*. Naples. 141–157.

Aubert, J.-J. 2007. "Dealing with the abyss: the nature and purpose of the Rhodian sea-law on jettison (*Lex Rhodia de iactu*, D 14.2) and the making of Justinian's *Digest*." In J. W. Cairns and P. J. du Plessis, eds., *Beyond dogmatics: law and society in the Roman world*. Edinburgh. 157–172.

Aubert, J.-J. 2010. "Productive investments in agriculture: *instrumentum fundi* and *peculium* in the later Roman republic." In J. Carlsen and E. Lo Cascio, eds., *Agricoltura e scambi nell'Italia tardo-repubblicana*. Bari. 167–185.

Aubert, J.-J. 2014a². "The republican economy and Roman law: regulation, promotion, or reflection?" In H. Flower, ed., *Cambridge companion to the Roman republic*. Cambridge. 167–186.

Aubert, J.-J. 2014b. "For swap or sale? The Roman law of barter." In C. Apicella, M.-L. Haack and Fr. Lerouxel, eds., *Les affaires de Monsieur Andreau: économie et société du monde romain*. Bordeaux. 109–121.

Aubert, J.-J. 2015. "Commerce." In D. Johnston, ed., *The Cambridge companion to Roman law*. Cambridge. 213–245.

Aubert, J.-J. and Raepsaet, G. (2011). "Un 'mandat' inscrit sur une sigillée argonnaise à Liberchies-*Geminiacum*." *L'Antiquité classique* 80: 139–156.

Camodeca, G. (1999). *Tabulae Pompeianae Sulpiciorum* (TPSulp.)*: edizione critica dell'archivio puteolano dei Sulpicii*. 2 vols. Rome.

Carlsen, J. 1995. Vilici *and Roman estate managers until AD 284*. Rome.

Chandezon, C. 2011. "Some aspects of large estate management in the Greek world during classical and Hellenistic times." In Z. H. Archibald, J. K. Davies and V. Gabrielsen, eds., *The economies of Hellenistic societies, third to first centuries BC*. Oxford. 96–121.

Coudry, M. (2004). "Loi et société: la singularité des lois somptuaires de Rome." *Cahiers du Centre Gustave Glotz* 15: 135–171.

Coudry, M. 2012. "Lois somptuaires et regimen morum." In J.-L. Ferrary ed., Leges publicae: *la legge nell'esperienza giuridica romana.* Pavia. 489–513.

Dubouloz, J. (2008). "Propriété et exploitation des entrepôts à Rome et en Italie (Ier–IIIe siècles)." *Les Mélanges de l'École française de Rome—Antiquité* 120: 277–294.

Dubouloz, J. 2011. *La propriété immobilière à Rome et en Italie (Ier–Ve siècles): organisation et transmission des* praedia urbana. Rome.

du Plessis, P. J. 2012. *Letting and hiring in Roman legal thought: 27 BCE–284 CE.* Leiden/Boston.

France, J. 2001. Quadragesima Galliarum: *l'organisation douanière des provinces alpestres, gauloises et germaniques de l'empire romain.* Rome.

France, J. (2008). "Les personnels et la gestion des entrepôts impériaux dans le monde romain." *Revue des études anciennes* 110: 483–507.

Giffard, A.-E. and Villers, R. 1970³. *Droit romain et ancien droit français (obligations).* Paris.

Harris, R. Forthcoming. "The organization of Rome to India trade: loans and agents in the Muziris Papyrus." In G. Dari-Mattiacci ed., *Roman law and economics.* Oxford.

Jakab, E. (2014). "*Horrea*, sûretés et commerce maritime dans les archives des Sulpicii." In J. Hallebeek et al., eds., Inter cives necnon peregrinos: *essays in honour of Boudewijn Sirks.* Göttingen. 331–349.

Johnston, D. 1999. *Roman law in context.* Cambridge.

MacCormack, G. (1994). "*Dolus, culpa, custodia* and *diligentia*: criteria of liability or content of obligation." *Index* 22: 189–209.

Mantovani, D. 2012. "*Legum multitudo* e diritto privato: revisione critica della tesi di Giovanni Rotondi." In J.-L. Ferrary ed., Leges publicae: *la legge nell'esperienza giuridica romana.* Pavia. 707–767.

Meyer, E. A. 2004. *Legitimacy and law in the Roman world:* tabulae *in Roman belief and practice.* Cambridge.

Miceli, M. 2008. *Studi sulla "rappresentanza" nel diritto romano.* Palermo.

Morelli, F. (2011). "Dal Mar Rosso ad Alessandria: il 'verso' (ma anche il 'recto') del 'papiro di Muziris' (SB XVIII 13167)." *Tyche* 26: 199–233.

Petrucci, A. (2002). "Ulteriori osservazioni sulla protezione dei contraenti con gli *institores* ed i *magistri navis* nel diritto romano dell'età commerciale." *Iura* 53: 17–56.

Rathbone, D. W. 2000. "The Muziris papyrus (SB XVIII): financing Roman trade with India," in *Alexandrian studies II in honour of Mostafa el Abbadi* (= *Bulletin de la Société d'Archéologie d'Alexandrie* 46). Alexandria. 39–50.

Rickman, G. 1971. *Roman granaries and store buildings.* Cambridge.

Rickman, G. 1998. "Problems of transport and storage of goods for distribution: 'les traces oubliées'." In C. Moatti ed., *La mémoire perdue: recherches sur l'administration romaine* (*CEFR* 243). Rome. 317–324.

Robaye, R. 1987. *L'obligation de garde: essai sur la responsabilité contractuelle en droit romain.* Brussels.

Virlouvet, C. (2006). "Encore à propos des *horrea Galbana* de Rome: entrepôts ou ergastules?" *Cahiers du Centre Gustave Glotz* 17: 23–60.

Virlouvet, C. (2007). "Entrepôts de stockage, entrepôts et marché: pour une typologie des *horrea* dans l'Afrique du Nord antique. Journée d'étude, Aix-en-Provence, Maison méditerranéenne des sciences de l'Homme, 13 octobre 2006." *Antiquités africaines* 43: 163–264.

Voci, P. (1990). "*Diligentia, custodia, culpa*: i dati fondamentali." *Studia et Documenta Historiae et Iuris* 56: 29–143.

Wacke, A. (1980). "Rechtsfragen der römischen Lagerhausvermietung: Zur formularmässigen Haftungsfreizeichnung eines horrearius für eingebrachte Kostbarkeiten." *Labeo* 26: 299–324 abridged and revised version in "Roman legal aspects of the letting of warehouses (the validity of an exemption clause regarding valuables)," in *Estudios de derecho romano y moderno*. Arganda del Rey/Madrid 1996. 441–464.

Zimmermann, R. 1990. *The law of obligations: Roman foundations of the civilian tradition*. Oxford.

CHAPTER 48

URBAN LANDLORDS AND TENANTS

PAUL J. DU PLESSIS

48.1 Introduction

With a population of close to a million inhabitants and a steady stream of itinerant visitors, the city of Rome was, by the end of the Republic, the largest of the ancient world by a considerable margin (Stambaugh 1988, 89). At this time, it was experiencing a wave of immigration, mainly from the Italian mainland, one of a number of successive waves of immigration that had taken place since the conclusion of the Second Punic War (Moatti 2013, 78). These intermittent population surges had a profound effect on the urban landscape of the city: the authorities had to reconsider fundamental issues of food supply, sanitation and, above all, housing, in order to accommodate new arrivals. In theory, several solutions to the housing problem were available, but in practice the preferred solution of the elite who owned the land was to create mass housing in the form of tenement buildings for Rome's growing population. This choice, it will be argued, was not merely based on the topography of Rome and the physical constraints of the city, but was in fact rooted in economic concerns. This chapter will focus on the rise of mass housing as a form of habitation in Rome and in the cities of the Empire (although the focus will be on the former, for which most information is available, rather than the latter) (on the related issue of urbanism and the complex distinction between urban and rural more generally in the Roman world see Erdkamp 2013, 241–242, 245–246). It will, like chapter 47 by Aubert, focus on the economics of such mass housing using legal and other sources in an attempt to provide a social context in which these rules operated. To that extent, the approach followed in this chapter in analysing the ancient city is both topographical and typological (Stambaugh 1988, 2).

At the start, the limits of this chapter should be made clear. First, there is an issue of terminology. While Roman legal sources use the term *insula* to describe such mass housing, the precise meaning of the term is open to interpretation (Morley 2013, 33). It was clearly not a technical term in law and the sources suggest that it had a spectrum of meanings, ranging from elegant "apartment buildings" with clearly identifiable apartments (*cenacula*) spread over a number of floors around an inner courtyard, to the much more squalid and dangerously unstable buildings inherited by Cicero from the banker M. Cluvius (*Att.* 14.9.1, discussed by Frier 1978). The latter buildings were often hastily and poorly constructed and housing the very lowest (often transient) members of society (for a cautious account of the height of [and therefore size of] *insulae* see Storey 2013, 156–159). In light of this, it is perhaps best to define an *insula* with reference to its alternative, the Roman *domus*. Whereas the *domus* was a single residential unit housing the *familia*, an *insula* was mass housing that could potentially house a number of *familiae* (see generally Wallace-Hadrill 1994; Storey 2013, 151; a useful comparison may drawn with the *fundus* as a legal concept with economic facets, on which see de Neeve 1984).

In second place, there is an issue of the volume and nature of the evidence. While writers such as Diodorus Siculus, Martial and Juvenal provide vivid accounts of the trials and inconveniences of city living, the typicality and representative nature of their experience should be approached with care. At the lower end of the social spectrum, city living was clearly an ordeal, and the sources suggest squalid, crowded conditions. This stands in sharp contrast to the elegant remains uncovered in locations like Ostia that were clearly inhabited by a better sort of tenant. It is therefore important to remember that mass housing did not come in only one size or form. It could consist of a number of different configurations depending on the size, location and geography of the town or city, and catered to a diverse group of tenants from different social groups.

Furthermore, with the exception of cities such as Pompeii, Herculaneum, Ostia and a few cities in the Greek East (e.g. Ephesus), it can be difficult to identify *insulae* from the archaeological record, especially at the lower end of the spectrum. It must not be forgotten that, at this lower end, domestic and industrial space was far more "fluid and dynamic" (and therefore less clearly demarcated: Storey 2013, 161). As Frier (1980) pointed out, archaeological remains tell us little about the legal rules that applied to such mass housing (for similar problems with commercial premises see Broekaert and Zuiderhoek 2013, 322). To understand these, we must look at the legal evidence as redacted in Justinian's compilation of the sixth century AD. But such evidence has its own problems. The legal material contained in Justinian's compilation is but a fraction of the original source material and is, as Frier has shown, more concerned with the upper end of the social spectrum than the lower. If, as Morley (2013, 32) has suggested, Rome during this period alone had nearly 50,000 *insulae*, their footprint in Roman law (and its application) must have been far greater than is visible in the remaining legal sources. To that end, one must be aware that the legal sources present a "normative" picture of what *should* happen. The *insula* of the legal sources is therefore a construct, which in reality may not have existed in such form anywhere and at any time in the history of the Roman Empire, much like the idealised "ancient city" created by Moses Finley in his seminal, if controversial work *The Ancient Economy* (Finley 1973).

48.2 The Economics of Ownership of *Insulae*

This brings us to the law that applied to *insulae*, as can be gleaned from Roman legal sources. Given the normative nature of the legal rules in question, we will also employ a normative construction of an *insula*; that is, an average example of mass housing that contains both residential and commercial space. At the outset, it should be noted that the legal sources rarely mention commercial space in the discussion of *insulae*. This may be significant in itself, but more research is required to explain this absence. It seems fitting to start at the top, namely with the owners of such *insulae*, since it is here that issue of economics come to the fore most clearly. To that end, two examples from the personal life of Cicero are instructive (Frier 1978). The first is a cluster of properties that Cicero owned on the Argiletum and Aventine. His correspondence with Atticus (*Att.* 12.32.2) regarding these properties is mainly concerned with using the rental income from them to fund the studies of his son. As Frier has shown (Frier 1978, 1 n. 2), Cicero treated these properties, which were located in different parts of the city, as a single asset (compare the comment on *fundus* above). This grouping together may have been, as Frier surmised (Frier 1978, 1 n. 2), because the properties had originally formed part of his wife's dotal property, which he had retained after the divorce to provide maintenance for his son. The second property came from an inheritance. Cicero had accepted the inheritance and subsequently, upon visiting the property, had discovered that some parts of it were near collapse (*Att.* 16.1.5). Nevertheless, he remained optimistic that he could make a profit from the building through rental income.

So what do these to examples reveal? Cicero, a *novus homo* of some wealth, owned a number of these buildings. To him, they were primarily financial assets that could be utilised in order to draw rental income to fund other endeavours (such as the education of his son). As an owner, Cicero does not appear to have been particularly concerned with the welfare of the tenants living in the collapsing building he had inherited from M. Cluvius. His tone is completely business-like when he observes "*non solum inquilini sed mures etiam migraverunt*" (not only the tenants, but also the mice have run away) (*Att.* 14.9.1). One should not judge Cicero too harshly for his tone in this letter, though. After all, he had only recently inherited the property and, in reality, it will have been one of a number than he owned, therefore making any sentimental attachment to the property or its inhabitants unlikely. It was also not a very good neighbourhood. Nonetheless, his comment raises an important point. For most upper-class Romans who owned *insulae*, they were first and foremost economic assets to be utilised financially. Like other assets of this stripe—warehouses, shops, ships and the like—their owners were mainly interested in the profit that these assets could make.

This then brings us neatly to the issue of the management of these assets rather than the details of how they operated etc. It is a well-established and often repeated *topos* that upper class Romans did not, as a rule, manage their assets personally. While a certain level of financial oversight concerning the accounts of the *familia* formed part and parcel of the responsibilities of a *diligens pater familias*, numerous sources reveal that these individuals used a number of strategies to manage their assets (and not only those located at a distance). One form of management was what might be termed in-house management. Here, the owner could use his slaves in one of two ways; first he could appoint a trusted slave as *institor* (a business agent) specifically to oversee the management of the *insula* and to deal with the tenants, or secondly the *insula* could be given to the slave as part of his *peculium* to manage for profit independently of the oversight of his master as the owner (compare the example of the slaves managing a warehouse on behalf of their owner in the Sulpicii tablets, discussed by Aubert, ch. 47). In both instances the slave would be termed an *insularius* (e.g. D.50.16.166; D.50.16.203). A wide range of possible motives for choosing one form of management over another exist (e.g. can we really envisage that large urban *familiae* all lived under one roof?), but legally the former exposed the owner to a greater level of financial risk than the latter, since in that case the owner's liability was limited to the extent of the *peculium* (see Aubert, ch. 47). It should also be remembered that *insulae* often came with staff (*instrumentum*) that the *insularius* was expected to oversee, as can be seen from Pomponius's definition of *familia urbana* in D.50.16.166: *non multum abest a vilico insularius: autem urbanorum numero est* (an *insularius* is not vastly different from a *vilicus*, apart from the fact that he counts among the urban [*familia*]). The comparison between *vilicus* and *insularius* here is telling and suggests a management role. The presence of a servile *instrumentum* within an *insula* could give rise to added complications if they were not properly supervised, especially in relation to theft of the tenants' property, a delict for which their owner would be liable.

The second form of management consisted of using free persons (either free born or freed) to manage the *insula* on the owner's behalf. Again, the owner could appoint his freedmen as *insularii* of his properties. The legal ramifications of such an appointment would depend on the legal nature of it and whether the *operae* of the freedman formed part of the scenario. Far more interesting, from a legal perspective, was the indirect management of *insulae* using third parties, "venture capitalists", from out with the *familia* (a pattern also visible in other assets such as warehouses and ships) (Cardascia 1982; du Plessis 2006 and 2012). In this case, the relationship between the owner of the *insula* and the "venture capitalist" was purely commercial. The latter rented the tenement from its owner, usually for a period of five years, with a view to exploit it financially through subletting (du Plessis 2006). Indirect management of this kind had a number of legal advantages. First and foremost, it removed any legal liability of the owner of the building *qua* the tenants. His only legal obligations were towards the primary tenant and they extended primarily to ensuring that the building was and remained in a condition fit for purpose (along with making any necessary repairs during the primary tenant's contractual term). An associated benefit of this type of arrangement is visible in the patterns of rental payment visible in the sources. As Frier has shown, primary tenants usually paid rent in five annual instalments at the start of each year (Frier 1977). They then recovered the initial financial outlay from their tenants (however they agreed to pay—daily, weekly etc.). Such an arrangement was beneficial to the owner for two reasons. First, it implied a steady fixed annual income at the start of each rental year for a period of five years; and second, it relieved the owner of the burden of having to chase after tenants for their rent. Given the amounts recorded in Cicero's correspondence as well as (seemingly fictional) amounts given in the Digest (e.g. D.19.2.30pr), it is clear that the primary tenant, who rented the entire *insula* from its owner with a view to exploiting it financially, required significant financial resources (du Plessis 2012, 158–159). Not only did he have to stump up the first rental instalment at the start of the contract, but the Digest also clearly implies that his prorated rental payments in instalments to the owner of the building was underwritten by real security (e.g. D.13.7.11.5). What form this real security took one can only speculate, but it has to be remembered that the object of the security had to be something that could sustain its value for the duration of the debt (compare here the rather exotic case mentioned in D.20.4.9, where someone who had rented baths used a single slave called Eros as security for the entire rent).

No contract detailing the letting of an *insula* to a primary tenant has been preserved. Although certain rental notices (collected in *FIRA* e.g. *FIRA* III 144, "This lodging is available for rent, it contains a dining room with three couches") exist, scholars are mostly reliant on individual texts from the Digest in which contract clauses that may have been included in such contracts are discussed. Given the normativity of many of these discussions, it is not really possible to draw many firm conclusions. What we can infer from the texts, however, is that a contract of this kind was first and foremost a commercial venture. To that extent, the owner (as landlord) had to ensure that the building was in a fit state of repair to enable the tenant to let out spaces within it. This also implies that the owner was responsible for maintenance. The primary tenant, on the other hand, was mainly obliged to pay the rent on time and according to the provisions stipulated in the agreement. He was also obliged to ensure that the building did not suffer any damage (normal wear and tear excepted) through the actions of the tenants (see below regarding conflagration). To what extent contracts of this kind were "relational" is difficult to tell, especially since we do not have any actual contracts for the letting of a tenement building. It stands to reason that such an arrangement would have been financially beneficial to the owner of the tenement. While this is not the place to enter into the debate about the liquidity of the upper classes and their lack of capital (despite having great landed wealth), it seems conceivable that the commercial arrangement between owner and primary tenant would have involved certain vested interests. If the owner, like Cicero in the example cited, was counting on the money for a number of years (since it was in a sense already pre-allocated for his son's education) his relationship with the primary tenant would have been more than strictly commercial (compare the discussion by Kehoe, ch. 49, about vested interests in agricultural tenancy).

This may also go some way to explaining the existence of a rather strange remedy, termed *deductio ex mercede*: D.19.2.27pr *Habitatores non, si paulo minus commode aliqua parte caenaculi uterentur, statim deductionem ex mercede facere oportet* (Inhabitants of an *insula*, ought not immediately make a deduction from the rent if their use of a part of the apartment has been slightly reduced). This remedy, which seems to have parallels in other areas of the contract of letting and hiring (e.g. *remissio mercedis* in agricultural tenancy, see extensively Capogrossi Colognesi 2005), seems to be based on a distortion of the contractual equivalence between use and payment of rent (du Plessis 2005). It catered for cases where the tenant's use of the property had been affected, but not to the point that it warranted the dissolution of the contract. By employing a deduction of rent, the contract could be salvaged through an adjustment of the rental price to reflect the disturbance. Who the "*habitatores*" in this text are, we cannot tell, but it seems inconceivable that they were low-status, itinerant tenants. The thought of them having the temerity to make a unilateral deduction of their rent is inconceivable in a system such as that of the Romans where status and social position had a profound impact on the availability of legal relief. Whoever these inhabitants were (possibly high-status tenants or even primary tenants), the owner wanted them to stay and was willing to accept a temporary reduction of rent to make that happen.

As for the contractual arrangements between primary tenants and those to whom he had let spaces within the *insula*, information is even scarcer since no contracts of this kind have survived. It is important to remember, as we move further down the contractual ladder, that much would have depended on the nature of the *insula* itself. Using Frier's premise concerning the "target audience" of the Roman law of letting and hiring, one must assume that better-off tenants would have utilised the law in a different way from those at the bottom of the social spectrum. We are therefore largely reliant on the matters raised in juristic discussions in the Digest, knowing full well that the lived reality, especially at the bottom end of the social spectrum, must have been very different.

Let us take the issue of the contract first. The Digest implies that the primary tenant contracted with each tenant living in the *insula*. Since we have no examples, it is difficult to speculate as to the form that such a contract would have taken, especially for short-term, transient tenants. I have argued elsewhere, using the mutilated inscriptions relating to the rental of warehouses (discussed by Aubert, ch. 47), that a similar regime may have been in use in *insulae*. Thus, the contract between primary and secondary tenants consisted of a set of "rules of the house" (a *lex contractus*) perhaps inscribed in stone and prominently displayed, supplemented by chirographs recording the fact of the lease and drawn up by the *insularius* (du Plessis 2012, 19–21). Such an arrangement, visible when comparing the epigraphic *lex horreorum* with the practice reflected in the Sulpicii tablets, has distinct practical advantages. The main one is that the "rules of the house" could contain all of the important provisions relating to the maintaining of the *insula* (issues regarding fires, sanitation, litter etc.), which could then be incorporated into the individual agreements. It also means that such individual leases could take on a standard "boilerplate" form.

There are three issues relating to such contracts that I wish to highlight specifically. The first relates to the ever-present danger of conflagration: D.19.2.11.1 *Si hoc in locatione convenit "ignem ne habeto" et habuit, tenebitur etiam si fortuitus casus admisit incendium, quia non debuit ignem habere. aliud est enim ignem innocentem habere: permittit enim habere, sed innoxium, ignem.* (If it has been agreed in the contract that "one shall not have a fire" and someone did have one, he will be held liable even if the conflagration occurred by accident, since he should not have had one. But the matter is different if it was agreed that he could have "an innocent fire", for then he is allowed to have one, provided it is harmless.) This enigmatic text contains two rules. The first, an absolute prohibition on having a fire, has the feel of a provision that would have been included in the "rules of the house" (the rather formal Latin is also indicative). Any tenant who contravened this rule would be liable even when a fire occurred accidentally. The legal effect of this provision is therefore to expand the tenant's usual contractual liability (*dolus* or *culpa*) also to include *casus fortuitus*. But why should this be so? If, as surmised above, the "rules of the house" contain "high-level" matters that could affect the liability of the primary tenant *qua* the owner of the building, any contravention would therefore imperil the contractual position of the primary tenant (du Plessis 2013). As for the final part of this text, it would appear that in certain circumstances, an owner might be willing to permit secondary tenants to have fires, provided they are "innocent fires". What lies behind this exception is anyone's guess. It may have something to do with the existence of commercial premises forming part of an *insula* or with the changes in building regulations after Nero's great fire (combined with the increased presence of fire-fighting personnel and equipment). The way in which fires are dealt with here again underscores the commercial nature of the *insula* as an asset to be exploited for economic gain.

The second issue relates to the payment of rent by individual tenants. As noted above, it was in the interest of the primary tenant to ensure full payment of the rent by his tenants to enable him to make the rental payment to the owner of the building. Roman law assisted the landlord in securing payment of rent by granting him a hypothec over the *invecta et illata* of the tenant (du Plessis 2012, 158–159). In a difficult text about when payment has legally been made, we are given the following information: D.13.7.11.5 … *Plane in eam dumtaxat summam invecta mea et illata tenebuntur, in quam cenaculum conduxi: non enim credibile est hoc convenisse, ut ad universam pensionem insulae frivola mea tenebuntur.* (Clearly my *invecta et illata* is only bound to the extent that I have rented the apartment, for it is inconceivable that it has been agreed that my "odds and sods" are bound in respect of the rent of the entire *insula*.) What this text clearly shows is that there was no direct relationship in law between the owner of the tenement and the secondary tenants. His only relationship was with the primary tenant who had rented the entire building from him. He had no interest in the secondary tenants (compare Cicero's statement above). Their goods were only deemed to be real security to the extent of their rent due to the primary tenant. He had no legal claim over them. The Latin *frivola mea* clearly implies that the stakes were high and the amounts large when it came to the primary tenant.

The final issue to note is that of security of tenure (du Plessis 2012, 160–161). In Roman law, letting and hiring as a consensual contract operated solely in the law of contracts (compare Epstein, ch. 39). A lease did not grant the tenant any limited real rights (possession) over the property as in many modern civil-law systems. The rights acquired by the tenant were solely contractual—use and enjoyment of the property in return for the payment of the agreed rent (a sort of dynamic equivalent *quid pro quo* expressed through the term *synallagma*). Since *insulae* were economic assets, they sometimes transferred from one owner to another with "sitting tenants". Take the example from Cicero's properties that he had inherited from M. Cluvius. Such a transfer could potentially imperil the primary tenant who had a lot invested in the property. Should the new owner decide to use the property for other purposes, the primary tenant had little protection at law. We see a good example of this in the following text: D.19.2.7 (Paul. 32 ad ed.) *Si tibi alienam insulam locavero quinquaginta tuque eandem sexaginta Titio locaveris et Titius a domino prohibitus fuerit habitare,* … (If I let an *insula* to you for 50, you then let it to Titius for 60 and he is prohibited from inhabiting it by the owner …). This very clearly shows the complications involved where absentee owners were involved. In law, the tenant who had been evicted had little recourse against the owner who evicted him. His main (nay only) remedy lay against his landlord, i.e. the primary tenant. It has been suggest by Kaser that this could be resolved by an ancillary *pactum* to the contract (see du Plessis 2012, 160–161 for a full discussion). This is based on a reading of D.19.2.25.1 (Gai. 10 ad ed. provinc.)

Thus, a primary tenant could protect himself against his lack of security of tenure by adding this *pactum* to his contract with the building owner. Should the tenement change hands during the term of his lease, the primary tenant could, if evicted, bring suit against the previous owner for the loss suffered through eviction of his tenants.

So, in the normative world of the law, the relationship between landlord and tenant was a harmonious one based on mutual rights and duties arising from their contract. To what extent the lived reality corresponded to this normative world is impossible to establish though the picture painted by the Latin authors of evicted tenants sleeping under a bridge, of belongings being turfed out onto the street unceremoniously (and then destroyed by an officious aedile) and of a tenant slinking off at night to avoid having to pay rent suggest something altogether different. Again, social status would have had a significant impact on the tenant's access to legal relief. Indeed, one gets the distinct impression that the only tenants that mattered were the better sort of tenant and, more importantly, primary tenants, since owners had a vested interest in their remaining.

48.3 Living in an *Insula*

This then brings us to the *insula* itself and the law applicable to such mass housing. We are again here largely reliant on a normative picture constructed from the legal sources. First, the issue of construction: the appearance of mass housing in Rome during the second half of the Republic must be read in the context of the general development of the urban landscape of Rome. Initially, many of these buildings were not made from the best materials, leading to both collapse and fire. Indeed, Cicero's comment about his inherited tenement is quite telling. The fact that parts of the building were teetering on the brink of collapse did not seem to worry him all that much. He remained confident that matters could be fixed by calling in the architects and that he could still generate a respectable income from it. He also did not seem to be overly concerned by the departure of the tenants, leading one to suspect either that there was a steady supply of willing tenants or that the matter was one to be dealt with by the primary tenant and therefore not really of concern to the owner. Building regulations seem to have improved as part of Augustus's city-wide programme of urban renewal, and further regulations, specifically related to conflagration, were progressively introduced during the course of the Empire (Dumser 2013, 139). Nevertheless, collapse and fire remain stock themes in Roman legal texts on the contract of lease, and Martial's quip about being able to touch his neighbour from the window of his apartment in the adjacent building across the road (Mart. 1.86) suggest that some buildings remained less than sturdy.

One final aspect to explore is how *insulae* and their inhabitants engaged with the civic administration of the city. The *Tabula Heracleensis* contains numerous provisions about the maintenance of streets in front of shops and *insulae*, and empowers aediles to let out the cleaning of said streets at auction should the inhabitants fail to clean said streets (Stambaugh 1988, 44, 114; Laurence 2013, 251). The cost of the contract had to be paid by the inhabitants. Apart from issues of cleaning and maintaining streets, they also crop up in relation to issues of "quasi-delictual" liability (the wording of the Praetorian provision is located in D.9.3.1pr). Take the following example: D.44.7.5.5 *Is quoque, ex cuius cenaculo (vel proprio ipsius vel conducto vel in quo gratis habitabat) deiectum effusumve aliquid est ita, ut alicui noceret, quasi ex maleficio teneri videtur* (He also, from whose apartment, whether it be his or which he has rented or in which he resides for free, something has been thrown down or poured out so that it has caused someone else damage, is deemed to be liable under quasi delict). If something has been thrown down or poured out from an apartment so as to harm another (*ut alicui noceret*), the inhabitant of the apartment is held liable under quasi-delict even if they did not personally throw down or pour out things.

This text by Gaius implies a building of a better kind with clearly defined apartments, but as the legal texts demonstrate, it is not always possible to work out who did the throwing or pouring (D.9.3.1.1—D.9.3.5pr). This clearly shows that these rules were designed to apply not only to buildings housing the better sort, but also to those at the lower end of the social spectrum. (Compare the suggestion in Suet. *Caes.* 41 following the interpretation of Moatti 2013, 81–82 that registers of people living in *insulae* were taken by the authorities for the purposes of assessing liability for taxes.)

One final observation regarding conflagration is required. As part of the civic reorganisation of the city of Rome undertaken by Augustus, the office of the prefect of the city was created to oversee city administration (Robinson 1992). Given the preponderance of mass housing, it comes as little surprise that this office also had an impact on *insulae*. As already mentioned in relation to conflagration, matters of keeping fires in a building could be specifically prohibited by the "rules of the house". The motivations for doing so could go further than merely preventing fire or protecting the asset. Take the following text: D. 1.15. 4 *Imperatores Severus et Antoninus Iunio Rufino praefecto vigilum ita rescripserunt: "insularios et eos, qui neglegenter ignes apud se habuerint, potes fustibus vel flagellis caedi iubere: eos autem, qui dolo fecisse incendium convincentur, ad Fabium Cilonem praefectum urbi amicum nostrum remittes* (The Emperors Severus and Antoninus to Iunius Rufus the prefect of the watch: you are permitted to beat with clubs or whips *insulariii* and those who have maintained fires carelessly; but those who are suspected of having caused a fire deliberately, you will remit them to our friend, Fabius Cilo the prefect of the city). Notice who could potentially be in trouble here: not only the tenants who kept fires carelessly, but also the *insularius*! Of course, given the dating of this text, one should not assume that beatings were meted out in all cases, since by this time the distinction between *humiliores* and *honestiores* had long since become entrenched in matters of punishment. Nonetheless, what we see here is another layer of civic oversight in the maintaining of an *insula*. It also shows quite deftly the interaction between the offices of the prefect of the watch (in charge of fire prevention) and the prefect of the city (in charge of general civic administration) (Lott 2013, 171, 175).

48.4 Conclusion

So what does this all amount to? In this chapter I have provided a brief overview of some of the main legal features of the letting of *insulae*. I have chosen this focus precisely because it demonstrates some of the most important economic aspects of the contract of letting and hiring as a commercial contract. This focus necessarily excluded other types of urban property such as "shop houses" (*tabernae*), probably the most common form of habitation in the ancient city, or inns of whatever description, but in fairness these deserve a proper treatment of their own, especially the latter (Frier 1977; Storey 2013, 154). This chapter has made two larger points. First, letting and hiring was a commercial contract. In the case of the letting of *insulae* (much like that of warehouses discussed by Aubert), it was utilised by the owners of these mass housing units as a means to generate an income in money. Urban properties such as these could produce a rental income that was on a par with, if not higher than, those produced from tenanted agricultural land. But unlike agricultural tenancy, the vested interests of the owner/landlord extended primarily to the primary tenant. The fate of secondary tenants was of little concern, perhaps reflecting the reality that many of them were transient. As Frier (1980) has already shown, the normative world of the Roman tenant only reflected reality to a certain extent. It is clear that the lived reality, especially at the lower end of the social spectrum, was very different, and one can but speculate whether these individuals would have had access to justice provided for by the contract of letting and hiring in the same way as financially wealthier tenants. One suspects not. Finally, it must not be forgotten that tenancy was an expression of power. The owner of the land on which the *insula* stood was the only person designated owner. Horizontal division of ownership was not a feature of Roman law, and tenants only acquired a contractual right through tenancy. Since so much of Roman prestige was attached to the ownership of land, it stands to reason that the law protected the interest of the owner, often at the expense of the tenant, even if (as has been argued) the law was written also with a better sort of tenant in mind.

Bibliography

Broekaert, W. and Zuiderhoek, A. 2013. "Industries and services." In P. Erdkamp, ed., *The Cambridge companion to ancient Rome*. Cambridge. 317–335.

Capogrossi Colognesi, L. 2005. Remissio mercedis: *una storia tra logiche di sistema e autorità della norma*. Naples.

Cardascia, G. 1982. "Sur une fonction de la sous-location en droit romain," in *Studi in onore di Arnaldo Biscardi*. Milan. Vol. 2: 365–388.

de Neeve, P. (1984). "*Fundus* as economic unit." *Tijdschrift voor Rechtsgeschiedenis* 52: 3–19.

Dumser, E. 2013. "The urban topography of Rome." In P. Erdkamp, ed., *The Cambridge companion to ancient Rome*. Cambridge. 131–150.

du Plessis, P. J. (2005). "A new argument for *deductio ex mercede*." *Fundamina* 11: 69–80.

du Plessis, P. J. (2006). "Janus in the Roman law of urban lease." *Historia: Zeitschrift Für Alte Geschichte* 55: 48–63.

du Plessis, P. J. 2012. *Letting and hiring in Roman legal thought: 27 BCE–284 CE*. Leiden.

du Plessis, P. J. 2013. "Notes on a fire." In F. Sturm, ed., Liber Amicorum *Guido Tsuno*. Frankfurt am Main. 309–316.

Erdkamp, P. 2013. "Urbanism." In W. Scheidel, ed., *The Cambridge companion to the Roman economy*. Cambridge. 241–265.

Finley, M. 1973. *The ancient economy*. Berkeley.

Frier, B. W. (1977). "The rental market in early imperial Rome." *Journal of Roman Studies* 67: 27–37.

Frier, B. W. (1978). "Cicero's management of his urban properties." *The Classical Journal* 74: 1–6.

Frier, B. W. 1980. *Landlords and tenants in imperial Rome*. Princeton.

Laurence, R. 2013. "Traffic and land transportation in and near Rome." In P. Erdkamp, ed.,. *The Cambridge companion to ancient Rome*. Cambridge. 246–261.

Lott, J. 2013. "Regions and neighbourhoods." In P. Erdkamp, ed., *The Cambridge companion to ancient Rome*. Cambridge. 169–189.

Moatti, C. 2013. "Immigration and cosmopolitanization." In P. Erdkamp, ed., *The Cambridge companion to ancient Rome*. Cambridge. 77–92.

Morley, N. 2013. "Population size and social structure." In P. Erdkamp, ed., *The Cambridge companion to ancient Rome*. Cambridge. 29–44.

Robinson, O. F. 1992. *Ancient Rome: city planning and administration*. London/New York.

Stambaugh, J. 1988. *The ancient Roman city*. Baltimore.

Storey, G. R. 2013. "Housing and domestic architecture." In P. Erdkamp, ed., *The Cambridge companion to ancient Rome*. Cambridge. 151–168.

Wallace-Hadrill, A. 1994. *Houses and society in Pompeii and Herculaneum*. Princeton.

CHAPTER 49

TENURE OF LAND AND AGRICULTURAL REGULATION

DENNIS P. KEHOE

49.1 Introduction

The legal institutions surrounding land played a crucial role in shaping the most important relationships defining the Roman economy, since, as in other pre-industrial societies, it was dominated by agriculture. These legal institutions affected the fortunes of all the groups who were involved in the cultivation of land, including both estate owners and small private landowners, farm tenants and agricultural labourers, and so were an important factor in the capacity of the Roman economy to change and grow, as well as in the distribution of wealth across society. To consider the large landowners who comprised the elite classes of the Roman Empire, the laws defining ownership of land affected these groups' incentives to invest in land, and so influenced the ability of the Empire's agrarian economy to produce the surpluses needed to sustain the urban populations and urban economies across the Empire. Likewise, many of these same landowners depended on farm tenants to cultivate the land from which they derived their wealth and social privileges. Thus the law's treatment of tenancy affected the fortunes of much of the Empire's population, as well as the ways in which landowners could profit from their land. Finally, the largest landowner in the Roman Empire was the state itself. The Imperial treasury, or *fiscus*, controlled a vast and ever growing number of estates and other properties including mines and quarries in Italy and in the provinces. These lands provided an important source of revenue that supplemented those collected from private land in the provinces, so that the legal administration of this land represented an important factor affecting the Empire's agrarian economy. Land on Imperial estates was subject to legal rules somewhat different from those regulating private land, and the way in which land tenure was defined on Imperial land merits consideration alongside private land to provide a complete picture of the role that law played in the rural economy.

49.2 Privatisation of Land

The long-term trend in the Roman Empire was to define and protect private property rights to land. This process began in Italy during the Republican period, but continued in the provinces under the Principate. In archaic Rome, it is likely that a great deal of land was owned corporately by kinship groups, or *gentes*. In this circumstance, the head of the *gens*, or possibly the *pater familias* in a smaller kinship group, would exercise considerable discretion in allocating land among the group's members. Although this is a matter of debate, it is likely that there was individually owned land in archaic Rome, although a great deal of land remained communal, as it did in later periods, when it was used for pasture (Roselaar 2010, 36–37). A gradual process led to the development of a legal category of private land over which the owner exercised full control, with the ability, within certain limits, to use it as he or she saw fit, and to alienate it by sale or gift, or to use it as collateral for a loan (Kaser 1971, 121). As Rome extended its power in Italy, it confiscated a great deal of the land occupied by the towns it brought under its control. This public land, or *ager publicus*, comprised a considerable portion of the land in Italy. Much of it was left in the hands of its original owners and their successors, but without a formal legal title recognised in Roman law. The one protection that such occupiers might have from the perspective of Roman law was access to the interdicts that protected lawful protection (Roselaar 2010, 94, 119–121; Kaser 1971, 387–388). Some of this land, called *ager censorius*, was leased out to occupiers who paid an annual charge, or *vectigal*, for it; the contracts issued by the censors probably involved middlemen who leased the right to collect the annual rent from the occupiers.

The major changes in the status of public land in Italy occurred in two phases, at the time of the Sextio-Licinian laws of 367 BC, and the Gracchan land reforms of 133–121 BC. What precisely this legislation involved remains a topic of considerable scholarly controversy, but both sets of laws set limits on the occupation of *ager publicus*. One purpose of the Gracchan reforms (133, 123–121 BC) was to increase the number of *assidui*, citizens with sufficient property to be able to perform military service. This was accomplished by placing restrictions on the amount of public land that could be occupied, and redistributing the excess to Roman citizens. This newly redistributed land became privatised; it was classified as *ager privatus vectigalisque*, since at first the occupiers were required to pay a rent for it, with restrictions on their rights to alienate it. Subsequent legislation soon removed the obligation to pay the *vectigal*, and in the *lex agraria* of 111 BC both the land that had been distributed in the Gracchan programme and the public land left in the hands of its occupiers were privatised (Roselaar 2010, 221–289).

This tendency toward privatisation of land in Italy, together with the legal remedies aimed at protecting private rights to land, responded to the needs of an increasingly commercialised agrarian economy. The substantial influx of wealth into Italy from the provinces, especially in the second century BC, resulted in prolonged economic change (Scheidel 2009, 67–70). The so-called villa-economy of Roman Italy featured compact estates, often cultivated with slave labour, that produced cash crops, in particular wine and olive oil, for growing markets in Rome and in other cities in Italy (Morley 1996; Marzano 2007). The establishment and protection of private rights to land enhanced the incentives that landowners had to invest in intensive agriculture (Roselaar 2010, 119–121). Roman legal policy also created private rights to other commodities connected with agriculture, including pasturing, access to roads, and water. The praedial or rustic servitudes represent a way of defining in terms of law reciprocal relationships that landowners in an agricultural community devised to share resources that were vital to agriculture but that were also disparately and unevenly distributed (Kaser 1971, 40–447; Bannon 2009, 47–100). A servitude represented a right, for example, to draw water, imposed on a "servient" property to benefit another "dominant" property. Servitudes were permanent rights, attached to the land rather than the persons who created them, and thus the holder of a servitude had an *in rem* claim to it.

Privatising land formed a major component of Rome's policy in administering the provinces. There, the full rights of ownership in Roman law, *dominium ex iure Quiritium*, was only available to Roman citizens who owned land that had Italian rights, or *ius Italicum*. This right would commonly be granted to Roman colonies, towns in the province in which all the citizens would also have Roman citizenship. Until the reign of Diocletian (284–305), land with *ius Italicum*, like land in Italy, was exempt from the taxes generally imposed on provincial land. The evidence for the development of private property in many provinces is indirect, in the form of archaeological remains of estates that produced foodstuffs for the market, including in Gaul, Germany, Spain, Africa and Syria (Hoffmann-Salz 2011; Woolf 1998, 142–168; Haley 2003; Pleket 1990, 7–118). In Egypt, papyrological evidence allows the process of the privatisation of land to be followed more closely. There the Romans inherited an agricultural system from the Ptolemies in which a great deal of land was under the control of the crown as royal land, *ge basilike*. Under Roman administration, katoecic land, originally assigned by the Ptolemies to support soldiers, became freely transferable, and for all intents and purposes private land (Rathbone 2007, 70–705). Beginning in the Julio-Claudian period, the Romans changed the types of taxes collected from privately held land, replacing periodically readjusted taxes with a much lower fixed rate (Monson 2012, 159–208). One aspect of protecting private rights to land involved its registration. In Egypt, each *nome* (an administrative division of the province) had a "property registry" or "bureau of acquisitions" (βιβλιοθήκη ἐγκτήσεων), where transactions involving property were recorded, including both sales and other changes in ownership, as well as liens. These efforts facilitated transactions involving land, since, with more certain knowledge about the status of land, people would be more able to buy and sell land as well as to use it as security in loans (Lerouxel 2015).

Another reform to safeguard property rights over provincial land was the "long-time prescription", or *longi temporis praescriptio*. This legal principle, first documented in a rescript issued in Egypt by the Emperor Septimius Severus (r. 193–211), protected lawful possessors of provincial land (different from Italic land, for which the rules of usucapion applied) against rival claims of ownership, say by people disputing an inheritance or past creditors. If the lawful possessor held the land for ten years, he would be protected from a suit from a rival claimant from the same city, and against a rival claimant from elsewhere if he held it for twenty years (Kaser 1971, 424–425; Oliver and Clinton 1989, no. 223 A, B [199–200 AD]). However, claims by the Imperial treasury, or *fiscus*, such as might arise in the case of tax arrears or debts connected with the performance of a civic liturgy, were not subject to this prescription. Quite possibly, the prescription represented an effort to respond to disorder following the Antonine plague in 165 and subsequent years that could have compromised records and led to disputes over land (Nörr 1969, 74–79). In Egypt, the policies described here helped to foster a class of landowners, similar to the curial classes in other cities in the Empire, to serve on the town councils created there at the beginning of the third century (Bowman and Rathbone 1992). In the third century, the development of large estates culminated in the immense properties of the Alexandrian magnate Aurelius Appianus and members of his circle, as documented in the Heroninos archive (Rathbone 1991).

49.3 Farm Tenancy

Farm tenancy was a major aspect of the Roman legal regulations that surrounded land. The formal law of farm tenancy, *locatio conductio*, probably dates to the second century BC, when the other remedies for consensual contracts were created, including sale (*emptio venditio*), partnership (*societas*) and mandate (*mandatum*) (Schiavone 2012, 133–153; de Neeve 1984). However, as de Ligt (2000) convincingly argues, as an economic institution farm tenancy was much older, since some form of it is characteristic of virtually all pre-industrial agrarian economies. Farm tenancy is to be distinguished from another form of land tenure, *precarium* (Steinwenter 1954). A person occupying land under *precarium* did so at the discretion of the landowner and had few rights—he could only stay on the land and cultivate it if the owner allowed this, and the owner could rescind his permission at any time. It is thought that in archaic Rome, landowners offered their clients access to land under this type of arrangement.

In its basic components, documented primarily in Digest 19.2 and 4.65 in the Code of Justinian, the classical Roman lease seems designed to answer the needs of landowners seeking to gain income from farms in which they had invested to profit from the burgeoning commercial agriculture in the late Republic (see section 49.2). The conventional unit leased to a tenant was a farm, generally called a *fundus* (Scheidel 1994). The term *fundus* is a very general one that refers to a farm as an individual autonomous unit of production, one that generally included a farmhouse, or *villa*. The leasing of a *fundus* can be contrasted with farm leases from Roman Egypt, which were generally for individual parcels of land or orchards. The conventional Roman farm lease was normally set for five years, and the tenant paid a rent in cash. The landlord's primarily obligation was to provide a farm that the tenant could cultivate (*frui*), whereas the tenant was required to cultivate the farm in accordance with the terms of the lease and pay the rent (*merces*). The tenant would be liable for any damage inflicted on the farm beyond what could be accounted for by wear and tear alone. The tenant was normally free to sublet the farm (unless a specific contractual provision forbade this). The landlord had ample leverage against an unsatisfactory tenant. The landlord could dismiss the tenant at the end of the lease period. If the tenant failed to pay the rent or damaged the farm, the landlord could proceed against the property that the tenant brought onto the farm, the *invecta inlata importata*, which were pledged as security for the rent and for the condition of the farm but did not pass into the possession of the landlord, in contrast to many other credit arrangements. Two legal remedies were created in the Republic to facilitate the efforts of landlords to enforce the terms of leases. One was the Salvian interdict (*interdictum Salvianum*), by which a creditor (in the case of a farm lease, the lessor) could claim possession of the pledged property, not only from the debtor (the tenant), but also from any other person possessing it. The *actio* (or *formula*) *Serviana*, probably introduced soon after the Salvian interdict, originally established a remedy for lessors to pursue the property of lessees pledged as security. Under the Principate, this remedy was extended to allow other types of creditors to pursue pledges (Kaser 1971, 464, 472).

What often determines the economic relationship between landowner and tenant, and thus affects the bargaining power of the two parties, is the way in which the costs of investment are shared (Foxhall 1990). We can gain some understanding of how the jurists envisioned the allocation of investment from a famous text in which Ulpian cites a letter of the late-first-century jurist Neratius (D.19.2.19.2) about what the landlord was expected to provide so that the tenant would have a farm that he could use (*frui*). In this text, the landlord was expected to provide buildings, storage facilities; wine presses and olive presses; in other words, the most expensive equipment, which was often fixed to the ground (Frier 1979; Balbo forthcoming). The tenant for his part was responsible for providing other equipment, such as ropes and tools. By implication, the tenant was normally expected to provide other movable capital, including draft animals and even slaves. In this type of lease, the tenant, paying a cash rent, would be involved in commercial agriculture. Roman farm tenancy, however, was far more complex than is suggested by this type of lease. Indeed, it is likely that many landowners, even in the period when commercial agriculture expanded in the late Republic, leased small plots of land to tenants with few resources of their own, who functioned as farm labourers (Launaro 2011, 17–177). Except for the very wealthiest ones, tenants would generally have been in a position of some economic dependence in relationship to their landlords (Lo Cascio 2009). But this is not to say that landowners could simply dictate terms to their tenants. For example, in the view of the first-century agronomist Columella (*Rust.* 1.7), tenants made the best contribution to the landowner's fortunes when they remained on the land for long periods cultivating it productively. In this circumstance, it would be less likely that the tenants would request remissions of rent. In the experience of the senator Pliny the Younger in the early second century, the income from his estates largely depended on the production of his tenants (Kehoe 1988; de Neeve 1990). However, he repeatedly confronted problems arising from his tenants' chronic indebtedness. Pliny's solution was not to replace his tenants, but to grant frequent remissions of rent, and when that did not solve the problem, to try to reduce the risk his tenants bore by replacing the traditional system of leasing for cash rents with sharecropping (*Ep.* 9.37, 10.8.5).

The question of risk, clearly a significant problem for both landowners and tenants, was a major focus for the Roman legal authorities as they sought to devise regulations for farm tenancy. Mediterranean agriculture was subject to frequent droughts, even at the micro-level, which could devastate the annual harvest (Horden and Purcell 2000, 175–230). The conventional Roman lease imposed the bulk of the risk on the tenant who, because he paid a rent in cash, was responsible for both the size of the harvest and the market price for the crops. Only when there was an unforeseen disaster, termed *vis maior*, was the tenant entitled to a remission of rent (Frier 1989–1990; du Plessis 2003; de Neeve 1983; Capogrossi Colognesi 2005, 3–104). The types of disaster that would qualify as *vis maior* included an unusual heat wave, an invasion by a hostile army, an earthquake, or an infestation by birds (D.19.2.15.1–3). But the normal hazards of farming, termed *vitia ex re*, did not entitle the tenant to a remission of rent, since, theoretically at least, he was supposed to take such risks into account when he negotiated his lease. The tenant's right to a remission has been interpreted as resulting from the landlord's failure to provide him with a farm that he could use (Capogrossi Colognesi 2005); alternatively, the tenant's right derived from the impossibility of his fulfilling his lease obligations (Frier 1989–1990). Although a diminished crop resulting from a drought, *sterilitas*, was formally regarded as a risk for which the tenant was supposed to account, one could leave him just as unable to pay his rent as a disaster that was considered *vis maior*. The Roman legal authorities, at least by the second century, developed a more flexible policy that took into account the fact that landowners often did grant remissions of rent for poor crops, much as Columella and Pliny discuss. Gaius states that the tenant would be entitled to a remission of rent "if the crops were damaged to a greater extent than was tolerable", *si laesi fuerint fructus plus quam tolerabile est* (D.19.2.25.6). Just how much damage the crops were to sustain was not specified; in later legal systems based on Roman law, a common rule, first articulated by Bartolus in the fourteenth century, was that the damage should exceed half of the crop (Capogrossi Colognesi 2005, 135–144).

In Roman law, however, the issue does not seem to have been whether the tenant had a right to claim a remission of rent for a poor harvest, but that landlords would be induced to grant them by social considerations or their own economic interests in maintaining working relationships with their tenants. So the task of the legal authorities was to determine what the rights and duties of landowners and tenants would be in this circumstance. The doctrine that the Roman government would follow was formulated by Papinian, as quoted by Ulpian (D.19.2.15.4), to the effect that a grant of a remission by the landlord in a poor year did not compromise his claim to the full rent for the lease period if later years proved more bountiful. This principle also informed a response by the Emperor Alexander Severus concerning a tenant's request for a remission of rent for a poor harvest (C.4.65.8, a. 231). The Roman approach, in contrast to later civilian systems, did not envision the grant of remission as ending the lease relationship between landowner and tenant, but quite the opposite, it seems to have been adapted to an economic reality in which the tenant occupied the land on a much longer-term basis than would be suggested by the terms of the conventional farm lease discussed above (Kehoe 2007, 109–128).

This concern to maintain productive relationships between landowners and tenants can be seen in the legal authorities' approach to another major issue in lease law, the tenant's security of tenure. In Roman law, the tenant lacked the right of possession, so that any new owner of a farm that a tenant was leasing would not be required to observe the terms of an existing lease. The tenant's only recourse would be against the original lessor, and his compensation would be monetary, without the new owner being compelled to allow him to stay on the farm. This lack of a right to possession has been seen as making the tenant's rights to the land insecure, and thus represented a stumbling block to the tenant's investment (Finley 1976, 109). To be sure, the tenant had the right to compensation for any improvements made to the farm that raised the value of the farm when the tenant left the lease. But it seems likely that such a legal claim would not by itself provide tenants with an incentive to invest if they viewed their tenure as short term. However, the rescript from Alexander Severus mentioned above concerning remission of rent recognised that the "custom of the region", *mos regionis*, might establish terms of tenure different from those in a conventional Roman farm lease. The Emperor Diocletian also referred to the custom of the region as authoritative for establishing tenure arrangements in two rescripts concerning the tenant's right to a remission of rent (C.4.65.18, a. 290; C.4.65.19, a. 293). These rescripts indicate that the Roman chancery was called upon repeatedly to adjudicate disputes arising from tenancy arrangements based more on local custom than on conventional Roman lease law. Some customary arrangements gave the tenure more security than we might expect under conventional lease law. Thus in the third century, the Emperor Gordian distinguished between tenants who were in leases for fixed periods and those who had perpetual leases (C.4.65.10, a. 239).

A convenient legal principle that allowed the Roman authorities to interpret such customary lease arrangements in terms of conventional law was the "tacit renewal of the lease", or *relocatio tacita*. According to this principle, if the tenant remained on his farm with the landowner's consent, the lease was considered to be renewed for an additional year under the same terms as had existed previously. In theory, by this principle, customary leases could be considered as formally renewed indefinitely. That this principle could in fact provide a legal description of long-term tenancy relationships is confirmed by a rescript of Valerian and Gallienus in which the emperors prohibited landowners from raising the rent or otherwise altering tenure arrangements of tenants in tacitly renewed leases (C.4.65.16, a. 260). In the fourth century, the Emperor Constantine issued a constitution that explicitly recognised the legal enforceability of customary tenure arrangements (C.11.50.1 [undated]). In this constitution, issued to the Vicar (the deputy praetorian prefect) for the eastern part of the Roman Empire, the emperor prohibited landowners from raising customary rents and also provided tenants with a legal basis to sue landowners who did this. The flexibility of Roman legal authorities in the third and fourth centuries suggests how they accommodated the needs of a broader community of citizens resulting from the *Constitutio Antoniniana*. The legal authorities incorporated "vulgar law", that is, legal principles based on provincial practices, into the law of the Empire (Levy 1956).

49.4 Land Tenure in the Provinces

Certainly the customary tenure arrangements discussed in section 49.3 included ones of provincial origin, but outside of Egypt we have little direct evidence for the terms of private farm leases. In Egypt, lease arrangements derived not from Roman legal norms but from a Graeco-Egyptian tradition. But we can gain some understanding of land in a province in which Roman law provided the basis for private legal relationships from the Imperial estates in Bagradas (modern Medjerda) valley in Africa Proconsularis. A famous series of inscriptions from the second century documents the conditions surrounding land tenure on these estates (Kehoe 2007, 56–72; Hoffmann-Salz 2011, 21–14; de Vos 2013).

The main cultivators, *coloni*, were sharecroppers. They paid one-third of the produce as rent for most crops, and they occupied their land under perpetual leaseholds. Their leases were based on a *lex Manciana*, in all likelihood an originally private tenure arrangement that was then adopted by the *fiscus* as the estates on which it was used came into Imperial control. In the second century, the Imperial administration offered a series of incentives to tenants who brought land under cultivation by planting vineyards, olive trees, and fruit trees, including perpetual leaseholds in accordance with the *lex Manciana* as well as initial rent-free seasons. An originally ad hoc programme to achieve this purpose became more uniform under the Emperor Hadrian, with the *lex Hadriana de rudibus agris*, or the "Hadrianic law concerning unused lands". Set above the *coloni* as the permanent cultivators of the land were middlemen, *conductores*. They leased from the *fiscus* the right to collect the rent from the *coloni* (generally six days each year) and to use the labour and draft animals of that group to cultivate additional lands. The Imperial administration pursued a similar policy of relying on small-scale cultivators on Imperial estates or state-owned land in other provinces. Thus in Asia Minor, a series of petitions to emperors from Imperial tenants in conflict with officials from nearby towns indicate that Imperial estates in that region were cultivated by small farmers with security of tenure (Hauken 1998). Similarly, in Egypt, the Roman administration leased out state-owned land to small-scale cultivators, who were largely secure in their tenure (Rowlandson 1996, 7–101).

To return to North Africa, it is not clear whether tenure arrangements on private land there were comparable to those documented on Imperial estates. The *lex Manciana* was a long-lasting tenure arrangement, as it provided the basis for the land tenure of *coloni* who came into conflict with emphyteutic possessors (see section 49.7) under the Emperor Constantine over water rights (C.11.63.1, a. 319; Weßel 2003, 111–113). Moreover, under the Vandal regime in late-fifth-century North Africa, the *lex Manciana* established the basis of tenure on an estate in the pre-desert region. This is known from the Albertini Tablets, deeds of sale in which people who bought and sold cultivation rights, called *culturae Mancianae*, within a larger estate under the ownership of a private individual (Weßel 2003). The endurance of the *lex Manciana* suggests that it became a widespread form of tenure in North Africa, both on Imperial estates and even private land as well, possibly as Imperial estates over time returned to private ownership. Mattingly and Hitchner (1995, 195) suggest that some form of long-term land tenure like the *Manciana* is likely to have played a significant role in the development of olive culture as an important source of wealth in Roman North Africa.

49.5 Water Rights

The legal regulation of water rights was a significant issue in the provinces, where agriculture in many regions, not just in Egypt, but also in Spain and Africa among other places, required irrigation. In Italy, as we have seen, the Romans created private rights to water, in the form of servitudes, and such arrangements must also have existed in the provinces. But a different approach was needed with commonly owned water resources. A major difficulty with such resources is the so-called "tragedy of the commons", as individual users have no incentive to preserve it or to invest in its upkeep, since such efforts will mainly benefit others. Still, as Ostrom (1990) has shown, communities do find ways to allocate water and other common property so as to share and provide for investment for the future. In Egypt, the irrigation from the Nile flood was organised at the village level, with theoretically all cultivators in the village required to contribute to the maintenance of dikes and canals with labour and taxes. In Africa, a well-known inscription records how, in the early third century, an agricultural community at Lamasba shared water rights from a spring in a semi-arid area where the principal crops included olive trees and fruit trees (*CIL* VIII 18587 = 4440, *ILS* 5793; 218–222 AD). Each user had the right to the water from the spring for a certain amount of time, in proportion to the number of trees he or she cultivated, which were a convenient proxy for the amount of land under cultivation (Shaw 1982). This was certainly a method of allocating water recognised in Roman law, as the Emperors Marcus Aurelius and Lucius Verus issued a rescript prescribing this method of apportioning water from a public river, as long as no one could show that more had been apportioned to him under his own right (D.8.3.17). In Spain, an inscription called the *lex rivi Hiberiensis* records how a high-ranking Roman official under the Emperor Hadrian adjudicated a dispute between two communities who shared water from a channel of the Ebro River (Beltrán Lloris 2006). In this circumstance, disputes could arise if the community upstream were perceived as using too much water and compromising the interests of their neighbours downstream.

49.6 Transition to Late Antiquity

In late Antiquity, as the task to maintain tax revenues took on great urgency, the Roman government's policies built upon the practice of the *fiscus* and private landowners of relying on small-scale cultivators in long-term tenancy arrangements. Its fiscal policy had two major components that affected the legal status of land and its cultivators. The first involved rigorous and regular censuses of the land, with an increased effort to maintain accurate records of landownership across the Empire, so as to identify landowners who would be responsible for paying taxes and the extent of their responsibility (Jones 1964, 61–69, 411–469). As part of this effort, beginning in the reign of Diocletian, the Roman government developed a system of tax liability that, ideally at least, made taxes more uniform and equitable across the Empire. One element of this system was to assess the tax liability of land in terms of notional units, or *iuga*, that represented the land's productivity as opposed to the size of a parcel. Theoretically, tax rates could be set that would represent an equal burden on various types of land, even across provinces, although in practice it is hard to imagine that tax assessments could have been uniform. In addition, land was assessed in *capita*, units that represented the personnel, including tenants and slaves, as well as animals, attached to it. The systems of *iugatio* and *capitatio* were gradually implemented in the Roman Empire in the fourth century, although eventually taxing on the basis of *capita* was abandoned.

The second component of the Empire's fiscal policy involved imposing greater responsibility on landowners to collect and pay taxes. One implication of this policy was that farmers were required to remain on their land, in their village of origin, their *origo*, or *idia*. This obligation was not an innovation of the late Imperial government, but it was applied more rigorously and uniformly in late Antiquity. One innovation was to define as the *origo* an estate on which tenants and probably other permanent labourers resided for the long term, when they were not otherwise registered in the census records as landowners in their own right. The estate owner would be responsible for collecting and paying any taxes that such *coloni* owed, but they would remain bound to the estate. Constitutions in the fourth century indicate that the "bound colonate" was gradually imposed throughout the Empire. The institution of the bound colonate imposed obligations on landowners, who could not dispossess *coloni*, change the terms of their tenure, or alienate the land without them (Kehoe 2007, 163–173; Lo Cascio 1997). The colonate represented a fiscal definition of certain categories of rural tenants and labourers, but the binding of *coloni* to the land carried with it a gradual legal, economic and social subordination of many tenants and labourers to their landlords. The importance of binding *coloni* to the fiscal concerns of the Imperial government can be seen in the repeated laws in late Antiquity imposing fines and other harsh punishments both on *coloni* who fled the estates to which they were bound and on landowners who harboured fugitive slaves. It seems clear that the law tended to counter market forces, since *coloni* with resources at their disposal might find better economic opportunities outside of the estate to which they were bound. But if *coloni* fled and took up tenure on a new estate, any contractual relationship with a new landowner would necessarily be outside the reach of the law. This situation would tend to undermine the law's authority in the rural economy.

The increasing fiscal responsibilities that landowners bore in late Antiquity and the binding of *coloni* were components of a gradual but long-term transformation in the countryside that altered the balance of power between powerful landowners and the Imperial government. The Imperial government, for all its power, struggled to counter the growing power of landowners and to maintain the authority of its legal and fiscal institutions. One area of the law in which this struggle can be seen is in the phenomenon of rural patronage, or *patrocinium* (Krause 1987; Grey 2011). Landowners who played a major role in collecting taxes and organising liturgies could also use their position to offer protection to farmers against fiscal charges; sometimes in exchange for protection they might take over land of vulnerable rural residents. A series of Imperial laws at the end of the fourth and early fifth centuries suggest the level of concern that the Imperial government had over this problem. At the same time, as Harries (1999, 77–98; cf. Humfress 2007, 29–61) argues, the government's legal institutions remained authoritative in the countryside, and were perhaps more authoritative than they had been under the Principate.

49.7 Long-Term Leasing and *Emphyteusis*

It was a common phenomenon for municipalities under the Principate to own substantial amounts of land, and they would often lease them on a perpetual basis. The rent was a *vectigal*, to be distinguished from *merces*, the rent in a conventional private lease, and the land was called *ager vectigalis*. The holders of such land would maintain their rights as long as they paid the rent, and they also enjoyed the right of possession and an *in rem* claim, in contrast to conventional private tenants (D.6.3.1, 3; D.6.3.2; Roselaar 2010, 139). By the third century, this form of long-term leasing became codified under a new contractual form, *emphyteusis* (C.4.66). In *emphyteusis*, land would be assigned to an emphyteutic possessor, *emphyteuticarius*, on a perpetual basis, in exchange for an annual rent, or *canon* (Kaser 1971, 223–225). The Roman legal authorities recognised the commonalities that *emphyteusis* shared with sale and lease, but they classified it as a distinct contract (Zeno, C.4.66.1, a. 476–484; Inst.3.24.3). The emphyteutic possessor would be comparable to an owner, in that his rights would remain secure, and he enjoyed the right of possession over the property. The emphyteutic possessor could sell, bequeath or otherwise alienate his rights to others. At the same time, *emphyteusis* shared common characteristics with leasing, since the possessor's rights depended on the payment of the annual rent. However, the possessor could only lose his rights after failing to pay the rent for three consecutive years (C.4.66.2, a. 529). State-owned and private land could be assigned under *emphyteusis*, as was land belonging to the Church, which in late Antiquity was a major institutional landowner.

The perpetual and alienable rights to municipal land and land held under emphyteutic leases meant that there were many people who held secure rights to land, but without being the owners in a formal sense. In this connection, we can think of the cultivators in Vandal-period Africa who bought and sold parcels of land within a large estate that were subject to Mancian tenures. Since, as seems clear, private landowners also leased out land on a long-term basis to tenants in customary land-tenure arrangements, there could be ambiguities about the precise nature of the tenants' rights to their land. A series of constitutions in the third century and continuing into late Antiquity indicate that some of these private tenants claimed rights to their land on the basis of the long-term prescription, by which a lawful possessor of provincial land could establish a prescriptive right to it after the passage of the requisite number of years. However, the consistent policy of the Roman legal authorities was to deny such tenants rights of possession, and by extension, the possibility of taking advantage of the long-time prescription (e.g. C.7.30.1, a. 226; Kehoe 2007, 135–137). The Roman government insisted on interpreting the rights and duties of landowners and tenants in terms of the conventions of the classical Roman farm lease, but the existence of disputes involving tenants' claiming the protection of the long-time prescription suggests how much more complex the actual conditions of land tenure in the countryside were.

49.8 Conclusion

This survey suggests that the forms of land tenure that existed in the Roman Empire varied considerably from province to province, and there are many areas where there is little evidence for the conditions under which land was cultivated, whether by slaves, tenants, wage labourers or some combination of all three. However, the responses of the legal authorities in matters involving land tenure focused primarily on allocating the costs of risk in agriculture between landowners and tenants, and accommodating long-term tenancy relationships within the conventions of Roman law. This situation suggests how important such relationships were to the Roman economy.

Bibliography

Balbo, M. Forthcoming. "Obblighi del padrone ed equipaggiamento del fittavolo nella riflessione dei giuristi." In D. Mantovani, ed., *Diritto romano e economia: due modi di pensare e organizzare il mondo (nei primi tre secoli dell'Impero)*. Pavia.

Bannon, C. 2009. *Gardens and neighbors: private water rights in Roman Italy*. Ann Arbor.

Beltrán Lloris, F. (2006). "An irrigation decree from Roman Spain: the *lex rivi Hiberiensis*." *Journal of Roman Studies* 96: 147–197.

Bowman, A. K., and Rathbone, D. (1992). "Cities and administration in Roman Egypt." *Journal of Roman Studies* 82: 107–127.

Capogrossi Colognesi, L. 2005. Remissio mercedis: *una storia tra logiche di sistema e autorità della norma*. Naples.

de Ligt, L. (2000). "Studies in legal and agrarian history II: tenancy under the Republic." *Athenaeum* 88: 377–391.

de Neeve, P. W. (1983). "*Remissio mercedis*." *Zeitschrift der Savigny-Stiftung für Rechtsgeschichte, romanistische Abteilung* 100: 296–339.

de Neeve, P. W. 1984. Colonus: *private farm-tenancy in Roman Italy during the Republic and the early principate*. Amsterdam.

de Neeve, P. W. (1990). "A Roman landowner and his estates: Pliny the Younger." *Athenaeum* 78: 363–402.

de Vos, M. 2013. "The rural landscape of Thugga: farms, presses, mills, and transport." In A. Bowman and A. Wilson, eds., *The Roman agricultural economy: organization, investment, and production*. Oxford. 143–218.

du Plessis, P. J. 2003. "A history of *remissio mercedis* and related legal institutions." PhD dissertation, University of Rotterdam.

Finley, M. I. 1976. "Private farm tenancy in Italy before Diocletian." In M. I. Finley, ed., *Studies in Roman property*. Cambridge. 103–121.

Foxhall, L. (1990). "The dependent tenant: land leasing and labour in Italy and Greece." *Journal of Roman Studies* 80: 97–114.

Frier, B. W. (1979). "Law, technology, and social change: the equipping of Italian farm tenancies." *Zeitschrift der Savigny-Stiftung für Rechtsgeschichte, romanistische Abteilung* 96: 204–228.

Frier, B. W. (1989–1990). "Law, economics, and disasters down on the Farm: *remissio mercedis* revisited." *Bulletino dell'Istituto di Diritto Romano "Vittorio Scialoja"*, 3rd series, 31–32: 237–270.

Grey, C. 2011. *Constructing communities in the late Roman countryside*. Cambridge.

Haley, E. W. 2003. Baetica felix: *people and prosperity in southern Spain from Caesar to Septimius Severus*. Austin.

Harries, J. 1999. *Law and empire in late antiquity*. Cambridge.

Hauken, T. 1998. *Petition and response: an epigraphic study of petitions to Roman emperors 181–249*. Bergen.

Hoffmann-Salz, J. 2011. *Die wirtschaftlichen Auswirkungen der römischen Eroberung: vergleichende Untersuchungen der Provinz Hispania Tarraconensis, Africa Proconsularis und Syria*, Historia Einzelschriften 218. Stuttgart.

Horden, P. and Purcell, N. 2000. *The corrupting sea: a study of Mediterranean history*. Oxford/Malden, Mass.

Humfress, C. 2007. *Orthodoxy and the courts in late antiquity*. Oxford.

Jones, A. H. M. 1964. *The later Roman Empire, 284–602*. 2 vols. Oxford/Norman. (Repr. Baltimore, 1992.)

Kaser, M. 1971². *Das römische Privatrecht: erster Abschnitt, das altrömische, das vorklassische und klassische Recht*. Munich.

Kehoe, D. P. (1988). "Allocation of risk and investment on the estates of Pliny the Younger." *Chiron* 18: 15–42.

Kehoe, D. P. 2007. *Law and the rural economy in the Roman Empire*. Ann Arbor.

Krause, J.-U. 1987. *Spätantike Patronatsformen im Westen des Römischen Reiches*. Munich.

Launaro, A. 2011. *Peasants and slaves: the rural population of Roman Italy (200 BC to AD 100)*. Cambridge.

Lerouxel, F. 2015. "The βιβλιοθήκη ἐγκτήσεων and transaction costs in the credit market of Roman Egypt (30 B.C.E. to ca. 170 C.E.)." In U. Yiftach-Firanko, D. Ratzan and D. Kehoe, eds., *Transaction costs in the ancient economy*. Ann Arbor. 162–184.

Levy, E. 1956. *Weströmisches Vulgarrecht: das Obligationenrecht*. Weimar.

Lo Cascio, E. ed., 1997. *Terre, proprietari e contadini dell'impero romano: dall'affitto agrario al colonato tardoantico*. Rome.

Lo Cascio, E. 2009. "Considerazioni sulla struttura e sulla dinamica dell'affitto agrario in età imperiale," in *Crescita e declino: studi di storia dell'economia romana*. Rome. 91–113.

Marzano, A. 2007. *Roman villas in central Italy: a social and economic history*. Leiden.

Mattingly, D. J., and Hitchner, R. B. (1995). "Roman Africa: an archaeological review." *Journal of Roman Studies* 85: 165–213.

Monson, A. 2012. *From the Ptolemies to the Romans: political and economic change in Egypt*. Cambridge.

Morley, N. 1996. *Metropolis and hinterland: the city of Rome and the Italian economy 200 B.C.–A.D. 200*. Cambridge.

Nörr, D. 1969. *Die Entstehung der* longi temporis praescriptio: *Studien zum Einfluß der Zeit im Recht und zur Rechtspolitik in der Kaiserzeit*. Cologne.

Oliver, J. H. and Clinton, K. 1989. *Greek constitutions of early Roman emperors from inscriptions and papyri*. Philadelphia.

Ostrom, E. 1990. *Governing the commons: the evolution of institutions for collective action*. Cambridge.

Pleket, H. W. 1990. "Wirtschaft." In F. Vittinghoff, ed., *Europäische Wirtschafts- und Sozialgeschichte in der römischen Kaiserzeit*. Stuttgart. 25–160.

Rathbone, D. 1991. *Economic rationalism and rural society in third-century A.D. Egypt: the Heroninos archive and the Appianus estate*. Cambridge.

Rathbone, D. 2007. "Roman Egypt." In W. Scheidel, I. Morris and R. Saller, eds., *The Cambridge economic history of the Greco-Roman world*. Cambridge. 698–719.

Roselaar, S. T. 2010. *Public land in the Roman Republic: a social and economic history of* ager publicus *in Italy, 396–89 BC*. Oxford.

Rowlandson, J. 1996. *Landowners and tenants in Roman Egypt: the social relations of agriculture in the Oxyrhynchite nome*. Oxford.

Scheidel, W. 1994. *Grundpacht und Lohnarbeit in der Landwirtschaft des römischen Italien*. Frankfurt.

Scheidel, W. (2009). "In search of Roman economic growth." *Journal of Roman Archaeology* 22: 46–70.

Schiavone, A. 2012. *The invention of law in the west*, transl. J. Carden and A. Shugaar. Cambridge.

Shaw, B. D. (1982). "Lamasba: an ancient irrigation community." *Antiquités africaines* 18: 61–103.

Steinwenter, A. (1954). "*Precarium*." *Paulys Realencyclopädie der classischen Altertumswissenschaft* 22.2: 1814–1827.

Weßel, H. 2003. *Das Recht der Tablettes Albertini*. Berlin.

Woolf, G. 1998. *Becoming Roman: the origins of provincial civilization in Gaul*. Cambridge.

CHAPTER 50

ROMAN LAW, MARKETS AND MARKET PRICES

LUUK DE LIGT

50.1 Introduction

The word "market" has multiple meanings. Used in a concrete sense, it refers either to the place at which goods and services are bought and sold or to the commercial activities taking place in such a location. Used abstractly, it may be used to denote the operation of the forces of supply and demand and to the way these forces affect the distribution of goods or services in smaller or larger geographical areas. The geographical areas in which these forces operate may also be called "markets".

The first part of this chapter deals with legal rules and administrative procedures relating to concrete markets. My principle aim here will be to make sense of a limited number of juridical sources, inscriptions and literary texts referring to applications for the right to hold markets (*ius nundinarum*) or for the privilege of immunity (*immunitas*) from market-taxes.

Legal rules governing markets in the abstract meaning of the term are a vast topic. In principle, any legal rule affecting the operation of markets for goods, labour markets or capital markets might be studied under this heading. Instead of attempting a general study of this type, I will focus on a handful of legal arrangements that made it possible for buyers or sellers to rescind contracts of sale that had been concluded in marketplaces. Finally, some attention will be given to governmental attempts to impose fixed or maximum prices, a topic that is covered more fully by Koops (ch. 46).

50.2 The Roman *Ius Nundinarum*: Problems and Solutions

In a fragment contained in book 50 of the Digest, the third-century jurist Herennius Modestinus refers to the ways in which the right to hold markets was obtained or lost:

Whenever the right to hold a market (*nundinae*) has been obtained from the emperor (*a principe*), the person who has obtained it loses the right to exercise it by not using it during the period of ten years. (D.50.11.1)

A passage from a letter sent by the Emperors Valentinian and Valens to the praetorian prefect Probus during the 360s or early 370s AD also refers to Imperial grants of the right to hold fairs or markets (*mercatus aut nundinae*). The fragment in question explains that those who have obtained an Imperial rescript giving them permission to hold fairs or markets "are not to harass any visitors by making any demands from them in connection with the merchandise of the traders, by exacting private sales taxes or fees for the use of commercial space, or by causing them trouble on account of some private debt" (C.4.60.1 [undated]).

While these passages leave no doubt that the *ius nundinarum* could be obtained from the emperor, two cases referred to in literary texts demonstrate that applications for the right to hold markets could also be addressed to the consuls or to the senate, at least during the first and early second centuries AD. According to Suetonius, the Emperor Claudius asked the consuls for permission to hold markets on his private estates (Suet. *Claud.* 12). Two letters contained in Pliny the Younger's correspondence refer to an application for the right to hold a rural market being submitted to the senate by Bellicius Sollers, a senator from Verona, and to the fierce opposition that this request aroused in the city of Vicetia, in whose territory the estate for which Bellicius wanted to obtain this right was presumably situated.[1] Finally, a famous North African inscription gives the text of a *senatus consultum*, issued in 138 AD, which permitted another senator, Lucilius Africanus, to hold twice-monthly markets on the *Saltus Beguensis*, a private estate that had been created on land previously belonging to the tribal confederacy of the Musulamii (Nollé 1982, 89–117).

One way of squaring these references to applications for the *ius nundinarum* being judged by the senate with the evidence for Imperial rescripts granting this right is to assume that the emperor took over a responsibility originally exercised by the senate. This was Mommsen's solution (Mommsen 1888, 1210; followed by Millar 1977, 350). Shaw has offered another explanation. In his view, the senate handled all applications for the *ius nundinarum* originating from the "public" or "senatorial" provinces whereas in all the other provinces the applicant needed to get permission from the emperor (Shaw 1981, 48). Unfortunately, the viability of either of these explanations is undermined by the existence of a substantial body of texts referring to applications for the right to hold markets being handled neither by the senate nor by the emperor but by provincial governors.

The earliest evidence for an application for the right to hold rural markets being submitted to a provincial governor is to be found in an epigraphic dossier consisting of six documents of which the earliest can be dated to 135 AD (*SEG* XLIV 977). The second of these documents is an announcement made by Titus Aurelius Fulvus Boeonius Antoninus, the later Emperor Antoninus Pius, in his capacity as governor of the province of Asia. The announcement explains that two men representing the village of Arhilla (or Arhilloi) have asked the governor to grant the village permission to hold an annual fair (*mercatus*) from

[1] Plin. *Ep.* 5.4 and 5.13. Herz (1997) argues that the market Bellicius wanted to establish must have been an annual fair rather than a high-frequency periodic market, but the term *nundinae* does not have this meaning in any literary or epigraphic text dating to the first two centuries AD.

19 to 25 October. Anyone wanting to oppose this request is invited to present himself before the governor, or before his successor, within thirty days.

The final document of this dossier is a letter written by the Roman landowner Asinius Rufus to the authorities of the city of Sardes.[2] Having described the village as "belonging to him as an ancestral possession", he urges the urban authorities, who are about to approach the emperor with the aim of obtaining certain "rights" (*dikaia*) for "the other fairs" held in the city's territory, to include the fair of Arhilla (or Arhilloi) in their petition.[3] As he explains, the urban authorities would put themselves in a bad light by petitioning the emperor in connection with all fairs except "the one granted by the emperor". The latter phrase clearly refers to the grant made by Aurelius Boeonius Antoninus during his term as governor.

Another epigraphic dossier from the province of Asia, datable to 209 AD, also refers to a governor granting the right to hold markets to a village (Nollé 1982, 11–58). The first nineteen lines of the inscription belong to a letter in which an unidentified person of high social standing urges the governor to grant the village of Mandragoreis permission to hold markets on the ninth, nineteenth and thirtieth day of each month. The second document contained in the dossier is an edict issued by the governor from which it appears that the request submitted by the representatives of the village was granted.

A third dossier relates to a request for the *ius nundinarum* that was submitted to a governor of Asia in 254 AD (Nollé 1982, 59–86). Having been approached by a certain Domitius Rufus, a member of the elite of the city of Sardes, the governor granted the village of Tetrapyrgia, which seems to have belonged to the territory of Philadelphia, the right to hold a market on the fifteenth and thirtieth day of each month.

Two inscriptions from the province of Numidia provide further references to provincial governors handling petition concerning periodic markets. During the second quarter of the third century AD two governors of this province gave the settlements of Castellum Tidditanorum and Castellum Mastarense permission to hold twice-monthly markets.[4] A third text, datable to the 280s AD, refers to a request concerning a domanial market. It appears from the text that a certain Munatius Flavianus had obtained a rescript from the Emperor Probus (before 282 AD), which gave him the right to hold "tax-free markets" (*nundinae immunes*). Between 287 and 289 AD, Munatius successfully asked the governor of Numidia to confirm this right (Nollé 1982, 119–129).

How can the evidence supplied by the inscriptions from Asia and Numidia be reconciled with the testimony of the Digest and the Justinianic Code? And how do we explain that only three years after the village of Arhilla obtained the right to hold an annual fair from the governor of Asia the friends of Lucilius Africanus directed their application for the *ius nundinarum* to the senate?

[2] It is tempting to identify the writer of the letter with the senator Asinius Rufus who lived in the early decades of the second century AD or with one of this senator's sons. See de Ligt 1996.

[3] Nollé and Eck 1996, 267–273, interpret the expression "belonging to me *e' progonôn*" as referring to a relationship of patronage rather than to an inherited right of ownership, but the fact that the village of the *Arhillenoi* is referred to as "the village and estate"(*chôros kai demos*) speaks against this reading.

[4] *CIL* VIII 19337 and *AE* 1942–43, 7. Recent discussions of the periodic markets of Roman North Africa include Zelener 2000; Chaouali 2002–2003; Meloni 2008 and Fentress 2009.

Part of the answer must be that procedures for obtaining the right to hold markets in the rural districts of Italy differed from those which had to be observed in the provinces. As the case of Bellicius Sollers shows, those wishing to obtain the *ius nundinarum* for rural estates in Italy had to submit their application to the senate. Since various political, administrative and juridical responsibilities originally exercised by the senate are known to have been taken over by the Emperor, Modestinus' reference to Imperial grants of the *ius nundinarum* might be explained as reflecting the standard procedure that was used in Italy in the early third century AD, and the same explanation might hold for the Imperial rescripts referred to in Valentian and Valens's letter to Probus. In the provinces a different procedure was followed. The epigraphic texts from Asia and Numidia leave no doubt that in these areas the provincial governor normally handled requests for the *ius nundinarum*.

As a next step we should try to account for the fact that the friends of Lucilius Africanus addressed their request to the senate rather than to the *proconsul Africae*. A convincing explanation can be found by giving due weight to the fact that Lucilius Africanus was a senator. During the Principate, men of senatorial status enjoyed various legal privileges. One of these was that any senator who became involved in a lawsuit as a defendant was entitled to have his case tried in Rome. The legal basis for this privilege was the fiction that, regardless of their place of origin or the place where they happened to live, senators were domiciled in Rome (Kaser 1966, 183). It seems reasonable to suppose that men belonging to this privileged class were not expected to leave Rome for the mundane purpose of submitting requests for the *ius nundinarum* to provincial governors. The obvious solution was to allow them to direct their applications to the senate.

The hypothesis that senators were allowed to bypass the provincial governor when applying for the right to hold markets might also be the key to the two passages from the *Corpus Iuris Civilis* referring to Imperial grants of the *ius nundinarum*. As we have just seen, these references *might* be explained by assuming that both of them deal with Italy. We should, however, consider the alternative possibility that both Modestinus and the Emperors Valentinian and Valens had in mind applicants of senatorial status. If the senate handled all applications for the *ius nundinarum* submitted by senators during the first and early second centuries AD, it is only a small step to posit a second stage in which such requests came to be handled by the emperor.

At first sight, the case of Munatius Flavianus might seem to undermine the validity of these suggestions. There is absolutely nothing to suggest that Munatius was a senator. How then do we explain that he took the step of obtaining an Imperial rescript before approaching the provincial governor? The obvious solution to this problem is that the Imperial rescript issued by the Emperor Probus had not given Munatius the right to hold a market but the privilege of *immunitas* for an existing periodic market (as argued by Charbonnel and Demougin 1976). The governor's role must have been to make sure that no taxes would be collected at the *nundinae* of Munatius's estate.

The evidence relating to the annual fair of Arhilla supports this interpretation. Some years after the village had obtained the right to hold an annual fair, the landowner Asinius Rufus took the step of urging the civic authorities of Sardes to include the newly established village fair in an application for unspecified "rights" they were about to submit to the emperor. It does not seem far-fetched to suppose that the "rights" the city of Sardes wanted to obtain for the fairs held in its territory included the privilege of immunity from Imperial market taxes, which only the emperor could grant.[5]

The relatively abundant evidence relating to applications for the right to hold markets not only illuminates the roles of the senate, the emperor and provincial governors, but also some of the criteria that guided them in dealing with these applications. The anonymous person who supported the application submitted by the village of Mandragoreis pointed out that the establishment of new periodic markets in this village would not cause any harm to the city or to the Imperial treasury. When submitting their application, the representatives of the village similarly stressed that their request entailed no harm for anyone, going on to point out that the schedule of the new market did not interfere with those of any existing markets. The latter consideration also appears in the letter in which the *proconsul Asiae* of 254 AD informs Domitius Rufus of his decision to permit the village of Tetrapyrgia to hold a monthly market. As the governor explains, his decision has been guided not only by the high esteem he has for Domitius but also by the fact that no other Maeonian city holds a market on the fifteenth day of the month (Nollé 1982, 12–15, 62–63).

After the spokesmen of the village of Arhilla had submitted their application for the right to hold an annual fair, Aurelius Boeonius Antoninus gave other interested parties the opportunity to oppose their request within thirty days. As far as we can tell, no one objected to the establishment of this particular market. The only example of a neighbouring community trying to prevent the creation of a new periodic market is the conflict between Bellicius Sollers and the city of Vicetia. Unfortunately, we are not told exactly why the *Vicetini* decided to oppose Bellicius' request for the right to hold domanial markets. One of their concerns might have been that the new market would have a negative impact on the urban food supply. Alternatively, they might have been worried about a possible drop in urban revenue from local tolls or market fees (de Ligt 1993, 205–217). Whatever the reason, or reasons, that prompted their protests, the authorities of Vicetia clearly expected the senate to take into account the harm that would be caused by the establishment of a new rural market.

A completely different consideration is alluded to in the *senatus consultum* concerning the domanial markets of the *Saltus Beguensis*. In this text the main provision granting the *ius nundinarum* is followed by the phrase "and those living in the vicinity as well as people coming from elsewhere will be permitted to gather and come together there only for the purpose of trade, without causing harm or inconvenience to anyone" (*CIL* VIII 11451, ll. 22–24). One scholar has interpreted this clause as evidence that the Roman authorities regarded all rural markets with suspicion (Shaw 1981, 46–48). It must, however, be remembered that the estate of Lucilius Africanus was situated in land that had formerly belonged to the Musulamii. Under Trajan the boundaries of the areas left to this tribal confederacy were redefined, and some of the land they had lost during the first century AD was now given to prominent Romans. There can be no doubt that this was an unusually sensitive area. Under normal circumstances provincial governors appear to have been structurally willing to grant the right to hold rural markets, as long as the establishment of the new

[5] de Ligt 1995, 49–53. Nollé and Eck 1996 reject this interpretation but fail to come up with any alternative reading of the term *dikaia*.

market did not interfere with the interests of other communities or individuals already having the *ius nundinarum*.

50.3 Roman Law, Market Transactions and Market Prices

Without a single exception, the textual evidence relating to grants of the *ius nundinarum* refers to rural periodic markets.[6] The obvious reason for this is that all settlements of urban status were assumed to have the right to hold markets. If we shift the focus of our investigations to the development of legal rules relating to commercial transactions concluded in marketplaces, the balance between city and country is reversed. Almost all of the evidence concerning the introduction of legal remedies offering protection to buyers who had paid too much for certain types of merchandise or relating to attempts to impose fixed or maximum prices refers to transactions concluded in urban markets or shops.

In Republican Rome, markets were supervised by four aediles. Originally two of these, the *aediles curules*, were elected from the patricians, but by the last century of the Republic the office had been opened up to plebeians. The other two aedileships could only be held by plebeians. Unlike their curule colleagues, they did not have edictal powers.

The responsibilities of the four aediles included control of weight and measures and general supervision of the quality of goods offered for sale and the prices charged for these goods. While control of weights and measures was based on objective criteria, it must have been less easy to assess whether the price of a particular item of merchandise was justified by its quality, and indeed the little evidence we have suggests that supervision of quality and market prices was exercised haphazardly and in a somewhat arbitrary fashion (cf. App. *Met.* 1.24–25).

Only in the case of the trade in slaves and draft animals did the *aediles curules* of Republican Rome use their edictal powers to introduce new legal remedies that altered the rules of the game between sellers and buyers (D.21.1). If someone had bought a slave or a draft animal suffering from a non-apparent disease or defect, for a price exceeding the slave or animal's market value, the aediles gave him two options. If he preferred to return the slave or animal and reclaim his money, he could sue the seller with the *actio redhibitoria*. Alternatively, if he preferred to keep the slave or animal, he could bring the *actio quanti minoris* and claim the difference between the purchase price and the market value. These legal remedies certainly existed by the early first century BC, but the majority view is that precursors of these actions had been created by the first decades of the second century BC (Jakab 1997, 128–129; Zimmermann 1990, 311 n. 113).

According to the version of the aedilician edict quoted in the Digest, the simple fact that the seller had failed to reveal the disease or defect sufficed to make him liable, regardless of whether he knew or should have known about it. In addition to this, the seller could be

[6] The African settlements of Castellum Tidditanorum and Castellum Mastarense were functional towns but lacked the juridical status of self-governing cities.

held liable if he had guaranteed that a slave possessed certain special qualities or that he was free from certain defects, or if he had behaved fraudulently in any other way.[7]

Why did the aediles think it necessary to create remedies that were available to people who had purchased a slave or draft animal, but not to buyers of any other goods? In a recent article drawing much of its inspiration from New Institutional Economics approaches to legal history, Frier and Kehoe observe that "one-off" transactions involving complex objects of sale and large amounts of money tend to attract considerable numbers of less scrupulous sellers. Sales of slaves and draft animals fit this description perfectly. Viewed in this light, the highly specific focus of the aedilician edict makes excellent sense (Frier and Kehoe 2007, 12–121).

Building on this observation, Frier and Kehoe infer that the presence of sellers trying to sell defective slaves or draft animals must have created an inefficient market in which wary buyers demanded large discounts, thereby discouraging sellers of high-quality slaves and animals from entering the market. In their view the aedilician edict must have been issued with the aim of addressing this problem. This is going one step too far. In a fragment from his commentary on the aedilician edict Ulpian explains that the aim of the edict is "to counter the dishonest tricks of sellers and to offer help to any buyers who have been deceived by them" (D.21.1.1.2). If Ulpian is to be believed, aedilician intervention was prompted by the wish to protect buyers of slaves or animals rather than to deal with market imperfections caused by asymmetrical information.

It seems reasonable to suppose that originally the protection offered by the aedilician edict applied only when a slave or draft animal had been bought in the marketplace. By the mid-first century AD, however, the edict was applied to sales of slaves that had taken place in other settings.[8] The extension of liability for latent defects to sellers of goods other than slaves or draft animals seems to have been a later development, and this extension was not achieved by widening the application of the aedilician edict as such. A passage from Ulpian's *Disputationes* states that the option of *redhibitio* is also available if a *fundus pestilens* has been sold (D.21.1.49). According to many older publications, all references to *redhibitiones* of goods other than slaves or animals must be regarded as post-classical interpolations and therefore as not representing the views of the jurists of the first to third centuries. However, it seems more likely that the jurists in question supported the idea that people who had bought any piece of movable property or real estate that was worth less than the purchase price because of the presence of latent defects could use the *actio empti* to return the purchased good and claim back the purchase price. In other words, Ulpian's text, as well as all other seemingly anomalous references to buyers being given the opportunity to claim either the purchase price or a discount corresponding to the difference between the purchase price and the market value of types of merchandise not referred to in the aedilician edict, are to be interpreted as referring to an extension of liability under the *actio empti*, the standard remedy available to all buyers, rather than to any extension of the scope of the aedilician edict itself (see the excellent discussion by Zimmermann 1990, 319–321).

[7] Kaser 1971, 569–570. The general clause concerning fraudulent behaviour is widely considered to be a relatively late addition.

[8] Crook 1967, 185–186. Zimmermann 1990, 319 is wrong to assert that up until the time of Hadrian the aedilician remedies were restricted to market transactions.

It seems significant that both the *aediles curules* and the classical jurists focused on those cases where a lack of knowledge about latent defects led to buyers paying more than the market value of the object of the sale. The inverse case, where the buyer had paid a price substantially lower than the market value, without acting fraudulently and without using violence, is dealt with in two rescripts bearing the name of the Emperor Diocletian. The first of these rescripts was issued in 285 AD, the other in 293 AD (C.4.44.2 and C.4.44.8). If the versions contained in the Justinianic Code are accepted as faithfully representing Diocletian's views, the latter ruled that someone who had sold a piece of farmland (*fundus*) for less than half its "just price" (*iustum pretium*) should be allowed to return the money and claim the sold property. Should the seller want to keep it, he must make up the full value. The scholarly literature uses the term *laesio enormis*, "enormous harm", to refer to such cases.

The authenticity of the text of Diocletian's rescripts has been endlessly debated.[9] It has been pointed out, for instance, that in the rescript of 285 AD the object of sale is first referred to as "a thing" (*res*) but subsequently as "a farm" (*fundus*). These and other linguistic oddities have been taken as proof that the original text must have been tampered with, either during the fourth or fifth centuries or by the Justinianic compilers. The current majority view is that none of these linguistic arguments is decisive.

Another reason why many legal historians find it difficult to accept the two rescripts as genuine is that not a single Imperial constitution issued during the fourth or fifth century refers to a sale of a piece of land being rescinded on the grounds that the purchase price was less than half the market value. In assessing the validity of this argument we must, however, consider the likelihood that attempts to determine the "just price" or "true value" of purchased goods must have become increasingly problematic as a result of the galloping inflation of the fourth century. On balance, there are no good reasons to reject Diocletian's rescript as inauthentic (cf. Koops, ch. 46). Of course, that conclusion is perfectly compatible with the view that *laesio enormis* did not become a generally recognised remedy before the publication of the Justinianic Code.

All of the legal remedies and juristic interpretations discussed so far belong to the realm of private law. In principle, magistrates and emperors also had the option of fixing prices or imposing price ceilings by means of public law regulations. Before (and after) the time of Diocletian such interventions appear to have been very rare and to have been confined to a handful of politically important cities.

Various emperors, including Tiberius, Nero and Commodus, are reported to have imposed maximum grain prices in the city of Rome during periods of severe food shortage (Tac. *Ann.* 2.87.1, 15.39.3; SHA *Comm.* 14.1–3). These measures were obviously motivated by the fact that keeping the citizen population of the capital city adequately supplied with basic foodstuffs was seen as a political priority. However, as Garnsey demonstrated more than twenty-five years ago, the standard response to the challenge posed by the

[9] Zimmermann 1990, 261 regards the Diocletianic rescripts as interpolated. Sirks (1985) suggests that the original versions of Diocletian's rescripts may have granted the possibility of *in integrum restitutio* in two cases in which the classical requirements for making this remedy available were not met, but this theory can be made to work only by assuming that the substance of both texts was changed as a result of interpolations. Pennitz (2002) accepts the two rescripts as genuinely Diocletianic.

expectations and demands of the *plebs frumentaria* of Rome was simply to bring in as much grain as possible and to award privileges to shippers serving the *annona* rather than to impose price controls (Garnsey 1988, 231–235).

Examples of emperors or provincial governors trying to impose food prices, or prices for other type of merchandise, are more difficult to find. The most famous example is Julian's attempt to impose maximum prices for grain, wine and vegetables in the Syrian city of Antioch during the food crisis of 362–363 AD (Julian. *Mis.* 368c–369c). It has been plausibly suggested that no Imperial intervention would have taken place should the emperor not have happened to be personally present in the city (Garnsey 1988, 247). An often-quoted passage from Ulpian's treatise "On the Duties of the Provincial Governor" refers to the existence of Imperial *mandata* ("instructions") urging provincial governors to take action against speculators who threaten the urban food supply (D.47.11.6). Erdkamp argues that provincial governors were expected to enforce these Imperial instructions systematically in all or most provincial communities. It seems, however, more likely that both during the Principate and during the late Empire local magistrates and town councils rather than Roman administrators took the lead in resolving or mitigating local food crises.[10] When the Pisidian city of Antioch suffered from severe food shortages in 92 or 93 AD, the governor of Pisidia intervened, issuing an edict that imposed a price ceiling of one *denarius* (about twice the normal price) for grain. It seems significant, however, that the inscription containing the edict starts with an explanatory preamble stating that the governor's intervention had been prompted by a letter from the *duoviri* and the decurions of the city (*AE* 1925, no. 126). There is nothing to suggest that the governor would have acted without this invitation.

Another text from the Digest refers to a rescript issued by Marcus Aurelius and Lucius Verus that forbids local town councils or magistrates to force any of their members to sell grain below the current market price. The underlying assumption is clearly that the local authorities will take the lead in resolving local food crises.[11] Instead of allowing local councils and magistrates to take every possible measure in dealing with such food shortages, the rescript actually restricts their freedom of action. This restrictive approach speaks volumes about Imperial policies and attitudes towards local food shortages.

The great exception to this general pattern is Diocletian's Price Edict, which introduced maximum prices not only for grain and other food items but for a very wide range of goods and services (Lauffer 1971). It is universally agreed that one of Diocletian's aims was to put an end to the never-ending price rises of the late third and early fourth centuries.[12]

[10] Erdkamp 2005, 313, arguing that the Imperial *mandata* concerning speculators were systematically applied because provincial governors were keen to prevent social unrest. For a more restrictive reading of the evidence which emphasises local initiative see de Ligt 2002, 20–21.

[11] D.48.12.3pr, discussed by Herz 1988, 107–108, Höbenreich 1997, 178–186, and Lo Cascio 2006, 230–231. Many local governments are known to have regulated food prices not only during food shortages but also at the time of major religious festivals. See de Ligt 1993, 64–65, 231, and Garnsey and van Nijf 1998.

[12] The exact motives that prompted the publication of the Price Edict must remain a matter of speculation. The preamble mentions the emperor's wish to protect the purchasing power of soldiers as the edict's primary goal. Since the maximum prices listed in the Edict were supposed to apply to compulsory purchases made by military personnel or government officials, we can be certain that considerations of fiscal and administrative expediency also played a part.

At the same time, the Price Edict reflects a strikingly novel conception of the emperor's role in controlling economic life as well as a high degree of confidence in the Imperial government's ability to enforce authoritarian measures affecting the behaviour of innumerable numbers of sellers.

As the events of the ensuing couple of months were to reveal, Diocletian's attempt to create price stability by introducing unchangeable maximum prices was completely unrealistic (cf. Koops, ch. 46).[13] Later emperors fell back on the traditional policy of keeping the most important cities of the Empire, which now included Constantinople, adequately supplied with the basic necessities of life, of which grain (and water) remained the most important. As in earlier periods, the favoured method used to achieve this aim was simply to ensure that sufficient amounts of grain were carried to these cities. Insofar as any attempts were made to impose fixed or maximum prices by means of public law regulations, as happened in Antioch in 362 AD, such measures were invariably prompted by food shortages. The geographical scope of these interventions was limited, and they were invariably of limited duration.

Bibliography

Carrié, M. and Rousselle, A. 1999. *L'Empire romain en mutation des Sévères à Constantin, 192–337*. Paris.

Chaouali, M. (2002–2003). "Les *nundinae* dans les grands domaines en Afrique du Nord à l'époque romaine." *Antiquités africaines* 38–39: 375–386.

Charbonnel, S. and Demougin, D. (1976). "Un marché en Numidie au IIIe siècle après J.-C." *Revue historique du droit français et étanger* 54: 559–568.

Crook, J. A. 1967. *Law and life of Rome: 90 B.C.–A.D. 212*. Ithaca.

de Ligt, L. 1993. *Fairs and markets in the Roman empire: economic and social aspects of periodic trade in a pre-industrial society*. Amsterdam.

de Ligt, L. (1995). "*Ius nundinarum* and *immunitas* in *I. Manisa* 523." *Epigraphica Anatolica* 24: 37–54.

de Ligt, L. (1996). "Further progress on *I. Manisa* 523." *Ancient Society* 27: 163–169.

de Ligt, L. 2002. "Restraining the rich, protecting the poor: symbolic aspects of Roman legislation." In W. Jongman and M. Kleijwegt, eds., *After the past: essays in honour of H. W. Pleket*. Leiden. 1–45.

Erdkamp, P. 2005. *The grain market in the Roman empire: a social, political and economic study*. Cambridge.

Garnsey, P. 1988. *Famine and food supply in the Graeco-Roman world: responses to risk and crisis*. Cambridge.

Garnsey, P. and van Nijf, O. 1998. "Contrôle des prix du grain à Rome et dans les cités de l'empire," in *La Mémoire perdue: recherches sur l'administration romaine*. Rome. 303–315.

Fentress, E. 2009. "Where were North African *nundinae* held?" In C. Gosden et al., eds., *Communities and connections: essays in honour of Barry Cunliffe*. Oxford. 125–141.

[13] Carrié and Rousselle 1999, 581, argue that the state must have been able to enforce the prices listed in the Edict in transactions carried out by government officials or military personnel, such as *adaeratio* or compulsory purchases.

Frier, B. W. and Kehoe, D. 2007. "Law and economic institutions." In W. Scheidel, I. Morris and R. Saller, eds., *The Cambridge economic history of the Greco-Roman world*. Cambridge. 113–143.

Herz, P. 1988. *Studien zur römischen Wirtschaftsgesetzgebung: die Lebensmittelversorgung*. Stuttgart.

Herz, P. 1997. "Zwei Marktplätze römischer Zeit und ihre Bedeutung: Vicetia, Marcelliana." In K. Ruffing and B. Tenger, eds., *Miscellanea oeconomica: Studien zur antiken Wirtschaftsgeschichte. Harald Winkel zum 65. Geburtstag*. St. Katharinen. 26–62.

Höbenreich, E. 1997. Annona: *Juristische Aspekte der stadtrömischen Lebensmittelversorgung im Prinzipat*. Graz.

Jakab, E. 1997. Praedicere *und* cavere *beim Marktkauf: Sachmängel im griechischen und römischen Recht*. Munich.

Kaser, M. 1966. *Das römische Zivilprozessrecht*. Munich.

Kaser, K. 1971[2]. *Das römische Privatrecht*, Vol. 1: *Das altrömische, das vorklassische und klassische Recht*. Munich.

Lauffer, S. 1971. Edictum Diocletiani de pretiis—*Diokletians Preisedikt*. Berlin.

Lo Cascio, E. 2006. "The role of the state in the Roman economy: making use the New Institutional Economics." In P. Bang, M. Ikeguchi and H. Ziche, eds., *Ancient economies, modern methodologies: archaeology, comparative history, models and institutions*. Bari. 215–234.

Meloni, L. 2008. "Le *nundinae* nel Nord Africa: produzione, merci e scambi nell'economia dei *vici*," in *L'Africa romana. Le ricchezze del Africa: risorse, produzioni, scambi*, Atti del XVII convegno di studio, Sevilla 14–17 dicembre 2006. Rome. Vol. 4: 2533–2545.

Millar, F. 1977. *The emperor in the Roman world (31 BC–AD 337)*. London.

Mommsen, T. 1888. *Römisches Staatsrecht*, Vol. III.2. Leipzig.

Nollé, J. 1982. Nundinas Instituere et Habere: *epigraphische Zeugnisse zur Einrichtung und Gestaltung von ländlichen Märkten in Afrika und in der Provinz Asia*. Hildesheim.

Nollé J. and Eck, W. (1996). "Der Brief des Asinius Rufus an die Magistrate von Sardeis. Zum Marktrechtsprivileg für die Gemeinde der *Arillenoi*." *Chiron* 26: 267–274.

Pennitz, M. 2002. "Zur Anfechtung wegen *laesio enormis* im römischen Recht." In M. Schermaier, M. Rainer and L. Winkel, eds., Iurisprudentia universalis: *Festschrift für Theo Mayer-Maly zum 70. Geburtstag*. Cologne. 575–589.

Shaw, B. D. (1981). "Rural markets in North Africa and the political economy of the Roman empire." *Antiquités africaines* 17: 37–83.

Sirks, A. J. B. (1985). "La *laesio enormis* en droit romain et byzantin." *Tijdschrift voor Rechtsgeschiedenis* 53: 291–307.

Zelener, Y. 2000. "Market dynamics in Roman North Africa." In E. Lo Cascio, ed., *Mercati permanenti e mercati periodici nel mondo romano. Atti degli Incontri capresi di storia dell'economia antica, Capri 13–15 ottobre 1997*. Bari. 223–235.

Zimmermann, R. 1990. *The law of obligations: Roman foundations of the civilian tradition*. Oxford.

INDEX

Introductory Note

References such as '178–9' indicate (not necessarily continuous) discussion of a topic across a range of pages. Wherever possible in the case of topics with many references, these have either been divided into sub-topics or only the most significant discussions of the topic are listed. Because the entire work is about 'Roman law' and 'Roman society', the use of these terms (and certain others that occur constantly throughout the book) as entry points has been restricted. Information will be found under the corresponding detailed topics.

abortion 428, 494
absens 250–1
absentee owners 629, 641
abuse, verbal 396–7
access to justice 266, 356–9, 644
accessio 522
accusations 119, 130, 273, 328, 337–9, 341–2, 368, 372, 428
acquisition of ownership 498, 538, 543, 545–6, 549
acquisitive prescription 538, 543
actio 192, 202, 318, 389–90, 574, 590, 596, 599, 602–5, 627
  and *obligatio* 576–7
actio de dolo 192, 318, 596, 603, 605
actio de in rem verso 389–90
actio de peculio 389–90
actio empti 590, 666
actio furti 192, 286, 604
actio incerti 585, 589
actio iniuriarum 323, 325, 396–7, 600
actio popularis 317–18
actio Publiciana 531–3
actio quod iussu 389–90
actio rei uxoriae 155, 425, 473
actiones, legis 159, 224–5, 228, 252, 284, 525, 542, 549, 582, 585–6
actiones adiecticiae qualitatis 390
actiones populares 313–18, 320
actiones utilis 482, 602–3
actions
  Aquilian 314–15, 602–3
  civil 217, 225, 372, 585, 591
  general 590, 603, 605
  legal 27, 121, 159, 284, 300, 367, 371, 425, 445, 621
  penal 250, 314–15, 319
  personal 572, 577
  popular 314–15, 317–18
  praetorian 326, 478, 602, 604
actors 75, 173, 330, 352–3, 355, 363, 367–8, 388, 394, 413
  legal 14, 443–5, 447, 449, 451, 453
acts 99–100, 112–13, 115–16, 322–6, 328–31, 371–2, 489–90, 570–1, 582–3, 596–8
  formal 581, 584
  legal 64, 106, 405, 425, 500
  private 248, 326, 404–5
adgnati 422, 424, 426
adjudication 14, 60, 171, 235–40, 242, 258, 289
administratio, libera 388, 390, 488
administration 101, 103, 107–8, 111, 121–2, 164–6, 168, 170, 488–9, 558–9
  civic 642–3
  free 388, 390, 488
  Imperial 79, 98–111, 151, 159, 162, 266, 352, 354, 626, 653
  of justice 31, 130, 266, 349, 356, 505
  local 124–5, 127, 129, 131, 133
  provincial 107, 111–13, 115, 117, 119, 121

administrative posts 151, 165–7, 171
administrative structures 6, 138, 164, 172–3
administrators 78, 151, 159, 164–5, 168, 339, 341, 468
adulterers 329–30
adulterium, *see* adultery
adultery 155, 206, 316, 318, 322, 328–30, 338, 421, 427–9, 438
  female 428–9
adulthood 434, 488–9
advisers 87, 102, 164, 169, 172, 358, 490, 584
  legal 121, 156, 160–1, 164, 168, 173, 341, 501
advocates 259, 277–81
aediles 87–8, 90, 92, 126–7, 166–7, 225–7, 230, 299–300, 612–13, 665–7
aedilician edict 226, 665–6
Aegyptus, province of, *see* Egypt
aequitas 155, 195
affectio 425, 476, 615
Africa 129, 164, 287, 648, 653–4
Africanus, Lucilius 661–4
agents 77, 117, 146, 302, 328, 503–4, 602, 622, 626, 628–30
  business 388, 637
ager privatus 556, 558, 647
ager publicus 526–7, 541, 556–7, 647
agnates 466–8, 505
agnatic and cognate relations 449, 466–9
agnatic ties 289, 449, 505
agreements 44, 113, 236–9, 271, 476–8, 482, 578–9, 585–7, 589–92, 631
agricultural land 513, 557, 644
agricultural regulation 646–57
agricultural tenancy 639, 644, 649–52
agriculture 157, 388, 487, 583, 623, 646, 648, 653, 656
  commercial 649–50
  intensive 648
Alexander Severus 66, 425, 429, 482, 614, 652
Alexandria 57, 60, 66, 161, 478, 503, 561, 622
alien communities 283, 292
alieni iuris 350, 419, 448, 600–1
aliens 102, 284, 286–9, 473
  resident 289, 403
ambiguities 46, 72, 153, 162, 210, 435, 469, 534, 627, 629
ambitus 228, 316, 336
amici 119, 168–70
Ammianus Marcellinus 342, 379
ancestors 85, 89, 274, 298, 467, 492, 575, 615
ancestral custom 71, 76, 371
animals 324, 326, 514, 518, 521, 526, 531, 599, 601–2, 665–6; *see also res mancipi*
  dangerous 313
  draft 650, 653, 665–6
animus 273, 280, 538–9, 545–7
annual magistracies 28, 227
Antioch 36, 160, 381, 668–9
Antoninus Pius 259, 265, 281, 304, 306, 428, 631, 661
Antonius Silvanus 501, 503, 507
apothecae 625, 630
appeal to the people 227, 334, 375
Appius Claudius 330–1
appointment 87, 99, 112, 140, 151, 504, 623, 627, 629–30, 638
appraisals 78, 224, 434, 609, 613, 616
Apuleius 272, 274–6, 278, 280, 300
Aquilian actions 314–15, 602–3
Arabia 160, 261, 428, 447
arable land 556–7
arbiter 130, 228, 241–3, 260, 327, 584–6
arbitration 113–15, 128, 234–43, 288
  and courts 234–43
arbitrators 113, 235–9, 241–2, 260, 584
archaic institutions 87, 588
archives 35, 271, 562, 628, 649
  property 554, 556, 560–2
arenas 47, 70, 75, 241, 436–7
argumentation 4, 28, 178, 181, 200–2, 209, 270, 272, 547
  argument and evidence 270–81
  rational 201–2, 212
  rhetorical 194, 202, 207, 211
aristocracy 95, 152, 220, 222, 229, 328, 336, 465, 524
  senatorial 221–3, 626
Aristotelian tradition 204–5
Aristotle 189–92, 196, 202, 271, 386
army 88, 90–1, 93, 288, 351, 353, 377, 553, 555, 611
arrest 77, 226, 230, 297–298, 299–301, 304, 380
arrest parties 300

arson 299, 312
Asia, province of 105, 108, 116, 261, 306, 661–3
Asia Minor 160, 300, 554, 653
assaults 228, 312, 329, 336, 394, 598, 600
assemblies 88–9, 93–5, 126–7, 129, 132, 137, 142, 220–1, 228, 230
popular 46, 85–8, 90, 93, 102–4, 106, 116, 126, 129, 220–1
assets 390, 446–50, 453, 498, 556, 560–1, 574–5, 637–8, 640–1, 643
liquid 520–1
associations 12, 139–40, 142–5, 305, 557, 579
social 12–13
associative law 137–8
assumptions 8–9, 15, 61, 181, 432–6, 440, 446–7, 450, 557–8, 562
Athenians 277, 280–1
attendants 297–8, 307, 444
atypical agreements 590
atypical contracts 590–1
auctions 226, 507, 558, 560, 613–14, 642
auctoritas 100, 271–80, 448, 525, 540
auditors 151, 153, 157–8
Augustan laws 353, 408, 425, 494
Augustus 98–104, 106–7, 117, 119, 169, 258–60, 302–3, 337–9, 378–9, 501–2
imperium 99–100
Aulus Gellius 71, 159, 327, 358, 598, 609
Aurelius, Marcus 47, 70, 103, 105, 108, 281, 341–2, 380, 428–9, 489
authorisation 50, 70, 337, 340, 351, 423, 425, 468, 488–9, 544
authorities 3–5, 130–1, 141–3, 151–3, 236, 238–9, 302–7, 403, 409, 427–8
local 285, 300, 305, 561, 668
autonomy 4–5, 71, 246, 284–5, 299, 453, 483–4, 526, 529
of law 4–5, 15–16
private 500, 502
Avidius Cassius 342

bad faith 242, 383, 518, 522, 527, 549
Baetica 31, 49, 51, 105, 107, 261, 349
bailees 516, 518
bailments 516–18
banditry 300, 302–4, 316, 371, 383, 631
bankruptcy 389, 507
bargaining power 612, 650
behaviour 13–14, 16, 280, 406, 408, 423–4, 427, 429, 433, 438
sexual 328, 420, 427
beliefs 4, 349, 352, 423, 432, 435–6, 439–40, 577
Bellicius Sollers 661, 663–4
beneficiaries 351, 411, 482, 520, 574–6, 578
bequests 210–11, 258, 341, 395, 403, 482, 488, 504, 556
Berytus 33, 160–1
best interests 89, 139, 145, 490, 493–5
bestiarii 367–8
biological sex 432–3, 435
birth 87–8, 133–4, 351–3, 359, 420–1, 449, 461, 464, 492, 498
Bithynia 126, 129, 144, 305, 354
Bithynia-Pontus 144, 304
Black, Donald 13–14
blood relation 476, 506
Boethius 159–60
bona fide contracts 522, 616
bona fides 516, 549, 612; *see also* good faith
bona vi rapta 313, 603
bones 324, 597–8, 609
bonorum possessio 426, 478, 505, 508, 538, 544–5
borrowers 520, 570, 587, 591, 614
boys 276, 329, 434, 466, 474, 489, 495
breach of contract 237, 520, 631
bribery 274, 306, 356
bronze tablets 45, 49, 105, 115, 337, 340
brothers 77, 424, 466–8, 499, 503, 505, 508
buildings 51, 94, 104, 131, 285, 625, 627, 635, 637–43, 650
public 127, 129, 164, 300, 626
business 130, 132, 251, 253, 389, 391, 504, 507, 624–5, 628
activities 388, 447, 578, 621–3
legal 170, 224–5, 251
life 390, 447, 621, 623
public 129, 222, 229, 443
business agents 388, 637
business managers 390, 627–9
buyers 420–1, 435–6, 516–17, 521–2, 525, 531, 533, 581, 586, 665–7

Caesar, Julius 116–17, 138, 140, 168–9, 219, 222, 312, 335, 337, 339
calendars 27, 44, 66, 221–2, 225
Campania 50, 230, 410, 623
Campus Martius 90, 94, 221
capacity 6, 422, 433–4, 444, 464, 474, 502, 542–3, 628, 630
capital 261–2, 302, 452, 475, 561, 612, 622, 639, 667
capital offences 334, 354
capital punishment 228–9, 325
Caracalla, Antoninus 57, 121–2, 142, 263, 278, 289, 340, 428, 548, 631
career, political 89–90, 92–3, 352
carmen 72–4, 79
Cassius 32, 157
Cassius, Avidius 342
Cassius Dio 103, 376, 379, 614
Cato 73–4, 154, 226, 274–5, 421, 423, 499, 530
causa 505, 539–40, 543, 546–7, 549, 576, 591–2
censors 86, 90–1, 94, 126, 224–5, 230, 298, 328, 352, 367
censorship 74, 87–8, 90
censuses 90, 128, 224, 226, 352, 403, 406, 561, 654
charioteers 394
charters 31, 120, 122, 287, 627
  epigraphic 119, 125, 129
  municipal 31, 49, 133, 287, 300
chattels 265, 323, 325, 514, 516, 518
childhood 392, 434, 490, 495–6
child-rearing 407–9
children 103, 106–7, 366–7, 406–8, 419–22, 424–6, 434, 436, 461–70, 505–8
  best interest of 493–5
  economic incapacity 488–91
  freeborn 492, 494
  illegitimate 478, 495
  legitimate 438, 461, 466–7, 469, 495
  male 419, 468
  newborn 492
  and parents 487–96
  status 64, 404, 494–5
choice of law 285, 288, 290–1
  across life histories 288–9
Christianisation 461–2
Christianity 342, 429, 463, 469
Christians 107, 277, 279–80, 304, 306, 341–2, 363, 371–2, 494, 618
Cicero, Marcus Tullius 29–30, 70–2, 75–6, 116–17, 152–4, 188, 196–7, 270–8, 280–1, 636–7
Cilicia 116–17, 160
cities 29–31, 91–4, 112–16, 144–5, 302–3, 635–7, 642–3, 648–9, 664–5, 667–9
  free 119, 144
citizen body 159, 364–5, 383, 403, 405, 408, 475
citizen status 106, 405, 407–8, 410
citizens 88–90, 95–6, 119–22, 130–4, 224–7, 286–9, 325–9, 350–1, 364–6, 377–81
  and foreigners 132–3
  male 94, 126, 327, 419, 434, 439–40, 464
  new 65, 405, 408, 427, 548
  private 92–3, 221, 229, 371, 404
citizenship 51, 106–7, 121–2, 132–3, 284–7, 289–90, 350, 352–5, 364–5, 402–9
  change of 288–9
  grants of 106, 222, 287, 478
  loss of 287–9
cives 114, 120–1, 556
civic administration 642–3
civic community 325, 330–1, 350, 475
civic duties 134, 434–5
civil actions 217, 225, 372, 585, 591
civil cases 117, 130, 241, 260, 319
civil law 152, 219, 223, 225, 285, 287, 289, 531, 533, 591–2
civil procedure 217, 245, 248, 254, 257, 262, 266, 357, 584, 586
  possession in 540–4
  Republican 245–57
civil rights 222, 366, 377
Civil Wars 91, 100, 102, 117, 219, 221, 229, 285, 302, 409
civil wrongs
  developments in Republican and classical Roman law 600–4
  origins of delictual obligations 596–9
  scope and function 596–605
civitas 86, 115, 124, 290–1, 350, 354, 526, 573–4, 576, 592
claimants 238, 248–50, 254, 263–4, 266, 500, 505, 527, 539, 541

claims 259, 264–6, 277–8, 330, 388, 390, 577–8, 584–6, 589–93, 665–7
classical jurists 36, 176, 235, 386, 477, 481, 541, 545, 623, 632
classical period 284–6, 474, 501–2, 505, 516, 524, 533, 543, 546, 548–9
classical Republic 219, 221, 223, 227–8
Claudius 101–2, 104, 106, 118, 170, 259, 279, 287, 661
clausulae arbitrariae 252, 542
clementia 374, 379, 384
clients 29, 32, 166, 182, 235, 259, 272–3, 275, 277–9, 297
Clodius Pulcher 75, 92, 138, 140, 377
Cnidos 119, 303
codes 13, 23–5, 27, 29, 31–3, 35, 37, 39, 73, 161
  Justinian's 258, 490, 631, 662, 667
  Theodosian 342
Codex Hermogenianus 36, 359
codification 10, 24–5, 33, 38, 58, 73, 176
  modern 24–5, 37
co-emperors 48, 121
coemptio 421, 425, 502, 583; *see also* marriage, *manus*
coercive powers 222, 229, 371, 374
cognitio 257–66, 318–19, 340, 354, 357, 380
co-heirs 575–6, 586
collective interests 312, 317, 319
collegia 137–43, 145–6, 303
  licit and illicit 140–4
colonies 30–1, 90, 125–6, 131, 274, 287–8, 526, 553, 628, 648
comitia 31, 45–6, 88, 93, 489
comitia calata 500
comitia centuriata 88, 94–5, 220–1, 224, 228, 403
comitia tributa 88, 94, 220, 222, 230
commentaries 28–9, 73, 78, 159, 177, 179, 181, 183–5, 627, 629–30
commerce 12, 63–4, 581–93
commercial agriculture 649–50
commercium 133, 350
Commodus 47, 279, 409, 429, 561, 667
communi consensu 430
communities 106–7, 114–15, 117, 119–21, 124–5, 128, 130–4, 299–300, 305–6, 502–4
  agricultural 648, 654
  civic 325, 330–1, 350, 475
  local 115, 120, 124, 131, 171, 353
  peregrine 115, 119, 125, 131
  political 325, 327–8, 350
  provincial 114, 119, 131, 289, 303, 350, 364, 668
compendiaria 625
compensation 315, 324–5, 390, 493, 523, 583, 592, 597–9, 602, 651
competence 102, 208, 221, 446–8
compilers 26, 38, 58, 444, 629
  Justinian's 25, 176, 327, 542, 573, 578, 667
complaints 303, 305, 356, 378, 392–3, 396, 612
compromissum 236–7, 241
concilium plebis 89, 220, 222, 230
concubinage 479, 481
concubines 393, 429, 479, 482, 503
condictio 576, 585, 589, 591
conduct 13, 15–16, 114, 227–8, 247–8, 352–3, 355, 359, 592, 598
  sexual 328, 433, 438–9
  standards of 303, 353
conductores 628, 630, 653
confiscation 230, 341, 557, 560
conflict resolution 235–6, 240–3
  methods 235–8, 241
  selection of method 239–41
conflicts 8–10, 13, 15, 99–101, 285–6, 289, 292, 447, 452, 653
confusio 522
consensual contracts 516, 531, 641, 649
consensus 76, 185, 328, 336–7, 396, 476, 481, 587, 597
consent 407, 422, 425, 427, 465, 476, 481, 483, 502, 519
  formless 476, 481
consorts in law 474–7
consorts in life 477–9
conspiracies 227, 318, 338, 374
  against the Emperor 378–9
conspirators 377–9
Constantine 36–8, 195, 263–4, 307, 362, 381, 409, 469, 483, 652–3
Constantinople 111, 160–2, 262, 380, 669
Constitutio Antoniniana 57, 63, 65–6, 353–4, 476, 548, 553, 652
constitutional structure 138–9, 141, 143, 145

constitutions 30–1, 37–8, 85–6, 95, 106–7, 260, 262–4, 617, 652, 655–6
 formation 86–9
 Imperial 36–8, 57–8, 62, 158, 262, 265, 285, 354–5, 388, 502
 Republican 71, 76, 89, 93
consular edicts 225
consular power 86–7, 98
consular year 91, 94, 112, 278
consuls 45, 86–7, 90–5, 98–100, 103–5, 112–14, 152, 220–4, 226–8, 259
 suffect 104, 341
consulship 74, 87–8, 90–2, 98, 104, 116, 241, 274, 277, 468
continuity 37, 66, 85, 189, 193, 195, 405, 411, 487, 491
contiones 28, 78, 93, 95–6, 221–2, 225
contracts 51–2, 571–2, 575–9, 581–93, 612–14, 617–18, 621–3, 627–8, 630–1, 638–42
 atypical 590–1
 bona fide 522, 616
 breach of 237, 520, 631
 hire and lease of 627, 630
 letting and hiring of 639, 643–4
 and *obligatio* 578–9
 of sale 61, 179, 452, 531–3, 581, 660
contractual practice 29, 64, 179, 445
contractual system 585–6, 591–2
contributions 15, 86, 154, 172, 212, 271, 275, 421, 425, 560–1
control 98, 100, 146, 279–80, 519–20, 548, 609–11, 613, 617–19, 647–8
 actual 528, 549
 effective 537–9
 factual 525, 534, 542
 imperial 161, 231, 653
 loss of 279–80
 physical 388, 525, 527, 538–9, 541, 546–7, 553
 social 13–14, 139, 395, 500, 507
conubium 106, 133, 350, 425, 474–6, 478
conventus 59–60, 118
conveyance 521, 581–2, 588
convictions 129–30, 137, 140, 276, 314, 338–9, 341, 355, 363, 367
co-owners 522, 560, 576
Coponius, Marcus 499–501, 503
corporal punishment 226–7, 350
corpus 538–9, 546–7, 603
Corpus Iuris Civilis 24, 37, 161–2, 419, 451, 663
corpus possidendi 388
costs 47–8, 50, 234, 239–40, 364, 370, 514, 517, 650, 656
councillors 129, 132, 134, 359
 town 352–3, 358
councils 86, 100, 120, 127, 129, 132, 342, 558
 local 50, 126, 128, 668
countryside 297, 300, 322, 393, 526, 528, 655–6
courts 74–5, 115–16, 238–40, 262–4, 266, 270–3, 280–1, 283–7, 289–90, 367–9
 appellate 129, 260, 263
 criminal 228, 352, 357
 hierarchy 262–3, 266
 jury 354, 378
 local 284, 290–1, 306
 permanent 91, 93–4, 228, 335, 354, 357
 and private arbitration 234–43
 public 312, 317–19
 standing 228–9, 340, 439
creativity 70
credibility 87, 275–6, 278
creditors 59, 266, 389–90, 507, 556, 562, 587–8, 611, 648, 650
credits 61, 143, 275, 326, 389, 452, 583–4, 586, 628
crimes 299, 303–5, 311, 314, 323–5, 327–9, 333–5, 337–43, 597, 599
 against the individual 322–31
 against the state 333–43
 Republic 333–7
 sexual 322–3, 325, 327–31, 427
criminal courts 228, 352, 357
criminal jurisdiction 130, 230, 302, 358
criminal law 9, 159, 224, 310–20, 363, 366, 374
 Roman formal categories 312–15
 substance of offences 315–19
criminal proceedings 45, 330, 358
criminal trials 30, 231
crops 324, 382, 612, 642, 651, 653–4
crudelitas 374, 379, 384
cruelty 304, 331, 374
culpa 602, 604, 631, 640
cultivation 514, 557–9, 646, 653–4
 rights 558, 653

cultivators 558, 653–4, 656
culture 9, 43, 71, 156, 310, 362, 367, 432–3, 495, 554
 legal 5–6, 9–11, 14, 16, 36, 38, 154, 164, 506, 609
 Roman 200–1, 362, 513, 581, 588
 rule-based 159, 162
cura minorum 64, 489–90
curator ventris 428, 494
curators 155, 428, 489
curule aediles, *see* aediles
custodia 179, 494, 516, 624, 627, 630
customers 625–7, 629–31
customs 4, 12, 15, 71, 85, 224, 291, 364, 427, 612

damage 277, 314–15, 368–9, 371, 388, 597–605, 609, 614–16, 623–4, 651; *see also damnum iniuria datum*; delict; *lex Aquilia*
 physical 371, 602
 to property 313, 315–16, 518, 599–600, 605, 616
 reparation of 596, 599–600, 604
damnum iniuria datum 313, 323, 601–2, 605; *see also lex Aquilia*
daughters 329–31, 419, 421–2, 465–6, 468, 490–1, 503, 505, 508, 600
 adulterous 329
de iniuriis aestimandis 600, 609
de pecuniis repetundis 228–9
death 45, 47, 104, 334, 421–3, 436, 464, 498–500, 505–6, 601–2
death penalty 94, 300, 334, 350, 355, 429, 599
debt slavery 224, 325
debtors 59, 62, 64, 264–5, 323, 437, 577–8, 586, 592, 601
debts 323–5, 389–90, 504, 507, 522, 531, 583, 585, 587, 592
decemviri 26–7, 87, 331
decemviri stlitibus iudicandis 230
declamation 76–8, 154
declamations, public 129, 201
decrees, senatorial 44–5, 98, 101–2, 104–5, 140, 142–3, 336, 338, 661, 664
decurions 50–1, 120, 129–30, 133, 351–2, 355, 366, 370, 668
defamation 312, 327, 338, 396, 600
defects 612–13, 665–6
 latent 226, 666–7
defences 71, 77, 253, 273, 376
 affirmative 252
 judicial 587, 589
defendants 207, 228, 248–50, 252, 263–4, 275–6, 279–80, 541–3, 584–6, 602–3
deference 279–80
degradation 322, 324–6, 329, 331, 408
delatores 106, 339
deliberative oratory 73, 76, 78
delicts 313–14, 316, 318, 353, 357, 571–2, 577–8, 583, 596–601, 604–5
delictual obligations 573
 origins 596–9
dependants 326, 330–1, 411, 488, 491
descendants 338, 352, 419, 422, 436, 505–6
 disinherited 508
detentio 545, 547
deterrents 342, 371–2
dictatorship 90, 93, 223, 375
dignitas 134, 152, 271–3, 276–7, 279–80, 351, 355, 365, 368, 370
dignity 279, 327, 336, 349, 351, 396
Diocletian 36–8, 48, 66, 121–2, 557, 562, 648, 652, 654, 667–9
 market interventions 617–18
Diocletian's edicts 49, 610, 612, 614, 618, 668
Dionysia 59, 61, 445–6, 452, 483
Dionysius 26–7, 86, 621
disabilities 249, 350, 366–7, 387, 403, 440, 447
discharge
 dishonourable 353, 367
 honourable 45, 289, 475, 478
discourse 71–3, 152–3, 177, 182–4, 328, 374
dishonour 86–7, 90, 355, 403–4, 407
dishonourable discharge 353, 367
disorder 36, 142, 299, 303, 649
disputants 113, 236–40, 242, 358
disputationes 180–1, 183, 185
dispute resolution 14, 113, 242, 283, 317
disputes 36, 113–15, 119–20, 128, 234–40, 242, 358, 410–11, 527, 654
distributive justice 362, 369
disturbances 144, 333, 380, 529, 538, 541, 639
divided interests 513, 517–21
divorce 155, 329–30, 422, 425, 428–30, 465, 479–83, 493–4, 560, 637
 unilateral 483

doctrine 3, 5, 10, 12–13, 32, 157, 208–9, 538–9, 543, 546
  history of 3, 5
documentary evidence 247, 532, 622
documents 44–52, 56–8, 60, 107, 141, 241, 246–7, 263–4, 627–8, 661
  legal 12, 43, 45, 52, 154, 356, 444, 500
  written 263–4, 271, 482, 588, 592
dolus 315–16, 318, 357, 596, 601, 603, 622, 631, 640
domanial markets 662, 664
domestic jurisdiction 328–9, 331
dominance 173, 538, 577
dominica potestas 388, 419
dominium 524, 526–8, 530–2, 534, 538, 541, 548, 553–4, 556, 588; *see also* ownership
dominium ex iure Quiritium 524, 541, 553, 588, 648
dominus 388–92, 404, 525, 528–9, 531, 533, 601–2, 625, 628, 631; *see also* owners
Domitian 107–8, 120, 128, 339
donations 58, 132, 473, 476–7, 479, 506, 527, 544
dowries 58, 421, 425, 451, 473, 478–9, 482–3, 556, 560–1, 577–8
draft animals 650, 653, 665–6
duoviri 120, 126–31, 237–40, 300, 668
duties 126, 365–6, 489–90, 515, 558, 569–71, 581–4, 588, 591–3, 597–8
  civic 134, 434–5
  moral 193, 259, 612
  social 577

eclecticism 188, 190, 192–3, 196–7
economic activities 48, 363, 452, 621, 623, 626
economic life 451, 488, 617, 669
economic loss 602–3
economic structure of property law 358, 513, 515, 517, 519, 521, 523, 545
economic transactions 402, 449, 582–3
economics 44, 49, 635, 637
economy 48, 319–20, 583–4, 591, 609–11, 613, 615, 617–19, 628, 646
edicta 32, 34, 45, 225
edictal powers 250, 665
edicts 28–9, 58–60, 106–7, 118–20, 179, 182–5, 225–6, 245–8, 250–1, 617–18
  aedilician 226, 665–6
  Diocletian's 49, 610, 612, 614, 618, 668
  perpetual 33
  praetorian 25, 28, 72, 76, 156, 158, 503, 505–6, 529, 533
  prefectural 58–60
  provincial 116, 118, 121, 141, 143, 261, 630
education 70, 188, 200–1, 272, 274, 278, 363, 391, 393–4, 411
  legal 32, 36, 151–3, 155, 157–62
  rhetorical 36, 155, 201, 204, 209
educative fictions 75–6
effective control 537–9
effects, legal 377, 422, 474–5, 478, 505, 577, 592, 640
Egypt 56–64, 66, 121, 261, 300–1, 501–2, 554–5, 561–2, 648–9, 652–4
  prefect of 58, 102, 108
Egyptians 61, 290, 476, 556
Ehrlich, Eugen 11–13
elected magistrates 129, 133, 220, 334
elections 90–1, 100–1, 112, 126, 129, 352
electoral bribery 140, 228, 316, 336
eliminatio 204–5
elites 78–9, 96, 152, 165, 201, 228–9, 351, 353–9, 363–6, 368–70
  local 160, 166, 300, 351, 354
  provincial 353, 524
  senatorial 101, 327, 626
  social 85, 90, 357
eloquence 79, 275, 277
emperors 101–8, 117–19, 127–30, 141–6, 169–73, 258–60, 300–7, 338–41, 378–81, 661–4; *see also individual emperors*
  conspiracies against 378–9
  law and imperial administration 98–111
  and military police 301–3
emphyteusis 534, 655–6
emphyteutic possessors 653, 656
Empire 31–6, 111–12, 117–19, 121–2, 124–5, 302–3, 337–8, 363–5, 379–84, 654–6
  coordination of police authorities 306–7
  early 157, 219, 226, 248, 257, 317, 487–8, 494
  high 276, 284, 290–1, 326, 362
  late 4, 129, 382, 668
  legal education 153–60
  legally marginalised groups 362–72

and *maiestas* 337–42
and provinces 117–21
riots 379–81
empirical analysis of law 12–14
employees 315, 604, 622, 625, 629
empowerment 227
emptio venditio 532–3, 588, 622, 649; *see also* sale; consensual contracts
enactments 25, 37, 103, 246, 336, 340, 483, 604, 610, 618
imperial 36, 342
enemies 206, 238, 301, 303, 334, 336–7, 377, 386, 428
external 334, 341
enforcement 86, 143, 241, 250, 259, 265, 363, 370, 583, 592
law 227, 230, 297–8, 306
enfranchisement of freedmen 402, 404–5, 409
enjoyment 525, 528, 533, 588, 590, 630, 641
peaceful 525, 527
enslavement 325, 356, 382, 386
enthymeme 202–4
epicheireme 202–3
epigraphic charters 119, 125, 129
epigraphic evidence 51, 138, 143, 395, 477, 479, 501, 503
epigraphy 43–53, 56
equality 26, 195, 328, 349, 368, 444–5, 589
equestrians 118, 166–70, 224, 229, 338, 351–4, 366, 403
equity 155, 195, 219, 240, 500, 506, 516
estate owners 436–7, 646, 655
estates 467–8, 499–508, 544, 546, 559, 646, 648, 650, 652–3, 655
imperial 118, 305, 307, 613, 646, 652–3
esteem, social 351–4, 358–9, 423
ethics 76, 191, 195, 569
etymology 190, 205, 335, 538, 569, 571
evidence 143–4, 164–6, 250–3, 261–2, 264–6, 270–1, 285–6, 290–1, 358, 661–5
and argument 270–81
documentary 247, 532, 622
explicit 170, 298
legal 143, 362, 404, 636
excellence 272, 275, 277, 529, 587
execution 61–2, 227, 230, 248–9, 265, 299, 377, 381, 392–3, 437–9
exercise of jurisdiction 114, 122, 299, 314
exile 74–5, 228–9, 355, 405, 427, 429, 439, 502
existimatio 322, 355, 396
expectations 12–13, 15–17, 238, 270–1, 280, 374, 378–9, 405, 501, 505
social 76, 466, 491, 493, 502, 507
expenses 130, 132, 247, 301, 356, 368, 370, 425, 644
expertise 44, 165, 172, 413, 462
legal 6, 165, 167–9, 172
experts 27, 33, 151, 168, 170, 177, 224, 290–1, 396
legal 3, 5, 61, 165, 170, 172
extortion 228–9, 274, 305–6, 316, 336, 358
extra ordinem 45, 257, 261, 371

fact-finding 15, 264
factional strife 140, 144, 380
false witness 325, 334
falsum 316, 318, 336, 339
familia 289, 350, 353, 355, 358, 366, 464, 488, 493, 636–8
family 461–70
imperial 338, 351, 366, 559, 626
rights and obligations of family members 465–6
family law 223, 351, 358, 369, 468
family members 229, 326, 393–4, 562
family property 468, 488, 498, 500
farm leases 649–52, 656
farm tenancy, *see* agricultural tenancy
farmers 557–8, 613, 653, 655
state 557–9
farms 240, 649–52
fathers 154–7, 328–30, 420–4, 426–7, 464–7, 478, 488, 490–4, 502–3, 506
father's power, *see patria potestas*
fault 330, 369, 429–30, 602, 631
intentional 601–2
fear 145, 297, 299, 349, 408, 516
fees 129, 259, 520, 618, 661
female adultery 428–9
female slaves 192, 420, 435–7, 448
festivals 128–9, 223, 467
fictions 49, 75–6, 78, 131, 286–8, 404, 528, 533, 586, 663
fideicommissum 258–60, 410, 490, 504
fideiussor 574–5

fides 94, 275, 357, 501, 504, 573, 577, 583, 586; *see also bona fides*; good faith
fiducia 51, 520, 587
filia familias 464–5
filius familias 464–5
fines 125, 130, 132, 313, 439, 610, 655
FIRA, *see Fontes Iuris Romani Anteiustiniani*
Fiscus 646, 648, 653–4
fixed penalties 600, 609
flamen 338, 421
Fontes Iuris Romani Anteiustiniani (FIRA) 298, 421–3, 548, 562, 597, 639
food shortages 667–9
force 24, 26, 275, 278, 426, 429, 612, 614, 618, 660
  armed 366–7
forced labour 428
forced sale 250, 614
foreigners 132, 192, 227, 283–4, 286, 288, 531–2, 582, 584, 587–8
  and citizens 132–3
forgery 312, 316, 336
formal manumission 406, 410
formalities 73, 105, 249, 258, 261, 443, 500–1, 516, 521, 525
formally rational law 10–12
former slaves 402–7, 410–12, 466; *see also* freedmen
formless consent 476, 481
formulary procedure 228, 248, 250, 252, 254, 257–63, 357, 584, 586, 591
formulas 78–9, 225, 237–8, 240, 242, 245–7, 259, 261, 538, 590
forum 27, 29, 31, 74–5, 93–4, 155–6, 223, 225, 273, 299
Fragmenta Vaticana 37–8
fraud 77, 318, 357, 363, 367, 612, 615, 617, 622, 631
free administration 388, 390, 488; *see also libera administratio; peculium*
free marriage 483
free persons 121, 331, 387, 391, 402, 419, 448, 477, 575, 603
free women 356, 387, 438, 448
freeborn children 492, 494
freeborn citizens 129, 466
freeborn status 494, 496
freedmen 50–1, 102, 326, 350, 352–4, 358, 366, 403–13, 475, 638; *see also* manumission
  enfranchisement 402, 404–5, 409
freedom 73, 95, 113, 116, 118, 395–6, 403–4, 406–7, 411–12, 502–3
  of contract 518, 521
  of speech 73–4
  of testation 502
freedwomen 408, 425, 477, 504
friends 119, 157, 168–9, 242, 266, 271, 273, 277, 304, 662–3
fugitive slaves 230, 387, 392, 655
functions 13, 28–9, 88, 90–2, 167–8, 170, 173, 516, 537–9, 596–7
  judicial 91, 93, 260, 340
  police 297–9, 301, 303, 305, 307
furtum 313, 320, 357, 597, 599–600, 603–5
furtum conceptum et oblatum 599
furtum manifestum 599, 604
furtum nec manifestum 599, 604

Gaius 32, 141–3, 159–60, 196, 251, 313, 387–8, 420–1, 500–1, 571–3
  Institutiones 157, 159, 161, 235, 252, 286, 572
Gallia Cisalpina 287–8, 570
games 74–5, 100, 133, 141, 154, 387, 665
  gladiatorial 47–8, 381, 618
Gellius, Aulus 71, 159, 327, 358, 598, 609
gender 350, 417, 423, 426, 429, 432–40, 445, 448, 463, 467
  definition 432–40
  by law 433–6
  norms 432, 436–7, 439
  tracing in Roman law 436–8
gendered notions 434, 436
general action 590, 603, 605
general administration 102, 230
general rules 107–8, 191, 194, 314, 467, 539, 543
generales leges 37–8
genus 28, 190, 205–6
Germanicus 101, 108, 340, 613
Germany 56, 164, 288, 648
gifts 47, 116, 127, 182, 258, 390, 392, 395, 479, 488
  marital 451

girls 51, 330–1, 434, 474, 489, 495
gladiators 48, 105, 274, 303, 353, 363, 367–8, 426–7
glory 272, 429
Gnomon of the *Idios Logos* 58, 62, 64, 502, 560
gods 91, 94, 156, 429, 582, 622, 631
gold 77–8, 114, 161, 353, 618, 629
good faith 184, 516, 522, 528, 543–4, 549, 581, 586, 589–90, 631; *see also bona fides*
goods 48–9, 51, 250–1, 612–16, 618, 622, 624, 626–7, 660, 665–8
government 91, 93, 95, 124, 126, 128, 145, 166, 172–3, 654–6
  local 124–5, 127–8, 131
  spending 611, 617–18
governors 92–3, 112–22, 127–30, 257–9, 261–3, 301–7, 364–5, 380–2, 661–4, 668
  jurisdiction 115–16, 132
  and military policing 303–5
  senatorial 101, 229
Gracchan reforms 647
Gracchus, Gaius 92, 115, 223, 227, 229, 301, 336, 375–6
grain 132, 300, 324, 420, 559, 562, 613, 627–8, 668–9
  supply 316, 318, 613
grandchildren 426, 488, 503, 505, 508
Greek 30, 36, 57, 63–5, 134, 144, 274, 276–7, 280, 555
Greek culture 188, 194, 200
Greek East 28, 300, 555, 636
Greek institutions 192, 555
Greek philosophy 188–97
guardians 64, 229, 300, 316, 422–3, 425–6, 428, 488–91, 502, 504
guardianship 64, 161, 274, 422–7, 436, 446–7, 466, 468, 470, 488–91
guards 300–1, 622
  harbour 300, 307
  prison 300, 305–6
  watchtower 300–1

habits 172, 273–4, 362, 364, 372
Hadrian 105–6, 169–70, 261, 306, 337, 339, 464, 466, 613–14, 653–4
handbooks 3, 6–7, 159, 212, 273, 275, 277, 310, 336, 487
  rhetorical 202, 204, 209, 211
Hannibalic War 90, 112–13
harm 317–18, 322, 324–8, 365, 368, 376, 494, 597, 602–4, 664
harshness 374
heirs 313, 408, 410, 422–3, 426, 435, 466–8, 498–508, 574–5, 583
  equal 77, 465
  universal 467, 506
hendiadys 71, 242
Herculaneum 50, 52, 105, 247, 339, 407, 636
hereditas 574–5
Hermagoras 207–9
Hermogenianus 36, 38
hierarchy 101, 168, 220, 263, 351–2, 355, 387, 407, 433
  social 86, 164, 297, 355, 437, 448
hire 520, 622, 627, 629–30
  contract of 520; *see also* consensual contracts
Hispania 92, 125–7, 340, 613
Hispania Citerior 91, 113, 115
Hispania Tarraconensis 118, 261, 554
Hispania Ulterior 91, 113–14
historians 4, 8–16, 189, 362–3, 372, 432, 463, 470, 549, 621
  legal 12, 16, 25, 33, 56, 219, 257, 462, 667
holders of *imperium* 112, 114–15, 118, 378
homes 152, 239–40, 326, 371, 514, 578
homicide 129, 228, 312, 316
homosexuality 474
honestiores 354–5, 357, 368–70, 643
honour 50, 90, 102, 125, 220, 236, 277, 396–7, 487, 491
honourable discharge 45, 289, 475, 478
Hopkins, Keith 16, 411
Horace 73–4, 77, 79
horrea 624–31
horrearius 624–5, 627–30
hostes 377, 383
house 206, 210–11, 327, 329–30, 420, 423, 427, 560, 581, 604
  rules of the 640, 643
household members 390, 395
household slaves 355, 395
households 322–3, 326–8, 391, 404, 407, 411, 413, 436, 464, 561
  imperial 354, 622

humanity/*humanitas* 188, 195
humiliores 354–5, 357, 363, 368–70, 643
husband and wife 425, 467, 473–84, 505–6
husbands 155, 328–30, 421–3, 425–30, 436–8, 448, 467–8, 473–4, 476–7, 482–3

ideology 4–5, 15, 24, 26, 37, 48, 71, 382–3, 427, 429
Idios Logos 58, 60, 64, 502, 560
ignominiosi 355
illegitimate children 478, 495
illicit *collegia* 140–2
imbalance 122, 358–9, 571
immovable property 541, 548
immunities 374–5, 613, 660, 664
Imperial administration 79, 98–111, 151, 159, 162, 266, 352, 354, 626, 653
Imperial chancellery 48, 63, 107, 178, 195, 444
Imperial constitutions 36–8, 57–8, 62, 158, 262, 265, 285, 354–5, 388, 502
Imperial control 161, 231, 653
Imperial court 168, 171–2, 178, 185
Imperial cult 338, 341, 354
Imperial enactments 36, 342
Imperial estates 118, 305, 307, 613, 646, 652–3
Imperial family 338, 351, 366, 559, 626
Imperial household 354, 622
Imperial period 114, 119, 121, 242, 257, 357–8, 379, 381, 402, 409
  early 76, 119, 299, 462–3, 559, 621
Imperial rescripts 35, 66, 183, 444, 446–7, 631, 652, 654, 661–3, 667–8
Imperial slaves 356, 631
Imperial treasury 339, 560, 646, 648, 664
imperium 87–8, 90–1, 93, 99–102, 107–8, 112–13, 115, 117, 226, 228–9
  Augustus 99–100
  holders of 112, 114–15, 118, 378
  proconsular 100
impunity 299, 377, 429
in ius vocare 263–4
in ius vocatio 248–9, 254
incentives 95, 236, 252, 408, 411, 610, 613, 646, 648, 652–4
incolae 133–4
income 131–2, 560, 642–3, 649–50
  sources of 132, 559
induction 178, 202, 204, 209
infames 355, 366–8, 372, 407
infamia 74, 130, 326, 339, 355, 357, 363, 367–8, 394
infanticide 492
inflation 49, 328, 617–18, 667
informal manumission 406
inheritance 61–4, 77, 366, 451–2, 466–9, 494–5, 498–508, 544, 575, 637; *see also* succession
  law 372, 468, 505, 508, 545
iniuria 313, 318, 320, 323–31, 357, 367, 396–7, 437, 598, 600–2
iniuria-contumelia 600–1, 605
injury 130, 317, 323–4, 434, 437, 508, 597, 601–2
  personal 597, 599–600, 603, 605, 609–10
innovations 46, 93, 257–8, 263, 506, 531, 602, 617, 655
  procedural 258, 260, 266, 325, 530
inscriptions 43–52, 105, 107, 141, 145, 165, 290–1, 477, 624–7, 662
institores 390–1, 570, 627, 637
institutional policing 297–8, 308
institutions 85–7, 92–4, 138–40, 241–2, 386–7, 425, 443, 540, 547–9, 583–5
  functioning 89–94
  Greek 192, 555
  legal 3, 6, 16, 44, 350, 428, 449, 582, 646, 655
  police 298, 300, 302, 307
  political 89, 319, 331, 338
  public 86, 98, 137
  Republic 85–96
  social 248, 463
insulae 529, 627, 636–44
  economics of ownership 636–42
  living in 642–3
insularius 627–8, 638, 640, 643
insult 316, 357, 437, 601
  indirect 600
intentional fault 601–2
intercolumnia 625, 628
interdict procedure 539, 547
interdicta 388, 538–41

interdictal possession 539–41, 543, 547
interdicts 248, 527–8, 538–9, 541, 545, 549, 647
interests 23, 137–8, 317, 364–5, 487–8, 491, 494, 517–22, 591–2, 641
  best 89, 139, 145, 490, 493–5
  collective 312, 317, 319
  divided 513, 517–18, 520–1
  economic 496, 651
  vested 639, 642, 644
international trade 584, 586, 596, 604
interpretation 3–4, 28–9, 77–8, 162, 184–5, 208, 210–11, 410–11, 481–2, 622–3
  strict 530, 623
intertium 52
intestacy 183, 466–8, 490, 499–500, 503–6
intestate succession 422, 467, 499, 503–6
investments 411, 514, 516–17, 557, 560, 629, 650, 654
Italian land 287, 534, 553, 611
Italy 89–91, 94–5, 100, 106–7, 126, 129–30, 302, 526, 646–8, 663
  peninsular 285, 461
iudex 228, 237–42, 257, 260–1, 286, 357–8, 390, 446, 542, 604
iudicia populi 93, 228–9, 334, 337, 375, 438
iudicia publica 312, 314, 316–18, 320
iudicium 226, 228, 238, 435, 446
Iulianus, Salvius, *see* Julian, lawyer
Iulius Paulus 160, 193, 533, 545–6, 613, 616
iura in re aliena 529, 532–4, 542
in iure 224, 228, 250–2, 254, 257, 525, 531, 533, 582, 587–8
in iure cessio 525, 531, 533, 543, 582, 587–8
iuris origo 26
iuris periti 9, 153
iuris prudentes 153, 166–7, 169, 172, 219, 410
ius agendi cum populo 220–1, 227, 230
ius civile 114, 120–2, 151–2, 190–1, 505–6, 526–7, 531–4, 548, 572–3, 585–6
ius gentium 184, 192, 196, 289, 371, 386, 577, 582, 584–5
ius honorarium 226, 534, 573, 585
ius Italicum 124, 133, 553, 648
Ius Latii 119
ius nundinarum 660–5
ius praetorium 226, 585
ius provocationis 221
ius publicum 99–102, 338
ius Quiritium 553, 582, 584–5
ius vitae necisque 461, 464, 491–2
iusta causa 525, 527–8
iustitia 196–7

Javolenus 479–80, 533
jewels 422–3, 428
Jewish revolt 383
Jews 300, 302, 341–2, 429
Jhering, Rudolph von 12, 549
joinder 251–3, 518
judges 52, 114–15, 130, 228–9, 241–3, 260–2, 276, 278–81, 357–8, 584–5
  appointment 235
  private 614, 616
judgment 76–7, 115–16, 237–8, 242, 257, 260, 264–5, 357–8, 543, 577–8
judicial functions 91, 93, 260, 340
judicial oratory 207, 253
judicial torture 154, 631
Julian
  emperor 160, 668
  lawyer 33, 118, 160, 164, 166, 194, 224, 247, 576, 668
Julius Caesar 116–17, 138, 140, 168–9, 219, 222, 312, 335, 337, 339
juries 76, 116, 119, 229, 270–1, 273, 278–80, 287, 356, 366
jurisdiction 29, 60–2, 111–18, 120–2, 130–3, 224–7, 237, 259–60, 283–4, 287–8
  civil 227–8
  criminal 130, 230, 302, 358
  domestic 328–9, 331
  exercise of 114, 122, 299, 314
  governors 115–16, 132
  local 118–20, 126, 130–1, 364
  provincial 116, 119, 122
  public 318–19
jurisdictional power 60, 102
jurisprudence 4–5, 38, 45, 63, 153, 159, 193, 210, 285–6, 533
jurisprudents, *see iuris prudentes*
jurists 25–9, 34–8, 169–71, 177–86, 188–97, 200–1, 209–12, 327–31, 433–5, 616–18

jurists (*Cont.*)
classical 36, 176, 235, 386, 477, 481, 541, 545, 623, 632
Republican 178, 190, 194–5, 225, 591, 603
rhetoric of 209–11
jurors 75, 228–9, 276, 357
jury courts 354, 378
justice 14–15, 24, 26, 29, 196, 234, 248, 266, 349, 356
access to 266, 356–9, 644
distributive 362, 369
substantive 4, 286, 292
Justinian 24–5, 38, 160–2, 178, 424–6, 429, 534, 537, 571, 603–4
codes 258, 490, 631, 662, 667
compilers 25, 176, 327, 542, 573, 578, 667
Digest 38, 157, 200, 322, 339, 410, 469, 623, 629
Institutes 33, 161, 259, 572, 576

katoikic land 559, 563, 648
κυριεία 555–6
killing 155, 207, 316, 320, 324, 329, 380–1, 420, 429, 601–2
kings 86–8, 112, 140, 369, 423, 557
kinship 56, 424, 463, 467, 469, 498
knights, *see equestrians; equites*
knowledge 9, 32–3, 35, 43–4, 193, 195–6, 200–1, 205, 208–10, 549
legal 4–5, 156, 161, 200, 291
κράτησις 555–6
κτήτορες 562–3

Labeo, M. Antistius 157, 181–2, 193, 210–11, 327–9, 331, 479, 533, 590, 629–30
labour 368, 514, 520, 522, 577, 612, 653–4
labourers 352, 355, 646, 655
laesio enormis 667
land 131, 133, 514–22, 526–7, 529, 534, 553–4, 556–60, 617, 646–57
agricultural 513, 557, 644
arable 556–7
categories 556–7
divided interests in 517, 519
Italian 287, 534, 553, 611
katoikic 559, 563, 648
ownership 532, 534, 561, 644
parcels of 518, 557–8, 656
possession 556–9
private 557–60, 646–8, 653, 656
privatisation 647–9
provincial 548, 554, 648, 656
public 50, 224, 226, 287, 527, 557, 647
state 557–9
temple 557–8
tenure 646–56
in provinces 652–3
landlords 520, 624–6, 628, 639, 641, 649–51, 655
urban 635–44
landowners 515, 522, 570, 646, 648–52, 654–6
language 36–7, 65–6, 71, 76, 79, 141–2, 146, 153–4, 190–1, 311
legal 47, 73–4, 388
lanistae 367
latent defects 226, 666–7
Latin literature 70–9
Latin right 119, 124, 133, 350
Latin status 410, 526
law enforcement 227, 230, 297–8, 306
law of nations 192
law of persons 159, 349–51, 359, 387, 556
lawsuits 14, 130, 133, 220, 238, 247–8, 251–3, 259, 288, 445–6
lawyers 8–11, 14, 29, 151–3, 155, 157–9, 161–2, 164–8, 170–3, 618
in administration 164–73
leases 494, 517–18, 520, 529, 590, 622–4, 626–30, 640–2, 649–53, 655–6
farm 649–52, 656
leasing 126, 224, 390, 649–51
legacies 403, 405, 410–11, 435, 438, 502–4, 507, 544, 572, 615–16
legal actions 27, 121, 159, 284, 300, 367, 371, 425, 445, 621
legal actors, women as 443–53
legal acts 64, 106, 405, 425, 500
legal advantage 356, 358–9, 638
legal advice 33, 170, 181, 356, 358–9, 478
legal advisers 121, 156, 160–1, 164, 168, 173, 341, 501
legal authority 5, 404, 433, 437, 440, 496, 650–2, 656
legal business 170, 224–5, 251
legal capacity 387–91, 422, 425, 444, 448, 450, 489, 498, 502, 504

legal content 44, 47, 52, 158, 492
legal culture 5–6, 9–11, 14, 16, 36, 38, 154, 164, 506, 609
legal discourse 156, 158, 176, 386, 412, 537, 579
legal documentation 44–51
legal documents 12, 43, 45, 52, 154, 356, 444, 500
legal education 32, 36, 151–62
 and Berytus 160–2
 Empire 153–60
 formalisation 160–2
 Republic 152–3
legal effects 377, 422, 474–5, 478, 505, 577, 592, 640
legal epigraphy 43–4, 52–3
legal evidence 143, 362, 404, 636
legal expertise 6, 165, 167–9, 172
legal experts 3, 5, 61, 165, 170, 172
legal fictions, *see* fictions
legal historians 12, 16, 25, 33, 56, 219, 257, 462, 667
legal information 29, 32, 34, 44
 organisation and access to 23–38
 Principate 32–5
 Republic 25–31
 towards a juristic canon 35–7
legal innovations 45, 182, 426
legal institutions 3, 6, 16, 44, 350, 428, 449, 582, 646, 655
legal instruments 44, 51, 56, 286–7, 335, 525, 528
legal knowledge 4–5, 156, 161, 200, 291
legal language 47, 73–4, 388
legal life 63, 177, 445, 461, 499, 502–3, 505, 507
legal literature 32, 34, 37, 57, 107, 176–8, 185, 388, 411, 489
 and imperial constitutions 57–8
legal norms 33, 106, 612, 652
legal order 26–7, 36, 63, 193, 474, 504
legal pluralism 15, 283–92
 choice of law across life histories 288–9
 fictions in Roman procedure 285–8
 in practice 290–1
 Republican history and later theory 284–5
legal powers 99, 130, 351, 366, 374, 525, 529
legal practice 6, 10, 12, 64–5, 191–2, 436, 444–5, 453, 475, 478
 after *Constitutio Antoniniana* 65–6
 before *Constitutio Antoniniana* 63–5
 peregrine 63
legal privilege 349–59, 663
legal processes 10, 13, 115, 120, 363, 365, 367, 371, 378, 444–5
legal protection 192, 365, 394, 478, 527
legal reasoning 154, 176–86
legal remedies 192, 249–50, 266, 357, 478, 495, 647, 650, 665, 667
legal rules 8–11, 15–16, 37, 349, 507, 513, 636, 646, 660, 665
 abstract 8, 10
legal scholars 172, 176, 432, 461, 542, 624
legal science 9–12, 14, 16–17, 25, 28, 64, 166, 195, 226
legal sociology 11–14, 463
legal statuses 74, 124, 133, 208, 272, 305, 349–59, 432, 434, 440
 local government structures 124–5
legal system 10–12, 14, 33–4, 356–8, 363–6, 369–72, 469, 517–18, 554, 581–2
legal teaching 33, 37, 152
legal traditions 3, 5, 9, 37, 63–5, 524, 554–5
legal training 8–9, 15, 74, 165, 170
legal transactions 350–1, 366, 445, 447–8, 451–2, 627
legal writing 9, 176–86
legally marginalised groups, Empire 362–72
legatees 210–11, 258, 502, 504, 507
legates 31, 92, 101, 118, 503
leges 11, 25–9, 32, 45, 98–9, 103–4, 226
 generales 37–8
 horreorum 624–7, 632
 maiestatis 335–7
 publicae 25, 30, 621
 regiae 26, 72, 220
legions 91, 101–2, 287, 340, 350, 495
legis actiones 159, 224–5, 228, 252, 284, 525, 542, 549, 582, 585–6
legislation 24–6, 30–1, 103, 222–3, 287, 325, 428, 489–90, 492, 494–5
 Augustan 74, 155, 329, 352, 427, 469, 491
legislative activities 6, 47, 222–3, 227
legislators 38, 86, 185, 194, 323, 330, 601
 intentions 184–5
legitimate children 438, 461, 466–7, 469, 495
lenders 520–1, 587, 591, 611, 614

Lenel, Otto 33, 59, 108, 119, 158, 226, 250, 252, 425
Lepidus, Aemilius 100, 224, 301
lessees 624, 627, 629, 650
lessors 627, 629, 650
letters 31–2, 107, 116, 140–1, 182, 184, 208–9, 271–2, 304–5, 661–2
letting 224, 587–9, 625–6, 639–41, 643–4
levitas 446, 451
lex Aelia Sentia 50, 103, 407–8, 475
lex Appuleia 335–6
lex Aquilia 315, 325, 368, 388, 546, 578, 596, 600–3, 609; *see also damnum iniuria datum*
lex contractus 624, 631, 640
lex Cornelia 246, 326–7, 336, 340
lex Falcidia 507, 616, 618
lex Fufia Caninia 103, 407–8
lex horreorum 625–7, 630
lex Irnitana 49–50, 52, 120–1, 130–1, 235, 261, 299, 475
lex Iulia 103, 138, 141, 328–30, 337, 339–42, 380, 425–9, 437, 439
Lex Iunia 406
lex maiestatis 338–41, 343
lex Manciana 653
lex Pompeia 404
lex provinciae 116, 225
lex Romana Visigothorum 429
lex Rupilia 114, 116–17
lex Sempronia 375–7, 621
liability 389–90, 450, 518, 577–8, 592–3, 597, 599, 604, 624, 629–31
  delictual 604
  legal 488, 577, 638
  quasi-delictual 604, 642
  standards of 191, 195, 631
  strict 604
  tax 556, 654
libera administratio 388, 390, 488; *see also peculium*
libertas 230, 350
liberty 27, 130, 137, 281, 326, 406–7, 409, 492
librarians 394, 396
Libri de officio proconsulis 185
libri decretorum 183–4
libri regularum 178, 182–3, 194
libri responsorum 178, 180–2, 184–5
Licinius Crassus, M. 222, 500
lictors 127, 299–300
Liebs, Detlef 33, 171–2, 177, 185, 252, 393
liens 542, 556, 562, 648
life
  economic 451, 488, 617, 669
  legal 63, 177, 445, 461, 499, 502–3, 505, 507
  political 4, 92–3, 475
  public 78, 95, 366
  social 11, 15, 363, 448, 506
life table 616
liquid assets 520–1
literary sources 9, 134, 138, 246, 252, 337–9, 358, 366, 484, 501
litigants 114, 231, 235, 237–8, 242, 245, 248, 252–4, 275, 286
litigation 14, 16, 228, 241, 245–7, 252–4, 357–9, 621, 623, 627
litis contestatio 251–2, 314, 576–7
Livy 31, 76–7, 86–7, 112, 140, 299, 330–1, 377, 438, 537–8
loans 518, 520, 578, 583, 587, 591, 611, 616, 622, 647–8
loca armaris 625
local administration 124–34
local authorities 285, 300, 305, 561, 668
local communities 115, 120, 124, 131, 171, 353
local councils 50, 126, 128, 668
local courts 284, 290–1, 306
local elites 160, 166, 300, 351, 354
local government 124–5, 127–8, 131
local government structures 124–9
local jurisdiction 118–20, 126, 130–1, 364
local law 114–15, 120–2, 131, 133, 289–92, 364, 447
local office 127–8, 132, 353
locatio conductio 259, 315, 520, 588–9, 591, 622, 627, 649; *see also* consensual contracts, hiring; letting; lessor; lessee
locator horrei 629–30
logic 28, 190, 194, 204, 211, 320, 534, 537, 597, 601
longi temporis praescriptio 548–9, 648, 656
long-term leasing 655
loss 73–4, 76, 324, 340–1, 368–9, 516–18, 589, 591, 602–3, 605
  of citizenship 287–9
  economic 602–3

loss of control 279–80
loyalty 32, 127, 145–6, 367, 392, 504
Lucian 499
Lucilius Africanus 661–4
Lucretia 423–4
Lycia 160, 563

Macedonia 31, 112–13
magister navis 390, 450
magisterial power 98–9, 298
magistracies 85, 87–94, 112, 222–4, 226–7, 230, 272, 289, 300, 366
  annual 28, 227
  junior 230, 352
  local 66, 125, 352
  major 223, 227
  non-annual 220, 223, 227, 230
magistrates 87–90, 92–6, 112–14, 126–7, 129–34, 182–5, 219–31, 237–42, 290–2, 375–8
  applying law 226–30
  civilian 306–7
  elected 129, 133, 220, 334
  former 94, 96, 117, 128, 133
  local 28, 105, 120, 126–8, 130–1, 134, 236, 307, 371, 668
  making law 220–6
  municipal 31, 33, 49, 120, 250
  plebeian 89, 221
  presiding 229, 290, 313, 357
maiestas 316, 318, 327, 333, 335–43, 358, 378
  later Empire 342
  under Empire 337–42
maiestas populi Romani 335–6, 340
maintenance 15, 92, 132, 494, 532, 546, 637, 639, 642, 654
  payments 446–7, 616
major magistracies 223, 227
mala carmina 73–4
male children 419, 468
male citizens 94, 126, 327, 419, 434, 439–40, 464
male line 350, 422, 424, 461, 466–7, 488
male slaves 420, 435, 448
management 31, 118, 446, 490, 519–21, 626, 630–1, 637–8
  indirect 626, 638
  of storage spaces 623–31
managers 370–1, 622, 624–5, 627–31
  business 390, 627–9
mancipatio 51, 421, 500–1, 516, 521–2, 524–6, 531–3, 543, 581–4, 587–8
mandata 34, 107–8, 231
manumission 49, 64, 126, 133, 392–4, 402–13, 477, 504, 615
  Augustan reforms 402, 406–10
  citizenship and familial integration 403–5
  formal 406, 410
  informal 406
  tax 615
  testamentary 103, 407–8, 410, 504
  under the Empire 410–13
manus 289, 388, 419, 422, 425–6, 437, 464, 467, 473, 505–6
  marriage 289, 350, 448, 470
Marcian 142, 159, 179, 194, 481, 484
Marcus Aurelius 47, 70, 103, 105, 108, 281, 341–2, 380, 428–9, 489
marginalisation 362–3, 365–6, 368, 370–2, 534, 603
marginalised groups 362–3, 365–7, 369, 371
Marius, C. 223, 327, 377
Mark Antony 140, 301
market prices 609–10, 613, 615, 618, 650, 660–9
  formation 611–14
market transactions 669
market value 412, 522, 616, 665–7
markets 51, 124, 127, 226, 584, 610–11, 613–14, 616, 618, 660–9
  domanial 662, 664
  periodic 662–5
marriage 353–4, 421–2, 425–6, 429, 463–4, 466–7, 469–70, 473–84, 489–90, 505–6
  dissolution of 481–3
  legal nature of 473, 479
  legitimate 464, 474
  modern theories on Roman law of marriage 479–81
  sibling 61
mass enslavements 374, 382
mass housing 635–7, 642–3
masters 326, 329, 387–93, 395–6, 404, 406–8, 411, 578, 601, 627–8
mater familias 436–7, 464

maternal authority 488
maximum prices 105, 610, 612–13, 617, 660, 665, 668–9
mediation 43, 235–41
mediators 235–9, 242–3
Mediterranean 86–7, 92, 94–5, 113, 406, 466, 475
membrum ruptum 597–8
merchandise 661, 665–6, 668
merchants 32, 48, 531, 590, 600, 612–13, 628
mercy 374, 379, 381, 393
Messius Saturninus 171
methodology 9, 14–15, 17, 71, 197, 201, 209, 240–1, 245
Mettius Rufus 58–9, 556, 562
military commands 111–12, 223, 305, 375
military forces 117, 376, 379, 381
military police 301–2, 305–7
  and emperors 301–3
  and governors 303–5
  Republican precedents 301
military service 89, 106, 377, 403, 489, 647
military tribunes 86–7
mines 129, 143, 305, 355, 515, 519, 646
minores 349, 467, 489
missio 250
models 25, 28, 76, 78, 92, 95, 125–6, 201–2, 546, 548
Modestinus, Herennius 77, 134, 159–60, 179, 339, 474, 481, 660, 663
modesty 446–7
Mommsen, Theodor 9, 11–12, 56, 141–2, 221, 310, 628, 630, 661
monarchy 25, 86–7, 95, 111, 117, 420
monetary reform 617–18
money 132, 411–12, 575–6, 584–5, 587–8, 590–2, 598–9, 611, 615, 665–7
moneylenders 611
moral behaviour, marginalisation 367–8
moral duties 193, 259, 612
moral offences 312, 601
mores 279, 396, 435, 446, 491, 540
mortgages 481, 516–17, 519–20, 575, 579
mos maiorum 71, 76–8, 85–6, 89, 492
mothers 155, 207, 423–4, 446, 467–9, 490, 492–3, 495, 506, 508
movable property 369, 386, 524, 527, 541, 666
Mucius Scaevola, Quintus
  Augur 152, 189, 377
  Pontifex 29, 153, 190, 438, 500, 570, 587, 589
Munatius Flavianus 662–3
munera 127–9, 132–3, 350
municipal charters 31, 49, 133, 287, 300
municipal laws 103, 130, 242, 610, 613
municipal magistrates 31, 33, 49, 120, 250
municipal statutes 33, 45, 317
municipia 31, 44, 49, 90, 120–1, 124–6, 131, 133, 237, 239
murder 119, 316, 325, 330, 336–7, 358
mutuum 587, 589, 591–2, 622

narrative analysis 177–8, 182, 184
narrative concentration 178–80
natura 192, 195–6, 419, 543
natural law 195–6, 386, 513
natural obligations 196, 573–4, 577
naturalis ratio 196
negotia 45, 51–2
negotiation 5, 238, 248, 253, 410, 413, 516, 617–18
neighbouring communities 621, 664
neighbours 238, 324, 521, 526, 574, 642, 654
Nero 105, 303, 351, 379, 612–13, 640, 667
Nerva 32, 104, 108, 339
newborn children 492
Nile Valley 554, 557
nomen gentilicium 404
nomikoi 61, 166, 171
nomina transcripticia 588, 622
nomoi 30–1
non-annual magistracies 220, 223, 227, 230
non-citizens 61, 64, 329, 350, 364–5, 368, 370, 475, 584
non-judicial oratory 208
non-Romans 113–14, 116, 225–7, 287, 364, 548, 621
normative order 10–12, 15, 537
norms 4–5, 76, 79, 92, 94, 234–5, 290–1, 409, 412, 432–4
  legal 33, 106, 612, 652
notarisation 62, 64
noxiam sarcire 597, 599

Numidia 662–3
nundinae 661, 663

oaths 86, 90, 226, 245, 248, 252–3, 271, 300, 558, 583
obligatio 569–79, 584, 587, 592–3, 597
  and *actio* 576–7
  and contract 578–9
  definitions 572–4, 576
  as relationship 574–5
  as thing 575–6
obligatio contracta 579, 588, 592
obligatio naturalis 577
obligationes consensu contractae 588–9
obligations 131, 465–7, 493–4, 530, 532–3, 571–5, 577–8, 586–8, 590–2, 598
  delictual 573, 596
  institutional structure 571–2
  law of 569, 588
  natural 196, 573–4, 577
  personal 533, 571–2
  sources of 61, 572
observers 182–4, 362, 461
Octavian 98, 100–2, 224, 301; *see also* Augustus
offences 311–12, 314–19, 322, 326, 333–4, 338, 341–2, 424, 428, 601–2
  capital 334, 354
  moral 312, 601
  public 312, 314–18
  sexual 310, 328, 439
  substance of 315–19
offenders 145, 181, 299, 437–9, 601
office 90–1, 99–101, 126–7, 133–4, 166–7, 170, 351–2, 374–5, 560, 643
  holders 50, 107–8, 167, 182
  local 127–8, 132, 353
  public 95, 350, 355, 359, 367–8, 445–6
officia 106, 108, 272, 304
officials 14, 16, 33–5, 60, 62, 102, 104, 120, 122, 258–9
operae 350, 412–13, 638
Opimius, L. 376
oral discussion 152, 157–8
oratio principis 47, 105
orators 75, 78, 89, 93, 95–6, 153, 156, 271, 273, 277
oratory 72, 78, 209, 247
  judicial 207, 253
  non-judicial 208
orders and status 351–6
ordo 278, 351–2, 355, 622
ordo decurionum 45, 50, 128
original owners 464, 515, 520, 522, 647
Ostia 302, 636
outlaws 304, 363, 370–2
overseers 392
Ovid 74–5, 428
Ovinian law 87
owners 388–91, 393–4, 420, 514–16, 518–19, 521–2, 525–6, 529, 627–31, 637–44
  absentee 629, 641
  estate 436–7, 646, 655
  original 464, 515, 520, 522, 647
  slave 307, 392, 405, 407, 411, 420, 615
ownership 514–15, 537, 539–42, 544, 547, 549, 553–4, 558, 560, 648
  acquisition of 498, 538, 543, 545–6, 549
  land 532, 534, 561, 644
  and power 524–34
  private 514, 526, 554, 559, 653
  rights 514–15, 525
  transfer of 388, 435, 516, 525, 532, 540, 543, 559

Papinian 38, 158–9, 161–2, 164, 166, 180, 182, 194, 545, 573
papyri 27, 36, 56–8, 63, 65, 300–1, 358–9, 444–5, 447, 622–3
papyrology 5, 43, 56–66
parcels of land 518, 557–8, 656
parental power 488, 491
parents 155, 259, 289, 313, 334, 394, 469, 474, 487–9, 491–5
  and children 487–96
parricide 334, 404, 428
partners 100, 329, 356, 391, 438, 522, 588, 622
partnership 130, 474, 522, 588–9, 622, 649
παράφερνα 560
pater familias 326, 419–20, 422, 436–8, 463–6, 488, 491–2, 498, 502, 505–6
paternal authority 464–5, 492
paternal power 289, 461–4, 466–7, 478, 488, 491

patria potestas 289, 419–20, 422, 461, 463–4, 467, 470, 475, 488, 491–3
patriarchy 434, 444
  and women 419–30
patricians 26, 86–7, 89–90, 99, 222, 334, 421, 467, 475, 665
patrimony 390, 422–3, 426, 490, 597, 601
patrocinium 655
patronage 152, 165, 359, 411
  emperor's 129, 352
  rural 655
patrons 31, 129, 236, 313, 325, 359, 366, 404, 407–13, 615
Patterson, Orlando 386, 393, 404
Paulus, Iulius 160, 193, 533, 545–6, 613, 616
peaceful enjoyment 525, 527
peculatus 316–17, 336
peculia 356, 367, 388–92, 395–6, 411–12, 448, 465, 478, 488, 637–8
  social repercussions 395
pecuniary penalties 422, 482, 599–600
pecus quadrupes 601–2
penal actions 250, 314–15, 319
penalties 226, 228, 236–7, 313–15, 324–5, 337, 339–41, 428–9, 598–9, 603–5
  pecuniary 422, 482, 599–600
  physical 596, 598–600
  public 428, 610
people's provinces 117–19
perduellio 228, 334–7, 339, 341, 376
peregrine communities 115, 119, 125, 131
peregrine law 59–62, 64, 66
peregrine towns 124
peregrines 61–2, 65, 286, 365, 382–3, 502, 504, 554, 561
periodic markets 662–5
permanent courts 91, 93–4, 228, 335, 354, 357
perpetual edicts 33
perpetual guardianship 435, 470
personal actions 572, 577
personal injuries 597, 599–600, 603, 605, 609–10
personal obligations 533, 571–2
personal rights 437, 465, 525
personal status 289, 291, 488
personality 284–5, 306, 350, 411, 581, 600
persons, law of 159, 349–51, 359, 387, 556
persuasion 151, 182, 202, 207, 209, 211, 270
petitioners 239, 248, 359, 464
petitioning 134, 369, 466, 662
petitions 34, 59–60, 151, 155, 164, 170, 358–9, 369, 444–5, 452
philosophers 151, 153, 157, 212, 302, 311, 327
philosophy 70, 73, 78–9, 157, 162, 177, 189, 200–1, 208, 327
physical assaults 598, 600
physical control 388, 525, 527, 538–9, 541, 546–7, 553
physical damage 371, 602
physical penalties 596, 598–600
pietas/piety 195, 278, 408–9, 412, 487, 491, 493, 498, 577
pimps 330, 367, 394, 427, 440, 628
pirates 76, 92, 274, 371
Piso Frugi, L. Calpurnius 114–15, 228
plagium 312, 315–16
plaintiffs 224, 228, 248–9, 252, 278, 357, 539, 541, 584–6, 603
plebeian magistrates 89, 221
plebeian tribunes 99, 222
plebeians 26, 86–90, 92–3, 99, 164, 219–23, 225–30, 368, 375, 665
pledge 265, 530–1, 587, 622–3, 626–7, 650
  rights of 562
Pliny 107, 144, 157, 304–6, 349, 354, 499, 501, 503, 613–14
  directives from Trajan 144–6
Plotinus 151, 157, 162
Plutarch 139–40, 154, 428, 483, 499
poenalis 313–15
poetry 36, 70, 72–4, 78–9
poets 74–5, 79, 327
  Augustan 73, 78
police
  arrangements 300–1
  civilian 306–7
  functions 297–308
  institutions 298, 300, 302, 307
  military 301–3, 305–7
policing 297–308, 320
  by civilian officials 298–301
  coordination of police authorities under Empire 306–7
  institutional 297–8, 308
  routine 301, 307
politeia 30–1, 194
political career 89–90, 92–3, 352
political change 78–9, 323

political community 325, 327–8, 350
political institutions 89, 319, 331, 338
political life 4, 92–3, 475
political power 73, 87, 100, 405, 466
political rights 31, 124, 419, 526
political treason 228
politics 73, 75–6, 78–9, 85, 95, 99–100, 107, 325, 327, 331
Polybius 30, 95, 221, 284, 621
pomerium 49, 94, 99–100, 221, 301, 375
Pompeii 129, 303, 426, 627, 636
Pompey 30–1, 89, 92, 274–5, 301
Pomponius 25–6, 29–30, 153, 157, 178, 189–90, 195, 284, 329, 369
pontiffs 27, 221, 224
Pontus 160, 503
popular actions 314–15, 317–18
popular assemblies 46, 85–8, 90, 93, 102–4, 106, 116, 126, 129, 220–1
popular participation 85–96
populus 75, 89, 336
Porphyry 151, 157–8
Porta Salaria 624–7, 630
positive law 4–5, 10, 15–16, 24, 173, 245, 374
posses 300, 378, 549
possessio 224, 388, 534, 537, 539–41, 543–9, 553–6
 towards a coherent use and concept of 544–7
possessio vel ususfructus 548
possession 499–500, 505–7, 514–16, 518–22, 525–8, 530–2, 537–43, 545–9, 650–1, 656
 acquisition of 388, 547
 archaeology of 540
 in civil procedure 540–4
 elements of 539
 functions of 538–9
 interdictal 539–41, 543, 547
 land 556–9
 law of 539, 542, 545, 548–9
 and provincial practice 553–63
 in Roman law 537–49
 terms and concepts 555–6
 types and concepts 546–7
 usucapion 539, 546–7, 549
 visions of 538–40
possessors 265, 388, 527–8, 538–9, 543–5, 549, 553, 656
 emphyteutic 653, 656
 initial/first 514–16
 lawful 648, 656
possessory titles 540, 544, 562–3
post-classical period 548–9
posts, administrative 151, 165–7, 171
potestas 92, 230, 366, 436, 464, 466–7, 494, 502, 505–6, 600–1
 dominica 388, 419
 tribunicia 46–7, 92, 99–100, 222
power 46, 90–2, 98–103, 226–7, 328–9, 464–6, 491–2, 507, 527–9, 582–5
 bargaining 612, 650
 coercive 222, 229, 371, 374
 consular 86–7, 98
 imperial 52, 121, 266, 291, 341
 jurisdictional 60, 102
 legal 99, 130, 351, 366, 374, 525, 529
 magisterial 98–9, 298
 and ownership 524–34
 paternal 289, 461–4, 466–7, 478, 488, 491
 political 73, 87, 100, 405, 466
 public 24, 366, 502
 state 9, 319, 374
praedial servitudes 529, 532–3
praefectus Aegypti 107, 118, 261, 452
praepositio 629–30
praesidial procurators 101
praetor fideicommissarius 259, 504
praetor peregrinus 91, 116, 192, 225, 227
praetor urbanus 115–16, 220, 222, 225, 227, 230, 238, 284; *see also* praetors
praetorian actions 326, 478, 602, 604
praetorian edicts 25, 28, 72, 76, 156, 158, 503, 505–6, 529, 533
praetorian jurisdiction 230
praetorian law 184, 222, 226, 326, 500–1
praetorian prefects 151, 160, 164, 263, 302, 352
praetorians 106, 225, 230, 287, 292, 302–3, 328, 330, 378–9, 572
praetors 89–91, 115–17, 220–2, 225–9, 238–40, 283–4, 505–8, 530–2, 584–5, 603–5
 urban 91, 113–14, 116, 118–20, 222, 225, 230, 250, 288, 406
pre-classical period 72, 291

prefects 58–60, 62, 101–2, 117, 164, 302, 563, 623, 643
prefectural edicts 58–60
prescription 15, 250, 543–4, 649
  acquisitive 538, 543
  long-term 656
presiding magistrates 229, 290, 313, 357
prestige 36, 90, 127–8, 134, 139, 270–81, 352, 356
  force of 271, 281
πρεσβύτεροι 558
pretrial activity 248, 251–4
price ceilings 618, 667–8
price setting 609–18
prices 48, 421, 521, 532, 582–3, 588, 609, 611–18, 665, 667–8
  fixed 325, 610, 613
  maximum 105, 610, 612–13, 617, 660, 665, 668–9
  purchase 524–5, 559, 665–7
priesthoods 100, 133, 222–3, 366, 403, 559–60
priests 47, 94, 100, 134, 299, 421, 581–2
primary tenants 638–42, 644
princeps 27–8, 46, 74, 98–101, 103, 105, 108, 303, 356, 379
Principate 138, 140, 188–9, 193, 298, 301–2, 378–9, 647, 650, 655
  early 189, 210, 327, 354, 378
  and Greek philosophy 193–7
  legal information 32–5
  licit and illicit *collegia* 140–4
principes 32, 34, 47, 126, 276, 349, 661
prison guards 300, 305–6
privacy 240–1, 319
private acts 248, 326, 404–5
private arbitration, *see* arbitration
private autonomy 500, 502
private citizens 92–3, 221, 229, 371, 404
private criminal law, *see* criminal law
private individuals 28–9, 35, 132, 396, 444, 526, 541, 613, 630
private judges 614, 616
private land 557–60, 646–8, 653, 656
private law 4–5, 28, 30, 57–8, 61–2, 64, 328, 331, 443, 558
private ownership 514, 526, 554, 559, 653
private property 131, 317, 500, 514, 525, 553, 562, 599, 648
private rights 647–8, 653
private transactions 58, 63, 561
privatisation 557, 647–8
privatisation of land 647–9
privileges 96, 99, 103, 285, 287, 354, 370, 393–4, 449–50, 663
Probus 662–3
procedural innovations 258–62, 266, 325, 530
procedure
  civil, *see* civil procedure
  fictions in 285–8
proconsular *imperium* 100
proconsuls 91, 99–102, 105–8, 113, 117, 119, 182–3, 365
procreation 408–9, 439, 475
procurators 58, 102, 117–18, 171, 307, 314, 352, 446, 503, 575
  financial 560
  praesidial 101–2
procurers 352–3, 476
professions 70, 79, 137, 259, 363, 367, 434
  honourable 126, 129
  legal 6, 266
profit 104, 330, 448, 489, 589, 613, 629, 637, 646, 649
profiteering 611–13, 618
promises 247, 250, 412, 426, 549, 576, 583–8, 592
  to appear 52, 247, 253
promisors 576, 582, 587, 592
proof 181, 257, 261, 265, 271–2, 505, 508, 533, 582–3, 617
property 205–6, 358–9, 487–91, 513–22, 527–32, 554–6, 562–3, 600–3, 637–9, 646–50; *see also dominium; dominium ex iure quiritium; possessio; iura in re aliena; res mancipi; traditio; mancipatio*
  acquisition 514
  children's 490–1
  damage to 313, 315–16, 518, 599–600, 605, 616
  divided interests 513, 517–21
  extent 514–15
  family 468, 488, 498, 500
  immovable 541, 548
  loss and recovery 515–16

movable 369, 386, 524, 527, 541, 666
voluntary transfers 516–17
property archive 554, 556, 560–3
property law, economic structure of 358, 513–23, 545
property rights 143, 250, 350, 500, 506, 513, 515, 519, 528
prophets 73, 560
prosecution 14, 74, 229–30, 273, 284, 326, 330, 340–2, 358, 366
open 313–14
prosecutors 207, 228–9, 278, 311, 313–15, 317, 376
prostitutes 329, 352–3, 358, 367–8, 395, 424, 427, 429, 438–40, 476
prostitution 312, 329, 394
protection 370–1, 393–4, 449–50, 493–5, 520, 531–3, 584–5, 590–2, 600–3, 655–6
judicial 584–5
legal 192, 365, 394, 478, 527
provinces 33, 90–4, 98–102, 106–8, 111–22, 261–3, 302–7, 553–5, 646–8, 652–4; *see also individual province names*
and Empire 117–21
senatorial 661
provincia, meaning of 112–13
provincial administration 107, 111–13, 115, 117, 119, 121
beginnings 111–17
provincial communities 114, 119, 131, 289, 303, 350, 364, 668
provincial edicts 116, 118, 121, 141, 143, 261, 630
provincial elites 353, 524
provincial governors, *see* governors
provincial jurisdiction 116, 119, 122
provincial land 548, 554, 648, 656
provincial practice 63, 262, 502, 652
and possession 553–63
provincial revolts 374, 381–3
provocatio 227, 334, 374–5, 377–8
proximus agnatus 466
prudentes 169, 589, 601–2
Ptolemies 61–2, 558, 648
puberty 423, 434, 489, 495, 499
public affairs 73, 78–9, 222, 225
public buildings 127, 129, 164, 300, 626
public business 129, 222, 229, 443
public courts 312, 317–19
public criminal law, *see* criminal law
public declamations 129, 201
public disorder 228, 316
public institutions 86, 98, 137
public interest 596
public jurisdiction 318–19
public land 50, 224, 226, 287, 527, 557, 647
public law 4, 9, 11–12, 31, 43, 222, 443, 617, 667, 669
public life 78, 95, 366
public offences 312, 314–18
public office 95, 350, 355, 359, 367–8, 445–6
public order 101, 139, 285, 297–308, 380, 478, 484
public penalties 428, 610
public power 24, 366, 502
public property 131–2, 224
public service 74, 90, 95, 127, 300
public slaves 132, 230, 298, 306, 392
public trials 142, 228, 230, 329, 353, 374, 427
public works 90–1, 127, 132, 226, 230, 355
publicity 229, 240–2, 379, 500, 531, 613
Punic Wars 90–1, 112–13, 284, 426, 527–8, 635
punishment 145, 286–7, 289, 304, 307, 366, 368, 378, 380–1, 392–3
capital 228–9, 325
corporal 226–7, 350
harsh 324, 392, 655
purchase 115, 369, 412, 421, 532–3, 540, 544, 560, 627
purchase prices 524–5, 559, 665–7
purchasers 179, 226, 369, 394, 500–1, 516, 559, 575, 581
Puteoli 130, 241, 252–3, 302, 628

quaestio 45, 115–16, 119, 228–9, 337, 340
quaestio de repetundis 115, 119
quaestiones 63, 158, 162, 180–3, 185, 226–7, 229, 375
quaestors 29, 89, 93–4, 116, 126–7, 164, 226, 230, 335
quaestorship 87–8, 93, 127, 224, 352
quasi-delicts 315, 596, 604–5
quasi-delictual liability 604, 642
quattuorviri 126
Quintilian 75–6, 202–9, 271, 273, 275, 278

Quintus Mucius Scaevola 29, 438, 500, 587
  Augur 152, 189, 377
  Pontifex 29, 153, 190, 438, 500, 570, 587, 589

rank 86, 236, 307, 349–52, 354–7, 359, 369, 393
  equestrian 101
  plebeian 467
  senatorial 352, 475
rapina 604
ratiocinatio 202, 204
rational argumentation 201–2, 212
real rights 533–4, 641
reasoning 140, 181, 193, 200–2, 209–10, 262, 480
  dialectical 181
  legal 154, 176–86
rebellion 374–84
rebels 273, 378, 382–3
recalcitrance 250
  summons and remedies for 249–51
recognition 10, 25, 53, 66, 139, 193, 365, 370, 527, 534
reconstruction 8–9, 11–12, 141, 323, 423, 462, 540, 624
re-enslavement 409
reforms 6, 48, 62, 102, 161, 231, 379, 406–8, 586, 648
  fiscal 48
  Gracchan 647
  monetary 618
regulae 37, 159–60, 191
regulations 71, 73, 101, 103–4, 129, 131, 140, 143–4, 438–9, 625
rei vindicatio 388, 515, 538–9, 542–3
relatives 104, 266, 271, 274, 426, 467–8, 493, 498, 503–5, 508
  male 448, 468, 490
reliability 43, 52, 404, 583, 629
religion 44, 52, 94, 141–2, 306, 342, 498
reluctance 145, 240, 403
  overcoming 254
reluctant defendants 245–54
remarriages 103, 341, 426, 469, 483, 490, 493
remedies, legal 192, 249–50, 266, 357, 478, 495, 647, 650, 665, 667
remissio mercedis 639
rent 51, 131, 369, 624–6, 630, 638–9, 641–2, 647, 649–53, 655–6
  remission of 611, 651–2
rental income 637, 643
repetundae 316–17, 336, 338, 358
repression 374–84
Republic 72–3, 85–96, 99–100, 116–19, 221–5, 227–9, 333–5, 337–8, 375–7, 423–4
  civil procedure 245–57
  classical 219, 221, 223, 227–8
  crimes against the state 333–7
  early 228, 375, 465, 530
  institutions and popular participation 85–96
  late 92, 94, 138–9, 188–93, 285, 375–7, 381–2, 467–9, 490–1, 649–50
  and Greek philosophy 189–93
  regulating *collegia* and electoral politics 139–40
  legal education 152–3
  legal information 25–31
  middle 270, 333
  and military policing 301
  sedition 375–7
Republican constitutions 71, 76, 89, 93
Republican jurists 178, 190, 194–5, 225, 591, 603
reputation 130, 270, 272, 276–7, 324, 349, 355, 365, 437, 600
res mancipi 386, 516, 524–5, 529, 531–2, 534, 540, 543, 582
res nec mancipi 516, 524–5, 531, 534, 540, 543, 582
res publica 45, 50, 98, 100, 285, 340, 376, 404, 491
rescripts, Imperial 35, 66, 183, 444, 446–7, 631, 652, 654, 661–3, 667–8
resistance 5, 71, 103, 254, 374–84, 387, 393
resources 144, 240, 359, 370, 379, 403, 648, 650, 653, 655
responsa 37, 57, 157–8, 161–2, 182, 185
restitution 76, 482, 542–4, 626
rhetoric 36, 70–1, 76, 153, 160, 162, 166, 194, 200–12, 272
  of jurists 209–11
  manuals 204, 209, 211
  and status 207–9
  teachers of 210–12

rhetorical argumentation 194, 202, 207, 211
rhetorical devices 182, 202, 208–9
rhetorical education 36, 155, 201, 204, 209
rhetorical handbooks 202, 204, 209, 211
rhetorical theory 201–2, 209, 211–12
rights 132–3, 369–70, 493–5, 517, 529–30, 532–4, 558–60, 647–9, 655–6, 662–3
 civil 222, 366, 377
 economic 422, 434
 personal 437, 465, 525
 of pledge 562
 political 31, 124, 419, 526
 private 647–8, 653
 property 143, 250, 350, 500, 506, 513, 515, 519, 528
 real 533–4, 641
riots 302–3, 316, 374–5, 379–82
robbery 357, 518, 596, 604–5, 630–1; *see also rapina*
Roman citizen colonies 124
Roman citizens, *see* citizens
Roman citizenship, *see* citizenship
Roman courts, *see* courts
Roman culture 200–1, 362, 513, 581, 588
Roman Egypt, *see* Egypt
Roman Empire, *see* empire
Roman government, *see* government
Roman institutions, *see* institutions
Roman jurisdiction, *see* jurisdiction
Roman Republic, *see* Republic
Romulus 86, 421, 483
routine policing 301, 307
rules of the house 640, 643
ruling class 85–6, 95, 368, 427
rural markets 664–5
rural patronage 655
rustic servitudes 529, 648

Sabinus 32, 162, 179, 183
sacrilegium 341–2
saevitia 368, 374, 379
safekeeping 518, 624–5, 627, 629–31; *see also custodia*
sale 251, 391–2, 435, 516–19, 531–3, 581, 586–90, 616–17, 647–9, 665–7; *see also consensual contracts; emptio venditio*
 contracts of 61, 179, 452, 531–3, 581, 660
 forced 250, 614
Sallust 78, 376
Salvius Iulianus, *see* Julian, lawyer
sanctions 248, 264, 316, 342, 392, 409, 430, 449, 526
Sardes 105, 662–3
satire 73, 77, 322
Saturninus, L. Appuleius 92, 223, 335–7, 376
Scaevola, Quintus Mucius 29, 438, 500, 587
 Augur 152, 189, 377
 Pontifex 29, 153, 190, 438, 500, 570, 587, 589
Schulz, Fritz 11, 176, 178, 185, 191, 193–4, 197, 246, 482–3
scribae 104, 167
scriptum et voluntas 208–9
SCU, *see senatus consultum ultimum*
secondary tenants 640–1, 644
security, state 333, 335, 341–2
security of tenure 641, 653
sedition 92, 137, 223, 316, 318, 374–5, 377, 380
 Republic 375–7
self-control 271, 280, 323
self-defence 297–8, 317, 381, 602
self-purchase 411–12
sellers 522, 525, 531–3, 581, 586, 590, 615, 617, 665–7, 669
senate 45–7, 85–7, 90–6, 104–6, 112–19, 140–3, 219–24, 333–40, 375–8, 661–4
senatorial aristocracy 221–3, 626
senatorial decrees 44–5, 98, 101–2, 104–5, 140, 142–3, 336, 338, 661, 664
senatorial elite 101, 327, 626
senatorial governors 101, 229
senatorial provinces 661
senatorial rank 352, 475
senatorial status 101, 303, 663
senators 86–7, 94, 98–9, 104–5, 352–3, 357–8, 366, 376–7, 661, 663
senatus consultum 44–5, 98, 101–2, 104–5, 140, 142–3, 336, 338, 661, 664
senatus consultum ultimum (SCU) 336–7, 376–8
senatus consultum Velleianum 446, 450, 574
Seneca 189, 193, 379, 428, 499
 the Elder 154–5, 370
sententiae 159–60, 182

Septimius Severus 57, 142, 193, 341, 428, 495, 648
services 48, 51, 93–4, 287, 289, 350, 408, 411–13, 615, 660
servitudes 519, 521, 529–30, 533, 542, 575, 648, 653
  praedial 529, 532–3
  rustic 529, 648
Servius Sulpicius Rufus 29, 153, 190–1, 589, 627
Servius Tullius 86, 88, 139
servus suis nummis emptus 412
settlements 124, 245, 324, 330, 382, 446, 597, 662, 665
sex, biological 432–3, 435
sexual behaviour 328, 420, 427
sexual conduct 328, 433, 438–9
sexual crimes 322–31, 427
sexual offences 310, 328, 439
sexuality 393, 433, 439
  legal regulation 438–40
ships 313, 315, 370, 531, 562, 637–8
sibling marriage 61
Silvanus, Antonius 501, 503, 507
sisters 77, 466–8, 505–6, 508, 626
skills 27, 58, 76, 153, 177, 211, 275, 394, 452
slave owners 307, 392, 405, 407, 411, 420, 615
slave rebellions 383
slave women 394, 420, 495
slavery 146, 195–6, 302, 322, 386–97, 403, 411, 492, 542
  debt 224, 325
  and social death 386–7
slaves 210–11, 322–7, 329–31, 386–97, 406–13, 419–20, 437–8, 464–7, 600–4, 665–6; *see also* freedman; manumission
  acquisition of property through 388–9
  female 192, 420, 435–7, 448
  freed 166, 350, 366, 407, 448, 464, 559
  fugitive 387, 392, 655
  household 355, 395
  Imperial 356, 631
  male 420, 435, 448
  master's liability for debts 389–90
  public 132, 230, 298, 306, 392
social context 9, 15, 17, 402, 537, 539, 596, 635
social control 13–14, 139, 395, 500, 507
social death, and slavery 386–7
social elites 85, 90, 357
social esteem 351–4, 358–9, 423
social expectations 76, 466, 491, 493, 502, 507
social hierarchy 86, 164, 297, 355, 437, 448
social institutions 248, 463
social life 11, 15, 363, 448, 506
social order 9, 13, 15, 227, 443–4, 448, 453
social position 240, 366, 391–5, 397, 639
social prestige 236, 239, 271, 353, 359
social status 6, 73, 152, 271, 349–59, 396–7, 503, 628, 642
societas 143, 588, 613, 622, 649
socio-legal history of Roman law 15–16
soldiers 106, 108, 301–7, 339, 341, 363, 379, 381, 478, 495
Sollers, Bellicius 661, 663–4
sons 154–6, 329–30, 465–6, 468–9, 499–500, 502–3, 505–6, 575, 583, 637
  emancipated 409, 505–6
sources, literary 9, 134, 138, 246, 252, 337–9, 358, 366, 484, 501
sovereigns 4–5, 25, 98, 290, 323, 325, 331
sovereignty 74, 317, 322–3, 325, 526
Spain 111, 115, 119–20, 164, 261, 285, 288, 648, 653–4
specificatio 522
sponsio 582–4, 592
spouses 58, 224, 421, 425, 429–30, 473, 476–7, 479, 481, 483
SPQR 85, 87, 89, 91, 93, 95
stability 10, 26, 33, 85, 92–4, 285, 334–5, 439, 514, 557
standards of liability 191, 195, 631
standing courts 228–9, 340, 439
state 10–13, 95, 235–8, 298, 305–7, 316–19, 333–43, 556–8, 610, 612–14
  structure 137–46
state control 24, 307, 394
state farmers 557–9
state land 557–9
state power 9, 319, 374
state security 333, 335, 341–2
stationarii 305, 307
statues 50, 133, 340–1, 522

status
  children 64, 404, 494–5
  doctrine 207–9, 211
  freeborn 494, 496
  legal 74, 124, 133, 208, 272, 305, 349–59, 432, 434, 440
  and orders 351–6
  and rhetoric 207–9
  senatorial 101, 303, 663
  social 6, 73, 152, 271, 349–59, 396–7, 503, 628, 642
statute law 4, 26, 30, 220–2, 227, 231, 286, 292, 621
statutes 70–2, 76–7, 104, 184–5, 245–6, 286–7, 329–30, 335–9, 380, 602
  municipal 33, 45, 317
stellionatus 316, 318–19
stipulatio 574–6, 578, 587–8
Stoicism 189–93, 195–6, 203, 205, 210
storage spaces, management 623–31
Stroux, Johannes 200–1
students 152, 154, 157, 160–2, 181–2, 202, 212, 243, 272, 462
  advanced 178, 181–2, 184
stuprum 328–31, 438–9
subordinates 117, 170, 327, 340
substantive justice 4, 286, 292
succession 65, 103–4, 157, 358, 426–7, 462, 466, 468, 502, 506–7; *see also* inheritance
  law of 58, 160, 498
  risk in 506–7
  testamentary 289, 499
successors 25, 32, 102–3, 107, 156, 422, 500, 505–6, 516, 521
Suetonius 103, 140, 260, 303, 449, 501, 661
suffect consuls 104, 341
sui heredes 422, 466–7, 505–7
Sulla 89–94, 116, 222, 224, 228, 320, 326–7, 352, 377, 439
Sulpicii 51–2, 92, 445, 628, 637, 640
Sulpicius Similis 58–9
summa honoraria 126
summons 248–9
  procedure 263–4
superiority 333, 335–6, 338
supervision 29, 120, 230, 319, 604, 665
syllogism 202–4, 209–10
syncretism 188–9, 197
Syria 101, 107, 340, 342, 554, 648
systematisation 10, 153, 156, 179, 194, 200, 208, 462, 543, 545–6
systems for declaration 561–2

tablets 26, 28, 47, 52, 106, 235, 339, 501, 503, 622–3
  wax 50, 52, 235, 247, 252, 339, 445, 501
tabulae 52, 271, 445, 476, 501–4
Tacitus 27, 30, 74, 79, 102, 281, 339–40, 351, 358, 611–12
taxes 118, 126, 132–3, 226, 234, 556–7, 559, 643, 648, 654–5
teachers 151, 153–4, 157, 160, 190, 279, 368, 392, 545
  of rhetoric 210–12
temple land 557–8
temples 91–4, 142, 230, 391, 557
tenancy, agricultural 639, 644, 649–52
tenants 368, 520–1, 531, 625–6, 628, 649–56
  primary 638–42, 644
  secondary 640–1, 644
  urban 635–44
tenements 521, 638–9, 641
tenuiores 141–2, 368
tenure 115, 221, 225, 651–3, 655
  security of 641, 653
territoriality 284–5, 290–1
Tertullian 35, 107, 424, 468, 490, 571
testamentary manumissions 103, 407–8, 410, 504
testamentary succession 289, 499
testaments 51, 62–4, 183, 406, 413, 422, 500–2
testation 435, 501–3, 507
testators 104, 210, 258, 422, 435, 498–500, 502–4, 507–8, 576
testimony 264–5, 271, 276–7, 280, 299, 341, 403, 662
theatre 74–5, 127, 129, 395
theatro populoque Romano 74–5
theft 130, 312–18, 320, 324, 357, 363, 367, 372, 437, 598–9; *see also furtum*
Theodosius 25, 37–8, 342

thieves 230, 286, 297, 300–1, 304, 369, 371, 570, 599
threats 326, 331, 333–5, 338, 340–1, 374–5, 377, 380, 383–4, 478
Tiberius 101, 223, 280, 302–3, 338, 340, 352, 611, 667
Tiberius Iulius Alexander 58–9
Titius 77–8, 154, 180, 477, 576, 641
titulus 43, 538–9, 546
toga 280, 439–40
tombs 51, 313–14, 316–18, 477
topoi 202, 204–7, 272, 301, 446, 450–1, 489, 500
torture 155, 271, 341, 374, 379, 392–3, 631
  judicial 154, 631
town councillors 352–3, 358
town councils 128–9, 133, 300, 649, 668
towns 50, 113, 124–34, 146, 297, 300, 303, 322, 647–8, 653
  peregrine 124
trade 48, 63–4, 133, 139, 291, 354, 369, 394, 621–32, 664–5
  international 584, 586, 596, 604
traditio 61, 516, 525, 532, 543, 545, 582, 588
training 17, 33, 76, 165, 391, 394, 411, 616
  of lawyers 151–62; *see also* legal education
Trajan 35, 105, 107–8, 144, 290, 304–5, 341, 560, 629, 664
  directives to Pliny 144–6
transactions 64, 389, 448–9, 517–18, 524–5, 569, 582–4, 588–91, 598, 627–8
  economic 402, 449, 582–3
  legal 350–1, 366, 445, 447–8, 451–2, 627
  private 58, 63, 561
transfer 318, 412, 425, 427, 503, 514, 516–17, 521, 531–3, 574–5
  of ownership 388, 435, 516, 525, 532, 540, 543, 559
  of property 516, 582, 590
transformations in public sphere 78–9
Transylvania 51, 623
treason, political 228
Trebatius Testa, C. 74, 168–9, 190
tresviri 126, 230, 299
trials 93–4, 130, 228–30, 271, 276, 278–80, 337–8, 340, 377–80, 585–6
  criminal 30, 231
  public 142, 228, 230, 329, 353, 374, 427
tribal assembly 89, 95, 221
tribunate 87–8, 92, 99, 223, 229, 331
tribunes 89, 92–3, 99, 221–3, 226–9, 273, 334, 336, 375, 377
  military 86–7
tribunicia potestas 46–7, 92, 99–100, 222
tribunii aerarii 229
Troesmis 103, 125, 129
trustees 258, 500–1, 504, 507, 520–1, 601
trusts 130, 503–4, 519, 521; *see also* *fideicommissum*
truth 44, 153, 184, 197, 270–1, 276–7, 279–81, 482, 499, 572
tutela 274, 350–1, 366, 446–7, 449, 466, 488–90
tutors 313, 422–3, 425, 443, 447, 449, 599
XII Tables 26–30, 72–4, 248–50, 323–7, 334, 421–3, 525–6, 528–9, 581, 596–600
typicality 585, 589–91, 636

Ulpian 105, 107–8, 159–60, 164, 183–5, 194–6, 341, 437, 476–7, 575–6
unified public sphere 72–3, 79
universal heirs 467, 506
universalis successio 506; *see also* succession
urban cohorts 302, 379
urban landlords 635–44
urban praetors 91, 113–14, 116, 118–20, 222, 225, 230, 250, 288, 406
urban servitudes 529
urban tenants 635–44
usucapion 421, 516, 528, 531–4, 538–41, 543–7, 549, 648
usufruct 192, 420, 490, 517, 519, 528–30, 532–3, 540, 542, 548
usus 421, 525, 528, 530, 540, 614
utility 8, 311, 375, 520, 530, 584

vadimonia 52, 247, 253
Valerius Eudaemon 59
Valerius Flaccus 115, 120
Valerius Maximus 76–7, 280, 328, 377, 508
validity 59, 476, 479, 583, 617, 630–1, 663, 667
valuation 323, 351, 522, 615–16
value 15–16, 76, 389–90, 516–17, 520–2, 589, 599–600, 603, 615–16, 618
  appraised 560–1

assessments at law 614–17
market 412, 522, 616, 665–7
monetary 391, 543
verbal abuse 396–7
verbal representation 180–2
Vespasian 46, 104, 107, 119, 338
veterans 106–7, 355, 561
auxiliary 106, 408
legionary 103
vicarious liability 451, 604
Vicetia 661, 664
victims 160, 297, 301, 305, 313, 322–7, 329–30, 393, 396, 597–9
vigiles 302
vilici 307, 628, 638
villages 131, 305, 356, 419, 558, 654–5, 662–4
vinculum 573, 597–8
vindication 538–9, 542–4, 549
violence 128, 137, 228, 304–5, 311, 316–18, 322–31, 356–7, 527, 603
vis 316, 336, 382
vis maior 631, 651
vis publica 228, 318
vocatus 249–51, 254
voting 93–5, 220, 222, 224, 228–9, 335–6, 366, 375, 377, 405

warehouses 560, 622, 637–8, 640, 643
wars 89, 94, 111–13, 221–2, 273, 285, 334, 383, 386, 426
Punic 90–1, 112–13, 284, 426, 527–8, 635
Social 273, 336, 526
watchtower guards 300–1
water 230, 340, 514, 648, 653–4, 669
rights 653–4
wax tablets 50, 52, 235, 247, 252, 339, 445, 501
wealth 88, 90, 239–40, 242, 273, 275, 351–4, 356, 370, 646–7
weapons 297, 317, 599
weavers 210–11, 354
Weber, Max 10–12, 15
widows 119, 425, 493, 532
childless 469
wills 103, 161, 318, 410, 437, 499–503, 506–7
wine 179, 395, 421, 587, 650, 668
witnesses 48, 51, 249, 264, 271–3, 275–80, 355, 357, 500–2, 582–4
prestigious 275, 280
wives 155, 329–30, 419, 421–3, 425–30, 436–7, 466–8, 473–81, 483, 505–6
women 338–40, 350, 362–3, 366, 419–29, 432–40, 443–53, 476–8, 481–4, 502
capacity of 443, 445
free 354, 395, 425, 427, 448, 481
as legal actors 443–53
and patriarchy 419–30
slave 394, 420, 495
wooden tablets 28, 503
workers 137, 143, 145, 170
wounding 514, 598, 601

Index Locorum

Act. Alex.
no. 4 iii.50–51 … 279
no. 8 iii.40–42 … 279
no. 11 iv.82–84 … 279
Act. Crisp. 5 … 279
Act. Max. 1.1 … 277
Act. Phil. 1.3, 4.1, 5.5, 6.2 and 4, 8.1 … 277
Act. Pion. 5.2–3, 6 … 277
Act. Scill. Mart. 14 … 279
Ad Herennium. See (Rhet.) ad Herennium
Act s 18 … 302
AE 1912, 36 … 628
AE 1925, 126 … 668
AE 1942–43, 7 … 662
AE 1949, 55 … 129
AE 1962, 92 … 106
AE 1971, 88 … 392
AE 1973, 146 … 263
AE 1975, 793 … 32
AE 1977, 801 … 105
AE 1979, 624 … 300
AE 1989, 683 … 105
AE 1996
685 … 125
885 … 101, 338
AE 1997, 1443 … 617
AE 1999
173 … 141
915 … 99, 106
AE 2006, 21 … 45
ll. 22–24 … 34
ll. 25–27 … 28
AE 2009, 1428 … 303
Aelius Aristides, Or. 50 … 128
Agennius Urbicus, 42.28–29 (Campbell) … 131
Amm. Marc.
19.12.17 … 378–9
29.1.18 … 378
Appian
B Civ.
1.60–61 … 377
4.120 … 300
5.132.547 … 302
Hisp.
38 … 382
41 … 382
43–44 … 382
49 … 382
68 … 382
71 … 382
87 … 382
96 … 383
98 … 382
Apul.
Apol.
1 … 278
2–3 … 280
2.8 … 302
4.7 … 35
6.9.10 … 45
11 … 278
16 … 277
24 … 274
25 … 278
28.1 … 571
36 … 278
38 … 278
57–58 … 275
61–62 … 275–6
68 … 490
72 … 275
78–83 … 272
87 … 272
90 … 275
92 … 484
Florida, 9.36 … 304
Met.
1.24–25 … 665

Apul (*Cont.*)
2.18 … 304
3.3 … 300
3.6 … 371
9.12 … 396
Aristotle
An. post. 1. 34 … 204
Eth. Nic.
III.1.4, 1110a4 … 192
V.2, 1131a2–9 … 569
Pol. III 9–10, 1280 a 31–1280 b 17 … 192
Rh.
1356a–1356b, 8–10 … 202
1357b, 19 … 204
ARS 147 … 303
Artem. Oneir. 1.35, 1.39–40, 1.48, 1.70, 1.77, 2.49–54 … 304
Asconius
Corn. 52 … 33
Scaur. 22C … 273
Augustinus
De civ. D.
1.19 … 423
2.9 … 324
Augustus (See also RGDA)
Res gestae … 100, 103
6.2 … 231
9 … 103
34 … 98
Aurel. Vict. Caes. 19.1–2 … 33
Avid. Cass.
7–14 … 379
7.6 … 378

Bas. 28.4.14 … 481
BGU
i 69 … 65
i 140 … 60, 478
i 301 … 64
i 326 … 503
i 19 … 27, 57
ii 388 … 560
ii 472 … 64
iii 729 … 64, 478
iii 741 … 65
iii 887 … 65
iii 888 … 62
iv 1024 … 359
v 1210 … 58, 560
vii 1563 … 59
vii 1578 … 60
vii 1662 … 64, 503
BKT
ix 201 … 57
x 16 … 57
Broughton MRR
1:
45–48 … 223
482 … 223
459 … 228
2: 126, 187–188, 190, 193–196, 214–215 and 217 … 223

Caesar
B Civ.
1.5 … 376
3.1 … 301
3.1.2–3 … 611
B Gall.
1.18 … 614
1.54.3 … 117
5.1.5 … 117
5.2.1 … 117
6.44 … 382
6.44.3 … 117
7.41 … 383
Cato Agr.
5.1 … 392
144.1 … 612
146–150 … 587
147 … 612
Catull. 51 … 73
ChLA iv 249 … 474
Cicero
Am.
1.1 … 152
37 … 375
Att.
6.1.8 … 225
6.1.15 … 116–17, 589
6.7.2 … 116
12.32.2 … 637
14.9.1 … 636–7
16.1.5 … 637
Balb. 20–22 … 285

Brut.
1.18.3 … 570
39.145 … 499
45.168 … 377
88 … 280
106 … 115, 228
114 … 281
152–153 … 153
184–193 … 280
Caecin.
12.35 … 326
18.51–53 … 499
104 … 274
Cael.
1 … 274
30–31 … 424
Cat.
1.4 … 376
4.10 … 377
Clu. … 489
11 … 274
41 … 489
57 … 277
95 … 273
154 … 273
196 … 274
202 … 270
Deiot.
16 … 274
26 … 274
39 … 278
De or. … 152, 272, 275, 278–9, 376, 492
1.40.181.9 … 492
1.45 … 189
1.180 … 499
1.186 … 225
1.188–189 … 152
1.223 … 270
1.231 … 279
2.100 … 271
2.106 … 376
2.116 … 271–2
2.132 … 376
2.134 … 376
2.165 … 376
2.182 … 278
2.182–183 … 273
2.184 … 273, 279
2.209 … 275
3.211 … 278
3.214 … 75
Div. Caec. 64 … 274
Fam.
5.2.8 … 377
5.20.2 … 116
10.12.3 … 220
13.11.3 … 125
Fin.
1.12 … 153, 193
2.20.66 … 423
4.74 … 273
Flacc.
6–24 … 277
8 … 274
9 … 276
9–10 … 277
9–12 … 280
24–25 … 274
34–36 … 277
36 … 277
40 … 277
42–53 … 277
64–66 … 277
66 … 280
86–91 … 382
90–93 … 277
92–93 … 382
94 … 382
100–101 … 274
101 … 278
104–106 … 274
Font.
14–16 … 277
21 … 275
27–33 … 277
28 … 280
37 … 274
40–41 … 274
44–46 … 277
Inv. rhet.
1.57–66 … 203
1.58 … 203
1.60 … 203
1.61 … 203
1.67–75 … 203
2.32–37 … 272

Cicero (*Cont.*)
2.33 ... 273
2.116–122 ... 211
2.122 ... 499
2.160 ... 196
2.177 ... 273
Leg.
1.13 ... 152
1.17 ... 25, 72
1.19 ... 72, 226
1.27 ... 273
2.15.37 ... 45
2.59 ... 72, 152
3.8 ... 226
3.10 ... 220, 226
3.23–24 ... 92
3.46 ... 30
Man. 60 ... 89
Mil.
37.101 ... 301
70 ... 376
73–78 ... 274
87 ... 274
99 ... 279
100 ... 278
Mur.
3 ... 278
15–54 ... 274
41 ... 220
78 ... 278
86 ... 278
90 ... 278
Off. ... 273, 287, 491, 581, 589, 612
1.22 ... 193
1.25.85 ... 491
1.71–72 ... 134
2.44–51 ... 272
3.50 ... 612
3.66–67 ... 581
3.69–70 ... 192, 196
3.70 ... 589
Orat. 25.86 ... 280
Part. or. 99 ... 253
Phil.
1.18 ... 30
2.69 ... 422
8.14 ... 376
Planc.
2 ... 279
3 ... 274
32 ... 274
60–62 ... 274
67 ... 274
Pis. 50, 61 and 90 ... 116
Q. Fr. 1.1.22 ... 116
Q. Rosc. Com.
4.10–11 ... 238
4.13 ... 589
5.14 ... 589
15 ... 279
17–19 ... 274
20 ... 274
42–44 ... 276
Quinct.
60 ... 250
72 ... 277
75 ... 276
80 ... 277
Rab. perd. ... 376
2 ... 274
12 ... 375
18 ... 280
Rab. post.
6 ... 279
34–36 ... 277
Rep.
1.43 ... 426
1.59 ... 272
2.1–2 ... 86
2.2 ... 30
2.39 ... 95
3.17 ... 423
4.8 ... 238
4.12 ... 324
5.1 ... 71
Rosc. Amer.
1–2 ... 280
10 ... 279
17 ... 274
24 ... 274
46 ... 278
59–61 ... 278
109–118 ... 274
133–135 ... 274

Sest.
5–17 … 274
18–26 … 274
39 … 377
119 … 279
Scaur.
13 … 274
22C … 273
28C … 275
38–45 … 277
46–50 … 274
Sull.
2 … 278
9–10 … 278
22–23 … 278
35 … 278
69–82 … 274
79 … 275, 280
81–82 … 278
117-127 … 75
Top.
2.10 … 406
3.14 … 583
4.23 … 421, 540
5.28 … 219
10.44 … 499
29 … 404
42 … 204
44–45 … 181
51 … 153, 270
52.194–53.199 … 499
54–55 … 203
73 … 275
Verr.
1.2 … 274, 278
1.11 … 274
1.14 … 274
1.16–25 … 274
1.42 … 274
2.1.6–7 … 274
2.1.39–40 … 274
2.1.47 … 274
2.1.73–85 … 380
2.1.82 … 382
2.1.83 … 271
2.1.90–94 … 489
2.1.109 … 226
2.1.153 … 274
2.2.12.31 … 267
2.2.31 … 261
2.2.31–32 … 192
2.2.32 … 114, 285
2.2.41 … 261
2.2.152 … 261
2.2.165 … 274
2.2.188 … 280
2.3.19 … 274
2.3.92 … 271
2.3.122–128 … 271
2.3.154–157 … 271
2.3.167–168 … 271
2.3.195 … 115
2.4.126–127 … 274
2.5.57 … 275
2.5.143–144 … 280
CIL
I.2 2527a … 479
II 1964 … 579
II 6278 … 618
IV 138 … 627
IX 3028 … 392
VI … 624
VI.2 625 … 477
VI.2 4370 … 477
VI.2 9366 … 477
VI.2 13268 … 477
VI 266 … 262
VI 1853 … 166
VI 5197 … 395
VI 10229 … 504
VI 10621 … 104
VI 18524 … 474, 484
VI 33747 … 624–6
VI 33860 … 625
VI 37795 … 626
VI 41118 … 58
VIII 7 … 126
VIII 8810 … 58
VIII 11451 … 664
VIII 11824 … 353
VIII 18587 … 654
VIII 19337 … 662
X 1874 … 50
X 4658 … 50

CIL (*Cont.*)
XI 3615 ... 126
XIII 5708 ... 504
XVI ... 106
XVI 24 ... 478
Codex
C. Cordi, 4 ... 24
C. Deo auctore
7 [a. 530] ... 24
11 ... 24
C. Haec
pr ... 24
2 ... 24
C. Omnem ... 33
7 ... 57, 161
C. Tanta
1. ... 176
9 ... 161
18 ... 118
20 ... 24
22 ... 24
1.12.2 ... 342
1.17.2.9 ... 161
2.12.18 ... 446
2.44.2.1 ... 449
2.57.1 ... 262
3.3 ... 424
3.4 ... 424
4.10.5 ... 614
4.20.9 ... 264, 275
4.25.2 ... 390
4.25.4 ... 451
4.29.6pr ... 446
4.33.3 ... 452
4.33.4 ... 452
4.43.1 ... 492
4.44.2 ... 617, 667
4.44.8 ... 617, 667
4.60.1 ... 661
4.65 ... 649
4.65.1 ... 631
4.65.4 ... 631
4.65.8 ... 651
4.65.10 ... 652
4.65.16 ... 652
4.65.18 ... 652
4.65.19 ... 652
4.66 ... 656
4.66.1 ... 656
4.66.2 ... 656
5.4.6 ... 476
5.17.5pr ... 483
5.24.1 ... 494
5.25.1 ... 259
5.31.6 ... 493
5.35.1 ... 446
5.4.9 ... 474
5.42 ... 489
5.46.2 ... 489
5.51.9 ... 489
5.60.3 ... 489
6.7.2 ... 409
6.30.18 ... 489
6.35 ... 393
6.56–57 ... 424
6.61.5 ... 36
7.4.17 ... 265
7.16.1 ... 492
7.30.1 ... 656
7.31.1.3 ... 549
7.39.3 ... 549
7.43.1 ... 264
7.62.6.1 ... 260
7.65.5.1 ... 265
7.71.4 ... 62
8.22.1 ... 265
8.38.2 ... 482
8.46.9 ... 493
8.51.1–3.3 ... 492
8.51.2pr ... 493
9.8.3 ... 379
9.8.4 ... 379
9.9 ... 427
9.9.4 ... 429
9.14.1pr ... 396
9.16.3 ... 371
9.17.1 ... 491
9.21.1 ... 403
10.50.1 ... 160
11.63.1 ... 653
Codex Theodosianus
1.1.5 ... 24, 38
1.4.1 ... 36
1.4.3 ... 38
2.4.2 ... 263
3.16.1 ... 483
3.3.1 ... 492
4.10.1 ... 409

4.8.6 … 492
5.10.1 … 492
5.35.1 … 425
5.35.2 … 426
6 … 24
8.18.1 … 34
9.1.3 … 34
9.5.1pr … 379
9.14.1 … 492
9.14.3 … 342
9.35.1 … 379
10.8.3 … 34
11.27.1 … 34
11.36.4 … 428
11.36.25 … 265
11.39.3 … 264, 275
12.1.6 … 495
12.5.2 … 34
12.6.16 … 626
14.3.10 … 34
14.4.4 … 34
16.1.2pr … 342
16.1.2.1 … 342
16.2.20 … 34
16.8.19 … 342
Coll.
2.5.1 … 194
3.3 … 393
3.3.1–3 … 393
3.3.2 … 391
3.3.5 … 392
4.2.2 … 439
9.2.2 … 355
10.7.11 … 599
10.9 … 631
Columella, Rust.
1.7 … 650
1.8.1 … 395
1.8.6 … 395
1.8.10 … 392
1.8.15 … 389
1.8.16–18 … 392
3.2.1 … 612
11.1.25 … 392
CPJ 158 a & b, 435 … 380
CPL
70–101 … 57
73 A and B … 57
120 … 65
208–209 … 474
246 … 623
247 … 623

Digesta
1.1.1.1 … 155, 197
1.1.1.3 … 477
1.1.3 … 193
1.1.4 … 386
1.1.6.1 … 194
1.1.7.1 … 4, 226
1.1.8 … 225
1.1.10pr … 196
1.1.10.1 … 196
1.1.11 … 194, 228
1.11–12 … 302
1.12.1.8 … 393
1.14.3 … 387
1.15 … 302
1.15.3.2 … 630–1
1.15.4 … 643
1.16.4.5 … 108
1.16.6.3 … 182
1.16.8 … 108, 304
1.16.9.4 … 279, 365
1.16.9.4–5 … 356
1.16.9.5 … 365
1.16.9.6 … 365
1.17.1 … 101, 107
1.18.1 … 304
1.18.3 … 304
1.18.4 … 108
1.18.6 … 303
1.18.6.2 … 365
1.18.6.4 … 365
1.18.8 … 257
1.18.9 … 257
1.18.13pr … 304, 380
1.18.19pr … 365
1.2.1 … 153, 176
1.2.2 … 25–30, 152–3, 157, 189–90, 284, 587
1.2.2pr … 25
1.2.2.2 … 26, 284
1.2.2.3 … 26
1.2.2.4 … 26, 152, 587
1.2.2.6 … 27
1.2.2.7 … 225
1.2.2.38 … 28
1.2.2.39 … 190

Digesta (*Cont.*)
1.2.2.39–40 … 189
1.2.2.41 … 30, 152, 190, 587
1.2.2.47–53 … 157
1.2.2.49 … 27–8
1.3.2 … 194
1.3.6 … 194
1.3.32–40 … 73
1.3.32pr … 291
1.3.34 … 291
1.5.3 … 387
1.5.4 … 193
1.5.4pr … 195
1.5.4.1 … 195, 386
1.5.4.2–3 … 386
1.5.5pr … 387
1.5.9 … 366, 433, 445
1.5.10 … 433
1.6.1.1 … 388
1.6.1.2 … 393
1.6.2 … 391, 393
1.6.9 … 350
1.8.1.1 … 575
1.22.1 … 33
2.1.7pr … 246
2.11.2.6–8 … 246
2.13.1pr … 253
2.13.1.1 … 29
2.13.1.3 … 247
2.13.4.3 … 390
2.13.12 … 366, 434, 452
2.14.1.3 … 195, 578
2.14.7pr-2 … 591
2.14.35 … 77
2.14.58 … 579
2.2–11 … 311
2.3 … 313
2.4 … 254, 313
2.4.22.1 … 254
2.5.2.1 … 250
2.6 … 250
2.7 … 313
2.8.15.1 … 541
3.1.1.5 … 279, 367, 447
3.1.2 … 367
3.1.8 … 158
3.2.1 … 355
3.2.4.3 … 394
3.2.11.3 … 341
3.3.67 … 575
3.4.1pr … 143
3.5.28–37 … 489
3.5.3pr. … 179
3.5.3.1 … 435
3.5.3.6–11 … 179
3.5.5.2 … 179
3.5.5.8(6) … 392
3.5.33 … 446
3.6 … 311, 313–14
4.1.7pr … 264
4.1.8 … 490
4.2.5 … 192
4.2.17 … 575
4.2.21.3 … 578
4.3.1.1 … 603
4.3.7.7 … 392
4.3.7.8 … 575
4.3.11.1 … 357
4.4.1pr-3 … 489
4.4.9.2 … 313
4.4.16.4 … 612
4.4.27.3 … 575
4.4.34.1 … 490
4.4.47.1 … 312
4.5.3.1 … 387
4.5.5.1 … 377–8
4.5.7.1 … 578
4.5.11 … 350
4.6.23.2 … 529
4.6.26.4 … 246
4.7.3pr … 370
4.8.3.3 … 236
4.8.7pr … 236
4.8.8 … 236
4.8.49pr … 367
4.9.1pr-8 … 370
5.1 … 315
5.1.12.2 … 386, 435, 446
5.1.19.1 … 578
5.1.21 … 253
5.1.53 … 613
5.1.57pr … 313
5.1.76 … 192
5.1.79pr … 263

5.1.79.1 … 27
5.2 … 312
5.3.20.6 … 105
5.3.27.1 … 394
6.1.24 … 541
6.1.28 … 394
6.1.62.1 … 158
6.1.68 … 265
6.2.11.1 … 533
6.3.1 … 656
6.3.1pr-1 … 131
6.3.2 … 656
6.3.3 … 656
7.1.5 … 576
7.1.15pr … 626
7.1.15.1 … 393–4, 396
7.1.15.2 … 394
7.1.68pr … 193, 420
7.7.6.1 … 388
7.7.6.2 … 615
7.8.4pr … 369
8.1.20 … 532
8.3.1.2 … 533
8.3.30 … 533
8.4.10 … 533
8.4.13pr … 533
8.5.8.5 … 370
8.5.10pr … 533
8.5.14pr … 533
8.5.16 … 532
8.6.19pr … 532
8.8.11.2 … 392
9.1 … 311
9.1.3 … 368
9.2 … 311
9.2.2 … 319
9.2.2pr … 601
9.2.5.3 … 368, 396, 602
9.2.5.3–7pr … 392, 396
9.2.5pr … 602
9.2.6 … 368
9.2.22.1 … 615
9.2.23.3 … 394
9.2.23.8 … 314, 319
9.2.27.5 … 601
9.2.28pr … 570
9.2.31 … 191, 195, 317, 602
9.2.33pr … 394, 615
9.2.39pr … 602
9.2.52.1 … 369
9.3 … 311, 318
9.3.1.10—9.3.5pr … 643
9.3.1pr … 642
9.3.5.13 … 314
9.2.5pr … 602
9.2.6 … 368
9.4.19pr … 578
10.2.22.5 … 159
10.2.24pr … 159
10.2.25.10 … 576
10.2.25.13 … 576
10.2.33 … 570
10.2.41 … 178
10.3.10.1 … 614
11.1.4pr … 575
11.1.11.4 … 279
11.3 … 315, 387, 395
11.3.1 … 387, 437
11.3.1.5 … 387, 395
11.3.2 … 395
11.3.5pr … 392
11.3.13.1 … 314
11.3.16 … 395
11.4 … 307
11.4.3 … 304
11.6 … 313, 315
11.6.3pr … 315
11.7.10 … 533
11.7.14.1 … 369
11.8.2 … 428
12.1.2.2 … 578
12.1.2.5 … 575
12.1.9.8 … 575
12.1.21 … 575
12.2.9.3 … 576
12.6.26.4 … 576
12.6.26.12 … 577
12.6.32.2 … 577
12.6.60 … 577
12.7.1pr … 576
12.7.3 … 576
12.7.5pr … 158, 312
13.4.8 … 574
12.6.26.4 … 576

Digesta (*Cont.*)
13.5.18.3 ... 576
13.6.17.3 ... 575
13.7.11.5 ... 638, 641
13.7.11.6 ... 575, 579
13.7.24pr ... 579
14.1.1.16 ... 450
14.1.5.1 ... 389
14.3.5.1 ... 627
14.3.7.1 ... 451
14.3.7.2 ... 570
14.3.11.2–4 ... 629
14.3.11.6 ... 629
14.3.20 ... 180
14.4.1pr ... 392
14.5.4.2 ... 313
14.5.8 ... 623
15.1–3 ... 389
15.1.3.4 ... 390
15.1.3.11 ... 578
15.1.4pr ... 390
15.1.4.6 ... 390
15.1.5.4 ... 390
15.1.7.1 ... 390
15.1.7.4 ... 390
15.1.8 ... 390
15.1.9.2 ... 390
15.1.11.2 ... 575
15.1.21pr ... 390, 392
15.1.29.1 ... 389
15.1.32pr ... 391, 395
15.1.32.2 ... 391
15.1.39 ... 390
15.1.44 ... 389
15.1.46 ... 390
15.1.47.6 ... 395
15.1.57.2 ... 390
15.1.74pr ... 389
15.3.3.5 ... 391
15.3.5pr ... 615
15.3.5.2 ... 390
15.3.7pr ... 395
15.3.10.8 ... 390
15.3.16 ... 390
15.4 ... 389
15.4.1.6 ... 390
15.4.3 ... 579
16.1.1.1 ... 450
16.1.4pr ... 450
16.1.11 ... 450
16.1.2.1 ... 574
16.1.2.2 ... 450
16.3.26.2 ... 575
16.3.27 ... 387, 395, 478, 482
16.3.31pr ... 184
17.1.1pr ... 579
17.1.22.4 ... 579
17.1.26pr ... 576
17.1.26.8 ... 369
17.1.27.1 ... 574
17.1.32 ... 579
17.1.45.2 ... 576
17.1.59.5 ... 579
17.2.30 ... 589
17.2.81 ... 158
17.6 ... 312
18.1.5 ... 387
18.1.6.1 ... 578
18.1.11.1 ... 436
18.1.39.1 ... 612
18.1.40.1 ... 533
18.1.66.1 ... 589
18.1.80.1 ... 532
18.2.13pr ... 586
18.4.2.8 ... 575
18.6.1pr ... 179
18.6.8.2 ... 533
19.1.3.2 ... 532
19.1.11.1 ... 586
19.1.11.5 ... 436
19.1.13.4 ... 391
19.1.25 ... 612
19.1.38.1 ... 586
19.1.43 ... 394
19.1.54pr ... 394
19.2 ... 649
19.2.7 ... 641
19.2.11.1 ... 640
19.2.13.4 ... 602
19.2.15.1–3 ... 651
19.2.15.2 ... 589
19.2.15.4 ... 651
19.2.19.2 ... 157, 650
19.2.22.3 ... 612
19.2.25.1 ... 641
19.2.25.6 ... 651

19.2.40 … 630
19.2.52 … 579
19.2.55pr … 631
19.2.60.6 … 629
19.2.60.9 … 630
19.5.5pr … 394, 615
19.5.9 … 576
19.5.14.3 … 311
20.1.4 … 481
20.1.6 … 319, 579, 615
20.1.8 … 393, 579
20.1.23.1 … 579
20.1.26.1 … 579
20.1.29pr … 579
20.1.34.1 … 579
20.3.3 … 157
20.3.4 … 579
20.4.9 … 638
20.4.21pr … 579
20.5.12.1 … 578
20.6.5.2 … 575–6
20.6.6pr … 576
20.6.11.1 … 579
21.1.1.2 … 666
21.1.1.8 … 312
21.1.1.9–10 … 387
21.1.4.2 … 395
21.1.17.14 … 387
21.1.17.18 … 313–14
21.1.17.3 … 392
21.1.17.4 … 392
21.1.17.5 … 392, 394
21.1.18pr … 386, 390
21.1.18.2 … 391
21.1.25.6 … 395
21.1.40 … 313
21.1.42 … 313
21.1.43.1 … 392
21.1.49 … 666
21.1.65 … 395
21.1.65pr … 387
21.2.10 … 532
21.2.39.3 … 492
21.2.46.1 … 532
21.2.51.3 … 575
21.2.6 … 290
22.1.3.3 … 489
22.1.11.1 … 575
22.1.28 … 420
22.1.28.1 … 193
22.5.1 … 276
22.5.2 … 276, 355
22.5.3pr … 276, 357
22.5.3.1–2 … 276
22.5.3.5 … 355
22.5.4 … 404
22.5.5 … 467
22.5.15.1 … 433
23–25 … 161
23.1.12 … 483
23.2.1 … 425
23.2.2 … 474
23.2.4 … 476
23.2.21 … 483
23.2.24 … 481
23.2.33 … 480
23.2.44 … 184, 352
23.2.57a … 479
23.2.65.1 … 476
23.3.21 … 482
23.3.39pr … 395
23.3.39.1 … 475
23.3.46pr … 575
23.3.56.1 … 425
23.3.58.1 … 575
23.3.68 … 576
23.3.76 … 576
23.5.10 … 578
24.1.3.8 … 390
24.1.32.12 … 481
24.1.32.13 … 476
25.4.1 … 428
25.5.5–7 … 259
25.7.3pr … 482
26 … 489
26–27 … 161
26.1.1 … 491
26.1.16pr … 434
26.1.18 … 434
26.2–5 … 490
26.5.13.1 … 158
26.5.13.2 … 489
26.7.5.10 … 489
26.7.7.14 … 158
26.7.12.3 … 491
26.7.37.2 … 158

Digesta (*Cont.*)
26.7.55.1 ... 599
26.10 ... 311, 315
26.10.1.6 ... 313
26.10.1.7 ... 493
26.10.3 ... 315
27.1.13pr ... 490
27.3 ... 311
27.3.1.19–24 ... 315
27.4 ... 491
27.9.3pr ... 579
27.9.3.1 ... 579
27.9.5.10 ... 579
27.9.5.13 ... 579
28–36 ... 161
28.1.20.6 ... 433
28.2.6pr ... 475
28.2.6.2 ... 433
28.2.11 ... 492
28.2.26 ... 59
28.3.6.6 ... 312
28.3.6.9 ... 380
28.5.4 ... 183–4
28.5.4pr-2 ... 183
28.5.35.3 ... 393
28.5.52pr ... 183
29.1.1pr ... 108
29.2.86.1 ... 341
29.2.97 ... 183
29.3.1.1 ... 247
29.5 ... 387, 393
29.5.1.28 ... 393
30.36pr ... 210
30.82pr ... 578
D.31.76.9 ... 341
31.29pr ... 259
31.45pr ... 435
32.35.2 ... 411
32.37.4 ... 576
32.41.2 ... 394
32.62 ... 435
33.7.5 ... 182
33.7.16.1 ... 153
33.7.19.1 ... 391
33.7.20.1 ... 390
33.8.16pr ... 391
33.8.22.1 ... 391
34.1.22.2 ... 578
34.2.25.9 ... 435
34.2.33 ... 438
34.3.7pr ... 576
34.3.21.1 ... 576
35.1.15 ... 476, 482
35.1.40.3 ... 193
35.1.59.2 ... 386
35.1.62.2 ... 493
35.2 ... 507
35.2.1pr ... 507
35.2.3.2 ... 616
35.2.9.1 ... 428
35.2.42 ... 616
35.2.45pr ... 616
35.2.45.1 ... 616
35.2.55 ... 616
35.2.62.1 ... 616
35.2.63.2 ... 615
35.2.63pr ... 394, 615–16
35.2.66pr ... 616
35.2.68 ... 498
35.2.68pr ... 616
35.2.73.1 ... 616
35.2.73.4 ... 616
35.3.1pr ... 616
36.1.4pr ... 507
36.1.23(22)pr ... 504
36.4.5.1 ... 570
37.1.3.1 ... 529
37.10.1.11 ... 494
37.10.3.5 ... 494
37.14.4 ... 341
37.14.17 ... 184
37.14.24 ... 178
37.15.1 ... 424
37.6.5pr ... 506
37.6.8 ... 159
37.9 ... 428
37.9.1.15 ... 494
37.9.1.21–26 ... 494
38.1.15.1 ... 575–6
38.5.1.15 ... 615
38.6.1.1–2 ... 505
38.10.10 ... 184
38.1.37pr ... 408
38.11.1.1 ... 480
38.16.1.3 ... 341
38.17 ... 424

38.17.2.34 ... 312
39.2.18.5 ... 574
39.2.26.4 ... 533
39.2.27 ... 180
39.3.1.23 ... 533
39.4.11.1 ... 541
39.5.12 ... 570
39.5.31pr ... 476
39.5.31.4 ... 341
39.5.35.1 ... 579
40.2.11 ... 394
40.2.13 ... 392
40.2.16pr ... 393
40.5 ... 410
40.7 ... 411
40.7.39.2 ... 391
40.8.2 ... 392
40.12.21pr-1 ... 314
41.10 ... 544
41.1.11 ... 547
41.1.37.1 ... 392
41.1–41.3 ... 545
41.1.43.1 ... 543
41.1.53 ... 547
41.1.59 ... 388
41.2.1.1 ... 541
41.2.1.9–13 ... 388
41.2.1.14 ... 388–9
41.2.1.16 ... 183
41.2.3.1 ... 546
41.2.3.3 ... 547
41.2.3.12 ... 389, 546
41.2.3.21–23 ... 545
41.2.3.23 ... 191, 195
41.2.8 ... 546
41.2.12pr ... 547
41.2.12.1 ... 541
41.2.17.1 ... 541
41.2.19.1 ... 546
41.2.24 ... 547
41.2.26 ... 543
41.2.34pr ... 546
41.2.41 ... 546
41.2.44.1 ... 389
41.2.44–46 ... 546
41.2.51 ... 546
41.2.52pr ... 548
41.4 ... 544
41.5 ... 544
41.5.2.1 ... 547
41.5.2.2 ... 547
41.5.3 ... 544
41.6 ... 544
41.7 ... 544
41.8 ... 544
41.9 ... 544
42.1.13.1 ... 265
42.1.15pr ... 265
42.2.7 ... 260
42.4.7.4 ... 393
42.4.7.17 ... 251
42.6.3pr ... 576
43.1.2.2 ... 541
43.1.2.3 ... 541
43.2.1pr ... 541
43.3.1.4 ... 253
43.3.2.4 ... 253
43.8.2.34 ... 313
43.8.5 ... 599
43.19.5.3 ... 533
43.20.3.4 ... 533
43.26.2 ... 529
43.30.1.3 ... 494
43.30.3.5–6 ... 494
44.6.3 ... 599
44.7.1pr ... 313, 572
44.7.3pr ... 574, 592
44.7.4 ... 313, 578, 597
44.7.5.4–6 ... 313
44.7.5.5 ... 642
44.7.5.6 ... 315
44.7.18 ... 576
44.7.49pr ... 313
44.7.52pr ... 570
45.1.2.3 ... 576
45.1.4.1 ... 586
45.1.56.2 ... 575
45.1.62 ... 570
45.1.76pr ... 576
45.1.95 ... 575
45.1.99pr ... 575
45.1.115.2 ... 158
45.1.126.2 ... 575, 577
45.1.140.2 ... 576
45.1.141.3 ... 575
45.3.1.2 ... 575

Digesta (*Cont.*)
45.3.2 ... 575
46.1.26 ... 576
46.1.27.4 ... 576
46.2.34pr ... 392
46.3.7 ... 314
46.3.22 ... 575
46.3.29 ... 576
46.3.35 ... 391
46.3.38.5 ... 579
46.3.69 ... 579
46.3.80 ... 587
46.3.94.3 ... 158
46.4.1 ... 570
46.8.17 ... 576
47.1 ... 311
47.1.2 ... 437
47.1.2.5 ... 437
47.2.21pr ... 194
47.2.22pr ... 495
47.2.52.26 ... 390
47.2.62(61).5 ... 389
47.2.62.8 ... 612
47.2.83pr ... 314
47.2.93 ... 314, 318
47.3.1pr ... 599
47.8.2.24 ... 313
47.8.2.27 ... 319
47.8.4.11 ... 616
47.9.1.1 ... 318
47.9.9 ... 597
47.10.1.2 ... 326
47.10.3.1 ... 326
47.10.13.7 ... 326
47.10.15.20 ... 326
47.10.15.39 ... 396
47.10.15.43 ... 396
47.10.15.44 ... 394, 396
47.10.45 ... 318
47.10.5pr ... 312, 326
47.10.7.2 ... 326
47.11.4 ... 428, 494
47.11.6 ... 668
47.11.6pr ... 613
47.12 ... 313
47.12.4 ... 317
47.12.8 ... 318
47.13.2 ... 312, 318
47.14.2 ... 318
47.15.2 ... 318
47.18.1pr ... 318
47.19.3 ... 318
47.20 ... 313
47.20.1 ... 318
47.20.3–4 ... 318
47.20.3.1 ... 314
47.20.3.1–2 ... 318
47.21 ... 104, 313–14
47.21.3.1 ... 104
47.22.1pr ... 142
47.22.2 ... 142
47.22.3 ... 142
47.22.3.1 ... 142
47.23 ... 314
48.1.1 ... 312
48.2.16 ... 355
48.2.20pr ... 312
48.3.2.1 ... 59
48.3.6pr-1 ... 306
48.3.6.1 ... 371
48.4.1pr ... 341
48.4.1.1 ... 341, 378, 380
48.4.2 ... 339
48.4.4pr ... 341
48.4.5.1–2 ... 341
48.4.7pr-2 ... 339
48.4.7.1 ... 341
48.4.11 ... 341
48.4.8 ... 339
48.5 ... 318, 427
48.5.12(11).3 ... 330
48.5.13 ... 328
48.5.14.1 ... 479
48.5.21(20)–23(22) ... 329
48.5.23(22).3 ... 330
48.5.23–24 ... 491
48.5.24(23)pr ... 329
48.5.25(24)pr ... 330
48.5.39(38).8 ... 429
48.5.44 (43) ... 480
48.6 ... 318
48.6.3pr–48.6.3.3 ... 380
48.6.5pr ... 380
48.6.10pr ... 380
48.7 ... 318
48.7.2 ... 318

48.7.4pr … 318, 357
48.7.5 … 318
48.7.8 … 318
48.8.2 … 491
48.8.3.4 … 318, 392
48.8.4.2 … 392
48.8.8 … 428
48.9 … 334, 404
48.9.5 … 491
48.10.1.4 … 318
48.10.28 … 579
48.12 … 318
48.12.3pr … 668
48.12.3.1 … 613
48.15 … 317
48.15.7 … 317
48.15.7pr … 312
48.18.10.1 … 341, 379
48.18.8pr … 59
48.19.13 … 354, 371
48.19.15 … 129
48.19.1pr … 312
48.19.16.10 … 371
48.19.27–28 … 129
48.19.28.3 … 380
48.19.28.13–14 … 354
48.19.28.15 … 304
48.19.28.16 … 355
48.19.9.11–12 … 129
48.19.39 … 494
49.1.10.3 … 158
49.1.16pr … 380
49.1.25 … 35
49.14.3.6 … 614
49.14.50 … 171
49.15.7.1 … 335
49.18.3 … 355
50.1.8 … 613
50.1.27.1 … 289
50.1.29 … 289
50.1.33 … 134
50.1.34 … 289
50.1.38.6 … 128
50.4.18.26 … 132
50.4.3.3 … 434
50.5.3 … 613
50.6.6(5).5 … 613
50.6.6(5).5.3 … 613
50.7.5.5 … 127
50.8.7(5)pr … 613
50.11.2 … 194
50.13.5pr … 322
50.13.5.1 … 355
50.15.4.2 … 133
50.16.1 … 451
50.16.13pr … 435
50.16.19 … 190, 464, 571, 575, 590
50.16.70 … 408
50.16.152 … 435
50.16.166 … 638
50.16.182 … 395
50.16.195.1–2 … 419
50.16.195.5 … 436
50.16.195pr … 435
50.16.199pr … 251
50.16.203 … 638
50.16.220.3 … 474
50.16.225 … 395
50.16.239.1 … 386
50.17.2pr … 445, 447
50.17.23 … 631
50.17.32 … 196
50.17.34 … 289
50.17.73 … 491
50.17.84.1 … 577
50.17.107 … 389
50.17.209 … 386
Dio. Cass.
36.38–40 … 33
37.26–28 … 376
37.42.1 … 377
38.14.4 … 377
40.50–54 … 301
40.52.2 … 275
42.50.4 … 611
42.51.1–3 … 611
47.14.4–5 … 614
47.17.3 … 614
48.9.5 … 611
49.12 … 302
51.21.5 … 611
53.12 … 117
54.3.2–3 … 280
54.3.5–6 … 378
54.4 … 301
54.7 … 303

Dio Cass., (*Cont.*)
54.11.5 … 382
54.21.8 … 278
54.30.4 … 280
54.31.3 … 382
54.34.7 … 382
55.14–22 … 379
55.18.1 … 378
55.18.5 … 378
55.18.6 … 378
55.19 … 378
55.19.2 … 378
56.1–29 … 103
56.16 … 383
56.18–25 … 383
57.19.2 … 378
58.21.4–5 … 611
59.21.4 … 378
59.25.5b … 378
59.26.4 … 379
59.28.11 … 381
60.15.6 … 378
60.17.8 … 618
60.21.4 … 382
62.2 … 383
62.7 … 383
62.9 … 383
62.11 … 383
62.29 … 474
63.13 … 474
63.27.2b … 378
69.2.5 … 378
72.13.4–5 … 380
72.22–30 … 342
73(74).8.5 … 378
78.17 … 302
80.15 … 474
Dio Chrys. Or. 31.162 … 130
Diod. Sic. 5.26.3 … 612
Dion. Hal. Ant. Rom.
2.10.1 … 359
2.25.5–6 … 328
2.25.6 … 421
2.26–27 … 420
2.27 … 492
4.24.6 … 408
4.66–77 … 423
5.70.2–3 … 375
10.3.4 … 27
ELRH U2 … 285
Epict. Diss.
4.1.91 … 304
4.13.5 … 302
Epit.Gai.1.1.7 … 394
Epit.Ulp. 3, 5–6 … 610
Eusebius
Hist. eccl.
3.33 … 107
8.14.3 … 380
Mart. Palest. 4.3.5 … 160

Festus
198M … 375
290 L … 86
Pauli Exc. 181L … 324
FIRA I
30 … 376
60 … 562
437, 438 … 548
FIRA I²
67 … 106
68 … 106
FIRA III … 64
17 … 474
47 … 501, 503
50 … 503
144 … 639
318 … 549
320–323 … 549
FIRA III²
143b … 627
145a … 624, 626
145b … 625
145c … 626
Firm. Mat. Err. prof. relig. 6.9 … 45
Flor.
1.24.1 … 26, 62
1.33.9 … 382
Frg. Dosith.
4–8 … 406
6 … 407
Fronto ad Anton.
Pium. 8.1 … 304
Front(inus) Aq.
100 f … 104
104 … 104
106 … 104
108 … 104

111 … 104
125 … 104
127 … 104
129 … 103
Fr.Vat. … 38
34 … 492
75–89 … 38
77 … 167
106–107 … 480
224 … 159
266–316 … 467

Gellius, NA
1.12 … 461
1.22.7 … 152
2.24.1–15 … 610
5.13.2.5 … 489
6.15.2 … 570
10.3.17 … 396
10.20 … 220
10.23 … 423
10.23.5 … 421
11.18.8 … 599
12.1.8–9 … 428
13.12–13 … 226
13.15.4 … 227
14.2 … 358
14.2.1 … 32
14.7.4–5 and 8 … 220
14.7.5 … 220
14.7.9 … 220
15.27.5 … 221
16.10.8 … 225
16.13.1–9 … 125
17.6 … 423
17.6.2 … 226
20.1.5–8 … 4
20.1.12 … 609
20.1.13 … 327, 598, 600

Hdn. 1.12.6–9 … 380
Hdt. 4.1–4 … 396
Horace
Ep.
1.14.15 … 395
1.16.48 … 304
2.1.23–27 … 79
2.1.153 … 74
2.2.50 … 73
Serm./Sat.
1.5.34–36 … 134
1.10.81–91 … 75
1.4.109–110 … 77
2.1 … 74
Hyginus, 82.35–84.2 … 131

IAM II, 94 … 289
IEph. 2.215 … 380
IEph. 21486 … 261
IHibis 4, 11–15 … 559
ILLRP no. 514 … 113
ILS
206 … 106, 287
311 … 105
1011 … 118
1015 … 118
1123 … 118
1151 … 118
1434 … 118
1452 … 118
1620 … 628
1621 … 628
2130 … 302
2691 … 118
3663 … 629
5723 … 627
5793 … 654
5913 … 625
6035 … 627
6043 … 104
6093–6116 … 129
6680 … 129
6780 … 129
7367 … 392
9430 … 105
IMagn. 114 … 380
Inscr. Ital. 13.1 … 375, 378
Institutes
1.1.2 … 33
1.2.4 … 34
1.6.5 … 394
1.8.2 … 391, 393
1.11.9 … 434
1.22pr … 489
1.23 … 490
1.23pr … 489
2.1 … 514
2.1.12 … 514

Institutes (*Cont.*)
2.2.2 ... 575
2.10.6 ... 433
2.23.1 ... 259
2.25pr ... 169
2.25.2 ... 589
3.3pr ... 468
3.4 ... 424
3.13pr ... 597
3.13pr-2 ... 572
3.24.3 ... 656
3.25.2 ... 589
4.3.16 ... 603
4.3.9 ... 314
4.4.3 ... 396
4.5 ... 604
4.6.1 ... 572
4.17.2 ... 252
4.18.10 ... 312
Institutes of Gaius
1.1 ... 196, 290
1.2 ... 219
1.2–7 ... 75
1.5 ... 59, 106
1.6 ... 225
1.8 ... 571
1.9 ... 307, 350, 387
1.10–11 ... 350
1.19 ... 350, 393–4
1.22 ... 406
1.27 ... 408
1.29 ... 51
1.29–30 ... 350
1.31 ... 407
1.32–34 ... 350
1.32b–34 ... 610
1.32c ... 613
1.39 ... 394
1.48–49 ... 350
1.52 ... 350, 388
1.52–54 ... 388
1.53 ... 392–3
1.55 ... 491
1.72 ... 435
1.82 ... 495
1.89 ... 495
1.112 ... 421
1.115a ... 58
1.119 ... 517, 583
1.122 ... 4
1.123 ... 583
1.128 ... 289
1.131 ... 289
1.132 ... 492
1.140 ... 583
1.142–143 ... 351
1.142–196 ... 489
1.144–145 ... 422
1.144–186 ... 490
1.145 ... 449
1.154–154a ... 196
1.158 ... 195, 289
1.159–163 ... 350
1.189 ... 196
1.190 ... 422, 435, 443
1.194 ... 425
1.196 ... 489
2.7 ... 548, 553
2.12–28 ... 545
2.14 ... 575
2.16 ... 531
2.40 ... 531
2.41–79 ... 545
2.42 ... 540
2.50 ... 420
2.66–70 ... 514
2.86–90 ... 488
2.95 ... 388
2.97–98 ... 498
2.101 ... 500
2.102 ... 500
2.104 ... 500
2.116–117 ... 501
2.118 ... 502
2.119–120 ... 179
2.122 ... 502
2.123–124 ... 488
2.156–157 ... 507
2.161–162 ... 507
2.163 ... 507
2.207 ... 58
2.213 ... 572
2.224 ... 407
2.226 ... 423

2.228 ... 407
2.274 ... 423
2.278 ... 259
2.281 ... 502
2.286 ... 427
2.287 ... 58
3.1 ... 505
3.1–17 ... 160
3.9 ... 505
3.17 ... 505
3.25–26 ... 4, 292
3.28 ... 4
3.32 ... 4
3.56 ... 406–7
3.63 ... 104
3.88 ... 313, 571
3.124 ... 610
3.149 ... 589
3.182 ... 604
3.189 ... 324
3.191 ... 599
3.195–208 ... 518
3.209 ... 604
3.215 ... 601
3.220 ... 326, 437
3.222 ... 396
4.1–5 ... 313
4.2 ... 572, 577, 592
4.9 ... 314
4.15 ... 130
4.16 ... 542
4.17b–20 ... 246
4.30 ... 225
4.30–187 ... 237
4.37 ... 192
4.37–38 ... 286
4.46 ... 250
4.48 ... 265
4.62 ... 425
4.70 ... 389
4.74 ... 391
4.75 ... 389
4.78–79 ... 157
4.79 ... 492, 583
4.83 ... 239
4.86-87 ... 239
4.93 ... 542
4.94 ... 542
4.103–104 ... 49
4.104–105 ... 284
4.114 ... 252
4.130–133 ... 252
4.139 ... 529
4.143–155 ... 545
4.148 ... 527
4.182 ... 357
4.183 ... 248
4.184 ... 250, 253
Isid. Etym.
5.1.5 ... 30
5.25.5 ... 395
Iuv.
2.37 ... 427
3.183–184 ... 618
3.306–308 ... 300
4.77 ... 407
6.115–135 ... 427
6.183–190 ... 427
6.224–240 ... 427
6.347–349 ... 427
8.79 ... 489
10.69–72 ... 378
10.100–102 ... 134
14.77 ... 304

John the Lydian
De mag.
1.38 ... 284
1.45 ... 284
John Chrys.
PG 53.112b–c ... 34
Joseph.
AJ
17.298 ... 382
19.24–26 ... 381
20.118–136 ... 380
BJ
2.232–246 ... 380
2.494–498 ... 380
2.77 ... 382

Leg. saec. 8 ... 490
lex coloniae genitivae (see also lex Urs.)
95.15–19 ... 404

lex de Gallia Cisalpina, 21-22 ... 239
lex Flavia municipalis
chs 21–13 ... 289
chs 91, 93 ... 287
lex Irn.
19.17–22 ... 300
20 ... 127, 300
21 ... 133
23 ... 405
24–25 ... 127
26 ... 300
29 ... 131
31 ... 128
60 ... 126
67–69 ... 132
72 ... 132
75 ... 613
76 ... 132
78 ... 132
79 ... 132
80 ... 128
81 ... 127
84 ... 120, 130, 237, 239, 610
85 ... 28, 33, 120
86 ... 129–30
91 ... 131
93 ... 120
94 ... 133
95 ... 131
97 ... 405
J ... 132
L ... 129
lex Malac.
51 ... 127
53 ... 133
54 ... 126, 129
59 ... 300
59–60 ... 126
63 ... 131
64–65 ... 126
66 ... 130, 132
67–69 ... 132
lex rivi hiberiensis III 35 ... 261
lex Romana Visigothorum ... 24, 429
lex Salp.
21 ... 133
25 ... 127
26.45.5–7 ... 300
lex Urs.
17 ... 128
61 ... 132
62 ... 127
70 ... 126
71 ... 127
81 ... 132
82 ... 131
95 ... 133
98 ... 133
105 ... 126, 128–9
124 ... 128
125 ... 127
126–127 ... 133
Lib.
Ep.
533 ... 160
1375 ... 160
1539 ... 160
Or.
19.8–24 ... 381
19.19 ... 381
48.22 ... 160
62.21 ... 160
Livy
1.8 ... 86
1.26.6 ... 72
1.43.10 ... 95
1.58.5–1.59.3 ... 423
2.18.8 ... 375
2.29 ... 375
3.4 ... 376
3.20 ... 221
3.25.9 ... 112
3.34.6 ... 26, 30
3.34.7 ... 26
3.44.2 ... 330
3.44.7 ... 331
3.45.4 ... 331
3.47.7 ... 331
3.50.5–6 ... 331
4.4.3 ... 86
4.6.2 ... 475
4.13 ... 375
4.13–16 ... 375
6.11–17 ... 375
6.30.3 ... 112
7.3.5 ... 87

8.18 … 423
8.22.2–4 … 438
8.33–35 … 375
9.20.10 … 31
9.46.5 … 27
9.46.5–6 … 225
10.31.9 … 438
24.44.1 … 112
25.2.9 … 438
26.1.7–10 … 284
27.22.2 … 112
28.24 … 383
28.32 … 383
30.27.1–5 … 222
34.1.3 … 423
34.9 … 382
34.21 … 382
34.3.2 … 423
35.5 … 383
39.8–19 … 45, 333, 376
39.14.6–8 … 45
39.18 … 45
39.18.1–3 … 227
39.18.7–9 … 45
40.37.4–5 … 423
44.1.3 … 112
Per. 55 … 382
Per. 77 … 377
Per. 103 … 377
Praef. 6 … 76
Praef. 10 … 76

Marcus Aurelius ad Fronto, Ep. 2.8 … 70
Mark 14:48 … 300
Martial
1.86 … 642
2.32 … 277
10.31 … 396
Matt. 26:55 … 300
MChr. 1 … 65

Nov.
72 … 490
89.14 … 490
134.10 … 429
Maior. 6.9 … 494
Theod.
1 [a. 438] … 24
2 [a. 447] … 24
12 … 494
Val.33 … 492

OGIS
484 … 132
669 … 58
4302a … 132
Ord. nob. urb. 20.36–41 … 134
ORF[3], 173 … 274
Oros. 4.20.14 … 423
Ovid
Am. 2.14 … 428
Fast. 2.685–856 … 423
Tr. 1.1.88 … 75
Tr. 3.1.82 … 75

Pal.
19 … 180
59 … 178
347 … 179
349 … 179
350 … 179
877 … 178
2145 … 182
2717 … 179
Paul (Ep. ad) Cor.
7.3–5 … 429
11.3 … 429
11.7 … 429
Paul (Ep. ad) Gal. 3.28 … 429
Paus.
7.16.9 … 31
8.30.9 … 31
P. Cair. Masp. i 67006v … 475
P. Col.
123 … 35, 57
viii 221 … 65
P. Duk. inv. 528 … 65
P. Dura 26 … 65
Pers. 5.90 … 32
I Peter 2:13–14 … 304
Petronius, Sat.
1–2 … 154
30 … 390
46 … 393
46.7 … 32
53 … 390, 392–3, 395

Petronius, Sat. (*Cont.*)
69 … 393
75 … 393, 396
75.4 … 395
76 … 391
76.1 … 393
111–12 … 304
P. Flor. i 56 … 62
P. Gen. ii 103–104 … 60
P. Giss. i 40 … 57, 65–6, 289
Phaedrus App. 15 … 304
P. Hamb.
i 63 … 65
i 97 … 64
Philo Leg. 361 … 279
Philostr.
VA
5.36 … 306
8.4 … 279
VS
555–556 … 274
559 … 277
560–561 … 280
P. Iand. vii 145 … 62
PIR III 323 … 625
Plautus
Asin. 131 … 299
Aul., 416 … 299
Amph.
3.2.47 … 422
155–160 … 299
Capt. 813–24 … 226
Merc., 419 … 226
Mostell. 253–254 … 392
Pers. 192 … 392
Poen. 843–844 … 395
Rud. 915–919 … 389
Stich. 426–428 … 395
Trin. 2.1.49 … 422
Truc.
2.1.6 … 569
5.1.64 … 569
Pliny (the Younger)
Ep. … 107, 157, 236, 341, 353–4, 393, 395–6, 405, 410, 499, 501, 503, 508, 614, 618, 661
1.19 … 129, 353
1.20.12 … 168
1.22.3 … 153
3.14 … 393
3.14.7 … 396
4.13 … 132
5.4 … 661
5.9.3–4 … 618
5.9.4 … 259
5.13 … 661
6.25 … 300
6.33 … 508
7.16.4 … 410
7.29.3 … 354
7.30.2 … 242
7.32.1 … 410
8.14 … 395
8.18 … 501
9.5 … 349
9.37 … 650
10.8.5 … 650
10.11.2 … 405
10.19 … 306
10.19–22 … 305
10.27–28 … 305
10.34 … 144
10.37–40 … 128, 132
10.54–55 … 614
10.65–66 … 121
10.75 … 503
10.77–78 … 305
10.79 … 129
10.79–80 … 59
10.92 … 144
10.93 … 144
10.96 … 354
10.96–97 … 341
10.109 … 290
10.113 … 290
Pliny (the Elder)
HN
3.30 … 125
7.128–129 … 394
17.7 … 599, 609
18 … 599
18.12 … 324
33.17 … 225
33.32 … 352
33.118 … 613
34.99. … 28
54.123 … 613

P. Lond.
ii 178 … 64, 478
iii 1164a … 64
v 1712 … 475
P. Lugd.Bat. XIII 14 … 503
Plutarch
Comp. Lys. et Sul. 3.2 … 439
Mor. 134–135 … 428
Vit.
Cic. 29 … 424
Cat. Mai. 9.6 … 499
Cat. Min.
2.5 … 154
19.4 … 275
C. Gracch.
4 … 375
16–17 … 376
Rom.
22 … 421
22.3 … 422
Sull. 8.2 … 610
Ti. Gracch. 20 … 375
P. Mich.
456r … 32
III 203 … 478
IX 546 … 65
VI 421 … 301
VII 434 … 474–5
VII 438 … 65
VII 475 … 475
XV 707 … 65
Polybius
3.22 … 284
3.40 … 383
3.67 … 383
6.11.11–12 … 95
6.11–18 … 221
6.16 … 223
11.29 … 383
11.31 … 383
39.5.2–3 … 30
39.5.5 … 31
Porph. ad Hor.
Epist. 2.1.152–155 … 324
Porph. Vita Plot.
5 … 157
13 … 151
15 … 157
P. Oxy.
1408 … 274
i 34 … 58
ii 237 … 61, 291–2, 483, 562
ii 237 viii 7–18 … 59
ii 237 viii 21–27 … 58
ii 237 viii 27–43 … 58
ii 244 … 64
ii 274 … 560, 562
iii 653 … 60
iv 706 … 61
iv 727 … 489
vi 899 … 59
vii 1020 … 35
vii 1033 … 301
ix 1201 … 60
ix 1201 l. 11 … 60
xvii 2103 … 57
xviii 2104 … 35
xxii 2339 … 380
xli 2951 … 65
xlii 3014 … 58
xlii 3015 … 61, 290
xlii 3016 … 261
xliii 3106 … 35
xliv 3208 … 623
P. Petaus 10 and 11 … 561
P. Ryl.
ii 75 … 62
iv 612 … 474–5
pseudo-Quintilian Declamationes minores 274.13 … 304
PSI
v 447 … 64
vi 729 … 65
vi 730 … 475
vii 743r frag. e … 261
ix 1027 … 64
xi 1182 … 57
P. Sijp. 15 … 305
P. Tebt. … 65
II 294 … 560
ll. 207–220 … 65
P. Tiberianus 11 … 475
P. Tor.Choach. 12 … 555
P. Turner 22 … 65
Publilius Syrus

PSI (*Cont.*)
596 Q44 … 393
616 Q64 … 393
P. Wisconsin I 14 … 503

Quintilian, Inst.
2.15.6 … 273
3.7.25 … 278
4.1.7 … 278
4.1.13 … 273
4.1.16–22 … 279
4.2.125 … 278
4.2.31–32 … 271
4.2.34 … 271
5.1.2 … 271
5.7.23–34 … 275
5.7.24 … 275
5.8.4–5.14.26 … 208
5.10.1–2 … 203
5.10.5–8 … 203
5.10.54–62 … 205
5.10.56–57 … 205
5.10.64 … 206
5.10.65 … 206
5.10.65–70 … 206
5.10.67 … 206–7
5.10.68 … 207
5.10.69 … 206–7
5.10.70 … 206
5.10.80–82 … 205
5.11.3 … 204
5.11.6 … 76
5.12.10 … 273
5.14.2 … 203
5.14.5 … 203
5.14.6 … 203
6.2.5 … 271
6.2.18 … 278
6.3.29–35 … 280
7.1.4–7.10.6 … 208
7.3.3–27 … 205
7.3.6 … 206
7.3.14 … 205
7.3.21 … 205
7.3.25 … 205
7.4.11 … 155
8.2.1 … 275
8.3.14 … 272
10.1.111–112 … 278
11.1.29 … 280
11.1.36 … 274–5
11.1.42 … 272
11.1.43–45 … 279
11.1.44-48 … 272
11.3.68–136 … 280
11.3.137–149 … 280
11.3.184 … 278
12.3.6 … 26
12.7.6 … 273
12.10.53 … 272

RDGE
7 … 113
43, ll. 9–10 … 31
67 … 119
Reg.Ulp.
1.10 … 406
1.11 … 408
3.4 … 407
20.13 … 367
RGDA 25 … 302
(Rhet.) Ad Herennium … 203, 272
1.8 … 272
2.5 … 272
2.9 … 275
2.11.17 … 336
2.25 … 272
3.10–15 … 272
4.25.35 … 336
4.60 … 279
1.9.14 … 77–8
336–339 … 203
RS
No. 2
ll. 29–31 … 287
l. 31 … 287
ll. 55 … 287
ll. 58–61 … 287
ll. 66–67 … 287
No. 7 … 337
No. 8 … 337
No. 25
ch. XCV … 404
No. 28
ch. XX … 288

ch. XXI … 49
ch. XXII … 49, 298, 570
No. 39
l. 29 … 46
l. 34 … 46
l. 36 … 46

Sall. Cat. 29 … 376
SB
i 1010 … 60
iv 7356 … 478
v 8011 … 474
x 10530 … 503
xvi 12609 … 65
xviii 13167 … 622, 633
xx 14710 … 61
SEG IV, 512 … 145
SEG IX, 8 … 119, 284–5, 303
SEG XVII
755 … 107
759 … 278
SEG XIX, 854 … 563
SEG XXXIII, 1177 … 563
SEG XXXVIII, 1462 … 128
SEG XLIV, 977 … 661
SEG XLIX, 1866 … 300
SEG LI, 1427 … 285
SEG LIV, 1625 … 285
Seneca (the Elder)
Controv.
1, Pref. 12 … 154
1.3.8 … 156
1.4.6 … 155
1.4.pr–1 … 155
1.13 … 155
2.1.20 … 156
2.3.13 … 155–6
2.5.10 … 155
4 praef. 10 … 393
10.1.2 … 370
Seneca (the Younger)
Ben.
3.7.1 … 263
3.18.1–3.22.1 … 193
3.19.1 … 393
5.24.1–3 … 278
Clem.
1.9–10 … 379
1.20 … 378
2.7 … 379
Ep. 48.10 … 29
Helv. 16.3 … 427–8
Ira
3.18 … 378
3.18–19 … 379
Oct. 846–850 … 380
Q Nat. 1.16.1 … 393
Sent.Paul.
2.17.6 … 391
2.18.3 … 631
2.20.1 … 479
2.27.1 … 429
3.4b.10a … 59
3.5 … 393
4.14.1 … 104
5, 1a, 1 … 613
5.1.1 … 492
5.6.15 … 483
5.6.16 … 393
5.26.1–2 … 380
5.29.2 … 379
SHA Alex.
22.7–8 … 614
39.3 … 626
SHA Ant. Pius
7.4 … 378
SHA Comm. 14.1–3 … 667
SHA Hadr.
4.3 … 378
7 … 378
11 … 302
18.7–10 … 392
18.8 … 394
18.10 … 302
21.7 … 125
SHA Heliogab. 10 … 474
SHA Marc.
24–25 … 379
24.9 … 378
SHA Sev.
12.1–4 … 58
18.3 … 613
SIG
543 … 403
674 … 31
888 … 35

Strabo
- 14.5.674 … 278
- 17.1.12 … 118
- 17.3 … 117

Suetonius
- Aug. … 117
  - 32 … 302
  - 33 … 260
  - 34.1 … 610
  - 34.2 … 103
  - 40.3–4 … 408
  - 43 … 302
  - 49 … 303
- Caes. (see also Iul.)
  - 41 … 643
  - 42.2 … 611
  - 43.2 … 610
- Calig.
  - 7 … 378
  - 41.1 … 31
- Claud.
  - 4.7 … 501
  - 12 … 661
  - 15 … 257
  - 18–19 … 449
  - 18.2 … 613
  - 25 … 302
  - 25.2 … 392
  - 37 … 378
- Dom. 7.1 … 618
- Iul.
  - 12 … 376
  - 43 … 301
  - 44.2. … 30
- Nero
  - 4 … 501
  - 17 … 130
  - 28–29 … 474
  - 49 … 378
- Tib.
  - 8 … 302
  - 8.1 … 378
  - 16 … 383
  - 20 … 383
  - 23 … 501
  - 34.1 … 610
  - 35 … 427
  - 37 … 302–3, 380
  - 54 … 378
  - 61 … 379

Tab. Her.
- 22 … 128
- 25 … 126
- ll. 108–125 … 353

Tacitus
- Agr. 14–16 … 383
- Ann.
  - 1.57 … 383
  - 1.58 … 383
  - 1.75.2 … 281
  - 2.2 … 358
  - 2.27–28 … 378
  - 2.29 … 277
  - 2.31 … 379
  - 2.59 … 613
  - 2.87.1 … 667
  - 2.88 … 383
  - 3.11 … 277
  - 3.24 … 439
  - 3.25.2 … 427
  - 3.27 … 30
  - 3.27.1. … 27
  - 3.33–34 … 423
  - 3.52 … 610
  - 4.15.2 … 102
  - 4.16 … 231
  - 4.67–69 … 302
  - 6.16–17 … 611
  - 11.1–3 … 378
  - 11.2 … 379
  - 11.5–7 … 618
  - 12.31 … 382
  - 12.43 … 380
  - 12.53.2 … 102
  - 12.60 … 102, 118
  - 12.60.1 … 102
  - 12.60.2 … 101–2
  - 12.69.4 … 102
  - 13.4 … 130, 379
  - 13.26–7 … 409
  - 13.31 … 612
  - 13.48 … 380
  - 14.17 … 303, 380
  - 14.29–39 … 383
  - 14.33 … 383

14.37 … 382
14.42–45 … 198, 393
14.45 … 380
14.61 … 380
15.18 … 613
15.22.1 … 105
15.39.3 … 667
15.44 … 371
15.58 … 378
15.69 … 378
15.73 … 378
16.18 … 378
Dial.
31 … 154
35 … 154
39.1 … 247
Hist.
4.13 … 382
11.7 … 259
Tert.
Ad nat. 1.10.16 … 45
Apol. 2 … 107
T.H.
6 … 253
6.13–15 … 52
13 … 253
14 … 253
89 … 28, 50, 475
Tit. Ulp.
5.2 … 474
6.6 … 425
6.7 … 425
11.28 … 489
13 … 352
13.2 … 329, 353
14 … 427
16.1 … 427
TPSulp … 623
1–19 … 253
25 … 263
27 … 239, 247
28 … 253
31 … 247
35 … 241
35–39 … 241
36 … 241
45 … 628
45.I.2.6 … 628
45.III.5 … 628
45.III.5.5 … 628
46 … 628
46.I.2.6 … 628
46.III.5.5 … 628
51–52 … 628
53 … 628
60 … 426
67–68 … 628
79 … 628
Twelve Tables. See XII Tables

Val. Max.
2.5.3 … 423
3.7.8 … 273
3.8.5 … 377
4.7.1 … 375
6.1.1 … 423
6.3.8 … 45
7.6 ext. 2 … 383
7.7.4 … 475
7.8.2 … 508
8.1. abs. 10 … 274
8.5.6 … 276
9.1.3 … 423
Varro
Rust.
1.16.2–3 … 612
1.16.5 … 392
1.69.1 … 612
2.2.5–6 … 587
2.3.5 … 587
2.4.5 … 587
2.5.10–11 … 587
Sat. Men. 188 … 249
Vell. Pat.
2.19 … 377
2.45.1 … 377
2.110–112 … 383
2.114 … 383
2.118.1 … 288
2.118–119 … 383
Vett. Val.
5.10 … 380
5.6.120–121 … 380

Xenophon Ephesiaca
2.13 … 300

XII Tables (*Cont.*)
XII Tables ... 26–30, 72–4, 77, 81, 87, 152–3, 159, 176, 220, 223, 226, 235, 248–50, 252, 254–5, 284, 297–8, 320, 323–7, 332, 334, 421–3, 466, 468, 480, 501–2, 505, 507, 525–6, 528–9, 540, 581, 583, 596–600, 605–6, 609, 621
1.1 ... 297
1.1-3 ... 77
1.13 ... 324
1.14 ... 324, 609
1.15 ... 324, 609
1.16 ... 324
1.17 ... 324
1.19 ... 324
1.22 ... 324
2.2 ... 284
2.3 ... 297
4.2 ... 583
4.2b ... 583
5.1 ... 422–3
5.2 ... 422
5.4 ... 422
6.1 ... 583
6.2 ... 334
6.3 ... 421
6.3 ... 540
6.8 ... 599
7.11 ... 583
7.12 ... 388, 583
7.8b ... 599
8 ... 599
8.1 ... 74, 324
8.2 ... 324
8.2, 3, 4 ... 597
8.4 ... 324, 598
8.4–5 ... 334
8.5 ... 324
8.6 ... 324, 599
8.9 ... 325
8.10 ... 325, 334, 597
8.11 ... 74, 325, 599
8.11-12 ... 334
8.12 ... 325, 599
8.12–14 ... 297
8.13 ... 298, 324
8.14 ... 599
8.15a ... 599
8.16 ... 599
8.19 ... 599
8.20 ... 599
9 ... 599
12.1 ... 583
12.4 ... 599

Zacharias of Mytilene, Vita Severi
53 ... 160
55–57 ... 160
Zonar. 9.17.1 ... 423